Five Hundred Years of
ENGLISH
POETRY

Five Hundred Years of
ENGLISH
POETRY

Chaucer to Arnold

·

Edited by Barbara Lloyd-Evans

PETER BEDRICK BOOKS
NEW YORK

For Gareth

'The best poetry is what we want; the best poetry will be found to have a power of forming, sustaining, and delighting us, as nothing else can.'

Matthew Arnold, 'The Study of Poetry'

First American edition published by
Peter Bedrick Books
2112 Broadway
New York, NY 10023

© Selection and editorial matter Barbara Lloyd-Evans 1989

Published by agreement with B. T. Batsford Ltd. London, England

Library of Congress Cataloging-in-Publication Data

Five hundred years of English poetry : Chaucer to Arnold / edited by
    Barbara Lloyd-Evans. — 1st American ed.
      p.   cm.
    Includes bibliographies and indexes.
    ISBN 0-87226-325-8. — ISBN 0-87226-215-4 (pbk.)
    1. English poetry.   I. Lloyd Evans, Barbara.
PR1175.F486   1989
821.008—dc20   89-42891
                                                                    CIP

Printed and bound in Great Britain
5 4 3 2 1

Contents

Preface   15

Geoffrey Chaucer (*c.*1343–1400)   17
  The Canterbury Tales
    General Prologue   18
    The Wife of Bath's Prologue and Tale
      The Prologue   39
      The Tale   58
    The Pardoner's Prologue and Tale
      The Introduction   68
      The Prologue   69
      The Tale   72
    The Nun's Priest's Tale
      The Introduction   84
      The Tale   85
  Notes   99

Edmund Spenser (*c.*1552–99)   105
  The Faerie Queene
    Book I   106
      Canto 1   107
      Canto 2   121
      Canto 3   132
      Canto 4   144
      Canto 5   157
      Canto 6   170
      Canto 7   182
      Canto 8   195
      Canto 9   208
      Canto 10   222
      Canto 11   239
      Canto 12   253
  Epithalamion   264
  Notes   274

John Donne (1572–1631)   281
  A Valediction: Of Weeping   282
  The Ecstasy   282
  The Relic   285
  A Nocturnal upon St Lucy's Day   286
  Song: Sweetest Love, I do not Go   287
  A Valediction: Forbidding Mourning   288

The Sun Rising 289
The Anniversary 290
Song: Go and Catch a Falling Star 291
The Canonization 292
The Good-Morrow 293
Holy Sonnets 294
  VII
  X
  XIV
Satire III 295
Notes 298

George Herbert (1593–1633) 301
The Pearl (Matt xiii.45) 301
Bitter-Sweet 303
Affliction 303
Jordan 305
The Collar 306
Easter 307
Discipline 307
Virtue 308
Love 309
Easter Wings 310
The Pulley 310
Notes 311

John Milton (1608–74) 312
L'Allegro 313
Il Penseroso 316
Comus 321
Lycidas 346
Paradise Lost
  Book I 350
  Book II 369
  Book IX 393
  Book X 420
Samson Agonistes 445
Notes 486

Andrew Marvell (1621–78) 495
The Coronet 496
Bermudas 496
The Definition of Love 498
The Mower to the Glow-worms 499
To His Coy Mistress 499
Notes 501

John Dryden (1631–1700)   502
  Absalom and Achitophel   503
  Absalom and Achitophel: The Second Part   526
  MacFlecknoe   529
  A Song for St Cecilia's Day, 1687   534
  Key to Absalom and Achitophel   536
  Notes   537

Alexander Pope (1688–1744)   541
  An Essay on Criticism   542
  Windsor Forest   544
  The Rape of the Lock
    Canto I   545
    Canto II   548
    Canto III   551
    Canto IV   556
    Canto V   560
  Ode on Solitude   563
  Epistle to Miss Teresa Blount   564
  An Essay on Man   565
  Epistle to Dr Arbuthnot   569
  The Dunciad   579
  Notes   581

Thomas Gray (1716–71)   586
  Ode on the Death of a Favourite Cat   587
  Elegy Written in a Country Churchyard   588
  Notes   594

Oliver Goldsmith (1730?–74)   593
  The Traveller   593
  The Deserted Village   596
  Song: When Lovely Woman Stoops to Folly   600

William Cowper (1731–1800)   601
  Light Shining Out of Darkness (from *Olney Hymns*)   601
  Simple Faith   602
  The Poplar Field   603
  The Task, Book VI
    The Winter Walk at Noon   604

George Crabbe (1754–1832)   608
  The Village, Book I   608
  The Borough
    Peter Grimes   610
  Notes   617

William Blake (1757–1827)   618
  Songs of Innocence
    Introduction   619
    The Shepherd   620
    The Ecchoing Green   620
    The Lamb   621
    The Little Black Boy   621
    The Blossom   622
    The Chimney Sweeper   623
    The Little Boy Lost   623
    The Little Boy Found   624
    Laughing Song   624
    A Cradle Song   624
    The Divine Image   625
    Holy Thursday   626
    Night   626
    Spring   628
    Nurse's Song   629
    Infant Joy   629
    A Dream   630
    On Another's Sorrow   630
  Songs of Experience
    Introduction   632
    Earth's Answer   632
    The Clod & the Pebble   633
    Holy Thursday   633
    The Little Girl Lost   634
    The Little Girl Found   636
    The Chimney Sweeper   637
    Nurse's Song   638
    The Sick Rose   638
    The Fly   638
    The Angel   639
    The Tyger   640
    My Pretty Rose-Tree   640
    Ah! Sun-flower   641
    The Lily   641
    The Garden of Love   641
    The Little Vagabond   642
    London   642
    The Human Abstract   643
    Infant Sorrow   643
    A Poison Tree   644
    A Little Boy Lost   644
    A Little Girl Lost   645
    To Tirzah   646

The School Boy 646
The Voice of the Ancient Bard 647
from Milton
    Jerusalem 648
from Jerusalem
    England! awake! awake! awake! 648
from For the Sexes
    To the Accuser who is the God of this World 649
Notes 649

William Wordsworth (1770–1850) 651
Expostulation and Reply 652
The Tables Turned 653
Lines Written in Early Spring 654
There Was a Boy 655
Lines Composed a Few Miles above Tintern Abbey 656
The 'Lucy' Poems
    Strange fits of passion 660
    She dwelt among the untrodden ways 660
    Three years she grew 661
    A slumber did my spirit seal 662
    I travelled among unknown men 662
Michael 663
Resolution and Independence 674
My Heart Leaps Up 678
Sonnets
    Composed upon Westminster Bridge, September 3, 1802 679
    It is a beauteous evening, calm and free 679
    The world is too much with us 679
I Wandered Lonely as a Cloud 680
The Solitary Reaper 681
Ode: Intimations of Immortality 682
Ode to Duty 688
The Prelude
    Book I 690
    Book II 705
The Excursion 716
Notes 719

Samuel Taylor Coleridge (1772–1832) 722
The Aeolian Harp 723
This Lime-Tree Bower My Prison 725
Kubla Khan 727
The Rime of the Ancient Mariner 728
Christabel 747
Frost at Midnight 765

Fears in Solitude   767
The Nightingale   773
Dejection: An Ode   776
The Pains of Sleep   780
To William Wordsworth   781
Metrical Feet   784
Notes   785

George Gordon, Lord Byron (1788–1824)   787
English Bards and Scotch Reviewers   788
Song: Maid of Athens   791
She Walks in Beauty   792
The Destruction of Sennacherib   792
When We Two Parted   793
Epistle to Augusta   794
So We'll Go No More A-roving   798
Childe Harold's Pilgrimage
   Canto III   799
   Canto IV   810
Don Juan, Canto I   813
The Vision of Judgement   826
On This Day I Complete My Thirty-sixth Year   850
Notes   852

Percy Bysshe Shelley (1792–1822)   855
Alastor   856
To Wordsworth   859
Hymn to Intellectual Beauty   859
Ozymandias   862
Julian and Maddalo   862
Sonnet: Lift not the Veil   871
Prometheus Unbound   871
The Mask of Anarchy   875
Love's Philosophy   883
Ode to the West Wind   884
The Sensitive Plant   886
The Cloud   895
To a Skylark   898
The Waning Moon   901
Epipsychidion   901
Adonais   905
To –   919
Song: Rarely, Rarely, Comest Thou   919
To Night   921
With Guitar, to Jane   922
To Jane   924
Notes   925

John Clare (1793–1864) 928
Pastoral Poetry 929
Sabbath Bells 932
The Fallen Elm 933
Badger 935
Gipsies 936
The Peasant Poet 937
I am 937
(John Clare) 938
The Silver Mist 938
Death's Memories 939
Secret Love 939
Love Lives beyond the Tomb 940
Notes 941

John Keats (1795–1821) 942
I Stood Tiptoe . . . 943
Epistle to George Keats 944
Sonnets
   To one who has been long in city pent 945
   On first looking into Chapman's *Homer* 945
   On the grasshopper and the cricket 946
Sleep and Poetry 946
Endymion 948
When I Have Fears . . . 951
Lines on the Mermaid Tavern 952
Hyperion 953
Ode: Bards of Passion and of Mirth 962
The Eve of St Agnes 963
La Belle Dame Sans Merci 974
Ode to Psyche 975
Ode to a Nightingale 977
Ode on a Grecian Urn 979
Ode on Melancholy 981
To Autumn 982
Lamia
   Part I 983
   Part II 992
This Living Hand 1000
Where Be Ye Going 1000
Old Meg 1001
A Song about Myself 1002
Notes 1003

Alfred, Lord Tennyson (1809–92)   1005
  Mariana   1005
  The Lotos-Eaters   1008
  The Lady of Shalott   1012
  Ulysses   1017
  Break, Break, Break   1020
  Songs from *The Princess*
    Sweet and low   1020
    The splendour falls   1020
    Now sleeps the crimson petal   1021
  In Memoriam A.H.H.   1021
  The Eagle   1040
  The Charge of the Light Brigade   1040
  The Brook   1042
  Maud   1043
  The Passing of Arthur   1046
  Merlin and the Gleam   1057
  Crossing the Bar   1061
  Notes   1062

Robert Browning (1812–89)   1064
  Song from *Pippa Passes*   1064
  My Last Duchess   1065
  Soliloquy of the Spanish Cloister   1066
  Porphyria's Lover   1068
  'How They Brought the Good News from Ghent to Aix' (16–)   1070
  The Lost Leader   1072
  Home Thoughts, from Abroad   1073
  The Bishop Orders His Tomb at St Praxed's Church   1074
  Meeting at Night   1077
  Parting at Morning   1077
  Love among the Ruins   1078
  Up at a Villa – Down in the City   1080
  Fra Lippo Lippi   1083
  Love in a Life   1092
  Life in a Love   1092
  The Last Ride Together   1093
  The Patriot   1096
  Memorabilia   1097
  'De Gustibus –'   1098
  Two in the Campagna   1099
  Abt Vogler   1102
  Caliban upon Setebos   1105
  Prospice   1112
  Notes   1113

Matthew Arnold (1822–88)   1115
  Resignation   1116
  Shakespeare   1122
  The Forsaken Merman   1123
  Isolation: To Marguerite   1127
  To Marguerite – Continued   1128
  Youth and Calm   1129
  The Buried Life   1129
  Dover Beach   1132
  Lines Written in Kensington Gardens   1133
  Requiescat   1135
  Stanzas from the Grande Chartreuse   1135
  The Scholar Gipsy   1138
  Philomela   1144
  Thyrsis   1145
  Growing Old   1152
  Notes   1153

List of Abbreviations   1155
A Note on the Text   1157
Versification, Verse Forms and Types of Poetry   1158
Glossary   1161
Index of First Lines   1193

Preface

English poetry is worth studying. Its value can only be fairly assessed by reading deeply and widely the works of the English poets over the centuries. This anthology seeks to provide a good basis for that study.

Firstly it is not a quirky personal anthology of favourite or unusual poems. It has as its centre the works of the major English poets from Chaucer to Matthew Arnold (except Shakespeare: see below); its purpose is to open windows onto that poetry, not onto the anthologiser.

Secondly all the poets chosen are in the mainstream of English poetry; all are covered by any formal educational approach or syllabi, each poet being well and fully represented.

Thirdly, as far as possible, the poems included are complete units (Books 1 and 2, 9 and 10 of 'Paradise Lost', Book 1 of 'The Faerie Queene' for example) rather than disconnected extracts. Occasionally length defeats the best of us (as for example, in Byron's 'Don Juan') but even here an attempt has been made to cover a whole span of the poem, for, to me, it is important that readers may be able to experience the ebb and flow of the total effect rather than be bounced artificially from one chosen titbit to another.

Similar considerations bulked large in my decision to omit Shakespeare. To include a few songs and sonnets would, I felt, duplicate other widely available volumes while at the same time not giving any sense of the majestic sweep of Shakespeare's genius. This could only be done, if at all, by wrenching large extracts from their proper context – the plays. And, on a purely practical level, it seemed not unreasonable to expect that most readers would have ready access to a copy of Shakespeare's complete works.

I have sought to provide an anthology, not only for the occasional dippers-in, but for the true student of English poetry. The gift of writing poetry may not be bestowed upon many of us, but the gift of reading it should be a birthright for us all. It is in the furtherance of that belief that this anthology was undertaken.

Stratford upon Avon
March 1989

B L-E

Geoffrey Chaucer

[c. 1343–1400]

The date of Ch.'s birth is much disputed – it is now believed to be between 1339–1346. In 1357 he was page to Lionel, later Duke of Clarence: 1359 was with Edward III's army in France, was captured and ransomed. He m. Philippa Roet, sister of John of Gaunt's third wife, possibly in 1366. Although she died in 1387, Ch. had Gaunt as his patron for the rest of his life. He held positions at court and often travelled abroad on the King's business – to Genoa, Florence, France and Lombardy. 1374 he was appointed Controller of Customs in the port of London, leasing a house in Aldgate. 1381 he was Knight of the Shire (MP) for Kent and in 1389 became the Clerk of the King's Works, being in charge of buildings and repairs to the Tower of London, Westminster Palace, and eight other royal residences and their gardens. His last post was as deputy forester of the royal forest of Petherton, Somerset. He was granted an annuity of £20 by Edward III which Henry IV, after his coronation, renewed, plus a further annuity of 40 marks and a butt of wine. The last recorded payment of his pension is for 5 June 1400. He was buried in Westminister Abbey where, 1555, a monument was erected to him.

The scheme for *The Canterbury Tales* was worked out probably about 1387 and, although exceeding 17,000 lines in verse and prose, it is incomplete, for only 23 of the 29 pilgrims tell stories, and only 24 tales are told (Ch. himself tells two): had the scheme been completed, there would have been four stories from each pilgrim. The order of the stories varies in different manuscripts and, as a result, the final arrangement of the narrative links and the prologues and epilogues to the stories is uncertain.

From **The Canterbury Tales**

General Prologue

Whan that Aprille with hise shoures° sote°   *showers/sweet*
The droghte of March hath perced to the rote,
And bathed every veyne in swich licour
Of which vertu° engendred is the flour;   *power*
Whan Zephirus eek° with his sweete breeth   *also*
Inspired hath in every holt° and heeth°   *wood/field*
The tendre croppes°, and the yonge sonne   *shoots*
Hath in the Ram[1] his halfe cours yronne°,   *run*
And smale fowles° maken melodye   *birds*
10 That slepen al the night with open iye°   *eye*
   (So priketh hem Nature in hir corages°):   *hearts*
Thanne longen folk to goon on pilgrimages,
And palmeres° for to seken straunge strondes°,   *pilgrims/foreign parts*
To ferne halwes°, couthe° in sondry londes;   *far off shrines/known*
And specially from every shires ende
Of Engelond° to Caunterbury° they wende,   *England/Canterbury*
The holy blisful martir[2] for to seeke,
That hem hath holpen° whan that they were seke°.   *helped/sick*
   Bifel that in that seson on a day,
20 In Southwerk° at the Tabard as I lay   *Southwark*
Redy to wenden° on my pilgrimage   *go*
To Caunterbury with ful devout corage,
At nyght was come into that hostelrye
Wel nine and twenty in a companye,
Of sondry folk, by aventure° yfalle   *by chance*
In felawship°, and pilgrimes were they alle   *companionship*
That toward Caunterbury wolden ryde.
The chambres° and the stables weren wyde,   *bedrooms*
And wel we weren esed° atte beste.   *accommodated*
30 And shortly, whan the sonne° was to reste,   *sun*
So hadde I spoken with hem everichon°   *everyone*
That I was of hir felawship anon°,   *at once*
And made forward° erly for to ryse,   *agreement*
To take oure wey theras° I yow devyse°.   *where/tell*
   But natheles°, whil I have tyme and space,   *nevertheless*
Er° that I ferther in this tale pace°,   *before/go on*
Me thynketh it acordaunt to resoun
To telle yow al the condicioun

Of ech of hem, so as it semed me,
40 And whiche° they weren, and of what degree,° *who/status*
And eek in what array that they were inne;
And at a knyght thanne wol I first biginne.

KNYGHT

A knyght ther was, and that a worthy man,
That fro the tyme that he first bigan
To riden out, he loved chivalrie,
Trouthe and honour, fredom and curteisie.³
Ful worthy° was he in his lordes werre,° *brave/war*
And therto hadde he riden, no man ferre,° *further*
As wel in Cristendom as in hethenesse,° *pagan lands*
50 And evere honoured for his worthynesse.
At Alisaundre°⁴ he was whan it was wonne. *Alexandria*
Ful ofte tyme he hadde the bord bigonne° *been head of table*
Aboven alle nacions in Pruce;° *Prussia*
In Lettow hadde he reysed,° and in Ruce,° *campaigned/Russia*
No Cristen man so ofte of his degree.
In Gernade° at the seege° eek hadde he be *Granada/siege*
Of Algezir,° and riden in Belmarye.° *Algeciras/Benmarin*
At Lyeys° was he, and at Satalye,° *Ayas/Attalia*
Whan they were wonne; and in the Grete See° *Mediterranean*
60 At many a noble armee° hadde he be. *assembly of forces*
At mortal batailles° hadde he been fiftene, *tournaments*
And foughten for oure feith at Tramissene° *Tremessen*
In lystes° thries, and ay slayn his foo.° *jousting areas/foe*
This ilke° worthy knyght hadde been also *same*
Somtyme° with the lord of Palatye° *formerly/Palatia*
Agayn° another hethen in Turkye. *against*
And everemore° he hadde a sovereyn prys,° *always/reputation*
And though that he were worthy, he was wys,° *prudent*
And of his port° as meeke as is a mayde. *behaviour*
70 He nevere yet no vilaynye ne sayde
In al his lyf unto no maner wight.° *anyone of any kind*
He was a verray,° parfit,° gentil knyght. *true/perfect*
But for to tellen yow of his array,° *equipage*
His hors° were gode, but he was nat gay.° *horses/gaudy*
Of fustian° he wered a gypoun° *thick cloth/tunic*
Al bismotered° with his habergeoun,° *rust-stained/coat of mail*
For he was late° ycome from his viage,° *recently/expedition*
And wente for to doon his pilgrimage.

SQUIER°

With hym ther was his sone, a young squier, squire
80 A lovyere, and a lusty° bacheler, *lively*
With lokkes crulle°, as they were layd in presse°. *curled/crimped*
Of twenty yeer of age he was, I gesse.
Of his stature he was of evene° lengthe, *moderate*
And wonderly deliver°, and greet of strengthe. *agile*
And he hadde been somtyme in chyvachie° *cavalry expeditions*
In Flaundres°, in Artoys°, and Picardye°,⁵ *Flanders/Artois/Picardy*
And born hym weel, as of so litel space°, *not been long in service*
In hope to stonden° in his lady grace. *stand well*
Embrouded° was he, as it were a mede° *embroidered/meadow*
Al ful of fresshe flowres, whyte and reede°. *red*
Syngyng he was, or floytinge° al the day. *playing flute or whistling*
He was as fressh as is the month of May.
Short was his gowne, with sleves longe and wyde.
Wel coude he sitte on hors and faire ryde.
He coude songes make, and wel endite°, *write poetry*
Juste° and eek daunce, and weel portraye° and write. *joust/draw*
So hoote he lovede, that by nightertale° *at night*
He slepte namore than dooth a nightingale.
Curteis he was, lowly°, and servysable°, *humble/useful*
100 And carf° biforn his fader at the table.⁶ *carved*

YEMAN° *yeoman*

A yeman hadde he, and servaunts namo° *no more*
At that tyme, for him liste° ride so; *he liked*
And he was clad in cote and hood of grene.
A sheef of pecok arwes, bright and kene°, *sharp*
Under his belt he bar° ful thriftily°, *bore/carefully*
(Wel coude he dresse° his takel° yemanly: *look after/gear*
His arwes drouped noght with fetheres lowe)
And in his hand he baar° a myghty bowe°. *bore/long bow*
A not-heed° hadde he, with a brown visage°. *close-cropped/face*
110 Of wodecraft° wel coude he al the usage. *woodcraft*
Upon his arm he bar a gay bracer°, *guard*
And by his syde, a swerd and a bokeler°, *small shield*
And on that other syde a gay daggere,
Harneised° wel, and sharp as point of spere; *mounted*
A Cristofre° on his brest, of silver shene°, *medal of St Christopher/shining*
An horn he bar, the bawdrik° was of grene. *shoulder strap*
A forster° was he soothly°, as I gesse. *forester/truly*

PRIORESSE

	Ther was also a nonne, a prioresse,	*nun*
	That of hir smiling was ful simple° and coy°	*sincere/shy*
120	Hire gretteste ooth° was but 'by Saint Loy.'	*oath*
	And she was cleped° Madame Eglentyne°	*called/ = sweetbriar*
	Ful wel she song the service divine,	
	Entuned° in hir nose ful semely°	*intoned/properly*
	And Frensh she spak ful faire and fetisly°	*elegantly*
	After the scole° of Stratford-atte-Bowe,⁷	*school*
	For Frensh of Paris was to hir unknowe.	
	At mete° wel ytaught was she withalle°	*meal-times/moreover*
	She leet° no morsel from hir lippes falle,	*let*
	Ne wette hir fingres in hir sauce depe;	
130	Wel coude she carie a morsel, and wel kepe°	*take care*
	That no drope ne fille° upon hir brist°	*fell/breast*
	In curteisie° was set ful muchel hir list°	*polite behaviour/liking*
	Hir overlippe wyped she so clene	
	That in hir coppe° ther was no ferthyng° sene	*cup/morsel*
	Of grece° whan she dronken hadde hir draughte.	*grease*
	Ful semely after hir mete she raughte°	*reached*
	And sikerly° she was of greet desport°	*certainly/bearing*
	And ful plesaunt, and amyable of port°	*behaviour*
	And peyned hire to countrefete cheere°	*manners*
140	Of court, and to been estatlich° of manere,	*dignified*
	And to ben holden digne° of reverence.	*worthy*
	But for to speken of hire conscience,	
	She was so charitable and so pitous°	*full of pity*
	She wolde wepe, if that she sawe a mous	
	Caught in a trappe, if it were deed° or bledde.	*dead*
	Of smale houndes hadde she that she fedde	
	With rosted flesh° or milk and wastel breed°	*meat/fine white bread*
	But sore wepte she, if any of hem were deed,	
	Or if men smoot° it with a yerde° smerte°	*struck/stick/sharply*
150	And al was conscience and tendre herte.	
	Ful semely° hir wimpel° pinched° was,	*becomingly/veil/pleated*
	Hir nose tretys° hir eyen greye as glas,	*well-formed*
	Hir mouth ful smal, and therto° softe and reed°	*also/red*
	But sikerly she hadde a fair forheed—	
	It was almoost a spanne brood, I trowe°	*guess*
	For, hardily° she was nat undergrowe.	*certainly*
	Ful fetis° was hir cloke, as I was war°	*elegant/aware*
	Of smal coral, aboute hire arm she bar	

A paire of bedes, gauded[8] al with grene,   *rosary*
160 And theron heng° a brooch of gold ful shene,   *hung/shining*
On which ther was first write a crowned A,
And after, *Amor vincit omnia.*[9]

NONNE AND III PREESTES

Another nonne with hir hadde she
That was hir chapeleyne, and preestes thre.   *chaplain*

MONK

A monk ther was, a fair for the maistrie,[10]
An outridere; that lovede venerie,   *hunting*
A manly man, to been an abbot able.
Ful many a deyntee° hors hadde he in stable,   *fine*
And whan he rood, men myghte his brydel heere   *rode*
170 Gynglen° in a whistlynge wynd als cleere,   *jingle*
And eek as loude, as dooth the chapel belle
Ther as° this lord was kepere[11] of the celle.   *where*
The reule° of Saint Maure° or of Saint Beneit,   *rule/Maurus/Benedict*
Bycause that it was old, and somdel streit°—   *somewhat strict*
This ilke° monk leet olde thynges pace,   *same/go their way*
And heeld after the newe world the space.   *stuck to the new ways*
He yaf nat of that text a pulled° hen   *plucked*
That seith that hunters beth nat holy men,[12]
Ne that a monk, whan he is reccheles,   *negligent*
180 Is likned til° a fissh that is waterlees.   *to*
This is to seyn, a monk out of his cloystre—   *say*
But thilke° text heeld he nat worth an oystre   *that same*
And I seyde his opinioun was good.
What sholde he studie, and make hymselven wood,   *mad*
Upon a book in cloystre alwey to poure,
Or swynken° with his handes, and laboure,   *work*
As Austyn° bit?°[12] How shal the world be served?   *St Augustine/bids*
Lat Austyn have his swink to him reserved!
Therfore, he was a pricasour° aright: *hard rider*
190 Grehoundes° he hadde as swift as fowel° in flight;   *greyhounds/birds*
Of priking° and of hunting for the hare   *tracking*
Was al his lust;° for no cost wolde he spare.   *pleasure*
I seigh° his sleves purfiled° at the hond   *saw/trimmed*
With grys, and that the fyneste of a lond.   *fur*
And for to festne° his hood under his chin,   *fasten*
He hadde of gold wroght a ful curious° pin   *elaborate*
A love-knotte in the gretter° ende ther was.   *larger*
His heed was balled, that shoon as any glas,   *bald*

And eek his face, as it hadde been anoint.
200 He was a lord ful fat, and in good poynt;°   condition
Hise eyen stepe,° and rollynge in his heed,   prominent
That stemed as a forneys of a leed;[13]
His bootes souple, his hors in greet estat.°   condition
Now certeinly he was a fair prelat.°   prelate
He was nat pale, as a forpyned goost.°   wasted-away ghost
A fat swan loved he best of any roost,°   roast
His palfrey° was as brown as is a berye.   saddle-horse

FRERE°   friar

A frere ther was, a wantown and a merye,
A limitour, a ful solempne° man.   pompous
210 In alle the ordres foure[14] is noon that can°   knows
So muche of daliaunce° and fair langage.   flirtation
He hadde maad ful many a mariage
Of yonge wommen at his owne cost.[15]
Unto his ordre he was a noble post.°   support
And wel biloved and famulier° was he   intimate
With frankeleyns° overal° in his contree,°   wealthy landowners/throughout/area
And with worthy wommen of the toun—
For he had power of confessioun,
As seyde hymself, more than a curat,°   parish priest
220 For of his ordre he was licenciat.°   licensed by his order
Ful swetely herde he confessioun,
And plesaunt was his absolucioun.
He was an esy man to yeve° penaunce   give
Ther as° he wiste° to have a good pitaunce.°   where/expected/donation
For unto a poure order for to yive
Is signe that a man is wel yshrive;°   shriven
For if he yaf,° he dorste make avaunt°   gave/dared boast
He wiste° that a man was repentaunt;   knew
For many a man so hard is of his herte,
230 He may nat wepe, althogh hym sore smerte.°   is very unhappy
Therefore, in stede of wepynge and preyeres,   prayers
Men moot° yeve silver to the povre freres.   may
His tipet° was ay farsed° ful of knyves   long sleeve/stuffed
And pynnes, for to yeven faire wyves.
And certeinly, he hadde a mery note;
Wel coude he singe, and pleyen on a rote;°   fiddle
Of yeddinges° he bar utterly the pris.°   ballads/prize
His nekke whit was as the flour-de-lys.°   lily
Therto, he strong was as a champioun.[16]
240 He knew the tavernes wel in every toun,

And everich hostiler° and tappestere	*innkeeper*
Bet than a lazar or a beggestere;°	*beggar*
For unto swich a worthy man as he	
Acorded nat, as by his facultee,°	*in view of his profession*
To have with sike° lazars aqueyntaunce.	*sick*
It is nat honeste,° it may nat avaunce;°	*it does no good/profit*
For to deelen with no swich poraille,°	*poor people*
But al with riche, and sellers of vitaille.°	*foodstuffs*
And overal ther as° profit sholde arise,	*wherever*
250 Curteis he was, and lowely° of servyse.	*humble*
Ther nas no man nowher so vertuous.°	*capable*
He was the beste beggere in his hous;°	*friary*
And yaf a certeyn ferme for the graunt[17]	
Noon of his bretheren cam ther in his haunt.	
For thogh a widwe° hadde noght a sho,°	*widow/shoe*
So plesaunt was his 'In principio,'[18]	
Yet wolde he have a ferthyng er he wente.	*farthing*
His purchas was wel bettre than his rente.[19]	
And rage° he coude, as it were right a whelp.°	*frolic/puppy*
260 In love-dayes[20] ther coude he muchel° help,	*greatly*
For ther he was nat lyk a cloisterer°	*member of a confined order*
With a thredbare cope,° as is a poure scoler,	*cloak*
But he was lyk a maister, or a pope.	
Of double worsted° was his semicope;°	*heavy woollen cloth/short cloak*
That rounded as a belle out of the presse.°	*mould*
Somwhat he lipsed, for his wantownesse,°	*affectation*
To make his English sweete upon his tonge;	
And in his harping, whan that he hadde songe,	
Hise eyen twynkled in his heed aryght,°	*finely*
270 As doon the sterres° in the frosty nyght.	*stars*
This worthy limitour was cleped° Huberd.	*called*

MARCHANT

A marchant was ther, with a forked berd,°	*beard*
In mottelee,° and hye on horse he sat,	*many coloured cloth*
Upon his heed a Flaundrish° bevere° hat,	*Flemish/beaver-fur*
His bootes clasped faire and fetisly.°	*elegantly*
His resons° he spak ful solempnely,°	*opinions/pompously*
Souninge° alway th'encrees of his winning.	*proclaiming*
He wolde the see° were kept° for any thing	*sea/patrolled*
Bitwixe Middelburgh° and Orewelle.°	*Middleburg/Orwell Haven*
280 Wel coude he in eschaunge sheeldes° selle.[21]	*French (écus) coins*
This worthy man ful wel his wit bisette.°	*employed*
Ther wiste° no wight that he was in dette,	*knew*

So estatly° was he of his governaunce,°   *impressive/dealings*
With his bargaynes, and with his chevisaunce.°   *profitable dealings*
Forsothe,° he was a worthy man withalle;   *in truth*
But sooth to seyn, I noot how men hym calle.

CLERK[22] OF OXENFORD

A clerk ther was of Oxenford° also,   *Oxford*
That unto logik[23] hadde longe ygo.
As leene was his hors as is a rake,
290 And he nas nat° right fat I undertake,   *was not*
But looked holwe, and therto sobrely.°   *grave*
Ful thredbare was his overeste courtepy,°   *outer short jacket*
For he hadde geten hym yet no benefice,°   *living*
Ne was so worldly for to have office.°   *a secular post*
For hym was lever° have at his beddes heed   *preferred*
Twenty bookes, clad in blak or reed,
Of Aristotle and his philosophie,
Than robes riche, or fithele,° or gay sautrie.°   *fiddle/psaltery*
But al be° that he was a philosophre,[24]   *despite*
300 Yet hadde he but litel gold in cofre.°   *coffer*
But al that he mighte of his freendes hente,°   *get*
On bookes and on lernynge he it spente,
And bisily gan for the soules preye°   *pray*
Of hem that yaf° hym wherwith to scoleye.°   *gave/study*
Of studie took he most cure° and most heede.   *care*
Noght o° word spak he more than was neede,   *one*
And that was seyd in forme and reverence,°   *with decorum and respect*
And short, and quyk,° and ful of hy sentence.°   *lively/moral significance*
Souninge° in moral vertu was his speche,   *resounding*
310 And gladly wolde he lerne and gladly teche.

SERGEANT OF LAWE°   *lawyer of high rank*

A sergeant of the lawe, war° and wys,°   *wary/prudent*
That often hadde been at the Parvys[25]
Ther was also, ful riche of excellence.
Discreet he was, and of greet reverence,°   *highly respected*
He semed swich, his wordes weren so wise.
Justice he was ful often in assise°   *assize courts*
By patente,° and by pleyn° commissioun.   *royal warrant/full*
For his science,° and for his heigh renoun,   *knowledge*
Of fees and robes hadde he many oon.
320 So greet a purchasour° was nowher noon: *speculator in land*
Al was fee simple° to hym in effect;   *owned outright*
His purchasing mighte nat been infect.°   *proved invalid*

Nowher so bisy a man as he ther nas,   *was not*
And yet he semed bisier than he was.
In termes° hadde he caas° and doomes° alle   *by heart/cases/judgements*
That from the tyme of Kyng William²⁶ were yfalle°   *had occurred*
Therto, he coude endite° and make a thing°   *compose/draw up a deed*
Ther coude no wight pinche° at his writyng;   *complain*
And every statut coude° he pleyn° by rote.   *know/wholly*
330 He rood but hoomly° in a medlee° cote   *unpretentiously/of mixed colour*
Girt with ceint° of silk, with barres° smale.   *belt/stripes*
Of his array telle I no lenger tale.

FRANKELEYN

A frankeleyn° was in his companye,   *wealthy landowner*
Whit was his beerd, as is the dayesye°   *daisy*
Of his complexioun he was sangwyn.²⁷
Wel loved he by the morwe° a sop in wyn;²⁸   *in the morning*
To liven in delit° was evere his wone°   *sensuous pleasure/wont*
For he was Epicurus owne sone,
That heeld opinioun that pleyn° delit   *full*
340 Was verraily° felicitee parfit°   *truly/perfect*
An housholdere, and that a greet° was he;   *great one*
Saint Julian he was in his contree°   *district*
His breed, his ale, was alweys after oon;°   *of the same high quality*
A bettre envyned° man was nowher noon;   *stocked with wine*
Withoute bake mete was never his hous
Of fish and flesh, and that so plentevous,
It snewed° in his hous of mete° and drynke,   *snowed/food*
Of alle deyntees° that men coude thynke.   *delicacies*
After° the sondry sesons of the yeer,   *according to*
350 So chaunged he his mete° and his soper.   *dinner*
Ful many a fat partrich hadde he in muwe°   *coop*
And many a breem° and many a luce° in stewe°   *carp/pike/fishpond*
Wo was his cook but if° his sauce were   *unless*
Poynaunt° and sharp, and redy al his geere.   *piquant*
His table dormant in his halle° alway   *living area*
Stood redy covered° al the longe day.   *set up*
At sessions° ther was he lord and sire;   *i.e. of the justices of the peace*
Ful ofte tyme he was knyght of the shire°   *local MP*
An anlas° and a gipser° al of silk   *dagger/purse*
360 Heeng at his girdel° whit as morne° milk.   *belt/morning*
A shirreve° hadde he been, and a countour°   *sheriff/auditor*
Was nowher swich a worthy vavasour°   *member of landed gentry*

HABERDASSHERE, CARPENTER, WEBBE, DYERE, TAPICER

An haberdasshere and a carpenter
A webbe,° a dyere and a tapycer,°— *weaver/tapestry-maker*
And they were clothed alle in o lyveree° *livery*
Of a solempne and a greet fraternitee.°²⁹ *guild*
Ful fresh and newe hir geere° apiked° was; *equipment/spick and span*
Hir knives were ychaped° noght with bras *mounted*
370 But al with silver; wroght ful clene and weel
Hire girdles and hir pouches everydeel.° *every part*
Wel semed ech of hem a fair burgeys° *burgher*
To sitten in a yeldhalle,° on a deÿs.° *guildhall/dais*
Everich,° for the wisdom that he can, *each*
Was shaply° for to been an alderman. *fit*
For catel° hadde they ynogh and rente,° *goods/income*
And eek hir wyves wolde it wel assente;
And elles certeyn were they to blame.
It is ful fair to been yclept° 'Madame', *addressed*
And goon to vigiliis° al bifore, *vigils*
380 And have a mantel royalliche ybore.

COOK

A cook they hadde with hem for the nones° *for the occasion*
To boille the chiknes with the marybones,° *marrow bones*
And poudre-marchant tart, and galyngale.° *i.e. spicy and sweet flavourings*
Wel coude he knowe° a draughte of Londoun° ale. *recognize/London*
He coude roste and sethe,° and broille and frye, *boil*
Maken mortreux,° and wel bake a pye. *stews*
But greet harm was it, as it thoughte° me, *I thought*
That on his shine° a mormal° hadde he. *shin/ulcer*
For blankmanger,° that made he with the beste. *savoury dish of chicken*

SHIPMAN

390 A shipman was ther, wonynge° fer by° weste; *living/in the*
For aught I woot,° he was of Dertemothe.° *know/Dartmouth*
He rood upon a rouncy,° as he couthe,° *nag/as best he could*
In a gowne of falding° to the knee. *coarse wool*
A daggere hangynge on a laas° hadde he *strap*
Aboute his nekke, under his arm adoun.
The hote somer hadde mad his hewe° al brown. *appearance*
And certeinly he was a good felawe.
Ful many a draughte of wyn had he ydrawe° *taken*

Fro Burdeux-ward, whil that the chapman° sleep.   *merchant*
400 Of nyce° conscience took he no keep°   *fastidious/heed*
If that he faught, and hadde the hyer° hond,   *upper*
By water he sente hem hoom to every lond.³⁰
But of his craft, to rekene wel his tydes,
His stremes,° and his daungers° hym bisides,°   *currents/hazards/around him*
His herberwe,° and his moone, his lodemenage,°   *anchorage/navigation*
Ther nas noon swich from Hull to Cartage°   *Cartagena*
Hardy he was and wys° to undertake.   *prudent*
With many a tempest hadde his berd been shake.
He knew wel alle the havenes,° as they were,   *harbours*
410 Fro Gootlond° to the Cape of Fynystere,°   *Gotland/Finisterre*
And every cryke° in Britaigne° and in Spayne.   *creek/Brittany*
His barge ycleped was the Maudelayne°   *Magdalene*

DOCTOUR OF PHISIK
With us ther was a doctour of phisik°   *medicine*
In al this world ne was ther noon hym lik,
To speke of phisik and of surgerye.
For he was grounded in astronomye,°   *astrology*
He kepte° his pacient a ful greet deel   *treated*
In houres, by his magyk natureel.³¹
Wel coude he fortunen the ascendent°   *assess the best time*
420 Of hise ymages for his pacient.
He knew the cause of everich° maladye,   *every*
Were it of hoot, or coold, or moyste, or drye,
And where they engendred, and of what humour.
He was a verray, parfit practisour°   *truly, perfect practitioner*
The cause yknowe,° and of his harm° the roote,   *known/illness*
Anon he yaf the sike man his boote°   *remedy*
Ful redy hadde he hise apothecaries
To sende hym drogges° and his letuaries,°   *drugs/ointments*
For ech of hem made other for to wynne,°   *brought returns for*
430 Hir frendshipe nas nat newe to bigynne.
Wel knew he the olde Esculapius,³²
And Deïscorides, and eek Rufus,
Olde Ypocras, Haly, and Galien,
Serapion, Razis, and Avicen,
Averrois, Damascien, and Constantyn,
Bernard, and Gatesden, and Gilbertyn.
Of his diete mesurable° was he,   *moderate*
For it was of no superfluitee,
But of greet norissing,° and digestible.   *nourishment*
440 His studie was but litel on the Bible°

In sangwin° and in pers° he clad was al,   *scarlet|Persian blue*
Lyned with taffata and with sendal;°   *silk*
And yet he was but esy of dispence;°   *expenditure*
He kepte that he wan in pestilence.°   *in plague time*
For gold in phisik is a cordial,°   *heart-warmer*
Therfore he lovede gold in special.

THE WYF OF BATHE

A good-wyf° was ther, of biside° Bathe,   *a woman of means|from near Bath*
But she was somdel° deef and that was scathe.°   *somewhat|pity*
Of clooth-makyng she hadde swich an haunt,°   *skill*
450 She passed° hem of Ypres and of Gaunt.°³³   *surpassed|Ghent*
In al the parisshe wif ne was ther noon
That to the offring³⁴ bifore hire sholde goon;   *go*
And if ther dide, certeyn so wrooth° was she   *angry*
That she was out of alle charitee.
Hir coverchiefs° ful fyne were of ground;°   *head-coverings|in texture*
I dorste swere they weyeden° ten pound   *weighed*
That on a Sonday were upon hir heed.
Hir hosen weren of fyn scarlet reed,   *red*
Ful streite yteyd,° and shoes ful moiste° and newe.   *tightly laced|soft*
460 Bold was hir face, and fair and reed° of hewe.   *red*
She was a worthy womman al hir lyve.
Housbondes at chirche dore³⁵ she hadde fyve,
Withouten other companye in youthe—
But therof nedeth nat to speke as nowthe.°   *just now*
And thries° hadde she been at Jerusalem;³⁶   *thrice*
She hadde passed many a straunge° strem;   *foreign*
At Rome she hadde been, and at Boloigne,°   *Boulogne*
In Galice° at Seint Jame, and at Coloigne;   *Galicia|Cologne*
She coude° much of wandrynge by the weye°;   *knew|straying from the path*
470 Gat-tothed° was she, soothly° for to seye.   *set wide apart|truly*
Upon an amblere° esily she sat,   *comfortable horse*
Ywimpled° wel, and on hir heed an hat   *veiled*
As brood is a bokeler° or a targe;°   *small round shields*
A foot-mantel° aboute hir hipes large,   *riding skirt*
And on hir feet a paire of spores° sharpe.   *spurs*
In felawschip wel coude she laughe and carpe.°   *chat*
Of remedies of love she knew per chaunce,
For she coude of that art the olde daunce.°   *all the tricks*

PERSOUN OF A TOUN

A good man was ther of religioun,
480 And was a poure persoun° of a toun,   *parson*

But riche he was of holy thoght and werk.
He was also a lerned man, a clerk,°   *cleric*
That Cristes gospel trewely° wolde preehe   *faithfully*
Hise parisshens° devoutly wolde he teche.   *parishioners*
Benigne he was, and wonder° diligent,   *wonderfully*
And in adversitee ful pacient.
And swich° he was ypreved° ofte sithes.°   *such/proved/times*
Ful looth were hym to cursen° for hise tithes,   *excommunicate*
But rather wolde he yeven,° out of doute,°   *give/surely*
490 Unto his poure parisshens aboute
Of his offring,[37] and eek of his substaunce.°   *property*
He coude in litel thyng have suffisaunce.°   *satisfaction*
Wyd was his parisshe, and houses fer asonder,
But he ne lefte° nat, for reyn ne thonder,   *neglected*
In siknesse nor in meschief,° to visite   *misfortune*
The ferreste° in his parisshe, muche and lite,°   *farthest/great and small*
Upon his feet, and in his hand a staf.
This noble ensample° to his sheep° he yaf,°   *example/flock/gave*
That first he wroghte,° and afterward he taughte.   *did*
500 Out of the gospel he tho° wordes caughte,°   *those/took*
And this figure he added eek therto,
That if gold ruste, what shal iren do?
For if a preest be foul, on whom we truste,
No wonder is a lewed° man to ruste.   *simple*
And shame it is, if a preest take keep,°   *heed*
A shiten° shepherde and a clene sheep.   *befouled*
Wel oghte a preest ensample for to yive,
By his clennesse, how that his sheep sholde live.
He sette nat his benefice to hyre[38]
510 And leet° his sheep encombred in the myre°   *leave/mire*
And ran to Londoun, unto Saint Poules,°   *St Paul's*
To seken hym a chaunterie[39] for soules,
Or with a bretherhed[40] to been withholde;
But dwelte at hoom, and kepte wel his folde,
So that the wolf ne made it nat miscarie.
He was a shepherde, and no mercenarie.
And though he holy were, and vertuous,
He was to synful men nat despitous,°   *contemptuous*
Ne of his speche daungerous° ne digne,°   *scornful/haughty*
520 But in his teching discreet and benygne.
To drawen folk to hevene by fairnesse,
By good ensample, was his bisynesse:
But it were° any persone obstinat,   *if there were*
What so he were, of heigh or lowe estat,

Hym wolde he snybben° sharply for the nonys.°   *rebuke/at any time*
A bettre preest I trowe° that nowher noon ys.   *believe*
He waited° after no pompe and reverence,°   *expected/deference*
·Ne maked hym a spiced° conscience.   *over-fastidious*
But Cristes loore° and hise apostles twelve   *teaching*
530° He taughte, but first he folwed it himselve.

PLOWMAN

With hym ther was a plowman, was his brother,
That hadde ylad° of dong ful many a fother.°   *carried/load*
A trewe swinker° and a good was he,   *toiler*
Lyvynge in pees° and parfit charitee.   *peace*
God loved he best with al his hole° herte   *whole*
At alle tymes, thogh hym gamed or smerte,° *made him happy or miserable*
And thanne his neighebore right as himselve.
He wolde thresshe, and therto dyke° and delve,   *dig ditches*
For Cristes sake, for every poure wight,
540 Withouten hire, if it lay in his might.
Hise tithes payed he ful faire and wel,
Bothe of his propre swink° and his catel.°   *own work/possessions*
In a tabard° he rood upon a mere.°   *short coat/mare*

Ther was also a reve and a millere,
A somnour, and a pardoner also,
A maunciple,⁴¹ and myself—ther were namo.°   *no more*

MILLER

The miller was a stout carl° for the nones.   *fellow*
Ful big he was of brawn, and eek of bones.
That proved wel, for overal ther° he cam,   *wherever*
550 At wrastling he wolde have alwey the ram.°   *i.e. as prize*
He was short-sholdred,° brood,° a thikke knarre.° *stocky/broad/thickhead*
Ther was no dore that he ne wolde heve of harre,° *hinges*
Or breke it at a renning° with his heed.°   *running/head*
His berd as any sowe or fox was reed,°⁴²   *red*
And therto brood, as though it were a spade.
Upon the cop° right of his nose he hade   *ridge*
A werte,° and theron stood a tuft of herys,°   *wart/hairs*
Reed as the bristles of a sowes erys.°   *ears*
Hise nosethirles° blake were and wyde.   *nostrils*
560 A swerd and a bokeler° bar he by his syde.   *small shield*
His mouth as greet was as a greet forneys.°   *furnace*
He was a janglere,° and a goliardeys,° *chatterer/teller of (dirty) jokes*
And that was moost of sinne and harlotries.°   *obscenities*

Wel coude he stelen corn, and tollen thries;[43]
And yet he hadde a thombe of gold, pardee.
A whit cote and a blew hood wered° he.   *wore*
A baggepipe wel coude he blowe and sowne,
And therwithal he broghte° us out of towne.   *with it he led*

MAUNCIPLE

A gentil maunciple was ther of a Temple,°   *an Inn of Court*
570 Of which achatours° mighte take exemple   *buyers*
For to be wise° in bying of vitaille,°   *prudent/victuals*
For whether that he payde, or took by taille,°   *on credit*
Algate° he wayted° so in his achat°   *always/watched/buying*
That he was ay biforn,° and in good staat.°   *ahead/financial position*
Now is nat that of God a ful fair grace
That swich a lewed° mannes wit shal pace°   *ignorant/surpass*
The wisdom of an heep of lerned men?
Of maistres° hadde he mo than thries ten   *masters*
That weren of lawe expert and curious,°   *cunning*
580 Of whiche ther weren a doseyne° in that hous   *dozen*
Worthy to been stiwardes of rente° and lond   *income*
Of any lord that is in Engelond,
To make hym lyve by his propre good;°   *own possessions*
In honour dettelees, but° he were wood,°   *unless/mad*
Or lyve as scarsly° as hym list desire;°   *frugally/it pleased him*
And able for to helpen al a shire
In any cas° that mighte falle° or happe;°   *event/befall*
And yet this manciple sette hir aller cappe.°   *made fools of them all*

REVE

The reve was a sclendre° colerik° man.   *slim/prone to anger*
590 His berd was shave as ny as ever he can;
His heer° was by his eres round yshorn;   *hair*
His top was dokked° lyk a preest biforn.   *cropped*
Ful longe were his legges, and ful lene,
Ylyk° a staf, ther was no calf ysene.°   *like/visible*
Wel coude he kepe a gerner° and a bynne;   *granary*
Ther was noon auditour coude of hym wynne.°   *get the better of*
Wel wiste° he by the droghte and by the reyn°   *knew/rain*
The yeldynge of his seed and of his greyn.°   *grain*
His lordes sheep, his neet,° his dayerye;°   *cattle/dairy*
600 His swyn, his hors, his stoor,° and his pultrye   *produce*
Was hoolly° in this reves governyng,   *wholly*
And by his covenant° yaf° the rekenyng,   *contract/gave*
Sin° that his lord was twenty yeer of age.   *since*

Ther coude no man bringe° hym in arrerage.°   *convict/being in arrears*
Ther nas baillif, ne herde,° nor other hyne,°   *shepherd/farm worker*
That he ne knew his sleighte° and his covyne.°   *cunning/deceit*
They were adrad° of hym as of the deeth.°   *afraid/death*
His wonyng° was ful faire upon an heeth;°   *house/common*
With grene trees shadwed was his place.
610 He coude° bettre than his lord purchace:°   *knew how to/buy*
Ful riche he was astored,° prively.°   *stocked up/secretly*
His lord wel coude he plesen subtilly,
To yeve and lene° hym of his owne⁴⁴ good,°   *lend/property*
And have a thank, and yet a cote and hood.
In youthe he hadde lerned a good mister:°   *trade(mystery)*
He was a wel good wrighte,° a carpenter.   *craftsman*
This reve sat upon a ful good stot,°   *a Norfolk breed of horse*
That was al pomely° grey, and highte° Scot.   *dapple/called*
A long surcote° of pers° upon he hade,°   *overcoat/blue/wore*
620 And by his syde he bar a rusty blade.
Of Northfolk° was this reve of which I telle,   *Norfolk*
Biside a toun men clepen Baldeswelle.
Tukked° he was, as is a frere,° aboute.   *tucked in by a belt/friar*
And ever he rood the hindreste° of oure route.°   *last/group*

SOMNOUR

A somnour was ther with us in that place,
That hadde a fyr-reed cherubinnes⁴⁵ face,
For sawcefleem° he was, with eyen narwe.   *pimply*
As hoot he was, and lecherous⁴⁶ as a sparwe,°   *sparrow*
With scalled° browes blake and piled° berd   *scabby/patchy*
630 Of his visage children were aferd.°   *afraid*
Ther nas quiksilver, litarge, ne brimstoon,
Boras, ceruce, ne oille of tartre noon,⁴⁷
Ne oynement that wolde clense and byte,
That hym myghte helpen of his whelkes° white,   *blotches*
Nor of the knobbes° sittinge on his chekes.   *lumps*
Wel loved he garleek, oynons, and eek lekes,
And for to drinken strong wyn, reed as blood.
Thanne wolde he speke and crie as he were wood.°   *mad*
And whan that he wel dronken hadde the wyn,
640 Than wolde he speke no word but Latyn.
A fewe termes hadde he, two or three,
That he had lerned out of som decree—
No wonder is, he herde it al the day;
And eek ye knowen wel how that a jay°   *jackdaw*
Can clepen 'Watte'⁴⁸ as wel as kan the Pope.

But whoso coude in other thyng hym grope°   examine
Thanne hadde he spent al his philosophie;°   learning
Ay° 'Questio quid iuris,'° wolde he crie.   always/I ask what is the law
He was a gentil harlot° and a kinde;   rascal
650 A bettre felawe sholde men noght fynde:
He wolde suffre° for a quart of wyn   permit
A good felawe to have his concubyn
A twelf monthe, and excuse hym atte fulle°.   completely
Ful prively a fynch eek coude he pulle.⁴⁹
And if he fond° owher° a good felawe,   found/anywhere
He wolde techen hym to have noon awe,°   fear
In swich° cas, of the erchedekenes curs°,   such/archdeacon's excommunication
But if° a mannes soule were in his purs;   unless
For in his purs he sholde ypunisshed be.
660 'Purs is the erchedekenes Helle,' seyde he.
But wel I woot° he lyed right indede;°   knew/really
Of cursing oghte ech gilty man him drede,
For curs wol slee° right as assoilling° saveth,   slay/absolution
And also war° hym of a Significavit.⁵⁰   beware
In daunger° hadde he at his owene gise°   in his power/disposal
The yonge girles of the diocise,
And knew hir conseil°, and was al hir reed°.   secrets/advisor
A gerland° hadde he set upon his heed   garland
As greet as it were for an ale-stake°.   inn sign
670 A bokeler° hadde he maad hym of a cake°.   small shield/loaf of bread

PARDONER

With hym ther was a gentil pardoner
Of Rouncivale, his freend and his compeer°,   companion
That streight was comen fro the court of Rome.
Ful loude he song 'Com hider, love, to me!'
This somnour bar to hym a stif° burdoun;°   strong/refrain or accompaniment
Was nevere tromp° of half so greet a soun.   trumpet
This pardoner hadde heer as yelow as wex,
But smothe it heng, as dooth a strike of flex;°   hank of flax
By ounces°, henge° hise lokkes that he hadde,   thin strands/hung
680 And therwith he hise shuldres overspradde;
But thinne it lay, by colpons°, oon and oon.   in rats' tails
But hood, for jolitee, ywered° he noon,   wore
For it was trussed up in his walet°.   pack
Hym thoughte he rood al of the newe jet;°   fashion
Dischevelee°, save his cappe, he rood al bare.   hair hanging loose
Swiche glaringe° eyen hadde he as an hare.   staring
A vernicle° hadde he sowed upon his cappe.   St Veronica badge

His walet lay biforn hym in his lappe,
Bretful° of pardoun, come from Rome al hoot.   *brimful*
690 A voys he hadde as smal as hath a goot.   *goat*
No berd hadde he, ne nevere sholde have;
As smothe it was as it were late yshave.
I trowe° he were a geldyng or a mare.   *believe*
But of his craft, fro Berwyk° into Ware,   *Berwick*
Ne was ther swich another pardoner.
For in his male° he hadde a pilwe-beer,°   *bag/pillow-case*
Which that he seyde was Oure Lady veyl.
He seyde he hadde a gobet of the seyl°   *sail*
That Seïnt Peter hadde, whan that he wente
700 Upon the see,° til Jesu Crist hym hente.°   *sea/called*
He hadde a croys of latoun,° ful of stones,   *cross of brassy metal*
And in a glas he hadde pigges bones.
But with thise relikes, whan that he fond°   *found*
A poure persoun° dwellynge upon lond,°   *parson/upcountry*
Upon a day he gat° hym more moneye   *got*
Than that the persoun gat in monthes tweye.
And thus, with feyned° flatery and japes,°   *false/jokes*
He made the persoun and the peple his apes.°   *dupes*
But trewely to tellen atte laste,
710 He was in chirche a noble ecclesiaste;
Wel coude he rede a lessoun or a storie,°   *Bible story*
But alderbest° he song an offertorie;⁵¹   *best of all*
For wel he wiste, whan that song was songe,
He moste° preche and wel affile° his tonge   *must/sharpen*
To wynne silver, as he ful wel coude;
Therfore he song so meriely° and loude.   *more merrily*

    Now have I told you shortly in a clause°   *small space*
Th'estat, th'array, the nombre, and eek the cause
Why that assembled was this companye
720 In Southwerk, at this gentil hostelrye
That highte the Tabard, faste° by the Belle.   *near*
But now is tyme to yow for to telle
How that we baren° us that ilke° nyght,   *what we did/same*
Whan we were in that hostelrie alight;
And after wol I telle of oure viage,°   *journey*
And al the remenaunt° of oure pilgrimage.   *rest*
    But first I pray yow, of youre curteisye,
That ye n'arette° it nat my vileinye,°   *attribute/lack of decorum*
Thogh that I pleynly speke in this matere,
730 To telle yow hir wordes and hir cheere;°   *behaviour*

Ne thogh I speke hir wordes proprely.° *exactly*
For this ye knowen also° wel as I, *as*
Whoso shal telle a tale after a man,
He moot reherce° as ny° as evere he kan *repeat/closely*
Everich° a word, if it be in his charge,° *every/responsibility*
Al° speke he never so rudeliche° or large,° *even though/roughly/broadly*
Or ellis° he moot° telle his tale untrewe, *else/will*
Or seyne° thyng, or fynde wordes newe. *falsify*
He may nat spare, althogh he were his brother;
740 He moot as wel seye o word as another.
Crist spak hymself ful brode° in holy writ, *plainly*
And wel ye woot no vileynye is it.
Eek Plato[52] seïth, whoso can hym rede,° *read*
'The wordes mote be cosin to the dede.'
Also I prey yow to foryeve° it me, *forgive*
Al° have I nat set folk in hir degree *although*
Heere in this tale, as that they sholde stonde.
My wit is short, ye may wel understonde.
    Greet chere made oure host° us everichon, *i.e. Harry Bailly, landlord of / the Tabard*
750 And to the soper sette he us anon.° *straight away*
He served us with vitaille° at the beste. *food and drink*
Strong was the wyn, and wel to drynke us leste.° *it pleased*

    A semely man oure hoste was withalle
For to han been a marchal° in an halle. *master of ceremonies*
A large man he was, with eyen stepe°— *prominent*
A fairer burgeys° was ther noon in Chepe°— *burgher/Cheapside*
Boold of his speche, and wys, and wel ytaught,
And of manhod hym lakkede right naught.
Eek therto he was right a mery man,
760 And after soper pleyen° he bigan, *divert*
And spak of mirthe, amonges othere thynges—
Whan that we hadde maad oure rekeninges°— *paid our bills*
And seyde thus: 'Now, lordinges, trewely,
Ye been to me right welcome, hertely.° *truly*
For by my trouthe, if that I shal nat lye,
I saugh nat this yeer so mery a companye
At ones in this herberwe° as is now. *inn*
Fayn° wolde I doon yow mirthe, wiste° I how. *gladly/knew*
And of a mirthe I am right now bithoght,
770 To doon yow ese,° and it shal coste noght. *pleasure*
    Ye goon to Caunterbury—God yow speede!
The blisful martir quite° yow youre mede!° *requite/reward*
And wel I woot, as ye goon by the weye,

Ye shapen° yow to talen° and to pleye;   *intend/gossip*
For trewely, confort° ne myrthe is noon   *comfort*
To ride by the weye doumb as the stoon.°   *stone*
And therfore wol I maken yow disport,
As I seyde erst, and doon yow som confort.   *before*
And if yow liketh alle, by oon assent,
780 For to stonden at° my jugement,   *by*
And for to werken° as I shal yow seye,   *do*
Tomorwe, whan ye riden by the weye,
Now, by my fader° soule that is deed,   *father's*
But if° ye be merye, I wol yeve yow myn heed.°   *unless/head*
Hold up youre hond, withouten more speche.'°

     Oure counseil was nat longe for to seche.°   *seek*
Us thoughte it was noght worth to make it wys,   *a fuss about it*
And graunted hym, withouten moore avys,   *deliberation*
And bad hym seye his verdit° as hym leste.   *verdict*
790 'Lordinges,' quod he, 'now herkneth for the beste;
But taak it nought, I prey yow, in desdeyn.°   *disdain*
This is the poynt, to speken short and pleyn,
That ech of yow, to shorte° with oure weye   *shorten*
In this viage,° shal telle tales tweye°   *journey/two*
To Caunterbury-ward, I mene it so,
And homward, he shal tellen othere two,
Of aventures that whilom° han bifalle.   *once upon a time*
And which of yow that bereth hym best of alle,
800 That is to seyn, that telleth in this cas
Tales of best sentence° and moost solas,   *meaning/delight*
Shal have a soper at oure aller° cost   *of all of us*
Heere in this place, sitting by this post,
Whan that we come agayn fro Caunterbury.
And for to make yow the more mery,
I wol myselven goodly° with yow ryde,   *willingly*
Right at myn owene cost, and be youre gyde.
And whoso wole my jugement withseye°   *gainsay*
Shal paye al that we spenden by the weye.
And if ye vouchesauf that it be so,
810 Tel me anon, withouten wordes mo,°   *more*
And I wol erly shape° me therfore.'   *prepare*
     This thyng was graunted, and oure othes swore
With ful glad herte, and preyden° hym also   *begged*
That he wolde vouchesauf for to do so,
And that he wolde been oure governour,
And of oure tales juge° and reportour,°   *judge/assessor*
And sette a soper, at a certeyn pris,°   *price*

And we wol° reuled been at his devys°   *will/decision*
In heigh and lowe;° and thus by oon assent   *everything*
820 We been acorded to his jugement.
And therupon the wyn was fet° anon;   *fetched*
We dronken, and to reste wente echon°   *each one*
Withouten any lenger taryinge.
      Amorwe,° whan that day gan for to springe,   *in the morning*
Up roos oure hoost and was oure aller cok,°   *was rooster for us all*
And gadrede° us togidre,° alle in a flok,   *gathered/together*
And forth we riden,° a litel moore than pas,°   *rode/walking pace*
Unto the Watering of Saint Thomas.
And there oure hoost bigan his hors areste,°   *pull up*
830 And seyde: 'Lordynges, herkneth, if yow leste!°   *it pleases you*
Ye woot youre forward,° and I it yow recorde.°   *agreement/recall*
If even-song and morwe-song accorde,⁵³
Lat se now who shal telle the firste tale.
As evere mote° I drynke wyn or ale,   *may*
Whoso be rebel to my jugement
Shal paye for al that by the wey is spent.
Now draweth cut,° er that we ferrer twinne;°   *lots/go further*
He which that hath the shorteste shal biginne.
Sire Knyght,' quod he, 'my mayster and my lord,
840 Now draweth cut, for that is myn accord.°   *decision*
Cometh neer,' quod he, 'my lady Prioresse.
And ye, sire Clerk, lat be youre shamefastnesse,°   *modesty*
Ne studieth noght.° Ley hond to, every man.'   *stop dreaming*
      Anon to drawen every wight bigan,
And shortly, for to tellen as it was,
Were it by aventure,° or sort,° or cas,°   *luck/fate/chance*
The sothe° is this, the cut fil° to the knyght,   *truth/fell*
Of which ful blithe and glad was every wyght,
And telle he moste° his tale, as was resoun,°   *must/right*
850 By forward° and by composicioun,°   *agreement/compact*
As ye han herd.⁵⁴ What nedeth wordes mo?
And whan this goode man saugh° that it was so,   *saw*
As he that wys° was and obedient   *sensible*
To kepe his forward by his free assent,
He seyde, 'Syn° I shal biginne the game,   *since*
What, welcome be the cut, a° Goddes name!   *in*
Now lat us ryde, and herkneth what I seye.'
      And with that word we ryden forth oure weye,
And he bigan with right a mery cheere°   *expression*
860 His tale anon, and seyde in this manere.⁵⁴ ·

                    *   *   *

The Wife of Bath's Prologue and Tale

PROLOGUE

Experience, though noon° auctoritee   *no*
Were in this world, is right ynough for me
To speke of wo that is in marriage;
For, lordinges, sith I twelve yeer was of age,
Thonked be God that is eterne on lyve,°   *alive*
Housbondes at chirchedore° I have had fyve;   *churchdoor (n.35)*
For I so ofte have ywedded be;
And alle were worthy men in hir degree.°   *position*
But me was told certeyn, nat longe agon° is,   *ago*
10 That sith° that Crist ne wente never but onis°   *since/once*
To wedding, in the Cane° of Galilee,⁵⁵   *Cana*
That by the same ensample° taughte he me   *example*
That I ne sholde wedded be but ones.
Herkne eek,° lo! which° a sharp word for the nones°   *also/what/for that*
Besyde a welle Jesus, God and man,   *occasion*
Spak in repreve° of the Samaritan:⁵⁶   *reproof*
'Thou hast yhad fyve housbondes,' quod he,
'And thilke° man, the which that hath now thee,   *that*
Is noght thyn housbond;' thus seyde he certeyn.
20 What that he mente therby, I can nat seyn;
But that I axe,° why that the fifthe man   *ask*
Was noon housbond to the Samaritan?
How manye mighte she have in mariage?
Yet herde I never tellen in myn age
Upon this nombre diffinicioun;°   *precise definition*
Men may devyne° and glosen⁵⁷ up and doun.   *guess*
But wel I woot expres,° withoute lye,°   *know/clearly*
God bad us for to wexe° and multiplye;   *increase*
That gentil° text can I wel understonde.   *noble*
30 Eek wel I woot he seÿde, myn housbonde
Sholde lete° fader and moder, and take me;⁵⁸   *leave*
But of no nombre mencion° made he,   *mention*
Of bigamye° or of octogamye;⁵⁹   *second marriage*
Why sholde men speke of it vileinye?°   *evil*
    Lo, here the wyse king, dan Salomon;⁶⁰
I trowe he hadde wyves mo° than oon.   *more*
As wolde God it leveful° were to me   *permitted*
To be refresshed° half so ofte as he!   *reinvigorated*
Which yifte° of God hadde he for alle his wyvis!   *what a gift*
40 No man hath swich,° that in this world alyve is.   *the like*

God woot,° this noble king, as to my wit,°   *knows/knowledge*
The firste night had many a mery fit°   *good old time*
With ech of hem, so wel was him on lyve!⁶¹
Blessed be God that I have wedded fyve
Of whiche I have pyked out the beste,
Both of here nether purs and of here cheste.⁶²
Diverse scoles° maken parfyt clerkes:°   *university schools/scholars*
And diverse practyk° in many sondry werkes   *practice*
Maketh the werkman parfit° sikerly;°   *perfect/truly*
50 Of five husbondes scoleying° am I.   *schooling*
Welcome the sixte, whan that ever he shal.°   *shall be*
Forsothe, I wol nat kepe me chaste in al;
Whan myn housbond is fro the world ygon,
Som Cristen man shal wedde me anon;
For thanne, th'Apostle seith,⁶³ that I am free
To wedde, a Goddes half°, wher it lyketh° me.   *in God's name/pleases*
He seith that to be wedded is no sinne;
Bet° is to be wedded than to brinne.°   *better/burn (with desire)*
What rekketh me°, thogh folk seye vileinye   *do I care*
60 Of shrewed° Lamech⁶⁴ and his bigamye?   *cursed*
I woot° wel Abraham was an holy man,   *know*
And Jacob eek, as ferforth° as I can;°   *far/know*
And ech of hem hadde wyves mo than two;
And many another holy man also.
    When saugh° ye ever, in any maner age,°   *saw/kind of*
That hye God defended° mariage.   *forbad*
By expres word? I pray you, telleth me;
Or wher comanded he virginitee?
I woot as wel as ye, it is no drede,°   *doubt*
70 Th'Apostel° whan he speketh of maydenhede;°   *St Paul/virginity*
He seyde, that precept therof hadde he noon.
Men may conseille a womman to been oon,°   *single*
But conseilling is no comandement;
He putte it in our owene jugement.
For hadde God comanded maydenhede,
Thanne hadde he dampned° wedding with the dede;°   *| same time* / *condemned/at the*
And certes,° if ther were no seed ysowe,°   *truly/sown*
Virginitee, wherof than sholde it growe?
Paul dorste nat comanden atte° leste   *at the*
80 A thing of which his maister yaf° noon heste.°   *gave/order*
The dart° is set up for virginitee;   *prize*
Cacche who so may, who renneth° best lat see.   *runs*
    But this word is nat take of° every wight,   *for*
But ther° as God list° give it of his might.   *where/pleases*

I woot wel, that th'Apostel was a mayde;°   *virgin*
But natheless, thogh that he wroot° and sayde,   *wrote*
He wolde° that every wight were swich° as he,   *wished/like him*
Al nis but conseil° to virginitee;   *it is nothing more than advice*
And for to been a wyf, he yaf me leve
90 Of indulgence;° so it is no repreve°   *permission/reproof*
To wedde me, if that my make° dye   *mate*
Withoute excepcioun° of bigamye°   *objection*
Al were it good no womman for to touche
He mente° as in his bed or in his couche,   *meant*
For peril is bothe fyr and tow t'assemble°   *put fire and flax together*
Ye knowe what this ensample may resemble°.   *signify*
This is al and som,° he heeld virginitee   *sum total*
More parfit than wedding in freletee°.   *weakness of the flesh*
Freletee clepe I,° but if° that he and she   *do I call it/unless*
100 Wolde leden° al hir lyf in chastitee.   *lead*
    I graunte it wel, I have noon envye,
Thogh maydenhede° preferre° bigamye;   *abstinence/surpass*
Hem lyketh° to be clene in body and goost,°   *pleases/spirit*
Of myn estaat° I nil nat make no boost.   *condition*
For wel ye knowe, a lord in his houshold,
He hath nat every vessel al of gold;
Somme been of tree,° and doon hir lord servyse.   *wood*
God clepeth° folk to him in sondry wyse,   *calls*
And everich hath of God a propre yifte,°   *his own gift*
110 Som this, som that—as him lyketh shifte.°   *provide*
    Virginitee is greet perfeccioun,
And continence eek with devocioun.
But Crist, that of perfeccioun is welle,°   *fountain-head*
Bad nat every wight he sholde go selle[65]
All that he hadde, and give it to the pore,
And in swich wyse folwe him and his fore.°   *footsteps*
He spak to hem that wolde live parfitly;°   *perfectly*
And lordinges, by your leve, that am nat I.
I wol bistowe the flour° of al myn age   *flower*
120 In the actes and in fruit of mariage.
    Telle me also, to what conclusioun°   *purpose*
Were members maad° of generacioun,   *made*
And of so parfit wis° a wright° ywroght?°[66]   *manner/creation/made*
Trusteth right wel, they wer nat maad for noght.
Glose° whoso wole, and seye bothe up and doun,   *interpret*
That they were maked for purgacioun°   *purging*
Of urine, and our bothe thinges smale
Were eek to knowe a femele° from a male,   *female*

And for noon other cause; sey ye no?
130 The experience woot wel it is noght so.
So that the clerkes be nat with me wrothe,° *angry*
I sey this, that they maked been for bothe,
This is to seye, for office,° and for ese *natural functions*
Of engendrure,° ther° we nat God displese. *begetting children|where*
Why sholde men elles in hir bokes sette,
That man shal yelde° to his wyf hir dette? *give*
Now wherwith sholde he make his payement,
If he ne used his sely° instrument? *natural*
Than were they maad, upon° a creäture, *in*
140 To purge uryne, and eek for engendrure.
But I seye noght that every wight is holde,° *bound*
That hath swich harneys° as I to yow tolde, *equipment*
To goon and usen hem in engendrure;
Than sholde men take of chastitee no cure.° *pay no attention to*
Crist was a mayde,° and shapen as a man, *virgin*
And many a saint, sith that the world bigan:
Yet lived they ever in parfit chastitee.
I nil envye no virginitee;
Lat hem be breed° of pured° whete seed, *bread|refined*
150 And lat us wyves hoten° barly breed; *be called*
And yet with barly breed, Mark[67] telle can,
Our Lord Jesu refresshed many a man.
In swich estaat as God hath cleped° us *called*
I wol persevere, I nam nat precious.° *choosy*
In wyfhode° I wol use myn instrument *being a wife*
As frely° as my Maker hath it sent. *generously*
If I be daungerous,° God yeve° me sorwe! *hard to please|give*
Myn housbond shal it have bothe eve and morwe,° *morning*
Whan that him list° com forth and paye his dette. *pleases*
160 An housbonde I wol have, I nil nat lette,° *be frustrated*
Which shal be bothe my dettour° and my thral,° *debtor|slave*
And have his tribulatioun withal° *moreover*
Upon his flessh, whyl that I am his wyf.
I have the power duringe al my lyf
Upon his propre° body, and noght he.° *own|not*
Right thus the Apostel tolde[68] it unto me;
And bad° our housbondes for to love us weel. *bade*
Al this sentence° me lyketh every deel.° *opinion|part*
Up sterte° the pardoner, and that anon,° *started|immediately*
170 'Now dame,' quod° he, 'by God and by Saint John, *said*
Ye been a noble prechour in this cas!
I was aboute to wedde a wyf; allas!

What° sholde I bye° it on my flesh so dere? *why/buy*
Yet hadde I lever° wedde no wyf to-yere!°' *rather/this year*
 'Abyde!' quod she, 'my tale is nat bigonne;
Nay, thou shalt drinken of another tonne° *barrel*
Er that I go,° shal savoure° wors than ale. *I've done/taste*
And whan that I have told thee forth my tale
Of tribulacioun in mariäge,
180 Of which I am expert in al myn age,
This to seyn, myself have been the whippe;
Than maystow chese° whether thou wolt sippe *can you choose*
Of thilke tonne° that I shal abroche.° *barrel/broach*
Bewar of it, er thou too ny° approache; *nigh*
For I shal telle ensamples mo than ten.
Whoso that nil° be war° by othere men, *will not/warned*
By him shul othere men corrected be.⁶⁹
The same wordes wryteth Ptholomee;°⁷⁰ *Ptolemy*
Rede in his *Almageste*, and take it there.
190 'Dame, I wolde praye yow, if your wil it were,'
Seyde this pardoner, 'as ye bigan,
Telle forth your tale, spareth for no man,
And teche us yonge men of your praktike.°' *practice*
 'Gladly,' quod she, 'sith it may yow lyke.° *please you*
But yet I praye to al this companye,
If that I speke after my fantasye,° *as I like*
As taketh not agrief° of that I seye; *amiss*
For myn entente nis but for to pleye.° *amuse*
 Now sires, now wol I telle forth my tale.
200 As ever mote I drinken wyn or ale,
I shal seye sooth, tho° housbondes that I hadde, *those*
As three of hem were gode° and two were badde, *good*
The three men were gode, and riche, and olde;
Unnethe° mighte they the statut° holde *scarcely/covenant*
In which that they were bounden unto me.
Ye woot° wel what I mene of this, pardee! *know*
As help me God, I laughe whan I thinke
How pitously anight I made hem swinke;° *labour*
And by my fey,° I tolde of it no stoor.° *faith/made nothing of it*
210 They had me yeven hir° gold and hir tresoor; *their*
Me neded nat do lenger° diligence *longer*
To winne hir love, or doon hem reverence.
They loved me so wel by God above,
That I ne tolde no dayntee of hir love!° *not set great store by*
A wys womman wol sette hir ever in oon:° *set her heart on one thing*
To gete hir love, theras° she hath noon. *where*

But sith I hadde hem hoolly° in myn hond,   *completely*
And sith they hadde me yeven° all hir lond,   *given/land*
What° sholde I taken heed hem for to plese,   *why*
220 But it° were for my profit and myn ese?   *unless*
I sette hem so a-werke,° by my fey,   *to work*
That many a night they songen° weilawey!°   *sang/alas!*
The bacoun was nat fet for hem, I trowe,
That som men han in Essex at Dunmowe.°⁷¹   *Dunmow*
I governed hem so wel, after° my lawe,   *according to*
That ech of hem ful blisful° was and fawe°   *happy/willing*
To bringe me gaye thinges fro the fayre.°   *fair*
They were ful glad whan I spak to hem fayre;
For God it woot, I chidde° hem spitously.°   *chided/unmercifully*
230   Now herkneth, how I bar me° proprely,   *behaved myself*
Ye wyse wyves, that can understonde.
Thus shulde ye speke and bere hem wrong on honde;°   *delude them*
For half so boldely can ther no man
Swere and lyen° as a womman can,   *lie*
I sey nat this by° wyves that ben wyse,°   *about/prudent*
But if° it be whan they hem misavyse.°   *unless/act ill-advisedly*
A wys wyf, if that she can hir good,°   *knows what's good for her*
Shal beren him on hond the cow° is wood,°⁷²   *jackdaw/mad*
And take witnesse of hir owene mayde
240 Of hir assent;° but herkneth how I sayde.   *agrees with her*
    "Sir olde kaynard,° is this thyn array°   *fool/your way*
Why is my neighebores wyf so gay?
She is honoured over al ther° she goth;°   *wherever/goes*
I sitte at hoom, I have no thrifty cloth.°   *good clothes*
What dostow° at my neigheboures hous?   *do you*
Is she so fair? artow° so amorous?   *are you*
What rowne° ye with our mayde? Benedicite!°   *whisper/bless me!*
Sir olde lechour, lat thy japes° be!   *tricks*
And if I have a gossib° or a freend,   *confident*
250 Withouten gilt,° thou chydest as a feend,°   *guilt/fiend*
If that I walke or pleye unto his hous!   *visit*
Thou comest hoom as dronken as a mous,
And prechest on thy bench, with yvel preef!°   *bad luck to you!*
Thou seist to me, it is a greet meschief°   *misfortune*
To wedde a poore womman, for costage;°   *expense*
And if that she be riche, of heigh parage,°   *birth*
Than seistow° that it is a tormentrye   *you say*
To suffre hir pryde and hir malencolye.°   *melancholy(indifference)*
And if that she be fair, thou verray knave,
260 Thou seyst that every holour° wol hir have;   *lecher*

She may no whyle in chastitee abyde,
That is assailled upon ech a side.
   Thou seyst, som folk desyre us for richesse,
Somme for our shap°, and somme for our fairnesse;   *shape*
And som, for she can outher° singe or daunce,   *either*
And som, for gentillesse° and daliaunce;°   *kindness/flirting*
Som, for hir handes and hir armes smale;°   *slender*
Thus goth al to the devel by° thy tale.   *according*
Thou seyst, men may nat kepe° a castel wal;   *hold*
270 It may so longe assailled been overal.°   *everywhere*
   And if that she be foul, thou seïst that she
Coveiteth° every man that she may se;   *wants*
For as a spaynel° she wol on him lepe,   *spaniel*
Til that she finde som man hir to chepe;°   *do business with*
Ne noon so grey goos° goth ther in the lake,   *goose*
As, seïstow°, that wol been withoute make.°   *you say/mate*
And seÿst, it is an hard thing for to welde°   *control*
A thing that no man wol, his thankes°, helde.°   *willingly/keep*
Thus seïstow, lorel°, whan thow goost to bedde;   *wretch*
280 And that no wys° man nedeth for to wedde,   *prudent*
Ne no man that entendeth° unto hevene.   *aims*
With wilde thonder-dint° and firy levene°   *thunderbolt/lighting*
Mote thy welked° nekke be to-broke!°   *withered/broken*
   Thow seÿst that dropping° houses, and eek smoke,   *leaking*
And chyding wyves, maken men to flee
Out of hir owene hous; a! Benedicite!
What eyleth° swich an old man for to chyde?   *ails*
   Thow seyst, we wyves wol our vyces hyde
Til we be fast°, and than we wol hem shewe;   *firmly married*
290 Wel may that be a proverbe of a shrewe!°   *scoundrel*
   Thou seïst, that oxen, asses, hors°, and houndes,   *horse*
They been assayed° at diverse stoundes;°   *tested/times*
Bacins°, lavours°, er that men hem bye,   *basins/washing bowls*
Spones and stoles°, and al swich housbondrye°,   *stools/household goods*
And so been° pottes, clothes, and array;°   *are/ornaments*
But folk of wyves maken noon assay
Til they be wedded; olde dotard shrewe!
And than, seïstow, we wol oure vices shewe.
  · Thou seïst also, that it displeseth me
300 But if that thou wolt preyse my beautee.
And but thou poure° alwey upon my face,   *gaze*
And clepe° me 'Faire dame' in every place;   *call*
And but thou make a feste° on thilke° day   *feast/that*
That I was born, and make me fresh and gay,

And but thou do to my norice° honour, — *nurse*
And to my chamberere° withinne my bour,° — *chambermaid/room*
And to my fadres° folk and his allyes;° — *father's/relatives*
Thus seïstow, olde barel ful of lyes!
 And yet of our apprentice Janekyn,
310 For his crisp heer,° shyninge as gold so fyn, — *curly hair*
And for he squiereth me bothe up and doun,
Yet hastow caught a fals suspecioun;
I wol° hym noght, thogh thou were deed° tomorwe. — *want/dead*
 But tel me this, why hydestow,° with sorwe,° — *do you hide, damn it*
The keyes of thy cheste awey fro me?
It is my good° as wel as thyn, pardee.° — *property/by God*
What wenestow° make an idiot of our dame? — *think you to*
Now by that lord, that called is Saint Jame,[73]
Thou shalt not bothe, thogh that thou were wood,° — *furious*
320 Be maister of my body and of my good;
That oon thou shalt forgo, maugree thyne yën;° — *damn your eyes*
What nedeth thee of me to enquere or spyën°? — *spy on*
I trowe, thou woldst loke° me in thy chiste!° — *lock/money-chest*
Thou sholdest seye, 'Wyf, go wher thee liste,° — *you please*
Tak your disport,° I wol nat leve° no talis;° — *pleasure/believe/tales*
I knowe yow for a trewe wyf, dame Alis.'
We love no man that taketh keep° or charge° — *heed/pays attention*
Wher that we goon, we wol° ben at our large.° — *want/liberty*
 Of alle men yblessed moot he be,
330 The wyse astrologien° Dan Ptholome,° — *astrologer/Ptolemy*
That seith this proverbe in his *Almageste*,
'Of alle men his wisdom is the hyeste,
That rekketh° never who hath the world° in honde.' — *care/wealth*
By this proverbe thou shalt understonde,
·Have thou ynogh,° what thar° thee recche° or care — *enough/need/worry*
How merily that othere folkes fare?
For certeyn, olde dotard, by your leve,
Ye shul have queynte[74] right ynough at eve.
He is to greet a nigard that wol werne° — *refuse*
340 A man to lighte his candle at his lanterne;
He shal have never the lasse° light, pardee; — *less*
Have thou ynough, thee thar° nat pleyne thee. — *need*
 Thou seÿst also, that if we make us gay
With clothing and with preciöus array,
That it is peril of our chastitee;
And yet, with sorwe, thou most enforce° thee, — *reinforce*
And seye thise wordes in the Apostle's name,
'In habit,° maad with chastitee and shame, — *clothes*

Ye wommen shul° apparaille yow,' quod he,[75]   *must*
350 'And noght in tressed heer° and gay perree°,   *braided hair|jewelry*
As perles, ne with gold, ne clothes riche;'
After thy text, ne after thy rubriche[76]
I wol nat wirche° as muchel° as a gnat.   *care|much*
Thou seydest this, that I was lyk a cat;
For whoso wolde senge° a cattes skin,   *singe*
Thanne wolde the cat wel dwellen in his in;°   *house*
And if the cattes skin be slyk and gay,
She wol nat dwelle in house half a day,
But forth she wole, er any day be dawed°,   *dawns*
360 To shewe hir skin, and goon a-caterwawed;°   *caterwauling*
This is to seye, if I be gay, sir shrewe,
I wol renne° out, my borel° for to shewe.   *run|clothes*
     Sire olde fool, what eyleth° thee to spyën?   *ails*
Thogh thou preye Argus, with his hundred yën°,   *eyes*
To be my warde-cors°, as he can° best,   *bodyguard|know how*
In feith, he shal nat kepe me but me lest;°   *wish*
Yet coude I make his berd°, so moot I thee°.   *outwit|prosper*
     Thou seydest eek, that ther ben thinges three,
The whiche thinges troublen al this erthe,
370 And that no wight ne may endure the ferthe;°   *fourth*
·O leve° sir shrewe, Jesu shorte thy lyf!   *dear*
Yet prechestow, and seyst, an hateful wyf
Yrekened° is for oon of thise meschances°.   *reckoned|misfortunes*
Been ther none othere maner resemblances
That ye may lykne your parables to,
But if° a sely° wyf be oon of tho°?   *unless|innocent|them*
     Thou lykenest eek wommanes love to helle,
To bareyne° land, ther° water may not dwelle.   *barren|where*
Thou lyknest it also to wilde fyr;[77]
380 The more it brenneth°, the more it hath desyr   *burus*
To consume every thing that brent° wol be.   *burnt*
Thou seyst, that right° as wormes° shende° a tree,   *just|grubs|destroy*
Right so a wyf destroyeth hir housbonde;
This knowe they that been to wyves bonde.°"   *bound*
     Lordinges, right thus, as ye have understonde,
Bar I stifly° myne olde housbondes on honde°,   *boldly|deluded*
That thus they seyden in hir dronkenesse;
And al was fals, but that I took° witnesse   *called as*
On Janekin and on my nece also.
390 O Lord, the peyne I dide hem and the wo,
Ful giltelees°, by Goddes swete pyne!°   *innocent|sufferings*
For as an hors I coude byte and whyne.[78]

I coude pleyne,° thogh I were in the gilt,   *complain*
Or elles oftentyme hadde I ben spilt.°   *ruined*
Whoso that first to mille comth, first grint;°   *grinds*
I pleyned first, so was our werre ystint.°   *stopped*
They were ful glad to excusen° hem ful blyve°   *exonerate themselves/quickly*
Of thing of which they never agilte hir lyve.°   *guilty in their lives*
    Of wenches wolde I beren him on honde,[79]
400 Whan that for syk unnethes° mighte he stonde.   *scarcely*
Yet tikled it his herte, for that he
Wende° that I hadde of him so greet chiertee.°   *thought/love*
I swoor that al my walkinge out by nighte
Was for to espye wenches that he dighte;°   *laid*
Under that colour° hadde I many a mirthe.°   *pretence/laugh*
For al swich wit is yeven° us in our birthe;   *given*
Deceite, weping, spinning God hath yive
To wommen kindely,° whyl° they may live.   *naturally/as long as*
And thus of o thing I avaunte me,°   *boast*
410 Atte ende I hadde the bettre in ech degree,°   *the upper hand in every way*
By sleighte,° or force, or by som maner thing,   *cunning*
As by continuel murmur° or grucching;°   *grumbling/grouching*
Namely° abedde hadden they meschaunce,°   *especially/a miserable time*
Ther wolde I chyde and do hem no plesaunce;°   *give them no enjoyment*
I wolde no lenger in the bed abyde,
If that I felte his arm over my syde,
Til he had maad his raunson° unto me;   *payment*
Than wolde I suffre him do his nycetee.°   *satisfy his desires*
And therfore every man this tale I telle,
420 Winne whoso may,° for al is for to selle.   *make profit where you can*
With empty hand men may none hawkes lure;
For winning° wolde I al his lust endure,   *profit*
And make me a feyned appetyt;
And yet in bacon° hadde I never delyt;°   *old dried meat/gratification*
That made me that ever I wolde hem chyde.
For thogh the Pope had seten° hem biside,   *sat*
I wolde nat spare hem at hir owene bord.°   *table*
For by my trouthe, I quitte° hem word for word.   *paid them back*
As help me verray God omnipotent,
430 Thogh I right now sholde make my testament,°   *will*
I ne owe hem nat a word that it nis quit.°   *been repaid*
I broghte it so aboute by my wit,
That they moste yeve it up, as for the beste;°   *make the best of it*
Or elles hadde we never been in reste.°   *at peace*
For thogh he loked as a wood leoun,°   *raging lion*
Yet sholde he faille of his conclusioun.°   *purpose*

Thanne wolde I seye, "Gode lief° tak keep°   *dear one/see*
How mekely loketh Wilkin oure sheep;[80]
Com neer, my spouse, lat me ba° thy cheke!   *kiss*
440 Ye sholde been al pacïent and meke,
And han a swete spyced° conscience,   *scrupulous*
Sith ye so preche of Jobes° pacience.   *Job's*
Suffreth alwey, sin° ye so wel can preche;   *since*
And but° ye do, certein we shal yow teche   *unless*
That it is fair° to have a wyf in pees.   *good*
Oon of us two moste bowen, douteless;
And sith a man is more resonable°   *rational*
Than womman is, ye moste been suffrable°   *patient*
What ayleth yow to grucche thus and grone?   *grouch*
450 Is it for ye wolde have my queynte[81] allone?
Why taak it al, lo, have it everydeel;°   *every bit*
Peter!° I shrewe° yow but° ye love it weel!   *by St Peter!/curse/unless*
For if I wolde selle my bele chose,[81]
I coude walke as fresh as is a rose;
But I wol kepe it for your owene tooth°   *enjoyment*
Ye be to blame, by God, I sey yow sooth."
    Swiche maner wordes hadde we on honde°   *exchanged*
Now wol I speken of my fourthe housbonde.
    My fourthe housbonde was a revelour,
460 This is to seyn, he hadde a paramour;°   *mistress*
And I was yong and ful of ragerye;°   *passion*
Stiborn° and strong, and joly as a pye°   *stubborn/magpie*
Wel coude I daunce to an harpe smale,
And singe, ywis° as any nightingale,   *I declare*
Whan I had dronke a draughte of swete wyn.
Metellius, the foule cherl, the swyn,
That with a staf birafte° his wyf hir lyf,   *bereft*
For° she drank wyn, thogh° I hadde been his wyf,   *because/if*
He sholde nat han daunted° me fro drinke;   *intimidated*
470 And, after wyn, on Venus moste° I thinke;   *mostly*
For al so siker° as cold engendreth hayl,   *as sure as*
A likerous° mouth moste han a likerous tayl.   *eager*
In womman vinolent° is no defence: *being tipsy*
This knowen lechours by experience.
    But, Lord Crist! whan that it remembreth me°   *I remember*
Upon my youthe, and on my jolitee,
It tikleth me aboute myn herte rote°   *bottom of*
Unto this day it dooth myn herte bote°   *good*
That I have had my world as in my tyme.
480 But age, allas! that al wol envenyme,°   *poison*

Hath me biraft° my beautee and my pith;°   *bereft/vitality*
Lat go, farewel, the Devil go therwith!
The flour is goon, ther is namore to telle,
The bren,° as I best can,° now moste I selle;   *bran/know how*
But yet to be right mery wol I fonde.°   *try*
Now wol I tellen of my fourthe housbonde.
    I seye, I hadde in herte greet despyt°   *contempt*
That he of any other had delyt.
But he was quit,° by God and by Saint Joce!   *paid back*
490 I made him of the same wode a croce;°   *staff*
Nat of my body in no foul manere,
But certeinly, I made folk swich chere,
That in his owene grece° I made him frye   *fat*
For angre, and for verray jalousye.
By God, in erthe I was his purgatorie,
For which I hope his soule be in glorie.
For God it woot, he sat ful ofte and song°   *sang*
Whan that his shoo ful bitterly him wrong.°   *pinched*
Ther was no wight, save God and he, that wiste,°   *knew*
500 In many wyse, how sore I him twiste.°   *tormented*
He deyde° whan I cam fro Jerusalem,   *died*
And lyth ygrave° under the rode-beem,⁸²   *buried*
Al° is his tombe noght so curious°   *although/elaborate*
As was the sepulcre of him, Darius,
Which that Appelles wroghte subtilly;°   *skilfully*
It nis but waste to burie him preciously.°   *expensively*
Lat him fare wel,° God yeve° his soule reste,   *go in peace/give*
He is now in the grave and in his cheste.°   *coffin*
    Now of my fifthe housbond wol I telle.
510 God lete his soule never come in helle!
And yet was he to me the moste shrewe;°   *vicious*
That fele I on my ribbes al by rewe,°   *each one*
And ever shal, unto myn ending day.
But in our bed he was so fresh° and gay,   *lively*
And therwithal so wel coude he me glose,°   *please*
Whan that he wolde han° my bele chose,   *have*
That thogh he hadde me bet° on every boon,°   *beaten/bone*
He coude winnen agayn my love anoon.°   *straightaway*
I trowe I loved him beste, for that he
520 Was of his love daungerous° to me.   *grudging*
We wommen han, if that I shal nat lye,
In this matere a queynte fantasye;°   *fancy*
Wayte what° thing we may nat lightly have,   *whatever*
Therafter wol we crye al day and crave.

Forbede us thing, and that desyren we;   *want*
Prees° on us faste,° and thanne wol we flee.   *pursue/hard*
With daunger° oute° we al our chaffare;°   *neglect/display/wares*
Greet prees° at market maketh dere ware,°   *demand/dear goods*
And too greet cheep° is holde at litel prys;°   *bargain/value*
530 This knoweth every womman that is wys.
   My fifthe housbonde, God his soule blesse!
Which that I took for love and no richesse,
He somtyme° was a clerk[83] of Oxenford,   *once*
And had left scole, and wente at hoom to bord
With my gossib,° dwellinge in oure toun,   *close friend*
God have hir soule! hir name was Alisoun.
She knew myn herte and eek my privetee°   *secrets*
Bet° than our parisshe preest, so moot I thee!°   *better/I can tell you*
To hir biwreyed° I my conseil° al.   *disclosed/secrets*
540 For had myn housbonde pissed on a wall,
Or doon a thing that sholde han cost his lyf,
To hir, and to another worthy wyf,
And to my nece, which that I loved weel,
I wolde han told his conseil every deel.°   *detail*
And so I dide ful often, God it woot,°   *knows*
That made his face ful often reed° and hoot°   *red/hot*
For verray shame, and blamed himself for he
Had told to me so greet a privetee.°   *secret*
   And so bifel that ones,° in a Lente,°   *one day/Lent*
550 So often tymes I to my gossib wente,
For ever yet I lovede to be gay,
And for to walke, in March, Averille,° and May,   *April*
Fro hous to hous, to here° sondry tales,   *hear*
That Jankin clerk, and my gossib Dame Alis,
And I myself, into the feldes wente.
Myn housbond was at London al that Lente;
I hadde the bettre leyser° for to pleye,°   *opportunity/amuse myself*
And for to see, and eek for to be seye°   *seen*
Of lusty° folk; what wiste° I wher my grace°   *lively/know/fortune*
560 Was shapen for to be, or in what place?
Therefore I made my visitaciouns,
To vigilies° and to processiouns,   *feasts*
To preching eek and to thise pilgrimages,
To pleyes of miracles and mariages,
And wered upon my° gaye scarlet gytes.°   *me/gowns*
Thise wormes, ne thise mothes, ne thise mites,
Upon my peril,° frete° hem never a deel;°   *upon my soul!/ate/part*
And wostow° why? for they were used weel.°   *do you know/often*

Now wol I tellen forth what happed me.
570 I seye, that in the feeldes walked we,
Til trewely we hadde swich daliance,   *pleasure*
This clerk and I, that of my purveyance°   *provision for the future*
I spak to him, and seyde him, how that he,
If I were widwe, sholde wedde me.
For certeinly, I sey for no bobance,   *boasting*
Yet was I never withouten purveyance
Of mariage, nof° othere thinges eek: *nor of/also*
I holde a mouses herte° nat worth a leek,   *life*
That hath but oon hol for to sterte° to,   *escape*
580 And if that faille, thanne is al ydo: *it is all up*
I bar him on honde, he hadde enchanted° me;   *pretended/bewitched*
My dame° taughte me that soutiltee: *mother/trick*
And eek I seyde, I mette° of him al night;   *dreamed*
He wolde han slayn me as I lay up-right,   *on my back*
And al my bed was ful of verray° blood,   *real*
But yet I hope that he shal do me good;
For blood bitokeneth° gold, as me was taught.   *betokens*
And al was fals, I dremed of it right naught,   *not at all*
But as I folwed ay° my dames lore,   *always/teaching*
590 As wel of this as of other thinges more.
But now sir, lat me see, what I shal seyn?
Aha! by God, I have my tale ageyn.
Whan that my fourthe housbond was on bere,   *bier*
I weep algate, and made sory chere,   *unceasingly/appearance*
As wyves moten, for it is usage,   *must/custom*
And with my coverchief covered my visage;
But for that I was purveyed of° a make,   *provided/mate*
I weep but smal, and that I undertake: *warrant*
To chirche was myn housbond born amorwe°   *in the morning*
600 With° neighebores, that for him maden sorwe;   *by*
And Jankin, oure clerk, was oon of tho.
As help me God, whan that I saugh him go
After the bere, me thoughte he hadde a paire
Of legges and of feet so clene° and faire,   *neat/handsome*
That al myn herte I yaf unto° his hold: *into/keeping*
He was, I trowe, a twenty winter old,
And I was fourty, if I shal seye sooth;
But yet I hadde alwey a coltes tooth: *young (colt's) appetite*
Gat-tothed° I was,[84] and that bicam me weel;   *with wide apart teeth*
610 I hadde the prente° of Seynt Venus' seel.[85]   *imprint/seal*
As help me God, I was a lusty° oon,   *lively*
And faire and riche, and yong, and wel bigoon;°   *provided*

And trewely, as myne housbondes tolde me,
I had the beste quoniam° mighte be.   *whatever*
For certes, I am al Venerien°   *of Venus*
In felinge°, and myn herte is Marcien°.   *feelings/of Mars*
Venus me yaf my lust, my likerousnesse°,   *eagerness*
And Mars yaf me my sturdy hardinesse°.   *boldness*
Myn ascendent was Taur°, and Mars therinne.   *Taurus–the bull*
620 Allas! allas! that ever love was sinne!
I folwed ay myn inclinacioun°   *bent*
By vertu of my constellacioun;[86]
That made me I coude noght withdrawe
My chambre of Venus from a good felawe.
Yet have I Martes mark upon my face,
And also in another privee° place.   *secret*
For, God so wis° be my savacioun°,   *may he be/salvation*
I ne loved never by no discrecioun,
But ever folwede myn appetyt;
630 Al were he short or long, or blak or whyt,
I took no kepe°, so that he lyked° me,   *heed/pleased*
How pore he was, ne eek of what degree.
      What sholde I seye, but, at the monthes ende,
This joly° clerk Jankin, that was so hende°,   *handsome/pleasant*
Hath wedded me with greet solempnitee°,   *ceremony*
And to him yaf I al the lond° and fee°   *property/money*
That ever was me yeven° therbifore;   *given*
But afterward repented me ful sore.
He nolde suffre° nothing of my list°.   *allow/pleasure*
640 By God, he smoot me ones° on the list°,   *once/cheek*
For that I rente° out of his book a leef,   *tore*
That of the strook myn ere wex al deef°.   *ear became deaf*
Stiborn° I was as is a leonesse,   *stubborn*
And of my tonge a verray jangleresse°,   *babbler*
And walke I wolde, as I had doon biforn°,   *before*
From hous to hous, although he had it sworn°.   *forbidden*
For which he oftentymes wolde preche,
And me of olde Romayn° gestes° teche,   *Roman/stories*
How he, Simplicius Gallus, lefte his wyf,
650 And hir forsook for terme° of al his lyf,   *duration*
Noght but for open-heeded° he hir say°   *hatless/saw*
Lokinge out at his dore° upon a day.   *door*
Another Romayn tolde he me by name,
That, for° his wyf was at a someres° game   *because/summer's*
Withoute his witing°, he forsook hir eke°.   *knowledge/also*
And than wolde he upon° his Bible seke   *in*

That ilke° proverbe of Ecclesiaste,[87]   *same*
Wher he comandeth and forbedeth faste,°   *absolutely*
Man shal nat suffre° his wyf go roule° aboute;   *allow/gad*
660 Than wolde he seye right thus, withouten doute,
    "Whoso that buildeth his hous al of salwes,°   *willow*
And priketh° his blinde hors over the falwes,   *rides/fields*
And suffreth his wyf to go seken halwes,°   *shrines*
    Is worthy to been hanged on the galwes°!"   *gallows*
But al for noght, I sette° noght an hawe°   *reckon/hawthorn berry*
Of his proverbes nof° his olde sawe,°   *nor of/sayings*
Ne I wolde nat of him corrected be.
I hate him that my vices telleth me,
And so do mo,° God woot! of us than I.   *more*
670 This made him with me wood° al outrely;°   *furious/utterly*
I nolde noght forbere° him in no cas.   *endure*
    Now wol I seye yow sooth, by Seint Thomas[88]
Why that I rente out of his book a leef,
For which he smoot me so that I was deef.
    He hadde a book that gladly, night and day,
For his desport° he wolde rede alway.°   *recreation/always*
He cleped° it Valerie and Theofraste,[89]   *called*
At whiche book he lough° alwey ful faste.°   *laughed/a great deal*
And eek ther was somtyme° a clerk at Rome,   *once*
680 A cardinal, that highte° Saint Jerome,   *called*
That made a book agayn° Jovinian,[90]   *against*
In whiche book eek ther was Tertulan,   *Tertullian*
Crisippus, Trotula, and Helowys,°   *Heloise*
That was abbesse nat fer° fro Parys;   *far*
And eek the Parables of Salomon,[91]
Ovydes Art,[92] and bokes many on,
And alle thise wer bounden in o volume.
And every night and day was his custume,°   *habit*
Whan he had leyser° and vacacioun°   *leisure/free time*
690 From other wordly occupacioun,
To reden on this book of wikked wyves.
He knew of hem mo° legendes and lyves   *more*
Than been of gode wyves in the Bible.
For trusteth wel, it is an impossible°   *impossibility*
That any clerk wol speke good of wyves,
But if° it be of holy seintes lyves,   *unless*
Ne of noon other womman never the mo.°   *nothing of any other women*
Who peyntede the leoun, tel me who?[93]
By God, if wommen hadde writen stories,
700 As clerkes han withinne hir oratories,°   *cells*

They wolde han writen of men more wikkednesse
Than all the mark° of Adam may redresse.   *in the image of = men*
The children of Mercurie° and of Venus[94]   *Mercury*
Been in hir wirking° ful contrarious;°   *occupations/opposed*
Mercurie loveth wisdom and science,°   *knowledge*
And Venus loveth ryot° and dispence.°   *wanton behaviour/extravagance*
And, for hir diverse disposicioun,
Ech falleth in otheres exaltacioun;[95]
And thus, God woot! Mercury is desolat
710 In Pisces, wher Venus is exaltat;
And Venus falleth ther Mercurie is reysed;°   *raised*
Therefore no womman of no clerk is preysed.
The clerk, whan he is old, and may noght do
Of Venus werkes worth° his olde sho,°   *that is worth/shoe*
Than sit° he doun, and writ° in his dotage   *sits/writes*
That wommen can nat kepe hir mariage!°   *marriage-vows*
    But now to purpos,° why I tolde thee   *the point*
That I was beten for a book, pardee.
Upon a night Jankin, that was our syre,°   *master*
720 Redde on his book, as he sat by the fyre,
Of Eva° first, that, for hir wikkednesse,   *Eve*
Was al mankinde broght to wrecchednesse,
For which that Jesu Crist himself was slayn,
That boghte° us with his hertes blood agayn.   *redeemed*
Lo, here expres° of womman may ye finde,   *made clear*
That womman was the los° of al mankinde.   *destruction*
    Tho° redde he me how Sampson loste his heres,°   *then/hair*
Slepinge, his lemman° kitte° hem with hir sheres;   *ladylove/cut*
Thurgh whiche tresoun loste he bothe his yën.°   *eyes*
730   Tho redde he me, if that I shall nat lyen,
Of Hercules and of his Dianyre,°   *Deianeira*
That caused him to sette himself afyre.
    Nothing forgat he the penaunce and wo
That Socrates had with hise wyves two;
How Xantippe caste pisse upon his heed;°   *head*
This sely° man sat stille, as he were deed;   *poor*
He wyped his heed, namore dorste° he seyn   *dared*
But 'Er that thonder stinte,° comth of a reyn.'   *stops*
    Of Phasipha,° that was the quene of Crete,   *Pasiphae*
740 For shrewednesse,° him thoughte the tale swete° *nastiness/fine*
Fy! spek° namore, it is a grisly thing,   *say*
Of hir horrible lust and hir lyking.°   *pleasure*
    Of Clitemistra,° for hir lecherye,   *Clytemnestra*
That falsly made hir housbond for to dye,

He redde it with ful good devocioun.
    He tolde me eek for what occasioun
Amphiorax° at Thebes loste his lyf;   *Amphiareus*
Myn housbond hadde a legende of his wyf,
Eriphilem, that for an ouche of gold   *Eriphyle*
750 Hath prively° unto the Grekes told   *secretly*
Wher that hir housbonde hidde him in a place,
For which he hadde at Thebes sory grace°.   *sad outcome*
    Of Livia tolde he me, and of Lucye,   *Lucilia*
They bothe made hir housbondes for to dye;
That oon for love, that other was for hate;
Livia hir housbond, on an even° late,   *evening*
Empoysoned hath, for that she was his fo.
Lucya, likerous,° loved hir housbond so,   *lecherous*
That, for° he sholde alwey upon hir thinke,   *so that*
760 She yaf him swich a maner° love drinke,   *kind of*
That he was deed, er it were by the morwe;° *dead/morning*
And thus algates° housbondes han sorwe.   *all ways*
    Than tolde he me, how oon Latumius
Compleyned to his felawe° Arrius,   *companion*
That in his gardin growed swich° a tree,   *such*
On which, he seyde, how that his wyves three
Hanged hemself for herte despitous°.   *bitterness of heart*
"O leve° brother," quod° this Arrius,   *dear/said*
"Yif me a plante° of thilke blissed tree,   *cutting*
770 And in my gardin planted shal it be!"
    Of latter date, of wyves hath he red,
That somme han slayn hir housbondes in hir bed,
And lete° hir lechour dighte° hir al the night   *let/lay*
Whyl that the corps° lay in the floor upright°. *body/on its back*
And somme han drive° nayles in hir brayn   *driven*
Whyl that they slepte, and thus they han hem slayn.
Somme han hem yeve° poysoun in hir drinke.   *given*
He spak more harm than herte may bithinke°.   *imagine*
And therwithal, he knew of mo° proverbes   *more*
780 Than in this world ther growen gras or herbes.
"Bet° is," quod he, "thyn habitacioun   *better*
Be with a leoun or a foul dragoun,
Than with a womman usinge° for to chyde.   *accustomed*
Bet is," quod he, "hye° in the roof abyde[96]   *high*
Than with an angry wyf doun in the hous;
They been so wikked and contrarious;
They haten° that hir housbondes loveth ay."   *hate*
He seyde, "A womman cast° hir shame away,   *throws*

When she cast of hir smok°"; and forthermo,   *clothes*
790 "A fair womman, but° she be chaast also,   *unless*
Is lyk a gold ring in a sowes nose."⁹⁷
Who wolde wenen°, or who wolde suppose   *imagine*
The wo that in myn herte was, and pyne°?   *torment*
    And whan I saugh he wolde never fyne°   *finish*
To reden on this cursed book al night,
Al sodeynly three leves have I plight°   *seized*
Out of his book, right as he radde°, and eke°,   *read/also*
I with my fist so took him on the cheke,
That in our fyr he fil° bakward adoun°.   *fell/down*
800 And he up stirte° as dooth a wood° leoun,   *jumped/raging*
And with his fist he smoot° me on the heed°,   *hit/head*
That in the floor I lay as I were deed.
And when he saugh how stille that I lay,
He was agast°, and wolde han fled his way,   *afraid*
Til atte laste out of my swogh° I breyde:°   *swoon/woke*
"O! hastow slayn me, false theef?" I seyde,
"And for my land thus hastow mordred° me?   *murdered*
Er I be deed, yet wol I kisse thee."
    And neer° he cam, and kneled faire adoun,   *closer*
810 And seyde, "Dere suster⁹⁸ Alisoun,
As help me God, I shal thee never smyte;
That I have doon, it is thyself to wyte°.   *blame*
Foryeve it me, and that I thee biseke°."   *beg*
And yet eftsones° I hit him on the cheke,   *again*
And seyde, "Theef, thus muchel° am I wreke;°   *much/revenged*
Now wol I dye, I may no lenger speke."
But atte laste, with muchel care° and wo,   *worry*
We fille acorded°, by us selven two.   *came to agreement*
He yaf me al the brydel° in myn hond   *bridle*
820 To han the governance of hous and lond,
And of his tonge°, and of his hond also;   *tongue*
And made him brenne° his book anon right tho°.   *burn/then*
And whan that I hadde geten° unto me,   *got*
By maistrie°, al the soveraynetee°,   *mastery/sovereignty*
And that he seyde, "Myn owene trewe wyf,
Do as thee lust° the terme° of al thy lyf,   *please/for the rest of*
Keep thyn honour, and keep eek myn estaat",
After that day we hadden never debaat.
God help me so, I was to him as kinde
830 As any wyf from Denmark unto Inde°,   *India*
And also trewe, and so was he to me.
I prey to God that sit° in magestee,   *sits*

So blesse his soule, for His mercy dere!
Now wol I seye my tale, if ye wol here.'   *hear*
The frere lough°, whan he hadde herd al this,   *laughed*
'Now, dame,' quod he, 'so have I joye or blis,
This is a long preamble of a tale!'
And whan the somnour herde the frere gale°,   *exclaim*
'Lo!' quod the somnour, 'Goddes armes two!
840 A frere wol entremette him evermo°.   *always be meddling*
Lo, gode men, a flye and eek a frere
Wol falle in every dish and eek matere.
What spekestow of preambulacioun°?   *making a preamble*
What! amble, or trotte, or pees,[99] or go sit doun;
Thou lettest° our disport° in this manere.'   *spoil/amusement*
   'Ye, woltow so, sir Somnour?' quod the frere,
'Now, by my feith, I shal, er that I go,
Telle of a somnour swich a tale or two,
That alle the folk shal laughen in this place.'
850 'Now elles°, Frere, I bishrewe° thy face,'   *unless/curse*
Quod this somnour, 'and I bishrewe me,
But if° I telle tales two or thre   *unless*
Of freres er I come to Sidingborne,   *Sittingbourne*
That I shal make thyn herte for to morne;
For wel I woot thy pacience is goon.'
   Our hoste cryde 'Pees!°' and that anoon!'°   *peace/immediately*
And seyde, 'Lat the womman telle hir tale
Ye fare as folk that dronken been of ale.
Do, dame, tel forth your tale, and that is best.'
860 'Al redy, sir,' quod she, 'right as yow lest°,   *please*
If I have licence of this worthy Frere.'
   'Yis, dame,' quod he, 'tel forth, and I wol here.'°   *listen*

TALE

In tholde dayes of the king Arthour°,   *Arthur*
Of which that Britons° speken greet honour,   *Bretons*
All was this land fulfild of fayerye.[100]
The elf-queen, with hir joly companye,
Daunced ful ofte in many a grene mede;°   *meadow*
This was the olde opinion, as I rede.
I speke of manye hundred yeres ago;
870 But now can no man see none elves mo.
For now the grete charitee and prayeres
Of limitours[101] and othere holy freres,
As thikke as motes in the sonne-beem,

That serchen every lond and every streem,
Blessinge halles, chambres, kichenes, boures°, — *bed-chambers*
Citees, burghes°, castels, hye toures, — *boroughs*
Thropes°, bernes°, shipnes°, dayeryes°; — *villages/barns/stables/dairies*
This maketh that ther been no fayeryes.
For ther as wont to walken was an elf,
880 Ther walketh now the limitour himself
In undermeles° and in morweninges°, — *mid-afternoon/mornings*
And seÿth his matins and his holy thinges
As he goth in his limitacioun°. — *district*
Wommen may go saufly° up and doun, — *safely*
In every bush, or under every tree;
Ther is noon other incubus[102] but he,
And he ne wol doon hem but dishonour.

    And so bifel it, that this King Arthour
Hadde in his hous a lusty bacheler,
890 That on a day cam rydinge fro river;° — *hawking by the river*
And happed° that, allone as she was born, — *it happened*
He saugh° a mayde walkinge him biforn, — *saw*
Of whiche mayde anon, maugree hir heed°, — *despite all her struggles*
By verray force he rafte° hir maydenheed; — *took*
For which oppressioun° was swich clamour — *violence*
And swich pursute° unto the King Arthour, — *appeal*
That dampned was this knight for to be deed° — *to death*
By cours of lawe, and sholde han lost his heed
Paraventure°, swich was the statut° tho; — *perhaps/law*
900 But that the quene and othere ladies mo
So longe preyeden the king of grace,
Til he his lyf him graunted in the place,
And yaf him to the quene al at hir wille,
To chese°, whether she wolde him save or spille.° — *choose/put to death*

    The quene thanketh the king with al hir might,
And after this thus spak she to the knight,
Whan that she saugh hir tyme°, upon a day: — *opportunity*
'Thou standest yet,' quod she, 'in swich array°, — *state*
That of thy lyf yet hastow no suretee°. — *certainty*
910 I grante thee lyf, if thou canst tellen me
What thing is it that wommen most desyren?
Be war, and keep thy nekke-boon° from yren°. — *neck-bone/iron (axe)*
And if thou canst nat tellen it anon°, — *immediately*
Yet wol I yeve° thee leve for to gon — *give*
A twelf-month and a day, to seche° and lere° — *seek/learn*
An answere suffisant in this matere.
And suretee° wol I han, er that thou pace°; — *pledge/leave*

Thy body for to yelden in this place.'
      Wo was this knight and sorwefully he syketh;°   *sighs*
920 But what! he may nat do al as him lyketh.
      And at the laste, he chees° him for to wende,°   *chose/leave*
      And come agayn, right at the yeres ende,
      With swich answere as God wolde him purveye;°   *provide*
      And taketh his leve, and wendeth forth his weye.
      He seketh every hous and every place,
      Wheras he hopeth for to finde grace,
      To lerne, what thing wommen loven most;
      But he ne coude arryven in no cost,°   *region*
      Wheras he mighte finde in this matere
930 Two creätures according in fere.°   *in agreement*
      Somme seyde,° wommen loven best richesse,   *said*
      Somme seyde, honour, somme seyde, jolynesse;°   *amourousness*
      Somme, riche array, somme seyden, lust° abedde,   *pleasure*
      And ofte tyme to be widwe and wedde.
      Somme seyde, that our hertes been most esed,
      Whan that we been yflatered and yplesed.
      He gooth ful ny the sothe,° I wol nat lye;   *truth*
      A man shal winne us best with flaterye;
      And with attendance, and with bisinesse,°   *attention*
940 Been we ylymed,° bothe more and lesse.   *ensnared*
      And somme seyn, how that we loven best
      For to be free, and do right as us lest,°   *pleases*
      And that no man repreve° us of our vyce,   *reprove*
      But seye that we be wyse, and no thing nyce.°   *foolish*
      For trewely, ther is noon of us alle,
      If any wight wol clawe us on the galle,°   *sore spot*
      That we nil kike,° for° he seith us sooth;°   *kick/since/truth*
      Assay, and he shal finde it that so dooth.°   *whoever does so*
      For be we never so vicious withinne,
950 We wol° been holden° wyse, and clene of sinne.   *wish/to be thought*
      And somme seyn, that greet delyt han we
      For to ben holden stable and eek secree,°   *discreet*
      And in o purpos stedefastly to dwelle,
      And nat biwreye° thing that men us telle,   *betray*
      But that tale is nat worth a rake-stele;°   *rake-handle*
      Pardee, we wommen conne nothing hele;°   *hide*
      Witnesse on Myda;° wol ye here the tale?   *Midas*
      Ovyde,° amonges othere thinges smale,   *Ovid*
      Seyde, Myda hadde, under his longe heres,
960 Growinge upon his heed two asses eres,   *head*
      The which vyce° he hidde, as he best mighte,   *defect*

Ful subtilly from every mannes sighte,
That, save his wyf, ther wiste of it namo.°   *no-one else*
He loved hir most, and trusted hir also;
He preyede hir, that to no creäture
She sholde tellen of his disfigure.
    She swoor him 'nay, for al this world to winne
She nolde° do that vileinye or sinne,   *would not*
To make hir housbond han so foul a name;
970 She nolde nat telle it for hir owene shame.'
But nathelees, hir thoughte° that she dyde,°   *it seemed to her|would die*
That she so longe sholde a conseil° hyde;   *secret*
Hir thoughte it swal° so sore aboute hir herte,   *swelled*
That nedely° som word hir moste asterte;°   *necessarily|escape*
And sith she dorste telle it to no man,
Doun to a mareys° faste° by she ran;   *marsh|near*
Til° she came there, hir herte was afyre,   *when*
And, as a bitore° bombleth° in the myre,°   *bittern|booms|mud*
She leyde hir mouth unto the water doun:
980 'Biwreye° me nat, thou water, with thy soun,'°   *betray|sound*
Quod she, 'to thee I telle it, and namo;°   *no-one else*
Myn housbond hath longe asses eres two!
Now is myn herte all hool,° now is it oute;   *whole*
I mighte no lenger kepe° it, out of doute.'   *keep secret*
Heer may ye se, thogh we a tyme abyde,
Yet out it moot,° we can no conseil hyde;   *must*
The remenant of the tale if ye wol here,
Redeth Ovyde, and ther ye may it lere.°   *learn*
    This knight, of which my tale is specially,
990 Whan that he saugh° he mighte nat come therby,   *saw*
This is to seye, what wommen loven moost,
Withinne his brest ful sorweful was the goost;°   *spirit*
But hoom he gooth, he mighte nat sojourne.°   *stay*
The day was come, that hoomward moste° he tourne,   *must*
And in his wey it happed him to ryde,
In al this care, under a forest syde,
Wheras he saugh° upon a daunce go   *saw*
Of ladies foure and twenty, and yet mo;
Toward the whiche daunce he drow ful yerne,°   *eagerly*
1000 In hope that som wisdom sholde he lerne,
But certeinly, er he came fully there,
Vanisshed was this daunce, he niste° where.   *knew not*
No creature saugh he that bar° lyf,   *was alive*
Save on the grene he saugh sittinge a wyf;°   *woman*
A fouler wight° ther may no man devyse.°   *creature|imagine*

Agayn° the knight this olde wyf gan ryse,   *before*
And seyde, 'Sir knight, heer-forth ne lyth° no wey. *lies*
Tel me, what that ye seken, by your fey?°   *faith*
Paraventure it may the bettre be;
1010 Thise olde folk can muchel thing,° quod she. *know a lot*
 'My leve mooder,' quod this knight certeyn,
'I nam° but deed,° but if° that I can seyn *am/dead/unless*
What thing it is that wommen most desyre;
Coude ye me wisse,° I wolde wel quyte° your hyre.' *let me know/pay*
 'Plighte me thy trouthe,° heer in myn hand,' quod she, *pledge*
'The nexte thing that I requere° thee,   *ask*
Thou shalt it do, if it lye in thy might;
And I wol telle it yow er it be night.'
'Have heer my trouthe,' quod the knight, 'I grante.'
1020 'Thanne,' quod she, 'I dar me wel avante,° *boast*
Thy lyf is sauf,° for I wol stonde therby, *safe*
Upon my lyf, the queen wol seye as I.
Lat see which is the proudeste of hem alle,
That wereth on a coverchief or a calle,° *head-covering*
That dar seye nay, of that I shal thee teche;
Lat us go forth withouten lenger speche.'
Tho rouned° she a pistel° in his ere, *whispered/message*
And bad him to be glad, and have no fere.° *fear*
 Whan they be comen to the court, this knight
1030 Seyde, 'He had holde° his day, as he hadde hight,° *kept to/promised*
And redy was his answere,' as he sayde.
Ful many a noble wyf, and many a mayde,
And many a widwe, for that they ben wyse,
The quene hirself sittinge as a justyse,° *judge*
Assembled been, his answere for to here;
And afterward this knight was bode° appere. *bidden*
 To every wight commanded was silence,
And that the knight sholde telle in audience,° *in front of all*
What thing that worldly wommen loven best.
1040 This knight ne stood nat stille° as doth a best,° *silent/beast*
But to his questioun anon° answerde *straightaway*
With manly voys, that al the court it herde:
 'My lige° lady, generally,° quod he, *liege/everywhere*
'Wommen desyren to have sovereyntee
As wel over hir housbond as hir love,
And for to been in maistrie° him above; *the upper hand*
This is your moste desyr, thogh ye me kille,
Doth as yow list, I am heer at your wille.'° *disposal*
 In al the court ne was ther wyf ne mayde,

1050 Ne widwe, that contraried° that he sayde,   *contradicted*
     But seyden, 'He was worthy han° his lyf.'   *to keep*
          And with that word up stirte° the olde wyf,   *started*
     Which that the knight saugh sittinge in the grene:
     'Mercy,' quod she, 'my sovereyn lady quene!
     Er that your court departe, do me right.
     I taughte this answere unto the knight;
     For which he plighte me his trouthe there,
     The firste thing I wolde of him requere,
     He wolde it do, if it lay in his might.
1060 Bifore the court than preye I thee, sir knight,'
     Quod she, 'that thou me take unto thy wyf;
     For wel thou wost° that I have kept° thy lyf.   *know/saved*
     If I sey fals, sey nay, upon thy fey!'°   *faith*
          This knight answerde, 'Allas! and weylawey!
     I woot right wel that swich was my biheste.°   *promise*
     For Goddes love, as chees° a newe requeste;   *choose*
     Tak al my good,° and lat my body go.'   *property*
          'Nay than,' quod she, 'I shrewe° us bothe two! *curse*
     For thogh that I be foul, and old, and pore,
1070 I nolde° for al the metal, ne for ore,   *want nothing*
     That under erthe is grave,° or lyth° above,   *buried/lies*
     But if° thy wyf I were, and eek thy love.'   *unless*
          'My love?' quod he; 'nay, my dampnacioun!
     Allas! that any of my nacioun°   *high birth*
     Sholde ever so foule disparaged° be!'   *disgraced*
     But al for noght, the ende is this, that he
     Constreyned° was, he nedes moste° hir wedde;   *forced/must*
     And taketh his olde wyf, and gooth to bedde.
          Now wolden som men seye, paraventure,
1080 That, for my necligence, I do no cure°   *take the trouble*
     To tellen yow the joye and al th'array°   *preparations*
     That at the feste was that ilke° day.   *that*
     To whiche thing shortly answere I shal;
     I seye, ther nas no joye ne feste at al,
     Ther nas° but hevinesse and muche sorwe;   *was not*
     For prively° he wedded hir on a morwe,°   *secretly/morning*
     And al day after hidde him as an oule;°   *owl*
     So wo was him, his wyf looked so foule.
          Greet was the wo the knight hadde in his thoght,
1090 Whan he was with his wyf abedde° ybroght;   *to bed*
     He walweth,° and he turneth to and fro.   *tosses*
     His olde wyf lay smylinge evermo,
     And seyde, 'O dere housbond, Benedicite!°   *bless me*

Fareth° every knight thus with his wyf as ye?   *behaves*
Is this the lawe of King Arthures hous?
Is every knight of his so dangerous?°   *hard to please*
I am your owene love and eek your wyf;
I am she, which that saved hath your lyf;
And certes, yet dide I yow never unright;°   *wrong*
1100 Why fare ye thus with me this firste night?
Ye faren lyk a man had lost his wit;
What is my gilt?° for Goddes love, tel me it,   *guilt*
And it shal been amended, if I may.'
      'Amended?' quod this knight, 'allas! nay, nay!
It wol nat been amended never mo!
Thou art so loothly,° and so old also,   *repulsive*
And therto comen of so lowe a kinde,°   *base stock*
That litel wonder is, thogh I walwe and winde.°   *toss and turn*
So wolde God myn herte wolde breste!'°   *break*
1110 'Is this,' quod she, 'the cause of your unreste?'
'Ye, certainly,' quod he, 'no wonder is.'
'Now, sire,' quod she, 'I coude amende al this,
If that me liste, er it were dayes three,
So wel ye mighte bere yow° unto me.   *so that you might behave respectfully*
But for ye speken of swich gentillesse[103]
As is descended out of old richesse,°   *wealth*
That therfore sholden ye be gentil men,
Swich arrogance is nat worth an hen.
Loke who that is most vertuous alway,
1120 Privee° and apert,° and most entendeth° ay   *in private|public|aims*
To do the gentil dedes that he can,
And tak him for the grettest° gentil man.   *greatest*
Crist wol,° we clayme of him our gentillesse,   *wishes that*
Nat of our eldres for hir old richesse.
For thogh they yeve us al hir heritage,
For which we clayme to been of heigh parage,°   *descent*
Yet may they nat biquethe,° for nothing,°   *bequeath|by no means*
To noon of us hir vertuous living,
That made hem gentil men ycalled be;
1130 And bad us folwen hem in swich degree.°   *in that state*
      Wel can the wyse poete of Florence,
That highte Dant,° spoken in this sentence;[104]   *is called Dante*
Lo in swich maner rym is Dantes tale:
"Ful selde° up ryseth by his branches smale   *seldom*
Prowesse° of man, for God, of his goodnesse,   *excellence*
Wol that of him we clayme our gentillesse";
For of our eldres may we nothing clayme

But temporel thing, that man may hurte° and mayme.   *damage*
        Eek every wight wot this as wel as I,
1140 If gentillesse were planted naturelly[105]
Unto a certeyn linage, doun the lyne,
Privee ne apert, than wolde they never fyne°   *cease*
To doon of gentillesse the faire offyce,
They mighte do no vileinye or vyce.
        Tak fyr,° and ber° it in the derkeste hous   *fire/bear*
Bitwix this and the mount of Caucasus,
And lat men shette° the dores and go thenne;°   *shut/thence*
Yet wol the fyr as faire lye° and brenne,°   *blaze/burn*
As twenty thousand men mighte it biholde;
1150 His office naturel° ay wol it holde,   *natural properties*
Up° peril of my lyf, til that it dye.   *upon*
        Heer may ye see wel, how that genterye°   *nobility*
Is nat annexed° to possessioun,°   *linked/hereditary wealth*
Sith folk ne doon hir operacioun°   *act*
Alwey, as dooth the fyr, lo! in his kinde.°   *according to their nature*
For, God it woot, men may wel often finde
A lordes sone° do shame and vileinye;   *son*
And he that wol han prys° of his gentrye°   *reputation/high birth*
For he was boren° of a gentil hous,   *born*
1160 And hadde hise eldres noble and vertuous,
And nil himselven do no gentil dedis,
Ne folwe his gentil auncestre that deed° is,   *dead*
He nis nat gentil, be he duk or erl;°   *earl*
For vileyns sinful dedes make a cherl.[106]
For gentillesse nis but renomee°   *renown*
Of thyne auncestres, for hir heigh bountee,°   *great goodness*
Which is a strange° thing to thy persone.   *foreign*
Thy gentillesse cometh fro God allone;
Than comth our verray gentillesse of grace,
1170 It was nothing biquethe us with our place.
        Thenketh how noble, as seith Valerius,
Was thilke Tullius Hostilius,
That out of povert° roos° to heigh noblesse.   *poverty/rose*
Redeth Senek,° and redeth eek Boëce;°   *Seneca/Boethius*
Ther shul ye seen expres that it no drede° is,   *doubt*
That he is gentil that doth gentil dedis;
And therfore, leve° housbond, I thus conclude,   *dear*
Al were it that myne auncestres were rude,°   *lowly*
Yet may the hye God, and so hope I,
1180 Grante me grace to liven vertuously.
        Thanne am I gentil, whan that I biginne

To liven vertuously and weyve° sinne.   *leave off*
   And theras ye of povert me repreve,
The hye God, on whom that we bileve,
In wilful° povert chees° to live his lyf.   *voluntary/chose*
And certes every man, mayden, or wyf,
May understonde that Jesus, Hevene king,
Ne wolde nat chese a vicious living.
Glad povert is an honest° thing, certeyn;   *honourable*
1190 This wol Senek and othere clerkes seyn.
Whoso that halt him payd of° his poverte,   *as satisfied with*
I holde him riche, al hadde he nat a sherte.°   *shirt*
He that coveyteth is a povre wight,°   *creature*
For he wolde han that is nat in his might.
But he that noght hath, ne coveyteth have,
Is riche, although ye holde him but a knave.
   Verray° povert, it singeth proprely;°   *true/is its own song*
Juvenal seith of povert merily:
"The povre man, whan he goth by the weye,
1200 Bifore the theves he may singe and pleye."
Povert is hateful good,° and, as I gesse,   *unattractive blessing*
A ful greet bringer out of bisiness;°   *diligence*
A greet amender eek of sapience°   *wisdom*
To him that taketh it in pacience.
Povert is this, although it seme elenge:°   *hard to bear*
Possessioun,° that no wight wol chalenge.   *a possession*
Povert ful ofte, whan a man is lowe,
Maketh° his God and eek himself to knowe.   *makes him*
Povert a spectacle° is, as thinketh me,   *eyeglass*
1210 Thurgh which he may his verray frendes see.
And therfore, sire, sin that I noght° yow greve,°   *should not/grieve*
Of my povert namore ye me repreve.°   *reproach*
   Now, sire, of elde° ye repreve me;   *old age*
And certes, sire, thogh noon auctoritee
Were in no book, ye gentils° of honour   *gentlemen*
Seyn that men sholde an old wight doon favour,
And clepe him fader,° for your gentillesse;
And auctours° shal I finden, as I gesse.   *authorities*
   Now ther ye seye, that I am foul and old,
1220 Than drede you noght to been a cokewold;°   *cuckold*
For filthe and elde,° also moot I thee,°   *old age/as I may thrive*
Been grete wardeyns° upon chastitee.   *guardians*
But nathelees, sin I knowe your delyt,°   *pleasure*
I shal fulfille your worldly appetyt.
   Chese now,' quod she, 'oon of thise thinges tweye,
To han me foul and old til that I deye,°   *die*

And be to yow a trewe humble wyf,
And never yow displese in al my lyf,
Or elles ye wol han° me yong and fair, *have*
1230 And take your aventure° of the repair° *chance/company*
That shal be to your hous, bycause of me,
Or in som other place, may wel be.
Now chese° yourselven, whether° that yow lyketh.' *choose/which*
  This knight avyseth him° and sore syketh? *considers/sighs*
But atte laste he seyde in this manere,
'My lady and my love, and wyf so dere,
I put me in your wyse governance;
Cheseth° yourself, which may be most plesance, *choose*
And most honour to yow and me also.
1240 I do no fors° the whether of the two; *not care*
For as yow lyketh? it suffiseth me.' *pleases you*
    'Thanne have I gete° of yow maistrye,' quod she, *got*
'Sin I may chese? and governe as me lest?'° *choose/please*
    'Ye, certes, wyf,' quod he, 'I holde it best.'
    'Kis me,' quod she, 'we be no lenger wrothe;
For, by my trouthe, I wol be to yow bothe,
This is to seyn, ye, bothe fair and good.
I prey to God that I mot sterven wood? *may die mad*
But° I to yow be also° good and trewe *unless/both*
1250 As ever was wyf, sin that the world was newe.
And, but° I be to morn° as fair to sene *unless/morning*
As any lady, emperyce? or quene, *empress*
That is bitwixe the est and eke the west,
Doth with my lyf and deeth right as yow lest? *please*
Cast up the curtin? loke how that it is.' *veil*
    And whan the knight saugh verraily al this,
That she so fair was, and so yong therto,
For joye he hente° hir in his armes two, *took*
His herte bathed in a bath of blisse;
1260 A thousand tyme arewe° he gan hir kisse. *in succession*
And she obeyed him in every thing
That mighte doon him plesance or lyking.
    And thus they live, unto hir lyves ende,
In parfit° joye; and Jesu Crist us sende *perfect*
Housbondes meke, yonge, and fresshe abedde,
And grace t'overbyde° hem that we wedde. *outlast*
And eek I preye Jesu shorte° hir lyves *shorten*
That wol nat be governed by hir wyves;
And olde and angry nigardes of dispence? *paying*
1270 God sende hem sone verray° pestilence. *soon true*

*   *   *

The Pardoner's[107] *Prologue and Tale*

INTRODUCTION

Oure hoste gan to swere as he were wood;° *mad*
'Harrow!°' quod he, 'by nayles and by blood!° *help!/of Christ*
This was a fals cherl° and a fals justise.[108] *churl*
As shamful deeth as herte may devyse
Come to thise juges° and hir advocats! *judges*
Algate° this sely° mayde is slayn, allas! *however/simple*
Allas! to dere° boghte she beautee! *dear*
Wherfore I seye al day,° as men may see *always*
That yiftes of Fortune or of Nature[109]
Ben cause of deeth to many a creäture.
Hire beautee was hire deth, I dar wel sayn.
Allas! so pitously as she was slayn!
Of bothe yiftes that I speke° of now *mention*
Men han ful ofte more harm than prow.° *profit*
But trewely, myn owene maister dere,
This is a pitous tale for to heere.
But nathelees, passe over, is no fors.° *matter*
I pray to God, so save they gentil cors,° *i.e. you*
And eek thyne urinals° and they jordanes,° *urine bottles/chamber pots*
Thyn ypocras,° and eek thy galianes,° *red spiced wine/medicines*
And every boist° ful of thy letuarie;[110] *box*
God blesse hem, and oure lady Seïnte Marie!
So mot I theen,° thou art a propre man, *thrive*
And lyk a prelat, by Saïnt Ronyan![111]
Seyde I nat wel? I can nat speke in terme;° *technically*
But wel I woot° thou doost myn herte to erme,° *know/grieve*
That I almost have caught a cardinacle.° *heart-attack*
By corpus bones!° but° I have triacle,° *God's body/unless/restorative*
Or elles a draughte of moiste and corny° ale, *malty*
Or but I here° anon° a mery tale, *hear/immediately*
Myn herte is lost for pitee of this mayde.
Thou bel amy,° thou Pardoner,' he seyde, *dear friend*
'Telle us som myrthe or japes° right anon.' *jokes*
'It shal be doon,' quod he, 'by Saint Ronyon!° *St Ronan*
But first,' quod he, 'heere at this alestake° *ale-sign*
I wol bothe drinke, and eten of a cake.°' *bread*
But right anon thise gentils gonne to crye,
'Nay, lat hym telle us of no ribaudye!° *ribaldry*
Telle us som moral thing, that we may lere° *learn*

40 Som wit,° and thanne wol we gladly here.°' *knowledge/hear*
   'I graunte, ywis,°' quod he, 'but I mot thinke *certainly*
   Upon som honest° thing while that I drinke.' *moral*

THE PROLOGUE

Radix malorum est Cupiditas: Ad Thimotheum, 6.[112]

'Lordings,' quod he, 'in chirches° whan I preche, *churches*
I peyne° me to han an hauteyn° speche, *take pains/high sounding*
And ringe it out as round as gooth a belle,
For I can° al by rote° that I telle. *know/by heart*
My theme° is alwey oon,° and ever was *text/one*
Radix malorum est Cupiditas.
   First I pronounce whennes° that I come,[113] *whence*
50 And than my bulles shewe I, alle and somme.° *one and all*
Our lige lordes seel° on my patente,° *seal/licence*
That shewe I first, my body to warente,° *warrant*
That no man be so bold, ne preest ne clerk,° *cleric*
Me to destourbe° of Cristes holy werk; *disturb*
And after that than telle I forth my tales:
Bulles of popes and of cardinales,
Of patriarkes,° and bishoppes I shewe; *patriarchs*
And in Latyn I speke a wordes fewe,
To saffron° with my predicacioun,° *colour/sermon*
60 And for to stire men to devocioun.
Than shewe I forth my longe cristal stones,° *glass containers*
Ycrammed ful of cloutes° and of bones; *rags*
Reliks° been they, as wenen° they, echoon.° *relics/believed/everyone*
Than have I in latoun° a sholder-boon° *brassy metal/bone*
Which that was of an holy Jewes shepe.
"Good men," seye I, "Tak of my wordes kepe;° *heed*
If that this boon° be wasshe in any welle,° *bone/pool or spring*
If cow, or calf, or sheep, or oxe swelle
That any worm hath ete, or worm° ystonge,° *snake/bitten*
70 Tak water of that welle, and wash his tonge,
And it is hool anon;° and forthermore, *healed immediately*
Of pokkes° and of scabbe, and every sore *pox*
Shal every sheep be hool, that of this welle
Drinketh a draughte. Tak kepe° eek what I telle, *note*
If that the good-man,° that the bestes oweth,° *worthy man/owns*
Wol every wike,° er that the cok him croweth, *week*
Fastinge, drinken of this welle a draughte,
As thilke° holy Jewe our eldres taughte,[114] *that same*

His bestes and his stoor° shal multiplye.   store
80 And, sirs, also it heleth° jalousye;   heals
For, though a man be falle in jalous rage,
Let maken with this water his potage°,   gruel
And never shal he more his wyf mistriste°,   mistrust
Though he the sooth° of hir defaute wiste;°   truth/knows
Al had° she taken° preestes two or three.   even though/i.e. as lovers
   Heer is a miteyn° eek°, that ye may see.   mitten /also
He that his hond wol° putte in this miteyn,   will
He shal have multiplying of his greyn°,   grain
Whan he hath sowen, be it whete° or otes°,   wheat/oats
90 So that° he offre pens°, or elles grotes.¹¹⁵   provided/pennies
   Good men and wommen, o° thing warne I yow,   one
If any wight° be in this chirche now,   creature
That hath doon sinne horrible, that he
Dar nat°, for shame, of it yshriven be°,   not/shriven
Or any womman, be she yong or old,
That hath ymaad hir housbond cokewold°,   cuckold
Swich folk shul have no power ne no grace
To offren° to my reliks in this place.   make offerings
And whoso findeth him out of swich° blame,   such
100 He wol com up and offre in Goddes name,
And I assoille° him by the auctoritee°   absolve/authority
Which that by bulle ygraunted was to me."
   By this gaude° have I wonne, yeer by yeer,   trick
An hundred mark sith I was Pardoner.
I stonde lyk a clerk° in my pulpet,   scholar
And whan the lewed peple is doun yset°,   seated
I preche, so as ye han herd bifore,
And telle an hundred false japes° more.   amusing stories
Than peyne I me° to strecche forth the nekke,   take care
110 And est and west upon the peple I bekke°,   nod my head
As doth a dowve° sitting on a berne°.   dove/barn
Myn hondes and my tonge goon so yerne°,   eagerly
That it is joye to see my bisinesse.
Of avaryce and of swich cursednesse
Is al my preching, for to make hem free°   willing
To yeve her° pens°, and namely° unto me.   their/pence/especially
For my entente is nat but° for to winne°,   only/gain
And nothing for correccioun of sinne.
I rekke° never, whan that they ben beried°,   care/buried
120 Though that her soules goon a blakeberied!¹¹⁶
For certes, many a predicacioun°   sermon
Comth oftetyme of yvel entencioun;°   intention

Som for plesaunce° of folk and flaterye,   *pleasure*
To been avaunced° by ipocrisye,   *promoted*
And som for veyne glorie,° and som for hate.°   *vainglory/hatred*
For, whan I dar non otherweyes debate,°   *attack*
Than wol I stinge him with my tonge smerte°   *sharply*
In preching, so that he shal nat asterte°   *escape*
To been defamed falsly, if that he
130 Hath trespased° to my brethren or to me.   *injured*
For, though I telle noght his propre° name,   *actual*
Men shal wel knowe that it is the same
By signes and by othere circumstances.
Thus quyte° I folk that doon us displesances;°   *pay back/offend us*
Thus spitte I out my venim under hewe°   *colour*
Of holynesse, to seme holy and trewe.
    But shortly myn entente I wol devyse;°   *describe*
I preche of nothing but° for coveityse.°117   *except/covetousness*
Therfor my theme is yet, and ever was—
140 *Radix malorum est cupiditas.*
Thus can I preche agayn that same vyce
Which that I use, and that is avaryce.
But, though myself be gilty in that sinne,
Yet can I maken other folk to twinne°   *turn*
From avaryce, and sore to repente.
But that is nat my principal entente.°   *intention*
I preche nothing but for coveityse;
Of this matere it oughte ynogh suffyse.°   *that's enough*
    Than telle I hem ensamples° many oon   *exempla*
150 Of olde stories, longe tyme agoon;°   *ago*
For lewed° peple loven tales olde;   *ignorant*
Swich thinges can they wel reporte° and holde.°   *repeat/remember*
What trowe° ye, the whyles I may preche,   *believe*
And winne gold and silver for° I teche,   *for what*
That I wol live in povert wilfully?°   *deliberately*
Nay, nay, I thoghte° it never trewely!   *that's not my idea*
For I wol preche and begge in sondry londes;°   *various lands*
I wol not do no labour with myn hondes,°   *hands*
Ne make baskettes, and live therby,
160 Because I wol nat beggen ydelly.°   *unsuccessfully*
I wol non of the apostles counterfete;°   *imitate*
I wol have money, wolle,° chese,° and whete,°   *wool/cheese/wheat*
Al were it yeven of the povrest page,°   *servant-boy*
Or of the povrest widwe in a village,
Al sholde hir children sterve° for famyne.   *starve to death*
Nay! I wol drinke licour of the vyne,

And have a joly wenche in every toun.
But herkneth, lordings, in conclusioun;   *listen*
Your lyking° is that I shal telle a tale.   *wish*
170 Now have I dronke a draughte of corny° ale;   *malty*
By God, I hope I shal yow telle a thing
That shal, by resoun, been at° your lyking.   *to*
For, though myself be a ful vicious man,
A moral tale yet I yow telle can,
Which I am wont to preche, for to winne.°   *get money*
Now holde your pees, my tale I wol beginne.'

THE TALE

In Flaundres° whylom° was a companye   *Flanders|once upon a time*
Of yonge folk, that haunteden° folye,   *went in for*
As ryot,° hasard,° stewes,° and tavernes,   *riotous living|gambling|brothels*
Wheras, with harpes, lutes, and giternes,°   *kind of guitar*
They daunce and pleye at dees° bothe day and night,   *dice*
And ete also and drinken over hir might,°   *capacity*
Thurgh which they doon the devel sacrifyse
Within that develes temple,° in cursed wyse   *i.e. the tavern*
By superfluitee° abhominable;   *overindulgence*
Hir othes° been so grete and so dampnable,   *swearing*
That it is grisly for to here hem swere;
Our blissed Lordes body they to-tere,°   *tear apart*
Hem thoughte Jewes rente° him noght ynough;[118]   *tore*
190 And ech of hem at otheres sinne lough.   *laughs*
And right anon than comen tombesteres°   *dancing girls*
Fetys° and smale,° and yonge fruytesteres,°   *neat|slim|fruit-sellers*
Singers with harpes, baudes,° wafereres,°   *bawds|wafer-sellers*
Whiche been the verray° develes officeres   *true*
To kindle and blowe the fyr of lecherye,
That is annexed° unto glotonye;   *linked*
The Holy Writ take I to my witnesse,[119]
That luxurie° is in wyn and dronkenesse.   *lust*
Lo, how that dronken Loth,[120] unkindely,°   *Lot|unnaturally*
200 Lay by his doghtres two, unwitingly;
So dronke he was, he niste° what he wroghte.°   *knew not|did*
Herodes,[121] whoso wel the stories soghte,°   *searches*
Whan he of wyn was replet at his feste,°   *feast*
Right at his owene table he yaf° his heste°   *gave|command*
To sleen° the Baptist John ful giltelees.°   *slay|innocent*
Senek[122] seith eek° a good word doutelees;   *also*
He seith, he can no difference finde

Bitwix a man that is out of his minde
And a man which that is dronkelewe,°   *drunk*
210 But that woodnesse,° yfallen in a shrewe,°   *madness/wretched man*
Persevereth lenger than doth dronkenesse.
O glotonye, ful of cursednesse,°   *evil*
O cause first of our confusioun,°   *downfall*
O original of our dampnacioun,°   *damnation*
Til Crist had boght° us with his blood agayn!   *redeemed*
Lo, how dere,° shortly for to sayn,   *dearly*
Aboght° was thilke° cursed vileinye;   *paid for/that same*
Corrupt was al this world for glotonye!
    Adam our fader,° and his wyf also,   *father*
220 Fro Paradys to labour and to wo
Were driven for that vyce, it is no drede;°   *doubt*
For whyl that Adam fasted, as I rede,[123]
He was in Paradys; and whan that he
Eet° of the fruyt defended° on the tree,   *ate/forbidden*
Anon° he was outcast to wo and peyne.   *immediately*
O glotonye, on thee wel oghte us pleyne!°   *complain*
O, wiste a man° how many maladyes   *if one only knew*
Folwen of excesse and of glotonyes,
He wolde been the more mesurable°   *moderate*
230 Of his diete, sittinge at his table.
Allas! the shorte° throte, the tendre° mouth,[124]   *little/soft*
Maketh that, Est and West, and North and South,
In erthe, in eir,° in water men to swinke°   *air/labour*
To gete a glotoun deyntee° mete and drinke!   *choice*
Of this matere,[125] o Paul,° wel canstow trete,°   *St Paul/speak*
'Mete unto wombe,° and wombe eek unto mete,   *stomach*
Shal God destroyen bothe,' as Paulus seith.
Allas! a foul thing is it, by my feith,
To seye° this word, and fouler is the dede,   *say*
240 Whan man so drinketh of the whyte and rede,°   *i.e. wine*
That of his throte he maketh his privee,°   *privy*
Thurgh thilke cursed superfluitee.°   *excess*
    The apostel[126] weping seith ful pitously,
'Ther walken many of whiche yow told have I,
I seye it now weping with pitous voys,
That they been enemys of Cristes croys,°   *cross*
Of whiche the ende is deeth, wombe is her god.'
O wombe! O bely! O stinking cod,°   *bag*
Fulfild° of donge° and of corrupcioun!   *filled/dung*
250 At either ende of thee foul is the soun.°   *sound*
How greet labour and cost is thee to finde!°   *provide for*

Thise cokes, how they stampe, and streyne, and grinde,   *cooks/pound*
And turnen substaunce into accident,[127]
To fulfille al thy likerous° talent!   *greedy*
Out of the harde bones knokke they
The mary, for they caste° noght awey   *marrow/throw*
That may go thurgh the golet° softe and swote;°   *gullet/sweetly*
Of spicerye, of leef, and bark, and rote°   *spices/root*
Shal been his sauce ymaked, by delyt°   *pleasure*
260   To make him yet a newer appetyt.
But certes, he that haunteth swich delyces°   *sensual pleasures*
Is deed, whyl that he liveth in tho° vyces.[128]   *dead/those*
     A lecherous thing is wyn, and dronkenesse
Is ful of stryving° and of wrecchednesse,   *strife*
O dronke man, disfigured is thy face,
Sour is thy breeth, foul artow° to embrace,   *art thou*
And thurgh thy dronke nose semeth the soun°   *noise*
As though thou seydest ay° 'Sampsoun, Sampsoun';°   *always/Samson*
And yet, God wot, Sampsoun drank never no wyn.   *knows*
270   Thou fallest, as it were a stiked swyn;°   *stuck pig*
Thy tonge is lost, and al thyn honest cure;°   *self-respect*
For dronkenesse is verray sepulture
Of mannes wit and his discrecioun.
In whom that drinke hath dominacioun,
He can no conseil° kepe, it is no drede.   *secret*
Now kepe yow fro the whyte and fro the rede,
And namely° fro the whyte wyn of Lepe,[129]   *especially*
That is to selle° in Fish-strete° or in Chepe.°   *for sale/Fish St/Cheapside*
This wyn of Spayne° crepeth subtilly[130]   *Spain*
280   In othere wynes, growing faste° by,   *near*
Of which ther ryseth swich fumositee,°   *exhalation*
That whan a man hath dronken draughtes three,
And weneth° that he be at hoom in Chepe,   *believes*
He is in Spayne, right at the toune of Lepe,
Nat at the Rochel, ne at Burdeux° toun;   *La Rochelle/Bordeaux*
And thanne wol he seye, 'Sampsoun, Sampsoun.'
     But herkneth, lordings, o word, I yow praye,
That alle the sovereyn actes, dar I seye,   *great deeds*
Of victories in the Olde Testament,
290   Thurgh verray God, that is omnipotent,
Were doon in abstinence and in preyere;°   *prayer*
Loketh° the Bible, and ther ye may it lere.°   *look at/learn*
     Loke, Attila, the grete conquerour,
Deyde in his sleep, with shame and dishonour,
Bledinge ay° at his nose in dronkenesse;   *continually*

A capitayn shoulde live in sobrenesse.
And over° al this, avyseth° yow right wel   *moreover/consider*
What was comaunded unto Lamuel¹³¹—
Nat Samuel, but Lamuel, seye I—
300 Redeth the Bible, and finde it expresly
Of wyn-yeving° to hem that han justyse°.   *wine-serving/judicial power*
Namore of this, for it may wel suffyse.
    And now that I have spoke of glotonye,
Now wol I yow defenden° hasardrye°.   *forbid/gambling*
Hasard is verray moder° of lesinges°,   *mother/lies*
And of deceite, and cursed forsweringes°,   *perjury*
Blaspheme of Crist, manslaughtre, and wast° also   *waste*
Of catel° and of tyme; and forthermo,   *property*
It is repreve° and contrarie of honour   *reproach*
310 For to ben holde a commune hasardour°.   *gambler*
And ever the hyër he is of estaat°,   *position*
The more is he holden desolaat°.   *disgraced*
If that a prince useth hasardrye,
In alle governaunce and policye
He is, as by commune opinioun,
Yholde° the lasse in reputacioun.   *held*
    Stilbon, that was a wys° embassadour,   *prudent*
Was sent to Corinthe°, in ful greet honour,   *Corinth*
Fro Lacidomie°, to make hir alliaunce.   *Sparta*
320 And whan he cam, him happede, par chaunce°,   *chance*
That alle the grettest° that were of that lond,   *greatest*
Pleyinge atte hasard° he hem fond.   *dice*
For which, as sone as it mighte be,
He stal° him hoom agayn to his contree,   *stole*
And seyde, 'Ther wol I nat lese° my name;   *lose*
Ne I wol nat take on me so greet defame°,   *dishonour*
Yow for to allye unto none hasardours.
Sendeth othere wyse embassadours;
For, by my trouthe, me were lever dye°,   *I would rather die*
330 Than I yow sholde to hasardours allye.
For ye that been so glorious in honours
Shul nat allyen yow with hasardours
As by my will, ne as by my tretee°.'   *treaty*
This wyse philosophre thus seyde he.
    Loke eek° that, to the king Demetrius¹³²   *also*
The king of Parthes°, as the book seith us,   *Parthians*
Sente him a paire of dees° of gold in scorn,   *dice*
For he hadde used hasard therbiforn;
For which he heeld his glorie or his renoun

340 At no value or reputacioun.
   Lordes may finden other maner pley°   *pastimes*
   Honeste ynough to dryve the day awey.°   *pass*
     Now wol I speke of othes° false and grete   *oaths*
   A word or two, as olde bokes trete.
   Gret swering is a thing abhominable,
   And false swering is yet more reprevable.°   *reprehensible*
   The heighe God forbad swering at al,
   Witnesse on Mathew;[133] but in special
   Of swering seith the holy Jeremye,
350 'Thou shalt seye sooth° thyn othes, and nat lye,   *truly*
   And swere in dome,° and eek in rightwisnesse';   *judgement*
   But ydel swering is a cursednesse.
   Bihold and see, that in the firste table°   *tablet*
   Of heighe Goddes hestes° honurable,[134]   *commandments*
   How that the seconde heste of Him is this—
   'Tak nat my name in ydel° or amis.°'   *in vain/wrongly*
   Lo, rather he forbedeth swich swering
   Than homicyde or many a cursed thing;
   I seye that, as by ordre, thus it stondeth;
360 This knoweth° that His hestes understondeth,° *he knows/understands*
   How that the second[135] heste of God is that.
   And forther-over,° I wol thee telle al plat,°   *furthermore/plainly*
   That vengeance shal nat parten° from his hous,   *leave*
   That° of his othes is too outrageous.°   *who/immoderate*
   'By Goddes precious herte, and by his nayles,
   And by the blode of Crist that is in Hayles;°   *Hailes*
   Seven is my chaunce,° and thyn is cink° and treye;° *throw/five/three*
   By Goddes armes, if thou falsly pleye,
   This dagger shal thurghout thyn herte go'—
370 This fruyt cometh of the bicched bones° two,   *damned dice*
   Forswering,° ire,° falsnesse, homicyde.   *perjury, anger*
   Now, for the love of Crist that for us dyde,
   Leveth° your othes, bothe grete and smale;   *give up*
   But, sirs, now wol I telle forth my tale.
     Thise ryotoures° three, of whiche I telle,   *revellers*
   Longe erst er° pryme[136] rong of any belle,   *before*
   Were set hem in a taverne for to drinke;
   And as they satte, they herde a belle[137] clinke
   Biforn a cors,° was caried to his grave;   *corpse*
380 That oon of hem gan callen to his knave,°   *servant*
   'Go bet,' quod he, 'and axe redily,°   *quickly/straight away*
   What cors is this that passeth heer forby;°   *nearby*
   And look° that thou reporte his name wel.'   *be sure*

'Sir,' quod this boy, 'it nedeth never-a-del°. *that's not necessary*
It was me told, er ye cam heer°, two houres; *here*
He was, pardee°, an old felawe° of youres; *truly/companion*
And sodeynly he was yslayn tonight°, *last night*
For-dronke°, as he sat on his bench upright; *blind drunk*
Ther cam a privee° theef, men clepeth° Deeth, *secret/call*
390   That in this contree al the peple sleeth°, *slayeth*
And with his spere° he smoot his herte atwo°, *spear/in two*
And wente his wey withouten wordes mo.
He hath a thousand slayn this pestilence:° *during this plague*
And, maister, er ye come in his presence,
Me thinketh that it were necessarie
For to be war° of swich an adversarie: *wary*
Beth redy for to meete him evermore.
Thus taughte me my dame°, I sey namore°.' *mother/no more*
'By sainte Marie,' seyde this taverner°, *innkeeper*
400   'The child seith sooth°, for he hath slayn this yeer, *truth*
Henne° over a myle, within a greet° village, *hence/great*
Both man and womman, child and hyne°, and page° *farm-worker/servant-boy/believe*
I trowe° his habitacioun be there;
To been avysed° greet wisdom it were, *forewarned*
Er that he dide a man a dishonour.'
'Ye Goddes armes,' quod this ryotour,
'Is it swich peril with him for to meete? *such*
I shal him seke by wey and eek by streete°, *highway and byeway*
I make avow to Goddes digne° bones! *noble*
410   Herkneth, felawes, we three been al ones;° *of one mind*
Lat ech of us holde up his hond til° other, *to the*
And ech of us bicomen otheres brother,
And we wol sleen° this false traytour Deeth; *slay*
He shal be slayn, which that so many sleeth,
By Goddes dignitee°, er it be night.' *glory*
   Togidres han thise three her trouthes plight°, *pledged their word of honour*
To live and dyen ech of hem for other,
As though he were his owene yboren° brother. *born*
And up they sterte° al dronken, in this rage, *started*
420   And forth they goon towardes that village,
Of which the taverner had spoke biforn,
And many a grisly° ooth than han they sworn, *horrible*
And Cristes blessed body they to-rente°— *tore apart*
'Deeth shal be deed°, if that they may him hente°. *dead/catch*
   Whan they han goon nat fully half a myle,
Right as they wolde han troden° over a style, *climbed*
An old man and a povre° with hem mette. *poor*

This olde man ful mekely° hem grette,°   *humbly/greeted*
And seyde thus, 'Now, lordes, God yow see!'°   *protect*
430   The proudest of thise ryotoures three
Answerde agayn, 'What! carl,° with sory grace,¹³⁸   *churl*
Why artow° al forwrapped° save thy face   *art thou/wrapped up*
Why livestow so longe in so greet age?'
        This olde man gan loke in his visage,
And seyde thus, 'For° I ne can nat finde   *because*
A man, though that I walked into Inde,°   *India*
Neither in citee nor in no village,
That wolde chaunge his youthe for myn age;
And therfore moot° I han myn age stille.   *must*
440   As longe time as it is Goddes wille.
        Ne deeth, allas! ne wol nat han my lyf;
Thus walke I, lyk a restelees caityf,°   *captive*
And on the ground, which is my modres°gate,   *mother's*
I knokke with my staf, bothe erly and late,
And seye, "Leve° moder, leet me in!   *dear*
Lo, how I vanish, flesh, and blood, and skin!
Allas! whan shul my bones been at reste?
Moder, with yow wolde I chaunge° my cheste,   *exchange*
That in my chambre longe tyme hath be,
450   Ye! for an heyre clowt° to wrappe me!"   *hair-shroud*
But yet to me she wol nat do that grace,
For which ful pale and welked° is my face.   *withered*
        But, sirs, to yow it is no curteisye
To speken to an old man vileinye,°   *roughness*
But° he trespasse in worde, or elles in dede,   *unless*
In Holy Writ ye may yourself wel rede,¹³⁹
"Agayns° an old man, hoor° upon his heed,   *before/white hairs*
Ye sholde aryse"; wherfor I yeve° yow reed,°   *give/advice*
Ne dooth unto an old man noon harm now,
460   Namore than ye wolde men dide to yow
In age, if that ye so longe abyde;
And God be with yow, wher ye go or ryde.°   *in whatever you do*
I moot go thider as I have to go.'°   *i.e. where I must*
        'Nay, olde cherl, by God, thou shalt nat so,'
Seyde this other hasardour anon;
'Thou partest nat so lightly,° by Saint John!   *easily*
Thou spak right now of thilke traitour Deeth,
That in this contree alle our frendes sleeth.°   *slayeth*
Have heer my trouthe,° as thou art his aspye,°   *i.e. listen to me/spy*
470   Tel wher he is, or thou shalt it abye,°   *pay for it*
By God, and by the holy sacrament!'°   *the Eucharist*

For soothly thou art oon of his assent,°   *following*
To sleen us yonge folk, thou false theef!'
   'Now, sirs,' quod he, 'if that yow be so leef°   *wishing*
To finde Deeth, turne up this crooked wey,
For in that grove I laft° him, by my fey,°   *left/faith*
Under a tree, and ther he wol abyde;
Nat for your boost° he wol him nothing hyde.   *boasting*
See ye that ook?° Right ther ye shul him finde.   *oak*
480 God save yow, that boghte agayn° mankinde,   *redeemed*
And yow amende!'° Thus seyde this olde man.   *reform*
And everich° of thise ryotoures ran,   *each*
Til he cam to that tree, and ther they founde
Of florins[140] fyne of golde ycoyned rounde
Wel ny an eighte busshels,° as hem thoughte.   *bushels*
No lenger thanne after Deeth they soughte,
But ech of hem so glad was of that sighte,
For that the florins been so faire and brighte,
That doun they sette hem by this precious hord.°   *hoard*
490 The worste of hem he spake the firste word.
   'Brethren,' quod he, 'tak kepe° what I seye;   *note*
My wit° is greet, though that I bourde° and pleye.   *wisdom/jest*
This tresor hath Fortune unto us yiven,°   *given*
In mirthe and jolitee our lyf to liven,
And lightly° as it comth, so wol we spende.   *easily*
Ey! Goddes precious dignitee!° who wende°   *reverence/expected*
To-day, that we sholde han so fair a grace?°   *favour*
But mighte this gold be caried fro this place
Hoom to myn hous, or elles unto youres—
500 For wel ye woot that al this gold is oures—
Than were we in heigh felicitee.
But trewely, by daye it may nat be;
Men wolde seyn° that we were theves stronge,°   *say/hardened*
And for our owene tresor doon us honge.°   *have us hanged*
This tresor moste ycaried be by nighte
As wysly° and as slyly as it mighte.   *carefully*
Wherfore I rede° that cut° among us alle   *advise/lots*
Be drawe, and lat se wher the cut wol falle;
And he that hath the cut with herte blythe
510 Shal renne° to the toune, and that ful swythe,°   *run/quickly*
And bringe us breed and wyn ful prively.°   *secretly*
And two of us shul kepen° subtilly   *guard*
This tresor wel; and, if he wol nat tarie,°   *delay*
Whan it is night, we wol this tresor carie
By oon assent,° wheras us thinketh best.'   *agreement*

That oon of hem the cut broughte in his fest,°   *closed hand*
And bad hem drawe, and loke wher it wol falle;
And it fil° on the yongeste of hem alle;   *fell*
And forth toward the toun he wente anon.
520 And also° sone as that he was gon,   *as*
That oon of hem spak thus unto that other,
'Thou knowest wel thou art my sworne brother,
Thy profit wol I telle thee anon.
Thou woost wel that our felawe is agon;°   *gone*
And heer is gold, and that ful greet plentee,
That shal departed° been among us three.   *shared*
But natheles, if I can shape° it so   *arrange*
That it departed were among us two,
Hadde I nat doon a freendes torn° to thee?'   *turn*
530   That other answerde, 'I noot° how that may be;   *know not*
He woot° how that the gold is with us tweye,   *knows*
What shal we doon, what shal we to him seye?'
'Shal it be conseil?'° seyde the firste shrewe,°   *secret/villain*
'And I shal tellen thee, in wordes fewe,
What we shal doon, and bringe it wel aboute.'
'I graunte,' quod that other, 'out of doute,
That, by my trouthe, I wol thee nat biwreye.°'   *betray*
'Now,' quod the firste, 'thou woost wel we be tweye,
And two of us shul strenger° be than oon.   *stronger*
540 Look whan that he is set,° and right anoon°   *seated/immediately*
Arys,° as though thou woldest with him pleye;   *arise*
And I shal ryve° him thurgh the sydes tweye   *stab*
Whyl that thou strogelest with him as in game,
And with thy dagger look thou do the same;
And than shal al this gold departed be,
My dere freend, bitwixen me and thee;
Than may we bothe our lustes° al fulfille,   *desires*
And pleye at dees° right at our owene wille.'   *dice*
And thus acorded° been thise shrewes° tweye   *agreed/villains*
550 To sleen° the thridde, as ye han herd me seye.   *slay*
   This yongest, which that wente unto the toun,
Ful ofte in herte he rolleth up and doun
The beautee of thise florins newe and brighte.
'O Lord!' quod he, 'if so were that I mighte
Have al this tresor to myself allone,
Ther is no man that liveth under the trone°   *throne*
Of God, that sholde live so mery as I!'
And atte laste the Feend,° our enemy,   *Devil*
Putte in his thought that he shold poyson beye,°   *buy*

560 With which he mighte sleen° his felawes tweye;   *slay*
For why the Feend fond him in swich lyvinge,°   *way of living*
That he had leve° him to sorwe bringe,   *leave*
For this was outrely° his fulle entente   *wholly*
To sleen hem bothe, and never to repente.
And forth he gooth, no lenger wolde he tarie,
Into the toun, unto a pothecarie,°   *apothecary*
And preyed him, that he him wolde selle
Som poyson, that he mighte his rattes quelle;°   *destroy*
And eek ther was a polcat° in his hawe,°   *polecat/yard*
570 That, as he seyde, his capouns° hadde yslawe,°   *chickens/slain*
And fayn° he wolde wreke° him, if he mighte,   *gladly/avenge*
On vermin, that destroyed° him by nighte.   *ruined*
    The pothecarie answerde, 'And thou shalt have
A thing that, also° God my soule save,   *as*
In al this world ther nis no creäture,
That ete or dronke hath of this confiture°   *mixture*
Noght but the mountance° of a corn° of whete,   *amount/grain*
That he ne shal his lyf anon forlete;°   *lose*
Ye, sterve° he shal, and that in lasse whyle   *die*
580 Than thou wolt goon a paas° nat but a myle;   *at walking pace*
This poyson is so strong and violent.'
    This cursed man hath in his hond yhent°   *taken*
This poyson in a box, and sith° he ran   *then*
Into the nexte strete, unto a man,
And borwed him large botels three;
And in the two his poyson poured he;
The thridde he kepte clene for his drinke.
For al the night he shoop° him for to swinke°   *intended/toil*
In caryinge of the gold out of that place.
590 And whan this ryotour, with sory grace,
Had filled with wyn his grete botels three,
To his felawes agayn repaireth he.
    What nedeth it to sermone of it more?
For right as they had cast° his deeth° bifore,   *plotted/death*
Right so they han him slayn, and that anon.
And whan that this was doon, thus spak that oon,°   *one*
'Now lat us sitte and drinke, and make us merie,
And afterward we wol his body berie.°'   *bury*
And with that word it happed him, par cas,°   *by chance*
600 To take the botel ther° the poyson was,   *where*
And drank, and yaf his felawe drinke also,
For which anon they storven° bothe two.   *died*
    But, certes, I suppose that Avicen°   *Avicenna*

Wroot never in no canon, ne in no fen,°   *section*
Mo wonder signes° of empoisoning   *symptoms*
Than hadde thise wrecches two, er° hir ending.   *before*
Thus ended been thise homicydes two,
And eek the false empoysoner also.

O cursed sinne, ful of cursednesse!
610 O traytours homicyde, o wikkednesse!
O glotonye, luxurie,° and hasardrye!°   *lechery/gambling*
Thou blasphemour of Crist with vileinye
And othes° grete, of usage° and of pryde!   *oaths/habit*
Allas! mankinde, how may it bityde,°   *happen*
That to thy creatour which that thee wroghte,°   *made*
And with his precious herte-blood thee boghte,°   *redeemed*
Thou art so fals and so unkinde,° allas!   *unnatural*
   Now, goode men, God forgeve yow your trespas,°   *sins*
And ware° yow fro the sinne of avaryce.   *guard*
620 Myn holy pardoun may yow alle waryce,°   *cure*
So that ye offre nobles[141] or sterlinges,
Or elles silver broches, spones,° ringes.   *spoons*
Boweth your heed° under this holy bulle!   *head*
Cometh up, ye wyves, offreth of your wolle!°   *wool*
Your name I entre heer in my rolle° anon;   *list*
Into the blisse of hevene shul ye gon;
I yow assoile,° by myn heigh power,   *absolve*
Yow that wol offre, as clene and eek as cleer
As ye were born and, lo, sirs, thus I preche.
630 And Jesu Crist, that is our soules leche,°   *physician*
So graunte yow his pardon to receyve;
For that is best; I wol yow nat deceyve.
   But sirs, o word forgat I in my tale,
I have relikes and pardon in my male,°   *bag*
As faire as any man in Engelond,
Whiche were me yeven by the popes hond.°   *hand*
If any of yow wol, of devocioun,
Offren, and han myn absolucioun,
Cometh forth anon, and kneleth heer adoun,
640 And mekely receyveth my pardoun:
Or elles, taketh pardon as ye wende,°   *go*
Al newe and fresh, at every tounes° ende,   *town's*
So that ye offren alwey newe and newe°   *again and again*
Nobles and pens,° which that be gode and trewe.°   *pence/genuine*
It is an honour° to everich° that is heer,   *good thing/for each*
That ye mowe° have a suffisant° pardoneer   *may/competent*

T'assoille° yow, in contree as ye ryde,   *absolve*
For aventures° which that may bityde°   *accidents/happen*
Peraventure° ther may falle oon or two   *perhaps*
650 Doun of his hors, and breke his nekke atwo°   *in two*
Look which a seuretee° is it to yow alle   *surety*
That I am in your felaweship yfalle,°   *fallen in with*
That may assoille yow, bothe more and lasse,°   *i.e. everybody*
Whan that the soule shal fro the body passe.
I rede° that our hoste heer shal biginne,   *advise*
For he is most envoluped° in sinne.   *enveloped*
Com forth, sir Hoste, and offre first anon,
And thou shalt kisse the reliks everichon,°   *everyone*
Ye, for a grote! unbokel° anon° thy purs.'   *unbuckle/immediately*

660 'Nay, nay,' quod he, 'than have° I Cristes curs!   *would I have*
Lat be,' quod he, 'it shal nat be, so theech!°   *may I thrive*
Thou woldest make me kisse thyn old breech,°   *breeches*
And swere it were a relik of a saint,
Thogh it were with thy fundement° depeint!°   *bottom/stained*
But by the croys which that Saint Eleyne fond,   *St Helen*
I wolde I hadde thy coillons° in myn hond   *testicles*
In stede of relikes or of seintuarie;°   *holy objects*
Lat cutte hem of,° I wol thee helpe hem carie;   *off*
Thay shul be shryned in an hogges tord.°'   *turd*
670   This pardoner answerde nat a word;
So wrooth he was, no word ne wolde he seye.
        'Now,' quod our host, 'I wol no lenger pleye°   *joke*
With thee, ne with noon other angry man.'
But right anon the worthy knight bigan,
Whan that he saugh that al the peple lough,°   *laugh*
'Namore of this, for it is right ynough;
Sir Pardoner, be glad and mery of chere;
And ye, sir Host, that been to me so dere,
I prey yow that ye kisse the Pardoner.[142]
680 And Pardoner, I prey thee, drawe thee neer,
And, as we diden, lat us laughe and pleye.'
Anon they kiste, and riden forth hir weye.

*   *   *

The Nun's Priest's Tale

THE INTRODUCTION

'Ho!' quod the knight, 'good sir, namore of this,
That ye han seyd is right ynough, ywis,
And mochel° more; for litel hevinesse°   *much/sadness*
Is right ynough to mochel° folk, I gesse.   *many*
I seye for me, it is a greet disese°   *pain*
Wheras men han ben in greet welthe and ese°,   *comfort*
To heren of hir sodeyn° fall, allas!   *sudden*
And the contrarie is joie and greet solas°,   *comfort*
As whan a man hath been in poore estaat°,   *state*
10 And clymbeth up, and wexeth° fortunat,   *becomes*
And ther abydeth in prosperitee,
Swich thing is gladsom, as it thinketh me,
And of swich thing were goodly for to telle.'
'Ye,' quod our hoste, 'by Seint Poules belle,   *St Paul's*
Ye seye right sooth; this monk, he clappeth° loude,   *prates*
He spak how 'Fortune covered with a cloude'
I noot° never what, and als° of a 'Tragedie'   *know not/also*
Right now ye herde, and parde!° no remedie   *by God*
It is for to biwaille°, ne compleyne   *bewail*
20 That that is doon; and als it is a peyne,
As ye han seyd°, to here° of hevinesse.   *said/hear*
Sir Monk, namore of this, so God yow blesse!
Your tale anoyeth° al this companye;   *upsets*
Swich talking is nat worth a boterflye°;   *butterfly*
For therin is ther no desport° ne game°.   *amusement/fun*
Wherfor, sir Monk, or Dan° Piers° by your name,   *master/Peter*
I preye yow hertely, telle us somwhat elles°,   *else*
For sikerly°, nere° clinking of your belles,   *truly/were it not*
That on your brydel hange on every syde,
30 By heven° king, that for us alle dyde°,   *heaven's/died*
I sholde er this han fallen doun for slepe,
Although the slough° had never been so depe;¹⁴³   *mire*
Than° had your tale al be told in vayn.   *then*
For certeinly, as that thise clerkes° seyn,   *scholars*
'Wheras° a man may have noon° audience,   *when/no*
Noght helpeth it to tellen his sentence°.'   *opinion*
And wel I woot the substance is in me°,   *I can understand*
If any thing shal wel reported be.
Sir, sey° somwhat of hunting, I yow preye.'   *say*
40 'Nay,' quod this monk, 'I have no lust° to pleye°;   *desire/jest*

Now let another telle, as I have told.'
Than spak our host, with rude° speche and bold,   *rough*
And seyde unto the nonnes preest anon,°   *immediately*
'Com neer,° thou preest, com hider,° thou Sir John,¹⁴⁴   *near/hither*
Tel us swich thing as may our hertes glade;°   *please*
Be blythe, though thou ryde upon a jade.°   *poor old horse*
What though thyn hors be bothe foule° and lene,°   *dirty/skinny*
If he wol serve thee, rekke° nat a bene;°   *care/bean*
Look that thyn herte be mery evermo.'
50   'Yis, sir,' quod he, 'yis, host, so mote I go,¹⁴⁵
But° I be mery, ywis,° I wol be blamed.'   *unless/indeed*
And right anon his tale he hath attamed,°   *begun*
And thus he seyde unto us everichon,
This swete preest, this goodly man, Sir John.

THE TALE

A povre° widwe, somdel stape° in age,   *poor/advanced*
Was whylom° dwelling in a narwe° cotage,   *once upon a time/little*
Bisyde a grove, stonding in a dale.°   *valley*
This widwe, of which I telle yow my tale,
Sin thilke° day that she was last a wyf,   *that very*
60   In pacience ladde° a ful simple lyf,   *led*
For litel was hir catel° and hir rente;°   *property/income*
By housbondrye,° of such as God hir sente,   *economy*
She fond° hirself, and eek° hir doghtren° two.   *looked after/also/daughters*
Three large sowes hadde she, and namo,°   *no more*
Three kyn,° and eek a sheep that highte Malle.°   *cows/called Molly*
Ful sooty was hir bour, and eek hir halle,¹⁴⁶
In which she eet° ful many a sclendre° meel.   *ate/frugal*
Of poynaunt sauce hir neded never a deel.°   *not a jot*
No deyntee morsel passed thurgh hir throte;
70   Hir dyete was accordant° to hir cote.°   *like/cottage*
Repleccioun° ne made hir never syk;°   *over-eating/sick*
Attempree° dyete was al hir phisyk,°   *moderate/medicine*
And exercyse, and hertes suffisaunce.°   *contentment*
The goute° lette° hir nothing for to daunce,   *gout/prevented*
Napoplexye° shente° nat hir heed°;   *nor apoplexy/ruined/head*
No wyn° ne drank she, neither whyt ne reed;   *wine*
Hir bord° was served most with whyt and blak,   *table*
Milk and brown breed,° in which she fond no lak,°   *bread/defect*
Seynd° bacoun, and somtyme an ey° or tweye,   *broiled/egg*
80   For she was, as it were, a maner deye.°   *kind of dairy woman*
A yerd° she hadde, enclosed al aboute   *yard*

With stikkes, and a drye dich° withoute,   *ditch*
In which she hadde a cok, hight° Chauntecleer,°   *called|Chanticleer*
In al the land, of crowing, nas° his peer.°   *there was not|equal*
His vois was merier than the mery orgon°   *organ*
On messe-dayes° that in the chirche gon;°   *mass-days|is played*
Wel sikerer° was his crowing in his logge,°   *surer|abode*
Than is a clokke, or an abbey orlogge.[147]
By nature knew he ech ascencioun
90 Of equinoxial[148] in thilke toun;
For whan degrees fiftene were ascended,
Thanne crew he, that it mighte nat ben amended.°   *bettered*
His comb was redder than the fyn coral,
And batailed,° as it were a castel° wal.   *crenellated|castle*
His bile° was blak, and as the jeet° it shoon;°   *bill|jet*
Lyk asur° were his legges, and his toon;°   *i.e. bright blue|toes*
His nayles° whytter than the lilie flour,   *claws*
And lyk the burned° gold was his colour.   *burnished*
This gentil° cok hadde in his governaunce   *noble*
100 Sevene hennes, for to doon al his plesaunce   *pleasure*
Whiche were his sustres° and his paramours,   *sisters*
And wonder lyk° to him, as of colours.   *like*
Of whiche the faireste hewed° on hir throte°   *coloured|throat*
Was cleped° faire damoysele[149] Pertelote.   *called*
Curteis° she was, discreet, and debonaire,°   *refined|gracious*
And compaignable,° and bar° hirself so faire,   *friendly|bore*
Sin thilke day that she was seven night old,
That trewely she hath the herte in hold°   *keeping*
Of Chauntecleer, loken° in every lith;°   *locked|limb*
110 He loved hir so, that wel was him therwith.°   *because of that*
But such a joye was it to here° hem singe,   *hear*
Whan that the brighte sonne gan to springe,°   *rise*
In swete accord, 'My lief° is faren° in londe.°' *love|gone|into the country*
For thilke° tyme, as I have understonde,°   *at that|heard*
Bestes and briddes° coude speke and singe.   *birds*
    And so befel,° that in a daweninge,°   *it happened|at dawn*
As Chauntecleer among his wyves alle
Sat on his perche, that was in the halle,[150]
And next him sat this faire Pertelote,
120 This Chauntecleer gan gronen° in his throte,   *groan*
As man that in his dreem is drecched° sore.   *upset*
And whan that Pertelote thus herde him rore,°   *roar*
She was agast,° and seyde, 'O herte dere,   *afraid*
What eyleth° yow, to grone in this manere?   *ails*
Ye been a verray° sleper,[151] fy for shame!'   *fine*

And he answerde and seyde thus, 'Madame,
I pray yow, that ye take it nat agrief:°   *amiss*
By God, me mette° I was in swich meschief°   *dreamed/trouble*
Right now, that yet° myn herte is sore afright.°   *still/frightened*
130 Now God,' quod he, 'my swevene recche aright,[152]
And keep my body out of foul prisoun!
Me mette,° how that I romed up and down   *dreamed*
Withinne our yerde, wheras° I sawe a beste,   *when*
Was lyk an hound, and wolde han maad areste°   *seized*
Upon my body, and wolde han had me deed.°   *killed*
His colour was bitwixe yellow and reed;°   *red*
And tipped was his tail, and bothe his eres,°   *ears*
With blak, unlyk the remnant° of his heres;°   *rest/hairs*
His snowte smal,° with glowinge eyen tweye.°   *narrow/two*
140 Yet of his look for fere° almost I deye;°   *fear/died*
This caused me my groning, douteles.'

'Avoy!' quod she, 'fy on yow, herteles!°   *coward*
Allas!' quod she, 'for, by that God above,
Now han ye lost myn herte and al my love;
I can nat love a coward, by my faith.
For certes,° what so any womman seith,   *indeed*
We alle desyren, if it mighte be,
To han housbondes hardy,° wyse, and free;°   *brave/generous*
And secree,° and no nigard, ne no fool,   *discreet*
150 Ne him that is agast° of every tool,°   *afraid/weapon*
Ne noon avauntour,° by that God above!   *braggart*
How dorste° ye seyn° for shame unto your love,   *dare/say*
That any thing mighte make yow aferd?°   *afraid*
Have ye no mannes herte, and han a berd?°   *beard*
Allas! and conne° ye been agast° of swevenis?°   *can/afraid/dreams*
Nothing, God wot, but vanitee,° in sweven is.   *emptiness*
Swevenes engendren° of replecciouns,°   *coming from/over-eating*
And ofte of fume,° and of complecciouns,[153]   *exhalations*
Whan humours been to habundant° in a wight.   *abundant*
160 Certes this dreem, which ye han met tonight,°   *last night*
Cometh of the grete superfluitee
Of youre rede colera,[154] pardee,
Which causeth folk to dreden in here° dremes   *their*
Of arwes,° and of fyr with rede lemes,°   *arrows/flames*
Of grete bestes, that they wol hem byte,
Of contek,° and of whelpes° grete and lyte;   *strife/dogs*
Right as the humour of malencolye°   *melancholy*
Causeth ful many a man, in sleep, to crye,
For fere of blake beres,° or boles° blake,   *bears/bulls*

170 Or elles, blake develes° wole hem take.   *devils*
    Of othere humours coude I telle also,
    That warken° many a man in sleep ful wo;   *bring*
    But I wol passe as lightly° as I can.   *quickly*
      Lo Catoun,° which that was so wys a man,   *Cato*
    Seyde he nat thus, ne do no fors° of dremes?   *take no notice of*
    Now, sire,' quod she, 'whan we flee° fro the bemes,°   *fly down/rafters*
    For Goddes love, as tak som laxatyf;
    Up° peril of my soule, and of my lyf,   *upon*
    I counseille yow the beste, I wol nat lye,
180 That bothe of colere and of malencolye
    Ye purge yow; and for° ye shul nat tarie,   *so that*
    Though in this toun is noon apothecarie,
    I shal myself to herbes techen° yow,   *direct*
    That shul ben for your hele,° and for your prow;°   *health/benefit*
    And in our yerd tho° herbes shal I finde,   *those*
    The whiche han of hir propretee, by kinde,°   *nature*
    To purgen yow binethe, and eek above.
    Forget not this, for Goddes owene love!
    Ye been ful colerik of compleccioun.[155]
190 Ware° the sonne in his ascencioun   *beware lest*
    Ne fynde yow nat repleet° of humours hote;   *over-full*
    And if it do, I dar wel leye° a grote,[156]   *wager*
    That ye shul have a fevere terciane,°   *tertian*
    Or an agu,° that may be youre bane.°   *ague/death*
    A day or two ye shul have digestyves[157]
    Of wormes, er ye take your laxatyves,
    Of lauriol,[158] centaure, and fumetere,
    Or elles of ellebor, that groweth there,
    Of catapuce, or of gaytres beryis,
200 Of erbe yve, growing in our yerd, ther mery is;°   *where it is pleasant*
    Pekke hem up right as they growe, and ete hem in.
    Be mery, housbond, for your fader° kin!   *father's*
    Dredeth° no dreem; I can say yow namore.°   *fear/no more*
      'Madame,' quod he, 'graunt mercy° of your lore.°   *thank you/teaching*
    But nathelees, as touching daun Catoun,
    That hath of wisdom such a greet renoun,
    Though that he bad no dremes for to drede,
    By God, men may in olde bokes rede
    Of many a man, more of auctoritee
210 Than ever Catoun was, so mote I thee,°   *thrive*
    That al the revers° seyn of his sentence,°   *opposite/opinion*
    And han wel founden by experience,
    That dremes ben significaciouns,

As wel of joye as tribulaciouns
That folk enduren in this lyf present.
Ther nedeth make of this noon argument;
The verray° preve° sheweth it in dede.   *true/test*
  Oon of the gretteste auctour°¹⁵⁹ that men rede   *authors*
Seith thus, that whylom° two felawes wente   *once upon a time*
220 On pilgrimage, in a ful good entente;°   *purpose*
And happed so thay come into a toun,
Wheras ther was swich congregacioun
Of peple, and eek so streit of herbergage,°   *shortage of lodgings*
That they ne founde as muche as o° cotage,   *one*
In which they bothe mighte ylogged° be.   *lodged*
Wherfor thay mosten,° of necessitee,   *must*
As for that night, departen° compaignye;   *part*
And ech of hem goth to his hostelrye,
And took his logging as it wolde falle.°   *luck would have it*
230 That oon of hem was logged in a stalle,
Fer° in a yerd, with oxen of the plough;   *far away*
That other man was logged wel ynough,
As was his aventure,° or his fortune,   *good luck*
That us governeth alle as in commune.°   *generally*
  And so bifel, that, longe er it were day,
This man mette° in his bed, theras he lay,   *dreamed*
How that his felawe gan upon him calle,
And seyde, "Allas! for in an oxes stalle
This night I shal be mordred° ther° I lye.   *murdered/where*
240 Now help me, dere brother, er I dye;
In alle haste com to me," he sayde.
This man out of his sleep for fere abrayde;°   *leapt*
But whan that he was wakned of his sleep,
He turned him, and took of this no keep;°   *notice*
Him thoughte his dreem nas but a vanitee.
Thus twyës° in his sleping dremed he.   *twice*
And atte thridde° tyme yet his felawe   *third*
Cam, as him thoughte, and seide, "I am now slawe;°   *slain*
Bihold my blody woundes, depe and wyde!
250 Arys° up erly in the morwe tyde,°   *arise/morning*
And at the west gate of the toun," quod he,
"A carte ful of donge° ther shaltow° see,   *dung/shalt thou*
In which my body is hid ful prively;°   *secretly*
Do° thilke carte aresten° boldely.   *have/stopped*
My gold caused my mordre° sooth to sayn";   *murder*
And tolde him every poynt° how he was slayn,   *detail*
With a ful pitous° face, pale of hewe.   *pitiful*

And truste wel, his dreem he fond° ful trewe; *found*
For on the morwe,° as sone° as it was day, *morning/soon*
260 To his felawes in° he took the way; *inn*
And whan that he cam to this oxes stalle,
After his felawe he bigan to calle.
    The hostiler° answered him anon, *innkeeper*
And seyde, "Sire, your felawe is agon,° *gone*
As sone as day he wente out of the toun."
This man gan fallen in suspecioun,
Remembring on his dremes that he mette.° *dreamed*
And forth he goth, no lenger wolde he lette,° *stay*
Unto the west gate of the toun, and fond
270 A dong carte, as it were to donge° lond, *manure*
That was arrayed° in the same wyse *disposed*
As he han herd the dede° man devyse;° *dead/describe*
And with an hardy herte he gan to crye
Vengeaunce and justice of this felonye:
"My felawe mordred° is this same night, *murdered*
And in this carte he lyth° gapinge upright.° *lies/on his back*
I crye out on the ministres,°" quod he, *officers*
"That sholden kepe° and reulen° this citee; *watch over/govern*
Harrow!° allas! her lyth° my felawe slayn!" *help!/lies*
280 What sholde I more unto this tale sayn?
The peple out sterte,° and caste the cart to grounde, *rushed out*
And in the middel of the dong they founde
The dede man, that mordred was al newe.° *recently*
    O blisful° God, that art so just and trewe! *blessed*
Lo, how that thou biwreyest° mordre alway! *uncovers*
Mordre wol out, that see we day by day.
Mordre is so wlatsom° and abhominable° *loathsome/inhuman*
To God, that is so just and resonable,
That he ne wol nat suffre it heled° be; *hidden*
290 Though it abyde a yeer, or two, or three,
Mordre wol out, this my conclusioun.
And right anoon, ministres of that toun
Han hent° the carter, and so sore him pyned,° *taken/tortured*
And eek the hostiler so sore engyned,° *racked*
That thay biknewe° hir wikkednesse anoon, *confessed*
And were anhanged° by the nekke-boon. *hanged*
    Here may men seen that dremes been to drede.° *fear*
And certes, in the same book I rede,° *read*
Right in the nexte chapitre after this,
300 (I gabbe° nat, so have I joye or blis,) *tell no lies*
Two men that wolde han passed over see,

For certeyn cause,° into a fer° contree,   *reason/distant*
If that the wind ne hadde been contrarie,°   *against them*
That made hem in a citee for to tarie,°   *remain*
That stood ful mery° upon an haven° syde.   *pleasant/harbour*
But on a day, agayn° the eventyde,   *towards*
The wind gan chaunge, and blew right as hem leste.°   *they needed*
Jolif° and glad they wente unto hir reste,   *happy*
And casten° hem ful erly for to saille;°   *intended*
310 But to that oo° man fil° a greet mervaille.   *one/fell*
That oon of hem, in sleping as he lay,
Him mette° a wonder dreem, agayn the day;°   *dreamed/before daylight*
Him thoughte a man stood by his beddes syde,
And him comaunded, that he sholde abyde,°   *stay*
And seyde him thus, "If thou to-morwe wende,°   *go*
Thou shalt be dreynt;° my tale is at an ende."   *drowned*
He wook,° and tolde his felawe what he mette,°   *woke/dreamed*
And preyde him his viage° for to lette;°   *journey/delay*
As for that day, he preyde him to abyde.
320 His felawe, that lay by his beddes syde,
Gan for to laughe, and scorned him ful faste.°   *volubly*
"No dreem," quod he, "may so myn herte agaste,°   *frighten*
That I wol lette° for to do my thinges.°   *stop/business*
I sette not a straw by thy dreminges,
For swevenes° been but vanitees and japes.   *dreams*
Men dreme alday° of owles or of apes,   *everyday*
And eke of many a mase° therwithal;°   *delusion/besides*
Men dreme of thing that nevere was ne shal.°   *shall be*
But sith I see that thou wolt heer abyde,
330 And thus forsleuthen° wilfully thy tyde,°   *idle away/tide*
God wot it reweth me;° and have good day."   *I am sorry*
And thus he took his leve, and wente his way.
But er that he hadde halfe his cours ysayled,
Noot I nat why, ne what mischaunce it ayled,
But casuelly° the shippes botme rente,°   *by accident/split open*
And ship and man under the water wente
In sighte of othere shippes it byside,
That with hem sayled at the same tyde.
And therfor, faire Pertelote so dere,
340 By swiche ensamples° olde maistow lere,°   *exempla/may you learn*
That no man sholde been to recchelees°   *regardless*
Of dremes, for I sey thee, douteless,
That many a dreem ful sore is for to drede.°   *fear*
    Lo, in the lyf of Saint Kenelm, I rede,
That was Kenulphus sone, the noble king

Of Mercenrike,° how Kenelm mette° a thing;   *Mercia/dreamed*
A lyte° er he was mordred, on a day,   *little while*
His mordre in his avisioun°¹⁶⁰ he say.°   *dream/saw*
His norice° him expounded every del°   *nurse/detail*
350 His sweven,° and bad him for to kepe him° wel   *dream/guard himself*
For° traisoun; but he nas but seven yeer old,   *for fear of*
And therfore litel tale hath he told°   *took little account*
Of any dreem, so holy was his herte.
By God, I hadde lever than my sherte,°   *give my shirt*
That ye had rad° his legende, as have I.   *read*
Dame Pertelote, I sey yow trewely,
Macrobeus, that writ the *Avisioun*
In Affrike of the worthy Cipioun,°   *Scipio*
Affermeth dremes, and seïth that they been
360 Warning of thinges that men after seen.
     And forthermore, I pray yow loketh wel
In the Olde Testament, of Daniel,¹⁶¹
If he held° dremes any vanitee.   *considered*
Reed eek of Joseph, and ther shul ye see
Wher° dremes ben somtyme, I sey nat alle,   *whether*
Warning of thinges that shul after falle.
Loke of Egipt the king, daun° Pharäo,°   *Lord/Pharaoh*
His bakere and his boteler° also,   *butler*
Wher° they ne felte noon effect in° dremes.   *whether/consequence of*
370 Whoso wol seken actes of sondry remes,°   *realms*
May rede of dremes many a wonder thing.
     Lo Cresus,° which that was of Lyde° king,   *Croesus/Lydia*
Mette° he nat that he sat upon a tree,   *dreamed*
Which signified he sholde anhanged° be?   *hanged*
Lo heer Andromacha,° Ectores° wyf,   *Andromache/Hector*
That day that Ector sholde lese° his lyf,   *lose*
She dremed on the same night biforn,
How that the lyf of Ector sholde be lorn,°   *lost*
If thilke day he wente into bataille;
380 She warned him, but it mighte nat availle;
He wente for to fighte nathelees,°   *nevertheless*
But he was slayn anoon° of Achilles.   *at once*
But thilke tale is al too long to telle,
And eek it is ny day, I may nat dwelle.
Shortly I seye, as for conclusioun,
That I shal han of this avisioun°   *vision*
Adversitee; and I seye forthermore,
That I ne telle of laxatyves no store,°   *set no store by*
For they ben venimous,° I woot it wel;   *poisonous*

390 I hem defye, I love hem never a del°.   *bit*
        Now let us speke of mirthe, and stinte° al this;   *stop*
    Madame Pertelote, so have I blis°,   *hope to go to heaven*
    Of o° thing God hath sent me large grace;   *one*
    For whan I see the beautee of your face,
    Ye ben so scarlet reed° about your yën°,   *red/eyes*
    It maketh al my drede for to dyen;°   *fade*
    For, also siker° as In principio,   *just as*
    Mulier est hominis confusio;[162]
    Madame, the sentence° of this Latin is: *meaning*
400 Womman is mannes joye and al his blis.
    For wan I fele anight° your softe syde,   *at night*
    Albeit that I may nat on you ryde,
    For that our perche is maad so narwe°, alas!   *narrow*
    I am so ful of joy and of solas°   *comfort*
    That I defye bothe sweven and dreem.'[163]
    And with that word he fley° down fro the beem°,   *flew/rafter*
    For it was day, and eek his hennes° alle;   *hens*
    And with a 'Chuk' he gan hem for to calle,
    For he had founde a corn, lay° in the yerd.   *lying*
410 Royal he was, he was namore aferd;°   *afraid*
    He fethered° Pertelote twenty tyme,   *embraced*
    And trad as ofte, er that it was pryme.[164]
    He loketh as it were a grim leoun;°   *lion*
    And on his toos° he rometh up and doun,   *toes*
    Him deyned° not to sette his foot to grounde.   *deigned*
    He chukketh, whan he hath a corn yfounde,
    And to him rennen° thanne his wyves alle.   *ran*
    Thus royal, as a prince is in his halle,
    Leve I this Chauntecleer in his pasture;°   *feeding*
420 And after wol I tell his adventure.
        Whan that the month in which the world bigan,
    That highte March, whan God first maked man,
    Was complet°, and ypassed were also,   *completed*
    Sin March bigan, thritty dayes and two,[165]
    Bifel that Chauntecleer, in al his pryde,
    His seven wyves walking by his syde,
    Caste up his eyen to the brighte sonne,
    That in the signe of Taurus hadde yronne
    Twenty degrees and oon, and somwhat more;
430 And knew by kynde°, and by noon other lore,   *nature*
    That it was pryme, and crew° with blisful stevene°.   *crowed/voice*
    'The sonne,' he sayde 'is clomben° up on hevene   *has climbed*
    Fourty degrees and oon, and more, ywis°.   *surely*

Madame Pertelote, my worldes blis,
Herkneth thise blisful briddes° how they singe,   *birds*
And see the fresshe floures how they springe;
Ful is myn herte of revel and solas.°   *comfort*
But sodeinly him fil° a sorweful cas;°   *befell/chance*
For ever the latter ende of joye is wo.
440 God woot that worldly joye is sone ago;°   *passed*
And if a rethor° coude faire endyte,°   *stylish author/write*
He in a cronique° saufly° mighte it wryte,   *chronicle/safely*
As for a sovereyn notabilitee.°   *great importance*
Now every wys man, lat him herkne me;
This storie is also° trewe, I undertake,   *as*
As is the book of Launcelot de Lake,
That° wommen holde in ful gret reverence.   *which*
Now wol I torne agayn to my sentence.°   *theme*
   A col°fox, ful of sly iniquitee,   *coal-black*
450 That in the grove hadde woned° yeres three,   *lived*
By heigh imaginacioun forncast,°   *predestined*
The same night thurghout the hegges° brast°   *hedges/burst*
Into the yerd, ther° Chauntecleer the faire   *where*
Was wont, and eek his wyves, to repaire;
And in a bed of wortes° stille he lay,   *vegetables*
Til it was passed undern° of the day,   *mid-morning*
Wayting his tyme° on Chauntecleer to falle,   *opportunity*
As gladly doon thise homicydes alle,
That in awayt liggen° to mordre° men.   *lie in wait/murder*
460 O false mordrer, lurking in thy den!
O newe Scariot,° newe Genilon!°   *Judas Iscariot/Ganelon*
False dissimilour, O Greek Sinon,
That broghtest Troye al outrely° to sorwe!   *completely*
O Chauntecleer, acursed be that morwe,°   *morning*
That thou into that yerd flough° fro the bemes!   *flew*
Thou were ful wel ywarned by thy dremes,
That thilke day was perilous to thee.
But what that God forwoot° mot° nedes be,   *foreknows/must*
After° the opinioun of certeyn clerkis.°   *according to/scholars*
470 Witnesse on him, that any perfit° clerk is,   *perfect*
That in scole is gret altercacioun
In this matere, and greet disputisoun,°   *dispute*
And hath ben of an hundred thousand men.
But I ne can not bulte° it to the bren,°   *sift/from the bran*
As can the holy doctour Augustyn,°   *St Augustine*
Or Boece,° or the bishop Bradwardyn,   *Boethius/Bradwardine*
Whether that Goddes worthy forwiting°   *foreknowledge*

Streyneth° me nedely° for to doon a thing,   *constrains/necessarily*
'Nedely' clepe I simple necessitee;
480 Or elles, if free choys be graunted me
To do that same thing, or do it noght,
Though God forwoot° it, er that it was wroght;   *foreknows*
Or if his witing° streyneth nevere a del   *foreknowledge*
But by necessitee condicionel.¹⁶⁶
I wol not han to do of swich matere;
My tale is of a cok, as ye may here,°   *hear*
That took his counseil of his wyf, with sorwe,°   *sad to say*
To walken in the yerd upon that morwe°   *morning*
That he had met° the dreem, that I yow tolde.   *dreamed*
490 Wommennes counseils° been ful ofte colde;°   *advice/comfortless*
Wommennes counseil broghte us first to wo,
And made Adam fro Paradys to go,
Ther as he was ful mery,° and wel at ese.   *content*
But for I noot,° to whom it mighte displese,   *know not*
If I counseil of wommen wolde blame,
Passe over, for I seyde it in my game.°   *jest*
Rede auctours, wher they trete of swich matere,
And what thay seyn of wommen ye may here.°   *hear*
Thise been the cokkes wordes, and nat myne;
500 I can noon harm of no womman divyne.°   *discover*
    Faire in the sond,° to bathe hir merily,   *dust*
Lyth° Pertelote, and alle hir sustres° by,   *lies/sisters*
Agayn° the sonne; and Chauntecleer so free°   *in/noble*
Song merier than the mermayde in the see;
For *Phisiologus* seith sikerly,¹⁶⁷
How that they singen wel and merily.
And so bifel that, as he caste his yë,°   *eye*
Among the wortes,° on a boterflye,°   *vegetables/butterfly*
He was war° of this fox that lay ful lowe.   *aware*
510 Nothing ne liste him thanne for to crowe,°   *no desire to crow*
But cryde anon, 'Cok, cok,' and up he sterte,°   *flies*
As man that was affrayed° in his herte.   *terrified*
For naturelly a beest desyreth flee
Fro his contrarie,° if he may it see,   *natural enemy*
Though he never erst° had seyn it with his yë.   *before*
    This Chauntecleer, whan he gan him espye,
He wolde han fled, but that the fox anon
Seyde, 'Gentil sire, allas! wher wol ye gon?
Be ye affrayed of me that am your freend?°   *friend*
520 Now certes, I were worse than a feend,   *fiend*
If I to yow wold° harm or vileinye.   *intended*

I am nat come your counseil° for t'espye;   *secrets*
But trewely, the cause of my cominge
Was only for to herkne how that ye singe.
For trewely ye have as mery a stevene°   *voice*
As any aungel hath, that is in hevene;
Therwith ye han in musik more felinge
Than hadde Boece,° or any that can singe.   *Boethius*
My lord your fader,° God his soule blesse!   *father*
530 And eek your moder, of hir gentilesse,°   *courtesy*
Han in myn hous ybeen, to my gret ese;°   *pleasure*
And certes, sire, ful fayn° wolde I yow plese.   *gladly*
But for men speke of singing, I wol saye,
So mote I brouke wel° myn eyen tweye,   *enjoy*
Save yow, I herde never man so singe,
As dide your fader in the morweninge;
Certes, it was of° herte, al that he song.°   *from the/sang*
And for to make his voys the more strong,
He wolde so peyne him, that with bothe his yën°   *eyes*
540 He moste winke,° so loude he wolde cryen,   *close*
And stonden on his tiptoon° therwithal,   *tiptoes*
And strecche forth his nekke long and smal.
And eek he was of swich discrecioun,°   *good judgement*
That ther nas no man in no regioun
That him in song or wisdom mighte passe.
I have wel rad° in *Daun Burnel the Asse*,[168]   *read*
Among his vers,° how that ther was a cok,   *verse*
For that a preestes sone yaf him a knok
Upon his leg, whyl he was yong and nyce,°   *foolish*
550 He made him for to lese° his benefyce.[169]   *lose*
But certeyn, ther nis no comparisoun
Bitwix the wisdom and discrecioun
Of youre fader, and of his subtiltee.
Now singeth, sire, for seïnte° charitee,   *holy*
Let see, conne° ye your fader countrefete°?'   *can/imitate*
This Chaunteeleer his winges gan to bete,°   *beat*
As man that coude his° tresoun° nat espye,   *i.e. the fox's/deceit*
So was he ravisshed with his° flaterye.   *i.e. the fox's*
    Allas! ye lordes, many a fals flatour°   *flatterer*
560 Is in your courtes, and many a losengeour,°   *fawner*
That plesen yow wel more, by my feith,
Than he that soothfastnesse° unto yow seith.   *truth*
Redeth Ecclesiaste[170] of flaterye;
Beth war, ye lordes, of hir trecherye.
    This Chauntecleer stood hye upon his toos,

Strecching his nekke, and heeld his eyen cloos,
And gan to crowe loude for the nones;°   *on this occasion*
And Daun Russel° the fox sterte up at ones,   *i.e. Master Red*
And by the gargat° hente° Chauntecleer,   *throat/seized*
570 And on his bak toward the wode° him beer,°   *wood/bore*
For yet ne was ther no man that him sewed.°   *pursued*
O destinee, that mayst nat been eschewed!°   *escaped*
Allas, that Chauntecleer fleigh° fro the bemes!   *flew*
Allas, his wyf ne roghte nat° of dremes!   *thought nothing*
And on a Friday[171] fil° al this meschaunce.°   *fell/mishap*
O Venus, that art goddesse of plesaunce,
Sin that thy servant was this Chauntecleer,
And in thy service dide al his power,
More for delyt, than world to multiplye,°   *increase the population*
580 Why woldestow° suffre him on thy day to dye?   *would you*
O Gaufred,° dere mayster soverayn,   *Geoffrey de Vinsauf*
That, whan thy worthy King Richard was slayn
With shot,° compleynedest his deth so sore,   *an arrow*
Why ne hadde I now thy sentence° and thy lore,°   *wisdom/learning*
The Friday for to chide, as diden ye?
For on a Friday soothly slayn was he.
Than wolde I shewe yow how that I coude pleyne°   *lament*
For Chauntecleres drede, and for his peyne.°   *distress*
    Certes, swich cry ne lamentacioun
590 Was never of ladies maad, whan Ilioun°   *Troy*
Was wonne, and Pirrus° with his streite° swerd,   *Pyrrhus/drawn*
Whan he hadde hent King Priam by the berd,
And slayn him, as saith us *Eneydos.*°   *the Aeneid*
As maden° alle the hennes in the clos,°   *made/enclosure*
Whan they had seyn° of Chauntecleer the sighte,   *seen*
But sovereynly° Dame Pertelote shrighte,°   *royally/shrieked*
Ful louder than dide Hasdrubales wyf,
Whan that hir housbond hadde lost his lyf,
And that the Romayns° hadde brend° Cartage;   *Romans/burnt*
600 She was so ful of torment and of rage,°   *frenzy*
That wilfully into the fyr she sterte,°   *leapt*
And brende° hirselven with a stedfast herte.   *burned*
O woful hennes, right so cryden ye,
As, whan that Nero brende° the citee   *burned*
Of Rome, cryden senatoures° wyves,   *senators'*
For that hir housbondes losten alle hir lyves;
Withouten gilt this Nero hath hem slayn.
Now wol I torne to my tale agayn.
    This sely° widwe, and eek hir doghtres two,   *simple*

610 Herden thise hennes crye and maken wo,   *hens*
    And out at dores sterten° they anoon,   *rushed/immediately*
    And syen° the fox toward the grove goon,   *saw*
    And bar° upon his bak the cok away;   *carrying*
    And cryden, 'Out! Harrow!° and weylaway!   *help!*
    Ha, ha, the fox!' and after him they ran,
    And eek with staves° many another man;   *sticks*
    Ran Colle our dogge, and Talbot, and Gerland,[172]
    And Malkin, with a distaf in hir hand;   *the servant girl*
    Ran cow and calf, and eek the verray hogges°   *hogs*
620 So were they fered for° berking of the dogges   *frightened by*
    And shouting of the men and wimmen eke,
    They ronne° so, hem thoughte hir herte breke.°   *ran/would burst*
    They yelleden as feendes° doon in helle;   *fiends*
    The dokes° cryden as men wolde hem quelle;°   *ducks/kill*
    The gees° for fere flowen° over the trees;   *geese/flew*
    Out of the hyve cam the swarm of bees;
    So hidous was the noyse, a! Benedicite!
    Certes, he Jakke Straw, and his meynee,   *truly/company*
    Ne made never shoutes half so shrille,
630 Whan that they wolden any Fleming kille,[173]
    As thilke day was maad upon the fox.
    Of bras thay broghten bemes, and of box,   *trumpets/boxwood*
    Of horn, of boon, in whiche they blewe and pouped,   *bone/tooted*
    And therwithal thay shryked° and they houped;   *shrieked*
    It semed as that heven sholde falle.
    Now, gode men, I pray yow herkneth alle!
        Lo, how fortune turneth° sodeinly   *overturns*
    The hope and pryde eek of hir enemy!
    This cok, that lay upon the foxes bak,
640 In al his drede, unto the fox he spak,
    And seyde, 'Sire, if that I were as ye,
    Yet sholde I seyn, as wis° God helpe me: *surely*
    "Turneth agayn, ye proude cherles° alle!   *churls*
    A verray pestilence upon yow falle!
    Now am I come unto this wodes° syde,   *wood's*
    Maugree your heed, the cok shal heer abyde;   *despite anything you can do*
    I wol him ete, in feith, and that anon."''   *eat/immediately*
    The fox answerde, 'In feith, it shal be don;'
    And as he spak that word, al sodeinly
650 This cok brak° from his mouth deliverly,   *broke away/nimbly*
    And heighe upon a tree he fleigh° anon.   *flew*
    And whan the fox saugh that he was ygon,
    'Allas!' quod he, 'O Chauntecleer, allas!

I have to yow,' quod he, 'ydoon trespas;   *wrong*
Inasmuche as I maked yow aferd,
Whan I yow hente; and broghte out of the yerd;   *caught*
But, sire, I dide it in no wikke° entente;°   *evil/intention*
Com doun, and I shal telle yow what I mente.
I shal seye sooth to yow, God help me so.'
660 'Nay than,' quod he, 'I shrewe° us bothe two,   *curse*
And first I shrewe myself, bothe blood and bones,
If thou bigyle° me ofter° than ones.   *deceive/more*
Thou shalt namore, thurgh thy flaterye,
Do° me to singe and winke with myn yë.   *get*
For he that winketh, whan he sholde see,
Al wilfully, God lat him never thee°!'   *thrive*
'Nay,' quod the fox, 'but God yeve him meschaunce,   *mischance*
That is so undiscreet of governaunce,   *self-control*
That jangleth° whan he sholde holde his pees.°   *babbles/peace*
670   Lo, swich it is for to be recchelees,   *reckless*
And necligent, and truste on flaterye.
But ye that holden this tale a folye,
As of a fox, or of a cok and hen,
Taketh the moralitee° good men.   *moral*
For Saint Paul[174] seith, that al that writen is,
To our doctryne° it is ywrite, ywis.   *edification*
Taketh the fruyt, and lat the chaf be stille.°   *remain*
      Now, gode God, if that it be thy wille,
As seith my Lord° so make us alle good men;   *i.e. Christ*
680 And bringe us to his heighe blisse. Amen.

NOTES

Chaucer

1 Zodiac sign, Aries, March 12 (old style dating) – April 18, is the date of the pilgrimage
   given in the *Man of Law's Tale*.
2 St Thomas Becket, murdered in Canterbury Cathedral, 1170: canonized, 1174.
3 truth = integrity: freedom = generosity of spirit: curteisye = courteous behaviour.
4 all battles fought, 1361–7, against the infidels, around the Mediterranean, in Russia
   and Lithuania.
5 Ch. himself had taken part (1369) in a campaign to Artois and Picardy: this refers to
   the crusade of the Bishop of Norwich.
6 carving meat was one of the duties of a squire.
7 i.e. French as it was spoken in the Benedictine nunnery near Stratford le Bow, East
   London.

8   every tenth bead, representing a 'Pater Noster'.

9   'love conquers all'.

10   a great one for having the upper hand.

11   a supervisor of outlying cells of the monastery.

12   St Jerome and St Augustine condemned hunting.

13   that glowed like a furnace under a cauldron.

14   there are four main orders of friars – 1. Carmelite (white dress), a begging order 2. Austin (black dress), groups of hermits forming an order following the rule of St Augustine 3. Iacobin – Dominican (black dress), following the rule of St Dominic 4. Minorites – Franciscans (grey dress), following the rule of St Francis. This friar is of a begging order with exclusive rights to beg in certain areas.

15   had provided dowries for.

16   literally – a knight, chosen for his prowess, in a fight to the death.

17   he paid for the monopoly of begging in his area.

18   used as a blessing to ward off evil (John I.1).

19   his pickings were better than his proper income.

20   days set aside for the amicable settling of disputes.

21   he does currency exchange deals.

22   an advanced student who was studying to go into holy orders: many scholars of the time were clerks.

23   logic and the study of Aristotle were a part of the course: the clerk here is beyond these elementary stages.

24   philosophy could also mean alchemy.

25   an area in front of the church where lawyers met their clients.

26   in the time of the Norman conquests.

27   his temperament was dominated by blood, as shown in his ruddy face.

28   bread dipped in wine.

29   they belonged to the parish guild which looked after its members – e.g. settling quarrels, seeing to their funerals, saying masses for the dead. To have become an alderman, each would have had to have a certain amount of property. Their wives would be as eager as the husbands for this status since it gave them pride of place on public occasions – e.g. vigils, which were ceremonies on the eve of a guild festival – when their fine clothes would be seen to best advantage.

30   threw his captives overboard to find their way home.

31   each sign of the zodiac has a particular influence on a part of the body, modified by the influence of whatever planet may be in the ascendancy. Each day is divided into parts and each division is under the influence of one planet. For medical assessment these influences were linked with the body's humours – hot, cold, wet, dry – which they could exaggerate or mitigate. The doctor's aim was to achieve for his patients as near a balance as he could between all these forces, for which various medicines, including some made up from precious stones and metals, were prescribed.

32   a list of the reputable medical authorities of the time. Aesculapius (god of medicine), Dioscorides (1st C.AD), Hippocrates (c.460BC) and Rufus (early 2nd C.AD), his commentator, were Greek: Galen (129?–199AD) practised in Greece and Rome: Hali, Serapion, Rhazes, Avicenna and Damascenus were Arabian: Bernard, Gatesden, Giobert were European: John of Gaddesden was of Merton College, Oxford (d. 1369).

33   Ypres and Ghent – cities of the Flemish wool trade: many Flemish weavers moved to England in the 14th C.

34 when gifts were offered in church.

35 the marriage ceremony at the church door, involving transfer of property, was followed by a nuptial mass at the altar.

36 the Wife of Bath's pilgrimages were to Jerusalem, Rome, Compostella and the Shrine of the Three Kings at Cologne.

37 whatever he was given at Mass was his to keep and use as he liked.

38 hire another at a low rate and pocket the difference.

39 an endowment for masses for the soul of the donor.

40 the guilds had their own priests, an easy, lucrative position.

41 reve = an estate manager (cf. l.589); somnour = summoner, who served summons to the ecclesiastical courts (cf. l.625); pardoner = one who dispensed papal pardons (cf. l.671); maunciple = a steward, here, to the Inns of Court in London (cf. l.569).

42 a red beard or redhead was not to be trusted (cf. Judas who was said to have had red hair): the miller was a rough, bad-tempered, lecherous thickhead.

43 the miller was paid a percentage of what he ground – this one got away with taking his portion three times: he could use his thumb to tip the scales in his favour – but he was honest as millers go!

44 i.e. his lord's.

45 the cherubim were of the 2nd order of angels, depicted in mediaeval mss. as having red faces.

46 the sparrow was associated with Venus and lechery.

47 all ointments for his skin diseases – here, probably, of sexual origin.

48 common name for a tamed jackdaw.

49 pluck a pigeon = have sex with.

50 a writ for imprisonment which the church courts could not impose.

51 sung by the choir while offerings were being made.

52 poss. from either Boethius, *De Consolatione Philosophiae* or the *Roman de la Rose* which Ch. translated.

53 if you agree this morning with what you said last night.

54 some mss. 'as ye may heere'.

55 John II.1.

56 John IV.16ff.

57 explain this way and that.

58 Matt.XIX.5.

59 i.e. in successive marriages.

60 dan = dominus, master: Solomon had 700 wives and 300 concubines (I Kings XI.3).

61 such a happy life he led.

62 for both their (lower purse) balls and their savings (coffers, where money was kept).

63 for the Wife's references here see I Cor. VII.1–40.

64 Gen.IV.19–24.

65 Matt.XIX.21.

66 poss. refers to created man but more probably to his reproductive organs.

67 John, not Mark,VI.9.

68 I Cor.VII.4.

69 he who won't learn from another's example will become an example himself.

70 in a collection of sayings attributed to Ptolemy.

71 the Dunmow Flitch, a side of bacon given to the married couple who had not quarrelled throughout the year.

72 i.e. will testify that the chough is mad: refers to the story of the bird that betrays to the husband his wife's misconduct with her lover, but the wife persuades him the bird is lying and he wrings its neck.

73 St James the Great.

74 vulgar word for the sexual parts of a woman (cunt): cf. more refined 'bele chose' l.453; the Wife veers between the rough and ready and the refined and affected in her language concerning sex.

75 I Timothy II.9.

76 headings used as directions.

77 naptha preparation which burns fiercely and is difficult to put out.

78 bite – in a bad temper, whinny, with pleasure, in a good.

79 I would pretend that he had a mistress.

80 i.e. he should be as meek as their ram, Wilkin.

81 see 74.

82 where the nave is separated from the choir.

83 see 22

84 a sign of boldness and lasciviousness.

85 a birth mark on the part of the body ruled by the planet in whose ascendancy one was born: Venus seal = a red mark on the thigh, in Taurus = on the neck, Mars = on the face and thigh or groin.

86 the result of the convocation of the stars is that the Wife is domineering, pleasure-loving and promiscuous.

87 Ecclesiasticus XXV.25.

88 Thomas Becket of Canterbury.

89 *The Letter of Valerius to Rufinus About Not Marrying*, Walter Map; *The Little Golden Book of Theophrastus on Marriage*: both anti-marriage tracts.

90 *A Letter Against Jovinian* (*see* Jovinian).

91 the parables of Solomon = the Book of Proverbs.

92 Ovid's *Ars Amatoria* recommends ways of succeeding in love, with anecdotes.

93 refers to the fable of a peasant showing a picture of a peasant killing a lion to a lion – who asks 'Who painted the picture anyway – man or lion?'

94 Venus = pleasure-loving; Mercury = studious or wisdom-loving: they are antagonistic.

95 as one planet is at its greatest power, the other is at its lowest.

96 Prov.XXI.9.

97 Prov.XI.22.

98 a term of affection.

99 either 'be still' or 'piss'.

100 supernatural beings (with size of ordinary people).

101 friars licensed to beg and hear confessions in a certain area.

102 an incubus begot children on women: a friar only dishonoured them.

103 no real equivalent in modern English for this word – it spans from birth status to nobility and gentleness of behaviour.

104 Dante, *Purgatorio* VII.121ff.

105 i.e. if gentilesse were an innate quality, passing naturally in a family from father to son, then no-one of them would ever do anything evil.

106 villeins and churls were the lowest rank in mediaeval society: their coarseness led to the terms 'villainous' and 'churlish.'

107 See 41.
108 refers to the Physician's 'Tale of Appius and Virginia.'
109 of nature, youth, beauty etc: of Fortune, wealth and rank.
110 electuary – a medicine in the form of a paste to be mixed with liquid or syrup.
111 either St Ronan (= St Ninian) or a pun on runnion = sexual organs.
112 the root of all evil is the love of money (I Timothy. VI.10).
113 the Papal Court in Rome: he could be licensed by either a papal bull (permit) or a bishop's letter with a seal.
114 poss. Jacob and Laban (Gen.XXX).
115 groat – silver coin worth 4 pennies;
mark – worth ⅔ of £1.
116 i.e. wandering about, to hell, for all he cares.
117 only preach for covetousness has two meanings – he only preaches about covetousness/or to satisfy his own covetousness.
118 the habit of swearing by the various parts of Christ's body.
119 Eph.V.18.
120 Gen.XIX.33.
121 Mark VI.17–29; Matt.XIV.1–11.
122 Seneca's 83rd Letter says that drunkenness is a brief form of madness.
123 an adaptation of a passage from St Jerome's *Against Jovinian* (*see* Jovinian).
124 in Jerome, the short pleasure of the throat.
125 I Cor.VI.13.
126 Phil.III.18.
127 substance = essential and permanent reality, accident = appearance, changeable and impermanent: cooks change the food (substance) preferring its taste, smell, appearance, etc. (accident).
128 I Tim.V.6.
129 poss. the light wine from there laced with spirit for export. Fish St. leads out of Thames St., where John Chaucer, (Ch.'s father) a vintner, had his house; near also the wharf where ships from France and Spain unloaded their wine. Chepe = Cheapside, originally = a market.
130 a dig at the practice of mixing wines, which was illegal.
131 Prov.XXXI.4–5.
132 a story from John of Salisbury's *Polycraticus*. Seneca also tells of a meeting between King Demetrius and a 'Stilbon philosophus'. Ch. seems to have mixed the two stories.
133 Matt.V.33–4; Jer.IV.2.
134 Exod.XX.2ff.
135 second commandment in the Vulgate Bible (St Jerome's) and third in the King James Bible.
136 some time between 6 a.m. and 9 or after sunrise: one of the appointed times for prayer.
137 the lich-bell, carried before a corpse to the funeral.
138 i.e. miserable old devil!
139 Lev.XIX.32.
140 florins were first minted in Florence, 1252, and called florins from the lily (flores = flowers) stamped on them: gold florins were minted in England in the reign of Edward III.
141 gold coins first minted by Edward II, worth half a mark (see 115); sterlings = English silver pence minted by the Norman Kings and, after, stamped with a star.
142 kissing was a common sign of peace-making.

143 mediaeval roads were full of pot-holes.

144 a nickname for a priest.

145 so may I enjoy the use of my legs.

146 Ch. describes the villager's house as though it were a great house where the bour = the private rooms/bedroom and the hall = the room where family and guests gathered and ate.

147 the public clock of an abbey.

148 the circle of the heavens making a complete revolution = a day; ascensioun = dawn.

149 a young lady of good family.

150 presumably of the cottage, see 146.

151 a fine sleeper you are!

152 may it be a dream of good fortune.

153 exhalation, cf. Pardoner's Tale l.239; complecciouns = complexion or temperament.

154 i.e. of the bile (hot and dry) and blood (hot and moist): choler was the humour of anger, hence the nightmares; melancholy was the humor of the black bile, situated in the liver.

155 see 154.

156 see 115.

157 to dissipate the bile.

158 laurel, centaury, fumitory – medicinal herbs used for purging choler and melancholy; black hellebore used to purge choler, white for phlegm, by vomiting; the fruit of celapneia and buckthorn (gaitrys) strong purges against choler; herb-ive (poss. buckthorn) for jaundice and tertian fever.

159 both Cicero and Valerius Maximus – and several mediaeval writers – tell this story.

160 term for a prophetic vision.

161 Dan.IV.5ff; Joseph – Gen.XXXVII.5ff; Pharaoh – Gen.XL–XLI.

162 just as, in the beginning, woman is man's downfall.

163 ?mere dreams and prophetic visions.

164 took her as often before prime – i.e. between 6–9 a.m.

165 Ch. mocking an elaborate rhetorical device?

166 on the question of necessity there were three positions: 1. God foreknows and fore-ordains all; 2. God foreknows, but free choice is left to man to do or not as he chooses; 3. God foreknows, but only 'conditional necessitiee'.
An example of simple necessity is – I am born, I die.
An example of conditional necessity is – I am born, I go on holiday.

167 the Bestiary was first written in Greek, 2nd C.; translated into Latin 4th–5th C.; it was attributed to Theobaldus; later translated into European languages; it contained descriptions of real and imaginary creatures with moral applications – e.g. mermaids (sirens) = wordly delights and seductions.

168 Master Burnellus, the hero of *The Mirror of Fools*, a satirical 12th C. poem by Nigel Wireker.

169 by not crowing and so the priest overslept.

170 Ecclesiasticus XII.10–11.

171 Friday, the day of Venus, considered a day of ill-luck – the day of Christ's crucifixion.

172 Colle (collie?) popular name for a dog: Talbot and Gerland poss. hunting dogs.

173 many Flemings, encouraged to come to London by Edward III, were massacred during the Peasants' Revolt: when the revolt failed, Jack Straw, with other leaders, was beheaded.

174 Rom.XV.4.

Edmund Spenser

[c.1552–1599]

He was probably born at East Smithfield, London; educated at the Merchant Taylors' School, where Mulcaster, who wrote two books on education promoting music, English literature, including the writing of English verse, and physical exercise in the curriculum, was headmaster; then to Pembroke Hall, Cambridge, where he made the acquaintance of Gabriel Harvey. 1579 he got a position in the Earl of Leicester's household where he became friends with Sir Philip Sidney to whom he dedicated his *Shepheardes Calendar*, 1579. That year it is possible he married Machabyas Chylde and also began writing *The Faerie Queene*. Appointed secretary to Lord Grey, the Lord Deputy of Ireland, he accompanied him to Ireland and 1588/9 acquired Kilcolman Castle, Co. Cork. The first three books of the *F.Q.* were registered in the Stationers' Register during his visit to London 1589 and were published 1590. His feelings about that visit and his unhappiness at having to return to Ireland and not receiving the court promotion he had hoped for are expressed in *Colin Clout Comes Home Again* and, with bitterness, in *Mother Hubbard's Tale*, 1591, the year in which he received an annual pension from the Queen of £50. 1594, he married Elizabeth Boyle. His sonnet sequence, *Amoretti*, is probably concerned with his courtship of Elizabeth, and *Epithalamion* celebrates their marriage. Books 4–6 of the *F.Q.* and his *Foure Hymnes* were published 1596 when he was again staying in London, at the house of the Earl of Essex. 1596/7 he returned to Ireland, depressed: in Oct. 1598 his house was burnt down in an insurrection, and he, with his family, was compelled to flee to Cork. He died in poverty in a lodging house in London, his funeral expenses being paid by the Earl of Essex. He is buried in Westminster Abbey near to the grave of his favourite poet, Chaucer, where, 1619, a monument was set up by Lady Anne Clifford.

From **The Faerie Queene**

Book I

Contayning
The Legend of the Knight of the Red Crosse
or
of Holinesse

1

Lo I the man, whose Muse whilome° did maske,   *lately*
  As time her taught, in lowly Shepheards weeds,[1]
  Am now enforst a far unfitter taske,
  For trumpets sterne to chaunge mine Oaten reeds,
  And sing of Knights and Ladies gentle deeds;
  Whose prayses having slept in silence long,
  Me, all too meane, the sacred Muse areeds°   *counsels*
  To blazon broad° emongst her learned throng: *abroad*
Fierce warres and faithfull loves shall moralize my song.

2

Helpe then, O holy Virgin[2] chiefe of nine,
  Thy weaker Novice to performe thy will,
  Lay forth out of thine everlasting scryne°   *chest for records*
  The antique rolles, which there lye hidden still,
  Of Faerie knights and fairest Tanaquill,[3]
  Whom that most noble Briton Prince so long
  Sought through the world, and suffered so much ill,
  That I must rue his undeserved wrong:
O helpe thou my weake wit, and sharpen my dull tong.

3

And thou most dreaded impe° of highest Jove,   *Cupid*
  Faire Venus sonne, that with thy cruell dart
  At that good knight so cunningly didst rove,°   *shoot*
  That glorious fire it kindled in his hart,
  Lay now thy deadly Heben° bow apart,   *ebony*
  And with thy mother milde come to mine ayde:
  Come both, and with you bring triumphant Mart,°   *Mars*
  In loves and gentle jollities arrayd,
After his murdrous spoiles and bloudy rage allayd.

4

And with them eke,° O Goddesse⁴ heavenly bright,   *also*
 Mirrour of grace and Majestie divine,
 Great Lady of the greatest Isle, whose light
 Like Phoebus lampe throughout the world doth shine,
 Shed thy faire beames into my feeble eyne,
 And raise my thoughts too humble and too vile,
 To thinke of that true glorious type° of thine,   *pattern*
 The argument of mine afflicted° stile: *humble*
The which to heare, vouchsafe, O dearest dred° a-while.   *object of awe*

CANTO 1⁵

The Patron of true Holinesse,
* Foule Errour doth defeate:*
Hypocrisie him to entrappe,
* Doth to his home entreate.*

I

A Gentle Knight was pricking° on the plaine,   *riding fast*
 Y cladd in mightie armes and silver shielde,⁶
 Wherein old dints of deepe wounds did remaine,
 The cruell markes of many a bloudy fielde;
 Yet armes till that time did he never wield:
 His angry steede⁷ did chide his foming bitt,
 As much disdayning to the curbe to yield:
 Full jolly° knight he seemd, and faire did sitt,   *brave*
As one for knightly giusts° and fierce encounters fitt.   *jousts*

2

But on his brest a bloudie Crosse he bore,
 The deare remembrance of his dying Lord,
 For whose sweete sake that glorious badge he wore,
 And dead as living ever him adored:
 Upon his shield the like was also scored,
 For soveraine hope, which in his helpe he had:
 Right faithfull true he was in deede and word,
 But of his cheere° did seeme too solemne sad;   *countenance*
Yet nothing did he dread, but ever was ydrad.°   *dreaded*

3

Upon a great adventure he was bond,
   That greatest Gloriana to him gave,
   That greatest Glorious Queene of Faerie lond,
   To winne him worship,° and her grace to have,   *honour*
   Which of all earthly things he most did crave;
   And ever as he rode, his hart did earne°   *yearn*
   To prove his puissance in battell brave
   Upon his foe, and his new force to learne;
Upon his foe, a Dragon[8] horrible and stearne.

4

A lovely Ladie[9] rode him faire beside,
   Upon a lowly Asse more white then snow,
   Yet she much whiter, but the same did hide
   Under a vele,[10] that wimpled° was full low,   *hung in folds*
   And over all a blacke stole she did throw,
   As one that inly mournd: so was she sad,
   And heavie sat upon her palfrey slow;
   Seemed in heart some hidden care she had,
And by her in a line° a milke white lambe[11] she lad.°   *lead/led*

5

So pure an innocent, as that same lambe,
   She was in life and every vertuous lore,
   And by descent from Royall lynage came
   Of ancient Kings and Queenes, that had of yore
   Their scepters stretcht from East to Westerne shore,
   And all the world in their subjection held;
   Till that infernall feend with foule uprore
   Forwasted all their land, and them expeld:
Whom to avenge, she had this Knight from far compeld.°   *summoned*

6

Behind her farre away a Dwarfe[12] did lag,
   That lasie seemd in being ever last,
   Or wearied with bearing of her bag
   Of needments at his backe. Thus as they past,
   The day with cloudes was suddeine overcast,
   And angry Jove an hideous storme of raine
   Did poure into his Lemans° lap so fast,   *mistress's*
   That every wight° to shrowd° it did constrain,   *creature/take shelter*
And this faire couple eke to shroud themselves were fain.°   *eager*

7

Enforst to seeke some covert nigh at hand,
  A shadie grove not far away they spide,
  That promist ayde the tempest to withstand:
  Whose loftie trees yclad with sommers pride,
  Did spred so broad, that heavens light did hide,[13]
  Not perceable with power of any starre:
  And all within were pathes and alleies wide,
  With footing worne, and leading inward farre:
Faire harbour that them seemes; so in they entred arre.

8

And foorth they passe, with pleasure forward led,
  Joying to heare the birdes sweete harmony,
  Which therein shrouded from the tempest dred,
  Seemd in their song to scorne the cruell sky.
  Much can° they prayse the trees[14] so straight and hy,   *did*
  The sayling Pine, the Cedar proud and tall,
  The vine-prop Elme, the Poplar never dry,
  The builder Oake, sole king of forrests all,
The Aspine good for staves, the Cypresse funerall.

9

The Laurell, meed° of mightie Conquerours   *reward*
  And Poets sage, the Firre that weepeth still,
  The Willow worne of forlorne Paramours,
  The Eugh° obedient to the benders will,   *yew*
  The Birch for shaftes, the Sallow° for the mill,   *willow*
  The Mirrhe sweete bleeding in the bitter wound,
  The warlike Beech, the Ash for nothing ill,
  The fruitfull Olive, and the Platane° round,   *plane tree*
The carver Holme,° the Maple seeldom inward sound.   *holm-oak*

10

Led with delight, they thus beguile the way,
  Untill the blustring storme is overblowne;
  When weening° to returne, whence they did stray,   *thinking*
  They cannot finde that path, which first was showne,
  But wander too and fro in wayes unknowne,
  Furthest from end then, when they neerest weene,
  That makes them doubt, their wits be not their owne:
  So many pathes, so many turnings seene,
That which of them to take, in diverse doubt they been.

11

At last resolving forward still to fare,
  Till that some end they finde or in or out,
  That path they take, that beaten seemd most bare,
  And like to lead the labyrinth about;°   *out of*
  Which when by tract they hunted had throughout,
  At length it brought them to a hollow cave,
  Amid the thickest woods. The Champion stout
  Eftsoones° dismounted from his courser brave,   *at once*
And to the Dwarfe a while his needlesse spere he gave.

12

'Be well aware,' quoth then that Ladie milde,
  'Least suddaine mischiefe ye too rash provoke:
  The danger hid, the place unknowne and wilde,
  Breedes dreadfull doubts: Oft fire is without smoke,
  And perill without show: therefore your stroke
  Sir knight with-hold,° till further triall made.'   *keep hold of*
  'Ah Ladie,' said he, 'shame were to revoke
  The forward footing for° an hidden shade: *because of*
Vertue gives her selfe light, through darkenesse for to wade.'

13

'Yea but,' quoth she, 'the perill of this place
  I better wot° then you, though now too late   *know*
  To wish you backe returne with foule disgrace,
  Yet wisedome warnes, whilest foot is in the gate,
  To stay the steppe, ere forced to retrate.°   *retreat*
  This is the wandring wood, this Errours[15] den,
  A monster vile, whom God and man does hate:
  Therefore I read° beware.' 'Fly fly,' quoth then   *advise*
The fearefull Dwarfe: 'this is no place for living men.'

14

But full of fire and greedy hardiment,°   *courage*
  The youthfull knight could not for ought be staide,
  But forth unto the darksome hole he went,
  And lookéd in: his glistring armor made
  A litle glooming light, much like a shade,
  By which he saw the ugly monster plaine,
  Halfe like a serpent horribly displaide,
  But th'other halfe did womans shape retaine,
Most lothsom, filthie, foule, and full of vile disdaine.

15

And as she lay upon the durtie ground,
  Her huge long taile her den all overspred,
  Yet was in knots and many boughtes° upwound, *coils*
  Pointed with mortall sting. Of her there bred
  A thousand yong ones, which she dayly fed,
  Sucking upon her poisonous dugs, eachone
  Of sundry shapes, yet all ill favored:
  Soone as that uncouth° light upon them shone, *unaccustomed*
Into her mouth they crept, and suddain all were gone.

16

Their dam upstart, out of her den effraide,
  And rushed forth, hurling her hideous taile
  About her cursed head, whose folds displaid
  Were stretcht now forth at length without entraile.° *coiling*
  She lookt about, and seeing one in mayle
  Armed to point,° sought backe to turne againe; *completely*
  For light she hated as the deadly bale,° *injury*
  Ay wont in desert darknesse to remaine,
Where plaine none might her see, nor she see any plaine.

17

Which when the valiant Elfe perceived, he lept
  As Lyon[16] fierce upon the flying pray,
  And with his trenchand° blade her boldly kept *sharp*
  From turning backe, and forced her to stay:
  Therewith enraged she loudly gan to bray,
  And turning fierce, her speckled taile advaunst,
  Threatning her angry sting, him to dismay:
  Who nought aghast, his mightie hand enhaunst:° *raised*
The stroke down from her head unto her shoulder glaunst.

18

Much daunted with that dint, her sence was dazd,
  Yet kindling rage, her selfe she gathered round,
  And all attonce her beastly body raizd
  With doubled forces high above the ground:
  Tho° wrapping up her wrethed sterne arownd, *then*
  Lept fierce upon his shield, and her huge traine° *tail*
  All suddenly about his body wound,
  That hand or foot to stirre he strove in vaine:
God helpe the man so wrapt in Errours endlesse traine.

19

His Lady sad to see his sore constraint,
  Cride out, 'Now now Sir knight, shew what ye bee,
  Add faith unto your force, and be not faint:
  Strangle her, else she sure will strangle thee.'
  That when he heard, in great perplexitie,
  His gall[17] did grate° for griefe° and high disdaine,   *become very upset/anger*
  And knitting all his force got one hand free,
  Wherewith he grypt her gorge° with so great paine,   *throat*
That soone to loose her wicked bands did her constraine.

20

Therewith she spewd out of her filthy maw
  A floud of poyson horrible and blacke,
  Full of great lumpes of flesh and gobbets raw.
  Which stunck so vildly, that it forst him slacke
  His grasping hold, and from her turne him backe:
  Her vomit full of bookes and papers[18] was,
  With loathly frogs and toades, which eyes did lacke,
  And creeping sought way in the weedy gras:
Her filthy parbreake° all the place defiled has.   *vomit*

21

As when old father Nilus gins to swell
  With timely° pride above the Aegyptian vale,   *in season*
  His fattie° waves do fertile slime outwell,   *enriching*
  And overflow each plaine and lowly dale:
  But when his later spring gins to avale°,   *subside*
  Huge heapes of mudd he leaves, wherein there breed
  Ten thousand kindes of creatures, partly male
  And partly female of his fruitfull seed;
Such ugly monstrous shapes elswhere may no man reed°.   *encounter*

22

The same so sore annoyed has the knight,
  That welnigh choked with the deadly stinke
  His forces faile, ne can no longer fight.
  Whose corage when the feend perceived to shrinke,
  She poured forth out of her hellish sinke
  Her fruitfull cursed spawne of serpents small,
  Deformed monsters, fowle, and blacke as inke,
  Which swarming all about his legs did crall,
And him encombred sore, but could not hurt at all.

23

As gentle Shepheard in sweete even-tide,
　　When ruddy Phoebus gins to welke° in west,　　　　　　*wane*
　　High on an hill, his flocke to vewen wide,
　　Markes which do byte their hasty supper best;
　　A cloud of combrous gnattes[19] do him molest,
　　All striving to infixe their feeble stings,
　　That from their noyance he no where can rest,
　　But with his clownish° hands their tender wings　　*rough country*
He brusheth oft, and oft doth mar their murmurings.

24

Thus ill bestedd°, and fearefull more of shame,　　　　　*situated*
　　Then of the certaine perill he stood in,
　　Halfe furious unto his foe he came,
　　Resolved in minde all suddenly to win,
　　Or soone to lose, before he once would lin;°　　　　　*cease*
　　And strooke at her with more then manly force,
　　That from her body full of filthie sin
　　He raft° her hatefull head without remorse;　　　　　*cut away*
A streame of cole black bloud forth gushed from her corse.

25

Her scattred brood, soone as their Parent deare
　　They saw so rudely falling to the ground,
　　Groning full deadly, all with troublous feare,
　　Gathred themselves about her body round,
　　Weening their wonted entrance to have found
　　At her wide mouth: but being there withstood
　　They flocked all about her bleeding wound,
　　And sucked up their dying mothers blood.
Making her death their life, and eke her hurt their good.

26

That detestable sight him much amazde,
　　To see th'unkindly Impes° of heaven accurst,　　　　*offspring*
　　Devoure their dam; on whom while so he gazd,
　　Having all satisfide their bloudy thurst,
　　Their bellies swolne he saw with fulnesse burst,
　　And bowels gushing forth: well worthy end
　　Of such as drunke her life, the which them nurst;
　　Now needeth him no lenger labour spend,
His foes have slaine themselves, with whom he should contend.[20]

27

His Ladie seeing all, that chaunst, from farre
  Approcht in hast to greet his victorie,
  And said, 'Faire knight, borne under happy starre,
  Who see your vanquisht foes before you lye:
  Well worthy be you of that Armorie,   *armour*
  Wherein ye have great glory wonne this day,
  And prooved your strength on a strong enimie,
  Your first adventure: many such I pray,
And henceforth ever wish, that like succeed it may.'

28

Then mounted he upon his Steede againe,
  And with the Lady backward sought to wend;°   *go*
  That path he kept, which beaten was most plaine,
  Ne ever would to any by-way bend,
  But still did follow one unto the end,
  The which at last out of the wood them brought.
  So forward on his way (with God to frend°)   *befriend*
  He passed forth, and new adventure sought;
Long way he travelled, before he heard of ought.

29

At length they chaunst to meet upon the way
  An aged Sire,[21] in long blacke weedes° yclad,   *garments*
  His feete all bare, his beard all hoarie gray,
  And by his belt his booke he hanging had;
  Sober he seemde, and very sagely sad,   *grave*
  And to the ground his eyes were lowly bent,
  Simple in shew, and voyde of malice bad,
  And all the way he prayed, as he went,
And often knockt his brest, as one that did repent.

30

He faire the knight saluted, louting° low,   *bowing*
  Who faire him quited,° as that courteous was: *returns the salute*
  And after asked him, if he did know
  Of straunge adventures, which abroad did pas.
  'Ah my deare Sonne,' quoth he, 'how should, alas,
  Silly° old man, that lives in hidden cell,   *simple*
  Bidding° his beades all day for his trespas,   *telling*
  Tydings of warre and worldly trouble tell?
With holy father sits not with such things to mell.°   *meddle*

31

But if of daunger which hereby doth dwell,
And homebred evill ye desire to heare,
Of a straunge man I can you tidings tell,
That wasteth all this countrey farre and neare.'
'Of such,' said he, 'I chiefly do inquere,
And shall you well reward to shew the place,
In which that wicked wight his dayes doth weare:°   *spend*
For to all knighthood it is foule disgrace,
That such a cursed creature lives so long a space.'

32

'Far hence,' quoth he, 'in wastfull° wildernesse   *desolate*
His dwelling is, by which no living wight
May ever passe, but thorough great distresse.'
'Now,' sayd the Lady, 'draweth toward night,
And well I wote, that of your later° fight   *know/recent*
Ye all forwearied be: for what so strong,
But wanting rest will also want of might?
The Sunne[22] that measures heaven all day long,
At night doth baite° his steedes the Ocean waves emong.   *refresh*

33

Then with the Sunne take Sir, your timely rest,
And with new day new worke at once begin:
Untroubled night they say gives counsell best.'
'Right well Sir knight ye have advised bin,'
Quoth then that aged man; 'the way to win
Is wisely to advise: now day is spent;
Therefore with me ye may take up your In°   *lodging*
For this same night.' The knight was well content:
So with that godly father to his home they went.

34

A little lowly Hermitage it was,
Downe in a dale, hard by a forests side,
Far from resort of people, that did pas
In travell to and froe: a little wyde°   *apart*
There was an holy Chappell edifyde,   *built*
Wherein the Hermite dewly wont° to say   *was accustomed*
His holy things each morne and eventyde:
Thereby a Christall streame did gently play,
Which from a sacred fountaine welled forth alway.

35

Arrived there, the little house they fill,
   Ne looke for entertainement, where none was:
   Rest is their feast, and all things at their will;
   The noblest mind the best contentment has.
   With faire discourse the evening so they pas:
   For that old man of pleasing wordes had store,
   And well could file his tongue as smooth as glas;
   He told of Saintes and Popes, and evermore
He strowd an Ave-Mary after and before.

36

The drouping Night thus creepeth on them fast,
   And the sad humour° loading their eye liddes,   *heaviness*
   As messenger of Morpheus on them cast
   Sweet slombring deaw, the which to sleepe them biddes.
   Unto their lodgings then his guestes he riddes:°   *takes*
   Where when all drownd in deadly° sleepe he findes,[23]   *death-like*
   He to his study goes, and there amiddes
   His Magick bookes and arts of sundry kindes,
He seekes out mighty charmes, to trouble sleepy mindes.

37

Then choosing out few wordes most horrible,
   (Let none them read) thereof did verses frame,
   With which and other spelles like terrible,
   He bad awake blacke Plutoes griesly Dame,[24]
   And cursed heaven, and spake reprochfull shame
   Of highest God, the Lord of life and light;
   A bold bad man, that dared to call by name
   Great Gorgon,[25] Prince of darknesse and dead night,
At which Cocytus quakes, and Styx is put to flight.

38

And forth he cald out of deepe darknesse dred
   Legions of Sprights, the which like little flyes
   Fluttring about his ever damned hed,
   A-waite whereto their service he applyes,
   To aide his friends, or fray° his enimies: *frighten*
   Of those he chose out two, the falsest twoo,
   And fittest for to forge true-seeming lyes;
   The one of them he gave a message too,
The other by him selfe staide other worke to doo.

39

He making speedy way through spersed° ayre,   *wide-spread*
   And through the world of waters wide and deepe,
   To Morpheus house doth hastily repaire.
   Amid the bowels of the earth full steepe,
   And low, where dawning day doth never peepe,
   His dwelling is; there Tethys his wet bed
   Doth ever wash, and Cynthia still doth steepe
   In silver deaw his ever-drouping hed,
Whiles sad Night over him her mantle black doth spred.

40

Whose double gates[26] he findeth locked fast,
   The one faire framed of burnisht Yvory,
   The other all with silver overcast;
   And wakefull dogges before them farre do lye,
   Watching to banish Care their enimy,
   Who oft is wont to trouble gentle Sleepe.
   By them the Sprite doth passe in quietly,
   And unto Morpheus comes, whom drowned deepe
In drowsie fit he findes: of nothing he takes keepe.°   *notice*

41

And more, to lulle him in his slumber soft,
   A trickling streame from high rocke tumbling downe
   And ever-drizling raine upon the loft,
   Mixt with a murmuring winde, much like the sowne°   *sound*
   Of swarming Bees, did cast him in a swowne°:   *swoon*
   No other noyse, nor peoples troublous cryes,
   As still are wont t'annoy the walled towne,
   Might there be heard: but carelesse Quiet lyes,
Wrapt in eternall silence farre from enemyes.

42

The messenger approching to him spake,
   But his wast° wordes returnd to him in vaine: *wasted*
   So sound he slept, that nought mought him awake.
   Then rudely he him thrust, and pusht with paine,
   Whereat he gan to stretch: but he againe
   Shooke him so hard, that forced him to speake.
   As one then in a dreame, whose dryer braine[27]
   Is tost with troubled sights and fancies weake,
He mumbled soft, but would not all his silence breake.

43

The Sprite then gan more boldly him to wake,
  And threatned unto him the dreaded name
  Of Hecate: whereat he gan to quake,
  And lifting up his lumpish° head, with blame   *dull*
  Halfe angry asked him, for what he came.
  'Hither,' quoth he, 'me Archimago sent,
  He that the stubborne Sprites can wisely tame,
  He bids thee to him send for his intent°   *purpose*
A fit false dreame, that can delude the sleepers sent.' *perception*

44

The God obayde, and calling forth straight way
  A diverse° dreame out of his prison darke,   *distracting*
  Delivered it to him, and downe did lay
  His heavie head, devoide of carefull carke,°   *sorrow*
  Whose sences all were straight benumbd and starke.°   *rigid*
  He backe returning by the Yvorie dore,
  Remounted up as light as chearefull Larke,
  And on his litle winges the dreame he bore
In hast unto his Lord, where he him left afore.

45

Who all this while with charmes and hidden artes,
  Had made a Lady of that other Spright,
  And framed of liquid ayre her tender partes[28]
  So lively,° and so like in all mens sight,   *lifelike*
  That weaker sence it could have ravisht quight:
  The maker selfe for all his wondrous witt,
  Was nigh beguiled with so goodly sight:
  Her all in white he clad, and over it
Cast a blacke stole, most like to seeme for Una fit.

46

Now when that ydle° dreame was to him brought,   *frivolous*
  Unto that Elfin knight he bad him fly,
  Where he slept soundly void of evill thought,
  And with false shewes abuse his fantasy,°   *imagination*
  In sort as he him schooled privily:
  And that new creature borne without her dew,°   *unnaturally*
  Full of the makers guile, with usage sly
  He taught to imitate that Lady trew,
Whose semblance she did carrie under feigned hew.°   *form*

47²⁹

Thus well instructed, to their worke they hast,
    And comming where the knight in slomber lay,
    The one upon his hardy head him plast,
    And made him dreame of loves and lustfull play,
    That nigh his manly hart did melt away,
    Bathed in wanton blis and wicked joy:
    Then seemed him his Lady by him lay,
    And to him playnd,° how that false winged boy   *complained*
Her chast hart had subdewd, to learne Dame pleasures toy.

48

And she her selfe of beautie soveraigne Queene,
    Faire Venus seemde unto his bed to bring
    Her, whom he waking evermore did weene
    To be the chastest flowre, that ay° did spring   *ever*
    On earthly braunch, the daughter of a king,
    Now a loose Leman° to vile service bound: *paramour*
    And eke the Graces seemed all to sing,
    Hymen io Hymen, dauncing all around,
Whilst freshest Flora her with Yvie girlond crownd.

49

In this great passion of unwonted° lust,   *unaccustomed*
    Or wonted feare of doing ought amis,
    He started up, as seeming to mistrust
    Some secret ill, or hidden foe of his:
    Lo there before his face his Lady is,
    Under blake stole hyding her bayted hooke,
    And as halfe blushing offred him to kis,
    With gentle blandishment and lovely looke,
Most like that virgin true, which for her knight him took.

50

All cleane dismayd to see so uncouth° sight,   *unpleasant*
    And halfe enraged at her shameless guise,
    He thought have slaine her in his fierce despight°:   *anger*
    But hasty heat tempring with sufferance wise,
    He stayde his hand, and gan himselfe advise
    To prove his sense, and tempt her faigned truth.
    Wringing her hands in wemens pitteous wise,
    Tho can° she weepe, to stirre up gentle ruth,°   *knew how to/pity*
Both for her noble bloud, and for her tender youth.

51

And said, 'Ah Sir, my liege Lord and my love,
  Shall I accuse the hidden cruell fate,
  And mightie causes wrought in heaven above,
  Or the blind God, that doth me thus amate, *dismay*
  For hoped love to winne me certaine hate?
  Yet thus perforce he bids me do, or die.
  Die is my dew: yet rew my wretched state
  You, whom my hard avenging destinie
Hath made judge of my life or death indifferently.

52

Your owne deare sake forst me at first to leave
  My Fathers kingdome,' There she stopt with teares;
  Her swollen hart her speach seemd to bereave,
  And then againe begun, 'My weaker yeares
  Captived to fortune and frayle worldly feares,
  Fly to your faith for succour and sure ayde:
  Let me not dye in languor and long teares.'
  'Why Dame,' quoth he, 'what hath ye thus dismayd?
What frayes° ye, that were wont to comfort me affrayd?' *frightens*

53

'Love of your self,' she said, 'and deare° constraint *dire*
  Lets me not sleepe, but wast the wearie night
  In secret anguish and unpittied plaint,
  Whiles you in carelesse sleepe are drowned quight.'
  Her doubtfull° words made that redoubted knight *dubious*
  Suspect her truth: yet since no'untruth he knew,
  Her fawning love with foule disdainefull spight
  He would not shend°, but said, 'Deare dame I rew°, *reproach/pity*
That for my sake unknowne such griefe unto you grew.

54

Assure your selfe, it fell not all to ground;
  For all so deare as life is to my hart,
  I deeme your love, and hold me to you bound;
  Ne let vaine feares procure° your needlesse smart, *cause*
  Where cause is none, but to your rest depart.'
  Not all content, yet seemd she to appease° *cease*
  Her mournefull plaintes, beguiled of her art,
  And fed with words, that could not chuse but please,
So slyding softly forth, she turnd as to her ease.

55

Long after lay he musing at her mood,
  Much grieved to thinke that gentle Dame so light,°   *frivolous*
For whose defence he was to shed his blood.
At last dull wearinesse of former fight
Having yrockt a sleepe his irkesome spright,°   *spirit*
That troublous dreame gan freshly tosse his braine,
With bowres, and beds, and Ladies deare delight:
But when he saw his labour all was vaine,
With that misformed spright he backe returnd againe.

CANTO 2[30]

The guilefull great Enchaunter parts
The Redcrosse Knight from Truth:
Into whose stead faire falshood steps,
And workes him woful ruth.°   *harm*

1

By this the Northerne wagoner[31] had set
  His sevenfold teme behind the stedfast starre,
That was in Ocean waves yet never wet,
But firme is fixt, and sendeth light from farre
To all, that in the wide deepe wandring arre:
And chearefull Chaunticlere with his note shrill
Had warned once, that Phoebus fiery carre
In hast was climbing up the Easterne hill,
Full envious that night so long his roome did fill.

2

When those accursed messengers of hell,
  That feigning dreame, and that faire-forged Spright
Came to their wicked maister, and gan tell
Their bootelesse° paines, and ill succeeding night: *unsuccessful*
Who all in rage to see his skilfull might
Deluded so, gan threaten hellish paine
And sad Proserpines wrath, them to affright.
But when he saw his threatning was but vaine,
He cast about, and searcht his balefull° bookes againe.   *death-bringing*

3

Eftsoones he tooke that miscreated faire,
  And that false other Spright, on whom he spred
  A seeming body of the subtile aire,
  Like a young Squire, in loves and lusty-hed
  His wanton dayes that ever loosely led,
  Without regard of armes and dreaded fight:
  Those two he tooke, and in a secret bed,
  Covered with darknesse and misdeeming° night,   *misleading*
Them both together laid, to joy in vaine delight.

4

Forthwith he runnes with feigned faithfull hast
  Unto his guest, who after troublous sights
  And dreames, gan now to take more sound repast,°   *rest*
  Whom suddenly he wakes with fearefull frights,
  As one aghast with feends or damned sprights,
  And to him cals, 'Rise rise unhappy Swaine,
  That here wex° old in sleepe, whiles wicked wights   *grows*
  Have knit themselves in Venus shamefull chaine;
Come see, where your false Lady doth her honour staine.'

5

All in amaze he suddenly up start
  With sword in hand, and with the old man went;
  Who soone him brought into a secret part,
  Where that false couple were full closely ment°   *joined*
  In wanton lust and lewd embracement:
  Which when he saw, he burnt with gealous fire,
  The eye of reason was with rage yblent,°   *blinded*
  And would have slaine them in his furious ire,
But hardly° was restreined of that aged sire.   *with difficulty*

6

Returning to his bed in torment great,
  And bitter anguish of his guiltie sight,
  He could not rest, but did his stout heart eat,
  And wast his inward gall with deepe despight,
  Yrkesome of life, and too long lingring night.
  At last faire Hesperus in highest skie
  Had spent his lampe, and brought forth dawning light,
  Then up he rose, and clad him hastily;
The Dwarfe him brought his steed: so both away do fly.[32]

7

Now when the rosy-fingred Morning faire,[33]
  Weary of aged Tithones saffron bed,
  Had spred her purple robe through deawy aire,
  And the high hils Titan° discovered,   *the sun*
  The royall virgin shooke off drowsy-hed,
  And rising forth out of her baser° bowre,   *humble*
  Lookt for her knight, who far away was fled,
  And for her Dwarfe, that wont to wait each houre;
Then gan she waile and weepe, to see that woefull stowre.° *plight*

8

And after him she rode with so much speede
  As her slow beast could make; but all in vaine:
  For him so far had borne his light-foot steede,
  Pricked with wrath and fiery fierce disdaine,
  That him to follow was but fruitlesse paine;
  Yet she her weary limbes would never rest,
  But every hill and dale, each wood and plaine
  Did search, sore grieved in her gentle brest,
He so ungently left her, whom she loved best.

9

But subtill Archimago, when his guests
  He saw divided into double parts,
  And Una wandring in woods and forrests,
  Th'end of his drift,° he praisd his divelish arts,   *plan*
  That had such might over true meaning harts;
  Yet rests not so, but other meanes doth make,
  How he may worke unto her further smarts:
  For her he hated as the hissing snake,
And in her many troubles did most pleasure take.

10

He then devisde himselfe how to disguise;
  For by his mightie science° he could take   *knowledge*
  As many formes and shapes in seeming wise,°   *guise*
  As ever Proteus to himselfe could make:
  Sometime a fowle, sometime a fish in lake,
  Now like a foxe,[34] now like a dragon fell,°   *fierce*
  That of himselfe he oft for feare would quake,
  And oft would flie away. O who can tell
The hidden power of herbes, and might of Magicke spell?

11

But now seemde best, the person to put on
　Of that good knight, his late beguiled guest:
　In mighty armes he was yclad anon,
　And silver shield: upon his coward brest
　A bloudy crosse, and on his craven crest
　A bounch of haires discolourd° diversly:　　　　　*many-coloured*
　Full jolly knight he seemde, and well addrest,
　And when he sate upon his courser free,
Saint George himself ye would have deemed him to be.

12

But he the knight, whose semblaunt° he did beare,　　*resemblance*
　The true Saint George was wandred far away,
　Still flying from his thoughts and gealous feare;
　Will was his guide, and griefe led him astray.
　At last him chaunst to meete upon the way
　A faithlesse Sarazin° all armed to point,　　　　　*Saracen*
　In whose great shield was writ with letters gay
　Sans foy°: full large of limbe and every joint　　*without faith*
He was, and cared not for God or man a point.

13

He had a faire companion of his way,
　A goodly Lady clad in scarlot red,[35]
　Purfled° with gold and pearle of rich assay,　　　*bordered*
　And like a Persian mitre on her hed
　She wore, with crownes and owches° garnished,　　*brooches*
　The which her lavish lovers to her gave;
　Her wanton palfrey all was overspred
　With tinsell trappings, woven like a wave,
Whose bridle rung with golden bels and bosses° brave.　*studs*

14

With faire disport° and courting dalliaunce　　　*entertainment*
　She intertainde her lover all the way:
　But when she saw the knight his speare advaunce,
　She soone left off her mirth and wanton play,
　And bad her knight addresse him to the fray:
　His foe was nigh at hand. He prickt with pride
　And hope to winne his Ladies heart that day,
　Forth spurred fast: adowne his coursers side
The red bloud trickling staind the way, as he did ride.

15

The knight of the Redcrosse when him he spide,
  Spurring so hote with rage dispiteous,   *unpitying*
  Gan fairely couch° his speare, and towards ride: *lower*
  Soone meete they both, both fell and furious,
  That daunted with their forces hideous,
  Their steeds do stagger, and amazed stand,
  And eke themselves too rudely rigorous,
  Astonied° with the stroke of their owne hand,   *stunned*
Do backe rebut,° and each to other yeeldeth land.   *recoil*

16

As when two rams stird with ambitious pride,
  Fight for the rule of the rich fleeced flocke,
  Their horned fronts so fierce on either side
  Do meete, that with the terrour of the shocke
  Astonied both, stand sencelesse as a blocke,
  Forgetfull of the hanging victory:
  So stood these twaine, unmoved as a rocke,
  Both staring fierce, and holding idely
The broken reliques of their former cruelty.

17

The Sarazin sore daunted with the buffe
  Snatcheth his sword, and fiercely to him flies;
  Who well it wards, and quyteth° cuff with cuff: *returns*
  Each others equall puissaunce envies,
  And through their iron sides with cruell spies°   *glances*
  Does seeke to perce: repining° courage yields   *angry*
  No foote to foe. The flashing fier flies
  As from a forge out of their burning shields,
And streames of purple bloud new dies the verdant fields.

18

'Curse on that Crosse,' quoth then the Sarazin,
  'That keepes thy body from the bitter fit°;   *death*
  Dead long ygoe I wote thou haddest bin,
  Had not that charme from thee forwarned° it: *protected*
  But yet I warne thee now assured sitt,
  And hide thy head.' Therewith upon his crest
  With rigour so outrageous he smitt,
  That a large share° it hewd out of the rest,   *piece*
And glauncing downe his shield, from blame°   *harm*
                him fairely blest.°   *preserved*

19

Who thereat wondrous wroth, the sleeping spark
  Of native vertue° gan eftsoones revive, *power*
  And at his haughtie helmet making mark,
  So hugely stroke, that it the steele did rive,
  And cleft his head. He tumbling downe alive,
  With bloudy mouth his mother earth did kis,
  Greeting his grave: his grudging° ghost did strive *complaining*
  With the fraile flesh: at last it flitted is,
Whither the soules do fly of men, that live amis.

20

The Lady when she saw her champion fall,
  Like the old ruines of a broken towre,
  Staid not to waile his woefull funerall,
  But from him fled away with all her powre;
  Who after her as hastily gan scowre° *run*
  Bidding the Dwarfe with him to bring away
  The Sarazins shield, signe of the conqueroure,
  Her soone he overtooke, and bad to stay,
For present cause was none of dread her to dismay.

21

She turning backe with ruefull countenaunce,
  Cride, 'Mercy mercy Sir vouchsafe to show
  On silly° Dame, subject to hard mischaunce, *simple*
  And to your mighty will.' Her humblesse low
  In so ritch weedes and seeming glorious show,
  Did much emmove his stout heroicke heart,
  And said, 'Deare dame, your suddein overthrow
  Much rueth° me; but now put feare apart, *grieves*
And tell, both who ye be, and who that tooke your part.'

22

Melting in teares, then gan she thus lament;
  'The wretched woman, whom unhappy howre
  Hath now made thrall to your commandement,
  Before that angry heavens list to lowre° *lour*
  And fortune false betraide me to your powre,
  Was (O what now availeth that I was!)
  Borne the sole daughter of an Emperour,[36]
  He that the wide West under his rule has,
And high hath set his throne, where Tiberis doth pas.

23

He in the first flowre of my freshest age,
 Betrothed me unto the onely haire°   *heir*
 Of a most mighty king, most rich and sage;
 Was never Prince[37] so faithfull and so faire,
 Was never Prince so meeke and debonaire°;   *courteous*
 But ere my hoped day of spousall shone,
 My dearest Lord fell from high honours staire,
 Into the hands of his accursed fone°,   *foes*
And cruelly was slaine, that shall I ever mone.

24

His blessed body spoild of lively breath,
 Was afterward, I know not how, convaid°   *conveyed*
 And fro me hid: of whose most innocent death
 When tidings came to me unhappy maid,
 O how great sorrow my sad soule assaid°.   *assailed*
 Then forth I went his woefull corse to find,
 And many yeares throughout the world I straid,
 A virgin widow, whose deepe wounded mind
With love, long time did languish as the striken hind.

25

At last it chaunced this proud Sarazin
 To meete me wandring, who perforce me led
 With him away, but yet could never win
 The Fort, that Ladies hold in soveraigne dread.
 There lies he now with foule dishonour dead,
 Who whiles he livde, was called proud Sans foy,[38]
 The eldest of three brethren, all three bred
 Of one bad sire, whose youngest is Sans joy°,   '*Without Joy*'
And twixt them both was borne the bloudy bold Sans loy°. '*Without Law*'

26

In this sad plight, friendlesse, unfortunate,
 Now miserable I Fidessa dwell,
 Craving of you in pitty of my state,
 To do none ill, if please ye not do well.'
 He in great passion all this while did dwell,
 More busying his quicke eyes, her face to view,
 Then his dull eares, to heare what she did tell;
 And said, 'Faire Lady hart of flint would rew°   *pity*
The undeserved woes and sorrowes, which ye shew.

27

Henceforth in safe assuraunce may ye rest,
   Having both found a new friend you to aid,
   And lost an old foe, that did you molest:
   Better new friend then an old foe is said.'
   With chaunge of cheare the seeming simple maid
   Let fall her eyen, as shamefast to the earth,
   And yeelding soft, in that she nought gain-said,°   *opposed*
   So forth they rode, he feining seemely merth,
And she coy lookes: so dainty they say maketh derth.[39]

28

Long time they thus together traveiled,
   Till weary of their way, they came at last,
   Where grew two goodly trees, that faire did spred
   Their armes abroad, with gray mosse overcast,
   And their greene leaves trembling with every blast,°   *breeze*
   Make a calme shadow far in compasse round:
   The fearefull Shepheard often there aghast°   *terrified*
   Under them never sat, ne wont there sound
His mery oaten pipe, but shund th'unlucky ground.

29

But this good knight soone as he them can spie,
   For the coole shade him thither hastly got:[40]
   For golden Phoebus now ymounted hie,
   From fiery wheeles of his faire chariot
   Hurled his beame so scorching cruell hot,
   That living creature mote it not abide;
   And his new Lady it endured not.
   There they alight, in hope themselves to hide
From the fierce heat, and rest their weary limbs a tide.°   *time*

30

Faire seemely pleasaunce each to other makes,
   With goodly purposes° there as they sit: *talk*
   And in his falsed° fancy he her takes   *deceived*
   To be the fairest wight, that lived yit;
   Which to expresse, he bends his gentle wit,
   And thinking of those braunches greene to frame
   A girlond for her dainty forehead fit,
   He pluckt a bough; out of whose rift there came
Small drops of gory bloud, that trickled downe the same.

31

Therewith a piteous yelling voyce was heard,
  Crying, 'O spare with guilty hands to teare
  My tender sides in this rough rynd embard,°   *imprisoned*
  But fly, ah fly far hence away, for feare
  Least to you hap, that happened to me heare,
  And to this wretched Lady, my deare love,
  O too deare love, love bought with death too deare.'
  Astond° he stood, and up his haire did hove,°   *astonished/rise*
And with that suddein horror could no member° move.   *limb*

32

At last whenas the dreadfull° passion   *full of dread*
  Was overpast, and manhood well awake,
  Yet musing at the straunge occasion,
  And doubting much his sence, he thus bespake;
  'What voyce of damned Ghost from Limbo lake,
  Or guilefull spright wandring in empty aire,
  Both which fraile men do oftentimes mistake,°   *mislead*
  Sends to my doubtfull eares these speaches rare,
And ruefull plaints, me bidding guiltlesse bloud to spare?'

33

Then groning deepe, 'Nor damned Ghost,' quoth he,
  'Nor guilefull sprite to thee these wordes doth speake,
  But once a man Fradubio,° now a tree,   *= Doubt*
  Wretched man, wretched tree; whose nature weake,[41]
  A cruell witch her cursed will to wreake,
  Hath thus transformd, and plast in open plaines,
  Where Boreas doth blow full bitter bleake,
  And scorching Sunne does dry my secret vaines:
For though a tree I seeme, yet cold and heat me paines.'

34

'Say on Fradubio then, or man, or tree,'
  Quoth then the knight, 'by whose mischievous arts
  Art thou misshaped thus, as now I see?
  He oft finds med'cine, who his griefe imparts;°   *discloses*
  But double griefs afflict concealing harts,
  As raging flames who striveth to suppresse.'
  'The author then,' said he, 'of all my smarts,
  Is one Duessa° a false sorceresse,   *i.e. two-faced*
That many errant° knights hath brought to wretchednesse.   *wandering* .

35

In prime of youthly yeares, when corage hot
  The fire of love and joy of chevalree
  First kindled in my brest, it was my lot
  To love this gentle Lady, whom ye see,
  Now not a Lady, but a seeming tree;
  With whom as once I rode accompanyde,
  Me chaunced of a knight encountred bee,
  That had a like° faire Lady by his syde,   *similar*
Like a faire Lady, but did fowle Duessa hyde.

36

Whose forged beauty he did take in hand,
  All other Dames to have exceeded farre;
  I in defence of mine did likewise stand,
  Mine, that did then shine as the Morning starre:
  So both to battell fierce arraunged arre,
  In which his harder fortune was to fall
  Under my speare: such is the dye° of warre: *luck (dice)*
  His Lady left as a prise martiall,°   *battle spoils*
Did yield her comely person, to be at my call.

37

So doubly loved of Ladies unlike faire,
  Th'one seeming such, the other such indeede,
  One day in doubt I cast° for to compare,   *decided*
  Whether° in beauties glorie did exceede;   *which*
  A Rosy[42] girlond was the victors meede:°   *reward*
  Both seemde to win, and both seemde won to bee,
  So hard the discord was to be agreede.
  Fraelissa° was as faire, as faire mote bee,   *Frailty*
And ever false Duessa seemde as faire as shee.

38

The wicked witch now seeing all this while
  The doubtfull ballaunce equally to sway,
  What not by right, she cast to win by guile,
  And by her hellish science raisd streight way
  A foggy mist, that overcast the day,
  And a dull blast, that breathing on her face,
  Dimmed her former beauties shining ray,
  And with foule ugly forme did her disgrace:
Then was she faire alone, when none was faire in place.[43]

39

Then cride she out, 'Fye, fye, deformed wight,
  Whose borrowed beautie now appeareth plaine
  To have before bewitched all mens sight;
  O leave her soone, or let her soone be slaine.'
  Her loathly visage viewing with disdaine,
  Eftsoones I thought her such, as she me told,
  And would have kild her; but with faigned paine,
  The false witch did my wrathfull hand withhold;
So left her, where she now is turnd to treen° mould.   *of a tree*

40

Thens forth I tooke Duessa for my Dame,
  And in the witch unweeting° joyd long time,   *not realising*
  Ne ever wist, but that she was the same,
  Till on a day (that day is every Prime,⁴⁴
  When Witches wont do penance for their crime)
  I chaunst to see her in her proper hew,°   *shape*
  Bathing her selfe in origane⁴⁵ and thyme:
  A filthy foule old woman I did vew,
That ever to have toucht her, I did deadly rew.

41

Her neather partes misshapen, monstruous,
  Were hidd in water, that I could not see,
  But they did seeme more foule and hideous,
  Than womans shape man would beleeve to bee.
  Thens forth from her most beastly companie
  I gan refraine, in minde to slip away,
  Soone as appeard safe opportunitie:
  For danger great, if not assured decay°   *destruction*
I saw before mine eyes, if I were knowne to stray.

42

The divelish hag by chaunges of my cheare°   *appearance*
  Perceived my thought, and drownd in sleepie night,
  With wicked herbes and ointments did besmeare
  My bodie all, through charmes and magicke might,
  That all my senses were bereaved quight:
  Then brought she me into this desert waste,
  And by my wretched lovers side me pight,°   *placed*
  Where now enclosd in wooden wals full faste,
Banisht from living wights, our wearie dayes we waste.'

43

'But how long time,' said then the Elfin knight,
  'Are you in this misformed house to dwell?'
  'We may not chaunge,' quoth he, 'this evil plight,
  Till we be bathed in a living well;[46]
  That is the terme prescribed by the spell.'
  'O how,' said he, 'mote I that well out find,
  That may restore you to your wonted well°?'   *well-being*
  'Time and suffised° fates to former kynd   *satisfied*
Shall us restore, none else from hence may us unbynd.'

44

The false Duessa, now Fidessa hight,°   *called*
  Heard how in vaine Fradubio did lament,
  And know well all was true. But the good knight
  Full of sad feare and ghastly dreriment,°   *grief*
  When all this speech the living tree had spent,
  The bleeding bough did thrust into the ground,
  That from the bloud he might be innocent,[47]
  And with fresh clay did close the wooden wound:
Then turning to his Lady, dead with feare her found.

45

Her seeming dead he found with feigned feare,
  As all unweeting° of that well she knew,[48]   *ignorant*
  And paynd himselfe with busie care to reare
  Her out of carelesse° swowne. Her eylids blew   *free from care*
  And dimmed sight with pale and deadly hew
  At last she up gan lift: with trembling cheare
  Her up he tooke, too simple and too trew,
  And oft her kist. At length all passed feare,[49]
He set her on her steede, and forward forth did beare.

CANTO 3 [50]

Forsaken Truth long seekes her love,
  And makes the Lyon mylde,
Marres blind Devotions mart,° and fals   *trade*
  In hand of leachour vylde.

I

Nought is there under heav'ns wide hollownesse,
  That moves more deare compassion of mind,
  Then beautie brought t'unworthy° wretchednesse   *undeserved*

Through envies snares or fortunes freakes unkind:
I, whether lately through her brightnesse blind,
Or through alleageance and fast fealtie,
Which I do owe unto all woman kind,
Feele my heart perst° with so great agonie,   *pierced*
When such I see, that all for pittie I could die.

2

And now it is empassioned so deepe,
   For fairest Unaes sake, of whom I sing,
   That my fraile eyes these lines with teares do steepe,
   To thinke how she through guilefull handeling,°   *treatment*
   Though true as touch,[51] though daughter of a king,
   Though faire as ever living wight was faire,
   Though nor in word nor deede ill meriting,
   Is from her knight divorced in despaire
And her due loves derived° to that vile witches share.   *diverted*

3

Yet she most faithfull Ladie all this while
   Forsaken, wofull, solitarie mayd
   Farre from all peoples prease,° as in exile,   *press*
   In wildernesse and wastfull deserts strayd,
   To seeke her knight; who subtilly betrayd
   Through that late vision, which th'Enchaunter wrought,
   Had her abandond. She of nought affrayd,
   Through woods and wastnesse wide him daily sought;
Yet wished tydings none of him unto her brought.

4

One day nigh wearie of the yrkesome way,
   From her unhastie beast she did alight,
   And on the grasse her daintie limbes did lay
   In secret shadow, farre from all mens sight:
   From her faire head her fillet° she undight,°   *headband/undid*
   And laid her stole aside. Her angels face
   As the great eye of heaven shyned bright,
   And made a sunshine in the shadie place;
Did never mortall eye behold such heavenly grace.[52]

5

It fortuned out of the thickest wood
   A ramping° Lyon rushed suddainly,   *raging*
   Hunting full greedie after salvage° blood;   *wild*

Soone as the royall virgin he did spy,
With gaping mouth at her ran greedily,
To have attonce devoured her tender corse:
But to the pray when as he drew more ny,
His bloudie rage asswaged with remorse,
And with the sight amazd, forgat his furious forse.

6

In stead thereof he kist her wearie feet,
And lickt her lilly hands with fawning tong,
As° he her wronged innocence did weet°   *as though/know*
O how can beautie maister the most strong,
And simple truth subdue avenging wrong?
Whose yeelded pride and proud submission,
Still dreading death, when she had marked long,
Her hart gan melt in great compassion,
And drizling teares did shed for pure affection.

7

'The Lyon Lord of everie beast in field,'
Quoth she, 'his princely puissance doth abate,
And mightie proud to humble weake does yield,
Forgetfull of the hungry rage, which late
Him prickt, in pittie of my sad estate°:   *condition*
But he my Lyon, and my noble Lord,
How does he find in cruell hart to hate
Her that him loved, and ever most adord,
As the God of my life? why hath he me abhord?'

8

Redounding° teares did choke th'end of her plaint,   *overflowing*
Which softly ecchoed from the neighbour wood;
And sad to see her sorrowfull constraint°   *distress*
The kingly beast upon her gazing stood;
With pittie calmd, downe fell his angry mood.
At last in close hart shutting up her paine,
Arose the virgin borne of heavenly brood°   *parents*
And to her snowy Palfrey got againe,
To seeke her strayed Champion, if she might attaine°   *reach*

9

The Lyon would not leave her desolate,
But with her went along, as a strong gard
Of her chast person, and a faithfull mate

Of her sad troubles and misfortunes hard:
Still° when she slept, he kept both watch and ward,   *always*
And when she wakt, he waited diligent,
With humble service to her will prepard:
From her faire eyes he tooke commaundement,
And ever by her lookes conceived her intent.

10

Long she thus traveiled through deserts wyde,
    By which she thought her wandring knight shold pas,
    Yet never shew of living wight espyde;
    Till that at length she found the troden gras,
    In which the tract° of peoples footing was   *track*
    Under the steepe foot of a mountaine hore°;   *grey*
    The same she followes, till at last she has
    A damzell spyde slow footing her before,
That on her shoulders sad a pot of water bore.

11

To whom approching she to her gan call,
    To weet, if dwelling place were nigh at hand;
    But the rude° wench her answered nought at all,   *ignorant*
    She could not heare, nor speake, nor understand;
    Till seeing by her side the Lyon stand,
    With suddaine feare her pitcher downe she threw,
    And fled away: for never in that land
    Face of faire Ladie she before did vew,
And that dread Lyons looke her cast in deadly hew.[53]

12

Full fast she fled, ne ever lookt behynd,
    As if her life upon the wager lay,[54]
    And home she came, whereas her mother blynd
    Sate in eternall night: nought could she say,
    But suddaine catching hold, did her dismay
    With quaking hands, and other signes of feare:
    Who full of ghastly fright and cold affray,°   *fear*
    Gan shut the dore. By this arrived there
Dame Una, wearie Dame, and entrance did requere.°   *request*

13

Which when none yeelded, her unruly Page
    With his rude clawes the wicket open rent,
    And let her in; where of his cruell rage

Nigh dead with feare, and faint astonishment,[55]
She found them both in darkesome corner pent;
Where that old woman day and night did pray
Upon her beades devoutly penitent;
Nine hundred *Pater nosters*[56] every day,
And thrise nine hundred *Aves* she was wont to say.

14

And to augment her painefull pennance more,
   Thrise every weeke in ashes she did sit,
   And next her wrinkled skin rough sackcloth wore,
   And thrise three times did fast from any bit°:   *bite of food*
   But now for feare her beads she did forget.
   Whose needlesse dread for to remove away,
   Faire Una framed words and count'nance fit:
   Which hardly° doen, at length she gan them pray,   *with difficulty*
That in their cotage small, that night she rest her may.

15

The day is spent, and commeth drowsie night,
   When every creature shrowded is in sleepe;
   Sad Una downe her laies in wearie plight,
   And at her feet the Lyon watch doth keepe:
   In stead of rest, she does lament, and weepe
   For the late losse of her deare loved knight,
   And sighes, and grones, and evermore does steepe°   *stain*
   Her tender brest in bitter teares all night,
All night she thinks too long, and often lookes for light.

16

Now when Aldeboran was mounted hie
   Above the shynie Cassiopeias chaire,
   And all in deadly sleepe did drowned lie,
   One knocked at the dore, and in would fare;
   He knocked fast, and often curst, and sware,
   That readie entrance was not at his call:
   For on his backe a heavy load he bare
   Of nightly stelths and pillage severall,°   *of various kinds*
Which he had got abroad by purchase° criminall.   *acquisition*

17

He was to weete° a stout and sturdie thiefe,   *in fact*
   Wont to robbe Churches of their ornaments,
   And poore mens boxes° of their due reliefe,   *alms boxes*

Which given was to them for good intents;
  The holy Saints of their rich vestiments
  He did disrobe, when all men carelesse slept,
  And spoild the Priests of their habiliments,°   *robes*
  Whiles none the holy things in safety kept;
Then he by cunning sleights in at the window crept.

                         18
And all that he by right or wrong could find,
  Unto this house he brought, and did bestow
  Upon the daughter of this woman blind,
  Abessa daughter of Corceca° slow;   *= blindness of heart*
  With whom he whoredome usd, that few did know,
  And fed her fat with feast of offerings,
  And plentie, which in all the land did grow;
  Ne spared he to give her gold and rings:
And now he to her brought part of his stolen things.

                         19
Thus long the dore with rage and threats he bet,°   *beat*
  Yet of those fearefull women none durst rize,
  The Lyon frayed° them, him in to let: *frightened*
  He would no longer stay him to advize,°   *consider*
  But open breakes the dore in furious wize,
  And entring is; when that disdainfull beast
  Encountring fierce, him suddaine doth surprize,
  And seizing cruell clawes on trembling brest,
Under his Lordly foot him proudly hath supprest.

                         20
Him booteth not° resist, nor succour call,   *it is useless*
  His bleeding hart is in the vengers° hand,   *avenger's*
  Who streight him rent in thousand peeces small,
  And quite dismembred hath: the thirstie land
  Drunke up his life; his corse left on the strand.°   *ground*
  His fearefull friends weare out the wofull night,
  Ne dare to weepe, nor seeme to understand
  The heavie hap,° which on them is alight,°   *lot/fallen*
Affraid, least to themselves the like mishappen might.

                         21
Now when broad day the world discovered° has,   *disclosed*
  Up Una rose, up rose the Lyon eke,
  And on their former journey forward pas,

In wayes unknowne, her wandring knight to seeke,
With paines farre passing that long wandring Greeke,[57]
That for his love refused deitie;
Such were the labours of this Lady meeke,
Still seeking him, that from her still did flie,
Then furthest from her hope, when most she weened nie°.   *near*

22

Soone as she parted thence, the fearefull twaine,
  That blind old woman and her daughter deare
  Came forth, and finding Kirkrapine° there slaine,   *= church robber*
  For anguish great they gan to rend their heare,
  And beat their brests, and naked flesh to teare.
  And when they both had wept and wayld° their fill,   *wailed*
  Then forth they ranne like two amazed deare,
  Halfe mad through malice, and revenging will,[58]
To follow her, that was the causer of their ill.

23

Whom overtaking, they gan loudly bray,
  With hollow howling, and lamenting cry,
  Shamefully at her rayling all the way,
  And her accusing of dishonesty,
  That was the flowre of faith and chastity;
  And still amidst her rayling, she° did pray,   *i.e. Corceca*
  That plagues, and mischiefs, and long misery
  Might fall on her, and follow all the way,
And that in endlesse error° she might ever stray.   *wandering*

24

But when she saw her prayers nought prevaile,
  She backe returned with some labour lost;
  And in the way as she did weepe and waile,
  A knight her met in mighty armes embost°,   *encased*
  Yet knight was not for all his bragging bost°,   *boast*
  But subtill Archimag, that Una sought
  By traynes° into new troubles to have tost:°   *wiles/thrown*
  Of that old woman tydings he besought,
If that of such a Ladie she could tellen ought.

25

Therewith she gan her passion to renew,
  And cry, and curse, and raile, and rend her heare,
  Saying, that harlot she too lately knew,

That causd her shed so many a bitter teare,
And so forth told the story of her feare:
Much seemed he to mone her haplesse chaunce,
And after for that Ladie did inquere;
Which being taught, he forward gan advaunce
His fair enchaunted steed, and eke his charmed launce.

26

Ere long he came, where Una traveild slow,
   And that wilde Champion wayting her besyde:
   Whom seeing such, for dread he durst not show
   Himselfe too nigh at hand, but turned wyde°   *aside*
   Unto an hill; from whence when she him spyde,
   By his like seeming shield, her knight by name
   She weend° it was, and towards him gan ryde: *thought*
   Approching nigh, she wist° it was the same,   *believed*
And with faire fearefull humblesse° towards him shee came.   *humility*

27

And weeping said, 'Ah my long lacked Lord,
   Where have ye bene thus long out of my sight?
   Much feared I to have been quite abhord,
   Or ought° have done, that ye displeasen might,   *aught*
   That should as death unto my deare hart light:[59]
   For since mine eye your joyous sight did mis,
   My chearefull day is turnd to chearelesse night,
   And eke my night of death the shadow is;
But welcome now my light, and shining lampe of blis.'

28

He thereto meeting° said, 'My dearest Dame,   *in the same manner*
   Farre be it from your thought, and fro my will,
   To thinke that knighthood I so much should shame,
   As you to leave, that have me loved still,
   And chose in Faery court of meere° goodwill,   *pure*
   Where noblest knights were to be found on earth:
   The earth shall sooner leave her kindly° skill   *natural*
   To bring forth fruit, and make eternall derth,
Then I leave you, my liefe,° yborne of heavenly berth.   *beloved*

29

And sooth to say, why I left you so long,
   Was for to seeke adventure in strange place,
   Where Archimago said a felon strong

To many knights did daily worke disgrace;
But knight he now shall never more deface°:   *defame*
Good cause of mine excuse; that mote° ye please   *may*
Well to accept, and evermore embrace
My faithfull service, that by land and seas
Have vowd you to defend, now then your plaint appease.'

30

His lovely° words her seemd due recompence   *loving*
    Of all her passed paines: one loving howre
    For many yeares of sorrow can dispence:°   *dispel*
    A dram of sweet is worth a pound of sowre°:   *sour*
    She has forgot, how many a wofull stowre°   *peril*
    For him she late endured; she speakes no more
    Of past: true is, that true love hath no powre
    To looken backe; his eyes be fixt before.
Before her stands her knight, for whom she toyld so sore.

31

Much like, as when the beaten marinere,
    That long hath wandred in the Ocean wide,
    Oft soust° in swelling Tethys saltish teare,   *soaked*
    And long time having tand° his tawney hide   *tanned*
    With blustring breath of heaven, that none can bide,
    And scorching flames of fierce Orions hound,[60]
    Soone as the port from farre he has espide,
    His chearefull whistle merrily doth sound,
And Nereus crownes with cups; his mates him pledg around.

32

Such joy made Una, when her knight she found;
    And eke th'enchaunter joyous seemd no lesse,
    Then the glad marchant, that does vew from ground
    His ship farre come from watrie wildernesse,
    He hurles out vowes, and Neptune oft doth blesse:
    So forth they past, and all the way they spent
    Discoursing of her dreadfull late distresse,
    In which he askt her, what the Lyon ment:
Who told her all that fell° in journey as she went.   *befell*

33

They had not ridden farre, when they might see
    One pricking towards them with hastie heat,
    Full strongly armd, and on a courser free,

That through his fiercenesse fomed all with sweat,
And the sharpe yron° did for anger eat,   *spur*
When his hot ryder spurd his chauffed° side;   *heated*
His looke was sterne, and seemed still to threat
Cruell revenge, which he in hart did hyde,
And on his shield *Sans loy* in bloudie lines was dyde.

34

When nigh he drew unto this gentle payre
And saw the Red-crosse, which the knight did beare,
He burnt in fire, and gan eftsoones prepare
Himselfe to battell with his couched speare.   *lowered*
Loth was that other, and did faint through feare,
To taste th'untryed dint of deadly steele;
But yet his Lady did so well him cheare,
That hope of new good hap he gan to feele;
So bent° his speare, and spurnd his horse with yron heele.   *aimed*

35

But that proud Paynim° forward came so fierce,   *pagan*
And full of wrath, that with his sharp-head speare
Through vainely crossed[61] shield he quite did pierce,
And had his staggering steede not shrunke for feare,
Through shield and bodie eke he should him beare°:   *have thrust*
Yet so great was the puissance of his push,
That from his saddle quite he did him beare:
He tombling rudely downe to ground did rush,
And from his gored wound a well of bloud did gush.

36

Dismounting lightly from his loftie steed,
He to him lept, in mind to reave° his life,   *take away*
And proudly said, 'Lo there the worthie meed
Of him, that slew Sansfoy with bloudie knife;
Henceforth his ghost freed from repining° strife,   *angry*
In peace may passen over Lethe lake,
When mourning altars purgd° with enemies life,   *cleansed*
The blacke infernall Furies doen aslake:°   *appease*
Life from Sansfoy thou tookst, Sansloy shall from thee take.'

37

Therewith in haste his helmet gan unlace,
Till Una cride, 'O hold that heavie hand,
Deare Sir, what ever that thou be in place:[62]

Enough is, that thy foe doth vanquisht stand
  Now at thy mercy: Mercie not withstand°:   *deny*
  For he is one the truest knight[63] alive,
  Though conquered now he lie on lowly land,
  And whilest him fortune favourd, faire did thrive
In bloudie field: therefore of life him not deprive.'

38

Her piteous words might not abate his rage,
  But rudely rending up his helmet, would
  Have slaine him straight: but when he sees his age,
  And hoarie head of Archimago old,
  His hastie hand he doth amazed hold,
  And halfe ashamed, wondred at the sight:
  For that old man well knew he, though untold,
  In charmes and magicke to have wondrous might,
Ne ever wont in field, ne in round lists[64] to fight.

39

And said, 'Why Archimago, lucklesse syre,
  What doe I see? what hard mishap is this,
  That hath thee hither brought to taste mine yre?
  Or thine the fault, or mine the error is,
  In stead of foe to wound my friend amis?'
  He answered nought, but in a traunce still lay,
  And on those guilefull dazed eyes of his
  The cloud of death did sit. Which doen away°,   *being gone*
He left him lying so, ne would no lenger stay.

40

But to the virgin comes, who all this while
  Amased stands, her selfe so mockt° to see   *deceived*
  By him, who has the guerdon° of his guile,   *reward*
  For so misfeigning° her true knight to bee: *pretending*
  Yet is she now in more perplexitie,
  Left in the hand of that same Paynim bold,
  From whom her booteth not° at all to flie;   *it is useless*
  Who by her cleanly garment catching hold,
Her from her Palfrey pluckt, her visage to behold.

41

But her fierce servant full of kingly awe
  And high disdaine, whenas his soveraine Dame
  So rudely handled by her foe he sawe,

With gaping jawes full greedy at him came,
  And ramping on his shield, did weene° the same   *think*
  Have reft away with his sharpe rending clawes:
  But he was stout, and lust did now inflame
  His corage more, that from his griping pawes
He hath his shield redeemed,° and foorth his swerd he drawes. *recovered*

42

O then too weake and feeble was the forse
  Of salvage beast, his puissance to withstand:
  For he was strong, and of so mightie corse,
  As ever wielded speare in warlike hand,
  And feates of armes did wisely° understand.   *skilfully*
  Eftsoones he perced through his chaufed° chest   *enraged*
  With thrilling point of deadly yron brand,°   *sword*
  And launcht° his Lordly hart: with death opprest   *pierced*
He roared aloud, whiles life forsooke his stubborne brest.[65]

43

Who now is left to keepe the forlorne maid
  From raging spoile of lawlesse victors will?
  Her faithfull gard removed, her hope dismaid,
  Her selfe a yeelded pray° to save or spill.°   *prey/destroy*
  He now Lord of the field, his pride to fill,
  With foule reproches, and disdainfull spight
  Her vildly entertaines,° and will or nill,   *treats*
  Beares her away upon his courser light:
Her prayers nought prevaile, his rage is more of might.

44

And all the way, with great lamenting paine,
  And piteous plaints she filleth his dull° eares,   *unlistening*
  That stony hart could riven have in twaine,
  And all the way she wets with flowing teares:
  But he enraged with rancor, nothing heares:
  Her servile beast yet would not leave her so,
  But followes her farre off, ne ought he feares,
  To be partaker of her wandring woe,
More mild in beastly kind, then that her beastly foe.[66]

CANTO 4 [67]

To sinfull house of Pride, Duessa
  guides the faithfull knight,
Where brothers death to wreak° Sansjoy   *avenge*
  doth chalenge him to fight.

1

Young knight, what ever that dost armes professe,
  And through long labours huntest after fame,
  Beware of fraud, beware of ficklenesse,
  In choice, and change of thy deare loved Dame,
  Least thou of her beleeve too lightly blame,
  And rash misweening° doe thy hart remove: *misunderstanding*
  For unto knight there is no greater shame,
  Then lightnesse and inconstancie in love;
That doth this Redcrosse knights ensample plainly prove

2

Who after that he had faire Una lorne°,   *lost*
  Through light misdeeming° of her loialtie,   *misjudging*
  And false Duessa in her sted had borne,
  Called Fidess', and so supposd to bee;
  Long with her traveild, till at last they see
  A goodly building,[68] bravely garnished°,   *decked out*
  The house of mightie Prince it seemd to bee;
  And towards it a broad high way that led,
All bare through peoples feet, which thither traveiled.

3

Great troupes of people traveild thitherward
  Both day and night, of each degree and place°,   *rank*
  But few returned, having scaped hard°,   *with difficulty*
  With balefull beggerie, or foule disgrace,
  Which ever after in most wretched case,
  Like loathsome lazars°, by the hedges lay.   *lepers*
  Thither Duessa bad him bend his pace:
  For she is wearie of the toilesome way,
And also nigh consumed is the lingring day.

4

A stately Pallace built of squared bricke,
  Which cunningly was without morter laid,
  Whose wals were high, but nothing strong, nor thick,

And golden foile all over them displaid,
That purest skye with brightnesse they dismaid:
High lifted up were many loftie towres,
And goodly galleries farre over laid°   *placed above*
Full of faire windowes, and delightfull bowres;
And on the top a Diall° told the timely howres.   *clock*

5

It was a goodly heape° for to behould,   *structure*
   And spake the praises of the workmans wit°;   *skill*
   But full great pittie, that so faire a mould°   *building*
   Did on so weake foundation ever sit:
   For on a sandie hill, that still did flit,°   *give way*
   And fall away, it mounted was full hie,
   That every breath of heaven shaked it:
   And all the hinder parts, that few could spie,
Were ruinous and old, but painted cunningly.

6

Arrived there they passed in forth right;
   For still to all the gates stood open wide,
   Yet charge of them was to a Porter hight°   *committed*
   Cald Malvenu, who entrance none denide:
   Thence to the hall, which was on every side
   With rich array and costly arras dight°:   *decked out*
   Infinite sorts of people did abide
   There waiting long, to win the wished sight
Of her, that was the Lady of that Pallace bright.

7

By them they passe, all gazing on them round,[69]
   And to the Presence° mount; whose glorious vew   *reception room*
   Their frayle amazed senses did confound:
   In living Princes court none ever knew
   Such endlesse richesse, and so sumptuous shew;
   Ne Persia selfe, the nourse of pompous pride
   Like ever saw. And there a noble crew
   Of Lordes and Ladies stood on every side,
Which with their presence faire, the place much beautifide.

8

High above all a cloth of State was spred,
   And a rich throne, as bright as sunny day,
   On which there sate most brave embellished

With royall robes and gorgeous array,
  A mayden Queene, that shone as Titans ray,   *(the sun)*
  In glistring gold, and peerelesse precious stone:
  Yet her bright blazing beautie did assay°   *attempt*
  To dim the brightnesse of her glorious throne,
As envying her selfe, that too exceeding shone.

9

Exceeding shone, like Phoebus fairest child,[70]
  That did presume his fathers firie wayne,   *chariot*
  And flaming mouthes of steedes unwonted° wilde   *unusually*
  Through highest heaven with weaker hand to rayne;
  Proud of such glory and advancement vaine,
  While flashing beames do daze his feeble eyen,
  He leaves the welkin° way most beaten plaine,   *heavenly*
  And rapt° with whirling wheeles, inflames the skyen,   *carried away*
With fire not made to burne, but fairely for to shyne.

10

So proud she shyned in her Princely state,
  Looking to heaven; for earth she did disdayne,
  And sitting high; for lowly° she did hate: *humility*
  Lo underneath her scornefull feete, was layne
  A dreadfull Dragon with an hideous trayne,   *tail*
  And in her hand she held a mirrhour bright,
  Wherein her face she often vewed fayne,
  And in her selfe-loved semblance tooke delight;
For she was wondrous faire, as any living wight.

11

Of griesly Pluto she the daughter was,
  And sad Proserpina the Queene of hell;
  Yet did she thinke her pearelesse worth to pas
  That parentage, with pride so did she swell,
  And thundring Jove, that high in heaven doth dwell,
  And wield the world, she claymed for her syre,
  Or if that any else did Jove excell:
  For to the highest she did still aspyre,
Or if ought higher were then that, did it desyre.

12

And proud Lucifera men did her call,
  That made her selfe a Queene,[71] and crownd to be,
  Yet rightfull kingdome she had none at all,

Ne heritage of native soveraintie,
But did usurpe with wrong and tyrannie
Upon the scepter, which she now did hold:
Ne ruld her Realmes with lawes, but pollicie,°   *political finesse*
And strong advizement of six wisards old,
That with their counsels bad her kingdome did uphold.

13

Soone as the Elfin knight in presence came,
  And false Duessa seeming Lady faire,
  A gentle Husher,° Vanitie by name   *usher*
  Made rowme, and passage for them did prepaire:
  So goodly brought them to the lowest staire
  Of her high throne, where they on humble knee
  Making obeyssance, did the cause declare,
  Why they were come, her royall state to see,
To prove° the wide report of her great Majestee.   *confirm*

14

With loftie eyes, halfe loth to looke so low,
  She thanked them in her disdainefull wise,
  Ne other grace vouchsafed them to show
  Of Princesse worthy, scarse them bad arise.
  Her Lordes and Ladies all this while devise°   *prepare*
  Themselves to setten forth to straungers sight:
  Some frounce° their curled haire in courtly guise,   *deck out*
  Some prancke° their ruffes, and others trimly dight   *prink out*
Their gay attire: each others greater pride does spight.

15

Goodly they all that knight do entertaine,
  Right glad with him to have increast their crew:
  But to Duess' each one himselfe did paine
  All kindnesse and faire courtesie to shew;
  For in that court whylome° her well they knew: *once*
  Yet the stout Faerie° mongst the middest° crowd   *i.e. the knight/in the*
  Thought all their glorie vaine in knightly vew,   *centre of*
  And that great Princesse too exceeding prowd,
That to strange knight no better countenance allowd.

16

Suddein upriseth from her stately place
  The royall Dame, and for her coche° doth call: *coach*
  All hurtlen° forth, and she with Princely pace,   *rush*

As faire Aurora in her purple pall,°   cloak
Out of the East the dawning day doth call:
So forth she comes: her brightnesse brode° doth blaze;   abroad
The heapes of people thronging in the hall,
Do ride each other, upon her to gaze:
Her glorious glitterand° light doth all mens eyes amaze.   glittering

17

So forth she comes, and to her coche does clyme,
  Adorned all with gold, and girlonds° gay,   garlands
  That seemd as fresh as Flora in her prime,
  And strove to match, in royall rich array,
  Great Junoes golden chaire, the which they say
  The Gods stand gazing on, when she does ride
  To Joves high house through heavens bras°-paved way   brass
  Drawne of faire Pecocks, that excell in pride,
And full of Argus eyes their tailes dispredden wide.

18

But this was drawne of six unequall beasts,[72]
  On which her six sage Counsellours did ryde,
  Taught to obay their bestiall beheasts,
  With like conditions to their kinds° applyde: natures
  Of which the first, that all the rest did guyde,
  Was sluggish Idlenesse the nourse of sin;
  Upon a slouthfull Asse he chose to ryde,
  Arayd in habit blacke, and amis° thin,   hood
Like to an holy Monck, the service to begin.

19

And in his hand his Portesse° stil he bare,   breviary
  That much was worne, but therein little red,
  For of devotion he had little care,
  Still drownd in sleepe, and most of his dayes ded;
  Scarse could he once uphold his heavie hed,
  To looken, whether it were night or day:
  May seeme the wayne was very evill led,
  When such an one had guiding of the way,
That knew not, whether right he went, or else astray.

20

From worldly cares himselfe he did esloyne,°   withdraw
  And greatly shunned manly exercise,
  From every worke he chalenged essoyne,°   exemption

For contemplation sake: yet otherwise,
His life he led in lawlesse riotise;
By which he grew to grievous malady;
For in his lustlesse° limbs through evill guise°   *feeble/way of living*
A shaking fever raignd continually:
Such one was Idlenesse, first of this company.

21

And by his side rode loathsome Gluttony,
   Deformed creature, on a filthie swyne,
   His belly was up-blowne with luxury,
   And eke with fatnesse swollen were his eyne,
   And like a Crane his neeke was long and fyne,°   *thin*
   With which he swallowd up excessive feast,
   For want whereof poore people oft did pyne°;   *waste away*
   And all the way, most like a brutish beast,
He spued up his gorge,° that all did him deteast.   *i.e. vomited*

22

In greene vine leaves he was right fitly clad;
   For other clothes he could not weare for heat,
   And on his head an yvie girland had,
   From under which fast trickled downe the sweat:
   Still as he rode, he somewhat° still did eat,   *something*
   And in his hand did beare a bouzing° can,   *drinking*
   Of which he supt so oft, that on his seat
   His dronken corse he scarse upholden can,
In shape and life more like a monster, than a man.

23

Unfit he was for any worldly thing,
   And eke unhable once° to stirre or go   *at all*
   Not meet to be of counsell to a king,
   Whose mind in meat and drinke was drowned so,   -
   That from his friend he seldome knew his fo:
   Full of diseases was his carcas blew,°   *livid*
   And a dry dropsie[73] through his flesh did flow:
   Which by misdiet daily greater grew:
Such one was Gluttony, the second of that crew.

24

And next to him rode lustfull Lechery,
   Upon a bearded Goat, whose rugged haire,
   And whally° eyes (the signe of gelosy,)   *green*

Was like the person selfe, whom he did beare:
Who rough, and blacke, and filthy did appeare,
Unseemely man to please faire Ladies eye;
Yet he of Ladies oft was loved deare,
When fairer faces were bid standen by°:   *aside*
O who does know the bent of womens fantasy?

25

In a greene gowne he clothed was full faire,
  Which underneath did hide his filthinesse,
  And in his hand a burning hart he bare,[74]
  Full of vaine follies, and new fanglenesse:
  For he was false, and fraught° with ficklenesse,   *riddled*
  And learned had to love with secret lookes,
  And well could daunce, and sing with ruefulnesse,
  And fortunes tell, and read in loving bookes°,   *books about love*
And thousand other wayes, to bait his fleshly hookes.

26

Inconstant man, that loved all he saw,
  And lusted after all, that he did love,
  Ne would his looser life be tide to law,
  But joyd weake wemens hearts to tempt and prove
  If from their loyall loves he might them move;
  Which lewdnesse fild° him with reprochful paine   *filled*
  Of that fowle evill°, which all men reprove,   *i.e. syphilis*
  That rots the marrow, and consumes the braine:
Such one was Lecherie, the third of all this traine.

27

And greedy Avarice by him did ride,
  Upon a Camell[75] loaden all with gold;
  Two iron coffers hong on either side,
  With precious mettall full, as they might hold,
  And in his lap an heape of coine he told°;   *counted*
  For of his wicked pelfe° his God he made,   *hoard*
  And unto hell him selfe for money sold;
  Accursed usurie was all his trade,
And right and wrong ylike in equall ballaunce waide.[76]

28

His life was nigh unto deaths doore yplast,[77]
  And thred-bare cote, and cobled° shoes he ware,   *patched*
  Ne scarse good morsell all his life did tast,

But both from backe and belly[78] still did spare,
  To fill his bags, and richesse to compare°;   *acquire*
  Yet chylde ne kinsman living had he none
  To leave them to; but thorough daily care
  To get, and nightly feare to lose his owne,
He led a wretched life unto him selfe unknowne.[79]

29

Most wretched wight, whom nothing might suffise,
  Whose greedy lust did lacke in greatest store,
  Whose need had end, but no end covetise°,   *covetousness*
  Whose wealth was want, whose plenty made him pore,
  Who had enough, yet wished ever more;
  A vile disease, and eke in foote and hand
  A grievous gout tormented him full sore,
  That well he could not touch, nor go, nor stand:
Such one was Avarice, the fourth of this faire band.

30

And next to him malicious Envie rode,
  Upon a ravenous wolfe, and still did chaw
  Betweene his cankred° teeth a venemous tode,[80]   *rotten*
  That all the poison ran about his chaw°;   *jaw*
  But inwardly he chawed his owne maw°   *liver*
  At neighbours wealth, that made him ever sad;
  For death it was, when any good he saw,
  And wept, that cause of weeping none he had,
But when he heard of harme, he wexed wondrous glad.

31

All in a kirtle of discolourd say[81]
  He clothed was, ypainted full of eyes;
  And in his bosome secretly there lay
  An hatefull Snake, the which his taile uptyes°   *coils*
  In many folds, and mortall sting implyes°.   *enwraps*
  Still as he rode, he gnasht his teeth, to see
  Those heapes of gold with griple° Covetyse,   *greedy*
  And grudged at the great felicitie
Of proud Lucifera, and his owne companie.

32

He hated all good workes and vertuous deeds,
  And him no lesse, that any like did use°,   *practise*
  And who with gracious bread the hungry feeds,

His almes for want of faith he doth accuse;
So every good to bad he doth abuse°:   *pervert*
And eke the verse of famous Poets witt
He does backebite, and spightfull poison spues
From leprous mouth on all, that ever writt:
Such one vile Envie was, that fifte in row did sitt.

33

And him beside rides fierce revenging Wrath,
    Upon a Lion, loth for to be led;
    And in his hand a burning brond° he hath,   *sword*
    The which he brandisheth about his hed;
    His eyes did hurle forth sparkles fiery red,
    And stared sterne on all, that him beheld,
    As ashes pale of hew and seeming ded;
    And on his dagger still his hand he held,
Trembling through hasty rage, when choler° in him sweld.   *anger*

34

His ruffin° raiment all was staind with blood,   *disorderly*
    Which he had spilt, and all to rags yrent,°   *torn*
    Through unadvized rashnesse woxen wood°;   *mad*
    For of his hands he had no governement;°   *control*
    Ne cared for° bloud in his avengement: *grieved over*
    But when the furious fit was overpast,
    His cruell facts° he often would repent;   *deeds*
    Yet wilfull man he never would forecast,
How many mischieves should ensue his heedlesse hast.

35

Full many mischiefes follow cruell Wrath;
    Abhorred bloudshed, and tumultuous strife,
    Unmanly° murder, and unthrifty scath,°   *inhuman/harm*
    Bitter despight, with rancours rusty knife,
    And fretting griefe the enemy of life;
    All these, and many evils moe° haunt ire,   *more*
    The swelling Splene,[82] and Frenzy raging rife,
    The shaking Palsey, and Saint Fraunces fire.[83]
Such one was Wrath, the last of this ungodly tire.°   *procession*

36

And after all, upon the wagon beame
    Rode Sathan,° with a smarting whip in hand,   *Satan*
    With which he forward lasht the laesie teme,

So oft as Slowth still in the mire did stand.
Huge routs° of people did about them band,   *crowds*
Showting for joy, and still before their way
A foggy mist[84] had covered all the land;
And underneath their feet, all scattered lay
Dead sculs and bones of men, whose life had gone astray.

37

So forth they marchen in this goodly sort,
To take the solace° of the open aire,   *pleasure*
And in fresh flowring fields themselves to sport;
Emongst the rest rode that false Lady faire,
The fowle Duessa, next unto the chaire
Of proud Lucifera, as one of the traine:
But that good knight would not so nigh repaire,°   *approach*
Him selfe estraunging from their joyaunce vaine,
Whose fellowship seemd far unfit for warlike swaine.

38

So having solaced themselves a space
With pleasaunce of the breathing° fields yfed,   *i.e. for exercise*
They backe returned to the Princely Place;
Whereas an errant knight in armes ycled,°   *clad*
And heathnish shield, wherein with letters red
Was writ *Sans joy*, they new arrived find:
Enflamed with fury and fiers hardy-hed,°   *audacity*
He seemd in hart to harbour thoughts unkind,
And nourish bloudy vengeaunce in his bitter mind.[85]

39

Who when the shamed shield of slaine Sans foy
He spide with that same Faery champions page,
Bewraying° him, that did of late destroy   *revealing*
His eldest brother, burning all with rage
He to him leapt, and that same envious gage°   *pledge*
Of victors glory from him snatcht away:
But th'Elfin knight, which ought° that warlike wage,°   *owned/token*
Disdaind to loose the meed° he wonne in fray,   *reward*
And him rencountring° fierce, reskewd the   *engaging in battle*
    noble pray.

40

Therewith they gan to hurtlen° greedily,   *rush*
Redoubted battaile ready to darrayne,°   *prepare*
And clash their shields, and shake their swords on hy,

That with their sturre they troubled all the traine;
Till that great Queene upon eternall paine
Of high displeasure, that ensewen might,
Commaunded them their fury to refraine,
And if that either to that shield had right,
In equall lists they should the morrow next it fight.

41

'Ah dearest Dame,' quoth then the Paynim° bold,   *Pagan*
'Pardon the errour of enraged wight,
Whom great griefe made forget the raines to hold
Of reasons rule, to see this recreant knight,
No knight, but treachour full of false despight
And shamefull treason, who through guile hath slayn
The prowest° knight, that ever field did fight,   *noblest*
Even stout Sans foy (O who can then refrayn?)
Whose shield he beares renverst,° the more to heape disdayn. *reversed*

42

And to augment the glorie of his guile,
His dearest love the faire Fidessa loe
Is there possessed of the traytour vile,
Who reapes the harvest sowen by his foe,
Sowen in bloudy field, and bought with woe:
That brothers hand shall dearely well requight
So be, O Queene, you equall° favour showe.'   *impartial*
Him litle answerd th'angry Elfin knight;
He never meant with words, but swords to plead his right.

43

But threw his gauntlet as a sacred pledge
His cause in combat the next day to try:
So been they parted both, with harts on edge,
To be avenged each on his enimy.
That night they pas in joy and jollity,
Feasting and courting both in bowre and hall;
For Steward was excessive Gluttonie,
That of his plenty poured forth to all:
Which doen, the Chamberlain Slowth did to rest them call.

44

Now whenas darkesome night had all displayd
Her coleblacke curtein over brightest skye,
The warlike youthes on dayntie couches layd,

Did chace away sweet sleepe from sluggish eye,
To muse on meanes of hoped victory.
But whenas Morpheus had with leaden mace
Arrested all that courtly company,
Up-rose Duessa from her resting place,
And to the Paynims lodging comes with silent pace.

45

Whom broad awake she finds, in troublous fit,   *condition*
  Forecasting, how his foe he might annoy,
  And him amoves° with speaches seeming fit°:   *arouses/suitable*
  'Ah deare Sans joy, next dearest to Sans foy,
  Cause of my new griefe, cause of my new joy,
  Joyous, to see his ymage in mine eye,
  And greeved, to thinke how foe did him destroy,
  That was the flowre of grace and chevalrye;
Lo his Fidessa to thy secret faith I flye.'

46

With gentle wordes he can° her fairely greet,   *knew how to*
  And bad say on the secret of her hart.
  Then sighing soft, 'I learne that litle sweet
  Oft tempred is,' quoth she, 'with muchell° smart: *much*
  For since my brest was launcht° with lovely dart   *pierced*
  Of deare Sansfoy, I never joyed howre,
  But in eternall woes my weaker hart
  Have wasted, loving him with all my powre,
And for his sake have felt full many an heavie stowre.°   *conflict*

47

At last when perils all I weened past,
  And hoped to reape the crop of all my care,
  Into new woes unweeting I was cast,
  By this false faytor,° who unworthy ware   *traitor*
  His worthy shield, whom he with guilefull snare
  Entrapped slew, and brought to shamefull grave.
  Me silly° maid away with him he bare,   *simple*
  And ever since hath kept in darksome cave,
For that° I would not yeeld, that to Sans foy I gave.   *because*

48

But since faire Sunne hath sperst° that lowring clowd,   *dispersed*
  And to my loathed life now shewes some light,
  Under your beames I will me safely shroud,

From dreaded storme of his disdainfull spight:
To you th'inheritance belongs by right
Of brothers prayse, to you eke longs° his love.   *belongs*
Let not his love, let not his restlesse spright
Be unrevenged, that calles to you above
From wandring Stygian shores, where it doth endlesse move.'

49

Thereto said he, 'Faire Dame be nought dismaid
  For sorrowes past; their griefe is with them gone:
  Ne yet of present perill be affraid;
  For needlesse feare did never vantage° none,   *give advantage*
  And helplesse hap° it booteth not to mone.   *unavoidable chance*
  Dead is Sans foy, his vitall paines are past,
  Though greeved ghost for vengeance deepe do grone:
  He lives, that shall him pay his dewties° last,   *rites*
And guiltie Elfin bloud shall sacrifice in hast.'

50

'O but I feare the fickle freakes,° quoth shee,   *whims*
  'Of fortune false, and oddes of armes in field.'
  'Why dame,' quoth he, 'what oddes can ever bee,
  Where both do fight alike, to win or yield?'
  'Yes but,' quoth she, 'he beares a charmed shield,
  And eke enchaunted armes, that none can perce,
  Ne none can wound the man, that does them wield.'
  'Charmd or enchaunted,' answerd he then ferce,
'I no whit reck,° ne you the like need to reherce°:   *care/recount*

51

But faire Fidessa, sithens° fortunes guile,   *since*
  Or enimies powre hath now captived you,
  Returne from whence ye came, and rest a while
  Till morrow next, that I the Elfe subdew,
  And with Sans foyes dead dowry you endew.°'   *endow*
  'Ay me, that is a double death,' she said,
  'With proud foes sight my sorrow to renew:
  Where ever yet I be, my secrete aid
Shall follow you.' So passing forth she him obaid.

CANTO 5

The faithfull knight in equall field
subdewes his faithlesse foe,
Whom false Duessa saves, and for
his cure to hell does goe.

1

The noble hart, that harbours vertuous thought,
  And is with child of glorious great intent,
  Can never rest, untill it forth have brought
  Th'eternall brood of glorie excellent:
  Such restlesse passion did all night torment
  The flaming corage of that Faery knight,
  Devizing, how that doughtie turnament
  With greatest honour he atchieven might;
Still did he wake, and still did watch for dawning light.

2

At last the golden Orientall gate
  Of greatest heaven gan to open faire,
  And Phoebus fresh, as bridegrome to his mate,
  Came dauncing forth, shaking his deawie haire:
  And hurld his glistring beames through gloomy aire.
  Which when the wakeful Elfe perceived, streight way
  He started up, and did him selfe prepaire,
  In sun-bright armes, and battailous° array: *warlike*
For with that Pagan proud he combat will that day.

3

And forth he comes into the commune hall,
  Where earely waite him many a gazing eye,
  To weet° what end to straunger knights may fall.   *learn*
  There many Minstrales maken melody,
  To drive away the dull melancholy,
  And many Bardes, that to the trembling chord
  Can tune their timely° voyces cunningly,   *in time*
  And many Chroniclers, that can record
Old loves, and warres for Ladies doen by many a Lord.

4

Soone after comes the cruell Sarazin,
  In woven maile all armed warily,
  And sternly lookes at him, who not a pin

Does care for looke of living creatures eye.
They bring them wines of Greece and Araby,
And daintie spices fetcht from furthest Ynd,
To kindle heat of corage privily°:   *secretly*
And in the wine a solemne oth they bynd
T'observe the sacred lawes of armes, that are assynd°.   *assigned*

5

At last forth comes that far renowmed Queene,
   With royall pomp and Princely majestie;
   She is ybrought unto a paled° greene,   *fenced*
   And placed under stately canapee°,   *canopy*
   The warlike feates of both those knights to see.
   On th'other side in all mens open vew
   Duessa placed is, and on a tree
   Sans-foy his shield is hangd with bloudy hew:
Both those the lawrell girlonds° to the victor dew.   *garlands*

6

A shrilling trompet sownded from on hye,
   And unto battaill bad them selves addresse:
   Their shining shieldes about their wrestes° they tye,   *wrists*
   And burning blades about their heads do blesse°,   *brandish*
   The instruments of wrath and heavinesse:
   With greedy force each other doth assayle,
   And strike so fiercely, that they do impresse
   Deepe dinted furrowes in the battred mayle;
The yron walles to ward their blowes are weake and fraile.

7

The Sarazin was stout, and wondrous strong,
   And heaped blowes like yron hammers great:
   For after bloud and vengeance he did long.
   The knight was fiers, and full of youthly heat:
   And doubled strokes, like dreaded thunders threat:
   For all for prayse and honour he did fight.
   Both stricken strike, and beaten both do beat,
   That from their shields forth flyeth firie light,
And helmets hewen deepe, shew marks of eithers might.

8

So th'one for wrong, the other strives for right:
   As when a Gryfon[86] seized° of his pray,   *having caught*
   A Dragon fiers encountreth in his flight,

Through widest ayre making his ydle way,
That would his rightfull ravine° rend away: *booty*
With hideous horrour both together smight,
And souce° so sore, that they the heavens affray: *strike*
The wise Southsayer seeing so sad sight,
Th'amazed vulgar tels of warres and mortall fight.

9

So th'one for wrong, the other strives for right,
And each to deadly shame would drive his foe:
The cruell steele so greedily doth bight
In tender flesh, that streames of bloud down flow,
With which the armes, that earst° so bright did show,   *before*
Into a pure vermillion now are dyde:
Great ruth in all the gazers harts did grow,
Seeing the gored woundes to gape so wyde,
That victory they dare not wish to either side.

10

At last the Paynim chaunst to cast his eye,
His suddein° eye, flaming with wrathfull fyre,   *flashing*
Upon his brothers shield, which hong thereby:
Therewith redoubled was his raging yre,
And said, 'Ah wretched sonne of wofull syre,
Doest thou sit wayling by black Stygian lake,[87]
Whilest here thy shield is hangd for victors hyre,°   *reward*
And sluggish german° doest thy forces slake,°   *brother/abate*
To after-send his foe, that him may overtake?

11

Goe caytive° Elfe, him quickly overtake,   *base*
And soone redeeme from his long wandring woe;
Goe guiltie ghost, to him my message make,
That I his shield have quit° from dying foe.'   *redeemed*
Therewith upon his crest he stroke him so,
That twise he reeled, readie twise to fall;
End of the doubtfull battell deemed tho°   *then*
The lookers on, and lowd to him gan call
The false Duessa, 'Thine the shield, and I, and all.'

12

Soone as the Faerie heard his Ladie speake,
Out of his swowning dreame he gan awake,
And quickning° faith, that earst was woxen weake,   *enlivening*

The creeping deadly cold away did shake:
Tho moved with wrath, and shame, and Ladies sake,
Of all attonce he cast° avengd to bee,   *resolved*
And with so'exceeding furie at him strake,
That forced him to stoupe upon his knee;
Had he not stouped so, he should have cloven bee.

13

And to him said, 'Goe now proud Miscreant,
Thy selfe thy message doe° to german deare,   *take*
Alone he wandring thee too long doth want:
Goe say, his foe thy shield with his doth beare.'
Therewith his heavie hand he high gan reare,
Him to have slaine; when loe a darkesome clowd
Upon him fell: he no where doth appeare,
But vanisht is. The Elfe him cals alowd,
But answer none receives: the darknes him does shrowd.

14

In haste Duessa from her place arose,
And to him running said, 'O prowest° knight,   *noblest*
That ever Ladie to her love did chose,
Let now abate the terror of your might,
And quench the flame of furious despight,
And bloudie vengeance; lo th'infernall powres
Covering your foe with cloud of deadly night,
Have borne him thence to Plutoes balefull bowres.
The conquest yours, I yours, the shield, and glory yours.'

15

Not all so satisfide, with greedie eye
He sought all round about, his thirstie blade
To bath in bloud of faithlesse enemy;
Who all that while lay hid in secret shade:
He standes amazed, how he thence should fade.
At last the trumpets Triumph sound on hie,
And running Heralds humble homage made,
Greeting him goodly with new victorie,
And to him brought the shield, the cause of enmitie.

16

Wherewith he goeth to that soveraine Queene,
And falling her before on lowly knee,
To her makes present of his service seene°:   *skilful*

Which she accepts, with thankes, and goodly gree,°   *favour*
Greatly advauncing° his gay chevalree.   *praising*
So marcheth home, and by her takes the knight,
Whom all the people follow with great glee,
Shouting, and clapping all their hands on hight,
That all the aire it fils, and flyes to heaven bright.

17

Home is he brought, and laid in sumptuous bed:
    Where many skilfull leaches° him abide,°   *doctors/attend*
    To salve his hurts, that yet still freshly bled.
    In wine and oyle they wash his woundes wide,
    And softly can embalme° on every side.   *anoint*
    And all the while, most heavenly melody
    About the bed sweet musicke did divide,°   *descant*
    Him to beguile of griefe and agony:
And all the while Duessa wept full bitterly.

18

As when a wearie traveller that strayes
    By muddy shore of broad seven-mouthed Nile,
    Unweeting of the perillous wandring wayes,
    Doth meet a cruell craftie Crocodile,
    Which in false griefe hyding his harmefull guile,
    Doth weepe full sore, and sheddeth tender teares:
    The foolish man, that pitties all this while
    His mournefull plight, is swallowed up unwares,
Forgetfull of his owne, that mindes anothers cares.

19

So wept Duessa untill eventide,
    That° shyning lampes in Joves high house were light: *when*
    Then forth she rose, ne lenger would abide,
    But comes unto the place, where th'Hethen knight
    In slombring swownd° nigh voyd of vitall spright,   *swoon*
    Lay covered with inchaunted cloud all day:
    Whom when she found, as she him left in plight,
    To wayle his woefull case she would not stay,
But to the easterne coast of heaven makes speedy way.

20

Where griesly Night, with visage deadly sad,
    That Phoebus chearefull face durst never vew,
    And in a foule blacke pitchie mantle clad,

She findes forth comming from her darkesome mew,°   *cave*
Where she all day did hide her hated hew.
Before the dore her yron charet° stood,   *chariot*
Alreadie harnessed for journey new;
And coleblacke steedes yborne of hellish brood,
That on their rustie bits did champ, as they were wood.°   *mad*

21

Who when she saw Duessa sunny bright,
    Adornd with gold and jewels shining cleare,
    She greatly grew amazed at the sight,
    And th'unacquainted light began to feare:
    For never did such brightnesse there appeare,
    And would have backe retyred to her cave,
    Untill the witches speech she gan to heare,
    Saying, 'Yet O thou dreaded Dame, I crave
Abide, till I have told the message, which I have.'

22

She stayd, and foorth Duessa gan proceede,
    'O thou most auncient Grandmother of all,
    More old than Jove, whom thou at first didst breede,
    Or that great house of Gods caelestiall,
    Which wast begot in Daemogorgons hall,°   *i.e. in chaos*
    And sawst the secrets of the world unmade,
    Why suffredst thou thy Nephewes° deare to fall   *grandchildren*
    With Elfin sword, most shamefully betrade?
Lo where the stout Sansjoy doth sleepe in deadly shade.

23

And him before, I saw with bitter eyes
    The bold Sansfoy shrinke underneath his speare;
    And now the pray of fowles in field he lyes,
    Nor wayld° of friends, nor laid on groning beare,[88]   *mourned*
    That whylome° was to me too dearely deare.   *once*
    O what of Gods then boots it to be borne,
    If old Aveugles sonnes so evill heare°?   *are spoken of*
    Or who shall not great Nightes children scorne,
When two of three her Nephews are so fowle forlorne?

24

Up then, up dreary Dame, of darknesse Queene,
    Go gather up the reliques of thy race,
    Or else goe them avenge, and let be seene,

That dreaded Night in brightest day hath place,
And can the children of faire light deface:°   *destroy*
Her feeling speeches some compassion moved
In hart, and chaunge in that great mothers face:
Yet pittie in her hart was never proved°   *felt*
Till then: for evermore she hated, never loved.

25

And said, 'Deare daughter rightly may I rew°   *rue*
  The fall of famous children borne of mee,
  And good successes, which their foes ensew:°   *ensue*
  But who can turne the streame of destinee,
  Or breake the chayne of strong necessitee,
  Which fast is tyde to Joves eternall seat?[289]
  The sonnes of Day he favoureth, I see,
  And by my ruines thinkes to make them great:
To make one great by others losse, is bad excheat.°   *gain*

26

Yet shall they not escape so freely all;
  For some shall pay the price of others guilt:
  And he the man that made Sansfoy to fall,
  Shall with his owne bloud price° that he hath split.   *pay for*
  But what art thou, that telst of Nephews kilt?'
  'I that do seeme not I, Duessa am,'
  Quoth she, 'how ever now in garments gilt,
  And gorgeous gold arayd I to thee came;
Duessa I, the daughter of Deceipt and Shame.'

27

Then bowing downe her aged backe, she kist
  The wicked witch, saying; 'In that faire face
  The false resemblance of Deceipt, I wist°   *know*
  Did closely lurke; yet so true-seeming grace
  It carried, that I scarse in darkesome place
  Could it discerne, though I the mother bee
  Of falshood, and root of Duessaes race,
  O welcome child, whom I have longd to see,
And now have seene unwares. Lo now I go with thee.'

28

Then to her yron wagon she betakes,
  And with her beares the fowle welfavourd° witch: *attractive*
  Through mirkesome° aire her readie way she makes.   *murky*

Her twyfold° Teme, of which two blacke as pitch,   *two fold*
And two were browne, yet each to each unlich°,   *unlike*
Did softly swim away, ne ever stampe,
Unlesse she chaunst their stubborne mouths to twitch;
Then foming tarre, their bridles they would champe,
And trampling the fine element°, would fiercely rampe°.   *air/rage*

29

So well they sped, that they be come at length
   Unto the place, whereas the Paynim lay,
   Devoid of outward sense, and native strength,
   Coverd with charmed cloud from vew of day,
   And sight of men, since his late luckelesse fray.
   His cruell wounds with cruddy° bloud congealed,   *clotted*
   They binden up so wisely, as they may,
   And handle softly, till they can be healed:
So lay him in her charet°, close in night concealed.   *chariot*

30

And all the while she stood upon the ground,
   The wakefull dogs[90] did never cease to bay,
   As giving warning of th'unwonted sound,
   With which her yron wheeles did them affray,
   And her darke griesly looke them much dismay;
   The messenger of death, the ghastly Owle
   With drearie shriekes did also her bewray°;   *betray*
   And hungry Wolves continually did howle,
At her abhorred face, so filthy and so fowle.

31

Thence turning backe in silence soft they stole,
   And brought the heavie corse with easie pace
   To yawning gulfe of deepe Avernus hole.[91]
   By that same hole an entrance darke and bace
   With smoake and sulphure hiding all the place,
   Descends to hell: there creature never past,
   That backe returned without heavenly grace;
   But dreadfull Furies, which their chaines have brast°, *burst apart*
And damned sprights sent forth to make ill° men aghast.   *evil*

32

By that same way the direfull dames doe drive
   Their mournefull charet, fild with rusty blood,
   And downe to Plutoes house are come bilive°:   *quickly*

Which passing through, on every side them stood
The trembling ghosts with sad amazed mood,
Chattring their yron teeth, and staring wide
With stonie eyes; and all the hellish brood
Of feends infernall flockt on every side,
To gaze on earthly wight, that with the Night durst ride.

33

They pas the bitter waves of Acheron,
    Where many soules sit wailing woefully,
    And come to fiery flood of Phlegeton,
    Whereas the damned ghosts in torments fry,
    And with sharpe shrilling shriekes doe bootlesse cry,
    Cursing high Jove, the which them thither sent.
    The house of endlesse paine is built thereby,
    In which ten thousand sorts of punishment
The cursed creatures doe eternally torment.

34

Before the threshold dreadfull Cerberus
    His three deformed heads did lay along,°   *stretched out*
    Curled with thousand adders venemous,
    And lilled° forth his bloudie flaming tong: *lolled*
    At them he gan to reare his bristles strong,
    And felly gnarre,° untill dayes enemy   *fiercely snarl*
    Did him appease; then downe his taile he hong
    And suffered them to passen quietly:
For she in hell and heaven had power equally.

35

There was Ixion turned on a wheele,
    For daring tempt the Queene of heaven to sin;
    And Sisyphus an huge round stone did reele°   *roll*
    Against an hill, ne might from labour lin°;   *cease*
    There thirstie Tantalus hong by the chin;
    And Tityus fed a vulture on his maw°;   *liver*
    Typhoeus joynts were stretched on a gin,°   *rack*
    Theseus condemned to endlesse slouth by law,
And fifty sisters[92] water in leake° vessels draw.   *leaky*

36

They all beholding worldly wights in place,°   *there*
    Leave off their worke, unmindfull of their smart,
    To gaze on them; who forth by them doe pace,

Till they be come unto the furthest part:
Where was a Cave ywrought by wondrous art,
Deepe, darke, uneasie, dolefull, comfortlesse,
In which sad Aesculapius farre a part
Emprisond was in chaines remedilesse,
For that Hippolytus rent corse he did redresse.°   *restore*

37

Hippolytus a jolly huntsman was,
    That wont in charet chace the foming Bore;
He all his Peeres in beautie did surpas,
But Ladies love as losse of time forbore°:   *gave up*
    His wanton stepdame[93] loved him the more,
But when she saw her offred sweets refused
    Her love she turnd to hate, and him before
His father fierce of treason false accused,
And with her gealous termes his open eares abused.

38

Who all in rage his Sea-god syre[94] besought,
    Some cursed vengeance on his sonne to cast:
From surging gulf two monsters straight were brought,
With dread whereof his chasing steedes aghast,
Both charet swift and huntsman overcast.
    His goodly corps on ragged cliffs yrent,
Was quite dismembred, and his members chast
Scattered on every mountaine, as he went,
That of Hippolytus was left no moniment.°   *trace*

39

His cruell stepdame seeing what was donne,
    Her wicked dayes with wretched knife did end,
In death avowing th'innocence of her sonne.
Which hearing his rash Syre, began to rend
His haire, and hastie tongue, that did offend:
Tho gathering up the relicks of his smart[95]
By Dianes meanes, who was Hippolyts frend,
    Them brought to Aesculape, that by his art
Did heale them all againe, and joyned every part.

40

Such wondrous science° in mans wit to raine   *knowledge*
    When Jove avizd° that could the dead revive,   *perceived*
    And fates expired[96] could renew againe,

Of endlesse life he might him not deprive,
But unto hell did thrust him downe alive,
With flashing thunderbolt ywounded sore:
Where long remaining, he did alwaies strive
Himselfe with salves to health for to restore,
And slake the heavenly fire, that raged evermore.

41

There auncient Night arriving, did alight
  From her nigh wearie waine,° and in her armes   *chariot*
  To Aesculapius brought the wounded knight:
  Whom having softly disarayd° of armes,   *undressed*
  Tho° gan to him discover° all his harmes,   *then/disclose*
  Beseeching him with prayer, and with praise,
  If either salves, or oyles, or herbes, or charmes
  A fordonne° wight from dore of death mote raise,   *ruined*
He would at her request prolong her nephews daies.

42

'Ah Dame,' quoth he, 'thou temptest me in vaine,
  To dare the thing, which daily yet I rew,
  And the old cause of my continued paine
  With like attempt to like end to renew.
  Is not enough, that thrust from heaven dew°   *due*
  Here endlesse penance for one fault I pay,
  But that redoubled crime with vengeance new
  Thou biddest me to eeke?° Can Night defray°   *also/destroy*
The wrath of thundring Jove, that rules both night and day?'

43

'Not so,' quoth she, 'but sith that heavens king
  From hope of heaven hath thee excluded quight,
  Why fearest thou, that canst not hope for thing,
  And fearest not, that more thee hurten might,
  Now in the powre of everlasting Night?
  Goe to then, O thou farre renowmed sonne
  Of great Apollo, shew thy famous might
  In medicine, that else° hath to thee wonne   *already*
Great paines, and greater praise, both never to be donne.°' *ended*

44

Her words prevaild: And then the learned leach
  His cunning hand gan to his wounds to lay,
  And all things else, the which his art did teach:

Which having seene, from thence arose away
The mother of dread darknesse, and let stay
Aveugles sonne there in the leaches cure,
And backe returning tooke her wonted way,
To runne her timely race,[97] whilst Phoebus pure
In westerne waves his wearie wagon did recure.°   *refresh*

45

The false Duessa leaving noyous° Night,   *harmful*
  Returnd to stately pallace of dame Pride;
  Where when she came, she found the Faery knight
  Departed thence, albe° his woundes wide   *although*
  Not throughly heald, unreadie were to ride.
  Good cause he had to hasten thence away;
  For on a day his wary Dwarfe had spide,
  Where in a dongeon deepe huge numbers lay
Of caytive° wretched thrals,° that wayled night and day.   *captive/*
                                                                   slaves

46

A ruefull sight, as could be seene with eie;
  Of whom he learned had in secret wise
  The hidden cause of their captivitie,
  How mortgaging their lives to Covetise,
  Through wastfull Pride, and wanton Riotise,
  They were by law of that proud Tyrannesse
  Provokt with Wrath, and Envies false surmise,
  Condemned to that Dongeon mercilesse,
Where they should live in woe, and die in wretchednesse.

47

There was that great proud king of Babylon,[98]
  That would compell all nations to adore,
  And him as onely God to call upon,
  Till through celestiall doome° throwne out of dore,   *judgement*
  Into an Oxe he was transformed of yore:
  There also was king Croesus, that enhaunst°   *exalted*
  His heart too high through his great riches store;
  And proud Antiochus, the which advaunst°   *lifted*
His cursed hand gainst God, and on his altars daunst.°   *danced*

48

And them long time before, great Nimrod was,
  That first the world with sword and fire warrayd°;   *made war*
  And after him old Ninus farre did pas°   *surpass*

In princely pompe, of all the world obayd;
There also was that mightie Monarch[99] layd
Low under all, yet above all in pride,
That name of native° syre did fowle upbrayd,   *natural*
And would as Ammons sonne be magnifide,
Till scornd of God and man a shamefull death he dide.

49

All these together in one heape were throwne,
  Like carkases of beasts in butchers stall.
  And in another corner wide were strowne
  The antique ruines of the Romaines fall:
  Great Romulus the Grandsyre of them all,
  Proud Tarquin, and too lordly Lentulus,
  Stout Scipio, and stubborne Hanniball,
  Ambitious Sylla, and sterne Marius,
High Caesar, great Pompey, and fierce Antonius.

50

Amongst these mighty men were wemen mixt,
  Proud wemen, vaine, forgetfull of their yoke:
  The bold Semiramis, whose sides transfixt
  With sonnes owne blade, her fowle reproches spoke;
  Faire Sthenoboea, that her selfe did choke
  With wilfull cord, for wanting of her will;[100]
  High minded Cleopatra, that with stroke
  Of Aspes sting her selfe did stoutly kill:
And thousands moe the like, that did that dongeon fill.

51

Besides the endlesse routs of wretched thralles,
  Which thither were assembled day by day,
  From all the world after their wofull falles,
  Through wicked pride, and wasted wealthes decay.
  But most of all, which in that Dongeon lay
  Fell from high Princes courts, or Ladies bowres,
  Where they in idle pompe, or wanton play,
  Consumed had their goods, and thriftlesse howres,
And lastly throwne themselves into these heavy stowres.°   *plights*

52

Whose case whenas the carefull Dwarfe had tould,
  And made ensample of their mournefull sight
  Unto his maister, he no lenger would

There dwell in perill of like painefull plight,
But early rose, and ere that dawning light
Discovered had the world to heaven wyde,
He by a privie Posterne° tooke his flight,   gate
That of no envious eyes he mote be spyde:
For doubtlesse death ensewd, if any him descryde.

53

Scarse could he footing find in that fowle way,
For many corses, like a great Lay-stall°   dung-heap
Of murdred men which therein strowed lay,
Without remorse, or decent funerall:
Which all through that great Princesse pride did fall
And came to shamefull end. And them beside
Forth ryding underneath the castell wall,
A donghill of dead carkases he spide,
The dreadfull spectacle° of that sad house of Pride.   example

CANTO 6

From lawlesse lust by wondrous grace
fayre Una is releast:
Whom salvage nation does adore,
and learnes her wise beheast°.   bidding

1

As when a ship, that flyes faire under saile,
An hidden rocke escaped hath unwares,
That lay in waite her wrack for to bewaile,[101]
The Marriner yet halfe amazed stares
At perill past, and yet in doubt ne dares
To joy at his foole-happie° oversight: lucky
So doubly is distrest twixt joy and cares
The dreadlesse courage of this Elfin knight,
Having escapt so sad ensamples in his sight.

2

Yet sad he was that his too hastie speed
The faire Duess had forst him leave behind;
And yet more sad, that Una his deare dreed°   revered one
Her truth had staind with treason so unkind°;   unnatural
Yet crime in her could never creature find,

But for his love, and for her owne selfe sake,
She wandred had° from one to other Ynd,   *would have*
Him for to seeke, ne ever would forsake,
Till her unwares the fierce Sansloy did overtake.

3
Who after Archimagoes fowle defeat,
  Led her away into a forrest wilde,
  And turning wrathfull fire to lustfull heat,
  With beastly sin thought her to have defilde,
  And made the vassall of his pleasures vilde°   *vile*
  Yet first he cast by treatie, and by traynes,   *entreaty/tricks*
  Her to perswade, that stubborne fort to yilde:
  For greater conquest of hard love he gaynes,
That workes it to his will, then he that it constraines.

4
With fawning wordes he courted her a while,
  And looking lovely, and oft sighing sore,   *lovingly*
  Her constant hart did tempt with diverse guile:
  But wordes, and lookes, and sighes she did abhore,
  As rocke of Diamond stedfast evermore.
  Yet for to feed his fyrie lustfull eye,
  He snatcht the vele, that hong her face before;
  Then gan her beautie shine, as brightest skye,
And burnt his beastly hart t'efforce° her chastitye.   *violate*

5
So when he saw his flatt'ring arts to fayle,
  And subtile engines bet from batteree,   *repelled*
  With greedy force he gan the fort assayle,
  Whereof he weend possessed soone to bee,
  And win rich spoile of ransackt chastetee.
  Ah heavens, that do this hideous act behold,
  And heavenly virgin thus outraged see,
  How can ye vengeance just so long withhold,
And hurle not flashing flames upon that Paynim bold?

6
The pitteous maiden carefull° comfortlesse,   *full of care*
  Does throw out thrilling shriekes, and shrieking cryes,
  The last vaine helpe of womens great distresse,
  And with loud plaints importuneth the skyes,
  That molten starres do drop like weeping eyes;

And Phoebus flying so most shamefull sight,
His blushing face in foggy cloud implyes,
And hides for shame. What wit of mortall wight
Can now devise to quit° a thrall° from such a plight?   *free/slave*

7

Eternall providence exceeding° thought,   *transcending*
Where none appeares can make her selfe a way:
A wondrous way it for this Lady wrought,
From Lyons clawes to pluck the griped pray.
Her shrill outcryes and shriekes so loud did bray,
That all the woodes and forestes did resownd;
A troupe of Faunes and Satyres far away[102]
Within the wood were dauncing in a rownd,
Whiles old Sylvanus slept in shady arber sownd.

8

Who when they heard that pitteous strained voice,
In hast forsooke their rurall meriment,
And ran towards the far rebownded noyce,
To weet, what wight so loudly did lament.
Unto the place they come incontinent°:   *immediately*
Whom when the raging Sarazin espide,
A rude, misshapen, monstrous rablement,
Whose like he never saw, he durst not bide,
But got his ready steed, and fast away gan ride.

9

The wyld woodgods arrived in the place,
There find the virgin dolefull desolate,
With ruffled rayments, and faire blubbred° face,   *tear-stained*
As her outrageous foe had left her late,
And trembling yet through feare of former hate;
All stand amazed at so uncouth° sight,   *unusual*
And gin to pittie her unhappie state,
All stand astonied at her beautie bright,
In their rude eyes unworthie° of so wofull plight.   *undeserving*

10

She more amazed, in double dread doth dwell;
And every tender part for feare does shake:
As when a greedie Wolfe through hunger fell
A seely° Lambe farre from the flocke does take,   *simple*
Of whom he meanes his bloudie feast to make,

A Lyon spyes fast running towards him,
The innocent pray in hast he does forsake,
Which quit° from death yet quakes in every lim   *released*
With chaunge of feare, to see the Lyon looke so grim.

11

Such fearefull fit assaid° her trembling hart,   *affected*
Ne word to speake, ne joynt to move she had:
The salvage nation feele her secret smart,
And read her sorrow in her count'nance sad;
Their frowning forheads with rough hornes yclad,
And rusticke horror all a side doe lay,
And gently grenning° shew a semblance glad   *grinning*
To comfort her, and feare to put away,
Their backward bent knees teach her humbly to obay.[103]

12

The doubtfull Damzell dare not yet commit
Her single person to their barbarous truth,
But still twixt feare and hope amazd does sit,
Late learnd what harme to hastie trust ensu'th,
They in compassion of her tender youth,
And wonder of her beautie soveraine,
Are wonne with pitty and unwonted ruth,
And all prostrate upon the lowly plaine,
Do kisse her feete, and fawne on her with countenance faine°.   *glad*

13

Their harts she ghesseth by their humble guise°   *manner*
And yieldes her to extremitie of time,[104]
So from the ground she fearelesse doth arise.
And walketh forth without suspect of crime:
They all as glad, as birdes of joyous Prime°   *springtime*
Thence lead her forth, about her dauncing round,
Shouting, and singing all a shepheards ryme,
And with greene braunches strowing all the ground,
Do worship her, as Queene, with olive girlond cround.[105]

14

And all the way their merry pipes they sound,
That all the woods with doubled Eccho ring,
And with their horned feet do weare° the ground,   *trample*
Leaping like wanton kids in pleasant Spring.
So towards old Sylvanus they her bring;

Who with the noyse awaked, commeth out,
  To weet° the cause, his weake steps governing,   *learn*
  And aged limbs on Cypresse stadle° stout,   *staff*
And with an yvie twyne his wast is girt about.

15

Far off he wonders, what them makes so glad,
  Or Bacchus merry fruit they did invent,[106]
  Or Cybeles franticke rites have made them mad;
  They drawing nigh, unto their God present
  That flowre of faith and beautie excellent.
  The God himselfe vewing that mirrhour° rare,[107]   *reflection*
  Stood long amazd, and burnt in his intent°;   *gaze*
  His owne faire Dryope now he thinkes not faire,
And Pholoe fowle, when her to this he doth compaire.

16

The woodborne people fall before her flat,
  And worship her as Goddesse of the wood;
  And old Sylvanus selfe bethinkes not, what
  To thinke of wight so faire, but gazing stood,
  In doubt to deeme her borne of earthly brood;
  Sometimes Dame Venus selfe he seemes to see,
  But Venus never had so sober mood;
  Sometimes Diana he her takes to bee,
But misseth bow, and shaftes, and buskins° to her knee.   *boots*

17

By vew of her he ginneth to revive
  His ancient love, and dearest Cyparisse,
  And calles to mind his pourtraiture alive,[108]
  How faire he was, and yet not faire to this,
  And how he slew with glauncing dart amisse
  A gentle Hynd°, the which the lovely boy   *deer*
  Did love as life, above all worldly blisse;
  For griefe whereof the lad n'ould° after joy,   *could not*
But pynd away in anguish and selfe-wild annoy°.   *grief*

18

The wooddy Nymphes, faire Hamadryades
  Her to behold do thither runne apace,
  And all the troupe of light-foot Naiades,
  Flocke all about to see her lovely face:
  But when they vewed have her heavenly grace,

They envie her in their malitious mind,
  And fly away for feare of fowle disgrace:
  But all the Satyres scorne their woody kind,
And henceforth nothing faire, but her on earth they find.

19

Glad of such lucke, the luckelesse lucky maid,
  Did her content to please their feeble eyes,
  And long time with that salvage people staid,
  To gather breath in many miseries.
  During which time her gentle wit she plyes,
  To teach them truth, which worshipt her in vaine,   *foolishly*
  And made her th'Image of Idolatryes;
  But when their bootlesse zeale she did restraine
From her own worship, they her Asse would worship fayn.   *eagerly*

20

It fortuned a noble warlike knight
  By just occasion to that forrest came,
  To seeke his kindred, and the lignage right,
  From whence he tooke his well deserved name:
  He had in armes abroad wonne muchell fame,
  And fild far landes with glorie of his might,
  Plaine, faithfull, true, and enimy of shame,
  And ever loved to fight for Ladies right,
But in vaine glorious frayes he litle did delight.

21

A Satyres sonne yborne in forrest wyld,
  By straunge adventure as it did betyde,   *happen*
  And there begotten of a Lady myld,
  Faire Thyamis the daughter of Labryde,[109]
  That was in sacred bands of wedlocke tyde
  To Therion, a loose unruly swayne;
  Who had more joy to raunge the forrest wyde,
  And chase the salvage° beast with busie payne,   *wild/care*
Then serve his Ladies love, and wast° in pleasures vayne.   *waste time*

22

The forlorne mayd did with loves longing burne,
  And could not lacke° her lovers company,   *be without*
  But to the wood she goes, to serve her turne,
  And seeke her spouse, that from her still does fly,
  And followes other game and venery:[110]

A Satyre chaunst her wandring for to find,
And kindling coles of lust in brutish eye,
The loyall links of wedlocke did unbind,
And made her person thrall unto his beastly kind.

23

So long in secret cabin there he held
  Her captive to his sensuall desire,
  Till that with timely fruit her belly sweld,
  And bore a boy unto that salvage sire:
  Then home he suffred her for to retire,
  For ransome leaving him the late borne childe;
  Whom till to ryper yeares he gan aspire,°   *reach*
  He noursled up in life and manners wilde,
Emongst wild beasts and woods, from lawes of men
                          exilde.

24

For all he taught the tender ymp,° was but   *child*
  To banish cowardize and bastard° feare;   *base*
  His trembling hand he would him force to put
  Upon the Lyon and the rugged Beare,[111]
  And from the she Beares teats her whelps to teare;
  And eke wyld roring Buls he would him make
  To tame, and ryde their backes not made to beare;
  And the Robuckes in flight to overtake,
That every beast for feare of him did fly and quake.

25

Thereby so fearelesse, and so fell he grew,
  That his owne sire and maister of his guise°   *mode of life*
  Did often tremble at his horrid vew,°   *appearance*
  And oft for dread of hurt would him advise,
  The angry beasts not rashly to despise,
  Nor too much to provoke; for he would learne°   *teach*
  The Lyon stoup to him in lowly wise,
  (A lesson hard) and make the Libbard° sterne   *leopard*
Leave roaring, when in rage he for revenge did earne.°   *yearn*

26

And for to make his powre approved° more,   *proven*
  Wyld beasts in yron yokes he would compell;
  The spotted Panther, and the tusked Bore,
  The Pardale° swift, and the Tigre cruell;   *panther or leopard*
  The Antelope, and Wolfe both fierce and fell;

And them constraine in equall teme to draw.[112]
  Such joy he had, their stubborne harts to quell,
  And sturdie courage tame with deadfull aw,
That his beheast they feared, as a tyrans law.

27

His loving mother came upon a day
  Unto the woods, to see her little sonne;
  And chaunst unwares to meet him in the way,
  After his sportes, and cruell pastime donne,
  When after him a Lyonesse did runne,
  That roaring all with rage, did lowd requere°   *demand*
  Her children deare, whom he away had wonne°:   *taken*
  The Lyon whelpes she saw how he did beare,
And lull in rugged armes, withouten childish feare.

28

The fearefull Dame all quaked at the sight,
  And turning backe, gan fast to fly away,
  Until with love revokt° from vaine affright,   *withdrawn*
  She hardly° yet perswaded was to stay,   *with difficulty*
  And then to him these womanish words gan say;
  'Ah Satyrane, my dearling, and my joy,
  For love of me leave off this dreadfull play;
  To dally thus with death, is no fit toy,
Go find some other play-fellowes, mine own sweet boy.'

29

In these and like delights of bloudy game
  He trayned was, till ryper yeares he raught,°   *reached*
  And there abode, whilst any beast of name
  Walkt in that forest, whom he had not taught
  To feare his force: and then his courage haught°   *high*
  Desird of forreine foemen to be knowne,
  And far abroad for straunge adventures sought:
  In which his might was never overthrowne,
But through all Faery lond his famous worth was blown.[113]

30

Yet evermore it was his manner faire,
  After long labours and adventures spent,
  Unto those native woods for to repaire,°   *return*
  To see his sire and ofspring° auncient.   *origin*
  And now he thither came for like intent;

Where he unwares the fairest Una found,
Straunge Lady, in so straunge habiliment,°   *attire*
Teaching the Satyres, which her sat around,
Trew sacred lore, which from her sweet lips did redound.°   *flow*

31

He wondred at her wisedome heavenly rare,
  Whose like in womens wit he never knew;
  And when her curteous deeds he did compare,
  Gan her admire, and her sad sorrowes rew,
  Blaming of Fortune, which such troubles threw,
  And joyd to make proofe of her crueltie
  On gentle Dame, so hurtlesse,° and so trew: *harmless*
  Thenceforth he kept her goodly company,
And learnd her discipline of faith and veritie.

32

But she all vowd unto the Redcrosse knight,
  His wandring perill closely° did lament,   *privately*
  Ne in this new acquaintaunce could delight,
  But her deare heart with anguish did torment,
  And all her wit in secret counsels spent,
  How to escape. At last in privie wise°   *secretly*
  To Satyrane she shewed her intent;
  Who glad to gain such favour, gan devise,
How with that pensive Maid he best might thence arise.°   *depart*

33

So on a day when Satyres all were gone,
  To do their service to Sylvanus old,
  The gentle virgin left behind alone
  He led away with courage stout and bold.
  Too late it was, to Satyres to be told,
  Or ever hope recover her againe:
  In vaine he seekes that having cannot hold.
  So fast he carried her with carefull paine,°   *pains*
That they the woods are past, and come now to the plaine.

34

The better part now of the lingring day,
  They traveild had, when as they farre espide
  A wearie wight forwandring° by the way,   *wandering*
  And towards him they gan in hast to ride,
  To weet of newes, that did abroad betide,

Or tydings of her knight of the Redcrosse.
But he them spying, gan to turne aside,
For feare as seemd, or for some feigned losse;
More greedy they of newes, fast towards him do crosse.

35

A silly° man,[114] in simple weedes forworne,   *simple/worn out*
  And soild with dust of the long dried way;
  His sandales were with toilesome travell torne,
  And face all tand with scorching sunny ray,
  As he had traveild many a sommers day,
  Through boyling sands of Arabie and Ynde;
  And in his hand a Jacobs° staffe, to stay   *pilgrim's*
  His wearie limbes upon: and eke behind,
His scrip° did hang, in which his needments he did bind.   *bag*

36

The knight approching nigh, of him inquerd
  Tydings of warre, and of adventures new;
  But warres, nor new adventures none he herd.
  Then Una gan to aske, if ought he knew,
  Or heard abroad of that her champion trew,
  That in his armour bare a croslet° red.   *small cross*
  'Aye me, Deare dame,' quoth he, 'well may I rew
  To tell the sad sight, which mine eies have red°:   *seen*
These eyes did see that knight both living and eke ded.'

37

That cruell word her tender hart so thrild,°   *pierced*
  That suddein cold did runne through every vaine,
  And stony horrour all her sences fild
  With dying fit, that downe she fell for paine.
  The knight her lightly reared up againe,
  And comforted with curteous kind reliefe:
  Then wonne from death, she bad him tellen plaine
  The further processe° of her hidden griefe;   *account*
The lesser pangs can beare, who hath endured the chiefe.

38

Then gan the Pilgrim thus, 'I chaunst this day,
  This fatall day, that shall I ever rew,
  To see two knights in travell on my way
  (A sory sight) arraunged in battell new,[115]
  Both breathing vengeaunce, both of wrathfull hew:

My fearefull flesh did tremble at their strife,
To see their blades so greedily imbrew,°   thrust
That drunke with bloud, yet thristed after life:
What more? the Redcrosse knight was slaine with Paynim knife.'

                                39
'Ah dearest Lord,' quoth she, 'how might that bee,
    And he the stoutest knight, that ever wonne°?'   lived
    'Ah dearest dame,' quoth he, 'how might I see
    The thing, that might not be, and yet was donne?'
    'Where is,' said Satyrane, 'that Paynims° sonne,   pagan's
    That him of life, and us of joy hath reft?'
    'Not far away,' quoth he, 'he hence doth wonne°   remain
    Foreby a fountaine, where I late him left
Washing his bloudy wounds, that through the steele were cleft.'

                                40
Therewith the knight thence marched forth in hast,
    Whiles Una with huge heavinesse opprest,
    Could not for sorrow follow him so fast;
    And soone he came, as he the place had ghest,
    Whereas that Pagan proud him selfe did rest,
    In secret shadow by a fountaine side:
    Even he it was, that earst would have supprest°   ravished
    Faire Una: whom when Satyrane espide,
With fowle reprochfull words he boldly him defide.

                                41
And said, 'Arise thou cursed Miscreaunt,
    That hast with knightlesse guile and trecherous train°   tricks
    Faire knighthood fowly shamed, and doest vaunt
    That good knight of the Redcrosse to have slain:
    Arise, and with like treason now maintain
    Thy guilty wrong, or else thee guilty yield.'
    The Sarazin this hearing, rose amain,
    And catching up in hast° his three square° shield,   haste/triangular
And shining helmet, soone him buckled to° the field.   for

                                42
And drawing nigh him said, 'Ah misborne° Elfe,   base-born
    In evill houre thy foes thee hither sent,
    Anothers wrongs to wreake° upon thy selfe: avenge
    Yet ill thou blamest me, for having blent°   defiled
    My name with guile and traiterous intent;

That Redcrosse knight, perdie,° I never slew, *truly*
But had he beene, where earst his armes were lent,[116]
Th'enchaunter vaine his errour should not rew:
But thou his errour shalt, I hope now proven trew.'

43

Therewith they gan, both furious and fell,
　To thunder blowes, and fiersly to assaile
　Each other bent° his enimy to quell,　　　　　　*determined*
　That with their force they perst both plate and maile,
　And made wide furrowes in their fleshes fraile,
　That it would pitty° any living eie.　　　　　　*bring pity to*
　Large floods of bloud adowne their sides did raile°:　*flow*
　But floods of bloud could not them satisfie:
Both hungred after death: both chose to win, or die.

44

So long they fight, and fell revenge pursue,
　That fainting each, themselves to breathen let,
　And oft refreshed, battell oft renue:
　As when two Bores with rancling malice met,
　Their gory sides fresh bleeding fiersly fret,°　　　　*tear at*
　Til breathlesse both them selves aside retire,
　Where foming wrath, their cruell tuskes they whet,°　*sharpen*
　And trample th'earth, the whiles they may respire;
Then backe to fight againe, new breathed and entire.°　*refreshed*

45

So fiersly, when these knights had breathed once,
　They gan to fight returne, increasing more
　Their puissant force, and cruell rage attonce,
　With heaped strokes more hugely, then before,
　That with their drerie° wounds and bloudy gore　　　*bloody*
　They both deformed,° scarsely could be known.　　　*disfigured*
　By this sad Una fraught with anguish sore,
　Led with their noise, which through the aire was thrown,
Arrived, where they in erth their fruitles bloud had sown.

46

Whom all so soone as that proud Sarazin
　Espide, he gan revive the memory
　Of his lewd lusts, and late attempted sin,
　And left the doubtfull° battell hastily,　　　　　*uncertain*
　To catch her, newly offred to his eie:

But Satyrane with strokes him turning, staid,
  And sternely bad him other businesse plie,
  Then hunt the steps of pure unspotted Maid:
Wherewith he all enraged, these bitter speaches said.

47

'O foolish faeries sonne, what furie mad
  Hath thee incenst, to hast thy dolefull fate?
  Were it not better, I that Lady had,
  Then that thou hadst repented it too late?
  Most sencelesse man he, that himselfe doth hate,
  To love another. Lo then for thine ayd
  Here take thy lovers token on thy pate.'
  So they to fight; the whiles the royall Mayd
Fled farre away, of that proud Paynim sore afrayd.

48

But that false Pilgrim, which that leasing° told,   *falsehood*
  Being in deed old Archimage, did stay
  In secret shadow, all this to behold,
  And much rejoyced in their bloudy fray:
  But when he saw the Damsell passe away°   *leave*
  He left his stond°, and her persewd apace,   *place*
  In hope to bring her to her last decay°.   *destruction*
  But for to tell her lamentable cace,
And eke this battels end, will need another place.

CANTO 7 [117]

The Redcrosse knight is captive made
By Gyaunt proud opprest,
Prince Arthur meets with Una great-
ly with those newes distrest.

1

What man so wise, what earthly wit so ware°,   *wary*
  As to descry° the crafty cunning traine°,   *discover/snare*
  By which deceipt doth maske in visour faire,
  And cast° her colours dyed deepe in graine°,   *dispense/thoroughly*
  To seeme like Truth, whose shape she well can faine°, *feign*
  And fitting gestures to her purpose frame,
  The guiltlesse man with guile to entertaine?
  Great maistresse of her art was that false Dame,
The false Duessa, cloked with Fidessaes name.

2

Who when returning from the drery Night,
   She fownd not in that perilous house of Pryde,
   Where she had left, the noble Redcrosse knight,
   Her hoped pray, she would no lenger bide,
   But forth she went, to seeke him far and wide.
   Ere long she fownd, whereas he wearie sate,
   To rest him selfe, foreby° a fountaine side,   *near*
   Disarmed all of yron-coted Plate;   *armour*
And by his side his steed the grassy forage ate.

3

He feedes upon the cooling shade, and bayes°   *bathes*
   His sweatie forehead in the breathing wind,
   Which through the trembling leaves full gently playes
   Wherein the cherefull birds of sundry kind
   Do chaunt sweet musick, to delight his mind:
   The Witch approching gan him fairely greet,
   And with reproch of carelesnesse unkind
   Upbrayd, for leaving her in place unmeet;   *unsuitable*
With fowle words tempring faire, soure gall with hony sweet.

4

Unkindnesse past, they gan of solace treat;   *talk*
   And bathe in pleasaunce of the joyous shade,
   Which shielded them against the boyling heat,
   And with greene boughes decking a gloomy glade,
   About the fountaine like a girlond made;
   Whose bubbling wave did ever freshly well,
   Ne ever would through fervent° sommer fade: *hot*
   The sacred Nymph,[118] which therein wont to dwell,
Was out of Dianes favour, as it then befell.

5

The cause was this: one day when Phoebe° fayre   *i.e. Diana*
   With all her band was following the chace,
   This Nymph, quite tyred with heat of scorching ayre
   Sat downe to rest in middest of the race:
   The goddesse wroth gan fowly her disgrace;   *revile*
   And bad the waters, which from her did flow,
   Be such as she her selfe was then in place: *there*
   Thenceforth her waters waxed dull and slow,
And all that drunke thereof, did faint and feeble grow.

6

Hereof this gentle knight unweeting was,
  And lying downe upon the sandie graile,°   *gravel*
  Drunke of the streame, as cleare as cristall glas;
  Eftsoones his manly forces gan to faile,
  And mightie strong was turnd to feeble fraile.
  His chaunged powres at first themselves not felt,
  Till crudled° cold his corage° gan assaile,   *congealed/heart*
  And chearefull° bloud in faintnesse chill did melt,   *full of courage*
And which like a fever fit through all his body swelt.°   *raged*

7

Yet goodly court he made still to his Dame,
  Pourd out in loosnesse on the grassy grownd,
  Both carelesse of his health, and of his fame:
  Till at the last he heard a dreadfull sownd,
  Which through the wood loud bellowing, did rebownd,
  That all the earth for terrour seemd to shake,
  And trees did tremble. Th'Elfe therewith astownd,°   *astounded*
  Upstarted lightly from his looser make,°   *companion*
And his unready weapons gan in hand to take.

8

But ere he could his armour on him dight,°   *put*
  Or get his shield, his monstrous enimy
  With sturdie steps came stalking in his sight,
  An hideous Geant° horrible and hye,   *i.e. Orgoglio*
  That with his talnesse seemd to threat the skye,
  The ground eke groned under him for dreed;
  His living like saw never living eye,
  Ne durst behold: his stature did exceed
The hight of three the tallest sonnes of mortall seed.

9

The greatest Earth his uncouth mother was,
  And blustring Aeolus his boasted sire,
  Who with his breath, which through the world doth pas,
  Her hollow womb did secretly inspire,°   *breathe into*
  And fild her hidden caves with stormie yre,
  That she conceived, and trebling the dew time,
  In which the wombes of women do expire,°   *give birth*
  Brought forth this monstrous masse of earthly slime,
Puft up with emptie wind, and fild with sinfull crime.

10

So growen great through arrogant delight
   Of th'high descent, whereof he was yborne,
   And through presumption of his matchlesse might,
   All other powres and knighthood he did scorne,
   Such now he marcheth to this man forlorne,
   And left to losse°: his stalking steps are stayde°   *destruction/supported*
   Upon a snaggy Oke, which he had torne
   Out of his mothers bowelles, and it made
His mortall mace, wherewith his foemen he dismayde.

11

That when the knight he spide, he gan advance
   With huge force and insupportable mayne°,   *power*
   And towardes him with dreadfull fury praunce;
   Who haplesse, and eke hopelesse, all in vaine
   Did to him pace, sad battaile to darrayne°,   *take up*
   Disarmd, disgrast, and inwardly dismayde,[119]
   And eke so faint in every joynt and vaine,   */ weakness*
   Through that fraile° fountaine, which him feeble made,   *causing*
That scarsely could he weeld his bootlesse° single blade°. *useless/sword*

12[120]

The Geaunt strooke so maynly° mercilesse,   *violently*
   That could have overthrowne a stony towre,
   And were not heavenly grace, that him did blesse°,   *preserve*
   He had beene pouldred all, as thin as flowre:
   But he was wary of that deadly stowre°,   *encounter*
   And lightly lept from underneath the blow:
   Yet so exceeding was the villeins powre,
   That with the wind it did him overthrow,
And all his sences stound°, that still he lay full low.   *stunned*

13

As when that divelish yron Engin° wrought   *cannon*
   In deepest Hell, and framd by Furies skill,
   With windy Nitre and quick° Sulphur fraught°, *inflammable/filled*
   And ramd with bullet round, ordaind to kill,
   Conceiveth fire, the heavens it doth fill
   With thundring noyse, and all the ayre doth choke,
   That none can breath, nor see, nor heare at will,
   Through smouldry cloud of duskish stincking smoke,
That th'onely breath[121] him daunts, who hath escapt the stroke.

14

So daunted when the Geaunt saw the knight,
  His heavie hand he heaved up on hye,
  And him to dust thought to have battred quight,
  Untill Duessa loud to him gan crye;
  'O great Orgoglio, greatest under skye,
  O hold thy mortall hand for Ladies sake,
  Hold for my sake, and do him not to dye,
  But vanquisht thine eternall bondslave make,
And me thy worthy meed° unto thy Leman° take.'   *reward/mistress*

15

He hearkned, and did stay from further harmes,
  To gayne so goodly guerdon,° as she spake: *prize*
  So willingly she came into his armes,
  Who her as willingly to grace° did take,   *favour*
  And was possessed of his new found make.°   *companion*
  Then up he tooke the slombred sencelesse corse,
  And ere he could out of his swowne awake,
  Him to his castle brought with hastie forse,
And in a Dongeon deepe him threw without remorse.

16

From that day forth Duessa was his deare,
  And highly honourd in his haughtie eye,
  He gave her gold and purple pall° to weare,   *robe*
  And triple crowne[122] set on her head full hye,
  And her endowd with royall majestye:
  Then for to make her dreaded more of men,
  And peoples harts with awfull terrour tye,
  A monstrous beast ybred in filthy fen
He chose, which he had kept long time in darksome den.

17

Such one it was, as that renowmed Snake[123]
  Which great Alcides in Stremona slew,
  Long fostred in the filth of Lerna lake,
  Whose many heads out budding ever new,
  Did breed him endlesse labour to subdew:
  But this same Monster much more ugly was;
  For seven great heads out of his body grew,
  An yron brest, and backe of scaly bras,
And all embrewd° in bloud, his eyes did shine as glas.   *stained*

18

His tayle was stretched out in wondrous length,
   That to the house of heavenly gods it raught,°   *reached*
   And with extorted powre, and borrowed strength,
   The ever-burning lamps from thence it brought,
   And prowdly threw to ground, as things of nought;
   And underneath his filthy feet did tread
   The sacred things, and holy heasts° foretaught.   *commands*
   Upon this dreadfull Beast with sevenfold head
He set the false Duessa, for more aw and dread.

19

The wofull Dwarfe, which saw his maisters fall,
   Whiles he had keeping of his grasing steed,
   And valiant knight become a caytive° thrall,   *captive*
   When all was past, tooke up his forlorne weed,°   *equipment*
   His mightie armour, missing most at need°;   *when needed most*
   His silver shield, now idle maisterlesse;
   His poynant° speare, that many made to bleed,   *sharp*
   The ruefull moniments° of heavinesse,   *memorials*
And with them all departes, to tell his great distresse.

20

He had not travaild long, when on the way
   He wofull Ladie, wofull Una met,
   Fast flying from the Paynims greedy pray,°   *booty*
   Whilest Satyrane him from pursuit did let°:   *prevent*
   Who when her eyes she on the Dwarfe had set,
   And saw the signes, that deadly tydings spake,
   She fell to ground for sorrowfull regret,
   And lively breath her sad brest did forsake,
Yet might her pitteous hart be seene to pant and quake.

21

The messenger of so unhappie newes,
   Would faine have dyde: dead was his hart within,
   Yet outwardly some little comfort shewes:
   At last recovering hart, he does begin
   To rub her temples, and to chaufe her chin,
   And every tender part does tosse and turne:
   So hardly° he the flitted life does win,°   *with difficulty/reach*
   Unto her native prison° to retourne: *i.e. the body*
Then gins her grieved ghost° thus to lament and mourne.   *spirit*

22

'Ye dreary instruments° of dolefull sight,   *i.e. eyes*
    That doe this deadly spectacle behold,
    Why do ye lenger feed on loathed light,
    Or liking find to gaze on earthly mould°,   *form*
    Sith cruell fates[124] the carefull° threeds unfould,   *full of care*
    The which my life and love together tyde?
    Now let the stony dart of senselesse cold
    Perce to my hart, and pas through every side,
And let eternall night so sad sight fro me hide.

23

O lightsome day, the lampe of highest Jove,
    First made by him, mens wandring wayes to guyde,
    When darknesse he in deepest dongeon drove,
    Henceforth thy hated face for ever hyde,
    And shut up heavens windowes shyning wyde:
    For earthly sight can nought but sorrow breed,
    And late repentance, which shall long abyde.
    Mine eyes no more on vanitie shall feed,
But seeled up with death, shall have their deadly meed.'   *reward*

24

Then downe againe she fell unto the ground;
    But he her quickly reared up againe:
    Thrise did she sinke adowne in deadly swownd,
    And thrise he her revived with busie paine:
    At last when life recovered had the raine°,   *rule*
    And over-wrestled his strong enemie,
    With foltring tong, and trembling every vaine,
    'Tell on,' quoth she, 'the wofull Tragedie,
The which these reliques sad present unto mine eie.

25

Tempestuous fortune hath spent all her spight,
    And thrilling sorrow throwne his utmost dart;
    Thy sad tongue cannot tell more heavy plight,
    Then that I feele, and harbour in mine hart:
    Who hath endured the whole, can beare each part.
    If death it be, it is not the first wound,
    That launched° hath my brest with bleeding smart.   *pierced*
    Begin, and end the bitter balefull stound°;   *sorrow*
If lesse, then that I feare, more favour I have found.'

26

Then gan the Dwarfe the whole discourse declare,
  The subtill traines of Archimago old;
  The wanton loves of false Fidessa faire,
  Bought with the bloud of vanquisht Paynim bold:
  The wretched payre tranformed to treen mould°;   *shape of trees*
  The house of Pride, and perils round about;
  The combat, which he with Sansjoy did hould;
  The lucklesse conflict with the Gyant stout,
Wherein captived, of life or death he stood in doubt.

27

She heard with patience all unto the end,
  And strove to maister sorrowfull assay°,   *affliction*
  Which greater grew, the more she did contend,
  And almost rent her tender hart in tway;
  And love fresh coles unto her fire did lay:
  For greater love, the greater is the losse.
  Was never Ladie loved dearer day,
  Then she did love the knight of the Redcrosse;
For whose deare sake so many troubles her did tosse.

28

At last when fervent sorrow slaked was,
  She up arose, resolving him to find
  Alive or dead: and forward forth doth pas,
  All as the Dwarfe the way to her assynd°:   *showed*
  And evermore in constant carefull mind
  She fed her wound with fresh renewed bale°;   *grief*
  Long tost with stormes, and bet° with bitter wind,   *beaten*
  High over hils, and low adowne the dale,
She wandred many a wood, and measurd many a vale.

29

At last she chaunced by good hap to meet
  A goodly knight,[125] faire marching by the way
  Together with his Squire, arayed meet°:   *properly accoutred*
  His glitterand° armour shined farre away,   *glittering*
  Like glauncing light of Phoebus brightest ray;
  From top to toe no place appeared bare,
  That deadly dint° of steele endanger may: *blow*
  Athwart his brest a bauldrick° brave he ware,   *shoulder belt*
That shynd, like twinkling stars, with stons most pretious rare.

30

And in the midst thereof one pretious stone
　　Of wondrous worth, and eke of wondrous mights,
　　Shapt like a Ladies head,[126] exceeding shone,
　　Like Hesperus emongst the lesser lights,°　　　　　*stars*
　　And strove for to amaze the weaker sights;
　　Thereby his mortall blade full comely hong[127]
　　In yvory sheath, ycarved with curious slights°;　　*patterns*
　　Whose hilts were burnisht gold, and handle strong
Of mother pearle, and buckled with a golden tong.°　*strap*

31

His haughtie° helmet, horrid° all with gold,　　*proud/bristling*
　　Both glorious brightnesse, and great terrour bred;
　　For all the crest a Dragon[128] did enfold
　　With greedie pawes, and over all did spred
　　His golden wings: his dreadfull hideous hed
　　Close couched° on the bever,° seemed to throw　　*lying/helmet*
　　From flaming mouth bright sparkles fierie red,
　　That suddeine horror to faint harts did show;
And scaly tayle was stretcht adowne his backe full low.

32

Upon the top of all his loftie crest,
　　A bunch of haires discolourd° diversly,　　*many-coloured*
　　With sprincled pearle, and gold full richly drest,
　　Did shake, and seemed to daunce for jollity,
　　Like to an Almond tree ymounted hye
　　On top of greene Selinis all alone,
　　With blossomes brave bedecked daintily;
　　Whose tender locks do tremble every one
At every little breath, that under heaven is blowne.

33

His warlike shield all closely covered was,
　　Ne might of mortall eye be ever seene;
　　Not made of steele, nor of enduring bras,
　　Such earthly metals soone consumed bene:
　　But all of Diamond perfect pure and cleene°　　*clear*
　　It framed was, one massie entire mould,
　　Hewen out of Adamant° rocke with engines° keene,　*diamond-hard/*
　　That point of speare it never percen could,　　*machines*
Ne dint of direfull sword divide the substance would.

34

The same to wight he never wont disclose,
   But° when as monsters huge he would dismay,   *except*
   Or daunt unequall armies of his foes,
   Or when the flying heavens he would affray°;   *frighten*
   For so exceeding shone his glistring ray,
   That Phoebus golden face it did attaint°,   *darken*
   As when a cloud his beames doth over-lay;
   And silver Cynthia wexed pale and faint,
As when her face is staynd with magicke arts constraint°.   *power*

35

No magicke arts hereof had any might,
   Nor bloudie wordes of bold Enchaunters call,
   But all that was not such, as seemd in sight,
   Before that shield did fade, and suddeine fall:
   And when him list the raskall routes° appall,   *rabbles*
   Men into stones therewith he could transmew°,   *transform*
   And stones to dust, and dust to nought at all;
   And when him list the prouder lookes subdew,
He would them gazing blind, or turne to other hew°.   *shape*

36

Ne let it seeme, that credence this exceedes,
   For he that made the same, was knowne right well
   To have done much more admirable deedes.
   It Merlin was, which whylome° did excell   *once upon a time*
   All living wightes in might of magicke spell:
   Both shield, and sword, and armour all he wrought
   For this young Prince, when first to armes he fell°;   *came*
   But when he dyde, the Faerie Queene it brought
To Faerie lond, where yet it may be seene, if sought.[129]

37

A gentle youth, his dearely loved Squire°   *i.e. Timias*
   His speare of heben° wood behind him bare,   *ebony*
   Whose harmefull head, thrice heated in the fire,
   Had riven many a brest with pikehead square;
   A goodly person, and could menage° faire   *control*
   His stubborne steed with curbed canon bit,[130]
   Who under him did trample as the aire°,   *as light as air*
   And chauft°, that any on his backe should sit;   *chafed*
The yron rowels° into frothy foam he bit.   *part of the bit*

38

When as this knight nigh to the Ladie drew,
  With lovely° court he gan her entertaine;   *loving*
  But when he heard her answeres loth, he knew
  Some secret sorrow did her heart distraine°:   *oppress*
  Which to allay, and calme her storming paine,
  Faire feeling words he wisely gan display,
  And for her humour fitting purpose faine,[131]
  To tempt the cause it selfe for to bewray;
Wherewith emmoved, these bleeding words she gan to say.

39

'What worlds delight, or joy of living speech
  Can heart, so plunged in sea of sorrowes deepe,
  And heaped with so huge misfortunes, reach?
  The carefull° cold beginneth for to creepe,   *full of care*
  And in my heart his yron arrow steepe,
  Soone as I thinke upon my bitter bale:°   *injury*
  Such helplesse harmes yts better hidden keepe,
  Then rip up griefe, where it may not availe,
My last left comfort is, my woes to weepe and waile.'

40

'Ah Ladie deare,' quoth then the gentle knight,
  'Well may I weene, your griefe is wondrous great;
  For wondrous great griefe groneth in my spright,
  Whiles thus I heare you of your sorrowes treat.
  But wofull Ladie let me you intrete,
  For to unfold the anguish of your hart:
  Mishaps are maistred by advice discrete,
  And counsell mittigates the greatest smart;
Found never helpe, who never would his hurts impart.'

41

'O but,' quoth she, 'great griefe will not be tould,
  And can more easily be thought, then said.'
  'Right so,' quoth he, 'but he, that never would,
  Could never: will to might gives greatest aid.'
  'But griefe,' quoth she, 'does greater grow displaid,
  If then it find not helpe, and breedes despaire.'
  'Despaire breedes not,' quoth he, 'where faith is staid°.'   *firm*
  'No faith so fast,' quoth she, 'but flesh does paire°.'   *weaken*
'Flesh may empaire,' quoth he, 'but reason can repaire.'

42

His goodly reason, and well guided speach
    So deepe did settle in her gratious thought,
    That her perswaded to disclose the breach,
    Which love and fortune in her heart had wrought,
    And said; 'Faire Sir, I hope good hap hath brought
    You to inquire the secrets of my griefe,
    Or that your wisedome will direct my thought,
    Or that your prowesse can me yield reliefe:
Then heare the storie sad, which I shall tell you briefe.

43

The forlorne Maiden, whom your eyes have seene
    The laughing stocke of fortunes mockeries,
    Am th'only daughter of a King and Queene,
    Whose parents deare, whilest equall° destinies   *impartial*
    Did runne about° and their felicities   *existed*
    The favourable heavens did not envy,
    Did spread their rule through all the territories,
    Which Phison and Euphrates floweth by,
And Gehons golden waves doe wash continually.

44

Till that their cruell cursed enemy,
    An huge great Dragon horrible in sight,
    Bred in the loathly lakes of Tartary,°   *Tartarus*
    With murdrous ravine,° and devouring might   *destruction*
    Their kingdome spoild, and countrey wasted quight:
    Themselves, for feare into his jawes to fall,
    He forst to castle strong to take their flight,
    Where fast embard° in mightie brasen° wall,   *imprisoned/brass-like*
He has them now foure yeres besieged to make them thrall.

45

Full many knights adventurous and stout
    Have enterprizd° that Monster to subdew;   *attempted*
    From every coast that heaven walks about,
    Have thither come the noble Martiall crew,
    That famous hard atchievements still pursew,
    Yet never any could that girlond win,
    But all still shronke,° and still he greater grew: *shrank away*
    All they for want of faith, or guilt of sin,
The pitteous pray of his fierce crueltie have bin.

46

At last yledd with farre reported praise,
    Which flying fame throughout the world had spred,
    Of doughtie knights, whom Faery land did raise,
    That noble order hight° of Maidenhed,[132]   *called*
    Forthwith to court of Gloriane I sped,
    Of Gloriane great Queene of glory bright,
    Whose kingdomes seat Cleopolis[133] is red°,   *named*
    There to obtaine some such redoubted knight,
That Parents deare from tyrants powre deliver might.

47

It was my chance (my chance was faire and good)
    There for to find a fresh unproved knight,
    Whose manly hands imbrewed° in guiltie blood   *stained*
    Had never bene, ne ever by his might
    Had throwne to ground the unregarded° right: *unrespected*
    Yet of his prowesse proofe he since hath made
    (I witnesse am) in many a cruell fight;
    The groning ghosts of many one dismaide
Have felt the bitter dint of his avenging blade.

48

And ye the forlorne reliques of his powre,
    His byting sword, and his devouring speare,
    Which have endured many a dreadfull stowre°,   *plight*
    Can speake his prowesse, that did earst you beare,
    And well could rule: now he hath left you heare,
    To be the record of his ruefull losse,
    And of my dolefull disaventurous deare°:   *injury*
    O heavie record of the good Redcrosse,
Where have you left your Lord, that could so well you tosse°? *wield*

49

Well hoped I, and faire beginnings had,
    That he my captive languour° should redeeme,   *despair*
    Till all unweeting, an Enchaunter bad
    His sence abusd, and made him to misdeeme
    My loyalty, not such as it did seeme;
    That rather death desire, then such despight.[134]
    Be judge ye heavens, that all things right esteeme,
    How I him loved, and love with all my might,
So thought I eke of him, and thinke I thought aright.

50

Thenceforth me desolate he quite forsooke,
  To wander, where wilde fortune would me lead,
  And other bywaies he himselfe betooke,
  Where never foot of living wight did tread,
  That brought not backe the balefull body dead,[135]
  In which him chaunced false Duessa meete,
  Mine onely° foe, mine onely deadly dread,   *particular*
  Who with her witchcraft and misseeming° sweete,   *deception*
Inveigled him to follow her desires unmeete°   *improper*

51

At last by subtill sleights she him betraid
  Unto his foe, a Gyant huge and tall,
  Who him disarmed, dissolute° dismaid,   *weak*
  Unwares surprised, and with mightie mall°   *club*
  The monster mercilesse him made to fall,
  Whose fall did never foe before behold;
  And now in darkesome dungeon, wretched thrall,
  Remedilesse, for aie° he doth him hold;   *ever*
This is my cause of griefe, more great, then may be told.'

52

Ere she had ended all, she gan to faint:
  But he her comforted and faire bespake,
  'Certes, Madame, ye have great cause of plaint,
  That stoutest heart, I weene, could cause to quake.
  But be of cheare, and comfort to you take:
  For till I have acquit° your captive knight,   *freed*
  Assure your selfe, I will you not forsake.'
  His chearefull words revived her chearelesse spright,
So forth they went, the Dwarfe them guiding ever right.

CANTO 8 [136]

Faire virgin to redeeme her deare
  brings Arthur to the fight:
Who slayes the Gyant, wounds the beast,
  and strips Duessa quight.

1

Ay me, how many perils doe enfold
  The righteous man, to make him daily fall?
  Were not, that heavenly grace doth him uphold,

And stedfast truth acquite him out of all.
Her love is firme, her care continuall,
So oft as he through his owne foolish pride,
Or weaknesse is to sinfull bands° made thrall: *bonds*
Else should this Redcrosse knight in bands have dyde,
For whose deliverance she this Prince doth thither guide.

2

They sadly traveild thus, untill they came
  Nigh to a castle builded strong and hie:
  Then cryde the Dwarfe, 'lo yonder is the same,
  In which my Lord my liege doth lucklesse lie,
  Thrall to that Gyants hatefull tyrannie:
  Therefore, deare Sir, your mightie powres assay.'
  The noble knight alighted by and by°   *immediately*
  From loftie steede, and bad the Ladie stay,
To see what end of fight should him befall that day.

3

So with the Squire, th'admirer of his might,
  He marched forth towards that castle wall;
  Whose gates he found fast shut, ne living wight
  To ward° the same, nor answere commers call.   *guard*
  Then tooke that Squire an horne of bugle° small,   *wild ox*
  Which hong adowne his side in twisted gold,
  And tassels gay. Wyde wonders over all
  Of that same hornes great vertues weren told.
Which had approved° bene in uses manifold.[137]   *proven*

4

Was never wight, that heard that shrilling sound,
  But trembling feare did feele in every vaine;
  Three miles it might be easie heard around,
  And Ecchoes three answerd it selfe againe:
  No false enchauntment, nor deceiptfull traine
  Might once abide the terror of that blast,
  But presently° was voide and wholly vaine°:   *immediately/futile*
  No gate so strong, no locke so firme and fast,
But with that percing noise flew open quite, or brast.°   *burst*

5

The same before the Geants gate he blew,
  That all the castle quaked from the ground,
  And every dore of freewill open flew.

The Gyant selfe dismaied with that sownd,
Where he with his Duessa dalliance fownd,
In hast came rushing forth from inner bowre,
With staring countenance sterne, as one astownd,
And staggering steps, to weet, what suddein stowre°   *disturbance*
Had wrought that horror strange, and dared his dreaded powre.

6

And after him the proud Duessa came,
  High mounted on her manyheaded beast,
  And every head with fyrie tongue did flame,
  And every head was crowned on his creast,
  And bloudie mouthed with late cruell feast.
  That when the knight beheld, his mightie shild
  Upon his manly arme he soone addrest,°   *placed*
  And at him fiercely flew, with courage fild,
And eger greedinesse° through every member thrild.   *desire*

7

Therewith the Gyant buckled him to fight,[138]
  Inflamed with scornefull wrath and high disdaine,
  And lifting up his dreadfull club on hight,
  All armed with ragged snubbes° and knottie graine,   *knobbles*
  Him thought at first encounter to have slaine.
  But wise and warie was that noble Pere,
  And lightly leaping from so monstrous maine,°   *assault*
  Did faire avoide the violence him nere;
It booted nought, to thinke, such thunderbolts to beare.[139]

8

Ne shame he thought to shunne so hideous might:
  The idle° stroke, enforcing furious way,   *futile*
  Missing the marke of his misaymed sight
  Did fall to ground, and with his° heavie sway°   *its/force*
  So deepely dinted in the driven clay,
  That three yardes deepe a furrow up did throw:
  The sad earth wounded with so sore assay,°   *assault*
  Did grone full grievous underneath the blow,
And trembling with strange feare, did like an earthquake show.

9

As when almightie Jove in wrathfull mood,
  To wreake° the guilt of mortall sins is bent,   *punish*
  Hurles forth his thundring dart with deadly food,°   *feud*

Enrold in flames, and smouldring dreriment,
Through riven cloudes and molten firmament;
The fierce threeforked engin° making way,   *dart*
Both loftie towres and highest trees hath rent,
And all that might his angrie passage stay,
And shooting in the earth, casts up a mount of clay.

10

His boystrous° club, so buried in the ground,   *rough*
He could not rearen up againe so light,   *easily*
But that the knight him at avantage found,
And whiles he strove his combred clubbe to quight°   *free*
Out of the earth, with blade all burning bright
He smote off his left arme, which like a blocke
Did fall to ground, deprived of native might;
Large streames of bloud out of the truncked stocke
Forth gushed, like fresh water streame from riven rocke.[140]

11

Dismaied with so desperate deadly wound,
And eke impatient of° unwonted° paine,   *with/unaccustomed*
He loudly brayd with beastly yelling sound,
That all the fields rebellowed againe;
As great a noyse, as when in Cymbrian plaine
An heard of Bulles, whom kindly rage° doth sting,   *natural urge*
Do for the milkie mothers want° complaine,   *absence*
And fill the fields with troublous bellowing,
The neighbour woods around with hollow murmur ring.

12

That when his deare Duessa heard, and saw
The evill stownd, that daungered her estate,   *plight*
Unto his aide she hastily did draw
Her dreadfull beast, who swolne with bloud of late
Came ramping forth with proud presumpteous gate,
And threatned all his heads like flaming brands.
But him the Squire made quickly to retrate,
Encountring fierce with single° sword in hand,   *only*
And twixt him and his Lord did like a bulwarke stand.

13

The proud Duessa full of wrathfull spight,
And fierce disdaine, to be affronted so,
Enforst her purple beast with all her might

That stop° out of the way to overthroe,   *obstacle*
    Scorning the let° of so unequall foe: *hindrance*
    But nathemore° would that courageous swayne   *not at all*
    To her yeeld passage, gainst his Lord to goe,
    But with outrageous strokes did him restraine,
And with his bodie bard the way atwixt them twaine.

14

Then tooke the angrie witch her golden cup,[141]
    Which still she bore, replete with magick artes;
    Death and despeyre did many thereof sup,
    And secret poyson through their inner parts,
    Th'eternall bale° of heavie wounded harts;   *distress*
    Which after charmes and some enchauntments said,
    She lightly sprinkled on his weaker parts;
    Therewith his sturdie courage soone was quayd,°   *daunted*
And all his senses were with suddeine dread dismayd.

15

So downe he fell before the cruell beast,
    Who on his necke his bloudie clawes did seize,
    That life nigh crusht out of his panting brest:
    No powre he had to stirre, nor will to rize.
    That when the carefull° knight gan well avise,°   *full of care/notice*
    He lightly left the foe, with whom he fought,
    And to the beast gan turne his enterprise;
    For wondrous anguish in his hart it wrought,
To see his loved Squire into such thraldome brought.

16

And high advauncing his bloud-thirstie blade,
    Stroke one of those deformed heads so sore,
    That of his puissance proud ensample made;
    His monstrous scalpe° downe to his teeth it tore,   *skull*
    And that misformed shape mis-shaped more:
    A sea of bloud gusht from the gaping wound,
    That her gay garments staynd with filthy gore,
    And overflowed all the field around;
That over shoes in bloud he waded on the ground.

17

Thereat he roared for exceeding paine,
    That to have heard, great horror would have bred,
    And scourging th'emptie ayre with his long traine,

Through great impatience° of his grieved hed   *pain*
His gorgeous ryder from her loftie sted
Would have cast downe, and trod in durtie myre,
Had not the Gyant soone her succoured;
Who all enraged with smart and franticke yre,
Came hurtling in full fierce, and forst the knight retyre.

                                    18

The force, which wont in two to be disperst,
    In one alone left° hand he new unites,   *remaining*
    Which is through rage more strong then both were erst;
    With which his hideous club aloft he dites,°   *brandishes*
    And at his foe with furious rigour smites,
    That strongest Oake might seeme to overthrow:
    The stroke upon his shield so heavie lites,
    That to the ground it doubleth him full low:
What mortall wight could ever beare so monstrous blow?

                                    19

And in his fall his shield, that covered was,
    Did loose his vele by chaunce, and open flew:
    The light whereof, that heavens light did pas,°   *surpass*
    Such blazing brightnesse through the aier threw,
    That eye mote not the same endure to vew.
    Which when the Gyaunt spyde with staring eye,
    He downe let fall his arme, and soft withdrew
    His weapon huge, that heaved was on hye
For to have slaine the man, that on the ground did lye.

                                    20

And eke the fruitfull-headed° beast, amazed   *many-headed*
    At flashing beames of that sunshiny shield,
    Became starke blind, and all his senses dazed,
    That downe he tumbled on the durtie field,
    And seemed himselfe as conquered to yield.
    Whom when his maistresse proud perceived to fall,
    Whiles yet his feeble feet for faintnesse reeld,
    Unto the Gyant loudly she gan call,
'O helpe Orgoglio, helpe, or else we perish all.'

                                    21

At her so pitteous cry was much amooved
    Her champion stout, and for to ayde his frend,
    Againe his wonted angry weapon prooved°:   *tried*

But all in vaine: for he has read his end
In that bright shield, and all their forces spend
Themselves in vaine: for since that glauncing sight,
He hath no powre to hurt, nor to defend;
As where th'Almighties lightning brond does light,
It dimmes the dazed eyen, and daunts the senses quight.

22

Whom when the Prince, to battell new addrest,
And threatning high his dreadfull stroke did see,
His sparkling blade about his head he blest,°   *waved*
And smote off quite his right leg by the knee,
That downe he tombled; as an aged tree,
High growing on the top of rocky clift,
Whose hartstrings with keene steele nigh hewen be,
The mightie trunck halfe rent, with ragged rift
Doth roll adowne the rocks, and fall with fearefull drift.°   *force*

23

Or as a Castle reared high and round,
By subtile engins and malitious slight°   *trickery*
Is undermined from the lowest ground,
And her foundation forst,° and feebled quight,   *undermined*
At last downe falles, and with her heaped hight
Her hastie ruine does more heavie° make,   *overwhelming*
And yields it selfe unto the victours might;
Such was this Gyaunts fall, that seemd to shake
The stedfast globe of earth, as it for feare did quake.

24

The knight then lightly leaping to the pray,
With mortall steele him smot againe so sore,
That headlesse his unweldy bodie lay,
All wallowd in his owne fowle bloudy gore,
Which flowed from his wounds in wondrous store.
But soone as breath out of his breast did pas,
That huge great body, which the Gyaunt bore,
Was vanisht quite, and of that monstrous mas
Was nothing left, but like an emptie bladder was.

25

Whose grievous fall, when false Duessa spide,
Her golden cup she cast unto the ground,
And crowned mitre rudely threw aside;

Such percing griefe her stubborne hart did wound,
That she could not endure that dolefull stound,°   *attack*
But leaving all behind her, fled away:
The light-foot Squire her quickly turnd around,
And by hard meanes enforcing her to stay,
So brought unto his Lord, as his deserved pray.

26

The royall Virgin, which beheld from farre,
    In pensive plight, and sad perplexitie,
    The whole atchievement° of this doubtfull warre,   *outcome*
    Came running fast to greet his victorie,
    With sober gladnesse, and myld modestie,
    And with sweet joyous cheare him thus bespake;
    "Faire braunch of noblesse, flowre of chevalrie,
    That with your worth the world amazed make,
How shall I quite° the paines, ye suffer for my sake?   *requite*

27

And you° fresh bud of vertue springing fast,   *i.e. Timias*
    Whom these sad eyes saw nigh unto deaths dore,
    What hath poore Virgin for such perill past,
    Wherewith you to reward? Accept therefore
    My simple selfe, and service evermore;
    And he that high does sit, and all things see
    With equall° eyes, their merites to restore,°   *impartial/reward*
    Behold what ye this day have done for mee,
And what I cannot quite, requite with usuree.[142]

28

But sith the heavens, and your faire handeling
    Have made you maister of the field this day,
    Your fortune maister eke with governing,[143]
    And well begun end all so well, I pray,
    Ne let that wicked woman scape away;
    For she it is, that did my Lord bethrall,
    My dearest Lord, and deepe in dongeon lay,
    Where he his better dayes hath wasted all.
O heare, how piteous he to you for ayd does call.'

29

Forthwith he gave in charge unto his Squire,
    That scarlot whore to keepen carefully;
    Whiles he himselfe with greedie° great desire   *eager*

Into the Castle entred forcibly,
Where living creature none he did espye;
Then gan he lowdly through the house to call:
But no man cared to answere to his crye.
There raignd a solemne silence over all,
Nor voice was heard, nor wight was seene in bowre or hall.

30

At last with creeping crooked pace forth came
An old old man, with beard as white as snow,
That on a staffe his feeble steps did frame,   *support*
And guide his wearie gate both too and fro:
For his eye sight him failed long ygo,
And on his arme a bounch of keyes he bore,
The which unused rust did overgrow:
Those were the keyes of every inner dore,
But he could not them use, but kept them still in store.

31

But very uncouth° sight was to behold,   *strange*
How he did fashion his untoward° pace,   *awkward*
For as he forward mooved his footing old,
So backward still was turnd his wrincled face,[144]
Unlike to men, who ever as they trace,°   *walk*
Both feet and face one way are wont to lead.
This was the auncient keeper of that place,
And foster father of the Gyant dead;
His name Ignaro° did his nature right aread.°   *Ignorance|describe*

32

His reverend haires and holy gravitie
The knight much honord, as beseemed well,°   *was proper*
And gently askt, where all the people bee,
Which in that stately building wont to dwell.
Who answerd him full soft, he could not tell.
Againe he askt, where that same knight was layd,
Whom great Orgoglio with his puissaunce fell
Had made his caytive° thrall; againe he sayde, *captive*
He could not tell: ne ever other answere made.

33

Then asked he, which way he in might pas:
He could not tell, againe he answered.
Thereat the curteous knight displeased was,

And said, 'Old sire, it seemes thou hast not red°   *discovered*
How ill it sits with that same silver hed
In vaine to mocke, or mockt in vaine to bee:
But if thou be, as thou art pourtrahed
With natures pen, in ages grave degree,
Aread° in graver wise, what I demaund of thee.'   *tell*

34

His answere likewise was, he could not tell.
   Whose sencelesse speach, and doted° ignorance   *stupid*
   When as the noble Prince had marked well,
   He ghest his nature by his countenance,
   And calmd his wrath with goodly temperance.
   Then to him stepping, from his arme did reach
   Those keyes, and made himselfe free enterance.
   Each dore he opened without any breach°;   *forcing*
There was no barre to stop, nor foe him to empeach.°   *oppose*

35

There all within full rich arayd he found,
   With royall arras° and resplendent gold.   *tapestry*
   And did with store of every thing abound,
   That greatest Princes presence might behold.
   But all the floore (too filthy to be told)
   With blood of guiltlesse babes, and innocents trew,[145]
   Which there were slaine, as sheepe out of the fold,
   Defiled was, that dreadfull was to vew,
And sacred° ashes over it was strowed new.   *accursed*

36

And there beside of marble stone was built
   An Altare, carved with cunning imagery,
   On which true Christians bloud was often spilt,
   And holy Martyrs often doen to dye,[146]
   With cruell malice and strong tyranny:
   Whose blessed sprites from underneath the stone
   To God for vengeance cryde continually,
   And with great griefe were often heard to grone,
That hardest heart would bleede, to heare their piteous mone.

37

Through every rowme he sought, and every bowr,
   But no where could he find that wofull thrall°:   *prisoner*
   At last he came unto an yron doore,

That fast was lockt, but key found not at all
Emongst that bounch, to open it withall;
But in the same a little grate was pight,°   *placed*
Through which he sent his voyce, and lowd did call
With all his powre, to weet, if living wight
Were housed therewithin, whom he enlargen° might.   *free*

38

Therewith an hollow, dreary, murmuring voyce
These piteous plaints and dolours did resound;
'O who is that, which brings me happy choyce
Of death, that here lye dying every stound,°   *moment*
Yet live perforce in balefull darkenesse bound?
For now three Moones have changed thrice their hew,°   *shape*
And have beene thrice hid underneath the ground,
Since I the heavens chearefull face did vew,
O welcome thou, that doest of death bring tydings trew.'

39

Which when that Champion heard, with percing point
Of pitty deare° his hart was thrilled sore,   *grievous*
And trembling horrour ran through every joynt,
For ruth of gentle knight so fowle forlore°:   *lost*
Which shaking off, he rent that yron dore,
With furious force, and indignation fell;
Where entred in, his foot could find no flore,
But all a deepe descent, as darke as hell,
That breathed ever forth a filthie banefull smell.

40

But neither darkenesse fowle, nor filthy bands,
Nor noyous° smell his purpose could withhold,   *poisonous*
(Entire° affection hateth nicer° hands)   *genuine/over-fastidious*
But that with constant zeale, and courage bold,
After long paines and labours manifold,
He found the meanes that Prisoner up to reare;
Whose feeble thighes, unhable to uphold
His pined° corse, him scarse to light could beare,   *wasted*
A ruefull spectacle of death and ghastly drere.°   *wretchedness*

41

His sad dull eyes deepe sunck in hollow pits,
Could not endure th'unwonted sunne to view;
His bare thin cheekes for want of better bits,°   *food*

And empty sides deceived° of their dew,   *deprived/vital juices*
  Could make a stony hart his hap to rew;
  His rawbone armes, whose mighty brawned bowrs°   *muscles*
  Were wont to rive steele plates, and helmets hew,
  Were cleane consumed, and all his vitall powres
Decayd, and all his flesh shronk up like withered flowres.

42

Whom when his Lady saw, to him she ran
  With hasty joy: to see him made her glad,
  And sad to view his visage pale and wan,
  Who earst in flowres of freshest youth was clad.
  Tho° when her well of teares she wasted had,   *then*
  She said, 'Ah dearest Lord, what evill starre
  On you hath fround, and pourd his influence bad,
  That of your selfe ye thus berobbed arre,
And this misseeming hew° your manly looks doth marre?   *appearance*

43

But welcome now my Lord, in wele or woe,
  Whose presence I have lackt too long a day;
  And fie on Fortune mine avowed foe,
  Whose wrathfull wreakes° them selves do now alay.   *revenges*
  And for these wrongs shall treble penaunce pay
  Of treble good: good growes of evils priefe.°   *experience*
  The chearelesse man, whom sorrow did dismay,
  Had no delight to treaten° of his griefe;   *talk*
His long endured famine needed more reliefe.

44

'Faire Lady,' then said that victorious knight,°   *i.e. Arthur*
  'The things, that grievous were to do, or beare,
  Them to renew,° I wote, breeds no delight;   *recall*
  Best musicke breeds delight in loathing eare:
  But th'onely good, that growes of passed feare,
  Is to be wise, and ware° of like agein.°   *wary/again*
  This dayes ensample hath this lesson deare
  Deepe written in my heart with yron pen,
That blisse may not abide in state of mortall men.

45

Henceforth sir knight, take to you wonted strength,
  And maister these mishaps with patient might;
  Loe where your foe lyes stretcht in monstrous length,

And loe that wicked woman in your sight,
The roote of all your care, and wretched plight,
Now in your powre, to let her live, or dye.'
'To do her dye,° quoth Una, 'were despight,°   *kill/spiteful*
And shame t'avenge so weake an enimy;
But spoile° her of her scarlot robe, and let her fly.'   *despoil*

46

So as she bàd, that witch they disaraid,
    And robd of royall robes, and purple pall,
    And ornaments that richly were displaid;
    Ne spared they to strip her naked all.
    Then when they had despoild her tire° and call,°   *attire/netted cap*
    Such as she was, their eyes might her behold,
    That her misshaped parts did them appall,
    A loathly, wrinckled hag, ill favoured, old,
Whose secret filth good manners biddeth not be told.

47

Her craftie head was altogether bald,
    And as in hate of honorable eld,°   *age*
    Was overgrowne with scurfe and filthy scald°;   *scabs*
    Her teeth out of her rotten gummes were feld,°   *fallen*
    And her sowre breath abhominably smeld;
    Her dried dugs, like bladders lacking wind,
    Hong downe, and filthy matter from them weld;
    Her wrizled° skin as rough, as maple rind,   *wrinkled*
So scabby was, that would have loathd all womankind.

48

Her neather parts, the shame of all her kind,
    My chaster Muse for shame doth blush to write;
    But at her rompe° she growing had behind   *rump*
    A foxes taile, with dong all fowly dight;°   *smeared*
    And eke her feet most monstrous were in sight;
    For one of them was like an Eagles claw,
    With griping talaunts° armd to greedy fight,   *talons*
    The other like a Beares uneven° paw:[147]   *rough*
More ugly shape yet never living creature saw.

49

Which when the knights beheld, amazd they were,
    And wondred at so fowle deformed wight.
    'Such then,' said Una, 'as she seemeth here,

Such is the face of falshood, such the sight
Of fowle Duessa, when her borrowed light
Is laid away, and counterfesaunce° knowne.'   *deception*
Thus when they had the witch disrobed quight,
And all her filthy feature° open showne,   *appearance*
They let her goe at will, and wander wayes unknowne.

50

She flying fast from heavens hated face,
And from the world that her discovered wide,°   *everywhere revealed her*
Fled to the wastfull wildernesse apace,
From living eyes her open shame to hide,
And lurkt in rocks and caves long unespide.
But that faire crew of knights, and Una faire
Did in that castle afterwards abide,
To rest them selves, and weary powres repaire,
Where store they found of all, that dainty was and rare.

CANTO 9

His loves and lignage Arthur tells:
The Knights knit friendly bands:
Sir Trevisan flies from Despayre,
Whom Redcrosse knight withstands.

1

O goodly golden chaine, wherewith yfere°   *together*
The vertues linked are in lovely wize:
And noble minds of yore allyed were,
In brave poursuit of chevalrous emprize,°   *enterprise*
That none did other safety despize,
Nor aid envy° to him, in need that stands,   *begrudge*
But friendly each did others prayse devize
How to advaunce with favourable hands,
As this good Prince redeemd the Redcrosse knight from bands.

2

Who when their powres, empaird through labour long,
With dew° repast they had recured° well,   *due/restored*
And that weake captive wight now wexed strong,
Them list no lenger there at leasure dwell,
But forward fare, as their adventures fell,°   *befell*

But ere they parted, Una faire besought
That straunger knight his name and nation tell;
Least so great good, as he for her had wrought,
Should die unknown, and buried be in thanklesse thought.

3

'Faire virgin,' said the prince, 'ye me require
    A thing without the compas° of my wit: *scope*
    For both the lignage and the certain Sire,
    From which I sprong, from me are hidden yit.
    For all so soone as life did me admit
    Into this world, and shewed heavens light,
    From mothers pap I taken was unfit°:   *unsuitably*
    And streight delivered to a Faery knight,
To be upbrought in gentle thewes° and martiall might.   *manners*

4

Unto old Timon he me brought bylive°,   *immediately*
    Old Timon, who in youthly yeares hath beene
    In warlike feates th'expertest man alive,
    And is the wisest now on earth I weene;
    His dwelling is low in a valley greene,
    Under the foot of Rauran mossy hore°,   *grey*
    From whence the river Dee as silver cleene°   *clear*
    His tombling billowes rolls with gentle rore:
There all my dayes he traind me up in vertuous lore.

5

Thither the great Magicien Merlin came,
    As was his use, ofttimes to visit me:
    For he had charge my discipline to frame,
    And Tutours nouriture° to oversee.   *training*
    Him oft and oft I askt in privitie,
    Of what loines and what lignage I did spring:
    Whose aunswere bad me still assured bee,
    That I was sonne and heire unto a king,
As time in her just terme° the truth to light should bring.'   *at the proper*
                                                                   time

6

'Well worthy impe°,' said then the Lady gent°,   *child/gentle*
    'And Pupill fit for such a Tutours hand.
    But what adventure, or what high intent
    Hath brought you hither into Faery land,
    Aread° Prince Arthur, crowne of Martiall band?'   *tell*

'Full hard it is,' quoth he, 'to read° aright   *understand*
  The course of heavenly cause, or understand
  The secret meaning of th'eternall might,
That rules mens wayes, and rules the thoughts of living wight.

                              7

For whither he through fatall° deepe foresight   *ordained by fate*
  Me hither sent, for cause to me unghest,
  Or that fresh bleeding wound,¹⁴⁸ which day and night
  Whilome° doth rancle in my riven brest,   *continuously*
  With forced fury following his° behest,   *its*
  Me hither brought by wayes yet never found,
  You to have helpt I hold my selfe yet blest.'
  'Ah curteous knight,' quoth she, 'what secret wound
Could ever find, to grieve the gentlest hart on ground?'

                              8

'Deare Dame,' quoth he, 'you sleeping sparkes awake,
  Which troubled once, into huge flames will grow,
  Ne ever will their fervent fury slake,
  Till living moysture into smoke do flow,
  And wasted life do lye in ashes low.
  Yet sithens° silence lesseneth not my fire,   *since*
  But told it flames, and hidden it does glow,
  I will revele, what ye so much desire:
Ah Love, lay downe thy bow, the whiles I may respire.°   *breathe*

                              9

It was in freshest flowre of youthly yeares,
  When courage first does creepe in manly chest,
  Then first the coale of kindly° heat appeares   *natural*
  To kindle love in every living brest;
  But me had warnd old Timons wise behest,°   *bidding*
  Those creeping flames by reason to subdew,
  Before their rage grew to so great unrest,
  As miserable lovers use to rew,
Which still wex old in woe, whiles woe still wexeth new.

                              10

That idle name of love, and lovers life,
  As losse of time, and vertues enimy
  I ever scornd, and joyd to stirre up strife,
  In middest of their mournfull Tragedy,
  Ay wont to laugh, when them I heard to cry,

And blow the fire, which them to ashes brent°:   *burnt*
Their God himselfe,° grieved at my libertie,   *i.e. Cupid*
Shot many a dart at me with fiers intent,
But I them warded all with wary government.°   *self-control*

11

But all in vaine: no fort can be so strong,
  Ne fleshly brest can armed be so sound,
  But will at last be wonne with battrie long,
  Or unawares at disavantage found;
  Nothing is sure, that growes on earthly ground:
  And who most trustes in arme of fleshly might,
  And boasts, in beauties chaine not to be bound,
  Doth soonest fall in disaventrous° fight,   *disastrous*
And yeeldes his caytive neck to victours most despight.°   *greatest malice*

12

Ensample make of him your haplesse joy,
  And of my selfe now mated,° as ye see,   *overcome*
  Whose prouder vaunt that proud avenging boy°   *i.e. Cupid*
  Did soone pluck downe, and curbd my libertie.
  For on a day prickt° forth with jollitie   *urged*
  Of looser° life, and heat of hardiment,°   *freer/boldness*
  Raunging the forest wide on courser free,
  The fields, the floods, the heavens with one consent
Did seeme to laugh on me, and favour mine intent.

13

For-wearied with my sports, I did alight
  From loftie steed, and downe to sleepe me layd;
  The verdant gras my couch did goodly dight,°   *provide*
  And pillow was my helmet faire displayd:
  Whiles every sence the humour sweet embayd,°   *pervaded*
  And slombring soft my hart did steale away,
  Me seemed, by my side a royall Mayd
  Her daintie limbes full softly down did lay:
So faire a creature yet saw never sunny day.

14

Most goodly glee° and lovely blandishment°   *pleasure/cajolery*
  She to me made, and bad me love her deare,
  For dearely sure her love was to me bent,
  As when just time expired should appeare.
  But whether dreames delude, or true it were,

Was never hart so ravisht with delight,
Ne living man like words did ever heare,
As she to me delivered all that night;
And at her parting said, She Queene of Faeries hight°.   *was called*

15

When I awoke, and found her place devoyd,
And nought but pressed gras, where she had lyen,
I sorrowed all so much, as earst I joyd,
And washed all her place with watry eyen.
From that day forth I loved that face divine;
From that day forth I cast° in carefull mind,   *determined*
To seeke her out with labour, and long tyne°,   *suffering*
And never vow to rest, till her I find,
Nine monethes I seeke in vaine yet ni'll° that vow unbind.'   *will not*

16

Thus as he spake, his visage wexed pale,
And chaunge of hew great passion did bewray°;   *reveal*
Yet still he strove to cloke his inward bale°,   *grief*
And hide the smoke, that did his fire display,
Till gentle Una thus to him gan say;
'O happy Queene of Faeries, that hast found
Mongst many, one that with his prowesse may
Defend thine honour, and thy foes confound:
True Loves are often sown, but seldom grow on ground.'

17

'Thine, O then,' said the gentle Redcrosse knight,
'Next to that Ladies love, shalbe the place,
O fairest virgin, full of heavenly light,
Whose wondrous faith, exceeding earthly race,
Was firmest fixt in mine extremest case°.   *plight*
And you, my Lord, the Patrone° of my life,   *protector*
Of that great Queene may well gaine worthy grace:
For onely worthy you through prowes priefe°   *trial*
Yf living man mote worthy be, to be her liefe°.'   *beloved*

18

So diversly discoursing of their loves,
The golden Sunne his glistring head gan shew,
And sad remembraunce now the Prince amoves,
With fresh desire his voyage to pursew:
Als° Una earnd° her traveill to renew.   *also[yearned*

Then those two knights, fast friendship for to bynd,
And love establish each to other trew,
Gave goodly gifts, the signes of gratefull mynd,
And eke as pledges firme, right hands together joynd.

19

Prince Arthur gave a boxe of Diamond sure,   *perfect*
  Embowd° with gold and gorgeous ornament,   *encircled*
  Wherein were closd few drops of liquor pure,[149]
  Of wondrous worth, and vertue excellent,
  That any wound could heale incontinent°:   *immediately*
  Which to requite, the Redcrosse knight him gave   *repay*
  A booke, wherein his Saveours testament
  Was writ with golden letters rich and brave;
A worke of wondrous grace, and able soules to save.

20

Thus beene they parted, Arthur on his way
  To seeke his love, and th'other for to fight
  With Unaes foe, that all her realme did pray.   *prey upon*
  But she now weighing the decayed plight,
  And shrunken synewes of her chosen knight,
  Would not a while her forward course pursew,
  Ne bring him forth in face of dreadfull fight,
  Till he recovered had his former hew:
For him to be yet weake and wearie well she knew.

21

So as they traveild, lo they gan espy
  An armed knight towards them gallop fast,
  That seemed from some feared foe to fly,
  Or other griesly thing, that him agast.   *terrified*
  Still as he fled, his eye was backward cast,
  As if his feare still followed him behind;
  Als flew his steed, as he his bands had brast,   *burst*
  And with his winged heeles did tread the wind,
As he had beene a fole of Pegasus his kind.

22

Nigh as he drew, they might perceive his head
  To be unarmd, and curld uncombed heares
  Upstaring° stiffe, dismayd with uncouth dread;   *standing up*
· Nor drop of bloud in all his face appeares
  Nor life in limbe: and to increase his feares,

In fowle reproch of knighthoods faire degree,   *condition*
  About his neck an hempen rope he weares,
  That with his glistring armes does ill agree;
But he of rope or armes has now no memoree.

23

The Redcrosse knight toward him crossed fast,
  To weet, what mister° wight was so dismayd: *kind of*
  There him he finds all sencelesse and aghast,
  That of him selfe he seemd to be afrayd;
  Whom hardly he from flying forward stayd,
  Till he these wordes to him deliver might;
  'Sir knight, aread° who hath ye thus arayd,   *tell*
  And eke from whom make ye this hasty flight:
For never knight I saw in such misseeming° plight.'   *unseemly*

24

He answerd nought at all, but adding new
  Feare to his first amazment, staring wide
  With stony eyes, and hartlesse hollow hew°,   *expression*
  Astonisht stood, as one that had aspide
  Infernall furies, with their chaines untide.
  Him yet againe, and yet againe bespake
  The gentle knight; who nought to him replide,
  But trembling every joynt did inly quake,
And foltring tongue at last these words seemd forth to shake.

25

'For Gods deare love, Sir knight, do me not stay°;   *hinder*
  For loe he comes, he comes fast after mee.'
  Eft° looking backe would faine have runne away;   *again*
  But he him forst to stay, and tellen free
  The secret cause of his perplexitie:
  Yet nathemore° by his bold hartie speach,   *in no way*
  Could his bloud-frosen hart emboldned bee,
  But through his boldnesse rather feare did reach°,   *penetrate*
Yet forst, at last he made through silence suddein breach.

26

'And am I now in safetie sure,' quoth he,
  'From him, that would have forced me to dye?
  And is the point of death now turnd fro mee,
  That I may tell this haplesse history?'
  'Feare nought:' quoth he, 'no daunger now is nye.'

'Then shall I you recount a ruefull cace,'
Said he, 'the which with this unlucky eye
   I late beheld, and had not greater grace
Me reft from it, had bene partaker of the place.[150]

27

I lately chaunst (Would I had never Chaunst)
   With a faire knight to keepen companee,
   Sir Terwin hight, that well himselfe advaunst
   In all affaires, and was both bold and free,
   But not so happie as mote happie bee:
   He loved, as was his lot, as Ladie gent,
   That him againe° loved in the least degree: *in return*
   For she was proud, and of too high intent,°   *aspirations*
And joyd to see her lover languish and lament.

28

From whom returning sad and comfortlesse,
   As on the way together we did fare,
   We met that villen (God from him me blesse°)   *protect*
   That cursed wight, from whom I scapt why leare,°   *recently*
   A man of hell, that cals himselfe Despaire:
   Who first us greets, and after faire areedes°   *tells*
   Of tydings strange, and of adventures rare,
   So creeping close, as Snake in hidden weedes,
Inquireth of our states, and of our knightly deedes.

29

Which when he knew, and felt our feeble harts
   Embost° with bale,° and bitter byting griefe,   *hard-pressed/sorrow*
   Which love had launched with his deadly darts,
   With wounding words and termes of foule repriefe,°   *reproach*
   He pluckt from us all hope of due reliefe,
   That earst us held in love of lingring life;
   Then hopelesse hartlesse, gan the cunning thiefe
   Perswade us die, to stint° all further strife: *end*
To me he lent this rope, to him a rustie knife.

30

With which sad instrument of hastie death,
   That wofull lover, loathing lenger light,
   A wide way made to let forth living breath.
   But I more fearefull, or more luckie wight,
   Dismayd with that deformed dismall sight,

Fled fast away, halfe dead with dying feare:
Ne yet assured of life by you, Sir knight,
Whose like infirmitie like chaunce may beare:
But God you never let his charmed speeches heare.'[151]

31

'How may a man,' said he, 'with idle speech   *i.e. Redcrosse knight*
  Be wonne, to spoyle° the Castle of his health?'   *despoil*
'I wote,' quoth he, 'whom triall° late did teach,   *i.e. despair*
  That like would not° for all this worldes wealth: *i.e. do it again*
  His subtill tongue, like dropping honny, mealt'th°   *melts*
  Into the hart, and searcheth every vaine,   *vein*
  That ere one be aware, by secret stealth
  His powre is reft, and weaknesse doth remaine.   *taken away*
O never Sir desire to try° his guilefull traine.'   *test/cunning*

32

'Certes,' said he, 'hence shall I never rest,   *i.e. Redcrosse knight*
  Till I that treachours art have heard and tride;
  And you Sir knight, whose name mote° I request,   *might*
  Of grace do me unto his cabin guide.'
  'I that hight Trevisan,' quoth he, 'will ride
  Against my liking backe, to doe you grace:
  But nor for gold nor glee° will I abide   *glitter*
  By you, when ye arrive in that same place;
For lever° had I die, then see his deadly face.'   *rather*

33

Ere long they come, where that same wicked wight
  His dwelling has, low in an hollow cave,
  Farre underneath a craggie clift ypight,   *placed*
  Darke, dolefull, drearie, like a greedie grave,
  That still for carrion carcases doth crave:
  On top whereof aye dwelt the ghastly Owle,
  Shrieking his balefull note, which ever drave
  Farre from that haunt all other chearefull fowle;
And all about it wandring ghostes did waile and howle.

34

And all about old stockes° and stubs of trees,   *stumps*
  Whereon nor fruit, nor leafe was ever seene,
  Did hang upon the ragged rocky knees°:   *crags*
  On which had many wretches hanged beene,
  Whose carcases were scattered on the greene,

And throwne about the cliffs. Arrived there,
That bare-head knight for dread and dolefull teene,°   *grief*
Would faine have fled, ne durst approchen neare,
But th'other forst him stay, and comforted in feare.

35

That darkesome cave they enter, where they find
  That cursed man, low sitting on the ground,
  Musing full sadly in his sullein mind;
  His griesie° lockes, long growen, and unbound,   *grizzled*
  Disordred hong about his shoulders round,
  And hid his face; through which his hollow eyne
  Lookt deadly dull, and stared as astound;
  His raw-bone cheekes through penurie and pine,°   *torment*
Were shronke into his jawes, as° he did never dine.   *as if*

36

His garment nought but many ragged clouts,°   *shreds*
  With thornes together pind° and patched was,   *pinned*
  The which his naked sides he wrapt abouts:
  And him beside there lay upon the gras
  A d'rearie corse, whose life away did pas
  All wallowd in his owne yet luke-warme blood,
  That from his wound yet welled fresh alas;
  In which a rustie knife fast fixed stood,
And made an open passage for the gushing flood.

37

Which piteous spectacle, approving° trew   *proving*
  The wofull tale that Trevisan had told,
  When as the gentle Redcrosse knight did vew,
  With firie zeale he burnt in courage bold,
  Him to avenge, before his bloud were cold,
  And to the villein° said, 'Thou damned wight,   *villain, i.e. Despair*
  The author of this fact,° we here behold,   *deed*
  What justice can but judge against thee right,
With thine owne bloud to price° his bloud, here shed   *pay for*
                    in sight.'[152]

38

'What franticke fit,' quoth he,° 'hath thus distraught   *i.e. Despair*
  Thee, foolish man, so rash a doome° to give?   *judgement*
  What justice ever other judgement taught,
  But he should die, who merites not to live?
  None else to death this man despayring drive,

But his owne guiltie mind deserving death.
Is then unjust to each his due to give?
Or let him die, that loatheth living breath?
Or let him die at ease, that liveth here uneath?°   *uneasily*

39

Who travels by the wearie wandring way,
    To come unto his wished home in haste,
    And meetes a flood, that doth his passage stay,
    Is not great grace to helpe him over past,
    Or free his feet, that in the myre sticke fast?
    Most envious man, that grieves at neighbours good,
    And fond,° that joyest in the woe thou hast,   *foolish*
    Why wilt not let him passe, that long hath stood
Upon the banke, yet wilt thy selfe not passe the flood?

40

He there does now enjoy eternall rest
    And happie ease, which thou doest want and crave,
    And further from it daily wanderest:
    What if some litle paine the passage have,
    That makes fraile flesh to feare the bitter wave?
    Is not short paine well borne, that brings long ease,
    And layes the soule to sleepe in quiet grave?
    Sleepe after toyle, port after stormie seas,
Ease after warre, death after life does greatly please.'

41

The knight much wondred at his suddeine wit,
    And said, 'The terme of life is limited,
    Ne may a man prolong, nor shorten it;
    The souldier may not move from watchfull sted,°   *post*
    Nor leave his stand, untill his Captaine bed:°   *bids*
    'Who life did limit by almightie doome,'
    Quoth he,° 'knowes best the termes established;   *i.e Despair*
    And he, that points° the Centonell his roome,°   *appoints/station*
Doth license him depart at sound of morning droome.°   *drum*

42

Is not his deed, what ever thing is donne,
    In heaven and earth? did not he all create
    To die againe? all ends that was begonne,
    Their times in his eternall booke of fate
    Are written sure, and have their certaine date.

Who then can strive with strong necessitie,
That holds the world in his° still chaunging state,   *its*
Or shunne the death ordaynd by destinie?
When houre of death is come, let none aske whence, nor why.

43

The lenger life, I wote the greater sin,
　The greater sin, the greater punishment:
　All those great battels, which thou boast to win,
　Through strife, and bloud-shed, and avengement,
　Now praysd, hereafter deare thou shalt repent:
　For life must life, and bloud must bloud repay.
　Is not enough thy evill life forespent°?   *already spent*
　For he, that once hath missed the right way,
The further he doth goe, the further he doth stray.

44

Then do no further goe, no further stray,
　But here lie downe, and to thy rest betake,
　Th'ill to prevent, that life ensewen may.[153]
　For what hath life, that may it loved make,
　And gives not rather cause it to forsake?
　Feare, sicknesse, age, losse, labour, sorrow, strife,
　Paine, hunger, cold, that makes the hart to quake;
　And ever fickle fortune rageth rife,
All which, and thousands mo° do make a loathsome life.   *more*

45

Thou wretched man, of death hast greatest need,
　If in true ballance thou wilt weigh thy state:
　For never knight, that dared warlike deede,
　More lucklesse disaventures did amate°:   *dismay*
　Witnesse the dongeon deepe, wherein of late
　Thy life shut up, for death so oft did call;
　And though good lucke prolonged hath thy date,°   *lifespan*
　Yet death then, would the like mishaps forestall,
Into the which hereafter thou maiest happen fall.

46

Why then doest thou, O man of sin, desire
　To draw thy dayes forth to their last degree?
　Is not the measure of thy sinfull hire
　High heaped up with huge iniquitie,
　Against the day of wrath, to burden thee?

Is not enough, that to this Ladie milde
Thou falsed hast thy faith with perjurie,
And sold thy selfe to serve Duessa vilde,°   *vile*
With whom in all abuse thou hast thy selfe defilde?

47

Is not he just, that all this doth behold
From highest heaven, and beares an equall° eye?   *impartial*
Shall he thy sins up in his knowledge fold,
And guiltie be of thine impietie?
Is not his law, Let every sinner die:
Die shall all flesh? what then must needs be donne,
Is it not better to doe willinglie,
Then linger, till the glasse be all out ronne?
Death is the end of woes: die soone, O faeries sonne.'

48

The knight was much enmoved with his speach,
That as a swords point through his hart did perse,
And in his conscience made a secret breach.
Well knowing true all, that he did reherse,°   *relate*
And to his fresh remembrance did reverse°   *review*
The ugly vew of his deformed crimes,
That all his manly powres it did disperse,
As he were charmed with inchaunted rimes,
That oftentimes he quakt, and fainted oftentimes.

49

In which amazement, when the Miscreant
Perceived him to waver weake and fraile,
Whiles trembling horror did his conscience dant,°   *daunt*
And hellish anguish did his soule assaile,
To drive him to despaire, and quite to quaile,° *become dismayed*
He shewed him painted in a table° plaine,   *picture*
The damned ghosts, that doe in torments waile,
And thousand feends that doe them endlesse paine
With fire and brimstone, which for ever shall remaine.

50

The sight whereof so throughly him dismaid,
That nought but death before his eyes he saw,
And ever burning wrath before him laid,
By righteous sentence of th'Almighties law:
Then gan the villein him to overcraw,°   *exult over*

And brought unto him swords, ropes, poison, fire,
And all that might him to perdition draw;
And bad him choose, what death he would desire:
For death was due to him, that had provokt Gods ire.

51

But when as none of them he saw him take,
  He to him raught° a dagger sharpe and keene,   *offered*
  And gave it him in hand: his hand did quake,
  And tremble like a leafe of Aspin° greene,[154]   *aspen*
  And troubled bloud through his pale face was seene
  To come, and goe with tydings from the hart,
  As it a running messenger had beene.
  At last resolved to worke his finall smart,
He lifted up his hand, that backe againe did start.

52

Which when as Una saw, through every vaine
  The crudled° cold ran to her well of life°,   *congealing/heart*
  As in a swowne: but soone relived° againe,   *revived*
  Out of his hand she snatcht the cursed knife,
  And threw it to the ground, enraged rife°,   *deeply*
  And to him said, 'Fie, fie, faint harted knight,
  What meanest thou by this reprochfull strife?
  Is this the battell, which thou vaunst to fight
With that fire-mouthed Dragon, horrible and bright?

53

Come, come away, fraile, feeble, fleshly wight°,   *creature*
  Ne let vaine words bewitch thy manly heart,
  Ne divelish thoughts dismay thy constant spright.
  In heavenly mercies hast thou not a part?
  Why shouldst thou then despeire, that chosen art?
  Where justice growes, there grows eke greater grace,
  The which doth quench the brond of hellish smart,
  And that accurst hand-writing doth deface°.   *blot out*
Arise, Sir knight arise, and leave this cursed place.'

54

So up he rose, and thence amounted° streight.   *mounted*
  Which when the carle° beheld, and saw his guest   *churl, i.e. Despair*
  Would safe depart, for all his subtill sleight,
  He chose an halter from among the rest,
  And with it hung himselfe, unbid° unblest.   *not prayed for*

But death he could not worke himselfe thereby;
For thousand times he so himselfe had drest,°   *made ready*
Yet nathelesse it could not doe him die,
Till he should die his last, that is eternally.

CANTO 10[155]

Her faithfull knight faire Una brings
    to house of Holinesse,
Where he is taught repentance, and
    the way to heavenly blesse°.   *bliss*

I

What man is he, that boasts of fleshly might,
  And vaine assurance° of mortality,°   *certainty/mortal life*
  Which all so soone, as it doth come to fight,
  Against spirituall foes, yeelds by and by,°   *immediately*
  Or from the field most cowardly doth fly?
  Ne let the man ascribe it to his skill
  That thorough grace hath gained victory.
  If any strength we have, it is to ill,
But all the good is Gods, both power and eke will.

2

By that, which lately hapned, Una saw,
  That this her knight was feeble, and too faint;
  And all his sinews woxen weake and raw,°   *exposed*
  Through long enprisonment, and hard constraint,
  Which he endured in his late restraint,
  That yet he was unfit for bloudie fight:
  Therefore to cherish him with diets daint,°   *dainty foods*
  She cast to bring him where he chearen° might,   *be refreshed*
Till he recovered had his° late decayed plight.   *from his*

3

There was an auntient house[156] not farre away,
  Renowmd throughout the world for sacred lore,
  And pure unspotted life: so well they say
  It governd was, and guided evermore,
  Through wisedome of a matrone grave and hore°;   *grey-haired*
  Whose onely joy was to relieve the needes
  Of wretched soules, and helpe the helpelesse pore:
  All night she spent in bidding of her bedes,°   *saying her rosary*
And all the day in doing good and godly deedes.

4

Dame Caelia[157] men did her call, as thought
  From heaven to come, or thither to arise,
  The mother of three daughters, well upbrought
  In goodly thewes,° and godly exercise: *manners*
  The eldest two most sober, chast, and wise,
  Fidelia and Speranza virgins were,
  Though spousd,° yet wanting wedlocks solemnize;   *betrothed*
  But faire Charissa to a lovely fere°   *mate*
Was lincked, and by him had many pledges dere.[158]

5

Arrived there, the dore they find fast lockt;
  For it was warely° watched night and day,   *warily*
  For feare of many foes: but when they knockt,
  The Porter opened unto them streight way:
  He was an aged syre, all hory gray,
  With lookes full lowly cast, and gate full slow,
  Wont on a staffe his feeble steps to stay,
  Hight Humilta°. They passe in stouping low;   *humility*
For streight and narrow was the way, which he did show.[159]

6

Each goodly thing is hardest to begin,
  But entred in a spacious court they see,
  Both plaine, and pleasant to be walked in,
  Where them does meete a francklin° faire and free,   *landowner*
  And entertaines with comely courteous glee.
  His name was Zele, that him right well became,
  For in his speeches and behaviour hee
  Did labour lively to expresse the same,
And gladly did them guide, till to the Hall they came.

7

There fairely them receives a gentle Squire,
  Of milde demeanure, and rare courtesie,
  Right cleanly clad in comely sad° attire;   *sober*
  In word and deede that shewed great modestie,
  And knew his good° to all of each degree,   *proper behaviour*
  Hight Reverence. He them with speeches meet
  Does faire entreat; no courting nicetie,°   *affectation*
  But simple true, and eke unfained sweet,
As might become a Squire so great persons to greet.

8

And afterwards them to his Dame he leades,
    That aged Dame, the Ladie of the place:
    Who all this while was busie at her beades°:   *rosary*
    Which doen, she up arose with seemely grace,
    And toward them full matronely did pace.
    Where when that fairest Una she beheld,
    Whom well she knew to spring from heavenly race,
    Her hart with joy unwonted° inly sweld,   *unaccustomed*
As feeling wondrous comfort in her weaker eld°.   *old age*

9

And her embracing said, 'O happie earth,
    Whereon thy innocent feet doe ever tread,
    Most vertuous virgin borne of heavenly berth,
    That to redeeme thy woefull parents head,
    From tyrans rage, and ever-dying dread,[160]
    Hast wandred through the world now long a day;
    Yet ceasest not thy wearie soles to lead,
    What grace hath thee now hither brought this way?
Or doen thy feeble feet unweeting° hither stray?   *unwittingly*

10

Strange thing it is an errant° knight to see   *wandering*
    Here in this place, or any other wight,
    That hither turnes his steps. So few there bee,
    That chose the narrow path, or seeke the right:
    All keepe the broad high way, and take delight
    With many rather for to go astray,
    And be partakers of their evill plight,
    Then with a few to walke the rightest way;
O foolish men, why haste ye to your owne decay?'

11

'Thy selfe to see, and tyred limbs to rest,
    O matrone sage,' quoth she, 'I hither came,
    And this good knight his way with me addrest°,   *directed*
    Led with thy prayses and broad-blazed fame,
    That up to heaven is blowne.' The auncient Dame
    Him goodly greeted in her modest guise,
    And entertaynd them both, as best became,
    With all the court'sies, that she could devise,
Ne wanted ought, to shew her bounteous or wise.

12

Thus as they gan of sundry things devise,°   *talk*
   Loe two most goodly virgins came in place,
   Ylinked arme in arme in lovely° wise,   *loving*
   With countenance demure, and modest grace, ·
   They numbred even steps and equall pace:
   Of which the eldest, that Fidelia hight,
   Like sunny beames threw from her Christall[161] face,
   That could have dazd the rash beholders sight,
And round about her head did shine like heavens light.

13

She was araied all in lilly white,[162]
   And in her right hand bore a cup of gold,
   With wine and water fild up to the hight,°   *top*
   In which a Serpent did himselfe enfold,
   That horrour made to all, that did behold;
   But she no whit did chaunge her constant mood°:   *expression*
   And in her other hand she fast did hold
   A booke, that was both signd and seald with blood,
Wherein darke things were writ, hard to be understood.

14

Her younger sister, that Speranza hight,
   Was clad in blew,[163] that her beseemed well;
   Not all so chearefull seemed she of sight,
   As was her sister; whether dread did dwell,
   Or anguish in her hart, is hard to tell:
   Upon her arme a silver anchor lay,
   Whereon she leaned ever, as befell:
   And ever up to heaven, as she did pray,
Her stedfast eyes were bent, ne swarved other way.

15

They seeing Una, towards her gan wend,
   Whom them encounters with like courtesie;
   Many kind speeches they betwene them spend,
   And greatly joy each other well to see:
   Then to the knight with shamefast° modestie   *humble*
   They turne themselves, at Unaes meeke request,
   And him salute with well beseeming glee°;   *pleasure*
   Who faire them quites,° as him beseemed best,   *responds to*
And goodly gan discourse of many a noble gest.°   *feat of arms*

16

Then Una thus; 'But she your sister deare,
   The deare Charissa where is she become?
   Or wants she health, or busie is elsewhere?'
   'Ah no,' said they, 'but forth she may not come:
   For she of late is lightned of her wombe,
   And hath encreast the world with one sonne more,
   That her to see should be but troublesome.'
   'Indeede,' quoth she, 'that should her trouble sore,
But thankt be God, and her encrease so[164] evermore.'

17

Then said the aged Caelia, 'Deare dame,
   And you good Sir, I wote° that of your toyle,   *know*
   And labours long, through which ye hither came,
   Ye both forwearied° be: therefore a whyle   *worn out*
   I read° you rest, and to your bowres recoyle°.'   *advise/retire*
   Then called she a Groome, that forth him led
   Into a goodly lodge, and gan despoile°   *take off*
   Of puissant armes, and laid in easie bed;
His name was meeke Obedience rightfully ared°.   *described*

18

Now when their wearie limbes with kindly° rest,   *natural*
   And bodies were refresht with due repast,
   Faire Una gan Fidelia faire request,
   To have her knight into her schoolehouse plaste°,   *placed*
   That of her heavenly learning he might taste,
   And heare the wisedome of her words divine.
   She graunted, and that knight so much agraste°,   *favoured*
   That she him taught celestiall discipline°,   *holy laws*
And opened his dull eyes, that light mote in them shine.

19

And that her sacred Booke, with bloud[165] ywrit,
   That none could read, except she did them teach,
   She unto him disclosed every whit,
   And heavenly documents° thereout did preach,   *instruction*
   That weaker wit of man could never reach,
   Of God, of grace, of justice, of free will,
   That wonder was to heare her goodly speach:
   For she was able, with her words to kill,
And raise againe to life the hart, that she did thrill°.   *pierce*

20

And when she list poure out her larger spright,[166]
  She would commaund the hastie Sunne to stay,
  Or backward turne his course from heavens hight;
  Sometimes great hostes of men she could dismay,
  Dry-shod to passe, she parts the flouds in tway;
 And eke huge mountaines from their native seat
  She would commaund, themselves to beare away,
  And throw in raging sea with roaring threat.
Almightie God her gave such powre, and puissance great.

21

The faithfull knight now grew in litle space,
  By hearing her, and by her sisters lore,
  To such perfection of all heavenly grace,
  That wretched world he gan for to abhore,
  And mortall life gan loath, as thing forlore,   *forlorn*
  Greeved with remembrance of his wicked wayes,
  And prickt with anguish of his sinnes so sore,
  That he desirde to end his wretched dayes:
So much the dart of sinfull guilt the soule dismayes.[167]

22

But wise Speranza gave him comfort sweet,
  And taught him how to take assured hold
  Upon her silver anchor, as was meet;
  Else had his sinnes so great, and manifold
  Made him forget all that Fidelia told.
  In this distressed doubtfull agonie,
  When him his dearest Una did behold,
  Disdeining life, desiring leave to die,
She found her selfe assayld with great perplexitie.

23

And came to Caelia to declare her smart,
  Who well acquainted with that commune° plight,   *common*
  Which sinfull horror[168] workes in wounded hart,
  Her wisely comforted all that she might,
  With goodly counsell and advisement right;
  And streightway sent with carefull diligence,
  To fetch a Leach,° the which had great insight   *doctor*
  In that disease of grieved conscience,
And well could cure the same; His name was Patience.

24

Who comming to that soule-diseased knight,
  Could hardly him intreat°, to tell his griefe: *persuade*
  Which knowne, and all that noyd° his heavie spright *troubled*
  Well searcht, eftsoones he gan apply reliefe
  Of salves and med'cines, which had passing priefe°, *were well-tested*
  And thereto added words of wondrous might:
  By which to ease he him recured briefe°, *quickly*
  And much asswaged the passion° of his plight, *suffering*
That he his paine endured, as seeming now more light.

25

But yet the cause and root of all his ill,
  Inward corruption, and infected sin,
  Not purged nor heald°, behind remained still, *healed*
  And festring sore did rankle yet within,
  Close creeping twixt the marrow and the skin.
  Which to extirpe°, he laid him privily *root out*
  Downe in a darkesome lowly place farre in,
  Whereas he meant his corrosives to apply,
And with streight° diet tame his stubborne malady. *strict*

26

In ashes and sackcloth he did array
  His daintie corse, proud humors° to abate, *traits*
  And dieted with fasting every day,
  The swelling of his wounds to mitigate,
  And made him pray both earely and eke late:
  And ever as superfluous flesh did rot
  Amendment readie still at hand did wayt,
  To pluck it out with pincers firie whot°, *hot*
That soone in him was left no one corrupted jot.

27

And bitter Penance with an yron whip,
  Was wont him once to disple° every day: *discipline*
  And sharpe Remorse his heart did pricke and nip,
  That drops of bloud thence like a well did play;
  And sad Repentance used to embay
  His bodie in salt water smarting sore,
  The filthy blots of sinne to wash away.
  So in short space they did to health restore
The man that would not live, but earst° lay at deathes dore. *erstwhile*

28

In which his torment often was so great,
   That like a Lyon he would cry and rore,
   And rend his flesh, and his owne synewes eat.
   His owne deare Una hearing evermore
   His ruefull shriekes and gronings, often tore
   Her guiltlesse garments, and her golden heare,°   *hair*
   For pitty of his paine and anguish sore;
   Yet all with patience wisely she did beare;
For well she wist, his crime could else be never cleare.°   *cleansed*

29

Whom thus recovered by wise Patience,
   And trew Repentance they to Una brought:
   Who joyous of his cured conscience,
   Him dearely kist, and fairely eke besought
   Himselfe to chearish, and consuming thought
   To put away out of his carefull brest.
   By this Charissa, late in child-bed brought,
   Was woxen strong, and left her fruitfull nest;
To her faire Una brought this unacquainted guest.[169]

30

She was a woman in her freshest age,
   Of wondrous beauty, and of bountie° rare,   *virtue*
   With goodly grace and comely personage,
   That was on earth not easie to compare;
   Full of great love, but Cupids wanton snare
   As hell she hated, chast in worke and will;
   Her necke and breasts were ever open bare,
   That ay thereof her babes might sucke their fill;
The rest was all in yellow robes[170] arayed still.

31

A multitude of babes about her hong,
   Playing their sports, that joyd her to behold,
   Whom still she fed, whiles they were weake and young,
   But thrust them forth still, as they wexed old:
   And on her head she wore a tyre° of gold,   *headdress*
   Adornd with gemmes and owches° wondrous faire,   *jewels*
   Whose passing price uneath° was to be told,   *scarcely*
   And by her side there sate a gentle paire
Of turtle doves, she sitting in an yvorie chaire.

32

The knight and Una entring, faire her greet,
  And bid her joy of that her happie brood;
  Who them requites with court'sies seeming meet,°   *appropriate*
  And entertaines with friendly chearefull mood.
  Then Una her besought, to be so good,
  As in her vertuous rules to schoole her knight,
  Now after all his torment well withstood,
  In that sad° house of Penaunce, where his spright
Had past the paines of hell, and long enduring night.

33

She was right joyous of her just request,
  And taking by the hand that Faeries sonne,
  Gan him instruct in every good behest,
  Of love, and righteousnesse, and well to donne,°   *well-doing*
  And wrath, and hatred warely° to shonne,   *carefully*
  That drew on men Gods hatred, and his wrath,
  And many soules in dolours° had fordonne°:   *misery/ruined*
  In which when him she well instructed hath,
From thence to heaven she teacheth him the ready path.

34

Wherein his weaker wandring steps to guide,
  An auncient matrone she to her does call,
  Whose sober lookes her wisedome well descride°:   *revealed*
  Her name was Mercie, well knowne over all,
  To be both gratious, and eke liberall:
  To whom the carefull charge of him she gave,
  To lead aright, that he should never fall
  In all his wayes through this wide worldes wave,
That Mercy in the end his righteous soule might save.

35

The godly Matrone by the hand him beares
  Forth from her presence, by a narrow way,
  Scattred with bushy thornes, and ragged breares°;   *briars*
  Which still before him she removed away,
  That nothing might his ready passage stay:
  And ever when his feet encombred were,
  Or gan to shrinke, or from the right to stray,
  She held him fast, and firmely did upbeare,
As carefull Nourse her child from falling oft does reare.

36

Eftsoones unto an holy Hospitall,°   *sanctuary*
    That was fore° by the way, she did him bring,   *close*
    In which seven Bead-men¹⁷¹ that had vowed all
    Their life to service of high heavens king
    Did spend their dayes in doing godly thing:
    Their gates to all were open evermore,
    That by the wearie way were travelling,
    And one sate wayting ever them before,
To call in commers-by, that needy were and pore.

37

The first of them that eldest was, and best,°   *chief*
    Of all the house had charge and governement,
    As Guardian and Steward of the rest:
    His office was to give entertainement
    And lodging, unto all that came, and went:
    Not unto such, as could him feast againe,
    And double quite,° for that he on them spent,   *repay*
    But such, as want of harbour° did constraine: *shelter*
Those for Gods sake his dewty was to entertaine.

38

The second was as Almner° of the place,   *almoner*
    His office was, the hungry for to feed,
    And thristy give to drinke, a worke of grace:
    He feard not once him selfe to be in need,
    Ne cared to hoord for those, whom he did breede°:   *his family*
    The grace of God he layd up still in store,
    Which as a stocke he left unto his seede;
    He had enough, what need him care for more?
And had he lesse, yet some he would give to the pore.

39

The third had of their wardrobe custodie,
    In which were not rich tyres,° nor garments gay,   *dresses*
    The plumes of pride, and wings of vanitie,
    But clothes meet to keepe keene could° away,   *cold*
    And naked nature seemely to aray;
    With which bare wretched wights he dayly clad,
    The images of God in earthly clay;
    And if that no spare cloths to give he had,
His owne coate he would cut, and it distribute glad.

40

The fourth appointed by his office was,
  Poore prisoners to relieve with gratious ayd,
  And captives to redeeme with price of bras°,   *ransom money*
  From Turkes and Sarazins, which them had stayd°;   *imprisoned*
  And though they faultie were, yet well he wayd,
  That God to us forgiveth every howre
  Much more then that, why° they in bands were layd,   *for which*
  And he that harrowd hell with heavie stowre°,   *disturbance*
The faultie soules from thence brought to his heavenly bowre.

41

The fift had charge sicke persons to attend,
  And comfort those, in point of death which lay;
  For them most needeth comfort in the end,
  When sin, and hell, and death do most dismay
  The feeble soule departing hence away.
  All is but lost, that living we bestow°,   *arrange*
  If not well ended at our dying day.
  O man have mind of that last bitter throw°;   *throe*
For as the tree does fall, so lyes it ever low.

42

The sixt had charge of them now being dead,
  In seemely sort their corses to engrave°,   *bury*
  And deck with dainty flowres their bridall bed,
  That to their heavenly spouse both sweet and brave°   *fair*
  They might appeare, when he their soules shall save.
  The wondrous workemanship of Gods owne mould°,   *image*
  Whose face he made, all beasts to feare, and gave
  All in his hand, even dead we honour should.
Ah dearest God me graunt, I dead be not defould°.   *defiled*

43

The seventh now after death and buriall done,
  Had charge the tender Orphans of the dead
  And widowes ayd, least they should be undone°;   *ruined*
  In face of judgement he their right would plead,
  Ne ought the powre of mighty men did dread
  In their defence, nor would for gold or fee
  Be wonne their rightfull causes downe to tread:
  And when they stood in most necessitee,
He did supply their want, and gave them ever free°.   *freely*

44

There when the Elfin knight arrived was,
  The first and chiefest of the seven, whose care
  Was guests to welcome, towardes him did pas:
  Where seeing Mercie, that his steps up bare,°   *bore*
  And alwayes led, to her with reverence rare
  He humbly louted° in meeke lowlinesse,   *bowed*
  And seemely welcome for her did prepare:
  For of their order she was Patronesse,
Albe° Charissa were their chiefest founderesse.   *although*

45

There she awhile him stayes, him selfe to rest,
  That to the rest more able he might bee:
  During which time, in every good behest
  And godly worke of Almes and charitee
  She him instructed with great industree;
  Shortly therein so perfect he became,
  That from the first unto the last degree,
  His mortall life he learned had to frame
In holy righteousnesse, without rebuke or blame.

46

Thence forward by that painfull way they pas,
  Forth to an hill, that was both steepe and hy;
  On top whereof a sacred chappell was,
  And eke a litle Hermitage thereby,
  Wherein an aged holy man did lye,
  That day and night said his devotion,
  Ne other wordly busines did apply°;   *pursue*
  His name was heavenly Contemplation;
Of God and goodnesse was his meditation.

47

Great grace that old man to him given had;
  For God he often saw from heavens hight,
  All° were his earthly eyen both blunt° and bad,   *although/dim*
  And through great age had lost their kindly° sight,   *natural*
  Yet wondrous quick and persant° was his spright,°   *piercing/spirit*
  As Eagles eye, that can behold the Sunne:[172]
  That hill they scale with all their powre and might,
  That his frayle thighes nigh wearie and fordonne°   *exhausted*
Gan faile, but by her helpe the top at last he wonne.

48

There they do finde that godly aged Sire,
  With snowy lockes adowne his shoulders shed,
  As hoarie frost with spangles doth attire
  The mossy braunches of an Oke halfe ded.
  Each bone might through his body well be red°,   *seen*
  And every sinew seene through° his long fast: *because of*
  For nought he cared his carcas long unfed;
  His mind was full of spirituall repast,
And pyned° his flesh, to keepe his body low and chast.   *starved*

49

Who when these two approching he aspide,
  At their first presence grew agrieved sore,
  That forst him lay his heavenly thoughts aside;
  And had he not that Dame respected more°,   *greatly*
  Whom highly he did reverence and adore,
  He would not once have moved for the knight.
  They him saluted standing far afore°;   *before*
  Who well them greeting, humbly did requight,
And asked, to what end they clomb° that tedious height. *had climbed*

50

'What end,' quoth she, 'should cause us take such paine,
  But that same end, which every living wight
  Should make his marke, high heaven to attaine?
  Is not from hence the way, that leadeth right
  To that most glorious house, that glistreth bright
  With burning starres, and everliving fire,
  Whereof the keyes[173] are to thy hand behight°   *entrusted*
  By wise Fidelia? she doth thee require,
To shew it to this knight, according° his desire.'   *granting*

51

'Thrise happy man,' said then the father grave,
  'Whose staggering steps thy steady hand doth lead,
  And shewes the way, his sinfull soule to save.
  Who better can the way to heaven aread°,   *direct*
  Then thou thy selfe, that was both borne and bred
  In heavenly throne, where thousand Angels shine?
  Thou doest the prayers of the righteous sead° *seed (offspring)*
  Present before the majestie divine
And his avenging wrath to clemencie incline.

52

Yet since thou bidst, thy pleasure shalbe donne.
  Then come thou man of earth, and see the way,
  That never yet was seene of Faeries sonne,
  That never leads the traveiler astray,
  But after labours long, and sad delay,
  Brings them to joyous rest and endlesse blis.
  But first thou must a season fast and pray,
  Till from her bands the spright assoiled° is,   *freed*
And have her strength recured° from fraile infirmitis.'   *recovered*

53

That done, he leads him to the highest Mount,[174]
  Such one, as that same mighty man of God,
  That bloud-red billowes[175] like a walled front
  On either side disparted with his rod,
  Till that his army dry-foot through them yod,°   *passed*
  Dwelt fortie dayes upon;[176] where writ in stone
  With bloudy letters by the hand of God,
  The bitter doome of death and balefull mone
He did receive, whiles flashing fire about him shone.

54

Or like that sacred hill,[177] whose head full hie,
  Adornd with fruitfull Olives all arownd,
  Is, as it were for endlesse memory
  Of that deare Lord, who oft thereon was fownd,
  For ever with a flowring girlond crownd:
  Or like that pleasaunt Mount,[178] that is for ay
  Through famous Poets verse each where° renownd,   *everywhere*
  On which the thrise three learned Ladies play
Their heavenly notes, and make full many a lovely lay.

55

From thence, far off he unto him did shew
  A litle path, that was both steepe and long,
  Which to a goodly Citie[179] led his vew;
  Whose wals and towres were builded high and strong
  Of perle and precious stone, that earthly tong
  Cannot describe, nor wit of man can tell;
  Too high a ditty° for my simple song;   *theme*
  The Citie of the great king hight° it well,   *called*
Wherein eternall peace and happinesse doth dwell.

56

As he thereon stood gazing, he might see
   The blessed Angels to and fro descend[180]
   From highest heaven, in gladsome companee,
   And with great joy into that Citie wend,
   As commonly° as frend does with his frend.   *easily*
   Whereat he wondred much, and gan enquere,
   What stately building durst so high extend
   Her loftie towres unto the starry sphere,
And what unknowen nation there empeopled° were.   *settled*

57

'Faire knight,' quoth he, 'Hierusalem that is,
   The new Hierusalem, that God has built
   For those to dwell in, that are chosen his,
   His chosen people purged from sinfull guilt,
   With pretious bloud, which cruelly was spilt
   On cursed tree, of that unspotted lam,
   That for the sinnes of all the world was kilt°:   *killed*
   Now are they Saints all in that Citie sam,°   *together*
More deare unto their God, then younglings to their dam.'

58

'Till now,' said then the knight, 'I weened well,
   That great Cleopolis,[181] where I have beene,
   In which that fairest Faerie Queene doth dwell,
   The fairest Citie was, that might be seene;
   And that bright towre all built of christall cleene,
   Panthea, seemd the brightest thing, that was:
   But now by proofe all otherwise I weene;
   For this great Citie that does far surpas,
And this bright Angels towre quite dims that towre of glas.'

59

'Most trew,' then said the holy aged man;
   'Yet is Cleopolis for earthly frame,°   *structure*
   The fairest peece, that eye beholden can:
   And well beseemes all knights of noble name,
   That covet in th'immortall booke of fame
   To be eternized, that same to haunt,°   *frequent*
   And doen their service to that soveraigne Dame,[182]
   That glorie does to them for guerdon° graunt: *reward*
For she is heavenly borne, and heaven may justly vaunt.°   *boast of it*

60

And thou faire ymp, sprong out from English race,
  How ever now accompted° Elfins sonne,   *accounted*
  Well worthy doest thy service for her grace,°   *favour*
  To aide a virgin desolate foredonne.
  But when thou famous victorie hast wonne,
  And high emongst all knights hast hong thy shield,
  Thenceforth the suit° of earthly conquest shonne,   *pursuit*
  And wash thy hands from guilt of bloudy field:
For bloud can nought but sin, and wars but sorrowes yield.

61

Then seeke this path, that I to thee presage,°   *fore-show*
  Which after all to heaven shall thee send;
  Then peaceably thy painefull pilgrimage
  To yonder same Hierusalem do bend,
  Where is for thee ordaind a blessed end:
  For thou emongst those Saints, whom thou doest see,
  Shalt be a Saint, and thine owne nations frend
  And Patrone: thou Saint George shalt called bee,
Saint George of mery England, the signe of victoree.'

62

'Unworthy wretch,' quoth he,° 'of so great grace,   *i.e. Redcrosse*
  How dare I thinke such glory to attaine?'
  'These that have it attaind, were in like cace,'
  Quoth he, 'as wretched, and lived in like paine.'
  'But deeds of armes must I at last be faine,°   *willing*
  And Ladies love to leave so dearly bought?'
  'What need of armes, where peace doth ay remaine,'
  Said he, 'and battailes none are to be fought?
As for loose loves are vaine, and vanish into nought.'

63

'O let me not,' quoth he, 'then turne againe
  Backe to the world, whose joyes so fruitlesse are;
  But let me here for aye in peace remaine,
  Or streight away on that last long voyage fare,
  That nothing may my present hope empare.°   *impaire*
  'That may not be,' said he, 'ne maist thou yit
  Forgot that royall maides bequeathed care,
  Who did her cause into thy hand commit,
Till from her cursed foe thou have her freely quit.°   *freed*

64

'Then shall I soone,' quoth he, 'so God me grace,
  Abet° that virgins cause disconsolate,   *uphold*
  And shortly backe returne unto this place,
  To walke this way in Pilgrims poore estate.
  But now aread° old father, why of late   *explain*
  Didst thou behight° me borne of English blood,   *call*
  Whom all a Faeries sonne doen nominate?'
  'That word shall I,' said he, 'avouchen° good,   *prove*
Sith to thee is unknowne the cradle of thy brood.

65

For well I wote, thou springst from ancient race
  Of Saxon kings, that have with mightie hand
  And many bloudie battailes fought in place
  High reard their royall throne in Britane land,
  And vanquisht them, unable to withstand:
  From thence a Faerie thee unweeting reft°,   *stole*
  There as thou slepst in tender swadling band,
  And her base Elfin brood there for thee left.
Such men do Chaungelings call, so chaungd by Faeries theft.

66

Thence she thee brought into this Faerie lond,
  And in an heaped furrow did thee hyde,
  Where thee a Ploughman all unweeting fond,
  As he his toylesome teme that way did guyde,
  And brought thee up in ploughmans state to byde°, *remain*
  Whereof Georgos[183] he thee gave to name;
  Till prickt with courage, and thy forces pryde,
  To Faery court thou cam'st to seeke for fame,
And prove thy puissaunt armes, as seemes thee best became.'

67

'O holy Sire,' quoth he, 'how shall I quight°   *requite*
  The many favours I with thee have found,
  That hast my name and nation red° aright,   *told*
  And taught the way that does to heaven bound?'
  This said, adowne he looked to the ground,
  To have returnd, but dazed were his eyne,
  Through passing° brightnesse, which did quite confound *surpassing*
  His feeble sence, and too exceeding shyne.
So darke are earthly things compard to things divine.

68

At last whenas himselfe he gan to find,   *recover*
  To Una back he cast him to retire;
  Who him awaited still with pensive mind.
  Great thankes and goodly meed° to that good syre,   *reward*
  He thence departing gave for his paines hyre.°   *recompense*
  So came to Una, who him joyed to see,
  And after litle rest, gan him desire,
  Of her adventure mindfull for to bee.
So leave they take of Caelia, and her daughters three.

CANTO 11[184]

The knight with that old Dragon fights
* two days incessantly:*
The third him overthrowes, and gayns
* most glorious victory.*

1

High time now gan it wex° for Una faire,   *become*
  To thinke of those her captive Parents deare,
  And their forwasted° kingdome to repaire°:   *laid to waste/restore*
  Whereto whenas they now approched neare,
  With hartie words her knight she gan to cheare,
  And in her modest manner thus bespake;
  'Dear knight, as deare, as ever knight was deare,
  That all these sorrowes suffer for my sake,
High heaven behold the tedious toyle, ye for me take.

2

Now are we come unto my native soyle,
  And to the place, where all our perils dwell;
  Here haunts that feend, and does his dayly spoyle,
  Therefore henceforth be at your keeping° well,   *on your guard*
  And ever ready for your foeman fell.
  The sparke of noble courage now awake,
  And strive your excellent selfe to excell;
  That shall ye evermore renowmed make,
Above all knights on earth, that batteill undertake.'

3

And pointing forth, 'Lo yonder is,' said she,
  'The brasen towre in which my parents deare
  For dread of that huge feend emprisond be,

Whom I from far see on the walles appeare,
Whose sight my feeble soule doth greatly cheare:
And on the top of all I do espye
The watchman wayting tydings glad to heare,
That O my parents might I happily
Unto you bring, to ease you of your misery.'

4

With that they heard a roaring hideous sound,
 That all the ayre with terrour filled wide,
 And seemed uneath° to shake the stedfast ground.   *almost*
Eftsoones° that dreadfull Dragon[185] they espide,   *forthwith*
 Where stretcht he lay upon the sunny side
 Of a great hill, himselfe like a great hill.
 But all so soone, as he from far descride
 Those glistring armes, that heaven with light did fill,
He roused himselfe full blith,° and hastned them untill.° *happily/towards*

5

Then bad the knight his Lady yede aloofe,°   *go above*
 And to an hill her selfe with draw aside,
 From whence she might behold that battailles proof°   *outcome*
 And eke be safe from daunger far descryde:
 She him obayd, and turnd a little wyde.°   *aside*
 Now O thou sacred Muse,° most learned Dame,   *i.e. Clio*
 Faire ympe of Phoebus, and his aged bride,°   *i.e. Memory*
 The Nourse of time, and everlasting fame,
That warlike hands ennoblest with immortall name;

6

O gently come into my feeble brest,
 Come gently, but not with that mighty rage,
 Wherewith the martiall troupes thou doest infest,°   *arouse*
 And harts of great Heroës doest enrage,
 That nought their kindled courage may aswage,°   *lessen*
 Soone as thy dreadfull trompe° begins to sownd;   *trumpet*
 The God of warre with his fiers equipage°   *equipment*
 Thou doest awake, sleepe never he so sownd,
And scared nations doest with horrour sterne astownd.°   *appal*

7

Faire Goddesse lay that furious fit° aside,   *strain of music*
 Till I of warres and bloudy Mars do sing,[186]
 And Briton fields with Sarazin bloud bedyde,

Twixt that great faery Queene and Paynim king,
That with their horrour heaven and earth did ring,
A worke of labour long, and endlesse prayse:
But now a while let downe that haughtie° string,   *noble*
And to my tunes thy second tenor[187] rayse,
That I this man of God his godly armes may blaze°   *proclaim*

8

By this the dreadfull Beast drew nigh to hand,
  Halfe flying, and halfe footing in his hast,
  That with his largenesse measured much land,
  And made wide shadow under his huge wast;
  As mountaine doth the valley overcast.
  Approching nigh, he reared high afore°   *in front*
  His body monstrous, horrible, and vast,
  Which to increase his wondrous greatnesse more,
Was swolne with wrath, and poyson, and with bloudy gore.

9

And over, all with brasen scales was armd,[188]
  Like plated coate of steele, so couched neare°,   *closely set*
  That nought mote perce, ne might his corse be harmd
  With dint of sword, nor push of pointed speare;
  Which as an Eagle, seeing pray appeare,
  His aery plumes doth rouze°, full rudely dight°,   *shake/ruffled up*
  So shaked he, that horrour was to heare,
  For as the clashing of an Armour bright,
Such noyse his rouzed scales did send unto the knight.

10

His flaggy° wings when forth he did display,   *drooping*
  Were like two sayles, in which the hollow wynd
  Is gathered full, and worketh speedy way:
  And eke the pennes°, that did his pineons bynd,   *feathers*
  Were like mayne-yards°, with flying canvas lynd,   *mainyards*
  With which whenas him list the ayre to beat,
  And there by force unwonted passage find,
  The cloudes before him fled for terrour great,
And all the heavens stood still amazed with his threat.

11

His huge long tayle wound up in hundred foldes,
  Does overspred his long bras-scaly backe,
  Whose wreathed boughts° when ever he unfoldes,   *coils*

And thicke entangeld knots adown does slacke,
Bespotted as with shields of red and blacke,
It sweepeth all the land behind him farre,
And of three furlongs does but litle lacke;
And at the point two stings in-fixed arre,
Both deadly sharpe, that sharpest steele exceeden farre.

12

But stings and sharpest steele did far exceed°   *were exceeded by*
  The sharpnesse of his cruell rending clawes;[189]
  Dead was it sure, as sure as death in deed,
  What ever thing does touch his ravenous pawes,
  Or what within his reach he ever drawes.
  But his most hideous head my toung to tell
  Does tremble: for his deepe devouring jawes
  Wide gaped, like the griesly mouth of hell,
Through which into his darke abisse all ravin° fell.   *prey*

13

And that° more wondrous was, in either jaw   *what*
  Three ranckes of yron teeth enraunged were,
  In which yet trickling bloud and gobbets° raw   *bits of food*
  Of late devoured bodies did appeare,
  That sight thereof bred cold congealed feare:
  Which to increase, and all atonce to kill,
  A cloud of smoothering smoke and sulphur seare°   *searing*
  Out of his stinking gorge° forth steemed still,   *throat*
That all the ayre about with smoke and stench did fill.

14

His blazing eyes, like two bright shining shields,
  Did burne with wrath, and sparkled living fyre;
  As two broad Beacons, set in open fields,
  Send forth their flames farre off to every shyre,
  And warning give, that enemies conspyre,
  With fire and sword the region to invade;
  So flamed his eyne with rage and rancorous yre:
  But farre within, as in a hollow glade,
Those glaring lampes were set, that made a dreadfull shade.

15

So dreadfully he towards him did pas,°   *pace*
  Forelifting up aloft his speckled brest,
  And often bounding on the brused gras,

As for great joyance of his newcome guest.
Eftsoones° he gan advance his haughtie crest,   *forthwith*
As chauffed° Bore° his bristles doth upreare,   *angry/boar*
And shoke° his scales to battell readie drest;°   *shook/prepared*
　That made the Redcrosse knight nigh quake for feare,
As bidding bold defiance to his foeman neare.[190]

16

The knight gan fairely couch° his steadie speare,   *lower, for battle*
　And fiercely ran at him with rigorous might:
　The pointed steele arriving rudely theare,
　His harder° hide would neither perce, nor bight,   *too hard*
　But glauncing by forth passed forward right;
　Yet sore amoved with so puissant push,
　The wrathfull beast about him turned light,°   *quickly*
　And him so rudely passing by, did brush
With his long tayle, that horse and man to ground did rush.

17

Both horse and man up lightly rose againe,
　And fresh encounter towards him addrest:
　But th'idle stroke yet backe recoyld in vaine,
　And found no place his deadly point to rest.
　Exceeding rage enflamed the furious beast,
　To be avenged of so gret despight°;   *injury*
　For never felt his imperceable brest
　So wondrous force, from hand of living wight;
Yet had he proved° the powre of many a puissant knight.   *tested*

18

Then with his waving wings displayed wyde,
　Himselfe up high he lifted from the ground,
　And with strong flight did forcibly divide
　The yielding aire, which nigh too feeble found
　Her flitting partes, and element unsound,
　To beare so great a weight: he cutting way
　With his broad sayles, about him soared round:
　At last low stouping with unweldie sway,°   *force*
Snatcht up both horse and man, to beare them quite away.

19

Long he them bore above the subject° plaine,   *below*
　So farre as Ewghen° bow a shaft may send,   *yew*
　Till struggling strong did him at last constraine,

To let them downe before his flightes end:
As hagard hauke presuming to contend
With hardie fowle, above his hable° might,   *powerful*
His wearie pounces° all in vaine doth spend,   *talons*
To trusse° the pray too heavie for his flight;   *carry off*
Which comming downe to ground, does free it selfe by fight.

20

He so disseized of his gryping grosse,°   *heavy burden*
  The knight his thrillant° speare againe assayd   *piercing*
  In his bras-plated body to embosse,°   *thrust*
  And three mens strength unto the stroke he layd;
  Wherewith the stiffe beame° quaked, as affrayd,   *spear*
  And glauncing from his scaly necke, did glyde
  Close under his left wing, then broad displayd.
  The percing steele there wrought a wound full wyde,
That with the uncouth smart the Monster lowdly cryde.

21

He cryde, as raging seas are wont to rore,
  When wintry storme his wrathfull wreck does threat,
  The rolling billowes beat the ragged shore,
  As they the earth would shoulder from her seat,
  And greedie gulfe does gape, as he would eat
  His neighbour element in his revenge:
  Then gin the blustring brethren° boldly threat   *winds*
  To move the world from off his stedfast henge.°   *axis*
And boystrous battell make, each other to avenge.

22

The steely head stucke fast still in his flesh,
  Till with his cruell claws he snatcht the wood,
  And quite a sunder broke. Forth flowed fresh
  A gushing river of blacke goarie blood,
  That drowned all the land, whereon he stood;
  The streame thereof would drive a water-mill.
  Trebly augmented was his furious mood
  With bitter sense° of his deepe rooted ill,   *feeling*
That flames of fire he threw forth from his large nosethrill.

23

His hideous tayle then hurled he about,
  And therewith all enwrapt the nimble thyes
  Of his° froth-fomy steed, whose courage stout   *i.e. Redcrosse's*

Striving to loose the knot, that fast him tyes,
Himselfe in streighter bandes too rash implyes;   *quickly entangles*
That to the ground he is perforce constraynd
To throw his rider: who can° quickly ryse   *does*
From off the earth, with durty bloud distaynd;   *stained*
For that reprochfull fall right fowly he disdaynd.

24

And fiercely tooke his trenchand° blade in hand,   *piercing*
  With which he stroke so furious and so fell,
  That nothing seemd the puissance could withstand:
  Upon his crest the hardned yron fell,
  But his more hardned crest was armd so well,
  That deeper dint therein it would not make;
  Yet so extremely did the buffe him quell,   *daunt*
  That from thenceforth he shund the like to take,
But when he saw them come, he did them still forsake.   *avoid*

25

The knight was wrath to see his stroke beguyld,   *foiled*
  And smote againe with more outrageous might;
  But backe againe the sparckling steele recoyld,
  And left not any marke, where it did light;
  As if in Adamant rocke it had bene pight.   *placed*
  The beast impatient of his smarting wound,
  And of so fierce and forcible despight,   *anger*
  Thought with his wings to stye° above the ground;   *rise*
But his late wounded wing unserviceable found.

26

Then full of griefe and anguish vehement,
  He lowdly brayd, that like was never heard,
  And from his wide devouring oven sent
  A flake° of fire, that flashing in his beard,   *flash*
  Him all amazd, and almost made affeard:
  The scorching flame sore swinged° all his face,   *singed*
  And through his armour all his bodie seard,
  That he could not endure so cruell cace,   *condition*
But thought his armes to leave, and helmet to unlace.

27

Not that great Champion° of the antique world,   *i.e. Hercules*
  Whom famous Poetes verse so much doth vaunt,
  And hath for twelve huge labours high extold,

So many furies and sharpe fits did haunt,
When him the poysoned garment did enchaunt
With Centaures bloud, and bloudie verses charmed,
As did this knight twelve thousand dolours° daunt,   *sufferings/brave*
Whom fyrie steele now burnt, that earst° him armed,   *before*
That erst him goodly armed, now most of all him harmed.

28

Faint, wearie, sore, emboyled, grieved, brent°   *burnt*
With heat, toyle, wounds, armes, smart, and inward fire
That never man such mischiefes did torment;
Death better were, death did he oft desire,
But death will never come, when needes require.
Whom so dismayd when that his foe beheld,
He cast to suffer him no more respire,°   *respite*
But gan his sturdie sterne° about to weld,°   *tail/wield*
And him so strongly stroke, that to the ground him feld.

29

It fortuned (as faire it then befell)
Behind his backe unweeting,° where he stood,   *unnoticed*
Of auncient time there was a springing well[191],
From which fast trickled fourth a silver flood,
Full of great vertues, and for med'cine good.
Whylome,° before that cursed Dragon got   *once upon a time*
That happie land, and all with innocent blood
Defyld those sacred waves, it rightly hot°   *called*
The Well of Life, ne yet his° vertues had forgot.   *its*

30

For unto life the dead it could restore,
And guilt of sinfull crimes cleane wash away,
Those that with sicknesses were infected sore,
It could recure, and aged long decay
Renew, as one were borne that very day.
Both Silo this, and Jordan did excell,
And th'English Bath, and eke the german Spau,
Ne can Cephise, nor Hebrus match this well:
Into the same the knight backe overthrowen, fell.[192]

31

Now gan the golden Phoebus for to steepe
His fierie face in billowes of the west,
And his faint steedes watred in Ocean deepe,

Whiles from their journall° labours they did rest,   *daily*
When that infernall Monster, having kest°   *cast*
  His wearie foe into that living well,
  Can° high advance his broad discoloured brest,   *did*
  Above his wonted pitch,° with countenance fell,°   *height/fierce*
And clapt his yron wings, as victor he did dwell.

32

Which when his pensive Ladie saw from farre,
  Great woe and sorrow did her soule assay,°   —   *assail*
  As weening that the sad end of the warre,
  And gan to highest God entirely° pray,   *wholeheartedly*
  That feared chance from her to turne away;
  With folded hands and knees full lowly bent
  All night she watcht, ne once adowne would lay
  Her daintie limbs in her sad dreriment,
But praying still did wake, and waking did lament.[193]

33

The morrow next gan early to appeare,
  That° Titan° rose to runne his daily race;   *when/i.e. the sun*
  But early ere the morrow next gan reare
  Out of the sea faire Titans deawy face,
  Up rose the gentle virgin from her place,
  And looked all about, if she might spy
  Her loved knight to move his manly pace:[194]
  For she had great doubt of his safety,
Since late she saw him fall before his enemy.

34

At last she saw, where he upstarted brave
  Out of the well, wherein he drenched lay;
  As Eagle[195] fresh out of the Ocean wave,
  Where he hath left his plumes all hoary gray,
  And deckt himselfe with feathers youthly gay,
  Like Eyas° hauke up mounts unto the skies,   *newly-fledged*
  His newly budded pineons to assay,
  And marveiles at himselfe, still as he flies:
So new this new-borne knight to battell new did rise.

35

Whom when the damned feend so fresh did spy,
  No wonder if he wondred at the sight,
  And doubted, whether his late enemy

It were, or other new supplied knight.
He, now to prove his late renewed might,
High brandishing his bright deaw-burning[196] blade,
Upon his crested scalpe so sore did smite,
That to the scull a yawning wound it made:
The deadly dint his dulled senses all dismaid.

36

I wote not, whether the revenging steele
   Were hardned with that holy water dew,
   Wherein he fell, or sharper edge did feele,
   Or his baptized hands now greater° grew   *stronger*
   Or other secret vertue did ensew;
   Else never could the force of fleshly arme,
   Ne molten mettall in his bloud embrew°:   *thrust*
   For till that stownd° could never wight him harme,   *moment*
By subtilty, nor slight°, nor might, nor mighty charme.   *trickery*

37

The cruell wound enraged him so sore,
   That loud he yelded° for exceeding paine;   *yelled*
   As hundred ramping Lyons seemed to rore,
   Whom ravenous hunger did thereto constraine:
   Then gan he tosse aloft his stretched traine°,   *tail*
   And therewith scourge the buxome° aire so sore,   *unresisting*
   That to his force to yeelden it was faine°;   *forced*
   Ne ought° his sturdie strokes might stand afore°,   *anything/up to*
That high trees overthrew, and rocks in peeces tore.

38

The same advauncing high above his head,
   With sharpe intended° sting so rude him° smot,[197]   *extended/i.e.*
   That to the earth him drove, as stricken dead,   *Redcrosse*
   Ne living wight would have him life behot°:   *considered*
   The mortall sting his angry needle shot
   Quite through his shield, and in his shoulder seasd,
   Where fast it stucke, ne would there out be got:
   The griefe thereof him wondrous sore diseasd°,   *distressed*
Ne might his ranckling paine with patience be appeasd.

39

But yet more mindfull of his honour deare,
   Then of the grievous smart, which him did wring°,   *trouble*
   From loathed soile he can° him lightly reare,   *did*

And strove to loose the farre° infixed sting: *deeply*
  Which when in vaine he tryde with struggeling,
  Inflamed with wrath, his raging blade he heft,°   *raised*
  And strooke so strongly, that the knotty string
  Of his huge taile he quite a sunder cleft,
Five joynts thereof he hewd, and but the stump him left.

40

Hart cannot thinke, what outrage, and what cryes,
  With foule enfouldred° smoake and flashing fire,   *i.e. like thunder-clouds*
  The hell-bred beast threw forth unto the skyes,
  That all was covered with darknesse dire:
  Then fraught with rancour, and engorged° ire,   *choking*
  He cast at once him to avenge for all,
  And gathering up himselfe out of the mire,
  With his uneven wings did fiercely fall
Upon his sunne-bright shield,[198] and gript it fast withall.

41

Much was the man encombred with his hold,
  In feare to loose his weapon in his paw,
  Ne wist yet, how his talants° to unfold;   *talons*
  Nor harder was from Cerberus greedie jaw
  To plucke a bone, then from his cruell claw
  To reave° by strength the griped gage° away: *tear/prize*
  Thrise he assayd it from his foot to draw,
  And thrise in vaine to draw it did assay,
It booted nought to thinke, to robbe him of his pray.

42

Tho° when he saw no power might prevaile,   *then*
  His trustie sword[199] he cald to his last aid,
  Wherewith he fiercely did his foe assaile,
  And double blowes about him stoutly laid,
  That glauncing fire out of the yron plaid;
  As sparckles from the Andvile° use to fly,   *anvil*
  When heavie hammers on the wedge are swaid°;   *struck*
  Therewith at last he forst him to unty
One of his grasping feete, him to defend thereby.

43

The other foot, fast fixed on his shield,
  Whenas no strength, nor stroks mote him constraine
  To loose, ne yet the warlike pledge to yield,

He smot thereat with all his might and maine,
That nought so wondrous puissance might sustaine;
Upon the joynt the lucky steele did light,
And made such way, that hewd it quite in twaine;
The paw yet missed not his minisht° might,   *reduced*
But hong still on the shield, as it at first was pight°.   *placed*

44

For griefe thereof, and divelish despight°,   *anger*
    From his infernall fournace forth he threw
    Huge flames, that dimmed all the heavens light,
    Enrold in duskish smoke and brimstone blew;
    As burning Aetna from his boyling stew°   *cauldron*
    Doth belch out flames, and rockes in peeces broke,
    And ragged ribs of mountaines molten new,
    Enwrapt in coleblacke clouds and filthy smoke,
That all the land with stench, and heaven with horror choke.

45

The heate whereof, an harmefull pestilence
    So sore him noyd°, that forst him to retire   *troubled*
    A little backward for his best defence,
    To save his bodie from the scorching fire,
    Which he from hellish entrailes did expire°.   *breathe out*
    It chaunst (eternall God that chaunce did guide)
    As he recoyled backward, in the mire
    His nigh forwearied feeble feet did slide,
And downe he fell, with dread of shame sore terrifide.

46

There grew a goodly tree him faire beside,[200]
    Loaden with fruit and apples rosie red,
    As they in pure vermilion had beene dide,
    Whereof great vertues over all were red°:   *known everywhere*
    For happie life to all, which thereon fed,
    And like eke everlasting did befall:
    Great God it planted in that blessed sted°   *place*
    With his almightie hand, and did it call
The Tree of Life, the crime of our first fathers fall.

47

In all the world like was not to be found,
    Save in that soile, where all good things did grow,
    And freely sprong out of the fruitfull ground,

As incorrupted Nature did them sow,
Till that dread Dragon all did overthrow.
Another like faire tree eke grew thereby,
Whereof who so did eat, eftsoones did know
Both good and ill: O mornefull memory:
That tree through one mans fault hath doen° us all to dy. *caused*

48

From that first tree forth flowd, as from a well,
A trickling streame of Balme,[201] most soveraine
And daintie deare,° which on the ground still fell, *very precious*
And overflowed all the fertill plaine,
As it had deawed bene with timely° raine: *seasonable*
Life and long health that gratious° ointment gave, *of grace*
And deadly woundes could heale, and reare againe
The senselesse corse appointed° for the grave. *destined*
Into that same he fell: which did from death him save.

49

For nigh thereto the ever damned beast
Durst not approch, for he was deadly made,[202]
And all that life preserved, did detest:
Yet he it oft adventured° to invade. *ventured*
By this the drouping day-light gan to fade,
And yeeld his roome to sad succeeding night,
Who with her sable mantle gan to shade
The face of earth, and wayes of living wight,
And high her burning torch set up in heaven bright.

50

When gentle Una saw the second fall
Of her deare knight, who wearie of long fight,
And faint through losse of bloud, moved not at all,
But lay as in a dreame of deepe delight,
Besmeard with pretious Balme, whose vertuous° might *power-giving*
Did heale his wounds, and scorching heat alay,
Againe she stricken was with sore affright,
And for his safetie gan devoutly pray;
And watch the noyous° night, and wait for joyous day. *harmful*

51

The joyous day gan early to appeare,
And faire Aurora from the deawy bed
Of aged Tithone gan her selfe to reare,

With rosie cheekes, for shame as blushing red;
Her golden lockes for haste were loosely shed
About her eares, when Una her did marke
Clymbe to her charet,° all with flowers spred,   *chariot*
From heaven high to chase the chearelesse darke;
With merry note her loud salutes the mounting larke.

52

Then freshly up arose the doughtie knight,
  All healed of his hurts and woundes wide,
  And did himselfe to battell readie dight°;   *prepare*
  Whose early foe awaiting him beside
  To have devourd, so soone as day he spyde,
  When now he saw himselfe so freshly reare,
  As if late fight had nought him damnifyde,°   *hurt*
  He woxe dismayd, and gan his fate to feare;
Nathlesse° with wonted rage he him advaunced neare.   *nevertheless*

53

And in his first encounter, gaping wide,
  He thought attonce him to have swallowd quight,
  And rusht upon him with outragious pride;
  Who him r'encountring fierce, as hauke in flight,
  Perforce rebutted° backe. The weapon bright   *forced*
  Taking advantage of his open jaw,[203]
  Ran through his mouth with so importune° might,
  That deepe emperst his darksome hollow maw,
And back retyrd,° life bloud forth with all did draw.   *withdrawn*

54

So downe he fell, and forth his life did breath,
  That vanisht into smoke and cloudes swift;
  So downe he fell, that th'earth him underneath
  Did grone, as feeble so great load to lift;
  So downe he fell, as an huge rockie clift,
  Whose false° foundation waves have washt away,   *insecure*
  With dreadfull poyse° is from the mayneland rift,   *power*
  And rolling downe, great Neptune doth dismay;
So downe he fell, and like an heaped mountaine lay.

55

The knight himselfe even trembled at his fall,
  So huge and horrible a masse it seemed;
  And his deare Ladie, that beheld it all,

Durst not approch for dread, which she misdeemed,   *misjudged*
But yet at last, when as the direfull feend
She saw not stirre, off-shaking vaine affright
She nigher drew, and saw that joyous end:
    Then God she praysd, and thankt her faithfull knight,
That had atchieved so great a conquest by his might.[204]

CANTO 12[205]

Faire Una to the Redcrosse knight
    betrouthed is with joy:
Though false Duessa it to barre
    her false sleights doe imploy.

1

Behold I see the haven nigh at hand,
    To which I meane my wearie course to bend;
    Vere° the maine shete, and beare up° with the land, *shift/steer towards*
    The which afore is fairely to be kend,   *discovered*
    And seemeth safe from stormes, that may offend;
    There this faire virgin wearie of her way
    Must landed be, now at her journeyes end:
    There eke my feeble barke° a while may stay,   *ship*
Till merry wind and weather call her thence away.

2

Scarsely had Phoebus in the glooming East
    Yet harnessed his firie-footed teeme,
    Ne reard above the earth his flaming creast,
    When the last deadly smoke aloft did steeme,
    That signe of last outbreathed life did seeme
    Unto the watchman on the castle wall;
    Who thereby dead that balefull Beast did deeme,
    And to his Lord and Ladie lowd gan call,
To tell, how he had seene the Dragons fatall fall.

3

Uprose with hastie joy, and feeble speed
    That aged Sire, the Lord of all that land,
    And looked forth, to weet, if true indeede
    Those tydings were, as he did understand,
    Which whenas true by tryall he out fond,   *found*

He bad to open wyde his brazen gate,
Which long time had bene shut, and out of hond°   *at once*
Proclaymed joy and peace through all his state;
For dead now was their foe, which them forrayed° late.   *harried*

4

Then gan triumphant Trompets sound on hie,
That sent to heaven the ecchoed report
Of their new joy, and happie victorie
Gainst him, that had them long opprest with tort°,   *wrong*
And fast imprisoned in sieged fort.
Then all the people, as in solemne feast,
To him assembled with one full consort°,   *company*
Rejoycing at the fall of that great beast,
From whose eternall bondage now they were releast.

5

Forth came that auncient Lord and aged Queene,
Arayd in antique robes downe to the ground,
And sad° habiliments right well beseene°;   *sober/as befit them*
A noble crew about them waited round
Of sage and sober Peres, all gravely gownd;
Whom farre before did march a goodly band
Of tall young men, all hable armes to sownd°,   *wield*
But now they laurell[206] braunches bore in hand;
Glad signe of victorie and peace in all their land.

6

Unto that doughtie Conquerour they came,
And him before themselves prostrating low,[207]
Their Lord and Patrone loud did him proclame,
· And at his feet their laurell boughes did throw.
Soone after them all dauncing on a row
The comely virgins came, with girlands dight,
As fresh as flowres in medow greene do grow,
When morning deaw upon their leaves doth light:
And in their hands sweet Timbrels° all upheld on hight.   *tambourines*

7

And them before, the fry° of children young   *swarm*
Their wanton° sports and childish mirth did play,   *playful*
And to the Maydens sounding tymbrels sung
In well attuned notes, a joyous lay,
And made delightfull musicke all the way,

Untill they came, where that faire virgin stood;
As faire Diana in fresh sommers day
Beholds her Nymphes, enraunged° in shadie wood,   *gathered*
Some wrestle, some do run, some bathe in christall flood.

8

So she beheld those maydens meriment
  With chearefull vew; who when to her they came,
  Themselves to ground with gratious humblesse bent,
  And her adored by honorable name,
  Lifting to heaven her everlasting fame:
  Then on her head they set a girland greene,
  And crowned her twixt earnest and twixt game°;   *joke*
  Who in her selfe-resemblance well beseene,²⁰⁸
Did seeme such, as she was, a goodly maiden Queene.

9

And after, all the raskall many° ran,   *crowd*
  Heaped together in rude rablement°,   *rough confusion*
  To see the face of that victorious man:
  Whom all admired, as from heaven sent,
  And gazd upon with gaping wonderment.
  But when they came, where that dead Dragon lay,
  Stretcht on the ground in monstrous large extent,
  The sight with idle° feare did them dismay,   *groundless*
Ne durst approch him nigh, to touch, or once assay.

10

Some feard, and fled; some feard and well it faynd°;   *disguised*
  One that would wiser seeme, then all the rest,
  Warnd him not touch, for yet perhaps remaynd
  Some lingring life within his hollow brest,
  Or in his wombe might lurke some hidden nest
  Of many Dragonets, his fruitfull seed;
  Another said, that in his eyes did rest
  Yet sparckling fire, and bad thereof take heed;
Another said, he saw him move his eyes indeed.

11

One mother, when as her foolehardie chyld
  Did come too neare, and with his talants° play,   *claws*
  Halfe dead through feare, her litle babe revyld°,   *rebuked*
  And to her gossips° gan in counsell say;   *women friends*
  'How can I tell, but that his talants may

Yet scratch my sonne, or rend his tender hand?'
So diversly themselves in vaine they fray°; *frighten*
Whiles some more bold, to measure him nigh stand,
To prove° how many acres he did spread of land. *assess*

12

Thus flocked all the folke him round about,
The whiles that hoarie° king, with all his traine, *grey-haired*
Being arrived, where that champion stout
After his foes defeasance° did remaine, *defeat*
Him goodly greetes, and fair does entertaine,
With princely gifts of yvorie and gold,
And thousand thankes him yeelds for all his paine.
Then when his daughter deare he does behold,
Her dearely doth imbrace, and kisseth manifold°. *many*

13

And after to his Pallace he them brings,
With shaumes°, and trompets, and with Clarions sweet; *oboes*
And all the way the joyous people sings,
And with their garments strowes the paved street:
Whence mounting up, they find purveyance° meet *provision*
Of all, that royall Princes court became°, *befitted*
And all the floore was underneath their feet
Bespred with costly scarlot of great name°. *quality*
On which they lowly sit, and fitting purpose° frame. *conversation*

14

What needs me tell their feast and goodly guize°, *behaviour*
In which was nothing riotous nor vaine?
What needs of daintie dishes to devize°, *describe*
Of comely services, or courtly trayne°? *assembly*
My narrow leaves cannot in them containe
The large discourse of royall Princes state.
Yet was their manner then but bare and plaine:
For th'antique world excesse and pride did hate;
Such proud luxurious pompe is swollen up but late.

15

Then when with meates and drinkes of every kinde
Their fervent appetites they quenched had,
That auncient Lord gan fit occasion finde,
Of straunge adventures, and of perils sad,
Which in his travell him befallen had,

For to demaund of his renowmed guest:
Who then with utt'rance grave, and count'nance sad,
From point to point, as is before exprest,
Discourst his voyage long, according his request.

16

Great pleasure mixt with pittifull° regard,   *compassionate*
    That godly King and Queene did passionate°   *moved to passion*
    Whiles they his pittifull adventures heard,
    That oft they did lament his lucklesse state,
    And often blame the too importune° fate,   *heavy*
    That heapd on him so many wrathfull wreakes°:   *painful events*
    For never gentle knight, as he of late,
    So tossed was in fortunes cruell freakes;
And all the while salt teares bedeawd the hearers cheaks.   ,

17

Then said that royall Pere in sober wise°;   *manner*
    'Deare Sonne, great beene the evils, which ye bore
    From first to last in your late enterprise,
    That I note°, whether prayse, or pitty more: *know not*
    For never living man, I weene, so sore
    In sea of deadly daungers was distrest;
    But since now safe ye seised° have the shore,   *reached*
    And well arrived are, (high God be blest)
Let us devize of ease and everlasting rest.'

18

'Ah dearest Lord,' said then that doughty knight,
    'Of ease or rest I may not yet devize;
    For by the faith, which I to armes have plight°,   *pledged*
    I bounden am streight after this emprize°,   *enterprise*
    As that your daughter can ye well advize,
    Backe to returne to that great Faerie Queene,
    And her to serve six yeares[209] in warlike wize,
    Gainst that proud Paynim° king, that workes her teene°: *pagan/grief*
Therefore I ought crave pardon, till I there have beene.'

19

'Unhappie falles that hard necessitie,'
    Quoth he, 'the troubler of my happie peace,
    And vowed foe of my felicitie;
    Ne I against the same can justly preace°   *contend*
    But since that band° ye cannot now release,   *bond*

Nor doen undo: (for vowes may not be vaine)
Soone as the terme of those six yeares shall cease,
Ye then shall hither backe returne againe,
The marriage to accomplish vowd betwixt you twain.[210]

20

Which for my part I covet to performe,
In sort° as through the world I did proclame,   *the manner*
That who so kild that monster most deforme,
And him in hardy battaile overcame,
Should have mine onely daughter to his Dame,°   *wife*
And of my kingdome heire apparaunt bee:
Therefore since now to thee perteines° the same,   *belongs*
By dew desert of noble chevalree,
Both daughter and eke kingdome, lo I yield to thee.'

21

Then forth he called that his daughter faire,
The fairest Un' his onely daughter deare,
His onely daughter, and his onely heyre;
Who forth proceeding with sad° sober cheare,°   *solemn/countenance*
As bright as doth the morning starre appeare
Out of the East, with flaming lockes bedight,
To tell that dawning day is drawing neare,
And to the world does bring long wished light;
So faire and fresh that Lady shewd her selfe in sight.

22

So faire and fresh, as freshest flowre in May;
For she had layd her mournefull stole aside,
And widow-like sad wimple° throwne away,   *veil*
Wherewith her heavenly beautie she did hide,
Whiles on her wearie journey she did ride;
And on her now a garment she did weare,
All lilly white, withoutten spot, or pride,°   *ornament*
That seemd like silke and silver woven neare,°   *closely*
But neither silke nor silver therein did appeare.[211]

23

The blazing brightnesse of her beauties beame,
And glorious light of her sunshyny face
To tell, were as to strive against the streame.
My ragged rimes are all too rude and bace,
Her heavenly lineaments for too enchace.°   *delineate*

Ne wonder; for her owne deare loved knight,
  All° were she dayly with himselfe in place,   *although*
  Did wonder much at her celestiall sight:
Oft had he seene her faire, but never so faire dight.°   *adorned*

24

So fairely dight, when she in presence came,
  She to her Sire made humble reverence,
  And bowed low, that her right well became,
  And added grace unto her excellence:
  Who with great wisedome, and grave eloquence
  Thus gan to say. But eare he thus had said,
  With flying speede, and seeming great pretence,°   *intentions*
  Came running in, much like a man dismaid,
A Messenger with letters, which his message said.

25

All in the open hall amazed stood,
  At suddeinnesse of that unwarie° sight,   *unexpected*
  And wondred at his breathlesse hastie mood.
  But he for nought would stay his passage right,°   *direct*
  Till fast° before the king he did alight;   *close*
  Where falling flat, great humblesse he did make,
  And kist the ground, whereon his foot was pight°;   *placed*
  Then to his hands that writ° he did betake,°   *document/deliver*
Which he disclosing,° red thus, as the paper spake.   *opening out*

26

'To thee, most mighty king of Eden faire,
  Her greeting sends in these sad lines addrest,
  The wofull daughter, and forsaken heire
  Of that great Emperour of all the West;
  And bids thee be advized for the best,
  Ere thou thy daughter linck in holy band
  Of wedlocke to that new unknowen guest:
  For he already plighted his right hand
Unto another love, and to another land.

27

To me sad mayd, or rather widow sad,
  He was affiaunced long time before,
  And sacred pledges he both gave, and had,
  False erraunt° knight, infamous, and forswore°:   *wandering/forsworn*
  Witnesse the burning Altars, which° he swore,   *by which*

And guiltie° heavens of his bold perjury, *made guilty*
Which though he hath polluted oft of yore,
Yet I to them for judgement just do fly,
And them conjure° t'avenge this shamefull injury. *entreat*

28

Therefore since mine he is, or° free or bond, *either*
Or false or trew, or living or else dead,
Withhold, O soveraine Prince, your hasty hond
From knitting league with him, I you aread°; *advise*
Ne weene° my right with strength adowne to tread, *think*
Through weakenesse of my widowhed, or woe:
For truth is strong, her rightfull cause to plead,
And shall find friends, if need requireth soe,
So bids thee well to fare, Thy neither friend, nor foe, Fidessa.'

29

When he these bitter byting words had red,
The tydings straunge did him abashed make,
That still he sate long time astonished
As in great muse, ne word to creature spake.
At last his solemne silence thus he brake,
With doubtfull eyes fast fixed on his guest;
'Redoubted knight, that for mine onely sake
Thy life and honour late adventurest,° *ventures*
Let nought be hid from me, that ought to be exprest.

30

What meane these bloudy vowes, and idle threats,
Throwne out from womanish impatient mind?
What heavens? what altars? what enraged heates
Here heaped up with termes of love unkind,° *unnatural*
My conscience cleare° with guilty bands would bind? *clean*
High God be witnesse, that I guiltlesse ame.
But if your selfe, Sir knight, ye faultie find,
Or wrapped be in loves of former Dame,
With crime do not it cover, but disclose the same.'

31

To whom the Redcrosse knight this answere sent,
'My Lord, my King, be nought hereat dismayd,
Till well ye wote by grave intendiment,° *consideration*
What woman, and wherefore doth me upbrayd
With breach of love, and loyalty betrayd.

It was in my mishaps, as hitherward
  I lately traveild, that unwares I strayd
  Out of my way, through perils straunge and hard;
That day should faile me, ere I had them all declard.

32

There did I find, or rather I was found
  Of this false woman, that Fidessa hight,
  Fidessa hight the falsest Dame on ground,
  Most false Duessa, royall richly dight,°   *adorned*
  That easie was t' invegle° weaker sight: *deceive*
  Who by her wicked arts, and wylie skill,
  Too false and strong for earthly skill or might,
  Unwares me wrought unto her wicked will,
And to my foe betrayd, when least I feared ill.'

33

Then stepped forth the goodly royall Mayd,
  And on the ground her selfe prostrating low,
  With sober countenaunce thus to him sayd;
  'O pardon me, my soveraigne Lord, to show
  The secret treasons, which of late I know
  To have bene wroght by that false sorceresse.
  She onely she it is, that earst did throw
  This gentle knight into so great distresse,
That death him did awaite in dayly wretchednesse.

34

And now it seemes, that she suborned hath
  This craftie messenger with letters vaine,
  To worke new woe and improvided scath,°   *unforeseen harm*
  By breaking of the band betwixt us twaine;
  Wherein she used hath the practicke° paine   *cunning*
  Of this false footman, clokt with simplenesse,
  Whom if ye please for to discover plaine,
  Ye shall him Archimago find, I ghesse,
The falsest man alive; who tries shall find no lesse.'

35

The king was greatly moved at her speach,
  And all with suddein indignation fraight,°   *filled*
  Bad on that Messenger rude hands to reach.
  Eftsoones the Gard, which on his state did wait,
  Attacht° that faitor° false, and bound him strait: *seized/traitor*

Who seeming sorely chauffed° at his band,　　　　　*angered*
　As chained Beare, whom cruell dogs do bait,
　With idle force did faine them to withstand,
And often semblaunce made to scape out of their hand.

36

But they him layd full low in dungeon deepe,
　And bound him hand and foote with yron chains.
　And with continuall watch did warely keepe;
　Who then would thinke, that by his subtile trains
　He could escape fowle death or deadly paines?²¹²
　Thus when that Princes wrath was pacifide,
　He gan renew the late forbidden banes°,　　　　　*banns*
　And to the knight his daughter deare he tyde,
With sacred rites and vowes for ever to abyde.

37

His owne two hands the holy knots did knit,
　That none but death for ever can devide;
　His owne two hands, for such a turne° most fit,　　　*task*
　The housling° fire did kindle and provide,　　　　*sacramental*
　And holy water thereon sprinckled wide,²¹³
　At which the bushy Teade° a groome did light,　　　*torch*
　And sacred lampe in secret chamber hide,
　Where it should not be quenched day nor night,
For feare of evill fates, but burnen ever bright.

38

Then gan they sprinckle all the posts with wine,
　And made great feast to solemnize that day;
　They all perfumde with frankencense divine,
　And precious odours fetcht from far away,
　That all the house did sweat with great aray:
　And all the while sweete Musicke did apply
　Her curious° skill, the warbling notes to play,　　　*ingenious*
　To drive away the dull Melancholy;
The whiles one sung a song of love and jollity.

39

During the which there was an heavenly noise²¹⁴
　Heard sound through all the Pallace pleasantly,
　Like as it had bene many an Angels voice,
　Singing before th'eternall maiesty,
　In their trinall triplicities on hye;

Yet wist no creature, whence that heavenly sweet
Proceeded, yet each one felt secretly
Himselfe thereby reft of his sences meet°,   *proper*
And ravished with rare impression in his sprite.

40

Great joy was made that day of young and old,
    And solemne feast proclaimd throughout the land,
    That their exceeding merth may not be told:
    Suffice it heare° by signes to understand   *here*
    The usuall joyes at knitting of loves band.
    Thrise happy man the knight himselfe did hold,
    Possessed of his Ladies hart° and hand,   *heart*
    And ever, when his eye did her behold,
His heart did seeme to melt in pleasures manifold.

41

Her joyous presence and sweet company
    In full content he there did long enjoy,
    Ne wicked envie, ne vile gealesy
    His deare delights were able to annoy:
    Yet swimming in that sea of blisfull joy,
    He nought forgot, how he whilome° had sworne,   *once*
    In case he could that monstrous beast destroy,
    Unto his Faerie Queene backe to returne:
The which he shortly did, and Una left to mourne.

42

Now strike your sailes ye jolly Mariners,
    For we be come unto a quiet rode°,   *sea passage*
    Where we must land some of our passengers,
    And light this wearie vessell of her lode.
    Here she a while may make her safe abode,
    Till she repaired have her tackles spent°,   *worn out*
    And wants supplide. And then againe abroad
    On the long voyage whereto she is bent:
Well may she speede and fairely finish her intent.

[1590]

Epithalamion[215]

Ye learned sisters° which have oftentimes   *the Muses*
Beene to me ayding, others to adorne:
Whom ye thought worthy of your gracefull rymes,
That even the greatest did not greatly scorne
To heare theyr names sung in your simple layes,
But joyed in theyr prayse.
And when ye list your owne mishaps to mourne,
Which death, or love, or fortunes wreck did rayse,
Your string could soone to sadder tenor° turne,   *mood*
10 And teach the woods and water to lament
Your dolefull dreriment.
Now lay those sorrowfull complaints aside,
And having all your heads with girland crownd,
Helpe me mine owne loves prayses to resound,
Ne let the same of any be envide:
So Orpheus did for his owne bride,
So I unto my selfe alone will sing,
The woods shall to me answer and my Eccho ring.

Early before the worlds light giving lampe,
20 His golden beame upon the hils doth spred,
Having disperst the nights unchearefull dampe,
Doe ye awake, and with fresh lusty hed
Go to the bowre° of my beloved love,   *room*
My truest turtle dove,
Bid her awake; for Hymen is awake,
And long since ready forth his maske to move,
With his bright Tead° that flames with many a flake,°   *torch/spark*
And many a bachelor to waite on him,
In theyr fresh garments trim.
30 Bid her awake therefore and soone her dight,°   *dress*
For lo the wished day is come at last,
That shall for al the paynes and sorrowes past,
Pay to her usury of long delight:
And whylest she doth her dight,
Doe ye to her of joy and solace° sing,   *pleasure*
That all the woods may answer and your eccho ring.

Bring with you all the Nymphes that you can heare°   *can hear you*
Both of the rivers and the forrests greene:
And of the sea that neighbours to her neare,
40 Al with gay girlands goodly wel beseene:°   *adorned*

And let them also with them bring in hand,
Another gay girland
For my fayre love of lillyes and of roses,
Bound truelove wize with a blew silke riband.[216]
And let them make great store of bridale poses,
And let them eeke bring store of other flowers
To deck the bridale bowers.
And let the ground whereas her foot shall tread,
For feare the stones her tender foot should wrong
50 Be strewed with fragrant flowers all along,
And diapred° lyke the discolored mead.°   *adorned/many-coloured meadows*
Which done, doe at her chamber dore awayt,
For she will waken strayt,°   *straightaway*
The whiles doe ye this song unto her sing,
The woods shall to you answer and your Eccho ring.

Ye Nymphes of Mulla[217] which with carefull heed,
The silver scaly trouts doe tend full well,
And greedy pikes which use therein to feed,
(Those trouts and pikes all others doo excell)
60 And ye likewise which keepe the rushy lake,
Where none doo fishes take,
Bynd up the locks the which hang scatterd light,
And in his waters which your mirror make,
Behold your faces as the christall bright,
That when you come whereas my love doth lie,
No blemish she may spie.
And eke ye lightfoot mayds which keepe the deere,
That on the hoary° mountayne use to towre,°   *frosty/frequent*
And the wylde wolves which seeke them to devoure,
70 With your steele darts doo chace from comming neer
Be also present heere,
To helpe to decke her and to help to sing,
That all the woods may answer and your eccho ring.

Wake, now my love, awake; for it is time,
The Rosy Morne long since left Tithones bed,
All ready to her silver coche° to clyme,   *coach*
And Phoebus gins to shew his glorious hed.
Hark how the cheerefull birds do chaunt theyr laies
And carroll of loves praise.
80 The merry Larke hir mattins° sings aloft.   *morning praise*
The thrush replyes, the Mavis° descant[218] playes,   *song thrush*
The Ouzell° shrills, the Ruddock° warbles soft,   *blackbird/robin*

So goodly all agree with sweet consent,
To this dayes merriment.
Ah my deere love why doe ye sleepe thus long,
When meeter° were that ye should now awake,   *more fitting*
T' awayt the comming of your joyous make,°   *mate*
And hearken to the birds lovelearned song,
The deawy leaves among.
90 For they of joy and pleasance to you sing,
That all the woods them answer and theyr eccho ring.

My love is now awake out of her dreame,
And her fayre eyes like stars that dimmed were
With darksome cloud, now shew theyr goodly beams
More bright then Hesperus his head doth rere.
Come now ye damzels, daughters of delight,
Helpe quickly her to dight,
But first come ye fayre houres which were begot
In Joves sweet paradice, of Day and Night,
100 Which doe the seasons of the yeare allot,
And all that ever in this world is fayre
Doe make and still° repayre.   *continually*
And ye three handmayds° of the Cyprian Queene,°   *the Graces|Venus*
The which doe still addorne her beauties pride,
Helpe to addorne my beautifullest bride:
And as ye her array, still throw betweene°   *at intervals*
Some graces° to be seene,   *pleasing qualities*
And as ye use to Venus, to her sing,
The whiles the woods shal answer and your eccho ring.

110 Now is my love all ready forth to come,
Let all the virgins therefore well awayt,
And ye fresh boyes that tend upon her groome
Prepare your selves; for he is comming strayt.
Set all your things in seemely good aray
Fit for so joyfull day,
The joyfulst day that ever sunne did see.
Faire Sun, shew forth thy favourable ray,
And let thy lifull heat not fervent be
For feare of burning her sunshyny face,
120 Her beauty to disgrace.°   *spoil*
O fayrst Phoebus, father of the Muse,
If ever I did honour thee aright,
Or sing the thing, that mote° thy mind delight,   *might*
Doe not thy servants simple boone refuse,

But let this day let this one day be myne,
Let all the rest be thine.
Then I thy soverayne prayses loud wil sing,
That all the woods shal answer and theyr eccho ring.

130 Harke how the Minstrels gin to shrill aloud
Their merry Musick that resounds from far,
The pipe, the tabor,° and the trembling Croud,°   *small drum|fiddle*
That well agree withouten breach or jar.
But most of all the Damzels doe delite,
When they their tymbrels° smyte,   *tambourines*
And thereunto doe daunce and carrol sweet,
That all the sences they doe ravish quite,
The whyles the boyes run up and downe the street,
Crying aloud with strong confused noyce,
As if it were one voyce.
140 *Hymen iô Hymen, Hymen* they do shout,
That even to the heavens theyr shouting shrill
Doth reach, and all the firmament doth fill,
To which the people standing all about,
As in approvance doe thereto applaud
And loud advaunce her laud,°   *praise*
And evermore they *Hymen Hymen* sing,
That al the woods them answer and theyr eccho ring.

Loe where she comes along with portly° pace   *stately*
Lyke Phoebe from her chamber of the East,
150 Arysing forth to run her mighty race,
Clad all in white, that seemes° a virgin best.   *suits*
So well it her beseemes that ye would weene
Some angell she had beene.
Her long loose yellow locks lyke golden wyre,
Sprinckled with perle, and perling° flowres a tweene,   *winding*
Doe lyke a golden mantle her attyre,
And being crowned with a girland greene,
Seeme lyke some mayden Queene.²¹⁹
Her modest eyes abashed to behold
160 So many gazers, as on her do stare,
Upon the lowly ground affixed are.
Ne dare lift up her countenance too bold,
But blush to heare her prayses sung so loud,
So farre from being proud.
Nathlesse doe ye still loud her prayses sing.
That all the woods may answer and your eccho ring.

Tell me ye merchants daughters did ye see
So fayre a creature in your towne before,
So sweet, so lovely, and so mild as she,
170 Adornd with beautyes grace and vertues store°,   *wealth*
Her goodly eyes lyke Saphyres shining bright,
Her forehead yvory white,
Her cheekes lyke apples which the sun hath rudded°,   *reddened*
Her lips lyke cherryes charming men to byte,
Her brest like to a bowle of creame uncrudded°,   *uncurdled*
Her paps lyke lyllies budded,
Her snowie necke lyke to a marble towre,
And all her body lyke a pallace fayre,
Ascending uppe with many a stately stayre.
180 To honors seat and chastities sweet bowre.
Why stand ye still ye virgins in amaze,
Upon her so to gaze,
Whiles ye forget your former lay to sing,
To which the woods did answer and your eccho ring.

But if ye saw that which no eyes can see,
The inward beauty of her lively spright°,   *spirit*
Garnisht with heavenly guifts of high degree,
Much more then would ye wonder at that sight,
And stand astonisht lyke to those which red°   *saw*
190 Medusaes mazeful° hed.²²⁰   *amazing*
There dwels sweet love and constant chastity,
Unspotted fayth and comely womanhood,
Regard of honour and mild modesty,
There vertue raynes as Queene in royal throne,
And giveth lawes alone.
The which the base affections²²¹ doe obay,
And yeeld theyr services unto her will,
Ne thought of thing uncomely ever may
Thereto approch to tempt her mind to ill.
200 Had ye once seene these her celestial threasures,
And unrevealed pleasures,
Then would ye wonder and her prayses sing,
That al the woods should answer and your eccho ring.

Open the temple gates unto my love,
Open them wide that she may enter in,
And all the postes adorne as doth behove°,   *is fitting*
And all the pillours deck with girlands° trim,   *garlands*
For to recyve this Saynt with honour dew,
That commeth in to you.

210 With trembling steps and humble reverence,
      She commeth in, before th' almighties vew,
      Of her ye virgins learne obedience,
      When so ye come into those holy places,
      To humble your proud faces:
      Bring her up to th' high altar, that she may
      The sacred ceremonies there partake,
      The which do endlesse matrimony make,
      And let the roring Organs loudly play
      The praises of the Lord in lively notes,
220 The whiles with hollow throates
      The Choristers the joyous Antheme sing,
      That al the woods may answere and their eccho ring.

      Behold whiles she before the altar stands
      Hearing the holy priest that to her speakes
      And blesseth her with his two happy hands,
      How the red roses flush up in her cheekes,
      And the pure snow with goodly vermill° stayne,   *vermilion*
      Like crimsin dyde in grayne,°   *thoroughly*
      That even th' Angels which continually,
230 About the sacred Altare doe remaine,
      Forget their service and about her fly,
      Ofte peeping in her face that seemes more fayre,
      The more they on it stare.
      But her sad° eyes still fastened on the ground,   *grave*
      Are governed with goodly modesty,
      That suffers not one looke to glaunce awry,
      Which may let in a little thought unsownd.
      Why blush ye love to give to me your hand,
      The pledge of all our band?°   *bond*
240 Sing ye sweet Angels, Alleluya sing,
      That all the woods may answere and your eccho ring.

      Now al is done; bring home the bride againe,
      Bring home the triumph of our victory,
      Bring home with you the glory of her gaine,°   *gaining her*
      With joyance bring her and with jollity.
      Never had man more joyfull day than this,
      Whom heaven would heape with blis.
      Make feast therefore now all this live long day,
      This day for ever to me holy is,
250 Poure out the wine without restraint or stay,
      Poure not by cups, but by the belly full,
      Poure out to all that wull,°   *will*

And sprinkle all the postes and wals with wine,
That they may sweat, and drunken be withall.
Crowne ye God Bacchus with a coronall,°   *garland*
And Hymen also crowne with wreathes of vine,
And let the Graces daunce unto the rest;
For they can doo it best:
The whiles the maydens doe theyr carroll sing,
260   To which the woods shal answer and theyr eccho ring.

Ring ye the bels, ye yong men of the towne,
And leave your wonted° labors for this day: *usual*
This day is holy; doe ye write it downe,
That ye for ever it remember may.
This day the sunne is in his chiefest hight,
With Barnaby the bright,[222]
From whence declining daily by degrees,
He somewhat loseth of his heat and light,
When once the Crab behind his back he sees.
270   But for this time it ill ordained was,
To chose the longest day in all the yeare,
And shortest night, when longest fitter weare:
Yet never day so long, but late° would passe.   *at last*
Ring ye the bels, to make it weare away,
And bonefiers make all day,
And daunce about them, and about them sing,
That all the woods may answer, and your eccho ring.

Ah when will this long weary day have end,
And lende me leave to come unto my love?
280   How slowly do the houres theyr numbers spend?
How slowly does sad Time his feathers move?
Hast thee O fayrest Planet° to thy home   *i.e. the sun*
Within the Westerne fome:
Thy tyred steedes long since have need of rest.
Long though it be, at last I see it gloome,
And the bright evening star with golden creast
Appeare out of the East.
Fayre childe of beauty, glorious lampe of love
That all the host of heaven in rankes doost lead,
290   And guydest lovers through the nightes dread,
How chearefully thou lookest from above,
And seemst to laugh atweene thy twinkling light
As joying in the sight
Of these glad many which for joy doe sing,
That all the woods them answer and their eccho ring.

Now ceasse ye damsels your delights forepast;
Enough is it, that all the day was youres:
Now day is doen, and night is nighing fast:
Now bring the Bryde into the brydall boures.
300 Now night is come, now soone her disaray,
And in her bed her lay;
Lay her in lillies and in violets,
And silken courteins over her display,
And odourd sheetes, and Arras coverlets.[223]
Behold how goodly my faire love does ly
In proud humility;
Like unto Maia, when as Jove her tooke,
In Tempe, lying on the flowry gras,
Twixt sleepe and wake, after she weary was,
310 With bathing in the Acidalian brooke.
Now it is night, ye damsels may be gon,
And leave my love alone,
And leave likewise your former lay to sing:
The woods no more shal answere, nor your eccho ring.

Now welcome night, thou night so long expected°   *looked for*
That long daies labour doest at last defray,°   *pay for*
And all my cares, which cruell love collected,
Hast sumd in one, and cancelled for aye:
Spread they broad wing over my love and me,
320 That no man may us see,
And in thy sable mantle us enwrap,
From feare of perill and foule horror free.
Let no false treason seeke us to entrap,
Nor any dread disquiet once annoy
The safety of our joy:
But let the night be calme and quietsome,
Without tempestuous storms or sad afray°:   *terror*
Lyke as when Jove with fayre Alcmena lay,
When he begot the great Tirynthian groome°:   *i.e. Hercules*
330 Or lyke as when he with thy selfe did lie,
And begot Majesty.
And let the mayds and yongmen cease to sing:
Ne let the woods them answer, nor theyr eccho ring.

Let no lamenting cryes, nor dolefull teares,
Be heard all night within nor yet without:
Ne let false whispers, breeding hidden feares,
Breake gentle sleepe with misconceived dout.°   *fear*
Let no deluding dreames, nor dreadful sights

Make sudden sad affrights;
340 Ne let housefyres, nor lightnings helpelesse harmes,
 Ne let the Pouke,° nor other evill sprights,   *Puck*
Ne let mischivous witches with theyr charmes,
 Ne let hob Goblins, names whose sence we see not,
  Fray° us with things that be not.   *frighten*
Let not the shriech Oule, nor the Storke be heard:²²⁴
 Nor the night Raven that still° deadly yels,   *continuously*
Nor damned ghosts cald up with mighty spels,
 Nor griesly vultures make us once affeard:
Ne let th' unpleasant Quyre of Frogs still croking
350 Make us to wish theyr choking.
 Let none of these theyr drery accents sing;
 Ne let the woods them answer, nor theyr eccho ring.

But let stil Silence trew night watches keepe,
 That scared peace may in assurance rayne,
And tymely sleep, when it is tyme to sleepe,
 May poure his limbs forth on your pleasant playne,
The whiles an hundred little winged loves,°   *cupids*
 Like divers fethered doves
 Shall fly and flutter round about your bed,
360 And in the secret darke, that none reproves,
 Their prety stealthes shal worke, and snares shal spread
To filch away sweet snatches of delight,
 Conceald through covert night.
Ye sonnes of Venus, play your sports at will,
 For greedy pleasure, carelesse of your toyes,°   *dallying*
Thinks more upon her paradise of joyes,
 Then what ye do, albe it good or ill.
All night therefore attend your merry play,
 For it will soone be day:
370 Now none doth hinder you, that say or sing,
Ne will the woods now answer, nor your Eccho ring.

Who is the same, which at my window peepes?
 Or whose is that faire face, that shines so bright,
Is it not Cinthia, she that never sleepes,
 But walkes about high heaven al the night?
O fayrest goddesse, do thou not envy
 My love with me to spy:
For thou likewise didst love, though now unthought,° *not thought of*
 And for a fleece of woll,° which privily,   *wool*
380 The Latmian shephard° once unto thee brought, *i.e. Endymion*

His pleasure with thee wrought.
Therefore to us be favourable now;
And sith of wemens labours thou hast charge,[225]
And generation goodly dost enlarge,
Encline thy will t' effect our wishfull vow,
And the chast wombe informe with timely seed,
That may our comfort breed:
Till which we cease our hopefull hap° to sing, fortune
Ne let the woods us answere, nor our Eccho ring.

390
And thou great Juno, which with awful° might awe-inspiring
The lawes of wedlock still dost patronize,
And the religion° of the faith first plight sanctity
With sacred rites hast taught to solemnize:
And eeke for comfort often called art
Of women in their smart,° pains
Eternally bind thou this lovely band,° bond
And all thy blessings unto us impart.
And thou glad Genius,[226] in whose gentle hand,
The bridale bowre and geniall° bed remaine, engendering
400 Without blemish or staine,
And the sweet pleasures of theyr loves delight
With secret ayde doest succour and supply,
Till they bring forth the fruitfull progeny,
Send us the timely fruit of this same night.
And thou fayre Hebe, and thou Hymen free,
Grant that it may so be.
Til which we cease your further prayse to sing,
Ne any woods shal answer, nor your Eccho ring.

And ye high heavens, the temple of the gods,
410 In which a thousand torches flaming bright
Doe burne, that to us wretched earthly clods,
In dreadful darknesse lend desired light;
And all ye powers which in the same° remayne, i.e. the heavens
More then we men can fayne,° imagine
Poure out your blessing on us plentiously,
And happy influence upon us raine,
That we may raise a large posterity,
Which from the earth, which they may long possesse,
With lasting happinesse,
420 Up to your haughty° pallaces may mount, noble
And for the guerdon° of theyr glorious merit
May heavenly tabernacles there inherit,

Of blessed Saints for to increase the count.
So let us rest, sweet love, in hope of this,
And cease till then our tymely joyes to sing,
The woods no more us answer, nor our eccho ring.

Song made in lieu of many ornaments,
With which my love should duly have bene dect,°   *adorned*
Which cutting off through hasty accidents,²²⁷
430 Ye would not stay your dew time to expect,°   *await*
But promist both to recompens,
Be unto her a goodly ornament,
And for short time an endlesse moniment.°   *memorial*

[1595]

NOTES

Spenser

There are three levels of meaning to be considered in reading *The Faerie Queene*: 1. the entertainment level – contained in the narrative and characters; 2. the moral and educative level – in the story, characters and situation; 3. the level of contemporary events, as in references to the relationship between the Church of England and Roman Catholicism, the court and its sycophants, and, of course, to the virgin queen – Elizabeth – herself, that surface from time to time; sometimes these are comic or satiric, sometimes romantic, even adulatory. In his consistent use of symbols and richness of apposite detail, Spenser is undoubtedly the most iconographic of English poets.

In these notes = is used to explain a reference, while = s is used where there a further symbolic meaning. Wherever possible such symbolism – of numbers or flowers, for example – is explained in the notes.

1 Sp.'s *The Shepheardes Calendar*, 1579.
2 = either Calliope, muse of heroic poetry, Clio, muse of history and fame, or Urania, muse of astronomy and knowledge; also = the Virgin Mary, leader of the nine degrees of angels; = s Q. Elizabeth.
3 Tanaquill = Gloriana = s Q. Elizabeth; Briton Prince = King Arthur.
4 = s Q. Elizabeth.
5 The number 1 is associated with the 'all alone' true God; the Redcrosse Knight = s the Virtue of Holiness – he is 'a tall, clownish [i.e. countryfied] young man' ('A Letter of the Authors').
6 armour = s the armour of a Christian (Ephes.VI.11ff.) including the shield of Faith: St George's shield traditionally white/silver with red cross.
7 = s untamed passion.

8   = s the devil (Rev.XII.9. and XX.2), combined with traditional stories of St George and the dragon.

9   = Una, daughter of Adam and Eve, rulers of all the world until the Fall; = s Truth and the Church of England.

10 veiled because after the Fall, sinning man not able to look at her naked brightness; for Neoplatonists = the dross which hides the truth.

11 lamb = s innocence and gentleness of Christ.

12 dwarf = s prudence? common sense? the flesh?

13 wood = s error ('errare' – to wander).

14 cf. Chaucer's *The Parlement of Foules*, 1.176 ff.

15 sayling = used for ships; vine-prop elms = s fidelity in love; poplar associated with weeping; fir weeps resin; willow = s unhappiness in love; shaftes = arrow shafts; willow grows in wet areas, hence the water-mill; myrrh bleeds a kind of gum, associated with Christ's birth and death, used in healing remedies; beech used occasionally in victory garlands; ash used for a multiplicity of purposes; olives = s peace and therefore fruitfulness; plane tree has a large round trunk; holm-oak good for carving.

16 the lion traditionally has reverence for virgins, protecting them.

17 the gall (spleen) is the seat of anger: it is not faith that brings Redcrosse new strength but his anger.

18 books and papers = s Catholic tracts and doctrines; frogs (believed poisonous) = s vices linked with the devil: 'eyes did lacke' i.e. they were spiritually blind.

19 gnats = s evil (Beelzebub is Lord of the Flies).

20 = s self-destructiveness of evil.

21 Archimago = s hypocrisy, with powers of black magic, a deceptive image-maker; = s sorcery of Catholic Church.

22 Redcrosse is linked with the sun and sun god: midsummer eve = s the sun of justice.

23 during sleep, reason is suppressed, so man at his most vulnerable.

24 i.e. Proserpine.

25 i.e. Demogorgon.

26 twin gates of sleep: one, through which true dreams pass, is silver (= s purity); the other, for false dreams, is ivory.

27 troubled sleep caused by lack of moisture in the brain.

28 Duessa (= falsehood) is made of 'liquid ayre', i.e. a product of the imagination and therefore not real.

29 n.b. all 'seem'd' – an illusion.

30 the number 2 signifies division and therefore evil.

31 the constellation Boötes, the waggoner and the seven stars of Ursa Major; stedfast star = the Pole Star = s constancy.

32 i.e. Holiness is separated from Truth by hypocrisy, illusion and lust.

33 Aurora: the cock heralds the end of night and its attendant black magic.

34 fox = s hypocrisy, cunning and the devil.

35 Duessa = the great whore of Babylon: = s the Pope and all his followers (Rev.XVII.4); Persian mitre = s Papal mitre; wanton palfry = s uncontrolled passions.

36 = s the Pope in Rome ('where Tiberis doth pas'): Papal power considered by the C. of E. as a continuation of the old Roman Empire; the C. of E. was the true Church; Elizabeth traced her position back to Emperor Constantine the Great, who renamed Byzantium as Constantinople (AD330) and made it the centre of his empire, not Rome.

37 the heir = Christ.
38 the degeneration is from faithlessness to lawlessness to joylessness (or loss of grace).
39 over-fastidiousness leads to poverty.
40 Redcrosse prefers shadows (= s lies) to the open sun (= s truth and true religion).
41 doubt allied to moral duplicity (Duessa/Fidessa = s Catholicism) results in stalemate, petrification, which can only be released by the water (baptism, John IV.14) of everlasting life.
42 rose = s frailty, mutability; dedicated to Venus; = s Tudor rose and white single rose both used by Queen Elizabeth I, one in her position as Queen, the other = s her virginity: Duessa = s the false deceiver, Mary, Queen of Scots.
43 when there was no other beautiful person nearby.
44 spring; when the annual penance of witches took place.
45 wild marjoram used as a cure for scabs, itch and scurvy.
46 = s the grace of God received in baptism.
47 Redcrosse is distancing himself from Fradubio, = s doubt.
48 she knew well.
49 all fear having gone.
50 the number 3 is the number of perfection, as exemplified in the Trinity.
51 as a touchstone, which tests the quality of gold.
52 unveiled truth too bright for mortal eye; sun = s God and Truth, Q. Elizabeth as the sun of the true religion; lion = s justice: Leo in the house of the sun links Christ (sun) and judgement (Leo) = s Christ as the true judge. Here Una, abandoned by her own lion (i.e. Redcrosse) is protected by a wild lion, = s natural justice.
53 made her turn pale.
54 as if her life were at stake.
55 terrified to the point of fainting.
56 'Our Father' and 'Hail Mary' both the opening words of prayers.
57 i.e. Odysseus who refused Calypso's offer of immortality because of his love for his wife, Penelope.
58 desire for revenge.
59 should be like death to my unhappy heart.
60 i.e. Sirius, the dog star.
61 had not the power of the true shield.
62 whatever rank you are.
63 the one truest.
64 jousting enclosures.
65 natural justice cannot withstand lawlessness.
66 milder, as a beast, than her human foe.
67 the number 4 is connected with the created universe – the four elements, seasons, winds, humours, etc; the square = s constancy, stability, virtue.
68 Lucifera's palace of pride and self-love; an illusion of stability and strength, with skin-deep attractions and ambitions at the mercy of time.
69 all around gazing on them.
70 Phaeton.
71 cf. Satan, = s Mary Queen of Scots.
72 the sins of the flesh – sloth, gluttony, lechery; the sins of the world – avarice; sins of the devil – envy, wrath: Lucifera = pride.
73 thirst-producing dropsy.
74 greene = Venus' colour: burning hart = love burning in lechery.

75 camel = s avarice.
76 made no difference between right and wrong.
77 avarice considered a sin of, particularly, old age.
78 i.e. clothes and food.
79 a solitary life.
80 wolf = s envy; toads were said to swell with envy.
81 dressed in a many-coloured garment with eyes everywhere.
82 the spleen is the seat of anger.
83 erysipelas, a skin disease.
84 mist = s ignorance and error.
85 Redcrosse, without Una, not proof against 'joylessness' (despair).
86 Redcrosse = the griffin (half lion, half eagle) = s a combination of choleric and destructive elements: he is still an imperfect knight but with the normal temperament for his age, the prime (20–40 years) being associated with summer, fire and choler though not, as here, to excess.
87 unless the dead were given their proper rites they had to wander the shore of the Styx until these were accomplished.
88 bier attended by mourners.
89 rope lowered by Zeus for the other gods to test his strength by trying to pull him out of heaven.
90 of the underworld; owl = s night and death; wolf = s the devil.
91 cf. the descent to the underworld of Aeneas (*Aeneid* VI) and Christ's harrowing of hell: for Neoplatonists = s the soul's descent into matter and mortality.
92 50 daughters of Danaus.
93 Phaedra.
94 Neptune.
95 the remnants of Hippolytus.
96 term of life, as dictated by the Fates, completed.
97 the passage of time.
98 Nebuchadnezzar (Dan.II and IV).
99 Alexander the Great.
100 not getting her wish.
101 cause/bring about: 'bewaile' poss. an error.
102 = s man's lower nature; here, nearer to natural man with instinctive code of honour: contemporary popular question was 'Is the savage bestial or innocent?' = s Q. Elizabeth and her subjects in pastoral arcadia.
103 teach their knees, which, naturally, being goat-like, bent backwards, to kneel.
104 present necessity.
105 olive was sacred to Faunus and the emblem of Athena the wise, = s peace.
106 wine from the grape
107 of heavenly beauty.
108 his appearance when he was alive.
109 Thyamis = s passion; Labryde = s turbulent, tempestuous; Therion = s wild beast.
110 deer hunting and sexual hunting/indulgence.
111 traditionally the wild man controlled the animals: lion = s wrath, bear = s wrath and lust; boar = s lust; leopard = s lust and deceit; panther = s lust: Bacchus rode a bull and his chariot was drawn by tigers, leopards and panthers.
112 to work together, side by side.
113 traditionally the wild man would become a knight.

114   i.e. Archimago again in disguise, cf. 29.
115   had just begun fighting.
116   'But had he (Redcrosse) been where only his armour was, Archimago would not have
      been sorry for the mistake, for Sans Loy would have killed Redcrosse. Now he, Sans
      Loy, hopes to make good that mistake by killing Redcrosse's substitute, Satyrane.'
117   the number 7 is the number of the deadly sins, the planets, the ages of man =s
      mortality and mutability.
118   i.e. Salmacis.
119   disarmed =s without God's protection; disgrast =s without God's grace; dismayde
      =s unmade, i.e. weak from drinking the water of the stream from the pool.
120   sts. 12–13 midpoint of Book I where Redcrosse (=fallen man) only saved by God's
      grace.
121   the blast alone.
122   Rev.XII.3–9, XVII.3: triple crown =s papal authority.
123   many-headed hydra slain by Hercules.
124   the three Fates who spin, weave and cut the thread of life.
125   Arthur =s magnificence, according to Sp. (see 'A Letter of the Authors') 'the
      perfection of all the rest and conteineth in it them all'.
126   i.e. of the Faerie Queene, cf. the image of the Virgin Mary imprinted on Arthur's
      shield.
127   the sword of Morddure =s justice.
128   a dragon was the emblem of Cadwallader, last of the Kings of Britain, and of Uther
      Pendragon, Arthur's father, Henry VII's ancestor.
129   i.e. virtue and faith still to be found in England.
130   a smooth round bit.
131   suited his approach to her grief.
132   the Order of the Garter, its patron St George.
133   =London
134   that preferred death to such dishonour.
135   none returned alive.
136   8 is the number of recognition: 50 sts. in this canto, 50 =s remission of sins.
137   Josh. VI.5.
138   victory of Christ over Satan; of the Church of England over Roman Catholicism.
139   it was useless to think such blows could be endured.
140   cf. Moses. Exod.XVII.6. and the crucifixion, John XIX.34.
141   Rev.XVII.4ff.; the giant, Rev.XII and XIII.
142   what I cannot repay may God repay with interest.
143   may your conduct continue to give you victory over your fate.
144   i.e. wilfully refusing to learn.
145   cf. Moloch to whom children were sacrificed; Pharoah, Exod. I.15.22; Herod, Matt.
      II.16: poss. ref. to the Massacre of St Bartholomew, 24 Aug. 1572, when Philip of
      Spain benefited from the massacre of the Huguenots in Paris.
146   Rev.VI.9–10
147   Rev.XIII.2
148   wound, i.e. of love.
149   divine grace.
150   would have shared my companion's fate.
151   may God never let you hear his enchanted arguments.

152 Redcrosse's anger leads him to demand an eye for an eye – he cannot withstand Despair's arguments.

153 that the rest of your life may bring.

154 aspen = s fear; traditionally one of the trees used to make the cross of the crucifixion.

155 10 is the number of perfection – of the 10 commandments.

156 the House of Holiness.

157 a heavenly Venus cf.30.

158 Faith, Hope and Charity, who was usually depicted with many children about her.

159 Matt. VII.14.

160 continuous fear of death.

161 crystal = s purity and durability of faith.

162 white robe = s purity; cup = s communion chalice; serpent – used by Moses to disperse the plague, Numb.XXI.9; traditionally St John is shown holding a chalice with a snake in it.

163 blue = colour of the heavens = s truth; silver anchor = s purity and hope; 'not so chearefull' because in hope there is always an element of apprehension.

164 may God give her increase in that way for evermore.

165 i.e. Christ's blood.

166 i.e. higher power: for examples of the triumph of faith see Josh.X.12–14, 2 Kings XX.10–11, Exod. XIV.21, Matt.XXI.21.

167 cf. Redcrosse with Despair, but here given Patience (to offset his choler and anger) to whom he confesses and from whom he receives absolution, accepts Penance and Repentance, and then finally finds Charity. Finally, with the aid of Contemplation, he is given a vision of the New Jerusalem.

168 horror of sin.

169 I.Cor.XIII.2.

170 yellow is the traditional colour of Hymen's dress and doves are sacred to Venus.

171 men who pray for others.

172 an eagle could look at the sun and not be blinded; oak is Jove's tree = endurance.

173 keys of heaven, Matt.XVI.19.

174 Mt Sinai, where Moses received the tablets of the Law, Exod.XXIV.12ff. Matt.XVII.1ff.

175 the crossing of the Red Sea, Exod.XIV.16ff.

176 Noah's flood lasted 40 days; Moses was 40 days on Mount Sinai; Christ was 40 days in the wilderness.

177 Mount of Olives.

178 Parnassus, home of the Muses.

179 the New Jerusalem, Rev.XXI.10ff.

180 Jacob's dream, Gen.XXVIII.12.

181 i.e. London.

182 i.e. Q. Elizabeth I.

183 georgos = ploughman.

184 11 is the number of sin.

185 Rev.XII.4,7,9.

186 Sp.'s projected epic 'Of politiche vertues in (Arthur's) person, after that he came to be king' or the later parts of *F.Q.* e.g. Book V.

187 bell, next to the tenor bell, which was the loudest of the peal.

188 for the description of the dragon cf. Ovid. *Metamorphoses* III.31ff; Dan.VII.7,19; Job XLI.15ff.

189 the attributes of the dragon cf. those of the hawk and the falcon = Mars' birds.
190 i.e. the dragon's signs of defiance.
191 Rev.XXII.1–2.
192 water – as for baptism in Siloam (John IX.7ff); the cleansing pools of Jordan (2 Kings V.10ff.) Cephisus (Pliny, *Historia Naturalis* II) and the pure waters of Hebrus (Horace, *Epistles* I.XVI.13) and the healing waters of Bath, England and Spa, Germany.
193 cf. Christ in Gethsemane.
194 was up and about.
195 the old eagle rises to the sun to burn off its old plumage and the film over its eyes, then renews itself by dipping into the spring three times = s regeneration by baptism.
196 with the reviving water of the well. cf.36.1.2.
197 to whom the 'he's and 'him's and 'his' refer in the following lines can only be deduced by their context.
198 the shield of faith.
199 the sword of the spirit = s the word of God, Ephes.VI.16–17.
200 Gen.II.9ff. – two trees were planted, one of life, the other of good and evil.
201 Rev.XXII.1ff: healing balm = s communion and the power of grace.
202 of the essence of.
203 dragon's jaws = hell's mouth.
204 Redcrosse's? God's?
205 12 is the number of grace and perfection: cf. Sp.'s *Epithalamion*.
206 laurel = s victory: Apollo's tree.
207 cf. the entry of Christ into Jerusalem, Matt.XXI.8.
208 in resembling her attractive self.
209 the six ages of the world which end in an unchanging eternity (Rev.XX.Iff.).
210 i.e. the marriage of Christ to his true bride, the Church, which can only be achieved at the end of time.
211 Rev.XIX.7–8.
212 Rev.XX.3.
213 fire (= male) and water (= female) were a part of ancient marriage ceremonies, carried out by sponsors who joined the hands of the couple.
214 earthly music links with the music of the spheres; trinall triplicities = 9 angelic orders: 9 = 3 × 3, the holy numbers of perfection – there are 9 degrees of angels.
215 published with the sonnet sequence, *Amoretti*, 1595; Epithalamion = lit. 'upon the bridal chamber' – a wedding song.
216 = s fidelity.
217 Mulla = the river Awbeg, near Sp.'s estate at Kilcolman, Ireland.
218 melody sung as descant to a plainsong tune.
219 i.e. Q. Elizabeth I.
220 the head – the seat of reason.
221 the lower emotions – the passions.
222 St Barnabas Day, June 11th (old style) when the sun is moving from Cancer (the crab) to Leo (the lion).
223 specially fine tapestries were made at Arras.
224 Deut.XIV.12–18.
225 *see* Lucina.
226 god of birth and generation.
227 poss. some re-arrangement of his wedding?

John Donne

[1572–1631]

Born into a Roman Catholic family: his father died when he was age 4 and his mother remarried – a Catholic physician, Dr John Syminges: educated at home by Catholic tutors and then at Hart Hall (now Hertford College) Oxford, 1583, a college favoured by Catholics as it had no chapel and therefore their Catholicism was less noticed. Debarred by his religion from taking a degree, he may have spent 1589–91 on the Continent. His earliest poems – his Satires and Elegies – belong to the 1590s. 1592, he was admitted to Lincoln's Inn as a law student. 1593 his brother died in prison after being arrested for sheltering a Catholic priest. D. renounced his Catholicism: sailed in attacks upon Spain and Spanish treasure ships with Essex, 1596, and Raleigh, 1597. Became Sir Thomas Egerton's secretary and, 1601, elected M.P. for Brackley, Northamptonshire. Because of his secret marriage to Ann More, Lady Egerton's niece, 1601, he was dismissed and imprisoned. For the next 14 years he had to live with the problems occasioned by his marriage – at first depending upon the good will of friends for support. *Holy Sonnets* was probably written 1610–11. Urged by James I he entered the Church of England, 1615 and James prevailed upon Cambridge to give him a D.D. He held livings at Keyston, Sevenoaks, Blunham and a readership in divinity at Lincoln's Inn. Ann died 1617 after the birth of their 13th child. In 1621 through the good offices of the Duke of Buckingham, he became the Dean of St Paul's and famed for his sermons. He died 31 March after having first, as Walton, his first biographer, relates had his portrait drawn wearing a shroud. His poems were collected by his son, John, and published 1633 (2nd, enlarged, edit., 1635) but the poems of *Songs and Sonnets* cannot be dated accurately.

A Valediction: Of Weeping

Let me pour forth
My tears before thy face, whilst I stay here,
For thy face coins° them, and thy stamp they bear,   *creates*
And by this mintage they are something worth,
    For thus they be
    Pregnant of thee;
Fruits of much grief they are, emblems of more;
When a tear falls, that thou falls which it bore,[1]
So thou and I are nothing then, when on a divers° shore.   *alien*

10   On a round ball
A workman that hath copies by, can lay
An Europe, Afric, and an Asia,
And quickly make that, which was nothing,[2] all,
    So doth each tear
    Which thee doth wear,
A globe, yea world, by that impression grow,
Till thy tears mixed with mine do overflow
This world; by waters sent from thee, my heaven dissolved so.

    O more than moon,[3]
20 Draw not up seas to drown me in thy sphere;
Weep me not dead, in thine arms, but forbear
To teach the sea what it may do too soon.
    Let not the wind
    Example find
To do me more harm than it purposeth;
Since thou and I sigh one another's breath,
Whoe'er sighs most is cruellest, and hastes the other's death.

[1633]

The Ecstasy

Where, like a pillow on a bed,
    A pregnant bank swelled up, to rest
The violet's[4] reclining head,
    Sat we two, one another's best.

Our hands were firmly cemented
   With a fast balm,[5] which thence did spring;
Our eye-beams twisted, and did thread
   Our eyes upon one double string;[6]

So to entergraft° our hands, as yet   *engrafted*
10   Was all our means to make us one,
And pictures in our eyes to get°   *beget*
   Was all our propagation.

As 'twixt two equal armies fate
   Suspends uncertain victory,
Our souls (which to advance their state
   Were gone out) hung 'twixt her and me.

And whilst our souls negotiate there,
   We like sepulchral statues lay;
All day the same our postures were,
20   And we said nothing, all the day.

If any, so by love refined
   That he soul's language understood,
And by good love were grown all mind,
   Within convenient distance stood,

He (though he knew not which soul spake,
   Because both meant, both spake the same)
Might thence a new concoction[7] take,
   And part far purer than he came.

This ecstacy doth unperplex
30   (We said) and tell us what we love,
We see by this, it was not sex,
   We see, we saw not what did move:

But as all several° souls contain   *separate*
   Mixture of things, they know not what,
Love, these mixed souls, doth mix again,
   And makes both one, each this and that.

A single violet transplant,
   The strength, the colour, and the size,
(All which before was poor and scant)
40   Redoubles still, and multiplies.

When love with one another so
    Interinanimates two souls,
That abler soul, which thence doth flow,
    Defects of loneliness controls.

We then, who are this new soul, know
    Of what we are composed, and made,
For th' atomies° of which we grow   *components*
    Are souls, whom no change can invade.

But, O alas! so long, so far
50   Our bodies why do we forbear?
They're ours, though they are not we; we are
    The intelligences, they the sphere.

We owe them thanks, because they thus
    Did us, to us, at first convey,
Yielded their forces°, sense, to us,   *powers*
    Nor are dross to us, but allay°.   *alloy*

On man heaven's influence works not so,
    But that it first imprints the air;[8]
So soul into the soul may flow,
60   Though it to body first repair.

As our blood labours to beget
    Spirits, as like souls as it can;
Because such fingers need° to knit   *are necessary*
    That subtle knot, which makes us man;[9]

So must pure lovers' souls descend
    T' affections°, and to faculties,   *feelings*
Which sense may reach and apprehend,
    Else a great prince in prison lies.

To' our bodies turn we then, that so
70   Weak men on love revealed may look;
Love's mysteries in souls do grow,
    But yet the body is his book.

And if some lover, such as we,
    Have heard this dialogue of one,[10]
Let him still mark us, he shall see
    Small change, when we're to bodies gone.

[1633]

The Relic[11]

When my grave is broke up again
Some second guest to entertain,
(For graves have learned that woman-head
To be to more than one a bed)
  And he that digs it, spies
A bracelet of bright hair about the bone,
  Will he not let us alone,
And think that there a loving couple lies
Who thought that this device might be some way
10 To make their souls, at the last busy day,
Meet at this grave, and make a little stay?

  If this fall in a time, or land,
  Where mis-devotion° doth command,   *idolatry*
  Then, he that digs us up, will bring
  Us to the Bishop and the King,
    To make us relics; then
Thou shalt be a Mary Magdalen,[12] and I
    A something else thereby;
All women shall adore us, and some men;
20 And since, at such times, miracles are sought,
I would that age were by this paper° taught   *poem*
What miracles we harmless lovers wrought.

  First, we loved well and faithfully,
  Yet knew not what we loved, nor why;
  Difference of sex no more we knew
  Than our guardian angels,[13] do;
    Coming and going we
Perchance might kiss, but not between those meals;
    Our hands ne'er touched the seals,
30 Which nature, injured by late law, sets free:[14]
These miracles we did; but now alas,
All measure, and all language, I should pass,
Should I tell what a miracle she was.

[1633]

A Nocturnal upon St Lucy's Day,
being the shortest day[15]

'Tis the year's midnight, and it is the day's,
Lucy's, who scarce seven hours herself unmasks;
   The sun is spent, and now his flasks°   *stars*
   Send forth light squibs,° no constant rays;   *small fireworks*
      The world's whole sap is sunk;
The general balm[16] th' hydroptic° earth hath drunk,   *thirsty*
Whither, as to the bed's-feet, life is shrunk,[17]
Dead and interr'd; yet all these seem to laugh,
Compar'd with me, who am their epitaph.

10 Study me then, you who shall lovers be
At the next world, that is, at the next spring:
   For I am every dead thing,
   In whom love wrought new alchemy.°   *basic change*
      For his art did express°   *squeeze out*
A quintessence even from nothingness,
From dull privations, and lean emptiness:
He ruined me, and I am re-begot
Of absence, darkness, death: things which are not.

All others, from all things, draw all that's good,
20 Life, soul, form, spirit, whence they being have;
   I, by love's limbeck,[18] am the grave
   Of all that's nothing. Oft a flood
      Have we two wept, and so
Drown'd the whole world, us two; oft did we grow
To be two chaoses, when we did show
Care to ought else; and often absences
Withdrew our souls, and made us carcasses.

But I am by her death (which word wrongs her)
. Of the first nothing,[19] the elixir° grown;   *quintessence*
30   Were I a man, that I were one,
   I needs must know; I should prefer,
      If I were any beast,
Some ends, some means; yea plants, yea stones detest
And love; all, all some properties° invest;   *are indued with*
If I an ordinary nothing were,
As shadow, a light, and body must be here.

But I am none; nor will my sun renew.
You lovers, for whose sake, the lesser sun
  At this time to the Goat is run
40   To fetch new lust, and give it you,
      Enjoy your summer all;
Since she enjoys her long night's festival,[20]
Let me prepare towards her,[21] and let me call
This hour her vigil, and her eve, since this
Both the year's and the day's deep midnight is.

[1633]

Song

    Sweetest love, I do not go
      For weariness of thee,
    Nor in hope the world can show
      A fitter love for me;
        But since that I
    Must die at last, 'tis best
    To use myself in jest
      Thus by fained° deaths to die.   *pretended*

    Yesternight the sun went hence,
10   And yet is here today,
    He hath no desire nor sense,
      Nor half so short a way:
        Then fear not me,
    But believe that I shall make
    Speedier journeys, since I take
      More wings and spurs than he.

    O how feeble is man's power,
      That if good fortune fall,
    Cannot add another hour,
20   Nor a lost hour recall!
        But come bad chance,
    And we join to it our strength,
    And we teach it art and length,
      Itself o'er us to' advance.

When thou sigh'st, thou sigh'st not wind,
   But sigh'st my soul away,
When thou weep'st, unkindly kind,
   My life's blood doth decay.
     It cannot be
30 That thou lov'st me, as thou sayst,
If in thine my life thou waste,
   Thou art the best of me.

Let not thy divining° heart   *foreseeing*
   Forethink me any ill,
Destiny may take thy part,
   And may thy fears fulfil.
     But think that we
Are but turned aside to sleep;
They who one another keep
40   Alive, ne'er parted be.

[1633]

A Valediction: forbidding Mourning

As virtuous men pass mildly away
   And whisper to their souls to go,
Whilst some of their sad friends do say
   'The breath goes now,' and some say, 'No':

So let us melt, and make no noise,
   No tear-floods, nor sigh-tempests move,
'Twere profanation of our joys
   To tell the laity° our love.   *non-lovers*

Moving of th' earth brings harms and fears,
10   Men reckon what it did and meant;
But trepidation of the spheres,[22]
   Though greater far, is innocent.

Dull sublunary[23] lovers' love
   (Whose soul is sense) cannot admit
Absence, because it doth remove
   Those things which elemented° it.   *are the elements of*

But we by a love so much refined°   *purified*
   That ourselves know not what it is,
Inter°-assured of the mind,   *mutually*
   Care less eyes, lips and hands to miss.

Our two souls therefore, which are one,
   Though I must go, endure not yet
A breach, but an expansion
Like gold to airy thinness beat.

If they be two, they are two so
   As stiff° twin compasses are two;   *firm*
Thy soul, the fixed foot, makes no show
   To move, but doth, if th' other do.

And though it in the centre sit,
30   Yet when the other far doth roam,
It leans, and hearkens after it,
   And grows erect, as that comes home.

Such wilt thou be to me, who must
   Like th' other foot, obliquely run;
Thy firmness° makes my circle just, °   *steadfastness/exact*
   And makes me end where I begun.

[1633]

The Sun Rising

   Busy old fool, unruly sun,
     Why dost thou thus,
Through windows and through curtains call on us?
Must to thy motions lovers' seasons run?
     Saucy pedantic wretch, go chide
     Late school-boys, and sour 'prentices,
   Go tell court-huntsmen[24] that the King will ride,
   Call country ants to harvest offices;   *duties*
   Love, all alike, no season knows, nor clime,
10 Nor hours, days, months, which are the rags of time.

Thy beams, so reverend and strong
　　Why shouldst thou think?
I could eclipse and cloud them with a wink,
But that I would not lose her sight so long:
　　If her eyes have not blinded thine,
　　Look, and tomorrow late, tell me,
Whether both the Indias[25] of spice and mine
Be where thou left'st them, or lie here with me.
Ask for those kings whom thou saw'st yesterday,
20　And thou shalt hear, 'All here in one bed lay.'

　　She is all states, and all princes I;
　　　　Nothing else is.
Princes do but play us; compared to this,
All honour's mimic,° all wealth alchemy.°　　　　　　　*imitation/counterfeit*
　　Thou, sun, art half as happy as we,
　　In that the world's contracted thus;
　　Thine age asks ease, and since thy duties be
To warm the world, that's done in warming us.
Shine here to us, and thou art everywhere;
30　This bed thy centre is, these walls thy sphere.[26]

[1633]

The Anniversary

All kings, and all their favourites,
　　All glory of honours, beauties, wits,
The sun itself, which makes times, as they pass,
Is elder by a year now than it was
When thou and I first one another saw:
All other things to their destruction draw,
　　Only our love hath no decay;
This, no tomorrow hath, nor yesterday,
Running it never runs from us away,
10　But truly keeps his first, last, everlasting day.

　　Two graves must hide thine and my corse;
　　If one might, death were no divorce.
Alas, as well as other princes, we
(Who prince enough in one another be)

Must leave at last in death these eyes and ears,
Oft fed with true oaths, and with sweet salt tears;
   But souls where nothing dwells but love
(All other thoughts being inmates°) then shall prove   *lodgers*
This, or a love increased there above,
20 When bodies to their graves, souls from their graves, remove.

   And then we shall be throughly blest;
   But we no more than all the rest.
Here upon earth we're kings, and none but we
Can be such kings, nor of such, subjects be;
Who is so safe as we? where none can do
Treason to us, except one of us two.
   True and false fears let us refrain,°   *curb*
Let us love nobly, and live, and add again
Years and years unto years, till we attain
30 To write threescore: this is the second of our reign.

[1633]

Song

Go, and catch a falling star,
   Get with child a mandrake root,[27]
Tell me where all past years are,
   Or who cleft the devil's foot;
Teach me to hear mermaids singing,
Or to keep off envy's stinging,
       And find
       What wind
Serves to advance an honest mind.

10 If thou beest born to strange sights,
   Things invisible to see,
Ride ten thousand days and nights
   Till age snow white hairs on thee;
Thou, when thou return'st, wilt tell me
All strange wonders that befell thee,
       And swear
       No where
Lives a woman true and fair.

If thou find'st one, let me know;
20   Such a pilgrimage were sweet.
Yet do not; I would not go,
    Though at next door we might meet.
Though she were true, when you met her,
And last, till you write your letter,
            Yet she
            Will be
False, ere I come, to two or three.

[1633]

The Canonization[28]

For God's sake hold your tongue, and let me love,
    Or chide my palsy, or my gout,
My five gray hairs, or ruined fortune flout;
With wealth your state, your mind with arts improve;
    Take you a course, get you a place,[29]
    Observe his honour,° or his grace°   *lord/bishop*
And the king's real, or his stamped face[30]
    Contemplate; what you will, approve,°   *try out*
        So you will let me love.

10 Alas, alas, who's injured by my love?
    What merchants' ships have my sighs drowned?
Who says my tears have overflow'd his ground?
When did my colds a forward spring remove?
    When did the heats which my veins fill
    Add one man to the plaguy° bill?[31]   *of the plague*
Soldiers find wars, and lawyers find out still
    Litigious men, which quarrels move,
        Though she and I do love.

Call us what you will, we are made such by love;
    Call her one, me another fly,°   *moth*
20 We're tapers too, and at our own cost die,[32]
And we in us find the eagle and the dove;
    The phoenix[33] riddle hath more wit
    By us, we two, being one, are it.

So, to one neutral thing both sexes fit.
   We die and rise the same, and prove
      Mysterious[34] by this love.

We can die by it, if not live by love,
   And if unfit for tombs or hearse
30 Our legend be, it will be fit for verse;
   And if no piece of chronicle we prove,
      We'll build in sonnets pretty rooms;
      As well a well-wrought urn becomes
The greatest ashes,[35] as half-acre tombs;
   And by these hymns all shall approve
      Us canonized for love;

And thus invoke us: 'You, whom reverend Love
   Made one another's hermitage;
You, to whom love was peace, that now is rage;
40 Who did the whole world's soul extract, and drove
   Into the glasses of your eyes,
      So made such mirrors, and such spies,
That they did all to you epitomize,
   Countries, towns, courts: beg° from above   *intercede for*
      A pattern of your love!'

[1633]

The Good-Morrow

I wonder, by my troth, what thou and I
Did, till we lov'd? were we not wean'd till then?
But sucked[36] on country pleasures, childishly?
Or snorted° we in the seven sleepers' den?[37]   *snored*
'Twas so; but this, all pleasures fancies be.   *(compared with)*
If ever any beauty I did see,
Which I desir'd, and got, 'twas but a dream of thee.

And now good-morrow to our waking souls,
Which watch not one another out of fear;
10 For love, all love of other sights controls,
And makes one little room, an everywhere.

Let sea-discoverers to new worlds have gone,
Let maps to others, worlds on worlds have shown,
Let us possess one world, each hath one, and is one.

My face in thine eye, thine in mine appears,
And true plain hearts do in the faces rest;
Where can we find two better hemispheres,
Without sharp north, without declining west?[38]
Whatever dies was not mixt equally;
20 If our two loves be one, or, thou and I
Love so alike, that none do slacken, none can die.[39]

[1633]

From **Holy Sonnets**

VII[40]

At the round earth's imagined corners, blow
    Your trumpets, angels, and arise, arise
    From death, you numberless infinities
Of souls, and to your scattered bodies go,
All whom the flood did, and fire shall o'erthrow,[41]
    All whom war, dearth, age, agues, tyrannies,
    Despair, law, chance hath slain, and you whose eyes
Shall behold God, and never taste death's woe.[42]
But let them sleep, Lord, and me mourn a space,
    For, if above all these, my sins abound,
'Tis late to ask abundance of thy grace,
    When we are there; here on this lowly ground
        Teach me how to repent; for that's as good
        As if thou hadst sealed my pardon, with thy blood.

X

Death, be not proud, though some have called thee
    Mighty and dreadful, for thou art not so;
    For, those, whom thou think'st thou dost overthrow,
Die not, poor Death, nor yet canst thou kill me;

From rest and sleep, which but thy pictures be,
   Much pleasure, then, from thee much more must flow,
   And soonest our best men with thee do go,
Rest of their bones, and soul's delivery.
Thou'rt slave to fate, chance, kings and desperate men,
   And dost with poison, war, and sickness dwell;
   And poppy, or charms, can make us sleep as well,
And better than thy stroke; why swell'st° thou then?   *(with pride)*
   One short sleep past, we wake eternally,
   And death shall be no more, Death, thou shalt die.[43]

XIV

Batter my heart, three-person'd God;[44] for you
   As yet but knock, breathe, shine, and seek to mend;
   That I may rise, and stand, o'erthrow me, and bend
Your force, to break, blow, burn, and make me new.
   I, like an usurpt town to another due,[45]
   Labour to admit you, but O, to no end.
   Reason, your viceroy in me, me should defend,
But is captiv'd and proves weak or untrue,
Yet dearly I love you, and would be lov'd fain,[46]
   But am betroth'd unto your enemy,[47]
Divorce me, untie, or break that knot again,
   Take me to you, imprison me, for I,
      Except you enthrall° me, never shall be free,   *make prisoner*
      Nor ever chaste, except you ravish me.

[1633]

Satire III

Kind pity chokes my spleen; brave scorn forbids
Those tears to issue which swell my eyelids;
I must not laugh, nor weep sins, and be wise,
Can railing then cure these worn° maladies?   *long-standing*
Is not our mistress, fair religion,
As worthy of all our souls' devotion,
As virtue was to the first blinded age?[48]
Are not heaven's joys as valiant° to assuage   *powerful*
Lusts, as earth's honour was to them?[49] Alas,

10 As we do them in means, shall they surpass
Us in the end,[50] and shall thy father's spirit
Meet blind philosophers[51] in heaven, whose merit
Of strict life may be imputed faith, and hear
Thee, whom he taught so easy ways and near°   *direct*
To follow, damned? O, if thou dar'st, fear this;
This fear great courage and high valor is.
Dar'st thou aid mutinous Dutch,[52] and dar'st thou lay
Thee in ships, wooden sepulchers, a prey
To leaders' rage, to storms, to shot, to dearth?
20 Dar'st thou dive seas and dungeons of the earth?
Hast thou courageous fire to thaw the ice
Of frozen north discoveries,[53] and thrice
Colder than salamanders,[54] like divine
Children in the oven, fires of Spain,[55] and the line,°   *equator*
Whose countries limbecks[56] to our bodies be,
Canst thou for gain bear? And must every he
Which cries not, 'Goddess!' to thy mistress, draw,
Or eat thy poisonous words?[57] Courage of straw!
O desperate coward, wilt thou seem bold, and
30 To thy foes and his (who made thee to stand
Sentinel in his world's garrison) thus yield,
And for forbidden wars,[58] leave th' appointed field?
Know thy foes: The foul Devil he is, whom thou
Strivest to please: for hate, not love, would allow[59]
Thee fain his whole realm to be quit; and as
The world's all parts wither away and pass,
So the world's self, thy other loved foe, is
In her decrepit wane,[60] and thou, loving this,
Dost love a withered and worn strumpet; last,
40 Flesh (itself's death) and joys which flesh can taste,
Thou lovest; and thy fair goodly soul, which doth
Give this flesh power to taste joy, thou dost loathe.
Seek true religion. O, where? Mirreus,
Thinking her unhoused here, and fled from us,
Seeks her at Rome; there, because he doth know
That she was there a thousand years ago.
He loves her rags so, as we here obey
The statecloth° where the Prince sat yesterday.   *canopy*
Crantz to such brave° loves will not be enthralled,   *showy*
50 But loves her only, who at Geneva is called
Religion – plain, simple, sullen,° young,   *obstinate*
Contemptuous, yet unhandsome; as among
Lecherous humors, there is one that judges

No wenches wholesome but coarse country drudges.
Graius stays still at home here, and because
Some preachers, vile ambitious bawds, and laws
Still new, like fashions, bid him think that she
Which dwells with us, is only perfect, he
Embraceth her whom his godfathers will
60 Tender° to him, being tender°, as wards still   *offer/impressionable*
Take such wives as their guardians offer, or
Pay values.[61] Careless° Phrygius doth abhor   *uncaring*
All, because all cannot be good, as one,
Knowing some women whores, dares marry none.
Graccus loves all as one, and thinks that so
As women do in divers countries go
In divers habits, yet are still one kind,
So doth, so is religion; and this blind-
ness too much light breeds; but unmoved thou
70 Of force must one, and forced but one allow;[62]
And the right, ask thy father which is she,[63]
Let him ask his; though truth and falsehood be
Near twins, yet truth a little elder is;
Be busy to seek her, believe me this,
He's not of none, nor worst, that seeks the best.
To adore, or scorn an image, or protest,
May all be bad; doubt wisely; in strange way
To stand inquiring right, is not to stray;
To sleep, or run wrong, is. On a huge hill,
80 Cragged and steep, Truth stands, and he that will
Reach her, about must, and about must go,
And what th' hill's suddenness resists, win so;
Yet strive so, that before age, death's twilight,
Thy soul rest, for none can work in that night.[64]
To will implies delay, therefore now do.
Hard deeds, the body's pains; hard knowledge too
The mind's endeavours reach, and mysteries
Are like the sun, dazzling, yet plain to all eyes.
Keep the truth which thou hast found; men do not stand
90 In so ill° case that God hath with his hand   *evil condition*
Signed kings' blank° charters to kill whom they hate, *unconditional*
Nor are they vicars, but hangmen to Fate.   *authority*
Fool and wretch, wilt thou let thy soul be tied
To man's laws, by which she shall not be tried
At the last day? O, will it then boot° thee   *serve*
To say a Philip, or a Gregory,
A Harry, or a Martin[65] taught thee this?

Is not this excuse for mere contraries
Equally strong? Cannot both sides say so?
100 That thou mayest rightly obey power, her bounds know;
Those passed, her nature and name is changed; to be
Then humble to her is idolatry.
As streams are, power is; those blest flowers that dwell
At the rough stream's calm head, thrive and do well,
But having left their roots, and themselves given
To the stream's tyrannous rage, alas, are driven
Through mills,° and rocks, and woods, and at last, almost   *watermills*
Consumed in going, in the sea are lost.
So perish souls, which more choose men's unjust
110 Power from God claimed, than God himself to trust.

[1669]

NOTES

Donne

1 her image that the tear reflects.
2 globe, i.e. the big O (nothing).
3 which controls seas and tides.
4 violet is the emblem of faithful love and truth.
5 moisture which was considered a natural inborn preservative against decay.
6 there were conflicting theories in D.'s time as to whether beams from the eye struck
    the object it looked on or the beams came from the object itself and imprinted an
    image on the eye of the beholder.
7 in alchemy – the purifying of metals by heat.
8 there was a belief that stars influenced man via the air so they would be working
    through a less pure medium.
9 cf. 'the spirits in a man which are the thin and active part of the blood, and so are of a
    kind of middle nature, between the soul and the body . . . and they do the office, to
    unite and apply the faculties of the soul to the organs of the body, and so there is man.'
    D. Sermons.II.261–2.
10 the single unit that lovers are.
11 this poem assumes that the beloved has given her lover a bracelet of plaited hair as a
    keepsake.
12 Mary Magdalen was traditionally depicted with golden hair.
13 who have no sexuality.
14 the laws (restricting the freedom of love) imposed since man's original and natural
    state.
15 this poem has possible connections with either the serious illness of D.'s patron, the
    Countess of Bedford, 1612 or that of his wife, 1611, or his wife's death, 1617. St Lucy's

Day was 13th Dec. – the shortest day in the year, when the sun entered the sign of Capricorn (the goat). Lucy = light.

16 cf. n.5.
17 one of the signs of imminent death, according to Hippocrates, was when the dying man huddled down to the foot of the bed.
18 vessels used for distilling by heat.
19 the nothingness before chaos.
20 i.e. of death.
21 for meeting.
22 a trembling of the celestial spheres believed to account for the variations in the movements of the planets.
23 below the moon and therefore subject to its inconsistencies.
24 alludes to James I's love of hunting: court huntsmen also = courtiers hunting love.
25 both the Indias – West Indies (gold), East Indies (spices).
26 the bed = the earth, round which the walls (the revolutions of the sun) mark the limits: sun was regarded as a source of sexual power.
27 large forked root of the mandrake plant believed to promote conception.
28 making saints of love's martyrs.
29 course = some way of advancing oneself: place = position at court.
30 i.e. on the coin of the realm.
31 printed list of deaths from the plague.
32 die – used also of an orgasm.
33 bird of which only one exists at a time, the new one rising from the fiery immolation of the old, therefore sexless.
34 beyond the range of natural things.
35 the ashes of the greatest.
36 children of well-to-do families were put out to wet-nurses to be suckled.
37 seven young Christians, taking refuge in a cave from the persecution of Decius, were walled up there and slept – only to be found alive nearly 200 years later.
38 sharp north – where love grows cold: declining west where it fades away.
39 it was believed death resulted from an imbalance of the properties of the body.
40 the nos. are those of the 1635 edit.
41 fire was to end the world, Rev.VI–XII.
42 I Cor.XV.51–2.
43 I Cor.XV.26,54.
44 the Holy Trinity.
45 i.e. owing duty to someone other than its occupier.
46 i.e. would like to be loved.
47 i.e. Satan.
48 before the revelation of Christianity.
49 non-Christian seekers after virtue.
50 reaching heaven they may, perhaps, in the end, surpass the Christian.
51 ancient moralists, e.g. the Stoics.
52 many English soldiers of fortune had helped the Dutch against their Spanish conquerors.
53 the north-west passage through to the Pacific.
54 lizard-like creatures believed to be able to withstand fire and live in it comfortably.
55 Shadrach, Meshach and Abednego who survived the fiery furnace Nebuchadnezzar ordered them into for refusing to agree to idol worship: fires of Spain – those of the Spanish inquisition.

56 cf. n.18.
57 swallow sickening insults.
58 those for wordly, not spiritual, gain: th'appointed field = this world as God's battlefield.
59 would gladly requite you, out of hate, with his whole kingdom.
60 the world was believed to be running down.
61 fines imposed if wards refused to marry the person chosen by their guardians.
62 one religion – necessarily accept one religion which never relinquish even under duress.
63 Deut.XXXII.7.
64 St John IX.4.
65 i.e. Philip II of Spain: Pope Gregory VII (who established papal infallibility) or Gregory XIV (Pope in Donne's time); Henry VIII; Martin Luther.

George Herbert

[1593–1633]

The younger brother of Lord Herbert of Cherbury: his father died when he was age three, and his mother, the friend and patron of Donne, married Sir John Danvers. He was educated at Westminster School, ?1604–9: Trinity College, Cambridge, where, 1609, he was King's Scholar. 1610, according to Walton, his first biographer, in a letter to his mother containing two sonnets he dedicated his poetry to God. His first published poems were two sets of memorial verses in Latin for a volume of elegies for Prince Henry, who died 1612. 1616, became a Fellow of Trinity, and, 1618, Reader in Rhetoric. By 1620 he was elected Public Orator at Cambridge: 1624, 1625 he was M.P. for Montgomery. By 1624 ordained deacon, and, 1626, became a canon of Lincoln Cathedral, with the prebendary of Leighton Bromswold, Huntingdonshire. 1629, married Jane Danvers, cousin of his stepfather, and they adopted two orphaned nieces: became rector of Bemerton, near Salisbury, Wiltshire, and was ordained. A great lover of music he would visit Salisbury Cathedral where the singing, he declared was 'Heaven on earth'. Ill with consumption, he sent his poems to his friend Ferrar (who had established a religious community at Little Gidding, near Leighton Bromswold) for publication should Ferrar think them of value, otherwise they were to be burnt. After his death, *The Temple*, 1633, included nearly all of his poems, which, he said, gave 'a picture of the many spiritual conflicts that have passed betwixt God and my soul, before I could subject mine to the will of Jesus, my Master'.

The Pearl (Matt XIII. 45)

I know the ways of Learning; both the head
And pipes that feed the press[1] and make it run;
What reason hath from nature borrowed,
Or of it self, like a good huswife, spun
In laws and policy; what the stars conspire,
What willing nature speaks, what forc'd by fire;[2]

Both th'old discoveries, and the new-found seas,
The stock and surplus, cause and history:
All these stand open, or I have the keys:
10   Yet I love thee.

I know the ways of Honour, what maintains
The quick returns of courtesy and wit:
In vies of favours whether° party gains,   *which*
When glory° swells the heart, and moldeth it   *ambition*
To all expressions both of hand and eye,
Which on the world a true-love-knot may tie,
And bear the bundle, wheresoe're it goes:
How many drams of spirit there must be
To sell my life unto my friends or foes:
20   Yet I love thee.

I know the ways of Pleasure, the sweet strains,
The lullings and the relishes° of it;   *musical flourishes*
The propositions of hot blood and brains;
What mirth and music mean; what love and wit
Have done these twenty hundred years and more:
I know the projects of unbridled store;°   *wealth*
My stuff is flesh, not brass; my senses live,
And grumble oft, that they have more in me
Than he that curbs them, being but one to five:
30   Yet I love thee.

I know all these, and have them in my hand:
Therefore not sealed,³ but with open eyes
I fly to thee, and fully understand
Both the main sale, and the commodities;
And at what rate and price I have thy love;
With all the circumstances that may move:
Yet through these labyrinths, not my grovelling wit,
But thy silk twist° let down from heav'n to me,   *thread*
Did both conduct and teach me, how by it
40   To climb to thee.

[1633]

Bitter-Sweet

Ah my dear angry Lord,
Since thou dost love, yet strike;
Cast down, yet help afford;
Sure I will do the like.

I will complain, yet praise;
I will bewail, approve;
And all my sour-sweet days
I will lament, and love.

[1633]

Affliction

When first thou didst entice to thee my heart
            I thought the service brave:
So many joys I writ down for my part,
            Besides what I might have
Out of my stock of natural delights,
Augmented with thy gracious benefits.

I looked on thy furniture[4] so fine,
            And made it fine to me:
Thy glorious household-stuff did me entwine
10   And 'tice me unto thee.
Such stars I counted mine: both heaven and earth
Paid me my wages in a world of mirth.

What pleasures could I want, whose King I served
            Where joys my fellows were?
Thus argued into hopes, my thoughts reserved
            No place for grief or fear.
Therefore my sudden soul caught at the place,
And made her youth and fierceness seek thy face.

And first thou gav'st me milk and sweetnesses;
20   I had my wish and way:
My days were strewed with flowers and happiness;

There was no month but May.
But with my years sorrow did twist and grow,
And made a party unawares for woe.

My flesh began unto my soul in pain,
        'Sicknesses cleave my bones;
Consuming agues dwell in every vein,
        And tune my breath to groans.'
Sorrow was all my soul; I scarce believed,
30 Till grief did tell me roundly, that I lived.

When I got health, thou took'st away my life,
        And more; for my friends die[5]:
My mirth and edge was lost; a blunted knife
        Was of more use than I.
Thus thin and lean, without a fence or friend,
I was blown through with every storm and wind.

Whereas my birth and spirit rather took
        The way that takes the town;
Thou didst betray me to a lingering book,
40   And wrap me in a gown.[6]
I was entangled in a world of strife
Before I had the power to change my life.

Yet, for° I threatened oft the siege to raise,   *because*
        Not simpering° all mine age,   *looking pleasant*
Thou often didst with academic praise
        Melt and dissolve my rage.
I took thy sweetened pill, till I came where
I could not go away, nor persevere.

Yet lest perchance I should too happy be
50   In my unhappiness,
Turning my purge to food, thou throwest me
        Into more sicknesses.
Thus doth thy power cross-bias[7] me, not making
Thine own gift good, yet me from my ways taking.

Now I am here, what thou wilt do with me
        None of my books will show:
I read, and sigh, and wish I were a tree;

                    For sure then I should grow
        To fruit or shade: at least some bird would trust
60 Her household to me, and I should be just.

        Yet, though thou troublest me, I must be meek;
                    In weakness must be stout.
        Well, I will change the service, and go seek
                    Some other master out.
        Ah, my dear God! though I am clean forgot,
        Let me not love thee, if I love thee not.

                                        [1633]

Jordan

        Who says that fictions only and false hair
        Become a verse? Is there in truth no beauty?
        Is all good structure in a winding stair?
        May no lines pass, except they do their duty
            Not to a true, but painted chair?

        Is it no verse, except enchanted groves
        And sudden arbours shadow coarse-spun lines?
        Must purling streams refresh a lover's loves?
        Must all be veiled while he that reads, divines,
            Catching the sense at two removes?

        Shepherds are honest people; let them sing:
        Riddle who list, for me, and pull for prime:[8]
        I envy no man's nightingale or spring;
        Nor let them punish me with loss of rhyme,
            Who plainly say, *My God, My King*.

                                        [1633]

The Collar

I struck the board,° and cried, 'No more!   table
                  I will abroad.°   go out
What? shall I ever sigh and pine?
My lines° and life are free; free as the road,   limits
   Loose as the wind, as large as store.⁹
          Shall I be still in suit°?   in service
   Have I no harvest but a thorn
   To let° me blood, and not restore   draw off
   What I have lost with cordial° fruit?   cherishing
10   Sure there was wine
Before my sighs did dry it: there was corn¹⁰
     Before my tears did drown it.
   Is the year only lost to me?
     Have I no bays¹¹ to crown it?
No flowers, no garlands gay? all blasted?
          All wasted?
   Not so, my heart: but there is fruit,
          And thou hast hands.
   Recover all thy sigh-blown age
20 On double pleasures: leave thy cold dispute
Of what is fit, and not. Forsake thy cage,
          Thy rope of sands,
Which petty thoughts have made, and made to thee
   Good cable, to enforce and draw,
          And be thy law,
While thou didst wink and wouldst not see.
          Away; take heed:
          I will abroad.
Call in thy death's head¹² there: tie up thy fears.
30   He that forbears
   To suit and serve his need,
          Deserves his load.'
But as I raved and grew more fierce and wild
          At every word,
   Methoughts I heard one calling, 'Child!'
     And I replied, 'My Lord'.

[1633]

Easter

I got me flowers to straw thy way,
  I got me boughs off many a tree;
But thou wast up by break of day,
  And brought'st thy sweets along with thee.

The sun arising in the East,
  Though he give light, and the East perfume;
If they should offer to contest
  With thy arising they presume.

Can there be any day but this,
  Though many suns to shine endeavour?
We count three hundred, but we miss:
  There is but one, and that one ever.

[1633]

Discipline

Throw away thy rod,
Throw away thy wrath:
      O my God,
Take the gentle path.

For my heart's desire
Unto thine is bent:
      I aspire
To a full consent.

Not a word or look
I affect to own,
      But by book,
And thy book alone.

Though I fail, I weep;
Though I halt in pace,
      Yet I creep
To the throne of grace.

Then let wrath remove;
Love will do the deed;
     For with love
20 Stony hearts will bleed.

Love is swift of foot,
Love's a man of war,
     And can shoot,
And can hit from far.

Who can 'scape his bow?
That which wrought on thee,
     Brought thee low,
Needs must work on me.

Throw away thy rod:
30 Though man frailties hath,
     Thou art God:
Throw away thy wrath.

[1633]

Virtue

Sweet day, so cool, so calm, so bright,
The bridal of the earth and sky:
The dew shall weep thy fall tonight,
     For thou must die.

Sweet rose, whose hue angry and brave
Bids the rash gazer wipe his eye:
Thy root is ever in its grave,
     And thou must die.

Sweet spring, full of sweet days and roses,
10 A box where sweets[13] compacted lie:
My music shows ye have your closes,[14]
     And all must die.

Only a sweet and virtuous soul,
Like seasoned timber never gives;
But though the whole world turn to coal,
    Then chiefly lives.

[1633]

Love

Love bade me welcome; yet my soul drew back,
    Guilty of dust and sin.
But quick-eyed Love, observing me grow slack
    From my first entrance in,
Drew nearer to me, sweetly questioning,
    If I lacked anything.

'A guest', I answered, 'worthy to be here.'
    Love said, 'You shall be he.'
'I, the unkind, ungrateful? Ah, my dear,
    I cannot look on thee.'
Love took my hand, and smiling did reply,
    'Who made the eyes but I?'

'Truth, Lord, but I have marred them; let my shame
    Go where it doth deserve.'
'And know you not', says Love, 'who bore the blame?'
    'My dear, then I will serve.'
'You must sit down', says Love, 'and taste my meat.'
    So I did sit and eat.

[1633]

Easter Wings [15]

Lord, who createdst man in wealth and store,
  Though foolishly he lost the same,
    Decaying more and more
      Till he became
        Most poor:
        With thee
        O let me rise
      As larks, harmoniously,
    And sing this day thy victories:
Then shall the fall further the flight in me.

My tender age in sorrow did begin;
  And still with sicknesses and shame
    Thou didst so punish sin,
      That I became
        Most thin.
        With thee
        Let me combine,
      And feel this day [16] thy victory;
    For, if I imp [17] my wing on thine,
Affliction shall advance the flight in me.

[1633]

The Pulley

When God at first made man,
Having a glass of blessings standing by,
'Let us', said he, 'pour on him all we can:
Let the world's riches, which dispersèd lie,
      Contract into a span.'   *lifespan*

So strength first made a way;
Then beauty flowed, then wisdom, honour, pleasure;
When almost all was out, God made a stay,
Perceiving that, alone of all his treasure,
      Rest in the bottom lay.

'For if I should', said he,
'Bestow this jewel also on my creature,
He would adore my gifts instead of me,
And rest in Nature, not the God of Nature:
             So both should losers be.

     Yet let him keep the rest,
But keep them with repining restlessness:
Let him be rich and weary, that at least,
If goodness lead him not, yet weariness
             May toss him to my breast.'

[1633]

NOTES

Herbert

1   of wine or printing presses = universities and scholars.
2   the alchemist's furnace.
3   in falconry, the bird's eyes were sewn shut in training.
4   both nature and church ceremony.
5   between 1624–5, three of H.'s patrons died – the Duke of Richmond, the Marquis of Hamilton, and King James. His mother died 1627.
6   of the scholar.
7   going off course – refers to the game of bowls.
8   draw for cards in the card-game primero.
9   as the plenty in store.
10 thorn, blood and wine all sacred images – here with both religious and secular overtones.
11 laurel wreath worn by the poet.
12 symbol of mortality.
13 things pleasing to the senses.
14 the end of a musical phrase.
15 originally printed sideways to give the effect on the page of wings.
16 Easter Day, when Christ conquered death.
17 to graft feathers on to a damaged wing.

John Milton

[1608–74]

His father was a scrivener and a composer of music. M. was born in
Bread Street, Cheapside, London, on 9 December. Educated at St
Paul's School, London; admitted to Christ's College, Cambridge,
1625, where he was known as the 'Lady of Christ's'; received a BA
1629, an MA 1630. While at Cambridge he was writing poetry in
both Latin and English and his first outstanding piece was 'On The
Morning of Christ's Nativity', written 1629. 'L'Allegro' and 'Il
Penseroso' may have been written at Cambridge or
Hammersmith, where the family moved, 1631/2. He studied
continuously at home after leaving the university and in 1634
provided a masque, *Comus*, for performance at Ludlow Castle for
the installation of the Earl of Bridgewater as Lord President of
Wales. 1635 the family moved to Horton, Buckinghamshire, where
M. wrote 'Lycidas'. 1637–9 he travelled through Europe, meeting
Galileo at his villa near Florence. At this time he seems to have been
contemplating a work on King Arthur. The next 20 years were
spent in political activity and pamphleteering in the defence of the
liberty of the responsible, rational individual in religious, social
and domestic areas. In June 1642 he m. Mary Powell, a Catholic
girl of 17. Within six weeks, on the understanding of her husband
that she return by the end of September, she returned to her family
near Oxford, and stayed there, possibly because of the outbreak of
the Civil War. M.'s subsequent pamphlet on – and for – divorce
achieved some notoriety. 1645 he published a volume of poetry; he
and his wife were reconciled, and, 1646, a daughter, Anne, was b.,
1648 a second daughter, Mary, and 1652 a third, Deborah. By
1652 M. was totally blind. His wife died 1652, after the birth of
their third daughter; 1656 he m. Katherine Woodcock (age 28)
who died two years later; 1663 he m. a third time, Elizabeth
Minshull, who survived him. With the establishment of the
Commonwealth under Cromwell he was appointed, 1649, Latin
secretary to the Council of State. He continued working on behalf
of the government until the Restoration, 1660, when he went
briefly into hiding, uncertain as to his fate. He was arrested, but at
the intercession of, it is said, D'Avenant the playwright, and
Marvell the poet, he was fined and released. By 1658 he had begun
work in earnest on *Paradise Lost* (which he had earlier contemplated
writing in dramatic form) and, according to Aubrey the biogra-

pher, he had finished it by 1663, although the copyright agreement was not signed until 1667. He received £5 down, a further £5 after the sale of 1,500 copies, and his widow relinquished all further claims to it for £8. *Samson Agonistes* was published 1671, with *Paradise Regained*, though it may have been written as early as 1647. He died from 'gout' and is buried beside his father in St Giles, Cripplegate.

L'Allegro[1]

Hence, loathéd Melancholy,
  Of Cerberus and blackest Midnight born,
In Stygian cave forlorn
  'Mongst horrid shapes, and shrieks, and sights unholy,
Find out some uncouth° cell,   *unknown*
  Where brooding darkness spreads his jealous wings,
And the night-raven sings;
  There under ebon shades and low-browed rocks,
As ragged as thy locks
10   In dark Cimmerian desert ever dwell.
But come, thou goddess fair and free,
  In heaven yclept° Euphrosyne,   *called*
And by men heart-easing Mirth,
  Whom lovely Venus at a birth
With two sister Graces more
  To ivy-crownèd Bacchus bore;
Or whether (as some sager sing)
  The frolic wind that breathes the spring,
Zephyr, with Aurora playing,
20 As he met her once a-Maying,
There on beds of violets blue,
  And fresh-blown° roses washed in dew,   *blooming*
Filled her with thee, a daughter fair,
  So buxom,° blithe, and debonair.°   *lively/elegant*
Haste thee, Nymph, and bring with thee
  Jest and youthful Jollity,
Quips and cranks,° and wanton wiles,   *jests*
  Nods and becks° and wreathèd smiles,   *beckonings*
Such as hang on Hebe's cheek,
30 And love to live in dimple sleek;
  Sport that wrinkled Care derides,

And Laughter holding both his sides.
Come, and trip it as ye go
On the light fantastic toe,
And in thy right hand lead with thee
The mountain nymph, sweet Liberty;
And if I give thee honour due,
Mirth, admit me of thy crew,
To live with her, and live with thee,
40 In unreproved pleasures free;
To hear the lark begin his flight,
And singing startle the dull night,
From his watch-tower in the skies,
Till the dappled dawn doth rise;
Then to come in spite° of sorrow   *despite*
And at my window bid good-morrow,
Through the sweet-briar or the vine,
Or the twisted eglantine,°   *briar*
While the cock with lively din
50 Scatters the rear of darkness thin,
And to the stack or the barn door
Stoutly struts his dames before;
Oft listening how the hounds and horn
Cheerly rouse the slumbering morn,
From the side of some hoar hill,
Through the high wood echoing shrill;
Sometime walking, not unseen,
By hedgerow elms, on hillocks green,
Right against the eastern gate,
60 Where the great sun begins his state,°   *progress*
Robed in flames and amber light,
The clouds in thousand liveries dight;°   *dressed*
While the ploughman near at hand
Whistles o'er the furrowed land,
And the milkmaid singeth blithe,
And the mower whets his scythe,
And every shepherd tells his tale
Under the hawthorn in the dale.
Straight mine eye hath caught new pleasures,
70 Whilst the landscape round it measures:
Russet lawns° and fallows gray,   *plains*
Where the nibbling flocks do stray;
Mountains on whose barren breast
The labouring clouds do often rest;
Meadows trim with daisies pied,°   *parti-coloured*

Shallow brooks and rivers wide.
Towers and battlements it sees
Bosomed high in tufted trees,
Where perhaps some beauty lies,
80 The cynosure° of neighbouring eyes.   *pole-star*
Hard by, a cottage chimney smokes
From betwixt two aged oaks,
Where Corydon and Thyrsis met
Are at their savoury dinner set
Of herbs and other country messes,
Which the neat-handed Phillis dresses;
And then in haste her bower she leaves,
With Thestylis to bind the sheaves;
Or if the earlier season lead,
90 To the tanned haycock in the mead.
Sometimes with secure° delight   *carefree*
The upland hamlets° will invite,   *villages*
When the merry bells ring round,
And the jocund rebecks° sound   *fiddles*
To many a youth and many a maid
Dancing in the chequered shade;
And young and old come forth to play
On a sunshine holiday,
Till the livelong daylight fail:
100 Then to the spicy nut-brown ale
With stories told of many a feat,
How fairy Mab the junkets² eat,°   *ate*
She was pinched and pulled, she said,
And he, by friar's lanthorn° led,   *will of the wisp*
Tells how the drudging goblin sweat
To earn his cream-bowl duly set,
When in one night, ere glimpse of morn,
His shadowy flail hath threshed the corn
That ten day-labourers could not end;
110 Then lies him down the lubber fiend,
And stretched out all the chimney's length,
Basks at the fire his hairy strength;
And crop-full out of doors he flings,
Ere the first cock his matin rings.
Thus done the tales, to bed they creep,
By whispering winds soon lulled asleep.
Towered cities please us then,
And the busy hum of men,
Where throngs of knights and barons bold

120 In weeds° of peace high triumphs hold,   *garments*
    With store of ladies, whose bright eyes
    Rain influence,³ and judge the prize
    Of wit or arms, while both contend
    To win her grace whom all commend.
    There let Hymen oft appear
    In saffron robe, with taper clear,
    And pomp, and feast, and revelry,
    With masque and antique pageantry:
    Such sights as youthful poets dream
130 On summer eves by haunted stream.
    Then to the well-trod stage anon,
    If Jonson's learnèd sock⁴ be on,
    Or sweetest Shakespeare, fancy's child,
    Warble his native wood-notes wild.
    And ever against eating cares
    Lap me in soft Lydian⁵ airs,
    Married to immortal verse,
    Such as the meeting soul may pierce
    In notes with many a winding bout⁶
140 Of linked sweetness long drawn out,
    With wanton heed and giddy cunning,
    The melting voice through mazes running,
    Untwisting all the chains that tie
    The hidden soul of harmony;
    That Orpheus' self may heave his head
    From golden slumber on a bed
    Of heaped Elysian flowers, and hear
    Such strains as would have won the ear
    Of Pluto, to have quite set free
150 His half-regained Eurydice.
    These delights if thou canst give,
    Mirth, with thee I mean to live.

                    ?1625–?1633 [1645]

Il Penseroso⁷

Hence, vain deluding joys,
    The brood of folly without father bred,
How little you bestead,°   *profit*
    Or fill the fixed mind with all your toys;°   *trifles*

Dwell in some idle brain,
　　And fancies fond° with gaudy shapes possess,　　　　　*foolish*
As thick and numberless
　　As the gay motes that people the sunbeams,
Or likest hovering dreams,
10　　The fickle pensioners° of Morpheus' train.　　　　　*attendants*
But hail, thou Goddess sage and holy,
Hail, divinest Melancholy,
Whose saintly visage is too bright
To hit° the sense of human sight,　　　　　　　　　　*wound*
And therefore to our weaker view
O'erlaid with black, staid Wisdom's hue;
Black, but such as in esteem
Prince Memnon's sister° might beseem　　　　　　　　*Himera*
Or that starred Ethiop queen° that strove　　　　　　*Cassiopeia*
20　To set her beauty's praise above
The sea-nymphs, and their powers offended.
Yet thou art higher far descended:
Thee bright-haired Vesta long of yore
To solitary Saturn bore;
His daughter she (in Saturn's reign
Such mixture was not held a stain).
Oft in glimmering bowers and glades
He met her, and in secret shades
Of woody Ida's inmost grove,
30　While yet there was no fear of Jove.
Come, pensive Nun, devout and pure,
Sober, steadfast, and demure,
All in a robe of darkest grain,°　　　　　　　　　　*colour*
Flowing with majestic train,
And sable stole of cypress lawn°　　　　　　　　　*fine black cloth*
Over thy decent shoulders drawn.
Come, but keep thy wonted state,
With even step and musing gait,
And looks commercing with the skies,
40　Thy rapt soul sitting in thine eyes;
There held in holy passion still,
Forget thyself to marble, till
With a sad° leaden downward cast　　　　　　　　　*serious*
Thou fix them on the earth as fast.
And join with thee calm Peace and Quiet,
Spare Fast, that oft with gods doth diet,
And hears the Muses in a ring
Aye round about Jove's altar sing.

And add to these retired Leisure,
50 That in trim gardens takes his pleasure;
But first, and chiefest, with thee bring
Him[8] that yon soars on olden wing,
Guiding the fiery-wheelèd throne,
The Cherub Contemplation;
And the mute Silence hist° along,   *call 'hist'*
'Less Philomel will deign a song,
In her sweetest, saddest plight,
Smoothing the rugged brow of Night,
While Cynthia checks her dragon yoke
60 Gently o'er th' accustomed oak.
Sweet bird, that shunn'st the noise of folly,
Most musical, most melancholy!
Thee, chauntress, oft the woods among
I woo to hear thy even-song;
And missing thee, I walk unseen
On the dry smooth-shaven green,
To behold the wandering moon
Riding near her highest noon,
Like one that had been led astray
70 Through the heaven's wide pathless way;
And oft, as if her head she bowed,
Stooping through a fleecy cloud.
Oft on a plat° of rising ground   *plot*
I hear the far-off curfew sound
Over some wide-watered shore,
Swinging slow with sullen° roar;   *solemn*
Of if the air will not permit,
Some still removed place will fit,
Where glowing embers through the room
80 Teach light to counterfeit a gloom,
Far from all resort of mirth,
Save the cricket on the hearth,
Or the bellman's° drowsy charm,   *nightwatchman's*
To bless the doors from nightly harm:
Or let my lamp at midnight hour
Be seen in some high lonely tower,[9]
Where I may oft outwatch the Bear,°   *Great Bear constellation*
With thrice great Hermes,[10] or unsphere
The spirit of Plato to unfold
90 What words or what vast regions hold
The immortal mind that hath forsook
Her mansion in this fleshly nook;

And of those daemons that are found
In fire, air, flood, or under ground,
Whose power hath a true consent°   *correspondence*
With planet or with element.
Sometime let gorgeous tragedy
In sceptred pall° come sweeping by,   *mantle*
Presenting Thebes, or Pelops' line,
100 Or the tale of Troy divine,[11]
Or what (though rare) of later age
Ennobled hath the buskined[12] stage.
But, O sad Virgin, that thy power
Might raise Musaeus from his bower,
Or bid the soul of Orpheus sing
Such notes as, warbled to the string,
Drew iron tears down Pluto's cheek
And made hell grant what love did seek;
Or call up him[13] that left half told
110 The story of Cambuscan bold,
Of Camball and of Algarsife,
And who had Canace to wife,
That owned the virtuous° ring and glass,   *powerful*
And of the wondrous horse of brass,
On which the Tartar king did ride;
And if aught else, great bards beside,
In sage and solemn tunes have sung,
Of tourneys and of trophies hung,
Of forests and enchantments drear,
120 Where more is meant than meets the ear.
Thus, Night, oft see me in thy pale career°,   *course*
Till civil-suited° Morn appear,   *simply-dressed*
Not tricked and frounced° as she was wont   *decked out*
With the Attic boy to hunt,
But kerchiefed in a comely cloud,
While rocking winds are piping loud,
Or ushered with a shower still,
When the gust hath blown his fill,
Ending on the rustling leaves,
130 With minute[14] drops from off the eaves.
And when the sun begins to fling
His flaring beams, me, Goddess, bring
To archèd walks of twilight groves,
And shadows brown that Sylvan loves,
Of pine or monumental oak,
Where the rude axe with heavèd stroke

Was never heard the nymphs to daunt,
Or fright them from their hallowed haunt.
There in close covert by some brook,
140 Where no profaner eye may look,
Hide me from day's garish° eye,   gaudy
While the bee with honied thigh,
That at her flowery work doth sing,
And the waters murmuring
With such consort° as they keep,   harmony
Entice the dewy-feathered Sleep;
And let some strange mysterious dream
Wave at his wings in airy stream
Of lively portraiture displayed,
150 Softly on my eyelids laid.
And as I wake, sweet music breathe
Above, about, or underneath,
Sent by some Spirit to mortals good,
Or the unseen Genius of the wood.
But let my due feet never fail
To walk the studious cloister's pale,°   enclosure
And love the high embowed° roof,   vaulted
With antique pillars' massy proof,
And storied windows richly dight,[15]
160 Casting a dim religious light.
There let the pealing organ blow
To the full-voiced quire below,
In service high and anthems clear,
As may with sweetness, through mine ear,
Dissolve me into ecstasies,
And bring all heaven before mine eyes.
And may at last my weary age
Find out the peaceful hermitage,
The hairy gown and mossy cell,
170 Where I may sit and rightly spell°   spell out
Of every star that heaven doth shew,
And every herb that sips the dew,
Till old experience do attain
To something like prophetic strain.
These pleasures, Melancholy, give,
And I with thee will choose to live.

?1625–?1633 [1645]

Comus¹⁶

The Persons
The Attendant Spirit, afterwards in the habit of Thyrsis
Comus with his crew
The Lady
First Brother
Second Brother
Sabrina the Nymph

The first scene discovers a wild wood.
[*The* **Attendant Spirit** *descends or enters*]

Spirit Before the starry threshold of Jove's court
My mansion is, where those immortal shapes
Of bright aërial Spirits live ensphered
In regions mild of calm and serene air,
Above the smoke and stir of this dim spot
Which men call earth, and with low-thoughted care,
Confined and pestered° in this pinfold° here,   *crowded in/animal pen*
Strive to keep up a frail and feverish being,
Unmindful of the crown that virtue gives,
10 After this mortal change,° to her true servants   *death*
Amongst the enthroned gods on sainted seats.
Yet some there be that by due steps aspire
To lay their just hands on that golden key
That opes the palace of Eternity:
To such my errand is, and but for such
I would not soil these pure ambrosial weeds°   *garments*
With the rank vapours of this sin-worn mould.
   But to my task. Neptune, besides the sway
Of every salt flood and each ebbing stream,
20 Took in, by lot, 'twixt high and nether Jove
Imperial rule of all the sea-girt isles
That like to rich and various gems inlay
The unadorned bosom of the deep,
Which he, to grace his tributary gods,
By course commits to several government,
And gives them leave to wear their sapphire crowns
And wield their little tridents,° but this isle,   *3-pronged spears*
The greatest and the best of all the main,
He quarters to his blue-haired deities;
30 And all this tract° that fronts the falling sun¹⁷   *area*
A noble peer of mickle° trust and power   *great*

Has in his charge, with tempered awe to guide
An old and haughty nation[18] proud in arms;
Where his fair offspring, nursed in princely lore,
Are coming to attend their father's state
And new-entrusted sceptre, but their way
Lies through the perplexed° paths of this drear wood,   *tangled*
The nodding horror of whose shady brows
Threats the forlorn and wandering passenger.
40 And here their tender age might suffer peril,
But that by quick command from sovereign Jove
I was dispatched for their defence and guard;
And listen why, for I will tell ye now
What never yet was heard in tale or song
From old or modern bard, in hall or bower.°   *dwelling*
    Bacchus, that first from out the purple grape
Crushed the sweet poison of misused wine,
After the Tuscan mariners transformed,
Coasting the Tyrrhene shore, as the winds listed,
50 On Circe's island fell (who knows not Circe,
The daughter of the Sun? whose charmed cup
Whoever tasted, lost his upright shape,
And downward fell into a groveling swine).
This nymph that gazed upon his clustering locks,
With ivy berries wreathed, and his blithe youth,
Had by him, ere he parted thence, a son
Much like his father, but his mother more,
Whom therefore she brought up and Comus named;
Who, ripe and frolic° of his full-grown age,   *happy in*
60 Roving the Celtic and Iberian fields,
At last betakes him to this ominous wood,
And, in thick shelter of black shades imbowered,
Excels his mother at her mighty art,
Offering to every weary traveller
His orient° liquor in a crystal glass,   *sparkling*
To quench the drouth of Phoebus, which as they taste
(For most do taste through fond intemperate thirst)
Soon as the potion works, their human countenance,
The express resemblance of the gods, is changed
70 Into some brutish form of wolf, or bear,
Or ounce,° or tiger, hog, or bearded goat,   *lynx*
All other parts remaining as they were;
And they, so perfect is their misery,
Not once perceive their foul disfigurement,
But boast themselves more comely than before

And all their friends, and native home forget
To roll with pleasure in a sensual sty.
Therefore when any favoured of high Jove
Chances to pass through this adventurous glade,
80 Swift as the sparkle of a glancing° star   *shooting*
I shoot from heaven to give him safe convoy,
As now I do; but first I must put off
These my sky-robes, spun out of Iris' woof,°   *rainbow coloured*
And take the weeds° and likeness of a swain°   *garments/servant*
That to the service of this house belongs,
Who with his soft pipe and smooth-dittied song
Well knows to still the wild winds when they roar,
And hush the waving woods, nor of less faith,[19]
And in this office of his mountain watch
90 Likeliest, and nearest to the present aid
Of this occasion. But I hear the tread
Of hateful steps; I must be viewless° now.   *unseen*

> [**Comus** *enters with a charming-rod in one hand,*
> *his glass in the other; with him a rout° of*   *rabble*
> *monsters headed like sundry sorts of wild beasts,*
> *but otherwise like men and women, their apparel*
> *glistering. They come in making a riotous and*
> *unruly noise, with torches in their hands.*]

Comus   The star[20] that bids the shepherd fold
Now the top of heaven doth hold,
And the gilded car° of day   *chariot*
His glowing axle doth allay°   *cool*
In the steep Atlantic stream,
And the slope sun his upward beam
Shoots against the dusky pole,
100 Pacing toward the other goal
Of his chamber in the east.
Meanwhile welcome joy and feast,
Midnight shout and revelry,
Tipsy dance and jollity.
Braid° your locks with rosy twine   *plait*
Dropping odours, dropping wine.
Rigour now is gone to bed,
And Advice with scrupulous head,
Strict Age, and sour Severity,
110 With their grave saws° in slumber lie.   *maxims*
We that are of purer fire
Imitate the starry quire,

Who in their nightly watchful spheres
Lead in swift round the months and years.
The sounds and seas with all their finny drove
Now to the moon in wavering morris° move,   *(the dance)*
And on the tawny sands and shelves
Trip the pert fairies and the dapper elves;
By dimpled brook and fountain brim
120 The wood-nymphs, decked with daisies trim,
Their merry wakes° and pastimes keep: *watches*
What hath night to do with sleep?
Night hath better sweets to prove,
Venus now wakes, and wakens Love.
Come, let us our rites begin;
'Tis only daylight that makes sin,
Which these dun° shades will ne'er report.   *blackish brown*
Hail, goddess of nocturnal sport,
Dark-veiled Cotytto, to whom the secret flame
130 Of midnight torches burns; mysterious dame,
That ne'er art called but when the dragon womb
Of Stygian darkness spits her thickest gloom,
And makes one blot of all the air,
Stay thy cloudy ebon chair
Wherein thou rid'st with Hecat', and befriend
Us thy vowed priests, till utmost end
Of all thy dues be done, and none left out
Ere the blabbing eastern scout,
The nice morn° on the Indian steep,°   *(Aurora)/(the Himalayas)*
140 From her cabined loop-hole peep,
And to the tell-tale Sun descry°   *reveal*
Our concealed solemnity.°   *rituals*
Come, knit hands, and beat the ground,
In a light fantastic round.

        [*The Measure*°]   *dance*

Break off, break off, I feel the different pace
Of some chaste footing near about this ground.
Run to your shrouds° within these brakes and trees;   *places of cover*
Our number may affright: some virgin sure
(For so I can distinguish by mine art)
150 Benighted in these woods. Now to my charms
And to my wily trains,° I shall ere long   *enticements*
Be well stocked with as fair a herd as grazed
About my mother Circe. Thus I hurl

My dazzling spells into the spongy air,
Of power to cheat the eye with blear° illusion   *confusing*
And give it false presentments,° lest the place   *appearance*
And my quaint habits° breed astonishment,   *clothes*
And put the damsel to suspicious flight,
Which must not be, for that's against my course;
160 I, under fair pretence of friendly ends,
And well-placed words of glozing° courtesy   *fawning*
Baited with reasons not unplausible,
Wind me into the easy-hearted man,
And hug him into snares. When once her eye
Hath met the virtue° of this magic dust,   *power*
I shall appear some harmless villager
Whom thrift keeps up about his country gear.°   *business*
But here she comes; I fairly° step aside,   *plainly*
And hearken, if I may, her business here.

[*The* **Lady** *enters*]

170 **Lady**   This way the noise was, if mine ear be true,
My best guide now. Methought it was the sound
Of riot and ill-managed merriment,
Such as the jocund flute or gamesome° pipe   *sportive*
Stirs up among the loose unlettered hinds,°   *farmhands*
When for their teeming° flocks, and granges° full,   *abundant/barns*
In wanton dance they praise the bounteous Pan,
And thank the gods amiss.° I should be loth   *wrongly*
To meet the rudeness and swilled° insolence   *drunken*
Of such late wássailers,° yet O where else   *revellers*
180 Shall I inform my unacquainted feet
In the blind mazes of this tangled wood?
My brothers, when they saw me wearied out
With this long way, resolving here to lodge
Under the spreading favour of these pines,
Stepped as they said to the next thicket side
To bring me berries, or such cooling fruit
As the kind hospitable woods provide.
They left me then when the grey-hooded Even,°   *evening*
Like a sad votarist in palmer's weed,°   *pilgrim's attire*
190 Rose from the hindmost wheels of Phoebus' wain.°   *chariot*
But where they are, and why they came not back,
Is now the labour of my thoughts; 'tis likeliest
They had engaged their wandering steps too far,
And envious darkness, ere they could return,
Had stole them from me; else, O thievish Night,

Why shouldst thou, but for some felonious end,
In thy dark lantern thus close up the stars
That Nature hung in heaven, and filled their lamps
With everlasting oil, to give due light
200 To the misled and lonely traveller?
This is the place, as well as I may guess,
Whence even now the tumult of loud mirth
Was rife, and perfect in my listening ear,
Yet naught but single° darkness do I find.   *total*
What might this be? A thousand fantasies
Begin to throng into my memory
Of calling shapes, and beckoning shadows dire,
And airy tongues that syllable men's names
On sands and shores and desert wildernesses.
210 These thoughts may startle well, but not astound
The virtuous mind, that ever walks attended
By a strong siding²¹ champion, Conscïence.
O welcome, pure-eyed Faith, white-handed Hope,
Thou hovering angel girt with golden wings,
And thou unblemished form of Chastity,
I see ye visibly, and now believe
That He, the supreme Good, to whom all things ill
Are but as slavish officers of vengeance,²²
Would send a glistering guardian if need were
220 To keep my life and honour unassailed.
Was I deceived, or did a sable° cloud   *dark*
Turn forth her silver lining on the night?
I did not err, there does a sable cloud
Turn forth her silver lining on the night,
And casts a gleam over this tufted grove.
I cannot halloo to my brothers, but
Such noise as I can make to be heard farthest
I'll venture, for my new-enlivened spirits
Prompt me; and they perhaps are not far off.

[*Song*]

230 *Sweet Echo, sweetest nymph that liv'st unseen*
     Within thy airy shell
     By slow Maeander's margent° green,   *bank*
And in the violet-embroidered vale
     Where the lovelorn nightingale
Nightly to thee her sad song mourneth well:
Canst thou not tell me of a gentle pair
     That likest thy Narcissus are?

                    O if thou have
               Hid them in some flowery cave,
240   *Tell me but where,*
          Sweet queen of parley°, daughter of the sphere;   *discourse*
          So mayest thou be translated to the skies,
     And give resounding grace° to all heaven's harmonies.   *trills*

     Comus [*Aside*]   Can any mortal mixture of earth's mould
     Breathe such divine enchanting ravishment?
     Sure something holy lodges in that breast,
     And with these raptures moves the vocal air
     To testify his hidden residence;
     How sweetly did they float upon the wings
250 Of silence, through the empty-vaulted night,
     At every fall° smoothing the raven down   *cadence*
     Of darkness till it smiled. I have oft heard
     My mother Circe with the Sirens three,
     Amidst the flowery-kirtled° Naiades,   *gowned*
     Culling their potent herbs and baleful drugs,
     Who as they sung would take the prisoned soul
     And lap it in Elysium; Scylla wept,
     And chid her barking waves into attention,
     And fell Charybdis murmured soft applause.
260 Yet they in pleasing slumber lulled the sense,
     And in sweet madness robbed it of itself;
     But such a sacred and home-felt° delight,   *artless*
     Such sober certainty of waking bliss,
     I never heard till now. I'll speak to her,
     And she shall be my Queen. Hail, foreign wonder,
     Whom certain these rough shades did never breed,
     Unless the goddess that in rural shrine
     Dwellest here with Pan or Sylvan, by blest song
     Forbidding every bleak unkindly fog
270 To touch the prosperous growth of this tall wood.
     Lady   Nay, gentle shepherd, ill is lost that praise
     That is addressed to unattending ears;
     Not any boast of skill, but extreme shift°   *effort*
     How to regain my severed company
     Compelled me to awake the courteous Echo
     To give me answer from her mossy couch.
     Comus   What chance, good lady, hath bereft you thus?
     Lady   Dim darkness and this leafy labyrinth.
     Comus   Could that divide you from near-ushering guides?
280 **Lady**   They left me weary on a grassy turf.

Comus   By falsehood, or discourtesy, or why?
Lady   To seek i' th' valley some cool friendly spring.
Comus   And left your fair side all unguarded, Lady?
Lady   They were but twain, and purposed quick return.
Comus   Perhaps forestalling night prevented them.
Lady   How easy my misfortune is to hit!
Comus   Imports their loss, beside the present need?
Lady   No less than if I should my brothers lose.
Comus   Were they of manly prime, or youthful bloom?
290   **Lady**   As smooth as Hebe's their unrazored lips.
Comus   Two such I saw, what time the laboured ox
In his loose traces from the furrow° came,   *ploughed field*
And the swinked° hedger at his supper sat;   *hard-working*
I saw them under a green mantling vine
That crawls along the side of yon small hill,
Plucking ripe clusters from the tender shoots;
Their port° was more than human, as they stood   *bearing*
I took it for a faëry vision
Of some gay creatures of the element,
300   That in the colours of the rainbow live
And play i' th' plighted° clouds. I was awe-strook,   *folded*
And as I passed, I worshipped; if those you seek,
It were a journey like the path to heaven
To help you find them.
Lady   Gentle villager,
What readiest way would bring me to that place?
Comus   Due west it rises from this shrubby point.
Lady   To find out that, good shepherd, I suppose,
In such a scant allowance of star-light,
Would overtask the best land-pilot's art
310   Without the sure guess of well-practised feet.
Comus   I know each lane and every alley green,
Dingle or bushy dell of this wild wood,
And every bosky bourn° from side to side   *bushy brook*
My daily walks and ancient neighbourhood,
And if your stray attendants be yet lodged,
Or shroud° within these limits, I shall know   *sheltered*
Ere morrow wake or the low-roosted lark
From her thatched pallet° rouse; if otherwise,   *straw bed*
I can conduct you, Lady, to a low
320   But loyal cottage, where you may be safe
Till further quest.
Lady   Shepherd, I take thy word,
And trust thy honest-offered courtesy,

Which oft is sooner found in lowly sheds
With smoky rafters, than in tap'stry halls
And courts of princes, where it first was named,
And yet is most pretended. In a place
Less warranted than this, or less secure,
I cannot be, that I should fear to change it.
Eye me, blest Providence, and square my trial
330 To my proportioned strength. Shepherd, lead on.
    [*Exeunt*]

    [*The two Brothers*]

Elder Brother   Unmuffle, ye faint stars, and thou, fair moon,
That wont'st to love the traveller's benison°   *benefit*
Stoop thy pale visage through an amber cloud,
And disinherit Chaos, that reigns here
In double night of darkness and of shades;
Of if your influence be quite dammed up
With black usurping mists, some gentle taper
Though a rush-candle from the wicker hole
Of some clay habitation, visit us
340 With thy long levelled rule of streaming light,
And thou shalt be our star of Arcady,
Or Tyrian cynosure°.   *the Pole-star*
Second Brother   Or if our eyes
Be barred that happiness, might we but hear   *|hurdles*
The folded flocks penned in their wattled cotes,°   *pens made of willow*
Or sound of pastoral reed with oaten° stops,   *of oat-straw*
Or whistle from the lodge, or village cock
Count the night-watches to his feathery dames,
'Twould be some solace yet, some little cheering,
In this close dungeon of innumerous boughs.
350 But O that hapless virgin, our lost sister,
Where may she wander now, whither betake her
From the chill dew, amongst rude burrs and thistles?
Perhaps some cold bank is her bolster° now,   *pillow*
Or 'gainst the rugged bark of some broad elm
Leans her unpillowed head fraught with sad fears.
What if in wild amazement and affright,
Or, while we speak, within the direful grasp
Of savage hunger or of savage heat?
Elder Brother   Peace, brother, be not over-exquisite[23]
360 To cast° the fashion of uncertain evils;   *forecast*
For grant they be so, while they rest unknown,
What need a man forestall his date of grief,

And run to meet what he would most avoid?
Or if they be but false alarms of fear,
How bitter is such self-delusion?
I do not think my sister so to seek,   *needing*
Or so unprincipled in virtue's book,
And the sweet peace that goodness bosoms ever,
As that the single want of light and noise
370 (Not being in danger, as I trust she is not)
Could stir the constant mood of her calm thoughts,
And put them into misbecoming plight.
Virtue could see to do what virtue would
By her own radiant light, though sun and moon
Were in the flat sea sunk. And wisdom's self
Oft seeks to sweet retired solitude,
Where with her best nurse, Contemplation,
She plumes her feathers, and lets grow her wings,
That in the various bustle of resort
380 Were all to-ruffled, and sometimes impaired.
He that has light within his own clear breast
May sit i' th' centre and enjoy bright day,
But he that hides a dark soul and foul thoughts
Benighted walks under the mid-day sun;
Himself is his own dungeon.

Second Brother   'Tis most true
That musing meditation most affects
The pensive secrecy of desert cell,
Far from the cheerful haunt of men and herds,
And sits as safe as in a senate-house;
390 For who would rob a hermit of his weeds,
His few books, or his beads, or maple dish,   *rosary*
Or do his grey hairs any violence?
But beauty, like the fair Hesperian tree
Laden with blooming gold, had need the guard
Of dragon-watch with unenchanted eye
To save her blossoms and defend her fruit
From the rash hand of bold Incontinence.
You may as well spread out the unsunned heaps
Of miser's treasure by an outlaw's den,
400 And tell me it is safe, as bid me hope
Danger will wink on opportunity,
And let a single helpless maiden pass
Uninjured in this wild surrounding waste.
Of night or loneliness it recks me not,   *I care not*
I fear the dread events that dog them both,

Lest some ill-greeting touch attempt the person
Of our unowned sister.

Elder Brother   I do not, brother,
Infer as if I thought my sister's state
Secure without all doubt or controversy;
410 Yet where an equal poise of hope and fear
Does arbitrate the event, my nature is
That I incline to hope rather than fear,
And gladly banish squint suspicïon.
My sister is not so defenceless left
As you imagine; she has a hidden strength
Which you remember not.

Second Brother   What hidden strength,
Unless the strength of heaven, if you mean that?

Elder Brother   I mean that too, but yet a hidden strength
Which, if heaven gave it, may be termed her own.
420 'Tis chastity, my brother, chastity:
She that has that is clad in complete steel,
And like a quivered²⁴ nymph with arrows keen
May trace huge forests and unharboured heaths,
Infamous hills and sandy perilous wilds,
Where, through the sacred rays of chastity,
No savage fierce, bandit, or mountaineer
Will dare to soil her virgin purity.
Yea, there where very desolation dwells,
By grots and caverns shagged with horrid shades,
430 She may pass on with unblenched° majesty,   *unshrinking*
Be it not done in pride or in presumption.
Some say no evil thing that walks by night
In fog or fire°, by lake or moorish fen,   *will o'the wisp*
Blue meagre hag, or stubborn unlaid° ghost   *unexorcised*
That breaks his magic chains at curfew time,
No goblin or swart° faëry of the mine,   *dark*
Hath hurtful power o'er true virginity.
Do ye believe me yet, or shall I call
Antiquity from the old schools° of Greece   *(of philosophy)*
440 To testify the arms of chastity?
Hence had the huntress Dian her dread bow,
Fair silver-shafted queen for ever chaste,
Wherewith she tamed the brinded° lioness   *streaked*
And spotted mountain pard°, but set at naught   *leopard*
The frivolous bolt of Cupid; gods and men
Feared her stern frown, and she was queen o' th' woods.
What was that snaky-headed Gorgon shield

That wise Minerva wore, unconquered virgin,
Wherewith she freezed her foes to cóngealed stone,
450 But rigid looks of chaste austerity,
And noble grace that dashed brute violence
With sudden adoration and blank awe?
So dear to heaven is saintly chastity
That when a soul is found sincerely so,
A thousand liveried angels lackey° her,   *attend*
Driving far off each thing of sin and guilt,
And in clear dream and solemn visïon
Tell her of things that no gross ear can hear,
Till oft converse with heavenly habitants
460 Begin to cast a beam on the outward shape,
The unpolluted temple of the mind,
And turns it by degrees to the soul's essence,
Till all be made immortal; but when lust,
By unchaste looks, loose gestures, and foul talk,
But most by lewd and lavish act of sin,
Lets in defilement to the inward parts,
The soul grows clotted by contagion,
Imbodies and imbrutes,²⁵ till she quite lose
The divine property of her first being.
470 Such are those thick and gloomy shadows damp
Oft seen in charnel vaults and sepulchres
Lingering, and sitting by a new-made grave,
As loth to leave the body that it loved,
And linked itself by carnal sensuality
To a degenerate and degraded state.
Second Brother   How charming is divine philosophy!
Not harsh and crabbed,° as dull fools suppose,   *peevish*
But musical as is Apollo's lute,
And a perpetual feast of nectared sweets,
Where no crude surfeit reigns.
480 **Elder Brother**   List! list, I hear
Some far-off halloo break the silent air.
Second Brother   Methought so too; what should it be?
Elder Brother   For certain,
Either some one like us night-foundered here,
Or else some neighbour woodman, or at worst,
Some roving robber calling to his fellows.
Second Brother   Heaven keep my sister! Again, again, and near!
Best draw, and stand upon our guard.
Elder Brother   I'll halloo;

If he be friendly, he comes well; if not,
Defense is a good cause, and Heaven be for us.

[*The* **Attendant Spirit**, *habited like a shepherd*]

490 That halloo I should know; what are you? speak.
Come not too near, you fall on iron stakes° else.   *swords*
Spirit   What voice is that? my young lord? speak again.
Second Brother   O brother, 'tis my father's shepherd, sure.
Elder Brother   Thyrsis, whose artful strains have oft delayed
The huddling brook to hear his madrigal,
And sweetened every musk-rose of the dale,
How camest thou here, good swain? Hath any ram
Slipped from the fold, or young kid lost his dam,
Or straggling wether° the pent° flock forsook?   *castrated ram/penned in*
500 How couldst thou find this dark sequestered nook?
Spirit   O my loved master's heir, and his next° joy,   *nearest*
I came not here on such a trivial toy
As a strayed ewe, or to pursue the stealth
Of pilfering wolf; not all the fleecy wealth
That doth enrich these downs is worth a thought
To this my errand, and the care it brought.
But O my virgin Lady, where is she?
How chance she is not in your company?
Elder Brother   To tell thee sadly, shepherd, without blame
510 Or our neglect, we lost her as we came.
Spirit   Ay me unhappy, then my fears are true.
Elder Brother   What fears, good Thyrsis? Prithee briefly shew.
Spirit   I'll tell ye. 'Tis not vain or fabulous°   *mythical*
(Though so esteemed by shallow ignorance)
What the sage poets, taught by the heavenly Muse,
Storied of old in high immortal verse
Of dire Chimeras and enchanted isles,
And rifted rocks whose entrance leads to hell,
For such there be, but unbelief is blind.
520   Within the navel° of this hideous wood,   *centre*
Immured in cypress shades, a sorcerer dwells,
Of Bacchus and of Circe born, great Comus,
Deep skilled in all his mother's witcheries,
And here to every thirsty wanderer
By sly enticement gives his baneful° cup,   *death-bringing*
With many murmurs° mixed, whose pleasing poison   *incantations*
The visage quite transforms of him that drinks,
And the inglorious likeness of a beast
Fixes instead, unmoulding reason's mintage

530 Charactered° in the face; this have I learnt   *imprinted*
    Tending my flocks hard by i' th' hilly crofts
    That brow° this bottom glade, whence night by night   *overlook*
    He and his monstrous rout are heard to howl
    Like stabled wolves, or tigers at their prey,
    Doing abhorred rites to Hecate
    In their obscured haunts of inmost bowers.
    Yet have they many baits and guileful spells
    To inveigle and invite the unwary sense
    Of them that pass unweeting° by the way.   *heedless*
540 This evening late, by then the chewing flocks
    Had ta'en their supper on the savoury herb
    Of knot-grass dew-besprent,° and were in fold,   *sprinkled*
    I sat me down to watch upon a bank
    With ivy canopied, and interwove
    With flaunting honeysuckle, and began,
    Wrapped in a pleasing fit of melancholy,
    To meditate° my rural minstrelsy,   *improvise*
    Till fancy had her fill. But ere a close°   *musical phrase*
    The wonted roar was up amidst the woods,
550 And filled the air with barbarous dissonance,
    At which I ceased, and listened them a while,
    Till an unusual stop of sudden silence
    Gave respite to the drowsy frighted steeds
    That draw the litter of close-curtained Sleep.
    At last a soft and solemn-breathing sound
    Rose like a steam of rich distilled perfumes,
    And stole upon the air, that even Silence
    Was took ere she was ware, and wished she might
    Deny her nature and be never more,
560 Still to be so displaced. I was all ear,
    And took in strains that might create a soul
    Under the ribs of Death, but O ere long
    Too well I did perceive it was the voice
    Of my most honoured lady, your dear sister.
    Amazed I stood, harrowed with grief and fear,
    And 'O poor hapless nightingale,' thought I,
    'How sweet thou sing'st, how near the deadly snare!'
    Then down the lawns° I ran with headlong haste   *glades*
    Through paths and turnings often trod by day,
570 Till guided by mine ear I found the place
    Where that damned wizard, hid in sly disguise
    (For so by certain signs I knew) had met
    Already, ere my best speed could prevent,

The aidless innocent Lady, his wished prey,
Who gently asked if he had seen such two,
Supposing him some neighbour villager;
Longer I durst not stay, but soon I guessed
Ye were the two she meant; with that I sprung
Into swift flight, till I had found you here;
But further know I not.

580 **Second Brother**   O night and shades,
How are ye joined with hell in triple knot
Against the unarmèd weakness of one virgin
Alone and helpless! Is this the confidence
You gave me, brother?

Elder Brother   Yes, and keep it still,
Lean on it safely; not a period°   *sentence*
Shall be unsaid, for me; against the threats
Of malice or of sorcery, or that power
Which erring men call chance, this I hold firm:
Virtue may be assailed, but never hurt,
590 Surprised by unjust force, but not enthralled,
Yea, even that which mischief meant most harm
Shall in the happy trial prove most glory.
But evil on itself shall back recoil,
And mix no more with goodness, when at last,
Gathered like scum, and settled to itself,
It shall be in eternal restless change
Self-fed and self-consumed; if this fail,
The pillared firmament is rottenness,
And earth's base built on stubble. But come, let's on.
600 Against the opposing will and arm of heaven
May never this just sword be lifted up;
But for that damned magician, let him be girt
With all the grisly legïons that troop
Under the sooty flag of Acheron,
Harpies and Hydras, or all the monstrous forms
'Twixt Africa and Ind, I'll find him out,
And force him to restore his purchase° back,   *prey*
Or drag him by the curls to a foul death,
Cursed as his life.

Spirit   Alas, good venturous youth,
610 I love thy courage yet, and bold emprise,[26]
But here thy sword can do thee little stead;
For other arms and other weapons must
Be those that quell the might of hellish charms.
He with his bare wand can unthread thy joints,

And crumble all thy sinews.
Elder Brother   Why, prithee, shepherd,
How durst thou then thyself approach so near
As to make this relation?
Spirit   Care and utmost shifts
How to secure the lady from surprisal°   *being taken unawares*
Brought to my mind a certain shepherd lad,
620 Of small regard to see to, yet well skilled
In every virtuous° plant and healing herb   *powerful*
That spreads her verdant leaf to the morning ray.
He loved me well, and oft would beg me sing;
Which when I did, he on the tender grass
Would sit, and hearken even to ecstasy,
And in requital ope his leathern scrip,°   *bag*
And show me simples° of a thousand names,   *herbs*
Telling their strange and vigorous faculties;
Amongst the rest a small unsightly root,
630 But of divine effect, he culled me out;
The leaf was darkish, and had prickles on it,
But in another country, as he said,
Bore a bright golden flower, but not in this soil:
Unknown, and like esteemed, and the dull swain
Treads on it daily with his clouted[27] shoon,°   *hobnailed shoes*
And yet more med'cinal is it than that moly
That Hermes once to wise Ulysses gave;
He called it haemony,[28] and gave it me,
And bade me keep it as of sovereign use
640 'Gainst all enchantments, mildew blast, or damp,
Or ghastly Furies' apparition;
I pursed it up, but little reckoning made,
Till now that this extremity compelled,
But now I find it true; for by this means
I knew the foul enchanter though disguised,
Entered the very lime-twigs[29] of his spells,
And yet came off. If you have this about you
(As I will give you when we go), you may
Boldly assault the necromancer's hall,
650 Where if he be, with dauntless hardihood
And brandished blade rush on him, break his glass,
And shed the luscious liquor on the ground,
But seize his wand, though he and his cursed crew
Fierce sign of battle make, and menace high,
Or like the sons of Vulcan vomit smoke,
Yet will they soon retire, if he but shrink.

Elder Brother   Thyrsis, lead on apace, I'll follow thee,
And some good angel bear a shield before us.

> *The scene changes to a stately palace, set out with all manner of*
> *deliciousness: soft music, tables spread with all dainties.* **Comus**
> *appears with his rabble, and the* **Lady** *set in an enchanted chair, to*
> *whom he offers his glass, which she puts by, and goes about to rise.*

Comus   Nay, lady, sit; if I but wave this wand,
660 Your nerves° are all chained up in alabaster,°   *sensations/marble*
And you a statue, or as Daphne was
Root-bound, that fled Apollo.
Lady   Fool, do not boast;
Thou canst not touch the freedom of my mind
With all thy charms, although this corporal rind
Thou hast immanacled, while heaven sees good.
Comus   Why are you vexed, lady? why do you frown?
Here dwell no frowns, nor anger; from these gates
Sorrow flies far: see, here be all the pleasures
That fancy can beget on youthful thoughts,
670 When the fresh blood grows lively, and returns
Brisk as the April buds in primrose season.
And first behold this cordial julep° here   *(sweet drink)*
That flames and dances in his crystal bounds
With spirits of balm and fragrant syrups mixed.
Not that Nepenthes° which the wife of Thone   *(pain-killing drug)*
In Egypt gave to Jove-born Helena
Is of such power to stir up joy as this,
To life so friendly, or so cool to thirst.
Why should you be so cruel to yourself,
680 And to those dainty limbs which Nature lent
For gentle usage and soft delicacy?
But you invert the covenants of her trust,
And harshly deal like an ill borrower
With that which you received on other terms,
Scorning the unexempt condition
By which all mortal frailty must subsist,
Refreshment after toil, ease after pain,
That have been tired all day without repast,
And timely rest have wanted; but, fair virgin,
This will restore all soon.
690 **Lady**   'Twill not, false traitor,
'Twill not restore the truth and honesty
That thou hast banished from thy tongue with lies.
Was this the cottage and the safe abode

Thou told'st me of? What grim aspects are these,
These ugly-headed monsters? Mercy guard me!
Hence with thy brewed enchantments, foul deceiver;
Hast thou betrayed my credulous innocence
With vizored falsehood and base forgery,°   *deception*
And wouldst thou seek again to trap me here
700   With lickerish³⁰ baits fit to ensnare a brute?
Were it a draught for Juno when she banquets,
I would not taste thy treasonous offer; none
But such as are good men can give good things,
And that which is not good is not delicious
To a well-governed and wise appetite.
Comus   O foolishness of men! that lend their ears
To those budge³¹ doctors of the Stoic fur,°   *(school of philosophy)*
And fetch their precepts from the Cynic tub,
Praising the lean and sallow Abstinence.
710   Wherefore did Nature pour her bounties forth
With such a full and unwithdrawing hand,
Covering the earth with odours, fruits, and flocks,
Thronging the seas with spawn innumerable,
But all to please and sate the curious taste?
And set to work millions of spinning worms,
That in their green shops weave the smooth-haired silk
To deck her sons, and that no corner might
Be vacant of her plenty, in her own loins
She hutched° the all-worshipped ore and precious gems   *housed*
720   To store her children with. If all the world
Should in a pet of temperance feed on pulse,°   *pulses*
Drink the clear stream, and nothing wear but frieze,°   *coarse cloth*
The All-giver would be unthanked, would be unpraised,
Not half his riches known, and yet despised;
And we should serve him as a grudging master,
As a penurious niggard of his wealth,
And live like Nature's bastards, not her sons,
Who would be quite surcharged with her own weight,
And strangled with her waste fertility;
730   The earth cumbered, and the winged air darked with plumes;
The herds would over-multitude their lords,
The sea o'erfraught would swell, and the unsought diamonds
Would so emblaze the forehead³² of the deep,°   *sea*
And so bestud with stars, that they below
Would grow inured to light, and come at last
To gaze upon the sun with shameless brows.
List, lady, be not coy, and be not cozened°   *cheated*

With that same vaunted name 'Virginity':
Beauty is Nature's coin, must not be hoarded,
740 But must be current, and the good thereof
Consists in mutual and partaken bliss,
Unsavoury in the enjoyment of itself.
If you let slip time, like a neglected rose
It withers on the stalk with languished head.
Beauty is Nature's brag, and must be shown
In courts, at feasts, and high solemnities
Where most may wonder at the workmanship;
It is for homely features to keep home,
They had their name thence; coarse complexions
750 And cheeks of sorry grain° will serve to ply   *colouring*
The sampler, and to tease° the housewife's wool.   *comb out*
What need a vermeil°-tinctured lip for that,   *vermilion*
Love-darting eyes, or tresses like the morn?
There was another meaning in these gifts,
Think what, and be advised; you are but young yet.
Lady   I had not thought to have unlocked my lips
In this unhallowed air, but that this juggler
Would think to charm my judgement, as mine eyes,
Obtruding false rules pranked° in reason's garb.   *decked out*
760 I hate when vice can bolt° her arguments,   *sort out*
And virtue has no tongue to check her pride.
Impostor, do not charge most innocent Nature,
As if she would her children should be riotous
With her abundance; she, good cateress,
Means her provision only to the good,
That live according to her sober laws
And holy dictate of spare Temperance.
If every just man that now pines with want
Had but a moderate and beseeming share
770 Of that which lewdly-pampered luxury
Now heaps upon some few with vast excess,
Nature's full blessings would be well dispensed
In unsuperfluous even proportion,
And she no whit encumbered with her store;
And then the Giver would be better thanked,
His praise due paid, for swinish gluttony
Ne'er looks to heaven amidst his gorgeous feast,
But with besotted base ingratitude
Crams, and blasphemes his Feeder. Shall I go on?
780 Or have I said enough? To him that dares
Arm his profane tongue with contemptuous words

Against the sun-clad power of Chastity,
Fain would I something say, yet to what end?
Thou hast nor ear nor soul to apprehend
The sublime notion and high mystery[33]
That must be uttered to unfold the sage
And serious doctrine of Virginity,
And thou art worthy that thou shouldst not know
More happiness than this thy present lot.
790 Enjoy your dear wit and gay rhetoric
That hath so well been taught her dazzling fence,°   art of fencing
Thou art not fit to hear thyself convinced.°   refuted
Yet should I try, the uncontrolled worth
Of this pure cause would kindle my rapt° spirits   transported
To such a flame of sacred vehemence
That dumb things would be moved to sympathize,
And the brute Earth would lend her nerves, and shake,
Till all thy magic structures, reared so high,
Were shattered into heaps o'er thy false head.
800 **Comus**　She fables not. I feel that I do fear
Her words set off by some superior power;
And though not mortal, yet a cold shuddering dew
Dips me all o'er, as when the wrath of Jove
Speaks thunder and the chains of Erebus
To some of Saturn's crew. I must dissemble,
And try her yet more strongly. Come, no more,
This is mere moral babble, and direct
Against the canon laws of our foundation;
I must not suffer this, yet 'tis but the lees°   dregs
810 And settlings of a melancholy blood;
But this will cure all straight; one sip of this
Will bathe the drooping spirits in delight
Beyond the bliss of dreams. Be wise, and taste.

　　　[*The* **Brothers** *rush in with swords drawn, wrest his glass out of his
　　　hand, and break it against the ground; his rout make sign of resistance,
　　　but are all driven in; the* **Attendant Spirit** *comes in*]

Spirit　What, have you let the false enchanter scape?
O ye mistook, ye should have snatched his wand
And bound him fast; without his rod reversed,
And backward mutters of dissevering° power,   breaking off
We cannot free the lady that sits here
In stony fetters fixed and motionless;
820 Yet stay, be not disturbed; now I bethink me,
Some other means I have which may be used,

Which once of Meliboeus[34] old I learnt,
The soothest shepherd that e'er piped on plains.
   There is a gentle Nymph not far from hence,
That with moist curb sways the smooth Severn stream;
Sabrina is her name, a virgin pure;
Whilom she was the daughter of Locrine,
That had the sceptre from his father Brute.
She, guiltless damsel, flying the mad pursuit
830 Of her enraged stepdame Gwendolen,
Commended her fair innocence to the flood
That stayed her flight with his cross-flowing course;
The water-nymphs that in the bottom played
Held up their pearled wrists and took her in,
Bearing her straight to aged Nereus' hall,
Who, piteous of her woes, reared her lank head,
And gave her to his daughters to imbathe
In nectared lavers° strewed with asphodel,[35]   *basins*
And through the porch and inlet of each sense
840 Dropped in ambrosial oils, till she revived
And underwent a quick immortal change,
Made goddess of the river. Still she retains
Her maiden gentleness, and oft at eve
Visits the herds along the twilight meadows,
Helping all urchin blasts°, and ill-luck signs   *infections brought by imps*
That the shrewd meddling elf delights to make,
Which she with precious vialed liquors heals;
For which the shepherds at their festivals
Carol her goodness loud in rustic lays,
850 And throw sweet garland wreaths into her stream
And pansies, pinks, and gaudy daffodils.
And, as the old swain[36] said, she can unlock
The clasping charm and thaw the numbing spell,
If she be right invoked in warbled song;
For maidenhood she loves, and will be swift
To aid a virgin such as was herself
In hard-besetting need: this will I try,
And add the power of some adjuring verse.

      [*Song*]
Sabrina fair,
860   *Listen where thou are sitting*
Under the glassy, cool, translucent wave,
   In twisted braids of lilies knitting
The loose train of thy amber-dropping hair;

> *Listen for dear honour's sake,*
> *Goddess of the silver lake,*
> *Listen and save.*

Listen and appear to us
In name of great Oceanus,
By the earth-shaking Neptune's mace,
870   And Tethys' grave majestic pace,
By hoary Nereus' wrinkled look,
And the Carpathian wizard's hook,
By scaly Triton's winding shell,
And old soothsaying Glaucus' spell,
By Leucothea's lovely hands,
And her son that rules the strands,
By Thetis' tinsel-slippered feet,
And the songs of Sirens sweet,
By dead Parthenope's dear tomb,
880   And fair Ligea's golden comb,
Wherewith she sits on diamond rocks
Sleeking her soft alluring locks;
By all the nymphs that nightly dance
Upon thy streams with wily glance,
Rise, rise, and heave thy rosy head
From thy coral-paven bed,
And bridle in thy headlong wave,
Till thou our summons answered have.
                         Listen and save.

    [**Sabrina** *rises, attended by water-nymphs, and sings*]

890   *By the rushy-fringed bank,*
Where grows the willow and the osier dank,
     My sliding chariot stays,[37]
Thick set with agate, and the azurn° sheen   azure
     Of turkis° blue, and emerald green,   turquoise
          That in the channel strays.
          Whilst from off the waters fleet
          Thus I set my printless feet
          O'er the cowslip's velvet head,
          That bends not as I tread.
900   *Gentle swain, at thy request*
               I am here.

Spirit   Goddess dear,
We implore thy powerful hand
To undo the charmed band

Of true virgin here distressed,
Through the force and through the wile
Of unblest enchanter vile.
Sabrina   Shepherd, 'tis my office best
To help ensnared chastity.
910 Brightest lady, look on me;
Thus I sprinkle on thy breast
Drops that from my fountain pure
I have kept of precious cure,
Thrice upon thy finger's tip,
Thrice upon thy rubied lip;
Next this marble venomed° seat,   *poisoned*
Smeared with gums of glutinous heat,
I touch with chaste palms moist and cold.
Now the spell hath lost his hold,
920 And I must haste ere morning hour
To wait in Amphitrite's bower.

[**Sabrina** *descends, and the* **Lady** *rises out of her seat*]

Spirit   Virgin, daughter of Locrine,
Sprung of old Anchises' line,
May thy brimmed waves for this
Their full tribute never miss
From a thousand petty rills,
That tumble down the snowy hills;
Summer drouth° or singed air   *drought*
Never scorch thy tresses fair,
930 Nor wet October's torrent flood
Thy molten crystal fill with mud,
May thy billows roll ashore
The beryl° and the golden ore,   *a precious stone*
May thy lofty head be crowned
With many a tower and terrace round,
And here and there thy banks upon
With groves of myrrh and cinnamon.
    Come, Lady, while heaven lends us grace,
Let us fly this cursed place,
940 Lest the sorcerer us entice
With some other new device.
Not a waste or needless sound
Till we come to holier ground;
I shall be your faithful guide
Through this gloomy covert° wide,   *thicket*
And not many furlongs thence

Is your father's residence,
Where this night are met in state
Many a friend to gratulate
950 His wished presence, and beside
All the swains that there abide
With jigs and rural dance resort;
We shall catch them at their sport,
And our sudden coming there
Will double all their mirth and cheer.
Come let us haste, the stars grow high,
But Night sits monarch yet in the mid sky.

*The scene changes, presenting Ludlow Town and the President's
Castle; then come in Country Dancers, after them the* **Attendant
Spirit**, *with the Two* **Brothers** *and the* **Lady**.

[*Song*]

Spirit   *Back, shepherds, back, enough your play
Till next sunshine holiday;*
960 *Here be without duck° or nod*   bow
*Other trippings to be trod
Of lighter toes, and such court guise
As Mercury did first devise
With the mincing° Dryades*   dainty
On the lawns and on the leas.

[*This second song presents them to their father and mother*]

*Noble Lord, and Lady bright,
I have brought ye new delight.
Here behold so goodly grown
Three fair branches of your own;*
970 *Heaven hath timely° tried their youth,*   at the right time
*Their faith, their patience, and their truth,
And sent them here through hard assays
With a crown of deathless praise,
    To triumph in victorious dance
O'er sensual folly and intemperance.*

[*The dances ended, the* **Spirit** *epilogises*]

Spirit   To the ocean now I fly,[38]
And those happy climes that lie
Where day never shuts his eye,
Up in the broad fields of the sky.
980 There I suck the liquid air
All amidst the gardens fair

Of Hesperus, and his daughters three
That sing about the golden tree:
Along the crisped shades and bowers
Revels the spruce and jocund spring;
The graces and the rosy-bosomed hours
Thither all their bounties bring,
That there eternal summer dwells,
And west winds with musky wing

990 About the cedarn° alleys fling   *cedar*
Nard° and cassia's° balmy smells.   *spikenard/(kind of cinnamon)*
Iris there with humid bow
Waters the odorous banks that blow°   *where blossom*
Flowers of more mingled hue
Than her purfled° scarf can shew,   *with embroidered edge*
And drenches with Elysian dew
(List, mortals, if your ears be true)
Beds of hyacinth and roses,
Where young Adonis oft reposes,

1000 Waxing well of his deep wound
In slumber soft, and on the ground
Sadly sits the Assyrian queen;[39]
But far above in spangled sheen
Celestial Cupid, her famed son, advanced,
Holds his dear Psyche sweet entranced
After her wandering labours long,
Till free consent the gods among
Make her his eternal bride,
And from her fair unspotted side

1010 Two blissful twins are to be born,
Youth and Joy; so Jove hath sworn.
    But now my task is smoothly done,
I can fly, or I can run
Quickly to the green earth's end,
Where the bowed welkin° slow doth bend,   *sky*
And from thence can soar as soon
To the corners of the moon.
    Mortals that would follow me,
Love Virtue, she alone is free;

1020 She can teach ye how to climb
Higher than the sphery chime;[40]
Or if Virtue feeble were,
Heaven itself would stoop to her.

Lycidas

In this monody the author bewails a learned friend,[41] *unfortunately drowned in his passage from Chester on the Irish Seas, 1637. And by occasion foretells the ruin of our corrupted clergy, then in their height.*[42]

Yet once more, O ye laurels,[43] and once more,
Ye myrtles brown, with ivy never sere,°   *withered*
I come to pluck your berries harsh and crude,
And with forced fingers rude
Shatter your leaves before the mellowing year.
Bitter constraint, and sad occasion dear,
Compels me to disturb your season due:
For Lycidas is dead, dead ere his prime,
Young Lycidas, and hath not left his peer.
10 Who would not sing for Lycidas? He knew
Himself to sing, and build the lofty rhyme.
He must not float upon his watery bier
Unwept, and welter° to the parching wind,   *tossed about*
Without the meed of some melodious tear.
   Begin then, Sisters of the sacred well[44]
That from beneath the seat of Jove doth spring,
Begin, and somewhat loudly sweep the string.
Hence with denial vain, and coy° excuse,   *evasive*
So may some gentle Muse
20 With lucky words favour my destined urn,
And as he[45] passes turn,
And bid fair peace be to my sable° shroud.   *dark*
For we were nursed upon the self-same hill,[46]
Fed the same flock, by fountain, shade, and rill.
   Together both, ere the high lawns° appeared   *plains*
Under the opening eyelids of the morn,
We drove afield, and both together heard
What time the grey-fly winds° her sultry horn,   *blows*
Battening° our flocks with the fresh dews of night,   *fattening*
30 Oft till the star that rose, at evening, bright
Toward heaven's descent had sloped his westering wheel.
Meanwhile the rural ditties were not mute,
Tempered to the oaten° flute;   *of oat-straw = pastoral*
Rough satyrs danced, and fauns with cloven heel
From the glad sound would not be absent long,
And old Damaetas[47] loved to hear our song.
   But O the heavy change, now thou art gone,
Now thou art gone, and never must return!

Thee, Shepherd, thee the woods and desert caves,
40 With wild thyme and the gadding° vine o'ergrown,   *wandering*
And all their echoes mourn.
The willows and the hazel copses green
Shall now no more be seen
Fanning their joyous leaves to thy soft lays.
As killing as the canker° to the rose,   *destructive worm*
Or taint-worm to the weanling° herds that graze,   *weaned young*
Or frost to flowers, that their gay wardrobe wear,
When first the white-thorn° blows,   *hawthorn/blossoms*
Such, Lycidas, thy loss to shepherd's ear.
50   Where were ye, Nymphs, when the remorseless deep
Closed o'er the head of your loved Lycidas?
For neither were ye playing on the steep[48]
Where your old bards, the famous Druids, lie,
Nor on the shaggy top of Mona high,
Nor yet where Deva spreads her wizard stream.
Ay me, I fondly dream,
Had ye been there, for what could that have done?
What could the Muse herself that Orpheus bore,[49]
The Muse herself, for her enchanting son
60 Whom universal nature did lament,
When by the rout that made the hideous roar
His gory visage down the stream was sent,
Down the swift Hebrus to the Lesbian shore?
    Alas! what boots° it with uncessant care   *profits*
To tend the homely slighted shepherd's trade,
And strictly meditate the thankless Muse?
Were it not better done as others use,
To sport with Amaryllis in the shade,
Or with the tangles of Neaera's hair?
70 Fame is the spur that the clear spirit doth raise
(That last infirmity of noble mind)
To scorn delights, and live laborious days;
But the fair guerdon° when we hope to find,   *reward*
And think to burst out into sudden blaze,
Comes the blind Fury[50] with the abhorred shears,
And slits the thin-spun life. 'But not the praise,'
Phoebus replied, and touched my trembling ears:
'Fame is no plant that grows on mortal soil,
Nor in the glistering foil°   *(setting for a gem)*
80 Set off to the world, nor in broad rumour lies,
But lives and spreads aloft by those pure eyes
And perfect witness of all-judging Jove;

As he pronounces lastly on each deed,
Of so much fame in heaven expect thy meed.°'   *reward*
     O fountain Arethuse, and thou honoured flood,
Smooth-sliding Mincius, crowned with vocal reeds,
That strain I heard was of a higher mood.
But now my oat° proceeds,   *flute*
And listens to the herald of the sea[51]
90 That came in Neptune's plea.
He asked the waves, and asked the felon winds,
What hard mishap hath doomed this gentle swain?
And questioned every gust of rugged wings
That blows from off each beaked promontory.
They knew not of his story,
And sage Hippotades their answer brings,
That not a blast was from his dungeon strayed;
The air was calm, and on the level brine
Sleek Panope with all her sisters played.
100 It was that fatal and perfidious bark,
Built in the eclipse,[52] and rigged with curses dark,
That sunk so low that sacred head of thine.
     Next Camus,[53] reverend sire, went footing slow,
His mantle hairy,[54] and his bonnet sedge°,   *(river plant)*
Inwrought with figures dim, and on the edge
Like to that sanguine flower° inscribed with woe.   *(the hyacinth)*
'Ah, who hath reft,' quoth he, 'my dearest pledge?'[55]
Last came, and last did go,
The Pilot[56] of the Galilean lake;
110 Two massy keys he bore of metals twain
(The golden opes, the iron shuts amain°)   *with great strength*
He shook his mitred locks, and stern bespake:
'How well could I have spared for thee, young swain,
Enow of such as for their bellies' sake
Creep and intrude and climb into the fold!
Of other care they little reckoning make
Than how to scramble at the shearer's feast,
And shove away the worthy bidden guest.
Blind mouths![57] that scarce themselves know how to hold
120 A sheep-hook,[58] or have learned aught else the least
That to the faithful herdman's art belongs!
What recks° it them? What need they? They are sped°;   *matters/satisfied*
And when they list°, their lean and flashy songs   *choose*
Grate on their scrannel° pipes of wretched straw,   *worthless*
The hungry sheep look up, and are not fed,
But swoln with wind, and the rank mist they draw,

Rot inwardly, and foul contagion spread,
Besides what the grim wolf[59] with privy paw
Daily devours apace, and nothing said;
130 But that two-handed engine[60] at the door
Stands ready to smite once, and smite no more.'
    Return, Alpheus, the dread voice is past
That shrunk thy streams; return, Sicilian Muse,
And call the vales, and bid them hither cast
Their bells and flowerets of a thousand hues.
Ye valleys low where the mild whispers use°   *frequent*
Of shades and wanton winds and gushing brooks,
On whose fresh lap the swart° star[61] sparely looks,   *dark*
Throw hither all your quaint enamelled eyes,
140 That on the green turf suck the honied showers,
And purple all the ground with vernal° flowers.   *spring*
Bring the rathe° primrose that forsaken dies,   *early*
The tufted crowtoe,° and pale jessamine,°   *wild hyacinth/jasmine*
The white pink, and the pansy freaked° with jet,   *freckled*
The glowing violet,
The musk-rose, and the well-attired woodbine,
With cowslips wan that hang the pensive head,
And every flower that sad embroidery wears.
Bid amaranthus° all his beauty shed,   *(an unfading flower)*
150 And daffadillies fill their cups with tears,
To strew the laureate hearse where Lycid lies.
For so to interpose a little ease,
Let our frail thoughts dally with false surmise;[62]
Ay me! whilst thee the shores and sounding seas
Wash far away, where'er thy bones are hurled,
Whether beyond the stormy Hebrides,
Where thou perhaps under the whelming° tide   *overwhelming*
Visit'st the bottom of the monstrous° world;   *sea-monsters'*
Or whether thou, to our moist vows denied,
160 Sleep'st by the fable of Bellerus old,
Where the great vision° of the guarded mount[63]   *visionary*
Looks toward Namancos and Bayona's hold:
Look homeward, Angel,° now, and melt with ruth;°   *(St Michael)/pity*
And, O ye dolphins,[64] waft the hapless youth.
    Weep no more, woeful shepherds, weep no more,
For Lycidas, your sorrow, is not dead,
Sunk though he be beneath the watery floor;
So sinks the day-star in the ocean bed,
And yet anon repairs his drooping head,
170 And tricks° his beams, and with new-spangled ore   *adorns*

Flames in the forehead of the morning sky:
So Lycidas sunk low, but mounted high,
Through the dear might of Him that walked the waves,[65]
Where, other groves and other streams along,
With nectar pure his oozy locks he laves,°   *washes*
And hears the unexpressive nuptial song[66]
In the blest kingdoms meek of joy and love.
There entertain him all the saints above,
In solemn troops and sweet societies
180   That sing, and singing in their glory move,
And wipe the tears for ever from his eyes.
Now, Lycidas, the shepherds weep no more;
Henceforth thou art the Genius° of the Shore,   *local spirit*
In thy large recompense, and shalt be good
To all that wander in that perilous flood.
      Thus sang the uncouth° swain to the oaks and rills,   *unlettered*
While the still morn went out with sandals grey;
He touched the tender stops of various quills,°   *(reeds of his pipe)*
With eager thought warbling his Doric lay.
190   And now the sun had stretched out all the hills,
And now was dropped into the western bay;
At last he rose, and twitched his mantle blue:[67]
Tomorrow to fresh woods, and pastures new.

1637 [1645]

Paradise Lost[68]

Book I[69]

Of man's first disobedience, and the fruit
Of that forbidden tree, whose mortal taste
Brought death into the world, and all our woe,
With loss of Eden, till one greater Man[70]
Restore us, and regain the blissful seat,
Sing heavenly Muse,[71] that on the secret top
Of Oreb, or of Sinai, didst inspire
That shepherd,[72] who first taught the chosen seed,
In the beginning how the heavens and earth
10   Rose out of chaos: or if Sion hill

Delight thee more, and Siloa's brook that flowed
Fast by the oracle of God;[73] I thence
Invoke thy aid to my adventurous song,
That with no middle flight intends to soar
Above the Aonian mount, while it pursues
Things unattempted yet in prose or rhyme.
And chiefly thou O Spirit, that dost prefer ·
Before all temples the upright heart and pure,
Instruct me, for thou know'st; thou from the first
20 Wast present, and with mighty wings outspread
Dove-like sat'st brooding on the vast abyss
And madest it pregnant:[74] what in me is dark
Illumine, what is low raise and support;
That to the highth of this great argument
I may assert eternal providence,
And justify° the ways of God to men.   *show the rightness of*
    Say first, for heaven hides nothing from thy view
Nor the deep tract of hell, say first what cause
Moved our grand parents in that happy state,
30 Favoured of heaven so highly, to fall off
From their creator, and transgress his will
For one restraint, lords of the world besides?
Who first seduced them to that foul revolt?
The infernal serpent° he it was, whose guile   *(Satan)*
Stirred up with envy and revenge, deceived
The mother of mankind, what time his pride
Had cast him out from heaven, with all his host
Of rebel angels, by whose aid aspiring
To set himself in glory above his peers,
40 He trusted to have equalled the most high,
If he opposed; and with ambitious aim
Against the throne and monarchy of God
Raised impious war in heaven and battle proud
With vain attempt. Him the almighty power
Hurled headlong flaming from the ethereal° sky[75]   *realm of pure air*
With hideous ruin° and combustion down   *destruction*
To bottomless perdition, there to dwell
In adamantine° chains and penal fire   *indestructible*
Who durst defy the Omnipotent to arms.
50 Nine times the space that measures day and night
To mortal men, he with his horrid crew
Lay vanquished, rolling in the fiery gulf
Confounded though immortal: but his doom
Reserved him to more wrath; for now the thought

Both of lost happiness and lasting pain
Torments him; round he throws his baleful eyes
That witnessed huge affliction and dismay
Mixed with obdurate pride and steadfast hate:
At once as far as angels' ken° he views   *field of vision*
60 The dismal situation waste and wild.
A dungeon horrible, on all sides round
As one great furnace flamed, yet from those flames
No light, but rather darkness visible[76]
Served only to discover sights of woe,
Regions of sorrow, doleful shades, where peace
And rest can never dwell, hope never comes[77]
That comes to all; but torture without end
Still urges,° and a fiery deluge, fed   *crushes*
With ever-burning sulphur unconsumed:
70 Such place eternal justice had prepared
For these rebellious, here their prison ordained
In utter darkness, and their portion set
As far removed from God and light of heaven
As from the centre thrice to the utmost pole.
O how unlike the place from whence they fell!
There the companions of his fall, o'erwhelmed
With floods and whirlwinds of tempestuous fire,
He soon discerns, and weltering° by his side   *tossing*
One next himself in power, and next in crime,
80 Long after known in Palestine, and named
Beelzebub. To whom the arch-enemy,
And thence in heaven called Satan, with bold words
Breaking the horrid silence thus began.
   'If thou beest he; but O how fallen! how changed
From him, who in the happy realms of light
Clothed with transcendent brightness didst outshine
Myriads though bright: if he whom mutual league,
United thoughts and counsels, equal hope
And hazard in the glorious enterprise,
90 Joined with me once, now misery hath joined
In equal ruin: in to what pit thou seest
From what highth fallen, so much the stronger proved
He with his thunder: and till then who knew
The force of those dire arms? Yet not for those,
Nor what the potent Victor in his rage
Can else inflict, do I repent or change,
Though changed in outward lustre, that fixed mind
And high disdain, from sense of injured merit,°   *deserving*

That with the mightiest raised me to contend,
100 And to the fierce contention brought along
Innumerable force of spirits armed
That durst dislike his reign, and me preferring,
His utmost power with adverse power opposed
In dubious battle on the plains of heaven,
And shook his throne. What though the field° be lost?   *battlefield*
All is not lost; the unconquerable will,
And study of revenge, immortal hate,
And courage never to submit or yield:
And what is else not to be overcome?
110 That glory never shall his wrath or might
Extort from me. To bow and sue for grace
With suppliant knee, and deify his power,
Who from the terror of this arm so late
Doubted° his empire, that were low indeed,   *feared for*
That were an ignominy and shame beneath
This downfall; since by fate the strength of gods
And this empyreal substance[78] cannot fail,
Since through experience of this great event
In arms not worse, in foresight much advanced,
120 We may with more successful hope° resolve   *hope of success*
To wage by force or guile eternal war
Irreconcilable, to our grand Foe,
Who now triumphs, and in the excess of joy
Sole reigning holds the tyranny of heaven.'
    So spake the apostate angel, though in pain,
Vaunting aloud, but racked with deep despair:
And him thus answered soon his bold compeer.
    'O prince, O chief of many thronèd powers,
That led the embattled seraphim to war
130 Under thy conduct, and in dreadful deeds
Fearless, endangered heaven's perpetual King;
And put to proof his high supremacy,
Whether upheld by strength, or chance, or fate,
Too well I see and rue the dire event,
That with sad overthrow and foul defeat
Hath lost us heaven, and all this mighty host
In horrible destruction laid thus low,
As far as gods and heavenly essences
Can perish: for the mind and spirit remains
140 Invincible, and vigour soon returns,
Though all our glory extinct,° and happy state   *extinguished·*
Here swallowed up in endless misery.

But what if He our conqueror, (whom I now
Of force° believe almighty, since no less   *perforce*
Than such could have o'erpowered such force as ours)
Have left us this our spirit and strength entire
Strongly to suffer and support our pains,
That we may so suffice° his vengeful ire,   *satisfy*
Or do Him mightier service as his thralls
150 By right of war, whate'er his business be
Here in the heart of hell to work in fire,
Or do his errands in the gloomy deep;
What can it then avail though yet we feel
Strength undiminished, or eternal being
To undergo eternal punishment?'
Whereto with speedy words the arch-fiend replied.
    'Fallen cherub, to be weak is miserable
Doing or suffering: but of this be sure,
To do aught good never will be our task,
160 But ever to do ill our sole delight,
As being the contrary to his high will
Whom we resist. If then his providence
Out of our evil seek to bring forth good,
Our labour must be to pervert that end,
And out of good still to find means of evil;
Which oft-times may succeed, so as perhaps
Shall grieve him, if I fail not,[79] and disturb
His inmost counsels from their destined aim.
But see the angry Victor hath recalled
170 His ministers of vengeance and pursuit
Back to the gates of heaven: the sulphurous hail
Shot after us in storm, o'erblown hath laid[80]
The fiery surge, that from the precipice
Of heaven received us falling, and the thunder,
Winged with red lightning and impetuous rage,
Perhaps hath spent his shafts, and ceases now
To bellow through the vast and boundless deep.
Let us not slip° the occasion, whether scorn,   *let slip*
Or satiate fury yield it from our Foe.
180 Seest thou yon dreary plain, forlorn and wild,
The seat of desolation, void of light,
Save what the glimmering of these livid flames
Casts pale and dreadful? Thither let us tend
From off the tossing of these fiery waves,
There rest, if any rest can harbour there,
And reassembling our afflicted° powers,   *downcast*

Consult how we may henceforth most offend°   *injure*
Our enemy, our own loss how repair,
How overcome this dire calamity,
190 What reinforcement we may gain from hope,
If not what resolution from despair.'
      Thus Satan talking to his nearest mate
With head uplift above the wave, and eyes
That sparkling blazed, his other parts besides
Prone on the flood, extended long and large
Lay floating many a rood°, in bulk as huge   *rod = 5½ yards*
As whom the fables name of monstrous size,
Titanian, or Earth-born, that warred on Jove,[81]
Briareos or Typhon, whom the den
200 By ancient Tarsus held, or that sea-beast
Leviathan, which God of all his works
Created hugest that swim the ocean stream:
Him haply slumbering on the Norway foam
The pilot of some small night-foundered skiff,
Deeming some island, oft, as seamen tell,
With fixed anchor in his scaly rind[82]
Moors by his side under the lea, while night
Invests° the sea, and wished morn delays: *engulfs*
So stretched out huge in length the arch-fiend lay
210 Chained on the burning lake, nor ever thence
Had risen or heaved his head, but that the will
And high permission of all-ruling heaven
Left him at large to his own dark designs,
That with reiterated crimes he might
Heap on himself damnation, while he sought
Evil to others, and enraged might see
How all his malice served but to bring forth
Infinite goodness, grace and mercy shown
On man by him seduced, but on himself
220 Treble confusion, wrath and vengeance poured.
Forthwith upright he rears from off the pool
His mighty stature; on each hand the flames
Driven backward slope their pointing spires, and rolled
In billows, leave i' the midst a horrid° vale.   *bristling*
Then with expanded wings he steers his flight
Aloft, incumbent° on the dusky air   *leaning on*
That felt unusual weight, till on dry land
He lights, if it were land that ever burned
With solid, as the lake with liquid fire;
230 And such appeared in hue°, as when the force[83]   *colour*

Of subterranean wind transports a hill
Torn from Pelorus, or the shattered side
Of thundering Aetna, whose combustible
And fuelled entrails thence conceiving fire,
Sublimed° with mineral fury, aid the winds,   *infused*
And leave a singed bottom all involved°   *entangled*
With stench and smoke: such resting found the sole
Of unblessed feet. Him followed his next° mate,   *closest*
Both glorying to have scaped the Stygian flood
240   As gods, and by their own recovered strength,
Not by the sufferance of supernal power.
      'Is this the region, this the soil, the clime,'
Said then the lost archangel, 'this the seat°   *place*
That we must change for heaven, this mournful gloom
For that celestial light? Be it so, since he
Who now is sovereign can dispose and bid
What shall be right: farthest from him is best
Whom reason hath equalled, force hath made supreme
Above his equals. Farewell happy fields
250   Where joy for ever dwells: hail horrors, hail
Infernal world, and thou profoundest hell
Receive thy new possessor: one who brings
A mind not to be changed by place or time.
The mind is its own place, and in itself
Can make a heaven of hell, a hell of heaven.
What matter where, if I be still the same,
And what I should be, all but less than He
Whom thunder hath made greater? Here at least
We shall be free; the Almighty hath not built
260   Here for his envy, will not drive us hence:
Here we may reign secure, and in my choice
To reign is worth ambition though in hell:
Better to reign in hell, than serve in heaven.
But wherefore let we then our faithful friends,
The associates and copartners of our loss
Lie thus astonished° on the oblivious° pool,   *stupefied/of oblivion*
And call them not to share with us their part
In this unhappy mansion, or once more
With rallied arms to try what may be yet
270   Regained in heaven, or what more lost in hell?'
      So Satan spake, and him Beelzebub
Thus answered. 'Leader of those armies bright,
Which but the Omnipotent none could have foiled,
If once they hear that voice, their liveliest pledge

Of hope in fears and dangers, heard so oft
In worst extremes, and on the perilous edge
Of battle when it raged, in all assaults
Their surest signal, they will soon resume
New courage and revive, though now they lie
280 Grovelling and prostrate on yon lake of fire,
As we erewhile, astounded and amazed,
No wonder, fallen such a pernicious highth.'
　　He scarce had ceased when the superior fiend
Was moving toward the shore; his ponderous shield
Ethereal temper,° massy, large, and round,　　　*tempered by ethereal flame*
Behind him cast; the broad circumference
Hung on his shoulders like the moon, whose orb
Through optic glass the Tuscan artist views[84]
At evening from the top of Fesole,
290 Or in Valdarno, to descry new lands,
Rivers or mountains in her spotty globe.
His spear, to equal which the tallest pine
Hewn on Norwegian hills, to be the mast
Of some great ammiral,° were but a wand,　　　*admiral's flagship*
He walked with to support uneasy steps
Over the burning marl, not like those steps
On heaven's azure, and the torrid clime
Smote on him sore besides, vaulted with fire;
Natheless he so endured, till on the beach
300 Of that inflamed sea, he stood and called
His legions, angel forms, who lay entranced
Thick as autumnal leaves that strew the brooks
In Vallombrosa, where the Etrurian shades
High overarched imbower; or scattered sedge
Afloat, when with fierce winds Orion armed
Hath vexed the Red Sea coast, whose waves o'erthrew
Busiris and his Memphian chivalry,
While with perfidious[85] hatred they pursued
The sojourners of Goshen, who beheld
310 From the safe shore their floating carcasses
And broken chariot wheels, so thick bestrewn
Abject° and lost lay these, covering the flood,　　　*cast down*
Under amazement of their hideous change.
He called so loud, that all the hollow deep
Of hell resounded. 'Princes, potentates,
Warriors, the flower of heaven, once yours, now lost,
If such astonishment as this can seize
Eternal spirits; or have ye chosen this place

After the toil of battle to repose
320 Your wearied virtue,° for the ease you find   *strength*
     To slumber here, as in the vales of heaven?
     Or in this abject posture have ye sworn
     To adore the Conqueror? who now beholds
     Cherub and seraph rolling in the flood
     With scattered arms and ensigns, till anon
     His swift pursuers from heaven gates discern
     The advantage, and descending tread us down
     Thus drooping, or with linked thunderbolts
     Transfix us to the bottom of this gulf.
330 Awake, arise, or be for ever fallen.'
        They heard, and were abashed, and up they sprung
     Upon the wing, as when men wont to watch
     On duty, sleeping found by whom they dread,
     Rouse and bestir themselves ere well awake.
     Nor did they not perceive the evil plight
     In which they were, or the fierce pains not feel;
     Yet to their general's voice they soon obeyed
     Innumerable. As when the potent rod
     Of Amram's son° in Egypt's evil day   *(Moses)*
340 Waved round the coast, up called a pitchy cloud
     Of locusts,[86] warping on the eastern wind,
     That o'er the realm of impious Pharaoh hung
     Like night, and darkened all the land of Nile:
     So numberless were those bad angels seen
     Hovering on wing under the cope° of hell   *canopy*
     'Twixt upper, nether, and surrounding fires;
     Till, as a signal given, the uplifted spear
     Of their great sultan waving to direct
     Their course, in even balance down they light
350 On the firm brimstone, and fill all the plain;
     A multitude, like which the populous north
     Poured never from her frozen loins, to pass
     Rhene or the Danaw,[87] when her barbarous sons
     Came like a deluge on the south, and spread
     Beneath Gibralter to the Lybian sands.
     Forthwith from every squadron and each band
     The heads and leaders thither haste where stood
     Their great commander; godlike shapes and forms
     Excelling human, princely dignities,
360 And powers that erst° in heaven sat on thrones;   *formerly*
     Though of their names in heavenly records now
     Be no memorial, blotted out and razed[88]

By their rebellion, from the books of life.
Nor had they yet among the sons of Eve
Got them new names, till wandering o'er the earth,
Through God's high sufferance for the trial of man,
By falsities and lies the greatest part
Of mankind they corrupted to forsake
God their creator, and the invisible
370 Glory of Him that made them, to transform
Oft to the image of a brute, adorned
With gay religions° full of pomp and gold,   *pagan rituals*
And devils to adore for deities:
Then were they known to men by various names,[89]
And various idols through the heathen world.
Say, Muse, their names then known, who first, who last,
Roused from the slumber, on that fiery couch,
At their great emperor's call, as next in worth
Came singly where he stood on the bare strand,
380 While the promiscuous° crowd stood yet aloof?   *mixed*
The chief were those who from the pit of hell
Roaming to seek their prey on earth, durst fix[90]
Their seats long after next the seat of God,
Their altars by his altar, gods adored
Among the nations round, and durst abide
Jehovah thundering out of Sion, throned
Between the cherubim; yea, often placed
Within his sanctuary itself their shrines,
Abominations; and with cursed things
390 His holy rites, and solemn feasts profaned
And with their darkness durst affront his light.
First Moloch, horrid king besmeared with blood
Of human sacrifice, and parents' tears,
Though for the noise of drums and timbrels° loud   *tambourines*
Their children's cries unheard, that passed through fire
To his grim idol. Him the Ammonite
Worshipped in Rabba and her watery plain,
In Argob and in Basan, to the stream
Of utmost Arnon. Nor content with such
400 Audacious neighbourhood, the wisest heart
Of Solomon he led by fraud to build
His temple right against the temple of God
On that opprobrious hill, and made his grove
The pleasant valley of Hinnom, Tophet thence
And black Gehenna called, the type of hell.
Next Chemos, the obscene dread of Moab's sons,

From Aroar to Nebo,[91] and the wild
Of southmost Abarim; in Hesebon
And Horonaim, Seon's realm, beyond
410   The flowery dale of Sibma clad with vines,
And Eleale to the Asphaltic Pool.°   (the Dead Sea)
Peor[92] his other name, when he enticed
Israel in Sittim, on their march from Nile,
To do him wanton rites; which cost them woe.[93]
Yet thence his lustful orgies he enlarged[94]
Even to that hill of scandal, by the grove
Of Moloch homicide, lust hard by hate;
Till good Josiah drove them thence to hell.
With these came they, who from the bordering flood
420   Of old Euphrates to the brook that parts[95]
Egypt from Syrian ground, had general names
Of Baalim and Ashtaroth; those male,
These feminine. For spirits when they please
Can either sex assume, or both; so soft
And uncompounded is their essence pure,
Not tied or manacled with joint or limb,
Nor founded on the brittle strength of bones,
Like cumbrous flesh; but in what shape they choose
Dilated or condensed, bright or obscure,
430   Can execute their airy purposes,
And works of love or enmity fulfil.
For those the race of Israel oft forsook[96]
Their living strength, and unfrequented left
His righteous altar, bowing lowly down
To bestial gods; for which their heads as low
Bowed down in battle, sunk before the spear
Of despicable foes. With these in troop
Came Astoreth, whom the Phoenicians called
Astarte, queen of heaven, with crescent horns;
440   To whose bright image nightly by the moon
Sidonian virgins paid their vows and songs,
In Sion also not unsung, where stood
Her temple on the offensive mountain, built
By that uxorious king, whose heart though large,
Beguiled by fair idolatresses, fell
To idols foul. Thammuz came next behind,
Whose annual wound in Lebanon allured
The Syrian damsels to lament his fate
In amorous ditties all a summer's day,
450   While smooth Adonis from his native rock

Ran purple to the sea, supposed with blood
Of Thammuz yearly wounded: the love-tale
Infected Sion's daughters with like heat,
Whose wanton passions in the sacred porch
Ezekiel saw,[97] when by the vision led
His eye surveyed the dark idolatries
Of alienated Judah. Next came one
Who mourned in earnest, when the captive ark[98]
Maimed his brute image, head and hands lopped off
460 In his own temple, on the groundsel° edge,   *door-sill*
Where he fell flat, and shamed his worshippers:
Dagon his name, sea monster, upward man
And downward fish: yet had his temple high
Reared in Azotus, dreaded through the coast
Of Palestine, in Gath and Ascalon
And Accaron and Gaza's frontier bounds.
Him followed Rimmon, whose delightful seat
Was fair Damascus, on the fertile banks
Of Abbana and Pharphar, lucid streams.
470 He also against the house of God was bold:
A leper once he lost and gained a king,[99]
Ahaz[100] his sottish conqueror, whom he drew
God's altar to disparage and displace
For one of Syrian mode, whereon to burn
His odious offerings, and adore the gods
Whom he had vanquished. After these appeared
A crew who under names of old renown,
Osiris, Isis, Orus and their train
With monstrous shapes[101] and sorceries abused
480 Fanatic Egypt and her priests, to seek
Their wandering gods disguised in brutish forms[102]
Rather than human. Nor did Israel scape
The infection when their borrowed gold composed
The calf in Oreb: and the rebel king[103]
Doubled that sin in Bethel and in Dan,
Likening his maker to the grazed ox,
Jehovah, who in one night when he passed[104]
From Egypt marching, equalled with one stroke
Both her first born and all her bleating gods.
490 Belial came last, than whom a spirit more lewd
Fell not from heaven, or more gross to love
Vice for itself: to him no temple stood
Or altar smoked; yet who more oft than he
In temples and at altars, when the priest

Turns atheist, as did Ely's sons,[105] who filled
With lust and violence the house of God.
In courts and palaces he also reigns
And in luxurious° cities, where the noise   *pleasure-seeking*
Of riot ascends above their loftiest towers,
500 And injury and outrage: and when night
Darkens the streets, then wander forth the sons
Of Belial, flown° with insolence and wine.   *elated*
Witness the streets of Sodom, and that night
In Gibeah, when the hospitable door
Exposed a matron to avoid worse rape.[106]
These were the prime in order and in might;
The rest were long to tell, though far renowned,
The Ionian gods, of Javan's issue held
Gods, yet confessed later than Heaven and Earth
510 Their boasted parents; Titan Heaven's first born
With his enormous brood, and birthright seized
By younger Saturn, he from mightier Jove
His own and Rhea's son like measure found;
So Jove usurping reigned: these first in Crete
And Ida known, thence on the snowy top
Of cold Olympus ruled the middle air
Their highest heaven; or on the Delphian cliff,
Or in Dodona, and through all the bounds
Of Doric land; or who with Saturn old
520 Fled over Adria to the Hesperian fields,
And o'er the Celtic roamed the utmost isles.°   *(Britain)*
All these and more came flocking; but with looks
Down cast and damp, yet such wherein appeared
Obscure some glimpse of joy, to have found their chief
Not in despair, to have found themselves not lost
In loss itself; which on his countenance cast
Like doubtful hue: but he his wonted pride
Soon recollecting, with high words, that bore
Semblance of worth, not substance, gently raised
530 Their fainting courage, and dispelled their fears.
Then straight commands that at the warlike sound
Of trumpets loud and clarions be upreared
His mighty standard; that proud honour claimed
Azazel as his right, a cherub tall:
Who forthwith from the glittering staff unfurled
The imperial ensign, which full high advanced
Shone like a meteor streaming to the wind
With gems and golden lustre rich imblazed,°   *emblazoned*

Seraphic arms and trophies: all the while
540 Sonorous metal blowing martial sounds:
At which the universal host upsent
A shout that tore hell's concave, and beyond
Frighted the reign° of Chaos and old Night.   *realm*
All in a moment through the gloom were seen
Ten thousand banners rise into the air
With orient colours waving: with them rose
A forest huge of spears: and thronging helms
Appeared, and serried shields in thick array
Of depth immeasurable: anon they move
550 In perfect phalanx° to the Dorian mood   *(a battle-formation)*
Of flutes and soft recorders; such as raised
To highth of noblest temper heroes old
Arming to battle, and in stead of rage
Deliberate valour breathed, firm and unmoved
With dread of death to flight or foul retreat,
Nor wanting power to mitigate and swage,°   *assuage*
With solemn touches, troubled thoughts, and chase
Anguish and doubt and fear and sorrow and pain
From mortal or immortal minds. Thus they
560 Breathing united force with fixed thought
Moved on in silence to soft pipes that charmed
Their painful steps o'er the burnt soil; and now
Advanced in view, they stand, a horrid° front   *bristling (with spears)*
Of dreadful length and dazzling arms, in guise
Of warriors old with ordered spear and shield,
Awaiting what command their mighty chief
Had to impose: he through the armed files
Darts his experienced eye, and soon traverse
The whole battalion views, their order due,
570 Their visages and stature as of gods,
Their number last he sums. And now his heart
Distends with pride, and hardening in his strength
Glories: for never since created man,
Met such embodied force, as named with these
Could merit more than that small infantry[107]
Warred on by cranes: though all the Giant brood[108]
Of Phlegra with the heroic race were joined
That fought at Thebes and Ilium, on each side
Mixed with auxiliar° gods; and what resounds   *supporting*
580 In fable or romance of Uther's son
Begirt with British and Armoric knights;
And all who since, baptized or infidel

Jousted in Aspramont or Montalban,
Damasco, or Marocco, or Trebisond,
Or whom Biserta sent from Afric shore
When Charlemain with all his peerage fell
By Fontarabbia. Thus far these beyond
Compare of mortal prowess, yet observed
Their dread commander: he above the rest
590   In shape and gesture proudly eminent
Stood like a tower; his form had yet not lost
All her original brightness, nor appeared
Less than archangel ruined, and the excess
Of glory obscured: as when the sun new risen
Looks through the horizontal misty air
Shorn of his beams, or from behind the moon
In dim eclipse disastrous° twilight sheds   *foretelling disaster*
On half the nations, and with fear of change
Perplexes monarchs. Darkened so, yet shone
600   Above them all the archangel: but his face
Deep scars of thunder had intrenched, and care
Sat on his faded cheek, but under brows
Of dauntless courage, and considerate° pride   *thoughtful*
Waiting revenge; cruel his eye, but cast°   *showed*
Signs of remorse and passion to behold
The fellows of his crime, the followers rather
(Far other once beheld in bliss) condemned
For ever now to have their lot in pain,
Millions of spirits for his fault amerced°   *deprived*
610   Of heaven, and from eternal splendours flung
For his revolt, yet faithful how they stood,
Their glory withered. As when heaven's fire
Hath scathed the forest oaks, or mountain pines,
With singed top their stately growth though bare
Stands on the blasted heath. He now prepared
To speak; whereat° their doubled ranks they bend   *at which*
From wing to wing, and half enclose him round
With all his peers: attention held them mute.
Thrice he essayed, and thrice in spite of scorn,
620   Tears such as angels weep, burst forth: at last
Words interwove with sighs found out their way.
    'O myriads of immortal spirits, O powers
Matchless, but with° the almighty, and that strife   *except by*
Was not inglorious, though the event was dire,
As this place testifies, and this dire change
Hateful to utter: but what power of mind

Foreseeing or presaging,° from the depth   *foreboding*
Of knowledge past or present, could have feared,
How such united force of gods, how such
630 As stood like these, could ever know repulse?
For who can yet believe, though after loss,
That all these puissant legions, whose exile
Hath emptied heaven, shall fail to re-ascend
Self-raised, and repossess their native seat?
For me be witness all the host of heaven,
If counsels different, or danger shunned
By me, have lost our hopes. But He who reigns
Monarch in heaven, till then as one secure
Sat on his throne, upheld by old repute,
640 Consent or custom, and his regal state
Put forth at full, but still his strength concealed,
Which tempted our attempt, and wrought our fall.
Henceforth his might we know, and know our own
So as not either to provoke, or dread
New war, provoked; our better part remains
To work in close design, by fraud or guile
What force effected° not: that He no less   *achieved*
At length from us may find, who overcomes
By force, hath overcome but half his foe.
650 Space may produce new worlds; whereof so rife°   *widespread*
There went a fame° in heaven that He ere long   *rumour*
Intended to create, and therein plant
A generation, whom his choice regard
Should favour equal to the sons of heaven:
Thither, if but to pry, shall be perhaps
Our first eruption, thither or elsewhere:
For this infernal pit shall never hold
Celestial spirits in bondage, nor the abyss
Long under darkness cover. But these thoughts
660 Full counsel must mature: peace is despaired,
For who can think submission? War then, war
Open or understood must be resolved.'
    He spake: and to confirm his words, out flew
Millions of flaming swords, drawn from the thighs
Of mighty cherubim; the sudden blaze
Far round illumined hell; highly they raged
Against the highest, and fierce with grasped arms
Clashed on their sounding shields the din of war,
Hurling defiance toward the vault of heaven.
670   There stood a hill not far whose grisly top

Belched fire and rolling smoke; the rest entire
Shone with a glossy scurf°, undoubted sign   *scaly crust*
That in his womb was hid metallic ore,
The work of sulphur.[109] Thither winged with speed
A numerous brigade hastened. As when bands
Of pioneers with spade and pickaxe armed
Forerun the royal camp, to trench a field,
Or cast a rampart. Mammon led them on,
Mammon, the least erected° spirit that fell   *upright*
680 From heaven, for even in heaven his looks and thoughts
Were always downward bent, admiring more
The riches of heaven's pavement, trodden gold,
Than aught divine or holy else enjoyed
In vision beatific°: by him first   *vision of God*
Men also, and by his suggestion taught,
Ransacked the centre, and with impious hands
Rifled the bowels of their mother earth
For treasures better hid. Soon had his crew
Opened into the hill a spacious wound
690 And digged out ribs of gold. Let none admire°   *wonder*
That riches grow in hell; that soil may best
Deserve the precious bane°. And here let those   *poison*
Who boast in mortal things, and wondering tell
Of Babel, and the works of Memphian kings
Learn how their greatest monuments of fame,
And strength and art are easily outdone
By spirits reprobate°, and in an hour   *rejected*
What in an age they with incessant toil
And hands innumerable scarce perform.
700 Nigh on the plain in many cells prepared,
That underneath had veins of liquid fire
Sluiced from the lake, a second multitude
With wondrous art founded the massy ore,[110]
Severing each kind, and scummed° the bullion dross: *took the scum off*
A third as soon had formed within the ground
A various mould, and from the boiling cells
By strange conveyance filled each hollow nook,
As in an organ from one blast of wind
To many a row of pipes the sound-board breathes.
710 Anon, out of the earth, a fabric huge
Rose like an exhalation, with the sound
Of dulcet° symphonies and voices sweet,   *harmonious*
Built like a temple, where pilasters° round   *shallow columns*
Were set, and Doric pillars overlaid

With golden architrave,° nor did there want   *moulding*
Cornice or frieze, with bossy° sculptures graven;   *in relief*
The roof was fretted° gold. Not Babylon,   *patterned*
Nor great Alcairo such magnificence
Equalled in all their glories, to enshrine
720 Belus or Serapis their gods, or seat
Their kings, when Egypt with Assyria strove
In wealth and luxury. The ascending pile°   *edifice*
Stood fixed her stately highth, and straight the doors
Opening their brazen folds discover wide
Within, her ample spaces, o'er the smooth
And level pavement: from the arched roof
Pendent by subtle magic many a row
Of starry lamps and blazing cressets° fed   *iron baskets used for torches*
With naphtha° and asphaltus° yielded light   *oil from asphalt/pitch*
730 As from a sky. The hasty multitude
Admiring entered, and the work some praise
And some the architect: his hand was known
In heaven by many a towered structure high,
Where sceptred angels held their residence,
And sat as princes, whom the supreme King
Exalted to such power, and gave to rule,
Each in his hierarchy, the orders bright.
Nor was his name unheard or unadored
In ancient Greece; and in Ausonian land°   *(Italy)*
740 Men called him Mulciber; and how he fell
From heaven, they fabled, thrown by angry Jove
Sheer o'er the crystal battlements; from morn
To noon he fell, from noon to dewy eve,
A summer's day; and with the setting sun
Dropped from the zenith like a falling star,
On Lemnos the Aegaean isle: thus they relate,
Erring; for he with this rebellious rout
Fell long before; nor aught availed him now
To have built in heaven high towers; nor did he scape
750 By all his engines,° but was headlong sent   *machinery*
With his industrious crew to build in hell.
Mean while the winged heralds by command
Of sovereign power, with awful ceremony
And trumpet's sound throughout the host proclaim
A solemn council forthwith to be held
At Pandaemonium,¹¹¹ the high capital
Of Satan and his peers: their summons called
From every band and squared regiment

By place or choice the worthiest; they anon
760 With hundreds and with thousands trooping came
Attended: all access was thronged, the gates
And porches wide, but chief the spacious hall
(Though like a covered field, where champions bold
Wont° ride in armed, and at the Soldan's° chair   *by custom/Sultan's*
Defied the best of paynim° chivalry   *pagan*
To mortal combat or career° with lance)   *combat*
Thick swarmed, both on the ground and in the air,
Brushed with the hiss of rustling wings. As bees
In spring time, when the sun with Taurus rides,
770 Pour forth their populous youth about the hive
In clusters; they among fresh dews and flowers
Fly to and fro, or on the smoothed plank,
The suburb of their straw-built citadel,
New rubbed with balm, expatiate° and confer   *move about*
Their state affairs. So thick the airy crowd
Swarmed and were straitened? till the signal given,   *confined*
Behold a wonder! they but now who seemed
In bigness to surpass Earth's giant sons
Now less than smallest dwarfs, in narrow room
780 Throng numberless, like that pygmean race
Beyond the Indian mount,[112] or faerie elves,
Whose midnight revels, by a forest side
Or fountain some belated peasant sees,
Or dreams he sees, while overhead the moon
Sits arbitress, and nearer to the earth
Wheels her pale course, they on their mirth and dance
Intent, with jocund music charm his ear;
At once with joy and fear his heart rebounds.
Thus incorporeal spirits to smallest forms
790 Reduced their shapes immense, and were at large,
Though without number still amidst the hall
Of that infernal court. But far within
And in their own dimensions like themselves
The great seraphic lords and cherubim
In close° recess and secret conclave sat   *closed*
A thousand demi-gods on golden seats,
Frequent and full. After short silence then
And summons read, the great consult began.

Book II[113]

High on a throne of royal state, which far
Outshone the wealth of Ormus and of Ind,
Or where the gorgeous East with richest hand
Showers on her kings barbaric pearl and gold,
Satan exalted sat, by merit raised
To that bad eminence; and from despair
Thus high uplifted beyond hope, aspires
Beyond thus high, insatiate to pursue
Vain war with heaven, and by success° untaught   *outcome*
10 His proud imaginations thus displayed.
        'Powers and dominions,° deities of heaven,   *orders of angels*
For since no deep within her gulf can hold
Immortal vigour, though oppressed and fallen,
I give not heaven for lost. From this descent
Celestial virtues° rising, will appear   *an order of angels*
More glorious and more dread than from no fall,
And trust themselves to fear no second fate:
Me though just right, and the fixed laws of heaven
Did first create your leader, next free choice,
20 With what besides, in counsel or in fight,
Hath been achieved of merit, yet this loss
Thus far at least recovered, hath much more
Established in a safe unenvied throne
Yielded with full consent. The happier state
In heaven, which follows dignity, might draw
Envy from each inferior; but who here
Will envy whom the highest place exposes
Foremost to stand against the Thunderer's aim
Your bulwark, and condemns to greatest share
30 Of endless pain? Where there is then no good
For which to strive, no strife can grow up there
From faction; for none sure will claim in hell
Precedence, none, whose portion is so small
Of present pain, that with ambitious mind
Will covet more. With this advantage then
To union, and firm faith, and firm accord,
More than can be in heaven, we now return
To claim our just inheritance of old,
Surer to prosper than prosperity
Could have assured us; and by what best way,
Whether of open war or covert guile,
We now debate: who can advise, may speak.'

He ceased, and next him Moloc, sceptred king
Stood up, the strongest and the fiercest spirit
That fought in heaven; now fiercer by despair:
His trust was with the Eternal to be deemed
Equal in strength, and rather than be less
Cared not to be at all; with that care lost
Went all his fear: of God, or hell, or worse
50 He recked not, and these words thereafter spake.
   'My sentence° is for open war: of wiles,   *decision*
More unexpert, I boast not: them let those
Contrive who need, or when they need, not now.
For while they sit contriving, shall the rest,
Millions that stand in arms, and longing wait
The signal to ascend, sit lingering here
Heaven's fugitives, and for their dwelling place
Accept this dark opprobrious den of shame,
The prison of his tyranny who reigns
60 By our delay? No, let us rather choose
Armed with hell flames and fury all at once
O'er heaven's high towers to force resistless way,
Turning our tortures into horrid° arms   *hideous*
Against the Torturer; when to meet the noise
Of his almighty engine He shall hear
Infernal thunder, and for lightning see
Black fire and horror shot with equal rage
Among his angels; and his throne itself
Mixed with Tartarean sulphur,° and strange fire,   *gunpowder*
70 His own invented torments. But perhaps
The way seems difficult and steep to scale
With upright wing against a higher foe.
Let such bethink them, if the sleepy drench
Of that forgetful lake benumb not still,
That in our proper motion we ascend
Up to our native seats; descent and fall
To us is adverse. Who but felt of late
When the fierce Foe hung on our broken rear
Insulting, and pursued us through the deep,
80 With what compulsion and laborious flight
We sunk thus low? The ascent is easy then;
The event is feared; should we again provoke
Our stronger, some worse way his wrath may find
To our destruction: if there be in hell
Fear to be worse destroyed: what can be worse
Than to dwell here, driven out from bliss, condemned

In this abhorred deep to utter woe;
Where pain of unextinguishable fire
Must exercise° us without hope of end   *torture*
90 The vassals of his anger, when the scourge
Inexorably, and the torturing hour
Call us to penance? More destroyed than thus
We should be quite abolished and expire.
What fear we then? what doubt we to incense
His utmost ire? which to the highth enraged,
Will either quite consume us, and reduce
To nothing this essential, happier far   *essence*
Than miserable to have eternal being:
Or if our substance be indeed divine,
100 And cannot cease to be, we are at worst
On this side nothing;[114] and by proof we feel
Our power sufficient to disturb his heaven,
And with perpetual inroads to alarm,
Though inaccessible, his fatal° throne: *by fate*
Which if not victory is yet revenge.'
    He ended frowning, and his look denounced
Desperate revenge, and battle dangerous
To less than gods. On the other side up rose
Belial, in act more graceful and humane;
110 A fairer person lost not heaven; he seemed
For dignity composed and high exploit:
But all was false and hollow; though his tongue
Dropt manna,[115] and could make the worse appear
The better reason, to perplex and dash
Maturest counsels: for his thoughts were low;
To vice industrious, but to nobler deeds
Timorous and slothful, yet he pleased the ear,
And with persuasive accent thus began.
    'I should be much for open war, O peers,
120 As not behind in hate; if what was urged
Main reason to persuade immediate war,
Did not dissuade me most, and seem to cast
Ominous conjecture on the whole success:
When he who most excels in fact° of arms,   *feat*
In what he counsels and in what excels
Mistrustful, grounds his courage on despair
And utter dissolution, as the scope
Of all his aim, after some dire revenge.
First, what revenge? The towers of heaven are filled
130 With armed watch, that render all access

Impregnable; oft on the bordering deep
Encamp their legions, or with obscure wing
Scout far and wide into the realm of night,
Scorning surprise. Or could we break our way
By force, and at our heels all hell should rise
With blackest insurrection, to confound
Heaven's purest light, yet our great Enemy,
All incorruptible would on his throne
Sit unpolluted, and the ethereal mould°   *form*
140 Incapable of stain would soon expel
Her mischief, and purge off the baser fire
Victorious. Thus repulsed, our final hope
Is flat despair: we must exasperate
The almighty Victor to spend all his rage,
And that must end us, that must be our cure,
To be no more; sad cure; for who would lose,
Though full of pain, this intellectual being,
Those thoughts that wander through eternity,
To perish rather, swallowed up and lost
150 In the wide womb of uncreated night
Devoid of sense and motion? and who knows,
Let this be good, whether our angry Foe
Can give it, or will ever? How He can
Is doubtful; that He never will is sure.
Will He, so wise, let loose at once his ire,
Belike° through impotence, or unaware,   *perhaps*
To give his enemies their wish, and end
Them in his anger, whom his anger saves
To punish endless? Wherefore cease we then?
160 Say they who counsel war; we are decreed,
Reserved and destined to eternal woe;
Whatever doing, what can we suffer more,
What can we suffer worse? Is this then worst,
Thus sitting, thus consulting, thus in arms?
What when we fled amain,° pursued and struck   *without delay*
With heaven's afflicting thunder, and besought
The deep to shelter us? This hell then seemed
A refuge from those wounds: or when we lay
Chained on the burning lake? That sure was worse.
170 What if the breath that kindled those grim fires
Awaked should blow them into sevenfold rage
And plunge us in the flames? or from above
Should intermitted° vengeance arm again   *suspended*
His red right hand[116] to plague us? what if all

Her stores were opened, and this firmament
Of hell should spout her cataracts of fire,
Impendent° horrors, threatening hideous fall   *overhanging*
One day upon our heads; while we perhaps
Designing or exhorting glorious war,
180 Caught in a fiery tempest shall be hurled
Each on his rock transfixed,° the sport and prey   *impaled*
Of racking whirlwinds, or for ever sunk
Under yon boiling ocean, wrapped in chains;
There to converse with everlasting groans,
Unrespited, unpitied, unreprieved,
Ages of hopeless end; this would be worse.
War therefore, open or concealed, alike
My voice dissuades; for what can force or guile
With Him, or who deceive his mind, whose eye
190 Views all things at one view? He from heaven's highth
All these our motions vain, sees and derides;
Not more almighty to resist our might
Than wise to frustrate all our plots and wiles.
Shall we then live thus vile, the race of heaven
Thus trampled, thus expelled to suffer here
Chains and these torments? Better these than worse
By my advice; since fate inevitable
Subdues us, and omnipotent decree,
The Victor's will. To suffer, as to do,
200 Our strength is equal, nor the law unjust[117]
That so ordains: this was at first resolved,
If we were wise, against so great a foe
Contending, and so doubtful what might fall.
I laugh, when those who at the spear are bold
And venturous, if that fail them, shrink and fear
What yet they know must follow, to endure
Exile, or ignominy, or bonds, or pain,
The sentence of their Conqueror: this is now
Our doom; which if we can sustain and bear,
210 Our supreme Foe in time may much remit
His anger, and perhaps thus far removed,
Not mind us not offending, satisfied
With what is punished; whence these raging fires
Will slacken, if his breath stir not their flames.
Our purer essence then will overcome
Their noxious vapour, or enured° not feel,   *accustomed*
Or changed at length, and to the place conformed
In temper° and in nature,° will receive   *psychologically/physically*

Familiar the fierce heat, and void of pain;
220 This horror will grow mild, this darkness light,
Besides what hope the never-ending flight
Of future days may bring, what chance, what change
Worth waiting, since our present lot appears
For happy though but ill, for ill not worst,
If we procure not to ourselves more woe.'
    Thus Belial with words clothed in reason's garb
Counselled ignoble ease, and peaceful sloth,
Not peace: and after him thus Mammon spake.
    'Either to disenthrone the King of heaven
230 We war, if war be best, or to regain
Our own right lost: Him to unthrone we then
May hope when everlasting fate shall yield
To fickle chance, and Chaos judge the strife:°   contest
The former vain to hope argues as vain
The latter: for what place can be for us
Within heaven's bound, unless heaven's Lord supreme
We overpower? Suppose He should relent
And publish grace to all, on promise made
Of new subjection; with what eyes could we
240 Stand in his presence humble, and receive
Strict laws imposed, to celebrate his throne
With warbled hymns, and to his Godhead sing
Forced hallelujahs; while He lordly sits
Our envied Sovereign, and his altar breathes
Ambrosial odours and ambrosial flowers,
Our servile offerings? This must be our task
In heaven, this our delight; how wearisome
Eternity so spent in worship paid
To whom we hate. Let us not then pursue
250 By force impossible, by leave obtained
Unacceptable, though in heaven, our state
Of splendid vassalage, but rather seek
Our own good from ourselves, and from our own
Live to ourselves, though in this vast recess,
Free, and to none accountable, preferring
Hard liberty before the easy yoke
Of servile pomp. Our greatness will appear
Then most conspicuous, when great things of small,
Useful of hurtful, prosperous of adverse
260 We can create, and in what place so e'er
Thrive under evil, and work ease out of pain
Through labour and endurance. This deep world

Of darkness do we dread? How oft amidst
Thick clouds and dark doth heaven's all-ruling Sire
Choose to reside, his glory unobscured,
And with the majesty of darkness round[118]
Covers his throne; from whence deep thunders roar
Mustering their rage, and heaven resembles hell?
As he our darkness, cannot we his light
270 Imitate when we please? This desert soil
Wants not her hidden lustre, gems and gold;
Nor want we skill or art, from whence to raise
Magnificence; and what can heaven show more?
Our torments also may in length of time
Become our elements,[119] these piercing fires
As soft as now severe, our temper changed
Into their temper; which must needs remove
The sensible° of pain. All things invite   *feeling*
To peaceful counsels, and the settled state
280 Of order, how in safety best we may
Compose° our present evils, with regard   *sort out*
Of what we are and where, dismissing quite
All thoughts of war: ye have what I advise.'
      He scarce had finished, when such murmur filled
The assembly, as when hollow rocks retain
The sound of blustering winds, which all night long
Had roused the sea, now with hoarse cadence lull
Seafaring men o'erwatched, whose bark by chance
Or pinnace anchors in a craggy bay
290 After the tempest: such applause was heard
As Mammon ended, and his sentence° pleased,   *decision*
Advising peace: for such another field
They dreaded worse than hell: so much the fear
Of thunder and the sword of Michael
Wrought still within them; and no less desire
To found this nether empire, which might rise
By policy, and long process of time,
In emulation opposite to heaven.
Which when Beelzebub perceived, than whom,
300 Satan except, none higher sat, with grave
Aspect he rose, and in his rising seemed
A pillar of state; deep on his front engraven
Deliberation sat and public° care;   *(for the state)*
And princely counsel in his face yet shone,
Majestic though in ruin: sage he stood
With Atlantean° shoulders fit to bear   *Atlas-like*

The weight of mightiest monarchies; his look
Drew audience and attention still as night
Or summer's noontide air, while thus he spake.
310   'Thrones and imperial powers, offspring of heaven
Ethereal virtues; or these titles now
Must we renounce, and changing style be called
Princes of hell? For so the popular vote
Inclines, here to continue, and build up here
A growing empire; doubtless; while we dream,
And know not that the King of heaven hath doomed
This place our dungeon, not our safe retreat
Beyond his potent arm, to live exempt
From heaven's high jurisdiction, in new league
320 Banded against his throne, but to remain
In strictest bondage, though thus far removed,
Under the inevitable curb, reserved°   *kept*
His captive multitude: for He, be sure
In heighth or depth, still first and last will reign
Sole King, and of his kingdom lose no part
By our revolt, but over hell extend
His empire, and with iron sceptre rule[120]
Us here, as with his golden those in heaven.
What sit we then projecting° peace and war?   *scheming*
330 War hath determined us,[121] and foiled with loss
Irreparable; terms of peace yet none
Vouchsafed or sought; for what peace will be given
To us enslaved, but custody severe,
And stripes, and arbitrary punishment
Inflicted? And what peace can we return,
But to our power[122] hostility and hate,
Untamed reluctance, and revenge though slow,
Yet ever plotting how the Conqueror least
May reap° his conquest, and may least rejoice   *achieve*
340 In doing what we most in suffering feel?
Nor will occasion want, nor shall we need
With dangerous expedition to invade
Heaven, whose high walls fear no assault or siege,
Or ambush from the deep. What if we find
Some easier enterprise? There is a place
(If ancient and prophetic fame in heaven
Err not) another world, the happy seat
Of some new race called Man, about this time
To be created like to us, though less
350 In power and excellence, but favoured more

Of Him who rules above; so was his will
Pronounced among the gods, and by an oath,
That shook heaven's whole circumference, confirmed.
Thither let us bend all our thoughts, to learn
What creatures there inhabit, of what mould,
Or substance, how endued,[123] and what their power,
And where their weakness, how attempted best,
By force or subtlety: though heaven be shut,
And heaven's high Arbitrator sit secure
360 In his own strength, this place may lie exposed
The utmost border of his kingdom, left
To their defence who hold it: here perhaps
Some advantageous act may be achieved
By sudden onset, either with hell fire
To waste his whole creation, or possess
All as our own, and drive as we were driven,
The puny habitants, or if not drive,
Seduce them to our party, that their God
May prove their foe[124], and with repenting hand
370 Abolish his own works. This would surpass
Common revenge, and interrupt his joy
In our confusion, and our joy upraise
In his disturbance; when his darling sons
Hurled headlong to partake with us, shall curse
Their frail original, and faded bliss,
Faded so soon. Advise if this be worth
Attempting, or to sit in darkness here
Hatching° vain empires.' Thus Beelzebub   *plotting*
Pleaded his devilish counsel, first devised
380 By Satan, and in part proposed: for whence,
But from the author of all ill could spring
So deep a malice, to confound the race
Of mankind in one root, and earth with hell   *(Adam)*
To mingle and involve, done all to spite
The great Creator? But their spite still serves
His glory to augment. The bold design
Pleased highly those infernal states, and joy
Sparkled in all their eyes; with full assent
They vote: whereat his speech he thus renews.
390 'Well have ye judged, well ended long debate,
Synod of gods, and like to what ye are,
Great things resolved, which from the lowest deep
Will once more lift us up, in spite of fate,
Nearer our ancient seat; perhaps in view

Of those bright confines, whence[125] with neighbouring arms
And opportune excursion we may chance
Re-enter heaven; or else in some mild zone
Dwell not unvisited of heaven's fair light
Secure, and at the brightening orient beam
400 Purge off this gloom; the soft delicious air,
To heal the scar of these corrosive fires
Shall breathe her balm. But first whom shall we send
In search of this new world, whom shall we find
Sufficient°? Who shall tempt with wandering feet   *capable*
The dark unbottomed infinite abyss
And through the palpable obscure[126] find out
His uncouth way, or spread his airy flight
Upborne with indefatigable wings
Over the vast abrupt° ere he arrive   *sudden depths*
410 The happy isle; what strength, what art can then
Suffice, or what evasion bear him safe
Through the strict sentries and stations° thick   *guardposts*
Of angels watching round? Here he had need
All circumspection, and we now no less
Choice in our suffrage° for on whom we send,   *selection*
The weight of all and our last hope relies.'
      This said, he sat; and expectation held
His look suspense, awaiting who appeared
To second, or oppose, or undertake
420 The perilous attempt: but all sat mute,
Pondering the danger with deep thoughts; and each
In other's countenance read his own dismay
Astonished: none among the choice and prime
Of those heaven-warring champions could be found
So hardy as to proffer or accept
Alone the dreadful voyage; till at last
Satan, whom now transcendent glory raised
Above his fellows, with monarchal pride
Conscious of highest worth, unmoved thus spake.
430 'O progeny of heaven, empyreal thrones,
With reason hath deep silence and demur°   *hesitation*
Seized us, though undismayed: long is the way
And hard, that out of hell leads up to light;
Our prison strong, this huge convex of fire,
Outrageous° to devour, immures° us round   *very ready/walls*
Ninefold, and gates of burning adamant°   *impenetrable stone*
Barred over us prohibit all egress.
These passed, if any pass, the void profound

Of unessential° night receives him next   *insubstantial*
440 Wide gaping, and with utter loss of being
    Threatens him, plunged in that abortive° gulf.   *formless and deadly*
    If thence he scape into whatever world,
    Or unknown region, what remains him° less   *for him*
    Than unknown dangers and as hard escape.
    But I should ill become this throne, O peers,
    And this imperial sovereignty, adorned
    With splendour, armed with power, if aught proposed
    And judged of public moment, in the shape
    Of difficulty or danger could deter
450 Me from attempting. Wherefore do I assume
    These royalties, and not refuse to reign,
    Refusing to accept as great a share
    Of hazard as of honour, due alike
    To him who reigns, and so much to him due
    Of hazard more, as he above the rest
    High honoured sits? Go therefore mighty powers,
    Terror of heaven, though fallen; intend° at home,   *consider*
    While here shall be our home, what best may ease
    The present misery, and render hell
460 More tolerable; if there be cure or charm
    To respite or deceive, or slack the pain
    Of this ill mansion: intermit° no watch   *omit*
    Against a wakeful foe, while I abroad
    Through all the coasts of dark destruction seek
    Deliverance for us all: this enterprise
    None shall partake with me.' Thus saying rose
    The monarch, and prevented all reply,
    Prudent, lest from his resolution raised
    Others among the chief might offer now
470 (Certain to be refused) what erst they feared;
    And so refused might in opinion stand
    His rivals, winning cheap the high repute
    Which he through hazard huge must earn. But they
    Dreaded not more the adventure than his voice
    Forbidding; and at once with him they rose;
    Their rising all at once was as the sound
    Of thunder heard remote. Towards him they bend
    With awful reverence prone; and as a god
    Extol him equal to the Highest in heaven:
480 Nor failed they to express how much they praised,
    That for the general safety he despised
    His own: for neither do the spirits damned

Lose all their virtue; lest bad men should boast
Their specious° deeds on earth, which glory excites,   *showy*
Or close° ambition varnished o'er with zeal.   *secret*
Thus they their doubtful consultations dark
Ended rejoicing in their matchless chief:
As when from mountain tops the dusky clouds
Ascending, while the north wind sleeps, o'erspread
490 Heaven's cheerful face, the louring element
Scowls o'er the darkened landscape snow, or shower;
If chance the radiant sun with farewell sweet
Extend his evening beam, the fields revive,
The birds their notes renew, and bleating herds
Attest their joy, that hill and valley rings.
O shame to men! Devil with devil damned
Firm concord holds, men only disagree
Of creatures rational, though under hope
Of heavenly grace and God proclaiming peace,
500 Yet live in hatred, enmity, and strife
Among themselves, and levy cruel wars,
Wasting the earth, each other to destroy:
As if (which might induce us to accord°)   *agree*
Man had not hellish foes enow° besides,   *enough*
That day and night for his destruction wait.
      The Stygian council thus dissolved; and forth
In order came the grand infernal peers,
Midst came their mighty paramount,° and seemed   *chief*
Alone the antagonist of heaven, nor less
510 Than hell's dread emperor with pomp supreme,
And God-like imitated state; him round
A globe of fiery seraphim enclosed
With bright emblazonry, and horrent° arms.   *bristling*
Then of their session ended they bid cry
With trumpets' regal sound the great result:
Toward the four winds four speedy cherubim
Put to their mouths the sounding alchemy°   *trumpets*
By herald's voice explained: the hollow abyss
Heard far and wide, and all the host of hell
520 With deafening shout returned them loud acclaim.
Thence more at ease their minds and somewhat raised
By false presumptuous° hope, the ranged powers   *proud*
Disband, and wandering, each his several way
Pursues, as inclination or sad choice
Leads him perplexed, where he may likeliest find
Truce to his restless thoughts, and entertain

The irksome hours, till this great chief return.
Part on the plain, or in the air sublime[127]
Upon the wing, or in swift race contend,
530 As at the Olympian games or Pythian fields;
Part curb their fiery steeds, or shun the goal[128]
With rapid wheels, or fronted brigades form.
As when to warn proud cities war appears[129]
Waged in the troubled sky, and armies rush
To battle in the clouds, before each van°   *advanced force*
Prick° forth the airy knights, and couch° their spears   *spur on/lower for*
Till thickest legions close with feats of arms   *attack*
From either end of heaven the welkin° burns.   *sky*
Others with vast Typhoean rage more fell°   *destructive*
540 Rend up both rocks and hills, and ride the air
In whirlwind; hell scarce holds the wild uproar.
As when Alcides from Oechalia crowned
With conquest, felt the envenomed robe, and tore
Through pain up by the roots Thessalian pines,
And Lichas from the top of Oeta threw
Into the Euboic sea. Others more mild,
Retreated in a silent valley, sing
With notes angelical to many a harp
Their own heroic deeds and hapless fall
550 By doom of battle; and complain that fate
Free virtue should enthral to force or chance.
Their song was partial, but the harmony
(What could it less when spirits immortal sing?)
Suspended hell, and took with ravishment
The thronging audience. In discourse more sweet
(For eloquence the soul, song charms the sense)
Others apart sat on a hill retired,
In thoughts more elevate, and reasoned high
Of providence, foreknowledge, will and fate,[130]
560 Fixed fate, free will, foreknowledge absolute,
And found no end, in wandering mazes lost.
Of good and evil much they argued then,
Of happiness and final misery,
Passion and apathy, and glory and shame,
Vain wisdom all, and false philosophy:
Yet with a pleasing sorcery could charm
Pain for a while or anguish, and excite
Fallacious hope, or arm the obdured° breast   *hardened*
With stubborn patience as with triple steel.
570 Another part in squadrons and gross bands,

On bold adventure to discover wide
That dismal world, if any clime perhaps
Might yield them easier habitation, bend
Four ways their flying march, along the banks
Of four infernal rivers that disgorge
Into the burning lake their baleful streams;
Abhorred Styx the flood of deadly hate,
Sad Acheron of sorrow, black and deep;
Cocytus, named of lamentation loud
580 Heard on the rueful stream; fierce Phlegethon
Whose waves of torrent fire inflame with rage.
Far off from these a slow and silent stream,
Lethe the river of oblivion rolls
Her watery labyrinth, whereof who drinks,
Forthwith his former state and being forgets,
Forgets both joy and grief, pleasure and pain.
Beyond this flood a frozen continent
Lies dark and wild, beat with perpetual storms
Of whirlwind and dire hail, which on firm land
590 Thaws not, but gathers heap, and ruin seems
Of ancient pile; all else deep snow and ice,
A gulf profound as that Serbonian bog
Betwixt Damiata and Mount Casius old,
Where armies whole have sunk:[131] the parching air
Burns frore,° and cold performs the effect of fire.   *frozen*
Thither by harpy-footed Furies haled,
At certain revolutions all the damned
Are brought: and feel by turns the bitter change
Of fierce extremes, extremes by change more fierce,
600 From beds of raging fire to starve in ice
Their soft ethereal warmth, and there to pine
Immovable, infixed, and frozen round,
Periods of time, thence hurried back to fire.
They ferry over this Lethean sound
Both to and fro, their sorrow to augment,
And wish and struggle, as they pass, to reach
The tempting stream, with one small drop to lose
In sweet forgetfulness all pain and woe,
All in one moment, and so near the brink;
610 But fate withstands, and to oppose the attempt
Medusa with Gorgonian terror guards
The ford, and of itself the water flies
All taste of living wight, as once it fled
The lip of Tantalus. Thus roving on

In confused march forlorn, the adventurous bands
With shuddering horror pale, and eyes aghast
Viewed first their lamentable lot,° and found   *fate*
No rest: through many a dark and dreary vale
They passed, and many a region dolorous,
620 O'er many a frozen, many a fiery alp,°   *mountain*
Rocks, caves, lakes, fens, bogs, dens, and shades of death,
A universe of death, which God by curse
Created evil, for evil only good,
Where all life dies, death lives, and nature breeds,
Perverse, all monstrous, all prodigious things,
Abominable, inutterable,° and worse   *unspeakable*
Than fables yet have feigned, or fear conceived,
Gorgons and Hydras, and Chimeras dire.
      Mean while the adversary of God and man,
630 Satan with thoughts inflamed of highest design,
Puts on swift wings, and towards the gates of hell
Explores his solitary flight; some times
He scours the right hand coast, some times the left,
Now shaves with level wing the deep, then soars
Up to the fiery concave° towering high.   *sky*
As when far off at sea a fleet descried
Hangs in the clouds, by equinoctial winds
Close sailing from Bengala, or the isles[132]
Of Ternate and Tidore, whence merchants bring
640 Their spicy drugs: they on the trading flood
Through the wide Ethiopian to the Cape
Ply stemming nightly toward the pole. So seemed
Far off the flying fiend: at last appear
Hell bounds high reaching to the horrid roof,
And thrice threefold the gates; three folds were brass,
Three iron, three of adamantine° rock,   *indestructible*
Impenetrable, impaled with circling fire,
Yet unconsumed. Before the gates there sat
On either side a formidable shape;
650 The one seemed woman to the waist, and fair,
But ended foul in many a scaly fold
Voluminous and vast, a serpent armed
With mortal sting: about her middle round
A cry° of hell hounds never ceasing barked   *pack*
With wide Cerberian° mouths full loud, and rung   *Cerberus-like*
A hideous peal: yet, when they list, would creep,
If aught disturbed their noise, into her womb,
And kennel there, yet there still barked and howled,

Within unseen. Far less abhorred than these
660 Vexed Scylla bathing in the sea that parts
Calabria from the hoarse Trinacrian shore:
Nor uglier follow the Night-hag, when called
In secret, riding through the air she comes
Lured with the smell of infant blood, to dance
With Lapland witches, while the labouring moon
Eclipses at their charms. The other shape,
If shape it might be called that shape had none
Distinguishable in member, joint, or limb,
Or substance might be called that shadow seemed,
670 For each seemed either; black it stood as night,
Fierce as ten Furies, terrible as hell,
And shook a dreadful dart;° what seemed his head   *spear*
The likeness of a kingly crown had on.
Satan was now at hand, and from his seat
The monster moving onward came as fast
With horrid strides, hell trembled as he strode.
The undaunted fiend what this might be admired,°   *wondered at*
Admired, not feared; God and his Son except,
Created thing nought valued he nor shunned;
680 And with disdainful look thus first began.
    'Whence and what art thou, execrable shape,
That darest, though grim and terrible, advance
Thy miscreated front athwart° my way   *across*
To yonder gates? Through them I mean to pass,
That be assured, without leave asked of thee:
Retire, or taste thy folly, and learn by proof,
Hell-born, not to contend with spirits of heaven.'
    To whom the goblin° full of wrath replied,   *evil spirit*
'Art thou that traitor angel, art thou he,
690 Who first broke peace in heaven and faith, till then
Unbroken, and in proud rebellious arms
Drew after him the third part of heaven's sons
Conjured against the highest, for which both thou
And they outcast from God, are here condemned
To waste eternal days in woe and pain?
And reckonest thou thyself with spirits of heaven,
Hell-doomed, and breathest defiance here and scorn
Where I reign king, and to enrage thee more,
Thy king and lord? Back to thy punishment,
700 False fugitive, and to thy speed add wings,
Lest with a whip of scorpions I pursue
Thy lingering, or with one stroke of this dart

Strange horror seize thee, and pangs unfelt before.'
   So spake the grisly terror, and in shape,
So speaking and so threatening, grew tenfold
More dreadful and deform:° on the other side   *deformed*
Incensed with indignation Satan stood
Unterrified, and like a comet burned,
That fires the length of Ophiucus huge
710 In the Arctic sky, and from his horrid hair[133]
Shakes pestilence and war. Each at the head
Levelled his deadly aim; their fatal hands
No second stroke intend, and such a frown
Each cast at the other, as when two black clouds
With heaven's artillery° fraught, come rattling on *(thunder and lightning)*
Over the Caspian, then stand front to front
Hovering a space, till winds the signal blow
To join their dark encounter in mid air:
So frowned the mighty combatants, that hell
720 Grew darker at their frown, so matched they stood;
For never but once more was either like
To meet so great a foe:[134] and now great deeds
Had been achieved, whereof all hell had rung,
Had not the snaky sorceress that sat
Fast by hell gate, and kept the fatal key,
Risen, and with hideous outcry rushed between.
   'O Father, what intends thy hand', she cried,
'Against thy only son? What fury, O son,
Possesses thee to bend that mortal dart
730 Against thy father's head? and know'st for whom;
For Him who sits above and laughs the while
At thee ordained his drudge, to execute
What e'er his wrath, which He calls justice, bids,
His wrath which one day will destroy ye both.'
   She spake, and at her words the hellish pest
Forbore, then these to her Satan returned:
   'So strange thy outcry, and thy words so strange
Thou interposest, that my sudden° hand   *hasty*
Prevented spares to tell thee yet by deeds
740 What it intends; till first I know of thee,
What thing thou art, thus double-formed, and why
In this infernal vale first met thou call'st
Me father, and that phantasm call'st my son?
I know thee not, nor ever saw till now
Sight more detestable than him and thee.'
   To whom thus the portress of hell gate replied.

'Hast thou forgot me then, and do I seem
Now in thine eye so foul, once deemed so fair
In heaven, when, at the assembly, and in sight
750 Of all the seraphim with thee combined
In bold conspiracy against heaven's King,
All on a sudden miserable pain
Surprised thee, dim thine eyes, and dizzy swum
In darkness, while thy head flames thick and fast
Threw forth, till on the left side opening wide,[135]
Likest to thee in shape and countenance bright,
Then shining heavenly fair, a goddess armed
Out of thy head I sprung: amazement seized
All the host of heaven; back they recoiled afraid
760 At first, and called me Sin, and for a sign
Portentous° held me; but familiar grown,   *ominous*
I pleased, and with attractive graces won
The most averse, thee chiefly, who full oft
Thy self in me thy perfect image viewing
Becamest enamoured, and such joy thou took'st
With me in secret, that my womb conceived
A growing burden. Mean while war arose,
And fields were fought in heaven; wherein remained
(For what could else) to our almighty Foe
770 Clear victory, to our part loss and rout
Through all the empyrean:[136] down they fell
Driven headlong from the pitch° of heaven, down   *high point*
Into this deep, and in the general fall
I also; at which time this powerful key
Into my hand was given, with charge to keep
These gates for ever shut, which none can pass
Without my opening. Pensive here I sat
Alone, but long I sat not, till my womb
Pregnant by thee, and now excessive grown
780 Prodigious motion felt and rueful throes.
At last this odious offspring whom thou seest
Thine own begotten, breaking violent way,
Tore through my entrails, that with fear and pain
Distorted, all my nether shape thus grew
Transformed: but he my inbred enemy
Forth issued, brandishing his fatal dart
Made to destroy: I fled, and cried out Death;
Hell trembled at the hideous name, and sighed
From all her caves, and back resounded Death.
790 I fled, but he pursued (though more, it seems,

Inflamed with lust than rage) and swifter far,
Me overtook his mother all dismayed,
And in embraces forcible and foul
Ingendering with me, of that rape begot
These yelling monsters that with ceaseless cry
Surround me, as thou sawest, hourly conceived
And hourly born, with sorrow infinite
To me, for when they list into the womb
That bred them they return, and howl and gnaw
800 My bowels, their repast;° then bursting forth   *meal*
Afresh with conscious terrors vex me round,
That rest or intermission none I find.
Before mine eyes in opposition sits
Grim Death my son and foe, who sets them on,
And me his parent would full soon devour
For want of other prey, but that he knows
His end with mine involved; and knows that I
Should prove a bitter morsel, and his bane,
When ever that shall be; so fate pronounced.
810 But thou, O Father, I forewarn thee, shun
His deadly arrow; neither vainly hope
To be invulnerable in those bright arms,
Though tempered heavenly, for that mortal dint,°   *blow*
Save He who reigns above, none can resist.'
     She finished, and the subtle fiend his lore
Soon learned, now milder, and thus answered smooth.
'Dear Daughter, since thou claim'st me for thy sire,
And my fair son here show'st me, the dear pledge
Of dalliance had with thee in heaven, and joys
820 Then sweet, now sad to mention, through dire change
Befallen us unforeseen, unthought of, know
I come no enemy, but to set free
From out this dark and dismal house of pain,
Both him and thee, and all the heavenly host
Of spirits that in our just pretences° armed   *claims*
Fell with us from on high: from them I go
This uncouth° errand sole, and one for all   *unknown*
My self expose, with lonely steps to tread
The unfounded° deep, and through the void immense   *bottomless*
830 To search with wandering quest a place foretold
Should be, and, by concurring signs, ere now
Created vast and round, a place of bliss
In the purlieus° of heaven, and therein placed   *borders*
A race of upstart creatures, to supply

Perhaps our vacant room, though more removed,
Lest heaven surcharged with potent° multitude   *powerful*
Might hap° to move new broils: be this or aught   *chance*
Than this more secret now designed, I haste
To know, and this once known, shall soon return,
840 And bring ye to the place where thou and Death
Shall dwell at ease, and up and down unseen
Wing silently the buxom° air, embalmed   *pliant*
With odours; there ye shall be fed and filled
Immeasurably, all things shall be your prey.'
He ceased, for both seemed highly pleased, and Death
Grinned horrible a ghastly smile, to hear
His famine should be filled, and blessed his maw°   *stomach*
Destined to that good hour: no less rejoiced
His mother bad, and thus bespake her sire.
850   'The key of this infernal pit by due,
And by command of heaven's all-powerful King
I keep, by him forbidden to unlock
These adamantine° gates; against all force   *indestructible*
Death ready stands to interpose his dart,
Fearless to be o'ermatched by living might.
But what owe I to his commands above
Who hates me, and hath hither thrust me down
Into this gloom of Tartarus profound,
To sit in hateful office here confined,
860 Inhabitant of heaven, and heavenly-born,
Here in perpetual agony and pain,
With terrors and with clamours compassed round
Of mine own brood, that on my bowels feed:
Thou art my father, thou my author,° thou   *creator*
My being gavest me; whom should I obey
But thee, whom follow? Thou wilt bring me soon
To that new world of light and bliss, among
The gods who live at ease, where I shall reign
At thy right hand voluptuous, as beseems
870 Thy daughter and thy darling, without end.'
    Thus saying, from her side the fatal key,
Sad instrument of all our woe, she took;
And towards the gate rolling her bestial train,
Forthwith the huge portcullis° high updrew   *a sliding grating*
Which but her self, not all the Stygian powers
Could once have moved; then in the key-hole turns
The intricate wards,° and every bolt and bar   *incisions in a key*
Of massy iron or solid rock with ease

Unfastens: on a sudden open fly
880 With impetuous recoil and jarring sound
The infernal doors, and on their hinges grate
Harsh thunder, that the lowest bottom shook
Of Erebus. She opened, but to shut
Excelled her power; the gates wide open stood,
That with extended wings a bannered° host   *with banners*
Under spread ensigns° marching might pass through   *standards*
With horse and chariots ranked in loose array;
So wide they stood, and like a furnace mouth
Cast forth redounding smoke and ruddy flame.
890 Before their eyes in sudden view appear
The secrets of the hoary deep, a dark
Illimitable ocean without bound,
Without dimension, where length, breadth, and highth,
And time and place are lost; where eldest Night[137]
And Chaos, ancestors of Nature, hold
Eternal anarchy, amidst the noise
Of endless wars, and by confusion stand.
For hot, cold, moist, and dry, four champions fierce
Strive here for mastery, and to battle bring
900 Their embryon° atoms; they around the flag   *embryonic*
Of each his faction,° in their several clans,   *group*
Light-armed or heavy, sharp, smooth, swift or slow,
Swarm populous, unnumbered as the sands
Of Barca or Cyrene's torrid soil,
Levied to side with warring winds,[138] and poise
Their lighter wings. To whom these most adhere,
He rules a moment; Chaos umpire sits,
And by decision more embroils the fray
By which he reigns: next him high arbiter
910 Chance governs all. Into this wild abyss,
The womb of nature and perhaps her grave,
Of neither sea, nor shore, nor air, nor fire,
But all these in their pregnant causes mixed
Confusedly, and which thus must ever fight,
Unless the Almighty Maker them ordain
His dark materials to create more worlds,
Into this wild abyss the wary fiend
Stood on the brink of hell and looked a while,
Pondering his voyage; for no narrow frith°   *strait*
920 He had to cross. Nor was his ear less pealed[139]
With noises loud and ruinous (to compare
Great things with small) than when Bellona storms,
With all her battering engines bent to raze

Some capital city; or less than if this frame
Of heaven were falling, and these elements
In mutiny had from her axle torn
The steadfast earth. At last his sail-broad vans°   *wings*
He spreads for flight, and in the surging smoke
Uplifted spurns the ground, thence many a league
930 As in a cloudy chair ascending rides
Audacious, but that seat soon failing, meets
A vast vacuity:° all unawares   *vacuum*
Fluttering his pennons vain plumb down he drops
Ten thousand fathom deep, and to this hour
Down had been falling, had not by ill chance
The strong rebuff of some tumultuous cloud
Instinct with fire and nitre hurried him
As many miles aloft: that fury stayed,
Quenched in a boggy Syrtis, neither sea,
940 Nor good dry land: nigh foundered, on he fares,
Treading the crude consistence,° half on foot,   *substance*
Half flying; behoves° him now both oar and sail.   *benefits*
As when a gryphon¹⁴⁰ through the wilderness
With winged course o'er hill or moory dale,
Pursues the Arimaspian, who by stealth
Had from his wakeful custody purloined°   *stolen*
The guarded gold: so eagerly the fiend
O'er bog or steep, through straight, rough, dense, or rare,
With head, hands, wings or feet pursues his way,
950 And swims or sinks, or wades, or creeps, or flies:
At length a universal hubbub wild
Of stunning sounds and voices all confused
Borne through the hollow dark assaults his ear
With loudest vehemence: thither he plies,
Undaunted to meet there what ever power
Or spirit of the nethermost abyss
Might in that noise reside, of whom to ask
Which way the nearest coast of darkness lies
Bordering on light; when straight behold the throne
960 Of Chaos, and his dark pavilion spread
Wide on the wasteful deep; with him enthroned
Sat sable-vested° Night, eldest of things,   *dark-clothed*
The consort of his reign; and by them stood
Orcus and Ades, and the dreaded name
Of Demogorgon; Rumour next and Chance,
And Tumult and Confusion all embroiled,
And Discord with a thousand various mouths.

To whom Satan turning boldly, thus. 'Ye powers
And spirits of this nethermost abyss,
970 Chaos and ancient Night, I come no spy,
With purpose to explore or to disturb
The secrets of your realm, but by constraint
Wandering this darksome desert, as my way
Lies through your spacious empire up to light,
Alone, and without guide, half lost, I seek
What readiest path leads where your gloomy bounds
Confine° with heaven; or if some other place   *border*
From your dominion won, the ethereal King
Possesses lately, thither to arrive
980 I travel this profound°, direct my course;   *deep*
Directed no mean recompense it brings
To your behoof°, if I that region lost,   *benefit*
All usurpation thence expelled, reduce
To her original darkness and your sway
(Which is my present journey) and once more
Erect the standard there of ancient Night.
Yours be the advantage all, mine the revenge.'
    Thus Satan; and him thus the anarch old
With faltering speech and visage incomposed°   *disordered*
990 Answered. 'I know thee, stranger, who thou art,
That mighty leading angel, who of late
Made head against heaven's King, though overthrown.
I saw and heard, for such a numerous host
Fled not in silence through the frighted deep
With ruin upon ruin, rout on rout,
Confusion worse confounded; and heaven gates
Poured out by millions her victorious bands
Pursuing. I upon my frontiers here
Keep residence; if all I can will serve,
1000 That little which is left so to defend,
Encroached on still through our intestine broils
Weakening the sceptre of old Night: first hell
Your dungeon stretching far and wide beneath;
Now lately heaven and earth, another world
Hung o'er my realm, linked in a golden chain
To that side heaven from whence your legions fell:
If that way be your walk, you have not far;
So much the nearer danger; go and speed°;   *succeed*
Havoc and spoil and ruin are my gain.'
1010   He ceased; and Satan stayed not to reply,
But glad that now his sea should find a shore,

With fresh alacrity and force renewed
Springs upward like a pyramid of fire
Into the wild expanse, and through the shock
Of fighting elements, on all sides round
Environed° wins his way; harder beset   *surrounded*
And more endangered, than when Argo passed
Through Bosporus, betwixt the jostling rocks:
Or when Ulysses on the larboard shunned
1020 Charybdis, and by the other whirlpool steered.
So he with difficulty and labour hard
Moved on, with difficulty and labour he;
But he once past, soon after when man fell,
Strange alteration! Sin and Death amain
Following his track, such was the will of heaven,
Paved after him a broad and beaten way
Over the dark abyss, whose boiling gulf
Tamely endured a bridge of wondrous length
From hell continued reaching the utmost orb
1030 Of this frail world; by which the spirits perverse°   *evil*
With easy intercourse° pass to and fro   *passage*
To tempt or punish mortals, except whom
God and good angels guard by special grace.
But now at last the sacred influence
Of light appears, and from the walls of heaven
Shoots far into the bosom of dim Night
A glimmering dawn; here Nature first begins
Her farthest verge, and Chaos to retire,
As from her outmost works, a broken foe,   *frontiers*
1040 With tumult less and with less hostile din,
That Satan with less toil, and now with ease
Wafts on the calmer wave by dubious light
And like a weather-beaten vessel holds
Gladly the port, though shrouds° and tackle torn;   *sails*
Or in the emptier waste, resembling air,
Weighs his spread wings, at leisure to behold
Far off the empyreal° heaven, extended wide   *celestial*
In circuit, undetermined square or round,
With opal towers and battlements adorned
1050 Of living sapphire, once his native seat;
And fast by hanging in a golden chain
This pendant world, in bigness as a star
Of smallest magnitude close by the moon.
Thither full fraught with mischievous revenge,
Accursed, and in a cursed hour he hies.

Book IX[141]

No more talk where God or angel guest
With man, as with his friend, familiar used
To sit indulgent, and with him partake
Rural repast, permitting him the while
Venial° discourse unblamed: I now must change   *permissible*
Those notes to tragic; foul distrust, and breach
Disloyal on the part of man, revolt,
And disobedience: on the part of heaven
Now alienated, distance and distaste,
10 Anger and just rebuke, and judgement given,
That brought into this world a world of woe,
Sin and her shadow Death, and Misery,
Death's harbinger: sad task, yet argument
Not less but more heroic than the wrath
Of stern Achilles on his foe pursued
Thrice fugitive about Troy wall; or rage
Of Turnus for Lavinia disespoused,
Or Neptune's ire or Juno's, that so long
Perplexed the Greek and Cytherea's son;°   *(Aeneas)*
20 If answerable style I can obtain
Of my celestial patroness,° who deigns   *(Urania)*
Her nightly visitation unimplored,
And dictates to me slumbering, or inspires
Easy my unpremeditated verse:
Since first this subject for heroic song
Pleased me long choosing, and beginning late;[142]
Not sedulous by nature to indite
Wars, hitherto the only argument
Heroic deemed, chief° mastery to dissect   *special*
30 With long and tedious havoc fabled knights
In battles feigned (the better fortitude
Of patience and heroic martyrdom
Unsung) or to describe races and games,
Or tilting furniture,° emblazoned shields,   *equipment*
Impreses° quaint, caparisons and steeds;   *emblems on shields*
Bases° and tinsel trappings, gorgeous knights   *trimmings for horses*
At joust and tournament; then marshalled feast
Served up in hall with sewers,° and seneschals;°   *waiters/stewards*
The skill of artifice or office mean,
40 Not that which justly gives heroic name
To person or to poem. Me of these
Nor skilled nor studious, higher argument

Remains, sufficient of it self to raise
That name, unless an age too late, or cold
Climate, or years[143] damp my intended wing
Depressed, and much they may, if all be mine,
Not hers who brings it nightly to my ear.
     The sun was sunk, and after him the star
Of Hesperus, whose office is to bring
50 Twilight upon the earth, short arbiter
Twixt day and night, and now from end to end
Night's hemisphere had veiled the horizon round:
When Satan who late fled before the threats
Of Gabriel out of Eden, now improved
In meditated fraud and malice, bent
On man's destruction, maugre° what might hap   *despite*
Of heavier on himself, fearless returned.
By night he fled, and at midnight returned
From compassing the earth, cautious of day,
60 Since Uriel, regent of the sun, descried°   *saw*
His entrance, and forewarned the cherubim
That kept their watch; thence full of anguish driven,
The space of seven continued nights he rode
With darkness, thrice the equinoctial line
He circled, four times crossed the car° of Night   *chariot*
From pole to pole, traversing each colure;°   *circle of longitude*
On the eighth returned, and on the coast averse°   *opposite*
From entrance or cherubic watch, by stealth
Found unsuspected way. There was a place,
70 Now not, though sin, not time, first wrought the change,
Where Tigris at the foot of Paradise[144]
Into a gulf shot under ground, till part
Rose up a fountain by the tree of life;
In with the river sunk, and with it rose
Satan involved in rising mist, then sought
Where to lie hid; sea he had searched and land
From Eden over Pontus, and the pool
Maeotis, up beyond the river Ob;
Downward as far antarctic; and in length
80 West from Orontes to the ocean barred
At Darien, thence to the land where flows
Ganges and Indus: thus the orb he roamed
With narrow search; and with inspection deep
Considered every creature, which of all
Most opportune might serve his wiles, and found
The serpent subtlest beast of all the field.

Him after long debate, irresolute°   *unresolved*
Of thoughts revolved°, his final sentence chose   *considered*
Fit vessel, fittest imp of fraud, in whom
90 To enter, and his dark suggestions hide
From sharpest sight: for in the wily snake,
Whatever sleights none would suspicious mark,
As from his wit and native subtlety
Proceeding, which, in other beasts observed,
Doubt might beget of diabolic power
Active within beyond the sense of brute.
Thus he resolved, but first from inward grief
His bursting passion into plaints thus poured:
'O earth, how like to heaven, if not preferred
100 More justly, seat worthier of gods, as built
With second thoughts, reforming what was old!
For what god after better worse would build?
Terrestrial heaven, danced round by other heavens
That shine, yet bear their bright officious lamps,
Light above light, for thee alone, as seems,
In thee concentring all their precious beams
Of sacred influence: as God in heaven
Is centre, yet extends to all, so thou
Centring receivest from all those orbs; in thee,
110 Not in themselves, all their known virtue appears
Productive in herb, plant, and nobler birth
Of creatures animate with gradual life
Of growth, sense, reason, all summed up in man.¹⁴⁵
With what delight could I have walked thee round,
If I could joy in aught, sweet interchange
Of hill, and valley, rivers, woods and plains,
Now land, now sea, and shores with forest crowned,
Rocks, dens, and caves; but I in none of these
Find place or refuge; and the more I see
120 Pleasures about me, so much more I feel
Torment within me, as from the hateful siege
Of contraries; all good to me becomes
Bane°, and in heaven much worse would be my state.   *cause of misery*
But neither here seek I, no nor in heaven
To dwell, unless by mastering heaven's supreme;
Nor hope to be my self less miserable
By what I seek, but others to make such
As I, though thereby worse to me redound:
For only in destroying I find ease
130 To my relentless thoughts; and him destroyed,

Or won to what may work his utter loss,
For whom all this was made, all this will soon
Follow, as to him linked in weal or woe;
In woe then, that destruction wide may range:
To me shall be the glory sole among
The infernal powers, in one day to have marred
What He almighty styled, six nights and days
Continued making, and who knows how long
Before had been contriving, though perhaps
140 Not longer than since I in one night freed
From servitude inglorious well-nigh half
The angelic name, and thinner left the throng
Of his adorers: He to be avenged,
And to repair his numbers thus impaired,
Whether such virtue spent of old now failed
More angels to create, if they at least
Are his created, or to spite us more,
Determined to advance into our room
A creature formed of earth, and him endow,
150 Exalted from so base original,
With heavenly spoils, our spoils: what He decreed
He effected; man He made, and for him built
Magnificent this world, and earth his seat,
Him lord pronounced, and, O indignity!
Subjected to his service angel wings,
And flaming ministers to watch and tend
Their earthly charge: of these the vigilance
I dread, and to elude, thus wrapped in mist
Of midnight vapour glide obscure, and pry
160 In every bush and brake, where hap° may find   *chance*
The serpent sleeping, in whose mazy folds
To hide me, and the dark intent I bring.
O foul descent! That I who erst contended
With gods to sit the highest, am now constrained
Into a beast, and mixed with bestial slime,
This essence to incarnate and imbrute,
That to the highth of deity aspired;
But what will not ambition and revenge
Descend to? Who aspires must down as low
170 As high he soared, obnoxious° first or last   *exposed*
To basest things. Revenge, at first though sweet,
Bitter ere long back on it self recoils;
Let it; I reck° not, so it light well aimed,   *care*
Since higher I fall short, on him who next

Provokes my envy, this new favourite
Of heaven, this man of clay, son of despite,[146]
Whom us the more to spite his Maker raised
From dust: spite then with spite is best repaid.'
    So saying, through each thicket dank or dry,
180 Like a black mist low creeping, he held on
His midnight search, where soonest he might find
The serpent: him fast sleeping soon he found
In labyrinth of many a round self-rolled,
His head the midst, well stored with subtle wiles:
Not yet in horrid° shade or dismal den,   *fearful*
Nor nocent° yet, but on the grassy herb   *harmful*
Fearless unfeared he slept: in at his mouth
The devil entered, and his brutal sense,
In heart or head, possessing, soon inspired
190 With act intelligential; but his sleep
Disturbed not, waiting close° the approach of morn.   *hidden*
Now when as sacred light began to dawn
In Eden on the humid flowers, that breathed
Their morning incense, when all things that breathe,
From the earth's great altar send up silent praise
To the creator, and his nostrils fill
With grateful smell, forth came the human pair
And joined their vocal worship to the choir
Of creatures wanting° voice; that done, partake   *lacking*
200 The season,° prime for sweetest scents and airs: *time of day*
Then commune how that day they best may ply
Their growing work: for much their work outgrew
The hands' dispatch of two, gardening so wide.
And Eve first to her husband thus began.
    'Adam, well may we labour still to dress
This garden, still to tend plant, herb and flower,
Our pleasant task enjoined, but till more hands
Aid us, the work under our labour grows,
Luxurious by restraint; what we by day
210 Lop overgrown, or prune, or prop, or bind,
One night or two with wanton growth derides,
Tending to wild. Thou therefore now advise
Or hear what to my mind first thoughts present,
Let us divide our labours, thou where choice
Leads thee, or where most needs, whether to wind
The woodbine[147] round this arbour, or direct
The clasping ivy where to climb, while I
In yonder spring° of roses intermixed   *grove*

With myrtle, find what to redress° till noon: *deal with*
220 For while so near each other thus all day
Our task we choose, what wonder if so near
Looks intervene and smiles, or object new
Casual discourse draw on, which intermits°   *interrupts*
Our day's work brought to little, though begun
Early, and the hour of supper comes unearned.'
     To whom mild answer Adam thus returned.
'Sole Eve, associate sole, to me beyond
Compare above all living creatures dear,
Well hast thou motioned° well thy thoughts employed   *proposed*
230 How we might best fulfil the work which here
God hath assigned us, nor of me shalt pass
Unpraised: for nothing lovelier can be found
In woman, than to study household good,
And good works in her husband to promote.
Yet not so strictly hath our Lord imposed
Labour, as to debar us when we need
Refreshment, whether food, or talk between,
Food of the mind, or this sweet intercourse
Of looks and smiles, for smiles from reason flow,
240 To brute denied, and are of love the food,
Love not the lowest end of human life.
For not to irksome toil, but to delight
He made us, and delight to reason joined.
These paths and bowers doubt not but our joint hands
Will keep from wilderness with ease, as wide
As we need walk, till younger hands ere long
Assist us: but if much converse¹⁴⁸ perhaps
Thee satiate, to short absence I could yield.
For solitude sometimes is best society,
250 And short retirement urges sweet return.
But other doubt possesses me, lest harm
Befall thee severed from me; for thou know'st
What hath been warned us, what malicious foe
Envying our happiness, and of his own
Despairing, seeks to work us woe and shame
By sly assault; and somewhere nigh at hand
Watches, no doubt, with greedy hope to find
His wish and best advantage, us asunder,
Hopeless to circumvent us joined, where each
260 To other speedy aid might lend at need;
Whether his first design be to withdraw
Our fealty from God, or to disturb

Conjugal love, than which perhaps no bliss
Enjoyed by us excites his envy more;
Or this, or worse, leave not the faithful side
That gave thee being, still shades thee and protects.
The wife, where danger or dishonour lurks,
Safest and seemliest by her husband stays,
Who guards her, or with her the worst endures.'
270　　To whom the virgin° majesty of Eve,　　　　　　　　　　　*chaste*
As one who loves, and some unkindness meets,
With sweet austere composure thus replied.
　　'Offspring of heaven and earth, and all earth's lord,
That such an enemy we have, who seeks
Our ruin, both by thee informed I learn,
And from the parting angel overheard
As in a shady nook I stood behind,
Just then returned at shut of evening flowers.
But that thou shouldst my firmness therefore doubt
280　To God or thee, because we have a foe
May tempt it, I expected not to hear.
His violence thou fear'st not, being such,
As we, not capable of death or pain,
Can either not receive, or can repel.
His fraud is then thy fear, which plain infers°　　　　　　　*implies*
Thy equal fear that my firm faith and love
Can by his fraud be shaken or seduced;
Thoughts, which how found they harbour in thy breast
Adam, misthought of her to thee so dear?'
290　　To whom with healing words Adam replied.
'Daughter of God and man, immortal Eve,
For such thou art, from sin and blame entire:°　　　　　*untouched by*
Not diffident° of thee do I dissuade　　　　　　　　　　*mistrustful*
Thy absence from my sight, but to avoid
The attempt it self, intended by our foe.
For he who tempts, though in vain, at least asperses°　　　*slanders*
The tempted with dishonour foul, supposed
Not incorruptible of faith, not proof
Against temptation: thou thy self with scorn
300　And anger wouldst resent the offered wrong,
Though ineffectual found: misdeem not then,
If such affront I labour to avert
From thee alone, which on us both at once
The enemy, though bold, will hardly dare,
Or daring, first on me the assault shall light.
Nor thou his malice and false guile contemn;

Subtle he needs must be, who could seduce
Angels; nor think superfluous others' aid.
I from the influence of thy looks receive
310 Access° in every virtue, in thy sight   *increase*
More wise, more watchful, stronger, if need were
Of outward strength; while shame, thou looking on,
Shame to be overcome or over-reached
Would utmost vigour raise, and raised unite.
Why shouldst not thou like sense within thee feel
When I am present, and thy trial choose
With me, best witness of thy virtue tried.'
    So spake domestic° Adam in his care   *(as home-protector)*
And matrimonial love; but Eve, who thought
320 Less° attributed to her faith sincere°,   *too little/pure*
Thus her reply with accent sweet renewed.
    'If this be our condition, thus to dwell
In narrow circuit straitened by a foe,
Subtle or violent, we not endued
Single with like defence, wherever met,
How are we happy, still in fear of harm?
But harm precedes not sin: only our foe
Tempting affronts us with his foul esteem
Of our integrity: his foul esteem
330 Sticks no dishonour on our front, but turns
Foul on himself; then wherefore shunned or feared
By us? Who rather double honour gain
From his surmise proved false, find peace within,
Favour from heaven, our witness, from the event.
And what is faith, love, virtue unassayed
Alone, without exterior help sustained?
Let us not then suspect our happy state
Left so imperfect by the maker wise,
As not secure to single or combined;
340 Frail is our happiness, if this be so,
And Eden were no Eden thus exposed.'
    To whom thus Adam fervently replied.
'O woman, best are all things as the will
Of God ordained them, his creating hand
Nothing imperfect or deficient left
Of all that He created, much less man,
Or aught that might his happy state secure,
Secure from outward force; within himself
The danger lies, yet lies within his power:
350 Against his will he can receive no harm.

But God left free the will, for what obeys
Reason, is free, and reason He made right,
But bid her well beware, and still erect,°   *always attentive*
Lest by some fair appearing good surprised
She dictate false, and misinform the will
To do what God expressly hath forbid.
Not then mistrust, but tender love enjoins,
That I should mind° thee oft, and mind thou me.   *remind*
Firm we subsist, yet possible to swerve,
360 Since reason not impossibly may meet
Some specious° object by the foe suborned,   *showy*
And fall into deception unaware,
Not keeping strictest watch, as she was warned.
Seek not temptation then, which to avoid
Were better, and most likely, if from me
Thou sever not: trial will come unsought.
Wouldst thou approve° thy constancy, approve   *prove*
First thy obedience; the other who can know,
Not seeing thee attempted, who attest?
370 But if thou think, trial unsought may find
Us both securer° than thus warned thou seem'st,   *more over-confident*
Go; for thy stay, not free, absents thee more;
Go in thy native innocence, rely
On what thou hast of virtue, summon all,
For God towards thee hath done his part, do thine.'
    So spake the patriarch of mankind, but Eve
Persisted, yet submiss,° though last, replied.   *submissive*
    'With thy permission then, and thus forwarned
Chiefly by what thy own last reasoning words
380 Touched only, that our trial, when least sought,
May find us both perhaps far less prepared,
The willinger I go, nor much expect
A foe so proud will first the weaker seek;
So bent, the more shall shame him his repulse.'
    Thus saying, from her husband's hand her hand[149]
Soft she withdrew, and like a wood-nymph light
Oread or dryad, or of Delia's train,
Betook her to the groves, but Delia's self
In gait surpassed and goddess-like deport,°   *bearing*
390 Though not as she with bow and quiver armed,
But with such gardening tools as art yet rude,
Guiltless of fire had formed, or angels brought.
To Pales, or Pomona thus adorned,
Likest she seemed, Pomona when she fled

Vertumnus, or to Ceres in her prime,
Yet virgin of Proserpina from Jove.
Her long with ardent look his eye pursued
Delighted, but desiring more her stay.
Oft he to her his charge of quick return
400 Repeated, she to him as oft engaged°   *promised*
To be returned by noon amid the bower,
And all things in best order to invite
Noontide repast, or afternoon's repose.
O much deceived, much failing, hapless Eve,
Of thy presumed return! Event° perverse!   *outcome*
Thou never from that hour in Paradise
Found'st either sweet repast, or sound repose;
Such ambush hid among sweet flowers and shades
Waited with hellish rancour imminent
410 To intercept thy way, or send thee back
Despoiled of innocence, of faith, of bliss.
For now, and since first break of dawn the fiend,
Mere serpent in appearance, forth was come,
And on his quest, where likeliest he might find
The only two of mankind, but in them
The whole included race, his purposed prey.
In bower and field he sought, where any tuft
Of grove or garden-plot more pleasant lay,
Their tendance° or plantation° for delight,   *care/planting*
420 By fountain or by shady rivulet
He sought them both, but wished his hap° might find   *chance*
Eve separate, he wished, but not with hope
Of what so seldom chanced, when to his wish,
Beyond his hope, Eve separate he spies,
Veiled in a cloud of fragrance, where she stood,
Half spied, so thick the roses¹⁵⁰ bushing round
About her glowed, oft stooping to support
Each flower of slender stalk, whose head though gay
Carnation, purple, azure, or specked with gold,¹⁵¹
430 Hung drooping unsustained, them she upstays
Gently with myrtle band, mindless the while,
Her self, though fairest unsupported flower,
From her best prop so far, and storm so nigh.
Nearer he drew, and many a walk traversed
Of stateliest covert°, cedar, pine, or palm,   *thicket*
Then voluble° and bold, now hid, now seen   *twisting easily*
Among thick-woven arborets° and flowers   *shrubs*
Embordered on each bank, the hand° of Eve: *handiwork*

Spot more delicious than those gardens feigned
440 Or of revived Adonis, or renowned
Alcinous, host of old Laertes' son,
Or that, not mystic, where the sapient king[152]
Held dalliance with his fair Egyptian spouse.
Much he the place admired, the person more.
As one who long in populous city pent,
Where houses thick and sewers annoy° the air,   *harm*
Forth issuing on a summer's morn to breathe
Among the pleasant villages and farms
Adjoined, from each thing met conceives delight,
450 The smell of grain, or tedded° grass, or kine°   *spread out to dry/cows*
Or dairy, each rural sight, each rural sound;
If chance with nymph-like step fair virgin pass,
What pleasing seemed, for her now pleases more,
She most, and in her look sums all delight.
Such pleasure took the serpent to behold
This flowery plat° the sweet recess of Eve   *patch*
Thus early, thus alone; her heavenly form
Angelic, but more soft, and feminine,
Her graceful innocence, her every air°   *manner*
460 Of gesture or least action overawed
His malice, and with rapine sweet bereaved
His fierceness of the fierce intent it brought:
That space the evil one abstracted stood
From his own evil, and for the time remained
Stupidly good, of enmity disarmed,
Of guile, of hate, of envy, of revenge;
But the hot hell that always in him burns,
Though in mid heaven,[153] soon ended his delight,
And tortures him now more, the more he sees
470 Of pleasure not for him ordained: then soon
Fierce hate he recollects, and all his thoughts
Of mischief, gratulating° thus excites.   *gloating*
     'Thoughts, whither have ye led me, with what sweet
Compulsion thus transported to forget
What hither brought us, hate, not love, nor hope
Of paradise for hell, hope here to taste
Of pleasure, but all pleasure to destroy,
Save what is in destroying, other joy
To me is lost. Then let me not let pass
480 Occasion which now smiles: behold alone
The woman, opportune° to all attempts,   *exposed*
Her husband, for I view far round, not nigh,

Whose higher intellectual more I shun,
And strength, of courage° haughty, and of limb   *valour*
Heroic built, though of terrestrial mould,
Foe not informidable, exempt from wound,
I not; so much hath hell debased, and pain
Enfeebled me, to what I was in heaven.
She fair, divinely fair, fit love for gods,
490 Not terrible, though terror be in love
And beauty, not approached by stronger hate,
Hate stronger, under show of love well feigned,
The way which to her ruin now I tend.'
      So spake the enemy of mankind, enclosed
In serpent, inmate bad, and toward Eve
Addressed his way, not with indented° wave,   *zigzagging*
Prone on the ground, as since, but on his rear,
Circular base of rising folds, that towered
Fold above fold a surging maze, his head
500 Crested aloft, and carbuncle° his eyes;   *reddish*
With burnished neck of verdant gold, erect
Amidst his circling spires,° that on the grass   *coils*
Floated redundant:° pleasing was his shape,   *overflowing*
And lovely, never since of serpent kind
Lovelier, not those that in Illyria changed
Hermione and Cadmus, or the god
In Epidaurus;¹⁵⁴ nor to which transformed
Ammonian Jove, or Capitoline was seen,
He with Olympias, this with her who bore
510 Scipio the height of Rome. With tract° oblique   *course*
At first, as one who sought access, but feared
To interrupt, sidelong he works his way.
As when a ship by skilful steersman wrought
Nigh river's mouth or foreland, where the wind
Veers oft, as oft so steers, and shifts her sail;
So varied he, and of his tortuous train
Curled many a wanton wreath in sight of Eve,
To lure her eye; she busied heard the sound
Of rustling leaves, but minded not, as used
520 To such disport before her through the field,
From every beast, more duteous at her call,
Than at Circean call the herd disguised.
He bolder now, uncalled before her stood;
But as in gaze admiring: oft he bowed
His turret crest, and sleek enamelled neck,
Fawning, and licked the ground whereon she trod.

His gentle dumb expression turned at length
The eye of Eve to mark his play; he glad
Of her attention gained, with serpent tongue
530 Organic, or impulse of vocal air,[155]
His fraudulent temptation thus began.
    'Wonder not, sovereign mistress, if perhaps
Thou canst, who art sole wonder, much less arm
Thy looks, the heaven of mildness, with disdain,
Displeased that I approach thee thus, and gaze
Insatiate, I thus single, nor have feared
Thy awful° brow, more awful thus retired.   *awe-inspiring*
Fairest resemblance of thy Maker fair,
Thee all things living gaze on, all things thine
540 By gift, and thy celestial beauty adore
With ravishment beheld, there best beheld
Where universally admired; but here
In this enclosure wild, these beasts among,
Beholders rude, and shallow to discern
Half what in thee is fair, one man except,
Who sees thee? And what is one? Who shouldst
        be seen
A goddess among gods, adorned and served
By angels numberless, thy daily train.'
    So glozed° the tempter, and his proem° tuned;   *flattered/preface*
550 Into the heart of Eve his words made way,
Though at the voice much marvelling; at length
Not unamazed she thus in answer spake.
'What may this mean? Language of man pronounced
By tongue of brute, and human sense expressed?
The first at least of these I thought denied
To beasts, whom God on their creation-day
Created mute to all articulate sound;
The latter I demur°, for in their looks   *doubt*
Much reason, and in their actions oft appears.
560 Thee, serpent, subtlest beast of all the field
I knew, but not with human voice endued;
Redouble then this miracle, and say,
How camest thou speakable of° mute, and how   *being*
To me so friendly grown above the rest
Of brutal° kind, that daily are in sight?   *animal*
Say, for such wonder claims attention due.'
    To whom the guileful tempter thus replied.
'Empress of this fair world, resplendent Eve,
Easy to me it is to tell thee all

570 What thou command'st, and right thou shouldst be obeyed:
I was at first as other beasts that graze
The trodden herb, of abject thoughts and low,
As was my food, nor aught but food discerned
Or sex, and apprehended nothing high:
Till on a day roving the field, I chanced
A goodly tree far distant to behold
Loaden with fruit of fairest colours mixed,
Ruddy and gold: I nearer drew to gaze;
When from the boughs a savoury odour blown,
580 Grateful to appetite, more pleased my sense
Than smell of sweetest fennel[156] or the teats
Of ewe or goat dropping with milk at even,
Unsucked of lamb or kid, that tend their play.
To satisfy the sharp desire I had
Of tasting those fair apples, I resolved
Not to defer; hunger and thirst at once,
Powerful persuaders, quickened at the scent
Of that alluring fruit, urged me so keen.
About the mossy trunk I wound me soon,
590 For high from ground the branches would require
Thy utmost reach or Adam's: round the tree
All other beasts that saw, with like desire
Longing and envying stood, but could not reach.
Amid the tree now got, where plenty hung
Tempting so nigh, to pluck and eat my fill
I spared not, for such pleasure till that hour
At feed or fountain never had I found.
Sated at length, ere long I might perceive
Strange alteration in me, to degree
600 Of reason in my inward powers, and speech
Wanted not long, though to this shape retained.
Thenceforth to speculations high or deep
I turned my thoughts, and with capacious mind
Considered all things visible in heaven,
Or earth, or middle, all things fair and good;
But all that fair and good in thy divine
Semblance, and in thy beauty's heavenly ray
United I beheld; no fair to thine
Equivalent or second, which compelled
610 Me thus, though importune perhaps, to come
And gaze, and worship thee of right declared
Sovereign of creatures, universal dame.'
     So talked the spirited sly snake; and Eve

Yet more amazed unwary thus replied.
  'Serpent, thy overpraising leaves in doubt
The virtue of that fruit, in thee first proved:
But say, where grows the tree, from hence how far?
For many are the trees of God that grow
In Paradise, and various, yet unknown
620 To us, in such abundance lies our choice,
As leaves a greater store of fruit untouched,
Still hanging incorruptible, till men
Grow up to their provision, and more hands   *what they provide*
Help to disburden nature of her birth.'
      To whom the wily adder, blithe and glad.
  'Empress, the way is ready, and not long,
Beyond a row of myrtles, on a flat,
Fast by a fountain, one small thicket past
Of blowing myrrh and balm; if thou accept
630 My conduct, I can bring thee thither soon.'
      'Lead then', said Eve. He leading swiftly rolled
In tangles, and made intricate seem straight,
To mischief swift. Hope elevates, and joy
Brightens his crest, as when a wandering fire,[157]
Compact° of unctuos° vapour, which the night   *composed/oily*
Condenses, and the cold environs round,
Kindled through agitation to a flame,
Which oft, they say, some evil spirit attends
Hovering and blazing with delusive light,
640 Misleads the amazed night-wanderer from his way
To bogs and mires, and oft through pond or pool,
There swallowed up and lost, from succour far.
So glistered the dire snake, and into fraud
Led Eve our credulous mother, to the tree
Of prohibition, root of all our woe;
Which when she saw, thus to her guide she spake.
      'Serpent, we might have spared our coming hither,
Fruitless to me, though fruit be here to excess,
The credit of whose virtue rest with thee,
650 Wondrous indeed, if cause of such effects.
But of this tree we may not taste nor touch;
God so commanded, and left that command
Sole daughter of His voice; the rest, we live
Law to our selves, our reason is our law.'
      To whom the tempter guilefully replied.
  'Indeed? Hath God then said that of the fruit
Of all these garden trees ye shall not eat,

Yet lords declared of all in earth or air?'
    To whom thus Eve yet sinless. 'Of the fruit
660 Of each tree in the garden we may eat,
But of the fruit of this fair tree amidst
The garden, God hath said, Ye shall not eat
Thereof, nor shall ye touch it, lest ye die.'
    She scarce had said, though brief, when now more bold
The tempter, but with show of zeal and love
To man, and indignation at his wrong,
New part puts on, and as to passion moved,
Fluctuates disturbed,[158] yet comely and in act
Raised, as of some great matter to begin.
670 As when of old some orator renowned
In Athens or free Rome, where eloquence
Flourished, since mute, to some great cause addressed,
Stood in himself collected, while each part,   *controlled*
Motion, each act won audience ere the tongue,
Sometimes in highth[159] began, as no delay
Of preface brooking through his zeal of right.
So standing, moving, or to highth upgrown
The tempter all impassioned thus began.
    'O sacred, wise, and wisdom-giving plant,
680 Mother of science, now I feel thy power   *knowledge*
Within me clear, not only to discern
Things in their causes, but to trace the ways
Of highest agents, deemed however wise.
Queen of this universe, do not believe
Those rigid threats of death; ye shall not die:
How should ye? By the fruit? It gives you life
To knowledge.[160] By the Threatener? Look on me,
Me who have touched and tasted, yet both live,
And life more perfect have attained than fate
690 Meant me, by venturing higher than my lot.
Shall that be shut to man, which to the beast
Is open? Or will God incense his ire
For such a petty trespass, and not praise
Rather your dauntless virtue, whom the pain
Of death denounced, whatever thing death be,
Deterred not from achieving what might lead
To happier life, knowledge of good and evil;
Of good, how just?[161] Of evil, if what is evil
Be real, why not known, since easier shunned?
700 God therefore cannot hurt ye, and be just;
Not just, not God; not feared then, nor obeyed:

Your fear it self of death removes the fear.[162]
Why then was this forbid? Why but to awe,
Why but to keep ye low and ignorant,
His worshippers; He knows that in the day
Ye eat thereof, your eyes that seem so clear,
Yet are but dim, shall perfectly be then
Opened and cleared, and ye shall be as gods,
Knowing both good and evil as they know.
710 That ye should be as gods, since I as man,
Internal[163] man, is but proportion meet,
I of brute human, ye of human gods.
So ye shall die perhaps, by putting off
Human, to put on gods, death to be wished,
Though threatened, which no worse than this can bring.
And what are gods that man may not become
As they, participating godlike food?
The gods are first, and that advantage use
On our belief, that all from them proceeds;
720 I question it, for this fair earth I see,
Warmed by the sun, producing every kind,
Them nothing: if they all things, who enclosed
Knowledge of good and evil in this tree,
That whoso eats thereof, forthwith attains
Wisdom without their leave? And wherein lies
The offence, that man should thus attain to know?
What can your knowledge hurt Him, or this tree
Impart against his will if all be his?
Or is it envy, and can envy dwell
730 In heavenly breasts? These, these and many more
Causes import your need of this fair fruit.
Goddess humane, reach then, and freely taste.'
    He ended, and his words replete with guile
Into her heart too easy entrance won:
Fixed on the fruit she gazed, which to behold
Might tempt alone, and in her ears the sound
Yet rung of his persuasive words, impregned
With reason, to her seeming, and with truth;
Mean while the hour of noon drew on, and waked
740 An eager appetite, raised by the smell
So savoury of that fruit, which with desire,
Inclinable now grown to touch or taste,
Solicited her longing eye; yet first
Pausing a while, thus to her self she mused.
    'Great are thy virtues, doubtless, best of fruits,

Though kept from man, and worthy to be admired,
Whose taste, too long forborne, at first assay
Gave elocution to the mute, and taught
The tongue not made for speech to speak thy praise:
750 Thy praise He also who forbids thy use,
Conceals not from us, naming thee the tree
Of knowledge, knowledge both of good and evil;
Forbids us then to taste, but his forbidding
Commends thee more, while it infers the good
By thee communicated, and our want:
For good unknown, sure is not had, or had
And yet unknown, is as not had at all.
In plain then, what forbids he but to know,
Forbids us good, forbids us to be wise?
760 Such prohibitions bind not. But if death
Bind us with after-bands, what profits then
Our inward freedom? In the day we eat
Of this fair fruit, our doom is, we shall die.
How dies the serpent? He hath eaten and lives,
And knows, and speaks, and reasons, and discerns,
Irrational till then. For us alone
Was death invented? Or to us denied
This intellectual food, for beasts reserved?
For beasts it seems: yet that one beast which first
770 Hath tasted, envies not, but brings with joy
The good befallen him, author unsuspect,[164]
Friendly to man, far from deceit or guile.
What fear I then, rather what know to fear
Under this ignorance of good and evil,
Of God or death, of law or penalty?
Here grows the cure of all, this fruit divine,
Fair to the eye, inviting to the taste,
Of virtue to make wise: what hinders then
To reach, and feed at once both body and mind?'
780   So saying, her rash hand in evil hour
Forth reaching to the fruit, she plucked, she ate:
Earth felt the wound, and nature from her seat
Sighing through all her works gave signs of woe,
That all was lost. Back to the thicket slunk
The guilty serpent, and well might, for Eve
Intent now wholly on her taste, naught else
Regarded, such delight till then, as seemed,
In fruit she never tasted, whether true
Or fancied so, through expectation high

790 Of knowledge, nor was godhead from her thought.
    Greedily she engorged without restraint,
    And knew not, eating, death: satiate at length,
    And heightened as with wine, jocund and boon,°   *merry*
    Thus to her self she pleasingly began.
        'O sovereign, virtuous, precious of all trees
    In Paradise, of operation blest
    To sapience,[165] hitherto obscured, infamed,
    And thy fair fruit let hang, as to no end
    Created; but henceforth my early care,
800 Not without song, each morning, and due praise
    Shall tend thee, and the fertile burden ease
    Of thy full branches offered free to all;
    Till dieted by thee I grow mature
    In knowledge, as the gods who all things know;
    Though others° envy what they cannot give;   *(gods)*
    For had the gift been theirs, it had not here
    Thus grown. Experience, next to thee I owe,
    Best guide; not following thee, I had remained
    In ignorance, thou open'st wisdom's way,
810 And giv'st access, though secret she retire,
    And I perhaps am secret;° heaven is high,   *hidden*
    High and remote to see from thence distinct
    Each thing on earth; and other care perhaps
    May have diverted from continual watch
    Our great Forbidder, safe with all his spies
    About him. But to Adam in what sort
    Shall I appear? Shall I to him make known
    As yet my change, and give him to partake
    Full happiness with me, or rather not,
820 But keep the odds of knowledge in my power
    Without copartner? So to add what wants
    In female sex, the more to draw his love,
    And render me more equal, and perhaps,
    A thing not undesirable, sometime
    Superior; for inferior who is free?
    This may be well: but what if God have seen,
    And death ensue? Then I shall be no more,
    And Adam wedded to another Eve,
    Shall live with her enjoying, I extinct;
830 A death to think. Confirmed then I resolve,
    Adam shall share with me in bliss or woe:
    So dear I love him, that with him all deaths
    I could endure, without him live no life.'

So saying, from the tree her step she turned,
But first low reverence done, as to the power
That dwelt within, whose presence had infused
Into the plant sciential° sap, derived   *of knowledge*
From nectar, drink of gods. Adam the while
Waiting desirous her return, had wove
840   Of choicest flowers a garland to adorn
Her tresses, and her rural labours crown,
As reapers oft are wont their harvest queen.
Great joy he promised to his thoughts, and new
Solace in her return, so long delayed;
Yet oft his heart, divine of something ill,
Misgave him; he the faltering measure° felt;   *(heart-beat)*
And forth to meet her went, the way she took
That morn when first they parted; by the tree
Of knowledge he must pass, there he her met,
850   Scarce from the tree returning; in her hand
A bough of fairest fruit that downy smiled,
New gathered, and ambrosial smell diffused.
To him she hasted, in her face excuse
Came prologue, and apology to prompt,[166]
Which with bland words at will she thus addressed.
   'Hast thou not wondered, Adam, at my stay?
Thee I have missed, and thought it long, deprived
Thy presence, agony of love till now
Not felt, nor shall be twice, for never more
860   Mean I to try, what rash untried I sought,
The pain of absence from thy sight. But strange
Hath been the cause, and wonderful to hear:
This tree is not as we are told, a tree
Of danger tasted, nor to evil unknown
Opening the way, but of divine effect
To open eyes, and make them gods who taste;
And hath been tasted such: the serpent wise,
Or not restrained as we, or not obeying,
Hath eaten of the fruit, and is become,
870   Not dead, as we are threatened, but thenceforth
Endued with human voice and human sense,
Reasoning to admiration,° and with me   *wonderfully*
Persuasively hath so prevailed, that I
Have also tasted, and have also found
The effects to correspond, opener mine eyes,
Dim erst, dilated spirits, ampler heart,
And growing up to godhead; which for thee

Chiefly I sought, without thee can despise.
For bliss, as thou hast part, to me is bliss,
880   Tedious, unshared with thee, and odious soon.
Thou therefore also taste, that equal lot
May join us, equal joy, as equal love;
Lest thou not tasting, different degree
Disjoin us, and I then too late renounce
Deity for thee, when fate will not permit.'
        Thus Eve with countenance blithe her story told;
But in her cheek distemper flushing glowed.
On the other side, Adam, soon as he heard
The fatal trespass done by Eve, amazed,
890   Astonied° stood and blank°, while horror chill   *stunned/speechless*
Ran through his veins, and all his joints relaxed;
From his slack hand the garland wreathed for Eve
Down dropped, and all the faded roses shed:
Speechless he stood and pale, till thus at length
First to himself he inward silence broke.
        'O fairest of creation, last and best
Of all God's works, creature in whom excelled
Whatever can to sight or thought be formed,
Holy, divine, good, amiable° or sweet!   *lovable*
900   How art thou lost, how on a sudden lost,
Defaced, deflowered, and now to death devote°?   *given up*
Rather how hast thou yielded to transgress
The strict forbiddance, how to violate
The sacred fruit forbidden? Some cursed fraud
Of enemy hath beguiled thee, yet unknown,
And me with thee hath ruined, for with thee
Certain my resolution is to die;
How can I live without thee, how forgo
Thy sweet converse and love so dearly joined,
910   To live again in these wild woods forlorn?
Should God create another Eve, and I
Another rib afford, yet loss of thee
Would never from my heart; no no, I feel
The link of nature draw me: flesh of flesh,
Bone of my bone thou art, and from thy state
Mine never shall be parted, bliss or woe.'
        So having said, as one from sad dismay
Recomforted, and after thoughts disturbed
Submitting to what seemed remediless,
920   Thus in calm mood his words to Eve he turned.
        'Bold deed thou hast presumed, adventurous Eve,

And peril great provoked, who thus hath dared
Had it been only coveting to eye
That sacred fruit, sacred to abstinence,
Much more to taste it under ban to touch.
But past who can recall, or done undo?
Not God omnipotent, nor fate, yet so
Perhaps thou shalt not die, perhaps the fact°   *deed*
Is not so heinous now, foretasted fruit,
930 Profaned first by the serpent, by him first
Made common and unhallowed ere our taste;
Nor yet on him found deadly, he yet lives,
Lives, as thou saidst, and gains to live as man
Higher degree of life, inducement strong
To us, as likely tasting to attain
Proportional ascent, which cannot be
But to be gods, or angels demi-gods.
Nor can I think that God, Creator wise,
Though threatening, will in earnest so destroy
940 Us his prime creatures, dignified so high,
Set over all his works, which in our fall,
For us created, needs with us must fail,
Dependent made; so God shall uncreate,
Be frustrate, do, undo, and labour lose,
Not well conceived of God, who though his power
Creation could repeat, yet would be loth
Us to abolish, lest the adversary
Triumph and say; Fickle their state whom God
Most favours, who can please Him long; me first
950 He ruined, now mankind; whom will He next?
Matter of scorn, not to be given the foe.
However I with thee have fixed my lot,
Certain to undergo like doom,° if death   *destiny*
Consort with thee, death is to me as life;
So forcible within my heart I feel
The bond of nature draw me to my own,
My own in thee, for what thou art is mine;
Our state cannot be severed, we are one,
One flesh; to lose thee were to lose my self.'
960   So Adam, and thus Eve to him replied.
'O glorious trial of exceeding love,
Illustrious evidence, example° high!   *manifestation*
Engaging me to emulate, but short
Of thy perfection, how shall I attain,
Adam, from whose dear side I boast me sprung,

And gladly of our union hear thee speak,
One heart, one soul in both; whereof good proof
This day affords, declaring thee resolved,
Rather than death or aught than death more dread
970 Shall separate us, linked in love so dear,
To undergo with me one guilt, one crime,
If any be, of tasting this fair fruit,
Whose virtue, for of good still good proceeds,
Direct, or by occasion° hath presented   *indirectly*
This happy trial of thy love, which else
So eminently never had been known.
Were it I thought death menaced would ensue
This my attempt, I would sustain alone
The worst, and not persuade thee, rather die
980 Deserted, than oblige° thee with a fact°   *penalise/deed*
Pernicious to thy peace, chiefly assured[167]
Remarkably, so late, of thy so true,
So faithful love unequalled; but I feel
Far otherwise the event°, not death, but life   *outcome*
Augmented, opened eyes, new hopes, new joys,
Taste so divine, that what of sweet before
Hath touched my sense, flat seems to this, and harsh.
On my experience, Adam, freely taste,
And fear of death deliver to the winds.'
990   So saying, she embraced him, and for joy
Tenderly wept, much won that he his love
Had so ennobled, as of choice to incur
Divine displeasure for her sake, or death.
In recompense (for such compliance° bad   *conformity*
Such recompense best merits) from the bough
She gave him of that fair enticing fruit
With liberal hand: he scrupled not to eat
Against his better knowledge, not deceived,
But fondly overcome with female charm.
1000 Earth trembled from her entrails, as again
In pangs, and Nature gave a second groan,
Sky loured and muttering thunder, some sad drops
Wept at completing of the mortal sin
Original; while Adam took no thought,
Eating his fill, nor Eve to iterate°   *repeat*
Her former trespass feared, the more to soothe
Him with her loved society, that now
As with new wine intoxicated both
They swim in mirth, and fancy that they feel

1010 Divinity within them breeding wings
   Wherewith to scorn the earth: but that false fruit
   Far other operation first displayed,
   Carnal desire inflaming, he on Eve
   Began to cast lascivious eyes, she him
   As wantonly repaid; in lust they burn:
   Till Adam thus gan Eve to dalliance move.
    'Eve, now I see thou art exact° of taste,   *perfect*
   And elegant,° of sapience no small part,   *refined*
   Since to each meaning savour we apply,
1020 And palate call judicious;[168] I the praise
   Yield thee, so well this day thou hast purveyed.
   Much pleasure we have lost, while we abstained
   From this delightful fruit, nor known till now
   True relish, tasting; if such pleasure be
   In things to us forbidden, it might be wished,
   For this one tree had been forbidden ten.
   But come, so well refreshed, now let us play,
   As meet is, after such delicious fare;
   For never did thy beauty since the day
1030 I saw thee first and wedded thee, adorned
   With all perfections, so inflame my sense
   With ardour to enjoy thee, fairer now
   Than ever, bounty of this virtuous tree.'
    So said he, and forbore not glance or toy
   Of amorous intent, well understood
   Of Eve, whose eye darted contagious fire.
   Her hand he seized, and to a shady bank,
   Thick overhead with verdant roof embowered
   He led her nothing loth; flowers were the couch,
1040 Pansies, and violets, and asphodel,
   And hyacinth, earth's freshest softest lap.
   There they their fill of love and love's disport
   Took largely, of their mutual guilt the seal,
   The solace of their sin, till dewy sleep
   Oppressed them, wearied with their amorous play.
   Soon as the force of that fallacious fruit,
   That with exhilarating vapour bland
   About their spirits had played, and inmost powers
   Made err, was now exhaled, and grosser sleep
1050 Bred of unkindly° fumes, with conscious° dreams *unnatural/guilty*
   Encumbered, now had left them, up they rose
   As from unrest, and each the other viewing,
   Soon found their eyes how opened, and their minds

How darkened; innocence, that as a veil
Had shadowed them from knowing ill, was gone,
Just confidence, and native righteousness
And honour from about them, naked left
To guilty shame; he covered, but his robe
Uncovered more. So rose the Danite strong[169]
1060 Herculean Samson from the harlot-lap
Of Philistean Dalilah, and waked
Shorn of his strength. They destitute and bare
Of all their virtue, silent, and in face
Confounded long they sat, as strucken mute,
Till Adam, though not less than Eve abashed,
At length gave utterance to these words constrained.
   'O Eve, in evil hour thou didst give ear
To that false worm, of whomsoever taught
To counterfeit man's voice, true in our fall,
1070 False in our promised rising; since our eyes
Opened we find indeed, and find we know
Both good and evil, good lost, and evil got,
Bad fruit of knowledge, if this be to know,
Which leaves us naked thus, of honour void,
Of innocence, of faith, of purity,
Our wonted ornaments now soiled and stained,
And in our faces evident the signs
Of foul concupiscence; whence evil store;
Even shame, the last° of evils; of the first   *latest*
1080 Be sure then. How shall I behold the face
Henceforth of God or angel, erst with joy
And rapture so oft beheld? Those heavenly shapes
Will dazzle now this earthly, with their blaze
Insufferably bright. O might I here
In solitude live savage, in some glade
Obscured, where highest woods impenetrable
To star or sunlight, spread their umbrage° broad   *shady foliage*
And brown as evening: cover me ye pines,
Ye cedars, with innumerable boughs
1090 Hide me, where I may never see them more.
But let us now, as in bad plight, devise
What best may for the present serve to hide
The parts of each from other, that seem most
To shame obnoxious,° and unseemliest seen,   *exposed*
Some tree whose broad smooth leaves together sewed,
And girded on our loins, may cover round
Those middle parts, that this new comer, shame,

There sit not, and reproach us as unclean.'
   So counselled he, and both together went
1100 Into the thickest wood, there soon they chose
The fig-tree,[170] not that kind for fruit renowned,
But such as at this day to Indians known
In Malabar or Decan spreads her arms
Branching so broad and long, that in the ground
The bended twigs take root, and daughters grow
About the mother tree, a pillared shade
High overarched, and echoing walks between;
There oft the Indian herdsman shunning heat
Shelters in cool, and tends his pasturing herds
1110 At loop-holes cut through thickest shade: those leaves
They gathered, broad as Amazonian targe,°   *shield*
And with what skill they had, together sewed,
To gird their waist, vain covering if to hide
Their guilt and dreaded shame; O how unlike
To that first naked glory. Such of late
Columbus found the American so girt
With feathered cincture,°[171] naked else and wild   *belt*
Among the trees on isles and woody shores.
   Thus fenced, and as they thought, their shame in part
1120 Covered, but not at rest or ease of mind
They sat them down to weep, nor only tears
Rained at their eyes, but high winds worse within
Began to rise, high passions, anger, hate,
Mistrust, suspicion, discord, and shook sore
Their inward state of mind, calm region once
And full of peace, now tossed and turbulent:
For understanding ruled not, and the will
Heard not her lore, both in subjection now
To sensual appetite, who from beneath[172]
1130 Usurping over sovereign reason claimed
Superior sway: from thus distempered breast,
Adam, estranged° in look and altered style,   *changed*
Speech intermitted° thus to Eve renewed.   *broken off*
   'Would thou hadst hearkened to my words, and stayed
With me, as I besought thee, when that strange
Desire of wandering this unhappy morn,
I know not whence possessed thee; we had then
Remained still happy, not as now, despoiled
Of all our good, shamed, naked, miserable.
1140 Let none henceforth seek needless cause to approve°   *give proof*
The faith they owe; when earnestly they seek

Such proof, conclude, they then begin to fail.'
　　To whom soon moved with touch of blame thus Eve.
'What words have passed thy lips, Adam severe,
Imput'st thou that to my default, or will
Of wandering, as thou call'st it, which who knows
But might as ill have happened thou being by,
Or to thy self perhaps: hadst thou been there,
Or here the attempt, thou couldst not have discerned
1150 Fraud in the serpent, speaking as he spake;
No ground of enmity between us known,
Why he should mean me ill, or seek to harm.
Was I to have never parted from thy side?
As good have grown there still a lifeless rib.
Being as I am, why didst not thou the head
Command me absolutely not to go,
Going into such danger as thou saidst?
Too facile° then thou didst not much gainsay,　　　　　　　　　*flexible*
Nay didst permit, approve, and fair dismiss.
1160 Hadst thou been firm and fixed in thy dissent,
Neither had I transgressed, nor thou with me.'
　　To whom then first incensed Adam replied.
'Is this the love, is this the recompense
Of mine to thee, ingrateful Eve, expressed
Immutable when thou wert lost, not I,
Who might have lived and joyed immortal bliss,
Yet willingly chose rather death with thee:
And am I now upbraided, as the cause
Of thy transgressing? Not enough severe,
1170 It seems, in thy restraint: what could I more?
I warned thee, I admonished thee, foretold
The danger, and the lurking enemy
That lay in wait; beyond this had been force,
And force upon free will hath here no place.
But confidence° then bore thee on, secure　　　　　　　*over-confidence*
Either to meet no danger, or to find
Matter° of glorious trial; and perhaps　　　　　　　　　*occasion*
I also erred in overmuch admiring
What seemed in thee so perfect, that I thought
1180 No evil durst attempt thee, but I rue
That error now, which is become my crime,
And thou the accuser. Thus it shall befall
Him who to worth in women overtrusting
Lets her will rule; restraint she will not brook,
And left to her self, if evil thence ensue,

She first his weak indulgence will accuse.'
    Thus they in mutual accusation spent
The fruitless hours, but neither self-condemning,
And of their vain contest appeared no end.

Book X[173]

Meanwhile the heinous and despiteful act
Of Satan done in Paradise, and how
He in the serpent, had perverted Eve,
Her husband she, to taste the fatal fruit,
Was known in heaven; for what can scape the eye
Of God all-seeing, or deceive His heart
Omniscient, who in all things wise and just,
Hindered not Satan to attempt the mind
Of man, with strength entire, and free will armed,
Complete to have discovered and repulsed
Whatever wiles of foe or seeming friend.
For still they knew, and ought to have still remembered
The high injunction not to taste that fruit,
Whoever tempted; which they not obeying,
Incurred, what could they less, the penalty,
And manifold° in sin, deserved to fall.   *having various forms*
Up into heaven from Paradise in haste
The angelic guards ascended, mute and sad
For man, for of his state by this they knew,
Much wondering how the subtle fiend had stolen
Entrance unseen. Soon as the unwelcome news
From earth arrived at heaven gate, displeased
All were who heard, dim sadness did not spare
That time celestial visages, yet mixed
With pity, violated not their bliss.
About the new-arrived, in multitudes
The ethereal people ran, to hear and know
How all befell: they, towards the throne supreme
Accountable, made haste to make appear,
With righteous plea, their utmost vigilance,
And easily approved;[174] when the most high
Eternal Father from his secret cloud,
Amidst in thunder uttered thus his voice.
    'Assembled angels, and ye powers returned

35 From unsuccessful charge, be not dismayed,
   Nor troubled at these tidings from the earth,
   Which your sincerest care could not prevent,
   Foretold so lately what would come to pass,
   When first this tempter crossed the gulf from hell.
40 I told ye then he should prevail and speed
   On his bad errand, man should be seduced
   And flattered out of all, believing lies
   Against his Maker; no decree of mine
   Concurring to necessitate his fall,
45 Or touch with lightest moment of impulse
   His free will, to her own inclining left
   In even scale. But fallen he is, and now
   What rests° but that the mortal sentence pass   *remains*
   On his transgression, death denounced that day,
50 Which he presumes already vain and void,
   Because not yet inflicted, as he feared,
   By some immediate stroke; but soon shall find
   Forbearance no acquittance ere day end.
   Justice shall not return as bounty scorned.[175]
   But whom send I to judge them? Whom but thee
   Vicegerent Son, to thee I have transferred
   All judgment, whether in heaven, or earth, or hell.
   Easy it might be seen that I intend
   Mercy colleague with justice, sending thee
60 Man's friend, his mediator, his designed
   Both ransom and redeemer voluntary,
   And destined man himself to judge man fallen.'
     So spake the Father, and unfolding bright
   Toward the right hand his glory, on the Son
   Blazed forth unclouded deity; he full
   Resplendent all his Father manifest
   Expressed, and thus divinely answered mild.
     'Father Eternal, thine is to decree,
   Mine both in heaven and earth to do thy will
70 Supreme, that thou in me thy Son beloved
   Mayst ever rest well pleased. I go to judge
   On earth these thy transgressors, but thou know'st,
   Whoever judged, the worst on me must light,
   When time shall be, for so I undertook
   Before Thee; and not repenting, this obtain
   Of right, that I may mitigate their doom°   *judgement*
   On me derived°; yet I shall temper so   *transferred*
   Justice with mercy, as may illustrate most

Them fully satisfied,[176] and Thee appease.
80 Attendance none shall need, nor train, where none
Are to behold the judgment, but the judged,
Those two; the third, best absent is condemned,
Convict° by flight, and rebel to all law,   *convicted*
Conviction to the serpent none belongs.'
  Thus saying, from his radiant seat He rose
Of high collateral[177] glory: Him thrones and powers,
Princedoms, and dominations ministrant°   *ministering*
Accompanied to heaven gate, from whence
Eden and all the coast in prospect lay.
90 Down he descended straight; the speed of gods
Time counts not, though with swiftest minutes winged.
Now was the sun in western cadence° low   *sinking*
From noon, and gentle airs due at their hour
To fan the earth now waked, and usher in
The evening cool when He from wrath more cool
Came the mild judge and intercessor both
To sentence man: the voice of God they heard
Now walking in the garden, by soft winds
Brought to their ears, while day declined, they heard,
100 And from his presence hid themselves among
The thickest trees, both man and wife, till God
Approaching, thus to Adam called aloud.
  'Where art thou Adam, wont with joy to meet
My coming seen far off? I miss thee here,
Not pleased, thus entertained with solitude,
Where obvious duty erewhile appeared unsought:[178]
Or come I less conspicuous, or what change
Absents thee, or what chance detains? Come forth.'
He came, and with him Eve, more loath, though first
110 To offend, discountenanced both, and discomposed;
Love was not in their looks, either to God
Or to each other, but apparent guilt,
And shame, and perturbation, and despair,
Anger, and obstinacy, and hate, and guile.
Whence Adam faltering long, thus answered brief.
  'I heard Thee in the garden, and of thy voice
Afraid, being naked, hid myself.' To whom
The gracious Judge without revile° replied.   *reviling*
  'My voice thou oft hast heard, and hast not feared,
120 But still rejoiced, how is it now become
So dreadful to thee? That thou art naked, who
Hath told thee? Hast thou eaten of the tree

Whereof I gave thee charge thou shouldst not eat?'
  To whom thus Adam sore beset replied.
'O heaven! In evil strait this day I stand
Before my Judge, either to undergo
My self the total crime, or to accuse
My other self, the partner of my life;
Whose failing, while her faith to me remains,
130 I should conceal, and not expose to blame
By my complaint; but strict necessity
Subdues me, and calamitous constraint
Lest on my head both sin and punishment,
However insupportable, be all
Devolved;° though should I hold my peace, yet Thou   *fallen*
Wouldst easily detect what I conceal.
This woman whom thou madest to be my help,
And gavest me as thy perfect gift, so good,
So fit, so acceptable, so divine,
140 That from her hand I could suspect no ill,
And what she did, whatever in it self,
Her doing seemed to justify the deed;
She gave me of the tree, and I did eat.'
  To whom the Sovereign Presence thus replied.
'Was she thy God, that her thou didst obey
Before his voice, or was she made thy guide,
Superior, or but equal, that to her
Thou didst resign thy manhood, and the place
Wherein God set thee above her made of thee,
150 And for thee, whose perfection far excelled
Hers in all real° dignity: adorned   *regal*
She was indeed, and lovely to attract
Thy love, not thy subjection, and her gifts
Were such as under government well seemed,
Unseemly to bear rule, which was thy part
And person,° hadst thou known thy self aright.'   *character*
  So having said, He thus to Eve in few:
'Say woman, what is this which thou hast done?'
  To whom sad Eve with shame nigh overwhelmed,
160 Confessing soon, yet not before her Judge
Bold or loquacious, thus abashed replied.
'The serpent me beguiled and I did eat.'
  Which when the Lord God heard, without delay
To judgment He proceeded on the accused
Serpent though brute, unable to transfer
The guilt on him who made him° instrument   *Satan*

Of mischief, and polluted from the end
Of his creation; justly then accursed,
As vitiated° in nature: more to know   *corrupt*
170 Concerned not man (since he no further knew)
Nor altered his offence; yet God at last
To Satan first in sin his doom applied,
Though in mysterious terms, judged as then best:
And on the serpent thus his curse let fall.[179]
    'Because thou hast done this, thou art accursed
Above all cattle, each beast of the field;
Upon thy belly grovelling thou shalt go,
And dust shalt eat all the days of thy life.
Between thee and the woman I will put
180 Enmity, and between thine and her seed;
Her seed shall bruise thy head, thou bruise his heel.'
    So spake this Oracle, then verified
When Jesus, son of Mary, second Eve,
Saw Satan fall like lightning down from heaven,[180]
Prince of the air; then rising from his grave,
Spoiled principalities and powers, triumphed
In open show, and with ascension bright
Captivity led captive through the air,
The realm it self of Satan long usurped,
190 Whom He shall tread at last under our feet;
Even He who now foretold his fatal bruise,
And to the woman thus his sentence turned.
    'Thy sorrow I will greatly multiply
By thy conception; children thou shalt bring
In sorrow forth, and to thy husband's will
Thine shall submit, he over thee shall rule.'
    On Adam last thus judgment He pronounced.
'Because thou hast hearkened to the voice of thy wife,
And eaten of the tree concerning which
200 I charged thee, saying: Thou shalt not eat thereof,
Cursed is the ground for thy sake, thou in sorrow
Shalt eat thereof all the days of thy life;
Thorns also and thistles it shall bring thee forth
Unbid, and thou shalt eat the herb of the field,
In the sweat of thy face shalt thou eat bread,
Till thou return unto the ground, for thou
Out of the ground wast taken, know° thy birth,   *understand*
For dust thou art, and shalt to dust return.'
    So judged He man, both judge and saviour sent,
210 And the instant stroke of death denounced that day

Removed far off; then pitying how they stood
Before Him naked to the air, that now
Must suffer change, disdained not to begin
Thenceforth the form of servant to assume,[181]
As when He washed his servants' feet so now
As Father of his family He clad
Their nakedness with skins of beasts, or slain,
Or as the snake with youthful coat repaid;
And thought not much to clothe his enemies:
220 Nor He their outward only with the skins
Of beasts, but inward nakedness, much more
Opprobrious, with his robe of righteousness,
Arraying° covered from his Father's sight.   *dressing*
To Him with swift ascent He up returned,
Into his blissful bosom reassumed
In glory as of old, to Him appeased
All, though all-knowing, what had passed with man
Recounted, mixing intercession sweet.
Meanwhile ere thus was sinned and judged on earth,
230 Within the gates of hell sat Sin and Death,
In counterview within the gates, that now
Stood open wide,[182] belching outrageous° flame   *fierce*
Far into chaos, since the fiend passed through,
Sin opening, who thus now to Death began.
    'O son, why sit we here each other viewing
Idly, while Satan our great author° thrives   *creator*
In other worlds, and happier seat provides
For us his offspring dear? It cannot be
But that success attends him; if mishap,
240 Ere this he had returned, with fury driven
By his avengers, since no place like this
Can fit his punishment, or their revenge.
Methinks I feel new strength within me rise,
Wings growing, and dominion given me large
Beyond this deep; whatever draws me on,
Or sympathy, or some connatural° force   *like*
Powerful at greatest distance to unite
With secret amity things of like kind
By secretest conveyance.° Thou my shade   *communication*
250 Inseparable must with me along:
For Death from Sin no power can separate.
But lest the difficulty of passing back
Stay his return perhaps over this gulf
Impassable, impervious, let us try

Advent'rous work, yet to thy power and mine
Not unagreeable, to found° a path   *build*
Over this main° from hell to that new world   *expanse*
Where Satan now prevails, a monument
Of merit high to all the infernal host,
260 Easing their passage hence, for intercourse,°   *trafficking*
Or transmigration, as their lot shall lead.
Nor can I miss the way, so strongly drawn
By this new felt attraction and instinct.'
    Whom thus the meagre shadow answered soon.
'Go whither fate and inclination strong
Leads thee, I shall not lag behind, nor err°   *go the wrong way*
The way, thou leading, such a scent I draw°   *inhale*
Of carnage, prey innumerable, and taste
The savour of death from all things there that live:
270 Nor shall I to the work thou enterprisest
Be wanting, but afford thee equal aid.'
    So saying, with delight he snuffed the smell
Of mortal change on earth. As when a flock
Of ravenous fowl, though many a league remote,
Against the day of battle, to a field,
Where armies lie encamped, come flying, lured
With scent of living carcasses designed
For death, the following day, in bloody fight.
So scented the grim feature, and upturned
280 His nostril wide into the murky air,
Sagacious° of his quarry from so far.   *quick to scent*
Then both from out hell gates into the waste
Wide anarchy of chaos damp and dark
Flew diverse, and with power (their power was great)
Hovering upon the waters; what they met
Solid or slimy, as in raging sea
Tossed up and down, together crowded drove
From each side shoaling towards the mouth of hell.
As when two polar winds blowing adverse
290 Upon the Cronian sea, together drive
Mountains of ice, that stop the imagined way[183]
Beyond Petsora eastward, to the rich
Cathaian coast. The aggregated soil
Death with his mace petrific,° cold and dry,   *petrifying*
As with a trident smote, and fixed as firm
As Delos floating once; the rest his look
Bound with Gorgonian rigor° not to move,   *stiffness*
And with asphaltic slime; broad as the gate,

Deep to the roots of hell the gathered beach
300   They fastened, and the mole° immense wrought on   *breakwater*
Over the foaming deep high arched, a bridge
Of length prodigious joining to the wall
Immovable of this now fenceless world
Forfeit to Death; from hence a passage broad,
Smooth, easy, inoffensive down to hell.
So, if great things to small may be compared,
Xerxes, the liberty of Greece to yoke,
From Susa his Memnonian palace high
Came to the sea, and over Hellespont
310   Bridging his way, Europe with Asia joined,
And scourged with many a stroke the indignant waves.
Now had they brought the work by wondrous art
Pontifical,° a ridge of pendent rock   *of bridge-building*
Over the vexed° abyss, following the track   *storm-ridden*
Of Satan, to the self same place where he
First lighted from his wing, and landed safe
From out of chaos to the outside bare
Of this round world: with pins of adamant
And chains they made all fast, too fast they made
320   And durable; and now in little space
The confines° met of empyrean heaven   *common boundaries*
And of this world, and on the left hand[184] hell
With long reach interposed; three several ways
In sight, to each of these three places led.
And now their way to earth they had descried,
To Paradise first tending, when behold
Satan in likeness of an angel bright
Betwixt the Centaur and the Scorpion steering
His zenith, while the sun in Aries rose:
330   Disguised he came, but those his children dear
Their parent soon discerned, though in disguise.
He after Eve seduced, unminded slunk
Into the wood fast by, and changing shape
To observe the sequel, saw his guileful act
By Eve, though all unweeting, seconded
Upon her husband, saw their shame that sought
Vain covertures;° but when he saw descend   *coverings*
The Son of God to judge them terrified
He fled, not hoping to escape, but shun
340   The present, fearing guilty what his wrath
Might suddenly inflict; that past, returned
By night, and listening where the hapless pair

Sat in their sad discourse, and various plaint,
Thence gathered his own doom, which understood
Not instant, but of future time. With joy
And tidings fraught, to hell he now returned,
And at the brink of Chaos, near the foot
Of this new wondrous pontifice° unhoped   *bridge*
Met who to meet him came, his offspring dear.
350 Great joy was at their meeting, and at sight
Of that stupendous bridge his joy increased.
Long he admiring stood, till Sin, his fair
Enchanting daughter, thus the silence broke.
    'O parent, these are thy magnific deeds,
Thy trophies, which thou view'st as not thine own,
Thou art their author and prime architect:
For I no sooner in my heart divined,
My heart, which by a secret harmony
Still moves with thine, joined in connection sweet,
360 That thou on earth hadst prospered, which thy looks
Now also evidence, but straight I felt
Though distant from thee worlds between, yet felt
That I must after thee with this thy son;
Such fatal consequence unites us three:
Hell could no longer hold us in her bounds,
Nor this unvoyageable gulf obscure
Detain from following thy illustrious track.
Thou hast achieved our liberty, confined
Within hell gates till now, thou us empowered
370 To fortify° thus far, and overlay   *strengthen*
With this portentous° bridge the dark abyss.   *prodigious*
Thine now is all this world, thy virtue° hath won   *power*
What thy hands builded not, thy wisdom gained
With odds° what war hath lost, and fully avenged   *advantage*
Our foil° in heaven; here thou shalt monarch reign,   *defeat*
There didst not; there let Him still Victor sway,
As battle hath adjudged, from this new world
Retiring, by his own doom alienated,
And henceforth monarchy with thee divide
380 Of all things parted by the empyreal bounds,
His quadrature,[185] from thy orbicular° world,   *spherical*
Or try thee now more dangerous to his throne.'
    Whom thus the prince of darkness answered glad.
'Fair daughter, and thou son and grandchild both,[186]
High proof ye now have given to be the race
Of Satan (for I glory in the name,[187]

Antagonist of heaven's almighty King)
Amply have merited of me, of all
The infernal empire, that so near heaven's door
390 Triumphal with triumphal act have met,
Mine with this glorious work, and made one realm
Hell and this world, one realm, one continent
Of easy thorough-fare. Therefore while I
Descend through darkness, on your road with ease
To my associate powers, them to acquaint
With these successes, and with them rejoice,
You two this way, among these numerous orbs
All yours, right down to Paradise descend;
There dwell and reign in bliss, thence on the earth
400 Dominion exercise and in the air,
Chiefly on man, sole lord of all declared,
Him first make sure your thrall, and lastly kill.
My substitutes I send ye, and create
Plenipotent° on earth, of matchless might   *with full authority*
Issuing from me: on your joint vigour now
My hold of this new kingdom all depends,
Through Sin to Death exposed by my exploit.
If your joint power prevails, the affairs of hell
No detriment need fear, go and be strong.'
410   So saying he dismissed them, they with speed
Their course through thickest constellations held
Spreading their bane; the blasted° stars looked wan,   *withered*
And planets, planet-strook, real eclipse
Then suffered. The other way Satan went down
The causey° to hell gate; on either side   *causeway*
Disparted° Chaos over built exclaimed,   *separated*
And with rebounding surge the bars assailed,
That scorned his indignation: through the gate,
Wide open and unguarded, Satan passed,
420 And all about found desolate; for those
Appointed to sit there, had left their charge,
Flown to the upper world; the rest were all
Far to the inland retired, about the walls
Of Pandaemonium, city and proud seat
Of Lucifer, so by allusion called,
Of that bright star to Satan paragoned.°   *compared*
There kept their watch the legions, while the grand
In council sat, solicitous what chance
Might intercept their emperor sent, so he
430 Departing gave command, and they observed.

As when the Tartar from his Russian foe
By Astracan over the snowy plains
Retires, or Bactrian sophy° from the horns   *(Persian King)*
Of Turkish crescent,[188] leaves all waste beyond
The realm of Aladule, in his retreat
To Tauris or Casbeen. So these the late
Heaven-banished host, left desert utmost hell
Many a dark league, reduced in careful watch
Round their metropolis, and now expecting
440 Each hour their great adventurer from the search
Of foreign worlds: he through the midst unmarked,
In show plebeian angel militant
Of lowest order, passed; and from the door
Of that Plutonian hall, invisible
Ascended his high throne, which under state°   *canopy*
Of richest texture spread, at the upper end
Was placed in regal lustre. Down a while
He sat, and round about him saw unseen:
At last as from a cloud his fulgent° head   *shining*
450 And shape star-bright appeared, or brighter, clad
With what permissive glory since his fall
Was left him, or false glitter: all amazed
At that so sudden blaze the Stygian throng
Bent their aspect, and whom they wished beheld,
Their mighty chief returned: loud was the acclaim:
Forth rushed in haste the great consulting peers,
Raised from their dark divan,° and with like joy   *council of state*
Congratulant° approached him, who with hand   *with congratulations*
Silence, and with these words attention won.
460   'Thrones, dominations, princedoms, virtues, powers,
For in possession such, not only of right,
I call ye and declare ye now, returned
Successful beyond hope, to lead ye forth
Triumphant out of this infernal pit
Abominable, accursed, the house of woe,
And dungeon of our tyrant: now possess,
As lords, a spacious world, to our native heaven
Little inferior, by my adventure hard
With peril great achieved. Long were to tell
470 What I have done, what suffered, with what pain
Voyaged the unreal,° vast, unbounded deep   *formless*
Of horrible confusion, over which
By Sin and Death a broad way now is paved
To expedite your glorious march; but I

Toiled out my uncouth° passage, forced to ride   *strange*
The untractable abyss, plunged in the womb
Of unoriginal Night and Chaos wild,
That jealous of their secrets fiercely opposed
My journey strange, with clamorous uproar
480 Protesting fate supreme; thence how I found
The new created world, which fame in heaven
Long had foretold, a fabric wonderful
Of absolute perfection, therein man
Placed in a paradise, by our exile
Made happy: him by fraud I have seduced
From his creator, and the more to increase
Your wonder, with an apple; he thereat
Offended, worth your laughter, hath given up
Both his beloved man and all this world,
490 To Sin and Death a prey, and so to us,
Without our hazard, labour, or alarm,
To range in, and to dwell, and over man
To rule, as over all he should have ruled.
True is, me also he hath judged, or rather
Me not, but the brute serpent in whose shape
Man I deceived: that which to me belongs,
Is enmity, which he will put between
Me and mankind; I am to bruise his heel;
His seed, when is not set, shall bruise my head:
500 A world who would not purchase with a bruise,
Or much more grievous pain? Ye have the account
Of my performance: what remains, ye gods,
But up and enter now into full bliss.'
    So having said, a while he stood, expecting
Their universal shout and high applause
To fill his ear, when contrary he hears
On all sides, from innumerable tongues
A dismal universal hiss, the sound
Of public scorn; he wondered, but not long
510 Had leisure, wondering at himself now more;
His visage drawn he felt to sharp and spare,
His arms clung to his ribs, his legs entwining
Each other, till supplanted down he fell
A monstrous serpent on his belly prone,
Reluctant, but in vain, a greater power
Now ruled him, punished in the shape he sinned,
According to his doom: he would have spoke,
But hiss for hiss returned with forked tongue

To forked tongue, for now were all transformed
520 Alike, to serpents all as accessories
To his bold riot:° dreadful was the din   *rebellion*
Of hissing through the hall, thick swarming now
With complicated monsters head and tail,
Scorpion and asp, and amphisbaena dire,[189]
Cerastes horned, hydrus, and ellops drear,
And dipsas (not so thick swarmed once the soil
Bedropped with blood of Gorgon, or the isle
Ophiusa) but still greatest he the midst,
Now dragon grown, larger than whom the sun
530 Ingendered in the Pythian vale on slime,
Huge Python, and his power no less he seemed
Above the rest still to retain; they all
Him followed issuing forth to the open field,
Where all yet left of that revolted rout
Heaven-fallen, in station stood or just array,[190]
Sublime° with expectation when to see   *uplifted*
In triumph issuing forth their glorious chief;
They saw, but other sight instead, a crowd
Of ugly serpents; horror on them fell,
540 And horrid sympathy; for what they saw
They felt themselves now changing; down their arms,
Down fell both spear and shield, down they as fast,
And the dire hiss renewed, and the dire form
Catched by contagion, like in punishment,
As in their crime. Thus was the applause they meant,
Turned to exploding hiss, triumph to shame
Cast on themselves from their own mouths. There stood
A grove hard by, sprung up with this their change,
His will Who reigns above, to aggravate
550 Their penance, laden with fair fruit, like that
Which grew in Paradise, the bait of Eve
Used by the tempter: on that prospect strange
Their earnest eyes they fixed, imagining
For one forbidden tree a multitude
Now risen, to work them further woe or shame;
Yet parched with scalding thirst and hunger fierce,
Though to delude them sent, could not abstain,
But on they rolled in heaps, and up the trees
Climbing, sat thicker than the snaky locks
560 That curled Megaera: greedily they plucked
The fruitage fair to sight, like that which grew
Near that bituminous lake° where Sodom flamed;   *(the Dead Sea)*

This more delusive, not the touch, but taste
Deceived; they fondly thinking to allay
Their appetite with gust,° instead of fruit   *relish*
Chewed bitter ashes, which the offended taste
With spattering noise rejected: oft they assayed,
Hunger and thirst constraining, drugged° as oft,   *sickened*
With hatefulest disrelish writhed their jaws
570   With soot and cinders filled; so oft they fell
Into the same illusion, not as man,
Whom they triumphed, once lapsed. Thus were they plagued
And worn with famine, long and ceaseless hiss,
Till their lost shape, permitted, they resumed,
Yearly enjoined, some say, to undergo
This annual humbling certain numbered days,
To dash their pride, and joy for man seduced.
However some tradition they dispersed
Among the heathen of their purchase got,
580   And fabled how the serpent, whom they called
Ophion with Eurynome, the wide-
Encroaching Eve perhaps, had first the rule
Of high Olympus, thence by Saturn driven
And Ops, ere yet Dictaean Jove was born.
Mean while in Paradise the hellish pair
Too soon arrived, Sin there in power before,
Once actual, now in body, and to dwell
Habitual habitant; behind her Death
Close following pace for pace, not mounted yet
590   On his pale horse: to whom Sin thus began.
    'Second of Satan sprung, all conquering Death,
What think'st thou of our empire now, though earned
With travail difficult, not better far
Than still at hell's dark threshold to have sat watch,
Unnamed, undreaded, and thy self half starved?'
    Whom thus the Sin-born monster answered soon.
'To me, who with eternal famine pine,
Alike is hell, or Paradise, or heaven,
There best, where most with ravine I may meet;
600   Which here, though plenteous, all too little seems
To stuff this maw, this vast unhide-bound° corpse.'   *emaciated*
    To whom the incestuous mother thus replied.
'Thou therefore on these herbs, and fruits, and flowers
Feed first, on each beast next, and fish, and fowl,
No homely morsels, and whatever thing
The scythe of time mows down, devour unspared,

Till I in man residing through the race,
His thoughts, his looks, words, actions all infect,
And season him thy last and sweetest prey.'
610   This said, they both betook them several ways,
Both to destroy, or unimmortal make
All kinds, and for destruction to mature
Sooner or later; which the Almighty seeing,
From his transcendent seat the saints among,
To those bright orders uttered thus his voice.
'See with what heat these dogs of hell advance
To waste and havoc yonder world, which I
So fair and good created, and had still
Kept in that state, had not the folly of man
620 Let in these wasteful furies, who impute
Folly to me, so doth the prince of hell
And his adherents, that with so much ease
I suffer them to enter and possess
A place so heavenly, and conniving seem
To gratify my scornful enemies,
That laugh, as if transported with some fit
Of passion, I to them had quitted° all,   *given up*
At random yielded up to their misrule;
And know not that I called and drew them thither
630 My hell-hounds, to lick up the draff° and filth   *dregs*
Which man's polluting sin with taint hath shed
On what was pure, till crammed and gorged, nigh burst
With sucked and glutted offal, at one sling
Of thy victorious arm, well-pleasing Son,
Both Sin, and Death, and yawning grave at last
Through Chaos hurled, obstruct the mouth of hell
For ever, and seal up his ravenous jaws.
Then heaven and earth renewed shall be made pure
To sanctity that shall receive no stain:
640 Till then the curse pronounced on both precedes.'
He ended, and the heavenly audience loud
Sung hallelujah, as the sound of seas,
Through multitude that sung: 'Just are thy ways,
Righteous are thy decrees on all thy works;
Who can extenuate° Thee? Next, to the Son,   *disparage*
Destined Restorer of mankind, by whom
New heaven and earth shall to the ages° rise,   *millenium*
Or down from heaven descend.' Such was their song,
While the Creator calling forth by name
650 His mighty angels gave them several charge,

As sorted best with present things. The sun
Had first his precept so to move, so shine,
As might affect the earth with cold and heat
Scarce tolerable, and from the north to call
Decrepit winter, from the south to bring
Solstitial summer's heat. To the blanc° moon   *pale*
Her office they prescribed, to the other five[191]
Their planetary motions and aspects
In sextile, square, and trine, and opposite,
660 Of noxious efficacy, and when to join
In synod unbenign, and taught the fixed
Their influence malignant when to shower,
Which of them rising with the sun, or falling,
Should prove tempestuous: to the winds they set
Their corners, when with bluster to confound
Sea, air, and shore, the thunder[192] when to roll
With terror through the dark aerial hall.
Some say he bid his angels turn askance[193]
The poles of earth twice ten degrees and more
670 From the sun's axle; they with labour pushed
Oblique the centric globe:° some say the sun   *(the earth)*
Was bid turn reins from the equinoctial road
Like distant breadth[194] to Taurus with the Seven
Atlantic Sisters,[195] and the Spartan Twins
Up to the tropic Crab; thence down amain°   *at full speed*
By Leo and the Virgin and the Scales,
As deep as Capricorn, to bring in change[196]
Of seasons to each clime;° else had the spring   *region*
Perpetual smiled on earth with vernant° flowers,   *vernal*
680 Equal in days and nights, except to those
Beyond the polar circles; to them day
Had unbenighted° shone, while the low sun   *unkindly*
To recompense his distance, in their sight
Had rounded still the horizon, and not known
Or east or west, which had forbid the snow
From cold Estotiland, and south as far
Beneath Magellan. At that tasted fruit
The sun, as from Thyestean banquet, turned
His course intended; else how had the world
690 Inhabited, though sinless, more than now,
Avoided pinching cold and scorching heat?
These changes in the heavens, though slow, produced
Like change on sea and land, sideral° blast,   *of the stars*
Vapour, and mist, and exhalation hot,

Corrupt and pestilent: now from the north
Of Norumbega, and the Samoed shore
Bursting their brazen dungeon, armed with ice
And snow and hail and stormy gust and flaw,
Boreas, and Caecias and Argestes loud
700 And Thrascias rend the woods and seas upturn;
With adverse blast upturns them from the south
Notus and Afer black with thunderous clouds
From Serraliona; thwart of these as fierce
Forth rush the Levant° and the Ponent° winds   *Eastern/Western*
Eurus and Zephir with their lateral noise,
Sirocco, and Libecchio. Thus began
Outrage from lifeless things; but Discord first
Daughter of Sin, among the irrational,
Death introduced through fierce antipathy:
710 Beast now with beast gan war, and fowl with fowl,
And fish with fish; to graze the herb all leaving,
Devoured each other; nor stood much in awe
Of man, but fled him, or with countenance grim
Glared on him passing: these were from without
The growing miseries, which Adam saw
Already in part, though hid in gloomiest shade,
To sorrow abandoned, but worse felt within,
And in a troubled sea of passion tossed,
Thus to disburden sought with sad complaint.
720   'O miserable of happy! Is this the end
Of this new glorious world, and me so late
The glory of that glory, who now become
Accurst of blessed, hide me from the face
Of God, whom to behold was then my highth
Of happiness: yet well, if here would end
The misery, I deserved it, and would bear
My own deservings; but this will not serve;
All that I eat or drink, or shall beget,
Is propagated° curse. O voice once heard   *handed down*
730 Delightfully, *Increase and multiply*,
Now death to hear! For what can I increase
Or multiply, but curses on my head?
Who of all ages to succeed, but feeling
The evil on him brought by me, will curse
My head, Ill fare our ancestor impure,
For this we may thank Adam; but his thanks
Shall be the execration; so besides
Mine own that bide upon me, all from me

Shall with a fierce reflux° on me redound,   *recoil*
740 On me, as on their natural centre, light,
Heavy, though in their place. O fleeting joys
Of Paradise, dear bought with lasting woes!
Did I request Thee, Maker, from my clay
To mould me man, did I solicit Thee
From darkness to promote me, or here place
In this delicious garden? As my will
Concurred not to my being, it were but right
And equal° to reduce me to my dust,   *just*
Desirous to resign, and render back
750 All I received, unable to perform
Thy terms too hard, by which I was to hold
The good I sought not. To the loss of that,
Sufficient penalty, why hast Thou added
The sense of endless woes? Inexplicable
Thy justice seems; yet to say truth, too late,
I thus contest; then should have been refused
Those terms whatever, when they were proposed:
Thou° didst accept them; wilt thou enjoy the good,   *(Adam)*
Then cavil the conditions? And though God
760 Made thee without thy leave, what if thy son
Prove disobedient, and reproved, retort,
Wherefore didst thou beget me? I sought it not:
Wouldst thou admit for his contempt of thee
That proud excuse? Yet him, not thy election,
But natural necessity begot.
God made thee of choice his own, and of his own
To serve Him, thy reward was of his grace,
Thy punishment then justly is at his will.
Be it so, for I submit, his doom° is fair,   *judgement*
770 That dust I am, and shall to dust return:
O welcome hour whenever! Why delays
His hand to execute what His decree
Fixed on this day? Why do I overlive,
Why am I mocked with death, and lengthened out
To deathless pain? How gladly would I meet
Mortality my sentence, and be earth
Insensible, how glad would lay me down
As in my mother's lap? There I should rest
And sleep secure; his dreadful voice no more
780 Would thunder in my ears, no fear of worse
To me and to my offspring would torment me
With cruel expectation. Yet one doubt

Pursues me still, lest all° I cannot die,   *wholly*
Lest that pure breath of life, the spirit of man
Which God inspired, cannot together perish
With this corporeal clod; then in the grave,
Or in some other dismal place who knows
But I shall die a living death? O thought
Horrid, if true! Yet why? It was but breath
790 Of life that sinned; what dies but what had life
And sin? The body properly hath neither.
All of me then shall die: let this appease
The doubt, since human reach no farther knows.
For though the Lord of all be infinite,
Is his wrath also? Be it, man is not so,
But mortal doomed. How can He exercise
Wrath without end on man whom death must end?
Can He make deathless death? That were to make
Strange contradiction, which to God Himself
800 Impossible is held, as argument°   *display*
Of weakness, not of power. Will He draw out,
For anger's sake, finite to infinite
In punished man, to satisfy his rigour
Satisfied never; that were to extend
His sentence beyond dust and nature's law,[197]
By which all causes else according still
To the reception of their matter act,
Not to the extent of their own sphere. But say
That death be not one stroke, as I supposed,
810 Bereaving° sense, but endless misery   *depriving of*
From this day onward, which I feel begun
Both in me, and without° me, and so last   *outside*
To perpetuity; ay me, that fear
Comes thundering back with dreadful revolution
On my defenceless head; both death and I
Am found eternal, and incorporate° both,   *united in one body*
Nor I on my part single,° in me all   *alone*
Posterity stands cursed: fair patrimony
That I must leave ye, sons; O were I able
820 To waste it all my self, and leave ye none!
So disinherited how would ye bless
Me now your curse! Ah, why should all mankind
For one man's fault thus guiltless be condemned,
If guiltless? But from me what can proceed,
But all corrupt, both mind and will depraved,
Not to do only, but to will the same

With me? How can they then acquitted stand
In sight of God? Him, after all disputes,
Forced, I absolve: all my evasions vain,[198]
830 And reasonings, though through mazes, lead me still
But to my own conviction: first and last
On me, me only, as the source and spring
Of all corruption, all the blame lights due;
So might the wrath. Fond wish! Couldst thou support
That burden heavier than the earth to bear
Than all the world much heavier, though divided
With that bad woman? Thus what thou desirest
And what thou fear'st, alike destroys all hope
Of refuge, and concludes thee miserable
840 Beyond all past example and future,
To Satan only like both crime and doom.
O conscience! into what abyss of fears
And horrors hast thou driven me; out of which
I find no way, from deep to deeper plunged!'
       Thus Adam to himself lamented loud
Through the still night, not now, as ere man fell,
Wholesome and cool, and mild, but with black air
Accompanied, with damps and dreadful gloom,
Which to his evil conscience represented
850 All things with double terror: on the ground
Outstretched he lay, on the cold ground, and oft
Cursed his creation, death as oft accused
Of tardy execution, since denounced°   *proclaimed*
The day of his offence. 'Why comes not death',
Said he, 'with one thrice acceptable stroke
To end me? Shall truth fail to keep her word,
Justice divine not hasten to be just?
But death comes not at call, justice divine
Mends not her slowest pace for prayers or cries.
860 O woods, O fountains, hillocks, dales and bowers,
With other echo late I taught your shades
To answer, and resound far other song.'
Whom thus afflicted when sad Eve beheld,
Desolate where she sat, approaching nigh,
Soft words to his fierce passion she assayed:
But her with stern regard he thus repelled.
       'Out of my sight, thou serpent, that name best
Befits thee with him leagued, thy self as false
And hateful; nothing wants, but that thy shape,
870 Like his, and colour serpentine, may show

Thy inward fraud, to warn all creatures from thee
Henceforth; lest that too heavenly form, pretended°   *devoted*
To hellish falsehood, snare them. But for thee
I had persisted happy, had not thy pride
And wandering vanity, when least was safe,
Rejected my forewarning, and disdained
Not to be trusted, longing to be seen
Though by the devil himself, him overweening°   *over-confident*
To over-reach, but with the Serpent meeting
880   Fooled and beguiled, by him thou, I by thee,
To trust thee from my side, imagined wise,
Constant, mature, proof against all assaults,
And understood not all was but a show
Rather than solid virtue, all but a rib
Crooked by nature, bent, as now appears,
More to the part sinister° from me drawn,   *left or corrupt*
Well if thrown out, as supernumerary
To my just° number found. O why did God,   *true*
Creator wise, that peopled highest heaven
890   With spirits masculine, create at last
This novelty on earth, this fair defect
Of nature, and not fill the world at once
With men as angels without feminine,
Or find some other way to generate
Mankind? This mischief had not then befallen,
And more that shall befall, innumerable
Disturbances on earth through female snares,
And strait conjunction with this sex: for either
He never shall find out fit mate, but such
900   As some misfortune brings him, or mistake,
Or whom he wishes most shall seldom gain
Through her perverseness, but shall see her gained
By a far worse, of if she love, withheld
By parents, or his happiest choice too late
Shall meet, already linked and wedlock-bound
To a fell adversary, his hate or shame:
Which infinite calamity shall cause
To human life, and household peace confound.'
     He added not, and from her turned, but Eve
910   Not so repulsed, with tears that ceased not flowing,
And tresses all disordered, at his feet
Fell humble, and embracing them, besought
His peace, and thus proceeded in her plaint.
     'Forsake me not thus, Adam, witness heaven

What love sincere, and reverence in my heart
I bear thee, and unweeting° have offended,   *unknowingly*
Unhappily deceived; thy suppliant
I beg, and clasp thy knees; bereave me not,
Whereon I live, thy gentle looks, thy aid,
920 Thy counsel in this uttermost distress
My only strength and stay: forlorn of thee,
Whither shall I betake me, where subsist?
While yet we live, scarce one short hour perhaps,
Between us two let there be peace, both joining,
As joined in injuries, one enmity
Against a foe by doom° express° assigned us,   *judgement/clear*
That cruel serpent: on me exercise not
Thy hatred for this misery befallen,
On me already lost, me than thy self
930 More miserable; both have sinned, but thou
Against God only, I against God and thee,
And to the place of judgment will return,
There with my cries importune heaven, that all
The sentence from thy head removed may light
On me, sole cause to thee of all this woe,
Me me only just object of his ire.'
      She ended weeping, and her lowly plight,
Immovable till peace obtained from fault
Acknowledged and deplored, in Adam wrought
940 Commiseration; soon his heart relented
Towards her, his life so late and sole delight,
Now at his feet submissive in distress,
Creature so fair his reconcilement seeking,
His counsel whom she had displeased, his aid;
As one disarmed, his anger all he lost,
And thus with peaceful words upraised her soon.
      'Unwary, and too desirous, as before,
So now of what thou know'st not, who desir'st
The punishment all on thy self; alas,
950 Bear thine own first, ill able to sustain
His full wrath whose thou feel'st as yet least part,
And my displeasure bear'st so ill. If prayers
Could alter high decrees, I to that place
Would speed before thee, and be louder heard,
That on my head all might be visited,
Thy frailty and infirmer sex forgiven,
To me committed and by me exposed.
But rise, let us no more contend, nor blame

Each other, blamed enough elsewhere, but strive
960 In offices of love, how we may lighten
Each other's burden in our share of woe;
Since this day's death denounced,° if aught I see,   *proclaimed*
Will prove no sudden, but a slow-paced evil,
A long day's dying to augment our pain,
And to our seed (O hapless seed!) derived.°   *passed on*
    To whom thus Eve, recovering heart, replied.
'Adam, by sad experiment I know
How little weight my words with thee can find,
Found so erroneous, thence by just event°   *consequence*
970 Found so unfortunate; nevertheless
Restored by thee, vile as I am, to place
Of new acceptance, hopeful to regain
Thy love, the sole contentment of my heart
Living or dying, from thee I will not hide
What thoughts in my unquiet breast are risen,
Tending to some relief of our extremes,
Or end, though sharp and sad, yet tolerable,
As in° our evils, and of easier choice.   *considering*
If care of our descent° perplex us most,   *descendants*
980 Which must be born to certain woe, devoured
By death at last, and miserable it is
To be to others cause of misery,
Our own begotten, and of our loins to bring
Into this cursed world a woeful race,
That after wretched life must be at last
Food for so foul a monster, in thy power
It lies, yet ere conception to prevent
The race unblest, to being yet unbegot.
Childless thou art, childless remain: so Death
990 Shall be deceived his glut, and with us two
Be forced to satisfy his ravenous maw.
But if thou judge it hard and difficult,
Conversing, looking, loving, to abstain
From love's due rights, nuptial embraces sweet,
And with desire to languish without hope,
Before the present object° languishing   *Eve*
With like desire, which would be misery
And torment less than none of what we dread,
Then both our selves and seed at once to free
1000 From what we fear for both, let us make short,
Let us seek death, or he not found, supply
With our own hands his office on our selves;

Why stand we longer shivering under fears,
That show no end but death, and have the power,
Of many ways to die the shortest choosing,
Destruction with destruction to destroy.'
     She ended here, or vehement despair
Broke off the rest; so much of death her thoughts
Had entertained, as dyed her cheeks with pale.
1010 But Adam with such counsel nothing swayed,
To better hopes his more attentive mind
Labouring had raised, and thus to Eve replied.
     'Eve, thy contempt of life and pleasure seems
To argue in thee something more sublime
And excellent than what thy mind contemns;
But self-destruction therefore sought, refutes
That excellence thought in thee, and implies,
Not thy contempt, but anguish and regret
For loss of life and pleasure overloved.
1020 Or if thou covet death, as utmost end
Of misery, so thinking to evade
The penalty pronounced, doubt not but God
Hath wiselier armed his vengeful ire than so
To be forestalled; much more I fear lest death
So snatched will not exempt us from the pain
We are by doom to pay; rather such acts
Of contumacy° will provoke the highest   *perversity*
To make death in us live: then let us seek
Some safer resolution, which methinks
1030 I have in view, calling to mind with heed
Part of our sentence, that thy seed shall bruise
The serpent's head; piteous amends, unless
Be meant, whom I conjecture, our grand foe
Satan, who in the serpent hath contrived
Against us this deceit: to crush his head
Would be revenge indeed; which will be lost
By death brought on our selves, or childless days
Resolved, as thou proposest; so our foe
Shall scape his punishment ordained, and we
1040 Instead shall double ours upon our heads.
No more be mentioned then of violence
Against our selves, and wilful barrenness,
That cuts us off from hope, and savours only
Rancour and pride, impatience and despite,
Reluctance° against God and his just yoke   *resistance*
Laid on our necks. Remember with what mild

And gracious temper He both heard and judged
Without wrath or reviling; we expected
Immediate dissolution, which we thought
1050 Was meant by death that day, when lo, to thee
Pains only in child-bearing were foretold,
And bringing forth, soon recompensed with joy,
Fruit of thy womb: on me the curse aslope°   *indirect*
Glanced on the ground, with labour I must earn
My bread; what harm? Idleness had been worse;
My labour will sustain me; and lest cold
Or heat should injure us, his timely care
Hath unbesought provided, and his hands
Clothed us unworthy, pitying while he judged;
1060 How much more, if we pray him, will his ear
Be open, and his heart to pity incline,
And teach us further by what means to shun
The inclement seasons, rain, ice, hail and snow,
Which now the sky with various face begins
To show us in this mountain, while the winds
Blow moist and keen, shattering the graceful locks
Of these fair spreading trees; which bids us seek
Some better shroud°, some better warmth to cherish   *cover*
Our limbs benumbed, ere this diurnal star°   *(the sun)*
1070 Leave cold the night, how we his gathered beams
Reflected, may with matter sere° foment°,   *dry/make heat*
Or by collision of two bodies grind
The air attrite° to fire, as late the clouds   *worn by friction*
Justling° or pushed with winds rude in their shock   *jostling*
Tine° the slant lightning, whose thwart flame driven down   *ignite*
Kindles the gummy bark of fir or pine,
And sends a comfortable heat from far,
Which might supply° the sun: such fire to use,   *replace*
And what may else be remedy or cure
1080 To evils which our own misdeeds have wrought,
He will instruct us praying, and of grace
Beseeching him, so as we need not fear
To pass commodiously this life, sustained
By Him with many comforts, till we end
In dust, our final rest and native home.
What better can we do, than to the place
Repairing where He judged us, prostrate fall
Before Him reverent, and there confess
Humbly our faults, and pardon beg, with tears[199]
1090 Watering the ground, and with our sighs the air

Frequenting, sent from hearts contrite, in sign   *filling*
Of sorrow, unfeigned, and humiliation meek.
Undoubtedly He will relent and turn
From his displeasure; in whose look serene,
When angry most He seemed and most severe,
What else but favour, grace, and mercy shone?'
   So spake our father penitent, nor Eve
Felt less remorse: they forthwith to the place
Repairing where He judged them prostrate fell
1100 Before him reverent, and both confessed
Humbly their faults, and pardon begged, with tears
Watering the ground, and with their sighs the air
Frequenting, sent from hearts contrite, in sign
Of sorrow unfeigned, and humiliation meek.

[1669]

Samson Agonistes[200]

A DRAMATIC POEM[201]

Characters:
Samson   Public Officer
Manoa, the father of Samson   Messenger
Dalila, his wife   Chorus of Danites
Harapha of Gath

The Scene, before the prison in Gaza

Samson   A little onward lend thy guiding hand
To these dark steps, a little further on,
For yonder bank hath choice of sun or shade;
There I am wont to sit, when any chance
Relieves me from my task of servile toil,
Daily in the common prison else enjoined° me,   *ordered*
Where I, a prisoner chained, scarce freely draw
The air imprisoned also, close and damp,
Unwholesome draught. But here I feel amends,
10 The breath of heaven fresh-blowing, pure and sweet,
With day-spring° born; here leave me to respire.°   *daybreak/breathe*
This day a solemn feast the people hold
To Dagon their sea-idol, and forbid

Laborious works; unwillingly this rest
Their superstition yields me; hence with leave
Retiring from the popular noise, I seek
This unfrequented place to find some ease,
Ease to the body some, none to the mind
From restless thoughts, that like a deadly swarm
20 Of hornets armed, no sooner found alone,
But rush upon me thronging, and present
Times past, what once I was, and what am now.
O wherefore was my birth from heaven foretold
Twice by an angel, who at last in sight
Of both my parents all in flames ascended
From off the altar, where an offering burned,
As in a fiery column charioting
His godlike presence, and from some great act
Or benefit revealed to Abraham's race°?   (the Jews)
30 Why was my breeding ordered and prescribed
As of a person separate²⁰² to God,
Designed for great exploits, if I must die
Betrayed, captived, and both my eyes put out,
Made of my enemies the scorn and gaze;
To grind in brazen fetters under task°   imposed work
With this heaven-gifted strength? O glorious strength,
Put to the labour of a beast, debased
Lower than bondslave! Promise was that I
Should Israel from Philistian yoke deliver;
40 Ask for this great deliverer now, and find him
Eyeless in Gaza at the mill with slaves,
Himself in bonds under Philistian yoke;
Yet stay, let me not rashly call in doubt
Divine prediction; what if all foretold
Had been fulfilled but through mine own default?
Whom have I to complain of but myself?
Who this high gift of strength committed to me,
In what part lodged, how easily bereft me,
Under the seal of silence could not keep
50 But weakly to a woman must reveal it,
O'ercome with importunity and tears.
O impotence of mind, in body strong!
But what is strength without a double share
Of wisdom? vast, unwieldy, burdensome,
Proudly secure°, yet liable to fall   over-confident
By weakest subtleties; not made to rule,
But to subserve where wisdom bears command.

God, when he gave me strength, to show withal
How slight the gift was, hung it in my hair.
60 But peace! I must not quarrel with the will
Of highest dispensation, which herein
Haply had ends above my reach to know:
Suffices that to me strength is my bane,
And proves the source of all my miseries,
So many, and so huge, that each apart
Would ask a life to wail; but chief of all,
O loss of sight, of thee I most complain!
Blind among enemies, O worse than chains,
Dungeon, or beggary, or decrepit age!
70 Light, the prime work of God, to me is extinct,[203]
And all her various objects of delight
Annulled, which might in part my grief have eased,
Inferior to the vilest now become
Of man or worm; the vilest here excel me,
They creep, yet see; I dark in light exposed
To daily fraud, contempt, abuse and wrong,
Within doors, or without, still as a fool,
In power of others, never in my own;
Scarce half I seem to live, dead more than half.
80 O dark, dark, dark, amid the blaze of noon,
Irrecoverably dark, total eclipse
Without all hope of day!
O first-created beam, and thou great Word,
'Let there be light, and light was over all';
Why am I thus bereaved thy prime decree?
The sun to me is dark
And silent as the moon,
When she deserts the night,
Hid in her vacant interlunar cave.
90 Since light so necessary is to life,
And almost life itself, if it be true
That light is in the soul,
She all in every part,[204] why was the sight
To such a tender ball as the eye confined?
So obvious and so easy to be quenched,
And not, as feeling, through all parts diffused,
That she might look at will through every pore?
Then had I not been thus exiled from light,
As in the land of darkness, yet in light,
100 To live a life half dead, a living death,
And buried; but O yet more miserable!

Myself my sepulchre, a moving grave,
Buried, not yet exempt
By privilege of death and burial
From worst of other evils, pains and wrongs,
But made hereby obnoxious° more   *exposed to*
To all the miseries of life,
Life in captivity
Among inhuman foes.
110 But who are these? For with joint pace I hear
The tread of many feet steering this way;
Perhaps my enemies who come to stare
At my affliction, and perhaps to insult,
Their daily practice to afflict me more.
Chorus   This, this is he; softly a while;
Let us not break in upon him.
O change beyond report, thought, or belief!
See how he lies at random, carelessly diffused°,   *spread out*
With languished head unpropped,
120 As one past hope, abandoned,
And by himself given over;
In slavish habit, ill-fitted weeds°   *clothes*
O'erworn and soiled;
Or do my eyes misrepresent? Can this be he,
That heroic, that renowned,
Irresistible Samson? Whom unarmed
No strength of man, or fiercest wild beast could withstand;
Who tore the lion, as the lion tears the kid,
Ran on embattled armies clad in iron,
130 And, weaponless himself
Made arms ridiculous, useless the forgery°   *forging*
Of brazen shield and spear, the hammered cuirass°,   *breastplate*
Chalybean-tempered steel, and frock of mail
Adamantean° proof;   *indestructible*
But safe he who stood aloof,
When insupportably° his foot advanced,   *not to be endured*
In scorn of their proud arms and warlike tools,
Spurned them to death by troops. The bold Ascalonite
Fled from his lion ramp°, old warriors turned   *aggressive stand*
140 Their plated° backs under his heel;   *in armour*
Or grovelling soiled their crested helmets in the dust.
Then with what trivial weapon came to hand,
The jaw of a dead ass, his sword of bone,
A thousand foreskins° fell, the flower of Palestine,[205] *(Philistines)*
In Ramath-lechi, famous to this day;

Then by main force pulled up, and on his shoulders bore
The gates of Azza,° post and massy bar,   *Gaza*
Up to the hill by Hebron, seat of giants old,
No journey of a Sabbath day, and loaded so;
150 Like whom° the Gentiles feign to bear up heaven.   *(Atlas)*
Which shall I first bewail,
Thy bondage or lost sight,
Prison within prison
Inseparably dark?
Thou art become (O worst imprisonment!)
The dungeon of thyself; thy soul
(Which men enjoying sight oft without cause complain)
Imprisoned now indeed,
In real darkness of the body dwells,
160 Shut up from outward light
To incorporate with gloomy night;
For inward light, alas,
Puts forth no visual beam.
O mirror of our fickle state,
Since man on earth unparalleled!
The rarer thy example stands,
By how much from the top of wondrous glory,
Strongest of mortal men,
To lowest pitch of abject fortune thou art fallen.
170 For him I reckon not in high estate
Whom long descent of birth
Or the sphere° of fortune raises;   *wheel*
But thee whose strength, while virtue was her mate,
Might have subdued the earth,
Universally crowned with highest praises.
Samson   I hear the sound of words, their sense the air
Dissolves unjointed ere it reach my ear.
Chorus   He speaks, let us draw nigh. Matchless in might,
The glory late of Israel, now the grief,
180 We come thy friends and neighbours not unknown
From Eshtaol and Zora's fruitful vale
To visit or bewail thee, or if better,
Counsel or consolation we may bring,
Salve to thy sores; apt words have power to 'suage°   *assuage*
The tumours of a troubled mind,
And are as balm to festered wounds.
Samson   Your coming, friends, revives me, for I learn
Now of my own experience, not by talk,
How counterfeit a coin they are who friends

190 Bear in their superscription° (of the most   *stamp on coin*
I would be understood); in prosperous days
They swarm, but in adverse withdraw their head,
Not to be found, though sought. Ye see, O friends,
How many evils have enclosed me round;
Yet that which was the worst now least afflicts me,
Blindness, for had I sight, confused with shame,
How could I once look up, or heave the head,
Who like a foolish pilot have shipwrecked
My vessel trusted to me from above,
200 Gloriously rigged; and for a word, a tear,
Fool, have divulged the secret gift of God
To a deceitful woman: tell me, friends,
Am I not sung and proverbed° for a fool *made into a proverb*
In every street, do they not say, how well
Are come upon him his deserts? yet why?
Immeasurable strength they might behold
In me, of wisdom nothing more than mean;°   *average*
This with the other should, at least, have paired,
These two proportioned ill drove me transverse.° *off course*
210 **Chorus** Tax not divine disposal, wisest men
Have erred, and by bad women been deceived;
And shall again, pretend they ne'er so wise.
Deject not then so overmuch thyself,
Who hast of sorrow thy full load besides;
Yet truth to say, I oft have heard men wonder
Why thou shouldst wed Philistian women rather
Than of thine own tribe fairer, or as fair,
At least of thy own nation, and as noble.
Samson The first I saw at Timna, and she pleased
220 Me, not my parents, that I sought to wed
The daughter of an infidel; they knew not
That what I motioned was of God; I knew
From intimate impulse, and therefore urged
The marriage on; that by occasion hence
I might begin Israel's deliverance,
The work to which I was divinely called;
She proving false, the next I took to wife
(O that I never had! fond wish too late)
Was in the vale of Sorec, Dalila,
230 That specious° monster, my accomplished snare.[206] *showy*
I thought it lawful from my former act,
And the same end; still watching to oppress
Israel's oppressors: of what now I suffer

She was not the prime cause, but I myself,
Who vanquished with a peal of words (O weakness!)
Gave up my fort of silence to a woman.
Chorus   In seeking just occasion to provoke
The Philistine, thy country's enemy,
Thou never wast remiss, I bear thee witness:
240 Yet Israel still serves with all his sons.
Samson   That fault I take not on me, but transfer
On Israel's governors, and heads of tribes,
Who seeing those great acts which God had done
Singly by me against their conquerors,
Acknowledged not, or not at all considered
Deliverance offered: I on the other side
Used no ambition° to commend my deeds;   *desire of honour*
The deeds themselves, though mute, spoke loud the doer;
But they persisted deaf, and would not seem
250 To count them things worth notice, till at length
Their lords the Philistines with gathered powers
Entered Judea seeking me, who then
Safe to the rock of Etham was retired,
Not flying, but forecasting in what place
To set upon them, what advantaged best;
Meanwhile the men of Judah, to prevent
The harass of their land, beset me round;
I willingly on some conditions came
Into their hands, and they as gladly yield me
260 To the uncircumcised a welcome prey,
Bound with two cords; but cords to me were threads
Touched with the flame: on their whole host I flew
Unarmed, and with a trivial weapon° felled   *(jawbone of an ass)*
Their choicest youth; they only lived who fled.
Had Judah that day joined, or one whole tribe,
They had by this° possessed the towers of Gath,   *now*
And lorded over them whom now they serve;
But what more oft in nations grown corrupt,
And by their vices brought to servitude,
270 Than to love bondage more than liberty,
Bondage with ease than strenuous liberty;
And to despise, or envy, or suspect
Whom God hath of his special favour raised
As their deliverer; if he aught begin,
How frequent to desert him, and at last
To heap ingratitude on worthiest deeds?
Chorus   Thy words to my remembrance bring

How Succoth and the fort of Penuel
Their great deliverer contemned,
280 The matchless Gideon in pursuit
Of Madian and her vanquished kings:
And how ingrateful Ephraim
Had dealt with Jephtha, who by argument,
Not worse than by his shield and spear,
Defended Israel from the Ammonite,
Had not his prowess quelled their pride
In that sore battle when so many died
Without reprieve adjudged to death,
For want of well pronouncing *Shibboleth.*
290 **Samson**   Of such examples add me to the roll;
Me easily indeed mine° may neglect   *(my people)*
But God's proposed deliverance not so.
Chorus   Just are the ways of God,
And justifiable to men;
Unless there be who think not God at all:
If any be, they walk obscure;
For of such doctrine never was there school,
But the heart of the fool,
And no man therein doctor but himself.
300   Yet more there be who doubt his ways not just,
As to his own edìcts, found contradicting,
Then give the reins to wandering thought,
Regardless of his glory's diminution;
Till by their own perplexities involved
They ravel° more, still less resolved,   *become entangled*
But never find self-satisfying solution.
    As if they would confine the interminable,°   *eternal*
And tie Him to his own prescript,°   *precepts*
Who made our laws to bind us, not Himself,
310 And hath full right to exempt
Whomso it pleases Him by choice
From national obstriction,° without taint   *obligation*
Of sin, or legal debt;²⁰⁷
For with his own laws He can best dispense.
    He would not else, who never wanted means,
Nor, in respect of the enemy, just cause,
To set his people free,
Have prompted this heroic Nazarite,
Against his vow of strictest purity,²⁰⁸
320 To seek in marriage that fallacious° bride,²⁰⁹   *deceitful*
Unclean, unchaste.

Down, reason, then, at least vain reasonings down,
Though reason here aver
That moral verdict quits her of unclean:
Unchaste was subsequent; her stain, not his.
    But see, here comes thy reverend sire
With careful° step, locks white as down,   *full of care*
Old Mánoa: advise
Forthwith how thou ought'st to receive him.
Samson   Ay me, another inward grief awaked
With mention of that name renews the assault.
Manoa   Brethren and men of Dan, for such ye seem,
Though in this uncouth° place; if old respect,   *strange*
As I suppose, towards your once gloried friend,
My son now captive, hither hath informed°   *directed*
Your younger feet, while mine cast back with age
Came lagging after; say if he be here.
Chorus   As signal° now in low dejected state,   *outstanding*
As erst° in highest, behold him where he lies.   *formerly*
340   **Manoa**   O miserable change! is this the man,
That invincible Samson, far renowned,
The dread of Israel's foes, who with a strength
Equivalent to angels' walked their streets,
None offering fight; who, single combatant,
Duelled° their armies ranked in proud array,   *fought as in a duel*
Himself an army, now unequal match
To save himself against a coward armed
At one spear's length? O ever-failing trust
In mortal strength! and oh what not in man
350   Deceivable and vain! Nay, what thing good
Prayed for, but often proves our woe, our bane?
I prayed for children, and thought barrenness
In wedlock a reproach; I gained a son,
And such a son as all men hailed me happy:
Who would be now a father in my stead?
O wherefore did God grant me my request,
And as a blessing with such pomp adorned?
Why are his gifts desirable, to tempt
Our earnest prayers, then given with solemn hand
360   As graces°, draw a scorpion's tail behind?   *favours*
For this did the angel twice descend? For this
Ordained thy nurture° holy, as of a plant   *upbringing*
Select and sacred, glorious for a while,
The miracle of men; then in an hour
Ensnared, assaulted, overcome, led bound,

Thy foes' derision, captive, poor, and blind,
Into a dungeon thrust, to work with slaves?
Alas, methinks whom God hath chosen once
To worthiest deeds, if he through frailty err,
370 He should not so o'erwhelm, and as a thrall°   *slave*
Subject him to so foul indignities,
Be it but for honour's sake of former deeds.
    Samson   Appoint° not heavenly disposition, father.   *prescribe*
Nothing of all these evils hath befallen me
But justly; I myself have brought them on,
Sole author I, sole cause: if aught seem vile,
As vile hath been my folly, who have profaned
The mystery of God given me under pledge
Of vow, and have betrayed it to a woman,
380 A Canaanite,[210] my faithless enemy.
This well I knew, nor was at all surprised,
But warned by oft experience: did not she
Of Timna first betray me, and reveal
The secret wrested from me in her highth
Of nuptial love professed, carrying it straight
To them who had corrupted her, my spies,
And rivals? In this other was there found
More faith? Who also in her prime of love,
Spousal embraces, vitiated with gold,
390 Though offered only, by the scent conceived
Her spurious first-born, treason against me.
Thrice she assayed with flattering prayer and sighs
And amorous reproaches to win from me
My capital[211] secret, in what part my strength
Lay stored, in what part summed;° that she might know: *collected*
Thrice I deluded her, and turned to sport
Her importunity, each time perceiving
How openly, and with what impudence,
She purposed to betray me, and (which was worse
400 Than undissembled hate) with what contempt
She sought to make me traitor to myself;
Yet the fourth time, when mustering all her wiles,
With blandished parleys,° feminine assaults,   *wheedling conversation*
Tongue-batteries, she surceased° not day nor night   *stopped*
To storm me over-watched,° and wearied out,   *too long awake*
At times when men seek most repose and rest,
I yielded, and unlocked her all my heart,
Who with a grain of manhood well resolved
Might easily have shook off all her snares;

410 But foul effeminacy held me yoked
    Her bondslave; O indignity, O blot
    To honour and religion! servile mind
    Rewarded well with servile punishment!
    The base degree to which I now am fallen,
    These rags, this grinding,° is not yet so base   *work at the mill*
    As was my former servitude, ignoble,
    Unmanly, ignominious, infamous,
    True slavery, and that blindness worse than this,
    That saw not how degenerately I served.
420 **Manoa**   I cannot praise thy marriage choices, son,
    Rather approved them not; but thou didst plead
    Divine impulsion prompting how thou might'st
    Find some occasion to infest° our foes.   *attack*
    I state not that; this I am sure, our foes
    Found soon occasion thereby to make thee
    Their captive, and their triumph; thou the sooner
    Temptation found'st, or over-potent charms,
    To violate the sacred trust of silence
    Deposited within thee; which to have kept
430 Tacit was in thy power; true; and thou bear'st
    Enough, and more, the burden of that fault;
    Bitterly hast thou paid, and still art paying,
    That rigid score.° A worse thing yet remains: *account*
    This day the Philistines a popular feast
    Here celebrate in Gaza, and proclaim
    Great pomp, and sacrifice, and praises loud
    To Dagon, as their god who hath delivered
    Thee, Samson, bound and blind into their hands,
    Them out of thine, who slew'st them many a slain.
440 So Dagon shall be magnified, and God,
    Besides whom is no god, compared with idols,
    Disglorified, blasphemed, and had in scorn
    By the idolatrous rout° amidst their wine;   *rabble*
    Which to have come to pass by means of thee,
    Samson, of all thy sufferings think the heaviest,
    Of all reproach the most with shame that ever
    Could have befallen thee and thy father's house.
    Samson   Father, I do acknowledge and confess
    That I this honour, I this pomp have brought
450 To Dagon, and advanced his praises high
    Among the heathen round; to God have brought
    Dishonour, obloquy,° and oped the mouths   *disgrace*
    Of idolists° and atheists; have brought scandal   *idolaters*

To Israel, diffidence° of God, and doubt   *distrust*
In feeble hearts, propense° enough before   *disposed*
To waver, or fall off and join with idols:
Which is my chief affliction, shame and sorrow,
The anguish of my soul, that suffers not
Mine eye to harbour sleep, or thoughts to rest.
460   This only hope relieves me, that the strife
With me hath end; all the contest is now
'Twixt God and Dagon; Dagon hath presumed,
Me overthrown, to enter lists with God,
His deity comparing and preferring
Before the God of Abraham. He, be sure,
Will not connive,° or linger, thus provoked,   *ignore*
But will arise and his great name assert:
Dagon must stoop, and shall ere long receive
Such a discomfit,° as shall quite despoil him   *defeat*
470   Of all these boasted trophies won on me,
And with confusion blank° his worshippers.   *bring to nothing*
Manoa   With cause this hope relieves thee, and these words
I as a prophecy receive; for God,
Nothing more certain, will not long defer
To vindicate the glory of his name
Against all competition, nor will long
Endure it doubtful whether God be Lord,
Or Dagon. But for thee what shall be done?
Thou must not in the meanwhile, here forgot,
480   Lie in this miserable loathsome plight[212]
Neglected. I already have made way
To some Philistian lords, with whom to treat
About thy ransom: well they may by this
Have satisfied their utmost of revenge
By pains and slaveries, worse than death, inflicted
On thee, who now no more canst do them harm.
Samson   Spare that proposal, father, spare the trouble
Of that solicitation; let me here,
As I deserve, pay on my punishment;
490   And expiate, if possible, my crime,
Shameful garrulity. To have revealed
Secrets of men, the secrets of a friend,
How heinous had the fact° been, how deserving   *deed*
Contempt, and scorn of all, to be excluded
All friendship, and avoided as a blab,
The mark of fool set on his front!°   *forehead*
But I God's counsel have not kept, his holy secret

Presumptuously have published, impiously,
Weakly at least, and shamefully: a sin
500 That Gentiles in their parables condemn
To their abyss and horrid pains confined.²¹³
Manoa   Be penitent and for thy fault contrite,
But act not in thy own affliction, son;
Repent the sin, but if the punishment
Thou canst avoid, self-preservation bids;
Or the execution° leave to high disposal,   *outcome*
And let another hand, not thine, exact
Thy penal forfeit from thyself; perhaps
God will relent, and quit° thee all his debt;   *cancel*
510 Who ever more approves and more accepts
(Best pleased with humble and filial submission)
Him who imploring mercy sues for life,
Than who self-rigorous chooses death as due;
Which argues over-just, and self-displeased
For self-offence, more than for God offended.
Reject not then what offered means who knows
But God hath set before us, to return thee
Home to thy country and his sacred house,
Where thou mayst bring thy offerings, to avert
520 His further ire, with prayers and vows renewed.
Samson   His pardon I implore; but as for life,
To what end should I seek it? When in strength
All mortals I excelled, and great in hopes
With youthful courage and magnanimous thoughts
Of birth from heaven foretold and high exploits,
Full of divine instinct, after some proof
Of acts indeed heroic, far beyond
The sons of Anak, famous now and blazed,°   *made public*
Fearless of danger, like a petty god
530 I walked about admired of all and dreaded
On hostile ground, none daring my affront.°   *provocation*
Then swollen with pride into the snare I fell
Of fair fallacious looks, venereal trains,°   *snares of love*
Softened with pleasure and voluptuous life;
At length to lay my head and hallowed pledge
Of all my strength in the lascivious lap
Of a deceitful concubine who shore° me   *sheared*
Like a tame wether, all my precious fleece,   *castrated ram*
Then turned me out ridiculous, despoiled,
540 Shaven, and disarmed among my enemies.
Chorus   Desire of wine and all delicious drinks,

Which many a famous warrior overturns,
Thou couldst repress, nor did the dancing ruby
Sparkling outpoured, the flavour, or the smell,
Or taste that cheers the heart of gods and men,
Allure thee from the cool crystalline stream.

Samson   Wherever fountain or fresh current flowed
Against° the eastern[214] ray, translucent, pure   *in the direction of*
With touch ethereal of heaven's fiery rod,
550 I drank, from the clear milky juice° allaying   *fresh water*
Thirst, and refreshed; nor envied them the grape
Whose heads that turbulent liquor fills with fumes.

Chorus   O madness, to think use of strongest wines
And strongest drinks our chief support of health,
When God with these forbidden made choice to rear
His mighty champion, strong above compare,
Whose drink was only from the liquid brook.

Samson   But what availed this temperance, not complete
Against another object more enticing?
560 What boots it° at one gate to make defence,   *use is it*
And at another to let in the foe,
Effeminately vanquished? By which means,
Now blind, disheartened, shamed, dishonoured, quelled,
To what can I be useful, wherein serve
My nation, and the work from heaven imposed,
But to sit idle on the household hearth,
A burdenous drone°? To visitants a gaze°   *idler/spectacle*
Or pitied object; these redundant° locks,   *overflowing*
Robustious° to no purpose, clustering down,   *robust*
570 Vain monument of strength; till length of years
And sedentary numbness craze° my limbs   *enfeeble*
To a contemptible old age obscure.
Here rather let me drudge and earn my bread,
Till vermin or the draff° of servile food   *leavings*
Consume me, and oft-invocated death
Hasten the welcome end of all my pains.

Manoa   Wilt thou then serve the Philistines with that gift
Which was expressly given thee to annoy° them?   *injure*
Better at home lie bed-rid, not only idle,
580 Inglorious, unemployed, with age outworn.
But God, who caused a fountain at thy prayer
From the dry ground to spring, thy thirst to allay
After the brunt of battle, can as easy
Cause light again within thy eyes to spring,
Wherewith to serve him better than thou hast;

And I persuade me so; why else this strength
Miraculous yet remaining in those locks?
His might continues in thee not for naught,
Nor shall his wondrous gifts be frustrate thus.

590 **Samson**   All otherwise to me my thoughts portend,
That these dark orbs no more shall treat with light,
Nor the other light of life continue long,
But yield to double darkness nigh at hand:
So much I feel my genial spirits[215] droop,
My hopes all flat; nature within me seems
In all her functions weary of herself;
My race of glory run, and race of shame,
And I shall shortly be with them that rest.

Manoa   Believe not these suggestions,° which proceed   *intimations*
600 From anguish of the mind and humours black,[216]
That mingle with thy fancy. I however
Must not omit a father's timely care
To prosecute the means of thy deliverance
By ransom or how else: meanwhile be calm,
And healing words from these thy friends admit.

Samson   O that torment should not be confined
To the body's wounds and sores,
With maladies innumerable
In heart, head, breast, and reins;°   *kidneys*
610 But must secret passage find
To the inmost mind,
There exercise all his fierce accidents,°   *symptoms*
And on her purest spirits prey,
As on entrails, joints, and limbs,
With answerable° pains, but more intense,   *corresponding*
Though void of corporal sense.
   My griefs not only pain me
As a lingering disease,
But finding no redress, ferment and rage,
620 Nor less than wounds immedicable°   *untreatable*
Rankle, and fester, and gangrene,
To black mortification.
Thoughts, my tormentors, armed with deadly stings
Mangle my apprehensive° tenderest parts,   *sensitive*
Exasperate, exulcerate,° and raise   *cause ulcers*
Dire inflammation which no cooling herb
Or med'cinal liquor can assuage,
Nor breath of vernal air from snowy alp.
Sleep hath forsook and given me o'er

630 To death's benumbing opium as my only cure.
Thence faintings, swoonings of despair,
And sense of heaven's desertion.
    I was his nursling once and choice delight,
His destined from the womb,
Promised by heavenly message. twice descending.
Under his special eye
Abstemious I grew up and thrived amain;
He led me on to mightiest deeds
Above the nerve° of mortal arm   strength
640 Against the uncircumcised, our enemies.
But now hath cast me off as never known,
And to those cruel enemies,
Whom I by his appointment had provoked,
Left me all helpless with the irreparable loss
Of sight, reserved alive to be repeated°   recited as
The subject of their cruelty or scorn.
Nor am I in the list of them that hope;
Hopeless are all my evils, all remediless;
This one prayer yet remains, might I be heard,
650 No long petition, speedy death,
The close of all my miseries, and the balm.
Chorus   Many are the sayings of the wise
In ancient and in modern books enrolled,
Extolling patience as the truest fortitude;
And to the bearing well of all calamities,
All chances incident to man's frail life,
Consolatories° writ   consolations
With studied argument, and much persuasion sought,
Lenient° of grief and anxious thought;   soothing
660 But with the afflicted in his pangs their sound
Little prevails, or rather seems a tune
Harsh, and of dissonant mood from his complaint,
Unless he feel within
Some source of consolation from above,
Secret refreshings that repair his strength,
And fainting spirits uphold.
    God of our fathers, what is man!
That thou towards him with hand so various,
Or might I say contrarious?
670 Temper'st thy providence through his short course,
Not evenly, as thou rul'st
The angelic orders and inferior creatures mute,
Irrational and brute.°   unreasoning

Nor do I name of men the common rout,°   *rabble*
That wandering loose about
Grow up and perish, as the summer fly,
Heads without name no more remembered;
But such as thou hast solemnly elected,
With gifts and graces eminently adorned
680   To some great work, thy glory,
And people's safety, which in part they effect;°   *produce*
Yet toward these thus dignified, thou oft
Amidst their highth of noon
Changest thy countenance and thy hand, with no regard
Of highest favours past
From thee on them, or them to thee of service.
    Nor only dost degrade them, or remit
To life obscured, which were a fair dismission,°   *dismissal*
But throw'st them lower than thou didst exalt them high,
690   Unseemly falls in human eye,
Too grievous for the trespass or omission;
Oft leav'st them to the hostile sword
Of heathen and profane, their carcasses
To dogs and fowls a prey, or else captíved,°   *taken captive*
Or to the unjust tribunals, under change of times,
And condemnation of the ingrateful multitude.
If these they scape, perhaps in poverty
With sickness and disease thou bow'st them down,
Painful diseases and deformed,
700   In crude° old age;   *harsh*
Though not disordinate,° yet causeless suffering   *intemperate*
The punishment of dissolute days, in fine,°   *short*
Just or unjust, alike seem miserable,
For oft alike, both come to evil end.
    So deal not with this once thy glorious champion,
The image of thy strength, and mighty minister.
What do I beg? How hast thou dealt already?
Behold him in this state calamitous, and turn
His labours, for thou canst, to peaceful end.
710   But who is this, what thing of sea or land?
Female of sex it seems,
That so bedecked, ornate, and gay,
Comes this way sailing
Like a stately ship
Of Tarsus, bound for the isles
Of Javan or Gadire,
With all her bravery on, and tackle trim,

Sails filled, and streamers waving,
Courted by all the winds that hold them play,
720 An amber scent of odorous perfume
Her harbinger, a damsel train behind;
Some rich Philistian matron she may seem,
And now at nearer view, no other certain
Than Dalila thy wife.
Samson   My wife, my traitress, let her not come near me.
Chorus   Yet on she moves, now stands and eyes thee fixed,
Like a fair flower surcharg'd with dew, she weeps
And words addressed seem into tears dissolved,
730 Wetting the borders of her silken veil:
But now again she makes address to speak.
Dalila   With doubtful feet and wavering resolution
I came, still dreading thy displeasure, Samson,
Which to have merited, without excuse,
I cannot but acknowledge; yet if tears
May expiate (though the fact° more evil drew   deed
In the perverse event° than I foresaw),   outcome
My penance hath not slackened, though my pardon
No way assured. But conjugal affection,
740 Prevailing over fear and timorous doubt,
Hath led me on, desirous to behold
Once more thy face, and know of thy estate;°   condition
If aught in my ability may serve
To lighten what thou suffer'st, and appease
Thy mind with what amends is in my power,
Though late, yet in some part to recompense
My rash but more unfortunate misdeed.
Samson   Out, out, hyena![217] These are thy wonted° arts,   usual
And arts of every woman false like thee,
750 To break all faith, all vows, deceive, betray;
Then as repentant to submit, beseech,
And reconcilement move° with feigned remorse,   propose
Confess, and promise wonders in her change,
Not truly penitent, but chief to try
Her husband, how far urged his patience bears,
His virtue or weakness which way to assail;
Then with more cautious and instructed skill
Again transgresses, and again submits;
That wisest and best men, full oft beguiled,
760 With goodness principled not to reject
The penitent, but ever to forgive,
Are drawn to wear out miserable days,

Entangled with a poisonous bosom snake,
If not by quick destruction soon cut off,
As I by thee, to ages an example.
Dalila   Yet hear me, Samson; not that I endeavour
To lessen or extenuate my offence,
But that on the other side if it be weighed
By itself, with aggravations° not surcharged,   *exaggerations*
770 Or else with just allowance counterpoised,
I may, if possible, thy pardon find
The easier towards me, or thy hatred less.
First granting, as I do, it was a weakness
In me, but incident to all our sex,
Curiosity, inquisitive, importune
Of° secrets, then with like infirmity   *soliciting*
To publish them, both common female faults;
Was it not weakness also to make known
For importunity, that is for naught,
780 Wherein consisted all thy strength and safety?
To what I did thou show'dst me first the way.
But I to enemies revealed, and should not.
Nor shouldst thou have trusted that to woman's frailty:
Ere I to thee, thou to thyself wast cruel.
Let weakness then with weakness come to parle,°   *speak*
So near related, or the same of kind;
Thine forgive mine, that men may censure thine
The gentler, if severely thou exact not
More strength from me than in thyself was found.
790 And what if love, which thou interpret'st hate,
The jealousy of love, powerful of sway
In human hearts, nor less in mine towards thee,
Caused what I did? I saw thee mutable°   *changeable*
Of fancy,° feared lest one day thou wouldst leave me   *affection*
As her at Timna, sought by all means therefore
How to endear, and hold thee to me firmest:
No better way I saw than by importuning
To learn thy secrets, get into my power
Thy key of strength and safety. Thou wilt say,
800 'Why then revealed?' I was assured by those
Who tempted me that nothing was designed[218]
Against thee but safe custody and hold:
That made for me;° I knew that liberty   *was in my interest*
Would draw thee forth to perilous enterprises,
While I at home sat full of cares and fears,
Wailing thy absence in my widowed bed;

Here I should still enjoy thee day and night,
Mine and love's prisoner, not the Philistines',
Whole to myself, unhazarded abroad,
810 Fearless at home of partners in my love.
These reasons in love's law have passed for good,
Though fond° and reasonless to some perhaps;   *foolish*
And love hath oft, well meaning, wrought much woe,
Yet always pity or pardon hath obtained.
Be not unlike all others, not austere
As thou art strong, inflexible as steel.
If thou in strength all mortals dost exceed,
In uncompassionate anger do not so.
Samson   How cunningly the sorceress displays
820 Her own transgressions, to upbraid me mine!
That malice, not repentance, brought thee hither,
By this appears: I gave, thou say'st, the example,
I led the way; bitter reproach, but true;
I to myself was false ere thou to me;
Such pardon therefore as I give my folly,
Take to thy wicked deed; which when thou seest
Impartial, self-severe, inexorable,
Thou wilt renounce thy seeking, and much rather
Confess it feigned° Weakness is thy excuse,   *dissembled*
830 And I believe it, weakness to resist
Philistian gold; if weakness may excuse,
What murtherer, what traitor, parricide,
Incestuous, sacrilegious, but may plead it?
All wickedness is weakness: that plea therefore
With God or man will gain thee no remission.
But love constrained thee? Call it furious rage
To satisfy thy lust: love seeks to have love;
My love how couldst thou hope, who took'st the way
To raise in me inexpiable hate,
840 Knowing, as needs I must, by thee betrayed?
In vain thou striv'st to cover shame with shame,
Or by evasions thy crime uncover'st more.
Dalila   Since thou determin'st weakness for no plea
In man or woman, though to thy own condemning,
Hear what assaults I had, what snares besides,
What sieges girt me round, ere I consented;
Which might have awed the best-resolved of men,
The constantest, to have yielded without blame.
It was not gold, as to my charge thou lay'st,
850 That wrought with me: thou know'st the magistrates

And princes of my country came in person,
Solicited, commanded, threatened, urged,
Adjured by all the bonds of civil duty
And of religion, pressed how just it was,
How honourable, how glorious to entrap
A common enemy, who had destroyed
Such numbers of our nation: and the priest
Was not behind, but ever at my ear,
Preaching how meritorious with the gods
860 It would be to ensnare an irreligious
Dishonourer of Dagon. What had I
To oppose against such powerful arguments?
Only my love of thee held long debate,
And combated in silence all these reasons
With hard contest. At length that grounded° maxim,   *basic*
So rife and celebrated in the mouths
Of wisest men, that to the public good
Private respects° must yield, with grave authority   *interests*
Took full possession of me and prevailed;
870 Virtue, as I thought, truth, duty, so enjoining.
Samson   I thought where all thy circling wiles would end,
In feigned religion, smooth hypocrisy.
But had thy love, still odiously pretended,
Been, as it ought, sincere, it would have taught thee
Far other reasonings, brought forth other deeds.
I before all the daughters of my tribe
And of my nation chose thee from among
My enemies, loved thee, as too well thou knewest,
Too well; unbosomed all my secrets to thee,
880 Not out of levity,[219] but overpowered
By thy request, who could deny thee nothing;
Yet now am judged an enemy. Why then
Didst thou at first receive me for thy husband,
Then, as since then, thy country's foe professed?
Being once a wife, for me thou wast to leave
Parents and country; nor was I their subject,
Nor under their protection, but my own;
Thou mine, not theirs. If aught against my life
Thy country sought of thee, it sought unjustly,
890 Against the law of nature, law of nations;
No more thy country, but an impious crew
Of men conspiring to uphold their state
By worse than hostile deeds, violating the ends
For which our country is a name so dear;

Not therefore to be obeyed. But zeal moved thee;
To please thy gods thou didst it; gods unable
To acquit themselves° and prosecute their foes   *discharge their duties*
But by ungodly deeds, the contradiction
Of their own deity, gods cannot be:
900 Less therefore to be pleased, obeyed, or feared.
These false pretexts and varnished colours° failing,   *superficial pretences*
Bare in thy guilt how foul must thou appear!
Dalila   In argument with men a woman ever
Goes by the worse°, whatever be her cause.   *comes off worst*
Samson   For want of words, no doubt, or lack of breath;
Witness when I was worried with thy peals°.   *noisy arguments*
Dalila   I was a fool, too rash, and quite mistaken
In what I thought would have succeeded best.
Let me obtain forgiveness of thee, Samson;
910 Afford me place to show what recompense
Towards thee I intend for what I have misdone,
Misguided; only what remains past cure
Bear not too sensibly°, nor still insist   *feelingly*
To afflict thyself in vain. Though sight be lost,
Life yet hath many solaces, enjoyed
Where other senses want not their delights
At home in leisure and domestic ease,
Exempt from many a care and chance to which
Eyesight exposes daily men abroad.
920 I to the lords will intercede, not doubting
Their favourable ear, that I may fetch thee
From forth this loathsome prison-house, to abide
With me, where my redoubled love and care
With nursing diligence, to me glad office,
May ever tend about thee to old age
With all things grateful° cheered, and so supplied,   *pleasant*
That what by me thou hast lost thou least shall miss,
Samson   No, no, of my condition take no care;
It fits not; thou and I long since are twain;
930 Nor think me so unwary or accurst
To bring my feet again into the snare
Where once I have been caught; I know thy trains°,   *lures*
Though dearly to my cost, thy gins°, and toils;   *snares*
Thy fair enchanted cup and warbling charms
No more on me have power, their force is nulled;°   *non-existent*
So much of adder's wisdom[220] I have learnt
To fence my ear against thy sorceries.
If in my flower of youth and strength, when all men

Loved, honoured, feared me, thou alone could hate me,
940   Thy husband, slight me, sell me, and forgo me,
How wouldst thou use me now, blind, and thereby
Deceivable, in most things as a child
Helpless, thence easily contemned, and scorned,
And last neglected? How wouldst thou insult
When I must live uxorious to thy will
In perfect thraldom, how again betray me,
Bearing my words and doings to the lords
To gloss° upon, and censuring, frown or smile?   *comment*
This gaol I count the house of liberty
950   To thine whose doors my feet shall never enter.
Dalila   Let me approach at least, and touch thy hand.
Samson   Not for thy life, lest fierce remembrance wake
My sudden rage to tear thee joint by joint.
At distance I forgive thee, go with that;
Bewail thy falsehood, and the pious works
It hath brought forth to make thee memorable
Among illustrious women, faithful wives;
Cherish thy hastened widowhood with the gold
Of matrimonial treason: so farewell.
960   **Dalila**   I see thou art implacable, more deaf
To prayers than winds and seas; yet winds to seas
Are reconciled at length, and sea to shore:
Thy anger, unappeasable, still rages,
Eternal tempest never to be calmed.
Why do I humble thus myself, and suing
For peace, reap nothing but repulse and hate?
Bid go with evil omen and the brand
Of infamy upon my name denounced?
To mix with thy concernments I desist
970   Henceforth, nor too much disapprove my own.
Fame, if not double-faced, is double-mouthed,
And with contrary blast proclaims most deeds;
On both his wings, one black, the other white,
Bears greatest names in his wild airy flight.
My name perhaps among the circumcised°   *(the Jews)*
In Dan°, in Judah, and the bordering tribes,   *(Samson's tribe)*
To all posterity may stand defamed,
With malediction mentioned°, and the blot   *cursed*
Of falsehood most unconjugal traduced°.   *censured*
980   But in my country where I most desire,
In Ekron, Gaza, Asdod, and in Gath,
I shall be named among the famousest

Of women, sung at solemn festivals,
Living and dead recorded, who, to save
Her country from a fierce destroyer, chose
Above the faith of wedlock bands, my tomb
With odours° visited and annual flowers: *spices*
Not less renowned than in Mount Ephraim
Jael, who with inhospitable guile
990 Smote Sisera sleeping, through the temples nailed.
Nor shall I count it heinous to enjoy
The public marks of honour and reward
Conferred upon me for the piety°   *devotion*
Which to my country I was judged to have shown.
At this whoever envies or repines,
I leave him to his lot, and like my own.
Chorus She's gone, a manifest serpent by her sting
Discovered in the end, till now concealed.
Samson So let her go; God sent her to debase me,
1000 And aggravate my folly who committed
To such a viper his most sacred trust
Of secrecy, my safety, and my life.
Chorus Yet beauty, though injurious, hath strange power,
After offence returning, to regain
Love once possessed, nor can be easily
Repulsed, without much inward passion° felt   *suffering*
And secret sting of amorous remorse.
Samson Love-quarrels oft in pleasing concord end,
Not wedlock-treachery endangering life.
1010 **Chorus** It is not virtue, wisdom, valour, wit,
Strength, comeliness of shape, or amplest merit
That woman's love can win or long inherit;°   *possess*
But what it is, hard is to say,
Harder to hit,
(Which way soever men refer it),
Much like thy riddle, Samson, in one day
Or seven, though one should musing sit;
    If any of these, or all, the Timnian bride
Had not so soon preferred
1020 Thy paranymph,° worthless to thee compared,   *bridegroom's companion*
Successor in thy bed,
Nor both° so loosely disallied°   *wives/broke*
Their nuptials, nor this last so treacherously
Had shorn the fatal harvest of thy head;
Is it for that° such outward ornament   *because*
Was lavished on their sex, that inward gifts

Were left for haste unfinished, judgment scant,
Capacity not raised to apprehend
Or value what is best
1030 In choice, but oftest to affect° the wrong?   *prefer*
Or was too much of self-love mixed,
Of constancy no root infixed,
That either they love nothing, or not long?
    Whate'er it be, to wisest men and best
Seeming at first all heavenly under virgin veil,
Soft, modest, meek, demure,
Once joined, the contrary she proves, a thorn
Intestine, far within defensive arms
A cleaving° mischief, in his way to virtue   *clinging*
1040 Adverse and turbulent; or by her charms
Draws him awry enslaved
With dotage, and his sense depraved
To folly and shameful deeds which ruin ends.
What pilot so expert but needs must wreck,
Embarked with such a steers-mate at the helm?
    Favoured of heaven who finds
One virtuous, rarely found,
That in domestic good combines:
Happy that house! his way to peace is smooth;
1050 But virtue which breaks through all opposition,
And all temptation can remove,
Most shines and most is acceptable above.
    Therefore God's universal law
Gave to the man despotic power
Over his female in due awe,
Nor from that right to part an hour,
Smile she or lour:°   *scowl*
So shall he least confusion draw
On his whole life, not swayed
1060 By female usurpation, nor dismayed.
    But had we best retire? I see a storm.
Samson   Fair days have oft contracted wind and rain.
Chorus   But this another kind of tempest brings.
Samson   Be less abstruse, my riddling days are past.
Chorus   Look now for no enchanting voice, nor fear
The bait of honied words; a rougher tongue
Draws hitherward; I know him by his stride,
The giant Harapha of Gath, his look
Haughty as is his pile° high-built and proud.   *(Gath)*
1070 Comes he in peace? What wind hath blown him hither

I less conjecture than when first I saw
The sumptuous Dalila floating this way;
His habit carries peace, his brow defiance.
Samson   Or peace or not, alike to me he comes.
Chorus   His fraught° we soon shall know, he now arrives.   *purpose*
Harapha   I come not, Samson, to condole thy chance,
As these perhaps, yet wish it had not been,
Though for no friendly intent. I am of Gath;
Men call me Harapha, of stock renowned
1080 As Og or Anak and the Emims old
That Kiriathaim held; thou knowest me now,
If thou at all art known.° Much I have heard   *have any knowledge*
Of thy prodigious might and feats performed
Incredible to me, in this displeased,
That I was never present on the place
Of those encounters where we might have tried
Each other's force in camp° or listed field:°   *battlefield/tournaments*
And now am come to see of whom such noise°   *rumour*
Hath walked° about, and each limb to survey,   *spread*
1090 If thy appearance answer loud report.
Samson   The way to know were not to see but taste.
Harapha   Dost thou already single° me? I thought   *challenge*
Gyves° and the mill had tamed thee. O that fortune   *leg-chains*
Had brought me to the field where thou art famed
To have wrought such wonders with an ass's jaw;
I should have forced thee soon with other arms,
Or left thy carcass where the ass lay thrown:
So had the glory of prowess been recovered
To Palestine, won by a Philistine
1100 From the unforeskinned° race, of whom thou bear'st   *circumcised*
The highest name for valiant acts; that honour,
Certain to have won by mortal duel° from thee.   *duel to the death*
I lose, prevented by thy eyes put out.
Samson   Boast not of what thou wouldst have done, but do
What then thou wouldst; thou seest it in thy hand.
Harapha   To combat with a blind man I disdain,
And thou hast need much washing to be touched.
Samson   Such usage as your honourable lords
Afford me, assassinated° and betrayed;   *waylaid*
1110 Who durst not with their whole united powers
In fight withstand me single and unarmed,
Nor in the house with chamber ambushes
Close-banded° durst attack me, no, not sleeping,   *secretly*
Till they had hired a woman with their gold,

Breaking her marriage faith to circumvent° me.   *get round*
Therefore without feigned shifts° let be assigned   *evasions*
Some narrow place enclosed, where sight may give thee,
Or rather flight, no great advantage on me;
Then put on all thy gorgeous arms, thy helmet
1120 And brigandine° of brass, thy broad habergeon,°   *body-armour/coat of mail*
Vant-brace° and greaves,° and gauntlet; add thy spear,   *fore-arm*
A weaver's beam, and seven-times-folded shield;   */ shield/thigh-armour*
I only with an oaken staff²²¹ will meet thee,
And raise such outcries on thy clattered iron,
Which long shall not withhold me from thy head,
That in a little time while breath remains thee,
Thou oft shall wish thyself at Gath to boast
Again in safety what thou wouldst have done
To Samson, but shalt never see Gath more.
1130 **Harapha**   Thou durst not thus disparage glorious arms²²²
Which greatest heroes have in battle worn,
Their ornament and safety, had not spells
And black enchantments, some magician's art,
Armed thee or charmed thee strong, which thou from heaven
Feign'dst at thy birth was given thee in thy hair,
Where strength can least abide, though all thy hairs
Were bristles ranged like those that ridge the back
Of chafed° wild boars, or ruffled porcupines.   *angry*
Samson   I know no spells, use no forbidden arts;²²³
1140 My trust is in the living God who gave me
At my nativity this strength, diffused
No less through all my sinews, joints and bones,
Than thine, while I preserved these locks unshorn,
The pledge of my unviolated vow.
For proof hereof, if Dagon be thy god,
Go to his temple, invocate his aid
With solemnest devotion, spread before him
How highly it concerns his glory now
To frustrate and dissolve these magic spells,
1150 Which I to be the power of Israel's God
Avow, and challenge Dagon to the test,
Offering to combat thee, his champion bold,
With the utmost of his godhead seconded:
Then thou shalt see, or rather to thy sorrow
Soon feel, whose God is strongest, thine or mine.
Harapha   Presume not on thy God, whate'er he be;
Thee he regards not, owns not, hath cut off
Quite from his people, and delivered up

Into thy enemies' hand; permitted them
1160 To put out both thine eyes and fettered send thee
Into the common prison, there to grind°   (i.e. grind corn)
Among the slaves and asses, thy comrádes,
As good for nothing else, no better service
With those thy boisterous° locks; no worthy match   thick-growing
For valour to assail, nor by the sword
Of noble warrior, so to stain his honour,
But by the barber's razor best subdued.
Samson   All these indignities, for such they are
From thine,° these evils I deserve and more,   (your people)
1170 Acknowledge them from God inflicted on me
Justly, yet despair not of his final pardon
Whose ear is ever open, and his eye
Gracious to re-admit the suppliant;
In confidence whereof I once again
Defy° thee to the trial of mortal fight,   challenge
By combat to decide whose god is God,
Thine or whom I with Israel's sons adore.
Harapha   Fair honour that thou dost thy God, in trusting
He will accept thee to defend his cause,
1180 A murderer, a revolter, and a robber.
Samson   Tongue-doughty° giant, how dost thou   bold of speech
    prove me these?
Harapha   Is not thy nation subject to our lords?
Their magistrates confessed it, when they took thee
As a league-breaker and delivered bound
Into our hands: for hadst thou not committed
Notorious murder on those thirty men
At Ascalon, who never did thee harm,
Then like a robber stripp'dst them of their robes?
The Philistines, when thou hadst broke the league,
1190 Went up with armed powers thee only seeking,
To others did no violence nor spoil.
Samson   Among the daughters of the Philistines
I chose a wife, which argued me no foe,
And in your city held my nuptial feast;
But your ill-meaning politician° lords,   cunning
Under pretence of bridal friends and guests,
Appointed to await me thirty spies,
Who threatening cruel death constrained the bride
To wring from me and tell to them my secret,
1200 That solved the riddle which I had proposed.
When I perceived all set on enmity,

As on my enemies, wherever chanced,
I used hostility, and took their spoil
To pay my underminers° in their coin.   *secret attackers*
My nation was subjected to your lords.
It was the force of conquest; force with force
Is well ejected when the conquered can.
But I a private person, whom my country
As a league-breaker gave up bound, presumed
1210 Single rebellion and did hostile acts.
I was no private but a person raised
With strength sufficient and command from heaven
To free my country; if their servile minds
Me, their deliverer sent, would not receive,
But to their masters gave me up for naught,
The unworthier they; whence to this day they serve.
I was to do my part from heaven assigned,
And had performed it if my known offence
Had not disabled me, not all your force.
1220 These shifts° refuted, answer thy appellant,°   *evasive arguments/challenger*
Though by his blindness maimed for high attempts,
Who now defies thee thrice to single fight,²²⁴
As a petty enterprise of small enforce.°   *effort*
Harapha   With thee, a man condemned, a slave enrolled,
Due by the law to capital punishment?
To fight with thee no man of arms will deign.
Samson   Cam'st thou for this, vain boaster, to survey me,
To descant° on my strength, and give thy verdict?   *discourse*
Come nearer, part not hence so slight informed;
1230 But take good heed my hand survey not thee.
Harapha   O Baal-zebub! can my ears unused°   *unaccustomed*
Hear these dishonours, and not render death?
Samson   No man withholds thee, nothing from thy hand
Fear I incurable; bring up thy van;°   *vanguard*
My heels are fettered, but my fist is free.
Harapha   This insolence other kind of answer fits.
Samson   Go, baffled coward, lest I run upon thee,
Though in these chains, bulk without spirit vast,
And with one buffet lay thy structure low,
1240 Or swing thee in the air, then dash thee down
To the hazard° of thy brains and shattered sides.   *danger*
Harapha   By Astaroth, ere long thou shalt lament
These braveries° in irons loaden on thee.   *bravado*
Chorus   His giantship is gone somewhat crestfallen,
Stalking with less unconscionable° strides,   *immoderate*

And lower looks, but in a sultry chafe.°   *temper*
Samson   I dread him not, nor all his giant brood,
Though fame divulge him father of five sons,[225]
All of gigantic size, Goliah chief.
1250 **Chorus**   He will directly to the lords, I fear,
And with malicious counsel stir them up
Some way or other yet further to afflict thee.
Samson   He must allege some cause, and offered fight
Will not dare mention, lest a question rise
Whether he durst accept the offer or not,
And that he durst not plain enough appeared.
Much more affliction than already felt
They cannot well impose, nor I sustain,
If they intend advantage of my labours,
1260 The work of many hands, which earns my keeping
With no small profit daily to my owners.
But come what will, my deadliest foe will prove
My speediest friend, by death to rid me hence,
The worst that he can give, to me the best.
Yet so it may fall out, because their end
Is hate, not help to me, it may with mine
Draw their own ruin who attempt the deed.
Chorus   Oh how comely it is and how reviving
To the spirits of just men long oppressed,
1270 When God into the hands of their deliverer
Puts invincible might
To quell the mighty of the earth, the oppressor,
The brute° and boisterous force of violent men,   *unreasoning*
Hardy and industrious to support
Tyrannic power, but raging to pursue
The righteous and all such as honour truth!
He all their ammunition
And feats of war defeats
With plain heroic magnitude of mind
1280 And celestial vigour armed;
Their armories and magazines contemns,
Renders them useless, while
With winged expedition
Swift as the lightning glance he executes
His errand on the wicked, who surprised
Lose their defence, distracted and amazed.°   *confused*
      But patience is more oft the exercise
Of saints, the trial of their fortitude,
Making them each his own deliverer,

1290 And victor over all
That tyranny or fortune can inflict;
Either of these is in thy lot,
Samson, with might endued
Above the sons of men; but sight bereaved
May chance to number thee with those
Whom patience finally must crown.
    This idol's day²²⁶ hath been to thee no day of rest,
Labouring thy mind
More than the working day thy hands;
1300 And yet perhaps more trouble is behind.
For I descry this way
Some other tending; in his hand
A sceptre or quaint° staff he bears,   *carved*
Comes on amain,° speed in his look.   *without delay*
By his habit I discern him now
A public officer, and now at hand.
His message will be short and voluble.°   *fluent*
Officer   Hebrews, the prisoner Samson here I seek.
Chorus   His manacles remark° him; there he sits.   *indicate*
1310 **Officer**   Samson, to thee our lords thus bid me say:
This day to Dagon is a solemn feast,
With sacrifices, triumph, pomp, and games;
Thy strength they know surpassing human rate,
And now some public proof thereof require
To honour this great feast, and great assembly;
Rise therefore with all speed and come along,
Where I will see thee heartened and fresh clad
To appear as fits before the illustrious lords.
Samson   Thou knowest I am an Hebrew, therefore tell them
1320 Our law forbids at their religious rites
My presence; for that cause I cannot come.
Officer   This answer, be assured, will not content them.
Samson   Have they not sword-players, and every sort
Of gymnic artists, wrestlers, riders, runners,
Jugglers and dancers, antics,° mummers,° mimics,   *clowns/actors*
But they must pick me out with shackles tired,
And over-laboured at their public mill,
To make them sport with blind activity?
Do they not seek occasion of new quarrels,
1330 On my refusal, to distress me more,
Or make a game of my calamities?
Return the way thou cam'st; I will not come.
Officer   Regard° thyself; this will offend them highly.   *look to*

Samson   Myself? My conscience and internal peace.
Can they think me so broken, so debased
With corporal servitude, that my mind ever
Will condescend to such absurd commands?
Although their drudge, to be their fool or jester,
And in my midst of sorrow and heart-grief
To show them feats and play before their god,   1340
The worst of all indignities, yet on me
Joined° with extreme contempt? I will not come.   *commanded*
Officer   My message was imposed on me with speed,
Brooks no delay; is this thy resolution?
Samson   So take it with what speed thy message needs.
Officer   I am sorry what this stoutness° will produce   *stubbornness*
Samson   Perhaps thou shalt have cause to sorrow indeed.
Chorus   Consider, Samson; matters now are strained
Up to the highth, whether to hold or break;
He's gone, and who knows how he may report   1350
Thy words by adding fuel to the flame?
Expect another message more imperious,
More lordly thundering than thou well wilt bear.
Samson   Shall I abuse this consecrated gift
Of strength, again returning with my hair
After my great transgression, so requite
Favour renewed, and add a greater sin
By prostituting holy things to idols;
A Nazarite in place abominable
Vaunting my strength in honour to their Dagon?   1360
Besides, how vile, contemptible, ridiculous,
What act more execrably unclean, profane?
Chorus   Yet with this strength thou serv'st the Philistines,
Idolatrous, uncircumcised, unclean.
Samson   Not in their idol-worship, but by labour
Honest and lawful to deserve my food
Of those who have me in their civil power.
Chorus   Where the heart joins not, outward acts defile not.
Samson   Where outward force constrains, the sentence°   *maxim*
holds;
But who constrains me to the temple of Dagon,   1370
Not dragging? The Philistian lords command.
Commands are no constraints. If I obey them,
I do it freely; venturing to displease
God for the fear of man, and man prefer,
Set God behind; which in his jealousy
Shall never, unrepented, find forgiveness.

Yet that He may dispense with me or thee,
Present in temples at idolatrous rites
For some important cause, thou need'st not doubt.

1380 **Chorus**   How thou wilt here come off surmounts my reach.

Samson   Be of good courage; I begin to feel
Some rousing motions° in me which dispose   *ideas or thoughts*
To something extraordinary my thoughts.
I with this messenger will go along,
Nothing to do, be sure, that may dishonour
Our law, or stain my vow of Nazarite.
If there be aught of presage° in the mind,   *foreboding*
This day will be remarkable in my life
By some great act, or of my days the last.

1390 **Chorus**   In time thou hast resolved; the man returns.

Officer   Samson, this second message from our lords
To thee I am bid say: art thou our slave,
Our captive, at the public mill our drudge,
And dar'st thou at our sending and command
Dispute thy coming? Come without delay;
Or we shall find such engines° to assail   *agents*
And hamper thee, as thou shalt come of° force,   *by*
Though thou wert firmlier fastened than a rock.

Samson   I could be well content to try their art,
1400 Which to no few of them would prove pernicious.
Yet knowing their advantages too many,
Because° they shall not trail me through their streets   *so that*
Like a wild beast, I am content to go.
Masters' commands come with a power resistless
To such as owe them absolute subjection;
And for a life who will not change his purpose?
(So mutable are all the ways of men.)
Yet this be sure, in nothing to comply
Scandalous or forbidden in our law.

1410 **Officer**   I praise thy resolution;° doff° these links.   *decision/cast off*
By this compliance thou wilt win the lords
To favour, and perhaps to set thee free.

Samson   Brethren, farewell; your company along
I will not wish, lest it perhaps offend them
To see me girt with friends; and how the sight
Of me as of a common enemy,
So dreaded once, may now exasperate them,
I know not. Lords are lordliest in their wine;
And the well-feasted priest then soonest fired
1420 With zeal, if aught° religion seem concerned;   *in any way*

No less the people on their holy-days
Impetuous, insolent, unquenchable;
Happen what may, of me expect to hear
Nothing dishonourable, impure, unworthy
Our God, our law, my nation, or myself;
The last of me or no I cannot warrant.
Chorus Go, and the holy One
Of Israel be thy guide
To what may serve his glory best, and spread his name
1430 Great among the heathen round;
Send thee the angel of thy birth, to stand
Fast by thy side, who from thy father's field
Rode up in flames after his message told
Of thy conception, and be now a shield
Of fire; that spirit that first rushed on thee
In the camp of Dan,
Be efficacious in thee now at need.
For never was from heaven imparted
Measure of strength so great to mortal seed,
1440 As in thy wondrous actions hath been seen.
But wherefore comes old Manoa in such haste
With youthful steps? Much livelier than erewhile
He seems: supposing here to find his son,
Or of him bringing to us some glad news?
Manoa Peace with you, brethren; my inducement hither
Was not at present here to find my son,
By order of the lords new parted hence
To come and play before them at their feast.
I heard all as I came, the city rings,
1450 And numbers thither flock; I had no will
Lest I should see him forced to things unseemly.
But that which moved my coming now was chiefly
To give ye part° with me what hope I have   *a share*
With good success° to work his liberty.   *outcome*
Chorus That hope would much rejoice us to partake
With thee; say, reverend sire; we thirst to hear.
Manoa I have attempted° one by one the lords,   *appealed to*
Either at home, or through the high street passing,
With supplication prone and father's tears
1460 To accept of ransom for my son their prisoner.
Some much averse I found and wondrous harsh,
Contemptuous, proud, set on revenge and spite;
That part most reverenced Dagon and his priests;
Others more moderate seeming, but their aim

Private reward, for which both God and state
They easily would set to sale; a third
More generous far and civil, who confessed
They had enough revenged, having reduced
Their foe to misery beneath their fears;
1470 The rest was magnanimity to remit,
If some convenient ransom were proposed.
What noise or shout was that? It tore the sky.
Chorus   Doubtless the people shouting to behold
Their once great dread, captive and blind before them,
Or at some proof of strength before them shown.
Manoa   His ransom, if my whole inheritance
May compass it, shall willingly be paid
And numbered down; much rather I shall choose
To live the poorest in my tribe, than richest,
1480 And he in that calamitous prison left.
No, I am fixed not to part hence without him.
For his redemption all my patrimony,
If need be, I am ready to forgo
And quit;° not wanting him, I shall want nothing.   *settle this account*
Chorus   Fathers are wont to lay up for their sons,
Thou for thy son art bent to lay out all;
Sons wont° to nurse their parents in old age,   *are accustomed*
Thou in old age car'st how to nurse thy son,
Made older than thy age through eyesight lost.
1490 **Manoa**   It shall be my delight to tend his eyes,
And view him sitting in the house, ennobled
With all those high exploits by him achieved,
And on his shoulders waving down those locks
That of a nation armed the strength contained.
And I persuade me God had not permitted
His strength again to grow up with his hair
Garrisoned round about him like a camp
Of faithful soldiery, were not his purpose
To use him further yet in some great service,
1500 Not to sit idle with so great a gift
Useless, and thence ridiculous, about him.
And since his strength with eyesight was not lost,
God will restore him eyesight to° his strength.   *along with*
Chorus   Thy hopes are not ill-founded nor seem vain
Of his delivery, and thy joy thereon
Conceived, agreeable to a father's love;
In both which we, as next,° participate.   *(of kin)*
Manoa   I know your friendly minds and – O what noise!

Mercy of heaven, what hideous noise was that!
1510 Horribly loud, unlike the former shout.
    Chorus   Noise call you it, or universal groan,
As if the whole inhabitation° perished?   *population*
Blood, death, and dreadful deeds are in that noise,
Ruin, destruction at the utmost point.
    Manoa   Of ruin indeed methought I heard the noise.
Oh it continues, they have slain my son.
    Chorus   Thy son is rather slaying them; that outcry
From slaughter of one foe could not ascend.
    Manoa   Some dismal accident it needs must be;
1520 What shall we do, stay here or run and see?
    Chorus   Best keep together here, lest running thither
We unawares run into danger's mouth.
This evil on the Philistines is fallen;
From whom could else a general cry be heard?
The sufferers then will scarce molest us here;
From other hands we need not much to fear.
What if his eyesight (for to Israel's God
Nothing is hard) by miracle restored,
He now be dealing dole° among his foes,   *grief*
1530 And over heaps of slaughtered walk his way?
    Manoa   That were a joy presumptuous to be thought.
    Chorus   Yet God hath wrought things as incredible
For his people of old; what hinders now?
    Manoa   He can I know, but doubt to think He will;
Yet hope would fain subscribe, and tempts belief.
A little stay will bring some notice hither.
    Chorus   Of good or bad so great, of bad the sooner;
For evil news rides post, while good news baits.[227]
And to our wish I see one hither speeding,
1540 A Hebrew, as I guess, and of our tribe
    Messenger   O whither shall I run, or which way fly
The sight of this so horrid spectacle
Which erst° my eyes beheld and yet behold;   *just now*
For dire imagination still pursues me.
But providence or instinct of nature seems,
Or reason though disturbed, and scarce consulted
To have guided me aright, I know not how,
To thee first reverend Manoa, and to these
My countrymen, whom here I knew remaining,
1550 As at some distance from the place of horror,
So in the sad event too much concerned.
    Manoa   The accident was loud, and here before thee

With rueful cry, yet what it was we hear not,
No preface needs, thou seest we long to know.
Messenger   It would burst forth, but I recover breath,
And sense distract°, to know well what I utter.   *distracted*
Manoa   Tell us the sum, the circumstance° defer.   *details*
Messenger   Gaza yet stands, but all her sons are fallen,
All in a moment overwhelmed and fallen.
1560 **Manoa**   Sad, but thou know'st to Israelites not saddest
The desolation of a hostile city.
Messenger   Feed on that first, there may in grief be
        surfeit°   *sickness from over eating*
Manoa   Relate by whom.
Messenger   By Samson.
Manoa   That still lessens
The sorrow, and converts it nigh to joy.
Messenger   Ah Manoa I refrain, too suddenly
To utter what will come at last too soon;
Lest evil tidings with too rude irruption°   *breaking*
Hitting thy aged ear should pierce too deep.
Manoa   Suspense in news is torture, speak them out.
1570 **Messenger**   Then take the worst in brief, Samson is dead.
Manoa   The worst indeed, O all my hopes defeated
To free him hence! but death who sets all free
Hath paid his ransom now and full discharge.
What windy joy this day had I conceived[228]
Hopeful of his delivery, which now proves
Abortive as the first-born bloom of spring
Nipped with the lagging rear of winter's frost.
Yet ere I give the reins to grief, say first,
How died he? death to life is crown or shame.
1580 All by him fell thou say'st, by whom fell he,
What glorious hand gave Samson his death's wound?
Messenger   Unwounded of his enemies he fell.
Manoa   Wearied with slaughter then or how? explain.
Messenger   By his own hands.
Manoa   Self-violence? what cause
Brought him so soon at variance with himself
Among his foes?
Messenger   Inevitable cause
At once both to destroy and be destroyed;
The edifice where all were met to see him
Upon their heads and on his own he pulled.
1590 **Manoa**   O lastly over-strong against thyself!
A dreadful way thou took'st to thy revenge.

More than enough we know; but while things yet
Are in confusion, give us if thou canst,
Eye-witness of what first or last was done,
Relation more particular and distinct.
Messenger   Occasions drew me early to this city,
And as the gates I entered with sunrise,
The morning trumpets festival proclaimed
Through each high street. Little I had despatched°   *done business*
1600   When all abroad was rumoured that this day
Samson should be brought forth to show the people
Proof of his mighty strength in feats and games;
I sorrowed at his captive state, but minded°   *determined*
Not to be absent at that spectacle.
The building was a spacious theatre,
Half round on two main pillars vaulted high,
With seats where all the lords, and each degree
Of sort, might sit in order to behold;
The other side was open, where the throng
1610   On banks° and scaffolds under sky might stand;   *benches*
I among these aloof obscurely stood.
The feast and noon grew high, and sacrifice
Had filled their hearts with mirth, high cheer, and wine,
When to their sports they turned. Immediately
Was Samson as a public servant brought,
In their state livery clad; before him pipes
And timbrels; on each side went armed guards,
Both horse and foot before him and behind
Archers, and slingers, cataphracts° and spears.   *armoured horsemen*
1620   At sight of him the people with a shout
Rifted the air, clamouring their god with praise,
Who had made their dreadful enemy their thrall°   *slave*
He, patient but undaunted, where they led him,
Came to the place; and what was set before him,
Which without help of eye might be assayed,
To heave, pull, draw, or break, he still performed,
All with incredible, stupendious force,
None daring to appear antagonist.
At length for intermission sake they led him
1630   Between the pillars; he his guide requested
(For so from such as nearer stood we heard),
As over-tired, to let him lean a while
With both his arms on those two massy pillars
That to the arched roof gave main support.
He unsuspicious led him; which when Samson

Felt in his arms, with head a while inclined,
And eyes fast fixed he stood, as one who prayed,
Or some great matter in his mind revolved°   *considered*
At last with head erect thus cried aloud:
1640 'Hitherto, lords, what your commands imposed
I have performed, as reason was, obeying,
Not without wonder or delight beheld,
Now of my own accord such other trial
I mean to show you of my strength, yet greater,
As with amaze° shall strike all who behold.'   *confusion*
Thus uttered, straining all his nerves he bowed;
As with the force of winds and waters pent
When mountains tremble° those two massy pillars   *(causing earthquakes)*
With horrible convulsion to and fro
1650 He tugged, he shook, till down they came and drew
The whole roof after them, with burst of thunder
Upon the heads of all who sat beneath,
Lords, ladies, captains, counsellors, or priests,
Their choice nobility and flower, not only
Of this but each Philistian city round,
Met from all parts to solemnize this feast.
Samson, with these inmixed, inevitably
Pulled down the same destruction on himself;
The vulgar only scaped who stood without.
1660 **Chorus**   O dearly bought revenge, yet glorious!
Living or dying thou hast fulfilled
The work for which thou wast foretold
To Israel, and now li'st victorious
Among thy slain self-killed,
Not willingly, but tangled in the fold
Of dire necessity, whose law in death conjoined°   *linked*
Thee with thy slaughtered foes, in number more
Than all thy life had slain before.
Semichorus   While their hearts were jocund and sublime,
1670 Drunk with idolatry, drunk with wine,
And fat regorged of bulls and goats,
Chanting their idol, and preferring
Before our living Dread who dwells
In Silo, his bright sanctuary,
Among them He a spirit of frenzy sent,
Who hurt their minds,
And urged them on with mad desire
To call in haste for their destroyer;
They only set on sport and play

1680 Unweetingly° importuned   *unwittingly*
    Their own destruction to come speedy upon them.
    So fond are mortal men
    Fallen into wrath divine,
    As their own ruin on themselves to invite,
    Insensate left, or to sense reprobate,°   *lost*
    And with blindness internal struck.
    Semichorus But he, though blind of sight,
    Despised and thought extinguished quite,
    With inward eyes illuminated,
1690 His fiery virtue roused
    From under ashes into sudden flame,
    And as an evening dragon° came,   *serpent*
    Assailant on the perched roosts
    And nests in order ranged
    Of tame villatic° fowl; but as an eagle   *barnyard*
    His cloudless thunder bolted° on their heads.   *threw down*
    So virtue, given for lost,
    Depressed, and overthrown, as seemed,
    Like that self-begotten bird[229]
1700 In the Arabian woods embost,°   *hidden*
    That no second knows nor third,
    And lay erewhile a holocaust,°   *fiery sacrifice*
    From out her ashy womb now teemed,°   *is born*
    Revives, reflourishes, then vigorous most
    When most unactive deemed,
    And though her body die, her fame survives,
    A secular bird, ages of lives.
    Manoa Come, come, no time for lamentation now,
    Nor much more cause; Samson hath quit himself
1710 Like Samson, and heroicly hath finished
    A life heroic, on his enemies
    Fully revenged; hath left them years of mourning,
    And lamentation to the sons of Caphtor
    Through all Philistian bounds. To Israel
    Honour hath left, and freedom: let but them
    Find courage to lay hold on this occasion;
    To himself and father's house eternal fame;
    And, which is best and happiest yet, all this
    With God not parted from him, as was feared,
1720 But favouring and assisting to the end.
    Nothing is here for tears, nothing to wail
    Or knock the breast, no weakness, no contempt,
    Dispraise, or blame, nothing but well and fair,

And what may quiet us in a death so noble.
Let us go find the body where it lies
Soaked in his enemies' blood, and from the stream
With lavers° pure and cleansing herbs wash off   *basins*
The clotted gore. I with what speed the while
(Gaza is not in plight° to say us nay)   *condition*
1730 Will send for all my kindred, all my friends,
To fetch him hence and solemnly attend
With silent obsequy° and funeral train   *funeral rites*
Home to his father's house: there will I build him
A monument, and plant it round with shade
Of laurel ever green, and branching palm,
With all his trophies hung, and acts enrolled
In copious legend, or sweet lyric song.
Thither shall all the valiant youth resort,
And from his memory inflame their breasts
1740 To matchless valour and adventures high;
The virgins also shall on feastful days
Visit his tomb with flowers, only bewailing
His lot unfortunate in nuptial choice,
From whence captivity and loss of eyes.
Chorus All is best, though we oft doubt,
What the unsearchable dispose
Of highest wisdom brings about,
And ever best found in the close.
Oft He seems to hide his face,
1750 But unexpectedly returns
And to his faithful champion hath in place
Bore witness gloriously; whence Gaza mourns,
And all that band° them to resist   *banded together*
His uncontrollable intent:
His servants He, with new acquist°   *acquisition*
Of true experience from this great event,
With peace and consolation hath dismissed,
And calm of mind, all passion spent.

?1647–70 [1671]

NOTES

Milton

1 the active man.
2 dish of curds and whey with cream.
3 as stars do
4 light shoes worn by actors in comedy.
5 music noted for its sweetness.
6 bouts rimée = rhymed verse.
7 the pensive man.
8 Ezek.I.4–6.
9 Isa.XXI.8.
10 Egyptian god, Thoth, in Greek identified with Hermes. Hermetic writings are concerned with philosophy, alchemy and black magic.
11 the city of Thebes, the descendants of Pelops, and the Trojan War provided material for many Greek tragedies.
12 the high boots worn by actors of tragedy.
13 Chaucer – *The Squire's Tale*.
14 falling each minute.
15 with huge solid pillars and highly decorated stained glass windows on which Biblical stories were represented.
16 a masque written for the members of the household of the newly created Lord President of Wales (the Earl of Bridgewater) where M.'s friend, Henry Lawes, was tutor to the children – Alice, age 15, John, 11 and Thomas, 9.
17 the tract is Wales and the bordering counties, which the Earl had charge of as the new Lord President.
18 haughty nation = Wales.
19 of less faith = less trustworthy: refers to the servant whose likeness he takes – Henry Lawes.
20 Venus or Hesperus, the evening star.
21 sides strongly.
22 things ill, sent as chastisement from God.
23 go into too great detail.
24 a nymph with a quiver of arrows.
25 those clogged down by flesh and brutish behaviour become, after death, ghosts.
26 boldness in the face of danger.
27 patched or hobnailed.
28 unknown – poss. M.'s invention; association of Haemonian (Thessaly) with magic: Coleridge suggests haemo-oinus, bloodwine, referring to the blood of Christ.
29 lime smeared on twigs for trapping birds.
30 pleasing to taste – lecherous.
31 who cause opinions to change.
32 the earth.
33 Cor. VI.13.
34 = Edmund Spenser.
35 undying flower growing in the Elysian Fields.
36 = Meliboeus.
37 i.e. the river water.
38 of the universe = the sky.
39 Venus, see glossary.

40 the music of the spheres.
41 Edward King, M.'s college friend.
42 added to the 1645 edition.
43 laurel is sacred to Apollo and the crown of the victor: myrtles sacred to Venus: ivy
    sacred to Bacchus, and crown of poets and scholars. 1341, Petrarch was crowned with
    ivy, laurel and myrtle. Edward King was a 'good scholar, fair poet and promising
    young clergyman'.
44 the muses at Aganippe, Mt Helicon, where there is an altar to Jove.
45 a male muse, a dead man (here, Milton) or Lycidas?
46 Christ's College, Cambridge.
47 poss. refers to a Cambridge don.
48 poss. Bardsey Island.
49 Calliope, see Glossary.
50 Atropos, see Glossary.
51 Triton, see Glossary.
52 an eclipse was regarded as a bad omen.
53 Camus = River Cam = Cambridge.
54 the academic gown with fur on its hood.
55 created from the blood of Hyacinth, killed accidentally by Apollo.
56 St Peter (Luke V.2–4, Matt. XVI.19) who, as first bishop, wore a mitre.
57 because they do not see the truth and take from others whom they themselves should
    be feeding.
58 the mark of the shepherd and the bishop.
59 the Roman Catholic Church, particularly the Jesuits, whose founder, Ignatius
    Loyola, bore arms which included two grey wolves.
60 this has been the subject of endless discussion. Poss. the sword of God in the hand of
    the avenger (Michael) – and hence poss. Cromwell and his Roundheads.
61 Sirius.
62 because King's body was missing.
63 St Michael, of St Michael's Mt, Cornwall.
64 they carried Palaemon (the protector of sailors) to a beach near Corinth.
65 Matt. XIV.25–6.
66 Rev. XIX.7.
67 blue is the colour of hope.
68 'The Verse':

    The measure is English heroic verse without rhyme, as that of Homer in Greek,
    and of Virgil in Latin; rhyme being no necessary adjunct or true ornament of
    poem or good verse, in longer works especially, but the invention of a barbarous
    age, to set off wretched matter and lame metre; graced indeed since by the use of
    some famous modern poets, carried away by custom, but much to their own
    vexation, hindrance, and constraint to express many things otherwise, and for
    the most part worse than else they would have expressed them. Not without
    cause therefore some both Italian and Spanish poets of prime note have rejected
    rhyme both in longer and shorter works, as have also long since our best English
    tragedies, as a thing of it self, to all judicious ears, trivial and of no true musical
    delight; which consists only in apt numbers, fit quantity of syllables, and the
    sense variously drawn out from one verse into another, not in the jingling sound
    of like endings, a fault avoided by the learned ancients both in poetry and all
    good oratory. This neglect then of rhyme so little is to be taken for a defect,

though it may seem so perhaps to vulgar readers, that it rather is to be esteemed an example set, the first in English, of ancient liberty recovered to heroic poem from the troublesome and modern bondage of rhyming.

69   M.'s summary ('The Argument') of Book 1

This first book proposes, first in brief, the whole subject, man's disobedience, and the loss thereupon of Paradise wherein he was placed: then touches the prime cause of his fall, the serpent, or rather Satan in the serpent; who revolting from God, and drawing to his side many legions of angels, was by the command of God driven out of heaven with all his crew into the great deep. Which action passed over, the poem hastes into the midst of things, presenting Satan with his angels now fallen into hell, described here, not in the centre (for heaven and earth may be supposed as yet not made, certainly not yet accursed) but in a place of utter darkness, fitliest called Chaos: here Satan with his angels lying on the burning lake, thunderstruck and astonished, after a certain space recovers, as from confusion, calls up him who next in order and dignity lay by him; they confer of their miserable fall. Satan awakens all his legions, who lay till then in the same manner confounded; they rise, their numbers, array of battle, their chief leaders named, according to the idols known afterwards in Canaan and the countries adjoining. To these Satan directs his speech, comforts them with hope yet of regaining heaven, but tells them lastly of a new world and new kind of creature to be created, according to an ancient prophecy or report in heaven; for that angels were long before this visible creation, was the opinion of many ancient Fathers. To find out the truth of this prophecy, and what to determine thereon he refers to a full council. What his associates thence attempt. Pandemonium the palace of Satan rises, suddenly built out of the deep: the infernal peers there sit in council.

70   Christ, Cor.XVI.21–22.
71   i.e. Urania; here linked with Christian holy inspiration.
72   Moses, Exod.XIX. 1: seed = the Israelites.
73   the Temple: M. parallels the spring on Mt Helicon, the haunt of the Muses, with the pool of Siloam, near the Temple of Jerusalem.
74   Gen.I.2.
75   Luke X.18, Rev. XX.1–2, Isa.XIV.12–15 and Homer *Iliad* I.591.
76   Job X.22.
77   Dante. *Inferno* III.9 – 'abandon all hope, ye who enter here'.
78   angels were believed to be formed from spiritual (not actual) fire cf. Ps. CIV.4.
79   if I am not mistaken.
80   as in 'laid the dust'.
81   giants – the children of Earth and Heaven, who rebelled against Jove (Zeus) as the Titans had against Uranus.
82   whales do not have scales!
83   volcanoes and earthquakes were believed to be caused by trapped winds and sulphurous fire.
84   Galileo, the astronomer whom M. visited at Fiesole, nr. Florence, 1638.
85   because he had given the Israelites permission to leave and then pursued them.
86   Exod. X.12–5.
87   Rhine and Danube were boundaries of the Roman Empire.
88   Rev.III.5.
89   Satan's 12 disciples, Moloch, Beelzebub (Baal), Ashtoreth, Thammuz, Dagon,

Osiris, Isis, (H)Orus, Belial, Titan, Saturn, Jove (Jupiter) are listed according to the areas in which they were worshipped – lines 381–418 amongst the Israelites; 419–476 in Syria and Phoenicia; 476–489 Egypt; 490–505 Belial has no location; 507–521 Greece and Rome.

90   II Kings XXI.4–5 and XVI.10 ff.

91   Num. XXXII and Isa. XV, XVI – all places named are east of the river Jordan and the Dead Sea, an area given by Moses to the tribes of Reuben and Gad: the cities were captured by the Israelites.

92   Baal was worshipped at Peor, Num. XXV.1–3.

93   the plague that killed 24,000, Num. XXV.9.

94   Peor is linked by St Jerome to Priapus, II Kings XXIII.5ff.

95   N.E. Syria to S.W. Canaan: the brook is Besor, I Sam. XXX.10.

96   Judges II.11–15.

97   Ezek. VIII.12.ff.

98   I Sam. V.1–4.

99   i.e. Naaman, II Kings V.1–19.

100   Ahaz, II Kings XVI. 10–15.

101   the Egyptian gods had animal forms – e.g. Isis, the horns of a cow, Horus, the head of a hawk.

102   the Golden Calf, Exod. XXXII.4ff.

103   Jeroboam, I Kings XII.28–9.

104   Exod. XII.12, Num. XXXIII.4.

105   Ely's sons = the Hebrew priests at Shiloh, I Sam. II.12–17.

106   Gen. XIX.6.ff.

107   i.e. the Pygmies, a race of dwarfs, constantly attacked by migrating cranes. Homer *Iliad* III.5–6.

108   a list of the most famous armies of fighting heroes – of the Greeks at Thebes; of the Greeks and Trojans at Troy; of King Arthur and the Knights of the Round Table; of King Charlemagne and his twelve paladins, including Roland, who fought against the Saracens.

109   sulphur was regarded, with mercury, as the principal active material of metals.

110   the ore is smelted, using the fire of the burning lake, then channelled off into the foundations; then, to music, Pandemonium rises.

111   Pandemonium i.e. pan = all, daemonium = assembly of demons.

112   Pygmies were located in the mountains beyond the source of the Ganges.

113   'The Argument' of Book 2:

    The consultation begun, Satan debates whether another battle be to be hazarded for the recovery of Heaven: some advise it, others dissuade: a third proposal is prefer'd, mention'd before by Satan, to search the truth of that prophesy or tradition in Heaven concerning another world, and another kind of creature equal or not much inferior to themselves, about this time to be created: their doubt who shall be sent on this difficult search: Satan their chief undertakes alone the voyage, is honour'd and applauded. The Council thus ended, the rest betake them several ways and to several employments, as their inclinations lead them, to entertain the time till Satan return. He passes on his journey to hell-gates, finds them shut, and who sat there to guard them, by whom at length they are open'd, and discover to him the great gulf between hell and heaven; with what difficulty he passes through, directed by Chaos, the power of that place, to the sight of this new world which he sought.

114 just short of being annihilated.
115 food supplied to the Israelites by God, Exod. XVI.14.
116 lines 174–186 reflect classical accounts (e.g. Horace, *Odes* I.2) of Jove's threat to overthrow the Titans.
117 this suggests a force – a natural law – greater than God's.
118 Exod. XIX.9.; Deut. IV.11.; II Chron. V.13, VI.1.
119 fallen angels were believed to occupy one or other of the four elements – fire, air, earth or water.
120 Ps. II.9.; Rev. II.27.
121 i.e. determined our fate.
122 to the limits of our power.
123 with what qualities endowed.
124 Gen. VI.5ff.
125 where, as armed neighbours and with opportune invasion, we may re-enter . . .
126 'felt darkness' of Exod. X.21.
127 Virgil. *Aen*. VI.642–665.
128 the pillars at each end of the low wall round which Roman charioteers raced.
129 portents said to have been seen in the sky before a disaster.
130 popular topics for discussion in M.'s time.
131 Ecclesiasticus XLIII.20–21.
132 the route of the East India Company from Malaya down the E. coast of Africa, round the Cape of Good Hope, to bring their spice to Europe.
133 a comet is a 'hairy' star – foretelling war and pestilence.
134 their meeting with Christ, who overcame them.
135 cf. the birth of Athene from the head of Zeus.
136 sphere of fire where angels live.
137 Chaos and Night are the disorderly matter out of which came the order of nature and the natural world and where the four elements – earth, air, fire and water – contend with, not complement, each other.
138 give some weight to fighting winds.
139 as if attacked by the sound of a peal of bells.
140 creature half-eagle, half-lion.
141 'The Argument' of Book 9:
     Satan having compassed the earth, with meditated guile returns as a mist by night into Paradise, enters into the serpent sleeping. Adam and Eve in the morning go forth to their labours, which Eve proposes to divide in several places, each labouring apart: Adam consents not, alleging the danger, lest that enemy, of whom they were forewarned, should attempt her found alone: Eve loth to be thought not circumspect or firm enough, urges her going apart, the rather desirous to make trial of her strength; Adam at last yields: the serpent finds her alone; his subtle approach, first gazing, then speaking, with much flattery extolling Eve above all other creatures. Eve wondering to hear the serpent speak, asks how he attained to human speech and such understanding not till now; the serpent answers, that by tasting of a certain tree in the garden he attained both to speech and reason, till then void of both: Eve requires him to bring her to that tree, and finds it to be the tree of knowledge forbidden: the serpent now grown bolder, with many wiles and arguments induces her at length to eat; she pleased with the taste deliberates a while whether to impart thereof to Adam or not, at last brings him of the fruit, relates what persuaded her to eat

> thereof: Adam at first amazed, but perceiving her lost, resolves through vehemence of love to perish with her; and extenuating the trespass eats also of the fruit: the effects thereof in them both; they seek to cover their nakedness; then fall to variance and accusation of one another.

142 It was not until he was about 40 years old that M. was able to concentrate on writing *P.L.*

143 three things might prevent his success – (a) the decline in contemporary culture (b) the cold climate which, it was believed, resulted in dull, melancholy minds or (c) M.'s age.

144 Gen. II.14.

145 man has properties of (a) growth, as in vegetation (b) sensation, as in animals (c) reason, peculiar to man himself.

146 created out of envy.

147 ivy and woodbine when entwined with the 'married elm' = true love: myrtle, rose = the frailty of human happiness: myrtle is associated with Venus who, when bathing, was spied upon and hid behind a myrtle bush.

148 both talking together and living together.

149 joined hands = faith, troth and concord, now broken.

150 cf. n.147.

151 the colours of Minerva, the virgin goddess.

152 Solomon, Song of Solomon VI.2, I Kings III.1.

153 Job I.6; II.1.

154 Aesculapius – son of Apollo, skilled in healing.

155 either the snake's tongue directly or by air vibrations.

156 milk from the teat, and fennel, traditionally favourite food of snakes; fennel = flattery.

157 will o'the wisp (*ignis fatuus*) – a phosphorescent light seen over moorland bogs, believed to be due to the spontaneous combustion of decaying matter.

158 squirms around like an actor moved to passion.

159 at the height of his passion.

160 in addition to.

161 i.e. if Eve gains knowledge of good, how is God just in forbidding it?

162 i.e of God. Fear of death implies an unjust God, but God cannot be unjust or He is no longer God, and no longer to be feared or obeyed.

163 the man inside the snake exterior.

164 its source is beyond suspicion.

165 i.e. given the power to bring wisdom.

166 with excuses written on her face, prompting her bland spoken words.

167 i.e. Eve has been assured of Adam's love.

168 Eve shows good taste in both food and wisdom (in choosing to eat the apple).

169 Judges XVI.

170 fig tree – cf. John Gerard's *Herbal* (1597) pp. 1330 ff. M.'s tree is a mixture of the Indian banyan and the banana trees.

171 in architecture the cincture divides the column from the capital and the base.

172 understanding and will are two divisions of the reason, the highest human faculty: from beneath = the lowest part of man which is ruled by the liver, where the lowest faculties are.

173 'The Argument' of Book 10:

> Man's transgression known, the guardian angels forsake Paradise, and return up to heaven to approve their vigilance, and are approved, God declaring that the

entrance of Satan could not be by them prevented. He sends his Son to judge the
transgressors, who descends and gives sentence accordingly; then in pity clothes
them both, and re-ascends. Sin and Death sitting till then at the gates of hell, by
wondrous sympathy feeling the success of Satan in this new world, and the sin by
man there committed, resolve to sit no longer confined in hell, but to follow
Satan their sire up to the place of man: to make the way easier from hell to this
world to and fro, they pave a broad highway or bridge over chaos, according to
the track that Satan first made; then preparing for earth, they meet him proud of
his success returning to hell; their mutual gratulation. Satan arrives at
Pandemonium, in full assembly relates with boasting his success against man;
instead of applause is entertained with a general hiss by all his audience,
transformed with himself also suddenly into serpents, according to his doom
given in Paradise; then deluded with a show of the forbidden tree springing up
before them, they greedily reaching to take of the fruit, chew dust and bitter
ashes. The proceedings of Sin and Death; God foretells the final victory of his Son
over them, and the renewing of all things; but for the present commands his
angels to make several alterations in the heavens and elements. Adam more and
more perceiving his fallen condition heavily bewails, rejects the condolement of
Eve; she persists and at length appeases him: then to evade the curse likely to fall
on their offspring, proposes to Adam violent ways which he approves not, but
conceiving better hope, puts her in mind of the late promise made them, that her
seed should be revenged on the serpent, and exhorts her with him to seek peace of
the offended Deity, by repentance and supplication.

174 those who were accountable made haste towards the supreme throne to offer their
     plea – a rightful one – of their greatest vigilance, and this was happily accepted.
175 justice is not to be offered a second time like a rejected gift.
176 the demands of both justice and mercy to be fully satisfied.
177 Christ as a pledge for mankind.
178 where formerly you did, unasked, your duty in meeting me.
179 finally God judges Satan, who was the first to sin, but does so in mysterious terms,
     thought best at that time. (Gen. III.14ff).
180 Luke X.18, Col. II.14ff, Eph. IV.8. Satan would always trouble mankind but he
     himself would be deposed by Mary (a second Eve)'s son, Jesus, in his harrowing of
     hell.
181 Phil. II.7
182 cf. Book II.649.
183 the North-east Passage to Cathay sought for by Hudson, 1608.
184 the sinister (evil) side.
185 cf. Book II.1048; Rev. XXI.16.
186 because he is the child of Satan's incestuous relationship with his daughter.
187 Satan = lit. 'adversary'.
188 the crescent battle formation of the Turks.
189 amphisbaena = serpent with a head at each end; cerastes = ram-headed monster with
     4 horns; hydrus = water snake; ellops = serpent, sometimes a swordfish;
     dipsas = serpent whose bite causes great thirst: many had emblematic significance –
     amphisbaena = inconsistency and adultery; cerastes = powerlust (see *The Book of
     Beasts*, ed. T.H. White).
190 either on guard or drawn up in military formation.
191 terms of astrology relating to the position of the planets – sextile = 60 degrees,

trine = 120, quartile = square, 90 degrees and opposite = 180; sextile and trine are considered harmonious, quartile and opposite disharmonious; in synod = in conjunction i.e. when the influence of two planets is equal and neutral; 'fixed' refers to the fixed stars.

192   i.e. the 4 elements – earth, air, fire and water.

193   the first relates to the heliocentric, the second to the geocentric theories of the cosmic system.

194   reining to one side the sun-chariot horses by the same number of degrees of decline.

195   the Pleiades – situated in the Taurus constellation; Spartan Twins = Gemini, Castor and Pollux; Leo, Virgin, the Scales – all signs of the Zodiac.

196   allowing for earth's climatic changes, unlike unchanging Eden.

197   i.e. God would be going against natural law were He as the agent to act according to his subject's capacities not his own.

198   the steps of repentance include (a) conviction of sin (b) contrition (c) confession (d) departure from evil (e) conversion to good. Adam reaches (a) but then falls into despair.

199   Adam completes the three stages of expiation – attrition, contrition, and repentance.

200   the story is based on Judges XIII–XVI

201   The following extracts are taken from M.'s prefatory note to *S.A.*

Of that sort of Dramatic Poem which is called Tragedy.

Tragedy, as it was anciently composed, hath ever been held the gravest, moralest, and most profitable of all other poems: therefore said by Aristotle to be of power by raising pity and fear, or terror, to purge the mind of those and such like passions, that is to temper and reduce them to just measure with a kind of delight, stirred up by reading or seeing those passions well imitated. Nor is nature wanting in her own effects to make good his assertion: for so in physic things of melancholic hue and quality are used against melancholy, sour against sour, salt to remove salt humours. . . .Heretofore men in highest dignity have laboured not a little to be thought able to compose a tragedy. . . . This is mentioned to vindicate tragedy from the small esteem, or rather infamy, which in the account of many it undergoes at this day with other common interludes: happening through the poet's error of intermixing comic stuff with tragic sadness and gravity; or introducing trivial and vulgar persons, which by all judicious hath been counted absurd; and brought in without discretion, corruptly to gratify the people. . . . [the] Chorus is here introduced after the Greek manner, not ancient only, but modern, and still in use among the Italians. In the modelling therefore of this poem, with good reason, the ancients and Italians are rather followed, as of much more authority and fame. The measure of verse used in the Chorus is of all sorts, called by the Greeks monostrophic . . . without regard had to strophe, antistrophe or epode, which were a kind of stanzas framed only for the music, then used with the Chorus that sung; not essential to the poem, and therefore not material. . . . Division into act and scene referring chiefly to the stage (to which this work was never intended) is here omitted. It suffices if the whole drama be found not produced beyond the fifth act.

Of the style and uniformity, and that commonly called the plot, whether intricate or explicit, which is nothing indeed but such economy, or disposition of the fable as may stand best with verisimilitude and decorum, they only will best judge who are not unacquainted with Aeschylus, Sophocles, and Euripides, the three tragic poets unequalled yet by any, and the best rule to all who endeavour to write tragedy. The circumscription of time wherein the whole drama begins and ends, is according to ancient rule, and best example, within the space of 24 hours.

202 Nazar is the Hebrew for 'to separate oneself', Num. VI.1ff.
203 by 1652 M. was almost totally blind.
204 Augustine's doctrine held that the soul was whole in every part of the body.
205 the Philistines were uncircumcised.
206 one that has accomplished its purpose.
207 obligation and duty owed to (Moses') law.
208 marriage to a Gentile for a Nazarite was considered unclean.
209 the woman of Timna.
210 the Philistines had conquered Canaan.
211 a pun – the most important, and appertaining to his head.
212 nothing of this in the Bible or tradition.
213 as were Tantalus and Prometheus.
214 water flowing eastward was believed to have life-giving power.
215 vital regenerative power.
216 of the four humours, black bile was the source of melancholy.
217 it was believed the hyena could counterfeit the human voice, luring men out to devour them.
218 Dalilah is lying, Judges XVI.5.
219 M. considered levity a vice, opposed to the virtue of gravity.
220 Ps. LVIII.4–5.
221 I Sam. XVII.7: the beam is the wooden roller in a loom: the shield, cf. the shield of Ajax, Homer *Iliad* 7.220.
222 Samson's challenge and Harapha's reply follow the rules of mediaeval combat, cf. Selden, *Duello* (1610) and *Anti-Duello* (1632).
223 cf. oath taken in mediaeval combats not to use magic or charms but to trust in God.
224 cf. mediaeval custom of challenging three times (as at the coronation of Charles II) before combat: men such as robbers, traitors and slaves had no right to single combat.
225 II Sam. XXI.16–22.
226 not holi(y)-day but idol-day.
227 is slow because of taking refreshment on the journey.
228 a false pregnancy – mere flatulence.
229 the phoenix which re-creates itself in its own fiery immolation.

Andrew Marvell

[1621–78]

The son of the Rev. Andrew Marvell, he was born in Holderness, Yorkshire: the family moved to Hull, where his father became a lecturer at Holy Trinity Church: educated at Hull Grammar school; Trinity College, Cambridge, B.A. 1539. In 1637 he contributed Greek and Latin verses to a volume celebrating the birth of a daughter to Charles I. *c.* 1639 he came under Catholic influence. 1641 his father was drowned crossing the Humber and Marvell left Cambridge for London. 1643–7 he travelled on the Continent, so avoiding the Civil War in England. 1649, he returned to London: 1649 his poems to Lovelace and on the death of Lord Hastings published. 1650 he wrote 'An Horatian Ode upon Cromwell's Return from Ireland'. 1650–4 he acted as tutor, first to Mary Fairfax, daughter of Lord Fairfax, the Parliamentarian general, and then to William Dutter, Cromwell's ward, when he probably wrote 'Bermudas'. 1653–4 Milton recommended him as his assistant in the Latin Secretaryship, an appointment made in 1657, when M. withdrew through blindness: it is reported that he protected M. at the Restoration. His elegy for Cromwell was published 1658 and, in 1659, he became M.P. for Hull. From 1662 he was often abroad on political business and published tracts and satires against the corruption at court, popery in England and individuals such as Clarendon. He died in his home in Great Russell St, London, from medical treatment for a tertian ague. 1681 *Miscellaneous Poems* published by Mary Marvell – actually Mary Palmer, his housekeeper. Famed in his lifetime as a patriot and satirist, particularly in support of Cromwell and the Parliamentarians: his poetry was not really recognized in England until after the 1914–18 war when Grierson published his *Metaphysical Lyrics* and T.S. Eliot his 'Andrew Marvell'.

The Coronet

When for the thorns with which I long, too long,
   With many a piercing wound,
   My Savior's head have crown'd,
I seek with garlands to redress that wrong;
   Through every garden, every mead,
I gather flowers (my fruits are only flowers)
   Dismantling all the fragrant towers°   high headdresses
That once adorn'd my shepherdess's head.
And now when I have summ'd up all my store,
10   Thinking (so I myself deceive)
   So rich a chaplet° thence to weave   head garland
As never yet the king of glory wore;
   Alas I find the serpent old
   That, twining° in his speckled breast,   entwining
   About the flowers disguised does fold,
   With wreaths° of fame and interest.   coils
Ah, foolish man, that would'st debase with them,
And mortal glory, heaven's diadem!
   But Thou who only couldst the serpent tame,
20 Either his slippery knots at once untie,
And disentangle all his winding snare:
Or shatter too with him my curious frame:[1]
And let these wither, so that he may die,
Though set with skill and chosen out with care,
That they, while Thou or both their spoils dost tread,
May crown thy feet, that could not crown thy head.

[1681]

Bermudas[2]

   Where the remote Bermudas ride,[3]
In th' ocean's bosom unespied,
From a small boat that rowed along,
The listening winds received this song:
   'What should we do but sing His praise,
That led us through the watery maze
Unto an isle so long unknown,[4]
And yet far kinder than our own?

Where He the huge sea monsters wracks,°   *wrecks*
10 That lift the deep upon their backs;
    He lands us on a grassy stage,
    Safe from the storms, and prelate's rage.
    He gave us this eternal spring
    Which here enamels everything,
    And sends the fowls to us in care,
    On daily visits through the air;
    He hangs in shades the orange bright,
    Like golden lamps in a green night,
    And does in the pomegranates close
20 Jewels more rich than Ormus shows;
    He makes the figs our mouths to meet,
    And throws the melons at our feet;
    But apples° plants of such a price,   *pineapples*
    No tree could ever bear them twice;
    With cedars, chosen by His hand,
    From Lebanon, He stores the land;
    And makes the hollow seas, that roar,
    Proclaim the ambergris⁵ on shore;
    He cast (of which we rather boast)
30 The Gospel's pearl upon our coast,
    And in these rocks for us did frame
    A temple, where to sound His name.
    O! let our voice His praise exalt,
    Till it arrive at heaven's vault,
    Which, thence (perhaps) rebounding, may
    Echo beyond the Mexique Bay.'
        Thus sung they in the English boat,⁶
    An holy and a cheerful note;
    And all the way, to guide their chime,
40 With falling oars they kept the time.

[1681]

The Definition of Love

My love is of a birth as rare
As 'tis for object strange and high:
It was begotten by Despair
Upon Impossibility.

Magnanimous Despair alone
Could show me so divine a thing,
Where feeble Hope could ne'er have flown
But vainly flapped its tinsel wing.

And yet I quickly might arrive
10 Where my extended° soul is fixt,°   *stretching out/intent upon*
But Fate does iron wedges drive,
And always crowds itself betwixt.

For Fate with jealous eye does see
Two perfect loves; nor lets them close:°   *unite*
Their union would her ruin be,
And her tyrannic power depose.[7]

And therefore her decrees of steel
Us as the distant poles[8] have placed,
(Though Love's whole world on us doth wheel[9])
20 Not by themselves° to be embraced.   *each other*

Unless the giddy heaven fall,
And earth some new convulsion tear;
And, us to join, the world should all
Be cramped into a planisphere.[10]

As lines° so loves oblique may well   *meridians*
Themselves in every angle greet:[11]
But ours so truly parallel,
Though infinite, can never meet.

Therefore the Love which us doth bind
30 But Fate so enviously debars,
Is the conjunction of the mind,
And opposition of the stars.[12]

The Mower to the Glow-worms

Ye living lamps, by whose dear light
The nightingale does sit so late
And studying all the summer night,
Her matchless songs does meditate;

Ye country comets, that portend[13]
No war, nor prince's funeral,
Shining unto no higher end
Than to presage the grasses' fall;

Ye glow-worms, whose officious° flame   attentive
To wandering mowers shows the way,[14]
That in the night have lost their aim,
And after foolish fires° do stray;   will o' the wisps

Your courteous lights in vain you waste,
Since Juliana here is come,
For she my mind hath so displaced
That I shall never find my home.

[1681]

To His Coy Mistress

Had we but world enough, and time,
This coyness, Lady, were no crime.
We would sit down and think which way
To walk and pass our long love's day.
Thou by the Indian Ganges' side
Shouldst rubies[15] find: I by the tide
Of Humber would complain. I would
Love you ten years before the Flood,
And you should, if you please, refuse
10   Till the conversion of the Jews.[16]
My vegetable[17] love should grow
Vaster than empires, and more slow;
An hundred years should go to praise
Thine eyes and on thy forehead gaze;
Two hundred to adore each breast;

But thirty thousand to the rest;
An age at least to every part,
And the last age should show your heart;
For, Lady, you deserve this state,°   *dignity*
20 Nor would I love at lower rate.
      But at my back I always hear
Time's wingéd chariot hurrying near;
And yonder all before us lie
Desarts° of vast eternity.   *deserts*
Thy beauty shall no more be found,
Nor, in thy marble vault, shall sound
My echoing song: then worms shall try
That long preserved virginity,
And your quaint° honour¹⁸ turn to dust,   *over-fastidious*
30 And into ashes all my lust:
The grave's a fine and private place,
But none, I think, do there embrace.
      Now therefore, while the youthful hue
Sits on thy skin like morning dew,
And while thy willing soul transpires°   *breathes out*
At every pore with instant fires,
Now let us sport us while we may,
And now, like amorous birds of prey,
Rather at once our time devour
40 Than languish in his slow-chapt° power.   *devouring*
Let us roll all our strength and all
Our sweetness up into one ball,
And tear our pleasures with rough strife
Thorough° the iron gates of life: *through*
Thus, though we cannot make our sun
Stand still,¹⁹ yet we will make him run.

[1681]

NOTES

Marvell

1   elaborately wrought construction.

2   in July 1653 M. went to live at Eton, as tutor to Cromwell's ward, William Dutton, in the house of John Oxenbridge who had visited the Bermudas twice.

3   like a ship at sea.

4   discovered by Juan Bermudez, 1515: for M.'s description see: Waller: *The Battle of the Summer Islands* (Bermudas), 1645, and Capt. John Smith: *The General History of Virginia, New England, and the Summer Islands*, 1624.

5   secretion of sperm whale used in perfume.

6   cf. *A Plaine Description of the Bermudas, now called the Summer Islands*, 1613 where there is a description of Richard More's landing party rowing ashore singing psalms.

7   it was believed that an equal mixture of pure elements brought a stability that could defy even fate.

8   either terrestrial or celestial.

9   their relationship forms an axis for the world of love.

10   defined by Johnson as 'a sphere projected on a plane' – as is the three-dimensional sphere flattened into two dimensions, so that the poles were brought together.

11   oblique lines and imperfect love meet at an angle; parallel lines and perfect love meet only at infinity.

12   their minds are united but fate and the stars that determine their destinies keep them apart.

13   comets were believed to be signs of approaching disaster.

14   according to Pliny, glow-worms were substitutes for the stars, appearing only when the hay was ready for cutting, to light the reapers in their work.

15   rubies are talismans to protect virginity.

16   i.e. the end of time, just before Judgement Day.

17   vegetation, which, according to Johnson, 'lacked life' thus distinguishing it from the animal.

18   reputation, chastity.

19   as Zeus did when, to prolong his enjoyment of Alcmene, he made one night last a whole week.

John Dryden

[1631–1700]

He was educated at Westminster School and Trinity College, Cambridge; inherited a small estate, which, with his prolific writings, kept him. His first major poem was *Heroique Stanzas*, 1658, on the death of Cromwell: 1660 he celebrated the King's return with *Astraea Redux* and *To His Sacred Majesty*: m. Lady Elizabeth Howard, 1633, to whose brother he had written verses. In 1667 *Annus Mirabilis* was published but his early writing was mostly plays. In 1668 he became Poet Laureate and Historiographer Royal, and wrote his first major critical work – *Of Dramatick Poesie*. His principal opponent in the literary world was Thomas Shadwell, whom he attacked in *MacFlecknoe*, 1682. His best known satires appeared in the 1680s – *Absalom and Achitophel*, 1681; *The Medall*; 200 lines for Tate's *The Second Part of Absalom and Achitophel*, as well as *Religio Laici* (a defence of the Anglican Church) in 1682. With James II's accession D. became a Catholic, writing *The Hind and the Panther*, 1687, in support of his new beliefs. In 1689, with the Revolution and the accession of William III and Mary II to the throne, D. refused to take the oath of allegiance and was dismissed from his court positions: he returned to playwriting and then to translating the Classics – including Homer, Theocritus, Horace, the whole of Virgil – and Chaucer. 1685 he turned again to satire, producing, 1693, *The Origin and Progress of Satire*. His last achievement was *Fables Ancient and Modern*, 1700. He is buried in Westminster Abbey.

Absalom and Achitophel[1]

In pious times[2], ere priest-craft did begin,
Before polygamy was made a sin;
When man on many multiplied his kind,
Ere one to one was, cursedly, confined;
When nature prompted and no law denied
Promiscuous use of concubine and bride;
Then Israel's monarch,° after heaven's own heart,   *David**
His vigorous warmth did, variously, impart
To wives and slaves; and, wide as his command,
10 Scattered his Maker's image through the land.
Michal, of royal blood, the crown did wear;
A soil ungrateful to the tiller's care.
Not so the rest; for several mothers bore
To God-like David several sons before.
But since like slaves his bed they did ascend,
No true succession could their seed attend.
Of all this numerous progeny was none
So beautiful, so brave as Absalom.
Whether, inspired by some diviner lust,
20 His father got him with a greater gust;
Or that his conscious destiny made way
By manly beauty to imperial sway.
Early in foreign fields[3] he won renown,
With kings and states allied to Israel's crown.
In peace the thoughts of war he could remove,
And seemed as he were only born for love.
Whate'er he did was done with so much ease,
In him alone 'twas natural to please:
His motions all accompanied with grace,
30 And paradise was opened in his face.
With secret joy indulgent David viewed
His youthful image in his son renewed;
To all his wishes nothing he denied,
And made the charming Annabel his bride.
What faults he had (for who from faults is free?),
His father could not or he would not see.
Some warm excesses, which the law forbore,
Were construed youth that purged by boiling o'er;
And Amnon's murder,[4] by a specious name,
40 Was called a just revenge for injured fame.
Thus praised and loved the noble youth remained,
While David undisturbed in Sion reigned.

*See p.536 for a key to the names in the poem.

But life can never be sincerely blest;
Heav'n punishes the bad, and proves° the best.   *tests*
The Jews, a headstong, moody, murm'ring race,
As ever tried th' extent and stretch of grace;
God's pampered people whom, debauched with ease,
No king could govern, nor no god could please
(Gods they had tried of every shape and size,
50 That god-smiths could produce, or priests devise):
These Adam-wits,⁵ too fortunately free,
Began to dream they wanted liberty;
And when no rule, no precedent, was found
Of men, by laws less circumscribed and bound
They led their wild desires to woods and caves,
And thought that all but savages were slaves.
They who, when Saul was dead, without a blow
Made foolish Ishbosheth the crown forgo;
Who banished David did from Hebron⁶ bring
60 And, with a general shout, proclaimed him King:
Those very Jews, who at their very best
Their humour more than loyalty expressed,
Now wondered why so long they had obeyed
An idol-monarch° which their hands had made;   *Cromwell*
Thought they might ruin him they could create,
Or melt him to that golden calf, a state.°   *the Commonwealth*
But these were random bolts; no formed design
Nor interest made the factious crowd to join.
The sober part of Israel, free from stain,
70 Well knew the value of a peaceful reign,
And, looking backward with a wise affright,
Saw seams of wounds, dishonest to the sight;
In contemplation of whose ugly scars
They cursed the memory of civil wars.
The moderate sort of men, thus qualified,
Inclined the balance to the better side;
And David's mildness managed it so well
The bad found no occasion to rebel.
But when to sin our biased nature leans
80 The careful devil is still at hand with means,
And providently pimps for ill desires:
The good old cause° revived, a plot requires.   *the Commonwealth*
Plots, true or false, are necessary things
To raise up commonwealths and ruin kings.
    Th' inhabitants of old Jerusalem
Were Jebusites; the town so called from them,

And theirs the native right –
But when the chosen people° grew more strong   *Protestants*
The rightful cause at length became the wrong;
90 And every loss the men of Jebus bore,
They still were thought God's enemies the more.
Thus worn and weakened, well or ill content,
Submit they must to David's government.
Impoverished and deprived of all command,
Their taxes doubled as they lost their land;
And, what was harder yet to flesh and blood,
Their gods disgraced and burnt like common wood.
This set the heathen priesthood in a flame;
For priests of all religions are the same:
100 Of whatsoe'er descent their godhead be,
Stock, stone, or other homely pedigree,
In his defence his servants are as bold
As if he had been born of beaten gold.
The Jewish rabbins, though their enemies,
In this conclude them honest men and wise;
For 'twas their duty, all the learned think,
T' espouse his cause by whom they eat and drink.
From hence began that plot,[7] the nation's curse,
Bad in itself, but represented worse;
110 Raised in extremes, and in extremes decried;
With oaths affirmed, with dying vows denied;
Not weighed or winnowed by the multitude,
But swallowed in the mass, unchewed and crude.
Some truth there was, but dashed and brewed with lies
To please the fools and puzzle all the wise.
Succeeding times did equal folly call,
Believing nothing, or believing all.
Th' Egyptian rites the Jebusites embraced,
Where gods were recommended by their taste;
120 Such sav'ry deities must needs be good
As served at once for worship and for food.[8]
By force they could not introduce these gods,
For ten to one in former days was odds;
So fraud was used (the sacrificer's trade):
Fools are more hard to conquer than persuade.
Their busy teachers mingled with the Jews,
And raked for converts even the court and stews;
Which Hebrew priests the more unkindly took
Because the fleece accompanies the flock.
130 Some thought they God's anointed meant to slay

By guns, invented since full many a day.
Our author swears it not; but who can know
How far the devil and Jebusites may go?
This plot, which failed for want of common sense,
Had yet a deep and dangerous consequence;
For as when raging fevers boil the blood,
The standing lake soon floats into a flood,
And ev'ry hostile humour, which before
Slept quiet in its channels, bubbles o'er;
140 So, several factions from this first ferment
Work up to foam, and threat the government.
Some by their friends, more by themselves, thoughtwise,
Opposed the pow'r to which they could not rise;
Some had in courts been great, and thrown from thence,
Like fiends, were hardened in impenitence;
Some, by their monarch's fatal mercy grown,
From pardon'd rebels, kinsmen to the throne,
Were raised in pow'r and public office high:
Strong bands, if bands ungrateful men could tie.
150 Of these the false Achitophel was first:
A name to all succeeding ages cursed.
For close designs, and crooked counsels fit;
Sagacious, bold, and turbulent of wit;
Restless, unfixed in principles and place;[9]
In pow'r unpleased, impatient of disgrace;
A fiery soul, which working out its way,
Fretted the pigmy-body to decay,[10]
And o'er-informed the tenement of clay.
A daring pilot in extremity;
160 Pleased with the danger, when the waves went high
He sought the storms; but, for a calm unfit,
Would steer too nigh the sands to boast his wit.
Great wits are sure to madness near allied,
And thin partitions do their bounds divide;
Else why should he, with wealth and honour blest,
Refuse his age the needful hours of rest?
Punish a body which he could not please;
Bankrupt of life, yet prodigal of ease?
And all to leave, what with his toil he won,
170 To that unfeathered, two-legged thing, a son;[11]
Got while his soul did huddled notions try,
And born a shapeless lump, like anarchy.
In friendship false, implacable in hate;
Resolved to ruin or to rule the state:

To compass this the triple bond[12] he broke,
The pillars of the public safety shook,
And fitted Israel for a foreign yoke.
Then, seized with fear, yet still affecting fame,
Usurped a patriot's[13] all-atoning name;
180 So easy still it proves in factious times,[14]
With public zeal to cancel private crimes.
How safe is treason, and how sacred ill,
Where none can sin against the people's will;
Where crowds can wink and no offence be known,
Since in another's guilt they find their own.
Yet, fame deserved, no enemy can grudge:
The statesman we abhor but praise the judge.[15]
In Israel's courts ne'er sat an Abbethdin
With more discerning eyes or hands more clean;
190 Unbribed, unsought, the wretched to redress;
Swift of dispatch, and easy of access.
Oh, had he been content to serve the crown
With virtues only proper to the gown;
Or had the rankness of the soil been freed
From cockle° that oppressed the noble seed;   *weeds*
David for him his tuneful harp had strung,
And heav'n had wanted one immortal song.
But wild ambition loves to slide, not stand;
And fortune's ice prefers to virtue's land.
200 Achitophel, grown weary to possess
A lawful fame and lazy happiness,
Disdained the golden fruit to gather free,
And lent the crowd his arm to shake the tree.[16]
Now, manifest of crimes, contrived long since,
He stood at bold defiance with his prince;
Held up the buckler of the people's cause
Against the crown, and skulked behind the laws.
The wished occasion of the plot he takes;
Some circumstances finds, but more he makes.[17]
210 By buzzing emissaries fills the ears
Of list'ning crowds with jealousies and fears
Of arbitrary counsels brought to light,
And proves the King himself a Jebusite.[18]
Weak arguments! which yet he knew full well
Were strong with people easy to rebel;
For, governed by the moon, the giddy Jews
Tread the same track when she the prime renews;
And once in twenty years, their scribes record,

By natural instinct they change their lord.
220 Achitophel still wants a chief, and none
Was found so fit as warlike Absalom.
Not that he wished his greatness to create
(For politicians neither love nor hate),
But for he knew his title not allowed
Would keep him still depending on the crowd;
That kingly power, thus ebbing out, might be
Drawn to the dregs of a democracy.
Him he attempts with studied arts to please,
And sheds his venom, in such words as these:
230   'Auspicious Prince! at whose nativity
Some royal planet ruled the southern sky;
Thy longing country's darling and desire;
Their cloudy pillar and their guardian fire;[19]
Their second Moses, whose extended wand
Divides the seas and shows the promised land;
Whose dawning day, in every distant age,
Has exercised the sacred prophets' rage;
The people's pray'r, the glad diviners' theme,
The young men's vision, and the old men's dream!
240 Thee, Saviour, thee, the nation's vows confess,
And, never satisfied with seeing, bless.
Swift unbespoken pomps thy steps proclaim,
And stammering babes are taught to lisp thy name.
How long wilt thou the general joy detain,
Starve and defraud the people of thy reign?
Content ingloriously to pass thy days,
Like one of virtue's fools that feeds on praise,
Till thy fresh glories, which now shine so bright,
Grow stale and tarnish with our daily sight.
250 Believe me, royal youth, thy fruit must be
Or gathered ripe or rot upon the tree.
Heav'n has to all allotted, soon or late,
Some lucky revolution of their fate,
Whose motions, if we watch and guide with skill
(For human good depends on human will),
Our fortune rolls as from a smooth descent
And from the first impression takes the bent;°   direction
But if unseized, she glides away like wind
And leaves repenting folly far behind.
260 Now, now she meets you with a glorious prize,
And spreads her locks before her as she flies.
Had thus old David, from whose loins you spring,

Not dared, when fortune called him, to be King,
At Gath an exile he might still remain;
And heav'n's anointing oil had been in vain.
Let his successful youth your hopes engage;
But shun th' example of declining age:
Behold him setting in his western skies,
The shadows length'ning as the vapours rise.
270 He is not now as when on Jordan's sand
The joyful people thronged to see him land,
Cov'ring the beach and black'ning all the strand;
But, like the Prince of Angels from his height,
Comes tumbling downward with diminished light;
Betrayed by one poor plot to public scorn
(Our only blessing since his cursed return);
Those heaps of people, which one sheaf did bind,
Blown off and scattered by a puff of wind.
What strength can he to your designs oppose,
280 Naked of friends, and round beset with foes?
If Pharaoh's doubtful succour he should use,
A foreign aid would more incense the Jews;
Proud Egypt would dissembled friendship bring,
Foment the war but not support the King.
Nor would the royal party e'er unite
With Pharaoh's arms t' assist the Jebusite;
Or if they should, their interest soon would break,
And, with such odious aid, make David weak.
All sorts of men, by my successful arts
290 Abhorring kings, estrange their altered hearts
From David's rule; and 'tis the general cry,
Religion, commonwealth, and liberty.
If you, as champion of the public good,
Add to their arms a chief of royal blood,
What may not Israel hope? and what applause
Might such a general gain by such a cause?
Not barren praise alone, that gaudy flow'r,
Fair only to the sight, but solid pow'r;
And nobler is a limited command,
300 Giv'n by the love of all your native land,
Than a successive title, long and dark,
Drawn from the mouldy rolls of Noah's ark.'
    What cannot praise effect in mighty minds
When flattery soothes and when ambition blinds!
Desire of pow'r, on earth a vicious weed,
Yet, sprung from high, is of celestial seed;

In God 'tis glory; and when men aspire,
'Tis but a spark too much of heav'nly fire.
Th' ambitious youth, too covetous of fame,
310 Too full of angel's metal° in his frame,   *mettle*
Unwarily was led from virtue's ways;
Made drunk with honour, and debauched with praise
Half loath and half consenting to the ill
(For loyal²⁰ blood within him struggled still),
He thus replied: 'And what pretence have I
To take up arms for public liberty?
My father governs with unquestioned right,
The faith's defender and mankind's delight;
Good, gracious, just, observant of the laws;
320 And heav'n by wonders has espoused his cause.
Whom has he wronged in all his peaceful reign?
Who sues for justice to his throne in vain?
What millions has he pardoned of his foes,
Whom just revenge did to his wrath expose?
Mild, easy, humble, studious of our good;
Inclin'd to mercy, and averse from blood.
If mildness ill with stubborn Israel suit,
His crime is God's beloved attribute.
What could he gain his people to betray,
330 Or change his right for arbitrary sway?
Let haughty Pharaoh curse with such a reign
His fruitful Nile, and yoke a servile train!
If David's rule Jerusalem displease,
The dog-star heats their brains to this disease.
Why then should I, encouraging the bad,
Turn rebel and run popularly mad?
Were he a tyrant, who by lawless might
Oppressed the Jews and raised the Jebusite,
Well might I mourn; but nature's holy bands
340 Would curb my spirits and restrain my hands.
The people might assert their liberty,
But what was right in them, were crime in me.
His favour leaves me nothing to require;
Prevents my wishes and out-runs desire.
What more can I expect while David lives?
All but his kingly diadem he gives;
And that,' but there he paused; then sighing said,
'Is justly destined for a worthier head.
For when my father from his toils shall rest
350 And late augment the number of the blest,

His lawful issue shall the throne ascend;
Or the collat'ral line where that shall end.
His brother, though oppressed with vulgar spite,
Yet dauntless and secure of native right,
Of every royal virtue stands possessed;
Still dear to all the bravest, and the best.
His courage foes, his friends his truth proclaim;
His loyalty the King, the world his fame.
His mercy ev'n th' offending crowd will find,
360 For sure he comes of a forgiving kind.
Why should I then repine at heaven's decree,
Which gives me no pretence to royalty?
Yet oh! that fate, propitiously inclined,
Had raised my birth, or had debased my mind;
To my large soul not all her treasure lent,
And then betrayed it to a mean descent.
I find, I find my mounting spirits bold,
And David's part disdains my mother's mould.
Why am I scanted by a niggard-birth?
370 My soul disclaims the kindred of her earth,
And, made for empire, whispers me within:
"Desire of greatness is a god-like sin.'"
    Him staggering so when hell's dire agent found,
While fainting virtue scarce maintained her ground,
He pours fresh forces in, and thus replies:
'Th' eternal God, supremely good and wise,
Imparts not these prodigious gifts in vain;
What wonders are reserved to bless your reign?
Against your will your arguments have shown,
380 Such virtue's only giv'n to guide a throne.
Not that your father's mildness I contemn;
But manly force becomes the diadem.
'Tis true, he grants the people all they crave,
And more perhaps than subjects ought to have;
For lavish grants suppose a monarch tame,
And more his goodness than his wit proclaim.
But when should people strive their bonds to break,
If not when kings are negligent or weak?
Let him give on till he can give no more,
390 The thrifty Sanhedrin shall keep him poor;
And every shekel which he can receive
Shall cost a limb of his prerogative.
To ply him with new plots shall be my care;
Or plunge him deep in some expensive war,

Which, when his treasure can no more supply,
He must, with the remains of kingship, buy.
His faithful friends our jealousies and fears
Call Jebusites and Pharaoh's pensioners;
Whom, when our fury from his aid has torn,
400   He shall be naked left to public scorn.
The next successor, whom I fear and hate,
My arts have made obnoxious to the state;
Turned all his virtues to his overthrow,
And gained our elders to pronounce a foe.[21]
His right, for sums of necessary gold,
Shall first be pawned, and afterwards be sold;
Till time shall ever-wanting David draw
To pass your doubtful title into law.
If not, the people have a right supreme
410   To make their kings; for kings are made for them.
All empire is no more than pow'r in trust,
Which, when resumed, can be no longer just.
Succession, for the general good designed,
In its own wrong a nation cannot bind;
If altering that the people can relieve,
Better one suffer than a nation grieve.
The Jews well know their pow'r: ere Saul they chose,
God was their king, and God they durst depose.
Urge now your piety, your filial name,
420   A father's right, and fear of future fame;
The public good, that universal call,
To which even heav'n submitted, answers all.
Nor let his love enchant your generous mind;
'Tis nature's trick to propagate her kind.
Our fond begetters, who would never die,
Love but themselves in their posterity.
Or let his kindness by th' effects be tried,
Or let him lay his vain pretence aside.
God said he loved your father; could he bring
430   A better proof than to anoint him King?
It surely show'd he loved the shepherd well
Who gave so fair a flock as Israel.
Would David have you thought his darling son?
What means he then, to alienate the crown?
The name of godly he may blush to bear;
'Tis after God's own heart to cheat his heir.
He to his brother gives supreme command,
To you a legacy of barren land;

Perhaps th' old harp on which he thrums his lays,
440 Or some dull Hebrew ballad in your praise.
Then the next heir, a prince severe and wise,
Already looks on you with jealous eyes;
Sees through the thin disguises of your arts,
And marks your progress in the people's hearts.
Though now his mighty soul its grief contains,
He meditates revenge who least complains;
And like a lion, slumb'ring in the way,
Or sleep-dissembling while he waits his prey,
His fearless foes within his distance draws,
450 Constrains his roaring and contracts his paws;
Till at the last, his time for fury found,
He shoots with sudden vengeance from the ground;
The prostrate vulgar passes o'er and spares,
But with a lordly rage his hunters tears.
Your case no tame expedients will afford;
Resolve on death, or conquest by the sword,
Which for no less a stake than life you draw;
And self-defence is nature's eldest law.
Leave the warm people no considering time,
460 For then rebellion may be thought a crime.
Prevail yourself of what occasion gives,
But try your title while your father lives;
And that your arms may have a fair pretence,
Proclaim you take them in the King's defence,
Whose sacred life each minute would expose
To plots from seeming friends and secret foes.
And who can sound the depth of David's soul?
Perhaps his fear his kindness may control;
He fears his brother, though he loves his son,
470 For plighted vows too late to be undone.
If so, by force he wishes to be gained,
Like women's lechery to seem constrained.
Doubt not; but when he most affects the frown
Commit a pleasing rape upon the crown.
Secure his person to secure your cause:
They who possess the prince, possess the laws.'
　　He said, and this advice above the rest
With Absalom's mild nature suited best.
Unblamed of life (ambition set aside),
480 Not stained with cruelty, nor puffed with pride,
How happy had he been if destiny
Had higher placed his birth, or not so high!

His kingly virtues might have claimed a throne,
And blest all other countries but his own;
But charming greatness since so few refuse,
'Tis juster to lament him than accuse.
Strong were his hopes a rival to remove,
With blandishments to gain the public love;
To head the faction while their zeal was hot,
490 And popularly prosecute the plot.
To further this, Achitophel unites
The malcontents of all the Israelites,
Whose differing parties he could wisely join
For several ends to serve the same design.
The best, and of the princes some were such,
Who thought the pow'r of monarchy too much;
Mistaken men, and patriots in their hearts,
Not wicked but seduced by impious arts.
By these the springs of property were bent
500 And wound so high they cracked the government.
The next for interest sought t' embroil the state,
To sell their duty at a dearer rate,
And make their Jewish markets of the throne;
Pretending public good to serve their own.
Others thought kings an useless heavy load,
Who cost too much and did too little good;
These were for laying honest David by
On principles of pure good husbandry.
With them joined all th' haranguers of the throng
510 That thought to get preferment by the tongue.
Who follow next a double danger bring,
Not only hating David, but the King;
The Solymaean rout; well versed of old
In godly faction, and in treason bold;
Cow'ring and quaking at a conqu'ror's sword,
But lofty to a lawful prince restored;
Saw with disdain an ethnic plot begun,
And scorned by Jebusites to be outdone.
Hot Levites[22] headed these; who pulled before
520 From th' ark, which in the Judge's days[23] they bore,
Resumed their cant and with a zealous cry
Pursued their old beloved theocracy;[24]
Where Sanhedrin and priest enslaved the nation,
And justified their spoils by inspiration:
For who so fit for reign as Aaron's race,
If once dominion they could found in grace?

These led the pack; though not of surest scent
Yet deepest mouthed against the government.
A numerous host of dreaming saints succeed,
530 Of the true old enthusiastic breed;
'Gainst form and order they their pow'r employ;
Nothing to build and all things to destroy.
But far more numerous was the herd of such
Who think too little and who talk too much.
These, out of mere instinct, they knew not why,
Adored their father's god, and property;
And by the same blind benefit of fate
The devil and the Jebusite did hate.
Born to be saved,[25] even in their own despite,
540 Because they could not help believing right.
Such were the tools; but a whole hydra more
Remains of sprouting heads too long to score.
Some of their chiefs were princes of the land.
In the first rank of these did Zimri stand:
A man so various that he seemed to be
Not one, but all mankind's epitome.
Stiff in opinions, always in the wrong,
Was everything by starts and nothing long;
But in the course of one revolving moon
550 Was chemist, fiddler, statesman, and buffoon.
Then all for women, painting, rhyming, drinking;
Besides ten thousand freaks that died in thinking.
Blest madman, who could every hour employ
With something new to wish or to enjoy!
Railing and praising were his usual themes;
And both (to show his judgement) in extremes;
So over violent, or over civil,
That every man with him was god or devil.
In squandering wealth was his peculiar art:
560 Nothing went unrewarded, but desert.
Beggared by fools, whom still he found° too late;   *found out*
He had his jest, and they had his estate.
He laughed himself from court; then sought relief
By forming parties, but could ne'er be chief;
For, spite of him, the weight of business fell
On Absalom and wise Achitophel.
Thus, wicked but in will, of means bereft,
He left not faction but of that was left.
    Titles and names 'twere tedious to rehearse
570 Of lords below the dignity of verse.

Wits, warriors, commonwealthsmen, were the best;
Kind husbands and mere nobles all the rest.
And, therefore, in the name of dullness be
The well-hung[26] Balaam and cold Caleb free.
And canting Nadab let oblivion damn,
Who made new porridge for the paschal Lamb.[27]
Let friendship's holy band some names assure;
Some their own worth, and some let scorn secure.
Nor shall the rascal rabble here have place,
580 Whom kings no titles gave, and God no grace.
Not bull-faced Jonas, who could statutes draw
To mean rebellion, and make treason law.
But he, though bad, is followed by a worse;
The wretch who heav'n's anointed dared to curse:
Shimei, whose youth did early promise bring
Of zeal to God and hatred to his King,
Did wisely from expensive sins refrain,
And never broke the sabbath, but for gain;
Nor ever was he known an oath to vent,
590 Or curse, unless against the government.
Thus, heaping wealth by the most ready way
Among the Jews, which was to cheat and pray,
The city, to reward his pious hate
Against his master, chose him magistrate.
His hand a vare° of justice did uphold;   *wand*
His neck was loaded with a chain of gold.
During his office treason was no crime:
The sons of Belial[28] had a glorious time;
For Shimei, though not prodigal of pelf,°   *wealth*
600 Yet loved his wicked neighbour as himself.
When two or three were gathered to declaim
Against the monarch of Jerusalem,
Shimei was always in the midst of them.
And if they cursed the King when he was by
Would rather curse than break good company.
If any durst his factious friends accuse,
He packed a jury of dissenting Jews;[29]
Whose fellow-feeling in the godly cause
Would free the suffering saint from human laws.
610 For laws are only made to punish those
Who serve the King, and to protect his foes.
If any leisure time he had from pow'r
(Because 'tis sin to misemploy an hour),
His bus'ness was, by writing,[30] to persuade

That kings were useless and a clog to trade;
And, that his noble style he might refine,
No Rechabite[31] more shunned the fumes of wine.
Chaste were his cellars, and his shrieval board
The grossness of a city feast abhorred;
620 His cooks, with long disuse, their trade forgot:
Cool was his kitchen though his brains were hot.
Such frugal virtue malice may accuse,
But sure 'twas necessary to the Jews;
For towns once burnt[32] such magistrates require
As dare not tempt God's providence by fire.
With spiritual food he fed his servants well,
But free from flesh that made the Jews rebel;
And Moses' laws° he held in more account   *Ten Commandments*
For forty days of fasting in the Mount.
630 To speak the rest, who better are forgot,
Would tire a well-breathed witness of the plot;
Yet, Corah, thou shalt from oblivion pass:
Erect thyself, thou Monumental Brass,
High as the serpent of thy metal made,[33]
While nations stand secure beneath thy shade.
What though his birth were base, yet comets rise
From earthy vapours ere they shine in skies.
Prodigious actions may as well be done
By weaver's issue as by prince's son.
640 This arch-attestor for the public good
By that one deed ennobles all his blood.
Who ever asked the witnesses' high race
Whose oath with martyrdom did Stephen grace?
Ours was a Levite and, as times went then,
His tribe were God-Almighty's gentlemen.
Sunk were his eyes, his voice was harsh and loud,
Sure signs he neither choleric was nor proud;
His long chin proved his wit; his saint-like grace
A church vermilion and a Moses' face.[34]
650 His memory, miraculously great,
Could plots exceeding man's belief repeat;
Which, therefore, cannot be accounted lies,
For human wit could never such devise.
Some future truths are mingled in his book,
But where the witness failed the prophet spoke.
Some things like visionary flights appear;
The spirit caught him up, the Lord knows where,
And gave him his rabbinical degree,
Unknown to foreign university.

660 His judgement yet his mem'ry did excel,
Which pieced his wondrous evidence so well;
And suited to the temper of the times,
Then groaning under Jebusitic crimes.
Let Israel's foes suspect his heav'nly call,
And rashly judge his wit apocryphal;
Our laws for such affronts have forfeits made:
He takes his life who takes away his trade.
Were I myself in witness Corah's place,
The wretch who did me such a dire disgrace
670 Should whet my memory, though once forgot,
To make him an appendix of my plot.
His zeal to heav'n made him his prince despise
And load his person with indignities;
But zeal peculiar privilege affords,
Indulging latitude to deeds and words.
And Corah might for Agag's murder call
In terms as coarse as Samuel used to Saul.[35]
What others in his evidence did join
(The best that could be had for love or coin),
680 In Corah's own predicament will fall;
For witness is a common name to all.
    Surrounded thus with friends of every sort,
Deluded Absalom forsakes the Court;
Impatient of high hopes, urged with renown,
And fired with near possession of a crown.
Th' admiring crowd are dazzled with surprise,
And on his goodly person feed their eyes.
His joy concealed, he sets himself to show,
On each side bowing popularly low;
690 His looks, his gestures, and his words he frames,
And with familiar ease repeats their names.
Thus, formed by nature, furnished out with arts,
He glides unfelt into their secret hearts;
Then with a kind compassionating look
And sighs bespeaking pity ere he spoke.
Few words he said, but easy those and fit;
More slow than Hybla drops° and far more sweet: *honey*
   'I mourn, my countrymen, your lost estate,
Though far unable to prevent your fate.
700 Behold a banished man,[36] for your dear cause
Exposed a prey to arbitrary laws!
Yet oh! that I alone could be undone,
Cut off from empire, and no more a son!

Now all your liberties a spoil are made;
Egypt and Tyrus intercept your trade,
And Jebusites your sacred rites invade.
My father, whom with reverence yet I name,
Charmed into ease, is careless of his fame,
And, bribed with petty sums of foreign gold,[37]
710 Is grown in Bathsheba's embraces old.
Exalts his enemies, his friends destroys,
And all his pow'r against himself employs.
He gives and let him give my right away,
But why should he his own and yours betray?
He, only he, can make the nation bleed,
And he alone from my revenge is freed.
Take then my tears', (with that he wiped his eyes)
''Tis all the aid my present pow'r supplies.
No court-informer can these arms accuse;
720 These arms may sons against their fathers use;
And, 'tis my wish, the next successor's reign
May make no other Israelite complain.'
   Youth, beauty, graceful action, seldom fail,
But common interest always will prevail;
And pity never ceases to be shown
To him who makes the people's wrongs his own.
The crowd (that still believe their kings oppress),
With lifted hands their young Messiah bless;
Who now begins his progress to ordain;
730 With chariots, horsemen, and a num'rous train.
From east to west his glories he displays,
And, like the sun, the promised land surveys.
Fame runs before him as the morning star,
And shouts of joy salute him from afar.
Each house receives him as a guardian god,
And consecrates the place of his abode.
But hospitable treats did most commend
Wise Issachar, his wealthy western friend.
This moving court, that caught the people's eyes
740 And seemed but pomp, did other ends disguise.
Achitophel had formed it with intent
To sound the depths, and fathom where it went,
The people's hearts; distinguish friends from foes;
And try their strength before they come to blows.
Yet all was coloured with a smooth pretence
Of specious love and duty to their prince.
Religion and redress of grievances,

Two names that always cheat and always please,
Are often urged; and good King David's life
750   Endangered by a brother and a wife.[38]
Thus, in a pageant show, a plot is made
And peace itself is war in masquerade.
Oh, foolish Israel! never warned by ill;
Still the same bait, and circumvented still!
Did ever men forsake their present ease,
In midst of health imagine a disease;
Take pains contingent mischiefs to foresee,
Make heirs for monarchs and for God decree?
What shall we think! Can people give away
760   Both for themselves and sons their native sway?
Then they are left defenceless to the sword
Of each unbounded arbitrary lord;
And laws are vain, by which we right enjoy,
If kings unquestioned can those laws destroy.
Yet, if the crowd be judge of fit and just,
And kings are only officers in trust,
Then this resuming cov'nant was declared
When kings were made, or is for ever barred:
If those who gave the sceptre could not tie
770   By their own deed their own posterity,
How then could Adam bind his future race?
How could his forfeit on mankind take place?
Or how could heavenly justice damn us all,
Who ne'er consented to our father's fall?
Then kings are slaves to those whom they command,
And tenants to their people's pleasure stand.
Add, that the pow'r for property allowed
Is mischievously seated in the crowd;
For who can be secure of private right
780   If sovereign sway may be dissolved by might?
Nor is the people's judgement always true,
The most may err as grossly as the few;
And faultless kings run down by common cry
For vice, oppression and for tyranny.
What standard is there in a fickle rout
Which, flowing to the mark, runs faster out?
Nor only crowds but Sanhedrins may be
Infected with this public lunacy;
And share the madness of rebellious times
790   To murder monarchs for imagined crimes.
If they may give and take whene'er they please

Not kings alone (the Godhead's images)
But government itself at length must fall
To nature's state, where all have right to all.
Yet grant our lords the people, kings can make,
What prudent men a settled throne would shake?
For whatsoe'er their sufferings were before,
That change they covet makes them suffer more.
All other errors but disturb a state;
800 But innovation is the blow of fate.
If ancient fabrics nod and threat to fall,
To patch the flaws and buttress up the wall
Thus far 'tis duty; but here fix the mark,
For all beyond it is to touch° our Ark.[39]   *commit sacrilege*
To change foundations, cast the frame anew,
Is work for rebels who base ends pursue;
At once divine and human laws control,
And mend the parts by ruin of the whole.
The tamp'ring world is subject to this curse,
810 To physic° their disease into a worse.   *treat*
    Now what relief can righteous David bring?
How fatal 'tis to be too good a king!
Friends he has few, so high the madness grows;
Who dare be such must be the people's foes.
Yet some there were, ev'n in the worst of days;
Some let me name, and naming is to praise.
    In this short file Barzillai first appears;
Barzillai crowned with honour and with years.
Long since the rising rebels he withstood
820 In regions waste beyond the Jordan's flood.
Unfortunately brave to buoy the state,
But sinking underneath his master's fate
In exile with his god-like prince he mourned;
For him he suffered and with him returned.
The court he practised, not the courtier's art.
Large was his wealth but larger was his heart,
Which well the noblest objects knew to choose,
The fighting warrior and recording muse.
His bed could once a fruitful issue boast;
830 Now more than half a father's name is lost.
His eldest hope, with every grace adorned,
By me (so heav'n will have it) always mourned
And always honoured, snatched in manhood's prime
B' unequal fates and providence's crime.
Yet not before the goal of honour won,

All parts fulfilled of subject and of son;
Swift was the race but short the time to run.
Oh, narrow circle but of pow'r divine,
Scanted in space, but perfect in thy line!
840 By sea, by land, thy matchless worth was known
Arms thy delight, and war was all thy own.
Thy force, infused, the fainting Tyrians propped,
And haughty Pharaoh found his fortune stopped.
Oh, ancient honour, oh, unconquered hand,
Whom foes unpunished never could withstand!
But Israel was unworthy of thy name:
Short is the date of all immoderate fame.
It looks as heav'n our ruin had designed,
And durst not trust thy fortune and thy mind.
850 Now, free from earth, thy disencumbered soul
Mounts up and leaves behind the clouds and starry pole;
From thence thy kindred legions may'st thou bring
To aid the guardian angel of thy King.
Here stop my muse, here cease thy painful flight;
No pinions can pursue immortal height.
Tell good Barzillai thou canst sing no more,
And tell thy soul she should have fled before;
Or fled she with his life, and left this verse
To hang on her departed patron's hearse?[40]
860 Now take thy steepy flight from heav'n, and see
If thou canst find on earth another he;
Another he would be too hard to find,
See then whom thou canst see not far behind.
Zadoc the priest,[41] whom, shunning pow'r and place,
His lowly mind advanced to David's grace.
With him the Sagan of Jerusalem,
Of hospitable soul and noble stem;
Him of the western dome,[42] whose weighty sense
Flows in fit words and heavenly eloquence.
870 The prophet's sons, by such example led,
To learning and to loyalty were bred;
For colleges on bounteous kings depend,
And never rebel was to arts a friend.
To these succeed the pillars of the laws,
Who best could plead and best can judge a cause.
Next them a train of loyal peers ascend.
Sharp judging Adriel, the muses' friend,
Himself a muse – in Sanhedrin's debate
True to his prince, but not a slave of state;

880 Whom David's love with honours did adorn
    That from his disobedient son were torn.
    Jotham[43] of piercing wit and pregnant thought,
    Endued by nature, and by learning taught
    To move assemblies, who but only tried
    The worse awhile then chose the better side,
    Nor chose alone but turned the balance too;
    So much the weight of one brave man can do.
    Hushai,[44] the friend of David in distress,
    In public storms of manly steadfastness;
890 By foreign treaties he informed his youth,
    And joined experience to his native truth.
    His frugal care supplied the wanting throne;
    Frugal for that but bounteous of his own.
    'Tis easy conduct when exchequers flow,
    But hard the task to manage well the low;
    For sovereign power is too depressed or high
    When kings are forced to sell or crowds to buy.
    Indulge one labour more, my weary muse,
    For Amiel, who can Amiel's praise refuse?
900 Of ancient race by birth but nobler yet
    In his own worth, and without title great.
    The Sanhedrin long time as chief he ruled,
    Their reason guided and their passion cooled;
    So dext'rous was he in the crown's defence,
    So formed to speak a loyal nation's sense,
    That as their band was Israel's tribes in small,
    So fit was he to represent them all.
    Now rasher charioteers the seat ascend,
    Whose loose careers his steady skill commend.
910 They, like th' unequal ruler of the day,
    Misguide the seasons and mistake the way;[45]
    While he withdrawn at their mad labour smiles,
    And safe enjoys the sabbath of his toils.
        These were the chief; a small but faithful band
    Of worthies, in the breach who dared to stand
    And tempt th' united fury of the land.
    With grief they viewed such powerful engines bent
    To batter down the lawful government;
    A numerous faction with pretended frights
920 In Sanhedrins to plume° the regal rights;   *pluck*
    The true successor from the court removed;
    The plot by hireling witnesses improved.
    These ills they saw and, as their duty bound,

They showed the King the danger of the wound;
That no concessions from the throne would please,
But lenitives° fomented the disease;   *soothing ointments*
That Absalom, ambitious of the crown,
Was made the lure to draw the people down;
That false Achitophel's pernicious hate
930 Had turned the plot to ruin church and state;
The council violent, the rabble worse;
That Shimei taught Jerusalem to curse.
    With all these loads of injuries oppressed,
And long revolving in his careful breast
Th' event of things, at last his patience tired,
Thus from his royal throne, by heav'n inspired,
The god-like David spoke; with awful fear
His train their Maker in their master hear.
    'Thus long have I, by native mercy swayed,
940 My wrongs dissembled, my revenge delayed;   *hidden*
So willing to forgive th' offending age,
So much the father did the King assuage.
But now so far my clemency they slight,
Th' offenders question my forgiving right.⁴⁶
That one was made for many, they contend;
But 'tis to rule, for that's a monarch's end.
They call my tenderness of blood, my fear,
Though manly tempers can the longest bear.
Yet, since they will divert my native course,
950 'Tis time to show I am not good by force.
Those heaped affronts that haughty subjects bring,
Are burdens for a camel, not a king;
Kings are the public pillars of the state,
Born to sustain and prop the nation's weight.
If my young Samson° will pretend a call   *Monmouth*
To shake the column, let him share the fall.
But oh, that yet he would repent and live!
How easy 'tis for parents to forgive!
With how few tears a pardon might be won
960 From nature, pleading for a darling son!
Poor pitied youth! by my paternal care
Raised up to all the height his frame could bear;
Had God ordained his fate for empire born,
He would have giv'n his soul another turn.
Gulled with a patriot's name, whose modern sense
Is 'one that would by law supplant his prince';
The people's brave, the politicians' tool;

Never was patriot yet but was a fool.
Whence comes it that religion and the laws
970 Should more be Absalom's than David's cause?
His old instructor,° ere he lost his place,   *Shaftesbury*
Was never thought endued with so much grace.
Good heav'ns, how faction can a patriot paint!
My rebel ever proves my people's saint.
Would *they* impose an heir upon the throne?
Let Sanhedrins be taught to give their own.
A king's at least a part of government,
And mine as requisite as their consent;
Without my leave a future king to choose
980 Infers a right the present to depose.
True, they petition me t' approve their choice,
But Esau's hands suit ill with Jacob's voice.[47]
My pious subjects for my safety pray,
Which to secure, they take my pow'r away.
From plots and treasons heav'n preserve my years,
But save me most from my petitioners.
Unsatiate as the barren womb or grave,
God cannot grant so much as they can crave.
What then is left but with a jealous eye
990 To guard the small remains of royalty?
The law shall still direct my peaceful sway,
And the same law teach rebels to obey.
Votes shall no more established pow'r control,
Such votes as make a part exceed the whole;
No groundless clamours shall my friends remove,
Nor crowds have pow'r to punish ere they prove;
For gods and god-like kings their care express
Still to defend their servants in distress.
Oh, that my pow'r to saving were confined!
1000 Why am I forced, like heav'n, against my mind
To make examples of another kind?
Must I at length the sword of justice draw?
Oh, cursed effects of necessary law!
How ill my fear they by my mercy scan;
Beware the fury of a patient man.
Law they require, let law then show her face;[48]
They could not be content to look on grace,
Her hinder parts, but with a daring eye
To tempt the terror of her front and die.
1010 By their own arts 'tis righteously decreed
Those dire artificers of death shall bleed.

Against themselves their witnesses will swear,
Till, viper-like, their mother-plot they tear;
And suck for nutriment that bloody gore
Which was their principle of life before.
Their Belial with their Belzebub will fight;
Thus on my foes my foes shall do me right.
Nor doubt th' event: for factious crowds engage
In their first onset all their brutal rage;
1020 Then let 'em take an unresisted course,
Retire and traverse and delude their force,
But when they stand all breathless, urge the fight
And rise upon 'em with redoubled might.
For lawful pow'r is still superior found
When long driv'n back, at length it stands the ground.'
   He said. Th' Almighty, nodding, gave consent,
And peals of thunder shook the firmament.
Henceforth a series of new time began,
The mighty years in long procession ran;
1030 Once more the god-like David was restored,
And willing nations knew their lawful lord.

[1681]

From *Absalom and Achitophel:*[49] *The Second Part*

Doeg, though without knowing how or why,
Made still a blundering kind of melody;
Spurred boldly on, and dashed through thick and thin
Through sense and nonsense, never out nor in;
Free from all meaning, whether good or bad,
And in one word, heroically mad.
He was too warm on picking-work to dwell
But faggoted° his notions as they fell,   *bundled together*
420 And if they rhymed and rattled all was well.
Spiteful he is not, though he wrote a satire,
For still there goes some thinking to ill-nature;
He needs no more than birds and beasts to think,
All his occasions are to eat and drink.
If he call rogue and rascal from a garret
He means you no more mischief than a parrot;
The words for friend and foe alike were made,

To fetter 'em in verse is all his trade.
For almonds he'll cry whore to his own mother,
430   And call young Absalom King David's brother.
Let him be gallows-free by my consent,
And nothing suffer since he nothing meant;
Hanging supposes human soul and reason,
This animal's below committing treason.
Shall he be hanged who never could rebel?
That's a preferment for Achitophel.
The woman that committed buggary
Was rightly sentenced by the law to die;
But 'twas hard fate that to the gallows led
440   The dog that never heard the statute read.
Railing in other men may be a crime,
But ought to pass for mere instinct in him;
Instinct he follows and no farther knows,
For to write verse with him is to *transprose*.
'Twere pity treason at his door to lay,
Who *makes heaven's gate a lock to its own key*.⁵⁰
Let him rail on, let his invective muse
Have four and twenty letters to abuse,
Which if he jumbles to one line of sense,
450   Indict him of a capital offence.
In fireworks give him leave to vent his spite,
Those are the only serpents he can write.
The height of his ambition is we know
But to be master of a puppet-show;
On that one stage his works may yet appear,
And a month's harvest keeps him all the year.
   Now stop your noses, readers, all and some,
For here's a tun of midnight-work to come,
Og⁵¹ from a treason tavern rolling home,
460   Round as a globe, and liquored ev'ry chink,
Goodly and great he sails behind his link;°   *boy carrying torch*
With all this bulk there's nothing lost in Og,
For ev'ry inch that is not fool is rogue:
A monstrous mass of foul corrupted matter,
As all the devils had spewed to make the batter.
When wine has given him courage to blaspheme,
He curses God, but God before cursed him;
And if man could have reason, none has more
That made his paunch so rich and him so poor.
470   With wealth he was not trusted, for heav'n knew
What 'twas of old to pamper up a Jew;

To what would he on quail and pheasant swell,
That ev'n on tripe⁵² and carrion could rebel?
But though heav'n made him poor (with rev'rence speaking)
He never was a poet of God's making;
The midwife laid her hand on his thick skull
With this prophetic blessing 'Be thou dull.'
Drink, swear and roar, forbear no lewd delight
Fit for thy bulk, do anything but write.
480 Thou art of lasting make like thoughtless men;
A strong nativity – but for the pen!
Eat opium, mingle arsenic in thy drink,
Still thou may'st live avoiding pen and ink.
I see, I see, 'tis counsel given in vain,
For treason botched in rhyme will be thy bane;°   *destruction*
Rhyme is the rock on which thou art to wreck,
'Tis fatal to thy fame and to thy neck.
Why should thy metre good king David blast?
A psalm of his will surely be thy last!
490 Dar'st thou presume in verse to meet thy foes,
Thou whom the penny pamphlet foiled in prose?
Doeg, whom God for mankind's mirth has made,
O'er-tops thy talent in thy very trade;
Doeg to thee, thy paintings are so coarse,
A poet is, though he's the poet's horse.
A double noose thou on thy neck dost pull,
For writing treason and for writing dull;
To die for faction is a common evil,
But to be hanged for nonsense is the devil.
500 Had'st thou the glories of thy King expressed,
Thy praises had been satire at the best;
But thou in clumsy verse, unlicked, unpointed,
Hast shamefully defied the Lord's anointed.
I will not rake the dunghill of thy crimes,
For who would read thy life that reads thy rhymes?
But of King David's foes be this the doom,
May all be like the young man Absalom;
And for my foes may this their blessing be,
509 To talk like Doeg, and to write like thee.

[1682]

MacFlecknoe

OR A SATIRE UPON THE TRUE-BLUE
PROTESTANT POET T. S.[53]

All human things are subject to decay,
And when Fate summons, monarchs must obey.
This Flecknoe found, who, like Augustus, young
Was called to Empire and had governed long;
In prose and verse was owned, without dispute
Through all the realms of Non-sense, absolute.
This aged prince, now flourishing in peace
And blest with issue of a large increase,
Worn out with business, did at length debate
10   To settle the succession of the state;
And pond'ring which of all his sons was fit
To reign and wage immortal war with wit,
Cried: ''Tis resolved; for nature pleads that he
Should only rule who most resembles me.
Shadwell alone my perfect image bears,
Mature in dullness from his tender years.
Shadwell alone, of all my sons, is he
Who stands confirmed in full stupidity.
The rest to some faint meaning make pretence,
20   But Shadwell never deviates into sense.
Some beams of wit on other souls may fall,
Strike through and make a lucid interval,
But Shadwell's genuine night admits no ray,
His rising fogs prevail upon the day.
Besides his goodly fabric fills the eye,
And seems designed for thoughtless majesty:
Thoughtless as monarch oaks that shade the plain
And, spread in solemn state, supinely reign.
Heywood and Shirley were but types of thee,
30   Thou last great prophet of tautology.
Even I, a dunce of more renown than they,
Was sent before but to prepare thy way;
And coarsely clad in Norwich drugget° came   coarse cloth
To teach the nations in thy greater name.
My warbling lute, the lute I whilom strung
When to King John of Portugal I sung,[54]
Was but the prelude to that glorious day
When thou on silver Thames did'st cut thy way
With well-timed oars before the Royal Barge,
40   Swelled with the pride of thy celestial charge;

And big with hymn, commander of an host,
The like was ne'er in Epsom blankets tossed.[55]
Methinks I see the new Arion sail,
The lute still trembling underneath thy nail,
At thy well-sharpened thumb from shore to shore
The treble squeaks for fear, the basses roar;
Echoes from Pissing-Alley 'Shadwell' call,
And 'Shadwell' they resound from Aston Hall.[56]
About thy boat the little fishes throng
50 As at the morning toast that floats along.
Sometimes as prince of thy harmonious band
Thou wield'st thy papers in thy threshing hand.
St André's feet ne'er kept more equal time,
Not ev'n the feet of thy own Psyche's rhyme
Though they in number as in sense excel;
So just, so like tautology they fell,
That, pale with envy, Singleton forswore
The lute and sword which he in triumph bore
And vowed he ne'er would act Villerius[57] more.'
60 Here stopped the good old sire, and wept for joy
In silent raptures of the hopeful boy.
All arguments, but most his plays, persuade
That for anointed dullness he was made.
    Close to the walls which fair Augusta° bind   *London*
(The fair Augusta much to fears inclined),[58]
An ancient fabric, raised t' inform the sight,   *building*
There stood of yore and Barbican it hight.
A watchtower once; but now, so Fate ordains,
Of all the pile an empty name remains.
70 From its old ruins brothel-houses rise,
Scenes of lewd loves and of polluted joys.
Where their vast courts the mother-strumpets keep
And, undisturbed by watch, in silence sleep.
Near these a Nursery[59] erects its head,
Where queens are formed and future heroes bred:
Where unfledged actors learn to laugh and cry,
Where infant punks their tender voices try,
And little Maximins[60] the gods defy.
Great Fletcher never treads in buskins° here,   *boots*
80 Nor greater Jonson dares in socks° appear;[61]   *low shoes*
But gentle Simkin° just reception finds   *a clown*
Amidst this monument of vanished minds;
Pure clinches° the suburban muse affords,   *puns*
And Panton° waging harmless war with words.   *a punster*
Here Flecknoe, as a place to fame well-known,

Ambitiously designed his Shadwell's throne.
For ancient Decker prophesied long since
That in this pile should reign a mighty prince,
Born for a scourge of wit and flail of sense;
90 To whom true dullness should some Psyches owe,
But worlds of Misers[62] from his pen should flow;
Humorists and hypocrites it should produce,
Whole Raymond families and tribes of Bruce.[63]
    Now Empress Fame had published the renown
Of Shadwell's coronation through the town.
Rowsed by report of fame the nations meet
From near Banhill and distant Watling Street.[64]
No Persian carpets spread th' imperial way,
But scattered limbs of mangled poets lay;
100 From dusty shops neglected authors come,
Martyrs of pies and relics of the bum.
Much Heywood, Shirley, Ogleby there lay,
But loads of Shadwell almost choked the way.
Bilked stationers° for Yeomen stood prepared,   *cheated publishers*
And Herringman was captain of the guard.
The hoary Prince in majesty appeared,
High on a throne of his own labours reared.
At his right hand our young Ascanius[65] sat,
Rome's other hope and pillar of the State.
110 His brows thick fogs, instead of glories, grace,
And lambent dullness played around his face.
As Hannibal did to the altars come,
Sworn by his sire a mortal foe to Rome;
So Shadwell swore, nor should his vow be vain,
That he till death true dullness would maintain,
And in his father's right and realm's defence
Ne'er to have peace with wit nor truce with sense.
The King himself the sacred unction made,
As King by office, and as priest by trade.
120 In his sinister° hand instead of ball°   *left/globe surmounted by a cross*
He placed a mighty mug of potent ale;
Love's Kingdom[66] to his right he did convey,
At once his sceptre and his rule of sway,
Whose righteous lore the Prince had practised young
And from whose loins recorded Psyche sprung.
His temples last with poppies[67] were o'erspread,
That nodding seemed to consecrate his head.
Just at that point of time, if fame not lie,
On his left hand twelve reverend owls did fly:
130 So Romulus, 'tis sung, by Tiber's brook

Presage of sway from twice six vultures took.
Th' admiring throng loud acclamations make,
And omens of his future empire take.
The sire then shook the honours of his head,
And from his brows damps of oblivion shed
Full on the filial dullness. Long he stood
Repelling from his breast the raging god;
At length burst out in this prophetic mood:
    'Heavens bless my son, from Ireland let him reign
140 To far Barbadoes on the western main;[68]
Of his dominion may no end be known,
And greater than his father's be his throne.
Beyond Love's Kingdom let him stretch his pen.'
He paused and all the people cried 'Amen.'
'Then thus,' continued he, 'my son, advance
Still in new impudence, new ignorance.
Success let others teach, learn thou from me
Pangs without birth and fruitless industry.
Let Virtuoso's[69] in five years be writ;
150 Yet not one thought accuse thy toil of wit.
Let gentle George in triumph tread the stage,[70]
Make Dorimant betray, and Loveit rage;
Let Cully, Cockwood, Fopling, charm the pit,
And in their folly show the writer's wit.
Yet still thy fools shall stand in thy defence,
And justify their author's want of sense.
Let 'em be all by thy own model made
Of dullness and desire no foreign aid,
That they to future ages may be known
160 Not copies drawn but issue of thy own.
Nay, let thy men of wit, too, be the same,
All full of thee and differing but in name;
But let no alien Sedley interpose
To lard with wit thy hungry Epsom prose.
And when false flowers of rhetoric thou would'st cull
Trust nature, do not labour to be dull
But write thy best and top; and in each line
Sir Formal's[71] oratory will be thine.
Sir Formal, though unsought, attends thy quill
170 And does thy northern dedications fill.[72]
Nor let false friends seduce thy mind to fame
By arrogating Jonson's[73] hostile name.
Let father Flecknoe fire thy mind with praise,
And uncle Ogleby thy envy raise.
Thou art my blood, where Jonson has no part;

What share have we in nature or in art?
Where did his wit on learning fix a brand
And rail at arts he did not understand?
Where made he love in Prince Nicander's[74] vein,
180 Or swept the dust in Psyche's humble strain?
Where sold he bargains, whip-stitch, kiss my arse,[75]
Promised a play and dwindled to a farce?
When did his muse from Fletcher scenes purloin,
As thou whole Eth'rege dost transfuse to thine?[76]
But so transfused as oils on waters flow,
His always floats above, thine sinks below.
This is thy province, this thy wondrous way,
New humours to invent for each new play;
This is that boasted bias of thy mind
190 By which one way, to dullness, 'tis inclined,
Which makes thy writings lean on one side still,
And, in all changes, that way bends thy will.
Nor let thy mountain belly make pretence
Of likeness;[77] thine's a tympany of sense.
A tun of man in thy large bulk is writ,
But sure thou'rt but a kilderkin° of wit.   *a small cask*
Like mine thy gentle numbers feebly creep,
Thy tragic muse gives smiles, thy comic sleep.
With whate'er gall thou sett'st thyself to write,
200 Thy inoffensive satires never bite.
In thy felonious heart though venom lies,
It does but touch thy Irish pen and dies.
Thy genius calls thee not to purchase fame
In keen iambics[78] but mild anagram;
Leave writing plays and choose for thy command
Some peaceful province in acrostic land.
There thou may'st wings[79] display and altars raise,
And torture one poor word ten thousand ways.
Or, if thou would'st thy diff'rent talents suit,
210 Set thy own songs and sing them to thy lute.'
He said, but his last words were scarcely heard,
For Bruce and Longville[80] had a trap prepared,
And down they sent the yet declaiming bard.
Sinking, he left his drugget robe behind;
Born upwards by a subterranean wind
The mantle[81] fell to the young prophet's part,
With double portion of his father's art.

A Song for St Cecilia's Day,[82] 1687

I

From harmony, from heavenly harmony
    This universal frame° began: *structure*
      When Nature underneath a heap
        Of jarring atoms lay,
        And could not heave her head,
The tuneful voice was heard from high:
        'Arise, ye more than dead.'
Then cold, and hot, and moist, and dry,
    In order to their stations° leap,   *proper positions*
10   And Music's power obey.
From harmony, from heavenly harmony
    This universal frame began:
    From harmony to harmony
Through all the compass of the notes it ran,
The diapason° closing full in Man.   *cadence*

II

What passion cannot Music raise and quell?
      When Jubal struck the corded shell,
    His listening brethren stood around,
    And, wondering, on their faces fell
20   To worship that celestial sound.
Less than a god they thought there could not dwell
      Within the hollow of that shell
      That spoke so sweetly and so well.
What passion cannot Music raise and quell?

III

    The Trumpet's loud clangour
      Excites us to arms,
    With shrill notes of anger
      And mortal alarms.
    The double double double beat
30   Of the thundering Drum
Cries: 'Hark! the foes come;
Charge, charge, 'tis too late to retreat.'

IV

    The soft complaining Flute
    In dying notes discovers
    The woes of hopeless lovers,
Whose dirge is whispered by the warbling Lute.

V

Sharp Violins proclaim
Their jealous pangs, and desperation,
Fury, frantic indignation,
40 Depth of pains, and height of passion,
For the fair, disdainful dame.

VI

But O! what art can teach,
What human voice can reach,
The sacred Organ's praise?
Notes inspiring holy love,
Notes that wing their heavenly ways
To mend the choirs above.

VII

Orpheus could lead the savage race;
And trees unrooted left their place,
50 Sequacious° of the lyre;   *following*
But bright Cecilia raised the wonder higher:
When to her Organ vocal breath was given,
An angel heard, and straight appeared,
Mistaking earth for heaven.

Grand Chorus

As from the power of sacred lays[83]
The spheres began to move,
And sung the great Creator's praise
To all the blest above;
So, when the last and dreadful hour
This crumbling pageant shall devour,
The Trumpet shall be heard on high,
The dead shall live, the living die,
And Music shall untune the sky.

[1687]

KEY TO *ABSALOM AND ACHITOPHEL*

Aaron's race	clergy/priesthood
Abethdin	presiding judge of Jewish Civil Court = Lord Chancellor
Absalom	James, Duke of Monmouth
Achitophel	Anthony Ashley Cooper, Earl of Shaftesbury
Adriel	John Sheffield, Earl of Mulgrave
Agag	Sir Edmund Berry Godfrey
Amiel	Edward Seymour
Amnon	Sir John Coventry
Annabel	Anne Scott, wife of the Duke of Monmouth
Balaam	Theophilus Hastings, Earl of Huntingdon
Barzillai	James Butler, Duke of Ormond
Bathsheba	Louise, Duchess of Portsmouth and Aubigny: Charles II's mistress
Caleb	Forde, Lord Grey
Corah	Titus Oates
David	Charles II
Doeg	Elkanah Settle
Egypt	France
Ethnic plot	Popish Plot
Gath	Brussels
Hebrew Priests	C. of E. clergy
Hebron	Scotland
Hushai	Laurence Hyde, Earl of Rochester
Ishbosheth	Richard Cromwell
Israel	England
Issachar	Thomas Thynne
Jebusites	Roman Catholics
Jerusalem	London
Jewish rabbins	Doctors of the C. of E.
Jews	English
Jonas	Sir William Jones
Jordan	English Channel or the Irish Sea
Jordan's sand	where Charles II landed, Dover, 26 May 1660
Jotham	George Savile, Marquis of Halifax
Levites	Presbyterian ministers
Michal	Catherine of Braganza, childless wife of Charles II
Nadab	William, Lord Howard of Escrick
Og	Thomas Shadwell
Pharoah	Louis XIV of France
Sagan	Henry Compton
Sanhedrin	Parliament
Saul	Oliver Cromwell
Shimei	Slingsby Bethel
Sion	London
Solymean rout	London rabble
Tyre, Tyrus	Holland
Zadoc	William Sancroft, Archbishop of Canterbury
Zimri	George Villiers, Duke of Buckingham

NOTES

Dryden

1 From: *To The Reader*.

'Tis not my intention to make an apology for my poem: some will think it needs no excuse, and others will receive none. The design, I am sure, is honest: but he who draws his pen for one party must expect to make enemies of the other. For wit and fool are consequents of Whig and Tory: and every man is a knave or an ass to the contrary side . . .

Yet if a poem have a genius, it will force its own reception in the world. For there's a sweetness in good verse, which tickles even while it hurts: and no man will be angry with him who pleases him against his will. The commendations of adversaries is the greatest triumph of a writer, because it never comes unless extorted. But I can be satisfied on more easy terms: if I happen to please the more moderate sort, I shall be sure of an honest party, and, in all probability, of the best judges, for the least concerned are commonly the least corrupt; and I confess I have laid in for these, by rebating the satire (where justice would allow it) from carrying too sharp an edge. They who can criticise so weakly as to imagine I have done my worst, may be convinced at their own cost that I can write severely with more ease than I can gently. I have but laughed at some men's follies when I could have declaimed against their vices; and other men's virtues I have commended as freely as I have taxed their crimes . . .

The violent on both sides will condemn the character of Absalom, as either too favourably or too hardly drawn. But they are not the violent whom I desire to please. The fault, on the right hand, is to extenuate, palliate and indulge, and, to confess freely, I have endeavoured to commit it. Besides the respect which I owe his birth, I have a greater for his heroic virtues, and David himself could not be more tender of the young man's life than I would be of his reputation. But since the most excellent natures are always the most easy, and, as being such, are the soonest being perverted by ill counsels, especially when baited with fame and glory, 'tis no more wonder that he withstood not the temptations of Achitophel than it was for Adam not to have resisted the two devils, the serpent and the woman. The conclusion of the story I purposely forbore to prosecute, because I could not obtain from myself to show Absalom unfortunate . . .

Were I the inventor, who am only the historian, I should certainly conclude the piece with the reconcilement of Absalom to David. And, who knows but this may come to pass? . . .

The true end of satire is the amendment of vices by correction. And he who writes honestly is no more an enemy to the offender than the physician to the patient, when he prescribes harsh remedies to an inveterate disease . . .

To conclude all, if the body politic have any analogy to the natural, in my weak judgement, an act of oblivion were as necessary in a hot, distempered state as an opiate would be in a raging fever.

2 *Absalom and Achitophel*.

In the year 1680 Dryden undertook the poem of Absalom and Achitophel at the desire of King Charles II.

For the Biblical story - see 2 Sam. XIII–XVIII.

Absalom and Achitophel was published in November 1681 when Lord Shaftesbury was in prison awaiting trial for high treason. In 1678, he had attempted to force the Exclusion Bill, which sought to exclude James, Duke of York (Charles's brother and legitimate heir since he and the Queen had no children) from the throne and to install on it James, Earl of Monmouth, instead. By 1679 Monmouth was very popular with both the people and the army: the Duke of York, a Roman Catholic, was disliked and lived in Brussels. Charles deprived Monmouth of his army position, banned him to Holland and recalled James.

In November 1679, Shaftesbury persuaded Monmouth to return to England, without Charles's permission. Charles had him banished by order in council, but Monmouth refused to leave and set out on a kind of 'royal' progress through the west country. On 2 July 1681, Charles had Shaftesbury arrested on an indictment of high treason. With his poem, published November 1681, Dryden hoped to bring about a reconciliation between Charles and Monmouth. However the indictment against Shaftesbury was thrown out by the jury on 24 November. Freed, Shaftesbury remained in London and with Monmouth and others planned a rebellion against Charles. On 22 September 1682, Monmouth was arrested and banished from court. He withdrew to Holland, whither in November, Shaftesbury also fled. Shaftesbury died in January 1683. Monmouth headed a rebellion against James II (after James's accession in 1685), was defeated and executed, 15 July 1685.

3 Monmouth had commanded the British forces under the French against the Dutch, 1672–3 and under the Dutch against the French, 1678.
4 an attack on Sir John Coventry, in which his nose was slit to the bone, by Monmouth after Coventry had made allusions to the King's love affairs in the House of Lords.
5 like Adam and Eve, free except being forbidden the tree of knowledge and life.
6 Charles was crowned in Scotland, 1 Jan. 1651, in England 23 April 1661, as David had reigned in Hebron before he had in Jerusalem, cf. 2 Sam. V.5.
7 the Popish Plot, Aug. 1676, when, according to Titus Oates, Charles II was to be killed and James made King supported by the Jesuits and the French.
8 refers to the Catholic doctrine of transubstantiation.
9 at the outbreak of the Civil War, Shaftesbury supported the King; in 1644 he changed sides and served under the Parliamentarians; he became estranged from Cromwell by 1654 and later actively supported the Restoration; by 1679 was chief supporter of the Exclusion Bill (1680 – to exclude James from the throne); eventually imprisoned by Charles on an indictment of high treason – at which point this poem was published.
10 Shaftesbury was of poor physique, small and sickly.
11 Shaftesbury's son lacked both character and ability.
12 the alliance between England, Sweden and Holland against France and its Catholic influence.
13 patriot = name taken by those who wished to see the Exclusion Bill passed.
14 180–191 lines added to the second edition.
15 Shaftesbury was Lord Chancellor 1672–3.
16 i.e. Shaftesbury's support of Monmouth.
17 charges were made against Shaftesbury of fabricating the Popish Plot.
18 something Shaftesbury did not do – though on his death-bed, Charles was said to have professed to being a Catholic.
19 Exod. XIII.21.
20 loyal – some editions have 'royal'.
21 refers to the Exclusion Bill, which was passed in the House of Commons but rejected by the Lords.
22 Presbyterian churchmen were forced to leave the C. of E. by the Act of Uniformity, 1662, which required total acceptance of the Book of Common Prayer.

23 Judges II.16.

24 the Protectorate, 1653–9.

25 refers to the Calvinist doctrine of the salvation of the elect.

26 verbal or sexual capacity.

27 William, Lord Howard, was said to have taken communion in 'lamb's wool' – ale poured on roasted apples and sugar.

28 I Sam. X.27, Deut. XIII.13.

29 by packing juries with Whigs, he could protect the Whigs and condemn the Tories.

30 poss. his tract *The Interest of Princes and States.*

31 Jerem. XXXV.14.

32 in the Great Fire of London.

33 Numb. XXI.6–9.

34 Exod. XXXIV.29–35.

35 I Sam. XV.

36 Monmouth was banished by the King, Sept. 1679, he returned Nov.

37 refers to France financing Charles II.

38 an attempt was made to involve both the Queen and the Duke of York in the Popish Plot.

39 the Ark of the Covenant.

40 friends might pin poems or epitaphs to the wooden structures used in funerals.

41 2 Sam. VIII.17.

42 John Dolben, Dean of Westminster: dome = that of Westminster Abbey: prophet's sons = the boys of Westminster School.

43 Judges IX.

44 2 Sam. XV–XVII.

45 cf. Phaeton.

46 the Whigs questioned the King's power to pardon or commute punishments in the cases of the Earl of Danby and Lord Stafford.

47 Gen. XXVII.22.

48 Exod. XXXIII. 20–3. Moses was only allowed to see the 'back parts' of God on Mt. Sinai.

49 *The Second Part of Absalom and Achitophel.* D. wrote lines 310–509 – the lines included here, 412–509, are satiric pictures of Settle (Doeg) and Shadwell (Og).

50 Settle's poem begins 'In gloomy times, when priestcraft bore the sway,
                          And made heaven's gate a lock to their own key . . .'

51 cf. MacFlecknoe.

52 the lining of a cow's stomach, cheap food.

53 In March 1682, after the jury had rejected the indictment against Shaftesbury for treason, a medal was struck to celebrate this with the bust of Shaftesbury on one side and a view of London Bridge and the Tower, with the sun rising above the Tower, on the other. D. published *The Medal, A Satire against Sedition,* it is said, at the request of Charles II himself. Shadwell then produced a riposte, *The Medal of John Bayes, a Satire against Folly and Knavery,* in which he abused D. *Mac Flecknoe* is D.'s reply.

54 Flecknoe boasted that the King of Portugal was his patron.

55 as was a character in Shadwell's *Epsom Wells* and MacFlecknoe's *The Virtuoso.*

56 Pissing Alley and Aston Hall both in London.

57 character of Davenant's *Siege of Rhodes.*

58 i.e. of Popish intrigue, rife in London.

59 the Nursery, a theatre, under patent from Charles II, 1664, to train actors and

actresses for the King's and the Duke's Companies; in Golden Lane, adjoining the Barbican, London.

60 a Roman emperor in D.'s *Tyrannic Love*, 1669 – a ranting hero.

61 buskins = high boots worn for tragedy; socks – low shoes worn for comedy.

62 Shadwell's adaption of Moliere's *L'Avare*.

63 Raymond = a character in Shadwell's *Humorists*: Bruce = in his *Virtuoso*.

64 Ban-hill, Watling Street, near the Nursery, London.

65 here Shadwell – to MacFlecknoe's Aeneas.

66 a pastoral tragi-comedy by MacFlecknoe.

67 sleep-inducing; also Shadwell took opium.

68 i.e. over an empty ocean.

69 Shadwell's play, first acted 1676.

70 Sir George Etherege and characters in several of his plays.

71 Sir Formal Trifle in Shadwell's *The Virtuoso*.

72 Shadwell's dedications of his plays to the Duke of Newcastle.

73 Shadwell praised Jonson as 'incomparably the best dramatic poet that ever was'.

74 in Shadwell's *Psyche*.

75 the catch phrases of Sir Samuel Hearty in *The Virtuoso*.

76 D. is suggesting plagiarism by Shadwell: cf. *Epsom Wells* with Etherege's *She Would if She Could*.

77 to Ben Jonson.

78 iambics were used for Greek satirical writing.

79 i.e. poems written in particular shapes, e.g. wings (cf. Herbert's 'Easter') or altars.

80 in *The Virtuoso* a trapdoor is opened under Sir Formal Trifle when he is making a speech.

81 2 Kings II.12–15.

82 St Cecilia's Day = 22 Nov., when the Music Society (1683 onwards) commissioned odes from poets to be set to music for public performance: this was set to music by Handel, 1739.

83 the music of the angels (sacred lays) set the spheres in motion (heavenly bodies) and the music of the spheres is praise sung continually by Nature to God.

Alexander Pope

[1688–1744]

He was the son of a London Catholic linen-draper: at 12 he had a
severe illness that stunted his growth: lived with his parents at
Binfield, Windsor Forest, and was self-educated. 1705 he met
Teresa and Martha Blount – the latter to be his close friend
(rumoured his mistress) throughout his life. First poems,
'Pastorals', (he says written when he was 16) were published in
Tonson's *Miscellany* Vol. VI, 1709. His friendship with the
dramatist Wycherley led him into London society and his *Essay on
Criticism*, 1711, and 'Messiah' published in the *Spectator*, 1712,
made him known amongst the Spectator group, which included
Addison, Steele and Lady Mary Montagu. His friendship with
Lady Montagu was to become a close one until it degenerated into
quarrels and vituperations when, after her secret marriage in 1712,
she left England with her husband for Turkey, 1716. In 1712, in
Lintot's *Miscellanies*, the first version of *The Rape of the Lock* was
published; republished, enlarged, two years later. 1713 saw the
publication of *Windsor Forest*. He moved away from the Addison
clique to join the Scriblerus Club, whose members included Swift,
Gay, and Arbuthnot. His satirical portrait of Addison (Atticus),
although written at this time, 1715, was not published until 1723,
four years after Addison's death. P.'s translations – of Homer's
Iliad, in heroic couplets, 1715, completed 1720, and of the *Odyssey*,
1725/6 (with the help of others) gave him financial security. In
1725 he published his edition of Shakespeare: Lewis Theobald
pointed out its errors in *Shakespeare Restored*, 1726 – so becoming the
hero of *The Dunciad*, a satire on dullness, the 1st vol. of which was
published anonymously in 1728, the enlarged edition in 1729. It
was Colley Cibber, however, who became Poet Laureate, 1730,
who was the hero of the completed version published 1743.
Between 1733–5 P. wrote several moral and philosophical poems
including *An Essay on Man*, 1733/4: 1733 he also published the first
of his satires in *Imitations of Horace*, followed by further imitations of
satires and epistles by Horace. It is the first that contains his fierce
attack on Lady Montagu as Sappho. *The Epistle to Arbuthnot*
appeared in its final form, 1735. The later years of his life he spent
editing (and amending) and publishing his earlier correspondence
– ensuring that it seemed to be published against his wishes –
disowning and discrediting Curll's publication, 'Literary Corre-

spondence', 1735, and similarly blaming Swift for a second publication, 1741. He was buried in Twickenham church. The first collected edition of his works published 1751.

From **An Essay on Criticism**

First follow Nature, and your judgment frame
By her just standard, which is still° the same: *always*
70 Unerring NATURE, still divinely bright,
One clear, unchang'd, and universal light,
Life, force, and beauty, must to all impart,
At once the source, and end, and test of art.
Art from that fund each just supply provides;
Works without show, and without pomp presides;
In some fair body thus th' informing soul
With spirits feeds, with vigour fills the whole,
Each motion guides, and ev'ry nerve sustains,
Itself unseen, but in th' effects, remains.
80 Some, to whom Heav'n in wit has been profuse,
Want as much more to turn it to its use;
For wit and judgment often are at strife,
Tho' meant each other's aid, like man and wife.
'Tis more to guide, than spur the muse's steed;
Restrain his fury, than provoke his speed;
The winged courser, like a gen'rous horse,
Shows most true mettle when you check his course.

     *   *   *

But true expression, like th' unchanging sun,
Clears, and improves whate'er it shines upon;
It gilds all objects, but it alters none.
Expression is the dress of thought, and still
Appears more decent, as more suitable;
320 A vile conceit in pompous words express'd,
Is like a clown in regal purple dress'd:
For different styles with different subjects sort,
As several garbs with country, town, and court.
Some by old words to fame have made pretence,
Ancients in phrase, mere moderns in their sense;
Such labour'd nothings, in so strange a style,
Amaze th' unlearn'd, and make the learned smile.

*   *   *

But most by numbers° judge a poet's song;   *metrical feet*
And smooth or rough, with them, is right or wrong:
In the bright muse, tho' thousand charms conspire,
340 Her voice is all these tuneful fools admire;
Who haunt Parnassus but to please their ear,
Not mend their minds; as some to church repair,
Not for the doctrine, but the music there.
These equal syllables alone require,
Tho' oft the ear the open vowels tire;
While expletives[1] their feeble aid do join,
And ten low words oft creep in one dull line:
While they ring round the same unvary'd chimes,
With sure returns of still expected rhymes;
350 Where'er you find 'the cooling western breeze',
In the next line, it 'whispers through the trees':
If crystal streams 'with pleasing murmurs creep',
The reader's threaten'd (not in vain) with 'sleep':
Then, at the last and only couplet fraught
With some unmeaning thing they call a thought,
A needless Alexandrine ends the song,
That, like a wounded snake, drags its slow length along.
Leave such to tune their own dull rhymes, and know
What's roundly smooth, or languishingly slow;
360 And praise the easy vigour of a line,
Where Denham's strength and Waller's sweetness join.
True ease in writing comes from art, not chance,
As those move easiest who have learn'd to dance.
'Tis not enough no harshness gives offense,
The sound must seem an echo to the sense;
Soft is the strain when zephyr gently blows,
And the smooth stream in smoother numbers flows:
But when loud surges lash the sounding shore,
The hoarse, rough verse should like the torrent roar.
370 When Ajax strives some rock's vast weight to throw,
The line too labours, and the words move slow;
Not so, when swift Camilla scours the plain,
Flies o'er th'unbending corn, and skims along the main.

*   *   *

Avoid extremes; and shun the fault of such
Who still are pleas'd too little or too much.
At ev'ry trifle scorn to take offence:

That always shows great pride, or little sense;
Those heads, as stomachs, are not sure the best
Which nauseate all, and nothing can digest.
390 Yet let not each gay turn° thy rapture move,   *display*
For fools admire, but men of sense approve:
As things seem large which we through mists descry,
Dullness is ever apt to magnify.

[1711]

From **Windsor Forest**

See! from the brake the whirring pheasant springs,
And mounts exulting on triumphant wings:
Short is his joy; he feels the fiery wound,
Flutters in blood, and panting beats the ground.
Ah! what avail his glossy, varying dyes,
His purple crest, and scarlet-circled eyes,
The vivid green his shining plumes unfold,
His painted wings, and breast that flames with gold?
    Nor yet, when moist Arcturus clouds the sky,
120 The woods and fields their pleasing toils deny.
To plains with well-breath'd beagles° we repair,   *hunting dogs*
And trace the mazes of the circling hare:
(Beasts, urg'd by us, their fellow-beasts pursue,
And learn of man each other to undo.)
With slaught'ring guns th' unwearied fowler° roves,   *birdcatcher*
When frosts have whiten'd all the naked groves;
Where doves in flocks the leafless trees o'ershade,
And lonely woodcocks haunt the wat'ry glade.
He lifts the tube,° and levels with his eye;   *shotgun*
130 Straight a short thunder breaks the frozen sky:
Oft, as in airy rings they skim the heath,
The clam'rous lapwings feel the leaden death:
Oft, as the mounting larks their notes prepare,
They fall, and leave their little lives in air.

[1713]

The Rape of the Lock[2]

An heroi-comical poem

Canto I

What dire offence from am'rous causes springs,
What mighty contests rise from trivial things,
I sing – This verse to Caryll, Muse! is due:
This, ev'n Belinda may vouchsafe to view:
Slight is the subject, but not so the praise,
If she inspire, and he approve my lays.
   Say what strange motive, Goddess! could compel
A well-bred lord t' assault a gentle belle?
O say what stranger cause, yet unexplor'd,
10 Could make a gentle belle reject a lord?
In tasks so bold, can little men engage,
And in soft bosoms, dwells such mighty rage?
   Sol through white curtains shot a tim'rous ray,
And ope'd those eyes that must eclipse the day:
Now lap-dogs give themselves the rousing shake,
And sleepless lovers, just at twelve, awake:
Thrice rung the bell, the slipper knock'd the ground,[3]   *handbell*
And the press'd watch[4] return'd a silver sound.
Belinda still her downy pillow prest,
20 Her guardian sylph prolong'd the balmy rest:
'Twas he had summon'd to her silent bed
The morning-dream that hover'd o'er her head,
A youth more glitt'ring than a birth-night beau,[5]
(That ev'n in slumber caus'd her cheek to glow)
Seem'd to her ear his winning lips to lay,
And thus in whispers said, or seem'd to say.
   'Fairest of mortals, thou distinguish'd care
Of thousand bright inhabitants of air!
If e'er one vision touch thy infant thought,
30 Of all the nurse and all the priest have taught,
Of airy elves by moonlight shadows seen,
The silver token, and the circled green,[6]
Or virgins visited by angel-pow'rs
With golden crowns and wreaths of heav'nly flow'rs;
Hear and believe! thy own importance know,
Nor bound thy narrow views to things below.

Some secret truths, from learned pride conceal'd,
To maids alone and children are reveal'd:[7]
What tho' no credit doubting wits may give?
40 The fair and innocent shall still believe.
Know then, unnumber'd spirits round thee fly,
The light militia of the lower sky:°   *air*
These, tho' unseen, are ever on the wing,
Hang o'er the box,° and hover round the ring.[8]   *theatre-box*
Think what an equipage° thou hast in air,   *horse-carriage*
And view with scorn two pages and chair.°   *sedan-chair*
As now your own, our beings were of old,
And once inclos'd in woman's beauteous mould;
Thence, by a soft transition, we repair
50 From earthly vehicles[9] to these of air.
Think not, when woman's transient breath is fled,
That all her vanities at once are dead;
Succeeding vanities she still regards,
And tho' she plays no more, o'erlooks the cards.
Her joy in gilded chariots,° when alive,   *coaches*
And love of ombre,° after death survive.   *(a card game)*
For when the fair in all their pride expire,
To their first elements[10] their souls retire:
The sprites of fiery termagants in flame
60 Mount up, and take a salamander's[11] name.
Soft yielding minds to water glide away,
And sip, with nymphs, their elemental tea.[12]
The graver prude sinks downward to a gnome,
In search of mischief still on earth to roam.
The light coquettes° in sylphs aloft repair,   *flirts*
And sport and flutter in the fields of air.
    Know farther yet; whoever fair and chaste
Rejects mankind, is by some sylph embrac'd:
For spirits, freed from mortal laws, with ease
70 Assume what sexes and what shapes they please.[13]
What guards the purity of melting maids,
In courtly balls, and midnight masquerades,
Safe from the treach'rous friend, the daring spark,°   *dandy*
The glance by day, the whisper in the dark,
When kind occasion prompts their warm desires,
When music softens, and when dancing fires?
'Tis but their sylph, the wise celestials know,
Though honour is the word with men below.
    Some nymphs there are, too conscious of their face,
80 For life predestin'd to the gnome's embrace.

These swell their prospects and exalt their pride,
When offers are disdain'd, and love deny'd;
Then gay ideas crowd the vacant brain,
While peers, and dukes, and all their sweeping train,
And garters, stars, and coronets appear,
And in soft sounds, 'your Grace' salutes their ear.
'Tis these that early taint the female soul,
Instruct the eyes of young Coquettes to roll,
Teach infant-cheeks a bidden blush to know,
90 And little hearts to flutter at a beau.
   Oft, when the world imagine women stray,
The sylphs through mystic mazes guide their way,
Through all the giddy circle they pursue,
And old impertinence° expel by new.   *folly*
What tender maid but must a victim fall
To one man's treat, but for another's ball?   *entertainment*
When Florio speaks, what virgin could withstand,
If gentle Damon did not squeeze her hand?
With varying vanities, from ev'ry part,
100 They shift the moving toyshop of their heart;   *[favours*
Where wigs with wigs, with sword-knots° sword-knots strive   *ribbon*
Beaux banish beaux, and coaches coaches drive.
This erring mortals levity may call,
Oh, blind to truth! the sylphs contrive it all.
   Of these am I, who thy protection claim,
A watchful sprite, and Ariel is my name.
Late, as I rang'd the crystal wilds of air,
In the clear mirror of thy ruling star
110 I saw, alas! some dread event impend,
Ere to the main this morning sun descend,
But heav'n reveals not what, or how, or where:
Warn'd by the sylph, oh pious maid, beware!
This to disclose is all thy guardian can:
Beware of all, but most beware of man!'
   He said; when Shock, who thought she slept too long,   *lap dog*
Leap'd up, and wak'd his mistress with his tongue.
'Twas then, Belinda, if report say true,
Thy eyes first open'd on a billet-doux;°   *love letter*
Wounds, charms, and ardours,[14] were no sooner read,
120 But all the vision vanish'd from thy head.
   And now, unveil'd, the toilet° stands display'd,   *dressing-table*
Each silver vase in mystic order laid.
First, rob'd in white, the nymph intent adores,
With head uncover'd, the cosmetic pow'rs.

A heav'nly image in the glass appears,
To that she bends, to that her eyes she rears;
Th' inferior priestess, at her altar's side,
Trembling begins the sacred rites of pride.
Unnumber'd treasures ope at once, and here
130 The various off'rings of the world appear;
From each she nicely culls with curious° toil,   *fastidious*
And decks the goddess with the glitt'ring spoil.
This casket India's glowing gems unlocks,
And all Arabia breathes from yonder box.
The tortoise here and elephant° unite,   *ivory*
Transform'd to combs, the speckled, and the white.
Here files of pins extend their shining rows,
Puffs, powders, patches,° Bibles, billet-doux.   *beauty spots*
Now awful beauty puts on all its arms;
140 The fair each moment rises in her charms,
Repairs her smiles, awakens ev'ry grace,
And calls forth all the wonders of her face;
Sees by degrees a purer blush arise,
And keener lightnings[15] quicken in her eyes.
The busy sylphs surround their darling care,
These set the head, and those divide the hair,
Some fold the sleeve, whilst others plait the gown;
And Betty's[16] prais'd for labours not her own.

Canto II

Not with more glories, in th' ethereal plain,
The sun first rises o'er the purpled main,
Than, issuing forth, the rival° of his beams   *Belinda*
Launch'd on the bosom of the silver Thames.
Fair nymphs, and well-drest youths around her shone,
But ev'ry eye was fix'd on her alone.
On her white breast a sparkling cross she wore,
Which Jews might kiss, and infidels adore.
Her lively looks a sprightly mind disclose,
10 Quick as her eyes, and as unfix'd as those:
Favours to none, to all she smiles extends;
Oft she rejects, but never once offends.
Bright as the sun, her eyes the gazers strike,
And, like the sun, they shine on all alike.
Yet graceful ease, and sweetness void of pride,
Might hide her faults, if belles had faults to hide:

If to her share some female errors fall,
Look on her face, and you'll forget 'em all.
　　This nymph, to the destruction of mankind,
20　Nourish'd two locks, which graceful hung behind
In equal curls, and well conspir'd to deck
With shining ringlets the smooth iv'ry neck.
Love in these labyrinths his slaves detains,
And mighty hearts are held in slender chains.
With hairy springes° we the birds betray,　　　　　　　　　*snares*
Slight lines of hair surprise the finny° prey,[17]　　　　　*with fins*
Fair tresses man's imperial race insnare,
And beauty draws us with a single hair.
　　Th' advent'rous Baron the bright locks admir'd;
30　He saw, he wish'd, and to the prize aspir'd.
Resolv'd to win, he meditates the way,
By force to ravish, or by fraud betray;
For when success a lover's toil attends,
Few ask, if fraud or force attain'd his ends.
　　For this, ere Phoebus rose, he had implor'd
Propitious Heav'n, and ev'ry pow'r ador'd,
But chiefly Love – to Love an altar built,
Of twelve vast French Romances, neatly gilt.
There lay three garters, half a pair of gloves,
40　And all the trophies of his former loves;
With tender billet-doux he lights the pyre,
And breathes three am'rous sighs to raise the fire.
Then prostrate falls, and begs with ardent eyes
Soon to obtain, and long possess the prize:
The pow'rs gave ear, and granted half his pray'r,[18]
The rest, the winds dispers'd in empty air.
　　But now secure the painted vessel glides,
The sun-beams trembling on the floating tides:
While melting music steals upon the sky,
50　And soften'd sounds along the waters die;
Smooth flow the waves, the zephyrs° gently play,　　　　*west winds*
Belinda smil'd, and all the world was gay.
All but the sylph – with careful thoughts opprest,
Th' impending woe sat heavy on his breast.
He summons straight his denizens° of air;　　　　　　　　*citizens*
The lucid squadrons round the sails repair;°　　　　　　　*gather*
Soft o'er the shrouds aërial whispers breathe,
That seem'd but zephyrs to the train° beneath.　　　　　　*retinue*
Some to the sun their insect-wings unfold,
60　Waft on the breeze, or sink in clouds of gold:

Transparent forms, too fine for mortal sight,
Their fluid bodies half dissolv'd in light.
Loose to the wind their airy garments flew,
Thin glitt'ring textures of the filmy dew,
Dipt in the richest tincture of the skies,
Where light disports in ever-mingling dyes;
While ev'ry beam new transient colours flings,
Colours that change whene'er they wave their wings.
Amid the circle, on the gilded mast,
70   Superior by the head, was Ariel plac'd;
His purple pinions op'ning to the sun,
He rais'd his azure wand, and thus begun.
      'Ye Sylphs and Sylphids,° to your chief give ear,   *female sylph*
Fays, Fairies, Genii, Elves, and Demons hear!
Ye know the spheres and various tasks assign'd
By laws eternal to th' aerial kind.
Some in the fields of purest ether play,
And bask and whiten in the blaze of day.
Some guide the course of wand'ring orbs on high,
80   Or roll the planets through the boundless sky.
Some less refin'd, beneath the moon's pale light
Pursue the stars that shoot athwart the night,
Or suck the mists in grosser air below,
Or dip their pinions in the painted bow,°   *rainbow*
Or brew fierce tempests on the wintry main,
Or o'er the glebe° distil the kindly rain.   *soil*
Others on earth o'er human race preside,
Watch all their ways, and all their actions guide:
Of these the chief the care of nations own,
90   And guard with arms divine the British throne.
      Our humbler province is to tend the fair,
Not a less pleasing, tho' less glorious care;
To save the powder from too rude a gale,
Nor let th' imprison'd essences exhale;
To draw fresh colours from the vernal flow'rs;
To steal from rainbows, e'er they drop in show'rs
A brighter wash;[19] to curl their waving hairs,
Assist their blushes, and inspire their airs;
Nay oft, in dreams, invention we bestow,
100   To change a flounce,° or add a furbelow.°   *dress trimming/fur trimming*
      This day, black omens threat the brightest fair
That e'er deserv'd a watchful spirit's care;
Some dire disaster, or by force, or slight;°   *sleight*
But what, or where, the Fates have wrapt in night.

Whether the nymph shall break Diana's law,
Or some frail china jar receive a flaw;
Or stain her honour, or her new brocade;° — *flowered silk*
Forget her pray'rs, or miss a masquerade;° — *masked ball*
Or lose her heart, or necklace, at a ball;
110 Or whether Heav'n has doom'd that Shock must fall.
Haste then, ye spirits! to your charge repair:
The flutt'ring fan be Zephyretta's care;
The drops° to thee, Brillante, we consign; — *diamond earrings*
And, Momentilla, let the watch be thine;
Do thou, Crispissa, tend her fav'rite lock;
Ariel himself shall be the guard of Shock.
  To fifty chosen sylphs, of special note,
We trust th' important charge, the petticoat;
Oft have we known that seven-fold[20] fence to fail,
120 Tho' stiff with hoops, and arm'd with ribs of whale;[21]
Form a strong line about the silver bound,
And guard the wide circumference around.
  Whatever spirit, careless of his charge,
His post neglects, or leaves the fair at large,
Shall feel sharp vengeance soon o'ertake his sins,
Be stop'd in vials, or transfix'd with pins;° — *hairpins*
Or plung'd in lakes of bitter washes lie,
Or wedg'd whole ages in a bodkin's eye:[22]
Gums and pomatums[23] shall his flight restrain,
130 While, clogg'd, he beats his silken wings in vain;
Or alum styptics° with contracting pow'r — *(astringent lotions)*
Shrink his thin essence like a rivell'd° flow'r: — *shrivelled*
Or, as Ixion fix'd, the wretch shall feel
The giddy motion of the whirling mill,[24]
In fumes of burning chocolate shall glow,
And tremble at the sea that froths below!'
  He spoke; the spirits from the sails descend;
Some, orb in orb, around the nymph extend;
Some thrid° the mazy ringlets of her hair; — *thread*
140 Some hang upon the pendants of her ear;
With beating hearts the dire event they wait,
Anxious, and trembling for the birth of Fate.

Canto III

Close by those meads, for ever crown'd with flow'rs,
Where Thames with pride surveys his rising tow'rs,

There stands a structure of majestic frame,
Which from the neighb'ring Hampton takes its name.
Here Britain's statesmen oft the fall foredoom
Of foreign tyrants, and of nymphs at home;
Here thou, great ANNA! whom three realms[25] obey,
Dost sometimes counsel take – and sometimes tea.
    Hither the heroes and the nymphs resort,
10 To taste awhile the pleasures of a court;
In various talk th' instructive hours they passed,
Who gave the ball, or paid the visit last;
One speaks the glory of the British Queen,
And one describes a charming Indian screen;
A third interprets motions, looks, and eyes;
At ev'ry word a reputation dies.
Snuff, or the fan, supply each pause of chat,
With singing, laughing, ogling, *and all that*.
    Mean while, declining from the noon of day,
20 The sun obliquely shoots his burning ray;
The hungry judges soon the sentence sign,
And wretches hang that jury-men may dine;
The merchant from th' Exchange° returns in peace,   *stock-exchange*
And the long labours of the toilet cease.
Belinda now, whom thirst of fame invites,
Burns to encounter two advent'rous knights,
At ombre[26] singly to decide their doom;
And swells her breast with conquests yet to come.
Straight the three bands prepare in arms to join,
30 Each band the number of the sacred nine.
Soon as she spreads her hand, th' aërial guard
Descend, and sit on each important card:
First Ariel perch'd upon a Matadore,[27]
Then each according to the rank they bore;
For sylphs, yet mindful of their ancient race,
Are, as when women, wond'rous fond of place.
    Behold, four Kings in majesty rever'd,
With hoary whiskers and a forky beard;
And four fair Queens whose hands sustain a flow'r,
40 Th' expressive emblem of their softer pow'r;
Four Knaves in garbs succinct,° a trusty band,   *brief*
Caps on their heads, and halberts° in their hand;   *battle-axes*
And particolour'd troops, a shining train,
Draw forth to combat on the velvet plain.°   *(card-table cloth)*
    The skilful nymph reviews her force with care:
'Let Spades be trumps!' she said, and trumps they were.

Now move to war her sable Matadores,
In show like leaders of the swarthy Moors.
Spadillio first, unconquerable Lord!
50   Led off two captive trumps, and swept the board.
As many more Manillio forc'd to yield,
And march'd a victor from the verdant field.
Him Basto follow'd, but his fate more hard
Gain'd but one trump and one plebeian card.
With his broad sabre next, a chief in years,
The hoary Majesty of Spades appears,
Puts forth one manly leg, to sight reveal'd,
The rest, his many-colour'd robe conceal'd.
The rebel Knave, who dares his prince engage,
60   Proves the just victim of his royal rage.
Ev'n mighty Pam,[28] that Kings and Queens o'er-threw
And mow'd down armies in the fights of Loo,
Sad chance of war! now destitute of aid,
Falls undistinguish'd by the victor Spade!
    Thus far both armies to Belinda yield;
Now to the Baron fate inclines the field.
His warlike Amazon her host invades,
Th' imperial consort of the crown of Spades.
The Club's black tyrant first her victim died,
70   Spite of his haughty mien, and barb'rous pride:
What boots the regal circle on his head,
His giant limbs, in state unwieldy spread;
That long behind he trails his pompous robe,
And, of all monarchs, only grasps the globe?
    The Baron now his Diamonds pours apace;
Th' embroider'd King who shows but half his face,
And his refulgent Queen, with pow'rs combin'd,
Of broken troops an easy conquest find.
Clubs, Diamonds, Hearts, in wild disorder seen,
80   With throngs promiscuous strow the level green.°   (the card table)
Thus when dispers'd a routed army runs,
Of Asia's troops, and Afric's sable sons,
With like confusion different nations fly,
Of various habit° and of various dye;   dress
The pierc'd battalions disunited fall,
In heaps on heaps; one fate o'erwhelms them all.
    The Knave of Diamonds tries his wily arts,
And wins (oh shameful chance!) the Queen of Hearts.
At this, the blood the virgin's cheek forsook,
90   A livid paleness spreads o'er all her look;

She sees, and trembles at th' approaching ill,
Just in the jaws of ruin, and Codille.°   *i.e. defeat*
And now, (as oft in some distemper'd state)
On one nice trick depends the gen'ral fate:
An Ace of Hearts steps forth: the King[29] unseen
Lurk'd in her hand, and mourn'd his captive Queen:
He springs to vengeance with an eager pace,
And falls like thunder on the prostrate Ace.
The nymph, exulting, fills with shouts the sky;
100 The walls, the woods, and long canals reply.
    O thoughtless mortals! ever blind to fate,
Too soon dejected, and too soon elate.
Sudden these honours shall be snatch'd away,
And curs'd for ever this victorious day.
    For lo! the board with cups and spoons is crown'd
The berries° crackle, and the mill turns round;   *coffee berries*
On shining altars of Japan° they raise   *lacquered tables*
The silver lamp; the fiery spirits blaze:
From silver spouts the grateful liquors glide,
110 While China's earth° receives the smoking tide: *china cups*
At once they gratify their scent and taste,
And frequent cups prolong the rich repast.
Straight hover round the fair her airy band;
Some, as she sipp'd, the fuming liquor fann'd,
Some o'er her lap their careful plumes display'd,
Trembling, and conscious of the rich brocade.
Coffee (which makes the politician[30] wise,
And see through all things with his half-shut eyes)
Sent up in vapours to the Baron's brain
120 New stratagems, the radiant lock to gain.
Ah cease, rash youth! desist ere 'tis too late,
Fear the just gods, and think of Scylla's fate!
Chang'd to a bird, and sent to flit in air,
She dearly pays for Nisus' injur'd hair!
    But when to mischief mortals bend their will,
How soon they find fit instruments of ill!
Just then, Clarissa drew with tempting grace
A two-edg'd weapon from her shining case:
So ladies in romance assist their knight,
130 Present the spear, and arm him for the fight.
He takes the gift with rev'rence, and extends
The little engine on his fingers' ends;
This just behind Belinda's neck he spread,
As o'er the fragrant steams she bends her head.

Swift to the lock a thousand sprites repair,
A thousand wings, by turns, blow back the hair;
And thrice they twitch'd the diamond in her ear;
Thrice she look'd back, and thrice the foe drew near.
Just in that instant, anxious Ariel sought
140   The close recesses of the virgin's thought;
As on the nosegay in her breast reclin'd,
He watch'd th' ideas rising in her mind,
Sudden he view'd, in spite of all her art,
An earthly lover lurking at her heart.
Amaz'd, confus'd, he found his pow'r expir'd,
Resign'd to fate, and with a sigh retir'd.
    The Peer now spreads the glitt'ring forfex° wide,   scissors
T'inclose the lock; now joins it, to divide.
Ev'n then, before the fatal engine clos'd,
150   A wretched sylph too fondly interpos'd;
Fate urg'd the sheers, and cut the sylph in twain,
(But airy substance soon unites again)[31]
The meeting points the sacred hair dissever
From the fair head, for ever, and for ever!
    Then flash'd the living lightning from her eyes,
And screams of horror rend th' affrighted skies.
Not louder shrieks to pitying heav'n are cast,
When husbands, or when lap-dogs breathe their last;
Or when rich china vessels, fall'n from high,
160   In glitt'ring dust and painted fragments lie!
    'Let wreaths of triumph now my temples twine',
(The victor cry'd) 'the glorious prize is mine!
While fish in streams, or birds delight in air,
Or in a coach-and-six the British fair,
As long as Atalantis shall be read,
Or the small pillow grace a lady's bed,
While visits[32] shall be paid on solemn days,
When num'rous wax-lights in bright order blaze,
While nymphs take treats, or assignations give,
170   So long my honour, name, and praise shall live!'
    What time would spare, from steel receives its date,
And monuments, like men, submit to fate!
Steel could the labour of the gods destroy,
And strike to dust th' imperial tow'rs of Troy;
Steel could the works of mortal pride confound,
And hew triumphal arches to the ground.
What wonder then, fair nymph! thy hairs should feel
The conqu'ring force of unresisted steel?

Canto IV

But anxious cares the pensive nymph oppress'd,
And secret passions labour'd in her breast.
Not youthful kings in battle seiz'd alive,
Not scornful virgins who their charms survive,
Not ardent lovers robb'd of all their bliss,
Not ancient ladies when refus'd a kiss,
Not tyrants fierce that unrepenting die,
Not Cynthia when her manteau's° pinn'd awry,   *a loose gown*
E'er felt such rage, resentment, and despair,
10   As thou, sad Virgin! for thy ravish'd hair.
        For, that sad moment, when the sylphs withdrew,
And Ariel weeping from Belinda flew,
Umbriel, a dusky, melancholy sprite,
As ever sully'd the fair face of light,
Down to the central earth, his proper scene,
Repair'd to search the gloomy Cave of Spleen.[33]
        Swift on his sooty pinions flits the gnome,
And in a vapour° reach'd the dismal dome.   *mist*
No cheerful breeze this sullen region knows,
20   The dreaded east is all the wind that blows.
Here in a grotto, shelter'd close from air,
And screen'd in shades from day's detested glare,
She sighs for ever on her pensive bed,
Pain at her side, and megrim° at her head.   *migraine*
        Two handmaids wait° the throne: alike in place,   *attend*
But diff'ring far in figure and in face.
Here stood Ill-nature like an ancient maid,
Her wrinkled form in black and white array'd;
With store of pray'rs, for mornings, nights, and noons
30   Her hand is fill'd; her bosom with lampoons.°   *personal abuse*
        There Affectation, with a sickly mien,
Shows in her cheek the roses of eighteen,
Practis'd to lisp, and hang the head aside,
Faints into airs, and languishes with pride,
On the rich quilt sinks with becoming woe,
Wrapt in a gown, for sickness, and for show.
The fair ones feel such maladies as these,
When each new night-dress gives a new disease.
        A constant vapour o'er the palace flies,
40   Strange phantoms rising as the mists arise;
Dreadful, as hermits' dreams in haunted shades,
Or bright, as visions of expiring maids.

Now glaring fiends, and snakes on rolling spires,°   *coils*
Pale spectres, gaping tombs, and purple fires:
Now lakes of liquid gold, Elysian scenes,
And crystal domes, and angels in machines.³⁴
    Unnumber'd throngs, on ev'ry side are seen,
Of bodies chang'd to various forms by Spleen.
Here living tea-pots stand, one arm held out,
50 One bent; the handle this, and that the spout:
A pipkin° there, like Homer's tripod³⁵ walks;   *cooking-pot*
Here sighs a jar, and there a goose-pie³⁶ talks;
Men prove with child, as pow'rful fancy works,
And maids turn'd bottles, call aloud for corks.
    Safe past the gnome through this fantastic band,
A branch of healing spleenwort³⁷ in his hand.
Then thus address'd the pow'r – 'Hail, wayward Queen!
Who rule the sex to fifty from fifteen:
Parent of vapours and of female wit,
60 Who give th' hysteric, or poetic fit,
On various tempers act by various ways,
Make some take physic, others scribble plays;
Who cause the proud their visits to delay,
And send the godly in a pet to pray;
A nymph there is, that all thy pow'r disdains,
And thousands more in equal mirth maintains.
But oh! if e'er thy gnome could spoil a grace,
Or raise a pimple on a beauteous face,
Like citron-waters° matrons cheeks inflame,   *brandy and lemon or orange*
70 Or change complexions at a losing game;
If e'er with airy horns³⁸ I planted heads,
Or rumpled petticoats, or tumbled beds,
Or caus'd suspicion when no soul was rude,
Or discompos'd the head-dress of a prude,
Or e'er to costive lap dog gave disease,
Which not the tears of brightest eyes could ease:
Hear me, and touch Belinda with chagrin,
That single act gives half the world the spleen.'
    The Goddess with a discontented air
80 Seems to reject him, tho' she grants his pray'r.
A wond'rous bag with both her hands she binds,
Like that where once Ulysses held the winds;
There she collects the force of female lungs,
Sighs, sobs, and passions, and the war of tongues.
A vial next she fills with fainting fears,
Soft sorrows, melting griefs, and flowing tears.

The gnome rejoicing bears her gifts away,
Spreads his black wings, and slowly mounts to day.
  Sunk in Thalestris' arms the nymph he found,
90 Her eyes dejected, and her hair unbound.
Full o'er their heads the swelling bag he rent,
And all the Furies issu'd at the vent.
Belinda burns with more than mortal ire,
And fierce Thalestris fans the rising fire.
'O wretched maid!' she spread her hands, and cry'd,
(While Hampton's echoes 'Wretched maid!' reply'd)
'Was it for this you took such constant care
The bodkin, comb, and essence to prepare?
For this your locks in paper durance bound?
100 For this with tort'ring irons° wreath'd around?   *hair-curlers*
For this with fillets° strain'd your tender head?   *head-bands*
And bravely bore the double loads of lead?[39]
Gods! shall the ravisher display your hair,
While the fops envy, and the ladies stare?
Honour forbid! at whose unrival'd shrine
Ease, pleasure, virtue, all, our sex resign.
Methinks already I your tears survey,
Already hear the horrid things they say,
Already see you a degraded toast,
110 And all your honour in a whisper lost!
How shall I, then, your helpless fame defend?
'Twill then be infamy to seem your friend!
And shall this prize, th' inestimable prize,
Expos'd through crystal to the gazing eyes,
And heighten'd by the diamond's circling rays,
On that rapacious hand for ever blaze?
Sooner shall grass in Hyde-park Circus grow,
And wits take lodgings in the sound of Bow;
Sooner let earth, air, sea, to Chaos fall,
120 Men, monkeys, lap-dogs, parrots, perish all!'
  She said; then raging to Sir Plume[40] repairs,
And bids her beau demand the precious hairs:
(Sir Plume of amber snuff-box justly vain,
And the nice° conduct of a clouded° cane)   *fastidious/dark-coloured*
With earnest eyes, and round unthinking face,
He first the snuff-box open'd, then the case,
And thus broke out – 'My Lord, why, what the devil!
Z – ds! damn the lock! 'fore Gad, you must be civil!
Plague on 't! 'tis past a jest – nay, prithee, pox!
130 Give her the hair' – he spoke, and rapp'd his box.
  'It grieves me much' (reply'd the Peer again)

'Who speaks so well should ever speak in vain.
But by this lock, this sacred lock I swear,
(Which never more shall join its parted hair;
Which never more its honours shall renew,
Clip'd from the lovely head where late it grew)
That while my nostrils draw the vital air,
This hand, which won it, shall for ever wear.'
He spoke, and speaking, in proud triumph spread
140   The long-contended honours of her head.
     But Umbriel, hateful gnome! forbears not so,
He breaks the vial whence the sorrows flow.
Then see! the Nymph in beauteous grief appears,
Her eyes half-languishing, half-drown'd in tears;
On her heav'd bosom hung her drooping head,
Which, with a sigh, she rais'd; and thus she said.
     'For ever curs'd be this detested day,
Which snatch'd my best, my fav'rite curl away!
Happy! ah ten times happy had I been,
150   If Hampton Court these eyes had never seen!
Yet am not I the first mistaken maid,
By love of courts to num'rous ills betray'd.
Oh had I rather un-admir'd remain'd
In some lone isle, or distant northern land;
Where the gilt chariot never marks the way,
Where none learn ombre, none e'er taste bohea°!   *black tea*
There kept my charms conceal'd from mortal eye,
Like roses, that in deserts bloom and die.
What mov'd my mind with youthful lords to roam?
160   O had I stay'd, and said my pray'rs at home!
'Twas this, the morning omens seem'd to tell:
Thrice from my trembling hand the patch-box° fell; *(for holding patches)*
The tott'ring china shook without a wind,
Nay Poll° sat mute, and Shock was most unkind!   *(the parrot)*
A sylph too warn'd me of the threats of fate,
In mystic visions, now believ'd too late!
See the poor remnants of these slighted hairs!
My hands shall rend what ev'n thy rapine spares:
These in two sable ringlets taught to break,
170   Once gave new beauties to the snowy neck;
The sister-lock now sits uncouth, alone,
And in its fellow's fate foresees its own;
Uncurl'd it hangs, the fatal shears demands,
And tempts, once more, thy sacrilegious hands.
Oh hadst thou, cruel! been content to seize
Hairs less in sight, or any hairs but these!'

Canto V

She said: the pitying audience melt in tears,
But Fate and Jove had stopp'd the Baron's ears.
In vain Thalestris with reproach assails,
For who can move when fair Belinda fails?
Not half so fix'd the Trojan could remain,
While Anna begg'd and Dido rag'd in vain.⁴¹
Then grave Clarissa⁴² graceful wav'd her fan;
Silence ensu'd, and thus the nymph began.
   'Say, why are beauties prais'd and honour'd most,
The wise man's passion, and the vain man's toast?
Why deck'd with all that land and sea afford
Why angels call'd, and angel-like adored?
Why round our coaches crowd the white-glov'd beaus?
Why bows the side-box from its inmost rows?⁴³
How vain are all these glories, all our pains,
Unless good sense preserve what beauty gains:
That men may say, when we the front-box grace,
'Behold the first in virtue as in face!'
Oh! if to dance all night, and dress all day,
Charm'd the small-pox, or chas'd old-age away;
Who would not scorn what housewife's cares produce,
Or who would learn one earthly thing of use?
To patch, nay ogle, might become a saint,
Nor could it sure be such a sin to paint.
But since, alas! frail beauty must decay,
Curl'd or uncurl'd, since locks will turn to grey;
Since painted, or not painted, all shall fade,
And she who scorns a man, must die a maid;
What then remains, but well our pow'r to use,
And keep good-humour still, whate'er we lose?
And trust me, dear! good-humour can prevail,
When airs, and flights, and screams, and scolding fail.
Beauties in vain their pretty eyes may roll;
Charms strike the sight, but merit wins the soul.'
   So spoke the Dame, but no applause ensu'd;
Belinda frown'd, Thalestris call'd her prude.
'To arms, to arms!' the fierce virago° cries,   *resolute woman*
And swift as lightning to the combat flies.
All side° in parties, and begin th' attack;   *take sides*
Fans clap, silks russle, and tough whalebones crack;
Heroes' and heroines' shouts confus'dly rise,
And base and treble voices strike the skies.

No common weapons in their hands are found,
Like gods they fight, nor dread a mortal wound.
   So when bold Homer makes the gods engage,
And heav'nly breasts with human passions rage;
'Gainst Pallas, Mars; Latona, Hermes arms,[44]
And all Olympus rings with loud alarms:
Jove's thunder roars, heav'n trembles all around,
50 Blue Neptune storms, the bellowing deeps resound:
Earth shakes her nodding tow'rs, the ground gives way,
And the pale ghosts start at the flash of day!
   Triumphant Umbriel on a sconce's° height   *branched candlestick*
Clapp'd his glad wings, and sat to view the fight:
Prop'd on their bodkin spears, the sprites survey
The growing combat, or assist the fray.
   While through the press enrag'd Thalestris flies,
And scatters death around from both her eyes,
A beau and witling° perish'd in the throng,   *petty pretender to wit*
60 One dy'd in metaphor, and one in song.
'O cruel nymph! a living death I bear,'
Cry'd Dapperwit,[45] and sunk beside his chair.
A mournful glance Sir Fopling[46] upwards cast,
'Those eyes are made so killing'[47] – was his last.
Thus on Maeander's flow'ry margin lies
Th' expiring swan, and as he sings he dies.
   When bold Sir Plume had drawn Clarissa down,
Chloe stepp'd in, and kill'd him with a frown;
She smil'd to see the doughty hero slain,
70 But, at her smile, the beau reviv'd again.
   Now Jove suspends his golden scales in air,
Weighs the men's wits against the lady's hair;
The doubtful beam long nods from side to side;
At length the wits mount up, the hairs subside.
   See fierce Belinda on the Baron flies,
With more than usual lightning in her eyes:
Nor fear'd the chief th' unequal fight to try,
Who sought no more than on his foe to die.
But this bold lord, with manly strength endu'd,
80 She with one finger and a thumb subdu'd:
Just where the breath of life his nostrils drew,
A charge of snuff the wily virgin threw;
The gnomes direct, to ev'ry atom just,
The pungent grains of titillating dust.
Sudden, with starting tears each eye o'erflows,
And the high dome re-echoes to his nose.

'Now meet thy fate!' incens'd Belinda cry'd,
And drew a deadly bodkin from her side,
(The same, his ancient personage to deck,[48]
90 Her great great grandsire wore about his neck,
In three seal-rings;° which after, melted down, *(for imprinting sealing-wax)*
Form'd a vast buckle for his widow's gown:
Her infant grandame's whistle next it grew,
The bells she jingled, and the whistle blew;
Then in a bodkin grac'd her mother's hairs,
Which long she wore, and now Belinda wears.)
     'Boast not my fall,' (he cry'd) 'insulting foe!
Thou by some other shalt be laid as low.
Nor think, to die dejects my lofty mind;
100 All that I dread is leaving you behind!
Rather than so, ah let me still survive,
And burn in Cupid's flames – but burn alive.'
     'Restore the lock!' she cries; and all around
'Restore the lock!' the vaulted roofs rebound.
Not fierce Othello in so loud a strain
Roar'd for the handkerchief that caus'd his pain.[49]
But see how oft ambitious aims are cross'd,
And chiefs contend 'till all the prize is lost!
The lock, obtain'd with guilt, and kept with pain,
110 In ev'ry place is sought, but sought in vain:
With such a prize no mortal must be blest,
So Heav'n decrees! with Heav'n who can contest?
     Some thought it mounted to the lunar sphere,
Since all things lost on earth are treasur'd there.
There heroes' wits are kept in pond'rous vases,[50]
And beaux' in snuff-boxes and tweezer-cases.[51]
There broken vows, and death-bed alms are found,
And lovers' hearts with ends of ribband bound,
The courtier's promises, and sick man's pray'rs,
120 The smiles of harlots, and the tears of heirs,
Cages for gnats, and chains to yoke a flea,
Dried butterflies, and tomes of casuistry.
     But trust the Muse – she saw it upward rise,
Tho' mark'd by none but quick, poetic eyes:
(So Rome's great founder° to the heav'ns withdrew,   *(i.e. Romulus)*
To Proculus alone confess'd in view)
A sudden star, it shot through liquid air,
And drew behind a radiant trail of hair.
Not Berenice's locks first rose so bright,

130 The heav'ns bespangling with dishevell'd light.
The sylphs behold it kindling as it flies,
    And pleas'd pursue its progress through the skies.
        This the beau monde shall from the Mall survey,
And hail with music its propitious ray;
This the bless'd lover shall for Venus take,
And send up vows from Rosamonda's lake;
This Partridge soon shall view in cloudless skies,
When next he looks through Galileo's eyes;°   *(telescope)*
And hence th' egregious wizard shall foredoom
140 The fate of Louis, and the fall of Rome.
        Then cease, bright Nymph! to mourn thy ravish'd hair,
Which adds new glory to the shining sphere!
Not all the tresses that fair head can boast,
Shall draw such envy as the lock you lost.
For, after all the murders of your eye,
When, after millions slain, yourself shall die;
When those fair suns shall set, as set they must,
And all those tresses shall be laid in dust,
This lock, the Muse shall consecrate to fame,
150 And 'midst the stars inscribe Belinda's name.

[1712: 1st version. 1714: 2nd version]

Ode on Solitude

Happy the man, whose wish and care
A few paternal acres bound,
Content to breathe his native air,
        In his own ground.

Whose herds with milk, whose fields with bread,
Whose flocks supply him with attire,
Whose trees in summer yield him shade,
        In winter fire.

Blest! who can unconcern'dly find
10 Hours, days, and years slide soft away,
In health of body, peace of mind,
        Quiet by day,

Sound sleep by night; study and ease
Together mix'd; sweet recreation,
And innocence, which most does please,
                With meditation.

Thus let me live, unseen, unknown;
Thus unlamented let me die;
Steal from the world, and not a stone
20   Tell where I lie.

[1717]

Epistle to Miss Teresa Blount

ON HER LEAVING THE TOWN AFTER THE CORONATION

As some fond Virgin, whom her mother's care
Drags from the town to wholesome country air,
Just when she learns to roll a melting eye,
And hear a spark,° yet think no danger nigh;   *dandy*
From the dear man unwilling she must sever,
Yet takes one kiss before she parts for ever:
Thus from the world fair Zephalinda° flew,   *i.e. Miss Blount*
Saw others happy, and with sighs withdrew;
Not that their pleasures caus'd her discontent,
10 She sigh'd not that they stay'd, but that she went.
    She went, to plain-work, and to purling° brooks,   *murmuring*
Old-fashion'd halls, dull Aunts, and croaking rooks:
She went from op'ra, park, assembly, play,
To morning-walks, and pray'rs three hours a-day;
To part her time 'twixt reading and bohea,°   *black tea*
To muse, and spill her solitary tea,
Or o'er cold coffee trifle with the spoon,
Count the slow clock, and dine exact at noon:
Divert her eyes with pictures in the fire,
20 Hum half a tune, tell stories to the squire;
Up to her godly garret after seven,
There starve and pray, for that's the way to heaven.
    Some squire, perhaps, you take delight to rack;°   *torture*
Whose game is whisk,° whose treat a toast in sack;°   *whist/sherry*

Who visits with a gun, presents you birds,
Then gives a smacking buss,° and cries, – No words!   *kiss*
Or with his hound comes hallooing from the stable,
Makes love with nods, and knees beneath a table;
Whose laughs are hearty, tho' his jests are coarse,
30   And loves you best of all things – but his horse.
      In some fair ev'ning, on your elbow laid,
You dream of triumphs in the rural shade;
In pensive thought recall the fancy'd scene,
See coronations rise on ev'ry green;
Before you pass th' imaginary sights
Of lords, and earls, and dukes, and garter'd knights,
While the spread fan o'ershades your closing eyes;
Then give one flirt,° and all the vision flies.   *flick of the fan*
Thus vanish sceptres, coronets, and balls,
40   And leave you in lone woods, or empty walls!
      So when your slave, at some dear idle time,
(Not plagu'd with head-aches, or the want of rhyme)
Stands in the streets, abstracted from the crew,
And while he seems to study, thinks of you;
Just when his fancy points° your sprightly eyes,   *pinpoints*
Or sees the blush of soft Parthenia rise,
Gay[52] pats my shoulder, and you vanish quite,
Streets, chairs,° and coxcombs rush upon my sight;   *sedan-chairs*
Vex'd to be still in town, I knit my brow,
50   Look sour, and hum a tune, as you may now.

[1717]

From **An Essay on Man**

Epistle I

      All are but parts of one stupendous whole,
Whose body, nature is, and God the soul;
That, chang'd thro' all, and yet in all the same,
270   Great in the earth, as in th' æthereal frame,
Warms in the sun, refreshes in the breeze,
Glows in the stars, and blossoms in the trees,
Lives thro' all life, extends thro' all extent,
Spreads undivided, operates unspent,

Breathes in our soul, informs our mortal part,
As full, as perfect, in a hair as heart;
As full, as perfect, in vile man that mourns,
As the rapt seraph that adores and burns;[53]
To him no high, no low, no great, no small;
280 He fills, he bounds, connects, and equals all.
    Cease then, nor order imperfection name:
Our proper bliss depends on what we blame.
Know thy own point: This kind, this due degree
Of blindness, weakness, Heav'n bestows on thee.
Submit – In this, or any other sphere,
Secure to be as blest as thou canst bear:
Safe in the hand of one disposing Pow'r,
Or in the natal, or the mortal° hour.   *of death*
All nature is but art, unknown to thee;
290 All chance, direction, which thou canst not see;
All discord, harmony, not understood;
All partial evil, universal good:
And, spite of pride, in erring reason's spite,
One truth is clear, WHATEVER IS, IS RIGHT.

Epistle II

Know then thyself, presume not God to scan,°   *examine in detail*
The proper study of mankind is man.
Plac'd on this isthmus of a middle state,
A being darkly wise, and rudely great:
With too much knowledge for the sceptic side,
With too much weakness for the stoic's pride,
He hangs between; in doubt to act, or rest;
In doubt to deem himself a god, or beast;
In doubt his mind or body to prefer;
10 Born but to die, and reas'ning but to err;
Alike in ignorance, his reason such,
Whether he thinks too little, or too much:
Chaos of thought and passion, all confus'd;
Still by himself abus'd, or disabus'd;
Created half to rise, and half to fall;
Great lord of all things, yet a prey to all;
Sole judge of truth, in endless error hurl'd:
The glory, jest, and riddle of the world!

*   *   *

Behold the child, by nature's kindly law,
Pleas'd with a rattle, tickled with a straw:
Some livelier play-thing gives his youth delight,
A little louder, but as empty quite:
Scarfs, garters,° gold, amuse his riper stage, *ribands to hold up stocking*
280 And beads° and pray'r-books are the toys of age: *rosary*
Pleas'd with this bauble still, as that before;
Till tir'd he sleeps, and life's poor play is o'er.

Epistle III

 Look round our world; behold the chain of love
Combining all below and all above.
See plastic⁵⁴ nature working to this end,
10 The single atoms each to other tend,
Attract, attracted to, the next in place
Form'd and impell'd its neighbour to embrace.
See matter next, with various life endu'd,
Press⁵⁵ to one centre still, the gen'ral good.
See dying vegetables life sustain,
See life dissolving vegetate again:
All forms that perish other forms supply,
(By turns we catch the vital breath, and die)
Like bubbles on the sea of matter born,
20 They rise, they break, and to that sea return.
Nothing is foreign: parts relate to whole;
One all-extending all-preserving soul
Connects each being, greatest with the least;
Made beast in aid of man, and man of beast;
All serv'd, all serving! nothing stands alone;
The chain holds on, and where it ends, unknown.

Epistle IV

 What's fame? A fancied life in others' breath,
A thing beyond us, ev'n before our death.
Just what you hear, you have, and what's unknown
240 The same (my Lord) if Tully's, or your own.
All that we feel of it begins and ends
In the small circle of our foes or friends;
To all beside as much an empty shade
An Eugene living, as a Caesar dead;

Alike or when, or where, they shone, or shine,
Or on the Rubicon, or on the Rhine.
A wit's a feather, and a chief's a rod;
An honest man's the noblest work of God.
Fame but from death a villain's name can save,
250 As justice tears his body from the grave,
When what t' oblivion better were resign'd,
Is hung on high, to poison half mankind.
All fame is foreign, but of true desert;
Plays round the head, but comes not to the heart:
One self-approving hour whole years out-weighs
Of stupid starers, and of loud huzzas;
And more true joy Marcellus exil'd feels,
Than Caesar with a senate at his heels.

            *   *   *

Come then, my friend,⁵⁶ my genius! come along;
O master of the poet, and the song!
And while the Muse now stoops, or now ascends,
To man's low passions, or their glorious ends,
Teach me, like thee, in various nature wise,
To fall with dignity, with temper rise;
Form'd by thy converse, happily to steer
380 From grave to gay, from lively to severe;
Correct with spirit, eloquent with ease,
Intent to reason, or polite to please.
Oh! while along the stream of time thy name
Expanded flies, and gathers all its fame,
Say, shall my little bark attendant sail,
Pursue the triumph, and partake the gale?
When statesmen, heroes, kings, in dust repose,
Whose sons shall blush their fathers were thy foes,
Shall then this verse to future age pretend°   *proclaim*
390 Thou wert my guide, philosopher, and friend?
That, urg'd by thee, I turn'd the tuneful art
From sounds to things, from fancy to the heart;
For wit's false mirror held up nature's light;
Show'd erring pride, WHATEVER IS, IS RIGHT;
That REASON, PASSION, answer one great aim;
That true SELF-LOVE and SOCIAL are the same;
That VIRTUE only makes our bliss below;
And all our knowledge is, OURSELVES TO KNOW.

                        [1733-4]

Epistle to Dr Arbuthnot[57]

P. Shut, shut the door, good John! fatigu'd I said,
Tie up the knocker, say I'm sick, I'm dead.
The dog-star° rages! nay, 'tis past a doubt,   *Sirius*
All Bedlam, or Parnassus, is let out:
Fire in each eye, and papers in each hand,
They rave, recite, and madden round the land.
    What walls can guard me, or what shades can hide?
They pierce my thickets, through my grot° they glide,[58]   *grotto*
By land, by water, they renew the charge,
10 They stop the chariot, and they board the barge.[59]
No place is sacred, not the church is free,
Ev'n Sunday shines no Sabbath-day to me:
Then from the Mint walks forth the man of rhyme,
Happy! to catch me, just at dinner-time.
    Is there a parson, much be-mus'd in beer,[60]
A maudlin poetess, a rhyming peer,
A clerk, foredoom'd his father's soul to cross,
Who pens a stanza, when he should engross°?   *prepare a legal document*
Is there, who, lock'd from ink and paper, scrawls
20 With desp'rate charcoal round his darken'd walls?[61]
All fly to TWIT'NAM,° and in humble strain   *Twickenham*
Apply to me, to keep them mad or vain.
Arthur,° whose giddy son neglects the laws,   *Moore*
Imputes to me and my damn'd works the cause:
Poor Cornus° sees his frantic wife elope,   *a cuckold*
And curses wit, and poetry, and Pope.
    Friend to my life! (which did not you prolong,
The world had wanted many an idle song)
What drop or nostrum° can this plague remove?   *drug*
30 Or which must end me, a fool's wrath or love?
A dire dilemma! either way I'm sped,°   *ruined*
If foes, they write, if friends, they read me dead.
Seiz'd and tied down to judge, how wretched I?
Who can't be silent, and who will not lie:
To laugh, were want of goodness and of grace,
And to be grave, exceeds all pow'r of face.
I sit with sad civility, I read
With honest anguish, and an aching head;
And drop at last, but in unwilling ears,
40 This saving counsel, 'Keep your piece nine years.'[62]
    'Nine years!' cries he, who high° in Drury-lane,   *(in a garret)*
Lull'd by soft zephyrs through the broken pane,

Rhymes ere he wakes, and prints before term° ends, *legal or publishing*
Oblig'd by hunger, and request of friends: *| season*
'The piece, you think, is incorrect? why take it,
I'm all submission, what you'd have it, make it.'
   Three things another's modest wishes bound,
My friendship, and a prologue, and ten pound.
   Pitholeon[63] sends to me: 'You know his Grace,
50 I want a patron; ask him for a place.'
Pitholeon libell'd me – 'But here's a letter
Informs you, Sir, 'twas when he knew no better.
Dare you refuse him? Curll invites to dine,
He'll write a journal, or he'll turn Divine.'[64]
   Bless me! a packet. – ''Tis a stranger sues,
A virgin tragedy, an orphan muse.'
If I dislike it, 'Furies, death and rage!'
If I approve, 'Commend it to the stage.'
There (thank my stars) my whole commission ends,
60 The play'rs and I are, luckily, no friends.
Fir'd that the house° reject him, ''Sdeath! I'll print it, *playhouse*
And shame the fools – Your int'rest, Sir, with Lintot.'
Lintot, dull rogue! will think your price too much:
'Not, Sir, if you revise it, and retouch.'
All my demurs but double his attacks;
At last he whispers, 'Do; and we go snacks°.' *share profits*
Glad of a quarrel, straight I clap the door,
Sir, let me see your works and you no more.
   'Tis sung, when Midas' ears began to spring
70 (Midas, a sacred person and a king),
His very minister who spy'd them first,
(Some say his Queen)[65] was forc'd to speak, or burst.
And is not mine, my friend, a sorer case,
When ev'ry coxcomb perks them in my face?
   A. Good friend, forbear! you deal in dang'rous things.
I'd never name queens, ministers, or kings;
Keep close to ears, and those let asses prick,
'Tis nothing ——
   P.   Nothing? if they bite and kick?
Out with it, Dunciad! let the secret pass,
80 That secret to each fool, that he's an ass:
The truth once told (and wherefore should we lie?)
The Queen of Midas slept, and so may I.
   You think this cruel? take it for a rule,
No creature smarts so little as a fool.
Let peals of laughter, Codrus! round thee break,

Thou unconcern'd canst hear the mighty crack:
Pit, box, and gall'ry in convulsions hurl'd,
Thou stand'st unshook amidst a bursting world.
Who shames a scribbler? break one cobweb through,
He spins the slight, self-pleasing thread anew:
Destroy his fib, or sophistry, in vain,
The creature's at his dirty work again,
Thron'd in the centre of his thin designs,
Proud of a vast extent of flimsy lines!
Whom have I hurt? has poet yet, or peer,
Lost the arch'd eye-brow, or Parnassian sneer?
And has not Colley° still his lord, and whore?   *Cibber*
His butchers, Henley, his free-masons, Moore?
Does not one table Bavius still admit?
Still to one bishop, Philips seem a wit?
Still Sappho[66]——
    A.   Hold! for God-sake – you'll offend,
No names – be calm – learn prudence of a friend:
I too could write, and I am twice as tall;
But foes like these ——
    P.   One flatt'rer's worse than all.
Of all mad creatures, if the learn'd are right,
It is the slaver° kills, and not the bite.   *saliva*
A fool quite angry is quite innocent:
Alas! 'tis ten times worse when they repent.
One dedicates in high heroic prose,
And ridicules beyond a hundred foes:
One from all Grubstreet will my fame defend,
And more abusive, calls himself my friend.
This prints my Letters,[67] that expects a bribe,
And others roar aloud, 'Subscribe, subscribe.'[68]
    There are, who to my person pay their court:
I cough like Horace, and, tho' lean, am short,[69]
Ammon's great son° one shoulder had too high,   *Alexander the Great*
Such Ovid's nose, and, 'Sir! you have an eye' –
Go on, obliging creatures, make me see,
All that disgrac'd my betters, met in me.
Say for my comfort, languishing in bed,
'Just so immortal Maro° held his head:'   *Virgil*
And when I die, be sure you let me know
Great Homer died three thousand years ago.
    Why did I write? what sin to me unknown
Dipt me in ink, my parents', or my own?
As yet a child, nor yet a fool to fame,

I lisp'd in numbers, for the numbers came.
I left no calling for this idle trade,
130 No duty broke, no father disobey'd.
The Muse but serv'd to ease some friend, not wife,
To help me through this long disease, my life,[70]
To second, Arbuthnot! thy art and care,
And teach the being you preserv'd, to bear.
    But why then publish? Granville, the polite[71]
And knowing Walsh would tell me I could write;
Well-natur'd Garth inflam'd with early praise,
And Congreve lov'd, and Swift endur'd my lays;
The courtly Talbot, Somers, Sheffield read,
140 Ev'n mitred Rochester would nod the head,
And St John's self (great Dryden's friends before)
With open arms receiv'd one poet more.
Happy my studies, when by these approv'd!
Happier their author, when by these belov'd!
From these the world will judge of men and books,
Not from the Burnets, Oldmixons, and Cookes.
    Soft were my numbers; who could take offence
While pure description held the place of sense?
Like gentle Fanny's[72] was my flow'ry theme,
150 A painted mistress, or a purling stream.
Yet then did Gildon draw his venal quill;
I wish'd the man a dinner, and sat still.
Yet then did Dennis rave in furious fret;
I never answer'd – I was not in debt.
If want provok'd, or madness made them print,
I wag'd no war with Bedlam or the Mint.
    Did some more sober critic come abroad;
If wrong, I smil'd; if right, I kiss'd the rod.
Pains, reading, study, are their just pretence,
160 And all they want is spirit, taste, and sense.
Commas and points they set exactly right,
And 'twere a sin to rob them of their mite.
Yet ne'er one sprig of laurel grac'd these ribalds,
From slashing Bentley down to piddling Tibbalds.   *Theobald*
Each wight who reads not, and but scans and spells,
Each word-catcher, that lives on syllables,
Ev'n such small critics some regard may claim,
Preserved in Milton's or in Shakespeare's name.
Pretty! in amber to observe the forms
170 Of hairs, or straws, or dirt, or grubs, or worms!
The things, we know, are neither rich nor rare,

But wonder how the devil they got there.
    Were others angry: I excus'd them too;
Well might they rage, I gave them but their due.
A man's true merit 'tis not hard to find;
But each man's secret standard in his mind,
That casting-weight pride adds to emptiness,
This, who can gratify? for who can guess?
The bard whom pilfer'd pastorals renown,
180 Who turns a Persian tale for half a crown,[73]
Just writes to make his barrenness appear,
And strains, from hard-bound° brains, eight lines a year;   *constipated*
He, who still wanting, tho' he lives on theft,
Steals much, spends little, yet has nothing left:
And he, who now to sense, now nonsense leaning,
Means not, but blunders round about a meaning:
And he, whose fustian's° so sublimely bad,   *bombast*
It is not poetry, but prose run mad:
All these, my modest satire bade translate,
190 And own'd that nine such poets made a Tate.
How did they fume, and stamp, and roar, and chafe!
And swear, not Addison himself was safe.
    Peace to all such! but were there one whose fires
True genius kindles, and fair fame inspires;
Blest with each talent and each art to please,
And born to write, converse, and live with ease:
Should such a man, too fond to rule alone,
Bear, like the Turk, no brother near the throne,[74]
View him with scornful, yet with jealous eyes,
200 And hate for arts that caus'd himself to rise;
Damn with faint praise, assent with civil leer,
And, without sneering, teach the rest to sneer;
Willing to wound, and yet afraid to strike,
Just hint a fault, and hesitate dislike;
Alike reserv'd to blame, or to commend,
A tim'rous foe, and a suspicious friend;
Dreading ev'n fools, by flatterers besieged,
And so obliging, that he ne'er oblig'd;
Like Cato, give his little senate laws,
210 And sit attentive to his own applause;
While wits and templars° ev'ry sentence raise,   *law students*
And wonder with a foolish face of praise –
Who but must laugh, if such a man there be?
Who would not weep, if Atticus° were he?   *Addison*
    What tho' my name stood rubric° on the walls,   *red letters*

Or plaister'd posts, with claps,[75] in capitals?
Or smoking forth, a hundred hawkers load,
On wings of winds came flying all abroad?
I sought no homage from the race that write;
220 I kept, like Asian monarchs, from their sight:
Poems I heeded (now be-rhym'd so long)
No more than thou, great George! a birthday song.
I ne'er with wits or witlings pass'd my days,
To spread about the itch of verse and praise;
Nor like a puppy, daggled° through the town,   *drag through mud*
To fetch and carry, sing-song up and down;
Nor at rehearsals sweat, and mouth'd, and cry'd,
With handkerchief and orange at my side;°   *(to dispel infection)*
230 But sick of fops, and poetry, and prate,
To Bufo° left the whole Castalian state.   *a toad = any patron*
     Proud as Apollo on his forked hill,
Sat full-blown Bufo, puff'd by ev'ry quill;
Fed with soft dedication all day long,
Horace and he went hand in hand in song.
His library (where busts of poets dead
And a true Pindar stood without a head)
Receiv'd of wits an undistinguish'd race,
Who first his judgment ask'd, and then a place:
Much they extoll'd his pictures, much his seat,°   *estate*
240 And flatter'd ev'ry day, and some days eat:
Till grown more frugal in his riper days,
He paid some bards with port, and some with praise,
To some a dry rehearsal[76] was assign'd,
And others (harder still) he paid in kind.[77]
Dryden alone (what wonder?) came not nigh,
Dryden alone escap'd this judging eye:
But still the great have kindness in reserve,
He help'd to bury whom he help'd to starve.
     May some choice patron bless each gray-goose quill°!   *quill pen*
250 May every Bavius have his Bufo still!
So when a statesman wants a day's defence,
Or envy holds a whole week's war with sense,
Or simple pride for flatt'ry makes demands,
May dunce by dunce be whistled off my hands!
Bless'd be the great! for those they take away,
And those they left me; for they left me Gay;
Left me to see neglected genius bloom,
Neglected die, and tell it on his tomb:
Of all thy blameless life, the sole return

260 My verse, and Queensberry weeping o'er thy urn!
    Oh let me live my own, and die so too!
(To live and die is all I have to do:)
Maintain a poet's dignity and ease,
And see what friends, and read what books I please:
Above a patron, tho' I condescend
Sometimes to call a minister my friend.
I was not born for courts or great affairs;
I pay my debts, believe, and say my pray'rs;
Can sleep without a poem in my head,
270 Nor know if Dennis be alive or dead.
    Why am I ask'd 'what next shall see the light?'
Heav'ns! was I born for nothing but to write?
Has life no joys for me? or (to be grave)
Have I no friend to serve, no soul to save?
'I found him close with Swift' — 'Indeed? no doubt'
(Cries prating Balbus) 'something will come out.'
'Tis all in vain, deny it as I will.
'No, such a genius never can lie still;'
And then for mine obligingly mistakes
280 The first lampoon Sir Will or Bubo[78] makes.
Poor guiltless I! and can I choose but smile,
When ev'ry coxcomb knows me by my style?
    Curst be the verse, how well soe'er it flow,
That tends to make one worthy man my foe,
Give virtue scandal, innocence a fear,
Or from the soft-ey'd virgin steal a tear!
But he who hurts a harmless neighbour's peace,
Insults fall'n worth, or beauty in distress,
Who loves a lie, lame slander helps about,
Who writes a libel, or who copies out:
That fop, whose pride affects a patron's name,
Yet, absent, wounds an author's honest fame:
Who can your merit selfishly approve,
And show the sense of it without the love;
Who has the vanity to call you friend,
Yet wants the honour, injur'd, to defend;
Who tells whate'er you think, whate'er you say,
And, if he lie not, must at least betray:
Who to the Dean and silver bell can swear,
300 And sees at Cannons[79] what was never there;
Who reads, but with a lust to misapply,
Makes satire a lampoon, and fiction, lie;
A lash like mine no honest man shall dread,

But all such babbling blockheads in his stead.
Let Sporus° tremble ——— *Lord Hervey*
    A.   What? that thing of silk,
Sporus, that mere white curd of ass's milk?
Satire or sense, alas! can Sporus feel?
Who breaks a butterfly upon a wheel?
    P. Yet let me flap this bug with gilded wings,
310 This painted child of dirt, that stinks and stings;
Whose buzz the witty and the fair annoys,
Yet wit ne'er tastes, and beauty ne'er enjoys:
So well-bred spaniels civilly delight
In mumbling of the game they dare not bite.
Eternal smiles his emptiness betray,
As shallow streams run dimpling all the way.
Whether in florid impotence he speaks,
And, as the prompter breathes, the puppet squeaks;
Or at the ear of Eve, familiar toad! *Queen Caroline*
320 Half froth, half venom, spits himself abroad,
In puns or politics, or tales, or lies,
Or spite, or smut, or rhymes, or blasphemies.
His wit all see-saw, between this and that,
Now high, now low, now master up, now miss,
And he himself one vile antithesis.
Amphibious thing! that, acting either part,
The trifling head, or the corrupted heart,
Fop at the toilet, flatt'rer at the board,
Now trips a lady, and now struts a lord.
330 Eve's tempter thus the Rabbins° have express'd, *Jewish scholars*
A cherub's face, a reptile all the rest,
Beauty that shocks you, parts that none will trust,
Wit that can creep, and pride that licks the dust.
    Not fortune's worshipper, nor fashion's fool,
Not lucre°'s madman, nor ambition's tool, *money*
Not proud, nor servile; be one poet's praise,
That, if he pleas'd, he pleas'd by manly ways:
That flatt'ry, even to kings, he held a shame,
And thought a lie in verse or prose the same.
340 That not in fancy's maze he wander'd long,
But stoop'd° to truth, and moraliz'd his song; *like a falcon*
That not for fame, but virtue's better end,
He stood° the furious foe, the timid friend, *withstood*
The damning critic, half-approving wit,
The coxcomb hit, or fearing to be hit;
Laugh'd at the loss of friends he never had,

The dull, the proud, the wicked, and the mad;
The distant threats of vengeance on his head,
The blow unfelt,[80] the tear he never shed;
350 The tale revived, the lie so oft o'erthrown,
Th' imputed trash, and dulness not his own;[81]
The morals blacken'd when the writings 'scape,
The libell'd person, and the pictur'd shape;[82]
Abuse, on all he lov'd, or lov'd him, spread,
A friend in exile, or a father, dead;[83]
The whisper, that to greatness still too near,
Perhaps yet vibrates on his sovereign's ear —
Welcome for thee, fair virtue! all the past:
For thee, fair virtue! welcome ev'n the last!
360   A. But why insult the poor, affront the great?
P. A knave's a knave, to me, in ev'ry state:
Alike my scorn, if he succeed or fail,
Sporus at court, or Japhet[84] in a jail,
A hireling scribbler, or a hireling peer,
Knight of the post° corrupt, or of the shire;   *professional witness*
If on a pillory, or near a throne,
He gain his prince's ear, or lose his own,
    Yet soft by nature, more a dupe than wit,
Sappho can tell you how this man was bit:
370 This dreaded sat'rist Dennis will confess
Foe to his pride, but friend to his distress:
So humble, he has knock'd at Tibbald's door,
Has drunk with Cibber, nay, has rhymed for Moore.
Full ten years slander'd, did he once reply?
Three thousand suns went down on Welsted's lie.
To please his mistress[85] one aspers'd his life;
He lash'd him not, but let her be his wife:
Let Budgell charge low Grub Street on his quill,
And write whate'er he pleas'd, except his will;
380 Let the two Curlls of town and court abuse
His father, mother, body, soul, and muse.
Yet why? that father held it for a rule,
It was a sin to call our neighbour fool:
That harmless mother thought no wife a whore;
Hear this, and spare his family, James Moore!
Unspotted names, and memorable long!
If there be force in virtue, or in song.
    Of gentle blood (part shed in honour's cause,
While yet in *Britain* honour had applause)
Each parent sprung ——

A.   What fortune, pray? ——

390   P.   Their own,
And better got, than Bestia's from the throne.
Born to no pride, inheriting no strife,
Nor marrying discord in a noble wife,
Stranger to civil and religious rage,
The good man walk'd innoxious through his age.
No courts he saw, no suits would ever try,
Nor dar'd an oath, nor hazarded a lie.
Unlearn'd, he knew no schoolman's subtle art,
No language but the language of the heart.
400 By nature honest, by experience wise,
Healthy by temp'rance, and by exercise;
His life, tho' long, to sickness passed unknown,
His death was instant, and without a groan,
O grant me thus to live, and thus to die!
Who sprung from kings shall know less joy than I.
     O friend! may each domestic bliss be thine!
Be no unpleasing melancholy mine:
Me, let the tender office long engage,
To rock the cradle of reposing age,[86]
410 With lenient arts extend a mother's breath,
Make languor smile, and smooth the bed of death,
Explore the thought, explain the asking eye,
And keep a while one parent from the sky!
On cares like these, if length of days attend,
May Heav'n, to bless those days, preserve my friend,
Preserve him social, cheerful, and serene,
And just as rich as when he serv'd a queen.
     A. Whether that blessing be deny'd or giv'n,
Thus far was right, the rest belongs to Heav'n.

[1735]

From **The Dunciad**

from *Book I*

Here she[87] beholds the chaos dark and deep,
Where nameless somethings[88] in their causes sleep,
'Till genial Jacob,[89] or a warm third day,[90]
Call forth each mass, a poem, or a play:
How hints, like spawn, scarce quick in embryo lie,
60 How new-born nonsense first is taught to cry,
Maggots half-form'd in rhyme exactly meet,
And learn to crawl upon poetic feet.
Here one poor word an hundred clenches° makes,   *puns*
And ductile° dulness new meanders takes;   *flexible*
There motley images her fancy strike,
Figures ill pair'd, and similes unlike.
She sees a mob of metaphors advance,
Pleas'd with the madness of the mazy dance:
How tragedy and comedy embrace;
70 How farce and epic get a jumbled race;
How time himself stands still at her command,
Realms shift their place, and ocean turns to land.
Here gay description Egypt glads with show'rs,[91]
Or gives to Zembla fruits, to Barca flow'rs;
Glitt'ring with ice here hoary hills are seen,
There painted vallies of eternal green,
In cold December fragrant chaplets° blow,   *head garlands*
And heavy harvests nod beneath the snow.

from *Book II*

Three college sophs,[92] and three pert templars° came,   *law students*
380 The same their talents, and their tastes the same;
Each prompt to query, answer, and debate,
And smit with love of poesy and prate.°   *prattle*
The pond'rous books two gentle readers bring;
The heroes sit, the vulgar form a ring
The clam'rous crowd is hush'd with mugs of Mum,°   *German beer*
'Till all, tun'd equal, send a gen'ral hum.
Then mount the clerks, and in one lazy tone
Thro' the long, heavy, painful page drawl on;
Soft creeping, words on words, the sense compose,

390 At ev'ry line they stretch, they yawn, they doze.
As to soft gales top-heavy pines bow low
Their heads, and lift them as they cease to blow:
Thus oft they rear, and oft the head decline,
As breathe, or pause, by fits, the airs divine.
And now to this side, now to that they nod,
As verse, or prose, infuse° the drowsy god.   *breathe in*

from *Book IV*

More she had spoke, but yawn'd – All nature nods:
What mortal can resist the yawn of gods?
Churches and chapels instantly it reach'd;
(St. James's first, for leaden Gilbert preach'd)
Then catch'd the schools; the Hall° scarce kept awake; *Westminster Hall*
610 The convocation[94] gap'd, but could not speak:
Lost was the nation's sense, nor could be found,
While the long solemn unison went round:
Wide, and more wide, it spread o'er all the realm;
Ev'n Palinurus nodded at the helm:
The vapour mild o'er each committee crept;
Unfinish'd treaties in each office slept;
And chiefless armies doz'd out the campaign;
And navies yawn'd for orders on the main.
     O Muse! relate (for you can tell alone,
620 Wits have short memories, and dunces none)
Relate, who first, who last resign'd to rest;
Whose heads she partly, whose completely blest;
What charms could faction, what ambition lull,
The venal quiet, and entrance the dull;
'Till drown'd was sense, and shame, and right, and wrong –
O sing, and hush the nations with thy song!

                    *   *   *

     In vain, in vain, – the all-composing hour
Resistless falls: the Muse obeys the pow'r.
She comes! she comes! the sable throne behold
630 Of Night primæval, and of Chaos old!
Before her, Fancy's gilded clouds decay,
And all its varying rainbows die away.
Wit shoots in vain its momentary fires,
The meteor drops, and in a flash expires.
As one by one, at dread Medea's strain,

The sick'ning stars fade off th' ethereal plain;
As Argus' eyes by Hermes' wand opprest,
Clos'd one by one to everlasting rest;
Thus at her felt approach, and secret might,
640 Art after Art goes out, and all is night.
See skulking *Truth* to her old cavern fled,
Mountains of casuistry heap'd o'er her head!
Philosophy, that lean'd on Heav'n before,
Shrinks to her second cause[95], and is no more.
Physic of Metaphysic begs defence,
And Metaphysic calls for aid on Sense!
See Mystery to Mathematics fly!
In vain! they gaze, turn giddy, rave, and die.
Religion blushing veils her sacred fires,
650 And unawares Morality expires.
Nor public flame, nor private, dares to shine;
Nor human spark is left, nor glimpse divine!
Lo! thy dread empire, Chaos is restor'd;
Light dies before thy uncreating word:
Thy hand, great Anarch°! lets the curtain fall;   *anarchist*
And universal darkness buries all.

[1743]

NOTES

Pope

1   words used to fill up line.

2   *The Rape of the Lock*, first version 1712, second, extended, version 1714, was originally
written in the hope of reconciling Lady Arabella Fermor and Lord Petre, a relative of
Pope's friend, Caryll, who 'raped' the lock, summer 1711. However, it was not
altogether successful. Sir George Brown (Sir Plume) was offended by it and Lady
Arabella herself was not altogether pleased with the portrait of herself in Belinda. It
has been suggested that she was the real subject of the satire. The 1712 version was
expanded by the addition of the 'machinery' (the world of sylphs, etc.), the card-
game and the cave of spleen. Clarissa's speech 'Sir, why are beauties . . .' was also
added.

   The poem is prefaced by the following letter of dedication:

To Mrs Arabella Fermor

Madam,
   It will be in vain to deny that I have some regard for this piece, since I dedicate it
to you. Yet you may bear me witness, it was intended only to divert a few young
ladies, who have good sense and good humour enough to laugh not only at their

sex's little unguarded follies, but at their own. But as it was communicated with the air of a secret, it soon found its way into the world. An imperfect copy having been offer'd to a bookseller, you had the good-nature for my sake to consent to the publication of one more correct: This I was forc'd to, before I had executed half my design, for the machinery was entirely wanting to complete it.

The machinery, Madam, is a term invented by the critics, to signify that part which the deities, angels, or demons, are made to act in a poem: For the ancient poets are in one respect like many modern ladies: let an action be never so trivial in itself, they always make it appear of the utmost importance. These machines I determin'd to raise on a very new and odd foundation, the Rosicrucian doctrine of spirits.

I know how disagreeable it is to make use of hard words before a lady; but 'tis so much the concern of a poet to have his works understood, and particularly by your sex, that you must give me leave to explain two or three difficult terms.

The Rosicrucians are a people I must bring you acquainted with. The best account I know of them is in a French book called *Le Comte de Gabalis*, which both in its title and size is so like a novel, that many of the fair sex have read it for one by mistake. According to these gentlemen, the four elements are inhabited by spirits which they call sylphs, gnomes, nymphs, and salamanders. The gnomes or demons of earth delight in mischief; but the sylphs, whose habitation is in the air, are the best condition'd creatures imaginable. For they say, any mortals may enjoy the most intimate familiarities with these gentle spirits, upon a condition very easy to all true adepts, an inviolate preservation of chastity.

As to the following cantos, all the passages of them are as fabulous, as the vision at the beginning, or the transformation at the end; (except the loss of your hair, which I always mention with reverence.) The human persons are as fictitious as the airy ones; and the character of Belinda, as it is now manag'd, resembles you in nothing but in beauty.

If this poem had as many graces as there are in your person, or in your mind, yet I could never hope it should pass through the world half so uncensur'd as you have done. But let its fortune be what it will, mine is happy enough, to have given me this occasion of assuring you that I am, with the truest esteem,

    Madam,

       Your most obedient, humble servant,

                                     A. POPE

3 to summon her maid.

4 a watch that chimed the hours and quarters when a projecting pin was pressed.

5 a young man at a birthday celebration.

6 silver token left by the fairies in the green grass circle where they were supposed to have danced.

7 Matt. XI.25.

8 fashionable drive in Hyde Park, London.

9 both the material form of the spirits and the carriages.

10 elements of earth, air, fire and water to which the souls of dead women returned according to their nature.

11 fabulous creature which could live in fire.

12 tea brewed from water, the sea-nymph's element: nb. tea then pronounced 'tay'.

13 cf. P.L.I.423.

14   wounds, charms, ardours reflect the affected language of the love-letter.
15   sometimes belladonna was used to make the eyes sparkle.
16   common name for a lady's maid.
17   cf. Butler on the trout – ''tis with a single hair pulled out'.
18   *Aeneid*. XI.759.
19   one used in cosmetics.
20   seven-fold shield of Ajax.
21   hoops and whalebones were used to make petticoats stand out.
22   large blunt-eyed needle used for threading ribbon.
23   ointment made of hog's lard.
24   for grinding chocolate.
25   Great Britain, Ireland and France (to which Britain still made claims).
26   a card-game for three players, played on velvet cloth; from a deck of cards (with no 8s, 9s or 10s) nine cards are dealt to each player, the rest left in a central pool; one player (ombre = the man) declares he will win more tricks than the other two individually; the game is to prevent this. Belinda (as ombre) discards and selects a new card from the pool; chooses trumps; wins the first four tricks; loses the next four, and, by winning the last, (thus avoiding the codille), takes the game.
27   matadore = three top trump cards – here, ace of spades (spadillo), deuce (two) of spades (manillio) and ace of clubs (basto).
28   Pam = Jack of Clubs – the highest card in this game.
29   King is highest card in a red suit, if it is not trumps.
30   coffee houses were frequented by, amongst others, amateur politicians.
31   cf. P.L. VI.336.
32   formal evening visits with lit torches.
33   cf. the visits to the underworld of Odysseus and Aeneas: spleen is the seat of melancholy.
34   i.e. as used for gods and goddesses to ascend and descend in the theatre.
35   a three-legged stool, which, in the *Iliad*, Vulcan made for the gods.
36   according to Pope, this alludes to a real situation.
37   a kind of fern, used as a purgative for melancholy.
38   sign of cuckolding.
39   on curling pins or on prisoners.
40   Sir George Brown, cousin of Arabella's mother.
41   i.e. Aeneas, whom Dido and her sister, Anna, pleaded with to stay in Carthage.
42   Clarissa – a new character introduced in later editions 'to open more clearly the moral of the poem' P.: parody of the *Iliad* XII.371.
43   at the theatre, gentlemen sat in the side boxes, ladies in the front boxes, with unmarried girls in the first row.
44   *Iliad* XX.90, where Mars fought against Pallas, Hermes against Latona and Jove threw thunderbolts.
45   a character in Wycherley's *Love in a Wood*.
46   a character in Etheredge's *Man of Mode*.
47   from a song in Buononcini's popular opera, *Camilla*.
48   *Iliad* II.129.
49   cf. Shakespeare's *Othello*, where Othello's distrust of Desdemona is aggravated by the loss of a handkerchief he had given her.
50   cf. Ariosto's *Orlando Furioso* XXXIV.68, where man's wit is kept in jars after being lost on earth through love, ambition, trade, the service of lords, etc.

51 cf. *Tatler* 142 'with seventeen several instruments in it, all necessary every hour of the day'.

52 cf. 'Epistle to Dr Arbuthnot', 256.

53 with the ardour of their love for God.

54 able to give shape or form.

55 it was believed that matter moves towards the centre of the earth.

56 Viscount Bolingbroke, 1678–1751, statesman, philosopher and friend of P.

57 John Arbuthnot, once physician to Queen Anne, was P.'s physician and friend: on his death-bed, he pleaded with P. to continue his 'noble disdain and abhorrence of vice' and to 'reform rather than chastise', warning him that he could be endangering his own safety. This, in the mode of Horace's *Epistles*, is P.'s defence of (and particularly himself) the satirist.

58 at Pope's house in Twickenham.

59 travelling from London to Twickenham.

60 Parson Eusden (= be-mused in) appointed Poet Laureate, 1718; later took holy orders: was known for being drunk.

61 i.e. in the madhouse.

62 cf. Horace, *Ars Poetica*, 388.

63 Leonard Welsted.

64 i.e. attack Pope in print or a sermon.

65 i.e. the alliance between the Queen and Walpole, with George II as Midas.

66 Lady Mary Wortley Montagu.

67 i.e. Curll.

68 money given towards publication.

69 P. was very small in stature.

70 P. suffered from a deformity of the spine, asthma, an eye disease and, in later life, dropsy.

71 all patrons or admirers of P.: Granville (Baron Lansdowne), Walsh (critic) and Garth, were all poets: Talbot (Duke of Shrewsbury), Lords Somers and Sheffield, the Duke of Buckingham, were patrons and statesmen: Congreve, Swift were writers: St John Bolingbroke was leader of the Opposition, a statesman and philosopher, whose ideas P. made use of in his *Essay on Man*: Burnett, Oldmixon and Cooke had all attacked P. or his writings.

72 John Hervey.

73 half-a-crown was the going price for a prostitute.

74 Turkish emperors killed their nearest kinsmen on ascending the throne.

75 copies of title pages pinned to boards outside booksellers.

76 one without port to drink.

77 with his own verses.

78 Sir William Yonge: Bubo = Bubb Dodington.

79 in his *Epistle to Burlington*, P. satirised Timon's villa and its obsequious dean: mischief makers suggested this was 'Canons', the home of the Duke of Chandos, a Whig M.P. and a supporter of the arts.

80 a fictitious account of an assault upon P. called 'A Pop upon Pope' 1728.

81 works were published as being by P. by Curll.

82 P. illustrated as a hunchback ape.

83 according to P. 'the Duke of Buckingham, Earl of Burlington, Lord Bathurst, Lord Bolingbroke, Bishop Atterbury, Dr Swift, Mr Gay, Dr Arbuthnot, his friends, his parents and his very nurse'.

84 Japhet Crook, a forger whose ears were cut off for his crime.

85 Mary Howard, maid of honour to Queen Caroline and mistress of George II.

86 the original of these lines was written at his mother's bedside, Sept. 1731, and sent to Aaron Hill, informing him of her illness: she died June 1733.

87 the goddess, Dulness, daughter of Chaos and Night.

88 i.e. things to be made into plays or poems.

89 Jacob Tonson.

90 the performance set apart for the author's benefit night.

91 in lower Egypt, soil was washed by the overflowing Nile, so needed no rain.

92 students in their second or third year.

93 i.e. the goddess, Dulness.

94 the Lower House of the Convocation of the Clergy, prorogued 1717.

95 philosophy to be explained by natural science, which is to be explained by metaphysics, which is to be explained by sense data.

Thomas Gray

[1716–71]

The son of a scrivener, Gray was born in London; educated at Eton, at the same time as Horace Walpole, and Peterhouse, Cambridge; after touring France and Italy, 1739–1741, he and Walpole quarrelled and separated; 1741, his father died and Gray began writing poetry in English (rather than Latin). In 1742 he moved to Cambridge, first to Peterhouse, then, 1756, to Pembroke College, and, about that time, he and Walpole were reconciled. His 'Ode on a Distant Prospect of Eton College' was published in 1747: his *Elegy*, possibly begun as early as 1746, was completed at Stoke Poges, where his mother and aunt had lived since his father's death. The 'Ode on the Death of a Favourite Cat' – one of Walpole's – was sent to Walpole in 1747. On Cibber's death, 1757, he was offered, but refused, the Poet Laureateship. The rest of his life was spent at Cambridge or travelling, as he indulged his interests in antiquities, botany, 'picturesque' scenery and the new discoveries in Old Norse and Welsh poetry.

Ode on the Death of a favourite Cat,[1] Drowned in a Tub of Goldfishes

'Twas on a lofty vase's side,
Where China's gayest art had dyed
  The azure flowers, that blow;°   *blossom*
Demurest of the tabby kind,
The pensive Selima reclined,
  Gazed on the lake below.

Her conscious tail her joy declared;
The fair round face, the snowy beard,
  The velvet of her paws,
10 Her coat, that with the tortoise vies,
Her ears of jet, and emerald eyes,
  She saw; and purred applause.

Still had she gazed; but 'midst the tide
Two angel forms were seen to glide,
  The genii° of the stream: *guardian spirits*
Their scaly armour's Tyrian[2] hue
Thro' richest purple to the view
  Betrayed a golden gleam.

The hapless nymph with wonder saw:
20 A whisker first and then a claw,
  With many an ardent wish,
She stretched in vain to reach the prize.
What female heart can gold despise?
  What cat's averse to fish?

Presumptuous maid! with looks intent
Again she stretched, again she bent,
  Nor knew the gulf between.
(Malignant Fate sat by, and smiled)
The slippery verge her feet beguiled,
30   She tumbled headlong in.

Eight times emerging from the flood
She mewed to every watry God,
  Some speedy aid to send.
No dolphin[3] came, no nereid° stirred   *sea-nymph*
Nor cruel *Tom*,° nor *Susan*° heard.   *servants*
  A favourite has no friend!

From hence, ye Beauties, undeceived,
Know, one false step is ne'er retrieved,
    And be with caution bold.
40 Not all that tempts your wandering eyes
And heedless hearts, is lawful prize;
    Nor all, that glisters, gold.

1747 [1748]

Elegy written in a Country Churchyard

The curfew tolls the knell of parting day,
The lowing herd wind slowly o'er the lea,
The plowman homeward plods his weary way,
And leaves the world to darkness and to me.

Now fades the glimmering landscape on the sight,
And all the air a solemn stillness holds,
Save where the beetle wheels his droning flight,
And drowsy tinklings lull the distant folds;

Save that from yonder ivy-mantled tower
10 The moping owl does to the moon complain
Of such, as wandering near her secret bower,
Molest her ancient solitary reign.

Beneath those rugged elms, that yew-tree's shade,
Where heaves the turf in many a mouldering heap,
Each in his narrow cell for ever laid,
The rude forefathers° of the hamlet° sleep.   *humble ancestors/small village*

The breezy call of incense-breathing morn,
The swallow twittering from the straw-built shed,
The cock's shrill clarion, or the echoing horn,
20 No more shall rouse them from their lowly bed.

For them no more the blazing hearth shall burn,
Or busy housewife ply her evening care:
No children run to lisp their sire's return,
Or climb his knees the envied kiss to share.

Oft did the harvest to their sickle yield,
Their furrow oft the stubborn glebe° has broke;   *field*
How jocund did they drive their team afield!
How bow'd the woods beneath their sturdy stroke!

Let not ambition mock their useful toil,
30   Their homely joys, and destiny obscure;
Nor grandeur hear with a disdainful smile,
The short and simple annals of the poor.

The boast of heraldry, the pomp of pow'r,
And all that beauty, all that wealth e'er gave,
Awaits alike th' inevitable hour.
The <u>paths of glory</u> lead but to the grave.

Nor you, ye proud, impute to these the fault,
If memory o'er their tomb no trophies° raise,   *carved memorials*
Where thro' the long-drawn isle and fretted° vault   *carved*
40   The pealing anthem swells the note of praise.

Can storied° urn or animated° bust   *with stories on it/given life*
Back to its mansion call the fleeting breath?
Can honour's voice provoke the silent dust,
Or flattery sooth the dull cold ear of death?

Perhaps in this neglected spot is laid
Some heart once pregnant with celestial fire;
Hands, that the rod of empire might have swayed,
Or waked to ectasy the living lyre.

But knowledge to their eyes her ample page,
50   Rich with the spoils of time, did ne'er unroll;
Chill penury repressed their noble rage,
And froze the genial current of the soul.

Full many a gem of purest ray serene,°   *bright*
The dark unfathomed caves of ocean bear:
Full many a flower is born to blush unseen,
And waste its sweetness on the desert air.

Some village Hampden, that with dauntless breast
The little tyrant of his fields withstood;
Some mute inglorious Milton here may rest,
60   Some Cromwell guiltless of his country's blood.

Th' applause of listening senates to command,
The threats of pain and ruin to despise,
To scatter plenty o'er a smiling land,
And read their history in a nation's eyes,

Their lot forbad: nor° circumscribed alone°   *not/only*
Their growing virtues, but their crimes confined;
Forbad to wade through slaughter to a throne,
And shut the gates of mercy on mankind,

The struggling pangs of conscious truth to hide,
70 To quench the blushes of ingenuous shame,
Or heap the shrine of luxury and pride
With incense kindled at the Muse's flame.

Far from the madding crowd's ignoble strife,
Their sober wishes never learned to stray;
Along the cool sequestered vale of life
They kept the noiseless tenor of their way.

Yet even these bones from insult to protect
Some frail memorial still erected nigh,
With uncouth rhymes and shapeless sculpture decked,
80 Implores the passing tribute of a sigh.

Their name, their years, spelt by th' unlettered Muse,
The place of fame and elegy supply:
And many a holy text around she strews,
That teach the rustic moralist to die.

For who to dumb forgetfulness a prey,
This pleasing anxious being e'er resigned,
Left the warm precincts of the cheerful day,
Nor cast one longing lingering look behind?

On some fond breast the parting soul relies,
90 Some pious drops° the closing eye requires;   *tears*
Even from the tomb the voice of nature cries,
Even in our ashes live their wonted fires.

For thee,° who mindful of th' unhonoured Dead   *the poet*
Dost in these lines their artless tale relate;
If chance, by lonely contemplation led,
Some kindred spirit shall inquire thy fate,

Haply some hoary-headed° swain° may say,   *grey-white haired/country youth*
'Oft have we seen him at the peep of dawn
Brushing with hasty steps the dews away
100 To meet the sun upon the upland lawn.

There at the foot of yonder nodding beech
That wreathes its old fantastic roots so high,
His listless length at noontide would he stretch,
And pore upon the brook that babbles by.

Hard by yon wood, now smiling as in scorn,
Muttering his wayward fancies he would rove,
Now drooping, woeful wan, like one forlorn,
Or crazed with care, or crossed in hopeless love.

One morn I missed him on the customed hill,
110 Along the heath and near his favourite tree;
Another came; nor yet beside the rill,
Nor up the lawn, nor at the wood was he;

The next with dirges due in sad array
Slow thro' the church-way path we saw him borne.
Approach and read (for thou can'st read) the lay,
Grav'd on the stone beneath yon aged thorn.'

THE EPITAPH

Here rests his head upon the lap of Earth
A Youth to Fortune and to Fame unknown.
Fair Science frowned not on his humble birth,
120 And Melancholy marked him for her own.

Large was his bounty, and his soul sincere,
Heaven did a recompence as largely send:
He gave to Misery all he had, a tear,
He gained from Heaven ('twas all he wished) a friend.

No farther seek his merits to disclose,
Or draw his frailties from their dread abode,
(There they alike in trembling hope repose,)
The bosom of his Father and his God.

1742–50 [1751]

NOTES

Gray

1 Written at Horace Walpole's request as an epitaph for one of his cats.

2 purple Phoenician dye from Tyre.

3 as did the one that saved the musician, Arion.

Oliver Goldsmith

[1730?–74]

The second son of an Anglo-Irish clergyman, he was born in Ireland, and spent his childhood there; educated at Trinity College, Dublin, he was eventually refused ordination and so went to Edinburgh to study medicine. In 1775–6 he was in France, Switzerland and Italy, coming home to support himself as a physician in Southwark and an usher (a kind of assistant teacher) in Peckham – though it is not clear whether he actually received a medical degree. He began writing for the *Monthly Review* and, by 1759, was contributing to many periodicals, including his own, *The Bee*, in October and November 1759. Samuel Johnson, whom he met in 1761, saved him from arrest for debt by selling, on his behalf, the ms. of *The Vicar of Wakefield*. He struggled to make his living by hack work including writing several biographies – but literary recognition came with *The Traveller*, 1764, much admired by Johnson and others. *The Deserted Village* was published in 1770. He figures in Boswell's *Life of Johnson* and, according to Garrick, the famous actor, he 'wrote like an angel but talked like poor Poll' (a parrot).

From *The Traveller or Prospect of Society*

My soul . . . , turn we to survey
Where rougher climes a nobler race display,
Where the bleak Swiss their stormy mansions tread,
And force a churlish soil for scanty bread;
No product here the barren hills afford,
170 But man and steel, the soldier and his sword.
No vernal blooms their torpid rocks array,
But winter lingering chills the laps of May;
No zephyr° fondly sues the mountain's breast,   *gentle breeze*
But meteors glare, and stormy glooms invest.

Yet still, even here, content can spread a charm,
Redress the clime, and all its rage disarm.
Though poor the peasant's hut, his feasts though small,
He sees his little lot, the lot of all;
Sees no contiguous palace rear its head
180   To shame the meanness of his humble shed;
No costly lord the sumptuous banquet deal
To make him loath his vegetable meal;
But calm, and bred in ignorance and toil,
Each wish contracting, fits him to the soil.
Chearful at morn he wakes from short repose,
Breasts the keen air, and carrols° as he goes;   *sings*
With patient angle trolls° the finny deep,   *fish with rod*
Or drives his vent'rous plow-share to the steep;
Or seeks the den where snow tracks mark the way,
190   And drags the struggling savage° into day.   *wild animal*
At night returning, every labour sped,
He sits him down the monarch of a shed;
Smiles by his chearful fire, and round surveys
His childrens looks, that brighten at the blaze:
While his lov'd partner, boastful of her hoard,
Displays her cleanly platter° on the board;   *wooden dish*
And haply too some pilgrim, thither led,
With many a tale repays the nightly bed.

$$* \quad * \quad *$$

Thine, Freedom, thine the blessings pictur'd here,°   *(in Britain)*
Thine are those charms that dazzle and endear;
Too blest indeed, were such without alloy,
But foster'd even by Freedom ills annoy:
That independence Britons prize too high,
340   Keeps man from man, and breaks the social tie;
The self-dependent lordlings stand alone,
All claims that bind and sweeten life unknown;

$$* \quad * \quad *$$

Yet think not, thus when Freedom's ills I state,
I mean to flatter kings, or court the great;
Ye powers of truth that bid my soul aspire,
Far from my bosom drive the low desire;
And thou fair freedom, taught alike to feel
The rabble's rage, and tyrant's angry steel;
Thou transitory flower, alike undone
By proud contempt, or favour's fostering sun,

Still may thy blooms the changeful clime endure,
370 I only would repress them to secure;
For just experience tells in every soil,
That those who think must govern those that toil,
And all that freedom's highest aims can reach,
Is but to lay proportion'd loads on each.
Hence, should one order disproportion'd grow,
Its double weight must ruin all below.
O then how blind to all that truth requires,
Who think it freedom when a part aspires!
Calm is my soul, nor apt to rise in arms,
380 Except when fast approaching danger warms:
But when contending chiefs blockade the throne,
Contracting regal power to stretch their own,
When I behold a factious band agree
To call it freedom, when themselves are free;
Each wanton judge new penal statutes draw,
Laws grind the poor, and rich men rule the law;
The wealth of climes, where savage nations roam,
Pillag'd from slaves, to purchase slaves at home;
Fear, pity, justice, indignation start,
390 Tear off reserve, and bare my swelling heart;
'Till half a patriot, half a coward grown,
I fly from petty tyrants to the throne.
Have we not seen, round Britain's peopled shore,
Her useful sons exchang'd for useless ore?
Seen all her triumphs but destruction haste,
400 Like flaring tapers brightening as they waste;
Seen opulence, her grandeur to maintain,
Lead stern depopulation in her train,
And over fields, where scatter'd hamlets rose,
In barren solitary pomp repose?
Have we not seen, at pleasure's lordly call,
The smiling long-frequented village fall;
Beheld the duteous son, the sire decay'd,
The modest matron, and the blushing maid,
Forc'd from their homes, a melancholy train,
410 To traverse climes beyond the western main;

*   *   *

Vain, very vain, my weary search to find
That bliss which only centres in the mind:
Why have I stray'd, from pleasure and repose,
To seek a good each government bestows?

In every government, though terrors reign,
Though tyrant kings, or tyrant laws restrain,
How small, of all that human hearts endure,
430 That part which laws or kings can cause or cure.
Still to ourselves in every place consign'd,
Our own felicity we make or find:
With secret course, which no loud storms annoy,
Glides the smooth current of domestic joy.
The lifted axe, the agonizing wheel,
Luke's iron crown, and Damien's bed of steel,
To men remote from power but rarely known,
Leave reason, faith and conscience all our own.

[1765]

From *The Deserted Village*

Sweet Auburn, loveliest village of the plain,
Where health and plenty cheered the labouring swain,
Where smiling spring its earliest visit paid,
And parting summer's lingering blooms delayed;
Dear lovely bowers of innocence and ease,
Seats of my youth, when every sport could please,
How often have I loitered o'er thy green,
Where humble happiness endeared each scene;
How often have I paused on every charm,
10 The sheltered cot,° the cultivated farm,   *cottage*
The never failing brook, the busy mill,
The decent° church that topt the neighbouring hill,   *suitable or modest*
The hawthorn bush, with seats beneath the shade,
For talking age and whispering lovers made.
How often have I blest the coming day,
When toil remitting lent its turn to play,
And all the village train from labour free
Led up their sports beneath the spreading tree,
While many a pastime circled in the shade,
20 The young contending as the old surveyed;
And many a gambol frolicked o'er the ground,
And slights° of art and feats of strength went round.   *small displays*
And still as each repeated pleasure tired,
Succeeding sports the mirthful band inspired;

The dancing pair that simply° sought renown   *innocently*
By holding out to tire each other down,
The swain mistrustless of his smutted face,
While secret laughter tittered round the place,
The bashful virgin's side-long looks of love,
30   The matron's glance that would those looks reprove.
These were thy charms, sweet village; sports like these,
With sweet succession, taught even toil to please;
These round thy bowers their cheerful influence shed,
These were thy charms – But all these charms are fled.

*   *   *

51   Ill fares the land, to hastening ills a prey,
Where wealth accumulates, and men decay;
Princes and lords may flourish, or may fade;
A breath can make them, as a breath has made,
But a bold peasantry, their country's pride,
When once destroyed, can never be supplied.

A time there was, ere England's griefs began,
When every rood° of ground maintained its man;   *quarter of an acre*
For him light labour spread her wholesome store,
60   Just gave what life required, but gave no more.
His best companions, innocence and health;
And his best riches, ignorance of wealth.
But times are altered; trade's unfeeling train
Usurp the land and dispossess the swain;
Along the lawn,° where scattered hamlets rose,   *plain*
Unwieldy wealth, and cumbrous pomp repose;
And every want to oppulence allied,
And every pang that folly pays to pride.
These gentle hours that plenty bade to bloom,
70   Those calm desires that asked but little room,
Those healthful sports that graced the peaceful scene,
Lived in each look, and brightened all the green;
These far departing seek a kinder shore,
And rural mirth and manners° are no more.   *customs*

*   *   *

Sweet was the sound when oft at evening's close,
Up yonder hill the village murmur rose;
There as I past with careless steps and slow,
The mingling notes came softened from below;
The swain responsive as the milk-maid sung,

The sober herd that lowed to meet their young;
The noisy geese that gabbled o'er the pool,
120 The playful children just let loose from school;
The watch-dog's voice that bayed the whispering wind,
And the loud laugh that spoke the vacant° mind,   *idle*
These all in sweet confusion sought the shade,
And filled each pause the nightingale had made.
But now the sounds of population fail,
No chearful murmurs fluctuate in the gale,
No busy steps the grass-grown foot-way tread,
For all the bloomy flush of life is fled.
All but yon widowed, solitary thing
130 That feebly bends beside the plashy spring;
She, wretched matron, forced, in age, for bread,
To strip the brook with mantling cresses° spread,   *covered with watercress*
To pick her wintry faggot° from the thorn,   *bundle of wood*
To seek her nightly shed, and weep till morn;
She only left of all the harmless train,
The sad historian of the pensive° plain.   *sad*

* * *

Beside yon straggling fence that skirts the way,
With blossomed furze unprofitably gay,°   *for decoration*
There, in his noisy mansion, skill'd to rule,
The village master taught his little school;
A man severe he was, and stern to view,
I knew him well, and every truant knew;
Well had the boding tremblers learned to trace
200 The day's disasters in his morning face;
Full well they laugh'd with counterfeited glee,
At all his jokes, for many a joke had he;
Full well the busy whisper circling round,
Conveyed the dismal tidings when he frowned;
Yet he was kind, or if severe in aught,
The love he bore to learning was in fault;
The village all declared how much he knew;
'Twas certain he could write, and cipher° too;   *calculate*
Lands he could measure, terms° and tides° presage°.   *set times/seasons/foretell*
210 And even the story ran that he could gauge°.   *measure contents of a vessel*
In arguing too, the parson owned° his skill,   *acknowledged*
For e'en tho' vanquished, he could argue still;
While words of learned length, and thundering sound,
Amazed the gazing rustics ranged around,
And still they gazed, and still the wonder grew,

That one small head could carry all he knew.
　　But past is all his fame. The very spot
Where many a time he triumphed, is forgot.

* 　 * 　 *

　O luxury! Thou curst by heaven's decree,
How ill exchanged are things like these for thee!
How do thy potions with insidious joy,
Diffuse their pleasures only to destroy!
Kingdoms by thee, to sickly greatness grown,
390 Boast of a florid vigour not their own.
At every draught more large and large they grow,
A bloated mass of rank unwieldy woe;
Till sapped their strength, and every part unsound,
Down, down they sink, and spread a ruin round.

* 　 * 　 *

　And thou, sweet Poetry, thou loveliest maid,
Still first to fly where sensual joys invade;
Unfit in these degenerate times of shame,
410 To catch the heart, or strike for honest fame;
Dear charming nymph, neglected and decried,
My shame in crowds, my solitary pride,
Thou source of all my bliss, and all my woe,
That found'st me poor at first, and keep'st me so;
Thou guide by which the nobler arts excell,
Thou nurse of every virtue, fare thee well.
Farewell, and, O, where'er thy voice be tried,
On Torno's cliffs, or Pambamarca's side,
Whether where equinoctial fervours glow,
420 Or winter wraps the polar world in snow,
Still let thy voice prevailing over time,
Redress the rigours of the inclement clime;
Aid slighted truth, with thy persuasive strain
Teach erring man to spurn the rage of gain;
Teach him that states of native strength possest,
Tho' very poor, may still be very blest;
That trade's proud empire hastes to swift decay,
As ocean sweeps the labour's mole° away;　　　　　*breakwater*
While self dependent power can time defy,
430 As rocks resist the billows and the sky.

[1770]

Song

from THE VICAR OF WAKEFIELD

When lovely woman stoops to folly,
    And finds too late that men betray,
What charm can sooth her melancholy,
    What art can wash her guilt away?

The only art her guilt to cover,
    To hide her shame from every eye,
To give repentance to her lover,
    And wring his bosom – is to die.

[1766]

William Cowper

[1731–1800]

He was the elder son of a rector in Hertfordshire; his mother died when he was six; educated privately and at Westminster School, he was called to the bar, 1754. A sensitive child who was bullied at school, he suffered from severe depression; this – probably aggravated by his love for his cousin Theodora, whom he hoped to marry – led to a suicide attempt. He was subject to religious melancholia and spent some of the time in the Collegium Insanorum at St Albans: in 1765 he went to live as a 'kind of adopted son' in the house of the Rev. Morley Unwin, and, on Morley's death, moved with Mary Unwin, Morley's widow, to Olney, where with the curate there, John Newton, he wrote the *Olney Hymns*, 1779. He became engaged to Mary but, during another bout of depression, he again attempted suicide. During a quieter period after this he wrote *John Gilpin*, 1782, and *The Task*, 1783–4, both at the suggestion of Lady Austen, who was his friend and neighbour. *The Poplar Field* was not published until after his death, and was written at Weston Underwood, where he had moved with Mary in 1786. From 1791 Mary suffered a series of strokes, dying in 1796, leaving Cowper in a state of depression from which he never wholly recovered.

Light Shining Out of Darkness
(from **Olney Hymns**)

God moves in a mysterious way,
　His wonders to perform;
He plants his footsteps in the sea,
　And rides upon the storm.

Deep in unfathomable mines
　Of never failing skill,
He treasures up his bright designs,
　And works his sovereign will.

Ye fearful saints fresh courage take,
10   The clouds ye so much dread
Are big with mercy, and shall break
      In blessings on your head.

Judge not the Lord by feeble sense,
      But trust him for his grace;
Behind a frowning providence,
      He hides a smiling face.

His purposes will ripen fast,
      Unfolding every hour;
The bud may have a bitter taste,
20   But sweet will be the flower.

Blind unbelief is sure to err,
      And Scan his work in vain;
God is his own interpreter,
      And he will make it plain.

[1779]

Simple Faith

Yon cottager who weaves at her own door,
Pillow and bobbins° all her little store,   *(on which lace is made)*
Content though mean, and cheerful, if not gay,
Shuffling her threads about the live-long day,
Just earns a scanty pittance, and at night
Lies down secure, her heart and pocket light;
She, for her humble sphere by nature fit,
Has little understanding, and no wit,
Receives no praise, but (though her lot be such,
10 Toilsome and indigent) she renders much;
Just knows, and knows no more, her Bible true,
A truth the brilliant Frenchman never knew;
And in that charter reads, with sparkling eyes,
Her title to a treasure in the skies.
   Oh happy peasant! Oh unhappy bard!
His the mere tinsel, hers the rich reward;

He praised perhaps for ages yet to come,
She never heard of half a mile from home;
He lost in errors his vain heart prefers,
She safe in the simplicity of hers.

[1782]

The Poplar Field

The poplars are felled, farewell to the shade
And the whispering sound of the cool colonnade,
The winds play no longer, and sing in the leaves,
Nor Ouse° on his bosom their image receives.　　　　　*(the river)*

Twelve years have elapsed since I first took a view
Of my favourite field and the bank where they grew,
And now in the grass behold they are laid,
And the tree is my seat that once lent me a shade.

The blackbird has fled to another retreat
Where the hazels afford him a screen from the heat,
And the scene where his melody charmed me before,
Resounds with his sweet-flowing ditty no more.

My fugitive years are all hasting away,
And I must ere long lie as lowly as they,
With a turf on my breast, and a stone at my head,
Ere another such grove shall arise in its stead.

'Tis a sight to engage me, if any thing can,
To muse on the perishing pleasures of man;
Though his life be a dream, his enjoyments, I see,
Have a being less durable even than he.

[1785]

From **The Task. Book VI**

The Winter Walk at Noon

The night was winter in his roughest mood;
The morning sharp and clear. But now at noon
Upon the southern side of the slant hills,
60 And where the woods fence off the northern blast,
The season smiles, resigning all its rage,
And has the warmth of May. The vault is blue
Without a cloud, and white without a speck
The dazzling splendour of the scene below.
Again the harmony comes o'er the vale;
And through the trees I view th' embattled tower°   *Emberton Church*
Whence all the music. I again perceive
The soothing influence of the wafted strains,
And settle in soft musings as I tread
70 The walk, still verdant, under oaks and elms,
Whose outspread branches overarch the glade.
The roof, though moveable through all its length
As the wind sways it, has yet well sufficed,
And, intercepting in their silent fall
The frequent flakes, has kept a path for me.
No noise is here, or none that hinders thought.
The redbreast warbles still, but is content
With slender notes, and more than half suppressed:
Pleased with his solitude, and flitting light
80 From spray to spray, where'er he rests he shakes
From many a twig the pendent drops of ice,
That twinkle in the withered leaves below.
Stillness, accompanied with sounds so soft,
Charms more than silence. Meditation here
May think down hours to moments. Here the heart
May give an useful lesson to the head,
And learning wiser grow without his books.
Knowledge and wisdom, far from being one,
Have oft-times no connexion. Knowledge dwells
90 In heads replete with thoughts of other men;
Wisdom in minds attentive to their own.
Knowledge, a rude unprofitable mass,
The mere materials with which wisdom builds,
Till smoothed and squared and fitted to its place,
Does but encumber whom it seems t' enrich.

Knowledge is proud that he has learned so much;
Wisdom is humble that he knows no more.
Books are not seldom talismans° and spells,   *objects with magical powers*
By which the magic art of shrewder wits
100 Holds an unthinking multitude enthralled.
Some to the fascination of a name
Surrender judgment, hood-winked. Some the style
Infatuates, and through labyrinths and wilds
Of error leads them by a tune entranced.
While sloth seduces more, too weak to bear
The insupportable fatigue of thought,
And swallowing, therefore, without pause or choice,
The total grist° unsifted, husks and all.   *supply of grain*
But trees, and rivulets whose rapid course
110 Defies the check of winter, haunts of deer,
And sheep-walks populous with bleating lambs,
And lanes in which the primrose ere her time
Peeps through the moss that clothes the hawthorn root,
Deceive no student. Wisdom there, and truth,
Not shy, as in the world, and to be won
By slow solicitation, seize at once
The roving thought, and fix it on themselves.

*   *   *

The Lord of all, himself through all diffused,
Sustains, and is the life of all that lives.
Nature is but a name for an effect
Whose cause is God. He feeds the secret fire
By which the mighty process is maintained,
Who sleeps not, is not weary; in whose sight
Slow circling ages are as transient days;
Whose work is without labour; whose designs
No flaw deforms, no difficulty thwarts;
230 And whose beneficence no charge exhausts.

*   *   *

But all are under one. One spirit – His
Who° wore the platted thorns with bleeding brows –   *(Christ)*
240 Rules universal nature. Not a flower
But shows some touch, in freckle, streak, or stain,
Of his unrivalled pencil? He inspires   *paintbrush*
Their balmy odours, and imparts their hues,
And bathes their eyes with nectar, and includes,
In grains as countless as the sea-side sands,

The forms with which he sprinkles all the earth.
Happy who walks with him! whom what he finds
Of flavour or of scent in fruit or flower,
Or what he views of beautiful or grand
250 In nature, from the broad majestic oak
To the green blade that twinkles in the sun,
Prompts with remembrance of a present God.
His presence, who made all so fair, perceived,
Makes all still fairer.

* * *

Who then, that has a mind well strung and tuned
To contemplation, and within his reach
A scene so friendly to his favourite task,
Would waste attention at the chequered board,°   *chess-board*
His hosts of wooden warriors to and fro
Marching and counter-marching, with an eye
As fixt as marble, with a forehead ridged
And furrowed into storms, and with a hand
270 Trembling, as if eternity were hung
In balance on his conduct of a pin?
Nor envies he aught more their idle sport,
Who pant with application misapplied
To trivial toys, and, pushing ivory balls°   *billiards*
Across a velvet level,° feel a joy   *billiard table*
Akin to rapture when the bawble finds
Its destined goal, of difficult access.

* * *

Here, unmolested, through whatever sign°   *(of the zodiac)*
The sun proceeds, I wander. Neither mist,
Nor freezing sky nor sultry, checking me,
Nor stranger intermeddling with my joy.
Even in the spring and play-time of the year,
300 That calls the unwonted villager abroad
With all her little ones, a sportive train,
To gather king-cups in the yellow mead,
And prink° their hair with daisies, or to pick   *decorate*
A cheap but wholesome salad from the brook,
These shades are all my own. The timorous hare,
Grown so familiar with her frequent guest,
Scarce shuns me; and the stock-dove, unalarmed,
Sits cooing in the pine-tree, nor suspends
His long love-ditty for my near approach.

310 Drawn from his refuge in some lonely elm
    That age or injury has hollowed deep,
    Where, on his bed of wool and matted leaves,
    He has outslept the winter, ventures forth
    To frisk awhile, and bask in the warm sun,
    The squirrel, flippant, pert, and full of play;
    He sees me, and at once, swift as a bird,
    Ascends the neighbouring beech; there whisks his brush,
    And perks his ears, and stamps and scolds aloud,
    With all the prettiness of feigned alarm,
320 And anger insignificantly fierce.

[1785]

George Crabbe

[1754-1832]

He was born at Aldeburgh, Suffolk, his father being a collector of
salt taxes; he was apprenticed to a doctor, when he met Sarah
Elmy ('Mira' in the poems) whom he married, some ten years
later, 1783; he practised as a local doctor in Aldeburgh but, 1770,
set out for London to become a writer. He was saved from
destitution by Edmund Burke, who helped him get *The Library*, a
poem in the style of Pope, published, 1781. Burke encouraged him
to take holy orders and, in 1781, he became curate at Aldeburgh
and, 1782-5, chaplain to the Duke of Rutland where he found time
and encouragement for his writing. 1783 *The Village* was published,
securing his reputation as a poet. He held a living in Leicestershire,
1789-1814, though he was an absentee vicar, spending his time in
Suffolk. In 1810 *The Borough* was published – a poem in 24 'letters'
concerned with life in a country town (Aldeburgh), which included
the tale of 'Peter Grimes'. 1813 Sarah died; the following year,
Crabbe was appointed vicar at Trowbridge, Wiltshire, where he
died.

From **The Village**. *Book I*

Fled are those times, when, in harmonious strains,
The rustic poet prais'd his native plains;
No shepherds now in smooth alternate verse,
10 Their country's beauty or their nymphs' rehearse;
Yet still for these we frame the tender strain,
Still in our lays, fond Corydons complain,
And shepherds' boys their amorous pains reveal,
The only pains, alas! they never feel.

       *   *   *

  Yes, thus the Muses sing of happy swains,
Because the Muses never knew their pains:
They boast their peasants' pipes; but peasants now
Resign their pipes and plod behind the plough;
And few amid the rural tribe have time,

To number syllables and play with rhyme;
Save honest Duck what son of verse could share
The poet's rapture and the peasant's care?
Or the great labours of the field degrade,
30   With the new peril of a poorer trade?
    From this chief cause these idle praises spring,
That, themes so easy, few forbear to sing;
For no deep thought the trifling subjects ask,
To sing of shepherds is an easy task;
The happy youth assumes the common strain,
A nymph his mistress and himself a swain;
With no sad scenes he clouds his tuneful prayer,
But all, to look like her, is painted fair.
    I grant indeed that fields and flocks have charms,
40   For him that gazes or for him that farms;
But when amid such pleasing scenes I trace
The poor laborious natives of the place,
And see the mid-day sun, with fervid ray,
On their bare heads and dewy temples play;
While some, with feebler heads and fainter hearts,
Deplore their fortune, yet sustain their parts,
Then shall I dare these real ills to hide,
In tinsel trappings of poetic pride?
    No; cast by fortune on a frowning coast,[1]
50   Which neither groves nor happy valleys boast;
Where other cares than those the Muse relates,
And other shepherds dwell with other mates;
By such examples taught, I paint the cot,°   *cottage*
As truth will paint it and as bards will not.
Nor you, ye poor, of letter'd scorn complain,
To you the smoothest song is smooth in vain;
O'ercome by labour and bow'd down by time,
Feel you the barren flattery of a rhyme?
Can poets sooth you, when you pine for bread,
60   By winding myrtles round your ruin'd shed?
Can their light tales your weighty griefs o'erpower,
Or glad with airy mirth the toilsome hour?
    Lo! where the heath, with withering brake grown o'er,
Lends the light turf° that warms the neighbouring poor;   *peat*
From thence a length of burning sand appears,
Where the thin harvest waves its wither'd ears;
Rank weeds, that every art and care defy,
Reign o'er the land and rob the blighted rye:
There thistles stretch their prickly arms afar,

70 And to the ragged infant threaten war;
    There poppies nodding, mock the hope of toil,
    There the blue bugloss° paints the sterile soil;   *plant with blue flowers*
    Hardy and high, above the slender sheaf,
    The slimy mallow° waves her silky leaf;   *marshplant*
    O'er the young shoot the charlock° throws a shade,   *plant with hairy stem*
    And clasping tares° cling round the sickly blade; *[and yellow flowers] weeds*
    With mingled tints the rocky coasts abound,
    And a sad splendour vainly shines around.
       So looks the nymph whom wretched arts adorn,
80 Betray'd by man, then left for man to scorn;
    Whose cheek in vain assumes the mimic rose,
    While her sad eyes the troubled breast disclose;
    Whose outward splendour is but folly's dress,
    Exposing most, when most it gilds distress.

                                              [1783]

From **The Borough**

Peter Grimes

    Old Peter Grimes made fishing his employ,
    His wife he cabin'd° with him and his boy,   *lodged*
    And seem'd that life laborious to enjoy:
    To town came quiet Peter with his fish,
    And had of all a civil word and wish.
    He left his trade upon the sabbath-day,
    And took young Peter in his hand to pray:
    But soon the stubborn boy from care broke loose,
    At first refused, then added his abuse:
10 His father's love he scorn'd, his power defied,
    But being drunk, wept sorely when he died.
       Yes! then he wept, and to his mind there came
    Much of his conduct, and he felt the shame, –
    How he had oft the good old man reviled,
    And never paid the duty of a child;
    How, when the father in his Bible read,
    He in contempt and anger left the shed:
    'It is the word of life,' the parent cried;
    – 'This is the life itself,' the boy replied;

20 And while old Peter in amazement stood,
   Gave the hot spirit to his boiling blood: –
   How he, with oath and furious speech, began
   To prove his freedom and assert the man;
   And when the parent check'd his impious rage,
   How he had cursed the tyranny of age, –
   Nay, once had dealt the sacrilegious blow
   On his bare head, and laid his parent low;
   The father groan'd – 'If thou art old,' said he,
   'And hast a son – thou wilt remember me:
30 Thy mother left me in a happy time,
   Thou kill'dst not her – Heav'n spares the double crime.'

                    *   *   *

      Now lived the youth in freedom, but debarr'd
   From constant pleasure, and he thought it hard;
   Hard that he could not every wish obey,
   But must awhile relinquish ale and play;
   Hard! that he could not to his cards° attend,   *gambling*
   But must acquire the money he would spend.
40   With greedy eye he look'd on all he saw,
   He knew not justice, and he laugh'd at law;
   On all he mark'd he stretch'd his ready hand;
   He fish'd by water, and he filch'd° by land: *stole*
   Oft in the night has Peter dropp'd his oar,
   Fled from his boat and sought for prey on shore;
   Oft up the hedge-row glided, on his back
   Bearing the orchard's produce in a sack,
   Or farm-yard load, tugg'd fiercely from the stack;
   And as these wrongs to greater numbers rose,
50 The more he look'd on all men as his foes.
      He built a mud-wall'd hovel, where he kept
   His various wealth, and there he oft-times slept;
   But no success could please his cruel soul,
   He wish'd for one to trouble and control;
   He wanted some obedient boy to stand
   And bear the blow of his outrageous hand;
   And hoped to find in some propitious hour
   A feeling creature subject to his power.
      Peter had heard there were in London then, –
60 Still have they being! – workhouse-clearing men,
   Who, undisturb'd by feelings just or kind,
   Would parish-boys² to needy tradesmen bind:°   *as apprentices*
   They in their want a trifling sum would take,

And toiling slaves, of piteous orphans, make.
   Such Peter sought, and when a lad was found,
The sum was dealt him, and the slave was bound.
Some few in town observed in Peter's trap
A boy, with jacket blue and woollen cap;
But none inquired how Peter used the rope,
70   Or what the bruise, that made the stripling° stoop;   *the young boy*
None could the ridges on his back behold,
None sought him shiv'ring in the winter's cold;
None put the question, – 'Peter, dost thou give
The boy his food? – What, man! the lad must live:
Consider, Peter, let the child have bread,
He'll serve thee better if he's stroked and fed.'
None reason'd thus – and some, on hearing cries,
Said calmly, 'Grimes is at his exercise.'
   Pinn'd°, beaten, cold, pinch'd, threaten'd, and abused – *pegged down*
80   His efforts punish'd and his food refused, –
Awake tormented, – soon aroused from sleep, –
Struck if he wept, and yet compell'd to weep,
The trembling boy dropp'd down and strove to pray,
Received a blow, and trembling turn'd away,
Or sobb'd and hid his piteous face; – while he,
The savage master, grinn'd in horrid glee:
He'd now the power he ever loved to show,
A feeling being subject to his blow.
   Thus lived the lad, in hunger, peril, pain,
90   His tears despised, his supplications vain:
Compell'd by fear to lie, by need to steal,
His bed uneasy and unbless'd his meal,
For three sad years the boy his tortures bore,
And then his pains and trials were no more.
   'How died he, Peter?' when the people said,
He growl'd – 'I found him lifeless in his bed;'
Then tried for softer tone, and sigh'd, 'Poor Sam is dead.'
Yet murmurs were there, and some questions ask'd, –
How he was fed, how punish'd, and how task'd?
100   Much they suspected, but they little proved,
And Peter pass'd untroubled and unmoved.

                    *   *   *

120   Then came a boy, of manners soft and mild;
Our seamen's wives with grief beheld the child;
All thought (the poor themselves) that he was one
Of gentle blood, some noble sinner's son,

Who had, belike, deceived some humble maid,
Whom he had first seduced and then betray'd:
However this, he seem'd a gracious lad,
In grief submissive and with patience sad.
     Passive he labour'd, till his slender frame
Bent with his loads, and he at length was lame:
130 Strange that a frame so weak could bear so long
The grossest insult and the foulest wrong;
But there were causes – in the town they gave
Fire, food, and comfort, to the gentle slave;
And though stern Peter, with a cruel hand,
And knotted rope, enforced the rude command,
Yet he consider'd what he'd lately felt,
And his vile blows with selfish pity dealt.
     One day such draughts° the cruel fisher made,   *catch of fish*
He could not vend° them in his borough-trade,   *sell*
140 But sail'd for London-mart:° the boy was ill,   *market*
But ever humbled to his master's will;
And on the river, where they smoothly sail'd,
He strove with terror and awhile prevail'd;
But new to danger on the angry sea,
He clung affrighten'd to his master's knee:
The boat grew leaky and the wind was strong,
Rough was the passage and the time was long;
His liquor fail'd, and Peter's wrath arose, –
No more is known – the rest we must suppose,
150 Or learn of Peter; – Peter says, he 'spied
The stripling's danger and for harbour tried;
Meantime the fish, and then th' apprentice died.'
     The pitying women raised a clamour round,
And weeping said, 'Thou hast thy 'prentice drown'd.'
     Now the stern man was summon'd to the hall,
To tell his tale before the burghers° all: *members of a borough*
He gave th' account; profess'd the lad he loved,
And kept his brazen features all unmoved.
     The mayor himself with tone severe replied,
160 'Henceforth with thee shall never boy abide;
Hire thee a freeman, whom thou durst not beat,
But who, in thy despite, will sleep and eat:
Free thou art now! – again shouldst thou appear,
Thou'lt find thy sentence, like thy soul, severe.'
     Alas! for Peter not a helping hand,
So was he hated, could he now command;
Alone he row'd his boat, alone he cast

His nets beside, or made his anchor fast;
To hold a rope or hear a curse was none;
170 He toil'd and rail'd; he groan'd and swore alone.
    Thus by himself compell'd to live each day,
To wait for certain hours the tide's delay;
At the same times the same dull views to see,
The bounding marsh-bank and the blighted tree;
The water only, when the tides were high,
When low, the mud half-cover'd and half-dry;
The sun-burnt tar that blisters on the planks,
And bank-side stakes in their uneven ranks;
Heaps of entangled weeds that slowly float,
180 As the tide rolls by the impeded boat.
    When tides were neap° and, in the sultry day,   *low*
Through the tall bounding mud-banks made their way,
Which on each side rose swelling, and below
The dark warm flood ran silently and slow;
There anchoring, Peter chose from man to hide,
There hang his head, and view the lazy tide
In its hot slimy channel slowly glide;
Where the small eels that left the deeper way
For the warm shore, within the shallows play;
190 Where gaping mussels, left upon the mud,
Slope° their slow passage to the fallen flood;   *move obliquely*
Here dull and hopeless he'd lie down and trace
How sidelong crabs had scrawl'd° their crooked race;   *(in the mud)*
Or sadly listen to the tuneless cry
Of fishing gull or clanging golden-eye;°   *wild duck*
What time the sea-birds to the marsh would come,
And the loud bittern, from the bulrush home,
Gave from the salt-ditch side the bellowing boom:
He nursed the feelings these dull scenes produce,
200 And loved to stop beside the opening sluice;°   *channel*
Where the small stream, confined in narrow bound,
Ran with a dull, unvaried, sadd'ning sound;
Where all, presented to the eye or ear,
Oppress'd the soul with misery, grief, and fear.

                    *   *   *

Cold nervous tremblings shook his sturdy frame,
And strange disease – he couldn't say the name;
Wild were his dreams, and oft he rose in fright,
Waked by his view of horrors in the night, –
Horrors that would the sternest minds amaze,

Horrors that demons might be proud to raise:
And though he felt forsaken, grieved at heart,
230 To think he lived from all mankind apart;
Yet, if a man approach'd, in terrors he would start.

*   *   *

Here when they saw him, whom they used to shun,
A lost, lone man, so harass'd and undone;
Our gentle females, ever prompt to feel,
Perceived compassion on their anger steal;
His crimes they could not from their memories blot,
260 But they were grieved, and trembled at his lot.
A priest too came, to whom his words are told;
And all the signs they shudder'd to behold.
'Look! look!' they cried; 'his limbs with horror shake,
And as he grinds his teeth, what noise they make!
How glare his angry eyes, and yet he's not awake:
See! what cold drops upon his forehead stand,
And how he clenches that broad bony hand.'

*   *   *

Then, as they watch'd him, calmer he became,
And grew so weak he couldn't move his frame,
280 But murmuring spake, – while they could see and hear
The start of terror and the groan of fear;
See the large dew-beads on his forehead rise,
And the cold death-drop glaze his sunken eyes;
Nor yet he died, but with unwonted force
Seem'd with some fancied being to discourse:
He knew not us, or with accustom'd art
He hid the knowledge, yet exposed his heart;
'Twas part confession and the rest defence,
A madman's tale, with gleams of waking sense.
290 'I'll tell you all,' he said, 'the very day
When the old man first placed them in my way:
My father's spirit – he who always tried
To give me trouble, when he lived and died –
When he was gone, he could not be content
To see my days in painful labour spent,
But would appoint his meetings, and he made
Me watch at these, and so neglect my trade.
'Twas one hot noon, all silent, still, serene,
No living being had I lately seen;
300 I paddled up and down and dipp'd my net,

But (such his pleasure) I could nothing get, –
A father's pleasure, when his toil was done,
To plague and torture thus an only son!
And so I sat and look'd upon the stream,
How it ran on, and felt as in a dream:
But dream it was not; no! – I fix'd my eyes
On the mid stream and saw the spirits rise;
I saw my father on the water stand,
And hold a thin pale boy in either hand;
310 And there they glided ghastly on the top
Of the salt flood, and never touch'd a drop:
I would have struck them, but they knew th' intent,
And smiled upon the oar, and down they went.
   Now, from that day, whenever I began
To dip my net, there stood the hard old man –
He and those boys: I humbled me and pray'd
They would be gone; – they heeded not, but stay'd:
Nor could I turn, nor would the boat go by,
But gazing on the spirits, there was I:
320 They bade me leap to death, but I was loth to die:
And every day, as sure as day arose,
Would these three spirits meet me ere the close;
To hear and mark them daily was my doom,
And 'Come,' they said, with weak, sad voices, 'come.'
To row away with all my strength I tried,
But there were they, hard by me in the tide,
The three unbodied forms – and 'Come,' still 'come,' they cried.
   Fathers should pity – but this old man shook
His hoary locks, and froze me by a look:
330 Thrice, when I struck them, through the water came
A hollow groan, that weaken'd all my frame:
'Father!' said I, 'have mercy:' – He replied,
I know not what – the angry spirit lied, –
'Didst thou not draw thy knife?' said he: 'Twas true,
But I had pity and my arm withdrew:
He cried for mercy which I kindly gave,
But he has no compassion in his grave.
   There were three places, where they ever rose,
The whole long river has not such as those,
340 Places accursed, where, if a man remain,
He'll see the things which strike him to the brain;
And there they made me on my paddle lean,
And look at them for hours; – accursed scene!
When they would glide to that smooth eddy-space,

Then bid me leap and join them in the place;
And at my groans each little villain sprite
Enjoy'd my pains and vanish'd in delight.
    In one fierce summer-day, when my poor brain
    Was burning hot, and cruel was my pain,
350 Then came this father-foe, and there he stood
With his two boys again upon the flood;
There was more mischief in their eyes, more glee
In their pale faces when they glared at me:
Still did they force me on the oar to rest,
And when they saw me fainting and oppress'd,
He, with his hand, the old man, scoop'd the flood,
And there came flame about him mix'd with blood;
He bade me stoop and look upon the place,
Then flung the hot-red liquor in my face;
360 Burning it blazed, and then I roar'd for pain,
I thought the demons would have turn'd my brain.
    Still there they stood, and forced me to behold
A place of horrors – they cannot be told –
Where the flood open'd, there I heard the shriek
Of tortured guilt – no earthly tongue can speak:
'All days alike! for ever!' did they say,
'And unremitted torments every day' –
Yes, so they said:' – But here he ceased and gazed
On all around, affrighten'd and amazed;
370 And still he tried to speak, and look'd in dread
Of frighten'd females gathering round his bed;
Then dropp'd exhausted, and appear'd at rest,
Till the strong foe the vital powers possess'd:
Then with an inward, broken voice he cried,
'Again they come,' and mutter'd as he died.

NOTES

Crabbe
1 in Suffolk, near Aldeburgh.
2 boys who were kept by the parish.

William Blake

[1757–1827]

He was the son of a London hosier, received no schooling, was apprentice to an engraver of the Society of Antiquaries, then a student at the Royal Academy of Arts. 1780 he met John Flaxman, a follower of Swedenborg, whose ideas greatly influenced Blake, who helped finance the publication of his first book – *Poetical Sketches*, 1783. 1782 he married Catherine Boucher, the daughter of a market-gardener, and, 1784, with help, set up a print shop. 1789 he engraved and published *Songs of Innocence* and *The Book of Thel*. 1790 he moved to Lambeth and continued to engrave his own and others' works, meeting prominent radicals such as Godwin, Paine, and Wollstonecraft. With the publication of *Visions of the Daughters of Albion*, 1793, his dual attack upon the materialism and the conditions of the working people of his time is shown in his visionary awareness and his political revolt against the establishment. In 1800 he moved to Felpham, Sussex, working for his patron, Hayley: a contretemps with a drunken soldier led to him being charged at Chichester with high treason, of which he was acquitted Jan. 1804. He returned to London to complete his *Milton*, 1804–8, and *Jerusalem: the Emanation of the Giant Albion*, 1804–20. 1809 his exhibition of his 'Canterbury Pilgrims' and other paintings was ridiculed in the *Examiner*. Neither his paintings nor his poetry found much understanding and his last years were hardly the culmination of the career he had hoped for. 1821 he was commissioned and, 1826, produced his illustrations for the Book of Job; 1824 he met a young painter, Samuel Palmer, and became the centre of a group of artists, the Ancients, who came to listen to him. He died, before completing the engravings for Dante's *Divine Comedy*, on 12 Aug 1827. He was generally believed to have been insane and it was not until the late 1860s that interest grew in his work, his reputation as a poet being secured by W.M. Rossetti's edition of his poems, 1874. His work as a painter and illustrator influenced the Art Nouveau movement in England in the 1880s.

Songs of Innocence and Experience[1]

SHOWING THE TWO CONTRARY STATES OF THE HUMAN SOUL

Songs of Innocence

Introduction

Piping down the valleys wild,
Piping songs of pleasant glee,
On a cloud I saw a child,
And he laughing said to me:

'Pipe a song about a Lamb.'
So I piped with merry chear.
'Piper, pipe that song again.'
So I piped, he wept to hear.

'Drop thy pipe, thy happy pipe,
Sing thy songs of happy chear.'
So I sung the same again
While he wept with joy to hear.

'Piper, sit thee down and write
In a book that all may read.'
So he vanish'd from my sight.
And I pluck'd a hollow reed,

And I made a rural pen,
And I stain'd the water clear,
And I wrote my happy songs
Every child may joy to hear.

The Shepherd

How sweet is the Shepherd's sweet lot!
From the morn to the evening he strays;
He shall follow his sheep all the day,
And his tongue shall be filled with praise.

For he hears the lamb's innocent call,
And he hears the ewe's tender reply;
He is watchful while they are in peace,
For they know when their Shepherd is nigh.

The Ecchoing Green

The Sun does arise,
And make happy the skies;
The merry bells ring
To welcome the Spring;
The sky-lark and thrush,
The birds of the bush,
Sing louder around
To the bells' chearful sound,
While our sports shall be seen
On the Ecchoing Green.

Old John with white hair
Does laugh away care,
Sitting under the oak
Among the old folk.
They laugh at our play,
And soon they all say:
'Such, such were the joys
When we all, girls and boys,
In our youth-time were seen
On the Ecchoing Green.'

Till the little ones weary
No more can be merry;
The sun does descend,
And our sports have an end.
Round the laps of their mothers
Many sisters and brothers,

Like birds in their nest,
Are ready for rest;
And sport no more seen
On the darkening Green.

The Lamb

Little Lamb, who made thee?
  Dost thou know who made thee?
Gave thee life & bid thee feed
By the stream & o'er the mead;
Gave thee clothing of delight,
Softest clothing, woolly, bright;
Gave thee such a tender voice,
Making all the vales rejoice?
  Little Lamb, who made thee?
  Dost thou know who made thee?

Little Lamb, I'll tell thee,
  Little Lamb, I'll tell thee:
He is called by thy name,
For he calls himself a Lamb.
He is meek & he is mild,
He became a little child:
I a child & thou a lamb,
We are called by his name.
  Little Lamb, God bless thee,
  Little Lamb, God bless thee.

The Little Black Boy[2]

My mother bore me in the southern wild,
And I am black, but O! my soul is white;
White as an angel is the English child,
But I am black, as if bereav'd of light.

My mother taught me underneath a tree,
And sitting down before the heat of day
She took me on her lap and kissed me,
And pointing to the east began to say:

'Look on the rising sun: there God does live,
And gives his light and gives his heat away;
And flowers and trees and beasts and men receive
Comfort in morning, joy in the noon day.

And we are put on earth a little space,
That we may learn to bear the beams of love;
And these black bodies and this sun-burnt face
Is but a cloud, and like a shady grove.

For when our souls have learn'd the heat to bear,
The cloud will vanish; we shall hear his voice,
Saying: "Come out from the grove, my love & care,
And round my golden tent like lambs rejoice."'

Thus did my mother say, and kissed me.
And thus I say to little English boy:
When I from black and he from white cloud free
And round the tent of God like lambs we joy,

I'll shade him from the heat, till he can bear
To lean in joy upon our father's knee;
And then I'll stand and stroke his silver hair,
And be like him, and he will then love me.

The Blossom

Merry, Merry Sparrow,
Under leaves so green,
A happy Blossom
Sees you swift as arrow
Seek your cradle narrow
Near my Bosom.

Pretty, Pretty Robin,
Under leaves so green,
A happy Blossom
Hears you sobbing, sobbing,
Pretty, Pretty Robin,
Near my Bosom.

The Chimney Sweeper

When my mother died I was very young,
And my father sold me while yet my tongue
Could scarcely cry "'weep!° 'weep! 'weep! 'weep!'   *sweep*
So your chimneys I sweep, & in soot I sleep.

There's little Tom Dacre, who cried when his head,
That curl'd like a lamb's back, was shav'd; so I said,
'Hush, Tom, never mind it, for when your head's bare,
You know that the soot cannot spoil your white hair.'

And so he was quiet, & that very night,
As Tom was asleeping he had such a sight,
That thousands of sweepers, Dick, Joe, Ned & Jack,
Were all of them lock'd up in coffins of black.

And by came an Angel who had a bright key,
And he open'd the coffins & set them all free;
Then down a green plain leaping, laughing they run,
And wash in a river and shine in the Sun.

Then naked & white, all their bags left behind,
They rise upon clouds, and sport in the wind;
And the Angel told Tom, if he'd be a good boy,
He'd have God for his father & never want joy.

And so Tom awoke; and we rose in the dark,
And got with our bags & our brushes to work.
Tho' the morning was cold, Tom was happy & warm;
So if all do their duty, they need not fear harm.[3]

The Little Boy Lost

'Father, father, where are you going?
O do not walk so fast.
Speak father, speak to your little boy,
Or else I shall be lost.'

The night was dark, no father was there;
The child was wet with dew;
The mire was deep, & the child did weep,
And away the vapour° flew.   *mist*

The Little Boy Found

The little boy lost in the lonely fen,
Led by the wand'ring light,
Began to cry, but God ever nigh,
Appear'd like his father in white.

He kissed the child & by the hand led
And to his mother brought,
Who in sorrow pale, thro' the lonely dale,
Her little boy weeping sought.

Laughing Song

When the green woods laugh with the voice of joy,
And the dimpling stream runs laughing by,
When the air does laugh with our merry wit,
And the green hill laughs with the noise of it,

When the meadows laugh with lively green,
And the grasshopper laughs in the merry scene,
When Mary and Susan and Emily[4]
With their sweet round mouths sing 'Ha, Ha, He!'

When the painted birds laugh in the shade
Where our table with cherries and nuts is spread,
Come live & be merry and join with me,
To sing the sweet chorus of 'Ha, Ha, He!'

A Cradle Song

Sweet dreams, form a shade
O'er my lovely infant's head,
Sweet dreams of pleasant streams
By happy silent moony beams.

Sweet sleep, with soft down
Weave thy brows an infant crown.
Sweet sleep, Angel mild,
Hover o'er my happy child.

Sweet smiles, in the night
Hover over my delight;
Sweet smiles, Mother's smiles,
All the livelong night beguiles.

Sweet moans, dovelike sighs,
Chase not slumber from thy eyes.
Sweet moans, sweeter smiles,
All the dovelike moans beguiles.

Sleep, sleep, happy child.
All creation slept and smil'd.
Sleep, sleep, happy sleep,
While o'er thee thy mother weep.

Sweet babe, in thy face
Holy image[5] I can trace.
Sweet babe, once like thee
Thy maker lay and wept for me,

Wept for me, for thee, for all,
When he was an infant small.
Thou his image ever see,
Heavenly face that smiles on thee,

Smiles on thee, on me, on all,
Who became an infant small.
Infant smiles are his own smiles;
Heaven & earth to peace beguiles.

The Divine Image

To Mercy, Pity, Peace, and Love
All pray in their distress;
And to these virtues of delight
Return their thankfulness.

For Mercy, Pity, Peace, and Love
Is God, our father dear,
And Mercy, Pity, Peace, and Love
Is Man, his child and care.

For Mercy has a human heart,
Pity, a human face,
And Love, the human form divine,
And Peace, the human dress.

Then every man of every clime
That prays in his distress,
Prays to the human form divine,
Love, Mercy, Pity, Peace.

And all must love the human form
In heathen, turk or jew.
Where Mercy, Love & Pity dwell
There God is dwelling too.

Holy Thursday

'Twas on a Holy Thursday, their innocent faces clean,
The children walking two & two, in red & blue & green[6],
Grey headed beadles[7] walk'd before, with wands as white as snow,
Till into the high dome of Paul's they like Thames' waters flow.

O what a multitude they seem'd, these flowers of London town!
Seated in companies[8] they sit with radiance all their own.
The hum of multitudes was there, but multitudes of lambs,
Thousands of little boys & girls raising their innocent hands.

Now like a mighty wind they raise to heaven the voice of song,
Or like harmonious thunderings the seats of heaven among.
Beneath them sit the aged men, wise guardians of the poor;
Then cherish pity, lest you drive an angel from your door.

Night

The sun descending in the west,
The evening star does shine;
The birds are silent in their nest,
And I must seek for mine.
The moon, like a flower
In heaven's high bower,
With silent delight
Sits and smiles on the night.

Farewell, green fields and happy groves,
Where flocks have took delight;
Where lambs have nibbled, silent moves
The feet of angels bright;
Unseen they pour blessing,
And joy without ceasing,
On each bud and blossom
And each sleeping bosom.

They look in every thoughtless[9] nest,
Where birds are cover'd warm;
They visit caves of every beast,
To keep them all from harm;
If they see any weeping
That should have been sleeping,
They pour sleep on their head
And sit down by their bed.

When wolves and tygers howl for prey,
They pitying stand and weep,
Seeking to drive their thirst[10] away
And keep them from the sheep;
But if they rush dreadful,
The angels, most heedful,
Receive each mild spirit,
New worlds to inherit.

And there the lion's ruddy eyes
Shall flow with tears of gold,
And pitying the tender cries,
And walking round the fold,
Saying, 'Wrath by his meekness,
And by his health sickness,
Is driven away
From our immortal day.

And now beside thee, bleating lamb,
I can lie down and sleep,
Or think on him[11] who bore thy name,
Graze after thee and weep.
For, wash'd in life's river,[12]
My bright mane for ever
Shall shine like the gold,
As I guard o'er the fold.'

Spring

Sound the Flute!
Now it's mute.
Birds delight
Day and Night;
Nightingale
In the dale,
Lark in Sky,
Merrily,
Merrily, Merrily to welcome in the Year.

Little Boy
Full of joy,
Little Girl
Sweet and small,
Cock does crow,
So do you;
Merry voice,
Infant noise,
Merrily, Merrily to welcome in the Year.

Little Lamb
Here I am,
Come and lick
My white neck,
Let me pull
Your soft Wool,
Let me kiss
Your soft face;
Merrily, Merrily we welcome in the Year.

Nurse's Song

When the voices of children are heard on the green
And laughing is heard on the hill,
My heart is at rest within my breast
And every thing else is still.

'Then come home, my children, the sun is gone down
And the dews[13] of night arise;
Come, come, leave off play, and let us away
Till the morning appears in the skies.'

'No, no, let us play, for it is yet day
And we cannot go to sleep;
Besides, in the sky, the little birds fly
And the hills are all cover'd with sheep.'

'Well, well, go & play till the light fades away
And then go home to bed.'
The little ones leaped & shouted & laugh'd
And all the hills ecchoed.

Infant Joy[14]

'I have no name;
I am but two days old.'
What shall I call thee?
'I happy am,
Joy is my name.'
Sweet joy befall thee!

Pretty joy!
Sweet joy but two days old,
Sweet joy I call thee:
Thou dost smile,
I sing the while,
Sweet joy befall thee.

A Dream

Once a dream did weave a shade
O'er my Angel-guarded bed,
That an Emmet° lost its way   *ant*
Where on grass methought I lay.

Troubled, 'wilder'd and forlorn,
Dark, benighted, travel-worn,
Over many a tangled spray
All heart-broke I heard her say:

'O my children! do they cry?
Do they hear their father sigh?
Now they look abroad to see,
Now return and weep for me.'

Pitying, I dropp'd a tear;
But I saw a glow-worm near,
Who replied: 'What wailing wight°   *person*
Calls the watchman of the night?

I am set to light the ground,
While the beetle goes his round:
Follow now the beetle's hum;
Little wanderer, hie° thee home.'   *hasten*

On Another's Sorrow

Can I see another's woe,
And not be in sorrow too?
Can I see another's grief,
And not seek for kind relief?

Can I see a falling tear,
And not feel my sorrow's share?
Can a father see his child
Weep, nor be with sorrow fill'd?

Can a mother sit and hear
An infant groan, an infant fear?
No, no, never can it be,
Never, never can it be!

And can he who smiles on all
Hear the wren with sorrows small,
Hear the small bird's grief & care,
Hear the woes that infants bear,

And not sit beside the nest,
Pouring pity in their breast;
And not sit the cradle near,
Weeping tear on infant's tear;

And not sit both night & day,
Wiping all our tears away?
O, no, never can it be,
Never, never can it be!

He doth give his joy to all;
He becomes an infant small;
He becomes a man of woe;
He doth feel the sorrow too.

Think not thou canst sigh a sigh
And thy maker is not by;
Think not thou canst weep a tear
And thy maker is not near.

O, he gives to us his joy
That our grief he may destroy;
Till our grief is fled & gone
He doth sit by us and moan.

[1789]

Songs of Experience

Introduction

Hear the voice of the Bard!
Who Present, Past, & Future sees,
Whose ears have heard
The Holy Word
That walk'd among the ancient trees,[15]

Calling the lapsed[16] Soul,
And weeping in the evening dew,
That might control
The starry pole,
And fallen, fallen light renew!

'O Earth, O Earth return!
Arise from out the dewy grass;
Night is worn,
And the morn
Rises from the slumberous mass.

Turn away no more.
Why wilt thou turn away?
The starry floor,
The wat'ry shore,
Is giv'n thee till the break of day.'

Earth's Answer

Earth rais'd up her head
From the darkness dread & drear.
Her light fled:
Stony dread!
And her locks cover'd with grey despair.

'Prison'd on wat'ry shore
Starry Jealousy does keep my den
Cold and hoar
Weeping o'er
I hear the father of the ancient men.[17]

Selfish father of men!
Cruel, jealous, selfish fear!
Can delight,
Chain'd in night,
The virgins of youth and morning bear?

Does spring hide its joy
When buds and blossoms grow?
Does the sower
Sow by night?
Or the plowman in darkness plow?

Break this heavy chain
That does freeze my bones around.
Selfish! vain!
Eternal bane!
That free Love with bondage bound.'

The Clod & the Pebble

'Love seeketh not Itself to please,
Nor for itself hath any care,
But for another gives its ease
And builds a Heaven in Hell's despair.'

  So sang a little Clod of Clay
  Trodden with the cattle's feet;
  But a Pebble of the brook
  Warbled out these metres meet:

'Love seeketh only Self to please,
To bind another to Its delight;
Joys in another's loss of ease,
And builds a Hell in Heaven's despite.'

Holy Thursday

Is this a holy thing to see
In a rich and fruitful land,
Babes reduc'd to misery,
Fed with cold and usurous[18] hand?

Is that trembling cry a song?
Can it be a song of joy?
And so many children poor?
It is a land of poverty!

And their sun does never shine,
And their fields are bleak & bare,
And their ways are fill'd with thorns;
It is eternal winter there.

For where-e'er the sun does shine,
And where-e'er the rain does fall,
Babe can never hunger there,
Nor poverty the mind appal.

The Little Girl Lost

In futurity
I prophetic see
That the earth from sleep
(Grave the sentence deep)

Shall arise and seek
For her maker meek,
And the desert wild
Become a garden mild.

In the southern clime,
Where the summer's prime
Never fades away,
Lovely Lyca lay.

Seven summers old
Lovely Lyca told.
She had wander'd long,
Hearing wild birds' song.

'Sweet sleep, come to me
Underneath this tree.
Do father, mother, weep,
Where can Lyca sleep?

Lost in desert wild
Is your little child.
How can Lyca sleep
If her mother weep?

If her heart does ache,
Then let Lyca wake;
If my mother sleep,
Lyca shall not weep.

Frowning, frowning night,
O'er this desert bright[19]
Let thy moon arise,
While I close my eyes.'

Sleeping Lyca lay,
While the beasts of prey,
Come from caverns deep,
View'd the maid asleep.

The kingly lion stood
And the virgin view'd;
Then he gambol'd round
O'er the hallow'd ground.

Leopards, tigers play
Round her as she lay,
While the lion old
Bow'd his mane of gold,

And her bosom lick,
And upon her neck
From his eyes of flame
Ruby tears there came;

While the lioness
Loos'd her slender dress,
And naked they convey'd
To caves the sleeping maid.

The Little Girl Found

All the night in woe
Lyca's parents go
Over vallies deep,
While the deserts weep.

Tired and woe-begone,
Hoarse with making moan,
Arm in arm seven days
They trac'd the desart ways.

Seven nights they sleep
Among shadows deep,
And dream they see their child
Starv'd in desert wild.

Pale thro' pathless ways
The fancied image strays,
Famish'd, weeping, weak,
With hollow piteous shriek.

Rising from unrest,
The trembling woman prest
With feet of weary woe;
She could no further go.

In his arms he bore
Her, arm'd with sorrow sore,
Till before their way
A couching lion lay.

Turning back was vain;
Soon his heavy mane
Bore them to the ground;
Then he stalk'd around,

Smelling to his prey.
But their fears allay
When he licks their hands,
And silent by them stands.

They look upon his eyes
Fill'd with deep surprise,
And wondering behold
A Spirit arm'd in gold.

On his head a crown,
On his shoulders down
Flow'd his golden hair.
Gone was all their care.

'Follow me,' he said;
'Weep not for the maid;
In my palace deep
Lyca lies asleep.'

Then they followed
Where the vision led,
And saw their sleeping child
Among tygers wild.

To this day they dwell
In a lonely dell,
Nor fear the wolvish howl
Nor the lion's growl.

The Chimney Sweeper

A little black thing among the snow,
Crying ''weep! 'weep!' in notes of woe!
'Where are thy father & mother, say?'
'They are both gone up to the church to pray.

Because I was happy upon the heath,
And smil'd among the winter's snow,
They clothed me in the clothes of death,
And taught me to sing the notes of woe.

And because I am happy & dance & sing,[20]
They think they have done me no injury;
And are gone to praise God & his Priest & King,
Who make up a heaven of our misery.'

Nurse's Song

When the voices of children are heard on the green
And whisp'rings are in the dale,
The days of my youth rise fresh in my mind,
My face turns green and pale.[21]

Then come home my children, the sun is gone down
And the dews of night arise;
Your spring & your day are wasted in play,
And your winter and night in disguise.

The Sick Rose[22]

O Rose, thou art sick.
The invisible worm,
That flies in the night
In the howling storm,

Has found out thy bed
Of crimson joy;
And his dark secret love
Does thy life destroy.

The Fly

Little Fly,
Thy summer's play
My thoughtless hand
Has brush'd away.

Am not I
A fly like thee?
Or art not thou
A man like me?

For I dance
And drink & sing,
Till some blind hand
Shall brush my wing.

If thought is life[23]
And strength & breath,
And the want
Of thought is death,

Then am I
A happy fly,
If I live
Or if I die.

The Angel

I Dreamt a Dream! what can it mean?
And that I was a maiden Queen,
Guarded by an Angel mild:
Witless woe was ne'er beguil'd!

And I wept both night and day,
And he wip'd my tears away,
And I wept both day and night,
And hid from him my heart's delight.

So he took his wings and fled;
Then the morn blush'd rosy red;
I dried my tears, & arm'd my fears
With ten thousand shields and spears.

Soon my Angel came again;
I was arm'd, he came in vain;
For the time of youth was fled
And grey hairs were on my head.

The Tyger

Tyger Tyger, burning bright
In the forests of the night,
What immortal hand or eye
Could frame thy fearful symmetry?

In what distant deeps or skies[24]
Burnt the fire of thine eyes?
On what wings dare he aspire?
What the hand dare sieze the fire?

And what shoulder, & what art,
Could twist the sinews of thy heart?
And when thy heart began to beat,
What dread hand? & what dread feet?

What the hammer? what the chain?
In what furnace was thy brain?
What the anvil? what dread grasp
Dare its deadly terrors clasp?

When the stars threw down their spears[25]
And water'd heaven with their tears,
Did he smile his work to see?[26]
Did he who made the Lamb make thee?

Tyger Tyger burning bright
In the forests of the night,
What immortal hand or eye
Dare frame thy fearful symmetry?

My Pretty Rose-Tree

A flower was offer'd to me,
Such a flower as May never bore;
But I said 'I've a Pretty Rose-tree,'
And I passed the sweet flower o'er.

Then I went to my Pretty Rose-tree,
To tend her by day and by night;
But my Rose turn'd away with jealousy,
And her thorns were my only delight.

Ah! Sun-flower[27]

Ah, Sun-flower! weary of time,
Who countest the steps of the Sun,
Seeking after that sweet golden clime
Where the traveller's journey is done;

Where the Youth pined away with desire,
And the pale Virgin shrouded in snow,
Arise from their graves and aspire
Where my Sun-flower wishes to go.

The Lily

The modest[28] Rose puts forth a thorn,
The humble Sheep a threat'ning horn;
While the Lily white shall in Love delight,
Nor a thorn nor a threat stain her beauty bright.

The Garden of Love

I went to the Garden of Love,
And saw what I never had seen;
A Chapel was built in the midst,
Where I used to play on the green.

And the gates of this Chapel were shut,
And 'Thou shalt not' writ over the door;
So I turn'd to the Garden of Love
That so many sweet flowers bore,

And I saw it was filled with graves,
And tomb-stones where flowers should be;
And Priests in black gowns were walking their rounds,
And binding with briars my joys & desires.

The Little Vagabond

Dear Mother, dear Mother, the Church is cold,
But the Ale-house is healthy & pleasant & warm;
Besides I can tell where I am used well,
Such usage in heaven will never do well.[29]

But if at the Church they would give us some Ale,
And a pleasant fire our souls to regale,
We'd sing and we'd pray all the live-long day,
Nor ever once wish from the Church to stray.

Then the Parson might preach & drink & sing,
And we'd be as happy as birds in the spring;
And modest dame Lurch, who is always at Church,
Would not have bandy children nor fasting nor birch.

And God, like a father rejoicing to see
His children as pleasant and happy as he,
Would have no more quarrel with the Devil or the Barrel,
But kiss him & give him both drink and apparel.

London

I wander thro' each charter'd° street   *documented*
Near where the charter'd Thames does flow,
And mark in every face I meet
Marks of weakness, marks of woe.

In every cry of every Man,
In every Infant's cry of fear,
In every voice, in every ban,
The mind-forg'd manacles I hear:

How the Chimney-sweeper's cry
Every black'ning Church appalls,
And the hapless Soldier's sigh
Runs in blood down Palace walls;

But most thro' midnight streets I hear
How the youthful Harlot's curse
Blasts the new born Infant's tear,
And blights with plagues the Marriage hearse.

The Human Abstract

Pity would be no more
If we did not make somebody Poor;
And Mercy no more could be
If all were as happy as we;

And mutual fear brings peace,
Till the selfish loves increase.
Then Cruelty knits a snare
And spreads his baits with care.

He sits down with holy fears
And waters the ground with tears;
Then Humility takes its root
Underneath his foot.

Soon spreads the dismal shade
Of Mystery[30] over his head,
And the Catterpiller and Fly
Feed on the Mystery;

And it bears the fruit of Deceit,
Ruddy and sweet to eat,
And the Raven his nest has made
In its thickest shade.

The Gods of the earth and sea
Sought thro' Nature to find this Tree;
But their search was all in vain:
There grows one in the Human Brain.

Infant Sorrow

My mother groan'd, my father wept;
Into the dangerous world I leapt,
Helpless, naked, piping loud,
Like a fiend hid in a cloud.

Struggling in my father's hands,
Striving against my swadling bands,
Bound and weary, I thought best
To sulk upon my mother's breast.

A Poison Tree[31]

I was angry with my friend;
I told my wrath, my wrath did end.
I was angry with my foe;
I told it not, my wrath did grow.

And I water'd it in fears,
Night & morning with my tears;
And I sunned it with smiles,
And with soft deceitful wiles.

And it grew both day and night,
Till it bore an apple bright;
And my foe beheld it shine,
And he knew that it was mine,

And into my garden stole
When the night had veil'd the pole.
In the morning glad I see
My foe outstretch'd beneath the tree.

A Little Boy Lost

'Nought loves another as itself,
Nor venerates another so,
Nor is it possible to Thought
A greater than itself to know.

And Father, how can I love you
Or any of my brothers more?
I love you like the little bird
That picks up crumbs around the door.'

The Priest sat by and heard the child;
In trembling zeal he seiz'd his hair;
He led him by his little coat;
And all admir'd the Priestly care.

And standing on the altar high,
'Lo, what a fiend is here!' said he,
'One who sets reason up for judge
Of our most holy Mystery.'

The weeping child could not be heard,
The weeping parents wept in vain;
They strip'd him to his little shirt,
And bound him in an iron chain;

And burn'd him in a holy place,
Where many had been burn'd before:
The weeping parents wept in vain.
Are such things done on Albion's° shore?   *England's*

A Little Girl Lost

*Children of the future Age
Reading this indignant page,
Know that in a former time
Love! sweet Love! was thought a crime.*

In the Age of Gold,
Free from winter's cold,
Youth and maiden bright
To the holy light,
Naked in the sunny beams delight.

Once a youthful pair,
Fill'd with softest care,
Met in garden bright,
Where the holy light
Had just remov'd the curtains of the night.

There in rising day,
On the grass they play;
Parents were afar,
Strangers came not near,
And the maiden soon forgot her fear.

Tired with kisses sweet,
They agree to meet
When the silent sleep
Waves o'er heaven's deep,
And the weary tired wanderers weep.

To her father white
Came the maiden bright;

But his loving look,
Like the holy book,
All her tender limbs with terror shook.

'Ona! pale and weak!
To thy father speak.
O the trembling fear!
O the dismal care!
That shakes the blossoms of my hoary hair.'

To Tirzah[32]

Whate'er is Born of Mortal Birth
Must be consumed with the Earth
To rise from Generation free;
Then what have I to do with thee?

The Sexes sprung from Shame & Pride,
Blow'd° in the morn, in evening died;   *bloomed*
But Mercy chang'd Death into Sleep;
The Sexes rose to work & weep.

Thou Mother of my Mortal part
With cruelty didst mould my Heart,
And with false self-deceiving tears
Didst bind my Nostrils, Eyes & Ears;

Didst close my Tongue in senseless clay,
And me to Mortal Life betray.
The Death of Jesus set me free:
Then what have I to do with thee?

The School Boy[33]

I love to rise in a summer morn,
When the birds sing on every tree;
The distant huntsman winds his horn,
And the sky-lark sings with me.
O! what sweet company.

But to go to school in a summer morn,
O! it drives all joy away;

Under a cruel eye outworn
The little ones spend the day
In sighing and dismay.

Ah! then at times I drooping sit,
And spend many an anxious hour;
Nor in my book can I take delight,
Nor sit in learning's bower,
Worn thro' with the dreary shower.°   *school lessons*

How can the bird that is born for joy
Sit in a cage and sing?
How can a child when fears annoy
But droop his tender wing,
And forget his youthful spring?

O! father & mother, if buds are nip'd
And blossoms blown away,
And if the tender plants are strip'd
Of their joy in the springing day
By sorrow and care's dismay,

How shall the summer arise in joy,
Or the summer fruits appear?
Or how shall we gather what griefs destroy,
Or bless the mellowing year
When the blasts of winter appear?

The Voice of the Ancient Bard³⁴

Youth of delight, come hither,
And see the opening morn,
Image of truth new born.
Doubt is fled, & clouds of reason,
Dark disputes & artful° teasing   *of art*
Folly is an endless maze,
Tangled roots perplex her ways,
How many have fallen there!
They stumble all night over bones of the dead,
And feel they know not what but care,
And wish to lead others when they should be led.

[1794]

from MILTON

Jerusalem

And did those feet in ancient time
Walk upon England's mountains green?
And was the holy Lamb of God
On England's pleasant pastures seen?

And did the Countenance Divine
Shine forth upon our clouded hills?
And was Jerusalem builded here
Among these dark Satanic Mills?

Bring me my Bow of burning gold!
Bring me my Arrows of desire!
Bring me my Spear! O clouds, unfold!
Bring me my Chariot of fire!

I will not cease from Mental Fight,
Nor shall my Sword sleep in my hand,
Till we have built Jerusalem
In England's green and pleasant land.

[1804]

from JERUSALEM

England! awake! awake! awake!
  Jerusalem thy Sister calls!
Why wilt thou sleep the sleep of death?
  And close her from thy ancient walls?

Thy hills & valleys felt her feet,
  Gently upon their bosoms move:
Thy gates beheld sweet Zion's ways;
  Then was a time of joy and love.

And now the time returns again:
  Our souls exult & London's towers,
Receive the Lamb of God to dwell
  In England's green and pleasant bowers.

[1804]

from FOR THE SEXES: THE GATES OF
PARADISE

*To the Accuser who is the God of this
World.*

Truly my Satan thou art but a Dunce,
And dost not know the Garment from the Man;
Every Harlot was a Virgin once,
Nor canst thou ever change Kate into Nan.

Tho thou art Worship'd by the Names Divine
Of Jesus & Jehovah: thou art still
The Son of Morn in weary Night's decline,
The lost Traveller's Dream under the Hill.

[1793]

NOTES

Blake

1 *Songs of Innocence* was originally published in 1789–90. The edition that combined the
two – *Innocence* and *Experience* – was first published in 1794. After that, although *Songs
of Innocence* was still printed by itself, *Songs of Experience* never was. A few of the poems
come from earlier writings, e.g. *An Island in the Moon*. In the original, each poem is set
within a coloured design – sometimes a pattern, sometimes a picture, and, for Blake,
this form of poem-picture made an artistic whole in which words, design and colour
formed one unit. The spelling and capitalisation of the original have been retained.

2 reflects the contemporary anti-slavery attitude, which culminated in the Abolition of
Slavery Act, 1807.

3 this is the boy speaker's comment: the poet is more concerned about Tom's ability to
cope with his situation after his vision of the angel and heaven.

4 earlier version had Edessa, Lyca, Emilie.

5 Holy image – of Christ.

6 different charity schools wore uniforms of different colours.

7 a parish official, who looked after relief for the poor and kept order in church.

8 stands were erected at St Paul's to accommodate this great choir.

9 in the sense of 'take no thought for the morrow'.

10 for blood.

11 Christ.

12 Rev. XXII.1–2; also John the Baptist's baptism (Matt. III.4–16) and Naaman's washing away of leprosy (2 Kings V.9–15).

13 dews were believed to be harmful to health.

14 Joy is an abstract noun – not used as a name in B.'s time. Could be used for male or female.

15 Gen. III.8.

16 i.e. fallen from innocence.

17 later called Urizen, the jealous selfish creator of the material world.

18 of an institution, calculating the return it will get.

19 in the moonlight.

20 on May Day celebrations, when sweeps and milkmaids in London danced.

21 green and pale = signs of envy and frustration.

22 rose = love, a young girl cf. the Virgin Mary – *Rosa sine spina* (Rose without a thorn).

23 lines 13–20 written later and inserted.

24 Gen. I.8.

25 Job XXXVIII.7.

26 Gen. I.10.

27 the sunflower's 'face' follows the sun, cf. Ovid. Met. IV where Clytie became a sunflower after being rejected by Hyperion.

28 in ms. lustful, envious, rejected in favour of 'modest' – suggesting this modesty a prudish self-protection.

29 in ms. Notebook 'makes all go to hell'.

30 symbolises the growth of religion, with the caterpillar and fly = the priesthood and the raven an omen of death.

31 in the Notebook, this is entitled *Christian Forebearance*.

32 found only in later copies of the poems, cf. John II.4; I Cor. XV.44ff.

33 transferred to *Songs of Experience* only in later copies.

34 transferred later to *Songs of Experience*.

William Wordsworth
[1770–1850]

He was born at Cockermouth, Cumbria, son of an attorney and attended the infants' school at Penrith. In 1778 his mother died, in 1783 his father. He was educated at Hawkshead Grammar School, 1779–87: attended St John's College, Cambridge, but did not find academia congenial. 1790 he went on a walking tour of France, the Alps and Italy, returning again to France 1791 for a year, when he was much influenced by French republicanism, and fell in love with Annette Vallon, by whom he had a daughter, born after his return to England. The same year war was declared between France and Britain and that, with the advent of the Reign of Terror (1793–4) in France, disillusioned him and a period of depression followed, when he wrote *The Borderers*, 1796–7, published 1842. In 1797 he received a legacy of £900 from a friend, Raisley Calvert, so that he might devote himself to poetry. With his sister, Dorothy, he settled first at Racedown, Dorset, then Alfoxden, Somerset, in order to be near Coleridge, living at Nether Stowey, whom he had met in 1795. The *Lyrical Ballads* was the product of this friendship. 1798–9 he spent the winter in Goslar, Germany, where he composed parts of *The Prelude* and the 'Lucy' poems. 1799 he returned to settle with D. in Dove Cottage, Grasmere. 1800 a second edition of the *Lyrical Ballads* was published with its celebrated, provocative Preface on poetic diction. 1802 he and D. visited Annette in France: later he married Mary Hutchinson: wrote *Resolution and Independence* and began his ode 'Intimations of Immortality', published in *Poems in Two Volumes*, 1807. He and Mary had five children, the first, John, b. 1803, two of whom died in childhood. He became estranged from Coleridge whose marriage was unhappy and who had fallen in love with W.'s sister-in-law, Sara, and whose deterioration through the use of opium had begun: though reconciled later, their relationship was never again the same. 1813 he was appointed Stamp Distributor for Westmorland (£400 per annum) and moved with his wife and family, and D., to Rydal Mount, Ambleside, where he lived for the rest of his life. He slowly settled into the 'grand old man of poetry' role, travelling and recording his journeys in his poetry: he was made Poet Laureate, 1843. The six volumes of his works, revised by him, were published 1849–50. He died at Rydal Mount and is buried in Grasmere churchyard. *The Prelude* was published posthumously, 1850.

Expostulation and Reply[1]

'Why, William, on that old grey stone,
Thus for the length of half a day,
Why, William, sit you thus alone,
And dream your time away?

Where are your books? – that light bequeathed
To Beings else forlorn and blind!
Up! up! and drink the spirit breathed
From dead men to their kind.

You look round on your Mother Earth,
10 As if she for no purpose bore you;
As if you were her first-born birth,
And none had lived before you!'

One morning thus, by Esthwaite lake,
When life was sweet, I knew not why,
To me my good friend Matthew spake,
And thus I made reply:

'The eye – it cannot choose but see;
We cannot bid the ear be still;
Our bodies feel, where'er they be,
20 Against or with our will.

Nor less I deem that there are Powers
Which of themselves our minds impress;
That we can feed this mind of ours
In a wise passiveness.

Think you, 'mid all this mighty sum
Of things for ever speaking,
That nothing of itself will come,
But we must still be seeking?

– Then ask not wherefore, here, alone,
30 Conversing as I may,
I sit upon this old grey stone,
And dream my time away.'

1798 [1798]

The Tables Turned

AN EVENING SCENE ON THE SAME
SUBJECT

Up! up! my Friend, and quit your books;
Or surely you'll grow double:
Up! up! my Friend, and clear your looks;
Why all this toil and trouble?

The sun, above the mountain's head,
A freshening lustre mellow
Through all the long green fields has spread,
His first sweet evening yellow.

Books! 'tis a dull and endless strife:
10 Come, hear the woodland linnet,
How sweet his music! on my life,
There's more of wisdom in it.

And hark! how blithe the throstle sings!
He, too, is no mean preacher:
Come forth into the light of things,
Let Nature be your Teacher.

She has a world of ready wealth,
Our minds and hearts to bless –
Spontaneous wisdom breathed by health,
20 Truth breathed by cheerfulness.

One impulse from a vernal wood
May teach you more of man,
Of moral evil and of good,
Than all the sages can.

Sweet is the lore which Nature brings;
Our meddling intellect
Mis-shapes the beauteous forms of things: –
We murder to dissect.

Enough of science and of art;
Close up those barren leaves;
Come forth and bring with you a heart
That watches and receives.

1798 [1798]

Lines Written in Early Spring

I heard a thousand blended notes,
While in a grove I sate reclined,
In that sweet mood when pleasant thoughts
Bring sad thoughts to the mind.

To her fair works did Nature link
The human soul that through me ran;
And much it grieved my heart to think
What man has made of man.

Through primrose tufts, in that green bower,
10 The periwinkle° trailed its wreaths;   *(evergreen plant with blue flowers)*
And 'tis my faith that every flower
Enjoys the air it breathes.

The birds around me hopped and played,
Their thoughts I cannot measure: —
But the least motion which they made,
It seemed a thrill of pleasure.

The budding twigs spread out their fan,
To catch the breezy air;
And I must think, do all I can,
20 That there was pleasure there.

If this belief from heaven be sent,
If such be Nature's holy plan,
Have I not reason to lament
What man has made of man?

1798 [1798]

There Was a Boy

There was a Boy; ye knew him well, ye cliffs
And islands of Winander°! – many a time   *Lake Windermere*
At evening, when the earliest stars began
To move along the edges of the hills,
Rising or setting, would he stand alone,
Beneath the trees, or by the glimmering lake;
And there, with fingers interwoven, both hands
Pressed closely palm to palm and to his mouth
Uplifted, he, as through an instrument,
10 Blew mimic hootings to the silent owls,
That they might answer him. – And they would shout
Across the watery vale, and shout again,
Responsive to his call, – with quivering peals,
And long halloos, and screams, and echoes loud
Redoubled and redoubled; concourse wild
Of jocund din! And, when there came a pause
Of silence such as baffled his best skill:
Then sometimes, in that silence, while he hung
Listening, a gentle shock of mild surprise
20 Has carried far into his heart the voice
Of mountain-torrents; or the visible scene
Would enter unawares into his mind
With all its solemn imagery, its rocks,
Its woods, and that uncertain heaven received
Into the bosom of the steady lake.
    This boy was taken from his mates, and died
In childhood, ere he was full twelve years old.
Pre-eminent in beauty is the vale
Where he was born and bred: the churchyard hangs
30 Upon a slope above the village-school;
And through that churchyard when my way has led
On summer-evenings, I believe that there
A long half-hour together I have stood
Mute – looking at the grave in which he lies!

1798 [1800]

Lines Composed a few miles above Tintern Abbey[2]
on Revisiting the Banks of the Wye during a Tour.
July 13, 1798

Five years have passed; five summers, with the length
Of five long winters! and again I hear
These waters, rolling from their mountain-springs
With a soft inland murmur.[3] Once again
Do I behold these steep and lofty cliffs,
That on a wild secluded scene impress
Thoughts of more deep seclusion; and connect
The landscape with the quiet of the sky.
The day is come when I again repose
10 Here, under this dark sycamore, and view
These plots of cottage ground, these orchard tufts,
Which at this season, with their unripe fruits,
Are clad in one green hue, and lose themselves
Mid groves and copses. Once again I see
These hedgerows, hardly hedgerows, little lines
Of sportive wood run wild; these pastoral farms,
Green to the very door; and wreaths of smoke
Sent up, in silence, from among the trees!
With some uncertain notice, as might seem
20 Of vagrant dwellers in the houseless woods,
Or of some Hermit's cave, where by his fire
The Hermit sits alone.

                    These beauteous forms,
Through a long absence, have not been to me
As is a landscape to a blind man's eye;
But oft, in lonely rooms, and 'mid the din
Of towns and cities, I have owed to them,
In hours of weariness, sensations sweet,
Felt in the blood, and felt along the heart;
And passing even into my purer mind,
30 With tranquil restoration – feelings too
Of unremembered pleasure; such, perhaps,
As have no slight or trivial influence
On that best portion of a good man's life,
His little, nameless, unremembered, acts
Of kindness and of love. Nor less, I trust,
To them I may have owed another gift,
Of aspect more sublime; that blessed mood,

In which the burthen of the mystery,
In which the heavy and the weary weight
40 Of all this unintelligible world,
Is lightened – that serene and blessed mood,
In which the affections gently lead us on –
Until, the breath of this corporeal frame
And even the motion of our human blood
Almost suspended, we are laid asleep
In body, and become a living soul;
While with an eye made quiet by the power
Of harmony, and the deep power of joy,
We see into the life of things.

               If this
50 Be but a vain belief, yet, oh! how oft –
In darkness and amid the many shapes
Of joyless daylight; when the fretful stir
Unprofitable, and the fever of the world,
Have hung upon the beatings of my heart –
How oft, in spirit, have I turned to thee,
O sylvan Wye! thou wanderer through the woods,
How often has my spirit turned to thee!

   And now, with gleams of half-extinguished thought,
With many recognitions dim and faint,
60 And somewhat of a sad perplexity,
The picture of the mind revives again;
While here I stand, not only with the sense
Of present pleasure, but with pleasing thoughts
That in this moment there is life and food
For future years. And so I dare to hope,
Though changed, no doubt, from what I was when first
I came among these hills; when like a roe
I bounded o'er the mountains, by the sides
Of the deep rivers, and the lonely streams,
70 Wherever nature led – more like a man
Flying from something that he dreads than one
Who sought the thing he loved. For nature then
(The coarser pleasures of my boyish days,
And their glad animal movements all gone by)
To me was all in all. – I cannot paint
What then I was. The sounding cataract
Haunted me like a passion; the tall rock,
The mountain, and the deep and gloomy wood,
Their colours and their forms, were then to me

80 An appetite; a feeling and a love,
    That had no need of a remoter charm,
    By thought supplied, nor any interest
    Unborrowed from the eye. – That time is past,
    And all its aching joys are now no more,
    And all its dizzy raptures. Not for this
    Faint° I, nor mourn nor murmur; other gifts   *become discouraged*
    Have followed; for such loss, I would believe,
    Abundant recompense. For I have learned
    To look on nature, not as in the hour
90 Of thoughtless youth; but hearing oftentimes
    The still, sad music of humanity,
    Nor harsh nor grating, though of ample power
    To chasten and subdue. And I have felt
    A presence that disturbs me with the joy
    Of elevated thoughts; a sense sublime
    Of something far more deeply interfused,
    Whose dwelling is the light of setting suns,
    And the round ocean and the living air,
    And the blue sky, and in the mind of man:
100 A motion and a spirit, that impels
    All thinking things, all objects of all thought,
    And rolls through all things. Therefore am I still
    A lover of the meadows and the woods,
    And mountains; and of all that we behold
    From this green earth; of all the mighty world
    Of eye, and ear – both what they half create,
    And what perceive; well pleased to recognize
    In nature and the language of the sense
    The anchor of my purest thoughts, the nurse,
110 The guide, the guardian of my heart, and soul
    Of all my moral being.

                    Nor perchance,
    If I were not thus taught, should I the more
    Suffer my genial spirits⁴ to decay:
    For thou art with me here upon the banks
    Of this fair river; thou my dearest Friend,
    My dear, dear Friend;⁵ and in thy voice I catch
    The language of my former heart, and read
    My former pleasures in the shooting lights
    Of thy wild eyes. Oh! yet a little while
120 May I behold in thee what I was once,
    My dear, dear Sister! and this prayer I make,

Knowing that Nature never did betray
The heart that loved her; 'tis her privilege,
Through all the years of this our life, to lead
From joy to joy: for she can so inform
The mind that is within us, so impress
With quietness and beauty, and so feed
With lofty thoughts, that neither evil tongues,
Rash judgments, nor the sneers of selfish men,
130 Nor greetings where no kindness is, nor all
The dreary intercourse of daily life,
Shall e'er prevail against us, or disturb
Our cheerful faith, that all which we behold
Is full of blessings. Therefore let the moon
Shine on thee in thy solitary walk;
And let the misty mountain winds be free
To blow against thee: and, in after years,
When these wild ecstasies shall be matured
Into a sober pleasure;[6] when thy mind
140 Shall be a mansion for all lovely forms,
Thy memory be as a dwelling place
For all sweet sounds and harmonies; oh! then,
If solitude, or fear, or pain, or grief
Should be thy portion, with what healing thoughts
Of tender joy wilt thou remember me,
And these my exhortations! Nor, perchance –
If I should be where I no more can hear
Thy voice, nor catch from thy wild eyes these gleams
Of past existence – wilt thou then forget
150 That on the banks of this delightful stream
We stood together; and that I, so long
A worshipper of Nature, hither came
Unwearied in that service; rather say
With warmer love – oh! with far deeper zeal
Of holier love. Nor wilt thou then forget,
That after many wanderings, many years
Of absence, these steep woods and lofty cliffs,
And this green pastoral landscape, were to me
More dear, both for themselves and for thy sake!

1798 [1798]

The 'Lucy' poems[7]

Strange fits of passion have I known:
And I will dare to tell,
But in the Lover's ear alone,
What once to me befell.

When she I loved looked every day
Fresh as a rose in June,
I to her cottage bent my way,
Beneath an evening-moon.

Upon the moon I fixed my eye,
10 All over the wide lea;
With quickening pace my horse drew nigh
Those paths so dear to me.

And now we reached the orchard-plot;
And, as we climbed the hill,
The sinking moon to Lucy's cot
Came near, and nearer still.

In one of those sweet dreams I slept,
Kind Nature's gentlest boon!
And all the while my eyes I kept
20 On the descending moon.

My horse moved on; hoof after hoof
He raised, and never stopped:
When down behind the cottage roof,
At once, the bright moon dropped.

What fond and wayward thoughts will slide
Into a Lover's head!
'O mercy!' to myself I cried,
'If Lucy should be dead!'

1799 [1800]

She dwelt among the untrodden ways
    Beside the springs of Dove,[8]

A Maid whom there were none to praise
  And very few to love:

A violet by a mossy stone
  Half hidden from the eye!
Fair as a star, when only one
  Is shining in the sky.

She lived unknown, and few could know
10   When Lucy ceased to be;
But she is in her grave, and oh,
  The difference to me!

1799 [1800]

_____

Three years she grew in sun and shower;
Then Nature said, 'A lovelier flower
  On earth was never sown;
This child I to myself will take;
She shall be mine, and I will make
  A lady of my own.

Myself will to my darling be
Both law and impulse: and with me
  The girl, in rock and plain,
10 In earth and heaven, in glade and bower,
Shall feel an overseeing power
  To kindle or restrain.

She shall be sportive as the fawn
That wild with glee across the lawn
  Or up the mountain springs;
And hers shall be the breathing balm,
And hers the silence and the calm
  Of mute insensate things.

The floating clouds their state shall lend
20 To her; for her the willow bend;
  Nor shall she fail to see
Even in the motions of the storm
Grace that shall mould the maiden's form
  By silent sympathy.

The stars of midnight shall be dear
To her; and she shall lean her ear
   In many a secret place
Where rivulets dance their wayward round,
And beauty born of murmuring sound
30   Shall pass into her face.

And vital feelings of delight
Shall rear her form to stately height,
   Her virgin bosom swell;
Such thoughts to Lucy I will give
While she and I together live
   Here in this happy dell.'

Thus Nature spake – The work was done –
How soon my Lucy's race was run!
   She died, and left to me
40 This heath, this calm and quiet scene;
The memory of what has been,
   And never more will be.

                  1799 [1800]

A slumber did my spirit seal;
   I had no human fears:
She seemed a thing that could not feel
   The touch of earthly years.

No motion has she now, no force;
   She neither hears nor sees;
Rolled round in earth's diurnal° course,   *daily*
   With rocks, and stones, and trees.

                  1799 [1800]

I travelled among unknown men,
   In lands beyond the sea;
Nor, England! did I know till then
   What love I bore to thee.

'Tis past, that melancholy dream!
   Nor will I quit thy shore
A second time; for still I seem
   To love thee more and more.

Among thy mountains did I feel
10   The joy of my desire;
And she I cherished turned her wheel
   Beside an English fire.

Thy mornings showed, thy nights concealed,
   The bowers where Lucy played;
And thine too is the last green field
   That Lucy's eyes surveyed.

1801 [1807]

Michael

A PASTORAL POEM[9]

If from the public way you turn your steps
Up the tumultuous brook of Greenhead Ghyll,[10]
You will suppose that with an upright path
Your feet must struggle; in such bold ascent
The pastoral mountains front you, face to face.
But, courage! for around that boisterous brook
The mountains have all opened out themselves,
And made a hidden valley of their own.
No habitation can be seen; but they
10 Who journey thither find themselves alone
With a few sheep, with rocks and stones, and kites°   *(birds of hawk*
That overhead are sailing in the sky.   *family)*
It is in truth an utter solitude;
Nor should I have made mention of this Dell
But for one object which you might pass by,
Might see and notice not. Beside the brook
Appears a straggling heap of unhewn stones!
And to that simple object appertains
A story – unenriched with strange events,
20 Yet not unfit, I deem, for the fireside,

Or for the summer shade. It was the first
Of those domestic tales that spake to me
Of Shepherds, dwellers in the valleys, men
Whom I already loved; – not verily
For their own sakes, but for the fields and hills
Where was their occupation and abode.
And hence this Tale, while I was yet a Boy
Careless of books, yet having felt the power
Of Nature, by the gentle agency
30 Of natural objects, led me on to feel
For passions that were not my own, and think
(At random and imperfectly indeed)
On man, the heart of man, and human life.
Therefore, although it be a history
Homely and rude, I will relate the same
For the delight of a few natural hearts;
And, with yet fonder feeling, for the sake
Of youthful Poets, who among these hills
Will be my second self when I am gone.

40   Upon the forest-side in Grasmere Vale
There dwelt a Shepherd, Michael was his name;
An old man, stout of heart, and strong of limb.
His bodily frame had been from youth to age
Of an unusual strength: his mind was keen,
Intense, and frugal, apt for all affairs,
And in his shepherd's calling he was prompt
And watchful more than ordinary men.
Hence had he learned the meaning of all winds,
Of blasts of every tone; and oftentimes,
50 When others heeded not, he heard the South
Make subterraneous music, like the noise
Of bagpipers on distant Highland hills.
The Shepherd, at such warning, of his flock
Bethought him, and he to himself would say,
'The winds are now devising work for me!'
And, truly, at all times, the storm, that drives
The traveller to a shelter, summoned him
Up to the mountains: he had been alone
Amid the heart of many thousand mists,
60 That came to him, and left him, on the heights.
So lived he till his eightieth year was past.
And grossly that man errs, who should suppose
That the green valleys, and the streams and rocks,

Were things indifferent to the Shepherd's thoughts.
Fields, where with cheerful spirits he had breathed
The common air; hills, which with vigorous step
He had so often climbed; which had impressed
So many incidents upon his mind
Of hardship, skill or courage, joy or fear;
70 Which, like a book, preserved the memory
Of the dumb animals, whom he had saved,
Had fed or sheltered, linking to such acts
The certainty of honourable gain;
Those fields, those hills – what could they less? had laid
Strong hold on his affections, were to him
A pleasurable feeling of blind love,
The pleasure which there is in life itself.

His days had not been passed in singleness.
His Helpmate was a comely matron, old –
80 Though younger than himself full twenty years.
She was a woman of a stirring life,
Whose heart was in her house: two wheels she had
Of antique form; this large, for spinning wool;
That small, for flax; and, if one wheel had rest,
It was because the other was at work.
The Pair had but one inmate in their house,
An only Child, who had been born to them
When Michael, telling o'er his years, began
To deem that he was old, – in shepherd's phrase,
90 With one foot in the grave. This only Son,
With two brave sheep-dogs tried in many a storm,
The one of an inestimable worth,
Made all their household. I may truly say,
That they were as a proverb in the vale
For endless industry. When day was gone,
And from their occupations out of doors
The Son and Father were come home, even then,
Their labour did not cease; unless when all
Turned to the cleanly supper-board, and there,
100 Each with a mess of pottage° and skimmed milk,   *(kind of soup)*
Sat round the basket piled with oaten cakes,
And their plain home-made cheese. Yet when the meal
Was ended, Luke (for so the Son was named)
And his old Father both betook themselves
To such convenient work as might employ
Their hands by the fire-side; perhaps to card°   *comb out*

Wool for the Housewife's spindle, or repair
Some injury done to sickle, flail, or scythe,
Or other implement of house or field.
110   Down from the ceiling, by the chimney's edge,
That in our ancient uncouth country style
With huge and black projection overbrowed
Large space beneath, as duly as the light
Of day grew dim the Housewife hung a lamp;
An aged utensil, which had performed
Service beyond all others of its kind.
Early at evening did it burn – and late,
Surviving comrade of uncounted hours,
Which, going by from year to year, had found,
120   And left, the couple neither gay perhaps
Nor cheerful, yet with objects and with hopes,
Living a life of eager industry.
And now, when Luke had reached his eighteenth year,
There by the light of this old lamp they sate,
Father and Son, while far into the night
The Housewife plied her own peculiar work,
Making the cottage through the silent hours
Murmur as with the sound of summer flies.
This light was famous in its neighbourhood,
130   And was a public symbol of the life
That thrifty Pair had lived. For, as it chanced,
Their cottage on a plot of rising ground
Stood single, with large prospect, north and south,
High into Easedale, up to Dunmail-Raise,
And westward to the village near the lake;
And from this constant light, so regular,
And so far seen, the House itself, by all
Who dwelt within the limits of the vale,
Both old and young, was named THE EVENING STAR.

140   Thus living on through such a length of years,
The Shepherd, if he loved himself, must needs
Have loved his Helpmate; but to Michael's heart
This son of his old age was yet more dear –
Less from instinctive tenderness, the same
Fond spirit that blindly works in the blood of all –
Than that a child, more than all other gifts
That earth can offer to declining man,
Brings hope with it, and forward-looking thoughts,
And stirrings of inquietude, when they

150 By tendency of nature needs must fail.
Exceeding was the love he bare to him,
His heart and his heart's joy! For oftentimes
Old Michael, while he was a babe in arms,
Had done him female service, not alone
For pastime and delight, as is the use
Of fathers, but with patient mind enforced
To acts of tenderness; and he had rocked
His cradle, as with a woman's gentle hand.

        And in a later time, ere yet the Boy
160 Had put on boy's attire, did Michael love,
Albeit of a stern unbending mind,
To have the Young-one in his sight, when he
Wrought in the field, or on his shepherd's stool
Sate with a fettered sheep before him stretched
Under the large old oak, that near his door
Stood single, and, from matchless depth of shade,
Chosen for the Shearer's covert from the sun,
Thence in our rustic dialect was called
The CLIPPING° TREE, a name which yet it bears.   *shearing*
170 There, while they two were sitting in the shade,
With others round them, earnest all and blithe,
Would Michael exercise his heart with looks
Of fond correction and reproof bestowed
Upon the Child, if he disturbed the sheep
By catching at their legs, or with his shouts
Scared them, while they lay still beneath the shears.

        And when by Heaven's good grace the boy grew up
A healthy Lad, and carried in his cheek
Two steady roses that were five years old;
180 Then Michael from a winter coppice cut
With his own hand a sapling, which he hooped
With iron, making it throughout in all
Due requisites a perfect shepherd's staff,°   *crook*
And gave it to the Boy; wherewith equipt
He as a watchman oftentimes was placed
At gate or gap, to stem or turn the flock;
And, to his office prematurely called,
There stood the urchin, as you will divine,
Something between a hindrance and a help;
190 And for this cause not always, I believe,
Receiving from his Father hire of praise;

Though nought was left undone which staff, or voice,
Or looks, or threatening gestures, could perform.

    But soon as Luke, full ten years old, could stand
Against the mountain blasts; and to the heights,
Not fearing toil, nor length of weary ways,
He with his Father daily went, and they
Were as companions, why should I relate
That objects which the Shepherd loved before
200 Were dearer now? that from the Boy there came
Feelings and emanations – things which were
Light to the sun and music to the wind;
And that the old Man's heart seemed born again?

    Thus in his Father's sight the Boy grew up:
And now, when he had reached his eighteenth year,
He was his comfort and his daily hope.
    While in this sort the simple household lived
From day to day, to Michael's ear there came
Distressful tidings. Long before the time
210 Of which I speak, the Shepherd had been bound
In surety for his brother's son, a man
Of an industrious life, and ample means;
But unforeseen misfortunes suddenly
Had prest upon him; and old Michael now
Was summoned to discharge the forfeiture,
A grievous penalty, but little less
Than half his substance. This unlooked-for claim,
At the first hearing, for a moment took
More hope out of his life than he supposed
220 That any old man ever could have lost.
As soon as he had armed himself with strength
To look his trouble in the face, it seemed
The Shepherd's sole resource to sell at once
A portion of his patrimonial fields.
Such was his first resolve; he thought again,
And his heart failed him. 'Isabel,' said he,
Two evenings after he had heard the news,
'I have been toiling more than seventy years,
And in the open sunshine of God's love
230 Have we all lived; yet, if these fields of ours
Should pass into a stranger's hand, I think
That I could not lie quiet in my grave.
Our lot is a hard lot; the sun himself

Has scarcely been more diligent than I;
And I have lived to be a fool at last
To my own family. An evil man
That was, and made an evil choice, if he
Were false to us; and, if he were not false,
There are ten thousand to whom loss like this
240　Had been no sorrow. I forgive him; – but
'Twere better to be dumb than to talk thus.

    When I began, my purpose was to speak
Of remedies and of a cheerful hope.
Our Luke shall leave us, Isabel; the land
Shall not go from us, and it shall be free;
He shall possess it, free as is the wind
That passes over it. We have, thou know'st,
Another kinsman – he will be our friend
In this distress. He is a prosperous man,
250　Thriving in trade – and Luke to him shall go,
And with his kinsman's help and his own thrift
He quickly will repair this loss, and then
He may return to us. If here he stay,
What can be done? Where every one is poor,
What can be gained?' At this the old Man paused,
And Isabel sat silent, for her mind
Was busy, looking back into past times.
There's Richard Bateman,[11] thought she to herself
He was a parish boy – at the church-door
260　They made a gathering for him, shillings, pence,
And halfpennies, wherewith the neighbours bought
A basket, which they filled with pedlar's wares;
And, with this basket on his arm, the lad
Went up to London, found a master there,
Who, out of many, chose the trusty boy
To go and overlook his merchandise
Beyond the seas; where he grew wondrous rich,
And left estates and monies to the poor,
And, at his birth-place, built a chapel floored
270　With marble, which he sent from foreign lands.
These thoughts, and many others of like sort,
Passed quickly through the mind of Isabel,
And her face brightened. The old Man was glad,
And thus resumed:– 'Well, Isabel! this scheme
These two days has been meat and drink to me.
Far more than we have lost is left us yet.
    We have enough – I wish indeed that I

Were younger; – but this hope is a good hope.
Make ready Luke's best garments, of the best
280 Buy for him more, and let us send him forth
To-morrow, or the next day, or to-night:
If he *could* go, the Boy should go tonight.'

Here Michael ceased, and to the fields went forth
With a light heart. The Housewife for five days
Was restless morn and night, and all day long
Wrought on with her best fingers to prepare
Things needful for the journey of her son.
But Isabel was glad when Sunday came
To stop her in her work: for, when she lay
290 By Michael's side, she through the last two nights
Heard him, how he was troubled in his sleep:
And when they rose at morning she could see
That all his hopes were gone. That day at noon
She said to Luke, while they two by themselves
Were sitting at the door, 'Thou must not go:
We have no other Child but thee to lose,
None to remember – do not go away,
For if thou leave thy Father he will die.'
The Youth made answer with a jocund voice;
300 And Isabel, when she had told her fears,
Recovered heart. That evening her best fare
Did she bring forth, and all together sat
Like happy people round a Christmas fire.

With daylight Isabel resumed her work;
And all the ensuing week the house appeared
As cheerful as a grove in Spring: at length
The expected letter from their kinsman came,
With kind assurances that he would do
His utmost for the welfare of the Boy;
310 To which, requests were added, that forthwith
He might be sent to him. Ten times or more
The letter was read over; Isabel
Went forth to show it to the neighbours round;
Nor was there at that time on English land
A prouder heart than Luke's. When Isabel
Had to her house returned, the old Man said,
'He shall depart to-morrow.' To this word
The Housewife answered, talking much of things
Which, if at such short notice he should go,
320 Would surely be forgotten. But at length
She gave consent, and Michael was at ease.

Near the tumultuous brook of Greenhead Ghyll,
In that deep valley, Michael had designed
To build a Sheep-fold; and, before he heard
The tidings of his melancholy loss,
For this same purpose he had gathered up
A heap of stones, which by the streamlet's edge
Lay thrown together, ready for the work.
With Luke that evening thitherward he walked:
330 And soon as they had reached the place he stopped,
And thus the old Man spake to him:– 'My son,
To-morrow thou wilt leave me: with full heart
I look upon thee, for thou art the same
That wert a promise to me ere thy birth,
And all thy life hast been my daily joy.
I will relate to thee some little part
Or our two histories; 'twill do thee good
When thou art from me, even if I should touch
On things thou canst not know of. – After thou
340 First cam'st into the world – as oft befalls
To new-born infants – thou didst sleep away
Two days, and blessings from thy Father's tongue
Then fell upon thee. Day by day passed on,
And still I loved thee with increasing love.
Never to living ear came sweeter sounds
Than when I heard thee by our own fireside
First uttering, without words, a natural tune;
While thou, a feeding babe, didst in thy joy
Sing at thy Mother's breast. Month followed month,
350 And in the open fields my life was passed
And on the mountains; else I think that thou
Hadst been brought up upon thy Father's knees.
But we were playmates, Luke: among these hills,
As well thou knowest, in us the old and young
Have played together, nor with me didst thou
Lack any pleasure which a boy can know.'
Luke had a manly heart; but at these words
He sobbed aloud. The old Man grasped his hand,
And said, 'Nay, do not take it so – I see
360 That these are things of which I need not speak.
– Even to the utmost I have been to thee
A kind and a good Father: and herein
I but repay a gift which I myself
Received at others' hands; for, though now old
Beyond the common life of man, I still
Remember them who loved me in my youth.

Both of them sleep together: here they lived,
As all their Forefathers had done; and, when
At length their time was come, they were not loth
370   To give their bodies to the family mould.
I wished that thou shouldst live the life they lived,
But 'tis a long time to look back, my Son,
And see so little gain from threescore years.
These fields were burthened when they came to me;
Till I was forty years of age, not more
Than half of my inheritance was mine.
I toiled and toiled; God blessed me in my work,
And till these three weeks past the land was free.
– It looks as if it never could endure
380   Another Master. Heaven forgive me, Luke,
If I judge ill for thee, but it seems good
That thou shouldst go.' At this the old Man paused;
Then pointing to the stones near which they stood,
Thus, after a short silence, he resumed:
'This was a work for us; and now, my Son,
It is a work for me. But, lay one stone –
Here, lay it for me, Luke, with thine own hands.
Nay, Boy, be of good hope; – we both may live
To see a better day. At eighty-four
390   I still am strong and hale; – do thou thy part;
I will do mine – I will begin again
With many tasks that were resigned to thee:
Up to the heights, and in among the storms,
Will I without thee go again, and do
All works which I was wont to do alone,
Before I knew thy face. – Heaven bless thee, Boy!
Thy heart these two weeks has been beating fast
With many hopes; it should be so – yes – yes –
I knew that thou couldst never have a wish
400   To leave me, Luke: thou hast been bound to me
Only by links of love: when thou art gone,
What will be left to us! – But I forget
My purposes. Lay now the corner-stone,
As I requested; and hereafter, Luke,
When thou art gone away, should evil men
Be thy companions, think of me, my Son,
And of this moment; hither turn thy thoughts,
And God will strengthen thee: amid all fear
And all temptation, Luke, I pray that thou
410   May'st bear in mind the life thy Fathers lived,

Who, being innocent, did for that cause
Bestir them in good deeds. Now, fare thee well –
When thou return'st, thou in this place wilt see
A work which is not here: a covenant
'Twill be between us; but, whatever fate
Befall thee, I shall love thee to the last,
And bear thy memory with me to the grave.'

    The Shepherd ended here; and Luke stooped down,
And, as his Father had requested, laid
420 The first stone of the Sheep-fold. At the sight
The old Man's grief broke from him; to his heart
He pressed his Son, he kissèd him and wept;
And to the house together they returned.
– Hushed was that House in peace, or seeming peace,
Ere the night fell: – with morrow's dawn the Boy
Began his journey, and, when he had reached
The public way, he put on a bold face;
And all the neighbours, as he passed their doors,
Came forth with wishes and with farewell prayers
430 That followed him till he was out of sight.
    A good report did from their Kinsman come,
Of Luke and his well-doing: and the Boy
Wrote loving letters, full of wondrous news,
Which, as the Housewife phrased it, were throughout
'The prettiest letters that were ever seen.'
Both parents read them with rejoicing hearts.
So, many months passed on: and once again
The Shepherd went about his daily work
With confident and cheerful thoughts; and now
440 Sometimes when he could find a leisure hour
He to that valley took his way, and there
Wrought at the Sheep-fold. Meantime Luke began
To slacken in his duty; and, at length,
He in the dissolute city gave himself
To evil courses: ignominy and shame
Fell on him, so that he was driven at last
To seek a hiding-place beyond the seas.

    There is a comfort in the strength of love;
'Twill make a thing endurable, which else
450 Would overset the brain, or break the heart:
I have conversed with more than one who well
Remember the old Man, and what he was

Years after he had heard this heavy news.
His bodily frame had been from youth to age
Of an unusual strength. Among the rocks
He went, and still looked up to sun and cloud,
And listened to the wind; and, as before,
Performed all kinds of labour for his sheep,
And for the land, his small inheritance.
460   And to that hollow dell from time to time
Did he repair, to build the Fold of which
His flock had need. 'Tis not forgotten yet
The pity which was then in every heart
For the old Man – and 'tis believed by all
That many and many a day he thither went,
And never lifted up a single stone.[12]

There, by the Sheep-fold, sometimes was he seen
Sitting alone, or with his faithful Dog,
Then old, beside him, lying at his feet.
470   The length of full seven years, from time to time,
He at the building of this Sheep-fold wrought,
And left the work unfinished when he died.
Three years, or little more, did Isabel
Survive her Husband: at her death the estate
Was sold, and went into a stranger's hand.
The Cottage which was named the EVENING STAR
Is gone – the ploughshare has been through the ground
On which it stood; great changes have been wrought
In all the neighbourhood:– yet the oak is left
480   That grew beside their door; and the remains
Of the unfinished Sheep-fold may be seen
Beside the boisterous brook of Greenhead Ghyll.

1800 [1800]

Resolution and Independence[13]

There was a roaring in the wind all night;
The rain came heavily and fell in floods;
But now the sun is rising calm and bright;
The birds are singing in the distant woods;

Over his own sweet voice the stock-dove broods;[14]
The jay makes answer as the magpie chatters;
And all the air is filled with pleasant noise of waters.

All things that love the sun are out of doors;
  The sky rejoices in the morning's birth;
10 The grass is bright with rain-drops; – on the moors
  The hare is running races in her mirth;
  And with her feet she from the plashy earth
Raises a mist; that, glittering in the sun,
Runs with her all the way, wherever she doth run.

I was a Traveller then upon the moor;
  I saw the hare that raced about with joy;
  I heard the woods and distant waters roar;
  Or heard them not, as happy as a boy:
  The pleasant season did my heart employ:
20 My old remembrances went from me wholly;
And all the ways of men, so vain and melancholy.

But, as it sometimes chanceth, from the might
  Of joy in minds that can no further go,
  As high as we have mounted in delight
  In our dejection do we sink as low;
  To me that morning did it happen so;
And fears and fancies thick upon me came;
Dim sadness – and blind thoughts, I knew not, nor could name.

I heard the sky-lark warbling in the sky;
30 And I bethought me of the playful hare:
  Even such a happy Child of earth am I;
  Even as these blissful creatures do I fare;
  Far from the world I walk, and from all care;
  But there may come another day to me –
Solitude, pain of heart, distress, and poverty.

My whole life I have lived in pleasant thought,
  As if life's business were a summer mood;
  As if all needful things would come unsought
  To genial faith, still rich in genial good;
40 But how can he[15] expect that others should
Build for him, sow for him, and at his call
Love him, who for himself will take no heed at all?

I thought of Chatterton, the marvellous Boy,
The sleepless Soul that perished in his pride;
Of Him[16] who walked in glory and in joy
Following his plough, along the mountain-side:
By our own spirits are we deified:
We Poets in our youth begin in gladness;
50 But thereof come in the end despondency and madness.

Now, whether it were by peculiar grace,
A leading from above, a something given,
Yet it befell that, in this lonely place,
When I with these untoward thoughts had striven,
Beside a pool bare to the eye of heaven
I saw a Man before me unawares:
The oldest man he seemed that ever wore grey hairs.

As a huge stone is sometimes seen to lie
Couched on the bald top of an eminence;
60 Wonder to all who do the same espy,
By what means it could thither come, and whence;
So that it seems a thing endued with sense:
Like a sea-beast crawled forth, that on a shelf
Of rock or sand reposeth, there to sun itself;

Such seemed this Man, not all alive nor dead,
Nor all asleep – in his extreme old age:
His body was bent double, feet and head
Coming together in life's pilgrimage;
As if some dire constraint of pain, or rage
70 Of sickness felt by him in times long past,
A more than human weight upon his frame had cast.

Himself he propped, limbs, body, and pale face,
Upon a long grey staff of shaven wood:
And, still as I drew near with gentle pace,
Upon the margin of that moorish flood
Motionless as a cloud the old Man stood,
That heareth not the loud winds when they call;
And moveth all together, if it move at all.

At length, himself unsettling, he the pond
80 Stirred with his staff, and fixedly did look
Upon the muddy water, which he conned,

As if he had been reading in a book:
And now a stranger's privilege I took;
And, drawing to his side, to him did say,
'This morning gives us promise of a glorious day'.

A gentle answer did the old Man make,
In courteous speech which forth he slowly drew:
And him with further words I thus bespake,
'What occupation do you there pursue?
90 This is a lonesome place for one like you.'
Ere he replied, a flash of mild surprise
Broke from the sable orbs of his yet-vivid eyes.

His words came feebly, from a feeble chest,
But each in solemn order followed each,
With something of a lofty utterance drest –
Choice word and measured phrase, above the reach
Of ordinary men; a stately speech;
Such as grave Livers do in Scotland use,
Religious men, who give to God and man their dues.

100 He told, that to these waters he had come
To gather leeches,[17] being old and poor:
Employment hazardous and wearisome!
And he had many hardships to endure:
From pond to pond he roamed, from moor to moor;
Housing, with God's good help, by choice or chance;
And in this way he gained an honest maintenance.

The old Man still stood talking by my side;
But now his voice to me was like a stream
Scarce heard; nor word from word could I divide;
110 And the whole body of the Man did seem
Like one whom I had met with in a dream;
Or like a man from some far region sent,
To give me human strength, by apt admonishment.

My former thoughts returned: the fear that kills;
And hope that is unwilling to be fed;
Cold, pain, and labour, and all fleshly ills;
And mighty Poets in their misery dead.
– Perplexed, and longing to be comforted,
My question eagerly did I renew,
120 'How is it that you live, and what is it you do?'

He with a smile did then his words repeat;
And said that, gathering leeches, far and wide
He travelled; stirring thus about his feet
The waters of the pools where they abide.
'Once I could meet with them on every side;
But they have dwindled long by slow decay;
Yet still I persevere, and find them where I may.'

While he was talking thus, the lonely place,
The old Man's shape, and speech – all troubled me:
130 In my mind's eye I seemed to see him pace
About the weary moors continually,
Wandering about alone and silently.
While I these thoughts within myself pursued,
He, having made a pause, the same discourse renewed.

And soon with this he other matter blended,
Cheerfully uttered, with demeanour kind,
But stately in the main; and when he ended,
I could have laughed myself to scorn to find
In that decrepit Man so firm a mind.
140 'God,' said I, 'be my help and stay secure;
I'll think of the Leech-gatherer on the lonely moor!'

1802 [1807]

My Heart Leaps Up

My heart leaps up when I behold
      A rainbow in the sky:
So was it when my life began;
So is it now I am a man;
So be it when I shall grow old,
      Or let me die!
The Child is father of the Man;
And I could wish my days to be
Bound each to each by natural piety.

1802 [1807]

Sonnets

COMPOSED UPON WESTMINSTER BRIDGE, SEPTEMBER 3, 1802[18]

Earth has not anything to show more fair:
   Dull would he be of soul who could pass by
   A sight so touching in its majesty:
This City now doth, like a garment, wear
The beauty of the morning; silent, bare,
   Ships, towers, domes, theatres, and temples lie
   Open unto the fields, and to the sky;
All bright and glittering in the smokeless air.
Never did sun more beautifully steep
   In his first splendour, valley, rock, or hill;
Ne'er saw I, never felt, a calm so deep!
   The river glideth at his own sweet will:
Dear God! the very houses seem asleep;
   And all that mighty heart is lying still!

1802 [1807]

It is a beauteous evening, calm and free,[19]
The holy time is quiet as a Nun
Breathless with adoration; the broad sun
Is sinking down in its tranquillity;
The gentleness of heaven broods o'er the Sea:
Listen! the mighty Being is awake,
And doth with his eternal motion make
A sound like thunder – everlastingly.
Dear Child![20] dear Girl! that walkest with me here,
If thou appear untouched by solemn thought,
Thy nature is not therefore less divine:
Thou liest in Abraham's bosom all the year;[21]
And worshipp'st at the Temple's inner shrine,
God being with thee when we know it not.

1802 [1807]

The world is too much with us; late and soon,
Getting and spending, we lay waste our powers;
Little we see in Nature that is ours;
We have given our hearts away, a sordid boon!°   *gift*
This Sea that bares her bosom to the moon,
The winds that will be howling at all hours,

And are up-gathered now like sleeping flowers,
For this, for everything, we are out of tune;
It moves us not. – Great God! I'd rather be
A Pagan suckled in a creed outworn;
So might I, standing on this pleasant lea,
Have glimpses that would make me less forlorn;
Have sight of Proteus rising from the sea;
Or hear old Triton blow his wreathéd horn.

1802–4 [1807]

I Wandered Lonely as a Cloud[22]

I wandered lonely as a cloud
That floats on high o'er vales and hills,
When all at once I saw a crowd,
A host, of golden daffodils;
Beside the lake, beneath the trees,
Fluttering and dancing in the breeze.

Continuous as the stars that shine
And twinkle on the Milky Way,
They stretched in never-ending line
10 Along the margin of a bay:
Ten thousand saw I at a glance,
Tossing their heads in sprightly dance.

The waves beside them danced, but they
Out-did the sparkling waves in glee:
A poet could not but be gay,
In such a jocund° company: merry
I gazed – and gazed – but little thought
What wealth the show to me had brought:

For oft, when on my couch I lie
20 In vacant or in pensive mood,
They flash upon that inward eye
Which is the bliss of solitude;
And then my heart with pleasure fills,
And dances with the daffodils.

1804 [1807]

The Solitary Reaper²³

Behold her, single in the field,
Yon solitary Highland Lass!
Reaping and singing by herself;
Stop here, or gently pass!
Alone she cuts and binds the grain,
And sings a melancholy strain;
O listen! for the vale profound
Is overflowing with the sound.

No nightingale did ever chaunt
10 More welcome notes to weary bands
Of travellers in some shady haunt,
Among Arabian sands:
A voice so thrilling ne'er was heard
In spring-time from the cuckoo-bird,
Breaking the silence of the seas
Among the farthest Hebrides.

Will no one tell me what she sings? –
Perhaps the plaintive numbers flow
For old, unhappy, far-off things,
20 And battles long ago:
Or is it some more humble lay,
Familiar matter of to-day?
Some natural sorrow, loss, or pain,
That has been, and may be again?

Whate'er the theme, the maiden sang
As if her song could have no ending;
I saw her singing at her work,
And o'er the sickle bending; –
I listened, motionless and still;
30 And, as I mounted up the hill,
The music in my heart I bore,
Long after it was heard no more.

1805 [1807]

Ode

Intimations of Immortality from Recollections of Early Childhood[24]

> The Child is Father of the Man;
> And I could wish my days to be
> Bound each to each by natural piety.[25]

I

There was a time when meadow, grove, and stream,
    The earth, and every common° sight,   *everyday*
        To me did seem
    Apparelled in celestial light,
The glory and the freshness of a dream.
It is not now as it hath been of yore; –
        Turn wheresoe'er I may,
          By night or day,
The things which I have seen I now can see no more.

II

10   The rainbow comes and goes,
        And lovely is the rose;
        The moon doth with delight
    Look round her when the heavens are bare;
        Waters on a starry night
        Are beautiful and fair;
    The sunshine is a glorious birth;
    But yet I know, where'er I go,
That there hath passed away a glory from the earth.

III

Now, while the birds thus sing a joyous song,
20   And while the young lambs bound
        As to the tabor's° sound,   *small drum*
To me alone there came a thought of grief:
A timely utterance[26] gave that thought relief,
        And I again am strong:
The cataracts blow their trumpets from the steep;

No more shall grief of mine the season wrong;
I hear the echoes through the mountains throng,
The winds come to me from the fields of sleep,
      And all the earth is gay;
30   Land and sea
      Give themselves up to jollity,
        And with the heart of May
      Doth every beast keep holiday; –
         Thou Child of Joy,
Shout round me, let me hear thy shouts, thou happy
                       Shepherd-boy!

              IV
Ye blessed Creatures, I have heard the call
      Ye to each other make; I see
The heavens laugh with you in your jubilee;
40   My heart is at your festival,
      My head hath its coronal,°   *garland*
The fullness of your bliss, I feel – I feel it all.
        O evil day! if I were sullen
        While Earth herself is adorning,
          This sweet May-morning,
        And the children are culling
          On every side,
      In a thousand valleys far and wide,
      Fresh flowers; while the sun shines warm,
50 And the Babe leaps up on his Mother's arm: –
        I hear, I hear, with joy I hear!
        – But there's a tree, of many, one,
A single field which I have looked upon,
Both of them speak of something that is gone:
         The pansy at my feet
         Doth the same tale repeat:
Whither is fled the visionary gleam?
Where is it now, the glory and the dream?

              V
Our birth is but a sleep and a forgetting:
The Soul that rises with us, our life's Star,
      Hath had elsewhere its setting,
        And cometh from afar:
      Not in entire forgetfulness,

And not in utter nakedness,
But trailing clouds of glory do we come
From God, who is our home:
Heaven lies about us in our infancy!
Shades of the prison-house begin to close
Upon the growing Boy,
70 But He beholds the light, and whence it flows,
He sees it in his joy;
The Youth, who daily farther from the east
Must travel, still is Nature's priest,
And by the vision splendid
Is on his way attended;
At length the Man perceives it die away,
And fade into the light of common day.

VI

Earth fills her lap with pleasures of her own;
Yearnings she hath in her own natural kind;
And, even with something of a Mother's mind,
And no unworthy aim,
The homely° Nurse doth all she can   *at-home-with*
To make her foster-child, her inmate Man,
Forget the glories he hath known,
And that imperial palace whence he came.

VII

Behold the Child[27] among his new-born blisses,
A six years' darling of a pigmy size!
See, where 'mid work of his own hand he lies,
Fretted° by sallies of his mother's kisses,   *bothered*
90 With light upon him from his father's eyes!
See, at his feet, some little plan or chart,
Some fragment from his dream of human life,
Shaped by himself with newly-learnèd art;
A wedding or a festival,
A mourning or a funeral;
And this hath now his heart,
And unto this he frames his song:
Then will he fit his tongue
To dialogues of business, love, or strife;
100 But it will not be long
Ere this be thrown aside,

And with new joy and pride
The little actor cons another part;
Filling from time to time his 'humorous stage'[28]
With all the Persons, down to palsied Age,
That Life brings with her in her equipage;
      As if his whole vocation
      Were endless imitation.

VIII

  Thou, whose exterior semblance doth belie
110   Thy soul's immensity;
Thou best Philosopher, who yet dost keep
Thy heritage, thou eye among the blind,
That, deaf and silent, read'st the eternal deep,
Haunted for ever by the eternal mind, –
      Mighty Prophet! Seer blest!
      On whom those truths do rest,
Which we are toiling all our lives to find,
In darkness lost, the darkness of the grave;
Thou, over whom thy Immortality
120 Broods like the day, a master o'er a slave,
A Presence which is not to be put by;[29]
Thou little Child, yet glorious in the might
Of heaven-born freedom on thy being's height,
Why with such earnest pains dost thou provoke
The years to bring the inevitable yoke,
Thus blindly with thy blessedness at strife?
Full soon thy soul shall have her earthly freight,
And custom lie upon thee with a weight,
Heavy as frost, and deep almost as life!

IX

130   O joy! that in our embers
      Is something that doth live,
      That nature yet remembers
      What was so fugitive!
The thought of our past years in me doth breed
Perpetual benediction: not indeed
For that which is most worthy to be blest –
Delight and liberty, the simple creed
Of childhood, whether busy or at rest,
With new-fledged hope still fluttering in his breast:–

140   Not for these I raise
           The song of thanks and praise;
       But for those obstinate questionings
       Of sense and outward things,
       Fallings from us, vanishings;
       Blank misgivings of a Creature
   Moving about in worlds not realized,
   High instincts before which our mortal Nature
   Did tremble like a guilty thing surprised:[30]
           But for those first affections,
150   Those shadowy recollections,
       Which, be they what they may,
   Are yet the fountain-light of all our day,
   Are yet a master-light of all our seeing;
       Uphold us, cherish, and have power to make
   Our noisy years seem moments in the being
   Of the eternal Silence: truths that wake,
               To perish never:
   Which neither listlessness, nor mad endeavour,
           Nor Man nor Boy,
160 Nor all that is at enmity with joy,
   Can utterly abolish or destroy!
       Hence in a season of calm weather
           Though inland far we be,
   Our souls have sight of that immortal sea
           Which brought us hither,
       Can in a moment travel thither,
   And see the children sport upon the shore,
   And hear the mighty waters rolling evermore.

                        X
   Then sing, ye birds, sing, sing a joyous song!
170   And let the young lambs bound
           As to the tabor's sound!
   We in thought will join your throng,
       Ye that pipe and ye that play,
       Ye that through your hearts to-day
       Feel the gladness of the May!
   What though the radiance which was once so bright
   Be now for ever taken from my sight,
       Though nothing can bring back the hour
   Of splendour in the grass, of glory in the flower;
180   We will grieve not, rather find

Strength in what remains behind;
In the primal sympathy
Which having been must ever be;
In the soothing thoughts that spring
Out of human suffering;
In the faith that looks through death,
In years that bring the philosophic mind.

XI

And O ye Fountains, Meadows, Hills, and Groves,
Forbode not any severing of our loves!
190 Yet in my heart of hearts I feel your might;
I only have relinquished one delight
To live beneath your more habitual sway.
I love the brooks which down their channels fret,
Even more than when I tripped lightly as they;
The innocent brightness of a new-born Day
        Is lovely yet;
The clouds that gather round the setting sun
Do take a sober colouring from an eye
That hath kept watch o'er man's mortality;
200 Another race hath been, and other palms° are won.   *victory tokens*
Thanks to the human heart by which we live,
Thanks to its tenderness, its joys, and fears,
To me the meanest° flower that blows° can give *most inconspicuous/blooms*
Thoughts that do often lie too deep for tears.

1803–6 [1807]

Ode to Duty

Jam non consilio bonus, sed more eo perductus, ut non tantum recte facere possim, sed nisi recte facere non possim.

SENECA[31]

Stern Daughter of the Voice of God![32]
O Duty! if that name thou love
Who are a light to guide, a rod
To check the erring, and reprove;
Thou, who art victory and law
When empty terrors overawe;
From vain temptations dost set free;
And calm'st the weary strife of frail humanity!

There are who ask not if thine eye
10 Be on them; who, in love and truth,
Where no misgiving is, rely
Upon the genial° sense of youth: *enlivening*
Glad Hearts! without reproach or blot;
Who do thy work, and know it not:
Oh! if through confidence misplaced
They fail, thy saving arms, dread Power! around them cast.

Serene will be our days and bright,
And happy will our nature be,
When love is an unerring light,
20 And joy its own security.
And they a blissful course may hold
Even now, who, not unwisely bold,
Live in the spirit of this creed;
Yet seek thy firm support, according to their need.

I, loving freedom, and untried,
No sport of every random gust,
Yet being to myself a guide,
Too blindly have reposed my trust;
And oft, when in my heart was heard
30 Thy timely mandate, I deferred
The task, in smoother walks to stray;
But thee I now would serve more strictly, if I may.

Through no disturbance of my soul,
Or strong compunction in me wrought,
I supplicate for thy control;
But in the quietness of thought:
Me this unchartered freedom tires;
I feel the weight of chance desires:
My hopes no more must change their name,
40 I long for a repose that ever is the same.

Stern Lawgiver! yet thou dost wear
The Godhead's most benignant grace;
Nor know we anything so fair
As is the smile upon thy face:
Flowers laugh before thee on their beds
And fragrance in thy footing treads;
Thou dost preserve the stars from wrong
And the most ancient heavens, through thee, are fresh and strong.

To humbler functions, awful Power!
50 I call thee: I myself commend
Unto thy guidance from this hour;
Oh, let my weakness have an end!
Give unto me, made lowly wise,
The spirit of self-sacrifice;
The confidence of reason[33] give;
And in the light of truth thy Bondman let me live!

1805 [1807]

The Prelude[34]

Book I

INTRODUCTION – CHILDHOOD AND SCHOOLTIME

O there is blessing in this gentle breeze,
A visitant that while it fans my cheek
Doth seem half-conscious of the joy it brings
From the green fields, and from yon azure sky.
Whate'er its mission, the soft breeze can come
To none more grateful than to me; escaped
From the vast city,° where I long had pined   *(London)*
A discontented sojourner: now free,
Free as a bird to settle where I will.
10 What dwelling shall receive me? in what vale
Shall be my harbour? underneath what grove
Shall I take up my home? and what clear stream
Shall with its murmur lull me into rest?
The earth is all before me.[35] With a heart
Joyous, nor scared at its own liberty,
I look about; and should the chosen guide
Be nothing better than a wandering cloud,
I cannot miss my way. I breathe again!
Trances of thought and mountings of the mind
20 Come fast upon me: it is shaken off,
That burthen of my own unnatural self,
The heavy weight of many a weary day
Not mine, and such as were not made for me.
Long months of peace (if such bold word accord
With any promises of human life),
Long months of ease and undisturbed delight
Are mine in prospect; whither shall I turn,
By road or pathway, or through trackless field,
Up hill or down, or shall some floating thing
30 Upon the river point me out my course?

　　Dear Liberty! Yet what would it avail
But for a gift that consecrates the joy?
For I, methought, while the sweet breath of heaven
Was blowing on my body, felt within
A correspondent breeze, that gently moved
With quickening virtue, but is now become

A tempest, a redundant energy,
Vexing its own creation. Thanks to both,
And their congenial powers, that, while they join
40 In breaking up a long-continued frost,
Bring with them vernal promises, the hope
Of active days urged on by flying hours, –
Days of sweet leisure, taxed with patient thought
Abstruse, nor wanting punctual service high,
Matins and vespers of harmonious verse![36]

Thus far, O Friend![37] did I, not used to make
A present joy the matter of a song,
Pour forth that day my soul in measured strains
That would not be forgotten, and are here
50 Recorded: to the open fields I told
A prophecy: poetic numbers came
Spontaneously to clothe in priestly robe
A renovated spirit singled out,
Such hope was mine, for holy services.
My own voice cheered me, and, far more, the mind's
Internal echo of the imperfect sound;
To both I listened, drawing from them both
A cheerful confidence in things to come.

Content and not unwilling now to give[38]
60 A respite to this passion, I paced on
With brisk and eager steps; and came, at length,
To a green shady place, where down I sate
Beneath a tree, slackening my thoughts by choice,
And settling into gentler happiness.
'Twas autumn, and a clear and placid day,
With warmth, as much as needed, from a sun
Two hours declined towards the west; a day
With silver clouds, and sunshine on the grass,
And in the sheltered and the sheltering grove
70 A perfect stillness. Many were the thoughts
Encouraged and dismissed, till choice was made
Of a known Vale,[39] whither my feet should turn,
Nor rest till they had reached the very door
Of the one cottage which methought I saw.
No picture of mere memory ever looked
So fair; and while upon the fancied scene
I gazed with growing love, a higher power
Than fancy gave assurance of some work

Of glory there forthwith to be begun,
80 Perhaps too there performed. Thus long I mused,
Nor e'er lost sight of what I mused upon,
Save when, amid the stately grove of oaks,
Now here, now there, an acorn, from its cup
Dislodged, through sere leaves rustled, or at once
To the bare earth dropped with a startling sound.
From that soft couch I rose not, till the sun
Had almost touched the horizon; casting then
A backward glance upon the curling cloud
Of city smoke, by distance ruralised;
90 Keen as a truant or a fugitive,
But as a pilgrim resolute, I took,
Even with the chance equipment of that hour,
The road that pointed toward the chosen Vale.
It was a splendid evening, and my soul
Once more made trial of her strength, nor lacked
Æolian[40] visitations; but the harp
Was soon defrauded, and the banded host
Of harmony dispersed in straggling sounds,
And lastly utter silence! 'Be it so;
100 Why think of any thing but present good?'
So, like a home-bound labourer I pursued
My way beneath the mellowing sun, that shed
Mild influence; nor left in me one wish
Again to bend the Sabbath of that time
To a servile yoke. What need of many words?
A pleasant loitering journey, through three days
Continued, brought me to my hermitage.
I spare to tell of what ensued, the life
In common things – the endless store of things,
110 Rare, or at least so seeming, every day
Found all about me in one neighbourhood –
The self-congratulation, and, from morn
To night, unbroken cheerfulness serene.
But speedily an earnest longing rose
To brace myself to some determined aim,
Reading or thinking; either to lay up
New stores, or rescue from decay the old
By timely interference: and therewith
Came hopes still higher, that with outward life
120 I might endue some airy phantasies
That had been floating loose about for years,
And to such beings temperately deal forth

The many feelings that oppressed my heart.
That hope hath been discouraged; welcome light
Dawns from the east, but dawns to disappear
And mock me with a sky that ripens not
Into a steady morning: if my mind,
Remembering the bold promise of the past,
Would gladly grapple with some noble theme,
130 Vain is her wish; where'er she turns she finds
Impediments from day to day renewed.

    And now it would content me to yield up
Those lofty hopes awhile, for present gifts
Of humbler industry. But, oh, dear Friend!
The poet, gentle creature as he is,
Hath, like the lover, his unruly times;
His fits when he is neither sick nor well,
Though no distress be near him but his own
Unmanageable thoughts: his mind, best pleased
140 While she as duteous as the mother dove
Sits brooding, lives not always to that end,
But like the innocent bird, hath goadings on
That drive her as in trouble through the groves;
With me is now such passion, to be blamed
No otherwise than as it lasts too long.

    When, as becomes a man who would prepare
For such an arduous work, I through myself
Make rigorous inquisition, the report
Is often cheering; for I neither seem
150 To lack that first great gift, the vital soul,[41]
Nor general truths, which are themselves a sort
Of elements and agents, under-powers,
Subordinate helpers of the living mind:
Nor am I naked of external things,
Forms, images, nor numerous other aids[42]
Of less regard, though won perhaps with toil
And needful to build up a poet's praise.
Time, place, and manners do I seek, and these
Are found in plenteous store, but nowhere such
160 As may be singled out with steady choice;
No little band of yet remembered names[43]
Whom I, in perfect confidence, might hope
To summon back from lonesome banishment,
And make them dwellers in the hearts of men
Now living, or to live in future years.

Sometimes the ambitious power of choice, mistaking
Proud spring-tide swellings for a regular sea,
Will settle on some British theme,[44] some old
Romantic tale by Milton left unsung;
170 More often turning to some gentle place
Within the groves of chivalry, I pipe
To shepherd swains, or seated harp in hand,
Amid reposing knights by a river side
Or fountain, listen to the grave reports
Of dire enchantments faced and overcome
By strong mind, and tales of warlike feats,
Where spear encountered spear, and sword with sword
Fought, as if conscious of the blazonry
That the shield bore, so glorious was the strife;
180 Whence inspiration for a song that winds
Through ever changing scenes of votive quest
Wrongs to redress, harmonious tribute paid
To patient courage and unblemished truth,
To firm devotion, zeal unquenchable,
And Christian meekness hallowing faithful loves.[45]
Sometimes, more sternly moved, I would relate
How vanquished Mithridates northward passed,
And, hidden in the cloud of years, became
Odin, the father of a race by whom
190 Perished the Roman Empire: how the friends
And followers of Sertorius, out of Spain
Flying, found shelter in the Fortunate Isles,
And left their usages, their arts and laws,
To disappear by a slow gradual death,
To dwindle and to perish one by one,
Starved in those narrow bounds: but not the soul
Of liberty, which fifteen hundred years
Survived, and, when the European came
With skill and power that might not be withstood,
200 Did, like a pestilence, maintain its hold
And wasted down by glorious death that race
Of natural heroes: or I would record
How, in tyrannic times, some high-souled man,
Unnamed among the chronicles of kings,
Suffered in silence for truth's sake: or tell,
How that one Frenchman,[46] through continued force
Of meditation on the inhuman deeds
Of those who conquered first the Indian Isles,
Went single in his ministry across
210 The ocean; not to comfort the oppressed,

But, like a thirsty wind, to roam about
Withering the oppressor: how Gustavus sought
Help at his need in Dalecarlia's mines:
How Wallace fought for Scotland; left the name
Of Wallace to be found, like a wild flower,
All over his dear country; left the deeds
Of Wallace, like a family of ghosts,
To people the steep rocks and river banks,
Her natural sanctuaries, with a local soul
220 Of independence and stern liberty.
Sometimes it suits me better to invent
A tale from my own heart, more near akin
To my own passions and habitual thoughts;
Some variegated story, in the main
Lofty, but the unsubstantial structure melts
Before the very sun that brightens it,
Mist into air dissolving! Then a wish,
My best and favourite aspiration, mounts
With yearning toward some philosophic song
230 Of truth that cherishes our daily life;
With meditations passionate from deep
Recesses in man's heart, immortal verse
Thoughtfully fitted to the Orphean° lyre;   *of Orpheus*
But from this awful burthen I full soon
Take refuge and beguile myself with trust
That mellower years will bring a riper mind
And clearer insight. Thus my days are past
In contradiction; with no skill to part
Vague longing, haply bred by want of power,
240 From paramount impulse not to be withstood,
A timorous capacity from prudence,
From circumspection, infinite delay.
Humility and modest awe themselves
Betray me, serving often for a cloak
To a more subtle selfishness; that now
Locks every function up in blank reserve,
Now dupes me, trusting to an anxious eye
That with intrusive restlessness beats off
Simplicity and self-presented truth.
250 Ah! better far than this, to stray about
Voluptuously through fields and rural walks,
And ask no record of the hours, resigned
To vacant musing, unreproved neglect
Of all things, and deliberate holiday.

Far better never to have heard the name
Of zeal and just ambition, than to live
Baffled and plagued by a mind that every hour
Turns recreant to her task; takes heart again,
Then feels immediately some hollow thought
260 Hang like an interdict upon her hopes.
This is my lot; for either still I find
Some imperfection in the chosen theme,
Or see of absolute accomplishment
Much wanting, so much wanting, in myself,
That I recoil and droop, and seek repose
In listlessness from vain perplexity,
Unprofitably travelling toward the grave,
Like a false steward who hath much received
And renders nothing back.
             Was it for this
270 That one, the fairest of all rivers, loved
To blend his murmurs with my nurse's song,
And, from his alder shades and rocky falls,
And from his fords and shallows, sent a voice
That flowed along my dreams? For this, didst thou,
O Derwent! winding among grassy holms°   *river banks*
Where I was looking on, a babe in arms,[47]
Make ceaseless music that composed my thoughts
To more than infant softness, giving me
Amid the fretful dwellings of mankind
280 A foretaste, a dim earnest, of the calm
That nature breathes among the hills and groves.

When he had left the mountains and received
On his smooth breast the shadow of those towers°   *(Cockermouth Castle)*
That yet survive, a shattered monument
Of feudal sway, the bright blue river passed
Along the margin of our terrace walk;
A tempting playmate whom we dearly loved.
Oh, many a time have I, a five years' child,
In a small mill-race severed from his stream,
290 Made one long bathing of a summer's day;
Basked in the sun, and plunged and basked again
Alternate, all a summer's day, or scoured
The sandy fields, leaping through flowery groves
Of yellow ragwort; or when rock and hill,
The woods, and distant Skiddaw's lofty height,
Were bronzed with deepest radiance, stood alone
Beneath the sky, as if I had been born

On Indian plains, and from my mother's hut
Had run abroad in wantonness, to sport
300 A naked savage, in the thunder shower.

    Fair seed-time had my soul, and I grew up
Fostered alike by beauty and by fear:
Much favoured in my birth-place, and no less
In that beloved Vale° to which erelong   *Esthwaite Water, Cumbria*
We were transplanted – there were we let loose
For sports of wider range. Ere I had told
Ten birth-days, when among the mountain slopes
Frost, and the breath of frosty wind, had snapped
The last autumnal crocus, 'twas my joy
310 With store of springes° o'er my shoulder hung   *snares*
To range the open heights where woodcocks run
Along the smooth green turf. Through half the night,
Scudding° away from snare to snare, I plied   *racing*
That anxious visitation; – moon and stars
Were shining o'er my head. I was alone,
And seemed to be a trouble to the peace
That dwelt among them. Sometimes it befell
In these night wanderings, that a strong desire
O'erpowered my better reason, and the bird
320 Which was the captive of another's toil
Became my prey; and when the deed was done
I heard among the solitary hills
Low breathings coming after me, and sounds
Of undistinguishable motion, steps
Almost as silent as the turf they trod.

    Nor less when spring had warmed the cultured° Vale,   *cultivated*
Roved we as plunderers where the mother-bird
Had in high places built her lodge; though mean
Our object° and inglorious, yet the end   *(collecting birds' eggs)*
330 Was not ignoble. Oh! when I have hung
Above the raven's nest, by knots of grass
And half-inch fissures in the slippery rock
But ill sustained, and almost (so it seemed)
Suspended by the blast that blew amain,
Shouldering the naked crag, oh, at that time
While on the perilous ridge I hung alone,
With what strange utterance did the loud dry wind
Blow through my ear! the sky seemed not a sky
Of earth – and with what motion moved the clouds!

340   Dust as we are, the immortal spirit grows
       Like harmony in music; there is a dark
       Inscrutable workmanship that reconciles
       Discordant elements, makes them cling together
       In one society. How strange that all
       The terrors, pains, and early miseries,
       Regrets, vexations, lassitudes interfused
       Within my mind, should e'er have borne a part,
       And that a needful part, in making up
       The calm existence that is mine when I
350   Am worthy of myself! Praise to the end!
       Thanks to the means which Nature deigned to employ;
       Whether her fearless visitings, or those
       That came with soft alarm, like hurtless light
       Opening the peaceful clouds; or she may use
       Severer interventions, ministry
       More palpable, as best might suit her aim.

           One summer evening (led by her) I found
       A little boat tied to a willow tree
       Within a rocky cave, its usual home.
360   Straight I unloosed her chain, and stepping in
       Pushed from the shore. It was an act of stealth
       And troubled pleasure, nor without the voice
       Of mountain-echoes did my boat move on;
       Leaving behind her still, on either side,
       Small circles glittering idly in the moon,
       Until they melted all into one track
       Of sparkling light. But now, like one who rows,
       Proud of his skill, to reach a chosen point
       With an unswerving line, I fixed my view
370   Upon the summit of a craggy ridge,
       The horizon's utmost boundary; for above
       Was nothing but the stars and the grey sky.
       She was an elfin pinnace; lustily
       I dipped my oars into the silent lake,
       And, as I rose upon the stroke, my boat
       Went heaving through the water like a swan;
       When, from behind that craggy steep till then
       The horizon's bound, a huge peak, black and huge,
       As if with voluntary power instinct
380   Upreared its head. I struck and struck again,
       And growing still in stature the grim shape
       Towered up between me and the stars, and still,

For so it seemed, with purpose of its own
And measured motion like a living thing,
Strode after me. With trembling oars I turned,
And through the silent water stole my way
Back to the covert° of the willow tree;   *covering*
There in her mooring-place I left my bark, –
And through the meadows homeward went, in grave
390 And serious mood; but after I had seen
That spectacle, for many days, my brain
Worked with a dim and undetermined sense
Of unknown modes of being; o'er my thoughts
There hung a darkness, call it solitude
Or blank desertion. No familiar shapes
Remained, no pleasant images of trees,
Of sea or sky, no colours of green fields;
But huge and mighty forms, that do not live
Like living men, moved slowly through the mind
400 By day, and were a trouble to my dreams.

   Wisdom and Spirit of the universe!
Thou soul that art the eternity of thought.
That givest to forms and images a breath
And everlasting motion, not in vain
By day or star-light thus from my first dawn
Of childhood didst thou intertwine for me
The passions that build up our human soul;
Not with the mean and vulgar works of man,
But with high objects, with enduring things –
410 With life and nature – purifying thus
The elements of feeling and of thought,
And sanctifying, by such discipline,
Both pain and fear, until we recognise
A grandeur in the beatings of the heart.
Nor was this fellowship vouchsafed to me
With stinted° kindness. In November days,   *begrudged*
When vapours rolling down the valley made
A lonely scene more lonesome, among woods,
At noon and 'mid the calm of summer nights,
420 When, by the margin of the trembling lake,
Beneath the gloomy hills homeward I went
In solitude, such intercourse was mine;
Mine was it in the fields both day and night,
And by the waters, all the summer long.

And in the frosty season, when the sun
Was set, and visible for many a mile
The cottage windows blazed through twilight gloom,
I heeded not their summons: happy time
It was indeed for all of us – for me
430 It was a time of rapture! Clear and loud
The village clock tolled six, – I wheeled about,
Proud and exulting like an untired horse
That cares not for his home. All shod with steel,
We hissed along the polished ice in games
Confederate, imitative of the chase°   hunting
And woodland pleasures, – the resounding horn,
The pack loud chiming, and the hunted hare.
So through the darkness and the cold we flew,
And not a voice was idle; with the din
440 Smitten, the precipices rang aloud;
The leafless trees and every icy crag
Tinkled like iron; while far distant hills
Into the tumult sent an alien sound
Of melancholy not unnoticed, while the stars
Eastward were sparkling clear, and in the west
The orange sky of evening died away.
Not seldom from the uproar I retired
Into a silent bay, or sportively
Glanced sideway, leaving the tumultuous throng,
450 To cut across the reflex of a star
That fled, and, flying still before me, gleamed
Upon the glassy plain; and oftentimes,
When we had given our bodies to the wind,
And all the shadowy banks on either side
Came sweeping through the darkness, spinning still
The rapid line of motion, then at once
Have I, reclining back upon my heels,
Stopped short; yet still the solitary cliffs
Wheeled by me – even as if the earth had rolled
460 With visible motion her diurnal round!
Behind me did they stretch in solemn train,
Feebler and feebler, and I stood and watched
Till all was tranquil as a dreamless sleep.

Ye Presences of Nature in the sky
And on the earth! Ye visions of the hills!
And souls of lonely places! can I think
A vulgar hope was yours when ye employed

Such ministry, when ye through many a year
Haunting me thus among my boyish sports,
470 On caves and trees, upon the woods and hills,
Impressed upon all forms the characters
Of danger or desire; and thus did make
The surface of the universal earth
With triumph and delight, with hope and fear,
Work like a sea?
                          Not uselessly employed,
Might I pursue this theme through every change
Of exercise and play, to which the year
Did summon us in his delightful round.

We were a noisy crew; the sun in heaven
480 Beheld not vales more beautiful than ours;
Nor saw a band in happiness and joy
Richer, or worthier of the ground they trod.
I could record with no reluctant voice
The woods of autumn, and their hazel bowers
With milk-white clusters hung; the rod and line,
True symbol of hope's foolishness, whose strong
And unreproved enchantment led us on
By rocks and pools shut out from every star,
All the green summer, to forlorn cascades
490 Among the windings hid of mountain brooks.
– Unfading recollections! at this hour
The heart is almost mine with which I felt
From some hill-top on sunny afternoons,
The paper kite high among fleecy clouds
Pull at her rein like an impetuous courser;
Or, from the meadows sent on gusty days,
Beheld her breast the wind, then suddenly
Dashed headlong, and rejected by the storm.

Ye lowly cottages wherein we dwelt,
500 A ministration of your own was yours;
Can I forget you, being as you were
So beautiful among the pleasant fields
In which ye stood? or can I here forget
The plain and seemly countenance with which
Ye dealt out your plain comforts? Yet had ye
Delights and exultations of your own.
Eager and never weary we pursued
Our home-amusements by the warm peat-fire

At evening, when with pencil, and smooth slate
510 In square divisions parcelled out and all
With crosses and with cyphers° scribbled o'er,   *noughts and crosses*
We schemed and puzzled, head opposed to head
In strife too humble to be named in verse:
Or round the naked table, snow-white deal,°   *fir or pine wood*
Cherry or maple, sate in close array,
And to the combat, loo or whist,⁴⁸ led on
A thick-ribbed army; not, as in the world,
Neglected and ungratefully thrown by
Even for the very service they had wrought,
520 But husbanded through many a long campaign.
Uncouth assemblage was it, where no few
Had changed their functions; some, plebeian cards
Which Fate, beyond the promise of their birth,⁴⁹
Had dignified, and called to represent
The persons of departed potentates.
Oh, with what echoes on the board they fell!
Ironic diamonds, – clubs, hearts, diamonds, spades,
A congregation piteously akin!
Cheap matter offered they to boyish wit,
530 Those sooty knaves, precipitated down
With scoffs and taunts, like Vulcan out of heaven:
The paramount ace, a moon in her eclipse,
Queens gleaming through their splendour's last decay,
And monarchs surly at the wrongs sustained
By royal visages. Meanwhile abroad
Incessant rain was falling, or the frost
Raged bitterly, with keen and silent tooth;
And, interrupting oft that eager game
From under Esthwaite's splitting fields of ice
540 The pent-up air, struggling to free itself,
Gave out to meadow grounds and hills a loud
Protracted yelling, like the noise of wolves
Howling in troops along the Bothnic Main.°   *Baltic Sea*

    Nor, sedulous as I have been to trace
How Nature by extrinsic passion first
Peopled the mind with forms sublime or fair,
And made me love them, may I here omit
How other pleasures have been mine, and joys
Of subtler origin; how I have felt,
550 Not seldom even in that tempestuous time,
Those hallowed and pure motions of the sense

Which seem, in their simplicity, to own
An intellectual charm; that calm delight
Which, if I err not, surely must belong
To those first-born affinities that fit
Our new existence to existing things,
And, in our dawn of being, constitute
The bond of union between life and joy.

    Yes, I remember when the changeful earth,
560 And twice five summers on my mind had stamped
The faces of the moving year, even then
I held unconscious intercourse with beauty
Old as creation, drinking in a pure
Organic pleasure from the silver wreaths
Of curling mist, or from the level plain
Of waters coloured by impending clouds.

    The sands of Westmoreland, the creeks and bays
Of Cumbria's rocky limits, they can tell
How, when the sea threw off his evening shade,
570 And to the shepherd's hut on distant hills
Sent welcome notice of the rising moon,
How I have stood, to fancies such as these
A stranger, linking with the spectacle
No conscious memory of a kindred sight,
And bringing with me no peculiar sense
Of quietness or peace; yet have I stood,
Even while mine eye hath moved o'er many a league
Of shining water, gathering as it seemed
Through every hair-breadth in that field of light
580 New pleasure like a bee among the flowers.

    Thus oft amid those fits of vulgar° joy   *common to all*
Which, through all seasons, on a child's pursuits
Are prompt attendants, 'mid that giddy bliss
Which, like a tempest, works along the blood
And is forgotten; even then I felt
Gleams like the flashing of a shield; – the earth
And common face of nature spake to me
Rememberable things; sometimes, 'tis true,
By chance collisions and quaint accidents
590 (Like those ill-sorted unions, work supposed
Of evil-minded fairies), yet not vain
Nor profitless, if haply they impressed

Collateral objects and appearances,
Albeit lifeless then, and doomed to sleep
Until maturer seasons called them forth
To impregnate and to elevate the mind.
– And if the vulgar joy by its own weight
Wearied itself out of the memory,
The scenes which were a witness of that joy
600   Remained in their substantial lineaments
Depicted on the brain, and to the eye
Were visible, a daily sight; and thus
By the impressive discipline of fear,
By pleasure and repeated happiness,
So frequently repeated, and by force
Of obscure feelings representative
Of things forgotten, these same scenes so bright,
So beautiful, so majestic in themselves,
Though yet the day was distant, did become
610   Habitually dear, and all their forms
And changeful colours by invisible links
Were fastened to the affections.
                       I began
My story early – not misled, I trust,
By an infirmity of love for days
Disowned by memory – ere the breath of spring
Planting my snowdrops among winter snows;
Nor will it seem to thee, O friend! so prompt
In sympathy, that I have lengthened out
620   With fond and feeble tongue a tedious tale.
Meanwhile, my hope has been, that I might fetch
Invigorating thoughts from former years;
Might fix the wavering balance of my mind,
And haply meet reproaches too, whose power
May spur me on, in manhood now mature,
To honourable toil. Yet should these hopes
Prove vain, and thus should neither I be taught
To understand myself, nor thou to know
With better knowledge how the heart was framed
630   Of him thou lovest; need I dread from thee
Harsh judgments, if the song be loth to quit
Those recollected hours that have the charm
Of visionary things, those lovely forms
And sweet sensations that throw back our life,
And almost make remotest infancy
A visible scene, on which the sun is shining?

One end at least hath been attained; my mind
Hath been revived, and if this genial mood
Desert me not, forthwith shall be brought down
640 Through later years the story of my life.
The road lies plain before me; — 'tis a theme
Single and of determined bounds; and hence
I choose it rather at this time, than work
Of ampler or more varied argument,
Where I might be discomfited and lost:
And certain hopes are with me, that to thee
This labour will be welcome, honoured Friend!

Book II

SCHOOL-TIME (CONTINUED)

Thus far, O friend! have we, though leaving much
Unvisited, endeavoured to retrace
The simple ways in which my childhood walked;
Those chiefly that first led me to the love
Or rivers, woods, and fields. The passion yet
Was in its birth, sustained as might befal
By nourishment that came unsought; for still
From week to week, from month to month, we lived
A round of tumult. Duly were our games
10 Prolonged in summer till the day-light failed:
No chair remained before the doors; the bench
And threshold steps were empty; fast asleep
The labourer, and the old man who had sate
A later lingerer; yet the revelry
Continued and the loud uproar: at last,
When all the ground was dark, and twinkling stars
Edged the black clouds, home and to bed we went,
Feverish with weary joints and beating minds.
Ah! is there one who ever has been young,
20 Nor needs a warning voice to tame the pride
Of intellect and virtue's self-esteem?
One is there, though the wisest and the best
Of all mankind, who covets not at times
Union that cannot be; — who would not give,
If so he might, to duty and to truth

The eagerness of infantine desire?
A tranquillising spirit presses now
On my corporeal frame, so wide appears
The vacancy between me and those days
30 Which yet have such self-presence in my mind,
That, musing on them, often do I seem
Two consciousnesses, conscious of myself
And of some other Being. A rude mass[50]
Of native rock, left midway in the square
Of our small market village, was the goal
Or centre of these sports; and when, returned
After long absence, thither I repaired,
Gone was the old grey stone, and in its place
A smart assembly-room usurped the ground
40 That had been ours. There let the fiddle scream,
And be ye happy! Yet, my Friends! I know
That more than one of you will think with me
Of those soft starry nights, and that old Dame
From whom the stone was named, who there had sate,
And watched her table with its huckster's° wares   *stallhoder's*
Assiduous, through the length of sixty years.

    We ran a boisterous course; the year span round
With giddy motion. But the time approached
That brought with it a regular desire
50 For calmer pleasures, when the winning forms
Of Nature were collaterally attached
To every scheme of holiday delight
And every boyish sport, less grateful else
And languidly pursued.
                    When summer came,
Our pastime was, on bright half-holidays,
To sweep along the plain of Windermere
With rival oars; and the selected bourne
Was now an island musical with birds
That sang and ceased not; now a sister isle
60 Beneath the oaks' umbrageous covert, sown
With lilies of the valley like a field;
And now a third small island, where survived
In solitude the ruins of a shrine
Once to Our Lady dedicate, and served
Daily with chaunted° rites. In such a race   *chanted*
So ended, disappointment could be none,
Uneasiness, or pain, or jealousy:

We rested in the shade, all pleased alike,
Conquered and conqueror. Thus the pride of strength,
70 And the vain-glory of superior skill,
Were tempered; thus was gradually produced
A quiet independence of the heart;
And to my Friend who knows me I may add,
Fearless of blame, that hence for future days
Ensued a diffidence and modesty,
And I was taught to feel, perhaps too much,
The self-sufficing power of solitude.

Our daily meals were frugal, Sabine fare![51]
More than we wished we knew the blessing then
80 Of vigorous hunger – hence corporeal strength
Unsapped by delicate viands; for, exclude
A little weekly stipend, and we lived
Through three divisions of the quartered year
In penniless poverty. But now to school
From the half-yearly holidays returned,
We came with weightier purses, that sufficed
To furnish treats more costly than the Dame
Of the old grey stone, from her scant board, supplied.
Hence rustic dinners on the cool green ground,
90 Or in the woods, or by a river side
Or shady fountain, while among the leaves
Soft airs were stirring, and the mid-day sun
Unfelt shone brightly round us in our joy.
Nor is my aim neglected if I tell
How sometimes, in the length of those half-years,
We from our funds drew largely; – proud to curb,
And eager to spur on, the galloping steed;
And with the cautious inn-keeper, whose stud
Supplied our want, we haply might employ
100 Sly subterfuge, if the adventure's bound
Were distant: some famed temple where of yore
The Druids worshipped, or the antique walls
Of that large abbey,[52] where within the Vale
Of nightshade, to St. Mary's honour built,
Stands yet a mouldering pile with fractured arch,
Belfry, and images, and living trees,
A holy scene! Along the smooth green turf
Our horses grazed. To more than inland peace
Left by the west wind sweeping overhead
110 From a tumultuous ocean, trees and towers

In that sequestered valley may be seen,
Both silent and both motionless alike;
Such the deep shelter that is there, and such
The safeguard for repose and quietness.

Our steeds remounted and the summons given,
With whip and spur we through the chauntry flew
In uncouth race, and left the cross-legged knight,
And the stone-abbot, and that single wren
Which one day sang so sweetly in the nave
120   Of the old church, that – though from recent showers
The earth was comfortless, and, touched by faint
Internal breezes, sobbings of the place
And respirations, from the roofless walls
The shuddering ivy dripped large drops – yet still
So sweetly 'mid the gloom the invisible bird
Sang to herself, that there I could have made
My dwelling-place, and lived for ever there
To hear such music. Through the walls we flew
And down the valley, and, a circuit made
130   In wantonness of heart, through rough and smooth
We scampered homewards. Oh, ye rocks and streams,
And that still spirit shed from evening air!
Even in this joyous time I sometimes felt
Your presence, when with slackened step we breathed
Along the sides of the steep hills, or when,
Lighted by gleams of moonlight from the sea,
We beat with thundering hoofs the level sand.

Midway on long Winander's eastern shore,
Within the crescent of a pleasant bay,
140   A tavern[53] stood; no homely-featured house,
Primeval like its neighbouring cottages,
But 'twas a splendid place, the door beset
With chaises, grooms, and liveries, and within
Decanters, glasses, and the blood-red wine.
In ancient times, or ere the Hall[54] was built
On the large island, had this dwelling been
More worthy of a poet's love, a hut,
Proud of its one bright fire and sycamore shade.
But – though the rhymes were gone that once inscribed
150   The threshold, and large golden characters,
Spread o'er the spangled sign-board, had dislodged
The old Lion and usurped his place, in slight

And mockery of the rustic painter's hand –
Yet, to this hour, the spot to me is dear
With all its foolish pomp. The garden lay
Upon a slope surmounted by a plain
Of a small bowling-green; beneath us stood
A grove, with gleams of water through the trees
And over the tree-tops; nor did we want
160   Refreshment, strawberries and mellow cream.
There, while through half an afternoon we played
On the smooth platform, whether skill prevailed
Or happy blunder triumphed, bursts of glee
Made all the mountains ring. But, ere night-fall,
When in our pinnace we returned at leisure
Over the shadowy lake, and to the beach
Of some small island steered our course with one,
The Minstrel of the Troop,[55] and left him there,
And rowed off gently, while he blew his flute
170   Alone upon the rock – oh, then, the calm
And dead still water lay upon my mind
Even with a weight of pleasure, and the sky,
Never before so beautiful, sank down
Into my heart, and held me like a dream!
Thus were my sympathies enlarged, and thus
Daily the common range of visible things
Grew dear to me: already I began
To love the sun; a boy I loved the sun,
Not as I since have loved him, as a pledge
180   And surety of our earthly life, a light
Which we behold and feel we are alive;
Nor for his bounty to so many worlds –
But for this cause, that I had seen him lay
His beauty on the morning hills, had seen
The western mountain touch his setting orb,
In many a thoughtless hour, when, from excess
Of happiness, my blood appeared to flow
For its own pleasure, and I breathed with joy.
And, from like feelings, humble though intense,
190   To patriotic and domestic love
Analogous, the moon to me was dear;
For I could dream away my purposes,
Standing to gaze upon her while she hung
Midway between the hills, as if she knew
No other region, but belonged to thee,
Yea, appertained by a peculiar right
To thee and thy grey huts, thou one dear Vale!

Those incidental charms which first attached
My heart to rural objects, day by day
200 Grew weaker, and I hasten on to tell
How Nature, intervenient° till this time   *extraneous*
And secondary, now at length was sought
For her own sake. But who shall parcel out
His intellect by geometric rules,
Split like a province into round and square?
Who knows the individual hour in which
His habits were first sown, even as a seed?
Who that shall point as with a wand and say
'This portion of the river of my mind
210 Came from yon fountain?' Thou, my Friend! art one
More deeply read in thy own thoughts; to thee
Science appears but what in truth she is,
Not as our glory and our absolute boast,
But as a succedaneum,° and a prop   *substitute*
To our infirmity. No officious slave
Art thou of that false secondary power
By which we multiply distinctions, then
Deem that our puny boundaries are things
That we perceive, and not that we have made.
220 To thee, unblinded by these formal arts,
The unity of all hath been revealed,
And thou wilt doubt with me, less aptly skilled
Than many are to range the faculties
In scale and order, class the cabinet
Of their sensations, and in voluble phrase
Run through the history and birth of each
As of a single independent thing.
Hard task, vain hope, to analyse the mind,
If each most obvious and particular thought,
230 Not in a mystical and idle sense,
But in the words of reason deeply weighed,
Hath no beginning.
                              Blest the infant Babe,
(For with my best conjecture I would trace
Our being's earthly progress,) blest the Babe,
Nursed in his Mother's arms, who sinks to sleep
Rocked on his Mother's breast; who with his soul
Drinks in the feelings of his Mother's eye!
For him, in one dear presence, there exists
A virtue which irradiates and exalts
240 Objects through widest intercourse of sense.

No outcast he, bewildered and depressed:
Along his infant veins are interfused
The gravitation and the filial bond
Of nature that connect him with the world.
Is there a flower, to which he points with hand
Too weak to gather it, already love
Drawn from love's purest earthly fount for him
Hath beautified that flower; already shades
Of pity cast from inward tenderness
250 Do fall around him upon aught that bears
Unsightly marks of violence or harm.
Emphatically such a Being lives,
Frail creature as he is, helpless as frail,
An inmate of this active universe.
For feeling has to him imparted power
That through the growing faculties of sense
Doth like an agent of the one great Mind
Create, creator and receiver both,
Working but in alliance with the works
260 Which it beholds. – Such, verily, is the first
Poetic spirit of our human life,
By uniform control of after years,
In most, abated or suppressed; in some,
Through every change of growth and of decay,
Pre-eminent till death.

　　　　　　　　From early days,
Beginning not long after that first time
In which, a Babe, by intercourse of touch
I held mute dialogues with my Mother's heart,
I have endeavoured to display the means
270 Whereby this infant sensibility,
Great birthright of our being, was in me
Augmented and sustained. Yet is a path
More difficult before me; and I fear
That in its broken windings we shall need
The chamois'° sinews, and the eagle's wing: 　　*(species of antelope)*
For now a trouble came into my mind
From unknown causes. I was left alone
Seeking the visible world, nor knowing why.
The props of my affections were removed,
280 And yet the building stood, as if sustained
By its own spirit! All that I beheld
Was dear, and hence to finer influxes
The mind lay open to a more exact

And close communion. Many are our joys
In youth, but oh! what happiness to live
When every hour brings palpable access
Of knowledge, when all knowledge is delight,
And sorrow is not there! The seasons came,
And every season wheresoe'er I moved
290   Unfolded transitory qualities,
Which, but for this most watchful power of love,
Had been neglected; left a register
Of permanent relations, else unknown.
Hence life, and change, and beauty, solitude
More active even than 'best society' –
Society made sweet as solitude
By inward concords, silent, inobtrusive,
And gentle agitations of the mind
From manifold distinctions, difference
300   Perceived in things, where, to the unwatchful eye,
No difference is, and hence, from the same source,
Sublimer joy; for I would walk alone,
Under the quiet stars, and at that time
Have felt whate'er there is of power in sound
To breathe an elevated mood, by form
Or image unprofaned; and I would stand,
If the night blackened with a coming storm,
Beneath some rock, listening to notes that are
The ghostly language of the ancient earth,
310   Or make their dim abode in distant winds.
Thence did I drink the visionary power;
And deem not profitless those fleeting moods
Of shadowy exultation: not for this,
That they are kindred to our purer mind
And intellectual life; but that the soul,
Remembering how she felt, but what she felt
Remembering not, retains an obscure sense
Of possible sublimity, whereto
With growing faculties she doth aspire,
320   With faculties still growing, feeling still
That whatsoever point they gain, they yet
Have something to pursue.
                              And not alone,
'Mid gloom and tumult, but no less 'mid fair
And tranquil scenes, that universal power
And fitness in the latent qualities
And essences of things, by which the mind

Is moved with feelings of delight, to me
Came, strengthened with a superadded soul,
A virtue not its own. My morning walks
330   Were early; – oft before the hours of school[56]
I travelled round our little lake, five miles
Of pleasant wandering. Happy time! more dear
For this, that one was by my side, a Friend,[57]
Then passionately loved; with heart how full
Would he peruse these lines! For many years
Have since flowed in between us, and, our minds
Both silent to each other, at this time
We live as if those hours had never been.
Nor seldom did I lift our cottage latch
340   Far earlier, ere one smoke-wreath had risen
From human dwelling, or the vernal thrush,
Was audible; and sate among the woods
Alone upon some jutting eminence,
At the first gleam of dawn-light, when the Vale,
Yet slumbering, lay in utter solitude.
How shall I seek the origin? where find
Faith in the marvellous things which then I felt?
Oft in these moments such a holy calm
Would overspread my soul, that bodily eyes
350   Were utterly forgotten, and what I saw
Appeared like something in myself, a dream,
A prospect in the mind.
                                    'Twere long to tell
What spring and autumn, what the winter snows,
And what the summer shade, what day and night,
Evening and morning, sleep and waking thought
From sources inexhaustible, poured forth
To feed the spirit of religious love
In which I walked with Nature. But let this
Be not forgotten, that I still retained
360   My first creative sensibility;
That by the regular action of the world
My soul was unsubdued. A plastic° power   *shaping*
Abode with me; a forming hand, at times
Rebellious, acting in a devious mood;
A local spirit of his own, at war
With general tendency, but, for the most,
Subservient strictly to external things
With which it communed. An auxiliar light
Came from my mind, which on the setting sun

370 Bestowed new splendour; the melodious birds,
The fluttering breezes, fountains that run on
Murmuring so sweetly in themselves, obeyed
A like dominion, and the midnight storm
Grew darker in the presence of my eye:
Hence my obeisance, my devotion hence,
And hence my transport.
                              Nor should this, perchance,
Pass unrecorded, that I still had loved
The exercise and produce of a toil,
Than analytic industry to me
380 More pleasing, and whose character I deem
Is more poetic as resembling more
Creative agency. The song would speak
Of that interminable building reared
By observation of affinities
In objects where no brotherhood exists
To passive minds. My seventeenth year was come;
And, whether from this habit rooted now
So deeply in my mind, or from excess
In the great social principle of life
390 Coercing all things into sympathy,
To unorganic natures were transferred
My own enjoyments; or the power of truth
Coming in revelation, did converse
With things that really are; I, at this time,
Saw blessings spread around me like a sea.
Thus while the days flew by, and years passed on,
From nature overflowing in my soul
I had received so much, that all my thoughts
Were steeped in feeling; I was only then
400 Contented, when with bliss ineffable
I felt the sentiment of Being spread
O'er all that moves and all that seemeth still;
O'er all that, lost beyond the reach of thought
And human knowledge, to the human eye
Invisible, yet liveth to the heart;
O'er all that leaps and runs, and shouts and sings,
Or beats the gladsome air; o'er all that glides
Beneath the wave, yea, in the wave itself,
And mighty depth of waters. Wonder not
410 If high the transport, great the joy I felt,
Communing in this sort through earth and heaven
With every form of creature, as it looked

Towards the uncreated with a countenance
Of adoration, with an eye of love.
One song they sang, and it was audible,
Most audible, then, when the fleshly ear,
O'ercome by humblest prelude of that strain,
Forgot her functions, and slept undisturbed.

If this be error, and another faith
420 Find easier access to the pious mind,
Yet were I grossly destitute of all
Those human sentiments that make this earth
So dear, if I should fail with grateful voice
To speak of you, ye mountains, and ye lakes
And sounding cataracts, ye mists and winds
That dwell among the hills where I was born.
If in my youth I have been pure in heart,
If, mingling with the world, I am content
With my own modest pleasures, and have lived
430 With God and Nature communing, removed
From little enmities and low desires,
The gift is yours; if in these times of fear,[58]
This melancholy waste of hopes o'erthrown,
If, 'mid indifference and apathy,
And wicked exultation when good men
On every side fall off, we know not how,
To selfishness, disguised in gentle names
Of peace and quiet and domestic love,
Yet mingled not unwillingly with sneers
440 On visionary minds; if, in this time
Of dereliction and dismay, I yet
Despair not of our nature, but retain
A more than Roman° confidence, a faith   *stoical*
That fails not, in all sorrow my support,
The blessing of my life; the gift is yours,
Ye winds and sounding cataracts! 'tis yours,
Ye mountains! thine, O Nature! Thou hast fed
My lofty speculations; and in thee,
For this uneasy heart of ours, I find
450 A never-failing principle of joy
And purest passion.
                    Thou, my Friend! wert reared
In the great city, 'mid far other scenes;
But we, by different roads, at length have gained
The self-same bourne.° And for this cause to thee   *boundary*

I speak, unapprehensive of contempt,
The insinuated scoff of coward tongues,
And all that silent language which so oft
In conversation between man and man
Blots from the human countenance all trace
460 Of beauty and of love. For thou hast sought
The truth in solitude, and, since the days
That gave thee liberty, full long desired,
To serve in Nature's temple, thou hast been
The most assiduous of her ministers;
In many things my brother, chiefly here
In this our deep devotion.
                                        Fare thee well!
Health and the quiet of a healthful mind
Attend thee! seeking oft the haunts of men,
And yet more often living with thyself,
470 And for thyself, so haply shall thy days
Be many, and a blessing to mankind.

By 1799 [1850]

From **The Excursion**[59]

PROSPECTUS

On Man, on Nature, and on Human Life,
Musing in solitude, I oft perceive
Fair trains of imagery before me rise,
Accompanied by feelings of delight
Pure, or with no unpleasing sadness mixed;
And I am conscious of affecting thoughts
And dear remembrances, whose presence soothes
Or elevates the mind, intent to weigh
The good and evil of our mortal state.
10 − To these emotions, whencesoe'er they come,
Whether from breath of outward circumstance,
Or from the soul − an impulse to herself −

I would give utterance in numerous° verse.   *metrical*
Of truth, of grandeur, beauty, love, and hope,
And melancholy fear subdued by faith;
Of blessed consolations in distress;
Of moral strength, and intellectual power;
Of joy in widest commonalty spread;
Of the individual mind that keeps her own
20 Inviolate retirement, subject there
To conscience only, and the law supreme
Of that Intelligence which governs all,
I sing – 'fit audience let me find though few!'

*   *   *

               Not Chaos, not
The darkest pit of lowest Erebus,
Nor aught of blinder vacancy, scooped out
By help of dreams – can breed such fear and awe
As fall upon us often when we look
40 Into our minds, into the mind of man –
My haunt, and the main region of my song.
– Beauty – a living presence of the earth,
Surpassing the most fair ideal forms
Which craft of delicate spirits hath composed
From earth's materials – waits upon my steps;
Pitches her tents before me as I move,
An hourly neighbour. Paradise, and groves
Elysian, Fortunate Fields – like those of old
Sought in the Atlantic main⁶⁰ – why should they be
50 A history only of departed things,
Or a mere fiction of what never was?
For the discerning intellect of Man,
When wedded to this goodly universe
In love and holy passion, shall find these
A simple produce of the common day.
– I, long before the blissful hour arrives,
Would chant, in lonely peace, the spousal verse°   *marriage song*
Of this great consummation – and, by words
Which speak of nothing more than what we are,
60 Would I arouse the sensual from their sleep
Of Death, and win the vacant and the vain
To noble raptures; while my voice proclaims
How exquisitely the individual mind
(And the progressive powers perhaps no less
Of the whole species) to the external world

Is fitted – and how exquisitely, too –
Theme this but little heard of among men –
The external world is fitted to the mind;
And the creation (by no lower name
70 Can it be called) which they with blended might
Accomplish – this is our high argument.°   *theme*
– Such grateful haunts foregoing, if I oft
Must turn elsewhere – to travel near the tribes
And fellowships of men, and see ill sights
Of madding passions mutually inflamed;
Must hear Humanity in fields and groves
Pipe solitary anguish; or must hang
Brooding above the fierce confederate storm
Of sorrow, barricadoed evermore
80 Within the walls of cities – may these sounds
Have their authentic comment; that even these
Hearing, I be not downcast or forlorn! –
Descend, prophetic Spirit! . . .
         . . . upon me bestow
A gift of genuine insight; that my song
With starlike virtue in its place may shine,
90 Shedding benignant influence, and secure,
Itself, from all malevolent effect
Of those mutations that extend their sway
Throughout the nether sphere°! – And if with this   *the earth*
I mix more lowly matter; with the thing
Contemplated, describe the Mind and Man
Contemplating; and who, and what he was –
The transitory being that beheld
The vision; when and where, and how he lived –
Be not this labour useless. If such theme
100 May sort with highest objects, then – dread power!
Whose gracious favour is the primal source
Of all illumination – may my life
Express the image of a better time,
More wise desires, and simpler manners – nurse
My heart in genuine freedom – all pure thoughts
Be with me – so shall thy unfailing love
Guide, and support, and cheer me to the end!

1798–1814 [1814]

NOTES

Wordsworth

The texts, based on the later revised edition, may vary from earlier published versions; the dates given are those of first publication.

1 '... arose out of conversation with a friend who was somewhat unreasonably attached to modern books and moral philosophy'. (Advertisement to *Lyrical Ballads*.) Possibly for William Hazlitt, who visited W. spring 1798.

2 the ruins of the medieval abbey in the valley of the River Wye, Monmouthshire.

3 cf. Immortality Ode, 162.

4 cf. *Samson Agonistes* (Milton), 594–8.

5 his sister, Dorothy, who accompanied him.

6 cf. I. Ode, 196–8.

7 first, second and fourth included, in this sequence, in L.B. 1800. No.3 later in volume. Order used here the date of composition. No sure evidence as to Lucy's identity, or identities.

8 several rivers with the name Dove in England.

9 'The character and circumstances of Luke were taken from a family to whom had belonged, many years before, the house we lived in at Town-end, along with its fields and woodlands, on the eastern shore of Grasmere.' I.F. cf. W.'s letter to Thomas Poole, April 1801.

10 a ravine of Dunmail Raise, near Grasmere.

11 'a story well-known in the country. The chapel is called Ings Chapel ... on the right-hand side of the road from Kendal to Ambleside in the Lake District.' W.

12 Matthew Arnold (of this line) it illustrates W.'s 'true and most characteristic form of expression ... nothing subtle ... no heightening, no study of poetic style ... yet it is an expression of the highest kind ...'

13 cf. Dorothy's Journal, 3 Oct. 1800: W.'s letter to Sara Hutchinson, 14 June 1802.

14 'the manner in which the bird reiterates and prolongs her soft note, as if herself delighting in it'. W.

15 Coleridge.

16 Robert Burns who died before achieving renown.

17 aquatic blood-sucking worms used by doctors for blood-letting.

18 composed 'on the roof of the coach on my way to France.' W.

19 written 'on the beach near Calais'. W.

20 probably W.'s daughter by Annette Vallon, Caroline.

21 Luke XVI.22.

22 cf. Dorothy's Journal, 15 April 1802.

23 suggested to W. by the following: '(we) passed a female who was reaping alone; she sang in Erse as she bended (sic) over her sickle; the sweetest human voice I ever heard.' (From the MS of *Tours to the British Mountains* by Thomas Wilkinson, 1824.)

24 two years elapsed between the writing of stanzas 1–4 and the 'remaining part'. Poem headed Ode, 1807, subtitle added 1815. 'Nothing was more difficult for me in childhood than to admit the notion of death as a state applicable to my own being ... it was not so much from the source of animal vivacity that my difficulty came, as from a sense of the indomitableness of the spirit within me ... With a feeling congenial to this, I was often unable to think of external things as having an external existence, and I communed with all that I saw as something not apart from, but inherent in, my own immaterial nature. Many times while going to school I have grasped a wall or a tree to

recall myself from the abysm of idealism to reality . . . to that dreamlike vividness and splendour which invests objects of sight in childhood, everyone, I believe, if he would look back, could bear testimony . . . I took hold of the notion of pre-existence as having sufficient foundation in humanity authorising me to make for my purpose the best use of it I could as a poet.' I.F.

25 from the last lines of 'My Heart Leaps Up'.
26 i.e. a poem.
27 Hartley Coleridge, S.T.'s son.
28 i.e. of the humours – differing temperaments. From Samuel Daniel's (1562–1619) dedicatory sonnet to *Musophilus*.
29 after this line, originally: 'To whom the grave

    Is but a lonely bed without sense or sight
    Of day or the warm light,
    A place of thought where we in waiting lie.'

W. omitted this and added line 117 on Coleridge's advice.
30 *Hamlet*, I.I.48.
31 from Seneca, *Moral Epistles*. CXX.10. 'Now (I am) not good by deliberation, but led by custom, so that not only do I behave properly but I cannot do otherwise than behave properly.'
32 cf. P.L. 9.652–3.
33 not merely analytical but moral
34 the poem was begun winter 1798–9 at Goslar, Germany. By the end of 1799, W. had finished most of Books I and II. Much of the rest was written 1804–5, when he completed the poem. He revised and re-touched it (for stylistic reasons) until he had altered nearly half of it. First published as a whole, 1850, three months after W.'s death. Present title and subtitle provided by his wife. Originally it was conceived as part of a long work on Man and Society to be called 'The Recluse'.
35 cf. P.L. 12.646.
36 lines 44–5 a late addition to the original poem.
37 Coleridge, to whom the poem was addressed.
38 lines 59–107 W.'s walk from Bristol to Racedown, Dorset, Sept. 1795, with, possibly, some details from his later walk to Dove Cottage, Grasmere.
39 where Dove Cottage is situated.
40 an Aeolian harp – an instrument so situated that when the wind blows it vibrates and musical sounds can be heard.
41 i.e. the power of the imagination.
42 sense impressions, both in receiving and remembering.
43 of mythology or history.
44 Milton had toyed with various themes (including that of King Arthur) before deciding on the theme of P.L.
45 a line added later.
46 Dominique des Gourges.
47 the Derwent flows north to Cockermouth, Cumbria, W.'s birthplace.
48 card-games – lines 520–35 describe the various playing cards.
49 some lower value cards used as higher ones, which through use had been damaged or lost.
50 the Stone of Rowe at Hawkshead (where W. attended school); at the head of Esthwaite Water.
51 Sabines – people over-run by the Romans = prisoner-of-war fare? simple farm fare.

52 Furness Abbey, 20 miles south of Hawkshead.
53 The White Lion, Bowness, Lake Windermere.
54 a large stone house (*c.*1770) on Belle Isle, Lake Windermere.
55 Robert Greenwood, later Senior Fellow of Trinity College, Cambridge.
56 school began 6 a.m. in summer, 7 a.m. in winter.
57 Rev. John Fleming of Rayrigg, Windermere, who was at St John's College with W.
58 cf. letter Coleridge to W. Sept. 1799 concerning the failure of the French Revolution.
59 part of the long philosophical poem W. never completed – to include *Prospectus*, *The Prelude*, and *The Excursion* and to be called 'The Recluse'.
60 the place of the blessed dead was linked with the lost Isle of Atlantis.

Samuel Taylor Coleridge

[1772–1832]

He was the youngest son of the Vicar of Ottery, Devon: his father died when he was young, and C. was sent to Christ's Hospital School where he met Leigh Hunt and Charles Lamb: 1792–4 he was at Jesus College, Cambridge, but politics (the French Revolution), drink and an unhappy love affair made him enlist: he was bought out by his brother under an insanity rule. 1794 his friendship with Southey led to the Pantisocracy scheme (to set up a commune in America). His first poems – sonnets – published in the *Morning Chronicle*: he and Southey collaborated in trying to raise money for the Pantisocracy, and they married sisters – Sara and Edith Fricker: C. quarrelled with Southey, and he and Sara moved to Clevedon, Somerset, where their first son, Hartley, b.: 1796 published *Poems on Various Subjects*. June 1797 he and William Wordsworth formed a close friendship that lasted for the next 14 years and resulted in the publication of the *Lyrical Ballads*, 1798. 1798–9 C. spent ten months in Germany (part of it with Wordsworth) studying the German philosophers. Returning to England, he wrote for the *Morning Post* and planned an extensive work on metaphysics. 1800 he moved to the Lake District, his marriage unhappy, and his love for Sara Hutchinson, W.'s future sister-in-law, deepening, his use of opium, now debilitating – all problems explored in 'Dejection: an Ode', 1802. C. began to compile his Notebooks in which he recorded daily entries on his life, work and dreams. 1808, after making an attempt to restore his health and position by taking a position as secretary to the Governor of Malta, he began a series of *Lectures on Poetry and Drama* and 1809–10 wrote and edited (with Sara Hutchinson's help) *The Friend*, a literary and political weekly paper. However the group broke up – Sara left for Wales, Dorothy Wordsworth became more intolerant of his behaviour, and he quarrelled with Wordsworth. 1813–14 he spent in London, extremely depressed, to be rescued by his friends, the Morgans, who took him to live in Calne, Wiltshire. By 1813–14 he had admitted his opium problem, submitting himself to treatment, and began writing again. 1816 *Christabel and Other Poems*, which included 'Kubla Khan' and 'The Pains of Sleep' was published: 1817, *Biographia Literaria* and the first collected edition of his poems – *Sibylline Leaves*. By spring 1816 he had found a home with Dr James Gillman, a young surgeon, in Highgate, London, where he remained for the rest of his life. There he wrote many prose works on philosophical, religious and literary subjects, and became the centre of a group of young disciples. Carlyle called him 'the sage of Highgate', Lamb 'an archangel slightly damaged'. He died of heart failure at Highgate – the echoes of his hypnotic way with words being captured in *Table Talk*, 1836.

The Aeolian Harp[1]

My pensive Sara! thy soft cheek reclined
Thus on mine arm, most soothing sweet it is
To sit beside our cot,° our cot o'ergrown   *cottage*
With white-flowered jasmin, and the broad-leaved myrtle,
(Meet emblems they of innocence and love!)
And watch the clouds, that late were rich with light,
Slow saddening round, and mark the star of eve
Serenely brilliant (such should wisdom be)
Shine opposite! How exquisite the scents
10 Snatched from yon bean-field°! and the world so hushed! *flowering broad*
The stilly murmur of the distant sea   *beans*
Tells us of silence.
                              And that simplest lute,°   *(the harp)*
Placed length-ways in the clasping casement,° hark!   *cottage window*
How by the desultory breeze caressed,
Like some coy maid half yielding to her lover,
It pours such sweet upbraiding,° as must needs   *reproaches*
Tempt to repeat the wrong! And now, its strings
Boldlier swept, the long sequacious° notes   *following each other*
Over delicious surges sink and rise,
20 Such a soft floating witchery of sound
As twilight elfins make, when they at eve
Voyage on gentle gales from fairy-land,
Where melodies round honey-dropping flowers,
Footless and wild, like birds of paradise,[2]
Nor pause, nor perch, hovering on untamed wing!
O the one Life within us and abroad,
Which meets all motion and becomes its soul,
A light in sound, a sound-like power in light
Rhythm in all thought, and joyance every where –
30 Methinks, it should have been impossible

Not to love all things in a world so filled;
Where the breeze warbles, and the mute still air
Is music slumbering on her instrument.

And thus, my love! as on the midway slope
Of yonder hill I stretch my limbs at noon,
Whilst through my half-closed eye-lids I behold
The sunbeams dance, like diamonds, on the main,
And tranquil muse upon tranquillity;
Full many a thought uncalled and undetained,
40   And many idle flitting phantasies,
Traverse my indolent and passive brain,
As wild and various as the random gales
That swell and flutter on this subject lute!
And what if all of animated nature
Be but organic harps diversely framed,
That tremble into thought, as o'er them sweeps
Plastic° and vast, one intellectual breeze,   *shaping*
At once the Soul of each, and God of all?
But thy more serious eye a mild reproof
50   Darts, O beloved Woman! nor such thoughts
Dim and unhallowed dost thou not reject,
And biddest me walk humbly with my God.
Meek Daughter in the family of Christ!
Well hast thou said and holily dispraised
These shapings of the unregenerate mind;
Bubbles that glitter as they rise and break
On vain philosophy's aye-babbling spring.
For never guiltless may I speak of him,
The Incomprehensible! save when with awe
60   I praise him, and with faith that inly feels;
Who with his saving mercies healed me,
A sinful and most miserable man,
Wildered and dark, and gave me to possess
Peace, and this cot, and thee, heart-honoured Maid!

1795 [1796]

This Lime-Tree Bower My Prison

Well, they³ are gone, and here must I remain,⁴
This lime-tree bower my prison! I have lost
Beauties and feelings, such as would have been
Most sweet to my remembrance even when age
Had dimmed mine eyes to blindness! They, meanwhile,
Friends, whom I never more may meet again,
On springy heath, along the hill-top edge,
Wander in gladness, and wind down, perchance,
To that still roaring dell, of which I told;
The roaring dell, o'erwooded, narrow, deep,
And only speckled by the mid-day sun;
Where its slim trunk the ash from rock to rock
Flings arching like a bridge; – that branchless ash,
Unsunned and damp, whose few poor yellow leaves
Ne'er tremble in the gale, yet tremble still,
Fanned by the water-fall! and there my friends
Behold the dark green file of long lank weeds,
That all at once (a most fantastic sight!)
Still nod and drip beneath the dripping edge
Of the blue clay-stone.

                              Now, my friends emerge
Beneath the wide wide Heaven – and view again
The many-steepled tract° magnificent   *expanse*
Of hilly fields and meadows, and the sea,
With some fair bark, perhaps, whose sails light up
The slip of smooth clear blue betwixt two Isles
Of purple shadow! Yes! they wander on
In gladness all; but thou, methinks, most glad,
My gentle-hearted Charles! for thou hast pined
And hungered after Nature, many a year,
In the great city pent, winning thy way
With sad yet patient soul, through evil and pain
And strange calamity!⁵ Ah! slowly sink
Behind the western ridge, thou glorious sun!
Shine in the slant beams of the sinking orb,
Ye purple heath-flowers! richlier burn, ye clouds!
Live in the yellow light, ye distant groves!
And kindle, thou blue ocean! So my friend
Struck with deep joy may stand, as I have stood,
Silent with swimming sense; yea, gazing round
On the wide landscape, gaze till all doth seem

Less gross than bodily; and of such hues
As veil the Almighty Spirit, when yet he makes
Spirits perceive his presence.
                              A delight
Comes sudden on my heart, and I am glad
As I myself were there! Nor in this bower,
This little lime-tree bower, have I not marked
Much that has soothed me. Pale beneath the blaze
Hung the transparent foliage; and I watched
Some broad and sunny leaf, and loved to see
50   The shadow of the leaf and stem above
Dappling its sunshine! And that walnut-tree
Was richly tinged, and a deep radiance lay
Full on the ancient ivy, which usurps
Those fronting elms, and now, with blackest mass
Makes their dark branches gleam a lighter hue
Through the late twilight: and though now the bat
Wheels silent by, and not a swallow twitters,
Yet still the solitary humble bee
Sings in the bean-flower! Henceforth I shall know
60   That Nature ne'er deserts the wise and pure;
No plot so narrow, be but Nature there,
No waste so vacant, but may well employ
Each faculty of sense, and keep the heart
Awake to love and beauty! and sometimes
'Tis well to be bereft of promised good,
That we may lift the soul, and contemplate
With lively joy the joys we cannot share.
My gentle-hearted Charles[6] ! when the last rook
Beat its straight path along the dusky air
70   Homewards, I blest it! deeming its black wing
(Now a dim speck, now vanishing in light)
Had crossed the mighty orb's dilated glory,
While thou stood'st gazing; or when all was still,
Flew creeking[7] o'er thy head, and had a charm
For thee, my gentle-hearted Charles, to whom
No sound is dissonant which tells of life.

                              June 1797 [1800]

Kubla Khan[8]

In Xanadu did Kubla Khan
A stately pleasure-dome decree:
Where Alph, the sacred river, ran
Through caverns measureless to man
   Down to a sunless sea.
So twice five miles of fertile ground
With walls and towers were girdled round:
And there were gardens bright with sinuous rills
Where blossomed many an incense-bearing tree;
10 And here were forests ancient as the hills,
Enfolding sunny spots of greenery.

But oh! that deep romantic chasm which slanted
Down the green hill athwart a cedarn° cover!   *of cedar wood*
A savage place! as holy and enchanted
As e'er beneath a waning moon was haunted
By woman wailing for her demon-lover!
And from this chasm, with ceaseless turmoil seething,
As if this earth in fast thick pants were breathing,
A mighty fountain momently was forced:
20 Amid whose swift half-intermitted burst
Huge fragments vaulted like rebounding hail,
Or chaffy grain beneath the thresher's flail:
And mid these dancing rocks at once and ever
It flung up momently the sacred river.
Five miles meandering with a mazy motion
Through wood and dale the sacred river ran,
Then reached the caverns measureless to man,
And sank in tumult to a lifeless ocean:
And 'mid this tumult Kubla heard from far
30 Ancestral voices prophesying war!

    The shadow of the dome of pleasure
    Floated midway on the waves;
    Where was heard the mingled measure
    From the fountain and the caves.
It was a miracle of rare device,
A sunny pleasure-dome with caves of ice!

    A damsel with a dulcimer°   *(stringed instrument)*
    In a vision once I saw:
    It was an Abyssinian maid,
40   And on her dulcimer she played,

Singing of Mount Abora.
Could I revive within me
Her symphony and song,
To such a deep delight 'twould win me
That with music loud and long,
I would build that dome in air,
That sunny dome! those caves of ice!
And all who heard should see them there,
And all should cry, Beware! Beware!
40 His flashing eyes, his floating hair!
Weave a circle round him thrice,
And close your eyes with holy dread,
For he on honey-dew hath fed,
And drunk the milk of Paradise.

1797 [1816]

The Rime of the Ancient Mariner[9]

Facile credo, plures esse Naturas invisibiles quam
visibiles in rerum universitate. Sed horum omnium
familiam quis nobis enarrabit, et gradus et
cognationes et discrimina et singulorum munera?
Quid agunt? quæ loca habitant? Harum rerum
notitiam semper ambivit ingenium humanum,
nunquam attigit. Juvat, interea, non diffiteor,
quandoque in animo, tanquam in tabula, majoris et
melioris mundi imaginem contemplari: ne mens
assuefactâ, hodiernæ vitæ minutiis se contrahat
nimis, et tota subsidat in pusillas cogitationes. Sed
veritati interea invigilandum est, modusque
servandus, ut certa ab incertis, diem a nocte,
distinguamus.

T. BURNET. ARCHÆOL. PHIL. p. 68.[10]

PART I

It is an ancient Mariner,
And he stoppeth one of three.
'By thy long grey beard and glittering eye,
Now wherefore stopp'st thou me?

An ancient Mariner meeteth three gallants bidden to a wedding-feast, and detaineth one.

The bridegroom's doors are opened wide,
10 And I am next of kin;
The guests are met, the feast is set:
May'st hear the merry din.'

He holds him with his skinny hand,
'There was a ship,' quoth he.
'Hold off! unhand me, grey-beard loon!'
Eftsoons° his hand dropt he.   *immediately*

He holds him with his glittering eye –   The wedding guest is
The wedding-guest stood still,   spellbound by the eye of
And listens like a three years' child: the old sea-faring man,
The Mariner hath his will.   and constrained to hear
                                                   his tale.

The wedding-guest sat on a stone:
He cannot choose but hear;
And thus spake on that ancient man,
20 The bright-eyed Mariner.

'The ship was cheered, the harbour cleared,
Merrily did we drop
Below the kirk,° below the hill,   *church*
Below the light house top.

The sun came up upon the left,[11]   The Mariner tells how
Out of the sea came he!   the ship sailed southward
And he shone bright, and on the right   with a good wind and fair
Went down into the sea.   weather, till it reached
                                                   the Line.

Higher and higher every day,
30 Till over the mast at noon –'
The wedding-guest here beat his breast,
For he heard the loud bassoon.

The bride hath paced into the hall,   The wedding guest
Red as a rose is she;   heareth the bridal music;
Nodding their heads before her goes   but the Mariner
The merry minstrelsy.   continueth his tale.

The wedding-guest he beat his breast,
Yet he cannot choose but hear;
And thus spake on that ancient man,
40 The bright-eyed Mariner.

'And now the storm-blast came, and he
Was tyrannous and strong:
He struck with his o'ertaking wings,
And chased us south along.

The ship driven by a storm toward the south pole.

With sloping masts and dipping prow,
As who pursued with yell and blow
Still treads the shadow of his foe,
And forward bends his head,
The ship drove fast, loud roared the blast,
50 And southward aye we fled.

The land of ice, and of fearful sounds where no living thing was to be seen.

And now there came both mist and snow,
And it grew wondrous cold:
And ice, mast-high, came floating by,
As green as emerald.

And through the drifts the snowy clifts
Did send a dismal sheen:
Nor shapes of men nor beasts we ken –
The ice was all between.

The ice was here, the ice was there,
60 The ice was all around:
It cracked and growled, and roared and howled,
Like noises in a swound°!   *swoon*

At length did cross an albatross,
Thorough the fog it came;
As if it had been a Christian soul,
We hailed it in God's name.

Till a great sea-bird, called the Albatross, came through the snow-fog, and was received with great joy and hospitality.

It ate the food it ne'er had eat,
And round and round it flew.
The ice did split with a thunder-fit;
70 The helmsman steered us through![12]

And lo! the Albatross proveth a bird of good omen, and followeth the ship as it returned northward through fog and floating ice.

And a good south wind sprung up behind;
The albatross did follow,
And every day, for food or play,
Came to the mariners' hollo!

In mist or cloud, on mast or shroud,
It perched for vespers nine;
Whiles all the night, through fog-smoke white,
Glimmered the white moon-shine.'

The ancient Mariner inhospitably killeth the pious bird of good omen.

'God save thee, ancient Mariner!
80 From the fiends, that plague thee thus! –
Why look'st thou so?' – 'With my cross-bow
I shot the albatross.'

PART II

'The sun now rose upon the right:
Out of the sea came he,
Still hid in mist, and on the left
Went down into the sea.

And the good south wind still blew behind,
But no sweet bird did follow,
Nor any day for food or play
90 Came to the mariners' hollo!

And I had done a hellish thing,
And it would work 'em woe:
For all averred, I had killed the bird
That made the breeze to blow.
Ah wretch! said they, the bird to slay,
That made the breeze to blow!

His shipmates cry out against the ancient Mariner, for killing the bird of good luck.

Nor dim nor red, like God's own head,
The glorious sun uprist:
Then all averred, I had killed the bird
100 That brought the fog and mist.
'Twas right, said they, such birds to slay,
That bring the fog and mist.

But when the fog cleared off, they justify the same, and thus make themselves accomplices in the crime.

The fair breeze blew, the white foam flew,
The furrow followed free;
We were the first that ever burst
Into that silent sea.

The fair breeze continues; the ship enters the Pacific Ocean, and sails northward, even till it reaches the Line.

Down dropt the breeze, the sails dropt down,
'Twas sad as sad could be;
And we did speak only to break
110   The silence of the sea!

The ship hath been suddenly becalmed.

All in a hot and copper sky,
The bloody sun, at noon,
Right up above the mast did stand,
No bigger than the moon.

Day after day, day after day,
We stuck, nor breath nor motion;
As idle as a painted ship
Upon a painted ocean.

Water, water, every where
120   And all the boards did shrink;
Water, water, every where
Nor any drop to drink.

And the Albatross begins to be avenged.

The very deep did rot: O Christ!
That ever this should be!
Yea, slimy things did crawl with legs
Upon the slimy sea.

About, about, in reel and rout
The death-fires danced at night;
The water, like a witch's oils,
130   Burnt green, and blue and white.

And some in dreams assured were
Of the Spirit that plagued us so;
Nine fathom deep he had followed us
From the land of mist and snow.

A spirit had followed them; one of the invisible inhabitants of this planet, neither departed souls nor angels; concerning whom the learned Jew, Josephus, and the Platonic Constantinopolitan, Michael Psellus, may be consulted. They are very numerous, and there is no climate or element without one or more.

And every tongue, through utter drought,
Was withered at the root;
We could not speak, no more than if
We had been choked with soot.

Ah! well a-day! what evil looks
140 Had I from old and young!
Instead of the cross, the albatross
About my neck was hung.'

The shipmates, in their sore distress, would fain throw the whole guilt on the ancient Mariner: in sign whereof they hang the dead sea-bird round his neck.

PART III

'There passed a weary time. Each throat
Was parched, and glazed each eye.
A weary time! a weary time,
How glazed each weary eye,
When looking westward, I beheld
A something in the sky.

The ancient Mariner beholdeth a sign in the element afar off.

At first it seemed a little speck,
150 And then it seemed a mist;
It moved and moved, and took at last
A certain shape, I wist.

knew

A speck, a mist, a shape, I wist!
And still it neared and neared:
As if it dodged a water-sprite,
It plunged and tacked and veered.

With throats unslaked, with black lips baked,
We could nor laugh nor wail;
Through utter drought all dumb we stood!
160 I bit my arm, I sucked the blood,
And cried, A sail! a sail!

At its nearer approach, it seemeth him to be a ship; and at a dear ransom he freeth his speech from the bonds of thirst.

With throats unslaked, with black lips baked,
Agape they heard me call:
Gramercy! they for joy did grin,
And all at once their breath drew in,
As they were drinking all.

A flash of joy;

See! see! (I cried) she tacks no more!
Hither to work us weal;
Without a breeze, without a tide,
170 She steadies with upright keel!

And horror follows. For can it be a ship that comes onward without wind or tide?

The western wave was all a-flame.
The day was well nigh done!
Almost upon the western wave
Rested the broad bright sun;
When that strange shape drove suddenly
Betwixt us and the sun.

And straight the sun was flecked with bars,   *It seemeth him but the*
(Heaven's Mother send us grace!)   *skeleton of a ship.*
As if through a dungeon-gate he peered
180 With broad and burning face.

Alas! (thought I, and my heart beat loud)
How fast she nears and nears!
Are those *her* sails that glance in the sun,
Like restless gossameres?

Are those *her* ribs through which the sun   *And its ribs are seen as*
Did peer, as through a grate?   *bars on the face of the*
And is that woman all her crew?   *setting Sun. The Spectre-*
Is that a Death? and are there two?   *woman and her Death-*
Is Death that woman's mate?   *mate, and no other on*
                                               board the skeleton-ship.

190 Her lips were red, her looks were free,   *Like vessel, like crew!*
Her locks were yellow as gold:
Her skin was as white as leprosy,
The night-mare life-in-death was she,
Who thicks man's blood with cold.

The naked hulk alongside came,   *Death and Life-in-death*
And the twain were casting dice;   *have diced for the ship's*
'The game is done! I've won, I've won!'   *crew, and she (the latter)*
Quoth she, and whistles thrice.   *winneth the ancient*
                                               Mariner.

The sun's rim dips; the stars rush out: *No twilight within the*
200 At one stride comes the dark;   *courts of the sun.*
With far-heard whisper, o'er the sea,
Off shot the spectre-bark.

We listened and looked sideways up!   *At the rising of the*
Fear at my heart, as at a cup,   *Moon.*
My life-blood seemed to sip!
The stars were dim, and thick the night,
The steersman's face by his lamp gleamed white;

From the sails the dew did drip –
Till clomb above the eastern bar
210 The horned moon, with one bright star
Within the nether tip.[13]

'One after one, by the star-dogged moon,
Too quick for groan or sigh,
Each turned his face with a ghastly pang,
And cursed me with his eye.

One after another,

Four times fifty living men,
(And I heard nor sigh nor groan)
With heavy thump, a lifeless lump,
They dropped down one by one.

His shipmates drop down dead.

220 The souls did from their bodies fly, –
They fled to bliss or woe!
And every soul, it passed me by,
Like the whizz of my cross-bow!'

But Life-in-Death begins her work on the ancient Mariner.

PART IV

'I fear thee, ancient Mariner!
I fear thy skinny hand!
And thou art long, and lank, and brown,
As is the ribbed sea-sand.[14]

The wedding guest feareth that a Spirit is talking to him.

I fear thee and thy glittering eye,
And thy skinny hand, so brown.' –
230 'Fear not, fear not, thou wedding-guest!
This body dropt not down.

But the ancient Mariner assureth him of his bodily life, and proceedeth to relate his horrible penance.

Alone, alone, all, all alone
Alone on a wide wide sea!
And never a saint took pity on
My soul in agony.

The many men, so beautiful!
And they all dead did lie:
And a thousand thousand slimy things
Lived on; and so did I.

He despiseth the creatures of the calm.

240 I looked upon the rotting sea,
    And drew my eyes away;
    I looked upon the rotting deck,
    And there the dead men lay.

    I looked to heaven, and tried to pray;
    But or ever a prayer had gusht,
    A wicked whisper came, and made
    My heart as dry as dust.

    I closed my lids, and kept them close,
    And the balls like pulses beat;
250 For the sky and the sea, and the sea and the sky
    Lay like a load on my weary eye,
    And the dead were at my feet.

    The cold sweat melted from their limbs,
    Nor rot nor reek did they:
    The look with which they looked on me
    Had never passed away.

    An orphan's curse would drag to hell
    A spirit from on high;
    But oh! more horrible than that
260 Is the curse in a dead man's eye!
    Seven days, seven nights, I saw that curse,
    And yet I could not die.

    The moving moon went up the sky,
    And no where did abide:
    Softly she was going up,
    And a star or two beside –

    Her beams bemocked the sultry main,
    Like April hoar-frost spread;
    But where the ship's huge shadow lay,
270 The charmed water burnt alway
    A still and awful red.

*And envieth that they
should live, and so many
lie dead.*

*But the curse liveth for
him in the eye of the
dead men.*

*In his loneliness and
fixedness he yearneth to-
wards the journeying
Moon, and the stars that
still sojourn, yet still move
onward; and every where
the blue sky belongs to
them, and is their ap-
pointed rest, and their
native country and their
own natural homes,
which they enter
unannounced, as lords
that are certainly ex-
pected and yet there is a
silent joy at their arrival.*

Beyond the shadow of the ship,
I watched the water-snakes:
They moved in tracks of shining white,
And when they reared, the elfish light
Fell off in hoary flakes.

By the light of the Moon he beholdeth God's creatures of the great calm.

Within the shadow of the ship
I watched their rich attire:
Blue, glossy green, and velvet black,
280 They coiled and swam; and every track
Was a flash of golden fire.

O happy living things! no tongue
Their beauty might declare:
A spring of love gushed from my heart,
And I blessed them unaware:
Sure my kind saint took pity on me,
And I blessed them unaware.

Their beauty and their happiness.

The selfsame moment I could pray;
And from my neck so free
290 The albatross fell off, and sank
Like lead into the sea.

He blesseth them in his heart.

The spell begins to break.

PART V

Oh sleep! it is a gentle thing,
Beloved from pole to pole!
To Mary Queen the praise be given!
She sent the gentle sleep from Heaven,
That slid into my soul.

The silly° buckets on the deck,
That had so long remained,
I dreamt that they were filled with dew,
300 And when I awoke, it rained.

simple

By grace of the holy Mother, the ancient Mariner is refreshed with rain.

My lips were wet, my throat was cold,
My garments all were dank;
Sure I had drunken in my dreams,
And still my body drank.

I moved, and could not feel my limbs:
I was so light – almost
I thought that I had died in sleep,
And was a blessed ghost.

And soon I heard a roaring wind:
310 It did not come anear;
But with its sound it shook the sails,
That were so thin and sere.

The upper air burst into life!
And a hundred fire-flags sheen,°
To and fro they were hurried about!
And to and fro, and in and out,
The wan stars danced between.

shone

And the coming wind did roar more loud,
And the sails did sigh like sedge;
320 And the rain poured down from one black cloud
The moon was at its edge.

The thick black cloud was cleft, and still
The moon was at its side:
Like waters shot from some high crag,
The lightning fell with never a jag,
A river steep and wide.

The loud wind never reached the ship,
Yet now the ship moved on!
Beneath the lightning and the moon
330 The dead men gave a groan.

They groaned, they stirred, they all uprose,
Nor spake, nor moved their eyes;
It had been strange, even in a dream,
To have seen those dead men rise.

The helmsman steered, the ship moved on;
Yet never a breeze up blew;
The mariners all 'gan work the ropes,
Where they were wont to do;
They raised their limbs like lifeless tools –
340 We were a ghastly crew.

The body of my brother's son
Stood by me, knee to knee:
The body and I pulled at one rope,
But he said nought to me.'

'I fear thee, ancient Mariner!'
'Be calm, thou wedding-guest!
'Twas not those souls that fled in pain,
Which to their corses came again,
But a troop of spirits blest:

But not by the souls of
the men, nor by demons
of earth or middle air,
but by a blessed troop of
angelic spirits, sent down
by the invocation of the
guardian saint.

350 For when it dawned – they dropped their arms,
And clustered round the mast;
Sweet sounds rose slowly through their mouths
And from their bodies passed.

Around, around, flew each sweet sound,
Then darted to the sun;
Slowly the sounds came back again,
Now mixed, now one by one.

Sometimes a-dropping from the sky
I heard the sky-lark sing;
360 Sometimes all little birds that are,
How they seemed to fill the sea and air
With their sweet jargoning!

And now 'twas like all instruments,
Now like a lonely flute;
And now it is an angel's song,
That makes the heavens be mute.

It ceased; yet still the sails made on
A pleasant noise till noon,
A noise like of a hidden brook
370 In the leafy month of June,
That to the sleeping woods all night
Singeth a quiet tune.

Till noon we quietly sailed on,
Yet never a breeze did breathe:
Slowly and smoothly went the ship,
Moved onward from beneath.

Under the keel nine fathom deep
From the land of mist and snow,
The spirit slid: and it was he
380 That made the ship to go.
The sails at noon left off their tune,
And the ship stood still also.

The sun, right up above the mast,
Had fixed her to the ocean:
But in a minute she 'gan stir,
With a short uneasy motion –
Backwards and forwards half her length
With a short uneasy motion.

Then like a pawing horse let go,
390 She made a sudden bound:
It flung the blood into my head,
And I fell down in a swound.

How long in that same fit I lay,
I have not to declare;
But ere my living life returned,
I heard, and in my soul discerned
Two voices in the air.

'Is it he?' quoth one, 'Is this the man?
By him who died on cross,
400 With his cruel bow he laid full low
The harmless Albatross.

The spirit who bideth by himself
In the land of mist and snow,
He loved the bird that loved the man
Who shot him with his bow.'

The other was a softer voice,
As soft as honey-dew:
Quoth he, 'The man hath penance done,
And penance more will do.'

The lonesome spirit from the south pole carries on the ship as far as the Line, in obedience to the angelic troop, but still requireth vengeance.

The Polar Spirit's fellow demons, the invisible inhabitants of the element, take part in his wrong; and two of them relate, one to the other, that penance long and heavy for the ancient Mariner hath been accorded to the Polar Spirit, who returneth southward.

PART VI

First Voice

410 'But tell me, tell me! speak again,
Thy soft response renewing –
What makes that ship drive on so fast?
What is the ocean doing?'

Second Voice

'Still as a slave before his lord,
The ocean hath no blast;
His great bright eye most silently
Up to the moon is cast –

If he may know which way to go;
For she guides him smooth or grim.
420 See, brother, see! how graciously
She looketh down on him.'

First Voice

'But why drives on that ship so fast,
Without or wave or wind?'

Second Voice

'The air is cut away before,
And closes from behind.

Fly, brother, fly! more high, more high!
Or we shall be belated:
For slow and slow that ship will go,
When the Mariner's trance is abated.'

430 'I woke, and we were sailing on
As in a gentle weather:
'Twas night, calm night, the moon was high;
The dead men stood together.

All stood together on the deck,
For a charnel-dungeon fitter:
All fixed on me their stony eyes,
That in the moon did glitter.

The Mariner hath been cast into a trance; for the angelic power causeth the vessel to drive northward faster than human life could endure.

The supernatural motion is retarded; the Mariner awakes, and his penance begins anew.

The pang, the curse, with which they died,
Had never passed away:
440 I could not draw my eyes from theirs,
Nor turn them up to pray.

And now this spell was snapped: once more   The curse is finally
I viewed the ocean green,   expiated.
And looked far forth, yet little saw
Of what had else been seen –

Like one, that on a lonesome road
Doth walk in fear and dread,
And having once turned round walks on,
And turns no more his head;
450 Because he knows, a frightful fiend
Doth close behind him tread.

But soon there breathed a wind on me,
Nor sound nor motion made:
Its path was not upon the sea,
In ripple or in shade.

It raised my hair, it fanned my cheek
Like a meadow-gale of spring –
It mingled strangely with my fears,
Yet it felt like a welcoming.

460 Swiftly, swiftly flew the ship,
Yet she sailed softly too:
Sweetly, sweetly blew the breeze –
On me alone it blew.

Oh! dream of joy! is this indeed   And the ancient Mariner
The light-house top I see?   beholdeth his native
Is this the hill? is this the kirk?   country.
Is this mine own countree?

We drifted o'er the harbour-bar,
And I with sobs did pray –
470 O let me be awake, my God!
Or let me sleep alway.

The harbour-bay was clear as glass,
So smoothly it was strewn!
And on the bay the moonlight lay,
And the shadow of the moon.

The rock shone bright, the kirk no less,
That stands above the rock:
The moonlight steeped in silentness
The steady weathercock.

480 And the bay was white with silent light,
Till rising from the same,
Full many shapes, that shadows were,
In crimson colours came.

The angelic spirits leave the dead bodies.

A little distance from the prow
Those crimson shadows were:
I turned my eyes upon the deck –
Oh, Christ! what saw I there!

And appear in their own forms of light.

Each corse lay flat, lifeless and flat,
And, by the holy rood°!
490 A man all light, a seraph-man,
On every corse there stood.

Christ's cross

This seraph-band, each waved his hand:
It was a heavenly sight!
They stood as signals to the land,
Each one a lovely light;

This seraph-band, each waved his hand,
No voice did they impart –
No voice; but oh! the silence sank
Like music on my heart.

500 But soon I heard the dash of oars,
I heard the pilot's cheer;
My head was turned perforce away,
And I saw a boat appear.

The pilot and the pilot's boy,
I heard them, coming fast:
Dear Lord in Heaven! it was a joy
The dead men could not blast.

I saw a third – I heard his voice:
It is the hermit good!
510 He singeth loud his godly hymns
That he makes in the wood.
He'll shrieve my soul, he'll wash away
The albatross's blood.'

PART VII

'This hermit good lives in that wood   The hermit of the wood.
Which slopes down to the sea.
How loudly his sweet voice he rears!
He loves to talk with marineres
That come from a far countree.

He kneels at morn, and noon, and eve –
520 He hath a cushion plump:
It is the moss that wholly hides
The rotted old oak-stump.

The skiff-boat neared: I heard them talk,
'Why, this is strange, I trow!
Where are those lights so many and fair,
That signal made but now?'

'Strange, by my faith!' the hermit said –   Approacheth the ship
'And they answered not our cheer!   with wonder.
The planks looked warped! and see those sails,
530 How thin they are and sere°!   *withered*
I never saw aught like to them,
Unless perchance it were

Brown skeletons of leaves that lag
My forest-brook along;
When the ivy-tod° is heavy with snow,   *bush*
And the owlet whoops to the wolf below,
That eats the she-wolf's young.'

'Dear Lord! it hath a fiendish look –'
(The pilot made reply)
540 'I am a-feared' – 'Push on, push on!'
Said the hermit cheerily.

The boat came closer to the ship,
But I nor spake nor stirred;
The boat came close beneath the ship,
And straight a sound was heard.

Under the water it rumbled on,
Still louder and more dread:
It reached the ship, it split the bay;
The ship went down like lead.

The ship suddenly sinketh.

The ancient Mariner is saved in the pilot's boat.

550 Stunned by that loud and dreadful sound,
Which sky and ocean smote,
Like one that hath been seven days drowned
My body lay afloat;
But swift as dreams, myself I found
Within the pilot's boat.

Upon the whirl, where sank the ship,
The boat spun round and round;
And all was still, save that the hill
Was telling of the sound.

560 I moved my lips – the pilot shrieked
And fell down in a fit;
The holy hermit raised his eyes,
And prayed where he did sit.

I took the oars: the pilot's boy,
Who now doth crazy go,
Laughed loud and long, and all the while
His eyes went to and fro.
'Ha! ha!' quoth he, 'full plain I see,
The Devil knows how to row.'

570 And now, all in my own countree,
I stood on the firm land!
The hermit stepped forth from the boat,
And scarcely he could stand.

'O shrieve me, shrieve me, holy man!'
The hermit crossed his brow.
'Say quick,' quoth he, 'I bid thee say –
What manner of man art thou?'

The ancient Mariner earnestly entreateth the hermit to shrieve him; and the penance of life falls on him.

Forthwith this frame of mine was wrenched
With a woful agony,
580 Which forced me to begin my tale;
And then it left me free.

Since then, at an uncertain hour,
That agony returns:
And till my ghastly tale is told,
This heart within me burns.

And ever and anon
throughout his future life
an agony constraineth
him to travel from land
to land.

I pass, like night, from land to land;
I have strange power of speech;
That moment that his face I see,
I know the man that must hear me:
590 To him my tale I teach.

What loud uproar bursts from that door
The wedding-guests are there:
But in the garden-bower the bride
And bride-maids singing are:
And hark the little vesper bell,
Which biddeth me to prayer!

O wedding-guest! this soul hath been
Alone on a wide wide sea:
So lonely 'twas, that God himself
600 Scarce seeméd there to be.

O sweeter than the marriage-feast,
'Tis sweeter far to me,
To walk together to the kirk
With a goodly company! –

To walk together to the kirk,
And all together pray,
While each to his great Father bends,
Old men, and babes, and loving friends,
And youths and maidens gay!

610 Farewell, farewell! but this I tell
To thee, thou wedding-guest!
He prayeth well, who loveth well
Both man and bird and beast.

And to teach, by his own
example, love and rever-
ence to all things that
God made and loveth.

He prayeth best, who loveth best
All things both great and small;
For the dear God who loveth us,
He made and loveth all.'

The Mariner, whose eye is bright,
Whose beard with age is hoar,
620 Is gone: and now the wedding-guest
Turned from the bridegroom's door.

He went like one that hath been stunned,
And is of sense forlorn:°   *deprived*
A sadder and a wiser man,
He rose the morrow morn.

1798 [1798 rev. 1817]

Christabel[15]

PART I

'Tis the middle of night by the castle clock,
And the owls have awakened the crowing cock;
Tu–whit! – Tu–whoo!
And hark, again! the crowing cock,
How drowsily it crew.
Sir Leoline, the Baron rich,
Hath a toothless mastiff bitch;
From her kennel beneath the rock
She maketh answer to the clock,
10 Four for the quarters, and twelve for the hour;
Ever and aye, by shine and shower,
Sixteen short howls, not over loud;
Some say, she sees my lady's shroud.

Is the night chilly and dark?
The night is chilly, but not dark.
The thin gray cloud is spread on high,
It covers but not hides the sky.
The moon is behind, and at the full;
And yet she looks both small and dull.

20 The night is chill, the cloud is gray:
'Tis a month before the month of May
And the Spring comes slowly up this way.

The lovely lady, Christabel
Whom her father loves so well,
What makes her in the wood so late,
A furlong from the castle gate?
She had dreams all yesternight
Of her own betrothed knight;
And she in the midnight wood will pray
30 For the weal° of her lover that's far away.   *benefit*

She stole along, she nothing spoke,
The sighs she heaved were soft and low,
And naught was green upon the oak,
But moss and rarest mistletoe:
She kneels beneath the huge oak tree,
And in silence prayeth she.

The lady sprang up suddenly,
The lovely lady, Christabel!
It moaned as near, as near can be,
40 But what it is, she cannot tell. –
On the other side it seems to be,
Of the huge, broad-breasted, old oak tree.
The night is chill; the forest bare;
Is it the wind that moaneth bleak?
There is not wind enough in the air
To move away the ringlet curl
From the lovely lady's cheek –
There is not wind enough to twirl
The one red leaf, the last of its clan,
50 That dances as often as dance it can,
Hanging so light, and hanging so high,
On the topmost twig that looks up at the sky.

Hush, beating heart of Christabel!
Jesu, Maria, shield her well!
She folded her arms beneath her cloak,
And stole to the other side of the oak.
        What sees she there?

There she sees a damsel bright,

Drest in a silken robe of white,
60 That shadowy in the moonlight shone:
The neck that made that white robe wan,
Her stately neck, and arms were bare;
Her blue-veined feet unsandal'd were,
And wildly glittered here and there
The gems entangled in her hair.
I guess, 'twas frightful there to see
A lady so richly clad as she —
Beautiful exceedingly!

Mary mother, save me now!
70 (Said Christabel,) And who art thou?

The lady strange made answer meet,
And her voice was faint and sweet:—
Have pity on my sore distress,
I scarce can speak for weariness:
Stretch forth thy hand, and have no fear!
Said Christabel, How camest thou here?
And the lady, whose voice was faint and sweet,
Did thus pursue her answer meet:—

My sire is of a noble line,
80 And my name is Geraldine:
Five warriors seized me yestermorn,
Me, even me, a maid forlorn:
They choked my cries with force and fright,
And tied me on a palfrey° white.   *lady's saddle-horse*
The palfrey was as fleet as wind,
And they rode furiously behind.

They spurred amain, their steeds were white:
And once we crossed the shade of night.
As sure as Heaven shall rescue me,
90 I have no thought what men they be;
Nor do I know how long it is
(For I have lain entranced° I wis)   *in a trance*
Since one, the tallest of the five,
Took me from the palfrey's back,
A weary woman, scarce alive.
Some muttered words his comrades spoke:
He placed me underneath this oak;
He swore they would return with haste;

Whither they went I cannot tell –
100 I thought I heard, some minutes past,
     Sounds as of a castle bell.
     Stretch forth thy hand (thus ended she),
     And help a wretched maid to flee.

     Then Christabel stretched forth her hand
     And comforted fair Geraldine:
     O well, bright dame! may you command
     The service of Sir Leoline;
     And gladly our stout chivalry
     Will he send forth and friends withal
110 To guide and guard you safe and free
     Home to your noble father's hall.

     She rose: and forth with steps they passed
     That strove to be, and were not, fast.
     Her gracious stars the lady blest,
     And thus spake on sweet Christabel:
     All our household are at rest,
     The hall as silent as the cell;
     Sir Leoline is weak in health,
     And may not well awakened be,
120 But we will move as if in stealth,
     And I beseech your courtesy,
     This night, to share your couch with me.

     They crossed the moat, and Christabel
     Took the key that fitted well;
     A little door she opened straight,
     All in the middle of the gate;
     The gate that was ironed° within and without,   *made of iron*
     Where an army in battle array had marched out.
     The lady sank, belike through pain,
130 And Christabel with might and main
     Lifted her up, a weary weight,
     Over the threshold of the gate:
     Then the lady rose again,
     And moved, as she were not in pain.

     So free from danger, free from fear,
     They crossed the court: right glad they were.
     And Christabel devoutly cried
     To the Lady by her side;

Praise we the Virgin all divine
140 Who hath rescued thee from thy distress!
Alas, alas! said Geraldine,
I cannot speak for weariness.
So free from danger, free from fear,
They crossed the court: right glad they were.

Outside her kennel the mastiff old
Lay fast asleep, in moonshine cold.
The mastiff old did not awake,
Yet she an angry moan did make!
And what can ail the mastiff bitch?
150 Never till now she uttered yell
Beneath the eye of Christabel.
Perhaps it is the owlet's scritch:°   screech
For what can ail the mastiff bitch?

They passed the hall, that echoes still,
Pass as lightly as you will!
The brands° were flat, the brands were dying,   torches
Amid their own white ashes lying;
But when the lady passed, there came
A tongue of light, a fit of flame;
160 And Christabel saw the lady's eye,
And nothing else saw she thereby,
Save the boss° of the shield of Sir Leoline tall,   metal stud in centre
Which hung in a murky old niche in the wall.
O softly tread, said Christabel,
My father seldom sleepeth well.

Sweet Christabel her feet doth bare,
And, jealous of the listening air,
They steal their way from stair to stair,
Now in glimmer, and now in gloom,
170 And now they pass the Baron's room,
As still as death with stifled breath!
And now have reached her chamber door;
And now doth Geraldine press down
The rushes of the chamber floor.

The moon shines dim in the open air,
And not a moonbeam enters here.
But they without its light can see
The chamber carved so curiously,

Carved with figures strange and sweet,
180 All made out of the carver's brain,
For a lady's chamber meet:
The lamp with twofold silver chain
Is fastened to an angel's feet.

The silver lamp burns dead and dim;
But Christabel the lamp will trim.
She trimmed the lamp, and made it bright,
And left it swinging to and fro,
While Geraldine, in wretched plight,
Sank down upon the floor below.

190 O weary lady, Geraldine,
I pray you, drink this cordial wine!
It is a wine of virtuous powers;
My mother made it of wild flowers.

And will your mother pity me,
Who am a maiden most forlorn?
Christabel answered – Woe is me!
She died the hour that I was born.
I have heard the grey-haired friar tell,
How on her death-bed she did say,
200 That she should hear the castle-bell
Strike twelve upon my wedding day.
O mother dear! that thou wert here!
I would, said Geraldine, she were!

But soon with altered voice, she said –
'Off, wandering mother! Peak and pine°!   *fade away*
I have power to bid thee flee.'
Alas! what ails poor Geraldine?
Why stares she with unsettled eye?
Can she the bodiless dead espy?
210 And why with hollow voice cries she,
'Off, woman, off! this hour is mine –
Though thou her guardian spirit be,
Off, woman, off! 'tis given to me.'

Then Christabel knelt by the lady's side,
And raised to heaven her eyes so blue –
Alas! said she, this ghastly ride –

Dear lady! it hath wildered you!
The lady wiped her moist cold brow,
And faintly said, ''tis over now!'

220 Again the wild-flower wine she drank:
Her fair large eyes 'gan glitter bright,
And from the floor whereon she sank,
The lofty lady stood upright;
She was most beautiful to see,
Like a lady of a far countree.

And thus the lofty lady spake –
All they, who live in the upper sky,
Do love you, holy Christabel!
And you love them, and for their sake
230 And for the good which me befell,
Even I in my degree will try,
Fair maiden, to requite you well.
But now unrobe yourself; for I
Must pray, ere yet in bed I lie.

Quoth Christabel, so let it be!
And as the lady bade, did she.
Her gentle limbs did she undress,
And lay down in her loveliness.

But through her brain of weal and woe
240 So many thoughts moved to and fro,
That vain it were her lids to close;
So half-way from the bed she rose,
And on her elbow did recline
To look at the lady Geraldine.

Beneath the lamp the lady bowed,
And slowly rolled her eyes around;
Then drawing in her breath aloud
Like one that shuddered, she unbound
The cincture° from beneath her breast: *girdle*
250 Her silken robe, and inner vest,
Dropt to her feet, and full in view,
Behold! her bosom and half her side –
A sight to dream of, not to tell!
O shield her! shield sweet Christabel!

Yet Geraldine nor speaks nor stirs;
Ah! what a stricken look was hers!
Deep from within she seems half-way
To lift some weight with sick assay,°   *effort*
And eyes the maid and seeks delay;
260 Then suddenly as one defied
Collects herself in scorn and pride,
And lay down by the Maiden's side! –
And in her arms the maid she took,
        Ah well-a-day!
And with low voice and doleful look
These words did say:
In the touch of this bosom there worketh a spell,
Which is lord of thy utterance, Christabel!
Thou knowest to-night, and wilt know to-morrow
270 This mark of my shame, this seal of my sorrow;
        But vainly thou warrest,°   *struggle*
            For this is alone in
          Thy power to declare,
            That in the dim forest
          Thou heard'st a low moaning,
And found'st a bright lady, surpassingly fair:
And didst bring her home with thee in love and in charity,
To shield her and shelter her from the damp air.

THE CONCLUSION TO PART I

It was a lovely sight to see
280 The lady Christabel, when she
Was praying at the old oak tree.
        Amid the jagged shadows
        Of mossy leafless boughs
        Kneeling in the moonlight,
        To make her gentle vows;
Her slender palms together prest,
Heaving sometimes on her breast;
Her face resigned to bliss or bale° –   *destruction*
Her face, oh call it fair not pale,
290 And both blue eyes more bright than clear,
Each about to have a tear.

With open eyes (ah woe is me!)
Asleep, and dreaming fearfully,
Fearfully dreaming, yet I wis,°   *certainly*
Dreaming that alone, which is –
O sorrow and shame! Can this be she,
The lady, who knelt at the old oak tree?
And lo! the worker of these harms,
That holds the maiden in her arms,
300   Seems to slumber still and mild,
As a mother with her child.

A star hath set, a star hath risen,
O Geraldine! since arms of thine
Have been the lovely lady's prison.
O Geraldine! one hour was thine –
Thou'st had thy will! By tairn° and rill,°   *tarn/stream*
The night-birds all that hour were still.
But now they are jubilant anew,
From cliff and tower, tu–whoo! tu–whoo!
310   Tu–whoo! tu–whoo! from wood and fell!

And see! the lady Christabel
Gathers herself from out her trance;
Her limbs relax, her countenance
Grows sad and soft; the smooth thin lids
Close o'er her eyes; and tears she sheds –
Large tears that leave the lashes bright!
And oft the while she seems to smile
As infants at a sudden light!

Yea, she doth smile, and she doth weep,
320   Like a youthful hermitess,
Beauteous in a wilderness,
Who, praying always, prays in sleep.
And, if she move unquietly,
Perchance, 'tis but the blood so free,
Comes back and tingles in her feet.
No doubt, she hath a vision sweet.
What if her guardian spirit 'twere?
What if she knew her mother near?
But this she knows, in joys and woes,
330   That saints will aid if men will call:
For the blue sky bends over all!

PART II

Each matin bell, the Baron saith,
Knells us back to a world of death.
These words Sir Leoline first said,
When he rose and found his lady dead:
These words Sir Leoline will say,
Many a morn to his dying day!

And hence the custom and law began,
That still at dawn the sacristan,   *sexton*
340 Who duly pulls the heavy bell,
Five and forty beads must tell
Between each stroke – a warning knell,
Which not a soul can choose but hear
From Bratha Head to Wyndermere.

Saith Bracy the bard, So let it knell!
And let the drowsy sacristan
Still count as slowly as he can!
There is no lack of such, I ween,   *believe*
As well fill up the space between.
350 In Langdale Pike and Witch's Lair,
And Dungeon-ghyll so foully rent,
With ropes of rock and bells of air
Three sinful sextons' ghosts are pent,
Who all give back, one after t'other,
The death-note to their living brother;
And oft too, by the knell offended,
Just as their one! two! three! is ended,
The devil mocks the doleful tale
With a merry peal from Borodale.

360 The air is still! through mist and cloud
That merry peal comes ringing loud;
And Geraldine shakes off her dread,
And rises lightly from the bed;
Puts on her silken vestments white,
And tricks her hair in lovely plight,
And nothing doubting of her spell
Awakens the lady Christabel.
'Sleep you, sweet lady Christabel?
I trust that you have rested well.'

370 And Christabel awoke and spied
    The same who lay down by her side –
    O rather say, the same whom she
    Raised up beneath the old oak tree!
    Nay, fairer yet! and yet more fair!
    For she belike hath drunken deep
    Of all the blessedness of sleep!
    And while she spake, her looks, her air
    Such gentle thankfulness declare,
    That (so it seemed) her girded vests
380 Grew tight beneath her heaving breasts.
    'Sure I have sinned!' said Christabel,
    'Now heaven be praised if all be well!'
    And in low faltering tones, yet sweet,
    Did she the lofty lady greet
    With such perplexity of mind
    As dreams too lively leave behind.

    So quickly she rose, and quickly arrayed
    Her maiden limbs, and having prayed
    That He, who on the cross did groan,
390 Might wash away her sins unknown,
    She forthwith led fair Geraldine
    To meet her sire, Sir Leoline.

    The lovely maid and the lady tall
    Are pacing both into the hall,
    And pacing on through page and groom,
    Enter the Baron's presence room.

    The Baron rose, and while he prest
    His gentle daughter to his breast,
    With cheerful wonder in his eyes
400 The lady Geraldine espies,
    And gave such welcome to the same,
    As might beseem so bright a dame!

    But when he heard the lady's tale,
    And when she told her father's name,
    Why waxed Sir Leoline so pale,
    Murmuring o'er the name again,
    Lord Roland de Vaux of Tryermaine?

Alas! they had been friends in youth;
But whispering tongues can poison truth;
410 And constancy lives in realms above;
And life is thorny; and youth is vain;
And to be wroth with one we love,
Doth work like madness in the brain.
And thus it chanced, as I divine,
With Roland and Sir Leoline.
Each spake words of high disdain
And insult to his heart's best brother:
They parted – ne'er to meet again!
But never either found another
420 To free the hollow heart from paining –
They stood aloof, the scars remaining,
Like cliffs which had been rent asunder;
A dreary sea now flows between; –
But neither heat, nor frost, nor thunder,
Shall wholly do away, I ween,
The marks of that which once hath been.

Sir Leoline, a moment's space,
Stood gazing on the damsel's face:
And the youthful Lord of Tryermaine
430 Came back upon his heart again.

O then the Baron forgot his age,
His noble heart swelled high with rage;
He swore by the wounds in Jesu's side,
He would proclaim it far and wide
With trump and solemn heraldry,
That they, who thus had wronged the dame,
Were base as spotted infamy!
'And if they dare deny the same,
My herald shall appoint a week,
440 And let the recreant traitors seek
My tourney° court – that there and then   *tournament*
I may dislodge their reptile souls
From the bodies and forms of men!'
He spake: his eye in lightning rolls!
For the lady was ruthlessly seized; and he kenned
In the beautiful lady the child of his friend!

And now the tears were on his face,
And fondly in his arms he took
Fair Geraldine, who met the embrace,
450 Prolonging it with joyous look.
Which when she viewed, a vision fell
Upon the soul of Christabel,
The vision of fear, the touch and pain!
She shrunk and shuddered, and saw again –
(Ah, woe is me! Was it for thee,
Thou gentle maid! such sights to see?)

Again she saw that bosom old,
Again she felt that bosom cold,
And drew in her breath with a hissing sound:
460 Whereat the Knight turned wildly round,
And nothing saw, but his own sweet maid
With eyes upraised, as one that prayed.

The touch, the sight, had passed away,
And in its stead that vision blest,
Which comforted her after-rest,
While in the lady's arms she lay,
Had put a rapture in her breast,
And on her lips and o'er her eyes
Spread smiles like light!
                With new surprise,
470 'What ails then my beloved child?'
The Baron said – His daughter mild
Made answer, 'All will yet be well!'
I ween, she had no power to tell
Aught else: so mighty was the spell.

Yet he, who saw this Geraldine,
Had deemed her sure a thing divine.
Such sorrow with such grace she blended,
As if she feared, she had offended
Sweet Christabel, that gentle maid!
480 And with such lowly tones she prayed,
She might be sent without delay
Home to her father's mansion.
                    'Nay!
Nay, by my soul!' said Leoline.
'Ho! Bracy, the bard, the charge be thine!
Go thou, with music sweet and loud,

And take two steeds with trappings proud,
And take the youth whom thou lov'st best
To bear thy harp, and learn thy song,
And clothe you both in solemn vest,
490   And over the mountains haste along,
Lest wandering folk, that are abroad,
Detain you on the valley road.

And when he has crossed the Irthing flood,
My merry bard! he hastes, he hastes
Up Knorren Moor, through Halegarth Wood,
And reaches soon that castle good
Which stands and threatens Scotland's wastes.

Bard Bracy! bard Bracy! your horses are fleet,
Ye must ride up the hall, your music so sweet,
More loud than your horses' echoing feet!
500   And loud and loud to Lord Roland call,
Thy daughter is safe in Langdale hall!
Thy beautiful daughter is safe and free –
Sir Leoline greets thee thus through me.
He bids thee come without delay
With all thy numerous array;
And take thy lovely daughter home:
And he will meet thee on the way
With all his numerous array
510   White with their panting palfreys' foam:
And by mine honour! I will say,
That I repent me of the day
When I spake words of fierce disdain
To Roland de Vaux of Tryermaine! –
– For since that evil hour hath flown,
Many a summer's sun hath shone;
Yet ne'er found I a friend again
Like Roland de Vaux of Tryermaine.'

The lady fell, and clasped his knees,
520   Her face upraised, her eyes o'erflowing;
And Bracy replied, with faltering voice,
His gracious Hail on all bestowing! –
'Thy words, thou sire of Christabel,
Are sweeter than my harp can tell;
Yet might I gain a boon of thee,
This day my journey should not be,

So strange a dream hath come to me;
That I had vowed with music loud
To clear yon wood from thing unblest,
530 Warned by a vision in my rest!
For in my sleep I saw that dove,
That gentle bird, whom thou dost love,
And call'st by thy own daughter's name –
Sir Leoline! I saw the same
Fluttering, and uttering fearful moan,
Among the green herbs in the forest alone.
Which when I saw and when I heard,
I wonder'd what might ail the bird;
For nothing near it could I see,
540 Save the grass and green herbs underneath the old tree.

And in my dream methought I went
To search out what might there be found;
And what the sweet bird's trouble meant,
That thus lay fluttering on the ground.
I went and peered, and could descry
No cause for her distressful cry;
But yet for her dear lady's sake
I stooped, methought, the dove to take,
When lo! I saw a bright green snake
550 Coiled around its wings and neck,
Green as the herbs on which it couched,
Close by the dove's its head it crouched;
And with the dove it heaves and stirs,
Swelling its neck as she swelled hers!
I woke; it was the midnight hour,
The clock was echoing in the tower;
But though my slumber was gone by,
This dream it would not pass away –
It seems to live upon my eye!
560 And thence I vowed this self-same day,
With music strong and saintly song
To wander through the forest bare,
Lest aught unholy loiter there.'

Thus Bracy said: the Baron, the while,
Half-listening heard him with a smile;
Then turned to Lady Geraldine,
His eyes made up of wonder and love;
And said in courtly accents fine,

'Sweet maid, Lord Roland's beauteous dove,
570   With arms more strong than harp or song,
Thy sire and I will crush the snake!'
He kissed her forehead as he spake,
And Geraldine, in maiden wise,
Casting down her large bright eyes,
With blushing cheek and courtesy fine
She turned her from Sir Leoline;
Softly gathering up her train,
That o'er her right arm fell again;
And folded her arms across her chest,
580   And couched her head upon her breast,
And looked askance at Christabel –
Jesu, Maria, shield her well!

A snake's small eye blinks dull and shy,
And the lady's eyes they shrunk in her head,
Each shrunk up to a serpent's eye,
And with somewhat of malice, and more of dread,
At Christabel she looked askance! –
One moment – and the sight was fled!
But Christabel in dizzy trance
590   Stumbling on the unsteady ground
Shuddered aloud, with a hissing sound;
And Geraldine again turned round,
And like a thing, that sought relief,
Full of wonder and full of grief,
She rolled her large bright eyes divine
Wildly on Sir Leoline.

The maid, alas! her thoughts are gone,
She nothing sees – no sight but one!
The maid, devoid of guile and sin,
600   I know not how, in fearful wise,
So deeply had she drunken in
That look, those shrunken serpent eyes,
That all her features were resigned
To this sole image in her mind;
And passively did imitate
That look of dull and treacherous hate!
And thus she stood, in dizzy trance,
Still picturing that look askance
With forced unconscious sympathy
610   Full before her father's view –

As far as such a look could be,
In eyes so innocent and blue!

And when the trance was o'er, the maid
Paused awhile, and inly prayed:
Then falling at the Baron's feet,
'By my mother's soul do I entreat
That thou this woman send away!'
She said: and more she could not say:
For what she knew she could not tell,
620 O'er-mastered by the mighty spell.

Why is thy cheek so wan and wild,
Sir Leoline? Thy only child
Lies at thy feet, thy joy, thy pride,
So fair, so innocent, so mild;
The same, for whom thy lady died!
O by the pangs of her dear mother
Think thou no evil of thy child!
For her, and thee, and for no other,
She prayed the moment ere she died:
630 Prayed that the babe for whom she died,
Might prove her dear lord's joy and pride!
     That prayer her deadly pangs beguiled,
          Sir Leoline!
     And wouldst thou wrong thy only child,
          Her child and thine?

Within the Baron's heart and brain
If thoughts, like these, had any share,
They only swelled his rage and pain,
And did but work confusion there.
640 His heart was cleft with pain and rage,
His cheeks they quivered, his eyes were wild,
Dishonoured thus in his old age;
Dishonoured by his only child,
And all his hospitality
To the wrong'd daughter of his friend
By more than woman's jealousy
Brought thus to a disgraceful end —
He rolled his eye with stern regard
Upon the gentle minstrel bard,
650 And said in tones abrupt, austere —
'Why, Bracy! dost thou loiter here?

I bade thee hence!' The bard obeyed;
And turning from his own sweet maid,
The aged knight, Sir Leoline,
Led forth the lady Geraldine!

1797–1800 [1816]

THE CONCLUSION TO PART II

A little child, a limber elf,
Singing, dancing to itself,
A fairy thing with red round cheeks,
That always finds, and never seeks,
660 Makes such a vision to the sight
As fills a father's eyes with light;
And pleasures flow in so thick and fast
Upon his heart, that he at last
Must needs express his love's excess
With words of unmeant bitterness.
Perhaps 'tis pretty to force together
Thoughts so all unlike each other;
To mutter and mock a broken charm,
To dally with wrong that does no harm.
670 Perhaps 'tis tender too and pretty
At each wild word to feel within
A sweet recoil of love and pity.
And what, if in a world of sin
(O sorrow and shame should this be true!)
Such giddiness of heart and brain
Comes seldom save from rage and pain,
So talks as it's most used to do.

Unfinished. 1801 [1816]

Frost at Midnight[16]

The frost performs its secret ministry,
Unhelped by any wind. The owlet's cry
Came loud – and hark, again! loud as before.
The inmates of my cottage, all at rest,
Have left me to that solitude, which suits
Abstruser musings: save that at my side
My cradled infant[17] slumbers peacefully.
'Tis calm indeed! so calm, that it disturbs
And vexes meditation with its strange
10 And extreme silentness. Sea, hill, and wood,
This populous village! Sea, and hill, and wood,
With all the numberless goings-on of life,
Inaudible as dreams! the thin blue flame
Lies on my low burnt fire, and quivers not;
Only that film, which fluttered on the grate,
Still flutters there, the sole unquiet thing.
Methinks, its motion in this hush of nature
Gives it dim sympathies with me who live,
Making it a companionable form,
20 Whose puny flaps and freaks° the idling spirit   *caprices*
By its own moods interprets, every where
Echo or mirror seeking of itself,
And makes a toy of thought.
                                    But O! how oft,
How oft, at school,[18] with most believing mind,
Presageful,° have I gazed upon the bars,   *full of foreboding*
To watch that fluttering stranger! and as oft
With unclosed lids, already had I dreamt
Of my sweet birth-place;[19] and the old church-tower,
Whose bells, the poor man's only music, rang
30 From morn to evening, all the hot Fair-day,
So sweetly, that they stirred and haunted me
With a wild pleasure, falling on mine ear
Most like articulate sounds of things to come!
So gazed I, till the soothing things I dreamt
Lulled me to sleep, and sleep prolonged my dreams!
And so I brooded all the following morn,
Awed by the stern preceptor's° face, mine eye   *teacher's*
Fixed with mock study on my swimming book:
Save if the door half opened, and I snatched
40 A hasty glance, and still my heart leaped up,

For still I hoped to see the *stranger's* face,
Townsman, or aunt, or sister more beloved,
My play-mate when we both were clothed alike![20]

    Dear Babe, that sleepest cradled by my side,
Whose gentle breathings, heard in this deep calm,
Fill up the interspersed vacancies
And momentary pauses of the thought!
My babe so beautiful! it thrills my heart
With tender gladness, thus to look at thee,
50 And think that thou shalt learn far other lore
And in far other scenes! For I was reared
In the great city, pent 'mid cloisters[21] dim,
And saw nought lovely but the sky and stars.
But thou, my babe! shalt wander like a breeze
By lakes and sandy shores, beneath the crags
Of ancient mountain, and beneath the clouds,
Which image in their bulk both lakes and shores
And mountain crags: so shalt thou see and hear
The lovely shapes and sounds intelligible
60 Of that eternal language, which thy God
Utters, who from eternity doth teach
Himself in all, and all things in himself.
Great universal Teacher! He shall mould
Thy spirit, and by giving make it ask.

    Therefore all seasons shall be sweet to thee,
Whether the summer clothe the general earth
With greenness, or the redbreast sit and sing
Betwixt the tufts of snow on the bare branch
Of mossy apple-tree, while the nigh thatch
70 Smokes[22] in the sun-thaw; whether the eve-drops fall   *eaves*
Heard only in the trances of the blast,
Or if the secret ministry of frost
Shall hang them up in silent icicles,
Quietly shining to the quiet Moon.

                      1798 [1798]

Fears in Solitude

WRITTEN IN APRIL, 1798, DURING THE
ALARM OF AN INVASION[23]

A green and silent spot, amid the hills,
A small and silent dell! O'er stiller place
No singing sky-lark ever poised himself.
The hills are heathy, save that swelling slope,
Which hath a gay and gorgeous covering on,
All golden with the never-bloomless furze,   *gorse*
Which now blooms most profusely: but the dell,
Bathed by the mist, is fresh and delicate
As vernal corn-field, or the unripe flax,
10 When, through its half-transparent stalks, at eve,
The level sunshine glimmers with green light.
Oh! 'tis a quiet spirit-healing nook!
Which all, methinks, would love; but chiefly he,
The humble man, who, in his youthful years,
Knew just so much of folly, as had made
His early manhood more securely wise!
Here he might lie on fern or withered heath,   *heather*
While from the singing-lark (that sings unseen
The minstrelsy that solitude loves best,)
20 And from the sun, and from the breezy air,
Sweet influences trembled o'er his frame;
And he, with many feelings, many thoughts,
Made up a meditative joy, and found
Religious meanings in the forms of nature!
And so, his sense gradually wrapt
In a half sleep, he dreams of better worlds,
And dreaming hears thee still, O singing-lark;
That singest like an angel in the clouds!

My God! it is a melancholy thing
30 For such a man, who would full fain preserve
His soul in calmness, yet perforce must feel
For all his human brethren – O my God!
It weighs upon the heart, that he must think
What uproar and what strife may now be stirring
This way or that way o'er these silent hills –
Invasion, and the thunder and the shout,
And all the crash of onset; fear and rage,
And undetermined conflict – even now,

Even now, perchance, and in his native isle:
40   Carnage and groans beneath this blessed sun!
We have offended, Oh! my countrymen!
We have offended very grievously,
And been most tyrannous. From east to west
A groan of accusation pierces Heaven!
The wretched plead against us; multitudes
Countless and vehement, the sons of God,
Our brethren! Like a cloud that travels on,
Steamed up from Cairo's swamps of pestilence,
Even so, my countrymen! have we gone forth
50   And borne to distant tribes slavery and pangs,
And, deadlier far, our vices, whose deep taint
With slow perdition murders the whole man,
His body and his soul! Meanwhile, at home,
All individual dignity and power
Engulfed in courts, committees, institutions,
Associations and societies,
A vain, speech-mouthing, speech-reporting guild,
One benefit-club for mutual flattery.
We have drunk up, demure as at a grace,
60   Pollutions from the brimming cup of wealth;
Contemptuous of all honourable rule,
Yet bartering freedom and the poor man's life
For gold, as at a market! The sweet words
Of Christian promise, words that even yet
Might stem destruction, were they wisely preached,
Are muttered o'er by men, whose tones proclaim
How flat and wearisome they feel their trade:
Rank° scoffers some, but most too indolent   *downright*
To deem them falsehoods or to know their truth.
70   Oh! blasphemous! the book of life is made
A superstitious instrument, on which
We gabble o'er the oaths we mean to break;
For all must swear – all and in every place,
College and wharf, council and justice-court;
All, all must swear, the briber and the bribed,
Merchant and lawyer, senator and priest,
The rich, the poor, the old man and the young;
All, all make up one scheme of perjury,
That faith doth reel; the very name of God
80   Sounds like a juggler's charm; and, bold with joy,
Forth from his dark and lonely hiding-place,

(Portentous sight!) the owlet Atheism,
Sailing on obscene wings athwart the noon,
Drops his blue-fringed lids, and holds them close,
And hooting at the glorious sun in Heaven,
Cries out, 'Where is it?'

                              Thankless too for peace,
(Peace long preserved by fleets and perilous seas)
Secure from actual warfare, we have loved
To swell the war-whoop, passionate for war!
90 Alas! for ages ignorant of all
Its ghastlier workings, (famine or blue plague,
Battle, or siege, or flight through wintry snows,)
We, this whole people, have been clamorous
For war and bloodshed; animating sports,
The which we pay for as a thing to talk of,
Spectators and not combatants! No guess
Anticipative of a wrong unfelt,
No speculation on contingency,
However dim and vague, too vague and dim
100 To yield a justifying cause; and forth,
(Stuffed out with big preamble, holy names,
And adjurations of the God in Heaven,)
We send our mandates for the certain death
Of thousands and ten thousands! Boys and girls,
And women, that would groan to see a child
Pull off an insect's leg, all read of war,
The best amusement for our morning-meal!
The poor wretch, who has learnt his only prayers
From curses, who knows scarcely words enough
110 To ask a blessing from his Heavenly Father,
Becomes a fluent phraseman, absolute
And technical in victories and defeats,
And all our dainty terms for fratricide;
Terms which we trundle smoothly o'er our tongues
Like mere abstractions, empty sounds to which
We join no feeling and attach no form!
As if the soldier died without a wound;
As if the fibres of this godlike frame
Were gored without a pang; as if the wretch
120 Who fell in battle, doing bloody deeds,
Passed off to Heaven, translated and not killed;
As though he had no wife to pine for him,
No God to judge him! Therefore, evil days

Are coming on us, O my countrymen!
And what if all-avenging Providence,
Strong and retributive, should make us know
The meaning of our words, force us to feel
The desolation and the agony
Of our fierce doings!

                    Spare us yet awhile,
130 Father and God! O! spare us yet awhile!
Oh! let not English women drag their flight
Fainting beneath the burthen of their babes,
Of the sweet infants, that but yesterday
Laughed at the breast! Sons, brothers, husbands, all
Who ever gazed with fondness on the forms
Which grew up with you round the same fire-side,
And all who ever heard the sabbath-bells
Without the infidel's scorn, make yourselves pure!
Stand forth! be men! repel an impious foe,
140 Impious and false, a light yet cruel race,
Who laugh away all virtue, mingling mirth
With deeds of murder; and still promising
Freedom, themselves too sensual to be free,
Poison life's amities, and cheat the heart
Of faith and quiet hope, and all that soothes
And all that lifts the spirit! Stand we forth;
Render them back upon the insulted ocean,
And let them toss as idly on its waves
As the vile sea-weed, which some mountain-blast
150 Swept from our shores! And oh! may we return
Not with a drunken triumph, but with fear,
Repenting of the wrongs with which we stung
So fierce a foe to frenzy!

                    I have told,
O Britons! O my brethren! I have told
Most bitter truth, but without bitterness.
Nor deem my zeal or factious or mis-timed;
For never can true courage dwell with them,
Who, playing tricks with conscience, dare not look
At their own vices. We have been too long
160 Dupes of a deep delusion! Some, belike,
Groaning with restless enmity, expect
All change from change of constituted power;
As if a Government had been a robe,

On which our vice and wretchedness were tagged
Like fancy-points and fringes, with the robe
Pulled off at pleasure. Fondly these attach
A radical causation to a few
Poor drudges of chastising Providence,
Who borrow all their hues and qualities
170 From our own folly and rank wickedness,
Which gave them birth and nursed them. Others, meanwhile,
Dote with a mad idolatry; and all
Who will not fall before their images,
And yield them worship, they are enemies
Even of their country!

                          Such have I been deemed –
But, O dear Britain! O my Mother Isle!
Needs must thou prove a name most dear and holy
To me, a son, a brother, and a friend,
A husband, and a father! who revere
180 All bonds of natural love, and find them all
Within the limits of thy rocky shores.
O native Britain! O my Mother Isle!
How shouldst thou prove aught else but dear and holy
To me, who from thy lakes and mountain-hills,
Thy clouds, thy quiet dales, thy rocks and seas,
Have drunk in all my intellectual life,
All sweet sensations, all ennobling thoughts,
All adoration of the God in nature,
All lovely and all honourable things,
190 Whatever makes this mortal spirit feel
The joy and greatness of its future being?
There lives nor form nor feeling in my soul
Unborrowed from my country. O divine
And beauteous island! thou hast been my sole
And most magnificent temple, in the which
I walk with awe, and sing my stately songs,
Loving the God that made me!

                          May my fears,
My filial fears, be vain! and may the vaunts
And menace of the vengeful enemy
200 Pass like the gust, that roared and died away
In the distant tree: which heard, and only heard
In this low dell, bowed not the delicate grass.

But now the gentle dew-fall sends abroad
The fruit-like perfume of the golden furze:
The light has left the summit of the hill,
Though still a sunny gleam lies beautiful,
Aslant the ivied° beacon. Now farewell,   *covered with ivy*
Farewell, awhile, O soft and silent spot!
On the green sheep-track, up the heathy hill,
210   Homeward I wind my way; and lo! recalled
From bodings that have well nigh wearied me,
I find myself upon the brow, and pause
Startled! And after lonely sojourning
In such a quiet and surrounded nook,
This burst of prospect, here the shadowy main,
Dim tinted, there the mighty majesty
Of that huge amphitheatre of rich
And elmy fields, seems like society –
Conversing with the mind, and giving it
220   A livelier impulse and a dance of thought!
And now, beloved Stowey! I behold
Thy church-tower, and, methinks, the four huge elms
Clustering, which mark the mansion of my friend;°   *Wordsworth*
And close behind them, hidden from my view,
Is my own lowly cottage, where my babe
And my babe's mother dwell in peace! With light
And quickened footsteps thitherward I tend,
Remembering thee, O green and silent dell!
And grateful, that by nature's quietness
230   And solitary musings, all my heart
Is softened, and made worthy to indulge
Love, and the thoughts that yearn for human kind.

1798 [1798]

The Nightingale

A CONVERSATION POEM. APRIL 1798

No cloud, no relique of the sunken day
Distinguishes the west, no long thin slip
Of sullen light, no obscure trembling hues.
Come, we will rest on this old mossy bridge!
You see the glimmer of the stream beneath,
But hear no murmuring: it flows silently,
O'er its soft bed of verdure. All is still,
A balmy night! and though the stars be dim,
Yet let us think upon the vernal showers
That gladden the green earth, and we shall find
A pleasure in the dimness of the stars.
And hark! the Nightingale begins its song,
'Most musical, most melancholy' bird![24]
A melancholy bird! Oh! idle thought!
In nature there is nothing melancholy.
But some night-wandering man whose heart was pierced
With the remembrance of a grievous wrong,
Or slow distemper, or neglected love,
(And so, poor wretch! filled all things with himself,
And made all gentle sounds tell back the tale
Of his own sorrow) he, and such as he,
First named these notes a melancholy strain.
And many a poet echoes the conceit;
Poet who hath been building up the rhyme
When he had better far have stretched his limbs
Beside a brook in mossy forest-dell,
By sun or moon-light, to the influxes
Of shapes and sounds and shifting elements
Surrendering his whole spirit, of his song
And of his fame forgetful! so his fame
Should share in Nature's immortality,
A venerable thing! and so his song
Should make all Nature lovelier, and itself
Be loved like Nature! But 'twill not be so;
And youths and maidens most poetical,
Who lost the deepening twilights of the spring
In ball-rooms and hot theatres, they still
Full of meek sympathy must heave their sighs
O'er Philomela's° pity-pleading strains.

the nightingale

40   My Friend, and thou, our Sister![25] we have learnt
        A different lore: we may not thus profane
        Nature's sweet voices, always full of love
        And joyance! 'Tis the merry nightingale
        That crowds, and hurries, and precipitates
        With fast thick warble his delicious notes,
        As he were fearful that an April night
        Would be too short for him to utter forth
        His love-chant, and disburthen° his full soul   *unburden*
        Of all its music!

                                And I know a grove
50   Of large extent, hard by a castle huge,
        Which the great lord inhabits not; and so
        This grove is wild with tangling underwood,
        And the trim walks are broken up, and grass,
        Thin grass and king-cups grow within the paths.
        But never elsewhere in one place I knew
        So many nightingales; and far and near,
        In wood and thicket, over the wide grove,
        They answer and provoke each other's song,
        With skirmish and capricious passagings,
60   And murmurs musical and swift jug jug,
        And one low piping sound more sweet than all –
        Stirring the air with such a harmony,
        That should you close your eyes, you might almost
        Forget it was not day! On moon-lit bushes,
        Whose dewy leaflets are but half disclosed,
        You may perchance behold them on the twigs,
        Their bright, bright eyes, their eyes both bright and full,
        Glistening, while many a glow-worm in the shade
        Lights up her love-torch.

                                A most gentle Maid,
70   Who dwelleth in her hospitable home
        Hard by the castle, and at latest eve
        (Even like a lady vowed and dedicate
        To something more than Nature in the grove)
        Glides through the pathways; she knows all their notes,
        That gentle maid! and oft a moment's space,
        What time the moon was lost behind a cloud,
        Hath heard a pause of silence; till the moon
        Emerging, hath awakened earth and sky
        With one sensation, and these wakeful birds

80 Have all burst forth in choral minstrelsy,
As if some sudden gale had swept at once
A hundred airy harps! And she hath watched
Many a nightingale perched giddily
On blossomy twig still swinging from the breeze,
And to that motion tune his wanton song
Like tipsy joy that reels with tossing head.

Farewell, O warbler! till to-morrow eve,
And you, my Friends! farewell, a short farewell!
We have been loitering long and pleasantly,
90 And now for our dear homes. – That strain again!
Full fain it would delay me! My dear babe,
Who, capable of no articulate sound,
Mars all things with his imitative lisp,
How he would place his hand beside his ear,
His little hand, the small forefinger up,
And bid us listen! And I deem it wise
To make him Nature's play-mate. He knows well
The evening-star; and once, when he awoke
In most distressful mood (some inward pain
100 Had made up that strange thing, an infant's dream. –)
I hurried with him to our orchard-plot,
And he beheld the moon, and, hushed at once,
Suspends his sobs, and laughs most silently,
While his fair eyes, that swam with undropped tears,
Did glitter in the yellow moon-beam! Well! –
It is a father's tale: But if that Heaven
Should give me life, his childhood shall grow up
Familiar with these songs, that with the night
He may associate joy. – Once more, farewell,
110 Sweet Nightingale! Once more, my friends! farewell.

1798 [1798]

Dejection: An Ode[26]

Late, late yestreen I saw the new moon,
With the old moon in her arms;
And I fear, I fear, my master dear!
We shall have a deadly storm.
Ballad of Sir Patrick Spence.

I

Well! If the Bard was weather-wise, who made
   The grand old ballad of Sir Patrick Spence,
   This night, so tranquil now, will not go hence
Unroused by winds, that ply a busier trade
Than those which mold yon cloud in lazy flakes,
Or the dull sobbing draft, that moans and rakes
Upon the strings of this Aeolian lute,[27]
     Which better far were mute.
   For lo! the new-moon winter-bright!
10   And overspread with phantom light,
    (With swimming phantom light o'erspread
    But rimmed and circled by a silver thread)
I see the old moon in her lap, foretelling
   The coming-on of rain and squally blast.
And oh! that even now the gust were swelling,
   And the slant night shower driving loud and fast!
Those sounds which oft have raised me, whilst they awed,
    And sent my soul abroad,
Might now perhaps their wonted° impulse give,   *accustomed*
20 Might startle this dull pain, and make it move and live!

II

A grief without a pang, void, dark, and drear,
   A stifled, drowsy, unimpassioned grief,
   Which finds no natural outlet, no relief,
    In word, or sigh, or tear –
O Lady![28] in this wan and heartless mood,
To other thoughts by yonder throstle wooed,
   All this long eve, so balmy and serene,
Have I been gazing on the western sky,
   And its peculiar tint of yellow green:
30 And still I gaze – and with how blank an eye!
And those thin clouds above, in flakes and bars,
That give away their motion to the stars;
Those stars, that glide behind them or between,

Now sparkling, now bedimmed, but always seen:
Yon crescent moon, as fixed as if it grew
In its own cloudless, starless lake of blue;
I see them all so excellently fair,
I see, not feel, how beautiful they are!

III

My genial spirits[29] fail;
40   And what can these avail
To lift the smothering weight from off my breast?
    It were a vain endeavour,
        Though I should gaze forever
On that green light that lingers in the west:
I may not hope from outward forms to win
The passion and the life, whose fountains are within.

IV

O Lady! we receive but what we give,
And in our life alone does Nature live:
Ours is her wedding garment, ours her shroud!
50   And would we aught behold, of higher worth,
Than that inanimate cold world allowed
To the poor loveless ever-anxious crowd,
    Ah! from the soul itself must issue forth
A light, a glory, a fair luminous cloud
        Enveloping the Earth –
And from the soul itself must there be sent
    A sweet and potent voice, of its own birth,
Of all sweet sounds the life and element!

V

O pure of heart! thou need'st not ask of me
60 What this strong music in the soul may be!
What, and wherein it doth exist,
This light, this glory, this fair luminous mist,
This beautiful and beauty-making power.
    Joy, virtuous Lady! Joy that ne'er was given,
Save to the pure, and in their purest hour,
Life, and Life's effluence, cloud at once and shower,
Joy, Lady! is the spirit and the power,
Which, wedding Nature to us, gives in dower
        A new Earth and new Heaven,
70 Undreamt of by the sensual and the proud –
Joy is the sweet voice, Joy the luminous cloud –

We in ourselves rejoice!
And thence flows all that charms or ear or sight,
    All melodies the echoes of that voice,
All colours a suffusion from that light.

VI

There was a time when, though my path was rough,
    This joy within me dallied with distress,
And all misfortunes were but as the stuff
    Whence Fancy made me dreams of happiness:
80 For hope grew round me, like the twining vine,
And fruits, and foliage, not my own, seemed mine.
But now afflictions bow me down to earth:
Nor care I that they rob me of my mirth;
        But oh! each visitation
Suspends what nature gave me at my birth,
    My shaping spirit of Imagination.
For not to think of what I needs must feel,
    But to be still and patient, all I can;
And haply by abstruse research to steal
90   From my own nature all the natural man –
    This was my sole resource, my only plan:
Till that which suits a part infects the whole,
And now is almost grown the habit of my soul.

VII

Hence, viper thoughts, that coil around my mind,
        Reality's dark dream!
I turn from you, and listen to the wind,
    Which long has raved unnoticed. What a scream
Of agony by torture lengthened out
That lute sent forth! Thou Wind, that rav'st without,
100   Bare crag, or mountain tairn,° or blasted tree,   *tarn*
Or pine grove whither woodman never clomb,°   *climbed*
Or lonely house, long held the witches' home,
    Methinks were fitter instruments for thee,
Mad lutanist! who in this month of showers,
Of dark-brown gardens, and of peeping flowers,
Mak'st devils' yule,30 with worse than wintry song,
The blossoms, buds, and timorous leaves among.
    Thou actor, perfect in all tragic sounds!
Thou mighty poet, e'en to frenzy bold!

110   What tell'st thou now about?
          'Tis of the rushing of an host in rout,
        With groans, of trampled men, with smarting wounds –
      At once they groan with pain, and shudder with the cold!
      But hush! there is a pause of deepest silence!
          And all that noise, as of a rushing crowd,
        With groans, and tremulous shudderings – all is over –
          It tells another tale, with sounds less deep and loud!
              A tale of less affright,
              And tempered with delight,
120   As Otway's self had framed the tender lay –
              'Tis of a little child
              Upon a lonesome wild,
        Not far from home, but she hath lost her way:
        And now moans low in bitter grief and fear,
        And now screams loud, and hopes to make her mother hear.

                              VIII
        'Tis midnight, but small thoughts have I of sleep:
        Full seldom may my friend such vigils keep!
        Visit her, gentle Sleep! with wings of healing,
          And may this storm be but a mountain birth,
130   May all the stars hang bright above her dwelling,
          Silent as though they watched the sleeping Earth!
              With light heart may she rise,
              Gay fancy, cheerful eyes,
          Joy lift her spirit, joy attune her voice;
        To her may all things live, from pole to pole,
          Their life the eddying of her living soul!
          O simple spirit, guided from above,
        Dear Lady! friend devoutest of my choice,
        Thus mayest thou ever, evermore rejoice.

                                                    1802 [1817]

The Pains of Sleep[31]

Ere on my bed my limbs I lay,
It hath not been my use to pray
With moving lips or bended knees;
But silently, by slow degrees,
My spirit I to Love compose,
In humble trust mine eye-lids close,
With reverential resignation,
No wish conceived, no thought exprest,
Only a *sense* of supplication;
A sense o'er all my soul imprest
That I am weak, yet not unblest,
Since in me, round me, every where
Eternal strength and wisdom are.

But yester-night I prayed aloud
In anguish and in agony,
Up-starting from the fiendish crowd
Of shapes and thoughts that tortured me:
A lurid light, a trampling throng,
Sense of intolerable wrong,
And whom I scorned, those only strong!
Thirst of revenge, the powerless will
Still baffled, and yet burning still!
Desire with loathing strangely mixed
On wild or hateful objects fixed.
Fantastic passions! maddening brawl!
And shame and terror over all!
Deeds to be hid which were not hid,
Which all confused I could not know,
Whether I suffered, or I did:
For all seemed guilt, remorse or woe,
My own or others still the same
Life-stifling fear, soul-stifling shame.

So two nights passed: the night's dismay
Saddened and stunned the coming day.
Sleep, the wide blessing, seemed to me
Distemper's° worst calamity.   *derangement of mind/body*
The third night, when my own loud scream
Had waked me from the fiendish dream,
O'ercome with sufferings strange and wild,
I wept as I had been a child;

And having thus by tears subdued
My anguish to a milder mood,
Such punishments, I said, were due
To natures deepliest stained with sin, –
For aye entempesting° anew   *creating a tempest*
The unfathomable hell within
The horror of their deeds to view,
To know and loathe, yet wish and do!
Such griefs with such men well agree,
50 But wherefore, wherefore fall on me?
To be beloved is all I need,
And whom I love, I love indeed.

1803 [1816]

To William Wordsworth

COMPOSED ON THE NIGHT AFTER HIS RECITATION OF A POEM ON THE GROWTH OF AN INDIVIDUAL MIND.

Friend of the wise! and teacher of the good!
Into my heart have I received that lay
More than historic, that prophetic lay
Wherein (high theme by thee first sung aright)
Of the foundations and the building up
Of a Human Spirit thou hast dared to tell
What may be told, to the understanding mind
Revealable; and what within the mind
By vital breathings secret as the soul
10 Of vernal growth, oft quickens in the heart
Thoughts all too deep for words! –

                          Theme hard as high!
Of smiles spontaneous, and mysterious fears,
(The first-born they of Reason and twin-birth)
Of tides obedient to external force,
And currents self-determined, as might seem,
Or by some inner Power; of moments awful,
Now in thy inner life, and now abroad,
When power streamed from thee, and thy soul received
The light reflected, as a light bestowed –

20 Of fancies fair, and milder hours of youth,
    Hyblean° murmurs of poetic thought   *bee-like*
    Industrious in its joy, in vales and glens
    Native or outland, lakes and famous hills!
    Or on the lonely high-road, when the stars
    Were rising; or by secret mountain-streams,
    The guides and the companions of thy way!

        Of more than Fancy, of the Social Sense
    Distending wide, and man beloved as man,
    Where France in all her towns lay vibrating[32]
30 Like some becalmed bark beneath the burst
    Of Heaven's immediate thunder, when no cloud
    Is visible, or shadow on the main.
    For thou wert there, thine own brows garlanded,
    Amid the tremor of a realm aglow,
    Amid a mighty nation jubilant,
    When from the general heart of human kind
    Hope sprang forth like a full-born Deity!
    – Of that dear Hope afflicted and struck down,
    So summoned homeward, thenceforth calm and sure
40 From the dread watch-tower of man's absolute self,
    With light unwaning on her eyes, to look
    Far on – herself a glory to behold,
    The Angel of the vision! Then (last strain)
    Of Duty, chosen Laws controlling choice,
    Action and joy! – An Orphic song indeed,
    A song divine of high and passionate thoughts
    To their own music chanted!

                                        O great Bard!
    Ere yet that last strain dying awed the air,
    With steadfast eye I viewed thee in the choir
50 Of ever-enduring men. The truly great
    Have all one age, and from one visible space
    Shed influence! They, both in power and act,
    Are permanent, and Time is not with *them*,
    Save as it worketh *for* them, they *in* it.
    Nor less a sacred roll, than those of old,
    And to be placed, as they, with gradual fame
    Among the archives of mankind, thy work
    Makes audible a linked lay of Truth,
    Of Truth profound a sweet continuous lay,
60 Not learnt, but native, her own natural notes!

Ah! as I listened with a heart forlorn,
The pulses of my being beat anew:
And even as life returns upon the drowned,
Life's joy rekindling roused a throng of pains —
Keen pangs of Love, awakening as a babe
Turbulent, with an outcry in the heart;
And fears self-willed, that shunned the eye of hope:
And hope that scarce would know itself from fear;
Sense of past youth, and manhood come in vain,
70 And genius given, and knowledge won in vain;
And all which I had culled in wood-walks wild,
And all which patient toil had reared, and all,
Commune with *thee* had opened out — but flowers
Strewed on my corse, and borne upon my bier,
In the same coffin, for the self-same grave!

    That way no more! and ill beseems it me,
Who came a welcomer in herald's guise,
Singing of glory, and futurity,
To wander back on such unhealthful road,
80 Plucking the poisons of self-harm! And ill
Such intertwine beseems triumphal wreaths
Strewed before *thy* advancing!

                    Nor do thou,
Sage Bard! impair the memory of that hour
Of thy communion with my nobler mind
By pity or grief, already felt too long!
Nor let my words import more blame than needs.
The tumult rose and ceased: for peace is nigh
Where wisdom's voice has found a listening heart.
Amid the howl of more than wintry storms,
90 The halcyon[33] hears the voice of vernal hours
Already on the wing.

                  Eve following eve,
Dear tranquil time, when the sweet sense of Home
Is sweetest! moments for their own sake hailed
And more desired, more precious for thy song,
In silence listening, like a devout child,
My soul lay passive, by thy various strain
Driven as in surges now beneath the stars,
With momentary stars of my own birth,
Fair constellated foam, still darting off

100   Into the darkness; now a tranquil sea,
      Outspread and bright, yet swelling to the moon.

      And when – O Friend! my comforter and guide!
      Strong in thyself, and powerful to give strength! –
      Thy long sustained Song finally closed,
      And thy deep voice had ceased – yet thou thyself
      Wert still before my eyes, and round us both
      That happy vision of beloved faces –
      Scarce conscious, and yet conscious of its close
      I sate, my being blended in one thought
110   (Thought was it? or aspiration? or resolve?)
      Absorbed, yet hanging still upon the sound –
      And when I rose, I found myself in prayer.

                                    1807 [1817]

Metrical Feet[34]

LESSON FOR A BOY

      Trōchēe trīps frŏm lōng tŏ shōrt;
      Frŏm lōng tŏ lōng iṅ sōlĕṁn sōrt
      Slōw Spōndēe stālks; strŏng fŏŏt! yĕt īll āblĕ
      Ĕvĕr to cōme ŭp wīth Dāctȳl trĭsȳllāblĕ.
      Ĭāmbĭcs mārch frŏm shŏrt tŏ lōng; –
      Wĭth ă lēāp ănd ă bōūnd thĕ swīft Ānăpæ̆sts thrōng;
      One syllable long, with one short at each side,
      Ămphībrăchȳs hāstes wĭth ă stātelȳ strīde; –
      First and last being long, middle short, Amphimacer
10   Strīkes hĭs thūndērĭng hōōfs līke ă prōūd hīgh-brĕd Rācer.
      If Derwent be innocent, steady, and wise,
      And delight in the things of earth, water, and skies;
      Tender warmth at his heart, with these metres to show it,
      With sound sense in his brains, may make Derwent a poet, –
      May crown him with fame, and must win him the love
      Of his father on earth and his Father above.
              My dear, dear child!
      Could you stand upon Skiddaw, you would not from its whole ridge
      See a man who so loves you as your fond S.T. COLERIDGE.

                                    Begun 1806 [1834]

NOTES

Coleridge

1   composed at Clevedon, Somerset, Aug. 1795 on C. and Sara's honeymoon: a harp whose strings vibrate in the wind.

2   birds of New Guinea with bright plumage and believed to have no feet, spending their life on the wing.

3   Charles and Mary Lamb and Wordsworth.

4   in June, 1797, some friends visited C. He had had an accident so could not go walking with them. One evening, when they left for a few hours, he composed this in the garden: sent in a letter to Southey, 17 July, 1797.

5   the inherited insanity in the Lamb family. Mary had killed her mother in a fit of insanity, Sept. 1796.

6   ref. to Charles was originally 'My sister and my Friends'. When C. and Wordsworth became estranged, C. altered it.

7   the noise of the feathers and wing shafts.

8   C. claimed he had a vivid dream in which he wrote not 'less than two to three hundred lines; if that, indeed, can be called composition in which all the images rose up before him as "things", with a parallel production of the correspondent expressions, without any sensation or consciousness of effort. On awakening he appeared to have a distinct recollection of the whole, and taking his pen, ink and paper, instantly and eagerly wrote down the lines . . . At this moment he was unfortunately called out by a person on business from Porlock . . . on his return to his room, found that . . . with the exception of some eight or ten scattered lines and images, all the rest had passed away . . .' 'Kubla Khan was composed in a sort of reverie.' C. note on the Crewe ms. Kubla Khan – first ruler (khan) of the Mongol dynasty, 13th-century China; place-names and topography fictitious, though the Alph, in classical legend, identified with the Nile. From *Purchas his Pilgrimage*. 1626. Bk.IV.ch. 13 (which C. was reading when he fell asleep) 'In Xamdu did Kublai Kan build a stately Palace, encompassing sixteen miles of plaine ground with a wall, wherein are fertile Meadows, pleasant Springs, delightful Streames, and all sorts of beasts of chase and game, and in the midst thereof a sumptuous house of pleasure.'

9   there are many variations between the 1798 version and the 1815–16 one, the text used here, when the marginal glosses were added.

10   *facile credo* . . . 'I can easily believe that there are more invisible than visible beings in the universe. But of their families, degrees, connections, distinctions and functions, who can tell us? How do they act? Where are they found? About such matters the human mind has always circled without attaining knowledge. Yet I do not doubt that sometimes it is well for the soul to contemplate as in a picture the image of a larger and better world, lest the mind habituated to the small concerns of daily life, limit itself too much and sink entirely into trivial thinking. But meanwhile we must be on the watch for the truth, avoiding extremes, so that we may distinguish certain from uncertain, day from night.' Burnet (17th-century theologian) *Archæologiae Philosophiae*.

11   that they are sailing south can be deduced from this.

12   round Cape Horn and then north.

13   as discussed by members of the Royal Society – 'An appearance of light. Like a star seen in the dark part of the Moon, on Friday the 7th of March, 1794.'

14   C. re lines 226–7 'I am indebted to Mr Wordsworth for these lines. It was on a delightful walk from Nether Stowey to Dulverton with him and his sister, in the

Autumn of 1797, that this poem was planned, and in part composed.'

15 Part I begun 1798: part II 1799: published 1816. The places mentioned such as Bratha Head, Windermere, Langdale Pike, Borrowdale, etc. are all areas in the Lake District.

16 written at Nether Stowey.

17 C.'s son, born 1797.

18 at Christ's Hospital School, London, where C. went, age 9, after his father died: such a flutter (stranger) foretold a visitor.

19 Ottery St Mary, Devon.

20 children of either sex were dressed alike – in skirts – until the boys were 'breeched' (put in trousers).

21 Christ's Hospital School, London.

22 the steam that rises as sun melts the snow on a thatched roof.

23 written at Nether Stowey: the threatened invasion was of England by France with whom England was at war.

24 from Milton: *Il Penseroso*.

25 William and Dorothy Wordsworth.

26 sent originally in a letter to Sara Hutchinson. For publication the original 340 lines were cut to 139, to form the Ode, personal revelations and references being left out. Readers are strongly recommended to read 'Letter to Sara Hutchinson'. As both could not be included, the Ode was chosen as the version C. himself chose to offer to the public, but for what is gained in smoothness of shape and general argument, there is an equal loss in intimacy and vitality – the difference, in fact, between a letter and an ode.

27 cf. note 1.

28 in the letter, Sara Hutchinson is addressed directly and by name as is Wordsworth.

29 not just good temper – more the vital creative energies of his imagination.

30 unnatural Christmas time (wintry weather) in spring.

31 earliest draft in a letter to Southey, Sept. 1803. Revised and published 1816. cf. Letter to Poole, Sept. 1803: 'God forbid my worst enemy should ever have the nights and the sleeps that I have had, night after night – surprised by sleep while I struggled to remain awake, starting up to bless my own loud screams that awakened me . . . till my repeated night-yells had made me a nuisance in my own house.' C. took opium (possibly the cause of these nightmares) initially to relieve neuralgia.

32 at the beginning of the French Revolution.

33 bird – the kingfisher – associated with nesting on the sea in the winter solstice and calming the wind and the sea.

34 begun for C.'s son Hartley and concluded for his younger brother, Derwent.

George Gordon, Lord Byron

[1788–1824]

He was the son of Capt. John Byron, who first eloped with and then
married Lady Carmarthen – they had a daughter, Augusta: then
married Catherine Gordon – B. was their child, born with a club
foot. 1789 the family moved to Aberdeen where B. was first
educated. 1798, after the deaths, in 1791 of B.'s father, in 1794 of
the fifth baron's grandson, and in 1798 of the baronet himself, B.
inherited the title: sent to Harrow school, and, 1805, to Cambridge.
He possibly first met his half-sister, Augusta, 1802. 1807 published
Hours of Idleness, which was attacked in the *Edinburgh Review*,
resulting in B.'s satire *English Bards and Scotch Reviewers*, 1809. That
year he took his seat in the House of Lords: then, to 1811, he
travelled in Portugal, Spain, Malta, Greece and the Levant: began
Childe Harold; wrote *The Maid of Athens*; swam the Hellespont and
became involved with the Greek struggle for freedom from the
Turks. March 1812 he had a great success with the publication of
Cantos 1 and 2 of *Childe Harold* and was lionised in London; he had an
affair with Lady Caroline Lamb, and formed a relationship with
Augusta. 1813 he wrote *The Bride of Abydos* (in seven days), *The
Corsair* (ten days); published *The Giaour*. 1814 Augusta had a child,
presumably by B. 1815 he married Annabella Milbanke, Lady
Melbourne's niece: daughter, Ada, born: published *Hebrew Melo-
dies*. Harrassed by debts, rumours of his incestuous relationship
with Augusta and that he was mad, led to his wife leaving him and a
legal separation arranged. Embittered, B. left England, 1816, for
Geneva, where the Shelleys were living: he wrote *The Prisoner of
Chillon*, two acts of *Manfred*, canto 3 of *C.H.* Claire Claremont
became his mistress and their daughter, Allegra, was born Jan.
1817. B. left for Venice, where third act of *Manfred* completed and
an Armenian dictionary published: then on to Rome, where he
began canto 4 of *C.H.*: returned to Venice and there wrote *Beppo*, in
which he first used the colloquial style that he later made so much
his own in *Don Juan*, begun 1818. 1819 the first two cantos of *D.J.*,
published anonymously, denounced by *Blackwood's* magazine as 'a
filthy and impious poem'. At this time he formed an attachment
with Teresa, Countess Guiccioli, whom he followed to Ravenna.
1820 he continued with cantos 3 and 4 of *D.J.*: 1821 Teresa left her
husband for B. and they joined the Shelleys at Pisa. B. became
interested in drama, writing several plays, but they were not well
received. 1822, Allegra, whom he had sadly neglected, died. With

the co-operation of Leigh Hunt, at Leghorn, *The Liberal* magazine was produced, in which his *The Vision of Judgement* and *Heaven and Earth* were published. Moving to Genoa, he wrote *Werner*, a poetic drama, and was engaged on *D.J.*: became increasingly preoccupied with Greece and its struggles: by July prepared to sail for Greece: Jan. 1824 arrived at Missolonghi where he formed the Byron Brigade. He died of fever there in April. Memorial services were held in Greece: the deans of Westminster and St Paul's refused his body: B.'s friend and executor John Hobhouse (who also burned B.'s memoirs immediately after his death) arranged for a brief lying in state in London, then interment in the family vault at Hucknall Torkard, near Newstead, Nottinghamshire.

From *English Bards and Scotch Reviewers*

When Vice triumphant holds her sov'reign sway,
Obey'd by all who nought beside obey;
When folly, frequent harbinger° of crime,   *herald*
30 Bedecks her cap with bells of every clime;
When knaves and fools combined o'er all prevail,
And weigh their justice in a golden scale;
E'en then the boldest start from public sneers,
Afraid of shame, unknown to other fears,
More darkly sin, by satire kept in awe,
And shrink from ridicule, though not from law.

Such is the force of wit! but not belong
To me the arrows of satiric song;
The royal vices of our age demand
40 A keener weapon, and a mightier hand.
Still there are follies, e'en for me to chase,
And yield at least amusement in the race:
Laugh when I laugh, I seek no other fame;
The cry is up, and scribblers are my game.
Speed Pegasus! – ye strains of great and small,
Ode, epic, elegy, have at you all!
I too can scrawl, and once upon a time
I poured along the town a flood of rhyme,
A schoolboy freak, unworthy praise or blame;
50 I printed – older children do the same,
'Tis pleasant, sure, to see one's name in print;
A book's a book, although there's nothing in't.

* * *

Time was, ere yet in these degenerate days
Ignoble themes obtain'd mistaken praise,
When sense and wit with poesy allied,
No fabled graces, flourish'd side by side;
From the same fount their inspiration drew,
And rear'd by taste, bloom'd fairer as they grew.
Then, in this happy isle, a Pope's[1] pure strain
110 Sought the rapt soul to charm, nor sought in vain;
A polish'd nation's praise aspired to claim,
And raised the people's, as the poet's fame.
Like him great Dryden[2] pour'd the tide of song,
In stream less smooth, indeed, yet doubly strong.
Then Congreve's scenes could cheer, or Otway's melt –
For nature then an English audience felt.
But why these names, or greater still, retrace,
When all to feebler bards resign their place?
Yet to such times our lingering looks are cast,
120 When taste and reason with those times are past.
Now look around, and turn each trifling page,
Survey the precious works that please the age;
This truth at least let satire's self allow,
No dearth of bards can be complain'd of now.
The loaded press beneath her labour groans,
And printers' devils° shake their weary bones;   *errand-boy*
While Southey's epics cram the creaking shelves,
And Little's° lyrics shine in hot-press'd twelves.   *i.e. Thomas Moore*
Thus saith the preacher: 'Nought beneath the sun
130 Is new,' yet still from change to change we run:
What varied wonders tempt us as they pass!
The cow-pox,[3] tractors, galvanism, and gas,
In turns appear, to make the vulgar stare,
Till the swoln bubble bursts – and all is air!
Nor less new schools of poetry arise,
Where dull pretenders grapple for the prize:
O'er taste awhile these pseudo-bards prevail;
Each country book-club bows the knee to Baal,
And, hurling lawful genius from the throne,
140 Erects a shrine and idol of its own;
Some leaden calf – but whom it matters not,
From soaring Southey down to grovelling Stott.

Behold! in various throngs the scribbling crew,
For notice eager, pass in long review:
Each spurs his jaded Pegasus apace,

And rhyme and blank maintain an equal race;
Sonnets on sonnets crowd, and ode on ode;
And tales of terror jostle on the road;
Immeasurable measures move along;
150 For simpering folly loves a varied song,
To strange mysterious dulness still the friend,
Admires the strain she cannot comprehend.
Thus Lays of Minstrels[4] – may they be the last! –
On half-strung harps whine mournful to the blast.
While mountain spirits prate to river sprites,
That dames may listen to the sound at nights;
And goblin brats, of Gilpin Horner's[5] brood,
Decoy young border-nobles through the wood,
And skip at every step, Lord knows how high,
160 And frighten foolish babes, the Lord knows why:
While high-born ladies in their magic cell,
Forbidding knights to read who cannot spell,
Despatch a courier to a wizard's grave,
And fight with honest men to shield a knave.

*   *   *

The time has been, when yet the muse was young,
190 When Homer swept the lyre, and Maro° sung,   *Virgil*
An epic scarce ten centuries could claim,
While awe-struck nations hail'd the magic name:
The work of each immortal bard appears
The single wonder of a thousand years.
Empires have moulder'd from the face of earth,
Tongues have expired with those who gave them birth,
Without the glory such a strain can give,
As even in ruin bids the language live.
Not so with us, though minor bards, content
200 On one great work a life of labour spent:
With eagle pinion soaring to the skies,
Behold the ballad-monger Southey rise!

1807–9 [1809]
Suppressed by Byron 1811

Song

ATHENS 1810[6]

Ζωή μου, σᾶς αγαπῶ.[7]

Maid of Athens, ere we part,
Give, oh give me back my heart!
Or, since that has left my breast,
Keep it now, and take the rest!
Hear my vow before I go,
Ζωή μου, σᾶς αγαπῶ.

By those tresses unconfined,
Woo'd by each Ægean wind;
10 By those lids whose jetty fringe
Kiss thy soft cheeks' blooming tinge;
By those wild eyes like the roe,
Ζωή μου, σᾶς αγαπῶ.

By that lip I long to taste;
By that zone-encircled waist;
By all the token-flowers[8] that tell
What words can never speak so well;
By love's alternate joy and woe,
Ζωή μου, σᾶς αγαπῶ.

20 Maid of Athens! I am gone:
Think of me, sweet! when alone.
Though I fly to Istambol,
Athens holds my heart and soul:
Can I cease to love thee? No!
Ζωή μου, σᾶς αγαπῶ.

1810 [1815]

She Walks in Beauty[9]

She walks in beauty, like the night
   Of cloudless climes and starry skies;
And all that's best of dark and bright
   Meet in her aspect and her eyes:
Thus mellowed to that tender light
   Which heaven to gaudy day denies.

One shade the more, one ray the less,
   Had half impaired the nameless grace
Which waves in every raven tress,
10   Or softly lightens o'er her face;
Where thoughts serenely sweet express
   How pure, how dear their dwelling-place.

And on that cheek, and o'er that brow,
   So soft, so calm, yet eloquent,
The smiles that win, the tints that glow,
   But tell of days in goodness spent,
A mind at peace with all below,
   A heart whose love is innocent.

1814 [1815]

The Destruction of Sennacherib

I

The Assyrian came down like the wolf on the fold
And his cohorts were gleaming in purple and gold;
And the sheen of their spears was like stars on the sea,
When the blue wave rolls nightly on deep Galilee.

II

Like the leaves of the forest when summer is green,
That host with their banners at sunset were seen:
Like the leaves of the forest when autumn hath blown,
That host on the morrow lay wither'd and strown.

III

For the Angel of Death spread his wings on the blast,
And breathed in the face of the foe as he passed;
And the eyes of the sleepers waxed deadly and chill,
And their hearts but once heaved, and for ever grew still!

IV

And there lay the steed with his nostril all wide,
But through it there rolled not the breath of his pride;
And the foam of his gasping lay white on the turf,
And cold as the spray of the rock-beating surf.

IV

And there lay the rider distorted and pale,
With the dew on his brow, and the rust on his mail:
And the tents were all silent, the banners alone,
The lances unlifted, the trumpet unblown.

VI

And the widows of Ashur° are loud in their wail,   *Assyria*
And the idols are broke in the temple of Baal;
And the might of the Gentile, unsmote by the sword,
Hath melted like snow in the glance of the Lord!

[1815]

When We Two Parted[10]

When we two parted
    In silence and tears,
Half broken-hearted
    To sever for years,
Pale grew thy cheek and cold,
    Colder thy kiss;
Truly that hour foretold
    Sorrow to this.

The dew of the morning
10   Sunk chill on my brow –
It felt like the warning
     Of what I feel now.
Thy vows are all broken,
     And light is thy fame:
I hear thy name spoken,
     And share in its shame.

They name thee before me,
     A knell to mine ear;
A shudder comes o'er me –
20   Why wert thou so dear?
They know not I knew thee,
     Who knew thee too well:–
Long, long shall I rue thee,
     Too deeply to tell.

In secret we met –
     In silence I grieve,
That thy heart could forget,
     Thy spirit deceive.
If I should meet thee
     After long years,
30 How should I greet thee?
     With silence and tears.

1815 [1816]

Epistle to Augusta[11]

I

My sister! my sweet sister! if a name
Dearer and purer were, it should be thine;
Mountains and seas divide us, but I claim
No tears, but tenderness to answer mine:
Go where I will, to me thou art the same –
A loved regret which I would not resign,
There yet are two things in my destiny, –
A world to roam through, and a home with thee.

II

The first were nothing – had I still the last,
10   It were the haven of my happiness;
But other claims and other ties thou hast,
    And mine is not the wish to make them less.
A strange doom is thy father's son's, and past
    Recalling, as it lies beyond redress;
      Reversed for him our grandsire's[12] fate of yore, –
He had no rest at sea, nor I on shore.

III

If my inheritance of storms hath been
    In other elements, and on the rocks
Of perils overlooked or unforeseen,
20   I have sustained my share of worldly shocks
The fault was mine; nor do I seek to screen
    My errors with defensive paradox;
      I have been cunning in mine overthrow,
The careful pilot of my proper woe.

IV

Mine were my faults, and mine be their reward.
    My whole life was a contest, since the day
That gave me being, gave me that which marred
    The gift, – a fate, or will, that walked astray;
And I at times have found the struggle hard,
30   And thought of shaking off my bonds of clay:
      But now I fain would for a time survive,
If but to see what next can well arrive.

V

Kingdoms and empires in my little day
    I have outlived, and yet I am not old;
And when I look on this, the petty spray
    Of my own years of trouble, which have roll'd
Like a wild bay of breakers, melts away:
    Something – I know not what – does still uphold
      A spirit of slight patience; – not in vain,
40 Even for its own sake, do we purchase pain.

VI

Perhaps the workings of defiance stir
    Within me – or perhaps a cold despair,
Brought on when ills habitually recur, –

Perhaps a kinder clime, or purer air,
(For even to this may change of soul refer,
And with light armour we may learn to bear,)
Have taught me a strange quiet, which was not
The chief companion of a calmer lot.

VII

I feel almost at times as I have felt
50   In happy childhood; trees, and flowers, and brooks,
Which do remember me of where I dwelt
Ere my young mind was sacrificed to books,
Come as of yore upon me, and can melt
My heart with recognition of their looks;
And even at moments I could think I see
Some living thing to love – but none like thee.

VIII

Here are the Alpine landscapes which create
A fund for contemplation; – to admire
Is a brief feeling of a trivial date;
60   But something worthier do such scenes inspire:
Here to be lonely is not desolate,
For much I view which I could most desire,
And, above all, a lake I can behold
Lovelier, not dearer, than our own of old.

IX

Oh that thou wert but with me! – but I grow
The fool of my own wishes, and forget
The solitude which I have vaunted so
Has lost its praise in this but one regret;
There may be others which I less may show; –
70   I am not of the plaintive mood, and yet
I feel an ebb in my philosophy,
And the tide rising in my alter'd eye.

X

I did remind thee of our own dear Lake,
By the old Hall which may be mine no more.
Leman's is fair; but think not I forsake
The sweet remembrance of a dearer shore:
Sad havoc Time must with my memory make,
Ere *that* or *thou* can fade these eyes before;
Though, like all things which I have loved, they are
80   Resign'd for ever, or divided far.

XI

The world is all before me; I but ask
Of Nature that with which she will comply –
It is but in her summer's sun to bask,
To mingle with the quiet of her sky,
To see her gentle face without a mask,
And never gaze on it with apathy.
    She was my early friend, and now shall be
My sister – till I look again on thee.

XII

I can reduce all feelings but this one;
90 And that I would not; – for at length I see
Such scenes as those wherein my life begun.
The earliest – even the only paths for me –
Had I but sooner learnt the crowd to shun,
I had been better than I now can be;
    The passions which have torn me would have slept;
I had not suffer'd, and *thou* hadst not wept.

XIII

With false Ambition what had I to do?
Little with Love, and least of all with Fame;
And yet they came unsought, and with me grew,
100 And made me all which they can make – a name.
Yet this was not the end I did pursue;
Surely I once beheld a nobler aim.
    But all is over – I am one the more
To baffled millions which have gone before.

XIV

And for the future, this world's future may
From me demand but little of my care;
I have outlived myself by many a day;
Having survived so many things that were;
My years have been no slumber, but the prey
110 Of ceaseless vigils; for I had the share
    Of life which might have fill'd a century,
Before its fourth in time had pass'd me by.

XV

And for the remnant which may be to come
I am content; and for the past I feel
Not thankless, – for within the crowded sum
Of struggles, happiness at times would steal,

And for the present, I would not benumb
My feelings further. – Nor shall I conceal
That with all this I still can look around,
120 And worship Nature with a thought profound.

XVI

For thee, my own sweet Sister, in thy heart
I know myself secure, as thou in mine;
We were and are – I am, even as thou art –
Beings who ne'er each other can resign;
It is the same, together or apart,
From life's commencement to its slow decline
We are entwined – let death come slow or fast,
The tie which bound the first endures the last!13

1816 [1831]

So We'll Go No More A-Roving14

So, we'll go no more a-roving
    So late into the night,
Though the heart be still as loving,
    And the moon be still as bright.

For the sword outwears its sheath,
    And the soul wears out the breast,
And the heart must pause to breathe,
    And love itself have rest.

Though the night was made for loving,
10   And the day returns too soon,
Yet we'll go no more a-roving
    By the light of the moon.

1817 [1830]

From **Childe Harold's Pilgrimage**

Canto III

2

Once more upon the waters! yet once more!
And the waves bound beneath me as a steed
That knows his rider. Welcome to their roar!
Swift be their guidance, wheresoe'er it lead!
Though the strain'd mast should quiver as a reed,
And the rent canvas fluttering strew the gale,
Still must I on; for I am as a weed,
Flung from the rock, on ocean's foam to sail
Where'er the surge may sweep, the tempest's breath prevail.

3

In my youth's summer I did sing of one[15],
The wandering outlaw of his own dark mind;
Again I seize the theme, then but begun,
And bear it with me, as the rushing wind
Bears the cloud onwards: in that tale I find
The furrows of long thought, and dried-up tears,
Which, ebbing, leave a sterile track behind,
O'er which all heavily the journeying years
Plod the last sands of life, – where not a flower appears.

4

Since my young days of passion – joy, or pain,
Perchance my heart and harp have lost a string,
And both may jar: it may be, that in vain
I would essay as I have sung to sing.
Yet, though a dreary strain, to this I cling;
So that it wean me from the weary dream
Of selfish grief or gladness – so it fling
Forgetfulness around me – it shall seem
To me, though to none else, a not ungrateful theme.

5

He, who grown aged in this world of woe,
In deeds, not years, piercing the depths of life,
So that no wonder waits him; nor below
Can love or sorrow, fame, ambition, strife,
Cut to his heart again with the keen knife

Of silent, sharp endurance: he can tell
Why thought seeks refuge in lone caves, yet rife
With airy images, and shapes which dwell
Still unimpair'd though old, in the soul's haunted cell.

6

'Tis to create, and in creating live
A being more intense, that we endow
With form our fancy, gaining as we give
The life we image, even as I do now.
What am I? Nothing: but not so art thou,
Soul of my thought! with whom I traverse earth,
Invisible but gazing, as I glow
Mix'd with thy spirit, blended with thy birth,
And feeling still with thee in my crush'd feelings' dearth.

7

Yet must I think less wildly: – I *have* thought
Too long and darkly, till my brain became,
In its own eddy boiling and o'er-wrought,
A whirling gulf of phantasy and flame:
And thus, untaught in youth my heart to tame,
My springs of life were poisoned. 'Tis too late!
Yet am I changed; though still enough the same
In strength to bear what time cannot abate,
And feed on bitter fruits without accusing fate.

8

Something too much of this:– but now 'tis past,
And the spell closes with its silent seal.
Long absent HAROLD re-appears at last;
He of the breast which fain no more would feel,
Wrung with the wounds which kill not, but ne'er heal;
Yet time, who changes all, had alter'd him
In soul and aspect as in age: years steal
Fire from the mind as vigour from the limb;
And life's enchanted cup but sparkles near the brim.

9

His had been quaffed too quickly, and he found
The dregs were wormwood; but he filled again,
And from a purer fount,[16] on holier ground,
And deem'd its spring perpetual; but in vain!
Still round him clung invisibly a chain

Which galled for ever, fettering though unseen,
And heavy though it clanked not; worn with pain,
Which pined although it spoke not, and grew keen,
Entering with every step he took through many a scene.

10

Secure in guarded coldness, he had mixed
Again in fancied safety with his kind,
And deem'd his spirit now so firmly fixed
And sheath'd with an invulnerable mind,
That, if no joy, no sorrow lurked behind;
And he, as one, might 'midst the many stand
Unheeded, searching through the crowd to find
Fit speculation; such as in strange land
He found in wonder-works of God and Nature's hand.

11

But who can view the ripened rose, nor seek
To wear it? who can curiously behold
The smoothness and the sheen of beauty's cheek,
Nor feel the heart can never all grow old?
Who can contemplate Fame through clouds unfold
The star which rises o'er her steep, nor climb?
Harold, once more within the vortex, rolled
On with the giddy circle, chasing time,
Yet with a nobler aim than in his youth's fond° prime.   *foolish*

12

But soon he knew himself the most unfit
Of men to herd with man; with whom he held
Little in common; untaught to submit
His thoughts to others, though his soul was quelled
In youth by his own thoughts; still uncompelled,
He would not yield dominion of his mind
To spirits against whom his own rebelled;
Proud though in desolation; which could find
A life within itself, to breathe without mankind.

13

Where rose the mountains, there to him were friends;
Where rolled the ocean, thereon was his home;
Where a blue sky, and glowing clime, extends,
He had the passion and the power to roam;
The desert, forest, cavern, breaker's foam,

Were unto him companionship; they spake
A mutual language, clearer than the tome
Of his land's tongue, which he would oft forsake
For Nature's pages glassed° by sunbeams on the lake.   *reflected*

14
Like the Chaldean,[17] he could watch the stars,
Till he had peopled them with beings bright
As their own beams; and earth, and earthborn jars,
And human frailties, were forgotten quite:
Could he have kept his spirit to that flight
He had been happy; but this clay will sink
Its spark immortal, envying it the light
To which it mounts, as if to break the link
That keeps us from yon heaven which woos us to its brink.

15
But in man's dwellings he became a thing
Restless and worn, and stern and wearisome,
Drooped as a wild-born falcon with clipt wing,
To whom the boundless air alone were home:
Then came his fit again, which to o'ercome,
As eagerly the barred-up bird will beat
His breast and beak against his wiry dome
Till the blood tinge his plumage, so the heat
Of his impeded soul would through his bosom eat.

16
Self-exiled Harold wanders forth again,
With nought of hope left, but with less of gloom;
The very knowledge that he lived in vain,
That all was over on this side the tomb,
Had made despair a smilingness assume,
Which, though 'twere wild, – as on the plundered wreck
When mariners would madly meet their doom
With draughts intemperate on the sinking deck, –
Did yet inspire a cheer, which he forbore to check.

17
Stop! – for thy tread is on an empire's dust!
An earthquake's spoil is sepulchred below!
Is the spot marked with no colossal bust?
Nor column trophied for triumphal show?
None; but the moral's truth tells simpler so,

As the ground was before, thus let it be; –
How that red rain° hath made the harvest grow!   *blood*
And is this all the world has gained by thee,
Thou first and last of fields! king-making victory?[18]

18

And Harold stands upon this place of skulls,
The grave of France, the deadly Waterloo!
How in an hour the power which gave annuls
Its gifts, transferring fame as fleeting too!
In 'pride of place'[19] here last the eagle° flew,   *i.e. Napoleon*
Then tore with bloody talon the rent plain,
Pierced by the shaft of banded nations through;
Ambition's life and labours all were vain;
He wears the shattered links of the world's broken chain.

*   *   *

21

There was a sound of revelry by night,
And Belgium's capital[20] had gather'd then
Her Beauty and her Chivalry, and bright
The lamps shone o'er fair women and brave men;
A thousand hearts beat happily; and when
Music arose with its voluptuous swell,
Soft eyes looked love to eyes which spake again,
And all went merry as a marriage bell;
But hush! hark! a deep sound strikes like a rising knell!

22

Did ye not hear it? – No; 'twas but the wind,
Or the car° rattling o'er the stony street;   *carriage*
On with the dance! let joy be unconfined;
No sleep till morn, when youth and pleasure meet
To chase the glowing hours with flying feet –
But hark! – that heavy sound breaks in once more,
As if the clouds its echo would repeat;
And nearer, clearer, deadlier than before!
Arm! Arm! it is – it is – the cannon's opening roar!

23

Within a windowed niche of that high hall
Sate Brunswick's[21] fated chieftain; he did hear
That sound the first amidst the festival,
And caught its tone with Death's prophetic ear;

And when they smiled because he deemed it near,
His heart more truly knew that peal too well
Which stretched his father on a bloody bier,
And roused the vengeance blood alone could quell;
He rushed into the field, and, foremost fighting, fell.

24

Ah! then and there was hurrying to and fro,
And gathering tears, and tremblings of distress,
And cheeks all pale, which but an hour ago
Blushed at the praise of their own loveliness;
And there were sudden partings, such as press
The life from out young hearts, and choking sighs
Which ne'er might be repeated; who could guess
If ever more should meet those mutual eyes,
Since upon night so sweet such awful morn could rise!

25

And there was mounting in hot haste: the steed,
The mustering squadron, and the clattering car,
Went pouring forward with impetuous speed,
And swiftly forming in the ranks of war;
And the deep thunder peal on peal afar;
And near, the beat of the alarming drum
Roused up the soldier ere the morning star;
While thronged the citizens with terror dumb,
Or whispering, with white lips – 'The foe! they come! they come!'

26

And wild and high the 'Cameron's gathering' rose!
The war-note of Lochiel, which Albyn's° hills   *Scotland*
Have heard, and heard, too, have her Saxon foes:–
How in the moon of night that pibroch[22] thrills,
Savage and shrill! But with the breath which fills
Their mountain-pipe, so fill the mountaineers
With the fierce native daring which instils
The stirring memory of a thousand years,
And Evan's,[23] Donald's fame rings in each clansman's ears!

27

And Ardennes waves above them her green leaves,
Dewy with nature's tear-drops as they pass,
Grieving, if aught inanimate e'er grieves,

Over the unreturning brave, – alas!
Ere evening to be trodden like the grass
Which now beneath them, but above shall grow
In its next verdure, when this fiery mass
Of living valour, rolling on the foe
And burning with high hope shall moulder cold and low.

28

Last noon beheld them full of lusty life,
Last eve in Beauty's circle proudly gay,
The midnight brought the signal-sound of strife,
The morn the marshalling in arms, – the day
Battle's magnificently stern array!
The thunder-clouds close o'er it, which when rent
The earth is covered thick with other clay,
Which her own clay shall cover, heaped and pent,
Rider and horse, – friend, foe, – in one red burial blent!

29

Their praise is hymned by loftier harps than mine:
Yet one I would select from that proud throng,
Partly because they blend me with his line,
And partly that I did his sire some wrong,
And partly that bright names will hallow song;
And his was of the bravest, and when showered
The death-bolts deadliest the thinned files along,
Even where the thickest of war's tempest lowered,
They reached no nobler breast than thine, young gallant Howard![24]

30

There have been tears and breaking hearts for thee,
And mine were nothing had I such to give;
But when I stood beneath the fresh green tree,
Which living waves where thou didst cease to live,
And saw around me the wide field revive
With fruits and fertile promise, and the Spring
Came forth her work of gladness to contrive,
With all her reckless birds upon the wing,
I turned from all she brought to those she could not bring.

31

I turned to thee, to thousands, of whom each
And one as all a ghastly gap did make
In his own kind and kindred, whom to teach

Forgetfulness were mercy for their sake;
The archangel's trump, not glory's, must awake
Those whom they thirst for; though the sound of fame
May for a moment soothe, it cannot slake
The fever of vain longing, and the name
So honoured but assumes a stronger, bitterer claim.

32

They mourn, but smile at length; and, smiling, mourn;
The tree will wither long before it fall;
The hull drives on, though mast and sail be torn;
The roof-tree sinks, but moulders on the hall
In massy hoariness; the ruined wall
Stands when its wind-worn battlements are gone;
The bars survive the captive they enthral;
The day drags through, though storms keep out the sun;
And thus the heart will break, yet brokenly live on

33

Even as a broken mirror, which the glass
In every fragment multiplies; and makes
A thousand images of one that was,
The same, and still the more, the more it breaks;
And thus the heart will do which not forsakes,
Living in shattered guise; and still, and cold,
And bloodless, with its sleepless sorrow aches,
Yet withers on till all without is old,
Showing no visible sign, for such things are untold.

34

There is a very life in our despair,
Vitality of poison, – a quick root
Which feeds these deadly branches; for it were
As nothing did we die; but life will suit
Itself to sorrow's most detested fruit,
Like to the apples on the Dead Sea's shore,[25]
All ashes to the taste: Did man compute
Existence by enjoyment, and count o'er
Such hours 'gainst years of life, – say, would he name threescore?

35

The psalmist numbered out the years of man:
They are enough; and if thy tale be *true*,

Thou, who didst grudge him even that fleeting span,
More than enough, thou fatal Waterloo!
Millions of tongues record thee, and anew
Their children's lips shall echo them, and say –
'Here, where the sword united nations drew,
Our countrymen were warring on that day!'
And this is much, and all which will not pass away.

*   *   *

77

Here[26] the self-torturing sophist, wild Rousseau,
The apostle of affliction, he who threw
Enchantment over passion, and from woe
Wrung overwhelming eloquence, first drew
The breath which made him wretched; yet he knew
How to make madness beautiful, and cast
O'er erring deeds and thoughts a heavenly hue
Of words, like sunbeams, dazzling as they past
The eyes, which o'er them shed tears feelingly and fast.

*   *   *

81

For then he was inspired, and from him came,
As from the Pythian's mystic cave of yore,
Those oracles[27] which set the world in flame,
Nor ceased to burn till kingdoms were no more:
Did he not this for France? which lay before
Bowed to the inborn tyranny of years?
Broken and trembling to the yoke she bore,
Till by the voice of him and his compeers
Roused up to too much wrath, which follows o'ergrown fears?

82

They made themselves a fearful monument!
The wreck of old opinions – things which grew,
Breathed from the birth of time: the veil they rent,
And what behind it lay, all earth shall view.
But good with ill they also overthrew,
Leaving but ruins, wherewith to rebuild
Upon the same foundation, and renew
Dungeons and thrones, which the same hour refilled
As heretofore, because ambition was self-willed.

83

But this will not endure, nor be endured!
Mankind have felt their strength, and made it felt.
They might have used it better, but, allured
By their new vigour, sternly have they dealt
On one another; pity ceased to melt
With her once natural charities. But they,
Who in oppression's darkness caved had dwelt,
They were not eagles, nourished with the day;
What marvel then, at times, if they mistook their prey?

84

What deep wounds ever closed without a scar?
The heart's bleed longest, and but heal to wear
That which disfigures it; and they who war
With their own hopes, and have been vanquished, bear
Silence, but not submission: in his lair
Fixed Passion holds his breath, until the hour
Which shall atone for years; none need despair:
It came, it cometh, and will come, – the power
To punish or forgive – in *one* we shall be slower.

85

Clear, placid Leman thy contrasted lake,
With the wild world I dwelt in, is a thing
Which warns me, with its stillness, to forsake
Earth's troubled waters for a purer spring.
This quiet sail is as a noiseless wing
To waft me from distraction; once I loved
Torn ocean's roar, but thy soft murmuring
Sounds sweet as if a sister's voice reproved,
That I with stern delights should e'er have been so moved.

86

It is the hush of night, and all between
Thy margin and the mountains, dusk, yet clear,
Mellowed and mingling, yet distinctly seen,
Save darken'd Jura, whose capt heights appear
Precipitously steep; and drawing near,
There breathes a living fragrance from the shore,
Of flowers yet fresh with childhood; on the ear
Drops the light drip of the suspended oar,
Or chirps the grasshopper one good-night carol more;

87

He is an evening reveller, who makes
His life an infancy, and sings his fill;
At intervals, some bird from out the brakes
Starts into voice a moment, then is still.
There seems a floating whisper on the hill,
But that is fancy, for the starlight dews
All silently their tears of love instil,
Weeping themselves away, till they infuse
Deep into Nature's breast the spirit of her hues.

*   *   *

92

The sky is changed! – and such a change! Oh night,
And storm, and darkness, ye are wondrous strong,
Yet lovely in your strength, as is the light
Of a dark eye in woman! Far along,
From peak to peak, the rattling crags among
Leaps the live thunder!²⁸ Not from one lone cloud,
But every mountain now hath found a tongue,
And Jura answers, through her misty shroud,
Back to the joyous alps, who call to her aloud!

93

And this is in the night: – Most glorious night!
Thou wert not sent for slumber! let me be
A sharer in thy fierce and far delight, –
A portion of the tempest and of thee!
How the lit lake shines, a phosphoric sea,
And the big rain comes dancing to the earth!
And now again 'tis black, – and now, the glee
Of the loud hills shakes with its mountain-mirth,
As if they did rejoice o'er a young earthquake's birth.

*   *   *

96

Sky, mountains, river, winds, lake, lightnings! ye!
With night, and clouds, and thunder, and a soul
To make these felt and feeling, well may be
Things that have made me watchful; the far roll
Of your departing voices, is the knoll
Of what in me is sleepless, – if I rest.
But where of ye, O tempests! is the goal?
Are ye like those within the human breast?
Or do ye find, at length, like eagles, some high nest?

97

Could I embody and unbosom now
That which is most within me, – could I wreak
My thoughts upon expression, and thus throw
Soul, heart, mind, passions, feelings, strong or weak,
All that I would have sought, and all I seek,
Bear, know, feel, and yet breathe – into *one* word,
And that one word were lightning, I would speak;
But as it is, I live and die unheard,
With a most voiceless thought, sheathing it as a sword.

1816 [1816]

Canto IV

93

What from this barren being do we reap?
Our senses narrow, and our reason frail,
Life short, and truth a gem which loves the deep,
And all things weighed in custom's falsest scale;
Opinion an omnipotence, – whose veil
Mantles the earth with darkness, until right
And wrong are accidents, and men grow pale
Lest their own judgments should become too bright,
And their free thoughts be crimes, and earth have too much light.

*　　*　　*

95

I speak not of men's creeds – they rest between
Man and his Maker – but of things allowed,
Averred, and known, and daily, hourly seen –
The yoke that is upon us doubly bowed,
And the intent of tyranny avow'd,
The edict of earth's rulers, who are grown
The apes of him who humbled once the proud,
And shook them from their slumbers on the throne:
Too glorious, were this all his mighty arm had done.

*　　*　　*

97

But France got drunk with blood to vomit crime,
And fatal have her Saturnalia been
To Freedom's cause, in every age and clime;
Because the deadly days which we have seen,
And vile ambition, that built up between
Man and his hopes an adamantine wall,
And the base pageant last upon the scene,[29]
Are grown the pretext for the eternal thrall
Which nips life's tree, and dooms man's worst – his second fall.

98

Yet, Freedom! yet thy banner, torn, but flying,
Streams like the thunder-storm *against* the wind;
Thy trumpet voice, though broken now and dying,
The loudest still the tempest leaves behind;
Thy tree hath lost its blossoms, and the rind,
Chopped by the axe, looks rough and little worth,
But the sap lasts, – and still the seed we find
Sown deep, even in the bosom of the north;
So shall a better spring less bitter fruit bring forth.

*   *   *

178

There is a pleasure in the pathless woods,
There is a rapture on the lonely shore,
There is society, where none intrudes,
By the deep sea, and music in its roar:
I love not Man the less, but Nature more,
From these our interviews, in which I steal
From all I may be, or have been before,
To mingle with the universe, and feel
What I can ne'er express, yet cannot all conceal.

179

Roll on, thou deep and dark blue ocean – roll!
Ten thousand fleets sweep over thee in vain;
Man marks the earth with ruin – his control
Stops with the shore; upon the watery plain
The wrecks are all thy deed, nor doth remain
A shadow of man's ravage, save his own,
When, for a moment, like a drop of rain,
He sinks into thy depths with bubbling groan,
Without a grave, unknelled, uncoffined, and unknown.

*   *   *

182

Thy shores are empires, changed in all save thee –
Assyria, Greece, Rome, Carthage, what are they?
Thy waters washed them power while they were free,
And many a tyrant since; their shores obey
The stranger, slave, or savage; their decay
Has dried up realms to deserts: – not so thou –
Unchangeable, save to thy wild waves' play,
Time writes no wrinkle on thine azure brow:
Such as creation's dawn beheld, thou rollest now.

183

Thou glorious mirror, where the Almighty's form
Glasses itself in tempests; in all time, –
Calm or convulsed, in breeze, or gale, or storm,
Icing the pole, or in the torrid clime
Dark-heaving – boundless, endless, and sublime,
The image of Eternity, the throne
Of the Invisible; even from out thy slime
The monsters of the deep are made; each zone
Obeys thee; thou goest forth, dread, fathomless, alone.

184

And I have loved thee, Ocean! and my joy
Of youthful sports was on thy breast to be
Borne, like thy bubbles, onward: from a boy
I wantoned with thy breakers – they to me
Were a delight; and if the freshening sea
Made them a terror – 'twas a pleasing fear,
For I was as it were a child of thee,
And trusted to thy billows far and near,
And laid my hand upon thy mane – as I do here.

185

My task is done, my song hath ceased, my theme
Has died into an echo; it is fit
The spell should break of this protracted dream.
The torch shall be extinguished which hath lit
My midnight lamp – and what is writ, is writ;
Would it were worthier! but I am not now
That which I have been – and my visions lit
Less palpably before me – and the glow
Which in my spirit dwelt is fluttering, faint, and low.

1817 [1818]

From **Don Juan**[30]

Canto I

I

I want a hero: an uncommon want,
  When every year and month sends forth a new one,
Till, after cloying the gazettes° with cant,°   *news-sheets/hypocrisy*
  The age discovers he is not the true one:
Of such as these I should not care to vaunt,
  I'll therefore take our ancient friend Don Juan –
We all have seen him, in the pantomime,[31]
Sent to the devil somewhat ere his time.

*   *   *

6

Most epic poets plunge 'in medias res'[32]
  (Horace makes this the heroic turnpike[33] road),
And then your hero tells, whene'er you please,
  What went before – by way of episode,
While seated after dinner at his ease,
  Beside his mistress in some soft abode,
Palace, or garden, paradise, or cavern,
Which serves the happy couple for a tavern.

7

That is the usual method, but not mine –
  My way is to begin with the beginning;
The regularity of my design
  Forbids all wandering as the worst of sinning,
And therefore I shall open with a line
  (Although it cost me half an hour in spinning)
Narrating somewhat of Don Juan's father,
And also of his mother, if you'd rather.

8

In Seville was he born, a pleasant city,
  Famous for oranges and women – he
Who has not seen it will be much to pity,
  So says the proverb – and I quite agree;
Of all the Spanish towns is none more pretty,
  Cadiz, perhaps – but that you soon may see:–
Don Juan's parents lived beside the river,
A noble stream, and called the Guadalquivir.

9

His father's name was José – *Don*, of course,
  A true Hidalgo, free from every stain   *of true Spanish stock*
Of Moor or Hebrew blood, he traced his source
  Through the most Gothic[34] gentlemen of Spain;
A better cavalier ne'er mounted horse,
  Or, being mounted, e'er got down again,
Than José, who begot our hero, who
Begot – but that's to come – Well, to renew:

10

His mother was a learned lady,[35] famed
  For every branch of every science known –
In every Christian language ever named,
  With virtues equalled by her wit alone:
She made the cleverest people quite ashamed,
  And even the good with inward envy groan,
Finding themselves very much exceeded
In their own way by all the things that she did.

*   *   *

12

Her favourite science was the mathematical,
  Her noblest virtue was her magnanimity;
Her wit (she sometimes tried at wit) was Attic all,
  Her serious sayings darkened to sublimity;
In short, in all things she was fairly what I call
  A prodigy – her morning dress was dimity,[36]
Her evening silk, or, in the summer, muslin,
And other stuffs, with which I won't stay puzzling.

13

She knew the Latin – that is, 'the Lord's prayer,'
  And Greek – the alphabet – I'm nearly sure;
She read some French romances here and there,
  Although her mode of speaking was not pure;
For native Spanish she had no great care,
  At least her conversation was obscure;
Her thoughts were theorems, her words a problem,
As if she deemed that mystery would en-noble 'em.

[Don Juan's father dies: his mother takes over his education, based on the Classics]

44

Juan was taught from out the best edition,
  Expurgated by learned men, who place,
Judiciously, from out the schoolboy's vision,
  The grosser parts; but, fearful to deface
Too much their modest bard by this omission,
  And pitying sore this mutilated case,
They only add them all in an appendix,
Which saves, in fact, the trouble of an index;

45

For there we have them all 'at one fell swoop,'
  Instead of being scattered through the pages;
They stand forth marshalled in a handsome troop,
  To meet the ingenuous youth of future ages,
Till some less rigid editor shall stoop
  To call them back into their separate cages,
Instead of standing staring all together,
Like garden gods – and not so decent either.

*[At sixteen, Juan is a handsome boy who notices and is noticed by a friend of
his mother's, Donna Julia, who, unfortunately . . .]*

62

Wedded she was some years, and to a man
  Of fifty, and such husbands are in plenty;
And yet, I think, instead of such a ONE
  'Twere better to have TWO of five-and-twenty,
Especially in countries near the sun:
  And now I think on't, 'mi vien in mente,'°   *it comes to my mind*
Ladies even of the most uneasy virtue
Prefer a spouse whose age is short of thirty.

63

'Tis a sad thing, I cannot choose but say,
  And all the fault of that indecent sun,
Who cannot leave alone our helpless clay,
  But will keep baking, broiling, burning on,
That howsoever people fast and pray,
  The flesh is frail, and so the soul undone:
What men call gallantry, and gods adultery,
Is much more common where the climate's sultry.

64

Happy the nations of the moral north!
   Where all is virtue, and the winter season
Sends sin, without a rag on, shivering forth
   ('Twas snow that brought Saint Anthony to reason);
Where injuries cast up what a wife is worth,
   By laying whate'er sum, in mulct,° they please on   *an imposed fine*
The lover, who must pay a handsome price,
Because it is a marketable vice.

*   *   *

69

Juan she saw, and, as a pretty child,
   Caressed him often – such a thing might be
Quite innocently done, and harmless styled,
   When she had twenty years, and thirteen he;
But I am not so sure I should have smiled
   When he was sixteen, Julia twenty-three;
These few short years make wondrous alterations,
Particularly amongst sun-burnt nations.

70

Whate'er the cause might be, they had become
   Changed; for the dame grew distant, the youth shy,
Their looks cast down, their greetings almost dumb,
   And much embarrassment in either eye;
There surely will be little doubt with some
   That Donna Julia knew the reason why,
But as for Juan, he had no more notion
Than he who never saw the sea or ocean.

[This upsets Juan]

90

Young Juan wandered by the glassy brooks,
   Thinking unutterable things; he threw
Himself at length within the leafy nooks
   Where the wild branch of the cork forest grew;
There poets find materials for their books,
   And every now and then we read them through
So that their plan and prosody are eligible,
Unless, like Wordsworth, they prove unintelligible.

91

He, Juan (and not Wordsworth), so pursued
  His self-communion with his own high soul,
Until his mighty heart, in its great mood,
  Had mitigated part, though not the whole
Of its disease; he did the best he could
  With things not very subject to control,
And turned, without perceiving his condition,
Like Coleridge, into a metaphysician.

92

He thought about himself, and the whole earth,
  Of man the wonderful, and of the stars,
And how the deuce they ever could have birth;
  And then he thought of earthquakes, and of wars,
How many miles the moon might have in girth,
  Of air-balloons, and of the many bars
To perfect knowledge of the boundless skies; –
And then he thought of Donna Julia's eyes.

[It all comes to a head, when . . .]

102

It was upon a day, a summer's day; –
  Summer's indeed a very dangerous season,
And so is spring about the end of May;
  The sun, no doubt, is the prevailing reason;
But whatsoe'er the cause is, one may say,
  And stand convicted of more truth than treason,
That there are months which nature grows more merry in, –
March has its hares, and May must have its heroine.

103

'Twas on a summer's day – the sixth of June: –
  I like to be particular in dates,
Not only of the age, and year, but moon;
  They are a sort of post-house, where the Fates
Change horses, making history change its tune,
  Then spur away o'er empires and o'er states,
Leaving at last not much besides chronology,
Excepting the post-obits° of theology.   *after death payments*

*   *   *

105

She sate, but not alone; I know not well
  How this same interview had taken place,
And even if I knew, I should not tell –
  People should hold their tongues in any case;
No matter how or why the thing befell,
  But there were she and Juan, face to face –
When two such faces are so, 'twould be wise,
But very difficult, to shut their eyes.

106

How beautiful she looked! her conscious heart
  Glowed in her cheek, and yet she felt no wrong,
Oh love! how perfect is thy mystic art,
  Strengthening the weak, and trampling on the strong!
How self-deceitful is the sagest part
  Of mortals whom thy lure hath led along! –
The precipice she stood on was immense,
So was her creed in her own innocence.

107

She thought of her own strength, and Juan's youth,
  And of the folly of all prudish fears,
Victorious virtue, and domestic truth,
  And then of Don Alfonso's fifty years:
I wish these last had not occurred, in sooth,
  Because that number rarely much endears,
And through all climes, the snowy and the sunny,
Sounds ill in love, whate'er it may in money.

108

When people say, 'I've told you *fifty* times,'
  They mean to scold, and very often do;
When poets say, 'I've written *fifty* rhymes,'
  They make you dread that they'll recite them too;
In gangs of *fifty*, thieves commit their crimes;
  At *fifty* love for love is rare, 'tis true,
But then, no doubt, it equally as true is,
A good deal may be bought for *fifty* Louis.°   *gold coins*

109

Julia had honour, virtue, truth, and love
  For Don Alfonso; and she inly swore,
By all the vows below to powers above,

She never would disgrace the ring she wore,
Nor leave a wish which wisdom might reprove;
    And while she pondered this, besides much more,
One hand on Juan's carelessly was thrown,
Quite by mistake – she thought it was her own;

*   *   *

112

I cannot know what Juan thought of this,
    But what he did, is much what you would do;
His young lip thanked it with a grateful kiss,
    And then, abashed at its own joy, withdrew
In deep despair, lest he had done amiss, –
    Love is so very timid when 'tis new:
She blushed, and frowned not, but she strove to speak,
And held her tongue, her voice was grown so weak.

113

The sun set, and up rose the yellow moon:
    The devil's in the moon for mischief; they
Who call'd her CHASTE, methinks, began too soon
    Their nomenclature; there is not a day,
The longest, not the twenty-first of June,
    Sees half the business in a wicked way,
On which three single hours of moonshine smile –
And then she looks so modest all the while.

114

There is a dangerous silence in that hour,
    A stillness, which leaves room for the full soul
To open all itself, without the power
    Of calling wholly back its self-control;
The silver light which, hallowing tree and tower,
    Sheds beauty and deep softness o'er the whole,
Breathes also to the heart, and o'er it throws
A loving languor, which is not repose.

115

And Julia sate with Juan, half embraced
    And half retiring from the glowing arm,
Which trembled like the bosom where 'twas placed;
    Yet still she must have thought there was no harm,
Or else 'twere easy to withdraw her waist;

But then the situation had its charm,
And then – God knows what next – I can't go on;
I'm almost sorry that I e'er begun.

116

Oh Plato! Plato! you have paved the way,
    With your confounded fantasies, to more
Immoral conduct by the fancied sway
    Your system feigns o'er the controlless core
Of human hearts, than all the long array
    Of poets and romancers: – You're a bore,
A charlatan, a coxcomb – and have been,
At best, no better than a go-between.

117

And Julia's voice was lost, except in sighs,
    Until too late for useful conversation;
The tears were gushing from her gentle eyes,
    I wish, indeed, they had not had occasion;
But who, alas! can love, and then be wise?
    Not that remorse did not oppose temptation;
A little still she strove, and much repented,
And whispering 'I will ne'er consent' – consented.

[Some time later]

120

Here my chaste Muse a liberty must take –
    Start not! still chaster reader – she'll be nice hence-
Forward, and there is no great cause to quake;
    This liberty is a poetic licence,
Which some irregularity may make
    In the design, and as I have a high sense
Of Aristotle and the Rules, 'tis fit
To beg his pardon when I err a bit.

121

This licence is to hope the reader will
    Suppose from June the sixth (the fatal day
Without whose epoch my poetic skill
    For want of facts would all be thrown away),
But keeping Julia and Don Juan still
    In sight, that several months have passed; we'll say
'Twas in November, but I'm not so sure
About the day – the era's more obscure.

122

We'll talk of that anon. – 'Tis sweet to hear
  At midnight on the blue and moonlit deep
The song and oar of Adria's° gondolier   *Venice*
By distance mellowed, o'er the waters sweep;
'Tis sweet to see the evening star appear;
  'Tis sweet to listen as the night-winds creep
From leaf to leaf; 'tis sweet to view on high
The rainbow, based on ocean, span the sky.

*[But sweetest of all is first love – man may be ingenious at discovering
things, but . . .]*

133

Man's a phenomenon, one knows not what,
  And wonderful beyond all wondrous measure;
'Tis pity though, in this sublime world, that
Pleasure's a sin, and sometimes sin's a pleasure;
Few mortals know what end they would be at,
  But whether glory, power, or love, or treasure,
The path is through perplexing ways, and when
The goal is gained, we die, you know – and then –

134

What then? – I do not know, no more do you –
  And so good night. – Return we to our story:
'Twas in November, when fine days are few,
  And the far mountains wax a little hoary,
And clap a white cape on their mantles blue;
  And the sea dashes round the promontory,
And the loud breaker boils against the rock,
And sober suns must set at five o'clock.

135

'Twas, as the watchmen say, a cloudy night;
  No moon, no stars, the wind was low or loud
By gusts, and many a sparkling hearth was bright
  With the piled wood, round which the family crowd;
There's something cheerful in that sort of light,
  Even as a summer sky's without a cloud:
I'm fond of fire, and crickets, and all that,
A lobster salad, and champagne, and chat.

136

'Twas midnight – Donna Julia was in bed,
  Sleeping, most probably, – when at her door

Arose a clatter might awake the dead,
  If they had never been awoke before,
And that they have been so we all have read,
  And are to be so, at the least, once more; –
The door was fastened, but with voice and fist
First knocks were heard, then 'Madam – Madam – hist!

137

For God's sake, Madam – Madam – here's my master,
  With more than half the city at his back –
Was ever heard of such a curst disaster!
  'Tis not my fault – I kept good watch – Alack!
Do pray undo the bolt a little faster –
  They're on the stair just now, and in a crack
Will all be here; perhaps he yet may fly –
Surely the window's not so *very* high!'

138

By this time Don Alfonso was arrived,
  With torches, friends, and servants in great number;
The major part of them had long been wived,
  And therefore paused not to disturb the slumber
Of any wicked woman, who contrived
  By stealth her husband's temples to encumber:
Examples of this kind are so contagious,
Were *one* not punished, *all* would be outrageous.

*   *   *

140

Poor Donna Julia! starting as from sleep
  (Mind – that I do not say – she had not slept)
Began at once to scream, and yawn, and weep;
  Her maid, Antonia, who was an adept,
Contrived to fling the bed-clothes in a heap,
  As if she had just now from out them crept:
I can't tell why she should take all this trouble
To prove her mistress had been sleeping double.

141

But Julia mistress, and Antonia maid,
  Appeared like two poor harmless women, who
Of goblins, but still more of men afraid,
  Had thought one man might be deterred by two,

And therefore side by side were gently laid,
    Until the hours of absence should run through,
And truant husband should return, and say,
'My dear, I was the first who came away.'

[Julia invites Don Alfonso to search the room]

143

He searched, *they* searched, and rummaged everywhere,
    Closet and clothes-press, chest and window-seat,
And found much linen, lace, and several pair
    Of stockings, slippers, brushes, combs, complete,
With other articles of ladies fair,
    To keep them beautiful, or leave them neat:
Arras° they pricked and curtains with their swords,   *wall tapestry*
And wounded several shutters, and some boards.

144

Under the bed they searched, and there they found –
    No matter what – it was not that they sought;
They opened windows, gazing if the ground
    Had signs or footmarks, but the earth said nought;
And then they stared each other's faces round:
    'Tis odd, not one of all these seekers thought,
And seems to me almost a sort of blunder,
Of looking *in* the bed as well as under.

145

During this inquisition Julia's tongue
    Was not asleep – 'Yes, search and search,' she cried,
'Insult on insult heap, and wrong on wrong!
    It was for this that I became a bride!
For this in silence I have suffered long
    A husband like Alfonso at my side;
But now I'll bear no more, nor here remain,
If there be law or lawyers in all Spain.'

*   *   *

153

'There is the closet, there the toilet, there
    The antechamber – search them under, over;
There is the sofa, there the great armchair,
    The chimney – which would really hold a lover.

I wish to sleep, and beg you will take care
   And make no further noise, till you discover
The secret cavern of this lurking treasure –
And when 'tis found, let me, too, have that pleasure.'

[Don Alfonso, finding nothing, leaves to see his friends off. Quickly Juan slips out from under the bedclothes to hide in the closet. Alfonso returns, but . . .]

180

Alfonso closed his speech, and begged her pardon,
   Which Julia half withheld, and then half granted,
And laid conditions, he thought very hard, on,
   Denying several little things he wanted:
He stood like Adam lingering near his garden,
   With useless penitence perplexed and haunted,
Beseeching she no further would refuse,
When, lo! he stumbled o'er a pair of shoes.

181

A pair of shoes! – what then? not much, if they
   Are such as fit with ladies' feet, but these
   (No one can tell how much I grieve to say)
   Were masculine; to see them, and to seize,
Was but a moment's act. – Ah! well-a-day!
   My teeth begin to chatter, my veins freeze –
Alfonso first examined well their fashion,
And then flew out into another passion.

182

He left the room for his relinquished sword,
   And Julia instant to the closet flew.
'Fly, Juan, fly! for heaven's sake – not a word –
   The door is open – you may yet slip through
The passage you so often have explored –
   Here is the garden-key – Fly – fly – Adieu!
Haste – haste! I hear Alfonso's hurrying feet –
Day has not broke – there's no one in the street.'

183

None can say that this was not good advice,
   The only mischief was, it came too late;
Of all experience 'tis the usual price,
   A sort of income-tax laid on by fate:
Juan had reached the room-door in a trice,

And might have done so by the garden-gate,
But met Alfonso in his dressing-gown,
Who threatened death – so Juan knocked him down.

[They fight; Juan loses the only garment he is wearing, and . . .]

188

Here ends this canto. – Need I sing, or say
   How Juan, naked, favoured by the night,
Who favours what she should not, found his way,
   And reached his home in an unseemly plight?
The pleasant scandal which arose next day,
   The nine days' wonder which was brought to light,
And how Alfonso sued for a divorce,
Were in the English newspapers, of course.

[Donna Inez sends Juan off to Europe]

191

She had resolved that he should travel through
   All European climes, by land or sea,
To mend his former morals, and get new,
   Especially in France and Italy
(At least this is the thing most people do)
   Julia was sent into a convent: she
Grieved, but, perhaps, her feelings may be better,
Shown in the following copy of her letter: –

[in which she declares her continuing love for Juan, and that . . .]

193

'I loved, I love you, for this love have lost
   State, station, heaven, mankind's, my own esteem,
And yet cannot regret what it hath cost,
   So dear is still the memory of that dream;
Yet, if I name my guilt, 'tis not to boast,
   None can deem harshlier of me than I deem:
I trace this scrawl because I cannot rest –
I've nothing to reproach or to request.

194

Man's love is of man's life a thing apart,
   'Tis woman's whole existence; man may range
The court, camp, church, the vessel, and the mart;

Sword, gown, gain, glory, offer in exchange
Pride, fame, ambition, to fill up his heart,
    And few there are whom these cannot estrange;
Men have all these resources, we but one,
To love again, and be again undone.'

            *   *   *

                199
This was Don Juan's earliest scrape; but whether
    I shall proceed with his adventures is
Dependent on the public altogether;
    We'll see, however, what they say to this,
Their favour in an author's cap's a feather,
    And no great mischief's done by their caprice;
And if their approbation we experience,
Perhaps they'll have some more a year hence.[37]

                                1818 [1819]

The Vision of Judgement[38]

            by Quevedo Redivivus
    Suggested by the composition so entitled
        by the author of 'Wat Tyler'.

    'A Daniel come to judgement! yea, a Daniel!
    I thank thee Jew, for teaching me that word.'
            Merchant of Venice IV.1.219.

                1
Saint Peter sat by the celestial gate:
    His keys were rusty, and the lock was dull,
So little trouble had been given of late;
    Not that the place by any means was full,
But since the Gallic era 'eighty-eight'[39]
    The devils had ta'en a longer, stronger pull,
And 'a pull altogether,' as they say
At sea – which drew most souls another way.

2

The angels all were singing out of tune,
  And hoarse with having little else to do,
Excepting to wind up the sun and moon,
  Or curb a runaway young star or two,
Or wild colt of a comet, which too soon
  Broke out of bounds o'er th' ethereal blue,
Splitting some planet with its playful tail,
As boats are sometimes by a wanton whale.

3

The guardian seraphs had retired on high,
  Finding their charges past all care below;
Terrestrial business filled nought in the sky
  Save the recording angel's black bureau;
Who found, indeed, the facts to multiply
  With such rapidity of vice and woe,
That he had stripped off both his wings in quills,
And yet was in arrear of human ills.

4

His business so augmented of late years,
  That he was forced, against his will no doubt,
(Just like those cherubs, earthly ministers,)
  For some resource to turn himself about,
And claim the help of his celestial peers,
  To aid him ere he should be quite worn out
By the increased demand for his remarks:
Six angels and twelve saints were named his clerks.

5

This was a handsome board – at least for heaven;
  And yet they had even then enough to do,
So many conquerors' cars were daily driven,
  So many kingdoms fitted up anew;
Each day too slew its thousands six or seven,
  Till at the crowning carnage, Waterloo,
They threw their pens down in divine disgust –
The page was so besmeared with blood and dust.

6

This by the way; 'tis not mine to record
  What angels shrink from: even the very devil
On this occasion his own work abhorr'd,

So surfeited with the infernal revel:
Though he himself had sharpened every sword,
   It almost quenched his innate thirst of evil.
(Here Satan's sole good work deserves insertion –
'Tis, that he has both generals in reversion.)[40]

                              7

Let's skip a few short years of hollow peace,
   Which peopled earth no better, hell as wont,
And heaven none – they form the tyrant's lease,
   With nothing but new names subscribed upon't;
'Twill one day finish: meantime they increase
   'With seven heads and ten horns,'[41] and all in front,
Like Saint John's foretold beast; but ours are born
Less formidable in the head than horn.

                              8

In the first year of freedom's second dawn[42]
   Died George the Third; although no tyrant, one
Who shielded tyrants, till each sense withdrawn
   Left him nor mental nor external sun:
A better farmer ne'er brushed dew from lawn,
   A worse king never left a realm undone!
He died – but left his subjects still behind,
One half as mad – and t'other no less blind.

                              9

He died! his death made no great stir on earth:
   His burial made some pomp; there was profusion
Of velvet, gilding, brass, and no great dearth
   Of aught but tears – save those shed by collusion.
For these things may be bought at their true worth;
   Of elegy there was the due infusion –
Bought also; and the torches, cloaks, and banners,
Heralds, and relics of old Gothic manners,

                              10

Formed a sepulchral melodrame. Of all
   The fools who flocked to swell or see the show,
Who cared about the corpse? The funeral
   Made the attraction, and the black the woe.
There throbbed not there a thought which pierced the pall;
   And when the gorgeous coffin was laid low,
It seemed the mockery of hell to fold
The rottenness of eighty years in gold.

11

So mix his body with the dust! It might
  Return to what it *must* far sooner, were
The natural compound left alone to fight
  Its way back into earth, and fire, and air;
But the unnatural balsams merely blight
  What nature made him at his birth, as bare
As the mere million's base unmummied clay –
Yet all his spices but prolong decay.

12

He's dead – and upper earth with him has done;
  He's buried; save the undertaker's bill,
Or lapidary° scrawl, the world is gone   *stone engraving*
  For him, unless he left a German will:
But where's the proctor who will ask his son?[43]
  In whom his qualities are reigning still,
Except that household virtue, most uncommon,
Of constancy to a bad, ugly woman.

13

'God save the king!' It is a large economy
  In God to save the like; but if he will
Be saving, all the better; for not one am I
  Of those who think damnation better still:
I hardly know too if not quite alone am I
  In this small hope of bettering future ill
By circumscribing, with some slight restriction,
The eternity of hell's hot jurisdiction.

14

I know this is unpopular; I know
  'Tis blasphemous; I know one may be damned
For hoping no one else may e'er be so;
  I know my catechism; I know we're crammed
With the best doctrines till we quite o'erflow;
  I know that all save England's church have shammed,
And that the other twice two hundred churches
And synagogues have made a *damned* bad purchase.

15

God help us all! God help me too! I am,
  God knows, as helpless as the devil can wish,
And not a whit more difficult to damn,
  Than is to bring to land a late-hooked fish,

Or to the butcher to purvey the lamb;
  Not that I'm fit for such a noble dish,
As one day will be that immortal fry
Of almost everybody born to die.

16

Saint Peter sat by the celestial gate,
  And nodded o'er his keys; when, lo! there came
A wondrous noise he had not heard of late –
  A rushing sound of wind, and stream, and flame;
In short, a roar of things extremely great,
  Which would have made aught save a saint exclaim;
But he, with first a start and then a wink,
Said, 'There's another star gone out, I think!'

17

But ere he could return to his repose,
  A cherub flapped his right wing o'er his eyes –
At which St. Peter yawned, and rubbed his nose:
  'Saint porter,' said the angel, 'prithee rise!'
Waving a goodly wing, which glowed, as glows
  An earthly peacock's tail, with heavenly dyes:
To which the saint replied, 'Well, what's the matter?
Is Lucifer come back with all this clatter?'

18

'No,' quoth the cherub; 'George the Third is dead.'
  'And who *is* George the Third?' replied the Apostle:
'*What George? what Third?*' 'The king of England,' said
  The angel. 'Well! he won't find kings to jostle
Him on his way; but does he wear his head?[44]
  Because the last we saw here had a tussle,
And ne'er would have got into heaven's good graces,
Had he not flung his head in all our faces.

19

He was, if I remember, king of France;
  That head of his, which could not keep a crown
On earth, yet ventured in my face to advance
  A claim to those of martyrs – like my own:
If I had had my sword, as I had once
  When I cut ears off, I had cut him down;
But having but my *keys*, and not my brand,
I only knocked his head from out his hand.

20

And then he set up such a headless howl,
   That all the saints came out and took him in;
And there he sits by St. Paul, cheek by jowl;
   That fellow Paul – the parvenù°! The skin   *upstart*
Of St. Bartholomew,⁴⁵ which makes his cowl
   In heaven, and upon earth redeemed his sin,
So as to make a martyr, never sped
Better than did this weak and wooden head.

21

But had it come up here upon its shoulders,
   There would have been a different tale to tell:
The fellow-feeling in the saint's beholders
   Seems to have acted on them like a spell,
And so this very foolish head heaven solders
   Back on its trunk: it may be very well,
And seems the custom here to overthrow
Whatever has been wisely done below.'

22

The angel answered, 'Peter! do not pout:
   The king who comes has head and all entire,
And never knew much what it was about –
   He did as doth the puppet – by its wire,
And will be judged like all the rest, no doubt:
   My business and your own is not to inquire
Into such matters, but to mind our cue –
Which is to act as we are bid to do.'

23

While thus they spake, the angelic caravan,
   Arriving like a rush of mighty wind,
Cleaving the fields of space, as doth the swan
   Some silver stream (say Ganges, Nile, or Inde,
Or Thames, or Tweed⁴⁶), and 'midst them an old man
   With an old soul, and both extremely blind,
Halted before the gate, and in his shroud
Seated their fellow traveller on a cloud.

24

But bringing up the rear of this bright host
   A Spirit of a different aspect waved
His wings, like thunder-clouds above some coast
   Whose barren beach with frequent wrecks is paved;

His brow was like the deep when tempest-tossed;
  Fierce and unfathomable thoughts engraved
Eternal wrath on his immortal face,
And *where* he gazed a gloom pervaded space.

25

As he drew near, he gazed upon the gate
  Ne'er to be entered more by him or sin,
With such a glance of supernatural hate,
  As made Saint Peter wish himself within;
He pattered with his keys at a great rate,
  And sweated through his apostolic skin:
Of course his perspiration was but ichor,[47]
Or some such other spiritual liquor.

26

The very cherubs huddled all together,
  Like birds when soars the falcon; and they felt
A tingling to the tip of every feather,
  And formed a circle like Orion's belt .
Around their poor old charge; who scarce knew whither
  His guards had led him, though they gently dealt
With royal manes (for by many stories,
And true, we learn the angels all are Tories).

27

As things were in this posture, the gate flew
  Asunder, and the flashing of its hinges
Flung over space an universal hue
  Of many-coloured flame, until its tinges
Reached even our speck of earth, and made a new
  Aurora borealis° spread its fringes   *northern lights*
O'er the North Pole; the same seen, when ice-bound,
By Captain Parry's crew, in 'Melville's Sound.'

28

And from the gate thrown open issued beaming
  A beautiful and mighty Thing of Light,
Radiant with glory, like a banner streaming
  Victorious from some world-o'erthrowing fight:
My poor comparisons must needs be teeming
  With earthly likenesses, for here the night
Of clay obscures our best conceptions, saving
Johanna Southcote, or Bob Southey raving.

29

'Twas the archangel Michael; all men know
   The make of angels and archangels, since
There's scarce a scribbler has not one to show,
   From the fiends' leader to the angels' prince;
There also are some altar-pieces, though
   I really can't say that they much evince
One's inner notions of immortal spirits;
But let the connoisseurs explain *their* merits.

30

Michael flew forth in glory and in good;
   A goodly work of him from whom all glory
And good arise; the portal past – he stood;
   Before him the young cherubs and saints hoary –
(I say *young*, begging to be understood
   By looks, not years; and should be very sorry
To state, they were not older than St. Peter,
But merely that they seemed a little sweeter).

31

The cherubs and the saints bowed down before
   That arch-angelic Hierarch, the first
Of essences angelical, who wore
   The aspect of a god; but this ne'er nursed
Pride in his heavenly bosom, in whose core
   No thought, save for his Master's service, durst
Intrude, however glorified and high;
He knew him but the viceroy of the sky.

32

He and the sombre, silent Spirit° met –   *(Satan)*
   They knew each other both for good and ill;
Such was their power, that neither could forget
   His former friend and future foe; but still
There was a high, immortal, proud regret
   In either's eye, as if 'twere less their will
Than destiny to make the eternal years
Their date of war, and their 'champ clos'° the spheres.   *combat area*

33

But here they were in neutral space: we know
   From Job, that Satan hath the power to pay
A heavenly visit thrice a year or so;

And that the 'sons of God'[48] like those of clay,
   Must keep him company; and we might show
     From the same book, in how polite a way
The dialogue is held between the Powers
Of Good and Evil – but 'twould take up hours.

34

And this is not a theologic tract,
   To prove with Hebrew and with Arabic,
If Job be allegory or a fact,
   But a true narrative; and thus I pick
From out the whole but such and such an act
   As sets aside the slightest thought of trick.
'Tis every tittle true, beyond suspicion,
And accurate as any other vision.

35

The spirits were in neutral space, before
   The gate of heaven; like eastern thresholds is[49]
The place where Death's grand cause is argued o'er,
   And souls despatched to that world or to this;
And therefore Michael and the other wore
   A civil aspect: though they did not kiss,
Yet still between his Darkness and his Brightness
There passed a mutual glance of great politeness.

36

The Archangel bowed, not like a modern beau,
   But with a graceful Oriental bend,
Pressing one radiant arm just where below
   The heart in good men is supposed to tend;
He turned as to an equal, not too low,
   But kindly; Satan met his ancient friend
With more hauteur, as might an old Castilian
Poor noble meet a mushroom rich° civilian.   *rich overnight*

37

He merely bent his diabolic brow
   An instant; and then raising it, he stood
In act to assert his right or wrong, and show
   Cause why King George by no means could or should
Make out a case to be exempt from woe
   Eternal, more than other kings, endued
With better sense and hearts, whom history mentions,
Who long have 'paved hell with their good intentions.'

38

Michael began: 'What wouldst thou with this man,
  Now dead, and brought before the Lord? What ill
Hath he wrought since his mortal race began,
  That thou canst claim him? Speak! and do thy will,
If it be just: if in this earthly span
  He hath been greatly failing to fulfil
His duties as a king and mortal, say,
And he is thine; if not, let him have way.'

39

'Michael!' replied the Prince of Air, 'even here,
  Before the gate of him thou servest, must
I claim my subject: and will make appear
  That as he was my worshipper in dust,
So shall he be in spirit, although dear
  To thee and thine, because nor wine nor lust
Were of his weaknesses; yet on the throne
He reigned o'er millions to serve me alone.

40

Look to *our* earth, or rather *mine*; it was,
  Once, more thy master's: but I triumph not
In this poor planet's conquest; nor, alas!
  Need he thou servest envy me my lot:
With all the myriads of bright worlds which pass
  In worship round him, he may have forgot
Yon weak creation of such paltry things:
I think few worth damnation save their kings, —

41

And these but as a kind of quit-rent,° to   *in lieu of other services*
  Assert my right as lord: and even had
I such an inclination, 'twere (as you
  Well know) superfluous; they are grown so bad,
That hell has nothing better left to do
  Than leave them to themselves: so much more mad
And evil by their own internal curse,
Heaven cannot make them better, nor I worse.

42

Look to the earth, I said, and say again:
  When this old, blind, mad, helpless, weak, poor worm
Began in youth's first bloom and flush to reign,
  The world and he both wore a different form,

And much of earth and all the watery plain
  Of ocean called him king: through many a storm
His isles had floated on the abyss of time;
For the rough virtues chose them for their clime.

43

He came to his sceptre young; he leaves it old:
  Look to the state in which he found his realm,
And left it; and his annals too behold,
  How to a minion first he gave the helm;⁵⁰
How grew upon his heart a thirst for gold,
  The beggar's vice, which can but overwhelm
The meanest hearts; and for the rest, but glance
Thine eye along America and France.

44

'Tis true, he was a tool from first to last
  (I have the workmen safe); but as a tool
So let him be consumed. From out the past
  Of ages, since mankind have known the rule
Of monarchs – from the bloody rolls amassed
  Of sin and slaughter – from the Cæsar's school,
Take the worst pupil; and produce a reign
More drenched with gore, more cumbered with the slain.

45

He ever warred with freedom and the free:
  Nations as men, home subjects, foreign foes,
So that they uttered the word "Liberty!"
  Found George the Third their first opponent. Whose
History was ever stained as his will be
  With national and individual woes?
I grant his household abstinence; I grant
His neutral virtues, which most monarchs want;

46

I know he was a constant consort; own
  He was a decent sire, and middling lord.
All this is much, and most upon a throne;
  As temperance, if at Apicius' board,
Is more than at an anchorite's supper shown.
  I grant him all the kindest can accord;
And this was well for him, but not for those
Millions who found him what oppression chose.

47

The New World shook him off; the Old yet groans
   Beneath what he and his prepared, if not
Completed: he leaves heirs on many thrones
   To all his vices, without what begot
Compassion for him – his tame virtues; drones
   Who sleep, or despots who have now forgot
A lesson which shall be re-taught them, wake
Upon the thrones of earth; but let them quake!

48

Five millions of the primitive, who hold
   The faith which makes ye great on earth, implored
A *part* of that vast *all* they held of old, –
   Freedom to worship – not alone your Lord,
Michael, but you, and you, Saint Peter! Cold
   Must be your souls, if you have not abhorred
The foe to Catholic participation°   *a right to hold office*
In all the license of a Christian nation.

49

True! he allowed them to pray God; but as
   A consequence of prayer, refused the law
Which would have placed them upon the same base
   With those who did not hold the saints in awe.'
But here Saint Peter started from his place,
   And cried, 'You may the prisoner withdraw:
Ere heaven shall ope her portals to this Guelph,[51]
While I am guard, may I be damned myself!

50

Sooner will I with Cerberus exchange
   My office (and *his* is no sinecure)
Than see this royal Bedlam bigot range
   The azure fields of heaven, of that be sure!'
'Saint!' replied Satan, 'you do well to avenge
   The wrongs he made your satellites endure;
And if to this exchange you should be given,
I'll try to coax *our* Cerberus up to heaven!'

51

Here Michael interposed: 'Good saint! and devil!
   Pray, not so fast; you both outrun discretion.
Saint Peter! you were wont to be more civil!
   Satan! excuse this warmth of his expression,

And condescension to the vulgar's level:
    Even saints sometimes forget themselves in session.
Have you got more to say?' – 'No.' – 'If you please,
I'll trouble you to call your witnesses.'

52

Then Satan turned and waved his swarthy hand,
    Which stirred with its electric qualities
Clouds farther off than we can understand,
    Although we find him sometimes in our skies;
Infernal thunder shook both sea and land
    In all the planets, and hell's batteries
Let off the artillery, which Milton mentions
As one of Satan's most sublime inventions.

53

This was a signal unto such damned souls
    As have the privilege of their damnation
Extended far beyond the mere controls
    Of worlds past, present, or to come; no station
Is theirs particularly in the rolls
    Of hell assigned; but where their inclination
Or business carries them in search of game,
They may range freely – being damned the same.

54

They're proud of this – as very well they may,
    It being a sort of knighthood, or gilt key
Stuck in their loins; or like to an 'entré'°   *right of access*
    Up the back stairs, or such freemasonry.[52]
I borrow my comparisons from clay,
    Being clay myself. Let not those spirits be
Offended with such base low likenesses;
We know their posts are nobler far than these.

55

When the great signal ran from heaven to hell –
    About ten million times the distance reckoned
From our sun to its earth, as we can tell
    How much time it takes up, even to a second,
For every ray that travels to dispel
    The fogs of London, through which, dimly beaconed,
The weathercocks are gilt some thrice a year,
If that the *summer* is not too severe:

56

I say that I can tell – 'twas half a minute;
  I know the solar beams take up more time
Ere, packed up for their journey, they begin it;
  But then their telegraph is less sublime,
And if they ran a race, they would not win it
  'Gainst Satan's couriers bound for their own clime.
The sun takes up some years for every ray
To reach its goal – the devil not half a day.

57

Upon the verge of space, about the size
  Of half-a-crown, a little speck appeared
(I've seen a something like it in the skies
  In the Ægean, ere a squall); it neared,
And, growing bigger, took another guise;
  Like an aërial ship it tacked, and steered,
Or *was* steered (I am doubtful of the grammar
Of the last phrase, which makes the stanza stammer; –

58

But take your choice): and then it grew a cloud;
  And so it was – a cloud of witnesses.
But such a cloud! No land e'er saw a crowd
  Of locusts numerous as the heavens saw these;
They shadowed with their myriads space; their loud
  And varied cries were like those of wild geese
(If nations may be likened to a goose),
And realised the phrase of 'hell broke loose.'

59

Here crashed a sturdy oath of stout John Bull,[53]
  Who damned away his eyes as heretofore:
There Paddy brogued 'By Jasus!' – 'What's your wull?'
The temperate Scot exclaimed: the French ghost swore
In certain terms I shan't translate in full,
  As the first coachman will; and 'midst the war,
The voice of Jonathan[54] was heard to express,
'*Our* president is going to war, I guess.'

60

Besides there were the Spaniard, Dutch, and Dane;
  In short, an universal shoal of shades,
From Otaheite's isle° to Salisbury Plain,

                                                        Tahiti

Of all climes and professions, years and trades,
Ready to swear against the good king's reign,
    Bitter as clubs in cards are against spades:
All summoned by this grand 'subpœna,' to
Try if kings mayn't be damned like me or you.

61

When Michael saw this host, he first grew pale,
    As angels can; next, like Italian twilight,
He turned all colours – as a peacock's tail,
    Or sunset streaming through a Gothic skylight
In some old abbey, or a trout not stale,
    Or distant lightning on the horizon *by* night,
Or a fresh rainbow, or a grand review
Or thirty regiments in red, green, and blue.

62

Then he addressed himself to Satan: 'Why –
    My good old friend, for such I deem you, though
Our different parties make us fight so shy,
    I ne'er mistake you for a *personal* foe;
Our difference is *political*, and I
    Trust that, whatever may occur below,
You know my great respect for you: and this
Makes me regret whate'er you do amiss –

63

Why, my dear Lucifer, would you abuse
    My call for witnesses? I did not mean
That you should half of earth and hell produce;
    'Tis even superfluous, since two honest, clean,
True testimonies are enough: we lose
    Our time, nay, our eternity, between
The accusation and defence: if we
Hear both, 'twill stretch our immortality.'

64

Satan replied, 'To me the matter is
    Indifferent, in a personal point of view:
I can have fifty better souls than this
    With far less trouble than we have gone through
Already; and I merely argued his
    Late majesty of Britain's case with you
Upon a point of form: you may dispose
Of him; I've kings enough below, God knows!'

65

Thus spoke the Demon (late called 'multifaced'
    By multo-scribbling Southey). 'Then we'll call
One or two persons of the myriads placed
    Around our congress, and dispense with all
The rest,' quoth Michael: 'Who may be so graced
    As to speak first? there's choice enough – who shall
It be?' Then Satan answer'd, 'There are many;
But you may choose Jack Wilkes as well as any.'

66

A merry, cock-eyed, curious-looking sprite
    Upon the instant started from the throng,
Dressed in a fashion now forgotten quite;
    For all the fashions of the flesh stick long
By people in the next world; where unite
    All the costumes since Adam's, right or wrong,
From Eve's fig-leaf down to the petticoat,
Almost as scanty, of days less remote.

67

The spirit looked around upon the crowds
    Assembled, and exclaimed, 'My friends of all
The spheres, we shall catch cold amongst these clouds;
    So let's to business: why this general call?
If those are freeholders I see in shrouds,
    And 'tis for an election that they bawl,
Behold a candidate with unturned coat!⁵⁵
Saint Peter, may I count upon your vote?'

68

'Sir,' replied Michael, 'you mistake; these things
    Are of a former life, and what we do
Above is more august; to judge of kings
    Is the tribunal met: so now you know.'
'Then I presume those gentlemen with wings,'
    Said Wilkes, 'are cherubs; and that soul below
Looks much like George the Third, but to my mind
A good deal older – Bless me! is he blind?'

69

'He is what you behold him, and his doom
    Depends upon his deeds,' the Angel said;
'If you have aught to arraign in him, the tomb
    Gives licence to the humblest beggar's head
To lift itself against the loftiest.' – 'Some,'

Said Wilkes, 'don't wait to see them laid in lead,
For such a liberty – and I, for one,
Have told them what I thought beneath the sun.'

70

'*Above* the sun repeat, then, what thou hast
    To urge against him,' said the Archangel. 'Why,'
Replied the spirit, 'since old scores are past,
    Must I turn evidence? In faith, not I.
Besides, I beat him hollow at the last,
    With all his Lords and Commons: in the sky
I don't like ripping up old stories, since
His conduct was but natural in a prince.

71

Foolish, no doubt, and wicked, to oppress
    A poor unlucky devil without a shilling;
But then I blame the man himself much less
    Than Bute and Grafton, and shall be unwilling
To see him punished here for their excess,
    Since they were both damned long ago, and still in
Their place below: for me, I have forgiven,
And vote his "habeas corpus" into heaven.'

72

'Wilkes,' said the Devil, 'I understand all this;
    You turned to half a courtier ere you died,
And seem to think it would not be amiss
    To grow a whole one on the other side
Of Charon's ferry; you forget that *his*
    Reign is concluded; whatsoe'er betide,
He won't be sovereign more: you've lost your labour,
For at the best he will but be your neighbour.

73

However, I knew what to think of it,
    When I beheld you in your jesting way,
Flitting and whispering round about the spit
    Where Belial, upon duty for the day,
With Fox's lard was basting William Pitt,
    His pupil; I knew what to think, I say:
That fellow even in hell breeds farther ills;
I'll have him *gagged* – 'twas one of his own bills.'

74

'Call Junius!' From the crowd a shadow stalked,
  And at the name there was a general squeeze,
So that the very ghosts no longer walked
  In comfort, at their own aërial ease,
But were all rammed, and jammed (but to be balked,
  As we shall see), and jostled hands and knees,
Like wind compressed and pent within a bladder,
Or like a human colic, which is sadder.

75

The shadow came – a tall, thin, grey-haired figure,
  That looked as it had been a shade on earth;
Quick in its motions, with an air of vigour,
  But nought to mark its breeding or its birth;
Now it waxed little, then again grew bigger,
  With now an air of gloom, or savage mirth;
But as you gazed upon its features, they
Changed every instant – to *what*, none could say.

76

The more intently the ghosts gazed, the less
  Could they distinguish whose the features were;
The Devil himself seemed puzzled even to guess;
  They varied like a dream – now here, now there;
And several people swore from out the press,
  They knew him perfectly; and one could swear
He was his father: upon which another
Was sure he was his mother's cousin's brother:

77

Another, that he was a duke, or knight,
  An orator, a lawyer, or a priest,
A nabob,° a man-midwife; but the wight   *wealthy man*
  Mysterious changed his countenance at least
As oft as they their minds; though in full sight
  He stood, the puzzle only was increased;
The man was a phantasmagoria in
Himself – he was so volatile and thin.

78

The moment that you had pronounced him *one*,
  Presto! his face changed, and he was another;
And when that change was hardly well put on,

It varied, till I don't think his own mother
(If that he had a mother) would her son
    Have known, he shifted so from one to t'other;
Till guessing from a pleasure grew a task,
At this epistolary 'Iron Mask.'[56]

79

For sometimes he like Cerberus would seem –
    'Three gentlemen at once' (as sagely says
Good Mrs. Malaprop[57]); then you might deem
    That he was not even *one*; now many rays
Were flashing round him; and now a thick steam
    Hid him from sight – like fogs on London days:
Now Burke, now Tooke, he grew to people's fancies,
And certes often like Sir Philip Francis.[58]

80

I've an hypothesis – 'tis quite my own;
    I never let it out till now, for fear
Of doing people harm about the throne,
    And injuring some minister or peer,
On whom the stigma might perhaps be blown;
    It is – my gentle public, lend thine ear!
'Tis, that what Junius we are wont to call
Was *really*, *truly*, nobody at all.

81

I don't see wherefore letters should not be
    Written without hands, since we daily view
Them written without heads; and books, we see,
    Are filled as well without the latter too:
And really till we fix on somebody
    For certain sure to claim them as his due,
Their author, like the Niger's mouth, will bother
The world to say if *there* be mouth or author.

82

'And who and what art thou?' the Archangel said.
    'For *that* you may consult my title-page,'
Replied this mighty shadow of a shade:
    'If I have kept my secret half an age,
I scarce shall tell it now.' – 'Canst thou upbraid,'
    Continued Michael, 'George Rex, or allege
Aught further?' Junius answer'd, 'You had better
First ask him for *his* answer to my letter:

83

My charges upon record will outlast
   The brass of both his epitaph and tomb.'
'Repent'st thou not,' said Michael, 'of some past
   Exaggeration? something which may doom
Thyself if false, as him if true? Thou wast
   Too bitter – is it not so? – in thy gloom
Of passion?' – 'Passion!' cried the Phantom dim,
'I loved my country, and I hated him.

84

What I have written, I have written: let
   The rest be on his head or mine!' So spoke
Old 'Nominis Umbra'; and while speaking yet,
   Away he melted in celestial smoke.
Then Satan said to Michael, 'Don't forget
   To call George Washington, and John Horne Tooke,
And Franklin;' – but at this time there was heard
A cry for room, though not a phantom stirred.

85

At length with jostling, elbowing, and the aid
   Of cherubim appointed to that post,
The devil Asmodeus to the circle made
   His way, and looked as if his journey cost
Some trouble. When his burden down he laid,
   'What's this?' cried Michael; 'why, 'tis not a ghost?'
'I know it,' quoth the incubus; 'but he°   *i.e. Southey*
Shall be one, if you leave the affair to me.

86

Confound the renegado! I have sprained
   My left wing, he's so heavy; one would think
Some of his works about his neck were chained
   But to the point; while hovering o'er the brink
Of Skiddaw (where as usual it still rained),
   I saw a taper, far below me, wink,
And stooping, caught this fellow at a libel –
No less on history than the Holy Bible.

87

The former is the devil's scripture, and
   The latter yours, good Michael: so the affair
Belongs to all of us, you understand.
   I snatched him up just as you see him there,

And brought him off for sentence out of hand:
   I've scarcely been ten minutes in the air –
At least a quarter it can hardly be:
I dare say that his wife is still at tea.'

88

Here Satan said, 'I know this man of old,
   And have expected him for some time here;
A sillier fellow you will scarce behold,
   Or more conceited in his petty sphere:
But surely it was not worth while to fold
   Such trash below your wing, Asmodeus dear:
We had the poor wretch safe (without being bored
With carriage) coming of his own accord.

89

But since he's here, let's see what he has done.'
   'Done!' cried Asmodeus, 'he anticipates
The very business you are now upon,
   And scribbles as if head clerk to the Fates.
Who knows to what his ribaldry may run,
   When such an ass as this, like Balaam's,[59] prates?'
'Let's hear,' quoth Michael, 'what he has to say:
You know we're bound to that in every way.'

90

Now the Bard, glad to get an audience, which
   By no means often was his case below,
Began to cough, and hawk, and hem, and pitch   *clear throat*
   His voice into that awful note of woe
To all unhappy hearers within reach
   Of poets when the tide of rhyme's in flow;
But stuck fast with his first hexameter,[60]
Not one of all whose gouty feet would stir.

91

But ere the spavin'd° dactyls[61] could be spurred   *limping*
   Into recitative, in great dismay
Both cherubim and seraphim were heard
   To murmur loudly through their long array;
And Michael rose ere he could get a word
   Of all his foundered verses under way,
And cried, 'For God's sake stop, my friend! 'twere best –
Non Di, non homines – you know the rest.'[62]

92

A general bustle spread throughout the throng,
    Which seemed to hold all verse in detestation;
The angels had of course enough of song
    When upon service; and the generation
Of ghosts had heard too much in life, not long
    Before, to profit by a new occasion:
The Monarch, mute till then, exclaimed, 'What! what!
Pye come again? No more – no more of that!'

93

The tumult grew; an universal cough
    Convulsed the skies, as during a debate,
When Castlereagh has been up long enough
    (Before he was first minister of state,
I mean – the *slaves hear now*); some cried 'Off, off!'
    As at a farce; till, grown quite desperate,
The Bard Saint Peter prayed to interpose
(Himself an author) only for his prose.

94

The varlet was not an ill-favoured knave;
    A good deal like a vulture in the face,
With a hook nose and a hawk's eye, which gave
    A smart and sharper-looking sort of grace
To his whole aspect, which, though rather grave,
    Was by no means so ugly as his case;
But that, indeed, was hopeless as can be,
Quite a poetic felony '*de se*.'°   *suicide*

95

Then Michael blew his trump, and stilled the noise
    With one still greater, as is yet the mode
On earth besides; except some grumbling voice,
    Which now and then will make a slight inroad
Upon decorous silence, few will twice
    Lift up their lungs when fairly overcrowed;
And now the Bard could plead his own bad cause,
With all the attitudes of self-applause.

96

He said – (I only give the heads) – he said,
    He meant no harm in scribbling; 'twas his way
Upon all topics; 'twas, besides, his bread,

Of which he buttered both sides; 'twould delay
Too long the assembly (he was pleased to dread),
　　And take up rather more time than a day,
To name his works – he would but cite a few –
'Wat Tyler' – 'Rhymes on Blenheim' – 'Waterloo.'

97

He had written praises of a regicide;
　　He had written praises of all kings whatever;
He had written for republics far and wide,
　　And then against them bitterer than ever;
For pantisocracy he once had cried[63]
　　Aloud, a scheme less moral than 'twas clever;
Then grew a hearty anti-jacobin –[64]
Had turned his coat – and would have turned his skin.

98

He had sung against all battles, and again
　　In their high praise and glory; he had called
Reviewing 'the ungentle craft,' and then
　　Become as base a critic as e'er crawled –[65]
Fed, paid, and pampered by the very men
　　By whom his muse and morals had been mauled:
He had written much blank verse, and blanker prose,
And more of both than anybody knows.

99

He had written Wesley's life: – here turning round
　　To Satan, 'Sir, I'm ready to write yours,
In two octavo volumes, nicely bound,
　　With notes and preface, all that most allures
The pious purchaser; and there's no ground
　　For fear, for I can choose my own reviewers:
So let me have the proper documents,
That I may add you to my other saints.'

100

Satan bowed, and was silent. 'Well, if you,
　　With amiable modesty, decline
My offer, what says Michael? There are few
　　Whose memoirs could be rendered more divine.
Mine is a pen of all work; not so new
　　As it was once, but I would make you shine
Like your own trumpet. By the way, my own
Has more of brass in it, and is as well blown.

101

But talking about trumpets, here's my Vision!
   Now you shall judge, all people; yes, you shall
Judge with my judgment, and by my decision
   Be guided who shall enter heaven or fall.
I settle all these things by intuition,
   Times present, past, to come, heaven, hell, and all,
Like King Alfonso.[66] When I thus see double
I save the Deity some worlds of trouble.'

102

He ceased, and drew forth an MS.; and no
   Persuasion on the part of devils, saints,
Or angels, now could stop the torrent; so
   He read the first three lines of the contents;
But at the fourth, the whole spiritual show
   Had vanished, with variety of scents,
Ambrosial and sulphureous, as they sprang,
Like lightning, off from his 'melodious twang.'

103

Those grand heroics acted as a spell:
   The angels stopped their ears and plied their pinions;
The devils ran howling, deafened, down to hell;
   The ghosts fled, gibbering, for their own dominions –
(For 'tis not yet decided where they dwell,
   And I leave every man to his opinions);
Michael took refuge in his trump – but, lo!
His teeth were set on edge, he could not blow!

104

Saint Peter, who has hitherto been known
   For an impetuous saint, upraised his keys,
And at the fifth line knocked the poet down;
   Who fell like Phaeton, but more at ease,
Into his lake, for there he did not drown;
   A different web being by the Destinies
Woven for the Laureate's final wreath, whene'er
Reform shall happen either here or there.

105

He first sank to the bottom – like his works,
   But soon rose to the surface – like himself;
For all corrupted things are buoyed like corks,
   By their own rottenness, light as an elf,

Or wisp that flits o'er a morass: he lurks,
   It may be, still, like dull books on a shelf,
In his own den, to scrawl some 'Life' or 'Vision,'
As Welborn[67] says – 'the devil turned precisian.'°   *Puritan*

106

As for the rest, to come to the conclusion
   Of this true dream, the telescope is gone
Which kept my optics free from all delusion,
   And showed me what I in my turn have shown;
All I saw farther, in the last confusion,
   Was, that King George slipped into heaven for one;
And when the tumult dwindled to a calm,
I left him practising the hundredth psalm.

1821 [1822]

On This Day I Complete My Thirty-sixth Year[68]

MISSOLONGHI, JAN. 22, 1824

'Tis time this heart should be unmoved,
   Since others it hath ceased to move:
Yet, though I cannot be beloved,
      Still let me love!

My days are in the yellow leaf;
   The flowers and fruits of love are gone;
The worm, the canker, and the grief
      Are mine alone!

The fire that on my bosom preys
10   Is lone as some volcanic isle;
No torch is kindled at its blaze –
      A funeral pile.

The hope, the fear, the jealous care,
   The exalted portion of the pain
And power of love, cannot share,
      But wear the chain.

But 'tis not *thus* – and 'tis not *here* –
   Such thoughts should shake my soul, nor *now*
Where glory decks the hero's bier,
20   Or binds his brow.

The sword, the banner, and the field,
   Glory and Greece, around me see!
The Spartan, borne upon his shield,[69]
           Was not more free.

Awake! (not Greece – she *is* awake!)
   Awake, my spirit! Think through *whom*
Thy life-blood tracks its parent lake,
           And then strike home!

Tread those reviving passions down,
30   Unworthy manhood! – unto thee
Indifferent should the smile or frown
           Of beauty be.

If thou regret'st thy youth, *why live?*
   The land of honourable death
Is here: – up to the field, and give
           Away thy breath!

Seek out – less often sought than found –
   A soldier's grave, for thee the best;
Then look around, and choose thy ground,
40   And take thy rest.

1824 [1824]

NOTES

Byron

1 Alexander Pope. qv.
2 John Dryden. qv.
3 a disease, the pustules of which appeared on a cow's udder, and were first used in a vaccine against the human variety of the disease: galvanism – electricity produced by chemical reaction, discovered 1798 by Galvani: gaslight used in England, 1792, for the first time.
4 *The Lay of the Last Minstrel* by Sir Walter Scott.
5 border legends used by Scott.
6 written at Athens, 1810, to Teresa Macri, aged 12.
7 'my life, I love you.'
8 flower arrangements were used to convey messages.
9 written June 1814 after B. saw his cousin, Anne Wilmot, for the first time.
10 written Aug–Sept. 1815; subject – Lady Frances Wedderburn Webster; there was a scandal about her relationship with Wellington in Paris, 1815.
11 written Aug. 16 when the rumours of his relationship with Augusta led to his departure from England.
12 Admiral John Byron, 1723–86.
13 the blood tie with Augusta (as opposed to the marriage tie).
14 written as part of a letter to Thomas Moore, 28 Feb. 1817.
15 i.e. Childe Harold; Cantos I and II took Childe Harold to Portugal and Spain, Gibraltar and Malta, and finally to Athens. Byron arrived there Dec. 1809. Cantos I and II were published in 1812.
16 i.e. of Greece.
17 a man of Chaldea, one skilled in the occult and astrology.
18 the Battle of Waterloo led to the Congress of Vienna, 1815, where the thrones of Europe were restored.
19 highest point of the flight.
20 Brussels: refers to the ball given by the Duchess of Richmond on the eve of the Battle of Quatre-Bras. Waterloo was fought on 15 June 1815.
21 Frederick, Duke of Brunswick, 1771–1815, killed at Quatre-Bras.
22 bagpipe music, usually a march or a dirge.
23 Sir Evan and Donald were of the Cameron clan, the head of which was called Lochiel: their rallying song was called 'Cameron's Gathering'.
24 Sir Frederick Howard, 1785–1815, B.'s cousin killed at Waterloo.
25 apples said to be attractive on the outside but tasting of ashes when eaten.
26 Geneva, where J.J. Rousseau was born.
27 the *Discours*, 1750 and 1753, and *Le Contrat Social*, 1762, which influenced the leaders of the French Revolution.
28 B. 'the thunder storms to which these lines refer occurred on the 13th of June, 1816, at midnight.'
29 the Congress of Vienna.
30 started July 1818 with 'no plan' in mind except a satiric attack on the literary modes of the day (particularly Wordsworth, Coleridge and Southey) and on the politics and ideology of England and Europe after the Congress of Vienna. The poem offers an interpretation of and a commentary on the social and political developments of the period in styles of writing that vary from the colloquial and comic to the serious and

highflown. It is impossible to include the whole epic here so extracts have been given to illustrate the many varied aspects of this poem – not the least of which is the narration – from Canto I.

Canto I is concerned with Don Juan's birth, upbringing and his first misdemeanour, an affair, for which he has to leave his homeland.

31 a popular stage production of *Don Juan*, based on Thomas Shadwell's *The Libertine*, 1787.

32 straight into the poem.

33 road with barrier across it for collecting tolls; here a point of no return.

34 from the late medieval period.

35 based on B.'s mother and his wife.

36 light cotton striped fabric.

37 B. ends the Canto considering contemporary poets, his own position as poet and his reasons for continuing his writing, with a final dig at the Lakeland Poets (Wordsworth, Coleridge, Southey).

38 B.'s parody of Southey's *A Vision of Judgement*, 1821, which was a celebration of George III and his ministers and all he stood for. In his Preface to his poem Southey attacked B. as the leader of a 'Satanic school' of poetry.
    From B.'s Preface:
    'Fools rush in where angels fear to tread' – Pope. If Mr Southey had not rushed in where he had no business, and where he never was before, and never will be again, the following poem would not have been written. It is not impossible that it may be as good as his own, seeing that it cannot, by any species of stupidity, natural or acquired, be worse. . . . to attempt to canonize a Monarch, who, whatever were his household virtues, was neither a successful nor a patriot king . . . like all other exaggeration necessarily begets opposition . . . Of his private virtues (although a little expensive to the nation) there can be no doubt . . . With regard to the supernatural personages treated of, I can only say that I know as much about them, and (as an honest man) have a better right to talk of them than Robert Southey. I have also treated them more tolerantly . . .'

39 1788 – the start of the French Revolution.

40 return of an estate to the grantor or lessor.

41 Rev. XII.3.

42 in 1820 when there were uprisings in Spain, Portugal and Greece.

43 George III hid the will of George II.

44 Louis was guillotined 1793.

45 St. Bartholomew was flayed alive.

46 rivers of India, Egypt, London and North Britain.

47 fluid in the veins of the gods.

48 Gen. VI.2.

49 justice was given in the gateways of Eastern cities.

50 John Stuart.

51 the house of Brunswick (the Georges) was descended from the Guelfs, a militant political party in Italy in the Middle Ages.

52 the Masons, a secret society.

53 represents England.

54 the U.S.A., see Turnbull.

55 one who has not changed sides.

56 the Man in the Iron Mask was imprisoned in the Bastille.

57 Sheridan's *The Rival*, IV.2.
58 Sir Philip Francis, one of those to whom Junius's *Letters* was attributed.
59 Num. XXII.28.
60 see 'Versification . . .' p. 1158
61 see 'Versification . . .' p. 1158
62 *non di* . . . neither gods nor men (can endure mediocre poets).
63 in 1795, Southey and Coleridge (who had married two sisters – Edith and Sarah Fricker) planned to set up a society based on equality of responsibility and benefit in America. Wordsworth also was involved.
64 a member of a revolutionary party in the French Revolution.
65 B. 'See Southey's Life of *Henry Kirke White*.'
66 B. 'King Alphonso (13th C.), of the Ptolemaic system. Had he been consulted about the creation of the world, he would have spared the Maker some absurdities.'
67 in Massinger's *A New Way to Pay Old Debts*.
68 written 22 Jun. 1824 at Missolonghi, (published just before B.'s death) with Louka Chalandritsanos, a Greek youth, who accompanied him, in mind.
69 Spartan dead were carried off the field on their shields.

Percy Bysshe Shelley

[1792–1822]

He was the eldest son of the M.P. (later a baronet) for Horsham, Sussex: educated at Syon House Academy, Eton and University College, Oxford – where he was known as 'Mad Shelley' and the 'Eton Atheist'. His first publications, privately, were several Gothic stories and poems, 1810–11: expelled from Oxford for circulating *The Necessity of Atheism*, written with his friend, T.J. Hogg: quarrelled with his father: eloped to Scotland with Harriet Westbrook, 16 years old, whom he married Aug. 1811, in Edinburgh. Atheist, anti-royalist, anti-tyranny, pro-reform and revolution, he expressed his early philosophy in *Queen Mab* and the notes, 1813. 1814 his marriage collapsed: eloped abroad with Mary Godwin and her 15-year-old stepsister, Jane Claire Clairmont; their travels through Europe are related in a combined journal, *History of a Six Weeks' Tour*, 1817: returned to London. He received an annuity of £1000 and found a house on the edge of Windsor Great Park. 1816 *Alastor* was published and he spent the summer at Geneva with Byron, where Mary began *Frankenstein* and Sh. wrote his 'Hymn to Intellectual Beauty' and 'Mont Blanc'. Autumn 1816 Harriet drowned herself in the Serpentine. Sh. immediately married Mary but failed to get the custody of his first two children. After a move to Great Marlow where he wrote *The Revolt of Islam*, 1818, harried by creditors, the family moved to Italy, first to Lucca, then Venice and Este (where he wrote 'Julian and Maddalo' and his daughter Clara died) then to Naples for the winter: by spring 1819 he was working on *Prometheus Unbound*: at Rome, his son William, his favourite, died and Mary suffered a breakdown. The family then settled in Tuscany, first near Livorno, then Florence, finally at Pisa, their home until 1822. Between 1819–20 he completed Act IV of *P.U.*; 'The Mask of Anarchy'; 'Ode to the West Wind'; 'Peter Bell The Third'; 'Ode to Naples', 'To Liberty'; 'To a Skylark'; 'The Cloud'; 'The Letter to Maria Gisborne'; 'Witch of Atlas'; *The Cenci*. 1820–1 he wrote several prose pieces including the *Defence of Poetry*. Spring, 1821, with the news of Keats' death, brought *Adonais*; a platonic love affair with Emilia Viviani resulted in *Epipsychidion*: the winter of 1821, at Pisa, with Trelawny, Edward and Jane Williams and Leigh Hunt, he wrote his last completed verse drama – *Hellas*, 1822. In April he moved to Lerici, beginning *The Triumph of Life*, as well as writing lyrics to Jane

Williams. He was at sea on 8 July with Edward Williams and a
boat-boy, returning from a visit to Byron at Livorno, when a
sudden squall blew up, sinking the boat and drowning its
occupants. His body was later found on the beach at Viareggio, a
copy of Sophocles in one pocket, in the other a copy of Keats' poems
'doubled back, as if the reader, in the act of reading, had hastily
thrust it away'. His ashes (except for his heart which Trelawny
retrieved from the fire and was later given to Mary) were buried in
the Protestant cemetery, Rome, where his son William had been
buried.

From *Alastor*[1]

50   There was a Poet whose untimely tomb
No human hands with pious reverence reared,
But the charmed eddies of autumnal winds
Built o'er his mouldering bones a pyramid
Of mouldering leaves in the waste wilderness:–
A lovely youth, – no mourning maiden decked
With weeping flowers, or votive cypress wreath,
The lone couch of his everlasting sleep:–
Gentle, and brave, and generous, – no lorn bard
Breathed o'er his dark fate one melodious sigh:
60   He lived, he died, he sung, in solitude.
Strangers have wept to hear his passionate notes,
And virgins, as unknown he passed, have pined
And wasted for fond love of his wild eyes.
The fire of those soft orbs has ceased to burn,
And Silence, too enamoured of that voice,
Locks its mute music in her rugged cell.

By solemn vision, and bright silver dream,
His infancy was nurtured. Every sight
And sound from the vast earth and ambient° air,   *surrounding*
70   Sent to his heart its choicest impulses.
The fountains of divine philosophy
Fled not his thirsting lips, and all of great,
Or good, or lovely, which the sacred past
In truth or fable consecrates, he felt
And knew. When early youth had passed, he left
His cold fireside and alienated home
To seek strange truths in undiscovered lands.
Many a wide waste and tangled wilderness

Has lured his fearless steps; and he has bought
80 With his sweet voice and eyes, from savage men,
His rest and food. Nature's most secret steps
He like her shadow has pursued.

*   *   *

. . . One darkest glen
452 Sends from its woods of musk-rose, twined with jasmine,
A soul-dissolving odour, to invite
To some more lovely mystery . . .

*   *   *

Hither the Poet came. His eyes beheld
470 Their own wan light through the reflected lines
Of his thin hair, distinct in the dark depth
Of that still fountain; as the human heart,
Gazing in dreams over the gloomy grave,
Sees its own treacherous likeness there. He heard
The motion of the leaves, the grass that sprung
Startled and glanced and trembled even to feel
An unaccustomed presence, and the sound
Of the sweet brook that from the secret springs
Of that dark fountain rose. A Spirit seemed
480 To stand beside him – clothed in no bright robes
Of shadowy silver or enshrining light,
Borrowed from aught the visible world affords
Of grace, or majesty, or mystery; –
But, undulating woods, and silent well,
And leaping rivulet, and evening gloom
Now deepening the dark shades, for speech assuming,
Held commune with him, as if he and it
Were all that was, – only . . . when his regard
Was raised by intense pensiveness, . . . two eyes,
490 Two starry eyes, hung in the gloom of thought,
And seemed with their serene and azure smiles
To beckon him.

Obedient to the light
That shone within his soul, he went, pursuing
The windings of the dell. – The rivulet
Wanton and wild, through many a green ravine
Beneath the forest flowed. Sometimes it fell
Among the moss with hollow harmony
Dark and profound. Now on the polished stones
It danced; like childhood laughing as it went:

500 Then, through the plain in tranquil wanderings crept,
Reflecting every herb and drooping bud
That overhung its quietness. – 'O stream!
Whose source is inaccessibly profound,
Whither do thy mysterious waters tend?
Thou imagest my life. Thy darksome stillness,
Thy dazzling waves, thy loud and hollow gulfs,
Thy searchless fountain, and invisible course
Have each their type in me: and the wide sky,
And measureless ocean may declare as soon
510 What oozy cavern or what wandering cloud
Contains thy waters, as the universe
Tell where these living thoughts reside, when stretched
Upon thy flowers my bloodless limbs shall waste
I' the passing wind!'

             *   *   *

                    . . . but thou° art fled –   *(the poet)*
Thou canst no longer know or love the shapes
Of this phantasmal scene, who have to thee
Been purest ministers, who are, alas!
Now thou art not. Upon those pallid lips
700 So sweet even in their silence, on those eyes
That image sleep in death, upon that form
Yet safe from the worm's outrage, let no tear
Be shed – not even in thought. Nor, when those hues
Are gone, and those divinest lineaments,
Worn by the senseless wind, shall live alone
In the frail pauses of this simple strain,
Let not high verse, mourning the memory
Of that which is no more, or painting's woe
Or sculpture, speak in feeble imagery
710 Their own cold powers. Art and eloquence,
And all the shows o' the world are frail and vain
To weep a loss that turns their lights to shade.
It is a woe too 'deep for tears,' when all
Is reft at once, when some surpassing Spirit,
Whose light adorned the world around it, leaves
Those who remain behind, not sobs or groans,
The passionate tumult of a clinging hope;
But pale despair and cold tranquility,
Nature's vast frame, the web of human things,
720 Birth and the grave, that are not as they were.

                                    1815 [1816]

To Wordsworth

Poet of Nature, thou hast wept to know
That things depart which never may return:
Childhood and youth, friendship and love's first glow,
Have fled like sweet dreams, leaving thee to mourn.
These common woes I feel. One loss is mine
Which thou too feel'st, yet I alone deplore.
Thou wert as a lone star, whose light did shine
On some frail bark in winter's midnight roar:
Thou hast like to a rock-built refuge stood
10 Above the blind and battling multitude:
In honoured poverty thy voice did weave
Songs consecrate to truth and liberty, –
Deserting these,[2] thou leavest me to grieve,
Thus having been, that thou shouldst cease to be.

[1816]

Hymn to Intellectual Beauty[3]

I

The awful shadow of some unseen Power
  Floats though unseen among us, – visiting
  This various world with as inconstant wing
As summer winds that creep from flower to flower, –
Like moonbeams that behind some piny mountain shower,
    It visits with inconstant glance
    Each human heart and countenance;
Like hues and harmonies of evening, –
    Like clouds in starlight widely spread, –
10   Like memory of music fled, –
    Like aught that for its grace may be
Dear, and yet dearer for its mystery.

II

Spirit of BEAUTY, that dost consecrate
  With thine own hues all thou dost shine upon
  Of human thought or form, – where art thou gone?
Why dost thou pass away and leave our state,
This dim vast vale of tears, vacant and desolate?

Ask why the sunlight not for ever
Weaves rainbows o'er yon mountain-river,
20 Why aught should fail and fade that once is shown,
Why fear and dream and death and birth
Cast on the daylight of this earth
Such gloom, – why man has such a scope
For love and hate, despondency and hope?

III

No voice from some sublimer world hath ever
To sage or poet these responses given –
Therefore the names of Demon, Ghost, and Heaven,
Remain the records of their vain endeavour,
Frail spells – whose uttered charm might not avail to sever,
30 From all we hear and all we see,
Doubt, chance, and mutability.
Thy light alone – like mist o'er mountains driven,
Or music by the night-wind sent
Through strings of some still instrument,
Or moonlight on a midnight stream,
Gives grace and truth to life's unquiet dream.

IV

Love, Hope, and Self-esteem, like clouds depart
And come, for some uncertain moments lent.
Man were immortal, and omnipotent,
40 Didst thou, unknown and awful as thou art,
Keep with thy glorious train° firm state within his heart.   *company*
Thou messenger of sympathies,
That wax and wane in lovers' eyes –
Thou – that to human thought art nourishment,
Like darkness to a dying flame!
Depart not as thy shadow came,
Depart not – lest the grave should be,
Like life and fear, a dark reality.

V

While yet a boy I sought for ghosts, and sped
50 Through many a listening chamber, cave and ruin,
And starlight wood, with fearful steps pursuing
Hopes of high talk with the departed dead.
I called on poisonous names⁴ with which our youth is fed:
I was not heard – I saw them not –
When musing deeply on the lot

Of life, at that sweet time when winds are wooing
        All vital things that wake to bring
        News of birds and blossoming, –
        Sudden, thy shadow fell on me;
60 I shrieked, and clasped my hands in ecstasy!⁵

VI

I vowed that I would dedicate my powers
    To thee and thine – have I not kept the vow?
    With beating heart and streaming eyes, even now
I call the phantoms of a thousand hours
Each from his voiceless grave: they have in visioned bowers
        Of studious zeal or love's delight
        Outwatched with me the envious night –
They know that never joy illumed my brow
        Unlinked with hope that thou wouldst free
70   This world from its dark slavery,
        That thou – O awful LOVELINESS,
Wouldst give whate'er these words cannot express.

VII

The day becomes more solemn and serene
    When noon is past – there is a harmony
    In autumn, and a lustre in its sky,
Which through the summer is not heard or seen,
As if it could not be, as if it had not been!
        Thus let thy power, which like the truth
        Of nature on my passive youth
80   Descended, to my onward life supply
        Its calm – to one who worships thee,
        And every form containing thee,
        Whom, SPIRIT fair, thy spells did bind
To fear° himself, and love all human kind.   *hold in awe*

1816 [1817]

Ozymandias

I met a traveller from an antique land
Who said: Two vast and trunkless legs of stone
Stand in the desert . . . Near them, on the sand,
Half sunk, a shattered visage lies, whose frown,
And wrinkled lip, and sneer of cold command,
Tell that its sculptor well those passions read
Which yet survive, stamped on these lifeless things,
The hand that mocked them, and the heart that fed:
And on the pedestal these words appear:
10 'My name is Ozymandias, king of kings:
Look on my works, ye Mighty, and despair!'
Nothing beside remains. Round the decay
Of that colossal wreck, boundless and bare
The lone and level sands stretch far away.

1817 [1818]

From *Julian and Maddalo*[6]

I rode one evening with Count Maddalo
Upon the bank of land° which breaks the flow   *the Lido*
Of Adria towards Venice: a bare strand
Of hillocks, heaped from ever-shifting sand,
Matted with thistles and amphibious weeds,
Such as from earth's embrace the salt ooze breeds,
Is this; an uninhabited sea-side,
Which the lone fisher, when his nets are dried,
Abandons; and no other object breaks
10 The waste, but one dwarf tree and some few stakes
Broken and unrepaired, and the tide makes
A narrow space of level sand thereon,
Where 'twas our wont to ride while day went down.
This ride was my delight. I love all waste
And solitary places; where we taste
The pleasure of believing what we see
Is boundless, as we wish our souls to be:
And such was this wide ocean, and this shore
More barren than its billows; and yet more
20 Than all, with a remembered friend I love

To ride as then I rode; – for the winds drove
The living spray along the sunny air
Into our faces; the blue heavens were bare,
Stripped to their depths by the awakening north;
And, from the waves, sound like delight broke forth
Harmonising with solitude, and sent
Into our hearts aëreal merriment.
So, as we rode, we talked; and the swift thought,
Winging itself with laughter, lingered not,
30 But flew from brain to brain, – such glee was ours,
Charged with light memories of remembered hours,
None slow enough for sadness: till we came
Homeward, which always makes the spirit tame.
This day had been cheerful but cold, and now
The sun was sinking, and the wind also.
Our talk grew somewhat serious, as may be
Talk interrupted with such raillery
As mocks itself, because it cannot scorn
The thoughts it would extinguish: – 'twas forlorn,
40 Yet pleasing, such as once, so poets tell,[7]
The devils held within the dales of Hell
Concerning God, freewill and destiny:
Of all that earth has been or yet may be,
All that vain men imagine or believe,
Or hope can paint or suffering may achieve,
We descanted,° and I (for ever still   *talk at length*
Is it not wise to make the best of ill?)
Argued against despondency, but pride
Made my companion take the darker side.
50 The sense that he was greater than his kind
Had struck, methinks, his eagle spirit blind
By gazing on its own exceeding light.
Meanwhile the sun paused ere it should alight,
Over the horizon of the mountains; – Oh,
How beautiful is sunset, when the glow
Of Heaven descends upon a land like thee,
Thou Paradise of exiles, Italy!
Thy mountains, seas, and vineyards, and the towers
Of cities they encircle! – it was ours
60 To stand on thee, beholding it: and then,
Just where we had dismounted, the Count's men
Were waiting for us with the gondola. –
As those who pause on some delightful way
Though bent on pleasant pilgrimage, we stood

Looking upon the evening, and the flood
Which lay between the city and the shore,
Paved with the image of the sky . . . the hoar
And aëry alps towards the North appeared
Through mist, an heaven-sustaining bulwark reared
70 Between the East and West; and half the sky
Was roofed with clouds of rich emblazonry
Dark purple at the zenith, which still grew
Down the steep West into a wondrous hue
Brighter than burning gold, even to the rent
Where the swift sun yet paused in his descent
Among the many-folded hills: they were
Those famous Euganean hills, which bear,
As seen from Lido thro' the harbour piles,
The likeness of a clump of peaked isles –
80 And then – as if the Earth and Sea had been
Dissolved into one lake of fire, were seen
Those mountains towering as from waves of flame
Around the vaporous sun, from which there came
The inmost purple spirit of light, and made
Their very peaks transparent. 'Ere it fade,'
Said my companion, 'I will show you soon
A better station – so, o'er the lagune°   lagoon
We glided; and from that funereal bark
I leaned, and saw the city, and could mark
90 How from their many isles, in evening's gleam,
Its temples and its palaces did seem
Like fabrics of enchantment piled to Heaven.
I was about to speak, when – 'We are even
Now at the point I meant,' said Maddalo,
And bade the gondolieri cease to row.
'Look, Julian, on the west, and listen well
If you hear not a deep and heavy bell.'
I looked, and saw between us and the sun
A building on an island; such a one
100 As age to age might add, for uses vile,
A windowless, deformed and dreary pile;
And on the top an open tower, where hung
A bell, which in the radiance swayed and swung;
We could just hear its hoarse and iron tongue:
The broad sun sunk behind it, and it tolled
In strong and black relief. – 'What we behold
Shall be the madhouse and its belfry tower,'
Said Maddalo, 'and ever at this hour

Those who may cross the water, hear that bell
110 Which calls the maniacs, each one from his cell,
To vespers.' – 'As much skill as need to pray
In thanks or hope for their dark lot have they
To their stern maker,' I replied. 'O ho!
You talk as in years past,' said Maddalo.
''Tis strange men change not. You were ever still
Among Christ's flock a perilous infidel,[8]
A wolf for the meek lambs – if you can't swim[9]
Beware of Providence.' I looked on him,
But the gay smile had faded in his eye.
120 'And such,' – he cried, 'is our mortality,
And this must be the emblem and the sign
Of what should be eternal and divine! –
And like that black and dreary bell, the soul,
Hung in a heaven-illumined tower, must toll
Our thoughts and our desires to meet below
Round the rent heart and pray – as madmen do
For what? they know not, – till the night of death
As sunset that strange vision, severeth
Our memory from itself, and us from all
130 We sought and yet were baffled.' I recall
The sense of what he said, although I mar
The force of his expressions. The broad star
Of day meanwhile had sunk behind the hill,
And the black bell became invisible,
And the red tower looked gray, and all between
The churches, ships and palaces were seen
Huddled in gloom; – into the purple sea
The orange hues of heaven sunk silently.
We hardly spoke, and soon the gondola
140 Conveyed me to my lodging by the way.
     The following morn was rainy, cold and dim:
Ere Maddalo arose, I called on him
And whilst I waited with his child[10] I played;
A lovelier toy sweet Nature never made,
A serious, subtle, wild, yet gentle being,
Graceful without design and unforeseeing,
With eyes – Oh speak not of her eyes! – which seem
Twin mirrors of Italian Heaven, yet gleam
With such deep meaning, as we never see
150 But in the human countenance: with me
She was a special favourite: I had nursed
Her fine and feeble limbs when she came first

To this bleak world; and she yet seemed to know
On second sight her ancient playfellow,
Less changed than she was by six months or so;
For after her first shyness was worn out
We sate there, rolling billiard balls about,
When the Count entered. Salutations past –
'The word you spoke last night might well have cast
160 A darkness on my spirit – if man be
The passive thing you say, I should not see
Much harm in the religions and old saws
(Tho' I may never own such leaden laws)
Which break a teachless nature to the yoke:
Mine is another faith' – thus much I spoke
And noting he replied not, added: 'See
This lovely child, blithe, innocent and free;
She spends a happy time with little care,
While we to such sick thoughts subjected are
170 As came on you last night – it is our will
That thus enchains us to permitted ill –
We might be otherwise – we might be all
We dream of happy, high, majestical.
Where is the love, beauty, and truth we seek
But in our mind? and if we were not weak
Should we be less in deed than in desire?'
'Ay, if we were not weak – and we aspire
How vainly to be strong!' said Maddalo:
'You talk Utopia.' 'It remains to know,'
180 I then rejoined, 'and those who try may find
How strong the chains are which our spirit bind;
Brittle perchance as straw . . . We are assured
Much may be conquered, much may be endured,
Of what degrades and crushes us. We know
That we have power over ourselves to do
And suffer – what, we know not till we try;
But something nobler than to live and die –
So taught those kings of old philosophy
Who reigned, before Religion made men blind;
190 And those who suffer with their suffering kind
Yet feel their faith, religion.' 'My dear friend,'
Said Maddalo, 'my judgement will not bend
To your opinion, though I think you might
Make such a system refutation-tight

As far as words go. I knew one like you
Who to this city came some months ago,
With whom I argued in this sort, and he
Is now gone mad, – and so he answered me, –
Poor fellow! but if you would like to go
200   We'll visit him, and his wild talk will show
How vain are such aspiring theories.'
'I hope to prove the induction otherwise,
And that a want of that true theory, still,
Which seeks a "soul of goodness" in things ill
Or in himself or others, has thus bowed
His being – there are some by nature proud,
Who patient in all else demand but this –
To love and be beloved with gentleness;
And being scorned, what wonder if they die
210   Some living death? this is not destiny
But man's own wilful ill.'
                    As thus I spoke
Servants announced the gondola, and we
Through the fast-falling rain and high-wrought sea
Sailed to the island where the madhouse stands.
We disembarked. The clap of tortured hands,
Fierce yells and howlings and lamentings keen,
And laughter where complaint had merrier been,
Moans, shrieks, and curses, and blaspheming prayers
Accosted us. We climbed the oozy stairs
220   Into an old courtyard. I heard on high,
Then, fragments of most touching melody,
But looking up saw not the singer there –
Through the black bars in the tempestuous air
I saw, like weeds on a wrecked palace growing,
Long tangled locks flung wildly forth, and flowing,
Of those who on a sudden were beguiled
Into strange silence, and looked forth and smiled
Hearing sweet sounds. – Then I: 'Methinks there were
A cure of these with patience and kind care,
230   If music can thus move . . . but what is he
Whom we seek here?' 'Of his sad history
I know but this,' said Maddalo: 'he came
To Venice a dejected man, and fame
Said he was wealthy, or he had been so;
Some thought the loss of fortune wrought him woe . . .'

           *   *   *

'Alas, what drove him mad?' 'I cannot say:
A lady came with him from France, and when
She left him and returned, he wandered then
About yon lonely isles of desert sand
Till he grew wild – he had no cash or land
250   Remaining, – the police had brought him here –
Some fancy took him and he would not bear
Removal; so I fitted up for him
Those rooms beside the sea, to please his whim,
And sent him busts and books and urns for flowers,
Which had adorned his life in happier hours,
And instruments of music – you may guess
A stranger could do little more or less
For one so gentle and unfortunate.'

                    *   *   *

270   Having said
These words we called the keeper, and he led
To an apartment opening on the sea –
There the poor wretch was sitting mournfully
Near a piano, his pale fingers twined
One with the other, and the ooze° and wind   *sea-mist*
Rushed through an open casement, and did sway
His hair, and starred it with the brackish spray;
His head was leaning on a music book,
And he was muttering, and his lean limbs shook;
280   His lips were pressed against a folded leaf
In hue too beautiful for health, and grief
Smiled in their motions as they lay apart –
As one who wrought from his own fervid heart
The eloquence of passion, soon he raised
His sad meek face and eyes lustrous and glazed
And spoke – sometimes as one who wrote, and thought
His words might move some heart that heeded not,
If sent to distant lands: and then as one
Reproaching deeds never to be undone
290   With wondering self-compassion; then his speech
Was lost in grief, and then his words came each
Unmodulated, cold, expressionless, –
But that from one jarred accent you might guess
It was despair made them so uniform:
And all the while the loud and gusty storm

Hissed through the window, and we stood behind
Stealing his accents from the envious wind
Unseen. I yet remember what he said
Distinctly: such impression his words made.

*   *   *

'It were
A cruel punishment for one most cruel,
440 If such can love, to make that love the fuel
Of the mind's hell; hate, scorn, remorse, despair:
But *me* – whose heart a stranger's tear might wear
As water-drops the sandy fountain-stone,
Who loved and pitied all things, and could moan
For woes which others hear not, and could see
The absent with the glance of phantasy,
And with the poor and trampled sit and weep,
Following the captive to his dungeon deep;
Me – who am as a nerve o'er which do creep
450 The else unfelt oppressions of this earth,
And was to thee the flame upon thy hearth,
When all beside was cold – that thou on me
Shouldst rain these plagues of blistering agony –
Such curses are from lips once eloquent
With love's too partial praise – let none relent
Who intend deeds too dreadful for a name
Henceforth, if an example for the same
They seek . . . for thou on me lookedst so, and so –
And didst speak thus . . . and thus . . . I live to show
460 How much men bear and die not!

*   *   *

Alas, love!
Fear me not . . . against thee I would not move
A finger in despite. Do I not live
That thou mayst have less bitter cause to grieve?
I give thee tears for scorn and love for hate;
And that thy lot may be less desolate
Than his on whom thou tramplest, I refrain
From that sweet sleep which medicines all pain.
500 Then, when thou speakest of me, never say
"He could forgive not." Here I cast away
All human passions, all revenge, all pride;
I think, speak, act no ill; I do but hide
Under these words, like embers, every spark

Of that which has consumed me – quick and dark
The grave is yawning . . . as its roof shall cover
My limbs with dust and worms under and over
So let Oblivion hide this grief . . . the air
Closes upon my accents, as despair
510 Upon my heart – let death upon despair!'
    He ceased, and overcome leant back awhile,
Then rising, with a melancholy smile
Went to a sofa, and lay down, and slept
A heavy sleep, and in his dreams he wept
And muttered some familiar name, and we
Wept without shame in his society.
I think I never was impressed so much;
The man who were not, must have lacked a touch
Of human nature . . . then we lingered not,
520 Although our argument was quite forgot,
But calling the attendants, went to dine
At Maddalo's; yet neither cheer nor wine
Could give us spirits, for we talked of him
And nothing else, till daylight made stars dim;
And we agreed his was some dreadful ill
Wrought on him boldly, yet unspeakable,
By a dear friend; some deadly change in love
Of one vowed deeply which he dreamed not of;
For whose sake he, it seemed, had fixed a blot
530 Of falsehood on his mind which flourished not
But in the light of all-beholding truth;
And having stamped this canker on his youth
She had abandoned him – and how much more
Might be his woe, we guessed not – he had store
Of friends and fortune once, as we could guess
From his nice habits and his gentleness;
These were now lost . . . it were a grief indeed
If he had changed one unsustaining reed
For all that such a man might else adorn.
540 The colours of his mind seemed yet unworn;
For the wild language of his grief was high,
Such as in measure were called poetry;
And I remember one remark which then
Maddalo made. He said: 'Most wretched men
Are cradled into poetry by wrong,
They learn in suffering what they teach in song.'

Sonnet

Lift not the veil which those who live
Call life: though unreal shapes be pictured there,
And it but mimic all we would believe
With colours idly spread, – behind, lurk Fear
And Hope, twin Destinies; who ever weave
Their shadows, o'er the chasm, sightless and drear.
I knew one who had lifted it – he sought,
For his lost heart was tender, things to love,
But found them not, alas! nor was there aught
The world contains, the which he could approve.
Through the unheeding many he did move,
A splendour among shadows, a bright blot
Upon this gloomy scene, a Spirit that strove
For truth, and like the Preacher, found it not.

1818 [1824]

From **Prometheus Unbound**[11]

Act I Sc 1

Prometheus:
The crawling glaciers pierce me with the spears
Of their moon-freezing crystals, the bright chains
Eat with their burning cold into my bones.
Heaven's winged hound, polluting from thy° lips   *(Jupiter's)*
His beak in poison not his own, tears up
My heart; and shapeless sights come wandering by,
The ghastly people of the realm of dream,
Mocking me: and the earthquake-fiends are charged
To wrench the rivets from my quivering wounds
40   When the rocks split and close again behind:
While from their loud abysses howling throng
The genii of the storm, urging the rage
Of whirlwind, and afflict me with keen hail.
And yet to me welcome is day and night,
Whether one breaks the hoar frost of the morn,
Or starry, dim, and slow, the other climbs
The leaden-coloured east; for then they lead

The wingless, crawling hours, one among whom
– As some dark priest hales the reluctant victim –
50 Shall drag thee, cruel King, to kiss the blood
From these pale feet, which then might trample thee
If they disdained not such a prostrate slave.
Disdain! Ah no! I pity thee. What ruin
Will hunt thee undefended through wide Heaven!
How will thy soul, cloven to its depth with terror,
Gape like a hell within! I speak in grief,
Not exultation, for I hate no more,
As then ere misery made me wise. The curse
Once breathed on thee I would recall. Ye mountains,
60 Whose many-voiced echoes, through the mist
Of cataracts, flung the thunder of that spell!
Ye icy springs, stagnant with wrinkling frost,
Which vibrated to hear me, and then crept
Shuddering through India! Thou serenest air,
Through which the sun walks burning without beams!
And ye swift whirlwinds, who on poised wings
Hung mute and moveless o'er yon hushed abyss,
As thunder, louder than your own, made rock
The orbed world! If then my words had power,
70 Though I am changed so that aught evil wish
Is dead within; although no memory be
Of what is hate, let them not lose it now!
What was that curse? for ye all heard me speak.

Act II Sc 5

Asia:
My soul is an enchanted boat,
Which, like a sleeping swan, doth float
Upon the silver waves of thy sweet singing;[12]
And thine doth like an angel sit
Beside a helm conducting it,
Whilst all the winds with melody are ringing.
It seems to float ever, for ever,
Upon that many-winding river,
80 Between mountains, woods, abysses,
A paradise of wildernesses!
Till, like one in slumber bound,

Borne to the ocean, I float down, around,
Into a sea profound, of ever-spreading sound:

    Meanwhile thy spirit lifts its pinions
    In music's most serene dominions;
Catching the winds that fan that happy heaven.
    And we sail on, away, afar,
    Without a course, without a star,
90 But, by the instinct of sweet music driven;
    Till through Elysian garden islets
    By thee, most beautiful of pilots,
    Where never mortal pinnace glided,
    The boat of my desire is guided:
Realms where the air we breathe is love,
Which in the winds and on the waves doth move,
Harmonizing this earth with what we feel above.

    We have passed Age's icy caves,
    And Manhood's dark and tossing waves,
100 And Youth's smooth ocean, smiling to betray:
    Beyond the glassy gulfs we flee
    Of shadow-peopled Infancy,
Through Death and Birth, to a diviner day;
    A paradise of vaulted bowers,
    Lit by downward-gazing flowers,
    And watery paths that wind between
    Wilderness calm and green,
Peopled by shapes too bright to see,
And rest, having beheld; somewhat like thee;
110 Which walk upon the sea, and chant melodiously!

Act III Sc 4

Spirit of the Hour:
    As I have said, I floated to the earth:
    It was, as it is still, the pain of bliss
    To move, to breathe, to be; I wandering went
    Among the haunts and dwellings of mankind,
    And first was disappointed not to see
    Such mighty change as I had felt within
130 Expressed in outward things; but soon I looked,
    And behold, thrones were kingless, and men walked
    One with the other even as spirits do,
    None fawned, none trampled; hate, disdain, or fear,

Self-love or self-contempt, on human brows
No more inscribed, as o'er the gate of hell,
'All hope abandon ye who enter here;'[13]
None frowned, none trembled, none with eager fear
Gazed on another's eye of cold command,
Until the subject of a tyrant's will
140   Became, worse fate, the abject of his own,
Which spurred him, like an outspent horse, to death.
None wrought his lips in truth-entangling lines
Which smiled the lie his tongue disdained to speak;
None, with firm sneer, trod out in his own heart
The sparks of love and hope till there remained
Those bitter ashes, a soul self-consumed,
And the wretch crept a vampire among men,
Infecting all with his own hideous ill;
None talked that common, false, cold, hollow talk
150   Which makes the heart deny the *yes* it breathes,
Yet question that unmeant hypocrisy
With such a self-mistrust as has no name.
And women, too, frank, beautiful, and kind
As the free heaven which rains fresh light and dew
On the wide earth, passed; gentle radiant forms,
From custom's evil taint exempt and pure;
Speaking the wisdom once they could not think,
Looking emotions once they feared to feel,
And changed to all which once they dared not be,
160   Yet being now, made earth like heaven; nor pride,
Nor jealousy, nor envy, nor ill shame,
The bitterest of those drops of treasured gall,
Spoilt the sweet taste of the nepenthe,° love.   *(drug for forgetting)*

Act IV Sc 4

Demogorgon:[14]
This is the day, which down the void abysm
At the Earth-born's° spell yawns for Heaven's despotism,   *(Prometheus)*
   And Conquest is dragged captive through the deep:
Love, from its awful throne of patient power
In the wise heart, from the last giddy hour
   Of dread endurance, from the slippery, steep,
560   And narrow verge of crag-like agony, springs
And folds over the world its healing wings.

Gentleness, Virtue, Wisdom, and Endurance,
These are the seals of that most firm assurance
    Which bars the pit over Destruction's strength;
And if, with infirm hand, Eternity,
Mother of many acts and hours, should free
    The serpent[15] that would clasp her with his length;
These are the spells by which to reassume
An empire o'er the disentangled doom.

570 To suffer woes which Hope thinks infinite;
To forgive wrongs darker than death or night;
    To defy Power, which seems omnipotent;
To love, and bear; to hope till Hope creates
From its own wreck the thing it contemplates;
    Neither to change, nor falter, nor repent;
This, like thy glory, Titan, is to be
Good, great and joyous, beautiful and free;
This is alone Life, Joy, Empire, and Victory.

1818/19 [1820]

From *The Mask of Anarchy*

WRITTEN ON THE OCCASION
OF THE MASSACRE[16] AT
MANCHESTER

1

As I lay asleep in Italy
There came a voice from over the sea,
And with great power it forth led me
To walk in the visions of Poesy.

2

I met Murder on the way –
He had a mask like Castlereagh –
Very smooth he looked, yet grim;
Seven blood-hounds followed him:

3

All were fat; and well they might
Be in admirable plight,
For one by one, and two by two,
He tossed them human hearts to chew
Which from his wide cloak he drew.

4

Next came Fraud, and he had on,
Like Eldon, an ermined gown;
His big tears, for he wept well,
Turned to mill-stones as they fell.

5

And the little children, who
Round his feet played to and fro,
Thinking every tear a gem,
Had their brains knocked out by them.

6

Clothed with the Bible, as with light,
And the shadows of the night,
Like Sidmouth, next, Hypocrisy
On a crocodile rode by.

7

And many more Destructions played
In this ghastly masquerade,
All disguised, even to the eyes,
Like Bishops, lawyers, peers, or spies.

8

Last came Anarchy: he rode
On a white horse, splashed with blood;
He was pale even to the lips,
Like Death in the Apocalypse.

9

And he wore a kingly crown;
And in his grasp a sceptre shone;
On his brow this mark I saw –
'I AM GOD, AND KING, AND LAW!'

10

With a pace stately and fast,
Over English land he passed,
Trampling to a mire of blood
The adoring multitude.

*   *   *

17

Lawyers and priests, a motley crowd,
To the earth their pale brows bowed;
Like a bad prayer not over loud,
Whispering – 'Thou° art law and God.' –   *Anarchy*

18

Then all cried with one accord,
'Thou art King, and God, and Lord;
Anarchy, to thee we bow,
Be thy name made holy now!'

19

And Anarchy, the skeleton,
Bowed and grinned to every one,
As well as if his education
Had cost ten millions to the nation.

*   *   *

22

When one fled past, a maniac maid,
And her name was Hope, she said:
But she looked more like Despair,
And she cried out in the air:

23

'My father Time is weak and gray
With waiting for a better day;
See how idiot-like he stands,
Fumbling with his palsied hands!

24

He has had child after child,
And the dust of death is piled
Over every one but me –
Misery, oh, misery!'

25

Then she lay down in the street,
Right before the horses' feet,
Expecting, with a patient eye,
Murder, Fraud, and Anarchy.

26

When between her and her foes
A mist, a light, an image rose,
Small at first, and weak, and frail
Like the vapour of a vale:

27

Till as clouds grow on the blast,
Like tower-crowned giants striding fast,
And glare with lightnings as they fly,
And speak in thunder to the sky,

28

It grew – a Shape arrayed in mail°   *armour*
Brighter than the viper's scale,
And upborne on wings whose grain
Was as the light of sunny rain.

29

On its helm, seen far away,
A planet, like the Morning's, lay;
And those plumes its light rained through
Like a shower of crimson dew.

30

With step as soft as wind it passed
O'er the heads of men – so fast
That they knew the presence there,
And looked, – but all was empty air.

31

As flowers beneath May's footstep waken,
As stars from Night's loose hair are shaken,
As waves arise when loud winds call,
Thoughts sprung where'er that step did fall.

32

And the prostrate multitude
Looked and ankle-deep in blood,
Hope, that maiden most serene,
Was walking with a quiet mien

*   *   *

34

A rushing light of clouds and splendour,
A sense awakening and yet tender
Was heard and felt – and at its close
These words of joy and fear arose

*   *   *

37

Hope speaks:
'Men of England, heirs of glory,
Heroes of unwritten story,
Nurslings of one mighty mother,
Hopes of her, and one another;

38

Rise like Lions after slumber
In unvanquishable number,
Shake your chains to earth like dew
Which in sleep had fallen on you –
Ye are many – they are few.

39

What is Freedom? – ye can tell
That which slavery is, too well –
For its very name has grown
To an echo of your own.

40

'Tis to work and have such pay
As just keeps life from day to day
In your limbs, as in a cell
For the tyrants' use to dwell,

41

So that ye for them are made
Loom, and plough, and sword, and spade,
With or without your own will bent
To their defence and nourishment.

42

'Tis to see your children weak
With their mothers pine and peak,
When the winter winds are bleak, –
They are dying whilst I speak.

43

'Tis to hunger for such diet
As the rich man in his riot
Casts to the fat dogs that lie
Surfeiting beneath his eye;

*   *   *

51

This is slavery – savage men,
Or wild beasts within a den
Would endure not as ye do –
But such ills they never knew.

52

What art thou Freedom? O! could slaves
Answer from their living graves
This demand – tyrants would flee
Like a dream's dim imagery:

53

Thou art not, as impostors say,
A shadow soon to pass away,
A superstition, and a name
Echoing from the cave of fame.

54

For the labourer thou art bread,
And a comely table spread
From his daily labour come
In a neat and happy home.

55

Thou art clothes, and fire, and food
For the trampled multitude –
No – in countries that are free
Such starvation cannot be
As in England now we see.

*   *   *

63

Science, Poetry, and Thought
Are thy lamps; they make the lot
Of the dwellers in a cot
So serene, they curse it° not.   *their condition*

64

Spirit, Patience, Gentleness,
All that can adorn and bless
Art thou – let deeds, not words, express
Thine exceeding loveliness.

65

Let a great Assembly be
Of the fearless and the free
On some spot of English ground
Where the plains stretch wide around.

66

Let the blue sky overhead,
The green earth on which ye tread,
All that must eternal be
Witness the solemnity.

67

From the corners uttermost
Of the bounds of English coast;
From every hut, village, and town
Where those who live and suffer moan
For others' misery or their own . . .

*   *   *

73

Let a vast assembly be,
And with great solemnity
Declare with measured words that ye
Are, as God has made ye, free –

74

Be your strong and simple words
Keen to wound as sharpened swords,
And wide as targes° let them be,   *shields*
With their shade to cover ye.

*   *   *

79

Stand ye calm and resolute,
Like a forest close and mute,
With folded arms and looks which are
Weapons of unvanquished war,

80

And let Panic, who outspeeds
The career of armed steeds
Pass, a disregarded shade
Through your phalanx undismayed.

81

Let the laws of your own land,
Good or ill, between ye stand
Hand to hand, and foot to foot,
Arbiters of the dispute,

82

The old laws of England – they
Whose reverend heads with age are gray,
Children of a wiser day;
And whose solemn voice must be
Thine own echo – Liberty!

83

On those who first should violate
Such sacred heralds in their state
Rest the blood that must ensue,
And it will not rest on you.

84

And if then the tyrants dare
Let them ride among you there,
Slash, and stab, and maim, and hew, –
What they like, that let them do.

85

With folded arms and steady eyes,
And little fear, and less surprise,
Look upon them as they slay
Till their rage has died away.

86

Then they will return with shame
To the place from which they came,
And the blood thus shed will speak
In hot blushes on their cheek.

*   *   *

90

And these words shall then become
Like Oppression's thundered doom
Ringing through each heart and brain,
Heard again – again – again –

91

"Rise like lions after slumber
In unvanquishable number –
Shake your chains to earth like dew
Which in sleep had fallen on you –
Ye are many – they are few." '

1819 [1832]

Love's Philosophy

I

The fountains mingle with the river
    And the rivers with the Ocean,
The winds of Heaven mix for ever
    With a sweet emotion;
Nothing in the world is single;
    All things by a law divine
In one spirit meet and mingle.
    Why not I with thine? –

II

See the mountains kiss high Heaven
10   And the waves clasp one another;
No sister-flower would be forgiven
    If it disdained its brother;
And the sunlight clasps the earth
    And the moonbeams kiss the sea:
What is all this sweet work worth
    If thou kiss not me?

1819 [1819]

Ode to the West Wind

I

O wild West Wind, thou breath of Autumn's being,
Thou, from whose unseen presence the leaves dead
Are driven, like ghosts from an enchanter fleeing,

Yellow, and black, and pale, and hectic red,
Pestilence-stricken multitudes: O thou,
Who chariotest to their dark wintry bed

The winged seeds, where they lie cold and low,
Each like a corpse within its grave, until
Thine azure sister of the Spring shall blow

10   Her clarion o'er the dreaming earth, and fill
(Driving sweet buds like flocks to feed in air)
With living hues and odours plain and hill:

Wild Spirit, which art moving everywhere;
Destroyer and preserver; hear, oh, hear!

II

Thou on whose stream, mid the steep sky's commotion,
Loose clouds like earth's decaying leaves are shed,
Shook from the tangled boughs of Heaven and Ocean,

Angels[17] of rain and lightning: there are spread
On the blue surface of thine aëry surge,
20   Like the bright hair uplifted from the head

Of some fierce Maenad, even from the dim verge
Of the horizon to the zenith's height,
The locks of the approaching storm. Thou dirge

Of the dying year, to which this closing night
Will be the dome of a vast sepulchre,
Vaulted with all thy congregated might

Of vapours, from whose solid atmosphere
Black rain, and fire, and hail will burst: oh, hear!

III

Thou who didst waken from his summer dreams
30 The blue Mediterranean, where he lay,
Lulled by the coil of his crystalline streams,

Beside a pumice isle in Baiae's bay,
And saw in sleep old palaces and towers
Quivering within the wave's intenser day,

All overgrown with azure moss and flowers
So sweet, the sense faints picturing them! Thou
For whose path the Atlantic's level powers

Cleave themselves into chasms, while far below
The sea-blooms and the oozy woods which wear
40 The sapless foliage of the ocean, know

Thy voice, and suddenly grow gray with fear,
And tremble and despoil themselves: oh, hear!

IV

If I were a dead leaf thou mightest bear;
If I were a swift cloud to fly with thee;
A wave to pant beneath thy power, and share

The impulse of thy strength, only less free
Than thou, O uncontrollable! If even
I were as in my boyhood, and could be

The comrade of thy wanderings over Heaven,
50 As then, when to outstrip thy skiey speed
Scarce seemed a vison; I would ne'er have striven

As thus with thee in prayer in my sore need.
Oh, lift me as a wave, a leaf, a cloud!
I fall upon the thorns of life! I bleed!

A heavy weight of hours has chained and bowed
One too like thee: tameless, and swift, and proud.

V

Make me thy lyre, even as the forest is:
What if my leaves are falling like its own!
The tumult of thy mighty harmonies

60 Will take from both a deep, autumnal tone,
Sweet though in sadness. Be thou, Spirit fierce,
My spirit! Be thou me, impetuous one!

Drive my dead thoughts over the universe
Like withered leaves to quicken a new birth!
And, by the incantation of this verse,

Scatter, as from an unextinguished hearth
Ashes and sparks, my words among mankind!
Be through my lips to unawakened earth

The trumpet of a prophecy! O, Wind,
70 If Winter comes, can Spring be far behind?

1819 [1820]

The Sensitive Plant

PART FIRST

A Sensitive Plant in a garden grew,
And the young winds fed it with silver dew,
And it opened its fan-like leaves to the light,
And closed them beneath the kisses of Night.

And the Spring arose on the garden fair,
Like the Spirit of Love felt everywhere;
And each flower and herb on Earth's dark breast
Rose from the dreams of its wintry rest.

But none ever trembled and panted with bliss

10 In the garden, the field, or the wilderness,
Like a doe in the noontide with love's sweet want,
As the companionless Sensitive Plant.

The snowdrop, and then the violet,
Arose from the ground with warm rain wet,
And their breath was mixed with fresh odour, sent
From the turf, like the voice and the instrument.

Then the pied wind-flowers° and the tulip tall,   *wood anemones*
And narcissi, the fairest among them all,
Who gaze on their eyes in the stream's recess,
20 Till they die of their own dear loveliness;

And the Naiad°like lily of the vale,   *water nymph*
Whom youth makes so fair and passion so pale
That the light of its tremulous bells is seen
Through their pavilions of tender green;

And the hyacinth purple, and white, and blue,
Which flung from its bells a sweet peal anew
Of music so delicate, soft, and intense,
It was felt like an odour within the sense;

And the rose like a nymph to the bath addressed,
30 Which unveiled the depth of her glowing breast,
Till, fold after fold, to the fainting air
The soul of her beauty and love lay bare:

And the wand-like lily, which lifted up,
As a Maenad, its moonlight-coloured cup,
Till the fiery star, which is its eye,
Gazed through clear dew on the tender sky;

And the jessamine faint, and the sweet tuberose,°   *lily-like plant*
The sweetest flower for scent that blows;
And all rare blossoms from every clime
40 Grew in that garden in perfect prime.

And on the stream whose inconstant bosom
Was pranked, under boughs of embowering blossom,
With golden and green light, slanting through
Their heaven of many a tangled hue,

Broad water-lilies lay tremulously,
And starry river-buds glimmered by,
And around them the soft stream did glide and dance
With a motion of sweet sound and radiance.

And the sinuous paths of lawn and of moss,
50 Which led through the garden along and across,
Some open at once to the sun and the breeze,
Some lost among bowers of blossoming trees,

Were all paved with daisies and delicate bells
As fair as the fabulous asphodels,[18]
And flow'rets which, drooping as day drooped too,
Fell into pavilions, white, purple, and blue,
To roof the glow-worm from the evening dew.

And from this undefiled paradise
The flowers (as an infant's awakening eyes
Smile on its mother, whose singing sweet
60 Can first lull, and at last must awaken it),

When Heaven's blithe winds had unfolded them,
As mine-lamps enkindle a hidden gem,
Shone smiling to Heaven, and every one
Shared joy in the light of the gentle sun;

For each one was interpenetrated
With the light and the odour its neighbour shed,
Like young lovers whom youth and love make dear
Wrapped and filled by their mutual atmosphere.

But the Sensitive Plant which could give small fruit
70 Of the love which it felt from the leaf to the root,
Received more than all, it loved more than ever,
Where none wanted but it, could belong to the giver,

For the Sensitive Plant has no bright flower;
Radiance and odour are not its dower;
It loves, even like Love, its deep heart is full,
It desires what it has not, the Beautiful!

The light winds which from unsustaining wings
Shed the music of many murmurings;

The beams which dart from many a star
80 Of the flowers whose hues they bear afar;

The plumed insects swift and free,
Like golden boats on a sunny sea,
Laden with light and odour, which pass
Over the gleam of the living grass;

The unseen clouds of the dew, which lie
Like fire in the flowers till the sun rides high,
Then wander like spirits among the spheres,
Each cloud faint with the fragrance it bears;

The quivering vapours of dim noontide,
90 Which like a sea o'er the warm earth glide,
In which every sound, and odour, and beam,
Move, as reeds in a single stream;

Each and all like ministering angels were
For the Sensitive Plant sweet joy to bear,
Whilst the lagging hours of the day went by
Like windless clouds o'er a tender sky.

And when evening descended from Heaven above,
And the Earth was all rest, and the air was all love,
And delight, though less bright, was far more deep,
100 And the day's veil fell from the world of sleep,

And the beasts, and the birds, and the insects were drowned
In an ocean of dreams without a sound;
Whose waves never mark, though they ever impress
The light sand which paves it, consciousness;

(Only overhead the sweet nightingale
Ever sang more sweet as the day might fail,
And snatches of its Elysian chant
Were mixed with the dreams of the Sensitive Plant); –

The Sensitive Plant was the earliest
110 Upgathered into the bosom of rest;
A sweet child weary of its delight,
The feeblest and yet the favourite,
Cradled within the embrace of night.

PART SECOND

There was a Power in this sweet place,
An Eve in this Eden; a ruling Grace
Which to the flowers, did they waken or dream,
Was as God is to the starry scheme.

A Lady, the wonder of her kind,
Whose form was upborne by a lovely mind
120 Which, dilating, had moulded her mien and motion
Like a sea-flower unfolded beneath the ocean,

Tended the garden from morn to even:
And the meteors of that sublunar Heaven,
Like the lamps of the air when Night walks forth,
Laughed round her footsteps up from the Earth!

She had no companion of mortal race,
But her tremulous breath and her flushing face
Told, whilst the morn kissed the sleep from her eyes,
That her dreams were less slumber than Paradise:

130 As if some bright Spirit for her sweet sake
Had deserted heaven while the stars were awake,
As if yet around her he lingering were,
Though the veil of daylight concealed him from her.

Her step seemed to pity the grass it pressed;
You might hear by the heaving of her breast,
That the coming and going of the wind
Brought pleasure there and left passion behind.

And wherever her aëry footstep trod,
Her trailing hair from the grassy sod
140 Erased its light vestige, with shadowy sweep,
Like a sunny storm o'er the dark green deep.

I doubt not the flowers of that garden sweet
Rejoiced in the sound of her gentle feet;
I doubt not they felt the spirit that came
From her glowing fingers through all their frame.

She sprinkled bright water from the stream
On those that were faint with the sunny beam;
And out of the cups of the heavy flowers
She emptied the rain of the thunder-showers.

150 She lifted their heads with her tender hands,
And sustained them with rods and osier°bands;   *willow*
If the flowers had been her own infants, she
Could never have nursed them more tenderly.

And all killing insects and gnawing worms,
And things of obscene and unlovely forms,
She bore, in a basket of Indian woof,°   *cloth*
Into the rough woods far aloof, –

In a basket, of grasses and wild-flowers full,
The freshest her gentle hands could pull
160 For the poor banished insects, whose intent,
Although they did ill, was innocent.

But the bee and the beamlike ephemeris°   *an insect which lives just a few*
Whose path is the lightning's, and soft moths that kiss   *hours*
The sweet lips of the flowers, and harm not, did she
Make her attendant angels be.

And many an antenatal tomb,
Where butterflies dream of the life to come,
She left clinging round the smooth and dark
Edge of the odorous cedar bark.

170 This fairest creature from earliest spring
Thus moved through the garden ministering
All the sweet season of Summertide,
And ere the first leaf looked brown – she died!

PART THIRD

Three days the flowers of the garden fair,
Like stars when the moon is awakened, were,
Or the waves of Baiae, ere luminous
She floats up through the smoke of Vesuvius.

And on the fourth, the Sensitive Plant
Felt the sound of the funeral chant,
180 And the steps of the bearers, heavy and slow,
And the sobs of the mourners, deep and low;

The weary sound and the heavy breath,
And the silent motions of passing death,
And the smell, cold, oppressive, and dank,
Sent through the pores of the coffin-plank;

The dark grass, and the flowers among the grass,
Were bright with tears as the crowd did pass;
From their sighs the wind caught a mournful tone,
And sate in the pines, and gave groan for groan.

190 The garden, once fair, became cold and foul,
Like the corpse of her who had been its soul,
Which at first was lovely as if in sleep,
Then slowly changed, till it grew a heap
To make men tremble who never weep.

Swift Summer into the Autumn flowed,
And frost in the mist of the morning rode,
Though the noonday sun looked clear and bright,
Mocking the spoil of the secret night.

The rose-leaves, like flakes of crimson snow,
200 Paved the turf and the moss below.
The lilies were drooping, and white, and wan,
Like the head and the skin of a dying man.

And Indian plants, of scent and hue
The sweetest that ever were fed on dew,
Leaf by leaf, day after day,
Were massed into the common clay.

And the leaves, brown, yellow, and gray, and red,
And white with the whiteness of what is dead,
Like troops of ghosts on the dry wind passed;
210 Their whistling noise made the birds aghast.

And the gusty winds waked the winged seeds,
Out of their birthplace of ugly weeds,
Till they clung round many a sweet flower's stem,
Which rotted into the earth with them.

The water-blooms under the rivulet
Fell from the stalks on which they were set;
And the eddies drove them here and there,
As the winds did those of the upper air.

Then the rain came down, and the broken stalks
220 Were bent and tangled across the walks;
And the leafless network of parasite bowers
Massed into ruin; and all sweet flowers.

Between the time of the wind and the snow
All loathliest weeds began to grow,
Whose coarse leaves were splashed with many a speck,
Like the water-snake's belly and the toad's back.

And thistles, and nettles, and darnels° rank,   *coarse grass*
And the dock, and henbane°, and hemlock° dank,   *poisonous plants*
Stretched out its long and hollow shank,
230 And stifled the air till the dead wind stank.

And plants, at whose names the verse feels loath,
Filled the place with a monstrous undergrowth,
Prickly, and pulpous°, and blistering, and blue,   *pulpy*
Livid, and starred with a lurid dew.

And agarics°, and fungi, with mildew and mould   *tree fungus*
Started like mist from the wet ground cold;
Pale, fleshy, as if the decaying dead
With a spirit of growth had been animated!

Spawn, weeds, and filth, a leprous scum,
240 Made the running rivulet thick and dumb,
And at its outlet flags° huge as stakes   *water-iris*
Dammed it up with roots knotted like water-snakes.

And hour by hour, when the air was still,
The vapours arose which have strength to kill,
At morn they were seen, at noon they were felt,
At night they were darkness no star could melt.

And unctuous meteors from spray to spray
Crept and flitted in broad noonday
Unseen; every branch on which they alit
250 By a venomous blight was burned and bit.

The Sensitive Plant, like one forbid,
Wept, and the tears within each lid
Of its folded leaves, which together grew,
Were changed to a blight of frozen glue.

For the leaves soon fell, and the branches soon
By the heavy axe of the blast were hewn;
The sap shrank to the root through every pore
As blood to a heart that will beat no more.

For Winter came: the wind was his whip:
260   One choppy finger was on his lip:
He had torn the cataracts from the hills
And they clanked at his girdle like manacles;

His breath was a chain which without a sound
The earth, and the air, and the water bound;
He came, fiercely driven, in his chariot-throne
By the tenfold blasts of the Arctic zone.

Then the weeds which were forms of living death
Fled from the frost to the earth beneath.
Their decay and sudden flight from frost
270   Was but like the vanishing of a ghost!

And under the roots of the Sensitive Plant
The moles and the dormice died for want:
The birds dropped stiff from the frozen air
And were caught in the branches naked and bare.

First there came down a thawing rain
And its dull drops froze on the boughs again;
Then there steamed up a freezing dew
Which to the drops of the thaw-rain grew;

And a northern whirlwind, wandering about
280   Like a wolf that had smelt a dead child out,
Shook the boughs thus laden, and heavy, and stiff,
And snapped them off with his rigid griff.°   talons

When Winter had gone and Spring came back
The Sensitive Plant was a leafless wreck;
But the mandrakes,[19] and toadstools, and docks, and darnels,
Rose like the dead from their ruined charnels.

CONCLUSION

Whether the Sensitive Plant, or that
Which within its boughs like a Spirit sat,
Ere its outward form had known decay,
290 Now felt this change, I cannot say.

Whether that Lady's gentle mind,
No longer with the form combined
Which scattered love, as stars do light,
Found sadness, where it left delight,

I dare not guess; but in this life
Of error, ignorance, and strife,
Where nothing is, but all things seem,
And we the shadows of the dream,

It is a modest creed, and yet
300 Pleasant if one considers it,
To own that death itself must be,
Like all the rest, a mockery.

That garden sweet, that lady fair,
And all sweet shapes and odours there,
In truth have never passed away:
'Tis we, 'tis ours, are changed; not they.

For love, and beauty, and delight,
There is no death nor change: their might
Exceeds our organs, which endure
310 No light, being themselves obscure.

1820 [1820]

The Cloud

I bring fresh showers for the thirsting flowers,
    From the seas and the streams;
I bear light shade for the leaves when laid
    In their noonday dreams.
From my wings are shaken the dews that waken

The sweet buds every one,
When rocked to rest on their mother's breast,
    As she dances about the sun.
I wield the flail of the lashing hail,
10   And whiten the green plains under,
And then again I dissolve it in rain,
    And laugh as I pass in thunder.

I sift the snow on the mountains below,
    And their great pines groan aghast;
And all the night 'tis my pillow white,
    While I sleep in the arms of the blast.
Sublime on the towers of my skiey bowers,
    Lightning my pilot sits;
In a cavern under is fettered the thunder,
20   It struggles and howls at fits;
Over earth and ocean, with gentle motion,
    This pilot is guiding me,
Lured by the love of the genii that move
    In the depths of the purple sea;
Over the rills, and the crags, and the hills,
    Over the lakes and the plains,
Wherever he dream, under mountain or stream,
    The Spirit he loves remains;
And I all the while bask in Heaven's blue smile,
30   Whilst he is dissolving in rains.

The sanguine Sunrise, with his meteor eyes,
    And his burning plumes outspread,
Leaps on the back of my sailing rack,°   *wind-driven clouds*
    When the morning star shines dead;
As on the jag of a mountain crag,
    Which an earthquake rocks and swings,
An eagle alit one moment may sit
    In the light of its golden wings.
And when Sunset may breathe, from the lit sea beneath,
40   Its ardours of rest and of love,
And the crimson pall of eve may fall
    From the depth of Heaven above,
With wings folded I rest, on mine aëry nest,
    As still as a brooding dove.

That orbed maiden with white fire laden,
    Whom mortals call the moon,

Glides glimmering o'er my fleece-like floor,
    By the midnight breezes strewn;
And wherever the beat of her unseen feet,
50   Which only the angels hear,
May have broken the woof° of my tent's thin roof,   *woven fabric*
    The stars peep behind her and peer;
And I laugh to see them whirl and flee,
    Like a swarm of golden bees,
When I widen the rent in my wind-built tent,
    Till the calm rivers, lakes, and seas,
Like strips of the sky fallen through me on high,
    Are each paved with the moon and these.

I bind the sun's throne with a burning zone°,   *girdle*
60   And the moon's with a girdle of pearl;
The volcanoes are dim, and the stars reel and swim,
    When the whirlwinds my banner unfurl.
From cape to cape, with a bridge-like shape,
    Over a torrent sea,
Sunbeam-proof, I hang like a roof, –
    The mountains its columns be.
The triumphal arch through which I march
    With hurricane, fire, and snow,
When the Powers of the air are chained to my chair,
70   Is the million-coloured bow;
The sphere-fire above its soft colours wove,
    While the moist Earth was laughing below.

I am the daughter of Earth and Water,
    And the nursling of the Sky;
I pass through the pores of the ocean and shores;
    I change, but I cannot die.
For after the rain when with never a stain
    The pavilion of Heaven is bare,
And the winds and sunbeams with their convex gleams
80   Build up the blue dome of air,
I silently laugh at my own cenotaph,
    And out of the caverns of rain,
Like a child from the womb, like a ghost from the tomb,
    I arise and unbuild it again.

1820 [1820]

To a Skylark

Hail to thee, blithe spirit!
    Bird thou never wert,
That from Heaven, or near it,
    Pourest thy full heart
In profuse strains of unpremeditated art.

Higher still and higher
    From the earth thou springest
Like a cloud of fire;
    The blue deep thou wingest,
10 And singing still dost soar, and soaring ever singest.

In the golden lightning
    Of the sunken sun,
O'er which clouds are bright'ning,
    Thou dost float and run;
Like an unbodied joy whose race is just begun.

The pale purple even
    Melts around thy flight;
Like a star of Heaven,
    In the broad daylight
20 Thou art unseen, but yet I hear thy shrill delight,

Keen as are the arrows
    Of that silver sphere,
Whose intense lamp narrows
    In the white dawn clear
Until we hardly see – we feel that it is there.

All the earth and air
    With thy voice is loud,
As, when night is bare,
    From one lonely cloud
30 The moon rains out her beams, and Heaven is overflowed.

What thou art we know not;
    What is most like thee?
From rainbow clouds there flow not
    Drops so bright to see
As from thy presence showers a rain of melody.

Like a Poet hidden
  In the light of thought,
Singing hymns unbidden,
  Till the world is wrought
40 To sympathy with hopes and fears it heeded not:

Like a high-born maiden
  In a palace-tower,
Soothing her love-laden
  Soul in secret hour
With music sweet as love, which overflows her bower:

Like a glow-worm golden
  In a dell of dew,
Scattering unbeholden
  Its aëreal hue
50 Among the flowers and grass, which screen it from the view!

Like a rose embowered
  In its own green leaves,
By warm winds deflowered,
  Till the scent it gives
Makes faint with too much sweet those heavy-winged thieves:

Sound of vernal showers
  On the twinkling grass,
Rain-awakened flowers,
  All that ever was
60 Joyous, and clear, and fresh, thy music doth surpass:

Teach us, Sprite or Bird,
  What sweet thoughts are thine:
I have never heard
  Praise of love or wine
That panted forth a flood of rapture so divine.

Chorus Hymeneal,°   *marriage song*
  Or triumphal chant,
Matched with thine would be all
  But an empty vaunt,
70 A thing wherein we feel there is some hidden want.

What objects are the fountains
   Of thy happy strain?
What fields, or waves, or mountains?
   What shapes of sky or plain?
What love of thine own kind? what ignorance of pain?

With thy clear keen joyance
   Languor cannot be:
Shadow of annoyance
   Never came near thee:
80 Thou lovest – but ne'er knew love's sad satiety.

Waking or asleep,
   Thou of death must deem
Things more true and deep
   Than we mortals dream,
Or how could thy notes flow in such a crystal stream?

We look before and after,
   And pine for what is not:
Our sincerest laughter
   With some pain is fraught;
90 Our sweetest songs are those that tell of saddest thought.

Yet if we could scorn
   Hate, and pride, and fear;
If we were things born
   Not to shed a tear,
I know not how thy joy we ever should come near.

Better than all measures
   Of delightful sound,
Better than all treasures
   That in books are found,
100 Thy skill to poet were, thou scorner of the ground!

Teach me half the gladness
   That thy brain must know,
Such harmonious madness
   From my lips would flow
The world should listen then – as I am listening now.

1820 [1820]

The Waning Moon

And like a dying lady, lean and pale,
Who totters forth, wrapped in a gauzy veil,
Out of her chamber, led by the insane
And feeble wanderings of her fading brain,
The moon arose up in the murky east,
A white and shapeless mass –

1820 [1824]

From *Epipsychidion*[20]

Verses addressed to the noble and unfortunate Lady Emilia V—.
now imprisoned in the convent of—

160   True Love in this differs from gold and clay,
That to divide is not to take away.
Love is like understanding, that grows bright,
Gazing on many truths; 'tis like thy light,
Imagination! which from earth and sky,
And from the depths of human fantasy,
As from a thousand prisms and mirrors, fills
The universe with glorious beams, and kills
Error, the worm, with many a sun-like arrow
Of its reverberated lightning. Narrow
170 The heart that loves, the brain that contemplates,
The life that wears, the spirit that creates
One object, and one form, and builds thereby
A sepulchre[21] for its eternity.

*   *   *

190   There was a Being whom my spirit oft
Met on its visioned wanderings, far aloft,
In the clear golden prime of my youth's dawn,
Upon the fairy isles of sunny lawn,
Amid the enchanted mountains, and the caves
Of divine sleep, and on the air-like waves
Of wonder-level dream, whose tremulous floor
Paved her light steps; – on an imagined shore,
Under the gray beak of some promontory

She met me, robed in such exceeding glory,
That I beheld her not. In solitudes
Her voice came to me through the whispering woods,
And from the fountains, and the odours deep
Of flowers, which, like lips murmuring in their sleep
Of the sweet kisses which had lulled them there,
Breathed but of *her* to the enamoured air;
And from the breezes whether low or loud,
And from the rain of every passing cloud,
And from the singing of the summer-birds,
And from all sounds, all silence. In the words
Of antique verse and high romance, – in form,
Sound, colour – in whatever checks that Storm
Which with the shattered present chokes the past;
And in that best philosophy, whose taste
Makes this cold common hell, our life, a doom
As glorious as a fiery martyrdom;
Her Spirit was the harmony of truth. –

*   *   *

In many mortal forms I rashly sought
The shadow of that idol of my thought.
And some were fair – but beauty dies away:
Others were wise – but honeyed words betray:
And One was true – oh! why not true to me?
Then, as a hunted deer that could not flee,
I turned upon my thoughts, and stood at bay,
Wounded and weak and panting; the cold day
Trembled, for pity of my strife and pain.
When, like a noonday dawn, there shone again
Deliverance. One stood on my path who seemed
As like the glorious shape which I had dreamed
As is the Moon, whose changes ever run
Into themselves, to the eternal Sun;
The cold chaste Moon, the Queen of Heaven's bright isles,
Who makes all beautiful on which she smiles,
That wandering shrine of soft yet icy flame
Which ever is transformed, yet still the same,
And warms not but illumines. Young and fair
As the descended Spirit of that sphere,
She hid me, as the Moon may hide the night
From its own darkness, until all was bright
Between the Heaven and Earth of my calm mind,
And, as a cloud charioted by the wind,

200

210

270

280

290

She led me to a cave in that wild place,
And sate beside me, with her downward face
Illumining my slumbers, like the Moon
Waxing and waning o'er Endymion.
And I was laid asleep, spirit and limb,
And all my being became bright or dim
As the Moon's image in a summer sea,
According as she smiled or frowned on me;
And there I lay, within a chaste cold bed:
300   Alas, I then was nor alive nor dead:–
For at her silver voice came Death and Life,
Unmindful each of their accustomed strife,
Masked like twin babes, a sister and a brother,
The wandering hopes of one abandoned mother,
And through the cavern without wings they flew,
And cried 'Away, he is not of our crew.'
I wept, and though it be a dream, I weep.

*   *   *

321   At length, into the obscure Forest came
The Vision I had sought through grief and shame . . .

*   *   *

Soft as an Incarnation of the Sun,
When light is changed to love, this glorious One
Floated into the cavern where I lay,
And called my Spirit, and the dreaming clay
Was lifted by the thing that dreamed below
340   As smoke by fire, and in her beauty's glow
I stood, and felt the dawn of my long night
Was penetrating me with living light:
I knew it was the Vision veiled from me
So many years – that it was Emily.

*   *   *

430   The blue Aegean girds this chosen home,[22]
With ever-changing sound and light and foam,
Kissing the sifted sands, and caverns hoar;
And all the winds wandering along the shore
Undulate with the undulating tide:
There are thick woods where sylvan forms abide;
And many a fountain, rivulet, and pond,
As clear as elemental diamond,
Or serene morning air; and far beyond,

The mossy tracks made by the goats and deer
440 (Which the rough shepherd treads but once a year)
Pierce into glades, caverns, and bowers, and halls
Built round with ivy, which the waterfalls
Illumining, with sound that never fails
Accompany the noonday nightingales;
And all the place is peopled with sweet airs;
The light clear element which the isle wears
Is heavy with the scent of lemon-flowers,
Which floats like mist laden with unseen showers,
And falls upon the eyelids like faint sleep;
450 And from the moss violets and jonquils peep,
And dart their arrowy odour through the brain
Till you might faint with that delicious pain.
And every motion, odour, beam, and tone,
With that deep music is in unison:
Which is a soul within the soul – they seem
Like echoes of an antenatal dream, –
It is an isle 'twixt Heaven, Air, Earth, and Sea,
Cradled, and hung in clear tranquillity;

*　　*　　*

560 And we will talk, until thought's melody
Become too sweet for utterance, and it die
In words, to live again in looks, which dart
With thrilling tone into the voiceless heart,
Harmonizing silence without a sound.
Our breath shall intermix, our bosoms bound,
And our veins beat together; and our lips
With other eloquence than words, eclipse
The soul that burns between them, and the wells
Which boil under our being's inmost cells,
570 The fountains of our deepest life, shall be
Confused in Passion's golden purity,
As mountain-springs under the morning sun.
We shall become the same, we shall be one
Spirit within two frames, oh! wherefore two?
One passion in twin-hearts, which grows and grew,
Till like two meteors of expanding flame,
Those spheres instinct with it become the same,
Touch, mingle, are transfigured; ever still
Burning, yet ever inconsumable:
580 In one another's substance finding food,
Like flames too pure and light and unimbued

To nourish their bright lives with baser prey,
Which point to Heaven and cannot pass away:
One hope within two wills, one will beneath
Two overshadowing minds, one life, one death,
One Heaven, one Hell, one immortality,
And one annihilation. Woe is me!
The winged words on which my soul would pierce
Into the height of love's rare Universe,
590   Are chains of lead around its flight of fire —
I pant, I sink, I tremble, I expire!

1821 [1821]

Adonais

AN ELEGY ON THE DEATH OF JOHN KEATS, AUTHOR OF *ENDYMION, HYPERION* etc [23]

Ἀστὴ πρὶν μὲν ἔλαμπες ἐνὶ ζωοῖσιν Ἑῷος[24]
νῦν δὲ θανὼν λάμπεις Ἕσπερος ἐν φθιμένοις. – PLATO.

1

I weep for Adonais – he is dead!
O, weep for Adonais! though our tears
Thaw not the frost which binds so dear a head!
And thou, sad Hour, selected from all years
To mourn our loss, rouse thy obscure compeers,
And teach them thine own sorrow, say: 'With me
Died Adonais; till the Future dares
Forget the Past, his fate and fame shall be
An echo and a light unto eternity!'

2

Where wert thou, mighty Mother, when he lay,
When thy Son lay, pierced by the shaft which flies
In darkness? where was lorn Urania
When Adonais died? With veiled eyes,
'Mid listening Echoes, in her Paradise
She sate, while one, with soft enamoured breath,
Rekindled all the fading melodies,
With which, like flowers that mock the corse beneath,
He had adorned and hid the coming bulk of Death.

3

Oh, weep for Adonais – he is dead!
Wake, melancholy Mother, wake and weep!
Yet wherefore? Quench within their burning bed
Thy fiery tears, and let thy loud heart keep
Like his, a mute and uncomplaining sleep;
For he is gone, where all things wise and fair
Descend; – oh, dream not that the amorous Deep
Will yet restore him to the vital air;
Death feeds on his mute voice, and laughs at our despair.

4

Most musical of mourners, weep again!
Lament anew, Urania! – He died,[25]
Who was the Sire of an immortal strain,
Blind, old, and lonely, when his country's pride,
The priest, the slave, and the liberticide,
Trampled and mocked with many a loathed rite
Of lust and blood; he went, unterrified,
Into the gulf of death; but his clear Sprite°   *spirit*
Yet reigns o'er earth; the third[26] among the sons of light.

5

Most musical of mourners, weep anew!
Not all to that bright station dared to climb;
And happier they their happiness who knew,
Whose tapers yet burn through that night of time
In which suns perished; others more sublime,
Struck by the envious wrath of man or god,
Have sunk, extinct in their refulgent prime;
And some[27] yet live, treading the thorny road,
Which leads, through toil and hate, to Fame's serene abode.

6

But now, thy youngest, dearest one, has perished –
The nursling of thy widowhood, who grew,
Like a pale flower by some sad maiden cherished,
And fed with true-love tears, instead of dew;
Most musical of mourners, weep anew!
Thy extreme hope, the loveliest and the last,
The bloom, whose petals nipped before they blew
Died on the promise of the fruit, is waste;
The broken lily lies – the storm is overpast.

7

To that high Capital, where kingly Death
Keeps his pale court in beauty and decay,
He came; and bought, with price of purest breath,
A grave among the eternal. – Come away!
Haste, while the vault of blue Italian day
Is yet his fitting charnel-roof! while still
He lies, as if in dewy sleep he lay;
Awake him not! surely he takes his fill
Of deep and liquid rest, forgetful of all ill.

8

He will awake no more, oh, never more! –
Within the twilight chamber spreads apace
The shadow of white Death, and at the door
Invisible Corruption waits to trace
His extreme way to her dim dwelling-place;
The eternal Hunger sits, but pity and awe
Soothe her pale rage, nor dares she to deface
So fair a prey, till darkness, and the law
Of change, shall o'er his sleep the mortal curtain draw.

9

Oh, weep for Adonais! – The quick Dreams,
The passion-winged Ministers of thought,
Who were his flocks, whom near the living streams
Of his young spirit he fed, and whom he taught
The love which was its music, wander not, –
Wander no more, from kindling brain to brain,
But droop there, whence they sprung; and mourn their lot
Round the cold heart, where, after their sweet pain,
They ne'er will gather strength, or find a home again.

10

And one with trembling hands clasps his cold head,
And fans him with her moonlight wings, and cries;
'Our love, our hope, our sorrow, is not dead;
See, on the silken fringe of his faint eyes,
Like dew upon a sleeping flower, there lies
A tear some Dream has loosened from his brain.'
Lost Angel of a ruined Paradise!
She knew not 'twas her own; as with no stain
She faded, like a cloud which had outwept its rain.

11

One from a lucid urn of starry dew
Washed his light limbs as if embalming them;
Another clipped her profuse locks, and threw
The wreath upon him, like an anadem,°   garland
Which frozen tears instead of pearls begem;°   decorate
Another in her wilful grief would break
Her bow and winged reeds, as if to stem
A greater loss with one which was more weak;
And dull the barbed fire against his frozen cheek.

12

Another Splendour on his mouth alit,
That mouth, whence it was wont to draw the breath
Which gave it strength to pierce the guarded wit,
And pass into the panting heart beneath
With lightning and with music: the damp death
Quenched its caress upon his icy lips;
And, as a dying meteor stains a wreath
Of moonlight vapour, which the cold night clips,°   embraces
It flushed through his pale limbs, and passed to its eclipse.

13

And others came . . . Desires and Adorations,
Winged Persuasions and veiled Destinies,
Splendours, and Glooms, and glimmering Incarnations
Of hopes and fears, and twilight Phantasies;
And Sorrow, with her family of Sighs,
And Pleasure, blind with tears, led by the gleam
Of her own dying smile instead of eyes,
Came in slow pomp; – the moving pomp might seem
Like pageantry of mist on an autumnal stream.

14

All he had loved, and moulded into thought,
From shape, and hue, and odour, and sweet sound,
Lamented Adonais. Morning sought
Her eastern watch-tower, and her hair unbound,
Wet with the tears which should adorn the ground,
Dimmed the aëreal eyes that kindle day;
Afar the melancholy thunder moaned,
Pale Ocean in unquiet slumber lay,
And the wild Winds flew round, sobbing in their dismay.

15

Lost Echo sits amid the voiceless mountains,
And feeds her grief with his remembered lay,
And will no more reply to winds or fountains,
Or amorous birds perched on the young green spray,
Or herdsman's horn, or bell at closing day;
Since she can mimic not his lips, more dear
Than those for whose disdain she pined away
Into a shadow of all sounds: – a drear
Murmur, between their songs, is all the woodmen hear.

16

Grief made the young Spring wild, and she threw down
Her kindling buds, as if she Autumn were,
Or they dead leaves; since her delight is flown,
For whom should she have waked the sullen year?
To Phoebus was not Hyacinth so dear
Nor to himself Narcissus, as to both
Thou, Adonais: wan they stand and sere
Amid the faint companions of their youth,
With dew all turned to tears; odour, to sighing ruth.

17

Thy spirit's sister, the lorn nightingale[28]
Mourns not her mate with such melodious pain;
Not so the eagle,[29] who like thee could scale
Heaven, and could nourish in the sun's domain
Her mighty youth with morning, doth complain,
Soaring and screaming round her empty nest,
As Albion° wails for thee: the curse of Cain[30]   *England*
Light on his° head who pierced thy innocent breast,   *the critic's*
And scared the angel soul that was its earthly guest!

18

Ah, woe is me! Winter is come and gone,
But grief returns with the revolving year;
The airs and streams renew their joyous tone;
The ants, the bees, the swallows reappear;
Fresh leaves and flowers deck the dead Seasons' bier;
The amorous birds now pair in every brake,°   *thicket*
And build their mossy homes in field and brere,°   *briar*
And the green lizard, and the golden snake,
Like unimprisoned flames, out of their trance awake.

19

Through wood and stream and field and hill and Ocean
A quickening life from the Earth's heart has burst
As it has ever done, with change and motion,
From the great morning of the world when first
God dawned on Chaos; in its stream immersed,
The lamps of Heaven flash with a softer light;
All baser things pant with life's sacred thirst;
Diffuse themselves; and spend in love's delight,
The beauty and the joy of their renewed might.

20

The leprous corpse, touched by this spirit tender,
Exhales itself in flowers of gentle breath;
Like incarnations of the stars, when splendour
Is changed to fragrance, they illumine death
And mock the merry worm that wakes beneath;
Nought we know, dies. Shall that alone which knows
Be as a sword consumed before the sheath
By sightless lightning?[31] — the intense atom glows
A moment, then is quenched in a most cold repose.

21

Alas! that all we loved of him should be,
But for our grief, as if it had not been,
And grief itself be mortal! Woe is me!
Whence are we, and why are we? of what scene
The actors or spectators? Great and mean
Meet massed in death, who lends what life must borrow.
As long as skies are blue, and fields are green,
Evening must usher night, night urge the morrow,
Month follow month with woe, and year wake year to sorrow.

22

He will awake no more, oh, never more!
'Wake thou,' cried Misery, 'childless Mother, rise
Out of thy sleep, and slake, in thy heart's core,
A wound more fierce than his, with tears and sighs.'
And all the Dreams that watched Urania's eyes,
And all the Echoes whom their sister's song
Had held in holy silence, cried: 'Arise!'
Swift as a Thought by the snake Memory stung,
From her ambrosial rest the fading Splendour sprung.

23

She rose like an autumnal Night, that springs
Out of the East, and follows wild and drear
The golden Day, which, on eternal wings,
Even as a ghost abandoning a bier,
Had left the Earth a corpse. Sorrow and fear
So struck, so roused, so rapt Urania;
So saddened round her like an atmosphere
Of stormy mist; so swept her on her way
Even to the mournful place where Adonais lay.

24

Out of her secret Paradise she sped,
Through camps and cities rough with stone, and steel,
And human hearts, which to her aery tread
Yielding not, wounded the invisible
Palms of her tender feet where'er they fell:
And barbed tongues, and thoughts more sharp than they,
Rent the soft Form they never could repel,
Whose sacred blood, like the young tears of May,
Paved with eternal flowers that undeserving way.

25

In the death-chamber for a moment Death,
Shamed by the presence of that living Might,
Blushed to annihilation, and the breath
Revisited those lips, and Life's pale light
Flashed through those limbs, so late her dear delight.
'Leave me not wild and drear and comfortless,
As silent lightning leaves the starless night!
Leave me not!' cried Urania: her distress
Roused Death: Death rose and smiled, and met her vain caress.

26

'Stay yet awhile! speak to me once again;
Kiss me, so long but as a kiss may live;
And in my heartless breast and burning brain
That word, that kiss, shall all thoughts else survive,
With food of saddest memory kept alive,
Now thou art dead, as if it were a part
Of thee, my Adonais! I would give
All that I am to be as thou now art!
But I am chained to Time, and cannot thence depart!

27

O gentle child, beautiful as thou wert,
Why didst thou leave the trodden paths of men
Too soon, and with weak hands though mighty heart
Dare the unpastured dragon in his den?
Defenceless as thou wert, oh, where was then
Wisdom the mirrored shield,³² or scorn the spear?
Or hadst thou waited the full cycle, when
Thy spirit should have filled its crescent sphere,
The monsters of life's waste had fled from thee like deer.

28

The herded wolves, bold only to pursue;
The obscene ravens, clamorous o'er the dead;
The vultures to the conqueror's banner true
Who feed where Desolation first has fed,
And whose wings rain contagion; – how they fled,
When, like Apollo, from his golden bow
The Pythian of the age³³ one arrow sped
And smiled! – The spoilers tempt no second blow,³⁴
They fawn on the proud feet that spurn them lying low.

29

The sun comes forth, and many reptiles spawn;
He sets, and each ephemeral insect then
Is gathered into death without a dawn,
And the immortal stars awake again;
So is it in the world of living men:
A godlike mind soars forth, in its delight
Making earth bare and veiling heaven, and when
It sinks, the swarms that dimmed or shared its light
Leave to its kindred lamps the spirit's awful night.'

30

Thus ceased she: and the mountain shepherds came,
Their garlands sere,° their magic mantles rent;   *withered*
The Pilgrim of Eternity,³⁵ whose fame
Over his living head like Heaven is bent,
An early but enduring monument,
Came, veiling all the lightnings of his song
In sorrow; from her wilds Ierne° sent   *Ireland*
The sweetest lyrist³⁶ of her saddest wrong,
And Love taught Grief to fall like music from his tongue.

31

Midst others of less note, came one frail Form,[37]
A phantom among men; companionless
As the last cloud of an expiring storm
Whose thunder is its knell; he, as I guess,
Had gazed on Nature's naked loveliness,
Actaeon-like, and now he fled astray
With feeble steps o'er the world's wilderness,
And his own thoughts, along that rugged way,
Pursued, like raging hounds, their father and their prey.

32

A pardlike Spirit beautiful and swift –   *leopard-like*
A Love in desolation masked; – a Power
Girt round with weakness; – it can scarce uplift
The weight of the superincumbent hour;
It is a dying lamp, a falling shower,
A breaking billow; – even whilst we speak
Is it not broken? On the withering flower
The killing sun smiles brightly: on a cheek
The life can burn in blood, even while the heart may break.

33

His head was bound with pansies overblown,
And faded violets, white, and pied, and blue;
And a light spear topped with a cypress cone,
Round whose rude shaft dark ivy-tresses grew
Yet dripping with the forest's noonday dew,
Vibrated, as the ever-beating heart
Shook the weak hand that grasped it; of that crew
He came the last, neglected and apart;
A herd-abandoned deer struck by the hunter's dart.

34

All stood aloof, and at his partial moan
Smiled through their tears; well knew that gentle band
Who in another's fate now wept his own,
As in the accents of an unknown land
He sung new sorrow; sad Urania scanned
The Stranger's mien, and murmured: 'Who art thou?'
He answered not, but with a sudden hand
Made bare his branded and ensanguined brow,
Which was like Cain's or Christ's – oh! that it should be so!

35

What softer voice is hushed over the dead?
Athwart what brow is that dark mantle thrown?
What form leans sadly o'er the white death-bed,
In mockery° of monumental stone,   *imitation*
The heavy heart heaving without a moan?
If it be He, who, gentlest of the wise,[38]
Taught, soothed, loved, honoured the departed one,
Let me not vex, with inharmonious sighs,
The silence of that heart's accepted sacrifice.

36

Our Adonais has drunk poison – oh!
What deaf and viperous murderer could crown
Life's early cup with such a draught of woe?
The nameless worm would now itself disown:
It felt, yet could escape, the magic tone
Whose prelude held° all envy, hate, and wrong,   *held off*
But what was howling in one breast alone,
Silent with expectation of the song,
Whose master's hand is cold, whose silver lyre unstrung.

37

Live thou, whose infamy is not thy fame!
Live! fear no heavier chastisement from me,
Thou noteless blot on a remembered name!
But be thyself, and know thyself to be!
And ever at thy season be thou free
To spill the venom when thy fangs o'erflow;
Remorse and Self-contempt shall cling to thee;
Hot Shame shall burn upon thy secret brow,
And like a beaten hound tremble thou shalt – as now.

38

Nor let us weep that our delight is fled
Far from these carrion kites that scream below;
He wakes or sleeps with the enduring dead;
Thou canst not soar where he is sitting now –
Dust to the dust! but the pure spirit shall flow
Back to the burning fountain whence it came,
A portion of the Eternal, which must glow
Through time and change, unquenchably the same,
Whilst thy cold embers choke the sordid hearth of shame.

39

Peace, peace! he is not dead, he doth not sleep –
He hath awakened from the dream of life –
'Tis we, who lost in stormy visions, keep
With phantoms an unprofitable strife,
And in mad trance, strike with our spirit's knife
Invulnerable nothings. – *We* decay
Like corpses in a charnel; fear and grief
Convulse us and consume us day by day,
And cold hopes swarm like worms within our living clay.

40

He has outsoared the shadow of our night;
Envy and calumny and hate and pain,
And that unrest which men miscall delight,
Can touch him not and torture not again;
From the contagion of the world's slow stain
He is secure, and now can never mourn
A heart grown cold, a head grown gray in vain;
Nor, when the spirit's self has ceased to burn,
With sparkless ashes load an unlamented urn.

41

He lives, he wakes – 'tis Death is dead, not he;
Mourn not for Adonais. – Thou young Dawn,
Turn all thy dew to splendour, for from thee
The spirit thou lamentest is not gone;
Ye caverns and ye forests, cease to moan!
Cease, ye faint flowers and fountains, and thou Air,
Which like a mourning veil thy scarf hadst thrown
O'er the abandoned Earth, now leave it bare
Even to the joyous stars which smile on its despair!

42

He is made one with Nature: there is heard
His voice in all her music, from the moan
Of thunder, to the song of night's sweet bird;[39]
He is a presence to be felt and known
In darkness and in light, from herb and stone,
Spreading itself where'er that Power may move
Which has withdrawn his being to its own;
Which wields the world with never-wearied love,
Sustains it from beneath, and kindles it above.

43

He is a portion of the loveliness
Which once he made more lovely: he doth bear
His part, while the one Spirit's plastic stress
Sweeps through the dull dense world, compelling there,
All new successions to the forms they wear;
Torturing th' unwilling dross that checks its flight
To its own likeness, as each mass may bear;
And bursting in its beauty and its might
From trees and beasts and men into the Heaven's light.

44

The splendours of the firmament of time
May be eclipsed, but are extinguished not;
Like stars to their appointed height they climb,
And death is a low mist which cannot blot
The brightness it may veil. When lofty thought
Lifts a young heart above its mortal lair,
And love and life contend in it, for what
Shall be its earthly doom, the dead live there
And move like winds of light on dark and stormy air.

45

The inheritors of unfulfilled renown
Rose from their thrones, built beyond mortal thought,
Far in the Unapparent. Chatterton
Rose pale, – his solemn agony had not
Yet faded from him; Sidney, as he fought
And as he fell and as he lived and loved
Sublimely mild, a Spirit without spot,
Arose; and Lucan, by his death approved:
Oblivion as they rose shrank like a thing reproved.

46

And many more, whose names on Earth are dark,
But whose transmitted effluence cannot die
So long as fire outlives the parent spark,
Rose, robed in dazzling immortality.
'Thou art become as one of us,' they cry,
'It was for thee yon kingless sphere has long
Swung blind in unascended majesty,
Silent alone amid an Heaven of Song.
Assume thy winged throne, thou Vesper° of our throng!'   *evening star*

47

Who mourns for Adonais? Oh, come forth,
Fond wretch! and know thyself and him aright.
Clasp with thy panting soul the pendulous Earth;
As from a centre, dart thy spirit's light
Beyond all worlds, until its spacious might
Satiate the void circumference: then shrink
Even to a point within our day and night;
And keep thy heart light lest it make thee sink
When hope has kindled hope, and lured thee to the brink.

48

Or go to Rome,[40] which is the sepulchre
Oh, not of him, but of our joy: 'tis nought
That ages, empires, and religions there
Lie buried in the ravage they have wrought;
For such as he can lend, – they borrow not
Glory from those who made the world their prey;
And he is gathered to the kings of thought
Who waged contention with their time's decay,
And of the past are all that cannot pass away.

49

Go thou to Rome, – at once the Paradise,
The grave, the city, and the wilderness;
And where its wrecks like shattered mountains rise,
And flowering weeds, and fragrant copses dress
The bones of Desolation's nakedness
Pass, till the spirit of the spot shall lead
Thy footsteps to a slope of green access
Where, like an infant's smile, over the dead
A light of laughing flowers along the grass is spread;

50

And gray walls moulder round, on which dull Time
Feeds, like slow fire upon a hoary brand;
And one keen pyramid[41] with wedge sublime,
Pavilioning the dust of him who planned
This refuge for his memory, doth stand
Like flame transformed to marble; and beneath,
A field is spread, on which a newer band
Have pitched in Heaven's smile their camp of death,
Welcoming him we lose with scarce extinguished breath.

51

Here pause: these graves are all too young[42] as yet
To have outgrown the sorrow which consigned
Its charge to each; and if the seal is set,
Here, on one fountain of a mourning mind,
Break it not thou! too surely shalt thou find
Thine own well full, if thou returnest home.
Of tears and gall. From the world's bitter wind
Seek shelter in the shadow of the tomb.
What Adonais is, why fear we to become?

52

The One remains, the many change and pass;
Heaven's light forever shines, Earth's shadows fly;
Life, like a dome of many-coloured glass,
Stains the white radiance of Eternity,
Until Death tramples it to fragments. – Die,
If thou wouldst be with that which thou dost seek!
Follow where all is fled! – Rome's azure sky,
Flowers, ruins, statues, music, words, are weak
The glory they transfuse with fitting truth to speak.

53

Why linger, why turn back, why shrink, my Heart?
Thy hopes are gone before: from all things here
They have departed; thou shouldst now depart!
A light is passed from the revolving year,
And man, and woman; and what still is dear
Attracts to crush, repels to make thee wither.
The soft sky smiles, – the low wind whispers near:
'Tis Adonais calls! oh, hasten thither,
No more let Life divide what Death can join together.

54

That Light whose smile kindles the Universe,
That Beauty in which all things work and move,
That Benediction which the eclipsing Curse
Of birth can quench not, that sustaining Love
Which through the web of being blindly wove
By man and beast and earth and air and sea,
Burns bright or dim, as each are mirrors of
The fire for which all thirst; now beams on me,
Consuming the last clouds of cold mortality.

55

The breath[43] whose might I have invoked in song
Descends on me; my spirit's bark is driven,
Far from the shore, far from the trembling throng
Whose sails were never to the tempest given;
The massy earth and sphered skies are riven!
I am borne darkly, fearfully, afar;
Whilst, burning through the inmost veil of Heaven,
The soul of Adonais, like a star,
Beacons from the abode where the Eternal are.

1821 [1821]

To—

Music, when soft voices die,
Vibrates in the memory –
Odours, when sweet violets sicken,
Live within the sense they quicken.

Rose leaves, when the rose is dead,
Are heaped for the beloved's bed;
And so thy thoughts, when thou art gone,
Love itself shall slumber on.

1821 [1824[

Song

I

Rarely, rarely, comest thou,
Spirit of Delight!
Wherefore hast thou left me now
Many a day and night?
Many a weary night and day
'Tis since thou art fled away.

II

How shall ever one like me
   Win thee back again?
With the joyous and the free
   Thou wilt scoff at pain.
Spirit false! thou hast forgot
   All but those who need thee not.

III

As a lizard with the shade
   Of a trembling leaf,
Thou with sorrow art dismayed;
   Even the sighs of grief
Reproach thee, that thou art not near,
And reproach thou wilt not hear.

IV

Let me set my mournful ditty
   To a merry measure;
Thou wilt never come for pity,
   Thou wilt come for pleasure;
Pity then will cut away
Those cruel wings, and thou wilt stay.

V

I love all that thou lovest,
   Spirit of Delight!
The fresh Earth in new leaves dressed,
   And the starry night;
Autumn evening, and the morn
When the golden mists are born.

VI

I love snow, and all the forms
   Of the radiant frost;
I love waves, and winds, and storms,
   Everything almost
Which is Nature's, and may be
Untainted by man's misery.

VII

I love tranquil solitude,
   And such society
As is quiet, wise, and good;

Between thee and me
What difference? but thou dost possess
The things I seek, not love them less.

VIII
I love Love – though he has wings,
   And like light can flee,
But above all other things,
   Spirit, I love thee –
Thou art love and life! Oh, come,
Make once more my heart thy home.

1821 [1824]

To Night

I
Swiftly walk o'er the western wave,
   Spirit of Night!
Out of the misty eastern cave,
Where, all the long and lone day-light,
Thou wovest dreams of joy and fear,
Which make thee terrible and dear, –
   Swift be thy flight!

II
Wrap thy form in a mantle gray,
   Star-inwrought!
Blind with thine hair the eyes of Day;
Kiss her until she be wearied out,
Then wander o'er city, and sea, and land,
Touching all with thine opiate wand –
   Come, long-sought!

III
When I arose and saw the dawn,
   I sighed for thee;
When light rode high, and the dew was gone,
And noon lay heavy on flower and tree,
And the weary Day turned to his rest,
Lingering like an unloved guest,
   I sighed for thee.

IV

Thy brother Death came, and cried,
    Wouldst thou me?
Thy sweet child Sleep, the filmy-eyed,
Murmured like a noontide bee,
Shall I nestle near thy side?
Wouldst thou me? – And I replied,
    No, not thee!

V

Death will come when thou art dead,
    Soon, too soon –
Sleep will come when thou art fled;
Of neither would I ask the boon
I ask of thee, beloved Night –
Swift be thine approaching flight,
    Come soon, soon!

1821 [1824]

With a Guitar, to Jane⁴⁴

Ariel to Miranda: Take
This slave of Music, for the sake
Of him who is the slave of thee,
And teach it all the harmony
In which thou canst, and only thou
Make the delighted spirit glow,
Till joy denies itself again,
And, too intense, is turned to pain;
For by permission and command
10 Of thine own Prince Ferdinand,
Poor Ariel sends this silent token
Of more than ever can be spoken;
Your guardian spirit, Ariel, who,
From life to life, must still pursue
Your happiness; – for thus alone
Can Ariel ever find his own.
From Prospero's enchanted cell,
As the mighty verses tell,
To the throne of Naples, he

20 Lit you o'er the trackless sea,
Flitting on, your prow before,
Like a living meteor.
When you die, the silent Moon,
In her interlunar swoon,
Is not sadder in her cell
Than deserted Ariel.
When you live again on earth,
Like an unseen star of birth,
Ariel guides you o'er the sea
30 Of life from your nativity.
Many changes have been run
Since Ferdinand and you begun
Your course of love, and Ariel still
Has tracked your steps, and served your will;
Now, in humbler, happier lot,
This is all remembered not;
And now, alas! the poor sprite is
Imprisoned, for some fault of his,
In a body like a grave; –
40 From you he only dares to crave,
For his service and his sorrow,
A smile to-day, a song to-morrow.

The artist who this idol wrought,
To echo all harmonious thought,
Felled a tree, while on the steep
The woods were in their winter sleep,
Rocked in that repose divine
On the wind-swept Apennine;
And dreaming, some of Autumn past,
50 And some of Spring approaching fast,
And some of April buds and showers,
And some of songs in July bowers,
And all of love; and so this tree, –
O that such our death may be! –
Died in sleep, and felt no pain,
To live in happier form again:
From which, beneath Heaven's fairest star,
The artist wrought this loved Guitar,
And taught it justly to reply,
60 To all who question skilfully,
In language gentle as thine own;
Whispering in enamoured tone

Sweet oracles of woods and dells,
And summer winds in sylvan cells;
For it had learned all harmonies
Of the plains and of the skies,
Of the forests and the mountains,
And the many-voiced fountains;
The clearest echoes of the hills,
70 The softest notes of falling rills,
The melodies of birds and bees,
The murmuring of summer seas,
And pattering rain, and breathing dew
And airs of evening; and it knew
That seldom-heard mysterious sound,
Which, driven on its diurnal round,
As it floats through boundless day,
Our world enkindles on its way. –
All this it knows, but will not tell
80 To those who cannot question well
The Spirit that inhabits it;
It talks according to the wit
Of its companions; and no more
Is heard than has been felt before,
By those who tempt it to betray
These secrets of an elder day:
But, sweetly as its answers will
Flatter hands of perfect skill,
It keeps its highest, holiest tone
90 For our beloved Jane alone.

1822 [1832]

To Jane

I

The keen stars were twinkling,
And the fair moon was rising among them,
    Dear Jane!
The guitar was tinkling,
But the notes were not sweet till you sung them
    Again.

II

As the moon's soft splendour
O'er the faint cold starlight of Heaven
　　Is thrown,
　So your voice most tender
To the strings without soul had then given
　　Its own.

III

The stars will awaken,
Though the moon sleep a full hour later,
　　To-night;
　No leaf will be shaken
Whilst the dews of your melody scatter
　　Delight.

IV

Though the sound overpowers,
Sing again, with your dear voice revealing
　　A tone
Of some world far from ours,
Where music and moonlight and feeling
　　Are one.

1822/32 [1839]

NOTES

Shelley

1 From the Preface: 'The poem entitled Alastor may be considered as allegorical of one of the most interesting situations of the human mind. It represents a youth of uncorrupted feelings and adventurous genius led forth by an imagination inflamed and purified through familiarity with all that is excellent and majestic, to the contemplation of the universe. He drinks deep of the fountains of knowledge, and is still insatiate . . . He imagines to himself the Being whom he loves . . . He seeks in vain for a prototype of his conception. Blasted by his disappointment, he descends to an untimely grave . . . The picture is not barren of instruction . . . Those who love not their fellow-beings live unfruitful lives, and prepare for their old age a miserable grave.'

2 W. relinquished the revolutionary ideas of his youth as he grew older.

3 i.e. beauty of spirit not the senses.

4 i.e. God, Christ (or spirits of the dead summoned by magic?).

5 as in a Sibylline trance.

6 From the Preface: Count Maddalo = Lord Byron. 'Count Maddalo is a Venetian nobleman of ancient family and of great fortune, who, without mixing much in the society of his countrymen resides chiefly at his magnificent palace in that city. He is a person of the most consummate genius, and capable, if he would direct his energies to such an end, of becoming the redeemer of his degraded country. But it is his weakness to be proud . . . his ambition preys on itself for want of objects which it can consider worthy of exertion . . . He is cheerful, frank and witty. His more serious conversation is a sort of intoxication; men are held by it as by a spell . . .'
   Julian = Shelley. 'Julian is an Englishman of good family, passionately attached to those philosophical notions which assert the power of man over his mind, and the immense improvements of which, by the extinction of certain moral superstitions, human society may yet be susceptible. Without concealing the evil in the world, he is for ever speculating how good may be made superior. He is a complete infidel, and a scoffer at all things reputed holy . . .'

7 P.L. II

8 S. was sent down from university for professing atheism.

9 B. was an excellent swimmer, S. refused to learn.

10 Allegra – the daughter of Byron and Claire Clairmont.

11 From the Preface: 'I was averse from a catastrophe so feeble as that of reconciling the Champion with the Oppressor of mankind . . . The only imaginary being resembling in any degree Prometheus, is Satan and Prometheus, in my judgement, is a more poetical character than Satan, because, in addition to courage, and majesty, and firm and patient opposition to omnipotent force, he is susceptible of being described as exempt from the taints of ambition, envy, revenge . . . Prometheus is, as it were, the type of highest perfection of moral and intellectual nature, impelled by the purest and the truest motives to the best and noblest ends.'

12 of a spirit 'voice in the air'.

13 Dante's *Inferno* – the inscription over the entrance to Hell.

14 Demogorgon has summoned up all the spirits of the universe to listen.

15 for S. 'good and evil run in cycles throughout history and experience' and so eternity is symbolised by a snake with its tail in its mouth. A snake is also for S. the symbol of good warring with evil that oppresses and deludes it.

16 the Peterloo Riots took place on 16 Aug. 1819, when a meeting in Manchester in favour of Parliamentary reform was broken up by the military, resulting in 11 deaths and many wounded.

17 in Greek = divine messengers.

18 plant of the lily genre, said to bloom eternally in the fields of the dead.

19 plant with root resembling the human form, said to shriek when pulled up.

20 This poem was published anonymously. Lady E. = Emilia Viviani.
    From the Advertisement: 'The writer of the following lines died at Florence as he was preparing for a voyage to one of the wildest of the Sporades . . . where he had fitted up the ruins of an old building, and where it was his hope to realise a scheme of life, suited perhaps to that happier and better world of which he is now an inhabitant but hardly practicable in this.'

21 i.e. as in marriage.

22 on an isle in the Ionian seas.

23 From the Preface: '. . . John Keats died at Rome of a consumption, in his twenty-fourth year . . . and was buried in the romantic and lonely cemetery of the Protestants . . under the pyramid which is the tomb of Cestius . . . The cemetery is an open space among the ruins, covered with violets and daisies. It might make one in love with death, to think that one should be buried in so sweet a place . . . The savage criticism on his (Keats') *Endymion*, which appeared in the *Quarterly Review*, produced the most violent effect on his susceptible mind: the agitation thus originated ended in the rupture of a blood-vessel in the lungs; a rapid consumption ensued and the succeeding acknowledgements from more candid critics of the true greatness of his powers were ineffectual to heal the wound . . .'

24 'Thou wert the morning star among the living/Ere thy fair light had fled,/Now, having died, thou art as Hesperus giving/New splendour to the dead'. S.'s translation.

25 i.e. Milton.

26 i.e. after Homer and Dante.

27 Wordsworth, Byron and Coleridge.

28 refers to Keats' 'Ode to a Nightingale'.

29 it was believed an eagle could restore its youth by flying near to the sun.

30 Cain was cursed for killing his brother Abel. Gen. III.11–12.

31 i.e. indiscriminate and unexpected.

32 Perseus used his shield as a mirror in order to kill the Medusa, whose look would have turned him to stone.

33 Apollo = Byron and his attack on reviewers in *English Bards and Scotch Reviewers*.

34 *Childe Harold* was universally acclaimed.

35 i.e. Byron.

36 i.e. Thomas Moore.

37 i.e. Shelley.

38 i.e. Leigh Hunt.

39 Keats' 'Ode to a Nightingale'.

40 where Keats is buried.

41 the tomb of Gaius Cestius, next to the Protestant cemetery, where Keats, and later Shelley, were buried.

42 Shelley's 3-year-old son, William, died and was interred there eighteen months before.

43 cf. 'Ode to the West Wind'.

44 Jane = Jane Williams whom S. loved. He was with her husband when they were drowned: the poem was given with the gift of a guitar: Prospero, Ariel, Miranda and Ferdinand – all characters in Shakespeare's *The Tempest* – Prospero the usurped Duke of Milan, wrecked with his daughter, Miranda (Jane) on an island, Ariel (S.) = his spirit servant, Ferdinand = Miranda's betrothed, son of the usurping Duke, Prospero's brother (Jane's husband, Edward).

John Clare
[1793–1864]

The son of a cottage farmer, (many of whom bore the brunt of the new Enclosure Acts and the rising prices caused by the Napoleonic wars), Clare was born and brought up in the village of Helpstone, Northamptonshire. Both he (with his wife and seven children) and his parents suffered continually from poverty, often being half-starved. He worked as a day-labourer, an uncertain day-to-day existence, only leaving Helpstone to move to Northborough, some three miles away, but a move that disturbed him greatly. His life was dominated by two things – putting aside the gnawing pressures of poverty and a growing family – his love for Mary Joyce and his poetry. Mary Joyce had been a close friend from boyhood, and certainly Clare loved her, though whether he actually sought to marry her and had been refused, is not known. By 1817 he had, however, given up all hopes of such a relationship and began to court Martha Turner (Patty) whose pregnancy led to their marriage in 1820.

That year also saw the publication of his first book of poems, *Poems Descriptive of Rural Life and Scenery*, which was an immediate success. However, interest was, as James Reeves puts it 'philanthropical rather than strictly poetical' and the novelty, amongst the better-off, of the 'peasant poet' soon wore off. Lionised and patronised briefly, he was then forgotten or ignored, and his subsequent volumes – *The Village Minstrel*, 1821, *The Shepherd's Calendar*, 1827 and *The Rural Muse*, 1835, were pooly received. By 1837, with the increasing stress of a large family, the lack of steady employment (other than writing poetry), his poverty and the failure of his books, his depression increased, his actions became erratic, his delusions more frequent, so that friends, fearing for his safety, put him into High Beech asylum, Epping Forest.

However, in 1841, missing his home and family and the area of countryside he knew so well, he ran away and walked home – a desperate journey of which he has left a searing account. He was home for six months before the local gentry, offended by his strange behaviour, had him certified insane, and he spent the rest of his life, bewildered and helpless (with no one knowing exactly what to do for him, let alone have the authority to do it) in Northampton General Lunatic Asylum. There he continued writing; he was, at first, visited by many, both those with genuine feeling for him and

the mere curiosity vultures, until, under new regulations, he was
shut up in the asylum grounds. During those last years, when:
     'I am: yet what I am none cares or knows'
he wrote many of his most intensely personal and moving poems.

Pastoral Poetry[1]

True poesy is not in words,
But images that thoughts express,
By which the simplest hearts are stirred
To elevated happiness.

Mere books would be but useless things
Where none had taste or mind to read,
Like unknown lands where beauty springs
And none are there to heed.

But poesy is a language meet
10 And fields are every one's employ,
The wild flower neath the shepherd's feet
Looks up and gives him joy;

A language that is ever green,
That feelings unto all impart,
As hawthorn blossoms soon as seen
Give May to every heart.

    *   *   *

An image to the mind is brought
Where happiness enjoys
An easy thoughtlessness of thought
And meets excess of joys.

The world is in that little spot
30 With him – and all beside
Is nothing, all a life forgot
In feelings satisfied.

And such is poesy, its power
May varied lights employ,
Yet to all mind it gives the dower
Of self creating joy.

And whether it be hill or moor,
I feel where e'er I go
A silence that discourses more
40 Than any tongue can do;

Unruffled quietness hath made
A peace in every place,
And woods are resting in their shade
Of social loneliness.

The storm from which the shepherd turns
To pull his beaver° down   *head-covering made of beaver furs*
While he upon the heath sojourns
Which autumn pleaches° brown,   *bleaches*

Is music aye, and more indeed,
50 To those of musing mind
Who through the yellow woods proceed
And listen to the wind.

The poet in his fitful glee,
And fancy's many moods,
Meets it as some strange melody
And poem of the woods.

                    *   *   *

And now a harp that flings around
The music of the wind,
The poet often hears the sound
When beauty fills the mind.

The morn with saffron strips and grey,
70 Or blushing to the view,
Like summer fields when run away
In weeds of crimson hue,

Will simple shepherds' hearts imbue
With nature's poesy,
Who inly fancy while they view
How grand must heaven be.

                    *   *   *

The old man, full of leisure hours,
Sits cutting at his door
Rude fancy sticks to tie his flowers
– They're sticks and nothing more

With many passing by his door,
But pleasure has its bent,
With him 'tis happiness, and more,
Heart satisfied content;

Those box edged borders that imprint
90   Their fragrance near his door
Hath been the comfort of his heart
For sixty years and more;

That mossy thatch above his head,
In winter's drifting showers,
To him and his old partner made
A music many hours;

It patted to their hearts a joy
That humble comfort made;
A little fire to keep them dry
100   And shelter over head,

And such, no matter what they call
Each, all are nothing less
Than poesy's power that gives to all
A cheerful blessednees.

So would I my own mind employ,
My own heart impress,
That poesy's self's a dwelling joy
Of humble quietness.

1824–32 [1935]

Sabbath Bells

I've often on a Sabbath day,
Where pastoral quiet dwells,
Lay down among the new mown hay
To listen distant bells
That beautifully flung the sound
Upon the quiet wind,
While beans in blossom breathed around
A fragrance oer the mind;

A fragrance and a joy beside
10   That never wears away,
The very air seems deified
Upon a Sabbath day;
So beautiful the flitting wrack°   *clouds driven by the wind*
Slow pausing from the eye,
Earth's music seemed to call them back,
Calm, settled in the sky;

And I have listened till I felt
A feeling not in words,
A love that rudest moods would melt
20   When those sweet sounds was² heard,
A melancholy joy at rest,
A pleasurable pain,
A love, a rapture of the breast,
That nothing will explain;

A dream of beauty that displays
Imaginary joys
That all the world in all its ways
Finds not to realize.
All idly stretched upon the hay
30   The wind-flirt fanning bye
How soft, how sweetly swept away
The music of the sky;

The ear, it lost and caught the sound
Swelled beautifully on,
A fitful melody around
Of sweetness heard and gone;
I felt such thoughts, I yearned to sing

The humming airs delight
That seemed to move the swallow's wing
40 Into a wilder flight;

The butterfly in wings of brown
Would find me where I lay
Fluttering and bobbing up and down
And settling on the hay;
The waving blossoms seemed to throw
Their fragrance to the sound,
While up and down, and loud and low
The bells were ringing round.

1824-32 [1979]

The Fallen Elm

Old elm that murmured in our chimney top
The sweetest anthem autumn ever made
And into mellow whispering calms would drop
When showers fell on thy many coloured shade,
And when dark tempests mimic thunder made,
While darkness came as it would strangle light
With the black tempest of a winter night
That rocked thee like a cradle to thy root, –
How did I love to hear the winds upbraid
10 Thy strength without – while all within was mute;
It seasoned comfort to our hearts desire,
We felt thy kind protection like a friend
And edged our chairs up closer to the fire
Enjoying comforts that was³ never penned.
Old favourite tree thou'st seen times changes lower,°   *lour*
Though change till now did never injure thee,
For time beheld thee as her sacred dower
And nature claimed thee her domestic tree;
Storms came and shook thee many a weary hour,
20 Yet stedfast to thy home thy roots hath been,
Summers of thirst parched round thy homely bower
Till earth grew iron – still thy leaves was⁴ green;
The childern° sought thee in thy summer shade,   *children*

And made their play house rings of sticks and stone;
The mavis° sang and felt himself alone   *song thrush*
While in thy leaves his early nest was made,
And I did feel his happiness mine own,
Nought heeding that our friendship was betrayed.
Friend[5] not inanimate – though stocks and stones
30 There are and many formed of flesh & bones –
Thou owned a language by which hearts are stirred
Deeper than by a feeling clothed in words,
And speakest now what's known of every tongue –
Language of pity and the force of wrong,
What cant assumes, what hypocrites will dare,
Speaks home to truth, and shows it what they are.
I see a picture which thy fate displays,
And learn a lesson from thy destiny.
Self-interest saw thee stand in freedom's ways,
40 So thy old shadow must a tyrant be;
Thou'st heard the knave abusing those in power
Bawl freedom loud and then oppress the free;
Thou'st sheltered hypocrites in many a shower
That when in power would never shelter thee;
Thou'st heard the knave supply his canting powers
With wrong's illusions when he wanted friends,
That bawled for shelter when he lived in showers,
And, when clouds vanished, made thy shade amends;
With axe at root he felled thee to the ground
50 And barked of freedom – O I hate the sound!
Time hears its visions speak, and age sublime
Had made thee a disciple unto time.
– It grows the cant term of enslaving tools
To wrong another by the name of right;
It grows the licence of o'erbearing fools
To cheat plain honesty by force of might;
Thus came enclosure – ruin was its guide,
But freedom's clapping hands enjoyed the sight,
Though comfort's cottage soon was thrust aside,
60 And workhouse prisons raised upon the site;
Een nature's dwellings, far away from men,
The common heath became the spoilers' prey,
The rabbit had not where to make his den,
And labour's only cow was drove away.
No matter – wrong was right & right was wrong
And freedom's bawl was sanction to the song.
– Such was thy ruin, music-making elm,

The rights of freedom was to injure thine,
As thou wert served, so would they overwhelm
70   In freedom's name the little that is mine;
And there are knaves that brawl for better laws,
And cant of tyranny in stronger powers,
Who glut their vile unsatiated maws
And freedom's birthright from the weak devours.

1824-32 [1920]

Badger

When midnight comes a host of dogs and men
Go out and track the badger to his den,
And put a sack within the hole, and lie
Till the old grunting badger passes by.
He comes and hears – they let the strongest loose.
The old fox hears the noise and drops the goose.
The poacher shoots and hurries from the cry,
And the old hare half wounded buzzes by.
They get a forked stick to bear him down
10   And clap° the dogs and take him to the town,   *seize quickly*
And bait° him all the day with many dogs,   *set dogs on*
And laugh and shout and fright the scampering hogs.
He runs along and bites at all he meets:
They shout and hollo down the noisy streets.

He turns about to face the loud uproar
And drives the rebels to their very door.
The frequent stone is hurled where'er they go;
When badgers fight, then every one's a foe.
The dogs are clapt and urged to join the fray;
20   The badger turns and drives them all away.
Though scarcely half as big, demure and small,
He fights with dogs for hours and beats them all.
The heavy mastiff, savage in the fray,
Lies down and licks his feet and turns away.
The bulldog knows his match and waxes cold,
The badger grins and never leaves his hold.
He drives the crowd and follows at their heels
And bites them through – the drunkard swears and reels.

The frighted women take the boys away,
30 The blackguard laughs and hurries on the fray.
He tries to reach the woods, an awkward race,
But sticks and cudgels quickly stop the chase.
He turns agen° and drives the noisy crowd   *again*
And beats the many dogs in noises loud.
He drives away and beats them every one,
And then they loose° them all and set them on.   *let go*
He falls as dead and kicked by boys and men,
Then starts and grins and drives the crowd agen;°   *again*
Till kicked and torn and beaten out he lies
40 And leaves his hold and cackles, groans, and dies.

1835–7 [1920]

Gipsies

The gipsies seek wide sheltering woods again,
With droves of horses flock to mark their lane,
And trample on dead leaves, and hear the sound,
And look and see the black clouds gather round,
And set their camps, and free from muck and mire,
And gather stolen sticks to make the fire.
The roasted hedgehog, bitter though as gall,
Is eaten up and relished by them all.
They know the woods and every fox's den
10 And get their living far away from men;
The shooters ask them where to find the game,
The rabbits know them and are almost tame.
The aged women, tawny with the smoke,
Go with the winds and crack the rotted oak.

1837–41 [1920]

The Peasant Poet

He loved the brook's soft sound,
    The swallow swimming by.
He loved the daisy-covered ground,
    The cloud-bedappled sky.
To him the dismal storm appeared
    The very voice of God;
And when the evening rack°⁶ was reared   *cloud-formation*
    Stood Moses with his rod.
And everything his eyes surveyed,
10   The insects in the brake,
Were creatures God Almighty made,
    He loved them for His sake –
A silent man in life's affairs,
    A thinker from a boy,
A peasant in his daily cares,
    A poet in his joy.

I am⁷

I am: yet what I am none cares or knows,
    My friends forsake me like a memory lost;
I am the self-consumer of my woes,
    They rise and vanish in oblivious host,
Like shades in love and death's oblivion lost;
And yet I am, and live with shadows tost°   *tossed*

Into the nothingness of scorn and noise,
    Into the living sea of waking dreams,
Where there is neither sense of life nor joys,
10   But the vast shipwreck of my life's esteems;
And e'en the dearest – that I loved the best –
Are strange – nay, rather stranger than the rest.

I long for scenes where man has never trod,
    A place where woman never smiled or wept;
There to abide with my Creator, God,
    And sleep as I in childhood sweetly slept:
Untroubling and untroubled where I lie,
The grass below – above the vaulted sky.

(John Clare)

I feel I am, I only know I am,
And plod upon the earth as dull and void;
Earth's prison chilled my body with its dram
Of dullness, and my soaring thoughts destroyed.
I fled to solitude from passion's dream,
But strife pursued: I only know I am.
I was a being created in the race
Of men, disdaining bounds of place and time;
A spirit that could travel o'er the space
10 Of earth and heaven like a thought sublime;
Tracing creation, like my Maker free,
A soul unshackled like eternity:
Spurning earth's vain and soul-debasing thrall –
But now I only know I am, that's all.

1842–64 [1920]

The Silver Mist

The silver mist more lowly swims
And each green-bosomed valley dims,
And o'er the neighbouring meadow lies
Like half-seen visions by dim eyes.
Green trees look grey, bright waters black,
The lated crow has lost her track
And flies by guess her journey home:
She flops along and cannot see
Her peaceful nest on oddling tree.
10 The lark drops down and cannot meet
The taller black-grown clumps of wheat.
The mists that rise from heat of day
Fade field and meadow all away.

1842–64 [1935]

Death's Memories

Death's memories are graves,
   Nor can they pass away:
Nature in every hillock saves
   A green plot o'er decay:
And daisies like to clumps of snow
Go each spring season there to blow.

Death's memories are graves,
   The all that nature granted,
Where the tall mallow° waves   *(a marsh plant)*
10   And the small flower blooms self-planted;
Where mothers sleep and babes lie still
And sunshine rests upon the hill.

Death's memories on tombs
   Keep fragments of decay,
Like wrecks of lumber-rooms
   Which Time throws out o' the way:
If common weeds were not to come,
The graves would be without a bloom.

1842–64 [1935]

Secret Love

I hid my love when young till I
Couldn't bear the buzzing of a fly;
I hid my love to my despite
Till I could not bear to look at light:
I dare not gaze upon her face
But left her memory in each place;
Where'er I saw a wild flower lie
I kissed and bade my love good-bye.

I met her in the greenest dells,
10 Where dewdrops pearl the wood bluebells;
The lost breeze kissed her bright blue eye,
The bee kissed and went singing by,
A sunbeam found a passage there,

A gold chain round her neck so fair;
As secret as the wild bee's song
She lay there all the summer long.

I hid my love in field and town
Till e'en the breeze would knock me down;
The bees seemed singing ballads o'er,
20 The fly's buzz[8] turned a lion's roar;
And even silence found a tongue,
To haunt me all the summer long;
The riddle nature could not prove
Was nothing else but secret love.

                    1842–64 [1935]

Love Lives Beyond the Tomb

Love lives beyond
The tomb, the earth, which fades like dew!
    I love the fond,
The faithful, and the true.

    Love lives in sleep,
The happiness of healthy dreams:
    Eve's dews may weep,
But love delightful seems.

    'Tis seen in flowers,
10 And in the morning's pearly dew;
    In earth's green hours,
And in the heaven's eternal blue.

    'Tis heard in spring
When light and sunbeams, warm and kind,
    On angel's wing
Bring love and music to the mind.

    And where is voice,
So young, so beautiful, and sweet
    As nature's choice,
20 Where spring and lovers meet?

Love lives beyond
The tomb, the earth, the flowers, and dew.
I love the fond,
The faithful, young, and true.

1842–64 [1873]

NOTES

Clare

1 In the original mss. of 'Pastoral Poetry', 'Sabbath Bells' and 'The Fallen Elm', there is no punctuation; 'and' is always written '&'.
2 was – sic.
3 ibid.
4 ibid.
5 i.e. the elm.
6 in some editions 'rock'.
7 in the mss. this and the next poem are linked; the second following on from the first.
8 in some transcriptions 'buzz' is 'bass' or 'Buss' – but it is obviously meant to echo line 2 as line 19 does line 12.

John Keats

[1795–1821]

He was the eldest son of a manager of livery stables in Moorfields, though by 1809 both his parents were dead: educated at Clarke's School, Enfield, and, 1810, apprenticed to an apothecary-surgeon. Greatly influenced by Spenser, his first poetry (c. 1814) included an 'Imitation of Spenser': 1815 transferred, as student, to Guy's Hospital: 1816 was licensed to practise as an apothecary but decided to write poetry instead. 1816 first published, in *The Examiner*, 'O solitude' and 'On First Looking into Chapman's Homer': wrote 'I stood tiptoe . . .' and began work on *Endymion*. His first volume of poems, 1817, reasonably reviewed but poor sales. In autumn a series of articles on the 'Cockney School of Poetry' was published in *Blackwood's Magazine*, with Hazlitt, Leigh Hunt and K. harshly attacked. He had met Shelley 1816 and now met and was influenced by Wordsworth and Hazlitt: spring 1818 *Endymion* published, and bitterly attacked in the autumn edition of *Blackwood's*: 'Isabella or The Pot of Basil' completed. July and August he toured, with his friend Charles Brown, Scotland and, briefly, Northern Ireland: Tom, his brother, became very ill, was nursed by K. and, in December, died. K. moved into Brown's house in Hampstead, now known as Keats' House, where he met Fanny Brawne, with whom he fell in love. Despite the fact that he was beset with financial problems and suffered frequent sore throats, in this year, 1818, he began the first version of *Hyperion*; wrote 'The Eve of St Agnes'; 'Eve of St Mark'; 'Ode to Psyche'; 'La Belle Dame sans Merci'; 'Ode to a Nightingale'; and, about the same time, the Odes 'On a Grecian Urn', 'On Melancholy', 'On Indolence'; *Lamia Part 1*; *Otho the Great* (with Brown); second version of *Hyperion – The Fall of Hyperion*; 'To Autumn'; *Lamia Part 2*. He became engaged to Fanny. Winter, 1819, he began 'The Cap and Bells' (unfinished): but K. became increasingly ill. His *Lamia, Isabella, The Eve of St Agnes and Other Poems*, published July 1820, was generally well received, but with some criticism from *Blackwood's*. Shelley invited him to Italy: September K. set off with Severn, his friend. They settled in Rome where, February 1821, K. died, and was buried in the Protestant cemetery there.

From *I stood tiptoe upon a little hill*

Here are sweet peas, on tip-toe for a flight:
With wings of gentle flush o'er delicate white,
And taper fingers catching at all things,
60 To bind them all about with tiny rings.

Linger awhile upon some bending planks
That lean against a streamlet's rushy banks,
And watch intently Nature's gentle doings:
They will be found softer than ring-dove's cooings.
How silent comes the water round that bend;
Not the minutest whisper does it send
To the o'erhanging sallows:° blades of grass   *willow trees*
Slowly across the chequered shadows pass.
Why, you might read two sonnets, ere they reach
70 To where the hurrying freshnesses aye preach
A natural sermon o'er their pebbly beds;
Where swarms of minnows show their little heads,
Staying their wavy bodies 'gainst the streams,
To taste the luxury of sunny beams
Tempered with coolness. How they ever wrestle
With their own sweet delight, and ever nestle
Their silver bellies on the pebbly sand.
If you but scantily hold out the hand,
That very instant not one will remain;
80 But turn your eye, and they are there again.

1816 [1817]

From *Epistle to George Keats*

        . . . Ah, my dear friend and brother,
110 Could I, at once, my mad ambition smother,
For tasting joys° like these, sure I should be   *i.e. the writing of poetry*
Happier, and dearer to society.
At times, 'tis true, I've felt relief from pain
When some bright thought has darted through my brain:
Through all that day I've felt a greater pleasure
Than if I'd brought to light a hidden treasure.
As to my sonnets, though none else should heed them,
I feel delighted, still, that you should read them.
Of late, too, I have had much calm enjoyment,
120 Stretched on the grass at my best loved employment
Of scribbling lines for you. These things I thought
While, in my face, the freshest breeze I caught.
E'en now I'm pillowed on a bed of flowers
That crowns a lofty clift, which proudly towers
Above the ocean-waves. The stalks, and blades,
Chequer my tablet° with their quivering shades.   *writing pad*
On one side is a field of drooping oats,
Through which the poppies show their scarlet coats;
So pert and useless, that they bring to mind
130 The scarlet coats that pester human-kind.
And on the other side, outspread, is seen
Ocean's blue mantle streaked with purple, and green.
Now 'tis I see a canvassed ship, and now
Mark the bright silver curling round her prow.
I see the lark down-dropping to his nest,
And the broad winged sea-gull never at rest;
For when no more he spreads his feathers free,
His breast is dancing on the restless sea.
Now I direct my eyes into the west,
140 Which at this moment is in sunbeams drest:
Why westward turn? 'Twas but to say adieu!
'Twas but to kiss my hand, dear George, to you!

                         Margate 1816 [1817]

Sonnets

To one who has been long in city pent,
  'Tis very sweet to look into the fair
  And open face of heaven, – to breathe a prayer
Full in the smile of the blue firmament.
Who is more happy, when, with heart's content,
  Fatigued he sinks into some pleasant lair
  Of wavy grass, and reads a debonair
And gentle tale of love and languishment?
Returning home at evening, with an ear
  Catching the notes of Philomel,° – an eye   *the nightingale*
Watching the sailing cloudlet's bright career,
  He mourns that day so soon has glided by:
E'en like the passage of an angel's tear
  That falls through the clear ether silently.

[1817]

On First Looking into Chapman's Homer

Much have I travelled in the realms of gold,
  And many goodly states and kingdoms seen;
  Round many western islands have I been
Which bards in fealty° to Apollo hold.   *allegiance*
Oft of one wide expanse had I been told
  That deep-browed Homer ruled as his demesne:°   *domain*
  Yet did I never breathe its pure serene
Till I heard Chapman speak out loud and bold:
Then felt I like some watcher of the skies
  When a new planet swims into his ken;[1]
Or like stout Cortez, when with eagle eyes
  He stared at the Pacific[2] – and all his men
Looked at each other with a wild surmise –
  Silent, upon a peak in Darien.

1816 [1817]

On the Grasshopper and Cricket[3]

The poetry of earth is never dead:
   When all the birds are faint with the hot sun,
   And hide in cooling trees, a voice will run
From hedge to hedge about the new-mown mead;
That is the Grasshopper's – he takes the lead
   In summer luxury, – he has never done
   With his delights; for when tired out with fun
He rests at ease beneath some pleasant weed.
The poetry of earth is ceasing never:
   On a lone winter evening, when the frost
     Has wrought a silence, from the stove there shrills
The Cricket's song, in warmth increasing ever,
   And seems to one in drowsiness half lost,
     The Grasshopper's among some grassy hills.

1816 [1817]

From *Sleep and Poetry*

O Poesy! for thee I hold my pen
That am not yet a glorious denizen°   *citizen*
Of thy wide heaven – Should I rather kneel
50 Upon some mountain-top until I feel
A glowing splendour round about me hung,
And echo back the voice of thine own tongue?
O Poesy! for thee I grasp my pen
That am not yet a glorious denizen
Of thy wide heaven; yet, to my ardent prayer,
Yield from thy sanctuary some clear air,
Smoothed for intoxication by the breath
Of flowering bays, that I may die a death
Of luxury, and my young spirit follow
60 The morning sun-beams to the great Apollo
Like a fresh sacrifice . . .

*   *   *

90 Life is the rose's hope while yet unblown;
The reading of an ever-changing tale;
The light uplifting of a maiden's veil;

A pigeon tumbling in clear summer air;
A laughing school-boy, without grief or care,
Riding the springy branches of an elm.

O for ten years, that I may overwhelm
Myself in poesy; so I may do the deed
That my own soul has to itself decreed.
Then will I pass the countries that I see
In long perspective, and continually
Taste their pure fountains. First the realm I'll pass
Of Flora, and old Pan: sleep in the grass,
Feed upon apples red, and strawberries,
And choose each pleasure that my fancy sees;
Catch the white-handed nymphs in shady places,
To woo sweet kisses from averted faces, –
Play with their fingers, touch their shoulders white
Into a pretty shrinking with a bite
As hard as lips can make it: till agreed,
A lovely tale of human life we'll read.

*   *   *

What though I am not wealthy in the dower
Of spanning wisdom; though I do not know
The shiftings of the mighty winds that blow
Hither and thither all the changing thoughts
Of man: though no great minist'ring reason sorts
Out the dark mysteries of human souls
To clear conceiving: yet there ever rolls
A vast idea before me, and I glean
Therefrom my liberty; thence too I've seen
The end and aim of Poesy.

*   *   *

For sweet relief I'll dwell
On humbler thoughts, and let this strange assay
Begun in gentleness die so away.
E'en now all tumult from my bosom fades:
I turn full hearted to the friendly aids
That smooth the path of honour; brotherhood,
And friendliness the nurse of mutual good.
The hearty grasp that sends a pleasant sonnet
Into the brain ere one can think upon it;
The silence when some rhymes are coming out;
And when they're come, the very pleasant rout:°

revelry

The message certain to be done to-morrow.
'Tis perhaps as well that it should be to borrow
Some precious book from out its snug retreat,
To cluster round it when we next shall meet.
Scarce can I scribble on; for lovely airs
Are fluttering round the room like doves in pairs;
Many delights of that glad day recalling,
330 When first my senses caught their tender falling.

[1817]

From **Endymion**[4]

BOOK I

A thing of beauty is a joy for ever:
Its loveliness increases; it will never
Pass into nothingness; but still will keep
A bower quiet for us, and a sleep
Full of sweet dreams, and health, and quiet breathing.
Therefore, on every morrow, are we wreathing
A flowery band to bind us to the earth,
Spite of despondence, of the inhuman dearth
Of noble natures, of the gloomy days,
10 Of all the unhealthy and o'er-darkened ways
Made for our searching: yes, in spite of all,
Some shape of beauty moves away the pall
From our dark spirits. Such the sun, the moon,
Trees old, and young, sprouting a shady boon°   blessing
For simple sheep; and such are daffodils
With the green world they live in; and clear rills
That for themselves a cooling covert make
'Gainst the hot season; the mid forest brake,
Rich with a sprinkling of fair musk-rose° blooms: fragrant rambling rose
20 And such too is the grandeur of the dooms
We have imagined for the mighty dead;
All lovely tales that we have heard or read:
And endless fountain of immortal drink,
Pouring unto us from the heaven's brink.

Nor do we merely feel these essences
For one short hour; no, even as the trees

That whisper round a temple become soon
Dear as the temple's self, so does the moon,
The passion poesy, glories infinite,
30   Haunt us till they become a cheering light
Unto our souls, and bound to us so fast,
That, whether there be shine, or gloom o'ercast,
They alway must be with us, or we die.

Therefore, 'tis with full happiness that I
Will trace the story of Endymion.
The very music of the name has gone
Into my being, and each pleasant scene
Is growing fresh before me as the green
Of our own valleys: so I will begin
40   Now while I cannot hear the city's din;
Now while the early budders are just new,
And run in mazes of the youngest hue
About old forests; while the willow trails
Its delicate amber; and the dairy pails
Bring home increase of milk. And, as the year
Grows lush in juicy stalks, I'll smoothly steer
My little boat, for many quiet hours,
With streams that deepen freshly into bowers.
Many and many a verse I hope to write,
50   Before the daisies, vermeil rimmed and white,
Hide in deep herbage; and ere yet the bees
Hum about globes of clover and sweet peas,
I must be near the middle of my story.
O may no wintry season, bare and hoary,
See it half finished: but let Autumn bold,
With universal tinge of sober gold,
Be all about me when I make an end.
And now at once, adventuresome, I send
My herald thought into a wilderness:
60   There let its trumpet blow, and quickly dress
My uncertain path with green, that I may speed
Easily onward, thorough flowers and weed.

                    *   *   *

Wherein lies happiness? In that which becks
Our ready minds to fellowship divine,
A fellowship with essence; till we shine,
780   Full alchemized,° and free of space. Behold   *transmuted*
The clear religion of heaven! Fold

A rose leaf round thy finger's taperness,
And soothe thy lips: hist, when the airy stress
Of music's kiss impregnates the free winds,
And with a sympathetic touch unbinds
Æolian⁵ magic from their lucid wombs:
Then old songs waken from enclouded tombs;
Old ditties sigh above their father's grave;
Ghosts of melodious prophecyings rave
790 Round every spot where trod Apollo's foot;
Bronze clarions awake, and faintly bruit,
Where long ago a giant battle was;
And, from the turf, a lullaby doth pass
In every place where infant Orpheus slept.
Feel we these things? – that moment have we stept
Into a sort of oneness, and our state
Is like a floating spirit's. But there are
Richer entanglements, enthralments far
More self-destroying, leading, by degrees,
800 To the chief intensity: the crown of these
Is made of love and friendship, and sits high
Upon the forehead of humanity.
All its more ponderous and bulky worth
Is friendship, whence there ever issues forth
A steady splendour; but at the tip-top,
There hangs by unseen film, an orbed drop
Of light, and that is love: its influence,
Thrown in our eyes, genders a novel sense,
At which we start and fret; till in the end,
810 Melting into its radiance, we blend,
Mingle, and so become a part of it, –
Nor with aught else can our souls interknit
So wingedly: when we combine therewith,
Life's self is nourished by its proper pith,
And we are nurtured like a pelican brood.
Aye, so delicious is the unsating food,
That men, who might have towered in the van
Of all the congregated world, to fan
And winnow from the coming step of time
820 All chaff of custom, wipe away all slime
Left by men-slugs and human serpentry,
Have been content to let occasion die,
Whilst they did sleep in love's Elysium.
And, truly, I would rather be struck dumb,
Than speak against this ardent listlessness:

For I have ever thought that it might bless
The world with benefits unknowingly;
As does the nightingale, upperched high,
And cloistered among cool and bunched leaves –
830 She sings but to her love, nor e'er conceives
How tiptoe Night holds back her dark-grey hood.
Just so may love, although 'tis understood
The mere commingling of passionate breath,
Produce more than our searching witnesseth:
What I know not: but who, of men, can tell
That flowers would bloom, or that green fruit would swell
To melting pulp, that fish would have bright mail,°   chain armour
The earth its dower of river, wood, and vale,
The meadows runnels,° runnels pebble-stones,   small streams
840 The seed its harvest, or the lute its tones,
Tones ravishment, or ravishment its sweet,
If human souls did never kiss and greet?

1817 [1818]

When I have fears

When I have fears that I may cease to be
    Before my pen has gleaned my teeming brain,
Before high-piled books, in charactery,°   handwriting
    Hold like rich garners the full ripened grain;
When I behold, upon the night's starred face,
    Huge cloudy symbols of a high romance,
And think that I may never live to trace
    Their shadows, with the magic hand of chance;
And when I feel, fair creature of an hour,⁶
    That I shall never look upon thee more,
Never have relish in the faery power
    Of unreflecting love; – then on the shore
Of the wide world I stand alone, and think
Till love and fame to nothingness do sink.

1818 [1848]

Lines on the Mermaid
Tavern[7]

Souls of Poets dead and gone,
What Elysium have ye known,
Happy field or mossy cavern,
Choicer than the Mermaid Tavern?
Have ye tippled drink more fine
Than mine host's Canary wine?
Or are fruits of Paradise
Sweeter than those dainty pies
Of venison? O generous food!
10   Drest as though bold Robin Hood
Would, with his maid Marian,
Sup and bowse° from horn and can.   *carouse*

I have heard that on a day
Mine host's sign-board flew away,
Nobody knew whither, till
An astrologer's old quill
To a sheepskin gave the story,
Said he saw you in your glory,
Underneath a new old sign
20   Sipping beverage divine,
And pledging with contented smack
The Mermaid in the Zodiac.

Souls of Poets dead and gone,
What Elysium have ye known,
Happy field or mossy cavern,
Choicer than the Mermaid Tavern?

1818 [1820]

From **Hyperion**[8]

BOOK I

Deep in the shady sadness of a vale
Far sunken from the healthy breath of morn,
Far from the fiery noon, and eve's one star,
Sat gray-haired Saturn, quiet as a stone,
Still as the silence round about his lair;
Forest on forest hung about his head
Like cloud on cloud. No stir of air was there,
Not so much life as on a summer's day
Robs not one light seed from the feathered grass,
10 But where the dead leaf fell, there did it rest.
A stream went voiceless by, still deadened more
By reason of his fallen divinity
Spreading a shade: the Naiad° mid her reeds   *water nymph*
Pressed her cold finger closer to her lips.

Along the margin-sand large foot-marks went,
No further than to where his feet had strayed,
And slept there since. Upon the sodden ground
His old right hand lay nerveless, listless, dead,
Unsceptred; and his realmless eyes were closed;
20 While his bowed head seemed list'ning to the Earth,
His ancient mother, for some comfort yet.

It seemed no force could wake him from his place;
But there came one,[9] who with a kindred hand
Touched his wide shoulders, after bending low
With reverence, though to one who knew it not.
She was a Goddess of the infant world;
By her in stature the tall Amazon
Had stood a pigmy's height: she would have ta'en
Achilles by the hair and bent his neck;
30 Or with a finger stayed Ixion's wheel.
Her face was large as that of Memphian° sphinx,   *of Memphis*
Pedestaled haply in a palace court,
When sages looked to Egypt for their lore.
But oh! how unlike marble was that face:
How beautiful, if sorrow had not made
Sorrow more beautiful than Beauty's self.
There was a listening fear in her regard,
As if calamity had but begun;

As if the vanward clouds of evil days
40 Had spent their malice, and the sullen rear
Was with its stored thunder labouring up.
One hand she pressed upon that aching spot
Where beats the human heart, as if just there,
Though an immortal, she felt cruel pain:
The other upon Saturn's bended neck
She laid, and to the level of his ear
Leaning with parted lips, some words she spake
In solemn tenour and deep organ tone:
Some mourning words, which in our feeble tongue
50 Would come in these like accents; O how frail
To that large utterance of the early Gods!
'Saturn, look up! – though wherefore, poor old King?
I have no comfort for thee, no not one:
I cannot say, "O wherefore sleepest thou?"
For heaven is parted from thee, and the earth
Knows thee not, thus afflicted, for a God;
And ocean too, with all its solemn noise,
Has from thy sceptre passed; and all the air
Is emptied of thine hoary majesty.
60 Thy thunder, conscious of the new command,
Rumbles reluctant o'er our fallen house;
And thy sharp lightning in unpractised hands
Scorches and burns our once serene domain.
O aching time! O moments big as years!
All as ye pass swell out the monstrous truth,
And press it so upon our weary griefs
That unbelief has not a space to breathe.
Saturn, sleep on: – O thoughtless, why did I
Thus violate thy slumbrous solitude?
70 Why should I ope thy melancholy eyes?
Saturn, sleep on! while at thy feet I weep.'

As when, upon a tranced summer-night,
Those green-robed senators of mighty woods,
Tall oaks, branch-charmed by the earnest stars,
Dream, and so dream all night without a stir,
Save from one gradual solitary gust
Which comes upon the silence, and dies off,
As if the ebbing air had but one wave;
So came these words and went; the while in tears
80 She touched her fair large forehead to the ground,
Just where her falling hair might be outspread

A soft and silken mat for Saturn's feet.
One moon, with alteration slow, had shed
Her silver seasons four upon the night,
And still these two were postured motionless,
Like natural sculpture in cathedral cavern;
The frozen God still couchant° on the earth,   *lying*
And the sad Goddess weeping at his feet:
Until at length old Saturn lifted up
90 His faded eyes, and saw his kingdom gone,
And all the gloom and sorrow of the place,
And that fair kneeling Goddess; and then spake,
As with a palsied tongue, and while his beard
Shook horrid° with such aspen°malady: *bristling/a tree with quivering leaves*
'O tender spouse of gold Hyperion,
Thea, I feel thee ere I see thy face;
Look up, and let me see our doom in it;
Look up, and tell me if this feeble shape
Is Saturn's; tell me, if thou hear'st the voice
100 Of Saturn; tell me, if this wrinkling brow,
Naked and bare of its great diadem,
Peers like the front of Saturn. Who had power
To make me desolate? whence came the strength?
How was it nurtured to such bursting forth,
While Fate seemed strangled in my nervous grasp?
But it is so; and I am smothered up,
And buried from all godlike exercise
Of influence benign on planets pale,
Of admonitions to the winds and seas,
110 Of peaceful sway above man's harvesting,
And all those acts which Deity supreme
Doth ease its heart of love in. – I am gone
Away from my own bosom: I have left
My strong identity, my real self,
Somewhere between the throne, and where I sit
Here on this spot of earth. Search, Thea, search!
Open thine eyes eterne, and sphere them round
Upon all space: space starred, and lorn of light;
Space regioned with life-air; and barren void;
120 Spaces of fire, and all the yawn of hell. –
Search, Thea, search! and tell me, if thou seest
A certain shape or shadow, making way
With wings or chariot fierce to repossess
A heaven he lost erewhile: it must – it must
Be of ripe progress – Saturn must be King.

Yes, there must be a golden victory;
There must be Gods thrown down, and trumpets blown
Of triumph calm, and hymns of festival
Upon the gold clouds metropolitan,
130 Voices of soft proclaim, and silver stir
Of strings in hollow shells; and there shall be
Beautiful things made new, for the surprise
Of the sky-children; I will give command:
Thea! Thea! Thea! where is Saturn?'

*   *   *

BOOK II

So ended Saturn; and the God of the Sea,   *Neptune*
Sophist and sage, from no Athenian grove,[10]
But cogitation in his watery shades,
170 Arose, with locks not oozy, and began,
In murmurs, which his first-endeavouring tongue
Caught infant-like from the far-foamed sands.
'O ye, whom wrath consumes! who, passion-stung,
Writhe at defeat, and nurse your agonies!
Shut up your senses, stifle up your ears,
My voice is not a bellows unto ire.
Yet listen, ye who will, whilst I bring proof
How ye, perforce, must be content to stoop:
And in the proof much comfort will I give,
180 If ye will take that comfort in its truth.
We fall by course of nature's law, not force
Of thunder, or of Jove. Great Saturn, thou
Hast sifted well the atom-universe;
But for this reason, that thou art the King,
And only blind from sheer supremacy,
One avenue was shaded from thine eyes,
Through which I wandered to eternal truth.
And first, as thou wast not the first of powers,
So art thou not the last; it cannot be:
190 Thou art not the beginning nor the end.
From chaos and parental darkness came
Light, the first fruits of that intestine broil,
That sullen ferment, which for wondrous ends
Was ripening in itself. The ripe hour came,
And with it light, and light, engendering
Upon its own producer, forthwith touched

The whole enormous matter into life.
Upon that very hour, our parentage,
The Heavens, and the Earth, were manifest:
200 Then thou first born, and we the giant race,
Found ourselves ruling new and beauteous realms.
Now comes the pain of truth, to whom 'tis pain;
O folly! for to bear all naked truths,
And to envisage circumstance, all calm,
That is the top of sovereignty. Mark well!
As Heaven and Earth are fairer, fairer far
Than Chaos and blank Darkness, though once chiefs;
And as we show beyond that Heaven and Earth
In form and shape compact and beautiful,
210 In will, in action free, companionship,
And thousand other signs of purer life;
So on our heels a fresh perfection treads,
A power more strong in beauty, born of us
And fated to excel us, as we pass
In glory that old Darkness: nor are we
Thereby more conquered, than by us the rule
Of shapeless Chaos. Say, doth the dull soil
Quarrel with the proud forests it hath fed,
And feedeth still, more comely than itself?
220 Can it deny the chiefdom of green groves?
Or shall the tree be envious of the dove
Because it cooeth, and hath snowy wings
To wander wherewithal and find its joys?
We are such forest-trees, and our fair boughs
Have bred forth, not pale solitary doves,
But eagles golden-feathered, who do tower
Above us in their beauty, and must reign
In right thereof; for 'tis the eternal law
That first in beauty should be first in might:
230 Yea, by that law, another race may drive
Our conquerors to mourn as we do now.
Have ye beheld the young God of the Seas,
My dispossessor? Have ye seen his face?
Have ye beheld his chariot, foam'd along
By noble winged creatures he hath made?
I saw him on the calmed waters scud,
With such a glow of beauty in his eyes,
That it enforced me to bid sad farewell
To all my empire: farewell sad I took,
240 And hither came, to see how dolorous fate

Had wrought upon ye; and how I might best
Give consolation in this woe extreme.
Receive the truth, and let it be your balm.'

*   *   *

       All eyes were on Enceladus's face,
And they beheld, while still Hyperion's name
Flew from his lips up to the vaulted rocks,
A pallid gleam across his features stern:
350 Not savage, for he saw full many a God
Wroth as himself. He° look'd upon them all,   (Enceladus)
And in each face he saw a gleam of light,
But splendider in Saturn's, whose hoar locks
Shone like the bubbling foam about a keel
When the prow sweeps into a midnight cove.
In pale and silver silence they remained,
Till suddenly a splendour, like the morn,
Pervaded all the beetling gloomy steeps,
All the sad spaces of oblivion,
360 And every gulf, and every chasm old,
And every height, and every sullen depth,
Voiceless, or hoarse with loud tormented streams:
And all the everlasting cataracts,
And all the headlong torrents far and near,
Mantled before in darkness and huge shade,
Now saw the light and made it terrible.
It was Hyperion. . . .

*   *   *

BOOK III

Thus in alternate uproar and sad peace,
Amazed were those Titans utterly.
O leave them, Muse! O leave them to their woes;
For thou art weak to sing such tumults dire:
A solitary sorrow best befits
Thy lips, and antheming a lonely grief.
Leave them, O Muse! for thou anon wilt find
Many a fallen old Divinity
Wandering in vain about bewildered shores.
10 Meantime touch piously the Delphic° harp,   of Delphi
And not a wind of heaven but will breathe
In aid soft warble from the Dorian¹¹ flute;

For lo! 'tis for the Father of all verse.°   *Apollo*
Flush every thing that hath a vermeil hue,
Let the rose glow intense and warm the air,
And let the clouds of even and of morn
Float in voluptuous fleeces o'er the hills;
Let the red wine within the goblet boil,
Cold as a bubbling well; let faint-lipped shells,
20 On sands, or in great deeps, vermilion turn
Through all their labyrinths; and let the maid
Blush keenly, as with some warm kiss surprised.
Chief isle of the embowered Cyclades,
Rejoice, O Delos, with thine olives green,
And poplars, and lawn-shading palms, and beech,
In which the Zephyr breathes the loudest song,
And hazels thick, dark-stemm'd beneath the shade:
Apollo is once more the golden theme!
Where was he, when the Giant of the Sun
30 Stood bright, amid the sorrow of his peers?
Together had he left his mother° fair   *Leto*
And his twin-sister° sleeping in their bower,   *Diana*
And in the morning twilight wandered forth
Beside the osiers° of a rivulet,   *willows*
Full ankle-deep in lilies of the vale.
The nightingale had ceased, and a few stars
Were lingering in the heavens, while the thrush
Began calm-throated. Throughout all the isle
There was no covert, no retired cave
40 Unhaunted by the murmurous noise of waves,
Though scarcely heard in many a green recess.
He listened, and he wept, and his bright tears
Went trickling down the golden bow he held.
Thus with half-shut suffused eyes he stood,
While from beneath some cumbrous boughs hard by
With solemn step an awful Goddess came,
And there was purport in her looks for him,
Which he with eager guess began to read
Perplexed, the while melodiously he said:
50 'How cam'st thou over the unfooted sea?
Or hath that antique mien and robed form
Moved in these vales invisible till now?
Sure I have heard those vestments sweeping o'er
The fallen leaves, when I have sat alone
In cool mid-forest. Surely I have traced
The rustle of those ample skirts about

These grassy solitudes, and seen the flowers
Lift up their heads, as still the whisper passed.
Goddess! I have beheld those eyes before,
60   And their eternal calm, and all that face,
Or I have dreamed.' – 'Yes,' said the supreme shape,
'Thou hast dreamed of me; and awaking up
Didst find a lyre all golden by thy side,
Whose strings touched by thy fingers, all the vast
Unwearied ear of the whole universe
Listened in pain and pleasure at the birth
Of such new tuneful wonder. Is't not strange
That thou shouldst weep, so gifted? Tell me, youth,
What sorrow thou canst feel; for I am sad
70   When thou dost shed a tear: explain thy griefs
To one who in this lonely isle hath been
The watcher of thy sleep and hours of life,
From the young day when first thy infant hand
Plucked witless the weak flowers, till thine arm
Could bend that bow heroic to all times.
Show thy heart's secret to an ancient power
Who hath forsaken old and sacred thrones
For prophecies of thee, and for the sake
Of loveliness new born.' – Apollo then,
80   With sudden scrutiny and gloomless eyes,
Thus answered, while his white melodious throat
Throbbed with the syllables. – 'Mnemosyne!
Thy name is on my tongue, I know not how;
Why should I tell thee what thou so well seest?
Why should I strive to show what from thy lips
Would come no mystery? For me, dark, dark,
And painful vile oblivion seals my eyes:
I strive to search wherefore I am so sad,
Until a melancholy numbs my limbs;
90   And then upon the grass I sit, and moan,
Like one who once had wings. – O why should I
Feel cursed and thwarted, when the liegeless air
Yields to my step aspirant? Why should I
Spurn the green turf as hateful to my feet?
Goddess benign, point forth some unknown thing:
Are there not other regions than this isle?
What are the stars? There is the sun, the sun!
And the most patient brilliance of the moon!
And stars by thousands! Point me out the way
100   To any one particular beauteous star,

And I will flit into it with my lyre
And make its silvery splendour pant with bliss.
I have heard the cloudy thunder: Where is power?
Whose hand, whose essence, what divinity
Makes this alarum in the elements,
While I here idle listen on the shores
In fearless yet in aching ignorance?
O tell me, lonely Goddess, by thy harp,
That waileth every morn and eventide,
110 Tell me why thus I rave, about these groves!
Mute thou remainest – mute! Yet I can read
A wondrous lesson in thy silent face:
Knowledge enormous makes a God of me.
Names, deeds, grey legends, dire events, rebellions,
Majesties, sovran voices, agonies,
Creations and destroyings, all at once
Pour into the wide hollows of my brain,
And deify me, as if some blithe wine
Or bright elixir peerless I had drunk,
120 And so become immortal.' – Thus the God,
While his enkindled eyes, with level glance
Beneath his white soft temples, stedfast kept
Trembling with light upon Mnemosyne.
Soon wild commotions shook him, and made flush
All the immortal fairness of his limbs;
Most like the struggle at the gate of death;
Or liker still to one who should take leave
Of pale immortal death, and with a pang
As hot as death's is chill, with fierce convulse
130 Die into life: so young Apollo anguished:
His very hair, his golden tresses famed
Kept undulation round his eager neck.
During the pain Mnemosyne upheld
Her arms as one who prophesied. – At length
Apollo shrieked; – and lo! from all his limbs
Celestial. . . .

Unfinished 1818/19 [1820]

Ode
Bards of Passion and of Mirth[12]

Bards of Passion and of Mirth,
Ye have left your souls on earth!
Have ye souls in heaven too,
Double-lived in regions new?
Yes, and those of heaven commune
With the spheres of sun and moon;
With the noise of fountains wond'rous,
And the parle of voices thund'rous;
With the whisper of heaven's trees
10 And one another, in soft ease
Seated on Elysian lawns
Browsed by none but Dian's fawns;
Underneath large blue-bells tented,
Where the daisies are rose-scented,
And the rose herself has got
Perfume which on earth is not;
Where the nightingale doth sing
Not a senseless, tranced thing,
But divine melodious truth;
20 Philosophic numbers smooth;
Tales and golden histories
Of heaven and its mysteries.

Thus ye live on high, and then
On the earth ye live again;
And the souls ye left behind you
Teach us, here, the way to find you,
Where your other souls are joying,
Never slumbered, never cloying.
Here, your earth-born souls still speak
30 To mortals, of their little week;
Of their sorrows and delights;
Of their passions and their spites;
Of their glory and their shame;
What doth strengthen and what maim.
Thus ye teach us, every day,
Wisdom, though fled far away.

Bards of Passion and of Mirth,
Ye have left your souls on earth!
Ye have souls in heaven too,
40   Double-lived in regions new!

1818 [1820]

The Eve of St. Agnes[13]

1

St. Agnes' Eve – Ah, bitter chill it was!
The owl, for all his feathers, was a-cold;
The hare limped trembling through the frozen grass,
And silent was the flock in woolly fold:
Numb were the Beadsman's° fingers, while he told   *man paid to pray*
His rosary, and while his frosted breath,
Like pious incense from a censer old,
Seemed taking flight for heaven, without a death,
Past the sweet Virgin's picture, while his prayer he saith.

2

His prayer he saith, this patient, holy man;
Then takes his lamp, and riseth from his knees,
And back returneth, meagre, barefoot, wan,
Along the chapel aisle by slow degrees:
The sculptured dead, on each side, seem to freeze,
Emprison'd in black, purgatorial rails:
Knights, ladies, praying in dumb orat'ries,°   *chapels*
He passeth by; and his weak spirit fails
To think how they may ache in icy hoods and mails.

3

Northward he turneth through a little door,
And scarce three steps, ere Music's golden tongue
Flattered to tears this aged man and poor;
But no – already had his deathbell rung:
The joys of all his life were said and sung:
His was harsh penance on St. Agnes' Eve:
Another way he went, and soon among
Rough ashes sat he for his soul's reprieve,
And all night kept awake, for sinners' sake to grieve.

4

That ancient Beadsman heard the prelude soft;
And so it chanced, for many a door was wide,
From hurry to and fro. Soon, up aloft,
The silver, snarling trumpets 'gan to chide:
The level chambers, ready with their pride,
Were glowing to receive a thousand guests:
The carved angels, ever eager-eyed,
Stared, where upon their heads the cornice rests,
With hair blown back, and wings put cross-wise on their breasts.

5

At length burst in the argent° revelry,   *silver*
With plume, tiara, and all rich array,
Numerous as shadows haunting faerily
The brain, new stuffed, in youth, with triumphs gay
Of old romance. These let us wish away,
And turn, sole-thoughted, to one Lady there,
Whose heart had brooded, all that wintry day,
On love, and winged St. Agnes' saintly care,
As she had heard old dames full many times declare.

6

They told her how, upon St. Agnes' Eve,
Young virgins might have visions of delight,
And soft adorings from their loves receive
Upon the honeyed middle of the night,
If ceremonies due they did aright;
As, supperless to bed they must retire,
And couch supine their beauties, lily white;
Nor look behind, nor sideways, but require
Of Heaven with upward eyes for all that they desire.

7

Full of this whim was thoughtful Madeline:
The music, yearning like a God in pain,
She scarcely heard: her maiden eyes divine,
Fixed on the floor, saw many a sweeping train°   *long skirt*
Pass by – she heeded not at all: in vain
Came many a tiptoe, amorous cavalier,
And back retired; not cooled by high disdain,
But she saw not: her heart was otherwhere:
She sighed for Agnes' dreams, the sweetest of the year.

8

She danced along with vague, regardless eyes,
Anxious her lips, her breathing quick and short:
The hallowed hour was near at hand: she sighs
Amid the timbrels, and the thronged resort
Of whisperers in anger, or in sport;
'Mid looks of love, defiance, hate, and scorn,
Hoodwinked° with faery fancy; all amort,°   *blinded/as if dead*
Save to St. Agnes and her lambs unshorn,[14]
And all the bliss to be before to-morrow morn.

9

So, purposing each moment to retire,
She lingered still. Meantime, across the moors,
Had come young Porphyro, with heart on fire
For Madeline. Beside the portal doors,
Buttressed from moonlight, stands he, and implores
All saints to give him sight of Madeline,
But for one moment in the tedious hours,
That he might gaze and worship all unseen;
Perchance speak, kneel, touch, kiss – in sooth such things have been.

10

He ventures in: let no buzzed whisper tell:
All eyes be muffled, or a hundred swords
Will storm his heart, Love's fev'rous citadel:
For him, those chambers held barbarian hordes,
Hyena foemen, and hot-blooded lords,
Whose very dogs would execrations howl
Against his lineage: not one breast affords
Him any mercy, in that mansion foul,
Save one old beldame,° weak in body and in soul.   *old woman*

11

Ah, happy chance! the aged creature came,
Shuffling along with ivory-headed wand,
To where he stood, hid from the torch's flame,
Behind a broad hall-pillar, far beyond
The sound of merriment and chorus bland:
He startled her; but soon she knew his face,
And grasped his fingers in her palsied hand,
Saying, 'Mercy, Porphyro! hie thee from this place:
They are all here to-night, the whole blood-thirsty race!

12

Get hence! get hence! there's dwarfish Hildebrand;
He had a fever late, and in the fit
He cursed thee and thine, both house and land:
Then there's that old Lord Maurice, not a whit
More tame for his gray hairs – Alas me! flit!
Flit like a ghost away.' – 'Ah, Gossip° dear,   *familiar friend*
We're safe enough; here in this arm-chair sit,
And tell me how' – 'Good Saints! not here, not here;
Follow me, child, or else these stones will be thy bier.'

13

He followed through a lowly arched way,
Brushing the cobwebs with his lofty plume,
And as she muttered 'Well-a – well-a-day!'
He found him in a little moonlight room,
Pale, latticed, chill, and silent as a tomb.
'Now tell me where is Madeline,' said he,
'O tell me, Angela, by the holy loom
Which none but secret sisterhood may see,
When they St. Agnes' wool are weaving piously.'

14

'St. Agnes! Ah! it is St. Agnes' Eve –
Yet men will murder upon holy days:
Thou must hold water in a witch's sieve,[15]
And be liege-lord of all the Elves and Fays,
To venture so: it fills me with amaze
To see thee, Porphyro! – St. Agnes' Eve!
God's help! my lady fair the conjuror plays
This very night: good angels her deceive!
But let me laugh awhile, I've mickle° time to grieve.'   *much*

15

Feebly she laugheth in the languid moon,
While Porphyro upon her face doth look,
Like puzzled urchin on an aged crone
Who keepeth closed a wond'rous riddle-book,
As spectacled she sits in chimney nook.
But soon his eyes grew brilliant, when she told
His lady's purpose; and he scarce could brook
Tears, at the thought of those enchantments cold,
And Madeline asleep in lap of legends old.

16

Sudden a thought came like a full-blown rose,
Flushing his brow, and in his pained heart
Made purple riot: then doth he propose
A stratagem, that makes the beldame start:
'A cruel man and impious thou art:
Sweet lady, let her pray, and sleep, and dream
Alone with her good angels, far apart
From wicked men like thee. Go, go! – I deem
Thou canst not surely be the same that thou didst seem.'

17

'I will not harm her, by all saints I swear,'
Quoth Porphyro: 'O may I ne'er find grace
When my weak voice shall whisper its last prayer,
If one of her soft ringlets I displace,
Or look with ruffian passion in her face:
Good Angela, believe me by these tears;
Or I will, even in a moment's space,
Awake, with horrid shout, my foemen's ears,
And beard them, though they be more fanged than wolves and bears.'

18

'Ah! why wilt thou affright a feeble soul?
A poor, weak, palsy-stricken, churchyard thing,
Whose passing-bell may ere the midnight toll;
Whose prayers for thee, each morn and evening,
Were never missed.' – Thus plaining, doth she bring
A gentler speech from burning Porphyro;
So woful, and of such deep sorrowing,
That Angela gives promise she will do
Whatever he shall wish, betide her weal or woe.

19

Which was, to lead him, in close secrecy,
Even to Madeline's chamber, and there hide
Him in a closet, of such privacy
That he might see her beauty unespied,
And win perhaps that night a peerless bride,
While legioned faeries paced the coverlet,
And pale enchantment held her sleepy-eyed.
Never on such a night have lovers met,
Since Merlin paid his Demon° all the monstrous debt.   *Vivien*

20

'It shall be as thou wishest,' said the Dame:
'All cates° and dainties shall be stored there   *provisions*
Quickly on this feast-night: by the tambour-frame°   *embroidery frame*
Her own lute thou wilt see: no time to spare,
For I am slow and feeble, and scarce dare
On such a catering trust my dizzy head.
Wait here, my child, with patience; kneel in prayer
The while: Ah! thou must needs the lady wed,
Or may I never leave my grave among the dead.'

21

So saying, she hobbled off with busy fear.
The lover's endless minutes slowly passed;
The dame returned, and whispered in his ear
To follow her; with aged eyes aghast
From fright of dim espial. Safe at last,
Through many a dusky gallery, they gain
The maiden's chamber, silken, hushed, and chaste;
Where Porphyro took covert, pleased amain.°   *greatly*
His poor guide hurried back with agues in her brain.

22

Her falt'ring hand upon the balustrade,
Old Angela was feeling for the stair,
When Madeline, St. Agnes' charmed maid,
Rose, like a missioned spirit, unaware:
With silver taper's light, and pious care,
She turned, and down the aged gossip led
To a safe level matting. Now prepare,
Young Porphyro, for gazing on that bed;
She comes, she comes again, like ring-dove frayed° and fled. *frightened*

23

Out went the taper as she hurried in;
Its little smoke, in pallid moonshine, died:
She closed the door, she panted, all akin
To spirits of the air, and visions wide:
No uttered syllable, or, woe betide!
But to her heart, her heart was voluble,
Paining with eloquence her balmy side;
As though a tongueless nightingale should swell
Her throat in vain, and die, heart-stifled, in her dell.

24

A casement high and triple-arched there was,
All garlanded with carven imag'ries
Of fruits, and flowers, and bunchs of knot-grass,°   *creeping plant with*
And diamonded with panes of quaint device,   *pink flowers*
Innumerable of stains and splendid dyes,
As are the tiger-moth's deep-damasked wings;
And in the midst, 'mong thousand heraldries,
And twilight saints, and dim emblazonings,
A shielded scutcheon° blushed with blood of queens and kings.
    inscription plate

25

Full on this casement shone the wintry moon,
And threw warm gules° on Madeline's fair breast,   *red*
As down she knelt for heaven's grace and boon;
Rose-bloom fell on her hands, together prest,
And on her silver cross soft amethyst,
And on her hair a glory, like a saint:
She seemed a splendid angel, newly drest,
Save wings, for heaven:– Porphyro grew faint:
She knelt, so pure a thing, so free from mortal taint.

26

Anon his heart revives: her vespers done,
Of all its wreathed pearls her hair she frees;
Unclasps her warmed jewels one by one;
Loosens her fragrant boddice; by degrees
Her rich attire creeps rustling to her knees:
Half-hidden, like a mermaid in sea-weed,
Pensive awhile she dreams awake, and sees,
In fancy, fair St. Agnes in her bed,
But dares not look behind, or all the charm is fled.

27

Soon, trembling in her soft and chilly nest,
In sort of wakeful swoon, perplexed she lay,
Until the poppied warmth of sleep oppressed
Her soothed limbs, and soul fatigued away;
Flown, like a thought, until the morrow-day;
Blissfully havened both from joy and pain;
Clasped like a missal° where swart paynims° pray;   *prayer-book/*
Blinded alike from sunshine and from rain,   *black pagans*
As though a rose should shut, and be a bud again.

28

Stol'n to this paradise, and so entranced,
Porphyro gazed upon her empty dress,
And listened to her breathing, if it chanced
To wake into a slumberous tenderness;
Which when he heard, that minute did he bless,
And breathed himself: then from the closet crept,
Noiseless as fear in a wide wilderness,
And over the hushed carpet, silent, stept,
And 'tween the curtains peeped, where, lo! – how fast she slept.

29

Then by the bed-side, where the faded moon
Made a dim, silver twilight, soft he set
A table, and, half anguished, threw thereon
A cloth of woven crimson, gold, and jet: –
O for some drowsy Morphean° amulet!°   *of Morpheus/charm*
The boisterous, midnight, festive clarion,
The kettle-drum, and far-heard clarinet,
Affray his ears, though but in dying tone:–
The hall door shuts again, and all the noise is gone.

30

And still she slept in azure-lidded sleep,
In blanched linen, smooth, and lavender'd,
While he from forth the closet brought a heap   */fruit*
Of candied apple, quince,° and plum, and gourd;   *yellow pear-shaped*
With jellies soother° than the creamy curd,   *smoother*
And lucent° syrops,° tinct° with cinnamon;   *shining/syrups/coloured*
Manna and dates, in argosy transferr'd
From Fez; and spiced dainties, every one,
From silken Samarcand to cedared Lebanon.

31

These delicacies he heaped with glowing hand
On golden dishes and in baskets bright
Of wreathed silver: sumptuous they stand
In the retired quiet of the night,
Filling the chilly room with perfume light. –
'And now, my love, my seraph fair, awake!
Thou art my heaven, and I thine eremite:°   *hermit*
Or I shall drowse beside thee, so my soul doth ache.'

32

Thus whispering, his warm, unnerved arm
Sank in her pillow. Shaded was her dream
By the dusk curtains:– 'twas a midnight charm
Impossible to melt as iced stream:
The lustrous salvers° in the moonlight gleam;   *serving dishes*
Broad golden fringe upon the carpet lies:
It seemed he never, never could redeem
From such a stedfast spell his lady's eyes;
So mused awhile, entoiled in woofed° phantasies.   *woven*

33

Awakening up, he took her hollow lute, –
Tumultuous, – and, in chords that tenderest be,
He played an ancient ditty, long since mute,
In Provence called, 'La belle dame sans merce':
Close to her ear touching the melody; –
Wherewith disturbed, she uttered a soft moan:
He ceased – she panted quick – and suddenly
Her blue affrayed eyes wide open shone:
Upon his knees he sank, pale as smooth-sculptured stone.

34

Her eyes were open, but she still beheld,
Now wide awake, the vision of her sleep:
There was a painful change, that night expelled
The blisses of her dream so pure and deep
At which fair Madeline began to weep
And moan forth witless words with many a sigh;
While still her gaze on Porphyro would keep;
Who knelt, with joined hands and piteous eye,
Fearing to move or speak, she looked so dreamingly.

35

'Ah, Porphyro!' said she, 'but even now
Thy voice was at sweet tremble in mine ear,
Made tuneable with every sweetest vow;
And those sad eyes were spiritual and clear:
How changed thou art! how pallid, chill, and drear!
Give me that voice again, my Porphyro,
Those looks immortal, those complainings dear!
Oh leave me not in this eternal woe,
For if thou diest, my Love, I know not where to go.'

36

Beyond a mortal man impassioned far
At these voluptuous accents, he arose,
Ethereal, flushed, and like a throbbing star
Seen mid the sapphire heaven's deep repose;
Into her dream he melted, as the rose
Blendeth its odour with the violet, –
Solution sweet: meantime the frost-wind blows
Like Love's alarum pattering the sharp sleet
Against the window-panes; St. Agnes' moon hath set.

37

'Tis dark: quick pattereth the flaw-blown° sleet: *squally*
'This is no dream, my bride, my Madeline!'
'Tis dark: the iced gusts still rave and beat:
'No dream, alas! alas! and woe is mine!
Porphyro will leave me here to fade and pine. –
Cruel! what traitor could thee hither bring?
I curse not, for my heart is lost in thine,
Though thou forsakest a deceived thing; –
A dove forlorn and lost with sick unpruned wing.'

38

'My Madeline! sweet dreamer! lovely bride!
Say, may I be for aye thy vassal blest?
Thy beauty's shield, heart-shaped and vermeil° dyed?   *vermilion*
Ah, silver shrine, here will I take my rest
After so many hours of toil and quest,
A famished pilgrim, – saved by miracle.
Though I have found, I will not rob thy nest
Saving of thy sweet self; if thou think'st well
To trust, fair Madeline, to no rude infidel.

39

Hark! 'tis an elfin-storm from faery land,
Of haggard° seeming, but a boon indeed: *wild-looking*
Arise – arise! the morning is at hand; –
The bloated wassaillers° will never heed:–   *revellers*
Let us away, my love, with happy speed;
There are no ears to hear, or eyes to see, –
Drowned all in Rhenish° and the sleepy mead:°   *wine/drink of malt and*
Awake! arise! my love, and fearless be,   *honey*
For o'er the southern moors I have a home for thee.'

40

She hurried at his words, beset with fears,
For there were sleeping dragons all around,
At glaring watch, perhaps, with ready spears –
Down the wide stairs a darkling way they found. –
In all the house was heard no human sound.
A chain-drooped lamp was flickering by each door;
The arras,° rich with horseman, hawk, and hound,   *wall-tapestry*
Fluttered in the besieging wind's uproar;
And the long carpets rose along the gusty floor.

41

They glide, like phantoms, into the wide hall;
Like phantoms, to the iron porch, they glide;
Where lay the Porter, in uneasy sprawl,
With huge empty flaggon by his side:
The wakeful bloodhound rose, and shook his hide,
But his sagacious eye an inmate owns:°   *recognises*
By one, and one, the bolts full easy slide:–
The chains lie silent on the footworn stones;–
The key turns, and the door upon its hinges groans.

42

And they are gone: aye, ages long ago
These lovers fled away into the storm.
That night the Baron dreamt of many a woe,
And all his warrior-guests, with shade and form
Of witch, and demon, and large coffin-worm,
Were long be-nightmared. Angela the old
Died palsy-twitched, with meagre face deform;
The Beadsman, after thousand aves° told,   *prayers*
For aye unsought for slept among his ashes cold.

1819 [1820]

La Belle Dame Sans Merci

A BALLAD[16]

I

O, what can ail thee, knight-at-arms,
    Alone and palely loitering?
The sedge has withered from the lake,
    And no birds sing.

II

O, what can ail thee, knight-at-arms,
    So haggard and so woe-begone?
The squirrel's granary is full,
    And the harvest's done.

III

I see a lily on thy brow,
    With anguish moist and fever dew;
And on thy cheeks a fading rose
    Fast withereth too.

IV

I met a lady in the meads,
    Full beautiful – a faery's child,
Her hair was long, her foot was light,
    And her eyes were wild.

V

I made a garland for her head,
    And bracelets too, and fragrant zone;°   *girdle*
She looked at me as she did love,
    And made sweet moan.

VI

I set her on my pacing steed,
    And nothing else saw all day long;
For sidelong would she bend, and sing
    A faery's song.

VII

She found me roots of relish sweet,
    And honey wild, and manna dew,[17]
And sure in language strange she said –
    'I love thee true'.

VIII

She took me to her elfin grot,°   *grotto*
　　And there she wept and sighed full sore,
And there I shut her wild wild eyes
　　With kisses four.

IX

And there she lulled me asleep
　　And there I dreamed – Ah! woe betide!
The latest dream I ever dreamed
　　On the cold hill side.

X

I saw pale kings and princes too,
　　Pale warriors, death-pale were they all;
They cried – 'La Belle Dame sans Merci
　　Hath thee in thrall!'

XI

I saw their starved lips in the gloam,
　　With horrid warning gaped wide,
And I awoke and found me here,
　　On the cold hill's side.

XII

And this is why I sojourn here
　　Alone and palely loitering,
Though the sedge has withered from the lake,
　　And no birds sing.

1819 [1820]

Ode to Psyche[18]

O Goddess! hear these tuneless numbers, wrung
　　By sweet enforcement and remembrance dear,
And pardon that thy secrets should be sung
　　Even into thine own soft-conched° ear: *shell-shaped but soft*
Surely I dreamt to-day, or did I see
　　The winged Psyche with awakened eyes?
I wandered in a forest thoughtlessly,
　　And, on the sudden, fainting with surprise,

Saw two fair creatures, couched side by side
In deepest grass, beneath the whisp'ring roof
Of leaves and trembled blossoms, where there ran
A brooklet, scarce espied:

'Mid hushed, cool-rooted flowers, fragrant-eyed,
Blue, silver-white, and budded Tyrian,[19]
They lay calm-breathing on the bedded grass;
Their arms embraced, and their pinions too;
Their lips touched not, but had not bade adieu,
As if disjoined by soft-handed slumber,
And ready still past kisses to outnumber
At tender eye-dawn of aurorean love:
The winged boy I knew;
But who wast thou, O happy, happy dove?
His Psyche true!

O latest born and loveliest vision far
Of all Olympus' faded hierarchy!
Fairer than Phœbe's sapphire-regioned star,
Or Vesper, amorous glow-worm of the sky;
Fairer than these, though temple thou hast none,
Nor altar heaped with flowers;
Nor virgin-choir to make delicious moan
Upon the midnight hours;
No voice, no lute, no pipe, no incense sweet
From chain-swung censer teeming;
No shrine, no grove, no oracle, no heat
Of pale-mouthed prophet dreaming.

O brightest! though too late for antique vows,
Too, too late for the fond believing lyre,
When holy were the haunted forest boughs,
Holy the air, the water, and the fire;
Yet even in these days so far retired
From happy pieties, thy lucent fans,°   *shining wings*
Fluttering among the faint Olympians,
I see, and sing, by my own eyes inspired.
So let me be thy choir, and make a moan
Upon the midnight hours;
Thy voice, thy lute, thy pipe, thy incense sweet
From swinged censer teeming;
Thy shrine, thy grove, thy oracle, thy heat
Of pale-mouthed prophet dreaming.

50 Yes, I will be thy priest, and build a fane°   *temple*
     In some untrodden region of my mind,
Where branched thoughts, new grown with pleasant pain,
     Instead of pines shall murmur in the wind:
Far, far around shall those dark-clustered trees
     Fledge the wild-ridged mountains steep by steep;
And there by zephyrs, streams, and birds, and bees,
     The moss-lain dryads° shall be lulled to sleep;   *wood-nymphs*
And in the midst of this wide quietness
A rosy sanctuary will I dress
60 With the wreathed trellis of a working brain,
     With buds, and bells, and stars without a name,
With all the gardener Fancy e'er could feign,
     Who breeding flowers, will never breed the same:
And there shall be for thee all soft delight
     That shadowy thought can win,
A bright torch, and a casement ope at night,
     To let the warm Love in!

April 1819 [1820]

Ode to a Nightingale

My heart aches, and a drowsy numbness pains
     My sense, as though of hemlock° I had drunk,   *poisonous plant*
Or emptied some dull opiate to the drains
     One minute past, and Lethe-wards had sunk:
'Tis not through envy of thy happy lot,
     But being too happy in thine happiness, –
          That thou, light-winged Dryad° of the trees,   *wood-nymph*
               In some melodious plot
     Of beechen green, and shadows numberless,
          Singest of summer in full-throated ease.

O, for a draught of vintage! that hath been
     Cooled a long age in the deep-delved earth,
Tasting of Flora and the country green,
     Dance, and Provençal song, and sunburnt mirth!
O for a beaker full of the warm South,
     Full of the true, the blushful Hippocrene,
          With beaded bubbles winking at the brim,

And purple-stained mouth;
    That I might drink, and leave the world unseen,
    And with thee fade away into the forest dim:

Fade far away, dissolve, and quite forget
    What thou among the leaves hast never known,
The weariness, the fever, and the fret
    Here, where men sit and hear each other groan;
Where palsy shakes a few, sad, last gray hairs,
    Where youth grows pale, and spectre-thin, and dies;[20]
      Where but to think is to be full of sorrow
        And leaden-eyed despairs,
      Where Beauty cannot keep her lustrous eyes,
        Or new Love pine at them beyond to-morrow.

Away! away! for I will fly to thee,
    Not charioted by Bacchus and his pards,°   *leopards*
But on the viewless wings of poesy,
    Though the dull brain perplexes and retards:
Already with thee! tender is the night,
    And haply the Queen-Moon is on her throne,
      Clustered around by all her starry Fays;°   *fairies*
        But here there is no light,
    Save what from heaven is with the breezes blown
      Through verdurous glooms and winding mossy ways.

I cannot see what flowers are at my feet,
    Nor what soft incense hangs upon the boughs,
But, in embalmed darkness, guess each sweet
    Wherewith the seasonable month endows
The grass, the thicket, and the fruit-tree wild;
    White hawthorn, and the pastoral eglantine;
      Fast fading violets covered up in leaves;
        And mid-May's eldest child,
    The coming musk-rose,° full of dewy wine,   *rose with white fragrant flower*
      The murmurous haunt of flies on summer eves.

Darkling° I listen; and, for many a time   *in the dark*
    I have been half in love with easeful Death,
Called him soft names in many a mused rhyme,
    To take into the air my quiet breath;
Now more than ever seems it rich to die,
    To cease upon the midnight with no pain,
      While thou art pouring forth thy soul abroad

In such an ecstasy!
Still wouldst thou sing, and I have ears in vain –
To thy high requiem become a sod.

Thou wast not born for death, immortal bird!
No hungry generations tread thee down;
The voice I hear this passing night was heard
In ancient days by emperor and clown:°   *peasant*
Perhaps the self-same song that found a path
Through the sad heart of Ruth,[21] when, sick for home,
She stood in tears amid the alien corn;
The same that oft-times hath
Charmed magic casements, opening on the foam
Of perilous seas, in faery lands forlorn.

Forlorn! the very word is like a bell
To toll me back from thee to my sole self!
Adieu! the fancy cannot cheat so well
As she is fam'd to do, deceiving elf.
Adieu! adieu! thy plaintive anthem fades
Past the near meadows, over the still stream,
Up the hill-side; and now 'tis buried deep
In the next valley-glades:
Was it a vision, or a waking dream?
Fled is that music:– Do I wake or sleep?

May 1819 [1820]

Ode on a Grecian Urn

Thou still unravished bride of quietness,
Thou foster-child of silence and slow time,
Sylvan historian, who canst thus express
A flowery tale more sweetly than our rhyme:
What leaf-fringed legend haunts about thy shape
Of deities or mortals, or of both,
In Tempe or the dales of Arcady?
What men or gods are these? What maidens loth?
What mad pursuit? What struggle to escape?
What pipes and timbrels? What wild ecstasy?

Heard melodies are sweet, but those unheard
  Are sweeter; therefore, ye soft pipes, play on;
Not to the sensual ear, but, more endeared,
  Pipe to the spirit ditties of no tone:
Fair youth, beneath the trees, thou canst not leave
  Thy song, nor ever can those trees be bare;
    Bold lover, never, never canst thou kiss,
Though winning near the goal – yet, do not grieve;
    She cannot fade, though thou hast not thy bliss,
      For ever wilt thou love, and she be fair!

Ah, happy, happy boughs! that cannot shed
  Your leaves, nor ever bid the Spring adieu;
And, happy melodist, unwearied,
  For ever piping songs for ever new;
More happy love! more happy, happy love!
  For ever warm and still to be enjoyed,
    For ever panting, and for ever young;
All breathing human passion far above,
    That leaves a heart high-sorrowful and cloyed,
      A burning forehead, and a parching tongue.

Who are these coming to the sacrifice?
  To what green altar, O mysterious priest,
Lead'st thou that heifer lowing at the skies,
  And all her silken flanks with garlands drest?
What little town by river or sea shore,
  Or mountain-built with peaceful citadel,
    Is emptied of this folk, this pious morn?
And, little town, thy streets for evermore
  Will silent be; and not a soul to tell
    Why thou art desolate, can e'er return.

O Attic° shape! Fair attitude! with brede°   *of Athens/embroidery*
  Of marble men and maidens overwrought,
With forest branches and the trodden weed;
  Thou, silent form, dost tease us out of thought
As doth eternity: Cold Pastoral!
  When old age shall this generation waste,
  Thou shalt remain, in midst of other woe
Than ours, a friend to man, to whom thou say'st,
  'Beauty is truth, truth beauty,' – that is all
    Ye know on earth, and all ye need to know.

May 1819 [1820]

Ode on Melancholy

No,[22] no, go not to Lethe, neither twist
　Wolf's-bane, tight-rooted, for its poisonous wine;
Nor suffer thy pale forehead to be kissed
　By nightshade, ruby grape of Proserpine;
Make not your rosary of yew-berries,
　Nor let the beetle,° nor the death-moth° be
　　Your mournful Psyche,° nor the downy owl
A partner in your sorrow's mysteries;
　For shade to shade will come too drowsily,
　　And drown the wakeful anguish of the soul.

But when the melancholy fit shall fall
　Sudden from heaven like a weeping cloud,
That fosters the droop-headed flowers all,
　And hides the green hill in an April shroud;
Then glut thy sorrow on a morning rose,
　Or on the rainbow of the salt sand-wave,
　　Or on the wealth of globed peonies;
Or if thy mistress some rich anger shows,
　Emprison her soft hand, and let her rave,
　　And feed deep, deep upon her peerless eyes.

She dwells with Beauty – Beauty that must die;
　And Joy, whose hand is ever at his lips
Bidding adieu; and aching Pleasure nigh,
　Turning to poison while the bee-mouth sips:
Ay, in the very temple of Delight
　Veiled Melancholy has her sovran° shrine,
　　Though seen of none save him whose strenuous tongue
Can burst Joy's grape against his palate fine;
His soul shall taste the sadness of her might,
　And be among her cloudy trophies hung.

*head moth
deathwatch beetle/death's
the soul*

sovereign

May/June 1819 [1820]

To Autumn[23]

Season of mists and mellow fruitfulness,
  Close bosom-friend of the maturing sun;
Conspiring with him how to load and bless
  With fruit the vines that round the thatch-eves run;
To bend with apples the mossed cottage-trees,
  And fill all fruit with ripeness to the core;
    To swell the gourd, and plump the hazel shells
  With a sweet kernel; to set budding more,
And still more, later flowers for the bees,
Until they think warm days will never cease,
    For Summer has o'er-brimmed their clammy cells.

Who hath not seen thee oft amid thy store?
  Sometimes whoever seeks abroad may find
Thee sitting careless on a granary floor,
  Thy hair soft-lifted by the winnowing wind;
Or on a half-reaped furrow sound asleep,
  Drowsed with the fume of poppies, while thy hook° *sickle*
    Spares the next swath° and all its twined flowers: *cut of corn*
And sometimes like a gleaner° thou dost keep *grain gatherer*
  Steady thy laden head across a brook;
  Or by a cider-press,° with patient look, *press for apples*
    Thou watchest the last oozings hours by hours.

Where are the songs of Spring? Ay, where are they?
  Think not of them, thou hast thy music too, –
While barred clouds bloom the soft-dying day,
  And touch the stubble-plains with rosy hue;
Then in a wailful choir the small gnats mourn
  Among the river sallows,° borne aloft *willows*
    Or sinking as the light wind lives or dies;
And full-grown lambs loud bleat from hilly bourn;° *domain*
  Hedge-crickets sing; and now with treble soft
  The red-breast whistles from a garden-croft;
    And gathering swallows twitter in the skies.

Sept. 1819 [1820]

Lamia

PART I

Upon a time, before the faery broods
Drove nymph and satyr from the prosperous woods,
Before king Oberon's bright diadem,
Sceptre, and mantle, clasped with dewy gem,
Frighted away the Dryads and the Fauns
From rushes green, and brakes, and cowslip'd lawns,
The ever-smitten Hermes empty left
His golden throne, bent warm on amorous theft:
From high Olympus had he stolen light,
10 On this side of Jove's clouds, to escape the sight
Of his great summoner, and made retreat
Into a forest on the shores of Crete.
For somewhere in that sacred island dwelt
A nymph, to whom all hoofed Satyrs knelt;
At whose white feet the languid Tritons poured
Pearls, while on land they withered and adored.
Fast by the springs where she to bathe was wont,
And in those meads where sometime she might haunt,
Were strewn rich gifts, unknown to any Muse,
20 Though Fancy's casket were unlocked to choose.
Ah, what a world of love was at her feet!
So Hermes thought, and a celestial heat
Burnt from his winged heels to either ear,
That from a whiteness, as the lily clear,
Blushed into roses 'mid his golden hair,
Fallen in jealous curls about his shoulders bare.

From vale to vale, from wood to wood, he flew,
Breathing upon the flowers his passion new,
And wound with many a river to its head,
30 To find where this sweet nymph prepared her secret bed:
In vain; the sweet nymph might nowhere be found,
And so he rested, on the lonely ground,
Pensive, and full of painful jealousies
Of the Wood-Gods, and even the very trees.
There as he stood, he heard a mournful voice,
Such as once heard, in gentle heart, destroys
All pain but pity: thus the lone voice spake:
'When from this wreathed tomb shall I awake!

When move in a sweet body fit for life,
40 And love, and pleasure, and the ruddy strife
Of hearts and lips! Ah, miserable me!'
The God, dove-footed, glided silently
Round bush and tree, soft-brushing, in his speed,
The taller grasses and full-flowering weed,
Until he found a palpitating snake,
Bright, and cirque-couchant° in a dusky brake.   *lying in coils*

She was a gordian° shape of dazzling hue,   *intricate*
Vermilion-spotted, golden, green, and blue;
Striped like a zebra, freckled like a pard,°   *leopard*
50 Eyed like a peacock,[24] and all crimson barred;°   *striped*
And full of silver moons, that, as she breathed,
Dissolved, or brighter shone, or interwreathed
Their lustres with the gloomier tapestries –
So rainbow-sided, touched with miseries,
She seemed, at once, some penanced lady elf,[25]
Some demon's mistress, or the demon's self.
Upon her crest she wore a wannish° fire   *pale*
Sprinkled with stars, like Ariadne's[26] tiar:
Her head was serpent, but ah, bitter-sweet!
60 She had a woman's mouth with all its pearls° complete: *teeth*
And for her eyes: what could such eyes do there
But weep, and weep, that they were born so fair?
As Proserpine still weeps for her Sicilian air.
Her throat was serpent, but the words she spake
Came, as through bubbling honey, for Love's sake,
And thus; while Hermes on his pinions lay,
Like a stooped falcon[27] ere he takes his prey.

'Fair Hermes, crowned with feathers, fluttering light,
I had a splendid dream of thee last night:
70 I saw thee sitting, on a throne of gold,
Among the gods, upon Olympus old,
The only sad one; for thou didst not hear
The soft, lute-fingered Muses chaunting clear,
Nor even Apollo when he sang alone,
Deaf to his throbbing throat's long, long melodious moan.
I dreamt I saw thee, robed in purple flakes,
Break amorous through the clouds, as morning breaks,
And, swiftly as a bright Phœbean dart,°   *sunbeam*
Strike for the Cretan isle; and here thou art!

80 Too gentle Hermes, hast thou found the maid?'
    Whereat the star° of Lethe not delayed   (Hermes)
    His rosy eloquence, and thus inquired:
    'Thou smooth-lipped serpent, surely high inspired!
    Thou beauteous wreath, with melancholy eyes,
    Possess whatever bliss thou canst devise,
    Telling me only where my nymph is fled, –
    Where she doth breathe!' 'Bright planet, thou hast said,'
    Returned the snake, 'but seal with oaths, fair God!'
    'I swear,' said Hermes, 'by my serpent rod,
90 And by thine eyes, and by thy starry crown!'
    Light flew his earnest words, among the blossoms blown.
    Then thus again the brilliance feminine:
    'Too frail of heart! for this lost nymph of thine,
    Free as the air, invisibly, she strays
    About these thornless wilds; her pleasant days
    She tastes unseen; unseen her nimble feet
    Leave traces in the grass and flowers sweet;
    From weary tendrils, and bowed branches green,
    She plucks the fruit unseen, she bathes unseen:
100 And by my power is her beauty veiled
    To keep it unaffronted, unassailed
    By the love-glances of unlovely eyes,
    Of Satyrs, Fauns, and bleared° Silenus' sighs.   dim-sighted
    Pale grew her immortality, for woe
    Of all these lovers, and she grieved so
    I took compassion on her, bade her steep
    Her hair in weïrd syrops°, that would keep   syrups
    Her loveliness invisible, yet free
    To wander as she loves, in liberty.
110 Thou shalt behold her, Hermes, thou alone,
    If thou wilt, as thou swearest, grant my boon!'
    Then, once again, the charmed God began
    An oath, and through the serpent's ears it ran
    Warm, tremulous, devout, psalterian°.   like a stringed instrument
    Ravished, she lifted her Circean° head,   like Circe
    Blushed a live damask°, and swift-lisping said,   deep red
    'I was a woman, let me have once more
    A woman's shape, and charming as before.
    I love a youth of Corinth – O the bliss!
120 Give me my woman's form, and place me where he is.
    Stoop, Hermes, let me breath upon thy brow,
    And thou shalt see thy sweet nymph even now.'

The God on half-shut feathers sank serene,
She breathed upon his eyes, and swift was seen
Of both the guarded nymph near-smiling on the green.
It was no dream; or say a dream it was,
Real are the dreams of Gods, and smoothly pass
Their pleasures in a long immortal dream.
One warm, flushed moment, hovering, it might seem
130 Dashed by the wood-nymph's beauty, so he burned;
Then, lighting on the printless verdure, turned
To the swooned serpent, and with languid arm,
Delicate, put to proof the lythe Caducean charm.
So done, upon the nymph his eyes he bent
Full of adoring tears and blandishment,
And towards her stept: she, like a moon in wane,
Faded before him, cowered, nor could restrain
Her fearful sobs, self-folding like a flower
That faints into itself at evening hour:
140 But the God fostering her chilled hand,
She felt the warmth, her eyelids opened bland,
And, like new flowers at morning song of bees,
Bloomed, and gave up her honey to the lees.
Into the green-recessed woods they flew;
Nor grew they pale, as mortal lovers do.

    Left to herself, the serpent now began
To change; her elfin blood in madness ran,
Her mouth foamed, and the grass, therewith besprent°,   *sprinkled*
Withered at dew so sweet and virulent;
150 Her eyes in torture fixed, and anguish drear,
Hot, glazed, and wide, with lid-lashes all sere°,   *withered*
Flashed phosphor and sharp sparks, without one cooling tear.
The colours all inflamed throughout her train,
She writhed about, convulsed with scarlet pain:
A deep volcanian° yellow took the place   *sulphur*
Of all her milder-mooned body's grace;
And, as the lava ravishes the mead,
Spoilt all her silver mail, and golden brede;
Made gloom of all her frecklings, streaks and bars,
160 Eclipsed her crescents, and licked up her stars:

So that, in moments few, she was undrest
Of all her sapphires, greens, and amethyst,
And rubious-argent: of all these bereft,   *like a ruby*
Nothing but pain and ugliness were left.

Still shone her crown; that vanished, also she
Melted and disappeared as suddenly;
And in the air, her new voice luting soft,
Cried, 'Lycius! gentle Lycius!' – Borne aloft
With the bright mists about the mountains hoar
170 These words dissolved: Crete's forests heard no more.

Whither fled Lamia, now a lady bright,
A full-born beauty new and exquisite?
She fled into that valley they pass o'er
Who go to Corinth from Cenchreas' shore;
And rested at the foot of those wild hills,
The rugged founts of the Peræan rills,
And of that other ridge whose barren back
Stretches, with all its mist and cloudy rack,
South-westward to Cleone. There she stood
180 About a young bird's flutter from a wood,
Fair, on a sloping green of mossy tread,
By a clear pool, wherein she passioned
To see herself escaped from so sore ills,
While her robes flaunted with the daffodils.

Ah, happy Lycius! – for she was a maid
More beautiful than ever twisted braid,
Or sighed, or blushed, or on spring-flowered lea
Spread a green kirtle° to the minstrelsy: *skirt*
A virgin purest lipped, yet in the lore
190 Of love deep learned to the red heart's core:
Not one hour old, yet of sciential° brain   *knowledgeable*
To unperplex bliss from its neighbour pain;
Define their pettish limits, and estrange
Their points of contact, and swift counterchange;
Intrigue with the specious chaos, and dispart
Its most ambiguous atoms with sure art;
As though in Cupid's college she had spent
Sweet days a lovely graduate, still unshent,°   *unspoilt*
And kept his rosy terms in idle languishment.

200 Why this fair creature chose so faerily
By the wayside to linger, we shall see;
But first 'tis fit to tell how she could muse
And dream, when in the serpent prison-house,
Of all she list, strange or magnificent:
How, ever, where she willed, her spirit went;

Whether to faint Elysium, or where
Down through tress-lifting waves the Nereids° fair   *sea-nymphs*
Wind into Thetis' bower by many a pearly stair;
Or where God Bacchus drains his cups divine,
210 Stretched out, at ease, beneath a glutinous pine;
Or where in Pluto's gardens palatine°   *palatial*
Mulciber's columns gleam in far piazzian line°.   *colonnade*
And sometimes into cities she would send
Her dream, with feast and rioting to blend;
And once, while among mortals dreaming thus,
She saw the young Corinthian Lycius
Charioting foremost in the envious race,
Like a young Jove with calm uneager face,
And fell into a swooning love of him.
220 Now on the moth-time of that evening dim
He would return that way, as well she knew,
To Corinth from the shore; for freshly blew
The eastern soft wind, and his galley now
Grated the quaystones with her brazen prow
In port Cenchreas, from Egina isle
Fresh anchored; whither he had been awhile
To sacrifice to Jove, whose temple there
Waits with high marble doors for blood and incense rare.
Jove heard his vows, and bettered his desire;
230 For by some freakful chance he made retire
From his companions, and set forth to walk,
Perhaps grown wearied of their Corinth talk:
Over the solitary hills he fared,
Thoughtless at first, but ere eve's star appeared
His phantasy was lost, where reason fades,
In the calmed twilight of Platonic° shades.   *philosophy's*
Lamia beheld him coming, near, more near –
Close to her passing, in indifference drear,
His silent sandals swept the mossy green;
240 So neighboured to him, and yet so unseen
She stood: he passed, shut up in mysteries,
His mind wrapped like his mantle, while her eyes
Followed his steps, and her neck regal white
Turned – syllabling thus, 'Ah, Lycius bright,
And will you leave me on the hills alone?
Lycius, look back! and be some pity shown.'
He did; not with cold wonder fearingly,
But Orpheus-like at an Eurydice;
For so delicious were the words she sung,

250 It seemed he had loved them a whole summer long:
And soon his eyes had drunk her beauty up,
Leaving no drop in the bewildering cup,
And still the cup was full, – while he, afraid
Lest she should vanish ere his lip had paid
Due adoration, thus began to adore;
Her soft look growing coy, she saw his chain so sure:
'Leave thee alone! Look back! Ah, Goddess, see
Whether my eyes can ever turn from thee!
For pity do not this sad heart belie –
260 Even as thou vanishest so shall I die.
Stay! though a Naiad of the rivers, stay!
To thy far wishes will thy streams obey:
Stay! though the greenest woods be thy domain,
Alone they can drink up the morning rain:
Though a descended Pleiad, will not one
Of thine harmonious sisters keep in tune
Thy spheres, and as thy silver proxy shine?
So sweetly to these ravished ears of mine
Came thy sweet greeting, that if thou shouldst fade
270 Thy memory will waste me to a shade:–
For pity do not melt!' – 'If I should stay,'
Said Lamia, 'here, upon this floor of clay,
And pain my steps upon these flowers too rough,
What canst thou say or do of charm enough
To dull the nice remembrance of my home?
Thou canst not ask me with thee here to roam
Over these hills and vales, where no joy is, –
Empty of immortality and bliss!
Thou art a scholar, Lycius, and must know
280 That finer spirits cannot breathe below
In human climes, and live. Alas! poor youth,
What taste of purer air hast thou to soothe
My essence? What serener palaces,
Where I may all my many senses please,
And by mysterious sleights a hundred thirsts appease?
It cannot be – Adieu!' So said, she rose
Tiptoe with white arms spread. He, sick to lose
The amorous promise of her lone complain,
Swooned, murmuring of love, and pale with pain.
290 The cruel lady, without any show
Of sorrow for her tender favourite's woe,
But rather, if her eyes could brighter be,
With brighter eyes and slow amenity,

Put her new lips to his, and gave afresh
The life she had so tangled in her mesh:
And as he from one trance was wakening
Into another, she began to sing,
Happy in beauty, life, and love, and every thing,
A song of love, too sweet for earthly lyres,
300 While, like held breath, the stars drew in their panting fires.
And then she whispered in such trembling tone,
As those who, safe together met alone
For the first time through many anguished days,
Use other speech than looks; bidding him raise
His drooping head, and clear his soul of doubt,
For that she was a woman, and without
Any more subtle fluid in her veins
Than throbbing blood, and that the self-same pains
Inhabited her frail-strung heart as his.
310 And next she wondered how his eyes could miss
Her face so long in Corinth, where, she said,
She dwelt but half retired, and there had led
Days happy as the gold coin could invent
Without the aid of love; yet in content
Till she saw him, as once she passed him by,
Where 'gainst a column he lent thoughtfully
At Venus' temple porch, 'mid baskets heaped
Of amorous herbs and flowers, newly reaped
Late on that eve, as 'twas the night before
320 The Adonian° feast; whereof she saw no more,   *of Adonis*
But wept alone those days, for why should she adore?
Lycius from death awoke into amaze,
To see her still, and singing so sweet lays;
Then from amaze into delight he fell
To hear her whisper woman's lore so well;
And every word she spake enticed him on
To unperplexed delight and pleasure known.
Let the mad poets say whate'er they please
Of the sweets of Faeries, Peris,° Goddesses,   *fairies of Persia*
330 There is not such a treat among them all,
Haunters of cavern, lake, and waterfall,
As a real woman, lineal indeed
From Pyrrha's pebbles or old Adam's seed.
Thus gentle Lamia judged, and judged aright,
That Lycius could not love in half a fright,
So threw the goddess off, and won his heart

More pleasantly by playing woman's part,
With no more awe than what her beauty gave,
That, while it smote, still guaranteed to save.
340 Lycius to all made eloquent reply,
Marrying to every word a twinborn sigh;
And last, pointing to Corinth, asked her sweet,
If 'twas too far that night for her soft feet.
The way was short, for Lamia's eagerness
Made, by a spell, the triple league decrease
To a few paces; not at all surmised
By blinded Lycius, so in her comprized.°   *wrapped up*
They passed the city gates, he knew not how,
So noiseless, and he never thought to know.

350   As men talk in a dream, so Corinth all,
Throughout her palaces imperial,
And all her populous streets and temples lewd,
Muttered, like tempest in the distance brewed,
To the wide-spreaded night above her towers.
Men, women, rich and poor, in the cool hours,
Shuffled their sandals o'er the pavement white
Companioned or alone; while many a light
Flared, here and there, from wealthy festivals,
And threw their moving shadows on the walls,
360 Or found them clustered in the corniced shade
Of some arched temple door, or dusky colonade.

    Muffling his face, of greeting friends in fear,
Her fingers he pressed hard, as one came near
With curled gray beard, sharp eyes, and smooth bald crown,
Slow-stepped, and robed in philosophic gown:
Lycius shrank closer, as they met and past,
Into his mantle, adding wings to haste,
While hurried Lamia trembled: 'Ah,' said he,
'Why do you shudder, love, so ruefully?
370 Why does your tender palm dissolve in dew?' –
'I'm wearied,' said fair Lamia: 'tell me who
Is that old man? I cannot bring to mind
His features: – Lycius! wherefore did you blind
Yourself from his quick eyes?' Lycius replied,
"Tis Apollonius sage, my trusty guide
And good instructor; but to-night he seems
The ghost of folly haunting my sweet dreams.'

While yet he spake they had arrived before
A pillared porch, with lofty portal door,
380 Where hung a silver lamp, whose phosphor glow
Reflected in the slabbed steps below,
Mild as a star in water; for so new,
And so unsullied was the marble hue,
So through the crystal polish, liquid fine,
Ran the dark veins, that none but feet divine
Could e'er have touched there. Sounds Æolian
Breathed from the hinges, as the ample span
Of the wide doors disclosed a place unknown
Some time to any, but those two alone,
390 And a few Persian mutes, who that same year
Were seen about the markets: none knew where
They could inhabit; the most curious
Were foiled, who watched to trace them to their house:
And but the flitter-winged verse must tell,   *fluttering*
For truth's sake, what woe afterwards befel,
'Twould humour many a heart to leave them thus,
Shut from the busy world of more incredulous.

June/July 1819

PART II

Love in a hut, with water and a crust,
Is – Love, forgive us! – cinders, ashes, dust;
Love in a palace is perhaps at last
More grievous torment than a hermit's fast:–
That is a doubtful tale from faery land,
Hard for the non-elect to understand.
Had Lycius lived to hand his story down,
He might have given the moral a fresh frown,
Or clenched it quite: but too short was their bliss
10 To breed distrust and hate, that make the soft voice hiss.
Beside, there, nightly, with terrific glare,
Love, jealous grown of so complete a pair,
Hovered and buzzed his wings, with fearful roar,
Above the lintel of their chamber door,
And down the passage cast a glow upon the floor.

For all this came a ruin: side by side
They were enthroned, in the even tide,

Upon a couch, near to a curtaining
Whose airy texture, from a golden string,
20 Floated into the room, and let appear
Unveiled the summer heaven, blue and clear,
Betwixt two marble shafts:– there they reposed,
Where use had made it sweet, with eyelids closed,
Saving a tythe° which love still open kept,   *a tenth*
That they might see each other while they almost slept;
When from the slope side of a suburb hill,
Deafening the swallow's twitter, came a thrill
Of trumpets – Lycius started – the sounds fled,
But left a thought a-buzzing in his head.
30 For the first time, since first he harboured in
.That purple-lined palace of sweet sin,
His spirit passed beyond its golden bourn
Into the noisy world almost forsworn.
The lady, ever watchful, penetrant,
Saw this with pain, so arguing a want
Of something more, more than her empery
Of joys; and she began to moan and sigh
Because he mused beyond her, knowing well
That but a moment's thought is passion's passing bell.[28]
40 'Why do you sigh, fair creature?' whispered he:
'Why do you think?' returned she tenderly:
'You have deserted me; – where am I now?
Not in your heart while care weighs on your brow:
No, no, you have dismissed me; and I go
From your breast houseless: aye, it must be so.'
He answered, bending to her open eyes,
Where he was mirrored small in paradise,
'My silver planet, both of eve and morn!
Why will you plead yourself so sad forlorn,
50 While I am striving how to fill my heart
With deeper crimson, and a double smart?
How to entangle, trammel up and snare
Your soul in mine, and labyrinth you there
Like the hid scent in an unbudded rose?
Aye, a sweet kiss – you see your mighty woes.
My thoughts! shall I unveil them? Listen then!
What mortal hath a prize, that other men
May be confounded and abashed withal,
But lets it sometimes pace abroad majestical,
60 And triumph, as in thee I should rejoice
Amid the hoarse alarm of Corinth's voice.

Let my foes choke, and my friends shout afar,
While through the thronged streets your bridal car
Wheels round its dazzling spokes.' – The lady's cheek
Trembled; she nothing said, but, pale and meek,
Arose and knelt before him, wept a rain
Of sorrows at his words; at last with pain
Beseeching him, the while his hand she wrung,
To change his purpose. He thereat was stung,
70 Perverse, with stronger fancy to reclaim
Her wild and timid nature to his aim:
Beside, for all his love, in self despite,
Against his better self, he took delight
Luxurious in her sorrows, soft and new.
His passion, cruel grown, took on a hue
Fierce and sanguineous as 'twas possible
In one whose brow had no dark veins to swell.
Fine was the mitigated fury, like
Apollo's presence when in act to strike
80 The serpent – Ha, the serpent! certes, she
Was none. She burnt, she loved the tyranny,
And, all subdued, consented to the hour
When to the bridal he should lead his paramour.
Whispering in midnight silence, said the youth,
'Sure some sweet name thou hast, though, by my truth,
I have not asked it, ever thinking thee
Not mortal, but of heavenly progeny,
As still I do. Hast any mortal name,
Fit appellation for this dazzling frame?
90 Or friends or kinsfolk on the citied earth,
To share our marriage feast and nuptial mirth?'
'I have no friends,' said Lamia, 'no, not one;
My presence in wide Corinth hardly known:
My parents' bones are in their dusty urns
Sepulchred, where no kindled incense burns,
Seeing all their luckless race are dead, save me,
And I neglect the holy rite for thee.
Even as you list invite your many guests;
But if, as now it seems, your vision rests
100 With any pleasure on me, do not bid
Old Apollonius – from him keep me hid.'
Lycius, perplexed at words so blind and blank,
Made close inquiry; from whose touch she shrank,
Feigning a sleep; and he to the dull shade
Of deep sleep in a moment was betrayed.

It was the custom then to bring away
The bride from home at blushing shut of day,
Veiled, in a chariot, heralded along
By strewn flowers, torches, and a marriage song,
110 With other pageants: but this fair unknown
Had not a friend. So being left alone,
(Lycius was gone to summon all his kin)
And knowing surely she could never win
His foolish heart from its mad pompousness,
She set herself, high-thoughted, how to dress
The misery in fit magnificence.
She did so, but 'tis doubtful how and whence
Came, and who were her subtle servitors.
About the halls, and to and from the doors,
120 There was a noise of wings till in short space
The glowing banquet-room shone with wide-arched grace.
A haunting music, sole perhaps and lone
Supportress of the faery-roof, made moan
Throughout, as fearful the whole charm might fade.
Fresh carved cedar, mimicking a glade
Of palm and plantain,° met from either side,   *(a tropical tree)*
High in the midst, in honour of the bride:
Two palms and then two plantains, and so on,
From either side their stems branched one to one
130 All down the aisled place; and beneath all
There ran a stream of lamps straight on from wall to wall.
So canopied, lay an untasted feast
Teeming with odours. Lamia, regal drest,
Silently paced about, and as she went,
In pale contented sort of discontent,
Missioned° her viewless servants to enrich   *commissioned*
The fretted° splendour of each nook and niche.   *decorated*
Between the tree-stems, marbled plain at first,
Came jasper° pannels; then anon, there burst   *(variety of quartz)*
140 Forth creeping imagery of slighter trees,
And with the larger wove in small intricacies.
Approving all, she faded at self-will,
And shut the chamber up, close, hushed and still,
Complete and ready for the revels rude,
When dreadful guests would come to spoil her solitude.

   The day appeared, and all the gossip rout.
O senseless Lycius! Madman! wherefore flout
The silent-blessing fate, warm cloistered hours,

And show to common eyes these secret bowers?
150 The herd approached; each guest, with busy brain,
Arriving at the portal, gazed amain,
And entered marveling: for they knew the street,
Remembered it from childhood all complete
Without a gap, yet ne'er before had seen
That royal porch, that high-built fair demesne;
So in they hurried all, mazed, curious and keen:
Save one, who looked thereon with eye severe,
And with calm-planted steps walked in austere;
'Twas Apollonius: something too he laughed,
160 As though some knotty problem, that had daft°   *troubled*
His patient thought, had now begun to thaw,
And solve and melt: — 'twas just as he foresaw.

He met within the murmurous vestibule
His young disciple. "'Tis no common rule,
Lycius,' said he, 'for uninvited guest
To force himself upon you, and infest
With an unbidden presence the bright throng
Of younger friends; yet must I do this wrong,
And you forgive me.' Lycius blushed, and led
170 The old man through the inner doors broad-spread;
With reconciling words and courteous mien
Turning into sweet milk the sophist's° spleen.°   *teacher of philosophy/*
                                                          ill-temper

Of wealthy lustre was the banquet-room,
Filled with pervading brilliance and perfume:
Before each lucid pannel fuming stood
A censer fed with myrrh and spiced wood,
Each by a sacred tripod held aloft,
Whose slender feet wide-swerved upon the soft
Wool-woofed carpets: fifty wreaths of smoke
180 From fifty censers their light voyage took
To the high roof, still mimicked as they rose
Along the mirrored walls by twin-clouds odorous.
Twelve sphered tables, by silk seats insphered,
High as the level of a man's breast reared
On libbard's° paws, upheld the heavy gold   *leopard's*
Of cups and goblets, and the store thrice told
Of Ceres' horn, and, in huge vessels, wine
Come from the gloomy tun° with merry shine.   *wine cask*
Thus loaded with a feast the tables stood,
190 Each shrining in the midst the image of a God.

When in an antichamber every guest
Had felt the cold full sponge to pleasure pressed,
By minist'ring slaves, upon his hands and feet,
And fragrant oils with ceremony meet
Poured on his hair, they all moved to the feast
In white robes, and themselves in order placed
Around the silken couches, wondering
Whence all this mighty cost and blaze of wealth could spring.

Soft went the music the soft air along,
200 While fluent Greek a voweled undersong
Kept up among the guests, discoursing low
At first, for scarcely was the wine at flow;
But when the happy vintage touched their brains,
Louder they talk, and louder come the strains
Of powerful instruments:– the gorgeous dyes,
The space, the splendour of the draperies,
The roof of awful richness, nectarous° cheer,   *of nectar*
Beautiful slaves, and Lamia's self, appear,
Now, when the wine has done its rosy deed,
210 And every soul from human trammels freed,
No more so strange; for merry wine, sweet wine,
Will make Elysian shades not too fair, too divine.
Soon was God Bacchus at meridian height;
Flushed were their cheeks, and bright eyes double bright:
Garlands of every green, and every scent
From vales deflowered, or forest-trees branch-rent,
In baskets of bright osiered gold were brought
High as the handles heaped, to suit the thought
Of every guest; that each, as he did please,
220 Might fancy-fit his brows, silk-pillowed at his ease.

What wreath for Lamia? What for Lycius?
What for the sage, old Apollonius?
Upon her aching forehead be there hung
The leaves of willow and of adder's tongue;
And for the youth, quick, let us strip for him
The thyrsus,° that his watching eyes may swim   *staff (= intoxication)*
Into forgetfulness; and, for the sage,
Let spear-grass and the spiteful thistle wage
War on his temples. Do not all charms fly
230 At the mere touch of cold philosophy?
There was an awful rainbow once in heaven:
We know her woof, her texture; she is given

In the dull catalogue of common things.
Philosophy will clip an Angel's wings,
Conquer all mysteries by rule and line,
Empty the haunted air, and gnomed° mine –   *worked by gnomes*
Unweave a rainbow, as it erewhile made
The tender-personed Lamia melt into a shade.

    By her glad Lycius sitting, in chief place,
240 Scarce saw in all the room another face,
Till, checking his love trance, a cup he took
Full brimmed, and opposite sent forth a look
'Cross the broad table, to beseech a glance
From his old teacher's wrinkled countenance,
And pledge him. The bald-head philosopher
Had fixed his eye, without a twinkle or stir
Full on the alarmed beauty of the bride,
Brow-beating her fair form, and troubling her sweet pride.
Lycius then pressed her hand, with devout touch,
250 As pale it lay upon the rosy couch:
'Twas icy, and the cold ran through his veins;
Then sudden it grew hot, and all the pains
Of an unnatural heat shot to his heart.
'Lamia, what means this? Wherefore dost thou start?
Know'st thou that man?' Poor Lamia answered not.
He gazed into her eyes, and not a jot
Owned they the lovelorn piteous appeal:
More, more he gazed: his human senses reel:
Some hungry spell that loveliness absorbs;
260 There was no recognition in those orbs.
'Lamia!' he cried – and no soft-toned reply.
The many heard, and the loud revelry
Grew hush; the stately music no more breathes;
The myrtle sickened in a thousand wreaths.
By faint degrees, voice, lute, and pleasure ceased;
A deadly silence step by step increased,
Until it seemed a horrid presence there,
And not a man but felt the terror in his hair.
'Lamia!' he shrieked; and nothing but the shriek
270 With its sad echo did the silence break.
'Begone, foul dream!' he cried, gazing again
In the bride's face, where now no azure vein
Wandered on fair-spaced temples; no soft bloom
Misted the cheek; no passion to illume
The deep-recessed vision: – all was blight;

Lamia, no longer fair, there sat a deadly white.
'Shut, shut those juggling° eyes, thou ruthless man! *manipulating*
Turn them aside, wretch! or the righteous ban
Of all the Gods, whose dreadful images
280 Here represent their shadowy presences,
May pierce them on the sudden with the thorn
Of painful blindness; leaving thee forlorn,
In trembling dotage to the feeblest fright
Of conscience, for their long offended might,
For all thine impious proud-heart sophistries,
Unlawful magic, and enticing lies.
Corinthians! look upon that grey-beard wretch!
Mark how, possessed, his lashless eyelids stretch
Around his demon eyes! Corinthians, see!
290 My sweet bride withers at their potency.'
'Fool!' said the sophist, in an under-tone
Gruff with contempt; which a death-nighing moan
From Lycius answered, as heart-struck and lost,
He sank supine beside the aching ghost.
'Fool! Fool!' repeated he, while his eyes still
Relented not, nor moved; 'from every ill
Of life have I preserved thee to this day,
And shall I see thee made a serpent's prey?'
Then Lamia breathed death breath; the sophist's eye,
300 Like a sharp spear, went through her utterly,
Keen, cruel, perceant,° stinging: she, as well *piercing*
As her weak hand could any meaning tell,
Motioned him to be silent; vainly so,
He looked and looked again a level – No!
'A Serpent!' echoed he; no sooner said,
Than with a frightful scream she vanished:
And Lycius' arms were empty of delight,
As were his limbs of life, from that same night.
On the high couch he lay! – his friends came round –
310 Supported him – no pulse, or breath they found,
And, in its marriage robe, the heavy body wound.

Sept. 1819 [1820]

This Living Hand[29]

This living hand, now warm and capable
Of earnest grasping, would, if it were cold
And in the icy silence of the tomb,
So haunt thy days and chill thy dreaming nights
That thou wouldst wish thine own heart dry of blood
So in my veins red life might stream again,
And thou be conscience-calmed – see here it is –
I hold it towards you.

1819/20 [1898]

Where Be Ye Going[30]

I

Where be ye going, you Devon Maid?
   And what have ye there in the Basket?
Ye tight little fairy just fresh from the dairy,
   Will ye give me some cream if I ask it?

II

I love your Meads, and I love your flowers,
   And I love your junkets° mainly,   *sweet dish of curds and whey*
But 'hind the door I love kissing more,
   O look not so disdainly.

III

I love your hills, and I love your dales,
   And I love your flocks a-bleating –
But O, on the heather to lie together,
   With both our hearts a-beating!

IV

I'll put your Basket all safe in a nook,
   Your shawl I hang up on the willow,
And we will sigh in the daisy's eye
And kiss on a grass green pillow.

1818 [1848]

Old Meg[31]

Old Meg she was a Gipsy,
  And lived upon the Moors:
Her bed it was the brown heath turf,
  And her house was out of doors.

Her apples were swart° blackberries,   *black*
  Her currants pods o' broom;
Her wine was dew of the wild white rose,
  Her book a churchyard tomb.

Her Brothers were the craggy hills,
10 Her Sisters larchen° trees –   *larch*
Alone with her great family
  She lived as she did please.

No breakfast had she many a morn,
  No dinner many a noon,
And 'stead of supper she would stare
  Full hard against the Moon.

But every morn of woodbine fresh
  She made her garlanding,
And every night the dark glen Yew
20 She wove, and she would sing.

And with her fingers old and brown
  She plaited Mats o' Rushes,
And gave them to the Cottagers
  She met among the Bushes.

Old Meg was brave as Margaret Queen[32]
  And tall as Amazon:
And old red blanket cloak she wore;
  A chip° hat had she on.   *made of wood fibre*
God rest her aged bones somewhere –
30 She died full long agone!

1818 [1848]

From *A Song About Myself* [33]

I

There was a naughty Boy,
  A naughty boy was he,
He would not stop at home,
  He could not quiet be –
    He took
    In his Knapsack
    A Book
    Full of vowels
    And a shirt
10   With some towels –
    A slight cap
    For night cap –
    A hair brush,
    Comb ditto,
    New Stockings
    For old ones
    Would split O!
    This Knapsack
    Tight at's back
20   He rivetted close
  And followed his Nose
    To the North,
    To the North,
  And follow'd his nose
    To the North.

IV

There was a naughty Boy,
  And a naughty Boy was he,
He ran away to Scotland
  The people for to see –
    Then he found
    That the ground
    Was as hard,
    That a yard
    Was as long,
10   That a song
    Was as merry,
    That a cherry
    Was as red –
    That lead

Was as weighty,
That fourscore
Was as eighty,
That a door
Was as wooden
20   As in England –
So he stood in his shoes
And he wonder'd,
He wonder'd,
He stood in his
Shoes and he wonder'd.

NOTES

Keats

1 possibly refers to the discovery of the planet Uranus, 30 March 1781.
2 it was Balboa who discovered the Pacific, 1513; was said to have been a stowaway on Cortes' expedition to Darien.
3 written in competition with Leigh Hunt who suggested the subject.
4 based on the Greek legend of the love of Cynthia, the moon, for Endymion, a shepherd boy.
5 an Æolian harp.
6 a lady K. met by chance in Vauxhall Gardens.
7 the Mermaid Tavern was the reputed haunt of Elizabethan poets and dramatists – Shakespeare, Jonson, etc.
8 the second generation of gods, the Titans, have been overthrown by the third, the Olympians. Saturn has lost his position to Jupiter: Hyperion has not yet lost his to Apollo, the god of the sun and poetry. The poem is unfinished because, according to K. 'There were too many Miltonic inversions in it.'
9 Thea, Hyperion's wife.
10 the academy of philosophy at Athens.
11 one for simple solemn music.
12 according to K. 'a sort of rondeau'.
13 St. Agnes' Eve was 20 Jan: Agnes was a 13th C. martyr and the saint of virgins. There was a legend that whosoever went to sleep after certain rituals on the eve of St. Agnes would dream of her future lover.
14 two lambs were shorn on St. Agnes' Day, their wool spun and woven by nuns to make an archbishop's cope.
15 to perform magic.
16 cf. letter to George and Georgiana Keats, 14 Feb.–3 May 1819.
17 cf. 'Kubla Khan' line 53.
18 see Keats' letter, no. 123, 14 Feb–3 May 1819, to Gregory and Georgiana Keats.

19 a purple dye came from Tyria.
20 K.'s brother, Tom, had died of tuberculosis, Dec. 1818.
21 Ruth. II.
22 the abrupt opening is because an earlier opening stanza was cancelled.
23 cf. letter to Reynolds, 21 Sept. 1819.
24 the marks like the 'eyes' of a peacock's tail.
25 a supernatural creature performing a penance.
26 tiara given to Ariadne by Bacchus, became a constellation.
27 with head thrust forward ready to strike.
28 bell which tolls for the dead.
29 written on a ms. page of K.'s last unfinished poem 'The Cap and Bells'.
30 from a letter to Haydon, 14 March 1818, Teignmouth. K. 'Here's some doggerel for you.'
31 in Keats' letter, no. 74 to Fanny Keats, 2-4 July 1818.
32 Queen Margaret, wife of Henry VI.
33 in the same letter as 'Old Meg'.

Alfred, Lord Tennyson

[1809–92]

Born Somersby, Lancashire: educated Trinity College, Cambridge, where he became acquainted with Arthur Hallam: won, 1829, the Chancellor's Prize for English Verse: 1827, *Poems by Two Brothers* published, with his brothers Charles and Frederick: 1830, *Poems Chiefly Lyrical*, unfavourably received: 1832 he visited the Continent with Hallam: 1833, Hallam died abroad and T. began his memorial poem for him – *In Memoriam. Poems*, 1833: 'Tithonus' written 1833 (pub. 1860): selections from the earlier volumes with revisions and new poems added, including 'Morte D'Arthur', 1842: 1845 T. received a civil list pension, £200 per annum. 1847, *The Princess* published and, 1850, *In Memoriam*, when he was appointed Poet Laureate. In 1850 m. Emily Sellwood, to whom he had been engaged for many years. They had one son, Hallam. By 1854 they were settled at Farringford, Isle of Wight and, in 1855, *Maud and Other Poems* published: 1859, the first four of *The Idylls of the King*. By this time he was very popular and continued publishing both volumes of poetry – *Enoch Arden*, 1864, *The Holy Grail and Other Poems*, 1870, *Gareth and Lynette*, 1872 – and plays. 1868, he built a new house at Haslemere, Surrey, and was made a peer in 1884. In his later years, his popularity waned, particularly with regard to his narrative and dramatic poetry, but as a lyricist he was – and is – regarded as a master. He is buried in Westminster Abbey and, in 1897, his son Hallam published *A Memoir*.

Mariana[1]

With blackest moss the flower-plots
  Were thickly crusted, one and all:
The rusted nails fell from the knots
  That held the pear to the gable-wall.
The broken sheds looked sad and strange:
  Unlifted was the clinking latch;
  Weeded and worn the ancient thatch
Upon the lonely moated grange.°   *country house*
  She only said, 'My life is dreary,

10   He cometh not,' she said;
            She said, 'I am aweary, aweary,
               I would that I were dead!'

Her tears fell with the dews at even;
     Her tears fell ere the dews were dried;
She could not look on the sweet heaven,
     Either at morn or eventide.
After the flitting of the bats,
     When thickest dark did trance° the sky,   *put into trance*
     She drew her casement-curtain by,
20 And glanced athwart° the glooming flats.   *across*
         She only said, 'The night is dreary,
            He cometh not,' she said;
         She said, 'I am aweary, aweary,
              I would that I were dead!'

Upon the middle of the night,
     Waking she heard the night-fowl crow:
The cock sung out an hour ere light:
     From the dark fen the oxen's low
Came to her: without hope of change,
30   In sleep she seemed to walk forlorn,
     Till cold winds woke the gray-eyed morn
About the lonely moated grange.
         She only said, 'The day is dreary,
            He cometh not,' she said;
         She said, 'I am aweary, aweary,
              I would that I were dead!'

About a stone-cast from the wall
     A sluice with blackened waters slept,
And o'er it many, round and small,
40   The clustered marish-mosses° crept.   *floating marsh-moss*
Hard by a poplar shook alway,
     All silver-green with gnarled bark:
     For leagues no other tree did mark
The level waste, the rounding gray.
         She only said, 'My life is dreary,
            He cometh not,' she said;
         She said, 'I am aweary, aweary,
              I would that I were dead!'

And ever when the moon was low,
50   And the shrill winds were up and away,
In the white curtain, to and fro,
    She saw the gusty shadow sway.
But when the moon was very low,
    And wild winds bound within their cell,
    The shadow of the poplar fell
Upon her bed, across her brow.
        She only said, 'The night is dreary,
            He cometh not,' she said;
        She said, 'I am aweary, aweary,
60   I would that I were dead!'

All day within the dreamy house,
    The doors upon their hinges creaked;
The blue fly sung in the pane; the mouse
    Behind the mouldering wainscot° shrieked,   *wood-panelling*
Or from the crevice peered about.
    Old faces glimmered through the doors,
    Old footsteps trod the upper floors,
Old voices called her from without.
        She only said, 'My life is dreary,
70   He cometh not,' she said;
        She said, 'I am aweary, aweary,
            I would that I were dead!'

The sparrow's chirrup on the roof,
    The slow clock ticking, and the sound
Which to the wooing wind aloof
    The poplar made, did all confound
Her sense; but most she loathed the hour
    When the thick-moted° sunbeam lay   *full of specks*
    Athwart the chambers, and the day
80 Was sloping toward his western bower.
        Then, said she, 'I am very dreary,
            He will not come,' she said;
        She wept, 'I am aweary, aweary,
            Oh God, that I were dead!'

[1830]

The Lotos-Eaters[2]

'Courage!' he said, and pointed toward the land,
'This mounting wave will roll us shoreward soon.'
In the afternoon they came unto a land
In which it seemed always afternoon.
All round the coast the languid air did swoon,
Breathing like one that hath a weary dream.
Full-faced above the valley stood the moon;
And like a downward smoke, the slender stream
Along the cliff to fall and pause and fall did seem.

10   A land of streams! some, like a downward smoke,
Slow-dropping veils of thinnest lawn,[3] did go;
And some through wavering lights and shadows broke,
Rolling a slumbrous sheet of foam below.
They saw the gleaming river seaward flow
From the inner land: far off, three mountain-tops,
Three silent pinnacles of aged snow,
Stood sunset-flushed: and, dewed with showery drops,
Up-clomb the shadowy pine above the woven copse.

The charmed sunset lingered low adown
20   In the red West: through mountain clefts the dale
Was seen far inland, and the yellow down
Bordered with palm, and many a winding vale
And meadow, set with slender galingale;°   *aromatic plant*
A land where all things always seemed the same!
And round about the keel with faces pale,
Dark faces pale against that rosy flame,
The mild-eyed melancholy Lotos-eaters came.

Branches they bore of that enchanted stem,
Laden with flower and fruit, whereof they gave
30   To each, but whoso did receive of them,
And taste, to him the gushing of the wave
Far far away did seem to mourn and rave
On alien shores; and if his fellow spake,
His voice was thin, as voices from the grave;
And deep-asleep he seemed, yet all awake,
And music in his ears his beating heart did make.

They sat them down upon the yellow sand,
Between the sun and moon upon the shore;

And sweet it was to dream of Fatherland,
40 Of child, and wife, and slave; but evermore
Most weary seemed the sea, weary the oar,
Weary the wandering fields of barren foam.
Then some one said, 'We will return no more;'
And all at once they sang, 'Our island home°   (Ithaca)
Is far beyond the wave; we will no longer roam.'

CHORIC SONG

I

There is sweet music here that softer falls
Than petals from blown roses on the grass,
Or night-dews on still waters between walls
Of shadowy granite, in a gleaming pass;
50 Music that gentlier on the spirit lies,
Than tired eyelids upon tired eyes;
Music that brings sweet sleep down from the blissful skies.
Here are cool mosses deep,
And through the moss the ivies creep,
And in the stream the long-leaved flowers weep,
And from the craggy ledge the poppy hangs in sleep.

II

Why are we weighed upon with heaviness,
And utterly consumed with sharp distress,
While all things else have rest from weariness?
60 All things have rest: why should we toil alone,
We only toil, who are the first of things,
And make perpetual moan,
Still from one sorrow to another thrown:
Nor ever fold our wings,
And cease from wanderings,
Nor steep our brows in slumber's holy balm;
Nor harken what the inner spirit sings,
'There is no joy but calm!'
Why should we only toil, the roof and crown of things?

III

70 Lo! in the middle of the wood,
The folded leaf is wooed from out the bud
With winds upon the branch, and there
Grows green and broad, and takes no care,
Sun-steeped at noon, and in the moon

Nightly dew-fed; and turning yellow
Falls, and floats adown the air.
Lo! sweetened with the summer light,
The full-juiced apple, waxing over-mellow,
Drops in a silent autumn night.
80 All its allotted length of days,
The flower ripens in its place,
Ripens and fades, and falls, and hath no toil,
Fast-rooted in the fruitful soil.

IV

Hateful is the dark blue sky,
Vaulted o'er the dark blue sea.
Death is the end of life; ah, why,
Should life all labour be?
Let us alone. Time driveth onward fast,
And in a little while our lips are dumb.
90 Let us alone. What is it that will last?
All things are taken from us, and become
Portions and parcels of the dreadful Past.
Let us alone. What pleasure can we have
To war with evil? Is there any peace
In ever climbing up the climbing wave?
All things have rest, and ripen toward the grave
In silence; ripen or fall and cease:
Give us long rest or death, dark death, or dreamful ease.

V

How sweet it were, hearing the downward stream,
100 With half-shut eyes ever to seem
Falling asleep in a half-dream!
To dream and dream, like yonder amber light,
Which will not leave the myrrh-bush on the height;
To hear each other's whispered speech;
Eating the Lotos day by day,
To watch the crisping ripples on the beach,
And tender curving lines of creamy spray;
To lend our hearts and spirits wholly
To the influence of mild-minded melancholy;
110 To muse and brood and live again in memory,
With those old faces of our infancy
Heaped over with a mound of grass,
Two handfuls of white dust, shut in an urn of brass!

VI

Dear is the memory of our wedded lives,
And dear the last embraces of our wives
And their warm tears: but all hath suffered change:
For surely now our household hearths are cold:
Our sons inherit us: our looks are strange:
And we should come like ghosts to trouble joy.
120 Or else the island princes over-bold
Have eat our substance, and the minstrel sings
Before them of the ten years' war in Troy,
And our great deeds, as half-forgotten things.
Is there confusion in the little isle?
Let what is broken so remain.
The Gods are hard to reconcile:
'Tis hard to settle order once again.
There *is* confusion worse than death,
Trouble on trouble, pain on pain,
130 Long labour unto aged breath,
Sore task to hearts worn out by many wars
And eyes grown dim with gazing on the pilot-stars.°   *used to steer boats by*

VII

But, propt on beds of amaranth° and moly,⁴   *unfading flower*
How sweet (while warm airs lull us, blowing lowly)
With half-dropt eyelid still,
Beneath a heaven dark and holy,
To watch the long bright river drawing slowly
His waters from the purple hill –
To hear the dewy echoes calling
140 From cave to cave through the thick-twined vine –
To watch the emerald-coloured water falling
Through many a woven acanthus-wreath divine!
Only to hear and see the far-off sparkling brine,
Only to hear were sweet, stretched out beneath the pine.

VIII

The Lotos blooms below the barren peak:
The Lotos blows by every winding creek:
All day the wind breathes low with mellower tone:
Through every hollow cave and alley lone
Round and round the spicy downs the yellow Lotus-dust is blown.
150 We have had enough of action, and of motion we,
Rolled to starboard, rolled to larboard,
                    when the surge was seething free,

Where the wallowing monster spouted his foam-fountains in the sea.
Let us swear an oath, and keep it with an equal mind,
In the hollow Lotos-land to live and lie reclined
On the hills like Gods together, careless of mankind.
For they lie beside their nectar, and the bolts are hurled
Far below them in the valleys, and the clouds are lightly curled
160 Round their golden houses, girdled with the gleaming world:
Where they smile in secret, looking over wasted lands,
Blight and famine, plague and earthquake,
                    roaring deeps and fiery sands,
Clanging fights, and flaming towns, and sinking ships,
                    and praying hands.
But they smile, they find a music centred in a doleful song
Steaming up, a lamentation and an ancient tale of wrong,
Like a tale of little meaning though the words are strong,
Chanted from an ill-used race of men that cleave the soil,
170 Sow the seed, and reap the harvest with enduring toil,
Storing yearly little dues of wheat, and wine and oil;
Till they perish and they suffer – some, 'tis whispered
                    – down in hell
Suffer endless anguish, others in Elysian valleys dwell,
Resting weary limbs at last on beds of asphodel.
Surely, surely, slumber is more sweet than toil, the shore
Than labour in the deep mid-ocean, wind and wave and oar;
Oh rest ye, brother mariners, we will not wander more.

                                         1830–2 [1832]

The Lady of Shalott[5]

PART I

On either side the river lie
Long fields of barley and of rye,
That clothe the wold° and meet the sky;   *open countryside*
And through the field the road runs by
    To many-towered Camelot;
And up and down the people go,
Gazing where the lilies blow
Round an island there below,
    The island of Shalott.

10 Willows whiten,[6] aspens° quiver,   *type of poplar tree*
    Little breezes dusk and shiver
    Through the wave that runs for ever
    By the island in the river
        Flowing down to Camelot.
    Four gray walls, and four gray towers,
    Overlook a space of flowers,
    And the silent isle imbowers
        The Lady of Shalott.

    By the margin, willow-veiled,
20 Slide the heavy barges trailed
    By slow horses; and unhailed
    The shallop° flitteth silken-sailed   *small open boat*
        Skimming down to Camelot:
    But who hath seen her wave her hand?
    Or at the casement seen her stand?
    Or is she known in all the land,
        The Lady of Shalott?

    Only reapers, reaping early
    In among the bearded barley,
30 Hear a song that echoes cheerly
    From the river winding clearly,
        Down to towered Camelot:
    And by the moon the reaper weary,
    Piling sheaves in uplands airy,
    Listening, whispers "Tis the fairy
        Lady of Shalott.'

PART II

    There she weaves by night and day
    A magic web with colours gay.
    She has heard a whisper say,
40 A curse is on her if she stay°   *i.e. stops weaving*
        To look down to Camelot.
    She knows not what the curse may be,
    And so she weaveth steadily,
    And little other care hath she,
        The Lady of Shalott.

And moving through a mirror clear
That hangs before her all the year,
Shadows of the world appear.
There she sees the highway near
50   Winding down to Camelot:
There the river eddy whirls,
And there the surly village-churls,
And the red cloaks of market girls,
      Pass onward from Shalott.

Sometimes a troop of damsels glad,
An abbot on an ambling pad;°   *horse*
Sometimes a curly shepherd-lad,
Or long-haired page in crimson clad,
      Goes by to towered Camelot;
60 And sometimes through the mirror blue
The knights come riding two and two:
She hath no loyal knight and true,
      The Lady of Shalott.

But in her web she still delights
To weave the mirror's magic sights,
For often through the silent nights
A funeral, with plumes and lights
      And music, went to Camelot:
Or when the moon was overhead,
70 Came two young lovers lately wed;
'I am half sick of shadows,' said
      The Lady of Shalott.

PART III

A bow-shot[7] from her bower-eaves,
He rode between the barley-sheaves,
The sun came dazzling through the leaves,
And flamed upon the brazen greaves°   *shin-armour*
      Of bold Sir Lancelot.
A red-cross knight for ever kneeled
To a lady in his shield,
80 That sparkled on the yellow field,
      Beside remote Shalott.

The gemmy° bridle glittered free,   *decorated with gems*
Like to some branch of stars we see
Hung in the golden Galaxy.
The bridle bells rang merrily
        As he rode down to Camelot:
And from his blazoned baldric° slung   *shoulder-sash*
A mighty silver bugle hung,
And as he rode his armour rung,
90   Beside remote Shalott.

All in the blue unclouded weather
Thick-jewelled shone the saddle-leather,
The helmet and the helmet-feather
Burned like one burning flame together,
        As he rode down to Camelot.
As often through the purple night,
Below the starry clusters bright,
Some bearded meteor, trailing light,
        Moves over still Shalott.

100 His broad clear brow in sunlight glowed;
On burnished hooves his war-horse trode;
From underneath his helmet flowed
His coal-black curls as on he rode,
        As he rode down to Camelot.
From the bank and from the river
He flashed into the crystal mirror,
'Tirra lirra,' by the river
        Sang Sir Lancelot.

She left the web, she left the loom,
110 She made three paces through the room,
She saw the water-lily bloom,
She saw the helmet and the plume,
        She looked down to Camelot.
Out flew the web and floated wide;
The mirror cracked from side to side;
'The curse is come upon me,' cried
        The Lady of Shalott.

PART IV

In the stormy east-wind straining,
The pale yellow woods were waning,
120 The broad stream in his banks complaining.
Heavily the low sky raining
    Over towered Camelot;
Down she came and found a boat
Beneath a willow left afloat,
And round about the prow she wrote
    The Lady of Shalott.

And down the river's dim expanse
Like some bold seër in a trance,
Seeing all his own mischance –
130 With a glassy countenance
    Did she look to Camelot.
And at the closing of the day
She loosed the chain, and down she lay;
The broad stream bore her far away,
    The Lady of Shalott.

Lying, robed in snowy white
That loosely flew to left and right –
The leaves upon her falling light –
Through the noises of the night
140   She floated down to Camelot:
And as the boat-head wound along
The willowy hills and fields among,
They heard her singing her last song,
    The Lady of Shalott.

Heard a carol, mournful, holy,
Chanted loudly, chanted lowly,
Till her blood was frozen slowly,
And her eyes were darkened wholly,
    Turned to towered Camelot.
150 For ere she reached upon the tide
The first house by the water-side,
Singing in her song she died,
    The Lady of Shalott.

Under tower and balcony,
By garden-wall and gallery,

A gleaming shape she floated by,
Dead-pale between the houses high,
        Silent into Camelot.
Out upon the wharfs they came,
160 Knight and burgher, lord and dame,
And round the prow they read her name,
        The Lady of Shalott.

Who is this? and what is here?
And in the lighted palace near
Died the sound of royal cheer;
And they crossed themselves for fear,
        All the knights at Camelot:
But Lancelot mused a little space;
He said, 'She has a lovely face;
170 God in his mercy lend her grace,
        The Lady of Shalott.'

May 1832 [1832: rev. 1842]

Ulysses[8]

It little profits that an idle king,
By this still hearth, among these barren crags,
Matched with an aged wife,° I mete and dole   *Penelope*
Unequal[9] laws unto a savage race,
That hoard, and sleep, and feed, and know not me.
I cannot rest from travel: I will drink
Life to the lees: all times I have enjoyed
Greatly, have suffered greatly, both with those
That loved me, and alone; on shore, and when
10 Through scudding drifts the rainy Hyades
Vext the dim sea: I am become a name;
For always roaming with a hungry heart
Much have I seen and known; cities of men
And manners, climates, councils, governments,
Myself not least, but honoured of them all;
And drunk delight of battle with my peers,
Far on the ringing plains of windy Troy.
I am a part of all that I have met;
Yet all experience is an arch wherethrough

20 Gleams that untravelled world, whose margin fades
For ever and for ever when I move.
How dull it is to pause, to make an end,
To rust unburnished, not to shine in use!
As though to breathe were life. Life piled on life
Were all too little, and of one to me
Little remains: but every hour is saved
From that eternal silence, something more,
A bringer of new things; and vile it were
For some three suns to store and hoard myself,
30 And this gray spirit yearning in desire
To follow knowledge like a sinking star,
Beyond the utmost bound of human thought.

This is my son, mine own Telemachus,
To whom I leave the sceptre and the isle –
Well-loved of me, discerning to fulfil
This labour, by slow prudence to make mild
A rugged people, and through soft degrees
Subdue them to the useful and the good.
Most blameless is he, centred in the sphere
40 Of common duties, decent not to fail
In offices of tenderness, and pay
Meet adoration to my household gods,
When I am gone. He works his work, I mine.

There lies the port; the vessel puffs her sail:
There gloom the dark broad seas. My mariners,
Souls that have toiled, and wrought, and thought with me –
That ever with a frolic welcome took
The thunder and the sunshine, and opposed
Free hearts, free foreheads – you and I are old;
50 Old age hath yet his honour and his toil;
Death closes all: but something ere the end,
Some work of noble note, may yet be done,
Not unbecoming men that strove with Gods.
The lights begin to twinkle from the rocks:
The long day wanes: the slow moon climbs: the deep
Moans round with many voices. Come, my friends,
'Tis not too late to seek a newer world.
Push off, and sitting well in order smite
The sounding furrows; for my purpose holds
60 To sail beyond the sunset, and the baths
Of all the western stars, until I die.
It may be that the gulfs will wash us down:

It may be we shall touch the Happy Isles,
And see the great Achilles, whom we knew.
Though much is taken, much abides; and though
We are not now that strength which in old days
Moved heaven and earth, that which we are, we are —
One equal temper of heroic hearts,
Made weak by time and fate, but strong in will
70   To strive, to seek, to find, and not to yield.

20 Oct. 1833 [1842]

Break, break, break

Break, break, break,
  On thy cold gray stones, O Sea!
And I would that my tongue could utter
  The thoughts that arise in me.

O well for the fisherman's boy,
  That he shouts with his sister at play!
O well for the sailor lad,
  That he sings in his boat on the bay!

And the stately ships go on
  To their haven under the hill;
But O for the touch of a vanish'd hand
  And the sound of a voice that is still!

Break, Break, Break,
  At the foot of thy crags, O Sea!
But the tender grace of a day that is dead
  Will never come back to me.

?1834 [1842]

From *The Princess*

SONGS

Sweet and low, sweet and low,
    Wind of the western sea,
Low, low, breathe and blow,
    Wind of the western sea!
Over the rolling waters go,
Come from the dying moon, and blow,
    Blow him again to me;
While my little one, while my pretty one, sleeps.

Sleep and rest, sleep and rest,
    Father will come to thee soon;
Rest, rest, on mother's breast,
    Father will come to thee soon;
Father will come to his babe in the nest,
Silver sails all out of the west
    Under the silver moon:
Sleep, my little one, sleep, my pretty one, sleep.

1849 [added 1850]

The splendour falls on castle walls[10]
    And snowy summits old in story:
The long light shakes across the lakes,
    And the wild cataract leaps in glory.
Blow, bugle, blow, set the wild echoes flying,
Blow, bugle; answer, echoes, dying, dying, dying.

O hark, O hear! how thin and clear,
    And thinner, clearer, farther going!
O sweet and far from cliff and scar
    The horns of Elfland faintly blowing!
Blow, let us hear the purple glens replying:
Blow, bugle; answer, echoes, dying, dying, dying.

O love, they die in yon rich sky,
    They faint on hill or field or river:
Our echoes roll from soul to soul,
    And grow for ever and for ever.

Blow, bugle, blow, set the wild echoes flying,
And answer, echoes, answer, dying, dying, dying.

[added 1850]

'Now sleeps the crimson petal, now the white;
Nor waves the cypress in the palace walk;
Nor winks the gold fin in the porphyry° font: *reddish-purple stone*
The fire-fly wakens: waken thou with me.

Now droops the milkwhite peacock like a ghost,
And like a ghost she glimmers on to me.

Now lies the Earth all Danaë to the stars,
And all thy heart lies open unto me.

Now slides the silent meteor on, and leaves
10   A shining furrow, as thy thoughts in me.

Now folds the lily all her sweetness up,
And slips into the bosom of the lake:
So fold thyself, my dearest, thou, and slip
Into my bosom and be lost in me.'

[1847]

From **In Memoriam A.H.H.**[11]

7

Dark house,[12] by which once more I stand
   Here in the long unlovely street,
   Doors, where my heart was used to beat
So quickly, waiting for a hand,

A hand that can be clasped no more –
   Behold me, for I cannot sleep,
   And like a guilty thing I creep
At earliest morning to the door.

He is not here; but far away
10   The noise of life begins again,
      And ghastly through the drizzling rain
On the bald street breaks the blank day.

11

Calm is the morn without a sound,
      Calm as to suit a calmer grief,
      And only through the faded leaf
The chestnut pattering to the ground:

Calm and deep peace on this high wold,
      And on these dews that drench the furze,
      And all the silvery gossamers
That twinkle into green and gold:

Calm and still light on yon great plain
10   That sweeps with all its autumn bowers,
      And crowded farms and lessening towers,
To mingle with the bounding main:

Calm and deep peace in this wide air,
      These leaves that redden to the fall;
      And in my heart, if calm at all,
If any calm, a calm despair:

Calm on the seas, and silver sleep,
      And waves that sway themselves in rest,
      And dead calm in that noble breast
20 Which heaves but with the heaving deep.

14

If one should bring me this report,
      That thou hadst touched the land to-day
      And I went down unto the quay,
And found thee lying in the port;

And standing, muffled round with woe,
      Should see thy passengers in rank
      Come stepping lightly down the plank,
And beckoning unto those they know;

And if along with thee should come
10   The man I held as half-divine,
     Should strike a sudden hand in mine,
And ask a thousand things of home;

And I should tell him all my pain,
     And how my life had drooped of late,
     And he should sorrow o'er my state
And marvel what possessed my brain;

And I perceived no touch of change,
     No hint of death in all his frame,
     But found him all in all the same,
I should not feel it to be strange.

27

I envy not in any moods
     The captive void of noble rage,
     The linnet born within the cage,
That never knew the summer woods:

I envy not the beast that takes
     His license in the field of time,
     Unfettered by the sense of crime,
To whom a conscience never wakes;

Nor, what may count itself as blest,
10   The heart that never plighted troth
     But stagnates in the weeds of sloth;
Nor any want-begotten rest.

I hold it true, whate'er befall;
     I feel it, when I sorrow most;
     'Tis better to have loved and lost
Than never to have loved at all.

28

The time draws near the birth of Christ:
     The moon is hid; the night is still;
     The Christmas bells from hill to hill
Answer each other in the mist.

Four voices of four hamlets round,
 From far and near, on mead and moor,
 Swell out and fail, as if a door
Were shut between me and the sound:

Each voice four[13] changes on the wind,
₁₀ That now dilate, and now decrease,
 Peace and goodwill, goodwill and peace,
Peace and goodwill, to all mankind.

This year I slept and woke with pain,
 I almost wished no more to wake,
 And that my hold on life would break
Before I heard those bells again:

But they my troubled spirit rule,
 For they controlled me when a boy;
 They bring me sorrow touched with joy,
₂₀ The merry merry bells of Yule.

30

With trembling fingers did we weave
 The holly round the Christmas hearth;
 A rainy cloud possessed the earth,
And sadly fell our Christmas-eve.

At our old pastimes in the hall
 We gambolled, making vain pretence
 Of gladness, with an awful sense
Of one mute Shadow° watching all.   *Hallam*

We paused: the winds were in the beech:
₁₀ We heard them sweep the winter land;
 And in a circle hand-in-hand
Sat silent, looking each at each.

Then echo-like our voices rang;
 We sung, though every eye was dim,
 A merry song we sang with him
Last year: impetuously we sang:

We ceased: a gentler feeling crept
   Upon us: surely rest is meet:
'They rest,' we said, 'their sleep is sweet,'
20 And silence followed, and we wept.

Our voices took a higher range;
   Once more we sang: 'They do not die
   Nor lose their mortal sympathy,
Nor change to us, although they change;

Rapt° from the fickle and the frail   *taken from*
   With gathered power, yet the same,
   Pierces the keen seraphic flame
From orb to orb, from veil to veil.'

Rise, happy morn, rise, holy morn,
30   Draw forth the cheerful day from night:
   O Father, touch the east, and light
The light that shone when Hope was born.

31

When Lazarus left his charnel-cave,[14]
   And home to Mary's house returned,
   Was this demanded – if he yearned
To hear her weeping by his grave?

'Where wert thou, brother, those four days?'
   There lives no record of reply,
   Which telling what it is to die
Had surely added praise to praise.

From every house the neighbours met,
10   The streets were filled with joyful sound,
   A solemn gladness even crowned
The purple brows of Olivet.

Behold a man raised up by Christ!
   The rest remaineth unrevealed;
   He told it not: or something sealed
The lips of that Evangelist.

34

My own dim life should teach me this,
　　That life shall live for evermore,
　　Else earth is darkness at the core,
And dust and ashes all that is;

This round of green, this orb of flame,
　　Fantastic beauty; such as lurks
　　In some wild Poet, when he works
Without a conscience or an aim.

What then were God to such as I?
10　　'Twere hardly worth my while to choose
　　Of things all mortal, or to use
A little patience ere I die;

'Twere best at once to sink to peace,
　　Like birds the charming serpent draws,
　　To drop head-foremost in the jaws
Of vacant darkness and to cease.

54

O, yet we trust that somehow good
　　Will be the final goal of ill,
　　To pangs of nature, sins of will,
Defects of doubt, and taints of blood;

That nothing walks with aimless feet;
　　That not one life shall be destroyed,
　　Or cast as rubbish to the void,
When God hath made the pile complete;

That not a worm is cloven in vain;
10　　That not a moth with vain desire
　　Is shrivelled in a fruitless fire,
Or but subserves another's gain.

Behold, we know not anything;
　　I can but trust that good shall fall
　　At last – far off – at last, to all,
And every winter change to spring.

So runs my dream; but what am I?
  An infant crying in the night;
  An infant crying for the light,
20 And with no language but a cry.

       55
The wish, that of the living whole
  No life may fail beyond the grave,
  Derives it not from what we have
The likest God within the soul?

Are God and Nature then at strife,
  That Nature lends such evil dreams?
  So careful of the type she seems,
So careless of the single life,

That I, considering everywhere
  Her secret meaning in her deeds,
  And finding that of fifty seeds
She often brings but one to bear,

I falter where I firmly trod,
  And falling with my weight of cares
  Upon the great world's altar-stairs
That slope thro' darkness up to God,

I stretch lame hands of faith, and grope,
  And gather dust and chaff, and call
  To what I feel is Lord of all,
And faintly trust the larger hope.

      56[15]
'So careful of the type?' but no.
  From scarped° cliff and quarried stone   *cut away*
  She° cries, 'A thousand types are gone;   *Nature*
I care for nothing, all shall go.

Thou makest thine appeal to me:
  I bring to life, I bring to death;
  The spirit does but mean the breath:
I know no more.' And he, shall he,

Man, her last work, who seemed so fair,
10   Such splendid purpose in his eyes,
     Who rolled the psalm to wintry skies,
Who built him fanes° of fruitless prayer,   *temples*

Who trusted God was love indeed
     And love Creation's final law —
     Tho' Nature, red in tooth and claw
With ravine, shrieked against his creed —

Who loved, who suffered countless ills,
     Who battled for the True, the Just,
     Be blown about the desert dust,
20 Or sealed within the iron hills?

No more? A monster then, a dream,
     A discord. Dragons of the prime,
     That tare each other in their slime,
Were mellow music matched with him.

O life as futile, then, as frail!
     O for thy voice to soothe and bless!
     What hope of answer, or redress?
Behind the veil, behind the veil.

57

Peace; come away: the song of woe
     Is after all an earthly song.
     Peace; come away: we do him wrong
To sing so wildly: let us go.

Come; let us go: your cheeks are pale;
     But half my life I leave behind.
     Methinks my friend is richly shrined;
But I shall pass, my work will fail.

Yet in these ears, till hearing dies,
10   One set slow bell will seem to toll
     The passing of the sweetest soul
That ever looked with human eyes.

I hear it now, and o'er and o'er,
   Eternal greetings to the dead;
   And 'Ave, Ave, Ave,' said,
'Adieu, adieu' for evermore.

91

When rosy plumelets tuft the larch,
   And rarely pipes the mounted thrush;
   Or underneath the barren bush
Flits by the sea-blue bird° of March;   *kingfisher*

Come, wear the form by which I know
   Thy spirit in time among thy peers;
   The hope of unaccomplished years
Be large and lucid round thy brow.

When summer's hourly-mellowing change
10   May breathe, with many roses sweet,
   Upon the thousand waves of wheat,
That ripple round the lonely grange;

Come: not in watches of the night,
   But where the sunbeam broodeth warm,
   Come, beauteous in thine after form
And like a finer light in light.

95

By night we lingered on the lawn,
   For underfoot the herb was dry;
   And genial warmth; and o'er the sky
The silvery haze of summer drawn;

And calm that let the tapers burn
   Unwavering: not a cricket chirred:
   The brook alone far-off was heard,
And on the board the fluttering urn:°   *tea urn*

And bats went round in fragrant skies,
10   And wheeled or lit the filmy shapes
   That haunt the dusk, with ermine° capes   *ermine moths*
And woolly breasts and beaded eyes;

While now we sang old songs that pealed
      From knoll to knoll, where, couched° at ease,   *lie down*
      The white kine° glimmered, and the trees   *cattle*
Laid their dark arms about the field.

But when those others, one by one,
      Withdrew themselves from me and night,
      And in the house light after light
20 Went out, and I was all alone,

A hunger seized my heart; I read
      Of that glad year which once had been,
      In those fallen leaves which kept their green,
The noble letters of the dead:

And strangely on the silence broke
      The silent-speaking words, and strange
      Was love's dumb cry defying change
To test his worth; and strangely spoke

The faith, the vigour, bold to dwell
30   On doubts that drive the coward back,
      And keen through wordy snares to track
Suggestion to her inmost cell.

So word by word, and line by line,
      The dead man touched me from the past,
      And all at once it seemed at last
The living soul was flashed on mine,

And mine in this was wound, and whirled
      About empyreal heights of thought,
      And came on that which is, and caught
40 The deep pulsations of the world,

Æonian° music measuring out   *everlasting*
      The steps of Time – the shocks of Chance –
      The blows of Death. At length my trance
Was cancelled, stricken through with doubt.

Vague words! but ah, how hard to frame
      In matter-moulded forms of speech,
      Or even for intellect to reach
Through memory that which I became:

Till now the doubtful dusk revealed
50   The knolls once more where, couched at ease,
      The white kine glimmered, and the trees
Laid their dark arms about the field:

And sucked from out the distant gloom
      A breeze began to tremble o'er
      The large leaves of the sycamore,
And fluctuate all the still perfume,

And gathering freshlier overhead,
      Rocked the full-foliaged elms, and swung
      The heavy-folded rose, and flung
60   The lilies to and fro, and said

'The dawn, the dawn,' and died away;
      And East and West, without a breath,
      Mixt their dim lights, like life and death,
To broaden into boundless day.

100[16]

I climb the hill: from end to end
      Of all the landscape underneath,
      I find no place that does not breathe
Some gracious memory of my friend;

No gray old grange, or lonely fold,
      Or low morass and whispering reed,
      Or simple stile from mead to mead,
Or sheepwalk up the windy wold;

Nor hoary knoll of ash and haw°   *hawthorn*
10   That hears the latest linnet trill,
      Nor quarry trenched along the hill
And haunted by the wrangling daw;°   *jackdaw*

Nor runlet tinkling from the rock;
      Nor pastoral rivulet that swerves
      To left and right through meadowy curves,
That feed the mothers of the flock;

But each has pleased a kindred eye,
      And each reflects a kindlier day;
      And, leaving these, to pass away,
20   I think once more he seems to die.

101

Unwatched, the garden bough shall sway,
  The tender blossom flutter down,
  Unloved, that beech will gather brown,
This maple burn itself away;

Unloved, the sun-flower, shining fair,
  Ray round with flames her disk of seed,
  And many a rose-carnation feed
With summer spice the humming air;

Unloved, by many a sandy bar,
10 The brook shall babble down the plain,
  At noon or when the lesser wain°   *haywain (constellation)*
Is twisting round the polar star;

Uncared for, gird° the windy grove,   *encircle*
  And flood the haunts of hern° and crake;°   *heron/corncrake*
  Or into silver arrows break
The sailing moon in creek and cove;

Till from the garden and the wild
  A fresh association blow,
  And year by year the landscape grow
20 Familiar to the stranger's child;

As year by year the labourer tills
  His wonted glebe,° or lops° the glades;   *cultivated land/cuts back*
  And year by year our memory fades
From all the circle of the hills.

102

We leave the well-beloved place
  Where first we gazed upon the sky;
  The roofs, that heard our earliest cry,
Will shelter one of stranger race.

We go, but ere we go from home,
  As down the garden-walks I move,
  Two spirits of a diverse love
Contend for loving masterdom.

One whispers, 'Here thy boyhood sung
10   Long since its matin song, and heard
    The low love-language of the bird
In native hazels tassel-hung."   *(with catkins)*

The other answers, 'Yea, but here
    Thy feet have strayed in after hours
    With thy lost friend among the bowers,
And this hath made them trebly dear.'

These two have striven half the day,
    And each prefers his separate claim,
    Poor rivals in a losing game,
20 That will not yield each other way.

I turn to go: my feet are set
    To leave the pleasant fields and farms;
    They mix in one another's arms
To one pure image of regret.

105[17]

Tonight ungathered let us leave
    This laurel, let this holly stand:
    We live within the stranger's land,
And strangely falls our Christmas-eve.

Our father's dust is left alone[18]
    And silent under other snows:
    There in due time the woodbine blows,
The violet comes, but we are gone.

No more shall wayward grief abuse
10   The genial hour with mask and mime;
    For change of place, like growth of time,
Has broke the bond of dying use.

Let cares that petty shadows cast,
    By which our lives are chiefly proved,
    A little spare the night I loved,
And hold it solemn to the past.

But let no footstep beat the floor,
    Nor bowl of wassail° mantle° warm;   *spiced wine/foam*
    For who would keep an ancient form
20 Through which the spirit breathes no more?

Be neither song, nor game, nor feast;
    Nor harp be touched, nor flute be blown;
    No dance, no motion, save alone
What lightens in the lucid east

Of rising worlds by yonder wood.
    Long sleeps the summer in the seed;
    Run out your measured arcs, and lead
The closing cycle rich in good.

106

Ring out, wild bells, to the wild sky,
    The flying cloud, the frosty light:
    The year is dying in the night;
Ring out, wild bells, and let him die.

Ring out the old, ring in the new,
    Ring, happy bells, across the snow:
    The year is going, let him go;
Ring out the false, ring in the true.

Ring out the grief that saps the mind,
10   For those that here we see no more;
    Ring out the feud of rich and poor,
Ring in redress to all mankind.

Ring out a slowly dying cause,
    And ancient forms of party strife;
    Ring in the nobler modes of life,
With sweeter manners, purer laws.

Ring out the want, the care, the sin,
    The faithless coldness of the times;
    Ring out, ring out my mournful rhymes,
20 But ring the fuller minstrel in.

Ring out false pride in place and blood,
  The civic slander and the spite;
  Ring in the love of truth and right,
Ring in the common love of good.

Ring out old shapes of foul disease;
  Ring out the narrowing lust of gold;
  Ring out the thousand wars of old,
Ring in the thousand years of peace.

Ring in the valiant man and free,
₃₀ The larger heart, the kindlier hand;
  Ring out the darkness of the land,
Ring in the Christ that is to be.

107

It is the day when he was born,[19]
  A bitter day that early sank
  Behind a purple-frosty bank
Of vapour, leaving night forlorn.

The time admits not flowers or leaves
  To deck the banquet. Fiercely flies
  The blast of North and East, and ice
Makes daggers at the sharpened eaves,

And bristles all the brakes and thorns
₁₀ To yon hard crescent, as she hangs
  Above the wood which grides° and clangs   *rubs together*
Its leafless ribs and iron horns

Together, in the drifts that pass[20]
  To darken on the rolling brine
  That breaks the coast. But fetch the wine,
Arrange the board and brim the glass;

Bring in great logs and let them lie,
  To make a solid core of heat;
  Be cheerful-minded, talk and treat
₂₀Of all things even as he were by;

We keep the day. With festal cheer,
  With books and music, surely we
  Will drink to him, whate'er he be,
And sing the songs he loved to hear.

108

I will not shut me from my kind,
  And, lest I stiffen into stone,
  I will not eat my heart alone,
Nor feed with sighs a passing wind:

What profit lies in barren faith,
  And vacant yearning, though with might
  To scale the heaven's highest height,
Or dive below the wells of Death?

What find I in the highest place,
10 But mine own phantom chanting hymns?
  And on the depths of death there swims
The reflex of a human face.

I'll rather take what fruit may be
  Of sorrow under human skies:
  'Tis held that sorrow makes us wise,
Whatever wisdom sleep with thee.

115

Now fades the last long streak of snow,
  Now burgeons every maze of quick°   *living things*
  About the flowering squares, and thick
By ashen roots the violets blow.

Now rings the woodland loud and long,
  The distance takes a lovelier hue,
  And drowned in yonder living blue
The lark becomes a sightless song.

Now dance the lights on lawn and lea,
10 The flocks are whiter down the vale,
  The milkier every milky sail
On winding stream or distant sea;

Where now the seamew pipes, or dives
  In yonder greening gleam, and fly
  The happy birds, that change their sky
To build and brood; that live their lives

From land to land; and in my breast
  Spring wakens too; and my regret
  Becomes an April violet,
20 And buds and blossoms like the rest.

116

Is it, then, regret for buried time
  That keenlier in sweet April wakes,
  And meets the year, and gives and takes
The colours of the crescent prime°?   *growing spring (T.)*

Not all: the songs, the stirring air,
  The life re-orient out of dust,
  Cry through the sense to hearten trust
In that which made the world so fair.

Not all regret: the face will shine
10   Upon me, while I muse alone;
  And that dear voice, I once have known,
Still speak to me of me and mine:

Yet less of sorrow lives in me
  For days of happy commune dead;
  Less yearning for the friendship fled,
Than some strong bond which is to be.

119

Doors, where my heart was used to beat
  So quickly, not as one that weeps
  I come once more; the city sleeps;
I smell the meadow in the street;

I hear a chirp of birds; I see
  Betwixt the black fronts long-withdrawn
  A light-blue lane of early dawn,
And think of early days and thee,

And bless thee, for thy lips are bland,
10   And bright the friendship of thine eye;
     And in my thoughts with scarce a sigh
I take the pressure of thine hand.

120

I trust I have not wasted breath:
    I think we are not wholly brain,
    Magnetic mockeries; not in vain,
Like Paul with beasts, I fought with Death;

Not only cunning casts in clay:
    Let Science prove we are, and then
    What matters Science unto men,
At least to me? I would not stay.

Let him, the wiser man who springs
10   Hereafter, up from childhood shape
     His action like the greater ape,
But I was *born* to other things.

124

That which we dare invoke to bless;
    Our dearest faith; our ghastliest doubt;
    He, They, One, All; within, without;
The Power in darkness whom we guess;

I found Him not in world or sun,
    Or eagle's wing, or insect's eye;
    Nor through the questions men may try,
The petty cobwebs we have spun:

If e'er when faith had fallen asleep,
10   I heard a voice 'believe no more'
     And heard an ever-breaking shore
That tumbled in the Godless deep;

A warmth within the breast would melt
    The freezing reason's colder part,
    And like a man in wrath the heart
Stood up and answered 'I have felt.'

No, like a child in doubt and fear:
  But that blind clamour made me wise;
  Then was I as a child that cries,
20 But, crying, knows his father near;

And what I am beheld again
  What is, and no man understands;
  And out of darkness came the hands
That reach through nature, moulding men.

129

Dear friend, far off, my lost desire
  So far, so near in woe and weal;
  O loved the most, when most I feel
There is a lower and a higher;

Known and unknown; human, divine;
  Sweet human hand and lips and eye;
  Dear heavenly friend that canst not die,
Mine, mine, for ever, ever mine;

Strange friend, past, present, and to be;
10 Loved deeplier, darklier understood;
  Behold, I dream a dream of good,
And mingle all the world with thee.

130

Thy voice is on the rolling air;
  I hear thee where the waters run;
  Thou standest in the rising sun,
And in the setting thou art fair.

What art thou then? I cannot guess;
  But though I seem in star and flower
  To feel thee some diffusive power,
I do not therefore love thee less:

My love involves the love before;
10 My love is vaster passion now;
  Though mixed with God and Nature thou,
I seem to love thee more and more.

Far off thou art, but ever nigh;
  I have thee still, and I rejoice;
  I prosper, circled with thy voice;
I shall not lose thee though I die.

1834–1850 [1850]

The Eagle
FRAGMENT

He clasps the crag with crooked hands;
Close to the sun in lonely lands,
Ringed with the azure world, he stands.

The wrinkled sea beneath him crawls;
He watches from his mountain walls,
And like a thunderbolt he falls.

by Oct. 1849 [1851]

The Charge of the Light Brigade[21]

I
Half a league, half a league,
  Half a league onward,
All in the valley of Death
  Rode the six hundred.
'Forward, the Light Brigade!
Charge for the guns!' he said:
Into the valley of Death
  Rode the six hundred.

II
'Forward, the Light Brigade!'
10 Was there a man dismayed?
Not though the soldier knew

Some one had blundered:
Their's not to make reply,
Their's not to reason why,
Their's but to do and die:
Into the valley of Death
   Rode the six hundred.

III
   Cannon to right of them,
   Cannon to left of them,
20 Cannon in front of them
     Volleyed and thundered;
Stormed at with shot and shell,
Boldly they rode and well,
Into the jaws of Death,
Into the mouth of Hell
   Rode the six hundred.

IV
Flashed all their sabres bare,
Flashed as they turned in air
Sabring the gunners there,
30 Charging an army, while
     All the world wondered:
Plunged in the battery-smoke
Right through the line they broke;
Cossack and Russian
Reeled from the sabre-stroke
   Shattered and sundered.
Then they rode back, but not
   Not the six hundred.

V
   Cannon to right of them,
40 Cannon to left of them,
Cannon behind them
     Volleyed and thundered;
Stormed at with shot and shell,
While horse and hero fell,
They that had fought so well
Came through the jaws of Death,
Back from the mouth of Hell,
All that was left of them,[22]
   Left of six hundred.

VI

50 When can their glory fade?
O the wild charge they made!
  All the world wondered.
Honour the charge they made!
Honour the Light Brigade,
  Noble six hundred!

2 Dec. 1854 [9 Dec. 1854]

From *The Brook*

I come from haunts of coot° and hern°   *(small water bird)|heron*
  I make a sudden sally,
And sparkle out among the fern,
  To bicker down a valley.

By thirty hills I hurry down,
  Or slip between the ridges,
By twenty thorps°, a little town,   *small villages*
  And half a hundred bridges.

Till last by Philip's farm I flow
10   To join the brimming river,
For men may come and men may go,
  But I go on for ever.

I chatter over stony ways,
  In little sharps and trebles,
I bubble into eddying bays,
  I babble on the pebbles.

With many a curve my banks I fret
  By many a field and fallow,
And many a fairy foreland set
20   With willow-weed and mallow°.   *(marsh plant)*

I chatter, chatter, as I flow
  To join the brimming river,
For men may come and men may go,
  But I go on for ever.

1854 [1855]

From *Maud: A Monodrama*

14

Maud has a garden of roses
And lilies fair on a lawn;
There she walks in her state
And tends upon bed and bower,
And thither I climbed at dawn
And stood by her garden-gate;
A lion ramps at the top,
He is claspt by a passion-flower.

Maud's own little oak-room
10 (Which Maud, like a precious stone
Set in the heart of the carven gloom,
Lights with herself, when alone
She sits by her music and books
And her brother lingers late
With a roystering company) looks
Upon Maud's own garden-gate:
And I thought as I stood, if a hand, as white
As ocean-foam in the moon, were laid
On the hasp of the window, and my Delight
20 Had a sudden desire, like a glorious ghost, to glide,
Like a beam of the seventh Heaven, down to my side,
There were but a step to be made.

The fancy flattered my mind,
And again seemed overbold;
Now I thought that she cared for me,
Now I thought she was kind
Only because she was cold.

I heard no sound where I stood
But the rivulet on from the lawn
30 Running down to my own dark wood;
Or the voice of the long sea-wave as it swelled
Now and then in the dim-gray dawn;
But I looked, and round, all round the house I beheld
The death-white curtain drawn;
Felt a horror over me creep,
Prickle my skin and catch my breath,
Knew that the death-white curtain meant but sleep,
Yet I shuddered and thought like a fool of the sleep of death.

22

Come into the garden, Maud,
  For the black bat, night, has flown,
Come into the garden, Maud,
  I am here at the gate alone;
And the woodbine spices are wafted abroad,
  And the musk of the rose is blown.

For a breeze of morning moves,
  And the planet of Love is on high,
Beginning to faint in the light that she loves
10 On a bed of daffodil sky,
To faint in the light of the sun she loves,
  To faint in his light and to die.

All night have the roses heard
  The flute, violin, bassoon;
All night has the casement jessamine stirred
  To the dancers dancing in tune;
Till a silence fell with the waking bird,
  And a hush with the setting moon.

I said to the lily, 'There is but one,
20 With whom she has heart to be gay.
When will the dancers leave her alone?
  She is weary of dance and play.'
Now half to the setting moon are gone,
  And half to the rising day;
Low on the sand and loud on the stone
  The last wheel echoes away.[23]

I said to the rose, 'The brief night goes
  In babble and revel and wine.
O young lord-lover, what sighs are those,
30 For one that will never be thine?
But mine, but mine,' so I sware to the rose,
  'For ever and ever, mine.'

And the soul of the rose went into my blood,
  As the music clashed in the hall;
And long by the garden lake I stood,
  For I heard your rivulet fall
From the lake to the meadow and on to the wood,
  Our wood, that is dearer than all;

From the meadow your walks have left so sweet
40   That whenever a March-wind sighs
He sets the jewel-print of your feet
    In violets blue as your eyes,
To the woody hollows in which we meet
    And the valleys of Paradise.

The slender acacia would not shake
    One long milk-bloom on the tree;
That white lake-blossom fell into the lake
    As the pimpernel dozed on the lea;
But the rose was awake all night for your sake,
50   Knowing your promise to me;
The lilies and roses were all awake,
    They sighed for the dawn and thee.

Queen rose of the rosebud garden of girls,
    Come hither, the dancers are done,
In gloss of satin and glimmer of pearls,
    Queen lily and rose in one;
Shine out, little head, sunning over with curls,
    To the flowers, and be their sun.

There has fallen a splendid tear
60   From the passion-flower at the gate.
She is coming, my dove, my dear;
    She is coming, my life, my fate.
The red rose cries, 'She is near, she is near;'
    And the white rose weeps, 'She is late;'
And the larkspur listens, 'I hear, I hear;'
    And the lily whispers, 'I wait.'

She is coming, my own, my sweet;
    Were it ever so airy a tread,
My heart would hear her and beat,
70   Were it earth in an earthy bed;
My dust would hear her and beat,
    Had I lain for a century dead,
Would start and tremble under her feet,
    And blossom in purple and red.

1854–5 [1855]

The Passing of Arthur[24]

That story which the bold Sir Bedivere,
First made and latest left of all the knights,
Told, when the man was no more than a voice
In the white winter of his age, to those
With whom he dwelt, new faces, other minds.

For on their march to westward, Bedivere,
Who slowly paced among the slumbering host,
Heard in his tent the moanings of the King:

'I found Him in the shining of the stars,
10 I marked Him in the flowering of His fields,
But in His ways with men I find Him not.
I waged His wars, and now I pass and die.
O me! for why is all around us here
As if some lesser god had made the world,
But had not force to shape it as he would,
Till the High God behold it from beyond,
And enter it, and make it beautiful?
Or else as if the world were wholly fair,
But that these eyes of men are dense and dim,
20 And have not power to see it as it is:
Perchance, because we see not to the close; —
For I, being simple, thought to work His will,
And have but stricken with the sword in vain;
And all whereon I leaned in wife[25] and friend
Is traitor to my peace, and all my realm
Reels back into the beast,° and is no more.   *anarchy*
My God, thou hast forgotten me in my death:
Nay — God my Christ — I pass but shall not die.'

Then, ere that last weird battle in the west,
30 There came on Arthur sleeping, Gawain killed
In Lancelot's war, the ghost of Gawain blown
Along a wandering wind, and past his ear
Went shrilling, 'Hollow, hollow all delight!
Hail, King! tomorrow thou shalt pass away.
Farewell! there is an isle of rest for thee.
And I am blown along a wandering wind,
And hollow, hollow, hollow all delight.'
And fainter onward, like wild birds that change

Their season in the night and wail their way
40 From cloud to cloud, down the long wind the dream
Shrilled; but in going mingled with dim cries
Far in the moonlight haze among the hills,
As of some lonely city sacked by night,
When all is lost, and wife and child with wail
Pass to new lords; and Arthur woke and called,
'Who spake? A dream. O light upon the wind,
Thine, Gawain, was the voice – are these dim cries
Thine? or doth all that haunts the waste and wild
Mourn, knowing it will go along with me?'

50   This heard the bold Sir Bedivere and spake:
'O me, my King, let pass whatever will,
Elves, and the harmless glamour of the field;
But in their stead thy name and glory cling
To all high places like a golden cloud
For ever: but as yet thou shalt not pass.
Light was Gawain in life, and light in death
Is Gawain, for the ghost is as the man;
And care not thou for dreams from him, but rise –
I hear the steps of Modred in the west,
60 And with him many of thy people, and knights
Once thine, whom thou hast loved, but grosser grown
Than heathen, spitting at their vows and thee.
Right well in heart they know thee for the King.
Arise, go forth and conquer as of old.'

    Then spake King Arthur to Sir Bedivere:
'Far other is this battle in the west
Whereto we move, than when we strove in youth,
And brake the petty kings, and fought with Rome,
Or thrust the heathen from the Roman wall,
70 And shook him through the north. Ill doom is mine
To war against my people and my knights.
The king who fights his people fights himself.
And they my knights, who loved me once, the stroke
That strikes them dead is as my death to me.
Yet let us hence, and find or feel a way
Through this blind haze, which ever since I saw
One lying in the dust at Almesbury,
Hath folded in the passes of the world.'

Then rose the King and moved his host by night,
80 And ever pushed Sir Modred, league by league,
Back to the sunset bound of Lyonnesse –
A land of old upheaven from the abyss
By fire, to sink into the abyss again;
Where fragments of forgotten peoples dwelt,
And the long mountains ended in a coast
Of ever-shifting sand, and far away
The phantom circle of a moaning sea.
There the pursuer could pursue no more,
And he that fled no further fly the King;
90 And there, that day when the great light of heaven
Burned at his lowest in the rolling year,
On the waste sand by the waste sea they closed.
Nor ever yet had Arthur fought a fight
Like this last, dim, weird battle of the west.
A deathwhite mist slept over sand and sea:
Whereof the chill, to him who breathed it, drew
Down with his blood, till all his heart was cold
With formless fear; and even on Arthur fell
Confusion, since he saw not whom he fought.
100 For friend and foe were shadows in the mist,
And friend slew friend not knowing whom he slew;
And some had visions out of golden youth,
And some beheld the faces of old ghosts
Look in upon the battle; and in the mist
Was many a noble deed, many a base,
And chance and craft and strength in single fights,
And ever and anon with host to host
Shocks, and the splintering spear, the hard mail hewn,
Shield-breakings, and the clash of brands, the crash
110 Of battleaxes on shattered helms, and shrieks
After the Christ, of those who falling down
Looked up to heaven, and only saw the mist;
And shouts of heathen and the traitor knights,
Oaths, insult, filth, and monstrous blasphemies,
Sweat, writhings, anguish, labouring of the lungs
In that close mist, and cryings for the light,
Moans of the dying, and voices of the dead.

Last, as by some one deathbed after wail
Of suffering, silence follows, or through death
120 Or deathlike swoon, thus over all that shore,
Save for some whisper of the seething seas,

A dead hush fell; but when the dolorous day
Grew drearier toward twilight falling, came
A bitter wind, clear from the North, and blew
The mist aside, and with that wind the tide
Rose, and the pale King glanced across the field
Of battle: but no man was moving there;
Nor any cry of Christian heard thereon,
Nor yet of heathen; only the wan wave
130 Brake in among dead faces, to and fro
Swaying the helpless hands, and up and down
Tumbling the hollow helmets of the fallen,
And shivered brands that once had fought with Rome,
And rolling far along the gloomy shores
The voice of days of old and days to be.

Then spake King Arthur to Sir Bedivere,
And whiter than the mist that all day long
Had held the field of battle was the King:

'Hearest thou this great voice that shakes the world,
140 And wastes the narrow realm whereon we move,
And beats upon the faces of the dead,
My dead, as though they had not died for me? –
O Bedivere, for on my heart hath fallen
Confusion, till I know not what I am,
Nor whence I am, nor whether I be King.
Behold, I seem but King among the dead.'

Then spake the bold Sir Bedivere: 'My King,
King everywhere! and so the dead have kings,
There also will I worship thee as King.
150 Yet still thy life is whole, and still I live
Who love thee; but who hates thee, he that brought
The heathen back among us, yonder stands,
Modred, unharmed, the traitor of thine house.'

Then spake the King: 'My house hath been my doom.
But call not thou this traitor of my house
Who hath but dwelt beneath one roof with me.
My house are rather they who sware my vows,
Yea, even while they brake them, owned me King.
And well for thee, saying in my dark hour,
160 When all the purport of my throne hath failed,
That quick or dead thou holdest me for King.
King am I, whatsoever be their cry;

And one last act of kinghood shalt thou see
Yet, ere I pass.' And uttering this the King
Made at the man: then Modred smote his liege
Hard on that helm which many a heathen sword
Had beaten thin; while Arthur at one blow,
Striking the last stroke with Excalibur,   *(Arthur's sword)*
Slew him, and all but slain himself, he fell.

170   So all day long the noise of battle rolled
Among the mountains by the winter sea;
Until King Arthur's Table, man by man,
Had fallen in Lyonnesse about their lord,
King Arthur. Then, because his wound was deep,
The bold Sir Bedivere uplifted him,
And bore him to a chapel nigh the field,
A broken chancel with a broken cross,
That stood on a dark strait of barren land:
On one side lay the Ocean, and on one
180   Lay a great water, and the moon was full.

Then spake King Arthur to Sir Bedivere:
'The sequel of today unsolders° all   *breaks apart*
The goodliest fellowship of famous knights
Whereof this world holds record. Such a sleep
They sleep – the men I loved. I think that we
Shall never more, at any future time,
Delight our souls with talk of knightly deeds,
Walking about the gardens and the halls
Of Camelot, as in the days that were.
190   I perish by this people which I made, –
Though Merlin sware that I should come again
To rule once more; but, let what will be, be,
I am so deeply smitten through the helm
That without help I cannot last till morn.
Thou therefore take my brand Excalibur,
Which was my pride: for thou rememberest how
In those old days, one summer noon, an arm
Rose up from out the bosom of the lake,
Clothed in white samite,° mystic, wonderful,   *silk*
200   Holding the sword – and how I rowed across
And took it, and have worn it, like a king;
And, wheresoever I am sung or told
In aftertime, this also shall be known:
But now delay not: take Excalibur,

And fling him far into the middle mere:°   *lake*
Watch what thou seëst, and lightly° bring me word.'   *quickly*

   To him replied the bold Sir Bedivere:
'It is not meet, Sir King, to leave thee thus,
Aidless, alone, and smitten through the helm –
210 A little thing may harm a wounded man;
Yet I thy hest° will all perform at full,   *command*
Watch what I see, and lightly bring thee word.'

   So saying, from the ruined shrine he stept,
And in the moon athwart the place of tombs,
Where lay the mighty bones of ancient men,
Old knights, and over them the sea-wind sang
Shrill, chill, with flakes of foam. He, stepping down
By zigzag paths, and juts of pointed rock,
Came on the shining levels of the lake.

220   There drew he forth the brand Excalibur,
And o'er him, drawing it, the winter moon,
Brightening the skirts of a long cloud, ran forth
And sparkled keen with frost against the hilt:
For all the haft twinkled with diamond sparks,
Myriads of topaz-lights, and jacinth-work
Of subtlest jewellery. He gazed so long
That both his eyes were dazzled as he stood,
This way and that dividing the swift mind,
In act to throw: but at the last it seemed
230 Better to leave Excalibur concealed
There in the many-knotted waterflags,°   *(iris-like flowers)*
That whistled stiff and dry about the marge.
So strode he back slow to the wounded King.

   Then spake King Arthur to Sir Bedivere:
'Hast thou performed my mission which I gave?
What is it thou hast seen? or what hast heard?'

   And answer made the bold Sir Bedivere:
'I heard the ripple washing in the reeds,
And the wild water lapping on the crag.'

240   To whom replied King Arthur, faint and pale:
'Thou hast betrayed thy nature and thy name,
Not rendering true answer, as beseemed

Thy fëalty,° nor like a noble knight: *oath of obedience*
For surer sign had followed, either hand,
Or voice, or else a motion of the mere.
This is a shameful thing for men to lie.
Yet now, I charge thee, quickly go again,
As thou art lief° and dear, and do the thing   *beloved*
I bade thee, watch, and lightly bring me word.'

250   Then went Sir Bedivere the second time
Across the ridge, and paced beside the mere,
Counting the dewy pebbles, fixed in thought;
But when he saw the wonder of the hilt,
How curiously and strangely chased,° he smote   *engraved*
His palms together, and he cried aloud:

'And if indeed I cast the brand away,
Surely a precious thing, one worthy note,
Should thus be lost for ever from the earth,
Which might have pleased the eyes of many men.
260   What good should follow this, if this were done?
What harm, undone? Deep harm to disobey,
Seeing obedience is the bond of rule.
Were it well to obey then, if a king demand
An act unprofitable, against himself?
The King is sick, and knows not what he does.
What record, or what relic of my lord
Should be to aftertime, but empty breath
And rumours of a doubt? But were this kept,
Stored in some treasure-house of mighty kings,
270   Some one might show it at a joust of arms,
Saying, "King Arthur's sword, Excalibur,
Wrought by the lonely maiden of the Lake.
Nine years she wrought it, sitting in the deeps
Upon the hidden bases of the hills."
So might some old man speak in the aftertime
To all the people, winning reverence.
But now much honour and much fame were lost.'

So spake he, clouded with his own conceit,
And hid Excalibur the second time,
280   And so strode back slow to the wounded King.

Then spoke King Arthur, breathing heavily:
'What is it thou hast seen? or what hast heard?'

And answer made the bold Sir Bedivere:
'I heard the water lapping on the crag,
And the long ripple washing in the reeds.'

To whom replied King Arthur, much in wrath:
'Ah, miserable and unkind, untrue,
Unknightly, traitor-hearted! Woe is me!
Authority forgets a dying king,
290 Laid widowed of the power in his eye
That bowed the will. I see thee what thou art,
For thou, the latest-left of all my knights,
In whom should meet the offices of all,
Thou wouldst betray me for the precious hilt;
Either from lust of gold, or like a girl
Valuing the giddy pleasure of the eyes.
Yet, for a man may fail in duty twice,
And the third time may prosper, get thee hence:
But, if thou spare to fling Excalibur,
300 I will arise and slay thee with my hands.'

Then quickly rose Sir Bedivere, and ran,
And, leaping down the ridges lightly, plunged
Among the bulrush beds, and clutched the sword,
And strongly wheeled and threw it. The great brand
Made lightnings in the splendour of the moon,
And flashing round and round, and whirled in an arch,
Shot like a streamer° of the northern morn,   *the Northern Lights*
Seen where the moving isles° of winter shock   *icebergs*
By night, with noises of the Northern Sea.
310 So flashed and fell the brand Excalibur:
But ere he dipt the surface, rose an arm
Clothed in white samite, mystic, wonderful,
And caught him by the hilt, and brandished him
Three times, and drew him under in the mere.
And lightly went the other to the King.

Then spoke King Arthur, drawing thicker breath:
'Now see I by thine eyes that this is done.
Speak out: what is it thou hast heard, or seen?'

And answer made the bold Sir Bedivere:
320 'Sir King, I closed mine eyelids, lest the gems
Should blind my purpose, for I never saw,
Nor shall see, here or elsewhere, till I die,

Not though I live three lives of mortal men,
So great a miracle as yonder hilt.
Then with both hands I flung him, wheeling him;
But when I looked again, behold an arm,
Clothed in white samite, mystic, wonderful,
That caught him by the hilt, and brandished him
Three times, and drew him under in the mere.'

330   And answer made King Arthur, breathing hard:
'My end draws nigh; 'tis time that I were gone.
Make broad thy shoulders to receive my weight,
And bear me to the margin; yet I fear
My wound hath taken cold, and I shall die.'

So saying, from the pavement he half rose,
Slowly, with pain, reclining on his arm,
And looking wistfully with wide blue eyes
As in a picture. Him Sir Bedivere
Remorsefully regarded through his tears,
340 And would have spoken, but he found not words;
Then took with care, and kneeling on one knee,
O'er both his shoulders drew the languid hands,
And rising bore him through the place of tombs.

But, as he walked, King Arthur panted hard,
Like one that feels a nightmare on his bed
When all the house is mute. So sighed the King,
Muttering and murmuring at his ear, 'Quick, quick!
I fear it is too late, and I shall die.'
But the other swiftly strode from ridge to ridge,
350 Clothed with his breath, and looking, as he walked,
Larger than human on the frozen hills.
He heard the deep behind him, and a cry
Before. His own thought drove him like a goad.
Dry° clashed his harness in the icy caves   *harsh*
And barren chasms, and all to left and right
The bare black cliff clanged round him, as he based
His feet on juts of slippery crag that rang
Sharp-smitten with the dint° of armed heels –   *blow*
And on a sudden, lo! the level lake,
360 And the long glories of the winter moon.

Then saw they how there hove a dusky barge,
Dark as a funeral scarf from stem to stern,
Beneath them; and descending they were ware
That all the decks were dense with stately forms,
Black-stoled, black-hooded, like a dream – by these
Three Queens[26] with crowns of gold: and from them rose
A cry that shivered to the tingling stars,
And, as it were one voice, an agony
Of lamentation, like a wind that shrills
370 All night in a waste land, where no one comes,
Or hath come, since the making of the world.

Then murmured Arthur, 'Place me in the barge.'
So to the barge they came. There those three Queens
Put forth their hands, and took the King, and wept.
But she, that rose the tallest of them all
And fairest, laid his head upon her lap,
And loosed the shattered casque,° and chafed his hands,   *helmet*
And called him by his name, complaining loud,
And dropping bitter tears against a brow
380 Striped with dark blood: for all his face was white
And colourless, and like the withered moon
Smote by the fresh beam of the springing east;
And all his greaves and cuisses° dashed with drops[27]   *thigh armour*
Of onset; and the light and lustrous curls –
That made his forehead like a rising sun
High from the daïs-throne – were parched with dust;
Or, clotted into points and hanging loose,
Mixed with the knightly growth that fringed his lips.
So like a shattered column lay the King;
390 Not like that Arthur who, with lance in rest,
From spur to plume a star of tournament,
Shot through the lists at Camelot, and charged
Before the eyes of ladies and of kings.

Then loudly cried the bold Sir Bedivere:
'Ah! my Lord Arthur, whither shall I go?
Where shall I hide my forehead and my eyes?
For now I see the true old times are dead,
When every morning brought a noble chance,
And every chance brought out a noble knight.
400 Such times have been not since the light that led
The holy Elders° with the gift of myrrh.   *(the Three Wise Men)*
But now the whole Round Table is dissolved

Which was an image of the mighty world,
And I, the last, go forth companionless,
And the days darken round me, and the years,
Among new men, strange faces, other minds.'

 And slowly answered Arthur from the barge:
'The old order changeth, yielding place to new,
And God fulfils himself in many ways,
410 Lest one good custom should corrupt the world.
Comfort thyself: what comfort is in me?
I have lived my life, and that which I have done
May He within himself make pure! but thou,
If thou shouldst never see my face again,
Pray for my soul. More things are wrought by prayer
Than this world dreams of. Wherefore, let thy voice
Rise like a fountain for me night and day.
For what are men better than sheep or goats
That nourish a blind life within the brain,
420 If, knowing God, they lift not hands of prayer
Both for themselves and those who call them friend?
For so the whole round earth is every way
Bound by gold chains about the feet of God.
But now farewell. I am going a long way
With these thou seëst – if indeed I go
(For all my mind is clouded with a doubt) –
To the island-valley of Avilion;[28]
Where falls not hail, or rain, or any snow,
Nor ever wind blows loudly; but it lies
430 Deep-meadowed, happy, fair with orchard lawns
And bowery hollows crowned with summer sea,
Where I will heal me of my grievous wound.'

 So said he, and the barge with oar and sail
Moved from the brink, like some full-breasted swan
That, fluting a wild carol ere her death,
Ruffles her pure cold plume, and takes the flood
With swarthy webs. Long stood Sir Bedivere
Revolving many memories, till the hull
Looked one black dot against the verge of dawn,
440 And on the mere the wailing died away.

 But when that moan had past for evermore,
The stillness of the dead world's winter dawn
Amazed him, and he groaned, 'The King is gone.'

And therewithal came on him the weird rhyme,
'From the great deep to the great deep he goes.'

Whereat he slowly turned and slowly clomb°   *climbed*
The last hard footstep of that iron crag;
Thence marked the black hull moving yet, and cried,
'He passes to be King among the dead,
450 And after healing of his grievous wound
He comes again; but – if he come no more –
O me, be yon dark Queens in yon black boat,
Who shrieked and wailed, the three whereat we gazed
On that high day, when, clothed with living light,
They stood before his throne in silence, friends
Of Arthur, who should help him at his need?'

Then from the dawn it seemed there came, but faint
As from beyond the limit of the world,
Like the last echo born of a great cry,
460 Sounds, as if some fair city were one voice
Around a king returning from his wars.

Thereat once more he moved about, and clomb
Even to the highest he could climb, and saw,
Straining his eyes beneath an arch of hand,
Or thought he saw, the speck that bare the King,
Down that long water opening on the deep
Somewhere far off, pass on and on, and go
From less to less and vanish into light.
And the new sun rose bringing the new year.

1869 [1869]

Merlin and the Gleam[29]

I

O young Mariner,
You from the haven
Under the sea-cliff,
You that are watching
The gray Magician
With eyes of wonder,

I am Merlin,
And *I* am dying,
I am Merlin
10   Who follow The Gleam.

II
Mighty the Wizard[30]
Who found me at sunrise
Sleeping, and woke me
And learned me Magic!
Great the Master,
And sweet the Magic,
When over the valley,
In early summers,
Over the mountain,
20   On human faces,
And all around me,
Moving to melody,
Floated The Gleam.

III
Once at the croak of a Raven[31] who crost it,
A barbarous people,
Blind to the magic,
And deaf to the melody,
Snarled at and cursed me.
A demon vext me,
30   The light retreated,
The landskip darkened,
The melody deadened,
The Master whispered
'Follow The Gleam.'

IV
Then to the melody,
Over a wilderness
Gliding, and glancing at
Elf of the woodland,
Gnome of the cavern,
40   Griffin and Giant,
And dancing of Fairies
In desolate hollows,
And wraiths of the mountain,
And rolling of dragons

By warble of water,
Or cataract music
Of falling torrents,
Flitted The Gleam.

V

Down from the mountain
50 And over the level,
And streaming and shining on
Silent river,
Silvery willow,
Pasture and plowland,
Innocent maidens,
Garrulous children,
Homestead and harvest,
Reaper and gleaner,
And rough-ruddy faces
60 Of lowly labour,
Slided The Gleam –

VI

Then, with a melody
Stronger and statelier,
Led me at length
To the city and palace
Of Arthur the king;
Touched at the golden
Cross of the churches,
Flashed on the Tournament,
70 Flickered and bickered
From helmet to helmet,
And last on the forehead
Of Arthur the blameless
Rested The Gleam.

VII

Clouds and darkness
Closed upon Camelot;
Arthur had vanished
I knew not whither,
The king who loved me,
80 And cannot die;
For out of the darkness
Silent and slowly

The Gleam, that had waned to a wintry glimmer
On icy fallow
And faded forest,
Drew to the valley
Named of the shadow,
And slowly brightening
Out of the glimmer,
90 And slowly moving again to a melody
Yearningly tender,
Fell on the shadow,
No longer a shadow,
But clothed with The Gleam.

VIII

And broader and brighter
The Gleam flying onward,
Wed to the melody,
Sang through the world;
And slower and fainter,
100 Old and weary,
But eager to follow,
I saw, whenever
In passing it glanced upon
Hamlet or city,
That under the Crosses
The dead man's garden,
The mortal hillock,
Would break into blossom;
And so to the land's
110 Last limit I came –
And can no longer,
But die rejoicing,
For through the Magic
Of Him the Mighty,
Who taught me in childhood,
There on the border
Of boundless Ocean,
And all but in Heaven
Hovers The Gleam.

IX

120 Not of the sunlight,
Not of the moonlight,
Not of the starlight!

O young Mariner,
Down to the haven,
Call your companions,
Launch your vessel,
And crowd your canvas,
And, ere it vanishes
Over the margin,
130 After it, follow it,
Follow The Gleam.

Aug. 1889 [1889]

Crossing the Bar[32]

Sunset and evening star,
    And one clear call for me!
And may there be no moaning of the bar,
    When I put out to sea,

But such a tide as moving seems asleep,
    Too full for sound and foam,
When that which drew from out the boundless deep
    Turns again home.

Twilight and evening bell,
10   And after that the dark!
And may there be no moaning of the bar,
    When I embark;

For tho' from out our bourne of Time and Place
    The flood may bear me far,
I hope to see my Pilot face to face
    When I have crost the bar.

Aug. 1889 [1889]

NOTES

Tennyson

1   cf. Shakespeare, *Measure for Measure*, III.212 ff.
2   source of story – *Odyssey*, IX.82–104.
3   fine linen or cotton, often used in 19th C. theatres to represent waterfalls.
4   magic herb given to Odysseus to ward off Circe's charms.
5   T. 'taken from an Italian novelette. The Lady of Shalott is evidently Lady Elaine of Morte D'Arthur but I do not think I had heard of the latter when I wrote the former. Shalott was a softer sound than Scalott.' cf. Malory XVIII.
6   the underside of willow leaves is silvery white.
7   as far as one could shoot an arrow.
8   sources – T. '*Odyssey*, XI.100–37, and Dante's *Inferno* XXVI'.
9   a primitive state of law, unequal in its effects.
10   written after 'hearing the echoes at Killarney in 1848'.
11   On 15 Sept. 1833, T.'s friend and his sister's fiancé, Arthur Henry Hallam, died in Vienna: T. received the news 1 Oct. 1833. His remains were brought back by sea and he was buried at Clevedon, Somerset, 3 Jan. 1834. Between then, and its publication in 1850, T. wrote this series of lyrics – a voyage of grief. The sections here are in the order of the 1850 edition, which was published anonymously, though an error in the first commercial announcement of the poem gave T. as its author.
12   67 Wimpole Street, Henry (Arthur's brother) Hallam's house.
13   each church had four bells.
14   John XI.31 ff.
15   nos. 56, 57 influenced by Charles Lydell's book on geology.
16   refers to T.'s move from Somersby in 1837.
17   refers to Christmas, 1837, when T. had moved to High Beech, Epping Forest.
18   his father was buried in Somersby.
19   1 Feb. 1811.
20   of snow, which, falling into the sea, seems to darken as it melts.
21   The charge took place on 25 Oct. 1854, during the Crimean War. The poem was written 'a few minutes after reading . . . *The Times* in which occurred the phrase "someone had blundered".' H.T., *A Memoir*, 1897.
22   only 195 returned.
23   of the guests' carriages.
24   founded on (according to H.T.) Malory's *Morte D'Arthur*, Layamon's *Brut*, Lady Charlotte Guest's translation of the *Mabinogion*, old chronicles, old French romances, Celtic folklore and his own imagination.
     Lines 170–440 were originally published as 'Morte D'Arthur', 1842: the rest was added and slight variations made for *The Holy Grail and Other Poems*, 1869. In the *Complete Works*, 1872, all these writings were brought together, with a new epilogue.
25   Arthur's wife, Guinevere, and his friend, Sir Lancelot, fell in love with each other, so betraying their fealty to King Arthur.
26   Morgan Le Fay (Arthur's sister), the Queen of Northgalis and the Queen of the Wastelands – but, according to T., 'they are much more'.
27   bloody from the battle.
28   'the Isles of the Blest' T.
29   'For those who cared to know about his literary history Tennyson wrote "Merlin and the Gleam".' The reading of the poem: Section 1. His boyhood awareness of the

magic of Merlin – the spirit of poetry: 2. refers to the poetry of his youth: 3. 'the harsh voice' – of unsympathetic reviews, 1832 and/or his inability to marry through poverty: 4. renewed inspiration from romantic fancy and nature, 'the early imagination': 5. period of the Eclogues and English Idylls: 6. 'human love and human heroism' when he 'began what he had already devised, his Epic of King Arthur': 7. the death of Hallam 'made him almost fail in this purpose': 8. 'finding a stronger faith than his own': 9. 'up to the end he faced death with the same earnest and unfailing courage he had always shown, but with an added sense of the awe and mystery of the Infinite'. The quotations are from H.T.'s *A Memoir*, 1897.

N.B. This analysis does not always follow exactly the chronological sequence of events (e.g. Hallam's death comes much earlier). The problem lies in the 17 year gap between Hallam's actual death and the publication of *In Memoriam*.

30 ?Sir Walter Scott. However cf. lines 114–5.

31 T.'s reviewers, or his family (his grandfather tried to dissuade him from writing poetry) or, in particular, Christopher North, the reviewer, who was associated with a raven.

32 T. 'I began and finished it in twenty minutes': the bar is the sandbank across the harbour mouth. At T.'s request this poem is used to close any edition of his poems.

Robert Browning

[1812–89]

He was brought up with his only sister in Camberwell, S.E.
London: influenced by his reading of Shelley, Keats and Byron,
and his mother's strong nonconformist religious beliefs: he enrolled
at London University, but stayed only one term. First publication,
Pauline (anon.). 1833/34 he travelled to Russia, and, 1838, paid his
first visit to Italy. *Paracelsus*, 1835, received critical praise, and,
after becoming friends with Macready, the actor, he wrote his first
stage play, *Stafford*, 1837. His next play, *Sordello*, was badly received
and affected his reputation for many years. 1845 he met Elizabeth
Barrett, whose *Poems*, 1844, he had read and admired. After
meeting secretly, they finally married and eloped to Italy, 1846.
There they had one son. Elizabeth died 1862. His *Men and Women*,
1855, and *Dramatis Personae*, 1864 were greatly admired and *The
Ring and the Book*, 1868, was a great success. From 1866 he lived with
his sister, partly in London – for 'the season' – and partly abroad.
He continued writing and publishing, including many collections
of his poems (1849, 1863, 1868, 1889). His last volume, *Asolando*,
1889, was published on 12 Dec., the day he died in Venice. He is
buried in Westminster Abbey.

Song[1]

(from *Pippa Passes*)

The year's at the spring
And day's at the morn;
Morning's at seven;
The hillside's dew-pearled;
The lark's on the wing;
The snail's on the thorn:
God's in his heaven –
All's right with the world!

[1841]

My Last Duchess

FERRARA[2]

That's my last Duchess painted on the wall,
Looking as if she were alive. I call
That piece a wonder, now: Fra Pandolf's[3] hands
Worked busily a day, and there she stands.
Will't please you sit and look at her? I said
'Fra Pandolf' by design, for never read
Strangers like you that pictured countenance,
The depth and passion of its earnest glance,
But to myself they turned (since none puts by
10   The curtain I have drawn for you, but I)
And seemed as they would ask me, if they durst,
How such a glance came there; so, not the first
Are you to turn and ask thus. Sir, 'twas not
Her husband's presence only, called that spot
Of joy into the Duchess' cheek; perhaps
Fra Pandolf chanced to say 'Her mantle laps
Over my Lady's wrist too much,' or 'Paint
Must never hope to reproduce the faint
Half-flush that dies along her throat:' such stuff
20   Was courtesy, she thought, and cause enough
For calling up that spot of joy. She had
A heart – how shall I say? – too soon made glad,
Too easily impressed; she liked whate'er
She looked on, and her looks went everywhere.
Sir, 'twas all one! My favour at her breast,
The dropping of the daylight in the West,
The bough of cherries some officious fool
Broke in the orchard for her, the white mule
She rode with round the terrace – all and each
30   Would draw from her alike the approving speech,
Or blush, at least. She thanked men, – good! but thanked
Somehow – I know not how – as if she ranked
My gift of a nine-hundred-years-old name
With anybody's gift. Who'd stoop to blame
This sort of trifling? Even had you skill
In speech – (which I have not) – to make your will
Quite clear to such an one, and say, 'Just this
Or that in you disgusts me; here you miss,
Or there exceed the mark' – and if she let
40   Herself be lessoned so, nor plainly set

Her wits to yours, forsooth, and made excuse,
– E'en then would be some stooping; and I choose
Never to stoop. Oh sir, she smiled, no doubt,
Whene'er I passed her; but who passed without
Much the same smile? This grew; I gave commands;
Then all smiles stopped together. There she stands
As if alive. Will't please you rise? We'll meet
The company below, then. I repeat,
The Count your Master's known munificence
50 Is ample warrant that no just pretence
Of mine for dowry will be disallowed;
Though his fair daughter's self, as I avowed
At starting, is my object. Nay, we'll go
Together down, Sir. Notice Neptune, though,
Taming a sea-horse, thought a rarity,
Which Claus of Innsbruck cast in bronze for me!

[1842]

Soliloquy of the Spanish Cloister

I

Gr-r-r – there go, my heart's abhorrence!
    Water your damned flower-pots, do!
If hate killed men, Brother Lawrence,
    God's blood, would not mine kill you!
What? your myrtle-bush wants trimming?
    Oh, that rose has prior claims –
Needs its leaden vase filled brimming?
    Hell dry you up with its flames!

II

At the meal we sit together:
10   *Salve tibi*°! I must hear   *good day to you*
Wise talk of the kind of weather,
    Sort of season, time of year:
Not a plenteous cork-crop: scarcely
    Dare we hope oak-galls;[4] *I doubt*
What's the Latin name for 'parsley'?
    What's the Greek name for Swine's Snout?

III

Whew! We'll have our platter burnished,
    Laid with care on our own shelf!
With a fire-new spoon we're furnished,
20   And a goblet for ourself,
Rinsed like something sacrificial
    Ere't is fit to touch our chaps° –   *lips*
Marked with L. for our initial!
    (He-he! There his lily snaps!)

IV

Saint, forsooth! While brown Dolores
    Squats outside the Convent bank
With Sanchicha, telling stories,
    Steeping tresses in the tank,
Blue-black, lustrous, thick like horsehairs,
30   –Can't I see his dead eye glow,
Bright as 'twere a Barbary corsair's?[5]
    (That is, if he'd let it show!)

V

When he finishes refection,°   *refreshments*
    Knife and fork he never lays
Cross-wise, to my recollection,
    As do I, in Jesu's praise.
I the Trinity[6] illustrate,
    Drinking watered orange-pulp –
In three sips the Arian[7] frustrate;
40   While he drains his at one gulp.

VI

Oh, those melons? If he's able
    We're to have a feast! so nice!
One goes to the Abbot's table,
    All of us get each a slice.
How go on your flowers? None double?
    Not one fruit-sort can you spy?
Strange! – And I, too, at such trouble,
    Keep them close-nipped on the sly!

VII

There's a great text in Galatians,[8]
50   Once you trip on it, entails
Twenty-nine distinct damnations,

One sure, if another fails:
　If I trip him just a-dying,
　　Sure of heaven as sure can be,
Spin him round and send him flying
　Off to hell, a Manichee?⁹

VIII

Or, my scrofulous° French novel　　　　　　　　*corrupting*
　On gray paper with blunt type!
Simply glance at it, you grovel
60　Hand and foot in Belial's gripe:
　If I double down its pages
　　At the woeful° sixteenth print,　　　　　　*bringing woe*
When he gathers his greengages,
　Ope a sieve and slip it in't?

IX

Or, there's Satan! – one might venture
　Pledge one's soul to him, yet leave
Such a flaw in the indenture°　　　　　　　　*agreement*
　As he'd miss till, past retrieve,
Blasted lay that rose-acacia
70　We're so proud of! *Hy, Zy, Hine.*¹⁰
'St, there's Vespers°! *Plena gratiâ*
　*Ave, Virgo!*¹¹ Gr-r-r – you swine!

[1842]

Porphyria's Lover

The rain set early in tonight,
　The sullen wind was soon awake,
It tore the elm-tops down for spite,
　And did its worst to vex the lake:
　I listened with heart fit to break.
When glided in Porphyria; straight
　She shut the cold out and the storm,
And kneeled and made the cheerless grate
　Blaze up, and all the cottage warm;
10　Which done, she rose, and from her form
Withdrew the dripping cloak and shawl,

And laid her soiled gloves by, untied
Her hat and let the damp hair fall,
   And, last, she sat down by my side
   And called me. When no voice replied,
She put my arm about her waist,
   And made her smooth white shoulder bare,
And all her yellow hair displaced,
   And, stooping, made my cheek lie there,
20   And spread, o'er all, her yellow hair,
Murmuring how she loved me – she
   Too weak, for all her heart's endeavour,
To set its struggling passion free
   From pride, and vainer ties dissever,
   And give herself to me for ever.
But passion sometimes would prevail,
   Nor could to-night's gay feast restrain
A sudden thought of one so pale
   For love of her, and all in vain:
30   So, she was come through wind and rain.
Be sure I looked up at her eyes
   Happy and proud; at last I knew
Porphyria worshipped me; surprise
   Made my heart swell, and still it grew
   While I debated what to do.
That moment she was mine, mine, fair,
   Perfectly pure and good: I found
A thing to do, and all her hair
   In one long yellow string I wound
40   Three times her little throat around,
And strangled her. No pain felt she;
   I am quite sure she felt no pain.
As a shut bud that holds a bee,
   I warily oped her lids: again
   Laughed the blue eyes without a stain.
And I untightened next the tress
   About her neck; her cheek once more
Blushed bright beneath my burning kiss:
   I propped her head up as before,
50   Only, this time *my* shoulder bore
Her head, which droops upon it still:
   The smiling rosy little head,
So glad it has its utmost will,
   That all it scorned at once is fled,
   And I, its love, am gained instead!

Porphyria's love: she guessed not how
   Her darling one wish would be heard.
And thus we sit together now,
   And all night long we have not stirred,
And yet God has not said a word!

[1842]

'How They Brought the Good News from Ghent to Aix' [16–]¹²

I

I sprang to the stirrup, and Joris, and he;
I galloped, Dirck galloped, we galloped all three;
'Good speed!' cried the watch, as the gate-bolts undrew;
'Speed!' echoed the wall to us galloping through;
Behind shut the postern,° the lights sank to rest,   *gate in city wall*
And into the midnight we galloped abreast.

II

Not a word to each other; we kept the great pace
Neck by neck, stride by stride, never changing our place;
I turned in my saddle and made its girths tight,
10 Then shortened each stirrup, and set the pique° right,   *part of bridle*
Rebuckled the cheek-strap, chained slacker the bit,
Nor galloped less steadily Roland a whit.

III

'Twas moonset at starting; but while we drew near
Lokeren,¹³ the cocks crew and twilight dawned clear;
At Boom, a great yellow star came out to see;
At Düffeld, 'twas morning as plain as could be;
And from Mecheln church-steeple we heard the half-chime,
So, Joris broke silence with, 'Yet there is time!'

IV

At Aerschot, up leaped of a sudden the sun,
20 And against him the cattle stood black every one,
To stare thro' the mist at us galloping past,

And I saw my stout galloper Roland at last,
With resolute shoulders, each butting away
The haze, as some bluff river headland its spray:

V

And his low head and crest, just one sharp ear bent back
For my voice, and the other pricked out on his track;
And one eye's black intelligence, – ever that glance
O'er its white edge at me, his own master, askance!
And the thick heavy spume-flakes which aye and anon
30 His fierce lips shook upwards in galloping on.

VI

By Hasselt, Dirck groaned; and cried Joris, 'Stay spur!
Your Roos galloped bravely, the fault's not in her,
We'll remember at Aix' – for one heard the quick wheeze
Of her chest, saw the stretched neck and staggering knees,
And sunk tail, and horrible heave of the flank,
As down on her haunches she shuddered and sank.

VII

So, we were left galloping, Joris and I,
Past Looz and past Tongres, no cloud in the sky;
The broad sun above laughed a pitiless laugh,
40 'Neath our feet broke the brittle bright stubble like chaff;
Till over by Dalhem a dome-spire sprang white,
And 'Gallop,' gasped Joris, 'for Aix is in sight!'

VIII

'How they'll greet us!' – and all in a moment his roan
Rolled neck and croup° over, lay dead as a stone;   °posterior
And there was my Roland to bear the whole weight
Of the news which alone could save Aix from her fate,
With his nostrils like pits full of blood to the brim,
And with circles of red for his eye-sockets' rim.

IX

Then I cast loose my buff°coat, each holster let fall,   °leather
50 Shook off both my jack-boots, let go belt and all,
Stood up in the stirrup, leaned, patted his ear,
Called my Roland his pet-name, my horse without peer;
Clapped my hands, laughed and sang, any noise, bad or good,
Till at length into Aix Roland galloped and stood.

X

And all I remember is – friends flocking round
As I sat with his head 'twixt my knees on the ground;
And no voice but was praising this Roland of mine,
As I poured down his throat our last measure of wine,
Which (the burgesses° voted by common consent)   *townsfolk*
60 Was no more than his due who brought good news from Ghent.

[1845]

*The Lost Leader*¹⁴

I

Just for a handful of silver he left us,
  Just for a riband to stick in his coat –
Found the one gift of which fortune bereft us,
  Lost all the others she lets us devote;
They, with the gold to give, doled him out silver,
  So much was theirs who so little allowed:
How all our copper had gone for his service!
  Rags – were they purple, his heart had been proud!
We that had loved him so, followed him, honoured him,
10   Lived in his mild and magnificent eye,
Learned his great language, caught his clear accents,
  Made him our pattern to live and to die!
Shakespeare was of us, Milton was for us,
  Burns, Shelley, were with us, – they watch from their graves!
He alone breaks from the van and the freemen,
  He alone sinks to the rear and the slaves!

II

We shall march prospering, – not thro' his presence;
  Songs may inspirit us, – not from his lyre;
Deeds will be done, – while he boasts his quiescence,
20   Still bidding crouch whom the rest bade aspire:
Blot out his name, then, record one lost soul more,
  One task more declined, one more footpath untrod,
One more triumph for devils and sorrow for angels,
  One wrong more to man, one more insult to God!
Life's night begins: let him never come back to us!
  There would be doubt, hesitation and pain,

Forced praise on our part – the glimmer of twilight,
   Never glad confident morning again!
Best fight on well, for we taught him – strike gallantly,
30   Menace our heart ere we master his own;
Then let him receive the new knowledge and wait us,
   Pardoned in heaven, the first by the throne!

[1845]

Home Thoughts, From Abroad

I

Oh, to be in England
Now that April's there,
And whoever wakes in England
Sees, some morning, unaware,
That the lowest boughs and the brushwood sheaf
Round the elm-tree bole are in tiny leaf,
While the chaffinch sings on the orchard bough
In England – now!

II

'And after April, when May follows,
10 And the whitethroat builds, and all the swallows!
Hark, where my blossomed pear-tree in the hedge
Leans to the field and scatters on the clover
Blossoms and dewdrops – at the bent spray's edge –
That's the wise thrush; he sings each song twice over,
Lest you should think he never could recapture
The first fine careless rapture!
And though the fields look rough with hoary dew,
All will be gay when noontide wakes anew
The buttercups, the little children's dower°   *inherited gift*
20 – Far brighter than this gaudy melon-flower!

[1845]

The Bishop orders his Tomb at St Praxed's Church[15]

ROME, 15–

Vanity, saith the preacher, vanity!
Draw round my bed: is Anselm keeping back?
Nephews – sons mine . . . ah God, I know not! Well –
She, men would have to be your mother once,
Old Gandolf envied me, so fair she was!
What's done is done, and she is dead beside,
Dead long ago, and I am Bishop since,
And as she died so must we die ourselves,
And thence ye may perceive the world's a dream.
10 Life, how and what is it? As here I lie
In this state-chamber, dying by degrees,
Hours and long hours in the dead night, I ask
'Do I live, am I dead?' Peace, peace seems all.
Saint Praxed's ever was the church for peace;
And so, about this tomb of mine. I fought
With tooth and nail to save my niche, ye know:
– Old Gandolf cozened me, despite my care;
Shrewd was that snatch from out the corner South·
He graced his carrion with, God curse the same!
20 Yet still my niche is not so cramped but thence
One sees the pulpit o' the epistle-side,[16]
And somewhat of the choir, those silent seats,
And up into the aery dome where live
The angels, and a sunbeam's sure to lurk:
And I shall fill my slab of basalt there,
And 'neath my tabernacle° take my rest   *sanctuary*
With those nine columns round me, two and two,
The odd one at my feet where Anselm stands:
Peach-blossom marble all, the rare, the ripe
30 As fresh-poured red wine of a mighty pulse.
– Old Gandolf with his paltry onion-stone,°   *cheap marble*
Put me where I may look at him! True peach,
Rosy and flawless: how I earned the prize!
Draw close: that conflagration of my church
– What then? So much was saved if aught were missed!
My sons, ye would not be my death? Go dig
The white-grape vineyard where the oil-press stood,
Drop water gently till the surface sink,
And if ye find . . . Ah God, I know not, I! . . .

40   Bedded in store of rotten fig-leaves soft,
     And corded up in a tight olive-frail,°   *rush basket*
     Some lump, ah God, of *lapis lazuli*,[17]
     Big as a Jew's head cut off at the nape,
     Blue as a vein o'er the Madonna's breast . . .
     Sons, all have I bequeathed you, villas, all,
     That brave Frascati villa with its bath,
     So, let the blue lump poise between my knees,
     Like God the Father's globe on both his hands
     Ye worship in the Jesu Church[18] so gay,
50   For Gandolf shall not choose but see and burst!
     Swift as a weaver's shuttle fleet° our years: *fly by*
     Man goeth to the grave, and where is he?
     Did I say basalt for my slab, sons? Black —
     'T was ever antique-black I meant! How else
     Shall ye contrast my frieze to come beneath?
     The bas-relief° in bronze ye promised me,   *sculpture*
     Those Pans and Nymphs ye wot of, and perchance
     Some tripod, thyrsus,[19] with a vase or so,
     The Saviour at his sermon on the mount,
60   Saint Praxed in a glory,° and one Pan   *halo*
     Ready to twitch the Nymph's last garment off,
     And Moses with the tables . . . but I know
     Ye mark me not! What do they whisper thee,
     Child of my bowels, Anselm? Ah, ye hope
     To revel down my villas while I gasp
     Bricked o'er with beggar's mouldy travertine[20]
     Which Gandolf from his tomb-top chuckles at!
     Nay, boys, ye love me — all of jasper,[21] then!
     'Tis jasper ye stand pledged to, lest I grieve.
70   My bath must needs be left behind, alas!
     One block, pure green as a pistachio-nut,
     There's plenty jasper somewhere in the world —
     And have I not Saint Praxed's ear to pray
     Horses for ye, and brown Greek manuscripts,
     And mistresses with great smooth marbly limbs?
     — That's if ye carve my epitaph aright,
     Choice Latin, picked phrase, Tully's every word,
     No gaudy ware like Gandolf's second line —
     Tully, my masters? Ulpian serves his need!
80   And then how I shall lie through centuries,
     And hear the blessed mutter of the mass,
     And see God made and eaten all day long,
     And feel the steady candle-flame, and taste

Good strong thick stupefying incense-smoke!
For as I lie here, hours of the dead night,
Dying in state and by such slow degrees,
I fold my arms as if they clasped a crook,
And stretch my feet forth straight as stone can point,
And let the bedclothes, for a mortcloth,° drop   coffin-covering
90   Into great laps and folds of sculptor's-work:
And as yon tapers dwindle, and strange thoughts
Grow, with a certain humming in my ears,
About the life before I lived this life,
And this life too, popes, cardinals and priests,
Saint Praxed at his sermon on the mount,
Your tall pale mother with her talking eyes,
And new-found agate urns as fresh as day,
And marble's language, Latin pure, discreet,
– Aha, ELUCESCEBAT[22] quoth our friend?
100 No Tully, said I, Ulpian at the best!
Evil and brief hath been my pilgrimage.
All *lapis*, all, sons! Else I give the Pope
My villas! Will ye ever eat my heart?
Ever your eyes were as a lizard's quick,
They glitter like your mother's for my soul,
Or ye would heighten my impoverished frieze,
Piece out its starved design, and fill my vase
With grapes, and add a vizor° and a Term,[23]   mask
And to the tripod ye would tie a lynx
110 That in his struggle throws the thyrsus down,
To comfort me on my entablature[24]
Whereon I am to lie till I must ask
'Do I live, am I dead?' There, leave me, there!
For ye have stabbed me with ingratitude
To death – ye wish it – God, ye wish it! Stone –
Gritstone,° a-crumble! Clammy squares which sweat   sandstone
As if the corpse they keep were oozing through –
And no more *lapis* to delight the world!
Well go! I bless ye. Fewer tapers there,
120 But in a row: and, going, turn your backs
– Ay, like departing altar-ministrants,
And leave me in my church, the church for peace,
That I may watch at leisure if he leers –
Old Gandolf, at me, from his onion-stone,
As still he envied me, so fair she was!

[1845]

Meeting at Night

I

The gray sea and the long black land;
And the yellow half-moon large and low;
And the startled little waves that leap
In fiery ringlets from their sleep,
As I gain the cove with pushing prow,
And quench its speed i' the slushy sand.

II

Then a mile of warm sea-scented beach;
Three fields to cross till a farm appears;
A tap at the pane, the quick sharp scratch
10 And blue spurt of a lighted match,
And a voice less loud, thro' its joys and fears,
Than the two hearts beating each to each!

[1845]

Parting at Morning

Round the cape of a sudden came the sea,
And the sun looked over the mountain's rim:
And straight was a path of gold for him,
And the need of a world of men for me.

[1845]

Love Among the Ruins

I

Where the quiet-coloured end of evening smiles,
    Miles and miles
On the solitary pastures where our sheep
    Half-asleep
Tinkle homeward thro' the twilight, stray or stop
    As they crop —
Was the site once of a city great and gay,
    (So they say)
Of our country's very capital, its prince
10   Ages since
Held his court in, gathered councils, wielding far
    Peace or war.

II

Now, — the country does not even boast a tree,
    As you see,
To distinguish slopes of verdure, certain rills
    From the hills
Intersect and give a name to, (else they run
    Into one)
Where the domed and daring palace shot its spires
20   Up like fires
O'er the hundred-gated circuit of a wall
    Bounding all,
Made of marble, men might march on nor be pressed,
    Twelve abreast.

III

And such plenty and perfection, see, of grass
    Never was!
Such a carpet as, this summer-time, o'erspreads
    And embeds
Every vestige of the city, guessed alone,°   *only*
30   Stock or stone —
Where a multitude of men breathed joy and woe
    Long ago;
Lust of glory pricked their hearts up, dread of shame
    Struck them tame;
And that glory and that shame alike, the gold
    Bought and sold.

IV

Now, – the single little turret that remains
  On the plains,
By the caper° overrooted, by the gourd   *(trailing shrub)*
40   Overscored,
While the patching houseleek'°s head of blossom winks   *(low-growing*
  Through the chinks –   *plant)*
Marks the basement whence a tower in ancient time
  Sprang sublime,
And a burning ring, all round, the chariots traced
  As they raced,
And the monarch and his minions and his dames
  Viewed the games.

V

And I know, while thus the quiet-coloured eve
50   Smiles to leave
To their folding, all our many-tinkling fleece
  In such peace,
And the slopes and rills in undistinguished gray
  Melt away –
That a girl with eager eyes and yellow hair
  Waits me there
In the turret whence the charioteers caught soul
  For the goal,
When the king looked, where she looks now, breathless, dumb
60   Till I come.

VI

But he looked upon the city, every side,
  Far and wide,
All the mountains topped with temples, all the glades'
  Colonnades,
All the causeys,° bridges, aqueducts, – and then,   *causeways*
  All the men!
When I do come, she will speak not, she will stand,
  Either hand
On my shoulder, give her eyes the first embrace
70   Of my face,
Ere we rush, ere we extinguish sight and speech
  Each on each.

VII

In one year they sent a million fighters forth
    South and North,
And they built their gods a brazen pillar high
    As the sky,
Yet reserved a thousand chariots in full force –
    Gold, of course.
Oh heart! oh blood that freezes, blood that burns!
80   Earth's returns
For whole centuries of folly, noise and sin!
    Shut them in,
With their triumphs and their glories and the rest!
    Love is best.

[1855]

Up at a Villa – Down in the City

(AS DISTINGUISHED BY AN ITALIAN PERSON OF QUALITY)

I

Had I but plenty of money, money enough and to spare,
The house for me, no doubt, were a house in the city-square;
Ah, such a life, such a life, as one leads at the window there!

II

Something to see, by Bacchus, something to hear, at least!
There, the whole day long, one's life is a perfect feast;
While up at a villa one lives, I maintain it, no more than a beast.

III

Well now, look at our villa! stuck like the horn of a bull
Just on a mountain-edge as bare as the creature's skull,
Save a mere shag of a bush with hardly a leaf to pull!
10   – I scratch my own, sometimes, to see if the hair's turned wool.

IV

But the city, oh the city – the square with the houses! Why?
They are stone-faced, white as a curd, there's something to take the
                                                                    eye!
Houses in four straight lines, not a single front awry;

You watch who crosses and gossips, who saunters, who hurries by;
Green blinds, as a matter of course, to draw when the sun gets high;
And the shops with fanciful signs which are painted properly.

V

What of a villa? Though winter be over in March by rights,
'Tis May perhaps ere the snow shall have withered well off the
heights:
You've the brown ploughed land before, where the oxen steam and
wheeze,
20 And the hills over-smoked behind by the faint grey olive-trees.

VI

Is it better in May, I ask you? You've summer all at once;
In a day he leaps complete with a few strong April suns.
'Mid the sharp short emerald wheat, scarce risen three fingers well,
The wild tulip, at end of its tube, blows out its great red bell
Like a thin clear bubble of blood, for the children to pick and sell.

VII

Is it ever hot in the square? There's a fountain to spout and splash!
In the shade it sings and springs; in the shine
such foam-bows²⁵ flash
On the horses with curling fish-tails, that prance and
paddle and pash
Round the lady atop in her conch – fifty gazers do not abash,
30 Though all that she wears is some weeds round her waist in a sort
of sash.

VIII

All the year long at the villa, nothing's to see though you linger,
Except yon cypress that points like Death's lean lifted forefinger.
Some think fireflies pretty, when they mix i' the corn and mingle,
Or thrid° the stinking hemp till the stalks of it seem a-tingle. *threaded*
Late August or early September, the stunning cicala is shrill,
And the bees keep their tiresome whine round the resinous
firs on the hill.
Enough of the seasons, – I spare you the months of the fever and
chill.

IX

Ere you open your eyes in the city, the blessed church-bells begin:
No sooner the bells leave off than the diligence° rattles in; *stagecoach*
40 You get the pick of the news, and it costs you never a pin.

By-and-by there's the travelling doctor gives pills, lets blood, draws
teeth;
Or the Pulcinello-trumpet breaks up the market beneath.   *puppet-show*
At the post-office such a scene-picture – the new play, piping hot!
And a notice how, only this morning, three liberal thieves were
shot.

Above it, behold the Archbishop's most fatherly of rebukes,
And beneath, with his crown and his lion, some little new law of
the Duke's!
Or a sonnet with flowery marge, to the Reverend Don So-and-so
Who is Dante, Boccaccio, Petrarca, Saint Jerome and Cicero,[26]
'And moreover,' (the sonnet goes rhyming,) 'the skirts of Saint Paul
has reached,
50 Having preached us those six Lent lectures more unctuous than
ever he preached.'
Noon strikes, – here sweeps the procession! our Lady[27] borne
smiling and smart
With a pink gauze gown all spangles, and seven swords
stuck in her heart!
Bang-whang-whang goes the drum, *tootle-te-tootle* the fife;
No keeping one's haunches still: it's the greatest pleasure in life.

X

But bless you, it's dear – it's dear! fowls, wine, at double the rate.
They have clapped a new tax upon salt, and what oil pays passing
the gate
It's a horror to think of. And so, the villa for me, not the city!
Beggars can scarcely be choosers: but still – ah, the pity, the pity!
Look, two and two go the priests, then the monks with cowls and
sandals,
60 And the penitents dressed in white shirts, a-holding the yellow
candles;
One, he carries a flag up straight, and another a cross with handles,
And the Duke's guard brings up the rear, for the better prevention
of scandals:
Bang-whang-whang goes the drum, *tootle-te-tootle* the fife.
Oh, a day in the city-square, there is no such pleasure in life!

[1855]

Fra Lippo Lippi[28]

I am poor brother Lippo, by your leave!
You need not clap your torches to my face.[29]
Zooks, what's to blame? you think you see a monk!
What, 'tis past midnight, and you go the rounds,
And here you catch me at an alley's end
Where sportive ladies leave their doors ajar?
The Carmine's my cloister: hunt it up,
Do, – harry out, if you must show your zeal,
Whatever rat, there, haps on his wrong hole,
10   And nip each softling of a wee white mouse,
Weke, weke, that's crept to keep him company!
Aha, you know your betters! Then, you'll take
Your hand away that's fiddling on my throat,
And please to know me likewise. Who am I?
Why, one, sir, who is lodging with a friend
Three streets off – he's a certain . . . how d'ye call?
Master – a . . . Cosimo of the Medici,
I' the house that caps the corner.[30] Boh! you were best!
Remember and tell me, the day you're hanged,
20   How you affected such a gullet's-gripe!
But you,[31] sir, it concerns you that your knaves
Pick up a manner nor discredit you:
Zooks, are we pilchards, that they sweep the streets
And count fair prize what comes into their net?
He's Judas to a tittle, that man is![32]
Just such a face! Why, sir, you make amends.
Lord, I'm not angry! Bid your hangdogs go
Drink out this quarter-florin to the health
Of the munificent House[33] that harbours me
30   (And many more beside, lads! more beside!)
And all's come square again. I'd like his face –
His, elbowing on his comrade in the door
With the pike and lantern, – for the slave that holds
John Baptist's head a-dangle by the hair
With one hand ('look you, now,' as who should say)
And his weapon in the other, yet unwiped!
It's not your chance to have a bit of chalk,
A wood-coal or the like or you should see!
Yes, I'm the painter, since you style me so.
40   What, brother Lippo's doings, up and down,
You know them and they take you? like enough!
I saw the proper twinkle in your eye –

'Tell you, I liked your looks at very first.
Let's sit and set things straight now, hip to haunch.
Here's spring come, and the nights one makes up bands
To roam the town and sing out carnival,
And I've been three weeks shut within my mew,°   cage
A-painting for the great man, saints and saints
And saints again. I could not paint all night –
50   Ouf! I leaned out of window for fresh air.
There came a hurry of feet and little feet,
A sweep of lute-strings, laughs, and whifts of song, –
Flower o' the broom,
Take away love, and our earth is a tomb!
Flower o' the quince,
I let Lisa go, and what good's in life since?
Flower o' the thyme – and so on. Round they went.
Scarce had they turned the corner when a titter
Like the skipping of rabbits by moonlight, – three slim shapes,
60   And a face that looked up . . . zooks, sir, flesh and blood,
That's all I'm made of! Into shreds it went,
Curtain and counterpane and coverlet,
All the bed-furniture – a dozen knots,
There was a ladder! Down I let myself,
Hands and feet, scrambling somehow, and so dropped,
And after them. I came up with the fun
Hard by Saint Laurence,³⁴ hail fellow, well met, –
Flower o' the rose,
If I've been merry, what matter who knows?
70   And so as I was stealing back again
To get to bed and have a bit of sleep
Ere I rise up to-morrow and go work
On Jerome³⁵ knocking at his poor old breast
With his great round stone to subdue the flesh,
You snap me of the sudden. Ah, I see!
Though your eye twinkles still, you shake your head –
Mine's shaved – a monk, you say – the sting's in that!
If Master Cosimo announced himself,
Mum's the word naturally; but a monk!
80   Come, what am I a beast for? tell us, now!
I was a baby when my mother died
And father died and left me in the street.
I starved there, God knows how, a year or two
On fig-skins, melon-parings, rinds and shucks,
Refuse and rubbish. One fine frosty day,
My stomach being empty as your hat,

The wind doubled me up and down I went.
Old Aunt Lapaccia[36] trussed me with one hand,
(Its fellow was a stinger as I knew)
90 And so along the wall, over the bridge,
By the straight cut to the convent. Six words there,
While I stood munching my first bread that month:
'So boy, you're minded,' quoth the good fat father
Wiping his own mouth, 'twas refection-time, —   *meal-time*
'To quit this very miserable world?
Will you renounce . . .' 'the mouthful of bread?' thought I;
By no means! Brief, they made a monk of me;
I did renounce the world, its pride and greed,
Palace, farm, villa, shop and banking-house,
100 Trash, such as these poor devils of Medici
Have given their hearts to — all at eight years old.
Well, sir, I found in time, you may be sure,
'Twas not for nothing — the good bellyful,
The warm serge and the rope that goes all round,
And day-long blessed idleness beside!
'Let's see what the urchin's fit for' — that came next.
Not overmuch their way, I must confess.
Such a to-do! They tried me with their books:
Lord, they'd have taught me Latin in pure waste!
110 *Flower o' the clove,*
All the Latin I construe is, 'amo' I love!
But, mind you, when a boy starves in the streets
Eight years together, as my fortune was,
Watching folk's faces to know who will fling
The bit of half-stripped grape-bunch he desires,
And who will curse or kick him for his pains, —
Which gentleman processional° and fine,   *dressed for a procession*
Holding a candle to the Sacrament,
Will wink and let him lift a plate and catch
120 The droppings of the wax to sell again,
Or holla for the Eight[37] and have him whipped, —
How say I? — nay, which dog bites, which lets drop
His bone from the heap of offal in the street, —
Why, soul and sense of him grow sharp alike,
He learns the look of things, and none the less
For admonition from the hunger-pinch.
I had a store of such remarks, be sure,
Which, after I found leisure, turned to use.
I drew men's faces on my copy-books,
130 Scrawled them within the antiphonary's marge,°   *music-book's margin*

Joined legs and arms to the long music-notes,
Found eyes and nose and chin for A's and B's,
And made a string of pictures of the world
Betwixt the ins and outs of verb and noun,
On the wall, the bench, the door. The monks looked black.
'Nay,' quoth the Prior, 'turn him out, d'ye say?
In no wise. Lose a crow and catch a lark.
What if at last we get our man of parts,
We Carmelites, like those Camaldolese
140 And Preaching Friars,[38] to do our church up fine
And put the front on it that ought to be!'
And hereupon he bade me daub away.
Thank you! my head being crammed, the walls a blank,
Never was such prompt disemburdening.
First, every sort of monk, the black and white,
I drew them, fat and lean: then, folks at church,
From good old gossips waiting to confess
Their cribs° of barrel-droppings, candle-ends, –   *petty thefts*
To the breathless fellow at the altar-foot,
150 Fresh from his murder, safe and sitting there
With the little children round him in a row
Of admiration, half for his beard and half
For that white anger of his victim's son
Shaking a fist at him with one fierce arm,
Signing° himself with the other because of Christ   *making the sign of the*
(Whose sad face on the cross sees only this   *cross*
After the passion of a thousand years)
Till some poor girl, her apron o'er her head,
(Which the intense eyes looked through) came at eve
160 On tiptoe, said a word, dropped in a loaf,
Her pair of earrings and a bunch of flowers
(The brute took growling), prayed, and so was gone.
I painted all, then cried" 'Tis ask and have;
Choose, for more's ready!' – laid the ladder flat,
And showed my covered bit of cloister-wall.
The monks closed in a circle and praised loud
Till checked, taught what to see and not to see,
Being simple bodies, – 'That's the very man!
Look at the boy who stoops to pat the dog!
170 That woman's like the Prior's niece who comes
To care about his asthma: it's the life!'
But there my triumph's straw-fire flared and funked;°   *went out*
Their betters took their turn to see and say:
The Prior and the learned pulled a face

And stopped all that in no time. 'How? what's here?
Quite from the mark of painting, bless us all!
Faces, arms, legs and bodies like the true
As much as pea and pea! it's devil's-game!
Your business is not to catch men with show,
180 With homage to the perishable clay,
But lift them over it, ignore it all,
Make them forget there's such a thing as flesh.
Your business is to paint the souls of men —
Man's soul, and it's a fire, smoke . . . no, it's not . . .
It's vapour done up like a new-born babe —
(In that shape when you die it leaves your mouth)
It's . . . well, what matters talking, it's the soul!
Give us no more of body than shows soul!
Here's Giotto, with his Saint a-praising God,
190 That sets us praising, — why not stop with him?
Why put all thoughts of praise out of our head
With wonder at lines, colours, and what not?
Paint the soul, never mind the legs and arms!
Rub all out, try at it a second time.
Oh, that white smallish female with the breasts,
She's just my niece . . . Herodias, I would say, —
Who went and danced and got men's heads cut off!
Have it all out!' Now, is this sense, I ask?
A fine way to paint soul, by painting body
200 So ill, the eye can't stop there, must go further
And can't fare worse! Thus, yellow does for white
When what you put for yellow's simply black,
And any sort of meaning looks intense
When all beside itself means and looks naught.
Why can't a painter lift each foot in turn,
Left foot and right foot, go a double step,
Make his flesh liker and his soul more like,
Both in their order? Take the prettiest face,
The Prior's niece . . . patron-saint — is it so pretty
210 You can't discover if it means hope, fear,
Sorrow or joy? won't beauty go with these?
Suppose I've made her eyes all right and blue,
Can't I take breath and try to add life's flash,
And then add soul and heighten them three-fold?
Or say there's beauty with no soul at all —
(I never saw it — put the case the same —)
If you get simple beauty and naught else,
You get about the best thing God invents:

That's somewhat: and you'll find the soul you have missed,
220 Within yourself, when you return Him thanks.
'Rub all out!' Well, well, there's my life, in short,
And so the thing has gone on ever since.
I'm grown a man no doubt, I've broken bounds:
You should not take a fellow eight years old
And make him swear to never kiss the girls.
I'm my own master, paint now as I please –
Having a friend, you see, in the Corner-house!°   *i.e. Medici Palace*
Lord, it's fast holding by the rings in front –
Those great rings serve more purposes than just
230 To plant a flag in, or tie up a horse!
And yet the old schooling sticks, the old grave eyes
Are peeping o'er my shoulder as I work,
The heads shake still – 'It's Art's decline, my son!
You're not of the true painters, great and old;
Brother Angelico's[39] the man, you'll find;
Brother Lorenzo stands his single peer:
Fag on at flesh, you'll never make the third!'
Flower o' the pine,
You keep your mistr . . . manners, and I'll stick to mine!
240 I'm not the third, then: bless us, they must know!
Don't you think they're the likeliest to know,
They with their Latin? So, I swallow my rage,
Clench my teeth, suck my lips in tight, and paint
To please them – sometimes do and sometimes don't;
For, doing most, there's pretty sure to come
A turn, some warm eve finds me at my saints –
A laugh, a cry, the business of the world –
(Flower o' the peach,
Death for us all, and his own life for each!)
250 And my whole soul revolves, the cup runs over,
The world and life's too big to pass for a dream,
And I do these wild things in sheer despite,
And play the fooleries you catch me at,
In pure rage! The old mill-horse, out at grass
After hard years, throws up his stiff heels so,
Although the miller does not preach to him
The only good of grass is to make chaff.
What would men have? Do they like grass or no –
May they or may n't they? all I want's the thing
260 Settled for ever one way. As it is,
You tell too many lies and hurt yourself:
You don't like what you only like too much,

You do like what, if given you at your word,
You find abundantly detestable.
For me, I think I speak as I was taught;
I always see the garden and God there
A-making man's wife: and, my lesson learned,
The value and significance of flesh,
I can't unlearn ten minutes afterwards.

270   You understand me: I'm a beast, I know.
But see, now – why, I see as certainly
As that the morning-star's about to shine,
What will hap some day. We've a youngster here
Comes to our convent, studies what I do,
Slouches and stares and lets no atom drop:
His name is Guidi[40] – he'll not mind the monks –
They call him Hulking Tom, he lets them talk –
He picks my practice up – he'll paint apace,
I hope so – though I never live so long,
280 I know what's sure to follow. You be judge!
You speak no Latin more than I, belike;
However, you're my man, you've seen the world
– The beauty and the wonder and the power,
The shapes of things, their colours, lights and shades,
Changes, surprises, – and God made it all!
– For what? Do you feel thankful, ay or no,
For this fair town's face, yonder river's line,
The mountain round it and the sky above,
Much more the figures of man, woman, child,
290 These are the frame to? What's it all about?
To be passed over, despised? or dwelt upon,
Wondered at? oh, this last of course! – you say.
But why not do as well as say, – paint these
Just as they are, careless what comes of it?
God's works – paint any one, and count it crime
To let a truth slip. Don't object, 'His works
Are here already; nature is complete:
Suppose you reproduce her – (which you can't)
There's no advantage! you must beat her, then.'
300 For, don't you mark? we're made so that we love
First when we see them painted, things we have passed
Perhaps a hundred times nor cared to see;
And so they are better, painted – better to us,
Which is the same thing. Art was given for that;
God uses us to help each other so,

Lending our minds out. Have you noticed, now,
Your cullion°'s hanging face? A bit of chalk,   *miserable wretch*
And trust me but you should, though! How much more,
If I drew higher things with the same truth!
310 That were to take the Prior's pulpit-place,
Interpret God to all of you! Oh, oh,
It makes me mad to see what men shall do
And we in our graves! This world's no blot for us,
Nor blank; it means intensely, and means good:
To find its meaning is my meat and drink.
'Ay, but you don't so instigate to prayer!'
Strikes in the Prior: 'when your meaning's plain
It does not say to folk – remember matins,°   *morning service*
Or, mind you fast next Friday!' Why, for this
320 What need of art at all? A skull and bones,
Two bits of stick nailed crosswise, or, what's best,
A bell to chime the hour with, does as well.
I painted a Saint Laurence six months since
At Prato, splashed the fresco in fine style:
'How looks my painting, now the scaffold's down?'
I ask a brother: 'Hugely,' he returns –
'Already not one phiz° of your three slaves   *face*
Who turn the Deacon off his toasted side,
But's scratched and prodded to our heart's content,
330 The pious people have so eased their own
With coming to say prayers there in a rage:
We get on fast to see the bricks beneath.
Expect another job this time next year,
For pity and religion grow i' the crowd –
Your painting serves its purpose!' Hang the fools!

– That is – you'll not mistake an idle word
Spoke in a huff by a poor monk, God wot,
Tasting the air this spicy night which turns
The unaccustomed head like Chianti wine!
340 Oh, the church knows! don't misreport me, now!
It's natural a poor monk out of bounds
Should have his apt word to excuse himself:
And hearken how I plot to make amends.
I have bethought me: I shall paint a piece
. . . There's for you! Give me six months, then go, see
Something in Sant' Ambrogio's! Bless the nuns!
They want a cast° o' my office. I shall paint   *sample*
God in the midst, Madonna and her babe,
Ringed by a bowery flowery angel-brood,

350 Lilies and vestments and white faces, sweet
As puff on puff of grated orris-root[41]
When ladies crowd to Church at midsummer.
And then in the front, of course a saint or two –
Saint John, because he saves the Florentines,
Saint Ambrose, who puts down in black and white
The convent's friends and gives them a long day,
And Job, I must have him there past mistake,
The man of Uz[42] (an Us without the z,
Painters who need his patience). Well, all these
360 Secured at their devotion, up shall come
Out of a corner when you least expect,
As one by a dark stair into a great light,
Music and talking, who but Lippo! I! –[43]
Mazed, motionless and moonstruck – I'm the man!
Back I shrink – what is this I see and hear?
I, caught up with my monk's-things by mistake,
My old serge gown and rope that goes all round,
I, in this presence, this pure company!
Where's a hole, where's a corner for escape?
370 Then steps a sweet angelic slip[44] of a thing
Forward, puts out a soft palm – 'Not so fast!'
– Addresses the celestial presence, 'nay –
He made you and devised you, after all,
Though he's none of you! Could Saint John[45] there draw –
His camel-hair make up a painting-brush?
We come to brother Lippo for all that,
Iste perfecit opus!'[46] So, all smile –
I shuffle sideways with my blushing face
Under the cover of a hundred wings
380 Thrown like a spread of kirtles° when you're gay   skirts
And play hot cockles,[47] all the doors being shut,
Till, wholly unexpected, in there pops
The hothead husband! Thus I scuttle off
To some safe bench behind, not letting go
The palm of her, the little lily thing
That spoke the good word for me in the nick,
Like the Prior's niece . . . Saint Lucy, I would say.
And so all's saved for me, and for the church
A pretty picture gained. Go, six months hence!
390 Your hand, sir, and good-bye: no lights, no lights!
The street's hushed, and I know my own way back,
Don't fear me! There's the gray beginning. Zooks!

[1855]

Love in a Life

I

Room after room,
I hunt the house through
We inhabit together.
Heart, fear nothing, for, heart, thou shalt find her –
Next time, herself! – not the trouble behind her
Left in the curtain, the couch's perfume!
As she brushed it, the cornice-wreath blossomed anew:
Yon looking-glass gleamed at the wave of her feather.

II

Yet the day wears,
10   And door succeeds door;
I try the fresh fortune –
Range the wide house from the wing to the centre
Still the same chance! she goes out as I enter.
Spend my whole day in the quest, – who cares?
But 'tis twilight, you see, – with such suites to explore,
Such closets to search, such alcoves to importune!

[1855]

Life in a Love

Escape me?
Never –
Beloved!
While I am I, and you are you,
    So long as the world contains us both,
    Me the loving and you the loth,
While the one eludes, must the other pursue.
My life is a fault at last, I fear:
    It seems too much like a fate, indeed!
10   Though I do my best I shall scarce succeed.
But what if I fail of my purpose here?
It is but to keep the nerves at strain,
    To dry one's eyes and laugh at a fall,

And, baffled, get up and begin again, –
  So the chase takes up one's life, that's all.
While, look but once from your farthest bound°   *boundary*
  At me so deep in the dust and dark,
Not sooner the old hope goes to ground
  Than a new one, straight to the self-same mark,
20   I shape me –
            Ever
            Removed!

[1855]

The Last Ride Together

I

I said – Then, dearest, since 'tis so,
Since now at length my fate I know,
Since nothing all my love avails,
Since all my life seemed meant for, fails,
  Since this was written and needs must be –
My whole heart rises up to bless
Your name in pride and thankfulness!
Take back the hope you gave, – I claim
Only a memory of the same,
10 – And this beside, if you will not blame,
  Your leave for one more last ride with me.

II

My mistress bent that brow of hers;
Those deep dark eyes where pride demurs
When pity would be softening through,
Fixed me a breathing-while or two
  With life or death in the balance: right!
The blood replenished me again;
My last thought was at least not vain:
I and my mistress, side by side
20 Shall be together, breathe and ride,
So, one day more am I deified.
  Who knows but the world may end to-night?

III

Hush! if you saw some western cloud
All billowy-bosomed, over-bowed
By many benedictions – sun's
And moon's and evening-star's at once –
   And so, you, looking and loving best,
Conscious grew, your passion drew
Cloud, sunset, moonrise, star-shine too,
30 Down on you, near and yet more near,
Till flesh must fade for heaven was here! –
Thus leant she and lingered – joy and fear!
   Thus lay she a moment on my breast.

IV

Then we began to ride. My soul
Smoothed itself out, a long-cramped scroll
Freshening and fluttering in the wind.
Past hopes already lay behind.
   What need to strive with a life awry?
Had I said that, had I done this,
40 So might I gain, so might I miss.
Might she have loved me? just as well
She might have hated, who can tell.
Where had I been now if the worst befell?
   And here we are riding, she and I.

V

Fail I alone, in words and deeds?
Why, all men strive and who succeeds?
We rode; it seemed my spirit flew,
Saw other regions, cities new,
   As the world rushed by on either side.
50 I thought, – All labour, yet no less
Bear up beneath their unsuccess.
Look at the end of work, contrast
The petty Done, the Undone vast,
This Present of theirs with the hopeful Past!
   I hoped she would love me; here we ride.

VI

What hand and brain went ever paired?
What heart alike conceived and dared?
What act proved all its thought had been?

What will but felt the fleshly screen?
60   We ride and I see her bosom heave.
There's many a crown for who can reach.
Ten lines, a statesman's life in each!
The flag stuck on a heap of bones,
A soldier's doing! what atones?
They scratch his name on the Abbey-stones.[48]
    My riding is better, by their leave.

VII

What does it all mean, poet? Well,
Your brains beat into rhythm, you tell
What we felt only; you expressed
70   You hold things beautiful the best,
    And pace them in rhyme so, side by side.
'Tis something, nay 'tis much: but then,
Have you yourself what's best for men?
Are you – poor, sick, old ere your time –
Nearer one whit your own sublime
Than we who never have turned a rhyme?
    Sing, riding's a joy! For me, I ride.

VIII

And you, great sculptor – so, you gave
A score of years to Art, her slave,
80   And that's your Venus, whence we turn
To yonder girl that fords the burn°!   *small stream*
    You acquiesce, and shall I repine?
What, man of music, you grown gray
With notes and nothing else to say,
Is this your sole praise from a friend,
'Greatly his opera's strains intend,
But in music we know how fashions end!'
    I gave my youth; but we ride, in fine.

IX

Who knows what's fit for us? Had fate
90   Proposed bliss here should sublimate°   *uplift*
My being – had I signed the bond –
Still one must lead some life beyond,
    Have a bliss to die with, dim-descried.
This foot once planted on the goal,
This glory-garland round my soul,
Could I descry such? Try and test!

I sink back shuddering from the quest.
Earth being so good, would heaven seem best?
　　Now, Heaven and she are beyond this ride.

X

100 And yet – she has not spoke so long!
What if Heaven be that, fair and strong
At life's best, with our eyes upturned
Whither life's flower is first discerned,
　　We, fixed so, ever should so abide?
What if we still ride on, we two
With life for ever old yet new,
Changed not in kind but in degree,
The instant made eternity, –
And Heaven just prove that I and she
　　Ride, ride together, for ever ride?

The Patriot

AN OLD STORY

I

It was roses, roses, all the way,
　　With myrtle mixed in my path like mad:
The house-roofs seemed to heave and sway,
　　The church-spires flamed, such flags they had,
A year ago on this very day.

II

The air broke into a mist with bells,
　　The old walls rocked with the crowd and cries.
Had I said, 'Good folk, mere noise repels –
　　But give me your sun from yonder skies!'
10 They had answered, 'And afterward, what else?'

III

Alack, it was I who leaped at the sun
　　To give it my loving friends to keep!
Naught man could do, have I left undone:
　　And you see my harvest, what I reap
This very day, now a year is run.

IV

There's nobody on the house-tops now –
    Just a palsied few at the windows set;
For the best of the sight is, all allow,
    At the Shambles' Gate[49] – or, better yet,
20 By the very scaffold's foot, I trow.

V

I go in the rain, and, more than needs,
    A rope cuts both my wrists behind;
And I think, by the feel, my forehead bleeds,
    For they fling, whoever has a mind,
Stones at me for my year's misdeeds.

VI

Thus I entered, and thus I go!
    In triumphs, people have dropped down dead.
'Paid by the World, what dost thou owe
    Me?' – God might question; now instead,
30 'Tis God shall repay: I am safer so.

[1855]

Memorabilia[50]

I

Ah, did you once see Shelley plain,
    And did he stop and speak to you
And did you speak to him again?
    How strange it seems and new!

II

But you were living before that,
    And also you are living after;
And the memory I started at –
    My starting moves your laughter.

III

I crossed a moor, with a name of its own
10   And a certain use in the world no doubt,
Yet a hand's-breadth of it shines alone
    'Mid the blank miles round about:

IV

For there I picked up on the heather
   And there I put inside my breast
A moulted feather, an eagle-feather!
   Well, I forget the rest.

[1855]

'*De Gustibus* —'[51]

I

Your ghost will walk, you lover of trees,
   (If our loves remain)
   In an English lane,
By a cornfield-side a-flutter with poppies.
Hark, those two in the hazel coppice —
A boy and a girl, if the good fates please,
   Making love, say, —
   The happier they!
Draw yourself up from the light of the moon,
And let them pass, as they will too soon,
   With the bean-flowers' boon,   *gift*
   And the blackbird's tune,
   And May, and June!

II

What I love best in all the world
Is a castle, precipice-encurled,
In a gash of the wind-grieved Apennine.
Or look for me, old fellow of mine,
(If I get my head from out the mouth
O' the grave, and loose my spirit's bands,
And come again to the land of lands) —
In a sea-side house to the farther South,
Where the baked cicalas die of drouth,
And one sharp tree — 'tis a cypress — stands,
By the many hundred years red-rusted,
Rough iron-spiked, ripe fruit-o'ercrusted,
My sentinel to guard the sands

To the water's edge. For, what expands
Before the house, but the great opaque
Blue breadth of sea without a break?
30 While, in the house, for ever crumbles
Some fragment of the frescoed walls,
From blisters where a scorpion sprawls.
A girl bare-footed brings, and tumbles
Down on the pavement, green-flesh melons,
And says there's news today – the king[52]
Was shot at, touched in the liver-wing,   *right arm*
Goes with his Bourbon arm in a sling:
– She hopes they have not caught the felons.
    Italy, my Italy!
40 Queen Mary's saying[53] serves for me –
    (When fortune's malice
    Lost her – Calais) –
Open my heart and you will see
Graved inside of it, 'Italy.'
Such lovers old are I and she:
So it always was, so shall ever be!

[1855]

Two in the Campagna

I

I wonder do you feel to-day
    As I have felt, since, hand in hand,
We sat down on the grass, to stray
    In spirit better through the land,
This morn of Rome and May?

II

For me, I touched a thought, I know,
    Has tantalized me many times,
(Like turns of thread the spiders throw
    Mocking across our path) for rhymes
10 To catch at and let go.

III

Help me to hold it! First it left
   The yellowing fennel, run to seed
There, branching from the brickwork's cleft,
   Some old tomb's ruin: yonder weed
Took up the floating weft,

IV

Where one small orange cup amassed
   Five beetles, – blind and green they grope
Among the honey-meal: and last,
   Everywhere on the grassy slope
20 I traced it. Hold it fast!

V

The champaign° with its endless fleece   *field*
   Of feathery grasses everywhere!
Silence and passion, joy and peace,
   An everlasting wash of air –
Rome's ghost since her decease.

VI

Such life here, through such lengths of hours,
   Such miracles performed in play,
Such primal naked forms of flowers,
   Such letting Nature have her way
30 While Heaven looks from its towers!

VII

How say you? Let us, O my dove,
   Let us be unashamed of soul,
As earth lies bare to heaven above!
   How is it under our control
To love or not to love?

VIII

I would that you were all to me,
   You that are just so much, no more.
Nor yours nor mine, nor slave nor free!
   Where does the fault lie? What the core
40 O' the wound, since wound must be?

IX

I would I could adopt your will,
   See with your eyes, and set my heart
Beating by yours, and drink my fill
   At your soul's springs, – your part my part
In life, for good and ill.

X

No. I yearn upward, touch you close,
   Then stand away. I kiss your cheek,
Catch your soul's warmth, – I pluck the rose
   And love it more than tongue can speak –
50 Then the good minute goes.

XI

Already how am I so far
   Out of that minute? Must I go
Still like the thistle-ball, no bar,
   Onward, whenever light winds blow,
Fixed by no friendly star?

XII

Just when I seemed about to learn!
   Where is the thread now? Off again!
The old trick! Only I discern –
   Infinite passion, and the pain
60 Of finite hearts that yearn.

[1855]

Abt Vogler

(AFTER HE HAS BEEN EXTEMPORIZING UPON THE MUSICAL INSTRUMENT OF HIS INVENTION)

I

Would that the structure brave, the manifold music I build,
   Bidding my organ obey, calling its keys to their work,
Claiming each slave of the sound, at a touch,
                      as when Solomon willed
   Armies of angels that soar, legions of demons that lurk,
Man, brute, reptile, fly, – alien of end and of aim,
   Adverse, each from the other heaven-high, hell-deep removed, –
Should rush into sight at once as he named the ineffable Name,
   And pile him a palace straight, to pleasure the princess he loved!

II

Would it might tarry like his, the beautiful building of mine,
10   This which my keys in a crowd pressed and importuned to raise!
Ah, one and all, how they helped, would dispart now
                      and now combine,
   Zealous to hasten the work, heighten their master his praise!
And one would bury his brow with a blind plunge down to hell,
   Burrow awhile and build, broad on the roots of things,
Then up again swim into sight, having based me my palace well,
   Founded it, fearless of flame, flat on the nether springs.

III

And another would mount and march, like
                the excellent minion° he was,   *servant*
   Ay, another and yet another, one crowd but with many a crest,
Raising my rampired° walls of gold as transparent as glass,   *with*
20   Eager to do and die, yield each his place to the rest: *ramparts*
For higher still and higher (as a runner tips with fire,
   When a great illumination surprises a festal night –
Outlining round and round Rome's dome from space to spire)
   Up, the pinnacled glory reached, and the pride
                     of my soul was in sight.

IV

In sight? Not half! for it seemed, it was certain,
                  to match man's birth,
   Nature in turn conceived, obeying an impulse as I;

And the emulous° heaven yearned down, made effort   *emulating*
                                     to reach the earth,
   As the earth had done her best, in my passion, to scale the sky:
Novel splendours burst forth, grew familiar and dwelt with mine,
30   Not a point nor peak but found and fixed its wandering star;
Meteor-moons, balls of blaze: and they did not pale nor pine,
   For earth had attained to heaven, there was no more near nor
                                     far.

V

Nay more; for there wanted not who walked in the glare and glow,
   Presences plain in the place; or, fresh from the Protoplast,   *the first*
Furnished for ages to come, when a kindlier   *created*
                            wind should blow,
   Lured now to begin and live, in a house to their liking at last;
Or else the wonderful Dead who have passed through the body and
                                   gone,
   But were back once more to breathe in an old world
                            worth their new:
What never had been, was now; what was, as it shall be anon;
   And what is, – shall I say, matched both? for I was made perfect
40   too.

VI

All through my keys that gave their sounds to a wish of my soul,
   All through my soul that praised as its wish flowed visibly forth,
All through music and me! For think, had I painted the whole,
   Why, there it had stood, to see, nor the process so wonder-worth:
Had I written the same, made verse – still, effect
                         proceeds from cause,
   Ye know why the forms are fair, ye hear how the tale is told;
It is all triumphant art, but art in obedience to laws,
   Painter and poet are proud in the artist-list enrolled:–

VII

But here is the finger of God, a flash of the will that can,
50   Existent behind all laws, that made them and, lo, they are!
And I know not if, save in this, such gift be allowed to man,
   That out of three sounds he frame, not a fourth sound, but a star.
Consider it well: each tone of our scale in itself is naught;
   It is everywhere in the world – loud, soft, and all is said:
Give it to me to use! I mix it with two in my thought:
   And there! Ye have heard and seen: consider and bow the head!

VIII

Well, it is gone at last, the palace of music I reared;
  Gone! and the good tears start, the praises that come too slow;
For one is assured at first, one scarce can say that he feared,
60   That he even gave it a thought, the gone thing was to go
Never to be again! But many more of the kind .
  As good, nay, better perchance: is this your comfort to me?
To me, who must be saved because I cling with my mind
  To the same, same self, same love, same God: ay,
                                  what was, shall be.

IX

Therefore to whom turn I but to thee, the ineffable Name?
  Builder and maker, thou, of houses not made with hands!
What, have fear of change from thee who art ever the same?
  Doubt that thy power can fill the heart that thy power expands?
There shall never be one lost good! What was, shall live as before;
70   The evil is null, is naught, is silence implying sound;
What was good shall be good, with, for evil, so much good more;
  On the earth the broken arcs; in the heaven, a perfect round.

X

All we have willed or hoped or dreamed of good shall exist;
  Not its semblance, but itself; no beauty, nor good, nor power
Whose voice has gone forth, but each survives for the melodist
  When eternity affirms the conception of an hour.
The high that proved too high, the heroic for earth too hard,
  The passion that left the ground to lose itself in the sky,
Are music sent up to God by the lover and the bard;
80   Enough that he heard it once: we shall hear it by-and-by.

XI

And what is our failure here but a triumph's evidence
  For the fulness of the days? Have we withered or agonized?
Why else was the pause prolonged but that singing
                            might issue thence?
  Why rushed the discords in but that harmony should be prized?
Sorrow is hard to bear, and doubt is slow to clear,
  Each sufferer says his say, his scheme of the weal and woe:
But God has a few of us whom he whispers in the ear;
  The rest may reason and welcome: 'tis we musicians know.

XII

Well, it is earth with me; silence resumes her reign:
90   I will be patient and proud, and soberly acquiesce.
Give me the keys. I feel for the common chord again,
    Sliding by semitones, till I sink to the minor, – yes,
And I blunt it into a ninth, and I stand on alien ground,
    Surveying awhile the heights I rolled from into the deep;
Which, hark, I have dared and done, for my resting-place is found,
    The C Major of this life:[54] so, now I will try to sleep.

[1864]

Caliban upon Setebos; or, Natural Theology in the Island[55]

'Thou thoughtest that I was altogether such a one as thyself'

[Will sprawl, now that the heat of day is best,
Flat on his belly in the pit's much mire,
With elbows wide, fists clenched to prop his chin.
And, while he kicks both feet in the cool slush,
And feels about his spine small eft-things° course,   *newt-like*
Run in and out each arm, and make him laugh:
And while above his head a pompion°plant,   *pumpkin*
Coating the cave-top as a brow its eye,
Creeps down to touch and tickle hair and beard,
10 And now a flower drops with a bee inside,
And now a fruit to snap at, catch and crunch, –
He looks out o'er yon sea which sunbeams cross
And recross till they weave a spider-web
(Meshes of fire, some great fish breaks at times)
And talks to his own self, howe'er he please,
Touching that other, whom his dam° called God.   *mother (Sycorax)*
Because to talk about Him, vexes – ha,
Could He but know! and time to vex is now,
When talk is safer than in winter-time.
20 Moreover Prosper and Miranda sleep[56]
In confidence he drudges at their task,
And it is good to cheat the pair, and gibe,
Letting the rank tongue blossom into speech.]

Setebos, Setebos, and Setebos!
'Thinketh, He dwelleth i' the cold o' the moon.

'Thinketh He made it, with the sun to match,
But not the stars; the stars came otherwise;
Only made clouds, winds, meteors, such as that:
Also this isle, what lives and grows thereon,
30   And snaky sea which rounds and ends the same.

'Thinketh, it came of being ill at ease:
He hated that He cannot change His cold,
Nor cure its ache. 'Hath spied an icy fish
That longed to 'scape the rock-stream where she lived,
And thaw herself within the lukewarm brine
O' the lazy sea her stream thrusts far amid,
A crystal spike 'twixt two warm walls of wave;
Only, she ever sickened, found repulse
At the other kind of water, not her life,
40   (Green-dense and dim-delicious, bred o' the sun)
Flounced back from bliss she was not born to breathe,
And in her old bounds buried her despair,
Hating and loving warmth alike: so He.

'Thinketh, He made thereat the sun, this isle,
Trees and the fowls here, beast and creeping thing:
Yon otter, sleek-wet, black, lithe as a leech;
Yon auk,° one fire-eye in a ball of foam,   *(sea-bird)*
That floats and feeds; a certain badger brown
He hath watched hunt with that slant white-wedge eye
50   By moonlight; and the pie° with the long tongue   *magpie*
That pricks deep into oakwarts° for a worm.   *galls on oak trees*
And says a plain word when she finds her prize,
But will not eat the ants; the ants themselves
That build a wall of seeds and settled stalks
About their hole – He made all these and more,
Made all we see, and us, in spite: how else?
He could not, Himself, make a second self
To be His mate; as well have made Himself;
He would not make what he mislikes or slights,
60   An eyesore to Him, or not worth His pains:
But did, in envy, listlessness or sport,
Make what Himself would fain, in a manner, be –
Weaker in most points, stronger in a few,
Worthy, and yet mere playthings all the while,

Things He admires and mocks too, – that is it.
Because, so brave, so better though they be,
It nothing skills° if He begin to plague.   *helps*
Look now, I melt a gourd-fruit into mash,
Add honeycomb and pods, I have perceived,
70   Which bite like finches when they bill and kiss, –
Then, when froth rises bladdery,[57] drink up all,
Quick, quick, till maggots scamper through my brain;
Last, throw me on my back i' the seeded thyme,
And wanton, wishing I were born a bird.
Put case, unable to be what I wish,
I yet could make a live bird out of clay:
Would not I take clay, pinch my Caliban
Able to fly? – for, there, see, he hath wings,
And great comb like the hoopoe's° to admire,   *bird with crest*
80   And there, a sting to do his foes offence,
There, and I will that he begin to live,
Fly to yon rock-top, nip me off the horns
Of grigs° high up that make the merry din,   *crickets*
Saucy through their veined wings, and mind me not.
In which feat, if his leg snapped, brittle clay,
And he lay stupid-like, – why, I should laugh;
And if he, spying me, should fall to weep,
Beseech me to be good, repair his wrong,
Bid his poor leg smartless or grow again, –
90   Well, as the chance were, this might take or else
Not take my fancy: I might hear his cry,
And give the mankin three sound legs for one,
Or pluck the other off, leave him like an egg,
And lessoned° he was mine and merely clay.   *taught*
Were this no pleasure, lying in the thyme,
Drinking the mash, with brain become alive,
Making and marring clay at will? So He.

'Thinketh, such shows nor right nor wrong in Him,
Nor kind, nor cruel: He is strong and Lord.
100   'Am strong myself compared to yonder crabs
That march now from the mountain to the sea;
'Let twenty pass, and stone the twenty-first,
Loving not, hating not, just choosing so.
'Say, the first straggler that boasts purple spots
Shall join the file, one pincer twisted off;
'Say, this bruised fellow shall receive a worm,
And two worms he whose nippers end in red;

As it likes me each time, I do: so He.

Well then, 'supposeth He is good in the main,
110 Placable° if His mind and ways were guessed,   *easily appeased*
But rougher than His handiwork, be sure!
Oh, He hath made things worthier than Himself,
And envieth that, so helped, such things do more
Than He who made them! What consoles but this?
That they, unless through Him, do naught at all,
And must submit: what other use in things?
'Hath cut a pipe of pithless elder-°joint   *elder tree*
That, blown through, gives exact the scream o' the jay
When from her wing you twitch the feathers blue:
120 'Sound this, and little birds that hate the jay
Flock within stone's throw, glad their foe is hurt:
'Put case such pipe could prattle and boast forsooth
"I catch the birds, I am the crafty thing,
I make the cry my maker cannot make
With his great round mouth; he must blow through mine!"
Would not I smash it with my foot? So He.

But wherefore rough, why cold and ill at ease?
Aha, that is a question! Ask, for that,
What knows, – the something over Setebos
130 That made Him, or He, may be, found and fought,
Worsted, drove off and did to nothing, perchance.
There may be something quiet o'er His head,
Out of His reach, that feels nor joy nor grief,
Since both derive from weakness in some way.
I joy because the quails come; would not joy
Could I bring quails here when I have a mind:
This Quiet, all it hath a mind to, doth.
'Esteemeth stars the outposts of its couch,
But never spends much thought nor care that way.
140 It may look up, work up, – the worse for those
It works on! 'Careth but for Setebos
The many-handed as a cuttle-fish,
Who, making Himself feared through what He does,
Looks up, first, and perceives he cannot soar
To what is quiet and hath happy life;
Next looks down here, and out of very spite
Makes this a bauble-world to ape yon real,
These good things to match those as hips° do grapes.   *dogrose berry*
'Tis solace making baubles, ay, and sport.
150 Himself peeped late, eyed Prosper at his books

Careless and lofty, lord now of the isle:
Vexed, 'stitched a book of broad leaves, arrow-shaped,
Wrote thereon, he knows what, prodigious words;
Has peeled a wand and called it by a name;
Weareth at whiles for an enchanter's robe
The eyed skin of a supple oncelot;°   *jaguar*
And hath an ounce° sleeker than youngling moke;°   *lynx/donkey*
A four-legged serpent he makes cower and couch,
Now snarl, now hold its breath and mind his eye,
160   And saith she is Miranda and my wife:
'Keeps for his Ariel[58] a tall pouch-bill crane
He bids go wade for fish and straight disgorge;
Also a sea-beast, lumpish, which he snared,
Blinded the eyes of, and brought somewhat tame,
And split its toe-webs, and now pens the drudge
In a hole o' the rock and calls him Caliban;
A bitter heart that bides its time and bites.
'Plays thus at being Prosper in a way,
Taketh his mirth with make-believes: so He.

170   His dam held that the Quiet made all things
Which Setebos vexed only: 'holds not so.
Who made them weak, meant weakness He might vex.
Had He meant other, while His hand was in,
Why not make horny eyes no thorn could prick,
Or plate my scalp with bone against the snow,
Or overscale my flesh 'neath joint and joint,
Like an orc's° armour? Ay, – so spoil His sport!   *(sea-monster)*
He is the One now: only He doth all.

'Saith, He may like, perchance, what profits Him.
180   Ay, himself loves what does him good; but why?
'Gets good no otherwise. This blinded beast
Loves whoso places flesh-meat on his nose,
But, had he eyes, would want no help, but hate
Or love, just as it liked him: He hath eyes.
Also it pleaseth Setebos to work,
Use all His hands, and exercise much craft,
By no means for the love of what is worked.
'Tasteth, himself, no finer good i' the world
When all goes right, in this safe summer-time,
190   And he wants little, hungers, aches not much,
Than trying what to do with wit and strength.
'Falls to make something: 'piled yon pile of turfs,

And squared and stuck there squares of soft white chalk,
And, with a fish-tooth, scratched a moon on each,
And set up endwise certain spikes of tree,
And crowned the whole with a sloth's skull a-top,
Found dead i' the woods, too hard for one to kill.
No use at all i' the work, for work's sole sake;
'Shall some day knock it down again: so He.

200 'Saith He is terrible: watch His feats in proof!
One hurricane will spoil six good months' hope.
He hath a spite against me, that I know,
Just as He favours Prosper, who knows why?
So it is, all the same, as well I find.
'Wove wattles[59] half the winter, fenced them firm
With stone and stake to stop she-tortoises
Crawling to lay their eggs here: well, one wave,
Feeling the foot of Him upon its neck,
Gaped as a snake does, lolled out its large tongue,
210 And licked the whole labour flat; so much for spite.
'Saw a ball flame down late (yonder it lies)
Where, half an hour before, I slept in the shade:
Often they scatter sparkles: there is force!
'Dug up a newt He may have envied once
And turned to stone, shut up inside a stone.
Please Him and hinder this? – What Prosper does?
Aha, if He would tell me how! Not He!
There is the sport: discover how or die!
All need not die, for of the things o' the isle
220 Some flee afar, some dive, some run up trees;
Those at His mercy, – why, they please Him most
When . . . when . . . well, never try the same way twice!
Repeat what act has pleased, He may grow wroth.°   *angry*
You must not know His ways, and play Him off,
Sure of the issue. 'Doth the like himself:
'Spareth a squirrel that it nothing fears
But steals the nut from underneath my thumb,
And when I threat, bites stoutly in defence:
'Spareth an urchin° that contrariwise,   *hedgehog*
230 Curls up into a ball, pretending death
For fright at my approach: the two ways please.
But what would move my choler° more than this,   *anger*
That either creature counted on its life
To-morrow and next day and all days to come,
Saying, forsooth, in the inmost of its heart,

'Because he did so yesterday with me,
And otherwise with such another brute,
So must he do henceforth and always.' – Ay?
Would teach the reasoning couple what 'must' means!
240 'Doth as he likes, or wherefore Lord? So He.

'Conceiveth all things will continue thus,
And we shall have to live in fear of Him
So long as He lives, keeps His strength: no change,
If He have done His best, make no new world
To please Him more, so leave off watching this, –
If He surprise not even the Quiet's self
Some strange day, – or, suppose, grow into it
As grubs grow butterflies: else, here are we,
And there is He, and nowhere help at all.

250 'Believeth with the life, the pain shall stop.
His dam held different, that after death
He both plagued enemies and feasted friends:
Idly! He doth His worst in this our life,
Giving just respite lest we die through pain,
Saving last pain for worst, – with which, an end.
Meanwhile, the best way to escape His ire
Is, not to seem too happy. 'Sees, himself,
Yonder two flies, with purple films and pink,
Bask on the pompion-bell above: kills both.
260 'Sees two black painful beetles roll their ball
On head and tail as if to save their lives:
Moves them the stick away they strive to clear.

Even so, 'would have Him misconceive, suppose
This Caliban strives hard and ails no less,
And always, above all else, envies Him;
Wherefore he mainly dances on dark nights,
Moans in the sun, gets under holes to laugh,
And never speaks his mind save housed as now:
Outside, 'groans, curses. If He caught me here,
270 O'erheard this speech, and asked 'What chucklest at?'
'Would, to appease Him, cut a finger off,
Or of my three kid yearlings burn the best
Or let the toothsome apples rot on tree,
Or push my tame beast for the orc to taste:
While myself lit a fire, and made a song
And sung it, '*What I hate, be consecrate*

To celebrate Thee and Thy state, no mate
For Thee; what see for envy in poor me?'
Hoping the while, since evils sometimes mend,
280 Warts rub away and sores are cured with slime,
That some strange day, will either the Quiet catch
And conquer Setebos, or likelier He
Decrepit may doze, doze, as good as die.

[What, what? A curtain o'er the world at once!
Crickets stop hissing; not a bird – or, yes,
There scuds His raven that has told Him all!
It was fool's play, this prattling! Ha! The wind
Shoulders the pillared dust, death's house o' the move,
And fast invading fires begin! White blaze –
290 A tree's head snaps – and there, there, there, there, there,
His thunder follows! Fool to gibe at Him!
Lo! 'Lieth flat and loveth Setebos!
'Maketh his teeth meet through his upper lip,
Will let those quails fly, will not eat this month
One little mess of whelks, so he may 'scape!]   (shellfish)

[1864]

Prospice[60]

Fear death? – to feel the fog in my throat,
    The mist in my face,
When the snows begin, and the blasts denote
    I am nearing the place,
The power of the night, the press of the storm,
    The post° of the foe;   sentry post
Where he stands, the Arch Fear in a visible form,
    Yet the strong man must go:
For the journey is done and the summit attained,
10   And the barriers fall,
Though a battle's to fight ere the guerdon° be gained,   reward
    The reward of it all.
I was ever a fighter, so – one fight more,
    The best and the last!
I would hate that death bandaged my eyes, and forbore,
    And bade me creep past.

No! let me taste the whole of it, fare like my peers
    The heroes of old,
Bear the brunt, in a minute pay glad life's arrears
20   Of pain, darkness and cold.
For sudden the worst turns the best to the brave,
    The black minute's at end,
And the elements' rage, the fiend-voices that rave,
    Shall dwindle, shall blend,
Shall change, shall become first a peace out of pain,
    Then a light, then thy breast,
O thou soul of my soul! I shall clasp thee again,
    And with God be the rest!

[1864]

NOTES

Browning

1 The irony of this song is that it is overheard by two murderers – Sebald and his mistress, Ottima, who have murdered Luca, Ottima's husband.

2 Alphonso II, Duke of Ferrara, was in 1564 negotiating for marriage with the niece of the Count of Tyrol. His 'last duchess' d.1561, age 17, believed to have been poisoned. B.'s poem possibly based on this.

3 Fra Pandolf, painter, Claus of Innsbruck, sculptor, are both fictitious.

4 diseased growth on oak trees, used in ink making.

5 a pirate from N. Africa.

6 i.e. God the Father, Christ the Son, and the Holy Ghost.

7 4th C. heresy denying the Trinity.

8 Gal. V.19–21, where 17 damnations listed.

9 4th C. heresy in which God and Satan were coeval in power.

10 meaning disputed, possibly a corruption of some medieval religious ritual.

11 Hail, Virgin, full of grace.

12 the incident is entirely fictional.

13 Lokeren, Boon, etc, towns between Ghent and Aix (Aachen).

14 William Wordsworth, who had just accepted the post of Poet Laureate which B. considered the final repudiation of W.'s earlier revolutionary spirit. With the Laureateship W. accepted a small pension.

15 a church in Rome; the characters are fictional.

16 S. side of the church from where the epistles are read.

17 blue, semi-precious stone.

18 a church in Rome.

19 staff carried by Bacchus.

20 a kind of limestone.

21 a precious form of quartz.

22 'he shone forth' – in inferior Latin.

23   a statue – a torso on a pedestal.

24   part of a classical temple, with an architrave, a frieze, and a cornice.

25   rainbows from the splashing foam.

26   Dante, Boccaccio, Petrarch – all Italian poets; St Jerome – a religious leader and writer; Cicero – a Roman author.

27   the statue of the Virgin Mary.

28   B. considered this artist a realist as opposed to earlier more traditional painters.

29   torches of the nightwatchmen who policed the streets at night.

30   the Medici-Ricardi Palace, built by Cosimo de Medici 1444–60. Lippi painted a nativity scene for the chapel.

31   the Captain of the group.

32   i.e. would be painted as Judas.

33   i.e. of Medici.

34   the Church of San Lorenzo.

35   on a painting of St. Jerome in the desert. Not painted by Lippi.

36   Lippi's foster-mother.

37   Florence's law was administered by eight elected officials.

38   the Dominican order of friars.

39   Fra Angelico; Fra Lorenzo Monaco.

40   Tommarco Guidi (Masaccio). B. thought he was Lippi's pupil, but more probably was his master.

41   root of iris – made into a perfume.

42   Job's birthplace.

43   in B.'s time man referred to (in Lippi's painting) thought to be Lippi, a self-portrait; now thought to be Francesco Marenghi who commissioned the painting.

44   St Lucy who is in the picture referred to.

45   Mark 1.6 'John was clothed with camel's hair'.

46   'This one accomplished the work'.

47   the game of Blind Man's Buff.

48   memorial stones in Westminster Abbey.

49   the shambles was the area of butchers' stalls in a town.

50   'memorable things'. B. had met a man in a bookshop who had known Shelley, whom B. admired greatly.

51   'De gustibus non est disputandum' – there is no arguing about tastes.

52   Ferdinand II (1810–59) King of the Two Sicilies.

53   Queen Mary (Tudor) – upset by the loss of Calais to the French in 1558, avowed that when she died they would find Calais written on her heart.

54   in extemporizing Vogler sinks to a minor key (a sad one) and then finally ends in C major – a key of resolution, acceptance and firmness.

55   this depiction of the character Caliban (from Shakespeare's *The Tempest*) owes as much to Darwin's *Origin of Species* as it does to Shakespeare. 'Thou thoughtest –' Ps. L.21.

56   in *The Tempest* Prospero is the usurped Duke of Milan; Miranda is his daughter whom Caliban tries to rape; Setebos is Caliban's mother's (Sycorax's) god.

57   bubbly?

58   the spirit servant to Prospero.

59   a frame of stakes interwoven with twigs.

60   'look ahead' – written shortly after Elizabeth Barrett Browning's death – to whom B. refers in the closing lines.

Matthew Arnold

[1822–88]

Son of Thomas, the well-known headmaster of Rugby School, he was educated at Rugby, Winchester, and Balliol College, Oxford: he became friends with A. H. Clough and won the Newdigate Prize for a poem on Cromwell: became a Fellow of Oriel College and, 1847, secretary to Lord Lansdowne. 1851, he was appointed Inspector of Schools and for the next 35 years he held that appointment. He travelled through England, and visited the Continent to study the educational system there, producing reports 1861, 1864, 1868, in which he wrote with approval of the more organised continental system. His first volume of poetry, *The Strayed Reveller and Other Poems*, was published in 1849 as by 'A.'. 1851 he married Fanny Wightman, and they had 6 children, 3 of whom predeceased him. Part of 'Dover Beach', 1867, was composed on his honeymoon. *Empedocles on Etna and Other Poems*, 1852, also appeared anonymously. 1853 he published a volume containing 'Sohrab and Rustum', 'The Scholar Gipsy', and 'Stanzas in Memory of the Author of "Obermann"' – which show how much he was influenced by Senancour's novel; in the Preface, he writes at length about the problems of writing poetry in the 'confusion of the present times'. *Poems 2nd Series*, 1855: *New Poems*, 1867, which included 'Thyrsis' and 'Rugby Chapel'. Increasingly he turned to prose and established a position as a leading critic. 1860 he became Professor of Poetry at Oxford and his lectures on poetry were published 1861. He died in Liverpool while awaiting the arrival of his daughter Lucy, who had married an American.

Resignation

TO FAUSTA[1]

To die be given us, or attain!
Fierce work it were, to do again.
So pilgrims, bound for Mecca, prayed
At burning noon; so warriors said,
Scarfed with the cross, who watch'd the miles
Of dust which wreathed their struggling files
Down Lydian mountains; so, when snows
Round Alpine summits, eddying, rose,
The Goth, bound Rome-wards; so the Hun,[2]
10 Crouched on his saddle, while the sun
Went lurid down o'er flooded plains
Through which the groaning Danube strains
To the drear Euxine; – so pray all,
Whom labours, self-ordained, enthrall;
Because they to themselves propose
On this side the all-common close
A goal which, gained, may give repose.
So pray they; and to stand again
Where they stood once, to them were pain;
20 Pain to thread back and to renew
Past straits, and currents long steer'd through.

But milder natures, and more free –
Whom an unblamed serenity
Hath freed from passions, and the state
Of struggle these necessitate;
Whom schooling of the stubborn mind
Hath made, or birth hath found, resigned –
These mourn not, that their goings pay
Obedience to the passing day.
30 These claim not every laughing Hour
For handmaid to their striding power;
Each in her turn, with torch upreared,
To await their march; and when appeared,
Through the cold gloom, with measured race,
To usher for a destined space
(Her own sweet errands all forgone)
The too imperious traveller on.
These, Fausta, ask not this; nor thou,
Time's chafing prisoner, ask it now!

40 We left, just ten years since, you say,
That wayside inn we left to-day.
Our jovial host, as forth we fare,
Shouts greeting from his easy chair.
High on a bank our leader stands,
Reviews and ranks his motley bands,
Makes clear our goal to every eye –
The valley's western boundary.
A gate swings to! our tide hath flowed
Already from the silent road.
50 The valley-pastures, one by one,
Are threaded, quiet in the sun;
And now beyond the rude stone bridge
Slopes gracious up the western ridge.
Its woody border, and the last
Of its dark upland farms is past –
Cool farms, with open-lying stores,
Under their burnished sycamores;
All past! and through the trees we glide,
Emerging on the green hill-side.
60 There climbing hangs, a far-seen sign,
Our wavering, many-coloured line;
There winds, upstreaming slowly still
Over the summit of the hill.
And now, in front, behold outspread
Those upper regions we must tread!
Mild hollows, and clear heathy swells,
The cheerful silence of the fells.
Some two hours' march with serious air,
Through the deep noontide heats we fare;
70 The red-grouse, springing at our sound,
Skims, now and then, the shining ground;
No life, save his and ours, intrudes
Upon these breathless solitudes.
O joy! again the farms appear.
Cool shade is there, and rustic cheer;
There springs the brook will guide us down,
Bright comrade, to the noisy town.
Lingering, we follow down; we gain
The town, the highway, and the plain.
80 And many a mile of dusty way,
Parched and road-worn, we made that day;
But, Fausta, I remember well,
That as the balmy darkness fell

We bathed our hands with speechless glee,
That night, in the wide-glimmering sea.

Once more we tread this self-same road,
Fausta, which ten years since we trod;
Alone we tread it, you and I,
Ghosts of that boisterous company.
90 Here, where the brook shines, near its head,
In its clear, shallow, turf-fringed bed;
Here, whence the eye first sees, far down,
Capped with faint smoke, the noisy town;
Here sit we, and again unroll,
Though slowly, the familiar whole.
The solemn wastes of heathy hill
Sleep in the July sunshine still;
The self-same shadows now, as then,
Play through this grassy upland glen;
100 The loose dark stones on the green way
Lie strewn, it seems, where then they lay;
On this mild bank above the stream,
(You crush them!) the blue gentians gleam.
Still this wild brook, the rushes cool,
The sailing foam, the shining pool!
These are not changed; and we, you say,
Are scarce more changed, in truth, than they.

The gipsies, whom we met below,
They, too, have long roamed to and fro;
110 They ramble, leaving, where they pass,
Their fragments on the cumbered grass.
And often to some kindly place
Chance guides the migratory race,
Where, though long wanderings intervene,
They recognise a former scene.
The dingy tents are pitched; the fires
Give to the wind their wavering spires;
In dark knots crouch round the wild flame
Their children, as when first they came;
120 They see their shackled beasts again
Move, browsing, up the gray-walled lane.
Signs are not wanting, which might raise
The ghost in them of former days –
Signs are not wanting, if they would;
Suggestions to disquietude.

For them, for all, time's busy touch,
While it mends little, troubles much.
Their joints grow stiffer – but the year
Runs his old round of dubious cheer;
130 Chilly they grow – yet winds in March,
Still, sharp as ever, freeze and parch;
They must live still – and yet, God knows,
Crowded and keen the country grows;
It seems as if, in their decay,
The law grew stronger every day.
So might they reason, so compare,
Fausta, times past with times that are.
But no! – they rubbed through yesterday
In their hereditary way,
140 And they will rub through, if they can,
To-morrow on the self-same plan,
Till death arrive to supersede,
For them, vicissitude and need.

The poet, to whose mighty heart
Heaven doth a quicker pulse impart,
Subdues that energy to scan
Not his own course, but that of man.
Though he move mountains, though his day
Be passed on the proud heights of sway,
150 Though he hath loosed a thousand chains,
Though he hath borne immortal pains,
Action and suffering though he know –
He hath not lived, if he lives so.
He sees, in some great-historied land,
A ruler of the people stand,
Sees his strong thought in fiery flood
Roll through the heaving multitude;
Exults – yet for no moment's space
Envies the all-regarded place.
160 Beautiful eyes meet his – and he
Bears to admire uncravingly;
They pass – he, mingled with the crowd,
Is in their far-off triumphs proud.
From some high station° he looks down,   *viewpoint*
At sunset, on a populous town;
Surveys each happy group, which fleets,
Toil ended, through the shining streets,
Each with some errand of its own –

And does not say: *I am alone.*
170 He sees the gentle stir of birth
When morning purifies the earth;
He leans upon a gate and sees
The pastures, and the quiet trees.
Low, woody hill, with gracious bound,
Folds the still valley almost round;
The cuckoo, loud on some high lawn,
Is answered from the depth of dawn;
In the hedge straggling to the stream,
Pale, dew-drenched, half-shut roses gleam;
180 But, where the farther side slopes down,
He sees the drowsy new-waked clown°   shepherd
In his white quaint-embroidered frock°   smock
Make, whistling, toward his mist-wreathed flock –
Slowly, behind his heavy tread,
The wet, flowered grass heaves up its head.
Leaned on his gate, he gazes – tears
Are in his eyes, and in his ears
The murmur of a thousand years.
Before him he sees life unroll,
190 A placid and continuous whole –
That general life, which does not cease,
Whose secret is not joy, but peace;
That life, whose dumb wish is not missed
If birth proceeds, if things subsist;
The life of plants, and stones, and rain,
The life he craves – if not in vain
Fate gave, what chance shall not control,
His sad lucidity of soul.

You listen – but that wandering smile,
200 Fausta, betrays you cold the while!
Your eyes pursue the bells of foam
Washed, eddying, from this bank, their home.
Those gipsies, so your thoughts I scan,
Are less, the poet more, than man.
They feel not, though they move and see;
Deeper the poet feels; but he
Breathes, when he will, immortal air,
Where Orpheus and where Homer are.
In the day's life, whose iron round
210 *Hems us all in, he is not bound;*
He leaves his kind, o'erleaps their pen,

And flees the common life of men.[3]
He escapes thence, but we abide —
Not deep the poet sees, but wide.

The world in which we live and move
Outlasts aversion, outlasts love,
Outlasts each effort, interest, hope,
Remorse, grief, joy; — and were the scope
Of these affections wider made,
220 Man still would see, and see dismayed,
Beyond his passion's widest range,
Far regions of eternal change.
Nay, and since death, which wipes out man,
Finds him with many an unsolved plan,
With much unknown, and much untried,
Wonder not dead, and thirst not dried,
Still gazing on the ever full
Eternal mundane spectacle —
This world in which we draw our breath,
230 In some sense, Fausta, outlasts death.

Blame thou not, therefore, him who dares
Judge vain beforehand human cares;
Whose natural insight can discern
What through experience others learn;
Who needs not love and power, to know
Love transient, power an unreal show;
Who treads at ease life's uncheered ways —
Him blame not, Fausta, rather praise!
Rather thyself for some aim pray
240 Nobler than this to fill the day;
Rather that heart, which burns in thee,
Ask, not to amuse, but to set free;
Be passionate hopes not ill resigned
For quiet, and a fearless mind.
And though fate grudge to thee and me
The poet's rapt security,
Yet they, believe me, who await
No gifts from chance, have conquered fate.
They, winning room to see and hear,
250 And to men's business not too near,
Through clouds of individual strife
Draw homeward to the general life.
Like leaves by suns not yet uncurled;

To the wise, foolish; to the world,
Weak; – yet not weak, I might reply,
Not foolish, Fausta, in His eye,
To whom each moment in its race,
Crowd as we will its neutral space,
Is but a quiet watershed
260 Whence, equally, the seas of life and death are fed.

Enough, we live! – and if a life,
With large results so little rife,
Though bearable, seem hardly worth
This pomp of worlds, this pain of birth;
Yet, Fausta, the mute turf we tread,
The solemn hills around us spread,
This stream which falls incessantly,
The strange-scrawl'd rocks,[4] the lonely sky,
If I might lend their life a voice,
270 Seem to bear rather than rejoice.
And even could the intemperate prayer
Man iterates, while these forbear,
For movement, for an ampler sphere,
Pierce Fate's impenetrable ear;
Not milder is the general lot
Because our spirits have forgot,
In action's dizzying eddy whirled,
The something[5] that infects the world.

?1843 . . . [1849]

Shakespeare

Others abide our question. Thou art free.
We ask and ask – Thou smilest and art still,
Out-topping knowledge. For the loftiest hill,
Who to the stars uncrowns his majesty,

Planting his stedfast footsteps in the sea,
Making the heaven of heavens his dwelling-place,
Spares but the cloudy border of his base
To the foiled searching of mortality;

And thou, who didst the stars and sunbeams know,
Self-schooled, self-scanned, self-honoured, self-secure,
Didst tread on earth unguessed at. – Better so!

All pains the immortal spirit must endure,
All weakness which impairs, all griefs which bow,
Find their sole speech in that victorious brow.

1 Aug. 1844 [1849]

The Forsaken Merman⁶

Come, dear children, let us away;
Down and away below!
Now my brothers call from the bay,
Now the great winds shoreward blow,
Now the salt tides seaward flow;
Now the wild white horses play,
Champ and chafe and toss in the spray.
Children dear, let us away!
This way, this way!

10 Call her once before you go –
Call once yet!
In a voice that she will know:
'Margaret! Margaret!'
Children's voices should be dear
(Call once more) to a mother's ear;
Children's voices, wild with pain –
Surely she will come again!
Call her once and come away;
This way, this way!
20 'Mother dear, we cannot stay!
The wild white horses foam and fret.'
Margaret! Margaret!

Come, dear children, come away down;
Call no more!
One last look at the white-walled town,
And the little grey church on the windy shore,

Then come down!
She will not come though you call all day;
Come away, come away!

30   Children dear, was it yesterday
We heard the sweet bells over the bay?
In the caverns where we lay,
Through the surf and through the swell,
The far-off sound of a silver bell?
Sand-strewn caverns, cool and deep,
Where the winds are all asleep;
Where the spent lights quiver and gleam,
Where the salt weed sways in the stream,
Where the sea-beasts, ranged all around,
40   Feed in the ooze of their pasture-ground;
Where the sea-snakes coil and twine,
Dry their mail and bask in the brine;
Where great whales come sailing by,
Sail and sail, with unshut eye,
Round the world for ever and aye?
When did music come this way?
Children dear, was it yesterday?

Children dear, was it yesterday
(Call yet once) that she went away?
40   Once she sate with you and me,
On a red gold throne in the heart of the sea,
And the youngest sate on her knee.
She combed its bright hair, and she tended it well,
When down swung the sound of a far-off bell.
She sighed, she looked up through the clear green sea;
She said: 'I must go, for my kinsfolk pray
In the little grey church on the shore to-day.
'Twill be Easter-time in the world – ah me!
And I lose my poor soul, Merman! here with thee.'
60   I said: 'Go up, dear heart, through the waves;
Say thy prayer, and come back to the kind sea-caves!'
She smiled, she went up through the surf in the bay.
Children dear, was it yesterday?

Children dear, were we long alone?
'The sea grows stormy, the little ones moan;
Long prayers,' I said, 'in the world they say;
Come!' I said; and we rose through the surf in the bay.
We went up the beach, by the sandy down
Where the sea-stocks bloom, to the white-walled town;
70 Through the narrow paved streets, where all was still,
To the little grey church on the windy hill.
From the church came a murmur of folk at their prayers,
But we stood without in the cold blowing airs.
We climbed on the graves, on the stones worn with rains,
And we gazed up the aisle through the small leaded panes.
She sate by the pillar; we saw her clear:
'Margaret, hist! come quick, we are here!
Dear heart,' I said, 'we are long alone;
The sea grows stormy, the little ones moan.'
80 But, ah, she gave me never a look,
For her eyes were sealed to the holy book!
Loud prays the priest; shut stands the door.
Come away, children, call no more!
Come away, come down, call no more!

Down, down, down!
Down to the depths of the sea!
She sits at her wheel in the humming town,
Singing most joyfully.
Hark what she sings: 'O joy, O joy,
90 For the humming street, and the child with its toy!
For the priest, and the bell, and the holy well;
For the wheel where I spun,
And the blessed light of the sun!'
And so she sings her fill,
Singing most joyfully,
Till the spindle drops⁷ from her hand,
And the whizzing wheel stands still.
She steals to the window, and looks at the sand,
And over the sand at the sea;
100 And her eyes are set in a stare;
And anon there breaks a sigh,
And anon there drops a tear,
From a sorrow-clouded eye,
And a heart sorrow-laden,

A long, long sigh;
From the cold strange eyes of a little Mermaiden
And the gleam of her golden hair.

  Come away, away children;
Come children, come down!
110 The hoarse wind blows coldly;
Lights shine in the town.
She will start from her slumber
When gusts shake the door;
She will hear the winds howling,
Will hear the waves roar.
We shall see, while above us
The waves roar and whirl,
A ceiling of amber,
A pavement of pearl,
120 Singing: 'Here came a mortal,
But faithless was she!
And alone dwell for ever
The kings of the sea.'

But, children, at midnight,
When soft the winds blow,
When clear falls the moonlight,
When spring-tides are low;
When sweet airs come seaward
From heaths starred with broom,
130 And high rocks throw mildly
On the blanched sands a gloom;
Up the still, glistening beaches,
Up the creeks we will hie,
Over banks of bright seaweed
The ebb-tide leaves dry.
We will gaze, from the sand-hills,
At the white, sleeping town;
At the church on the hill-side –
And then come back down.
140 Singing: 'There dwells a loved one,
But cruel is she!
She left lonely for ever
The kings of the sea.'

?1847-9 [1849]

Isolation: To Marguerite[8]

We were apart; yet, day by day,
I bade my heart more constant be.
I bade it keep the world away,
And grow a home for only thee;
Nor feared but thy love likewise grew,
Like mine, each day, more tried, more true.

The fault was grave! I might have known,
What far too soon, alas! I learned –
The heart can bind itself alone,
10 And faith may oft be unreturned.
Self-swayed our feelings ebb and swell –
Thou lov'st no more; – Farewell! Farewell!

Farewell! – and thou, thou lonely heart,
Which never yet without remorse
Even for a moment didst depart
From thy remote and sphered course
.To haunt the place where passions reign –
Back to thy solitude again!

Back! with the conscious thrill of shame
20 Which Luna° felt, that summer-night,   *the moon*
Flash through her pure immortal frame,
When she forsook the starry height
To hang over Endymion's sleep
Upon the pine-grown Latmian steep.

Yet she, chaste queen, had never proved
How vain a thing is mortal love,
Wandering in Heaven, far removed.
But thou hast long had place to prove
This truth – to prove, and make thine own:
30 'Thou hast been, shalt be, art, alone.'

Or, if not quite alone, yet they
Which touch thee are unmating things –
Ocean and clouds and night and day;
Lorn autumns and triumphant springs;
And life, and others' joy and pain,
And love, if love, of happier men.

Of happier men – for they, at least,
Have *dreamed* two human hearts might blend
In one, and were through faith released
40 From isolation without end
Prolonged; nor knew, although not less
Alone than thou, their loneliness.

?Sept./Oct. 1849 [1857]

To Marguerite – continued

Yes! in the sea of life enisled,
With echoing straits between us thrown,
Dotting the shoreless watery wild,
We mortal millions live *alone*.
The islands feel the enclasping flow,
And then their endless bounds they know.

But when the moon their hollows lights,
And they are swept by balms of spring,
And in their glens, on starry nights,
10 The nightingales divinely sing;
And lovely notes, from shore to shore,
Across the sounds and channels pour –

Oh! then a longing like despair
Is to their farthest caverns sent;
For surely once, they feel, we were
Parts of a single continent!
Now round us spreads the watery plain –
Oh might our marges° meet again!   edges

Who ordered, that their longing's fire
20 Should be, as soon as kindled, cooled?
Who renders vain their deep desire? –
A God, a God their severance ruled!
And bade betwixt their shores to be
The unplumbed, salt, estranging sea.

?Sept./Oct. 1849 [1852]

Youth and Calm

'Tis death! and peace, indeed, is here,
And ease from shame, and rest from fear.
There's nothing can dismarble now
·The smoothness of that limpid brow.
But is a calm like this, in truth,
The crowning end of life and youth,
And when this boon rewards the dead,
Are all debts paid, has all been said?
And is the heart of youth so light,
10   Its step so firm, its eye so bright,
Because on its hot brow there blows
A wind of promise and repose
From the far grave, to which it goes;
Because it hath the hope to come,
One day, to harbour in the tomb?
Ah no, the bliss youth dreams is one
For daylight, for the cheerful sun,
For feeling nerves and living breath –
Youth dreams a bliss on this side death.
20   It dreams a rest, if not more deep,
More grateful than this marble sleep;
It hears a voice within it tell:
Calm's not life's crown, though calm is well.
'Tis all perhaps which man acquires,
But 'tis not what our youth desires.

?1849–1851 [1852 as 'Lines Written by a Death Bed']

The Buried Life

Light flows our war of mocking words, and yet,
Behold, with tears mine eyes are wet!
I feel a nameless sadness o'er me roll.
Yes, yes, we know that we can jest,
We know, we know that we can smile!
But there's a something in this breast,
To which thy light words bring no rest,
And thy gay smiles no anodyne.°   pain-killing drug

Give me thy hand, and hush awhile,
10 And turn those limpid eyes on mine,
And let me read there, love! thy inmost soul.

Alas! is even love too weak
To unlock the heart, and let it speak?
Are even lovers powerless to reveal
To one another what indeed they feel?
I knew the mass of men concealed
Their thoughts, for fear that if revealed
They would by other men be met
With blank indifference, or with blame reproved;
20 I knew they lived and moved
Tricked in disguises, alien to the rest
Of men, and alien to themselves – and yet
The same heart beats in every human breast!

But we, my love! – doth a like spell benumb
Our hearts, our voices? – must we too be dumb?

Ah! well for us, if even we,
Even for a moment, can get free
Our heart, and have our lips unchained;
For that which seals them hath been deep-ordained!

30 Fate, which foresaw
How frivolous a baby man would be –
By what distractions he would be possessed,
How he would pour himself in every strife,
And well-nigh change his own identity –
That it might keep from his capricious play
His genuine self, and force him to obey
Even in his own despite his being's law,
Bade through the deep recesses of our breast
The unregarded river of our life
40 Pursue with indiscernible flow its way;
And that we should not see
The buried stream, and seem to be
Eddying at large in blind uncertainty,
Though driving on with it eternally.

But often, in the world's most crowded streets,
But often, in the din of strife,
There rises an unspeakable desire

After the knowledge of our buried life;
A thirst to spend our fire and restless force
50 In tracking out our true, original course;
A longing to inquire
Into the mystery of this heart which beats
So wild, so deep in us – to know
Whence our lives come and where they go.
And many a man in his own breast then delves,
But deep enough, alas! none ever mines.
And we have been on many thousand lines,
And we have shown, on each, spirit and power;
But hardly have we, for one little hour,
60 Been on our own line, have we been ourselves –
Hardly had skill to utter one of all
The nameless feelings that course through our breast,
But they course on for ever unexpressed.
And long we try in vain to speak and act
Our hidden self, and what we say and do
Is eloquent, is well – but 'tis not true!
And then we will no more be racked
With inward striving, and demand
Of all the thousand nothings of the hour
70 Their stupefying power;
Ah yes, and they benumb us at our call!
Yet still, from time to time, vague and forlorn,
From the soul's subterranean depth upborne
As from an infinitely distant land,
Come airs, and floating echoes, and convey
A melancholy into all our day.

Only – but this is rare –
When a beloved hand is laid in ours,
When, jaded with the rush and glare
80 Of the interminable hours,
Our eyes can in another's eyes read clear,
When our world-deafened ear
Is by the tones of a loved voice caressed –
A bolt is shot back somewhere in our breast,
And a lost pulse of feeling stirs again.
The eye sinks inward, and the heart lies plain,
And what we mean, we say, and what we would, we know.
A man becomes aware of his life's flow,
And hears its winding murmur; and he sees
90 The meadows where it glides, the sun, the breeze.

And there arrives a lull in the hot race
Wherein he doth for ever chase
That flying and elusive shadow, rest.
An air of coolness plays upon his face,
And an unwonted calm pervades his breast.
And then he thinks he knows
The hills where his life rose,
And the sea where it goes.

?1849–52 [1852]

Dover Beach

The sea is calm to-night.
The tide is full, the moon lies fair
Upon the straits; – on the French coast the light
Gleams and is gone; the cliffs of England stand,
Glimmering and vast, out in the tranquil bay.
Come to the window, sweet is the night-air!
Only, from the long line of spray
Where the sea meets the moon-blanched land,
Listen! you hear the grating roar
10 Of pebbles which the waves draw back, and fling,
At their return, up the high strand,
Begin, and cease, and then again begin,
With tremulous cadence slow, and bring
The eternal note of sadness in.

Sophocles long ago
Heard it on the Aegaean, and it brought
Into his mind the turbid ebb and flow
Of human misery; we
Find also in the sound a thought,
20 Hearing it by this distant northern sea.

The Sea of Faith
Was once, too, at the full, and round earth's shore
Lay like the folds of a bright girdle furled.
But now I only hear
Its melancholy, long, withdrawing roar,
Retreating, to the breath

Of the night-wind, down the vast edges drear
And naked shingles of the world.

Ah, love, let us be true
30   To one another! for the world, which seems
To lie before us like a land of dreams,
So various, so beautiful, so new,
Hath really neither joy, nor love, nor light,
Nor certitude, nor peace, nor help for pain;
And we are here as on a darkling plain
Swept with confused alarms of struggle and flight,
Where ignorant armies clash by night.

?Late June 1851 [1867]

Lines Written in Kensington Gardens

In this lone, open glade I lie,
Screened by deep boughs on either hand;
And at its end, to stay the eye,
Those black-crowned, red-boled pine-trees stand!

Birds here make song, each bird has his,
Across the girdling° city's hum.   encircling
How green under the boughs it is!
How thick the tremulous sheep-cries come!

Sometimes a child will cross the glade
10   To take his nurse his broken toy;
Sometimes a thrush flit overhead
Deep in her unknown day's employ.

Here at my feet what wonders pass,
What endless, active life is here!
What blowing daisies, fragrant grass!
An air-stirred forest, fresh and clear.

Scarce fresher is the mountain-sod
Where the tired angler lies, stretched out,
And, eased of basket and of rod,
20   Counts his day's spoil, the spotted trout.

In the huge world, which roars hard by,
Be others happy if they can!
But in my helpless cradle I
Was breathed on by the rural Pan.

I, on men's impious uproar hurled,
Think often, as I hear them rave,
That peace has left the upper world
And now keeps only in the grave.

Yet here is peace for ever new!
30 When I who watch them am away,
Still all things in this glade go through
The changes of their quiet day.

Then to their happy rest they pass!
The flowers upclose, the birds are fed,
The night comes down upon the grass,
The child sleeps warmly in his bed.

Calm soul of all things! make it mine
To feel, amid the city's jar,
That there abides a peace of thine,
40 Man did not make, and cannot mar.

The will to neither strive nor cry,
The power to feel with others give!
Calm, calm me more! nor let me die
Before I have begun to live.

1849-52 [1867]

Requiescat

Strew on her roses, roses,
    And never a spray of yew!
In quiet she reposes;
    Ah, would that I did too!

Her mirth the world required;
    She bathed it in smiles of glee.
But her heart was tired, tired,
    And now they let her be.

Her life was turning, turning,
10   In mazes of heat and sound.
But for peace her soul was yearning,
    And now peace laps her round.

Her cabined, ample spirit,
    It fluttered and failed for breath.
To-night it doth inherit
    The vasty hall of death.

?1849–53 [1853]

From *Stanzas from the Grande Chartreuse*[9]

For rigorous teachers seized my youth,
And purged its faith, and trimmed its fire,
Showed me the high, white star of Truth,
70 There bade me gaze, and there aspire.
Even now their whispers pierce the gloom:
What dost thou in this living tomb?

Forgive me, masters of the mind!
At whose behest I long ago
So much unlearnt, so much resigned –
I come not here to be your foe!
I seek these anchorites, not in ruth,   *monks/pity*
To curse and to deny your truth;

Nor as their friend, or child, I speak!
80 But as, on some far northern strand,
Thinking of his own Gods, a Greek
In pity and mournful awe might stand
Before some fallen Runic stone[10]—
For both were faiths, and both are gone.

Wandering between two worlds, one dead,
The other powerless to be born,
With nowhere yet to rest my head,
Like these, on earth I wait forlorn.
Their faith, my tears, the world deride –
90 I come to shed them at their side.

Oh, hide me in your gloom profound,
Ye solemn seats of holy pain!
Take me, cowled forms, and fence me round,
Till I possess my soul again;
Till free my thoughts before me roll,
Not chafed by hourly false control!

For the world cries your faith is now
But a dead time's exploded dream;
My melancholy, sciolists° say,   *intellectual impostors*
100 Is a passed mode, an outworn theme –
As if the world had ever had
A faith, or sciolists been sad!

Ah, if it *be* passed, take away,
At least, the restlessness, the pain;
Be man henceforth no more a prey
To these out-dated stings again!
The nobleness of grief is gone –
Ah, leave us not the fret alone!

But – if you cannot give us ease –
110 Last of the race of them who grieve
Here leave us to die out with these
Last of the people who believe!
Silent, while years engrave° the brow;   *furrow*
Silent – the best are silent now.

*   *   *

What helps it now, that Byron bore,
With haughty scorn which mocked the smart,
Through Europe to the Aetolian shore[11]
The pageant of his bleeding heart?
That thousands counted every groan,
And Europe made his woe her own?

What boots it, Shelley! that the breeze
140   Carried thy lovely wail away,
Musical through Italian trees
Which fringe thy soft blue Spezzian bay?[12]
Inheritors of thy distress
Have restless hearts one throb the less?

Or are we easier, to have read,
O Obermann! the sad, stern page,
Which tells us how thou hidd'st thy head
From the fierce tempest of thine age
In the lone brakes of Fontainebleau,
150   Or chalets near the Alpine snow?

Ye slumber in your silent grave! —
The world, which for an idle day
Grace to your mood of sadness gave,
Long since hath flung her weeds° away.   *mourning clothes*
The eternal trifler breaks your spell;
But we — we learnt your lore too well!

Years hence, perhaps, may dawn an age,
More fortunate, alas! than we,
Which without hardness will be sage,
160   And gay without frivolity.
Sons of the world, oh, speed those years;
But, while we wait, allow our tears!

*　　*　　*

The Scholar Gipsy[13]

Go, for they call you, shepherd, from the hill;
  Go, shepherd,[14] and untie the wattled cotes°!   *fences of the sheepfold*
    No longer leave thy wistful flock unfed,
    Nor let thy bawling fellows° rack their throats,   *bleating lambs*
    Nor the cropped herbage shoot another head.
      But when the fields are still,
    And the tired men and dogs all gone to rest,
      And only the white sheep are sometimes seen
      Cross and recross the strips of moon-blanched green,
10   Come, shepherd, and again begin the quest![15]

Here, where the reaper was at work of late –
  In this high field's dark corner, where he leaves
    His coat, his basket, and his earthen cruse,°   *water-jar*
    And in the sun all morning binds the sheaves,
      Then here, at noon, comes back his stores to use –
      Here will I sit and wait,
    While to my ear from uplands far away
      The bleating of the folded° flocks is borne,   *in the fold*
      With distant cries of reapers in the corn –
20   All the live murmur of a summer's day.

Screened is this nook o'er the high, half-reaped field,
  And here till sun-down, shepherd! will I be.
    Through the thick corn the scarlet poppies peep,
    And round green roots and yellowing stalks I see
      Pale pink convolvulus in tendrils creep;
      And air-swept lindens° yield   *lime-trees*
    Their scent, and rustle down their perfumed showers
      Of bloom on the bent grass where I am laid,
      And bower me from the August sun with shade;
30   And the eye travels down to Oxford's towers.

And near me on the grass lies Glanvil's book –
  Come, let me read the oft-read tale again!
    The story of the Oxford scholar poor,
    Of pregnant parts° and quick inventive brain,   *gifted*
      Who, tired of knocking at preferment's door,
      One summer-morn forsook
    His friends, and went to learn the gipsy-lore,
      And roamed the world with that wild brotherhood,
      And came, as most men deemed, to little good,
40   But came to Oxford and his friends no more.

But once, years after, in the country-lanes,
　　Two scholars, whom at college erst he knew,
　　　Met him, and of his way of life enquired;
　　Whereat he answered, that the gipsy-crew,
　　　His mates, had arts to rule as they desired
　　　　The workings of men's brains,
　　And they can bind them to what thoughts they will.
　　　'And I,' he said, 'the secret of their art,
　　　When fully learned, will to the world impart;
50　　But it needs heaven-sent moments for this skill.'

This said, he left them, and returned no more. –
　　But rumours hung about the country-side,
　　　That the lost Scholar long was seen to stray,
　　Seen by rare glimpses, pensive and tongue-tied,
　　　In hat of antique shape, and cloak of grey,
　　　　The same the gipsies wore.
　　Shepherds had met him on the Hurst[16] in spring;
　　　At some lone alehouse in the Berkshire moors,
　　　On the warm ingle-bench,° the smock-frocked boors°　*chimney-nook*
60　Had found him seated at their entering,　　　　　　　　*seat/farm workers*

But, 'mid their drink and clatter, he would fly.
　　And I myself seem half to know thy looks,
　　　And put the shepherds, wanderer! on thy trace;°　　　*track*
　　And boys who in lone wheatfields scare the rooks
　　　I ask if thou hast passed their quiet place;
　　　　Or in my boat I lie
　　Moored to the cool bank in the summer-heats,
　　　'Mid wide grass meadows which the sunshine fills,
　　　And watch the warm, green-muffled Cumner° hills,　　*Cumnor*
70　And wonder if thou haunt'st their shy retreats.

For most, I know, thou lov'st retired ground°!　　　　　*lonely areas*
　　Thee at the ferry Oxford riders blithe,
　　　Returning home on summer-nights, have met
　　Crossing the stripling Thames at Bablock-hithe,
　　　Trailing in the cool stream thy fingers wet,
　　　　As the punt's rope chops round;
　　And leaning backward in a pensive dream,
　　　And fostering in thy lap a heap of flowers
　　　Plucked in shy fields and distant Wychwood bowers,
80　And thine eyes resting on the moonlit stream.

And then they land, and thou art seen no more! —
   Maidens, who from the distant hamlets come
     To dance around the Fyfield elm in May,
   Oft through the darkening fields have seen thee roam,
     Or cross a stile into the public way.
       Oft thou hast given them store
   Of flowers — the frail-leafed, white anemony,
     Dark bluebells drenched with dews of summer eves,
     And purple orchises with spotted leaves —
90   But none hath words she can report of thee.

And, above Godstow Bridge, when hay-time's here
   In June, and many a scythe in sunshine flames,
     Men who through those wide fields of breezy grass
   Where black-winged swallows haunt the glittering Thames,
     To bathe in the abandoned lasher° pass,   *pool below a dam*
       Have often passed thee near
   Sitting upon the river bank o'ergrown;
     Marked thine outlandish garb, thy figure spare,
     Thy dark vague eyes, and soft abstracted air —
100   But, when they came from bathing, thou wast gone!

At some lone homestead in the Cumner hills,
   Where at her open door the housewife darns,
     Thou hast been seen, or hanging on a gate
   To watch the threshers in the mossy barns.
     Children, who early range these slopes and late
       For cresses from the rills,
   Have known thee eying, all an April-day,
     The springing pastures and the feeding kine;
     And marked thee, when the stars come out and shine,
110   Through the long dewy grass move slow away.

In autumn, on the skirts of Bagley Wood —
   Where most the gipsies by the turf-edged way
     Pitch their smoked tents, and every bush you see
   With scarlet patches tagged and shreds of grey,
     Above the forest-ground called Thessaly —
       The blackbird, picking food,
   Sees thee, nor stops his meal, nor fears at all;
     So often has he known thee past him stray,
     Rapt, twirling in thy hand a withered spray,
120   And waiting for the spark from heaven to fall.

And once, in winter, on the causeway chill
  Where home through flooded fields foot-travellers go,
    Have I not passed thee on the wooden bridge,
  Wrapt in thy cloak and battling with the snow,
    Thy face toward Hinksey and its wintry ridge?
      And thou hast climbed the hill,
  And gained the white brow of the Cumner range;
    Turned once to watch, while thick the snowflakes fall,
    The line of festal light in Christ-Church° hall –   *college*
130   Then sought thy straw in some sequestered grange.

But what – I dream! Two hundred years are flown
  Since first thy story ran through Oxford halls,
    And the grave Glanvil did the tale inscribe
  That thou wert wandered from the studious walls
    To learn strange arts, and join a gipsy-tribe;
      And thou from earth art gone
  Long since, and in some quiet churchyard laid –
    Some country-nook, where o'er thy unknown grave
    Tall grasses and white flowering nettles wave,
140   Under a dark, red-fruited yew-tree's shade.

– No, no, thou hast not felt the lapse of hours!
  For what wears out the life of mortal men?
    'Tis that from change to change their being rolls;
  'Tis that repeated shocks, again, again,
    Exhaust the energy of strongest souls
      And numb the elastic powers.
  Till having used our nerves with bliss and teen,°   *sorrow*
    And tired upon a thousand schemes our wit,
    To the just-pausing Genius we remit
150   Our worn-out life, and are – what we have been.

Thou hast not lived, why should'st thou perish, so?
  Thou hadst *one* aim, *one* business, *one* desire;
    Else wert thou long since numbered with the dead!
  Else hadst thou spent, like other men, thy fire!
    The generations of thy peers are fled,
      And we ourselves shall go;
  But thou possessest an immortal lot,
    And we imagine thee exempt from age
    And living as thou liv'st on Glanvil's page,
160   Because thou hadst – what we, alas! have not.

For early didst thou leave the world, with powers
　　Fresh, undiverted to the world without,
　　　Firm to their mark, not spent on other things;
　　Free from the sick fatigue, the languid doubt,
　　　Which much to have tried, in much been baffled, brings.
　　　　O life unlike to ours!
　　Who fluctuate idly without term or scope,
　　　Of whom each strives, nor knows for what he strives,
　　　And each half lives a hundred different lives;
170　Who wait like thee, but not, like thee, in hope.

Thou waitest for the spark from heaven! and we,
　　Light half-believers of our casual creeds,
　　　Who never deeply felt, nor clearly willed,
　　Whose insight never has borne fruit in deeds,
　　　Whose vague resolves never have been fulfilled;
　　　　For whom each year we see
　　Breeds new beginnings, disappointments new;
　　　Who hesitate and falter life away,
　　　And lose to-morrow the ground won to-day –
180　Ah! do not we, wanderer! await it too?

Yes, we await it! – but it still delays,
　　And then we suffer! and amongst us one,[17]
　　　Who most has suffered, takes dejectedly
　　His seat upon the intellectual throne;
　　　And all his store of sad experience he
　　　　Lays bare of wretched days;
　　Tells us his misery's birth and growth and signs,
　　　And how the dying spark of hope was fed,
　　　And how the breast was soothed, and how the head,
190　And all his hourly varied anodynes.　　　　　　　　*pain relievers*

This for our wisest![18] and we others pine,
　　And wish the long unhappy dream would end,
　　　And waive all claim to bliss, and try to bear;
　　With close-lipped patience for our only friend,
　　　Sad patience, too near neighbour to despair –
　　　　But none has hope like thine!
　　Thou through the fields and through the woods dost stray,
　　　Roaming the country-side, a truant boy,
　　　Nursing thy project in unclouded joy,
200　And every doubt long blown by time away.

O born in days when wits were fresh and clear,
   And life ran gaily as the sparkling Thames;
     Before this strange disease of modern life,
   With its sick hurry, its divided aims,
     Its heads o'ertaxed, its palsied hearts, was rife –
       Fly hence, our contact fear!
   Still fly, plunge deeper in the bowering wood!
     Averse, as Dido did[19] with gesture stern
     From her false friend's approach in Hades turn,
210   Wave us away, and keep thy solitude!

Still nursing the unconquerable hope,
   Still clutching the inviolable shade,
     With a free, onward impulse brushing through,
   By night, the silvered branches of the glade –
     Far on the forest-skirts, where none pursue,
       On some mild pastoral slope
   Emerge, and resting on the moonlit pales°   *fences*
     Freshen thy flowers as in former years
     With dew, or listen with enchanted ears,
220   From the dark dingles,° to the nightingales!   *wooded dells*

But fly our paths, our feverish contact fly!
   For strong the infection of our mental strife,
     Which, though it gives no bliss, yet spoils for rest;
   And we should win thee from thy own fair life,
     Like us distracted, and like us unblest.
       Soon, soon thy cheer would die,
   Thy hopes grow timorous, and unfixed thy powers.
     And thy clear aims be cross and shifting made;
     And then thy glad perennial youth would fade,
230   Fade, and grow old at last, and die like ours.

Then fly our greetings, fly our speech and smiles!
   – As some grave Tyrian trader, from the sea,
     Descried at sunrise an emerging prow
   Lifting the cool-haired creepers stealthily,
     The fringes of a southward-facing brow
       Among the Aegean isles;
   And saw the merry Grecian coaster come,
     Freighted with amber grapes, and Chian° wine,   *from Chios*
     Green, bursting figs, and tunnies steeped in brine –
240   And knew the intruders on his ancient home,

The young light-hearted masters of the waves –
   And snatched his rudder, and shook out more sail;
   And day and night held on indignantly
O'er the blue Midland waters with the gale,
   Betwixt the Syrtes° and soft Sicily,   *Gulf of Sidra*
     To where the Atlantic raves
  Outside the western straits; and unbent sails
   There, where down cloudy cliffs, through sheets of foam,
Shy traffickers, the dark Iberians come;
250   And on the beach undid his corded bales.

?1852–3 [1853]

Philomela[20]

Hark! ah, the nightingale –
The tawny-throated!
Hark, from that moonlit cedar what a burst!
What triumph! hark! – what pain!

O wanderer from a Grecian shore,
Still, after many years, in distant lands,
Still nourishing in thy bewildered brain
That wild, unquenched, deep-sunken, old-world pain –
Say, will it never heal?
10 And can this fragrant lawn
With its cool trees, and night,
And the sweet, tranquil Thames,
And moonshine, and the dew,
To thy racked° heart and brain   *torn apart*
Afford no balm?

Dost thou to-night behold,
Here, through the moonlight on this English grass,
The unfriendly palace in the Thracian wild?
Dost thou again peruse
20 With hot cheeks and seared eyes
The too clear web,° and thy dumb sister's shame?   *tapestry*
Dost thou once more assay
Thy flight, and feel come over thee,

Poor fugitive, the feathery change
Once more, and once more seem to make resound
With love and hate, triumph and agony,
Lone Daulis, and the high Cephissian vale?
Listen, Eugenia° –   = *well-born*
How thick the bursts come crowding through the leaves!
30 Again – thou hearest?
Eternal passion!
Eternal pain!

?1852–3 [1853]

Thyrsis[21]

A MONODY,[22] TO COMMEMORATE THE AUTHOR'S FRIEND, ARTHUR HUGH CLOUGH, WHO DIED AT FLORENCE, 1861

1

How changed is here each spot man makes or fills!
    In the two Hinkseys nothing keeps the same;
        The village street its haunted mansion[23] lacks,
    And from the sign is gone Sibylla's[24] name,
        And from the roofs the twisted chimney-stacks –
            Are ye too changed, ye hills?
    See, 'tis no foot of unfamiliar men
        To-night from Oxford up your pathway strays!
        Here came I often, often, in old days –
10   Thyrsis and I; we still had Thyrsis then.

2

Runs it not here, the track by Childsworth Farm[25],
    Past the high wood, to where the elm-tree crowns
        The hill behind whose ridge the sunset flames?
    The signal-elm, that looks on Ilsley Downs,
        The Vale, the three lone weirs, the youthful Thames? –
            This winter-eve is warm,
    Humid the air! leafless, yet soft as spring,
        The tender purple spray on copse and briers!
        And that sweet city with her dreaming spires,
20   She needs not June for beauty's heightening,

3

Lovely all times she lies, lovely to-night! –
 Only, methinks, some loss of habit's power
  Befalls me wandering through this upland dim.
 Once passed I blindfold here, at any hour;
  Now seldom come I, since I came with him.
   That single elm-tree bright
 Against the west – I miss it! is it gone?
  We prized it dearly; while it stood, we said,
  Our friend, the Gipsy-Scholar, was not dead;
30 While the tree lived, he in these fields lived on.

4

Too rare, too rare, grow now my visits here,
 But once I knew each field, each flower, each stick;
  And with the country-folk acquaintance made
 By barn in threshing-time, by new-built rick.
  Here, too, our shepherd-pipes we first assayed.
   Ah me! this many a year
 My pipe is lost, my shepherd's holiday!
  Needs must I lose them, needs with heavy heart
  Into the world and wave of men depart;
40 But Thyrsis of his own will went away.[26]

5

It irked him to be here, he could not rest.
 He loved each simple joy the country yields,
  He loved his mates; but yet he could not keep,
 For that a shadow loured on the fields,
  Here with the shepherds and the silly° sheep.   *simple*
   Some life of men unblest
 He knew, which made him droop, and filled his head.
  He went; his piping took a troubled sound
  Of storms that rage outside our happy ground;
50 He could not wait their passing, he is dead.

6

So, some tempestuous morn in early June,
 When the year's primal burst of bloom is o'er,
  Before the roses and the longest day –
 When garden-walks and all the grassy floor
  With blossoms red and white of fallen May
   And chestnut-flowers are strewn –
 So have I heard the cuckoo's parting cry,

From the wet field, through the vext garden-trees,
Come with the volleying rain and tossing breeze:
60   *The bloom is gone, and with the bloom go I!*

7

Too quick despairer, wherefore wilt thou go?
  Soon will the high Midsummer pomps come on,
    Soon will the musk carnations break and swell,
  Soon shall we have gold-dusted snapdragon,
    Sweet-William with his homely cottage-smell,
      And stocks in fragrant blow;
  Roses that down the alleys shine afar,
    And open, jasmine-muffled lattices,
    And groups under the dreaming garden-trees,
70   And the full moon, and the white evening-star.

8

He hearkens not! light comer, he is flown!
  What matters it? next year he will return,
    And we shall have him in the sweet spring-days,
  With whitening hedges, and uncrumpling fern,
    And blue-bells trembling by the forest-ways,
      And scent of hay new-mown.
  But Thyrsis never more we swains shall see;
    See him come back, and cut a smoother reed,
    And blow a strain the world at last shall heed –
80   For Time, not Corydon,[27] hath conquered thee!

9

Alack, for Corydon no rival now! –
  But when Sicilian shepherds lost a mate,
    Some good survivor with his flute would go,
  Piping a ditty sad for Bion's fate;
    And cross the unpermitted ferry's flow,
      And relax Pluto's brow,
  And make leap up with joy the beauteous head
    Of Proserpine, among whose crowned hair
    Are flowers, first opened on Sicilian air,
90   And flute his friend, like Orpheus, from the dead.

10

O easy access to the hearer's grace
  When Dorian° shepherds sang to Proserpine!   *of Doris in ancient Greece*
    For she herself had trod Sicilian fields,

She knew the Dorian water's gush divine,
  She knew each lily white which Enna yields,
    Each rose with blushing face;
She loved the Dorian pipe, the Dorian strain.
  But ah, of our poor Thames she never heard!
  Her foot the Cumner° cowslips never stirred;   *Cumnor*
100 And we should tease her with our plaint in vain!

11

Well! wind-dispersed and vain the words will be,
  Yet, Thyrsis, let me give my grief its hour
    In the old haunt, and find our tree-topped hill!
Who, if not I, for questing here hath power?
  I know the wood which hides the daffodil,
    I know the Fyfield tree,
I know what white, what purple fritillaries
  The grassy harvest of the river-fields,
  Above by Ensham, down by Sandford, yields,[28]
110 And what sedged brooks are Thames's tributaries;

12

I know these slopes; who knows them if not I? –
  But many a dingle° on the loved hill-side,   *wooded dell*
    With thorns once studded, old, white-blossomed trees,
Where thick the cowslips grew, and far descried
  High towered the spikes of purple orchises,
    Hath since our day put by
The coronals of that forgotten time;
  Down each green bank hath gone the ploughboy's team,
  And only in the hidden brookside gleam
120 Primroses, orphans of the flowery prime.

13

Where is the girl, who by the boatman's door,
  Above the locks, above the boating throng,
    Unmoored our skiff when through the Wytham flats,
Red loosestrife and blond meadow-sweet among
  And darting swallows and light water-gnats,
    We tracked the shy Thames shore?
Where are the mowers, who, as the tiny swell
  Of our boat passing heaved the river-grass,
  Stood with suspended scythe to see us pass? –
130 They all are gone, and thou art gone as well!

14

Yes, thou art gone! and round me too the night
  In ever-nearing circle weaves her shade.
    I see her veil draw soft across the day,
  I feel her slowly chilling breath invade
    The cheek grown thin, the brown hair sprent° with grey;   *sprinkled*
      I feel her finger light
Laid pausefully upon life's headlong train; –
  The foot less prompt to meet the morning dew,
  The heart less bounding at emotion new,
140 And hope, once crushed, less quick to spring again.

15

And long the way appears, which seemed so short
  To the less practised eye of sanguine youth;
    And high the mountain-tops, in cloudy air,
  The mountain-tops where is the throne of Truth,
    Tops in life's morning-sun so bright and bare!
      Unbreachable the fort
Of the long-battered world uplifts its wall;
  And strange and vain the earthly turmoil grows,
  And near and real the charm of thy repose,
150 And night as welcome as a friend would fall.

16

But hush! the upland hath a sudden loss
  Of quiet! – Look, adown the dusk hill-side,
    A troop of Oxford hunters going home,
  As in old days, jovial and talking, ride!
    From hunting with the Berkshire hounds they come.
      Quick! let me fly, and cross
Into yon farther field! – 'Tis done; and see,
  Backed by the sunset, which doth glorify
  The orange and pale violet evening-sky,
160 Bare on its lonely ridge, the Tree! the Tree!

17

I take the omen! Eve° lets down her veil,   *evening*
  The white fog creeps from bush to bush about,
    The west unflushes, the high stars grow bright,
  And in the scattered farms the lights come out.
    I cannot reach the signal-tree to-night,
      Yet, happy omen, hail!
Hear it from thy broad lucent Arno-vale[29]

(For there thine earth-forgetting eyelids keep
The morningless and unawakening sleep
170   Under the flowery oleanders pale),

18

Hear it, O Thyrsis, still our tree is there! –
Ah, vain! These English fields, this upland dim,
These brambles pale with mist engarlanded,
That lone, sky-pointing tree, are not for him;
To a boon southern country he is fled,
And now in happier air,
Wandering with the great Mother°'s train divine   *Earth Mother*
(And purer or more subtle soul than thee,
I trow, the mighty Mother doth not see)
180   Within a folding of the Apennine,

19

Thou hearest the immortal chants of old! –
Putting his sickle to the perilous grain
In the hot cornfield of the Phrygian king,
For thee the Lityerses-song again
Young Daphnis with his silver voice doth sing;
Sings his Sicilian fold,
His sheep, his hapless love, his blinded eyes –
And how a call celestial round him rang,
And heavenward from the fountain-brink he sprang,
190   And all the marvel of the golden skies.

20

There thou art gone, and me thou leavest here
Sole in these fields! yet will I not despair.
Despair I will not, while I yet descry
'Neath the mild canopy of English air
That lonely tree against the western sky.
Still, still these slopes, 'tis clear,
Our Gipsy-Scholar haunts, outliving thee!
Fields where soft sheep from cages pull the hay,
Woods with anemonies in flower till May,
200   Know him a wanderer still; then why not me?

21

A fugitive and gracious light he seeks,
Shy to illumine; and I seek it too.
This does not come with houses or with gold,

With place, with honour, and a flattering crew;
　　'Tis not in the world's market bought and sold –
　　　But the smooth-slipping weeks
Drop by, and leave its seeker still untired;
　　Out of the heed of mortals he is gone,
　　He wends unfollowed, he must house alone;
210 　Yet on he fares, by his own heart inspired.

22

Thou too, O Thyrsis, on like quest wast bound;
　　Thou wanderedst with me for a little hour!
　　　Men gave thee nothing; but this happy quest,
If men esteemed thee feeble, gave thee power,
　　If men procured thee trouble, gave thee rest.
　　　And this rude Cumner ground,
Its fir-topped Hurst, its farms, its quiet fields,
　　Here camst thou in thy jocund youthful time,
　　Here was thine height of strength, thy golden prime!
220 　And still the haunt beloved a virtue yields.

23

What though the music of thy rustic flute
　　Kept not for long its happy, country tone;
　　　Lost it too soon, and learnt a stormy note
Of men contention-tost, of men who groan,
　　Which tasked thy pipe too sore, and tired thy throat –
　　　It failed, and thou wast mute![30]
Yet hadst thou alway visions of our light,
　　And long with men of care thou couldst not stay,
　　And soon thy foot resumed its wandering way,
230 　Left human haunt, and on alone till night.

24

Too rare, too rare, grow now my visits here!
　　'Mid city-noise, not, as with thee of yore,
　　　Thyrsis! in reach of sheep-bells is my home.
　　– Then through the great town's harsh, heart-wearying roar,
　　Let in thy voice a whisper often come,
　　　To chase fatigue and fear:
Why faintest thou? I wandered till I died.
　　Roam on! The light we sought is shining still.
　　Dost thou ask proof? Our tree yet crowns the hill,
240 　*Our Scholar travels yet the loved hill-side.*

?1863–5 [1866]

Growing Old

What is it to grow old?
Is it to lose the glory of the form,
The lustre of the eye?
Is it for beauty to forego her wreath?
– Yes, but not this alone.

Is it to feel our strength –
Not our bloom only, but our strength – decay?
Is it to feel each limb
Grow stiffer, every function less exact,
10   Each nerve more loosely strung?

Yes, this, and more; but not
Ah, 'tis not what in youth we dreamed 'twould be!
'Tis not to have our life
Mellowed and softened as with sunset-glow,
A golden day's decline.

'Tis not to see the world
As from a height, with rapt prophetic eyes,
And heart profoundly stirred;
And weep, and feel the fulness of the past,
20   The years that are no more.

It is to spend long days
And not once feel that we were ever young;
It is to add, immured
In the hot prison of the present, month
To month with weary pain.

It is to suffer this,
And feel but half, and feebly, what we feel.
Deep in our hidden heart
Festers the dull remembrance of a change,
30   But no emotion – none.

It is – last stage of all –
When we are frozen up within, and quite
The phantom of ourselves,
To hear the world applaud the hollow ghost
Which blamed the living man.

1864–7 [1867]

NOTES

Arnold

1 Jane Arnold: Fausta = Fortunate: refers to a walk in the Lake District taken by members of the Arnold family in summer 1833.

2 the northern destructive raiders of Rome.

3 lines 211–12 added 1881.

4 the marks on rocks, the result of glacial movement.

5 the 'worm i' the bud' – the something that thwarts life's expectations.

6 story from George Borrow's review of J.M. Thiele's *Danske Folkesagn*, Universal Review 11.

7 1849 – 'shuttle falls': corrected because Clough questioned its technological accuracy.

8 'Isolation' and 'To Marguerite' probably written Sept./Oct. 1849: 'To Marguerite' first published 1852, but the two poems, in sequence, were first published 1857 and subsequently as part of a group of poems headed *Switzerland*. 'Marguerite' was thought to be a French girl A. met while at Thun, Switzerland, Sept. 1848 and 1849: cf. letters to Clough 29 Sept. 1848, 23 Sept. 1849: now suggested – Mary Calude of Ambleside, met when he was staying at Fox How.

9 A. visited the monastery of La Grande Chartreuse on his honeymoon, 7 Sept. 1851.

10 a stone inscribed with 'runes' – characters of ancient Germanic alphabet: i.e. the Greek feels pity for the old faiths that have gone.

11 the Grecian shore where he died.

12 Shelley was drowned in the Bay of Spezia.

13 based on a passage from Joseph Glanvil's *Vanity of Dogmatizing*, 1661.

14 A.H. Clough.

15 i.e. for the integrity and power needed to pursue, as a poet, his vision of truth.

16 Hurst, Berkshire Moors, Cumnor, Bablock-hythe, Wychwood, Fyfield, Godstow, Bagley Wood, Hinksey, Sandford, Wytham – all places near Oxford.

17 seems to refer to Tennyson and *In Memoriam*, but A., realising how sharp the comment was, insisted it referred to Goethe.

18 ironic: A. did not find much wisdom in Tennyson's poetry.

19 Dido refused to speak to Aeneas when they met on his descent to the underworld, cf. *Aeneid*, VI.450–71.

20 A. followed the Greek version of the legend (see Philomela), but realising how firmly established the link was between Philomela and the nightingale, used as title, Philomela, when it should have been Prokne, cf. line 21 where the Greek version is obviously in his mind: the sub-text in concerned with A.'s fear that he might not be able to continue writing poetry.

21 a name in the pastoral convention for a shepherd: A. and Clough had been close friends at Oxford and the hill with the elm tree had special significance for them: this poem and 'The Scholar Gipsy' are closely linked by content, theme and form.

22 a lament by a single mourner.

23 in N. Hinksey.

24 Sibylla Kerr who kept the Cross Keys Inn, died 1860.

25 usually known as Chilswell Farm.

26 Clough resigned his fellowship at Oxford, refusing to be constricted by the acceptance of the 39 Articles of the Church of England necessary for such an appointment.
27 in pastoral convention, Thyrsis and Corydon are rival poets: the Sicilian is Theocritus: Bion, his friend, for whom he wrote a lament.
28 see note 16.
29 Clough is buried in the Protestant Cemetery at Florence, where the River Arno flows.
30 Clough published no new poems in England after 1849.

List of Abbreviations

=   stands for
= s   symbolizes

Men and Women
A   Arnold
B   Byron
Br   Browning
Ch   Chaucer
Col   Coleridge
D   Dryden
H.T.   Hallam Tennyson
I.F.   Isobella Fenwick–W.W. dictated notes to her on his poems.
K   Keats
M   Milton
P   Pope
Sh   Shelley
Sp   Spenser
T   Tennyson
D.W.   Dorothy Wordsworth
W.W.   William Wordsworth

Poems
A.&A.   Absalom and Achitophel
A.M.   Ancient Mariner
C.H.   Childe Harold
Ch.   Christabel
C.T.   Canterbury Tales
D.J.   Don Juan
F.Q.   Faerie Queene
K.K.   Kubla Khan
I.M.   In Memoriam
I.Ode   Ode on Intimations of Immortality
L.B.   Lyrical Ballads
P.L.   Paradise Lost
Prel   Prelude
P.U.   Prometheus Unbound
R. of L.   Rape of the Lock
S.A.   Samson Agonistes
T.A.   Lines Written above Tintern Abbey

Books of the Bible/Religion
O.T.   Old Testament
Dan   Daniel
Eccl   Ecclesiastes
Exod   Exodus

Gen	Genesis
Heb	Hebrews
Isa	Isaiah
Jer	Jeremiah
Jon	Jonah
Josh	Joshua
Judg	Judges
Num	Numbers
Phil.	Philippians
Prov	Proverbs
Ps	Psalms
Sam	Samuel
N.T.	New Testament
Corin	Corinthians
Ephes	Ephesians
Matt	Matthew
Phil	Philippians
Rev	Revelations
St J	St John
Tim	Timothy
C. of E.	Church of England

A Note on the Text

Spelling and punctuation

In older poems 'v' and 'u' have been altered and 'f' changed to 's' where necessary to conform with modern usage. Punctuation has also been altered to conform with modern usage or to clarify meaning. Further changes have been made in the case of the following:

Chaucer: 'y's have been retained to distinguish long 'i' from short 'i' sounds

Milton: capital letters have been rationalized in accordance with modern usage

Spenser: the original spelling has been retained; in punctuation, inverted commas have occasionally been inserted to clarify meaning.

Elsewhere the use of capital letters and punctuation has, in many circumstances, been rationalized so that it will not impede today's reader.

Dates

The dates given without brackets at the ends of poems are the dates of composition, where known. Dates given in square brackets [ ] are dates of publication.

The poets are arranged chronologically in order of their dates of birth.

Glossary

N.B. the information given in the glossary is only that necessary for understanding references in the text.

Versification, Verse Forms and Types of Poetry

Rhythm
A sequence of syllables varied in emphasis (*stress*): the stressed and unstressed syllables are divided into *feet*; *scansion* is the analysis of the pattern of those feet; a *caesura* is a pause between two groups of rhythm patterns.

Scansion
The usual way of way of scanning is by marking the stressed and unstressed syllables. ' = stressed, ˘ unstressed.
So:
    ă căesŭră iš ă paúse bĕtwĕen twŏ gŕoups.

Metre
Poems are built up from rhythm patterns, of which the basic unit is the foot. The most common feet are:
    iambs (˘´) Thĕ bóy stoŏd ón thĕ búrniñg déck
    trochees (´˘) Jăck ańd Jĭll wĕnt úp thĕ hĭ'll
    anapaests (˘ ˘´) Thĕ Ássy̆riăn caḿe dŏwn lĭke ă wólf oñ thĕ fŏld
    dactyls (´˘˘). Whe're iš thĕ bóy whŏ loŏks áftĕr thĕ shĕep?
(See also Coleridge's poem 'Metrical Feet', p. ooo.)

Line length can vary from the brevity of
    (a) 'Break, break, break' to, for instance,
    (b) 'That, like a wounded snake, drags its slow length along.'
but each can be broken down into foot patterns. The varying line lengths are called:
    dimeter – 2 feet
    trimeter – 3 feet
    tetrameter – 4 feet
    pentameter – 5 feet
    hexameter – 6 feet, 6 iambic feet = an alexandrine
    heptameter – 7 feet
    octameter – 8 feet
line (a) above is a trimeter, line (b) a hexameter.
Strict conformity to one kind of metrical foot can be very monotonous, so poets vary the metrical feet they employ:
    Bre'ak, bre'ak, bre'ak,
    Oñ thy̆ co'ld gre'y̆ st'ones, O' se'a!
    Añd I' wo'uld thăt mĭy to'ngue co'uld ut'te'r
    Thĕ tho'ughts thă't ări'se iñ me'.
The carrying over of the metre between lines 3 and 4 is called *enjamb(e)ment*.

Rhyme

The repetition of words with the same sound. This can be at the ends of lines (end rhymes) or within the lines (internal rhymes):

> I bring fresh *showers* for the thirsting *flowers*,
>> From the seas and the *streams*;
> I bear light *shade* for the leaves when *laid*
>> In their noonday *dreams*.

Stanza

One line or several lines grouped together:

couplet	2 lines (when rhymed and used continuously = heroic verse)
tercet	3 lines
quatrain	4 lines
quintet	5 lines
sestet	6 lines
octave	8 lines
Spenserian	9 lines
ten-lined	10 lines

Traditional stanza forms

terza rima	3-lined – rhyming aba – bcb –cdc
ballad	4-lined – rhyming abcb with lines alternating 4 feet, 3 feet, 4 feet, 3 feet
rhyme royal	7-lined – iambic pentameter rhyming ababbcc
ottava rima	8-lined – rhyming abababcc
Spenserian	9-lined – 8 lines iambic pentameter, last line alexandrine, rhyming ababbcbcc
sonnet	14 lines iambic pentameter: Italian – divided into octave (8 lines) and sestet (6 lines) rhyming either abbaabba cdecde or abbaabba cdcdcd English (Shakespearean) – 3 quatrains – abab cdcd efef and a final couplet gg – with a break after each quatrain Spenserian – abab bcbc cdcd ee

ro(u)ndel	14 lines with 2 rhymes and repeated lines (capital letters)
	         ABabbaABababAB
	      or ABbaabABbabbaAB

villanelle	5 tercets and closing quatrain; the number of tercets can vary; the first 2 lines set the rhymes and are repeated: A^1bA^2 abA^1 abA^2 abA^1 abA^2 abA^1A^2 (see
free verse	where there is no readily perceptible pattern of formal scansion

Devices

alliteration	repetition of the first letter of a word
	e.g. Round the rugged rock the ragged rascal ran
assonance	repetition of sound
	e.g. Along the cliff to fall and pause and fall did
	seem (Tennyson, 'The Lotos-Eaters')
simile	a comparison introduced by 'like' or 'as'
	e.g. The ship went through the waves like a plough
metaphor	a comparison not introduced by 'like' or 'as'
	e.g. The ship ploughed through the waves
personification	when a non-human object is referred to in human terms
	e.g. She (the ship) ploughed through the waves

Types of poetry

didactic	where the aim is to teach or improve the reader
dramatic	where a character or characters directly tell their story or reveal their situation
epic	lengthy poems concerned with heroic deeds in which both the human and the supernatural are involved
lyric	originally written to be sung to the accompaniment of the lyre; a short poem expressing a thought or a feeling
narrative	telling a story in verse
occasional	written for a special occasion
satiric	verse which ridicules evil or folly

Glossary

Ab(b)ana Syrian river (II Kings V. 12).

Abessa =s Roman Catholic Church, associated with monasticism: daughter of Corceca.

Accaron (Ekron) Philistine city.

Acheron river of Hades; the river of woe.

Achilles Greek hero; fought at Troy where he chased Hector round the walls.

Acidalian brook Spenser's own invention.

Acteon a hunter who saw Diana bathing, was changed by her into a stag and killed by his own hounds.

Adam, first man.

    mark of in the image of.

Addison, Joseph 1672–1719; classical scholar; a contributor to the *Statesman* and *Spectator*; satirised by Pope as 'Atticus'.

Ades *see* Hades.

Adonis beloved of Venus; where he was killed by a boar when hunting; a hyacinth grew; rescued by Venus from Hades for six months each year.

Adria river flowing into the Adriatic.

Aegina Greek isle.

Aeneid Virgil's epic – the story of Aeneas.

Aeolian harp a stringed instrument which, when the wind blows across it, produces a kind of music.

Aeolus god of the winds.

Aesculapius son of Apollo; god of medicine; when visited and asked for help by the Romans, accompanied them back in the form of a serpent.

Aetna Etna, the volcano in Sicily.

Afer S.W. wind.

Afric Africa.

Ahaz king who had an altar built in the temple at Jerusalem like the one at Damascus (II Kings XVI. 10).

Aladule mountainous part of Armenia.

Albano town, S.E. of Rome.

Alcairo Cairo (Memphis).

Alcides *see* Hercules.

Alcinous king of Phaeacia, who kept gardens with trees in fruit and blossom at the same time; Odysseus was his guest.

Alcmena(e) on whom Zeus begot Hercules.

Aldeboran Aldebaran, star in the Taurus constellation; brought discord.

Alexander the Great; visited the temple of Ammon; died of a bout of excessive drinking.

Algarsife son of Cambuscan.

Algeciras town in Spain.

Alis Alice, the Wife of Bath's name.

Alisaundre Alexandria.

Almesbury where Guinevere took refuge in a nunnery after leaving Lancelot.

Alpheus river of Arcadia; *see* Arethusa.

Amalfi   Italian coastal town.

Amaranthus   immortal flower of paradise.

Amaryllis   name for a shepherdess in pastoral poetry.

Amazons   a tribe of female warriors.

Ambrogio, Sant'   a convent where Fra Lippo Lippi painted the Coronation of the Virgin, 1447.

Ambrose, St   4th C. Archbishop of Milan; patron saint of the church of Sant' Ambrogio.

Ammon   originally god of Thebes in Egypt.

    "   Jupiter   his temple was visited by Alexander the Great, whom some worshipped as Ammon's son.

Ammonites   a race descended from Lot; their chief city was Rabbah/Rabbath Ammon; their language akin to Hebrew.

Amphiareus   hid himself from going to the siege of Thebes, where it had been foretold he was to die; was betrayed by his wife for a necklace.

Amphiatus   character in Sydney's *Arcadia*.

Amphitrite   Neptune's wife.

Amram's son   Moses (Exod. VI. 20).

Amyntas   conventional name in pastoral poetry for a shepherd.

Anacreon   6th C. BC poet who wrote in a graceful style.

Anak   his sons were giants (Num. XII.23).

Anchises   father of Aeneas; great-grandfather of Locrine.

Andre, St   a French dancing master and choreographer for Shadwell's opera, *Psyche*, 1675.

Andromache   Hector's wife; her dream is recounted by Dares the Phrygian.

Angelico, Fra   1387–1455; Florentine religious painter.

Anna   Anne, Queen of England, 1702–14.

Anthony, St   ?251–356; a hermit who fought demons in the desert.

Antiochus   2nd C. BC; King of Syria who besieged Jerusalem.

Antonius   *c.* 82–30 BC; Marcus Antonius (Mark Anthony); Cleopatra's lover; defeated at the Battle of Actium, 31 BC; killed himself, believing Cleopatra to be dead.

Aonia   part of Boeotia, where Mt Helicon and the fountain of Aganippe were.

Aphrodite   *see* Venus.

Apicinus   Roman epicure.

Apollo   god of song and music; drove the chariot of the sun daily acoss the sky; he found an empty tortoise shell with three sinews which, when plucked, made music; killed the python that came out of the mud after the deluge of Deucalion, in commemoration of which the Pythian games were founded. In Homer, Apollo and Helos are separate gods; the later linking of the two a result of Egyptian influence.

Apennines   range of mountains in Italy.

Appius   the Roman magistrate who wanted a beautiful girl, Virginia, as his mistress; in a lawsuit, he adjudged her to be the slave of a dependent of his, but her father killed her to protect her chastity.

Arabia   famous for its perfume.

Arabian woods   the woods of Araby where the phoenix lived.

Arbuthnot, John   1667–1735; physician to Queen Anne; close friend of Swift.

Arcady   area in the Peloponnese; its people chiefly hunters and cattlemen, worshippers of Pan; often connected with the pastoral life.

Archimago =s hypocrisy; the power of black magic and the Roman Catholic Church.

Arcturus star, in the constellation Boötes, which brought stormy weather.

Arethusa pursued by Alpheus in river form to Sicily, where she escaped by becoming a fountain, but the two eventually mingled in the sea; Arethusa=nobility of justice, Alpheus=light of truth.

Argestes W.N.W. wind.

Argo Jason's boat, when he passed through the Bosphorus to fetch the Golden Fleece.

Argob on the east bank of the river Jordan.

Argos sometimes Agamemnon's kingdom of which Mycenae was the capital; often=the whole of the Peloponnesus.

Argus a monster with many eyes who guarded Io; killed by Hermes and turned into a peacock.

Arimaspians the one-eyed race, living in S. Russia, who stole the gold guarded by the gryphons.

Arion *c.* 700 BC; Greek musician; when returning to Corinth after winning a music competition was threatened by sailors; he was allowed to play once more and threw himself into the sea where dolphins carried him to shore.

Aristotle philosopher and critic whose *Poetics* set the 'rules' governing Greek tragedy and comedy.

Armorica Brittany.

Arnold, Jane Matthew Arnold's elder sister; in 1841–2 was engaged to George Cotton (assistant master at Rugby) but this was broken; her resulting depression affected her father, Dr Arnold, who died 12 June 1842; August 1850 she married W.E. Forster.

Arrius character in a story in Map's *Epistola Valerii*.

Arthur, King very probably real army leader or chieftain of the 5th or 6th C. who conquered areas of Scotland, Ireland, etc; hero of Malory's *Morte d'Arthur*; son of Uther Pendragon; tutored by Merlin; founder of the Knights of the Round Table; his wife Guinevere betrayed him by falling in love with Sir Lancelot, his great friend; after killing in battle the treacherous Modred, he was wounded and taken to Avalon; he died but legend has it that he will return in Britain's hour of need.

Art Nouveau decorative style in vogue in Europe and America, 1880s – *c.* 1914; cf. illustrations in *The Yellow Book* and Aubrey Beardsley's work.

Artois province in France.

Ascalon a Philistine city (Judges XIV. 19).

Ascanius Aeneas's son.

Ashdod a Philistine city.

Astoreth Phoenician moon-goddess; female counterpart of Baal.

Astoroth plural form of Astoreth.

Asia beloved of Prometheus, a nymph of the sea;=s the soul.

Aspramount (Aspromonte?) a place either in S. Italy or near Nice, France.

Astracan a Tartar kingdom on the lower Volga, near the Russian frontier.

Atlantean Atlas-like.

Atlantis *The New Atlantis* – memoirs, mostly scandalous, by Mrs Manley, 1633–1724.

Atlas   he held the world on his shoulders.

Atropos   one of the Fates, who cut the thread of life.

Attalia   on the S.E. coast of Asia Minor.

Attic Boy   Cephalus, *see* Aurora.

Attila   leader of the Huns who invaded Italy, 5th C. AD; died when he burst a blood vessel on his wedding night.

Auber, Daniel Francois Esprit   1782–1871; composer of operas.

Aubrey, John   1626–97; antiquary and biographer, chiefly remembered for *Brief Lives*, his entertaining, if at times inaccurate, lives of eminent people of his day.

Augustine, St   354–430; believed that monks should do manual work – 'laborare est orare'; supporter of predestination rather than free will (*Discussion with Pelagius*).

Augustus   title conferred first on Gaius Octavius, born 63 BC, in 27 BC, in recognition of his services to the state; and then on subsequent Roman emperors.

Aurora   goddess of the dawn, who loved Cephalus.

Ausonian land   old Greek name for Italy.

Avernus hole   entrance to Hades; a lake near Naples.

Aveugle   = blindness; the son of night.

Avicen   Avicenna, 980–1037; Muslim philosopher and scientist; wrote the *Book of the Cannon in Medicine*, each division of which is called a *fen*.

Ayas   Armenia.

Azazel   a fallen angel; name associated with 'scapegoat' (Lev. XVI 8ff.).

Azotus   *see* Ashdod.

Azza   Gaza.

Baal   sungod of the Philistines; as Beelzebub, god of the flies, a Philistine idol; as Baal-Peor, the idol worshipped at Peor.

Baalim   plural of Baal.

Bablockhithe   ferry over the river Thames, near Cumnor, Oxford.

Babel   the tower of (Gen. XI. 4–9).

Babylon   where the tower of Babel was erected and King Nebuchadnezzar's hanging gardens were (Dan. II, IV. 27).

Bacchus   (Dionysus) at first the god of religious ecstasy, later the god of wine; taken by sailors, he changed the mast into serpents, himself into a lion, maddening the sailors who jumped into the sea to become dolphins; his chariot is drawn by a leopard.

Bactrian   Persian.

Baiae   the Greek settlement W. of Naples.

Balbus   Lord Dupplin, a ceaseless talker.

Baldeswell   nr. Norfolk, England.

Balzac, Honoré de   1799–1850; French novelist.

Barca   desert area in N. Africa; second city of Cyrenaica, N. Africa.

Barnaby   St Barnabas day, 11 June (old calendar); the longest day in the year.

Bas(h)an   E. of Jordan.

Bath   in Avon, England; established as a healing spa in Roman times.

Bavius   poetaster; at enmity with Virgil.

Bayona   fortress town S. of Cape Finisterre.

Bear a constellation.

Bedivere knight of King Arthur's Round Table.

Beelzebub see Baal

Bedlam Bethlehem Hospital for the insane, London.

Belial worthlessness, or the spirit of evil (Deut. XIII. 13, Cor. VI. 15).

Belle an inn in Southwark, London.

Bellerus giant after whom Land's End (Bellarium) was named in Roman times.

Bellini, Vincenzo 1801–35; composer of operas.

Bellona goddess of war.

Benedict, St founder of the Benedictine order of monks.

Bengala Bengal.

Benmarin in N. Africa.

Bentley, Richard 1662–1742, editor of the classics, who 'freely' edited Milton.

Berenice Egyptian Queen whose locks, dedicated to her husband's safe return from war, were taken by Jupiter and turned into a constellation.

Berwick on the River Tweed, N. England.

Bestia corrupt Roman consul.

Bestiary a collection of stories about real and fantastic animals, with morals or parallels involved; derived from a Greek original, *Physiologus*.

Bethel, Slingsby 1617–97; Whig sheriff of London, who packed juries with enemies of the King; wrote against both Cromwell and Royalty (*see* Shimei).

Bion 1st C. BC Greek pastoral poet; lived in Sicily; a lament for him was written by his pupil and friend, Moschus.

Bis(z)erta in Tunisia; from where the King of Africa set out to attack Charlemagne's troops in France.

Blackwood's Magazine 1817–1980; montly periodical started as Tory rival to Whig *Edinburgh Review*; first known as *Edinburgh Monthly Magazine*, then *Blackwood's Edinburgh Magazine*; from 1906 as *Blackwood's Magazine*.

Blount, Martha 1690–1762, she (and her sister) close friends of Pope; later presumed to be his mistress; Pope dedicated his *Moral Essays* to her.

Boece Boethius; died 524; author of *De Consolatione Philosophiae*, which was translated by Chaucer; wrote the standard mediaeval textbook on music.

Boloigne Boulogne, France.

Bordeaux one of the chief ports of Gascony; in Chaucer's day it was under the English crown.

Boreas N. wind, associated with evil.

Boulevart applied to the outer fortification or rampart of a town.

Boulogne Boulogne, France or Bologna, Italy.

Bow bells, of Bow Church, London; an unfashionable area in 17th C.

Bradwardine, Thomas died 1349; Archbishop of Canterbury; supporter of predestination rather than free will.

Bretons people of Brittany.

Briareos third son of Uranus; giant with 50 heads, 100 arms; traditionally fought for Zeus against the Titans.

Briton Breton.

Briton Prince = King Arthur.

Brown, Charles 1771–1810; born in Philadelphia, USA; wrote Gothic novels admired by Keats and Shelley.

Brunswick   Frederick, Duke of, 1771–1815; was killed at the Battle of Quatre-Bras.

Brut(e)us   fabled Roman founder of Britain.

Buckingham   Duke of, *see* Villiers, George.

Budgell, Eustace   contributor to the *Spectator*; said that articles sent to the *Grub Street Journal* accusing him of forging a will to his own benefit were written by Pope.

Burdeaux   Bordeaux; great wine port in 14th C. France.

Burke, Edmund   1729–97; opposed the war in the American colonies

Burnel(1)   the asse; hero of the satirical poem, *Speculum Stultorum*, (*Mirror of Fools*) by Nigel Wireker, a monk of Canterbury.

Burns, Robert   1759–96; Scottish poet.

Busiris   legendary King of Egypt.

Bute   Earl of; a minister of George III.

Butler, James   Duke of Ormond, Lord Lieutenant of Ireland; fought for Charles I and supported Charles II; had 8 sons (6 dead by 1681) and 2 daughters.

Butler, Thomas   1634–80: son of James; distinguished soldier and courtier: died of a fever.

Cadiz   town in Spain.

Cadmus   he and his wife, Harmonia (Hermione) were metamorphosed by Zeus into serpents and taken to Elysium.

Caducean   refers to an enchanter's staff carried by e.g. Hermes or Mercury.

Caecias   E.N.E. wind.

Caelia   = heavenly.

Caesar, Julius   Roman general and dictator; 102–44 BC; murdered on the Ides of March by a conspiracy led by Brutus and Cassius.

Calliope   mother of Orpheus; muse of poetry.

Calvano   a mountain near Naples.

Camaldolenses   members of a religious sect living in the plain of Camaldoli in the Apennines.

Camball   younger son of Cambuscan.

Cambuscan   Genghis Khan, King of the Tartars, who had 2 sons – Camball, and Algarsife.

Camelot   King Arthur's legendary capital.

Cameron, David   was wounded at the Battle of Culloden, 1749.

Cameron, Sir Evan   fought at the Battle of Killiecrankie, 1689.

Campagna   the countryside around Rome.

Camus   the river Cam, Cambridge.

Canace   daughter of Cambuscan who married Camball (not Cambuscan's son)

Canterbury   in Kent, England; Thomas à Becket was murdered in the cathedral there.

Caphtor   Crete? Phoenicia?; the Philistines emigrated from there to Canaan.

Carpathian Wizard   Proteus, the sea-god, who carried a sheephook to control his sea-calves.

Cartegna   S.E. Spain.

Carthage   town of N. Africa.

Caryll, Sir John   he asked Pope to write *The Rape of the Lock*.

Casheen (Kasbin) formerly the capital of Persia, near Teheran.

Casius hills to the S. of Lake Serbonis.

Caspian a proverbially stormy sea.

Cassandra daughter of Hecuba and Priam, whose prophecies none believed.

Cassia a kind of cinnamon.

Cassiopeia wife of the Ethiopean King Cepheus; boasted herself more beautiful than the Nereids and as a result was transformed into a constellation.

Castalia a spring sacred to Apollo and the Muses.

Castlereagh, Robert Stewart, Viscount 1769–1822; eminent statesman whose repressive domestic policy seen to be responsible for the Peterloo Massacre; in a fit of insanity, he committed suicide.

Cathian of Cathay, regarded as a separate country. N. of China.

Cato, Dionysius author of a book of moral injunctions and precepts, *Disticha de Moribus Filium*, very popular in mediaeval times.

Caucasus a large mountain range from the Black Sea to the Caspian Sea.

Cecilia, St patroness of music; her day, 22 Nov., began to be celebrated in England in 1683, when the Musical Society commissioned odes from poets for setting to music.

Celtic(k) i.e. of France.

Cenchreas town on the isthmus of Corinth.

Centaur(s) half-man, half-horse; they were led by Chiron; lived in the region of Mt Pelion; Hercules killed most of them; = Sagittarius, the zodiac sign.

Cephise Cephisus, whose waters washed sheep white.

Cephissian vale the valley of the River Cephisus, running through Phocis.

Cerberus three-headed dog guarding the entrance to Hades.

Ceres goddess of corn and the harvest; usually represented with a torch which she used in her search for her daughter, Proserpine (Primavera), whom Pluto abducted.

Chalybeans they were famed for their metal work; lived on the shores of the Black Sea.

Chaos in Greek = formless matter, out of which the world was made; adapted by Milton into the Christian tradition.

Chapman, George ?1559–1634; translated Homer's *Iliad* and *Odyssey*

Charissa = Charity (spiritual love).

Chartreuse, la Grande Carthusian monastery near Grenoble, France.

Charybdis a rock with a whirlpool; Odysseus steered between it and Scylla, on which a monster lived who snatched two men off his boat.

Chatterton, Thomas 1752–70; a poet who, starving in a garret, committed suicide.

Cha(u)nticlere Chanticleer, the cock whose crowing heralds the dawn.

Cheapside an area in London.

Chemos a form of Moloch; also known as Peor/Baal Peor.

Chianti a region of Italy, S. of Florence, famed for its wines.

Chimeras monsters, part lion, part goat, part serpent, which breathed out fire.

Chiron son of Chronos and Philyra (a nymph); wise and just; famed as a teacher and healer; leader of the Centaurs.

Chloris she was pursued and raped by Jove; became known as Flora; also a name for a shepherdess in pastoral poetry.

Cibber, Colley 1617–1757; actor and playwright who wrote a vivid autobiography of his life in the theatre; 1713 became Poet Laureate; Pope later made him the hero of *The Dunciad*.

Cimmerians people who proverbially lived in caves.

Cipion = Scipio.

Cipres of Cyprus.

   lawn a black gauze.

Circe a sorceress; lived on the Isle of Aeaea, which (according to Homer) is somewhere in the Tyrrhenian Sea; she turned men into beasts; her magic was dispersed by reversing her wand.

Circean of Circe.

Clarendon, Edward Hyde, Earl of, 1609–74; Royalist, supporter of King Charles; in exile began his *Historical Narrative of the Rebellion and Civil Wars in England* (known as *The History of the Rebellion*); returned to England at the Restoration, but was impeached and fled to France.

Cleone on the road from Corinth to Argos.

Cleopatra Queen of Egypt; mistress first of Julius Caesar, then of Mark Antony; poisoned herself with an asp bite.

Cleopolis Clio, muse of history, associated with the moon = s earthly honour; = s famed city, i.e. London.

Clytemnestra Agamemnon's wife, who with the help of her lover, Aegisthus, murdered him after his return from the Trojan War.

Cocytus underground river associated with grief and weeping.

Codrus poet ridiculed by Virgil and Juvenal.

Compton, Henry 1632–1713, Bishop of London; superintended the education of the Duke of York's daughters.

Comus magician; son of Bacchus and Circe.

Congreve, William 1670–1729, playwright.

Cooper, Antony Ashley 1621–1683, Earl of Shrewsbury, *see* notes to *Absalom and Achitophel* – Dryden.

Corceca mother of Abessa; = blind of heart, spiritual blindness.

Correggio 1489–1534, Italian painter.

Cortez Spanish explorer; conqueror of Mexico.

Corydon boy's name in pastoral poetry.

Cosimo de Medici, 1389–1464, wealthy banker, patron of the arts; had great political power in Florence.

Cotytto Thracian goddess, whose rites were celebrated with licentious revelry.

Crisippus Jerome said it was absurd of C. to advise wise men to marry to placate the gods of marriage and procreation.

Christopher a medal in the likeness of St Christopher, patron saint of foresters and travellers.

Croesus 6th C. BC, last king of Lydia, renowned for his wealth.

Cromwell, Oliver 1599–1658, soldier, politician, general; 1653–8 Lord Protector of England.

Cromwell, Richard 1626–1658, son of Oliver and his successor as Lord Protector of England.

Cronian Sea Arctic Ocean.

Crook, Japhet a forger whose ears were cut off for his crime.

Cumnor Hills near Oxford, England.

Cupid Venus's son, god of love; fell in love with and eventually married Psyche.

Curll, Edmund 1675–1747, an unscrupulous bookseller.

Cybele earth-mother (Rhea); goddess of fertility, of wild nature; favoured especially by women; worshipped with orgiastic rites and dances.

Cyclades group of Greek islands.

Cymbrian modern Jutland; ?Wales.

Cynick tub refers to Diogenes, Greek philosopher, who is said to have lived in a tub.

Cynthia goddess of the moon, who fell in love with Endymion, a shepherd boy, on the slopes of Mt Latmos; depicted as driving a team of dragons.

Cyparisse son of Telephus; grieved over killing a stag and was changed into a cypress, linked with Sylvanus; *or* youth who fled from the attentions of Apollo and was saved by being changed into a cypress.

Cyprian Queen i.e. Venus as worshipped in Cyprus.

Cyrene Greek city on the coast opposite Crete.

Cytherea Venus as worshipped on the island of Cythera.

Cytherea's son Aeneas.

Dagon god of the Philistines, with temples at Gaza and Ashdod.

Damaetas a character in Sidney's *Arcadia*, a loutish clown.

Damasco Damascus.

Damien, Robert Francois a half-wit, who suffered torture before being put to death, March 1757, having tried to assassinate Louis XV.

Damon name for a young man in pastoral poetry.

Danae imprisoned in a house of bronze by her father; was visited by Jove in a shower of gold; their child was Perseus.

Danaus his 50 daughters were forced to marry, so they killed their husbands on their wedding night and were condemned for ever to fill a vessel, full of holes, with water.

Danaw Danube, river of Europe.

Daniel who was skilled in interpreting dreams (Dan. 1. 17).

Dante Alighieri 1265–1321; poet of Florence.

Daphne to escape from Apollo she changed into a tree.

Daphnis ideal shepherd of pastoral poetry; his mistress was taken to Phrygia by King Lityerses, who was killed by Hercules; the Lityerses song is an early example of a reaper's song; Daphnis was also beloved by a nymph who blinded him when he fell in love with a princess; Mercury, his father, took him to heaven, leaving a spring of water where Sicilians offered annual sacrifices.

Darien isthmus of Panama, with a peak called Darien.

Darius died 330 BC; King of Phrygia, defeated by Alexander the Great; tradition has it he ordered a magnificent tomb to be built for himself by Appelles, a Jewish craftsman.

Darlecarlian in the course of the war with Denmark, Gustavus II of Sweden retreated there where he became a miner and field labourer.

Dartmouth port in Devon, England.

Daulis town in Phocis.

Decan area near Goa, India.

Dekker, Thomas   1572–1632; playwright, satirised by Ben Jonson.

Deianeira   Hercules' wife; *see* Hercules.

Delia   *see* Diana.

Delos   Greek isle, in the Aegean, raised by Neptune; it floated free until Jove chained it to the sea-floor; birthplace of Apollo.

Delphian cliff   at Delphi, the seat of the oracle of Apollo.

Delphic choir   i.e. of poets.

Demeter   Rhea's daughter, mother of Proserpina.

Demetrius   poss, Demetrius Nicator, king of the Parthians, an Asian people.

Demogorgon   an infernal power; for Spenser, the Prince of Chaos and Darkness; for Shelley = eternity.

Denham, Sir John   1615–69; author of topographical poem, *Cooper's Hill*.

Dennis, John   1657–1742; censured Pope's *Essay on Criticism*.

Deva   River Dee, the haunt of magicians, whose changes of course were thought to foretell the country's fortunes.

Diana   goddess of the moon and hunting; born at Delos (Delia); commonly worshipped in woody places; associated with women and childbirth; usually depicted carrying a bow and quiver of arrows.

Dickens, Charles   1812–70; English novelist.

Dictaean   of Mt Dicte, on Crete, where Jove was brought up.

Doddington, Bubb   a dishonest political patron.

Dodona   in Epirus; seat of the oracle of Zeus.

Dorian mode   simple solemn music.

Doric   Greek dialect of pastoral writers – Theocritus, Bion, and Moschus.

"   **lay**   pastoral song.

Doris   area of ancient Greece.

D'Orsay, Count   a dandy, well-known in Victorian London.

Dowland, John   1563–1626; English lutenist; his *First Book of Songes or Ayres of Foure Partes with Tabletures for the Lute* published 1597.

Druid   ancient British priest and bard.

Drury Lane   area, in London, of theatres and prostitutes.

Dryades   wood nymphs.

Dryope   the beloved of Faunus/Sylvanus.

Duck, Stephen   1705–56; a poet; his *The Thatcher's Labour* gave a realistic picture of labouring life of the time; elsewhere his poetry is conventional pastoral poetry.

Duessa   = two-faced; in Spenser = s Catholic Church.

Dunmail Raise   in the Lake District, England.

Dunmow   in Essex, England, where the Dunmow flitch – a side of bacon – is competed for by happily married couples.

Easedale   in the Lake District, England.

Echo   loved Narcissus (who loved only his own reflection in a pool) and pined away into a mere voice; wandered everywhere, from the Meander in Phrygia, to the valley of nightingales, Athens.

Ecron   a Philistine city.

Eden   the garden where Adam and Eve lived.

Egremont   small town in the Lake District, England, where the Ennerdale River flows.

Eldon, John Scott 1st Earl of   1751–1838, lawyer and statesman, becoming finally Lord Chancellor; hated the Roman Catholics.

Eleyne *see* Helen.

Elysian Fields the fields of happiness where heroes and the souls of the blest live eternally.

Elysium the heaven of Roman gods.

Emims giants (Deut. II. 10–11; Gen. XIV. 5).

Enceladus a hundred-armed giant who rebelled against Jupiter.

Endymion beloved by the moon, Diana, she bore him 50 daughters.

Enna in Sicily.

Ephraim the Ephraimites refused to help Jeptha and the Gileadites in their quarrel with the Ephs; Jeptha's men used the word 'Shibboleth', which the Ephraimites could not pronounce, as a password to sort out possible spies and infiltrators (Judges XI, XII).

Epictetus Stoic philosopher; taught at Rome until AD 90, then at Nicopolis in Epirus, where Arrian took down his discourses.

Epicurus 342–270 BC, Greek philosopher whose belief that a virtuous life brought absence of pain was popularized as – 'pleasure is the true goal of living.'

Erebus lowest place in Hades/Hades itself.

Eshtaol Samson was buried between Zora and Eshtaol (Josh. XV. 33).

Estotiland today N.E. Labrador.

Et(h)am where Samson stayed in a cave (Judges V. 7).

Etherege, Sir George *c.* 1634–91; Restoration playwright.

Ethiopian sea off the E. coast of Africa; now part of the Indian Ocean.

Etna volcano on Sicily.

Etrurian from Tuscany, Italy.

Euboic Sea between E. coast of Greece and the Isle of Euboea.

Eugene Prince of Savoy, 1663–1736; a hero, with Marlborough, of the battles of Blenheim and Malplaquet.

Euphrates one of the four rivers flowing from Eden; = s justice.

Euphrosyne = Mirth; daughter of Venus and Bacchus, sister to Aglaia and Thalia.

Euronyme = wide-ruling; daughter of Ocean; yielded her power to Ops.

Eurus E.S.E. wind.

Eurydice Orpheus' wife, whom he tried to save from Hades but on looking back at her, lost her.

Eve Adam's wife; first woman.

Fairfield mountain near Ambleside, Lake District, England.

Faun rural deity; man with goat's ears, horns, hind legs and tail.

Faunus = Pan/Sylvanus.

Ferrar, Nicholas 1592–1637; he retired 1625 to Little Gidding to set up a religious community based on Anglican beliefs; close friend of George Herbert; after Herbert's death was entrusted with the ms. of his poems.

Fesole Fiesole, near Florence, Italy.

Fez in Morocco.

Fidelia = Faith.

Fidessa = faithlessness (Duessa).

Finistere (Finisterra) Cape Finisterre, in Brittany or Spain.

Fish Street where Chaucer's father lived in London.

Flaxman, John 1755–1826; sculptor and draughtsman influenced by classical reliefs and vases.

Fletcher, John 1579–1625; author of popular tragedies; collaborator with Francis Beaumont. *c.* 1584–1616.

Flora goddess of flowers; = s Queen Elizabeth I.

Florio name for a young man in pastoral poetry.

Fontainebleau near Paris.

Fontarrabia Fuenterrabia, on the frontier between Spain and France.

Fox, Charles James 1749–1806; opponent of Pitt and his policies.

Fradubio = Doubt; can only be freed from his condition by God's grace.

Fraelissa = Frailty.

Franklin, Benjamin 1706–90; American statesman and scientist.

Frascati town S. of Rome.

Furies spirits of revenge and discord; daughters of Acheron and Night; haunted the guilty.

Fyfield near Oxford, where an elm tree served as a maypole.

Fynystere *see* Finistere.

Gabriel an archangel.

Gadire Cadiz, S. coast of Spain.

Gaecias N.E. wind.

Galen (Galien) 2nd C. AD, Graeco-Roman doctor.

Galicia Spain.

Galileo 1564–1642; Italian astronomer and physicist.

Galli priests of Rhea.

Gallus Sulpicius Consul in Rome, 166 BC; figures in a story by Valerius Maximus.

Ganelon a traitor who caused the death of Roland and the defeat of Charlemagne.

Ganges a river in India.

Gargarus the highest part of Mt Ida.

Gath a Philistine town.

Gaunt Ghent, Flemish town, famous for fine cloth.

Gawain a knight of the Round Table, who died fighting for King Arthur.

Gay, John 1685–1732; poet and playwright; friend of Pope; wrote, 1728, *The Beggar's Opera*; befriended by the Duke and Duchess of Queensberry.

Gaza Philistine city in S.W. Palestine.

Gehenna valley of Hinnom, S.W. of Jerusalem; = a place of torment for the wicked (2 Kings XVI and XXIII).

Gehon *see* Gihon.

Geneva town of Switzerland; home of Calvin and his followers.

Geoffrey of Vinsauf 12th C. writer; his *Poetria Nova* contained a lament on King Richard I's death, which happened on a Friday.

Ghent *see* Gaunt.

Gideon rescued Israel from the Midianites (Judges VI. ii).

Gihon river of paradise; = s temperance.

Gilbert, Dr John became Archbishop of York.

Gildon, Charles 1665–1724; critic who censured *The Rape of the Lock*.

Giotto 1267–1337; great Florentine painter.

Giulio Romano 1492–1546; painter and architect; studied under Raphael, whom he succeeded as head of the Roman school of painting.

Glanvill, Joseph 1636–80; clergyman who wrote *The Vanity of Dogmatizing*, 1661.

Glaucus a sea-god and prophet.

Gloriana Queen of Faerie-land, for whom, in Spenser's *Faerie Queene*, Prince Arthur is seeking; the embodiment of divine beauty; = s Queen Elizabeth I.

Goat the sign of Capricorn, associated with lust.

Godfrey, Sir Edmund Barry 1621–78; took Oates' deposition about the Popish Plot and was found murdered 2 Oct. 1678, for which the Protestants accused the Catholics.

Godwin, William 1756–1836; atheist; believed in human beings acting according to their reason not by threat of institutions such as the church or the state; married 1. Mary Wollstonecraft 2. Mrs Clairmont; their daughter, Claire Clairmont, became Byron's mistress.

Goethe, Johann Wolfgang von 1749–1832; German poet, dramatist and philosopher.

Goliah Goliath, the giant whom David killed.

Gorgon *see* Demogorgon; Medusa.

Goshen area N. of the Nile where the Israelites settled (Gen. XLVII. 27).

Gothard Swiss mountain.

Gothic late mediaeval architectural style.

Gotland island in the Baltic.

des Gourges, Dominique died 1582; went to Florida to avenge the massacre of the French by the Spaniards (Hakluyt's *Voyages*).

Gracchus Roman family, renowned for its enlightened attitudes.

Graces the Three Graces – Aglaia, Thalia, Euphrosyne, personifying grace and beauty.

Grafton, Duke of a minister of George II.

Graius = a Greek; = s the Church of England, when attendance at church was compelled by act of law (the Act of Uniformity 1559).

Grasmere in the Lake District, England.

Granada town in Spain.

Grey, Lord died 1701; consented to an affair between his wife and the Duke of Monmouth.

Grub Street traditional haunt of hack writers.

Guadalquivir Spanish river.

Guiers Mort ('dead Guiers') a river which has its source near La Grande Chartreuse.

Guinevere King Arthur's wife, beloved of Lancelot.

Guizot, Francis G. statesman; he and Charles Montalembert were enemies; when the latter was elected to the Académie Française, the former had to make the official speech of welcome.

Gustavus I 1496–1560; drove the Danes out of Sweden.

Hades hell; the classical underworld.

Hailes Abbey in Gloucestershire; a phial of, reputedly, Christ's blood, which a sinner could not see, was kept there.

Hamadryades tree nymphs.

Hampden, John 1594–1642; refused to pay a tax levied by Charles I.

Hampton Court   on the Thames, near London.

Hannibal   247–183/4 BC; Carthaginian general who, age 9, swore eternal enmity to Rome.

Happy Isles   = Isles of the Blest, believed to be beyond the Pillars of Hercules (Gibraltar).

Harapha   lit. the giant; not in the Biblical story – created by Milton.

Harpies   birds with women's faces.

Hasdrubal   1. Hannibal's brother 2. King of Carthage who committed suicide when Rome burned Carthage, 146 BC.

Hasdrubal's wife   threw herself and her children into the flames when her husband was defeated by Scipio Minor.

Hastings, Theophilus   Earl of Huntingdon 1650–1701; at first a follower of Monmouth; later joined James II's party.

Hayley, William   1745–1820; popular poet whose *Ballads on Animals* was illustrated by Blake, his protégé; declined the Poet Laureateship, 1790.

Hebe   daughter of Juno; goddess of youth; cup-bearer of the gods.

Hebron   city of Arba, the father of Anak, whose children were giants.

Hecate   Queen of the underworld, associated with witchcraft and bad dreams; Circe used her charms against Scylla; hounds follow her across the sky pursuing the souls of the damned.

Hector   Trojan warrior, son of Priam and Hecuba; killed by Achilles at Troy.

Helen, St   mother of the Emperor Constantine; said to have discovered the cross of the Crucifixion, parts of which were distributed throughout the world; its discovery celebrated on 3 May.

Helen(a)   wife of Menelaus, who gave her husband a drug to dispel his grief.

Helicon, Mt   part of a range in Boeotia, Greece, between the Gulf of Corinth and Copais; abode of the Muses.

Héloise   young girl, beloved of Peter Abelard who was her tutor; they secretly married and had a son; she denied the marriage so as not to impede Abelard's ecclesiastical preferment and her uncle, enraged, caused him to be castrated; she became a nun in the convents of, first, Argenteuil, then later, Paraclete.

Henley, John   1692–1756; left the church to become an itinerant lecturer 'on any branch of knowledge, composition and elocution'; on Easter day, 1729, lectured on *the Religious History and Use of the Butchers' Calling*.

Hera   Queen of Heaven – Jove's wife; to whom peacocks were sacred.

Hercules   his second labour of the 12 was to destroy the Hydra of Lerna; he put on a poisoned robe sent to him by his wife, Deianeira, and in his agony, tore up trees and rocks and threw Lichas, his friend, into the sea; eventually on Mt Oeta in Thessaly, he built, and burned himself to death on, a funeral pyre.

Hermes   supposed author of the Third and Fourth Hermetic writings, regarded by the Neo-Platonists as the source of all knowledge.

Hermes   messenger of the gods, who guided the dead over the river Lethe; was said to be always falling in love.

Hermione   *see* Cadmus.

Herringman, Henry   publisher of both Pope and Shadwell until 1678.

Herod   ruler of Galilee (Matt. XIV. 1–9).

Herodias   instructed her daughter, Salome, to ask Herod for the head of John the Baptist as a reward for her dancing.

Hervey, John   vice-chamberlain to Walpole; enemy of Pope in politics and literature; a fop who drank ass's milk to remedy his physical frailty; was prominent in Court and close to Queen Caroline.

Hesperian Tree   on which the Golden Apples, guarded by the Hesperides and the dragon, Ladon, grew.

Hesperian Fields   in the western area = Italy.

Hesperus   evening star/morning star/planet = Venus.

Heywood, Thomas   ?1574–1641; dramatist; member of the Lord Admiral's Company (of actors) and later of the Queen's Players.

Hidalgo   of the lower nobility in Spain; of true Spanish stock.

Himera   Ethiopian princess.

Hinnom   valley watered by a stream from Siloam, where Topheth is (in Greek, Gehenna = Hell).

Hippocrene   a spring on Mt Helicon, sacred to the Muses.

Hippolytus   son of Theseus and Hippolyta.

Hippotades   Aeolus, god of the winds.

Homer   Greek, (?) author of *The Iliad* and *The Odyssey*.

Horace   65–8 BC; Latin poet.

Horeb   and Sinai; poss. the same mountain or twin peaks (Deut. IV. 10; Exod. XIX. 11).

Horner, Gilpin   a character in Wycherley's *The Country Wife*.

Howard, William   Lord ?1626–94; an Anabaptist minister who served under Cromwell; 1674 was discovered in secret correspondence with the Dutch; imprisoned; set free on confessing; 1681 imprisoned in the Tower, charged with writing *The Englishman Speaking Plain English in a Letter from a Friend to a Friend*, in which the deposition of the King and the exclusion of the Duke of York was advocated.

Hudson, Henry   died 1611; English navigator; explored the Hudson River (of New York, USA); 1610 discovered the Bay and Straits named after him, the inland Bay being connected by the Straits to the Atlantic Ocean.

Hull   port in Yorkshire, N. England.

Humber   river that flows past Hull; Marvell's home town.

Humilta   = Humility.

Hunt, Leigh   1784–1859; poet and editor; vigorous supporter of Keats, Shelley and Hazlitt.

Huntingdon   Earl of; *see* Hastings, Theophilus.

Hyacinth   beloved of Apollo; was killed by a discus.

Hyades   = the rainy ones; seven nymphs in the constellation Taurus, whose conjunction with the sun brings stormy weather.

Hyde, Laurence   1641–1711; later Earl of Rochester; Duke of York's confidant; became 1st Lord of the Treasury; patron of Dryden.

Hyde Park Circus   a fashionable place, in 17th C., for driving carriages; in London.

Hydrus   (hydra) a water snake with nine heads: when one was cut off, two replaced it.

Hymen   god of marriage.

Ida, Mt   mountain S. of Troy, where Jove was secretly reared; connected with the worship of Cybele (Rhea).

Idalian   of Ida.

Ilion Troy.

Illyria mountainous area on the E. coast of the Adriatic.

Inde India.

Indian steep = the Himalayas.

Indian mount = W. Himalayas.

Ionians Greeks; they were supposed to have been descended from Javan, the grandson of Noah.

Iris messenger of the gods; personification of the rainbow; wife of Zephyrus; mother of Eros.

Isles of the Blest Elysium; thought to be beyond the Pillars of Hercules (Gibraltar).

Ixion attempted to seduce Juno; for this he was condemned by Jove to be bound eternally to a turning wheel; father of the Centaurs.

Jacob he saw angels ascending and descending from heaven (Gen. XXVIII. 10–22).

Jacob's staff carried by pilgrims to the shrine of St James of Compostella, Spain.

Jael killed Sisera, the Canaanite general (Judges IV. 21).

James, Duke of York Charles II's brother and legitimate heir to the throne as Charles had no legitimate children; see also Monmouth.

James, St patron saint of Spain, whose shrine is at Santiago de Compostella.

Javan Noah's grandson; traditional ancestor of the Ionians (Greeks).

Jeptha led the people of Gilead against the Ammonites (Judges XI. 12–33).

Jeroboam led the revolt of the 10 tribes of Israel against Rehoboam (I Kings XII. 28–9).

Jerome, St c. 340–420; renowned for his asceticism and his learning; wrote the *Epistola Adversus Jovinianum*.

Jerusalem the Holy City; a place of pilgrimage.

Joce, St Jodicus, a Breton saint.

John, St John the Baptist; patron saint of Florence.

John, Sir common nickname for a priest.

Jones, Sir William prosecuted those involved in the Popish Plot; helped Shaftesbury get the Exclusion Bill (to exclude the Duke of York, the rightful heir as Charles II had no legitimate heirs, from the throne) through Parliament.

Jonson, Ben 1572–1637; player and playwright.

Jordan the river, which cleansed away sins (II Kings V. 10ff; Matt. III. 13).

Joseph had a coat of many colours and dreamed (Gen. XXXVII, XL, XII).

Josiah King of Judah (II Kings XXII; II Chron. XXXIV. 1–7).

Jove Saturn's son, who overthrew his father; spent his childhood on Mt Ida.

Ammonian Jove i.e. of Ammon, who in the form of a snake slept with Olympia, the mother of Alexander the Great.

Capitoline Jove (Jupiter Capitolinus) i.e. of Rome, who, as a snake, slept with Sempronia, mother of Scipio Africanus.

Jovinian died early 5th C.; unorthodox monk, who was condemned for denying that virginity was better than marriage, abstinence better than thankful eating.

Jubal 'father of all such as handle the harp and the organ' (Gen. IV. 21).

Judas Iscariot betrayer of Christ (Matt. XXVI. 14ff).

Julian, St patron saint of hospitality.

Junius wrote a series of letters attacking leading politicians and George III, under this pseudonym – described as 'nominis umbra' (the shade of a name).

Juno Hera, queen of heaven; *see* Turnus.

Jupiter *see* Jove.

Jura a mountain in the Alps.

Juvenal 1st C. AD, Latin satirist.

Kaukasous the Caucasus mountains.

Kenelm, St at age 7 became the King of Mercia; his dream, in which he saw himself sitting in a tree which a friend cut down, and his soul flying to heaven, was a true prophecy of his subsequent murder on his aunt's orders.

Kiriathim *see* Emims.

Kirkrapine = church robber.

Labryde father of Thyamis; = violent, tempestuous.

Lacidomye Lacedaemon; chief city of Sparta.

Lamb, Lady Caroline 1785–1828; married William Lamb, 2nd Viscount Melbourne; became infatuated with Byron; her novel – *Glenarvon* – (= Byron) had a brief success.

Lamech son of Methuselah; father of Noah (Gen. IV. 19–23).

Lamia female serpent granted human shape by Hermes; she seduced Lycius; Apollonius, Lycius' tutor, exposed her; she vanished and Lycius died.

Lamuel a king whose mother advised him against strong drink (Prov. XXXI. 4–5).

Lapland legendary stronghold of witches and sorcerers.

La Rochelle *see* Rochelle.

Latmus, Mt a mountain in Caria, S.W. Asia Minor.

Latumius poss. a corruption of Pacuvius, the name used in Walter Map's *Epistola Valerii*; the 'hanging tree' story had wide circulation, in Cicero and the *Gesta Romanorum* for example.

La(u)ncelot King Arthur's knight and friend who fell in love with Guinevere, Arthur's wife.

Laurent (Lawrence), St martyr roasted on a gridiron; legend has it that he urged his executioners to turn him over as he was done on one side.

Laurent, St a village near La Grande Chartreuse.

Lebanon noted for its cedar trees.

Leman a lake in Switzerland.

Lemnos an island in the Aegean Sea.

Lentulus consul of Rome, 49 BC; after the battle of Pharsalus, fled to Egypt, where he died.

Lepe near Cadiz, Spain.

Lerna, Lake near Argos, where lived the Hydra that Hercules slew.

Lethe river of forgetfulness in the underworld.

Lettow Lithuania.

Leucothea wife of Athames, who drowned and became a sea-nymph; protector of Odysseus.

Levant the east (sun-rising).

Leviathan a monster, thought of as a whale (Job. XLI).

Libecchio S.W. wind.

Libian sands i.e. of N. Africa.

Lichas *see* Hercules.

Ligea a siren.

Limbo the place of lost spirits.

Lintot(t), Bernard 1675–1736; bookseller and printer; published in *Miscellaneous Poems*, 1712, the first version of Pope's *The Rape of the Lock*; derided by Pope in *The Dunciad.*

Lippi, Fra Lippo 1406–69; Florentine painter; entered the Carmelite order as a boy; gave up his vows, June 1421, but continued to be clothed by the monastery until 1431.

Livia wife of Drusus; poisoned her husband for her lover, Sejanus, 23 AD.

Locrine son of Brut(e)us, legendary founder of Britain.

Lorenzo, Fra 1370–1425; a painter of the Giotto school.

Lot(Looth) who escaped from Sodom and Gomorrah (Gen. XIX ff.).

Loy, St St Eligius, patron saint of courtiers and goldsmiths.

Lucan 39–65 AD, young Latin poet who committed suicide rather than die under Nero's sentence.

Lucifer Satan; the planet Venus; the morning/evening star.

Lucifera woman ruler of the House of Pride in Spenser's *Faerie Queene.*

Lucilia wife of Lucretius, the poet; she gave him a love potion to keep him faithful to her but he died, poisoned by it.

Lucina goddess of 'light-bringing', hence of childbirth; her name used to invoke both Diana and Juno.

Luke Luke Dosa with his brother, George, led a popular revolution in Hungary; George was proclaimed king by the peasants, for which he, not Luke, was tortured with a red-hot crown.

Lydia the country between the Aegean sea and Mysia, Asia Minor, whose boundaries varied; divided by Tmolus, a range of mountains; known as Maeonia to Homer.

Lydian pleasant, enervating mode of music.

Lyonesse legendary region between Cornwall and the Scilly Isles.

Mab Queen of the Fairies.

Macrobius *c.* 400; wrote a commentary on *Somnium Scripionis* (*Dream of Scipio*), a part of Cicero's *De Republica.*

Madian Gideon's enemy (Judges VIII).

Maenad a Bacchante; woman inspired to ecstasy and frenzy by Dionysus.

Maeotis the inland sea of Azof.

Magellan straits at the S. tip of S. America.

Maia most beautiful of Atlas' daughters; mother, by Jove, of Mercury.

Majesty begot, according to Spenser, by Jove and Night.

Malabar in S.W. India.

Malkin diminutive of Matilda; common name for a servant.

Mall a walk by St James' Park, London.

Malvenu = unwelcome.

Mammon god of the things of the flesh.

Map, Walter *fl.* 1200; author of a collection of legends and anecdotes – *De Nugis Curialium*; poss. author of some satirical verses, as well as a large part of *Lancelot*, the lost Latin original of the Arthurian legend.

Marcellus opponent of Julius Caesar in whose death he was poss. involved.

Marcian under the influence of Mars.

Marius, Gaius 157–86 BC; consul and army commander; his antagonism to Sulla occasioned the First Civil War in Rome.

Marocco Morocco.

Mars god of war.

Mart = Mars.

Mary Magdalene who ministered to Christ (Luke XXIII. 49ff.).

Masaccio 1401–28; painted the frescoes in Santa Maria del Carmine, Florence.

Matthew for his record of Christ's teaching about vows (Matt. V. 33–4).

Maurus, St introduced the order of St Benedict to France.

Meander a winding river in Lydia, Asia Minor.

Medea Circe's niece, a witch.

Medusa one of three female monsters (the Gorgons), with snakes for hair who turned all to stone who looked at them; when Perseus, having slain her, returned with her head, the drops of blood that fell became snakes, which is why Libya is full of snakes.

Megaera one of the Furies, with snaky hair.

Memmonia see Susa.

Memnon Ethiopian prince.

Mercia Anglo-Saxon kingdom of England; overrun by the Danes, 9th C.

Mercury (Hermes) son of Zeus and Maia; born in a cave in Arcadia; the planet brings studiousness to those born under its influence.

Merlin the magician/wise man who tutored King Arthur; Vivien, the temptress, coaxed his spells from him.

Metellius a character from a collection of *exempla* by Valerius Maximus from Greek and Roman history.

Mexique Bay the Gulf of Mexico.

Michael, St an archangel, often depicted with his foot on a snake or dragon (= Satan).

Midas preferred Pan's music to Apollo's, so was given ass's ears; discovered by his barber who could not keep it a secret.

Middleburgh on the Isle of Walcheren, Netherlands.

Midland waters the sea between N. Africa and Sicily.

Mincius Virgil's native river (*Eclogues* VII. 12–3).

Minerva (Athena) the virgin goddess whose shield was the head of the Gorgon; the goddess of wisdom and chastity.

Mint a sanctuary for debtors in Southwark, London.

Mirreus a man of incense; = the Catholic Church.

Mithradates King of Pontus (Asia Minor); defeated Pompey, 66 BC; marched via the Black Sea to invade Italy from the north.

Mnemosyne goddess of memory.

Modred King Arthur's nephew who plotted and fought against him.

Moloch god of the Ammonites to whom children were sacrificed (II Kings XXIII. 10).

Moly white-flowered herb that Hermes gave to Ulysses to protect him against Circe's charms.

Mona Isle of Anglesey, off the Welsh coast.

Monmouth James Duke of, 1649–85; illegitimate son of Charles II and Lucy Walters; took his wife's name on their marriage.

Montague Lady Mary Wortley 1689–1762; author of *Turkish Letters* (published after her death); leading member of society; quarrelled with Pope who attacked her as Sappho in his *Imitations of Horace, Satire I*.

Montalban in Languedoc, S. France.

Montalembert, Charles *see* Guizot, F.G.

Moore, Arthur with his son, James, he plagiarised lines from Pope's 'The Rival Modes', 1727.

Moore, Thomas 1779–1852; the Irish poet.

Morpheus the god of sleep.

Moses who saw the burning bush and received the Laws on Mt Oreb, or its spur, Mt Sinai.

Mulciber Vulcan, the blacksmith god.

Musaeus semi-mythical Greek poet, contemporary with Orpheus.

Muses the nine goddesses who inspired the arts.

Naaman a captain in the Syrian army who was converted to the Hebrew religion after being cured of leprosy by bathing in the River Jordan, on the advice of Elisha (II Kings. V. 1–19).

Naiades water nymphs.

Namancos a mountain in N.W. Spain.

Narcissus he fell in love with his own reflection; *see* Echo.

Neaera girl's name in pastoral poetry.

Neptune (Poseidon) god of the sea; Odysseus incurred his anger by killing his son, Polyphemus, the one-eyed giant.

Nereids water nymphs.

Nereus god of the Aegean sea; a wise old man.

Nero to re-enact the burning of Troy he set fire to Rome, 64 AD.

Niger a river in Africa.

Night offspring of Chaos; gave birth to Deceit, Lies, Strife and Lawlessness.

Nilus the River Nile.

Nimrod the mighty hunter of the Lord; associated with the Tower of Babel (Gen. X. 8–9).

Ninus founder of Nineveh; married to Semiramis (Jonah III. 3).

Norfolk county in England.

Norumbega roughly, S.E. Canada and N.E. America.

Norus S. wind.

Oates, Titus contrived the Popish Plot, according to which Charles II was to be killed and James, Duke of York to be made King; an Anabaptist weaver who became a Church of England clergyman, then, 1672, a Catholic; while he was travelling in France and Spain, he claimed he had uncovered a Jesuit plot against the English government; during James II's reign he was pilloried, whipped and fined for perjury; under William III received a pension; claimed to have received a Doctorate of Divinity from Salamanca.

Ob Siberian river flowing into the Arctic Ocean.

Obermann *see* Senancour, Étienne Pivert de.

Oberon King of the Fairies.

Oceanus god of the ocean waters that encircle the earth.

Odysseus his travels, after the fall of Troy, are narrated in *The Odyssey*; *see also* Ulysses.

Oechalia a town in Thessaly or Messenia.

Oenone married to Paris who deserted her for Helen.

Oeta *see* Hercules.

Og King of Bashan (Deut. III. 11).

Ogilby, John 1600–76; published feeble verse translations of Homer, Virgil, Aesop.

Olivet a hill near Jerusalem.

Olympian games Greek national games, held every five years at Olympia.

Olympias *see* Jove.

Olympus, Mt mountain in Greece, the home of the gods.

Ophion = a serpent; yielded his control of Olympus to Saturn.

Ophiouchus a large constellation in the N. hemisphere.

Ophiusa = full of serpents; name given to several Greek islands, including Rhodes.

Ops mother of Jove.

Orcus (Pluto) the god of Hades.

Oread mountain nymphs.

Oreb where the golden calf was (Exod. XXX).

Orgoglio = freshly pride; offspring of earth; ruler of the winds; a giant faun/satyr (Gen. VI. 4).

Orion legendary Greek hunter; after death became a constellation which, in its ascendancy, brings bad weather.

Orion's hound the Dog Star – Sirius.

Ormus (H)ormuz; island town in Persian Gulf; centre of the jewellery trade.

Orontes river in Syria.

Orpheus mythical early Greek poet; his music could charm people, animals, trees and even stones; attempted to bring Eurydice back from Hades, but lost her by turning his head to look at her; was torn apart by the Thracian women, and his head was washed ashore at Lesbos, endowing the islanders there with the gift of song.

Orus (Horus) son of Isis and Osiris.

Orwell Haven a port near Ipswich, England.

Osiris Egyptian god, murdered by his brother, Set; cut up into pieces and scattered throughout the world; when Isis collected them together, Osiris was re-born.

Othello the Moor of Venice of Shakespeare's play, *Othello*.

Otway, Thomas 1652–85; playwright.

Ovid 43 BC – *c.* 17 AD; Latin poet famous for his love poetry; three times married – only the last a success; banished to Tomi (Constanza) by the Emperor Augustus; died in exile; his *Metamorphoses* frequently used as a source for mythological stories.

Oxenford Oxford.

Ozell, John an accountant; translator of French plays.

Ozymandias the Greek name for the Egyptian King Ramses II; said to have set up a large statue to himself.

Palatia Turkey.

Pales Roman goddess of pastures, flocks and herds.

Palestine   land of the Philistines.

Palinurus   pilot of Aeneas' boat; in *The Dunciad* = the Prime Minister, Walpole.

Pallas   one of the Titans.

Pambamarca   in Ecuador.

Pan   the god of nature, flocks and shepherds.

Panope   the greatest of the Nereids.

Panthea   the place of the gods; in Spenser = Westminster Palace or Greenwich.

Paphian   of Paphos; centre for worship of Aphrodite.

Parnassus   the abode of the Muses.

Parry, Sir William Edward,   1790–1855; explorer; describes Melville's Sound in his *Journal of a Voyage*, 1821.

Parthenia   a small river flowing E. of Olympia.

Partenope   a siren with a monument near Naples.

Parthes   Parthians, from the S.E. of the Caspian Sea.

Partridge, John   'a ridiculous star-gazer' who 'always predicted the downfall of the Pope and the King of France'.

Pasiphae   her relationship with a bull resulted in the Minotaur.

Paul's, St   the cathedral in London.

Pegasus   the winged horse which came from the blood of the beheaded Medusa.

Pelias   son of Poseidon and Tyro; sent Jason to Colchis for the Golden Fleece; finally cut to pieces and boiled by his own daughter (Peliades) who had been told, by Medea, that by doing this she could restore him.

Peleian   of Peleus.

Peleus   King of the Myrmidons in Thessaly.

Pelion   a range of mountains, N. coast of Thessaly.

Pella   village in the Piedmont area of Italy.

Pelops   see Milton 'Il Penseroso', li. 99 notes.

Pelorus   Cape Faro in N.W. Sicily.

Penelope   Odysseus' wife who waited for many years, refusing to remarry, for his return from Troy.

Pennel   *see* Succoth.

Peraean   a general term for an isthmus.

Percy (Piercy), Thomas   1729–1811; Bishop of Dromore; an antiquarian; collected the *Reliques of Ancient English Poetry*, 1765, which was attacked as unscholarly; very popular.

Perseus   *see* Danae.

Petsora   river in Siberia.

Phaedra   daughter of Minos; Theseus married her after the death of Hippolyta.

Phaeton   son of Phoebus, the sun god; asked to drive his father's chariot for a day – disastrously.

Pharaoh   the ruler of Egypt.

Pharphar   a river in Syria (II Kings. V. 12).

Philips, Ambrose   1675–1749; poet and secretary to Archbishop Boulton; author of *Persian Times*.

Phillis   popular girl's name in pastoral poetry.

Philoclea   a character in Sidney's *Arcadia*.

Philomela her sister, Procne, married Tereus, the King of Thrace; he fell in love with Philomela, raped her and cut out her tongue lest she should reveal what had happened; she wove the events into a tapestry, sent it to her sister, who, in revenge, killed her own son, Itys, serving him up in a pie to his father; Tereus pursued the sisters until he was turned into a hoopoe, and, according to the Greeks, Procne changed into a nightingale, Philomela into a swallow; according to the Roman version, vice-versa, due perhaps to a slip of the pen by Apollodorus of Athens who recorded the story in his *Bibliotheca*.

Phisiologus *see* Bestiary.

Phison a river of Paradise; = s Prudence (Gen. II. 11).

Phlegethon = a river of fire; one of the rivers of hell.

Phlegra where a battle took place between the gods and the giants; W. peninsula of N. Greece.

Phocis a mountainous region of N. Greece, a part of Thrace.

Phoebe *see* Diana.

Phoebus = bright or pure; god of inspiration, who warned Virgil against ambition by tweaking his ears (*Eclogues* VI. 3–4); *see also* Apollo.

Pholoe beloved of Pan.

Phrygians a people who had many gods as a result of their subjection to many different overlords.

Phthiatia (Phthia) home of Achilles; S.E. Thessaly.

Picardie Picardy, France.

Pindar Roman poet.

Pirocles a character in Sidney's *Arcadia*.

Pirrus *see* Pyrrhus.

Pisces the sign of the fish in the zodiac.

Pitholeon a 'foolish poet of Rhodes', Pope; = Leonard Welsted, poet, translator and clerk in the government.

Pitt, William Earl of Chatham; 1708–78; Whig statesman.

Plato 4th C. BC Greek philosopher.

Pleiad daughter of Atlas and Pleione; Pleiades – the 7 daughters who after death were placed in heaven and formed a group of stars.

Pluto god of the underworld who abducted Proserpina (Persephone) and made her his wife, allowing her to return to the earth for six months each year.

Pomona goddess of fruit; wooed and won by Vertumnus.

Pompey 106–48 BC; great Roman commander; was stabbed to death after his defeat in the Battle of Pharsalus, 48 BC.

Pontus the Black Sea.

Portsmouth and Aubigny, Duchess of 1649–1734; Charles II's mistress.

Prato a town near Florence where Fra Lippo Lippi painted some of his best pictures.

Priam King of the Trojans.

Promethean *see* Prometheus.

Prometheus he stole fire from the gods to give to men; was punished by Jupiter, being tied to a rock where, daily, a vulture tore out his liver.

Proserpina(e) (Persephone, Primavera) daughter of Ceres; *see* Pluto.

Proteus a sea-god who could change into whatever shape he wished; the old man of the sea who tended Neptune's flocks (seals); = s formlessness which is multiplicity which = evil.

Provençal of area in S. France associated with the troubadours.

Pruce   Prussia.

Psyche   beloved of Cupid; Venus, jealous of her beauty, sent Cupid to torment her; she was warned not to look at his face, but, in the light of a lamp, she did, and he deserted her; after many trials they were re-united and married; their child was Pleasure.

Ptolemy, Claudius   2nd C. AD; Greek astronomer; his chief work, *Almagest*, a treatise on astronomy.

Pugin, A.W.   1812–52; architect who favoured the Gothic style in church building.

Pye, Henry James   Poet Laureate before Southey.

Pyrrha   after the Flood, Deucalia and Pyrrha threw pebbles which became men and women.

Pyrrhus   who, with his naked sword, killed King Priam when Troy was sacked.

Pythian games   held at Delphi; next in importance to the Olympian Games; included artistic and musical competitions.

Python   after the Flood, from the mud, acted on by the sun, came a great snake – Python; Apollo killed it.

Quantocks   hills in Somerset, England.

Queensberry, Duke of   he befriended John Gay.

Quintus Sertorius   *c.* 122–72 BC; Roman general; governor of Ebro valley in Spain; tried to overcome Rome from the provinces; defeated by Sulla, he escaped to Mauritanea; returned to become master of most of Spain; when he was murdered most of his followers fled to the Canary Isles (the Fortunate Isles) where they fought to keep out the Spaniards; they were finally subdued by plague.

Rabba   Ammonite capital; captured by David (II Sam. XII).

Ram   the zodiac sign from 12 March – 21 April; a prize for wrestling.

Rauran   hill in Merionethshire, Wales; one of the seats of the Tudor Henry VII's ancestors.

Red Sea   (Hebrew) = the sea of sedge.

Rhea   Saturn's wife; mother of Jove; great mother of the gods.

Rhene   River Rhine.

Rimmon   Syrian god (II Kings XVI. 10).

Rochelle, La   port in Gascony, a part of France which once belonged to England.

Romaines   Romans.

Romayn   P. Sempronius Sophus, a character in Valerius Maximus' book of historical exempla.

Rome   in Spenser = the Catholic Church.

Romulus   who, with his twin brother, Remus, founded Rome, the site Romulus chose being visited by twice as many vultures as that chosen by his brother; was carried to heaven in a storm and deified.

Ronan, St   poss. St Ninian, who evangelised the Picts.

Rosamunda's Lake   a pond in St James's Park, London.

Rouncivale   Hospital of the Blessed Mary of Rouncivalle, near Charing Cross, London.

Royal Academy of Arts founded 1768, its patron George III, for an annual exhibition of contemporary art and the establishment of a school of art.

Rubicon Italian river boundary over which no Roman general could take his army; 49 BC Julius Caesar did, provoking civil war.

Ruce Russia.

Rydal Water in the Lake District, England.

Sabrina daughter of Locrine; grand-daughter of Brutus.

Salamon Solomon.

Salerno Italian coastal town.

Salmacis a nymph who fell in love with Hermaphroditus, who rejected her; as he swam she clung to him and the gods united them; those who enter her pool become weakened – half-man, half-woman.

Samarkand in S. Russia; noted for its silks.

Samoed Shore coastal area in N.E. Siberia.

Samson warrior betrayed by Dalilah, captured by his enemies and, now blind, made to turn millstones to grind corn for them (Judges XIII ff.).

Sancroft, William 1617–93; Archbishop of Canterbury.

Sans Foy = faithlessness.

Sans Joy = joylessness.

Sans Loy = lawlessness.

Sappho c. mid-7th C. BC, Greek lyric poet; she left Lesbos because of political troubles and went to Sicily, where she died.

Sarazin Saracen.

Saturn leader of the Titans, overthrowing his father, Uranus, and, in turn, overthrown by his son, Jove; god of melancholy, solitude and grave-diggers.

Satyrane the offspring of a satyr and Thyamis; has control over wild animals; = natural goodness and power.

Satyr Greek woodland deity with horse's ears and tail; Roman woodland deity with goat's ears, tail, legs and budding horns; linked with fertility rites.

Savile, George 1633–95; later Marquis of Halifax; tried to mediate between the Tories and the Whigs; his speech in the House of Commons turned the balance against the Exclusion Bill.

Scariot Judas Iscariot, the betrayer of Christ.

Scipio Africanus born c. 234 BC; commander of forces against Hannibal and Carthage; in his dream he was shown a vision of his future victory against Carthage.

Scorpion the zodiac sign.

Scylla (1) once a nymph whom Circe, through jealousy, changed so that her lower parts were surrounded by a knot of gaping dogs' heads; later changed into rock in the Straits of Messina, between Sicily and Italy.

Scylla (2) plucked a hair from the head of Nisus, her father, on which his safety depended; was turned into a sea-bird, forever pursued by an eagle.

Sedley, Sir Charles ? 1639–1701; wit and poet who contributed a prologue to Shadwell's *Epsom Wells*.

Selinis Philistine city.

Semiramis restored Babylon; killed by her son, Ninus, with whom she fell in love.

Senancour, Étienne Pivert de 1770–1846; his *Obermann* is a series of fictional letters on man and society.

Sennacherib   Assyrian king who unsuccessfully besieged Jerusalem (II King's XIX.8ff).

Seneca   *c.* 5 BC–65 AD; Roman philosopher and dramatist.

Serbonis   a lake near Damietta on the estuary of the Nile; bordered by quicksands.

Serapis   Egyptian god with temples at Alexandria and Memphis.

Serralione   Sierra Leone.

Settle, Elkanah   1648–1724; began life as a Tory; his reply to *Absalom and Achitophel*, entitled *Absalom Senior or Achitophel Transprosed* (sic), 1682, defended the Whigs.

Severn   river rising in Wales, flowing through Shropshire; Ludlow Castle stands beside it.

Severn, Joseph   1793–1879; painter and great friend of Keats whom he cared for in Italy and of whom he made several portraits and a death-mask.

Seville   town in Spain.

Seymour, Edward   1633–1708; speaker of the House of Commons, 1673–8; re-elected 1679 but the King refused to accept him.

Shadwell, Thomas   1640–92; once Dryden's friend, an ardent Whig; poor poet who wrote *The Medal of John Bayes, a Satire against Folly and Knavery* in answer to Dryden's *The Medal, a Satire against Sedition*; see notes to Dryden *MacFlecknoe.*

Shalott   variant of Astolat; see Tennyson note 2.

Sheffield, John   1648–1721; Earl of Mulgrave; patron of Dryden; 1679 Charles II gave him the governship of Hull and the Lord Lieutenancy of Yorkshire; wrote an 'Essay upon Poetry' and an 'Essay on Satire'.

Shibboleth   *see* Ephraim.

Shimei   a Benjamite who, as supporter of Saul, threw stones at David (II Sam. XVI. 5–13); when David was victorious welcomed him (II Sam. XIX. 18); later confined by Solomon within the walls of Jerusalem on pain of death because he could not be trusted (I Kings II. 36–37). In Dryden, *Absalom and Achitophel,* = Sheriff Slingsby Bethel (*see* Bethel).

Shirley, James   1596–1666; dramatist.

Sidmouth, Henry Addington, Viscount   1757–1844; his severe administration resulted in the hanging of 14 Luddites at York.

Sidney, Sir Philip   1554–1586; poet, critic, courtier and soldier; fatally wounded in battle.

Sidon(ia)   chief city of the Phoenicians on the coast of Syria; celebrated for glass, purple dye and wine (Deut. III. 9).

Silenus   shaggy bearded man with horse's ears who knows folklore secrets; daemon of fertility; old god of the woods.

Silo(am)   a pool with healing powers (John IX. 7ff.).

S(h)ilo(h)   where the tabernacle was set up (Judges XVIII. 1).

Silvanus   Roman god of uncultivated land; = Pan, Faunus.

Simois   river near Troy.

Sinai   where Moses received the tablets of the Law (Exod. III. 1).

Singleton, John   a musician of the Theatre Royal.

Sinon   Greek who persuaded the Trojans to take the wooden horse into Troy.

Sion Hill   *see* Zion.

Sirens   whose songs lured sailors to their death.

Sirius the Dog-star; in ascendancy in late summer, when the vegetation withers; in Rome this was the season of public recitals of poetry.

Sirocco hot Mediterranean wind.

Sisyphus condemned by Zeus to roll a rock up a hill from which it continually rolled down again.

Sittingbourne in Kent, 40 miles from London, 16 from Canterbury.

Skiddaw a mountain in the Lake District, England.

Smyrna one of the seven cities claiming to be Homer's birthplace.

Society of Antiquaries founded 1572; suppressed on the accession of James I; present society founded 1717/18.

Socrates 489–199 BC; Athenian philosopher; famous for his patience; had two wives, one called Xantippe.

Sodom town at the S. end of the Dead Sea (Gen. XIX. 24 ff.).

Solomon, King son of David; legend has it he received from Leah a ring made of brass and iron, engraved with the name of God; this gave him special magical powers which he used in the building of his palace and the temple at Jerusalem (I Kings XI).

Sophocles c. 496–405 BC, Athenian dramatist born at Colonnus.

Sophonisba daughter of Hasdrubal; betrothed to Masinissa but married Syphax.

Sophy the Shah, the Persian king; a sage.

Southcott, Joanna 1750–1814; a religious fanatic.

Southey, Robert 1774–1843; poet; appointed Poet Laureate 1813.

Southwark on the S. bank of the Thames, London; the beginning of the pilgrims' road to Canterbury.

Spectator periodical produced by Addison and Steele from 1 March 1711 to 6 Dec. 1712; revived by Addison 1714; appeared daily; very popular.

Sporus Nero's eunuch whom he publicly married; in Pope's *Epistle to Dr Arbuthnot* = Lord Hervey.

Sthenoboea (Anteia) wife of Proteus, king of the Argives, who tried to tempt Bellerophon; when he refused she told Proteus that he had tried to seduce her, and then killed herself.

Stilbon a character from John of Salisbury's *Polycraticus – Of the Follies of Courtiers*.

Stoic(k) a school of philosophy, c. 308 BC at Athens, teaching control of the emotions and indifference to pleasure or pain.

Stott, Robert pseudonym 'Hafiz'; poet of the *Morning Post*; according to Byron 'the most profound explorer of bathos'.

Stratford-atte-Bow suburb of London where there was a convent school.

Straw, Jack one of leaders of the Peasants' Revolt, 1381.

Stremona where Hercules slew the Hydra, which had ravaged the country of Lerna, near Argos.

Stuart, John, Earl of Bute; appointed Prime Minister, 1762.

Stygian of the Styx.

Styx river of the Underworld, over which the dead were ferried; = hatred.

Succoth a town where Gideon and his men were refused food (Judges VIII. 5).

Susa Memmonia, the winter seat of the Persian kings.

Swift, Jonathan 1667–1745; became eventually Dean of St Patrick's, Dublin; best known publication *Gulliver's Travels*, 1726; many alienated by his fierce satires; member, with Pope, Gay and Arbuthnot, of the Scriblerus Club.

Sylla, Cornelius died 78 BC; successful Roman commander; dissolute dictator.

Sylvan(us) the god of the woods.

Synon betrayed Troy, with the wooden horse, into Greek hands.

Syrtis, Major and Minor two gulfs in the Mediterranean off N. Africa.

Tabard an inn at Southwark, with a tabard (a short sleeveless coat) as its sign.

Tanaquil(1) wife of Tarquin Priscus, first of the Tarquin Kings of Rome; = Queen Elizabeth I (Spencer).

Tantalus punished by Zeus, having to stand, thirst-stricken, waist deep in water which receded as he tried to drink it.

Tarquin, Collatinus husband of Lucretia, whose beauty and virtue so inflamed Sextus that he raped her; after telling her husband and her father what had happened, she took her own life.

Tarshish port on the Guadalquivir, Spain; ships from = s pride.

Tarsus capital of Sicily.

Tartarus the place of the guilty; according to Homer as far beneath Hades as the earth is below heaven.

Tartary Tartarus.

Tate, Nahum 1652–1715; poet and playwright; successor to Dryden as Poet Laureate.

Tauris (Tabriz) in N.W. Persia.

Taurus zodiac sign of the bull.

Tempe a valley in Thessaly.

Termate a spice island in the Malay Straits.

Terni a waterfall in Italy.

Tertullian early Roman convert to Christianity; wrote treatises on chastity, monogamy and modesty.

Tethys wife of Oceanus.

Thalestris an Amazon (female warrior).

Thames the river, flowing from the Cotswolds, on which London stands.

Thammuz = Adonis.

Thea wife of Hyperion, a Titan who was father of the sun, the moon and the dawn.

Thebes chief city of Boeotia; reputed birthplace of Dionysius and Hercules; scene of the Oedipus tragedies.

Thebs see Milton 'Il Penseroso'. li. 99 notes.

Theobald, Lewis 1688–1744; poet, essayist, playwright and Shakespearean scholar; his *Shakespeare Restored* revealed inaccuracies in Pope's edition of *Shakespeare*, for which Pope ridiculed him in *The Dunciad*, whilst accepting many of his emendations in the 2nd edition of his *Shakespeare*.

Theophrastus *c.* 372–287 BC; Greek philosopher and naturalist; born at Erebos, on Lesbos; pupil of Plato and Aristotle; author of *Liber Aureolus de Nuptiliis*.

Therion husband of Thyamis; Greek = wild beast.

Theseus   poss. Poseidon's son; married Hippolyta (or Antiope); their son was Hippolytus; he fought the Amazons, slew the Minotaur and carried off Helen when she was a young girl; he attempted to carry off Persephone (Proserpina) from the Underworld, for which he was chained there until Hercules freed him.

Thestylis   popular name in pastoral poetry.

Thetis   one of the Nereids; a sea-goddess; mother of Achilles.

Thisb(a)e   town in Boeotia; famed for its wild pigeons.

Thone   Egyptian; he and his wife, Polydamna, entertained Menelaus and Helen on their way home from Troy.

Thracias   N.W. wind.

Thyamis   wife of Therion, a satyr; their child was Satyrane (Spenser).

Thyestes   seduced the wife of his brother Atreus, who in revenge served up one of Thyestes's own children to him at a banquet; an act which caused the sun to alter its course.

Thynne, Thomas   1648–82; he entertained Monmouth on his progress through England, 1680, at Longleat.

Thyrsis   a singer in the pastoral writings of Theocritus and Virgil; in the acting of Milton's *Comus* at Ludlow Castle played by Henry Lawes, the musician and tutor to the Earl's children.

Tibbald   *see* Theobald.

Tiberius   the river Tiber in Rome.

Tidore   a spice island in the Malay Straits.

Tigris   a river in Paradise (Gen. II. 14).

Tilphusa   a spring near Thebes; sacred to Apollo.

Timias   Arthur's squire; Greek = honour.

Tiresias   Theban soothsayer, blinded from age 7; fled with the Thebans after their defeat in the war of the Epigoni, but, according to some, was captured, and, drinking of the well of Tilphusa, died; said to have been buried nearby.

Tiryns   in Argolis, where Hercules lived.

Tirynthian groom   = Hercules.

Tirzah   1. daughter of Zelophedad (Num. XXVII.1, XXXVI.11; Josh. XVII.3ff.).

   2. ancient city in Canaan (I Kings XIV.17ff.).

Titans   usually 12; children of Heaven (Uranus) and Earth (Ge); Saturn, helped by his son, rebelled against Uranus, deposing him; then he himself was deposed by Jove; Apollo, the sun god, was also a Titan.

Tithone   husband of Aurora, for whom she requested eternal life but forgot to ask for eternal youth.

Tityus   punished for assaulting Leto (or Artemis); he was killed by Artemis (or Apollo); was cast into Tartarus, where vultures tore at his liver.

Tmolus   a mountain range in Lydia; at its foot, the city of Smyrna.

Tonson, Jacob   1657–1737; bookseller and publisher; acquired the copyright of *Paradise Lost* for £8; well-known for his *Miscellanies*, containing translations from the classics.

Tooke, John Horne   opposed the war in the American colonies.

Tophet   'place of burning'; in the valley of Hinnom, where sacrifices were offered to Moloch.

Torno   in Lapland.

Trebisond   a city in Asia Minor, renowned for its tournaments.

Tremessen   in N. Africa.

Trinacrian   = Sicilian.

Triton(s)   son(s) of Poseidon (Neptune) and Amphitrite, with fish tails and the forefeet of a horse, carrying conch-shells as trumpets to calm the waves.

Troas   the area around Troy.

Troy   believed to have been built by Apollo and Poseidon.

Trotula   poss. a gynaecologist or midwife practising at Salerno 11th C; credited with having written treatises on women's diseases, cosmetics and feminine passion.

Tullus, Hostilius   673–643 BC; third King of Rome who began life as a shepherd.

Tully   Cicero, 106–43 BC; Roman prose writer; known as a master of rhetoric.

Turnbull, Jonathan   1710–85; American politician.

Turnus   King of the Rutulians; accepted suitor of Lavinia; fought against Aeneas to whom Lavinia was given by her father, Latinus.

Typhoeus   a monster with 100 dragon heads, whom Jove overcame with a thunderbolt; was buried under Etna.

Typhon   monster son of Typhoeus.

Tyrian   of Tyre; Phoenician.

Ulpian   3rd C. AD; an inferior Latin writer.

Ulysses (Odysseus)   who once kept the winds in a bag (*Odyssey* X. 19).

Urania   i.e. Venus in her heavenly or spiritual aspect.

Uriel   = the light of God; by Milton, linked with the sun.

Uther Pendragon   King Arthur's father.

Valdarno   valley of the Arno, the river that passes through Florence.

Valerius Maximus   Roman historian of Tiberius's reign, *c.* AD 14–23: author of a book of *exempla*.

Vallombrosa   = 'a shady valley'; near Florence; visited by Milton, 1638.

Venus   Roman goddess of love; as Urania = heavenly love; as Pandemos = earthly love; as Cyprian Queen worshipped on Cyprus; when bathing was spied upon, so hid behind a myrtle bush; on her day, gardeners had a holiday.

Vertumnus   god connected with the progress of fruition; wooed and won Pomona.

Vesta   virgin daughter of Saturn.

Villiers, George   Duke of Buckingham, 1628–87 poet, dramatist, politician, wit and libertine; ridiculed by Dryden in his play *The Rehearsal*, 1671.

Virgil   Roman poet; author of the *Aeneid*.

Vivia(e)n   temptress in King Arthur's court who got Merlin's spells from him.

Viviana, Emilia   a 17-year-old heiress shut up in a convent at Pisa; Shelley's love for her expressed in 'Epipsychidion'.

Vogler, Abt   1749–1814; organist, composer and music teacher who invented a portable organ – the 'orchestrion'.

Vulcan   the fire god whose forge was under Mt Etna; he was thrown out of heaven by Jove.

Wallace, Sir William ?1272–1305; Scottish patriot who resisted the English; was taken prisoner by treachery and executed in London.

Walton, Izaak 1593–1683; biographer; author of *The Compleat Angler*, 1653.

Ware in Hertfordshire; or Kent, near Dover.

Washington, George 1732–99; first American president.

Watering of St Thomas a brook outside London where horses were watered.

Welsted, Leonard translator of Longinus; accused Pope (according to Pope) of causing a lady's death and of living in familiarity with the Duke of Chandos.

Westminster Hall the law courts in London.

Westmorland the coastal area of the Lake District, England.

Whitechapel area in London.

Wilkes, John (Jack) 1727–97; MP; popular hero in the cause of liberty.

Wollstonecraft, Mary 1759–97; wife of William Godwin; their daughter Mary married Shelley; author of *Thoughts on the Education of Daughters*, 1787, several novels, and *Vindications of the Rights of Man, and the Rights of Woman*, 1792.

Wood, Anthony 1632–95; historian and antiquary who received help from Aubrey; in *Athenae Oxoniensis*, 1681/2, he libelled the Earl of Clarendon, for which he was expelled from the University, 1693.

Wychwood a wood, 10 miles N. of Oxford.

Xantippe Socrates' second wife, who tormented him continually.

Xerxes 485–465 BC; King of Persia who made a bridge of boats over the Bosphorus to invade Greece; was eventually defeated at the Battle of Salamis.

Yinde India.

Yonge, Sir William politician and versifier.

Ypres Flemish town famous for its fine cloth.

Zembla Zemlya, islands off N. Russia.

Zephyr W. wind.

Zion the hill on which Jerusalem is built; a sanctuary and a place of ceremonial song and prophecy.

Zora where Samson was born (Judges XIII.2).

Index of First Lines

A flower was offer'd me 640
A gentle knight was pricking on the plaine 107
A green and silent spot, amid the hills 767
A little black thing among the snow 637
A little onward lend thy guiding hand 445
A povre widwe, somedel stape in age 85
A sensitive plant in a garden grew 886
A slumber did my spirit steal 662
A thing of beauty is a joy for ever 948
Ah, did you once see Shelley plain 1097
Ah my dear angry Lord 303
Ah, my dear friend and brother 944
Ah, sunflower, weary of time 641
All are but parts of one stupendous whole 565
All human things are subject to decay 529
All kings and all their favourites 290
All the night in woe 636
And did those feet in ancient time 648
And like a dying lady, lean and pale 901
Ariel to Miranda: Take 922
As I lay asleep in Italy 875
As some fond Virgin, whom her mother's care 564
As virtuous men pass mildly away 288
At the round earth's imagined corners, blow 294

Bards of Passion and of Mirth 962
Batter my heart, three-person'd God; for you 294
Before the starry threshold of Jove's court 321
Behold her, single in the field 681
Break, break, break 1020
Busy old fool, unruly sun 289
By night we lingered on the lawn 1029

Calm is the morn without a sound 1022
Can I see another's woe 630
Children of the future Age 645
Come, dear children, let us away 1123
Courage, he said, and pointed toward the land 1008

Dark house, by which once more I stand 1021
Dear friend, far off, my lost desire 1039
Dear Mother, dear Mother, the Church is cold 642
Death be not proud, though some have called thee 294
Death's memories are graves 939
Deep in the shady sadness of a vale 953
Doeg, though without knowing how or why 526
Doors, where my heart was used to beat 1037

Earth has not anything to show more fair 679
Earth rais'd up her head 632
England! awake! awake! awake! 648
Ere on my bed my limbs I lay 780
Escape me? 1092
Experience, though noon auctoritee 39

Father, father, where are you going? 623
Fear death? – to feel fog in my throat 1112
First follow Nature, and your judgement frame 542
Five years have passed, five summers, with the length 656
Fled are those times, when, in harmonious strains 608
For God's sake hold your tongue, and let me love 292
For rigorous teachers seized my youth 1135
From harmony, from heavenly harmony 534

Go, and catch a falling star 291
Go, for they call you, shepherd, from the hill 1138
God moves in a mysterious way 601
Gr-r-r – there go, my heart's abhorrence 1066

Had I but plenty of money, money enough and to spare 1080
Had we but world enough and time 499
Hail to thee, blithe spirit! 898
Half a league, half a league 1040
Happy the man, whose wish and care 563
Hark! ah, the nightingale 1144
He clasps the crag with crooked hands 1040
He loved the brook's soft sound 937
Hear the voice of the Bard! 632
Hence, loathed Melancholy 313

Hence, vain deluding joys 316
Here are sweet peas, on tip-toe for a flight 943
Here she beholds the chaos dark and deep 579
High on a throne of a royal state, which far 369
Ho! quod the Knight, good sir, namore of this 84
How changed is here each spot man makes or fills 1145
How sweet is the shepherd's sweet lot! 620

I am poor brother Lippo, by your leave! 1083
I am: yet what I am none cares or knows 937
I bring fresh showers for the thirsting flowers 895
I climb the hill: from end to end 1031
I come from haunts of coot and hern 1042
I Dreamt a Dream! what can it mean? 639
I envy not in any moods 1023
I feel I am, I only know I am 938
I got me flowers to straw thy way 307
I have no name 629
I heard a thousand blended notes 654
I hid my love when young till I 939
I know the ways of Learning; both the head 301
I love to rise in a summer morn 646
I met a traveller form an antique land 862
I rode one evening with Count Maddalo 862
I said – Then, dearest, since 'tis so 1093
I sprang to the stirrup, and Joris, and he 1070
I struck the board, and cried, No more! 306
I travelled among unknown men 662
I trust I have not wasted breath 1038
I've often on a Sabbath day 932
I wander through each charter'd street 642
I wandered lonely as a cloud 680
I want a hero: an uncommon want 813
I was angry with my friend 644
I weep for Adonais – he is dead! 905
I went to the Garden of Love 641
I will not shut me from my kind 1036
I wonder by my troth, what thou and I 293
I wonder, do you feel today 1099
If from the public way you turn your steps 663
If one should bring me this report 1022
In Flaundres whylom was a companye 72
In futurity 634

In pious times ere priest-craft did begin 503
In the Age of gold 645
In this lone, open glade I lie 1133
In tholde dayes of the King Arthour 58
In Xanadu did Kubla Khan 727
Is it then, regret for buried time 1037
Is this a holy thing to see 633
It is a beauteous evening, calm and free 679
It is an Ancient Mariner 728
It is the day when he was born 1035
It little profits that an idle king 1017
It was roses, roses, all the way 1096

Just for a handful of siler he left us 1072

Kind pity chokes my spleen; brave scorn forbids 295

Let me pour forth 282
Lift not the veil which those who live 871
Light flows our war of mocking words, and yet 1129
Little Fly 638
Little Lamb, who made thee 621
Lo I the man, whose Muse whilome did maske 106
Lord, who createdst men in wealth and store 310
Love bade me welcome; yet my soul drew back 309
Lordinges, quod he, in chirches whan I preche 69
Love lives beyond 940
. Love seeketh not Itself to please 633

Maid of Athens, ere we part 791
Maud has a garden of roses 1043
Meanwhile the heinous and despiteful act 420
Merry, Merry Sparrow 622
Much have I travelled in the realms of gold 945
Music, when soft voices die 919
My heart aches, and a drowsy numbness pains 977
My heart leaps up when I behold 678
My love is of a birth so rare 498
My mother bore me in the Southern wild 621
My mother groan'd, my father wept 643

My own dim life should teach me this 1026
My pensive Sara! thy soft cheek reclined 723
My sister! my sweet sister! if a name 794
My soul . . . turn we to survey 593

No cloud, no relique of the sunken day 773
No more talk where God or angel guest 393
No, no, go not to Lethe, neither twist 981
Nought loves another as itself 644
Now fades the last long streak of snow 1036
Now sleeps the crimson petal, now the white 1021

O Friend! O Teacher! God's great gift to me! 781
O Goddess! hear these tuneless numbers, wrung 975
O Poesy! for thee I hold my pen 946
O Rose, thou art sick 638
O there is a blessing in this gentle breeze 690
O, what can ail thee, knight-at-arms 974
O wild West Wind, thou breath of Autumn's being 884
O, yet we trust that somehow good 1026
O young Mariner 1057
Of man's first disobedience, and the fruit 350
Oh, to be in England 1073
Old elm that murmured in our chimney top 933
Old Meg she was a Gipsy 1001
Old Peter Grimes made fishing his employ 610
On either side the river lie 1012
On Man, on Nature, and on Human Life 716
Others abide our quesiton, Thou are free 1122
Once a dream did weave a shade 630
Once more upon the waters! yet once more 799
Our Hoste gan to swere as he were wood 68

P. Shut, shut the door, good John! fatigu'd I said 569
Peace; come away; the song of woe 1028
Piping down the valleys wild 619
Pity would be no more 643
Poet of Nature, Thou hast wept to know 859

Rarely, rarely comest thou 919
Ring out, wild bells, to the wild sky 1034

Room after room 1092
Round the cape of a sudden came the sea 1077

Saint Agnes' Eve – Ah, bitter chill it was 963
Saint Peter sat by the celestial gate 826
Season of mists and mellow fruitfulness 982
See! from the brake the whirring pheasant springs 544
She dwelt among untrodden ways 660
She walks in beauty, like the night 792
'So careful of the type?' but no 1027
So, we'll go no more a' roving 798
Souls of Poets dead and gone 952
Sound the Flute! 628
Stern Daughter of the Voice of God 688
Strange fits of passion have I known 660
Strew on her roses, roses 1135
Sunset and evening star 1061
Sweet and low, sweet and low 1020
Sweet Auburn, loveliest village of the plain 596
Sweet day, so cool, so calm, so bright 308
Sweet dreams, from a shade 624
Sweetest love, I do not go 287
Swiftly walk o'er the western wave 921

That story which the bold Sir Bedivere 1046
That's my last Duchess, painted on the wall 1065
That which we dare invoke to bless 1038
The Assyrian came down like the wolf on the fold 792
The awful shadow of some unseen Power 859
The crawling glaciers pierce me with the spears 871
The curfew tolls the knell of passing day 588
The fountains mingle with the river 883
The frost performs its secret ministry 765
The gipsies seek wide sheltering woods again 936
The gray sea and the long blank land 1077
The keen stars were twinkling 924
The little boy lost in the lonely fen 624
The modest Rose puts forth a thorn 641
The night was winter in his roughest mood 604
The poetry of earth is never dead 946
The poplars are felled, farewell to the shade 603
The rain set early in tonight 1068

The sea is calm to-night 1132
The silver mist more lowly swims 938
The splendour falls on castle walls 1020
The sun descending in the west 626
The Sun does arise 620
The time draws near the birth of Christ 1023
The wish, that of the living whole 1027
The world is too much with us; late and soon 679
The year's at the spring 1064
There was a Boy; ye knew him well, ye cliffs 655
There was a naughty Boy 1002
There was a Poet whose untimely tomb 856
There was a roaring in the wind all night 674
There was a time when meadow, grove, and stream 682
This living hand, now warm and capable 1000
Thou still unravished bride of quietness 979
Three years she grew in sun and shower 661
Throw away thy rod 307
Thus far, O friends! have we, though leaving much 705
Thy voice is on the rolling air 1039
'Tis death! and peace, indeed, is here 1129
'Tis the middle of the night by the castle clock 747
'Tis the year's midnight, and it is the day's 286
'Tis time this heart should be unmoved 850
To die be given us, or attain! 1116
To Mercy, Pity, Peace and Love 625
To one who has been long in city pent 945
Tonight ungathered let us leave 1033
Trochee trips from long to short 784
True love in this differs from gold and clay 901
True Poesy is not in words 929
Truly my Satan thou art but a Dunce 649
'Twas on a Holy Thursday, their innocent faces clean 626
'Twas on a lofty vase's side 587
Tyger, Tyger, burning bright 646

Unwatched, the garden bough shall sway 1032
Up! Up! my Friend, and quit your books 653
Upon a time, before the faery broods 983

Vanity, saith the preacher, vanity! 1074

We leave the well-beloved place 1032
We were apart; yet, day by day 1127
Well! If the Bard was weather-wise, who made 776
Well, they are gone, and here must I remain 725
Whan that Aprille with his showres sote 18
What dire offence from am'rous causes springs 545
What is it to grow old? 1152
Whate'er is Born of Mortal Birth 646
When first thou didst entice to thee my heart 303
When for the thorns with which I long, too long 496
When God at first made man 310
When I have fears that I may cease to be 951
When Lazarus lft his charnel-cave 1025
When lovely woman stoops to folly 600
When midnight comes a host of dogs and men 935
When my grave is broke up again 285
When my mother died I was very young 623
When rosy plumelets tuft the larch 1029
When the green woods laugh with the voice of joy 624
When the voices of children are heard on the green (Songs of I.) 629
When the voices of children are heard on the green (Songs of E.) 638
When vice triumphant holds her sov'reign sway 788
When we two parted 793
Where be ye going, you Devon Maid 1000
Where, like a pillow on a bed 282
Where the quiet-coloured end of evening smiles 1078
Where the remote Bermudas ride 496
Who says that fictions only and false hair 305
Why, William, on that old grey stone 652
'Will sprawl, now that the heat of day is best 1105
With blackest moss the flower-pots 1005
With trembling fingers did we weave 1024
Would that the structure brave, the manifold music I build 1102

Ye learned sisters which have oftentimes 264
Ye living lamps, by whose dear light 499
Yes! in the sea of life enisled 1128
Yet once more, O ye laurels, and once more 346
Yon cottager who weaves at her own door 602
Your ghost will walk, you lover of trees 1098
Youth of delight, come hither 647